The SAGE Handbook of

Social Gerontology

The SAGE Handbook of
Social Gerontology

Edited by
Dale Dannefer and
Chris Phillipson

Los Angeles | London | New Delhi
Singapore | Washington DC

First published 2010
This paperback edition first published 2013

SAGE Publications Ltd
1 Oliver's Yard
55 City Road
London EC1Y 1SP

SAGE Publications Inc.
2455 Teller Road
Thousand Oaks, California 91320

SAGE Publications India Pvt Ltd
B 1/I 1 Mohan Cooperative Industrial Area
Mathura Road
New Delhi 110 044

SAGE Publications Asia-Pacific Pte Ltd
3 Church Street
10-04 Samsung Hub
Singapore 049483

Library of Congress Control Number: 2009935290

British Library Cataloguing in Publication data

A catalogue record for this book is available from the British Library

ISBN 978-1-4129-3464-0
ISBN 978-1-4462-7047-9 (pbk)

Typeset by GLYPH International Pvt. Ltd., Bangalore, India
Printed by MPG Printgroup, UK
Printed on paper from sustainable resources

Contents

Notes on Contributors

Isabella Aboderin, PhD, is a Senior Research Fellow at the Oxford Institute of Ageing, University of Oxford where she leads the programme on Africa and co-ordinates the African Research on Ageing Network. Isabella is Africa Regional Chair of the International Association of Gerontology and Geriatrics. Her research interests centre on three areas: Ageing and development in sub-Saharan Africa, Intergenerational family support and social change in sub-Saharan Africa and Social and life course determinants of health in old age.

W. Andrew Achenbaum, a Professor of History and Social Work in the University of Houston's Graduate College of Social Work, holds the Gerson & Sabina David Professorship in Global Aging. He also is an adjunct professor of geriatric and palliative care and a senior fellow in the Institute of Spirituality and Health, both in the Houston, Texas Medical Center. A graduate of Amherst College, Achenbaum received his PhD from the University of Michigan, where he was a professor of history and deputy director of its Institute of Gerontology. An author of five books (most recently *Older Americans, Vital Communities*, Johns Hopkins, 2007) and co-editor of twelve others, Mr. Achenbaum is currently working on *Leaving a Legacy* with H. R. Moody and embarking on a biography of Robert N. Butler.

Ronald H. Aday, PhD, is Professor of Sociology at Middle Tennessee State University where he served for 25 years as the Director of Aging Studies. He received his PhD from Oklahoma State University with specialties in crime, corrections and gerontology. His lifelong work on aging and health issues in the field of corrections has contributed significantly to the public policy debate on older offenders. He has published extensively on the topic including Aging Prisoners: Crisis in American Corrections. His forthcoming co-authored books with Jennifer Krabill include *Older Women in Prison: Understanding the Lives of an Indivisible Population* and *Managing Geriatric Inmates: Best Practice Models*.

Graham Allan is Professor of Sociology at the University of Keele, UK. His research has focused principally on the sociology of informal relationships, including friendships, family ties, and community sociology. He has published widely in these areas. Recently he has acted as one of the Advisory Editors for George Ritzer's *Encyclopedia of Sociology*. He is also co-editor of the *Palgrave Studies in Family Sociology* book series.

Dawn E. Alley is Assistant Professor of Epidemiology and Preventive Medicine at the University of Maryland School of Medicine. She received her PhD in gerontology from the University of Southern California in 2006 and held a postdoctoral fellowship as a Robert Wood Johnson Foundation Health and Society Scholar at the University of Pennsylvania. Her research examines predictors of disability in late life, with a focus on obesity, stress, and socioeconomic health disparities. She has collaborated with investigators from multiple population-based longitudinal cohort studies of older persons, including the Health and Retirement Study, the InCHIANTI study, and the Health, Aging, and Body Composition study. She is currently working on a study examining the association between stress, metabolic syndrome, and physical function in older caregivers.

Duane F. Alwin is the Tracy Winfree and Ted H. McCourtney Professor of Sociology and Demography at Pennsylvania State University, where he currently directs the Center on Population Health and Aging. He received a PhD in sociology from the University of Wisconsin in 1972. He is a former chair of the Section on Aging and the Life Course of the American Sociological Association. His research interests include a wide range of phenomena concerned with the connection between human development, social structure, demography, and social change. His research has received continuous support from the National Institute on Aging since 1983. His current scholarship focuses on the implications of population processes for research on cognitive aging, as well as on the linkage between social structures and health inequalities. He has published extensively on these and related topics and is the recipient of numerous prestigious awards, grants, and special university honors.

Monika Ardelt, PhD, is Associate Professor of Sociology and the 2008 Colonel Allan R. and Margaret G. Crow Term Professor at the University of Florida. She is also a 1999 Brookdale National Fellow and a 2005 Positive Psychology Templeton Senior Fellow. She is a Founding Faculty Member and Member of the Advisory Committee of the Center for Spirituality and Health at the University of Florida. Dr. Ardelt received her Diploma (MA) in Sociology from the Johann Wolfgang Goethe-University of Frankfurt/Main in Germany and her PhD in Sociology from the University of North Carolina at Chapel Hill. Her research focuses on successful human development across the life course with particular emphasis on the relations between wisdom, religion, spirituality, aging well, and dying well.

Jan Baars is Professor of Interpretive Gerontology at the University for Humanistics in Utrecht and Professor of Philosophy of the Social Sciences and the Humanities at Tilburg University, The Netherlands. In the 80s he was one of the founders of Critical Gerontology, a paradigm which proved its continuing strength in *Aging, Globalization and Inequality: The New Critical Gerontology* (Baywood, 2006) which he edited with Dannefer, Phillipson and Walker. His other recent work analyzes the role of concepts of time in the study of aging, such as *Aging and Time* (Baywood, 2007) and *Aging: Living through Different Times* (forthcoming, Johns Hopkins University Press).

Robert H. Binstock, PhD, is Professor of Aging, Health, and Society at Case Western Reserve University. A former president of the Gerontological Society of America, he has served as director of a White House Task Force on Older Americans, and chair of the Gerontological Health Section of the American Public Health Association. He has frequently testified before the U.S. Congress. Most of Binstock's 300 publications deal with policies and politics affecting aging. His latest book is *Handbook of Aging and the Social Sciences* (7th edition, 2011) co-edited with Linda K. George.

Colette Browning, PhD, is Director of Monash Research for an Ageing Society and the Healthy Ageing Research Unit at Monash University. Her research focuses on psychosocial approaches to ageing, interventions to optimize healthy ageing, and ageing and culture. She is a Fellow of the Australian Psychological Society, Associate Editor of *Australian Psychologist* and serves on the editorial board of Gerontology. She has more than 100 publications on health and ageing and chronic illness.

Toni Calasanti, PhD, is a Professor of Sociology at Virginia Tech, where she is also a faculty affiliate of both the Center for Gerontology and Women's and Gender Studies. Chosen as the 2008–09 Petersen Visiting Scholar in Gerontology and Family Studies, Oregon State University, she is co-author of *Gender, Social Inequalities, and Aging* and co-editor of *Age Matters: Re-Aligning Feminist Thinking* (both with Kathleen Slevin), and has published in such journals as *Journal of Gerontology: Social Sciences*; *The Gerontologist*; *Social Forces*; *Journal of Aging Studies*; and *Men and Masculinities*. Her recent work focuses on age and gender in relation to spousal carework, and on the intersecting inequalities in relation to aging bodies and the anti-aging industry.

Alfred Chan is currently Chair Professor of Social Gerontology and Director of the Asia-Pacific Institute of Ageing Studies at Lingnan University. Professor Chan's writings on health and social care issues have been published in leading journals on social sciences. His recent works include an interpretation of intergenerational relationships, ageing and long-term care policies in Asia Pacific, the development of health and social-care measurements, quality-of-life and public service consumer satisfaction surveys.

Sheung-Tak Cheng is Chair Professor at the Department of Psychological Studies, Hong Kong Institute of Education. He has published over 70 articles in psychology and gerontology. His research is focused on the intergenerational transfer of social capital, in terms of how the interactions of older and younger people benefit each other, and in terms of younger persons' support to older persons when the latter become dependent. He is a fellow of the American Psychological Association and the Association for Psychological Science, and a recipient of the Outstanding International Psychologist Award from the American Psychological Association (Division 52).

Philippa Clarke is a Research Assistant Professor in the Institute for Social Research at the University of Michigan. Dr. Clarke's research interests are in social gerontology, social epidemiology, life course perspectives, disability, and population health. She is primarily interested in the social determinants of health at both the micro and macro levels of social reality and at the intersection of these levels as well. Her current work examines the social determinants of health trajectories over the adult life course; the role of the built environment in disability progression; and the mental health consequences of social policy changes in retirement.

Peter G. Coleman is Professor of Psychogerontology at the University of Southampton, England, a joint appointment between the Schools of Psychology and of Medicine. He received his PhD in the psychology of ageing from the University of London 1972 and subsequently worked for five years in the Department of Social Gerontology in the Institute of Applied Psychology, Nijmegen, The Netherlands. Most of his research relates to mental health issues, especially the functions of reminiscence and sources of self-esteem and meaning in later life. In more recent years he has focused on the role of religion and spirituality with ageing, and has received funding both from the Economic and Social Research and the Arts and Humanities Research Council (UK) for research on bereavement and spiritual belief, and on the role of ritual, secular as well as religious, in older people's lives. He has co-edited textbooks for the British Society of Gerontology, and made contributions to various handbooks on the subjects of Gerontology, Clinical Psychology and Spirituality. He is a Fellow of the British Psychological Society and an Academician of the Academy of Social Sciences (UK).

Eileen Crimmins, PhD, is the AARP Professor of Gerontology at the University of Southern California where she is currently the director of the USC/UCLA Center on Biodemography and Population Health. She received her PhD in Demography at the University of Pennsylvania. She has been on the Board of Councilors for the National Center for Health Statistics, and a member of several NIA Monitoring Committees. She has been Vice-President of the Population Association of America, Chair of the Section on Aging and the Life Course of the American Sociological Association, and Secretary-Treasurer of the Society for the Study of Social Biology. She serves as Associate Editor for a number of journals. She is a Co PI of the Health and Retirement Survey which is the major longitudinal survey in the United States on aging and health issues. Professor Crimmins currently works on two major areas: trends and differences in population health and the links between social, psychological, and behavioral characteristics and biological risk factors. Professor Crimmins and members of her Center have been instrumental in increasing the collection of data on biological risk in large populations. This has included involvement in the planning, collection, and assessment of data for many surveys around the world including: the Nihon University Longitudinal Study of Aging in Japan, the Mexican Family Life Study, and the Chinese Health and Retirement Study.

Dale Dannefer is Selah Chamberlain Professor of Sociology and chair of the Department of Sociology at Case Western Reserve University. Professor Dannefer received his PhD in Sociology from Rutgers University and has been a fellow at Yale University and at the Andrus Gerontology Center at USC, and a visiting scholar at the Max Planck Institute for Human Development and Education in Berlin. He is a recipient of the Matilda White Riley Distinguished Scholar Award of the Section on Aging and the Life Course of the American Sociological Association. He holds elected offices in both the Behavioral and Social Sciences section of the Gerontological Society of America and the Section of Aging and the Life Course of the ASA, and serves on the editorial boards of the *Journals of Gerontology Social Sciences and Social Forces*. Current research topics include life course theory, cumulative dis/advantage processes and the possibilities of participatory action research for facilitating culture change in long-term care.

Kathryn Douthit, PhD, is Chair and Associate Professor of Counseling and Human Development in the Margaret Warner Graduate School of Education and Human Development at the University of Rochester. Douthit's research interests, focused generally on social determinants of health, reflect her cross-disciplinary training in in immunology and human development. More specifically, Douthit's work explores the relationships between late life brain health and cumulative life course advantage and disadvantage.

Carroll L. Estes, PhD, is Professor of Sociology at the University of California, San Francisco (UCSF). She is Board Chair of both the National Committee to Preserve Social Security and Medicare and the National Committee Foundation. Dr. Estes is founding and first director of the UCSF Institute for

Health & Aging. She is past president of the Gerontological Society of America, the American Society on Aging, and the Association for Gerontology in Higher Education.

Michael Fine is Associate Professor, Head of the Department of Sociology and Deputy Director, Centre for Research on Social Inclusion, at Macquarie University, Sydney, Australia. He received his PhD in anthropology and sociology from the University of Sydney in 1988, for a study of nursing home care in the Netherlands. He researches, publishes and teaches in the fields of ageing, care, human services and social policy. His current research concerns theory and innovations in care; social isolation and social exclusion; and the aged care workforce. He holds or has held a number of significant national and international positions including Deputy-President of RC11 (the Research Committee on Ageing of the International Sociological Association), and President of the Australian Association of Gerontology (NSW Div). He is editorial advisor to a number of international journals and receives regular national and international invitations as a speaker, researcher and policy advisor. His recent book, *A Caring Society? Care and the Dilemmas of Human Service in the Twenty-First Century*, was published by Palgrave MacMillan in 2007.

Jennifer R. Fishman, PhD, is Assistant Professor in the Department of the Social Studies of Medicine and Biomedical Ethics Unit at McGill University. Fishman's sociological research centers on the empirical investigation of the commercialization and commodification of new biomedical technologies. Her work has appeared in the *American Sociological Review*, *Social Studies of Science*, and *Sociology of Health and Illness*. She is currently working on a project exploring the advent and implementation of 'personalized genomic medicine.'

Christine L. Fry is Professor of Anthropology Emerita at Loyola University of Chicago. Her continuing interests are in aging, community studies of older adults, the meaning of age and the life course, and cross-cultural studies of age. She was co-director of Project AGE (Jennie Keith co-director, Charlotte Ikels, Anthony Glascock, Jeanette Dickerson-Putman, Pat Draper and Henry Harpending, co-PIs). She has served as Chair of the Behavioral and Social Science section of GSA as well as Secretary of GSA. She was the founder-President of the Association for Anthropology and Gerontology (AAGE). Her publications focus on the life course; the meaning of age; the meaning of a good old age (well-being); cultural transformations, globalization and old age; and anthropological theories of age. She presently lives and writes in Bisbee, Arizona, the *Queen of the Copper Camps*.

Daniel R. George, PhD, teaches in the Department of Humanities at Penn State College of Medicine. He earned his DPhil and MSc in medical anthropology from Oxford University and earned his BA from The College of Wooster (Ohio). Along with Peter Whitehouse, Dr. George is co-author of *The Myth of Alzheimer's: What You Aren't Being Told About Today's Most Dreaded Diagnosis* (St. Martin's Press, 2008). His doctoral research evaluated whether intergenerational volunteering enhanced quality of life for persons with mild to moderate dementia.

Linda K. George is Professor of Sociology and Associate Director of the Center for the Study of Aging and Human Development at Duke University. She is the author/editor of seven books, more than 200 journal articles, and more than 80 book chapters. She is past President of the Gerontological Society of America and former editor of the Social Sciences section of the *Journal of Gerontology*. She has been Chair of the Aging and the Life Course Section and the Sociology of Mental Health Section of the American Sociological Association. She is co-editor of the *Handbook on Aging in the Social Sciences* (third to seventh editions). Her major research interests include: social factors and depression; the effects of stress and coping, especially the stress of caring for an impaired family member; the relationship between religion and health; and the effects of beliefs and expectancies on health. Among her awards are the Mentorship Award of the Behavioral and Social Sciences Section of the Gerontological Society of America, the Trinity College (Duke University) Distinguished Teaching Award, the John Templeton Prize (1998 and 1999) for Exemplary Papers at the Interface of Science and Human Values, the Kleemeier Award of the Gerontological Society of America in recognition of career contributions in aging research (2002), the Dean's Mentoring Award for Graduate Students (Duke University, 2005) and the Matilda White Riley award of the American Sociological Association for distinguished scholarship on aging and the life course (2004).

Caroline Glendinning is Research Director (Adults, Older People and Carers), in the Social Policy Research Unit, University of York, England, where she leads SPRU's DH-funded research programme on

Choice and Change across the Lifecourse. She is also Chair of the UK Social Policy Association; Associate Director of the National Institute for Health Research School for Social Care Research; and a Trustee of the Thalidomide Trust. Professor Glendinning has a long-standing interest in comparative research and is currently contributing to two cross-European studies of long-term care reform.

Jon Hendricks received the 2008 Kleemeier Award from the Gerontological Society of Ameria for his distinguished research. He has also been recognized by the Association of Gerontology in Higher Education with their Tibbitts Award and by GSA with its Kalish Outstanding Publication Award. He publishes on social issues affecting the aging process and has lectured internationally. Hendricks is currently co-Editor-in-Chief of the *Hallym International Journal of Aging*. Hendricks is affiliated with Oregon State University.

Martha Holstein, PhD, straddles the academic and policy worlds in her work on ethics, aging, and long-term care. She teaches ethics at Loyola University in Chicago and works on LTC policy with the Health and Medicine Policy Research Group also in Chicago. Once a book on ethics and aging is complete, a project shared with two colleagues, she will start work on a book that she's long wanted to write, one that is both personal and scholarly (if that's possible) and focused on being an aging woman. Interdisciplinary by inclination and training, her perspective is feminist and critical. As a relic of the 60s, her idealism is at war with her deepening cynicism about the possibilities for a better, more just society.

Katelin Isaacs is a Doctoral Candidate in the Department of Sociology at Duke University. Her research focuses on inequality throughout the life course with a particular emphasis on gender and retirement. Her dissertation project, titled 'Women's Retirement Insecurity Across U.S. Birth Cohorts,' uses longitudinal data to examine how women's earlier work and family experiences shape their access to subsequent economic resources in retirement, such as Social Security, occupational pensions, and private savings wealth. A National Institute of Aging training grant on the Social, Medical, and Economic Demography of Aging funds her research.

Marja Jylhä, MD, PhD, is Professor of Gerontology at the Tampere School of Public Health, University of Tampere and Director of the national graduate school Doctoral Programs in Public Health. Her interests in research include self-rated health, disability and mortality in old age; social determinants of health; longevity and the oldest-old; and old age as a stage of life in the modern society. She is the Principal Investigator of Tampere Longitudinal Study on Ageing (TamELSA), and Co-PI of the Vitality 90+ Study. At present, she is also actively involved in the European Research Area in Ageing Research (ERA-AGE) and FUTURAGE.

Eva Kahana, PhD, is Robson Professor of Humanities, Sociology, Applied Social Science, Medicine and Nursing, and is the Director of the Elderly Care Research Center. She received her doctorate in human development from the University of Chicago in 1968, and an honorary Doctorate of Humane Letters from Yeshiva University in 1991. Dr. Kahana has published extensively in the areas of stress, coping and adaptation of the aged.

Ruth Katz is Professor of Sociology and senior researcher at the Center for Research and Study of Aging and Head of the Graduate program at the Department of Human Services, the University of Haifa, Israel. Professor Katz received her PhD in Sociology from Tel-Aviv University, Israel and has been a visiting scholar at BYU, Utah and at the Center for Family Studies, Melbourn, Australia. She was on the international board of the Committee on Family Relations of the International Association of Sociology. She serves on the editorial boards of several international journals. She is the recipient of a large number of research grants from competitive national and international foundations like the Us-Israel Bi-National Foundation. She publishes extensively having close to 100 book chapters and articles as well as being co-editor of special issues for family journals. Current research topics include intergenerational family relations, caregiving, alternative family life styles, aging and immigration.

Stephen Katz is Professor of Sociology at Trent University in Peterborough, Canada. He is author of *Disciplining Old Age: The Formation of Gerontological Knowledge* (1996), *Cultural Aging: Life Course, Lifestyle and Senior Worlds* (2005), and numerous book chapters and articles on critical gerontology and the aging body. He is currently working on a critique of the functional aging body in relation to gerontological, neurological and pharmacological expertise on memory, cognitive impairment and the aging brain.

Sally Keeling teaches and supervises research in the postgraduate Gerontology programme of the University of Otago, Christchurch, New Zealand, where her research interests are in the areas of social support, family care, health and wellbeing of older people. She was President of the New Zealand Association of Gerontology (2002–05), and Director of the New Zealand Institute for Research on Ageing, Victoria University of Wellington (2007–09). Her original academic background is in social and cultural anthropology, and she has worked in the aged care and educational sector in senior management positions for many years. Her doctorate in Anthropology was attached to the Mosgiel Longitudinal Study of Ageing, from the University of Otago in 1998. She is involved with current national collaborative research projects including 'Health, Work and Retirement', the LILAC Study (Life and Living in advanced Age: a Cohort Study) and the NZ Longitudinal Study of Ageing.

Jessica Kelley-Moore is an Associate Professor of Sociology at Case Western Reserve University and faculty affiliate of the University Center for Aging and Health; Prevention Research Center; and Center for Reducing Health Disparities. Her research interests focus on social distribution of health disparities over the life course, particularly those related to disability, race, and geographic location.

Hal Kendig, PhD, is Head of the Ageing, Work, and Health Research Unit at the University of Sydney, and National Convenor of the ARC/NHMRC Research Network in Ageing Well. He leads research on Ageing Baby boomers in Australia and Socioeconomic Determinants of Health Inequalities over the Life Course. He is a Fellow of the Academy of Social Sciences of Australia and serves on the Editorial Board of the Journal of Gerontology (Social Sciences). He has more than 180 publications on health, social, and policy aspects of ageing.

Yuzhi Liu graduated from Department of Mathematics at Peking University and currently serves as deputy director of Center for Healthy Aging and Development of Peking University. Her research fields include healthy longevity, gender and family issues as well as research methods in demographic studies. She has published numerous articles in the fields and is active in related projects.

Liz Lloyd is a senior Lecturer in Social Gerontology in the School for Policy Studies in the University of Bristol. Her early career was in community work, including in older people's organizations. She turned to teaching and research and obtained her doctorate from the University of Bristol in 1996. She still maintains an active interest in service-provision, as a trustee of voluntary organizations. She teaches at undergraduate and postgraduate levels on health and social care policies and practices. Her specialist research interest is in the relationship between ageing and the ethics of care, particularly at the end of life. She has engaged in a range of collaborative research projects with colleagues in the UK as well as internationally and she is currently the Principle Investigator on a project in the UK New Dynamics of Ageing Programme, entitled 'Maintaining Dignity in Later Life: Older People's Experiences of Supportive Care'.

Peter Lloyd-Sherlock is Professor of Social Policy and International Development at the School of International Development, University of East Anglia. He previously held lectureships at the London School of Hygiene and Tropical Medicine and the University of Glasgow. Peter has led research projects on population ageing and older people in Argentina, Brazil, South Africa and Thailand. His published books include *Population Ageing and International: From Generalisation to Evidence* (Policy Press, 2010) and *Living Longer. Ageing, Development and Social Protection* (Zed Books/United Nations Research Institute for Social Development, 2004). He was lead author for the United Nations Department of Economic and Social Affairs Guide to the National Implementation of the Madrid International Plan of Action on Ageing (2008).

Ariela Lowenstein is Professor of Gerontology and Director, Center for Research and Study of Aging, the University of Haifa and Head, Dept. of Health Services Management at Max Stern Academic Yezreel College, Israel. Professor Lowenstein received her PhD in Sociology from The Hebrew University of Jerusalem, Israel and has been a fellow at The University of Massachustes Boston and at Kings' College London. She is a recipient of the Distinguished Scholar Rosali Wolf Award from the International Network for the Prevention of Elder Abuse and the recipient of a prize for Scholarly Life Achievements in Gerontology from the Israeli Gerontological Society. She serves on editorial boards of several international journals. She is the recipient of a large number of research grants from competitive national and international foundations including the European Commission. She publishes extensively, having close to

200 book chapters and articles as well as co-editor of four books and of special issues of gerontology journals. Current research topics include intergenerational family relations, caregiving, quality of life, elder abuse and neglect, aging and immigration, gerontological education.

Susan A. MacManus is Distinguished University Professor of Public Administration and Political Science in the Department of Government and International Affairs at the University of South Florida. Her book, *Young v. Old: Generational Combat in the 21st Century* (Westview Press) was designated an Outstanding Academic Book by Choice magazine in 1996. *Targeting Senior Voters*, published in August 2000 by Rowman & Littlefield, predicted problems with punch card ballots among senior citizens before the election and was the first book to focus on problems encountered by disabled voters. She served as Chair of the Florida Elections Commission from 1999 to 2003 and helped the Collins Center For Public Policy, Inc. draft Florida's Help America Vote Act state plan required by Congress to qualify for federal funding under the Help America Vote Act. She also served as an advisor to the Florida Division of Elections on the development of its statewide poll worker training manual. In 2008, MacManus was appointed by the U.S. Election Assistance Commission to two working groups: the Election Management Guidelines Development Working Group on Elderly and Disabled Voters in Long-Term Care Facilities and the Working Group on Media and Public Relations. She has long served as a political analyst for WFLA-TV – Tampa's NBC affiliate station.

Kyriakos S. Markides received his PhD in Sociology in 1976 from Louisiana State University. He is currently the Annie and John Gnitzinger Distinguished Professor of Aging and Director of the Division of Sociomedical Sciences, Department of Preventive Medicine and Community Health at the University of Texas Medical Branch in Galveston. Dr. Markides is the Editor of the *Journal of Aging and Health* which he founded in 1989. He is the author or co-author of over 290 publications most of which are on aging and health issues in the Mexican American population as well as minority aging issues in general. He is currently Principal Investigator of the Hispanic EPESE (Established Population for the Epidemiological Study of the Elderly), a longitudinal study of the health of older Mexican Americans from the five Southwestern states. Dr. Markides is credited with coining the term 'Hispanic Epidemiological Paradox' (with J. Coreil) which is currently the leading theme in Hispanic health. He is also the editor of the *Encyclopedia of Health and Aging* (SAGE, 2007). The Institute for Scientific Information (ISA) has listed Dr. Markides among the most highly cited social scientists in the world. Dr. Markides is the 2006 recipient of the Distinguished Mentorship Award of the Gerontological Society of America, and the 2009 Distinguished Professor Award in Gerontology and Geriatrics from UCLA.

Victor Marshall is Professor of Sociology, University of North Carolina at Chapel Hill, and a Senior Research Scientist at the UNC Institute on Aging. In addition to his interests in theorizing the life course and aging, his research focuses on aging workforce issues and the uses of the life course perspective to both understand and develop public policy.

Claudine McCreadie took a non-graduate diploma in Social Administration at the London School of Economics and, thanks to a suggestion from her tutor Professor Bleddyn Davies, went on to take a degree in Economics at Cambridge. She then had a research job, followed by a lectureship in Social Policy, at Birmingham University and a further research post at the Centre for Studies in Social Policy (later the Policy Studies Institute), before having a longish career break to bring up five children. After occasional Social Policy teaching at Royal Holloway College, she resumed her academic career as a part time Research Associate at the Age Concern Institute of Gerontology, King's College London, working closely with Professor Anthea Tinker on the very disparate topics of the mistreatment of older people, and older people's relationship to technology. Claudine retired in 2007.

Harry R. Moody, PhD, is Director of Academic Affairs at AARP in Wshington, DC. He edits a monthly e-newsletter, 'Human Values in Aging' and is the author of the textbook, *Aging: Concepts and Controversies* (Sage, 2009). He is completing another book *The New Aging Enterprise*.

Angela M. O'Rand is Professor of Sociology and Dean of Social Sciences at Duke University. She has been at Duke for over 30 years publishing research on life course processes related to education, family, work, pension acquisition, health and retirement. Her theoretical interests have focused primarily on cumulative processes of inequality, with a special interest in gender differences.

Frank Oswald is Professor for Interdisciplinary Ageing Research at the Goethe University Frankfurt, Germany. He was trained as a psychologist and received his PhD and habilitation in Psychology at the University of Heidelberg. His research interests are person-environment transaction, contexts of adult development, housing and relocation in old age. He was national project leader of the German part of the European study ENABLE-AGE on the relationships of housing and health. He is author/ co-author of several articles in the area of Environmental Gerontology and Psychology and Chair of the Society for Social and Behavioural Sciences in Gerontology of the German Society of Gerontology and Geriatrics.

David R. Phillips has been Chair Professor of Social Policy in Hong Kong since 1997 and was founder director of the Asia-Pacific Institute of Ageing Studies at Lingnan University, Hong Kong. His research and teaching interests include social gerontology, health and welfare. He has published extensively on ageing, demographic, and socio-epidemiological issues in the Asia-Pacific region and elsewhere. Recent edited books include *Ageing in the Asia-Pacific Region* (Routledge, 2000), *Ageing and Long-term Care – National Policies in the Asia-Pacific* (ISEAS, 2002, edited with Alfred Chan), and *Ageing and Place* (Routledge, 2005, 2008, edited with Gavin Andrews).

Chris Phillipson is Professor of Applied Social Studies and Social Geronology at Keele University. He served as Pro-Vice Chancellor for the University (2005–09) and was also founding Director of the Centre for Social Gerontology (1986–97). He has led a number of research studies in the field of ageing concerned with family and community life in old age, problems of social exclusion, and issues relating to urbanisation and migration. His recent books include *Ageing, Globalization and Inequality* (Baywood, 2006) and *The Futures of Old Age* (Sage, 2006.)

Dana Rosenfeld is Senior Lecturer in Sociology, and a member of the Institute for Life Course Studies and of the Center for Social Gerontology at Keele University, UK. After receiving her PhD in Sociology at the University of California, Los Angeles in 1999, she held a National Institute of Mental Health Postdoctoral Research Fellowship at the Department of Behavioral Science, University of Kentucky. A qualitative sociologist, her interests include identity in historical and interactional context (*The Changing of the Guard: Lesbian and Gay Elders, Identity, and Social Change*, Temple University Press, 2003); gender and sexuality; and health, illness and disability, particularly the experience and interactional management of invisible illness and disability. Dr. Rosenfeld is the lead editor of *Medicalized Masculinities* (Temple University Press, 2006), and is currently researching adherence to medical regimens, the overlaps between illness and disability, and ageing and AIDS. She is on the editorial boards of *Social Theory and Health* and the *Journal of Aging Studies*.

Leslie Roth is currently a graduate student in the Department of Sociology at Duke University. Her dissertation involves archival research into how minorities are constructed as risks to society through moral discourse. She hopes to show that moral discourse surrounding African Americans and Mexican immigrants leads to legislation that helps maintain boundaries around race and class.

Marja Saarenheimo is a psychologist and works as a project leader in the Central Union for the Welfare of the Aged in Finland. Her earlier positions include the University of Tampere, where she worked in the Department of psychology and at the School of Public Health. She has also coordinated the Research programme on ageing in the Academy of Finland in co-operation with Professor Marja Jylhä. Her research interests include geropsychology, mental health in later life, family caregiving, psychotherapy with the elderly, and autobiographical memory. Moreover, she has given courses on narrative and discoursive methods in psychology and social sciences, co-operating with several universities in Finland.

Thomas Scharf is Professor of Social Gerontology and Director of the Irish Centre for Social Gerontology at the National University of Ireland, Galway. He was previously Professor of Social Gerontology and Director of the Centre for Social Gerontology at Keele University, United Kingdom. His research encompasses the fields of social gerontology, social policy and political science, with a particular focus on aspects of disadvantage faced by older people. Thomas Scharf's most recent book is *Critical Perspectives on Ageing Societies* (co-edited with Miriam Bernard; Policy Press, 2007).

James H. Schulz is Professor of Economics Emeritus, Brandeis University. Author of The Economics of Aging (7th edition) and co-author of Aging Nation: The Economics and Politics of Growing Older in America.

Richard A. (Rick) Settersten, Jr. is Professor of Human Development and Family Sciences at Oregon State University. Settersten received his PhD in Human Development and Social Policy from Northwestern University and held fellowships at the Max Planck Institute for Human Development and Education in Berlin, Germany and the Institute for Policy Research at Northwestern. Before moving to OSU, he was Professor of Sociology at Case Western Reserve University. Settersten is a Fellow of the Gerontological Society of America and a member of the MacArthur Foundation Research Network on Transitions to Adulthood and Public Policy. A sociologist of the life course, his research has especially focused the first and last few decades of adult life. He is the author or editor of *On the Frontier of Adulthood*, *Invitation to the Life Course*, and *Lives in Time and Place*, among other books and journal issues.

Merril Silverstein is Professor of Gerontology and Sociology at the University of Southern California. His research focuses on aging within the context of family life. Topics of interest include intergenerational social support, grandparent-grandchild relations, migration in later life, public policy toward caregivers, and international-comparative perspectives on aging families. He has authored over one-hundred publications, three-quarters of which appear in peer-reviewed journals. Dr. Silverstein is principal investigator of the Longitudinal Study of Generations, a project that has tracked multigenerational families over four decades. He is also involved in funded research in China, Sweden, Israel, and the Netherlands. His research has been supported by grants from NIA, NICHD, NSF, Fogarty International Center, Binational Foundation, and AARP. He is a fellow of the Gerontological Society of America, the Brookdale National Fellowship Program, and the Fulbright International Senior Scholars Program. He currently serves as editor-in-chief of the *Journal of Gerontology: Social Sciences*.

Philip Taylor, PhD, joined Monash University in 2010 as Director of Research and Graduate Studies at its Gippsland campus. Prior to this he was Professor of Employment Policy at Swinburne University of Technology where he directed the Business, Work and Ageing Centre for Research. He has researched and written in the field of age and the labour market for over 20 years. He is currently leading major programmes of research at Swinburne considering the management of ageing workforces, and involving extensive employer-based research. His interests include the management of labour supply, individual orientations to work and retirement, employers' attitudes and practices towards older workers and international developments in public policies aimed at combating age barriers in the labour market and extending working life.

Leng Leng Thang is socio-cultural anthropologist with research interests on intergenerational programs, intergenerational relationships, aging and gender. Her field is Asia with a focus on Japan and Singapore. She serves on the editorial board of *Journal of Intergenerational Relationships* and is currently vice chair of International Consortium for Intergenerational Programs. She is Associate Professor and Head of Department of Japanese Studies, National University of Singapore.

Fleur Thomese is an Associate Professor in the Department of Sociology at VU University Amsterdam. After receiving her PhD there at the Faculty of Social and Cultural Sciences, focusing on neighborhoods and networks of older adults, she further developed her interest in interactions between individual and societal change. A modernization perspective is proving useful for understanding recent changes in neighborhoods, personal networks, and their associations. She is also exploring the use of evolutionary theory for understanding the way different social and cultural settings shape grandparenting and its effects on fertility. She greatly enjoys the interdisciplinary and international work environment of social gerontology.

Peter Uhlenberg is Professor of Sociology and Fellow of the Carolina Population Center at the University of North Carolina, Chapel Hill. He is former editor of *Social Forces*, Guest Editor of a forthcoming special issue of *Journal of Aging and Health* in honor of Charles Longino, and editor of *International Handbook of Population Aging* (2009). He was given the 2006 "Matilda White Riley Distinguished Scholar Award" by the Section on Aging and the Life Course of the American Sociological Association and is currently Chair of the section. He currently has 17 grandchildren.

Theo van Tilburg is Professor of Sociology and Social Gerontology at VU University Amsterdam. He is Director of the research program 'Social Context of Aging' and board member of the 'Longitudinal Aging Study Amsterdam', an ongoing interdisciplinary study into aspects of aging since 1991. He is editorial associate editor of *Personal Relationships*; and board member of *International Journal of Ageing and Later Life*; *Journal of Social and Personal Relationships*; *Journal of Gerontology: Social Sciences*. His research interests include the effects of personal network characteristics and social support on well-being and health; life-course developments in personal networks, related to deteriorating health and role loss; societal developments in composition and function of families and personal networks; cross-national studies in loneliness, including the evaluation of interventions.

Christina Victor is Professor of Gerontology and Public Health in the School of Health Sciences and Social Care and Director of the Doctorate in Public Health (DrPH) in the Graduate School at Brunel University. Christina's initial degree was in geography from Swansea University and she followed this with an M Phil from Nottingham. Her PhD was awarded by the Welsh National School of Medicine. Her major research interests are in social relationship in old age and later life, diversity and ageing and the use and evaluation of health services for older people. Christina has written over 180 journal articles and book chapters. Her books include *The Social World of Older People*, (with John Bond and Sasha Scambler-2009 Open University Press); *Ageing in a Consumer Society* (with Ian Jones, Paul Higgs, Richard Wiggins and Martyn Hyde, Policy Press, 2008) , *The Social Context of Ageing* (Routledge, 2005), and *Researching Ageing*, (with Anne Jamieson Open University Press, 2002). Her latest book, *Ageing, Health and Care* is due to be published in 2010 by Policy Press.

Azrini Wahidin is a Reader in Criminology and Criminal Justice at Queen's University, Belfast and was the Programme Director for the undergraduate degree programme in Criminology in the School of Sociology, Social Policy and Social Work. She has also held positions at Keele and Kent Universities before taking up her post at Queen's. She received her PhD in Criminology and Gerontology from Keele University. Her research examined the experiences of the ageing female prison population in England and Wales and she has written extensively in the area of prisons and managing the needs of the ageing prison population. She is an Associate Visiting Professor at the Univesiti Malaya and Middle Tennessee State University. Her key publications are: *Running Out of Time: Older Women in Prison, Criminology, Criminal Justice, Ageing, Crime and Society*, *Foucault and Ageing* and *Risk and Social Welfare*.

Hans-Werner Wahl received his PhD in psychology from the Free University of Berlin in 1989 and was from 1997 to 2005 Professor of Social and Environmental Gerontology at the German Centre for Research on Ageing at the University of Heidelberg. Since 2006, he is Professor of Psychological Aging Research at the Institute of Psychology, University of Heidelberg. His research interests include conceptual and empirical issues related to person-environment relations in later life, the management of age-related chronic conditions, and the understanding of the awareness of aging across the lifespan.

Alan Walker is Professor of Social Policy and Social Gerontology at the University of Sheffield, UK. He has been researching and writing on aspects of ageing and social policy for over 30 years. He is currently Director of the New Dynamics of Ageing Programme (http://www.newdynamics.group.shef.ac.uk/) funded by the AHRC, BBSRC, EPSRC, ESRC and MRC, and of the European Research Area in Ageing (http://www.shef.ac.uk/era-age/). Previously he directed the UK Growing Older Programme (http://www. shef.ac.uk/uni/projects/gop/index.htm) and the European Forum on Population Ageing (http://www.shef. ac.uk/ageingresearch). He also chaired the European Observatory on Ageing and Older People. In 2007 he was given Lifetime Achievement Awards by both the Social Policy Association and the British Society of Gerontology.

Steven P. Wallace, PhD, is professor at the UCLA School of Public Health, Vice-Chair of the Department of Community Health Sciences, and Associate Director of the UCLA Center for Health Policy Research. Dr. Wallace is a leading scholar nationally in the area of aging in communities of color, having published widely on topics including access to long-term care by diverse elderly, disparities in the consequences of health policy changes on racial/ethnic minority elderly, and the politics of aging. Professor Wallace is Co-PI of the coordinating center for NIA's Resource Centers for Minority Aging Research, a past chair of the Gerontological Health Section of the American Public Health Association, is and PI of several projects that provide community-based training on how to use data to advocate for improving access to care for underserved populations in California.

Tony Warnes is Emeritus Professor of Social Gerontology at the Sheffield Institute for Studies of Ageing, University of Sheffield and an Academician of the Academy of Social Sciences. From 1994 to 2000 he was Chair of the British Society of Gerontology, the association of social scientists with special interests in studies of older people, and he is Editor of *Ageing & Society* (Cambridge University Press). His long term research interests have been in the social demography of ageing societies, including health and social inequalities, and in improving care services for frail older people.

Peter J. Whitehouse, MD, PhD, (Psychology) is Professor of Neurology at Case Western Reserve University. He also holds or has held appointments in psychiatry, neuroscience, psychology, nursing, organizational behavior, cognitive science, bioethics, and history. He is evolving into an integrative narrative evolutionary health coach. His long-term interest is developing innovative clinical and learning environments to promote individual and collective health and wisdom. He is the author *The Myth of Alzheimer's* (St. Martin's Press, 2008).

Yi Zeng, PhD, is a Professor at the Center for Study of Aging and Human Development and Geriatric Division, Medical School of Duke University. He is also a Professor at China Center for Economic Research, National School of Development at Peking University, and Distinguished Research Scholar of the Max Planck Institute for Demographic Research. His main research interests are healthy aging, population and family households dynamics and policy analysis. Up to Nov. 30, 2009, he has had 62 articles published in peer-reviewed academic journals in North America and Europe, and 63 articles published in peer-reviewed academic journals in China. He has published nineteen books; among them, eight books were written in English (including three by Springer Publisher and one by the University of Wisconsin Press).

Yun Zhou is Professor of Sociology at Peking University of China. She received her PhD in Sociocultural Anthropology from Arizona State University in 1993 and has been teaching at Peking University since then. Her current research interests in the field of social gerontology include care-giving and care-receiving, gender and aging, as well as social policies for elderly. Professor Zhou published numerous articles on the related topics and is active in the field of aging studies.

Preface

The subject matter of the *SAGE Handbook of Social Gerontology* deals with one of the most enduring and complex issues of human societies: namely, ageing and its social, economic, and cultural determinants. In the 21st Century, ageing has become one of the most challenging issues worldwide, as population ageing is becoming an increasingly visible reality in all societies, and is occurring in a context of globalizing economies and rapid technical and cultural change. These concerns are discussed in this handbook from the standpoint of **social gerontology**, defined here as the application of social science disciplines (e.g., demography, economics, social anthropology, and sociology) to the study and understanding of ageing individuals and ageing populations and the interrelation of each with social forces and social change. Social gerontology is itself linked to the broad study of ageing, or **gerontology**, a multi-disciplinary and (increasingly) interdisciplinary approach drawing upon the behavioural, natural, and social sciences.

In recent decades, the scope of social gerontology has been stretched in a number of significant ways. For example, although the discourse surrounding ageing is often equated with the decades of later life, leading thinkers in gerontology have long recognized that ageing is a lifelong process and a complete understanding of ageing encompasses the full life course. A second example concerns the social significance of age itself, which varies dramatically across social and historical contexts. In particular, the social institutions of late modernity have developed a particular reliance on age as an organizing principle of society, thus making it an enduring feature of social structures even if it is a constantly changing feature of individuals.

Given the above background, the invitation from SAGE to the editors to produce a Handbook focusing on social gerontology was an exciting, albeit challenging, prospect. The opportunity provided was to produce a volume that presented a systematic overview of major advances in social gerontology, drawing upon theoretical and empirical studies undertaken over the past two decades. This period has been of considerable importance to furthering our understanding of social aspects of ageing, with the growth of funded research, the expansion of national societies concerned with the study of ageing, and the pooling of research findings across a variety of international organizations.

Given the above developments, three main objectives were set for the *SAGE Handbook of Social Gerontology*. First, a key concern was to provide a comprehensive assessment of the importance of 'social' aspects of ageing, in all its multi-dimensional and multi-disciplinary guises. Here, we were struck by the continuing relevance of a point made by Malcolm Johnson (2005: 23) in an earlier handbook, that:

> Despite the growing importance of research on the social features of life in the Third and Fourth Ages, which explore the positive potentialities of being an older person, these studies are overwhelmed by the sheer weight of inquiries about illnesses—physical and psychological—and the interventions which might ameliorate their consequences. An analysis of the hundreds of presentations at national and international conferences shows that programmes are little different in structure and balance of content from those of ten, twenty, or even thirty years ago.

Similarly, the dominance of medicalized and biologized approaches as explaining basic processes of ageing has tended to confine the 'social' to the 'ageing-as-problem' discourse—dealing with topics such as individual needs and attitudes at the micro-level, and at the macro-level, the economic and political implications of global population ageing. Yet evidence is mounting to demonstrate that at every social system level, from intimate dyads through work organizations to the state, social processes influence physiological as well as psychological processes of ageing.

Secondly, part of this expansion in the social science literature has itself been driven by the internationalization of research into ageing, with the emergence of major research centres specializing in gerontology across all continents of the world. This itself reflects the nature of population ageing as a global phenomenon, one raising different, kinds of issues for social and cultural systems in, for example, Asia, sub-Saharan Africa, Latin America, and Europe. In this context, a second objective of the *SAGE Handbook of Social Gerontology* has been to illustrate the different challenges associated with ageing by drawing on examples from across a wide range of countries. The task set by the editors was to develop a handbook that demonstrated both the vitality of social science research and the variety of emerging perspectives, these reflecting the complexity and heterogeneity of the different economic and cultural settings in which research is produced. Of course, it has only been possible to draw upon a selection of societies and cultures. We have, however, wherever possible, invited contributors to draw in research from a wide range of countries to illustrate their arguments, and we believe this has added a valuable dimension to the volume.

Thirdly, although contributors to the book come from a range of perspectives within social gerontology, there are underlying themes and concerns running through the different chapters in the *Handbook* and these reflect important developments within the discipline. Over the period from the 1980s through to the 2000s, social gerontology began to embrace a variety of approaches, with important contributions from feminism, social history, political economy, and developmental psychology. In some cases, as Katz (2003: 16) observes, social gerontology began to draw upon areas that were—from the 1990s at least—losing ground in the rest of the social sciences (the influence of Marxism in the area known as critical gerontology being one such example). In other instances, researchers drew upon perspectives from beyond gerontology—the application of cultural studies to the field of ageing representing a case in point. At the same time, the underlying question for all social science approaches to ageing remained that of exploring the basis of social integration in later life, with contrasting points of emphasis around questions of self and identity, the influence of economic relationships, and the impact of social differences (or cumulative advantage and disadvantage) over the life course. Awareness of the impact of globalization also brought significant challenges to social gerontology, with many of its traditional concerns now debated within the context of global and trans-national settings.

As the above summary would suggest, social gerontology itself contains a vast array of themes and concerns, all of these reflecting and building upon the varied concerns of older people and the institutions to which they are linked. At the same time, a shared concern of all the contributors is to examine the way in which social processes are involved in shaping age and the life course, and which also create alternative conceptions and visions about the future of old age (Baars et al., 2006). In bringing together different strands of thinking, the *SAGE Handbook of Social Gerontology* also demonstrates the distinctive contributions which social science can bring to the study of ageing. One illustration of this was provided by Matilda White Riley in her 1986 Presidential Address to the American Sociological Association, where she explored how her interest in the nature of ageing flowed from wider concerns with the impact of social and cultural change. She summarized the link between individual ageing on one side, and social change on the other, as follows:

> In studying age, we not only bring people (women as well as men) ... back into society, but recognise that *both* people and society undergo process and change. The aim is to understand each of the two dynamisms: (1) the *aging of people* in successive cohorts who grow up, grow old, die and are replaced by other people; and (2) the *changes in society* as people of different ages pass through the social institutions that are organized by age. The key to this understanding lies in the interdependence of aging and social change, as each transforms the other (Riley, 1987: 2).

Of course, this *Handbook* examines many complementary points to those raise by Riley, not least those concerned with issues of inequality and difference within cohorts, and the range of mechanisms—historical, economic, bio-social, and so on—that contribute to the social variations that are produced and reproduced in later life. But this idea of exploring the interconnections between ageing on one side, and social change (in all its manifestations) on the other side, provides the underlying pulse to many of the chapters in the handbook and is certainly a fundamental theme of social gerontology itself.

Finally, having set out the main objectives behind this handbook, we might just note how it relates to other such books within the field of ageing. Handbooks have themselves played an important role in providing reviews of sub-fields within the discipline. The first were devoted to surveying progress in gerontological research during the 1950s, and comprise Birren's (1959) *Handbook of Aging and the*

Individual, Tibbitts's (1960) *Handbook of Social Gerontology*, and Burgess's (1960) *Aging in Western Societies*. In the 1970s, a new set of handbooks were developed. These have undergone regular revision and are presently in their 6th editions: *Handbook of the Biology of Aging* (Masoro and Austed, 2006), *Handbook of the Psychology of Aging* (Birren et al., 2006), and *Handbook of Aging and the Social Sciences* (Binstock et al., 2006). At the same time more specialist handbooks were developed, such as the *Handbook of the Humanities and Aging*, edited by Cole et al. (1992), and the *Handbook of Theories of Aging* edited by Bengston et al. (2nd edn. 2009). Finally, *The Cambridge Handbook of Age and Ageing* (Johnson, 2005) aimed to provide an overview both of literature from the social and behavioural sciences as well as an assessment of key developments in biomedicine.

We see this volume as providing a complementary resource to the more recent Handbooks listed above. This volume is the first since Tibbitts's 1960 volume to set out the full scope of social gerontology, a field that has expanded hugely since that time across the full range of the social sciences. The specially commissioned essays have been written by leading international experts in their respective fields. The volume is organized into five parts, each exploring different aspects of research into social aspects of ageing:

1 *Disciplinary overviews:* the chapters in Section One aim to provide summaries of findings from key disciplinary areas within social gerontology, including demography, economics, epidemiology, environmental perspectives, history, social anthropology, and sociology.
2 *Social relationships and social differences:* the chapters in Section Two explore the key social institutions and social structures influencing the lives of older people. Topics here include social inequality, gender, and ageing, the role of religion, inter-generational ties, social networks, and friendships in later life.
3 *Individual characteristics and change in later life:* the chapters in Section Three examine different aspects of individual ageing, including self and identity, cognitive processes, the experience of time, age and wisdom, and also biosocial interactions and their impact on physical and psychological ageing.
4 *Comparative perspectives and cultural innovations:* the chapters in Section Four review variations in the experience of growing old from a range of social and cultural standpoints within and beyond late modernity. Topics include ageing and development, ageing in a global context, migration, and cross-cultural perspectives on grandparenthood.
5 *Policy issues:* Section Five, the final Section, examines some of the main policy concerns affecting older people across the world. Topics include developments in social policy, long-term care, technology and older people, end-of-life issues, work and retirement, crime and older people, and the politics of old age.

The SAGE Handbook of Social Gerontology thus draws together a range of multidisciplinary and interdisciplinary perspectives on ageing. The editors are immensely grateful for the dedication and hard work of contributors. The handbook was conceived as an attempt to draw together a fresh assessment of findings relating to social, economic, and cultural aspects of growing old, drawing upon some of the best researchers and scholars working in the field. We hope that this volume goes some way both to confirming the strength of research in social gerontology as well as stimulating consideration of new areas for theoretical and empirical development.

Dale Dannefer
Chris Phillipson
August 2009

REFERENCES

Baars, J., Dannefer, D., Phillipson, C., and Walker, A. (eds) (2006) *Aging, Globalization and Inequality.* Amityville, NY: Baywood.

Bengston, V.L., Gans, D., Putney, N.M., and Silverstein, M. (eds) (2009) *Handbook of Theories of Aging.* New York: Springer (1st edn. 1999).

Binstock, R., George, L., Cutler, S., Hendricks, J. and Schultz, J. (2006) (eds) *Handbook of Aging and the Social Social Sciences.* New York: Elsevier Academic Press (1st edn. 1976).

Birren, J. (ed.) (1959) *Handbook of Aging and the Individual.* Chicago: University of Chicago Press.

Birren, J., Schaie, W., Abeles, R., Gatz, M., and Salthouse, T. (2006) (eds) *Handbook of the Psychology of Aging.* New York: Elsevier Academic Press (1st edn. 1976).

Cole, T.R., Van Tassel, D.D., and Kastenbaum, R. (eds) (1992) *Handbook of the Humanities and Aging.* New York: Springer.

Burgess, E. (ed.) (1960) *Aging in Western Societies.* Chicago: University of Chicago Press.

Johnson, M. (ed.) (2005) in association with Bengston, V.L., Coleman, P., and Kirkwood, T. *The Cambridge Handbook of Age and Ageing.* Cambridge: Cambridge University Press.

Katz, S. (2003) 'Critical gerontological theory: intellectual fieldwork and the nomadic life of ideas', in S. Biggs, A. Lowenstein, and J. Hendricks (eds), *The Need for Theory: Critical Approaches to Social Gerontology.* Amityville, NY: Baywood, pp. 15–31.

Masoro, E. and Austed, S. (2006) (eds) *Handbook of the Biology of Aging.* New York: Elsevier Academic Press (1st edn. 1976)

Riley, M.W. (1987) 'On the significance of age in sociology', *American Sociological Review,* 52, 1–14.

Tibbitts, C. (ed.) (1960) *Handbook of Social Gerontology.* Chicago: University of Chicago Press.

Acknowledgements

This book is the product of dedicated work and deep collaboration, between many skilled and supportive colleagues – authors and editors, as well as critical readers and support staff. Without such collaboration, the volume would not have been possible to produce. We would like first to express our appreciation to the authors of these chapters, on whose cutting-edge expertise, careful scholarship the entire project rests. We would also like to thank those on both sides of the Atlantic, whose names are not so visible, but whose work has been critical, to the completion of this project. For work done in the USA, thanks go above all to Debra Klocker and also to Michelle Rizzuto in the Department of Sociology at CWRU. We also relied on the editorial expertise of Dale Dannefer's research assistants, Mary Ellen Stone, and Sherri Brown. For editorial work in the UK, many thanks to Sheila Allen, Sue Humphries and Jenny Liddle at Keele University, who provided substantial help and support. Finally, we are immensely grateful to Sage who have kept faith with the project and who have been consistently helpful and encouraging at all phases of the work.

Table 5.1 United Nations (2007) *World Population Ageing 2007*. Department of Economic and Social Affairs/Population Division. New York: United Nations. Reprinted with permission.

Table 5.2 United Nations (2007) *World Population Ageing 2007*. Department of Economic and Social Affairs/Population Division. New York: United Nations. Reprinted with permission.

Table 5.3 United Nations (2007) *World Population Ageing 2007*. Department of Economic and Social Affairs/Population Division. New York: United Nations. Reprinted with permission.

Table 5.8 United Nations (2005) *The Living Arrangements of Older People Around the World*. Department of Economic and Social Affairs/Population Division. New York: United Nations. (Available at http://www.un.org/esa/population/publications/livingarrangement/covernote.pdf). Reprinted with permission.

Table 5.9 United Nations (2005) *The Living Arrangements of Older People Around the World*. Department of Economic and Social Affairs/Population Division. New York: United Nations. (Available at http://www.un.org/esa/population/publications/livingarrangement/covernote.pdf). Reprinted with permission.

Table 5.10 United Nations (2005) *The Living Arrangements of Older People Around the World*. Department of Economic and Social Affairs/Population Division. New York: United Nations. (Available at http://www.un.org/esa/population/publications/livingarrangement/covernote.pdf). Reprinted with permission.

Tables 15.1 United Nations (2002) *World Population Aging 1950–2050*. Department of Economics and Social Affairs, Population Division. Reprinted with permission.

Table 15.3 United Nations (2002) *World Population Aging 1950–2050*. Department of Economics and Social Affairs, Population Division. Reprinted with permission.

Fundamental and Disciplinary Perspectives on Ageing

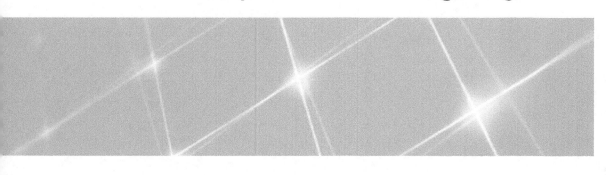

The Study of the Life Course: Implications for Social Gerontology

Dale Dannefer and
Richard A. Settersten, Jr.

INTRODUCTION

A leading policy expert of the American Association of Retired Persons (AARP), John Rother (2009), has observed that the life-course perspective is the 'missing element in the public policy debate' on ageing (2009). The significance of the life course has also been emphasized by Robert Butler, who joined colleagues to issue a call for a 'new paradigm' of gerontological and geriatric research and practice anchored in a life-course approach (Butler et al., 2008). Across multiple societies, the fields of medicine and epidemiology are being transformed by life-course methods as investigators probe the long-term effects of early nutritional status, toxin exposure and other risks on age-related diseases, which create differential patterns of ageing and outcomes in old age (e.g., Ben-Schlomo and Kuh, 2002; Gluckman and Hanson, 2006a, 2006b). In China and elsewhere, increasing public and governmental concern is focusing on old age by reference to earlier life-course events – specifically whether or not one's job provided retirement pension (see Chapters 32 and 43). In advanced industrial societies around the world, many older people are engaging in a diverse array of activities and social involvement that build on earlier life experiences and shape the nature of their lives as older

people – whether in continuing labor force participation, volunteering, or recreational or creative activities. In these and innumerable other examples, often from unexpected arenas of policy and research, there is a growing acknowledgment that ageing and old age cannot be understood, either at the individual or societal levels, without paying attention to the cumulated life practices and experiences of ageing individuals.

What is the significance of this expanding emphasis on the life course? Most fundamentally, it represents the recognition of mounting evidence that demonstrates that the physical, psychological, and social aspects of individual ageing are often not dictated by chronological age per se, but instead shaped by a host of factors that cumulate in individuals over decades of living. This is a significant departure from the conventional practice of thinking about age in normative terms – reflected in ideas like 'normal ageing' or natural 'stages' of life. We now know that, even in childhood and adolescence, age by itself is not enough to define individual lives (Rogoff, 2002). This is especially true in later life, when variability is greatest among age peers (Crystal and Shea, 2003; Nelson and Dannefer, 1992).

This emphasis marks a paradigmatic shift away from viewing ageing as a *general or immutable process of organismically governed change* and old age as a distinct phase of life to be understood on its own terms, and instead toward understanding ageing as an *experientially contingent reality* involving continuous interactions between the body, psyche, and social world. Thus, patterns of ageing are organized not only by organismically based changes but also are fundamentally dependent on one's social circumstances, opportunities and experiences over prior decades. Old age is no longer viewed as embodying a set of common and universal experiences, nor as a dark period of inevitable decline. Rather, old age is recognized as comprised of a set of experiences that are highly variable across individuals, groups, and nations, and highly contingent on health, wealth, social relationships, social policies, and other factors.

It is notable that this shift in the conception of ageing is now occurring in medicine, epidemiology and public health, and the policy sciences. Yet in no field is the emergence of the life-course perspective more significant than in research and theory in gerontology. Indeed, it was sociologists of ageing who first originated the life-course perspective and gave it conceptual structure (Cain, 1964; Clausen, 1972; Elder, 1974, 1975; Riley et al., 1972), just as psychologists of ageing did in originating the life-span perspective (e.g., Baltes, 1968; Schaie, 1965).[1]

What the life-course perspective brings to gerontology is the recognition that life experiences, which are inevitably organized by social relationships and societal contexts in which individuals are located, powerfully shape how people grow old. The life-course perspective seeks to make visible the significance of 'macro,' or 'distal,' social forces, including the social institutions and cultural practices that organize everyday life routines, and unique historical events and periods of social change (see Kohli, 2007; Mayer, 2004; Settersten and Gannon, 2005). The life-course perspective also emphasizes the power of *social ties*, the ways in which the lives of individuals are intimately affected by the circumstances and actions of others.

Finally, the life-course perspective shines a spotlight on the significance of age, not only as a property of individuals but also as a property of social structure. Comparative studies have revealed that the meanings of age and old age, and even the very awareness of age, vary historically and cross-culturally. Societies differ in how age is regarded, and the significance of age in societies may change over time. This clearly happened with the development of advanced industrial societies. The late 19th and 20th centuries saw a rise in 'age consciousness' (Chudacoff, 1989), as age became an increasingly central basis of social organization and regulation in arenas such as education and work. Age consciousness – a feature of a culture that is

distinct from the biological ageing of individuals – becomes part of the social environment that has an effect on how people age. It shapes their ideas about what is appropriate ageing through the production of age norms, which through the 20th century were increasingly calibrated to specific chronological age (e.g., Kett, 1977; Lawrence, 1984; Neugarten, 1979; Settersten and Hagestad, 1996). Research on the emergence of age consciousness has focused on the United States, but similar developments occurred in Europe and elsewhere (Gillis, 1974; Kohli, 1986a).

From the vantage point of life-course analysis, then, the concept of age is itself a central object of inquiry, not a taken-for-granted part of the world. Yet in everyday life, age often *is* precisely a taken-for-granted part of the world. When an idea or phenomenon that is social in origin is assumed to be an inevitable aspect of human nature, it is an idea that requires deconstruction. The social practice of mistakenly attributing social arrangements to human nature or other natural forces is called *naturalization*. When age becomes a central organizing reality of society, and a strong normative sense of 'age-appropriate behavior' and perceived danger of being 'off time' emerge in cultural beliefs and practices, age becomes naturalized. It is the task of sociological analysis to deconstruct the processes by which this occurs. This strong emphasis on social processes does not mean that we do not recognize the importance of ontogenetic, organismic processes. Instead, it reflects a growing recognition of the extent to which the organism itself is shaped by context and experience in the process of development (Loehlin, 2007; Perry and Svalavitz, 2006) and through the life course (Langa et al., 2008; see Douthit and Marquis, this volume).

AGE AND THE LIFE COURSE: HISTORICAL PERSPECTIVES AND FOUNDATIONAL PRINCIPLES

The concept of the life course was first articulated in sociology in Leonard Cain's (1964) classic paper, 'Life-Course and Social Structure.' Cain's paper offered an initial conceptualization of some of the key paradigmatic dimensions of the life course that would later become central to life-course analysis. Cain pointed to age as a feature of both individuals and social structure, and thus anticipated elaboration of the life course as a major basis of social organization. The articulation of age as a property of both social systems and individuals was given its most elegant and systematic formulation in Matilda Riley's initial presentation of the age stratification (Riley et al., 1972), of which the life course was an integral component (Clausen, 1972). Cain's early paper and the Riley approach laid the conceptual foundations for subsequent elaboration of the life course as a social institution, an idea that developed both in Europe (e.g., Kohli, 1986; Mayer, 1986) and in the United States (Dannefer and Uhlenberg, 1999; Hogan, 1981; Meyer, 1986; Settersten, 1999).

In the late 1960s and early 1970s, Glen Elder began to analyze data from several classic longitudinal studies, which led to the publication of his classic book *Children of the Great Depression* (1974, 1999) and a prolific programme of life-course research (see Elder and Johnson, 2003). Elder's work has consistently examined how discrete events and changes leave their imprint on the life courses of individuals and cohorts, and how their effects are mediated through family environments.

While Cain focused on the life course as systematically related to social institutions and foreshadowed the later elaboration of the life course as a full-blown feature of social structure, scholars like Elder, John Clausen, and others developed a predictive approach that sought to understand outcomes in later life as a consequence of early life experiences. Below, we discuss these two distinct approaches, which we call the 'personological' and the 'institutional.' But first it will be useful to set forth some general principles that apply to both of these approaches to the life course.

Life-course perspective, life-span development, and cohort analysis

Both the *life-course perspective* in sociology and a counterpart intellectual tradition in the discipline of psychology, *life-span development* (Baltes, 1968; Riegel, 1976), emerged as sites of intellectual excitement in the late 1960s and 1970s. Closely allied with a rapidly expanding new energy in the sociology of age (Riley, 1973, Riley et al., 1972), both of these traditions were initially catalyzed by the near-simultaneous introduction both in psychology (Baltes, 1968; Schaie, 1965) and sociology (Riley, 1973; Ryder, 1965) of cohort analysis as a radically new and essential methodological approach to understanding ageing.

An appreciation of cohort analysis is a key foundational element of the life-course perspective. Cohort analysis demonstrated the force of changing social conditions in altering patterns of development and ageing, and provided a method for linking lives and history. A cohort is generally defined as a collection of individuals who enter a system at a common time or time interval. In studies of individual development and ageing, the entry point is typically defined by the year of birth. Cohort entry provides an anchor point from which individual trajectories can be constructed and change can be tracked, allowing comparisons across multiple cohorts. Before cohort analysis, research on 'age change' (or maturational effects) and 'age differences' almost exclusively assumed that patterns of individual ageing could be inferred by examining cross-sectional (point in time) age differences. Comparing cross-sectional findings with longitudinal (over time) trajectories made clear that the two often bore little resemblance to each other, and that to infer biographical patterns from cross-sectional data entailed a risk of a *life-course fallacy* (Riley, 1973, Riley et al., 1972).

The introduction of cohort analysis had a cataclysmic impact. It stimulated interest and investment in longitudinal research, compelled a permanent state of caution regarding the casual use of cross-sectional data to infer maturational (age-based) changes, and brought with it a host of new methodological challenges and complexities. In short, it established a new methodological paradigm and standard for how to approach research on ageing.

Distinctively human features of ageing and development: organismic foundations of the life course

In this section, we discuss distinctive features of human development and ageing which, because of their universal and formative significance, comprise foundational principles for understanding life-course dynamics. 'Cohort effects' and other forms of environmental influence may be found for nonhuman species. However, the magnitude of the effects of experience and social context in shaping development and ageing is especially pervasive and enduring in the human case because of several distinct characteristics of *Homo sapiens*. It is because of these features that life-course experiences matter so much in shaping patterns of ageing, and it is because of them that one's chronological age and bodily processes of ageing cannot, by themselves, account for how human beings develop and age over the life course.

A primary element in these foundational characteristics is the inherently interactive and contingent character of human growth and development. Humans are, in psychologist Barbara Rogoff's

(2002) terms, 'hard-wired for flexibility.' As Berger and Luckmann emphasized in their classic sociological treatise, *The Social Construction of Reality* (1967), human beings are, from the beginning of life to the end of it, 'unfinished' by biological determinants, and are formed and continuously reformed in the course of everyday life. The flexibility and unfinished nature of the human organism are, of course, most apparent in the early years of life, when developments that will be decisive for later life outcomes are set in motion.

But these characteristics are not restricted to the early years. They continue throughout life, reflected in the potentials of older people for lifelong learning, curiosity, and the continued evolution of the self. The 'world-openness' (to use Berger and Luckmann's phrase) of adult and elder humans, is an indicator of *neoteny* (Bromhall, 2003; Dannefer, 1999; Gould, 1977). Neoteny (sometimes called 'juvenescence' [Montagu, 1989]) refers to the fact that, in comparison with other species, adult humans are much more like human children psychologically and even morphologically (Gould, 1977). Neoteny refers to the cluster of features that give this lifelong youthfulness to *Homo sapiens*.

Potentials for learning, change, and growth in adulthood and old age are therefore constitutional and universal features of human ageing. This is why, for example, nonagenarians and centenarians can continue to gain new knowledge and acquire new skills in a wide array of areas (e.g., Snowdon, 2002). Because of the inherent responsiveness of the human organism, and because human individuals are always located in culturally specific social contexts, patterns of physical and mental ageing are socially organized in ways that are meant to promote fundamental flexibility. This does not mean that there are no universal features of development or no developmental or organismic imperatives (Dannefer and Perlmutter, 1990). But it does mean that there is a more significant way in which individuals are involved in development – through their own actions in the world.

This point introduces a second distinctive principle for approaching the life course: the principle of human action as *world-construction*, and human beings as *world-constructing actors*. Acting in the world, individuals do more than simply 'produce their own development' (Lerner and Walls, 1999); they simultaneously co-constitute relationships with others and their own personhood (Dannefer, 1999; Mascolo et al., 1999). This continuously occurring interactive process is inescapably organized by social institutions and practices, beginning with the fundamental institution of language. To acknowledge that experiences and contexts shape individual life patterns and activity routines, and thus unavoidably *organize* the individual expression of agency, does not negate the significance of expressing agency. It clarifies that the expression of agency always operates within specific social settings – what Settersten (1999) called 'agency within structure.' Indeed, this recognition only enhances the significance of agency because it makes clear that agentic action is essential and constitutive of social relationships and social context.

These conditions begin at birth, as each of us enters the world and human community helpless and unstructured, with our entire being shaped by language and taken-for-granted practices of everyday life. Our actions, like those of others around us, largely conform to and reproduce those conventions. We are constituted within pre-existing systems of social relationships and, as our lives reflect the rhythms and characteristics of these systems, the systems are also reproduced.

Human world-construction, however, also has inherent impulses for innovation and change, deriving in part from the imagination and creativity of human consciousness. This is why human societies are unique in their ability to undergo change on scales of magnitude and rapidity that are unknown to other species. Of course, whether the actual change that occurs corresponds to the goals and intentions of those who implemented it is, however, another question. This can well be demonstrated by familiar experiences of the 'linked lives' – as when parental efforts at sanction and control backfire, leading to more radical but unintended change in a teenager's actions. This is a familiar illustration of the sociological principle of unintended consequences (Merton, 1968). Life-course processes thus cannot be separated from dynamics of stability and change.

These established principles have implications both for scholars who see ageing and the life course as determined by organismic processes (e.g, Gutmann, 1987; Levinson, 1997), and also for those who emphasize individual choice, freedom, and intentional action detached from social structure (e.g, Gilleard and Higgs, 2005). As organismic processes meet social environments, aspects of those environments open or close, accelerate or delay, and in many cases shape their expression. Moreover, such processes are largely mediated by the actor's conscious intentionality. Regarding choice, not only are the degree and types of options that individuals have facilitated or constrained by their circumstances, but their very desires and interests are also shaped by culturally (and often commercially) imposed definitions of what to strive for as 'the good life' (e.g., Ewen 1977; Ewen and Ewen, 1992; Schor, 2004).

DIMENSIONS OF LIFE-COURSE THEORIZING AND THEIR RELEVANCE FOR SOCIAL GERONTOLOGY

The life-course perspective encompasses several major types of phenomena and explanatory paradigms. One major paradigmatic approach – the *personological* – attempts to use key features of early life experience to predict and account for outcomes later in life, either for individuals or for populations. A second paradigmatic approach – the *institutional* – does not focus on individuals at all, but instead analyzes the life course as a social and political construct, often consisting of more or less explicitly defined age-graded stages that are reinforced in institutions, created by social policy, or legitimated by social and behavioral sciences. It therefore refers to a part of the social and cultural definition of reality that broadly organizes both people's lives and their 'knowledge' about age and ageing. We turn to each of these approaches below.

The personological paradigm

The role of early experience in shaping later-life outcomes

The personological paradigm is well exemplified in the influential research of Glen Elder, which has drawn heavily on the Berkeley Guidance, Berkeley Growth, and Oakland Growth Studies, begun in 1928–29. Elder brought great prominence to the life course as a field of study in North America and beyond, and his work has provided a nuanced view of how outcomes later in the life course may be affected by earlier life experiences. His work has especially demonstrated how the social conditions of one's youth and early adult years have a lasting influence in psychological and social characteristics. Elder's analysis of the intersection of biography and social change has also demonstrated the importance of timing – the effect of events may turn out to be quite different, depending on the age at which an individual encounters them.

The Oakland and Berkeley samples provided an exceptional lens for analyzing the role of timing in the nature of the effects of change because the samples were based on different birth cohorts. Since the Oakland sample was born in 1920–21 and the Berkeley samples in 1928–29 they were at very different ages when they encountered key events. Elder's landmark *Children of the Great Depression* (1974/1999) examines in detail the life-course patterns and outcomes of these study participants. The effects of the Depression differed for boys and girls, by social class, and by whether families were economically deprived. Boys in deprived households more often aspired to or entered adult roles earlier than peers, but showed little evidence of persistent disadvantage from the Depression.

In contrast, Oakland females were more vulnerable psychologically, especially those from deprived families. Elder found that they had to assume domestic responsibilities as their mothers sought work, they felt less well-dressed, more excluded and self-conscious, and they experienced more hurt feelings and mood swings. Relative to non-deprived girls, they married earlier and more frequently stopped working after marriage or childbirth.

Born nearly a decade later, Berkeley children had different experiences than their older Oakland counterparts (Elder and Caspi, 1990). As very young children, Berkeley subjects were dependent on the direct care of parents and vulnerable to family instability and conflict. Elder attributed their differential outcomes to the difference in their ages when hardship hit. Such findings have led life-course scholars to emphasize *timing* as a key determinant of how events shape life-course outcomes.

Another key finding of Elder's work relates to the interconnected nature of the Great Depression and military service during World War II (e.g., Elder and Chan, 1999). For example, the great majority (90 per cent) of Oakland men served in World War II. For many of those from deprived families, military service provided a chance to 'knife off' disadvantaged pasts, recalibrating one's position in relation to powerful structures of opportunity.

In later life, observed differences among age peers have been traced to such earlier experiences. Here, as in some of the analyses in *Children,* a notable theme of Elder's work has been that some degree of hardship in youth or early adulthood – so long as it is experienced on the foundation of some key forms of environmental support and resources – is correlated with positive outcomes later in the life course. For example, by the late 1960s, 40 years after the Great Depression, when the mothers of the Berkeley children had reached in old age, middle-class mothers who had experienced hardship and deprivation in the Depression years were faring better than any other subgroups in terms of psychological functioning, including middle-class mothers who were not deprived, while comparably deprived working-class mothers were faring the poorest of any group (Elder and Liker, 1982).

A popular interpretation for such findings proposes that coping skills and resilience may be nurtured in an effort to deal with hardship. Similar associations between teenage characteristics and late-life outcomes were also found by Clausen (1993), who also used data from the Berkley and Oakland studies. In offering interpretations for the differences observed in analyzing the diversity of life pathways, Elder, Clausen, and other life-course scholars have tended to emphasize individual choice-making as an irreducible component of individual lives, even though it is clear that childhood and subsequent experiences have produced differential risks that reverberate into later life, and which may have little or nothing to do with individual choice.

Critical perspectives on the personological paradigm

Any programme of research that is so extensive and so broad in its explanatory objectives as the personological approach to life-course studies is bound to generate controversy and critical analysis. Thus it is not surprising that, its unquestioned and influential contributions notwithstanding, a number of theoretical problems with this tradition of work have been identified, especially from a sociological perspective. Concerns have been raised over conceptual and measurement problems associated with the casual and uncritical use of the notion of 'agency' (see Dannefer, 1999; Dannefer and Uhlenberg, 1999; Settersten and Gannon, 2005; and also Chapter 22), a problem that has received a response in a recent effort by Hitlin and Elder (2007) to address the concept more systematically.

A second and more specific problem that characterizes much research in this tradition of life-course research is *Time One Encapsulation* (Dannefer and Kelley-Moore, 2009; see also Hagestad and Dannefer, 2001). This term refers to the practice of predicting later-life outcomes by measuring environmental factors only at the first observation period, or 'Time One,' without considering the continued explanatory potentials of similar (and likely correlated) social-causal factors later in the life course. For example, in the case just recounted of Elder's findings, we cannot know the extent to which the association between Time One causal factors (social status and hardship status in early life) and Time Two outcome (psychological functioning later in life) is a direct relationship, compared with the extent to which it is dependent upon the kind of work and family systems into which the individuals in question spent the intervening years. In subsequent work, Elder and associates have conducted some analyses that respond to this problem by including more proximate contextual variables (e.g.,Wilson et al., 2007).

The limitations on explanatory understanding imposed by Time One Encapsulation are made clear in recent research that takes a 'developmental origins' approach in medicine and epidemiology. This research focuses on the relationship between one's early environmental circumstances and subsequent lifestyle and disease processes (Gluckman and Hanson, 2006a, 2006b). An integral part of this approach is a systematic examination of the causal role of experiential factors in adulthood, and the health effects of a 'mismatch' between childhood and adult experiences. For example, individuals who survive nutritional deprivation in childhood have a good chance of developing into robust and resilient healthy adults – unless in adulthood they begin to engage in the stereotypically unhealthy patterns so characteristic today, including being sedentary and consuming high-fat diets, which lead to 'chronic positive energy balance,' which has devastating consequences for health (e.g., Gluckman and Hanson, 2006a, 2006b). Thus, health outcomes cannot be understood by looking at childhood lifestyle alone, but only by their interaction with practices in adulthood.

Another set of critical concerns about life-course analysis are methodological. For the study of ageing, early experiences are important to examine because of their potentially decisive importance, yet their effects are challenging to demonstrate. Extending back so many decades, the life course becomes an endogenous causal system that seeks to explain the present while overlooking more proximate social effects with which earlier events may be correlated, thus creating a risk of spurious interpretations. The goal of understanding lives over many decades makes demanding requests of theories, methods, and data that often cannot be accommodated. The longer lives are studied, the more difficult it becomes to trace connections, and the possible connections seem endless and tenuous. It is hard to know which variables are important, when they are important, how they might be arrayed in sequence, and what processes and mechanisms drive these connections. Variables are likely to be multiply confounded not only at single time points in time but also, especially, across multiple time points. These complexities aside, few longitudinal studies are long enough to explore connections between old age and earlier life periods, though major investments are now being made in these directions.

Population patterns over the life course

Another important tradition of work examines life-course outcomes, not at the level of individual but at the population level, where a cohort's collective transition behavior (e.g., Burkhauser et al.,

2009; Hogan, 1981; O'Rand and Henretta, 1999) or resource inequality characteristics are of interest (Dannefer and Kelley-Moore, 2009). One expanding tradition of such work was stimulated by observations of the diversity of the aged (e.g., Riley, 1980; Rowe and Kahn, 1987, 1997) and by the concern with an emergent 'two worlds of ageing' (Crystal, 1982). The observation that diversity and inequality tend to be greater among older people than any other age group prompted the question of why, and led some researchers to begin to examine processes that might account for this circumstance (Crystal and Shea, 2003; Crystal and Waehrer, 1996; Dannefer and Sell, 1988; Easterlin et al., 1993; Maddox and Douglass, 1974). Such analysts study inequality and other distributional characteristics of a property such as income or health within a cohort.

A noteworthy set of developments in this area revolve around the growing interest in the concept of cumulative advantage and disadvantage (Crystal and Shea, 2003; Dannefer, 2003, 2009; Ferraro and Shippee, 2009; see also Chapters 9, 20 and 25). Cumulative dis/advantage refers to the tendency for inequality to increase among age peers as they move through the life course. This approach has focused attention on the intersection between the processes of ageing over the life course and the *socioeconomic gradient*, which has established a strong connection between economic resources and health (e.g,. Link and Phelan, 1995; Marmot, 2004). The cumulative dis/advantage perspective suggests that the relatively high levels of observed diversity and inequality in old age partly reflect processes of social stratification that operate over the collective life course of each succeeding cohort as it ages. A piece of good news is that these are potentially modifiable processes; both public and private pension developments over the 20th century have had the effect of substantially reducing old age poverty compared to a century ago (see Chapter 3).

The institutional paradigm

A second major approach to the life course does not focus on patterns of individual change at all, but on the massively powerful social construction of life stages by social policy and cultural understanding. A simplified version of the institutionalized life course is exemplified by the 'three boxes of life' – schooling upfront, work in the middle, and retirement at the end. European scholars have placed more emphasis on this paradigm of life- course studies, analyzing the age-graded policies and practices that are the basis for a legally, culturally, and scientifically defined set of prescriptions for organizing lives and their impact in organizing and regulating individual experiences and opportunities based on age. This approach has also received considerable attention in the United States, which has examined historical shifts in the actual demography of specific transitions such as home-leaving, education, work, marriage and parenthood, and retirement, as well as the age-based social expectations related to them. From late 19th century through to the latter part of the 20th century, evidence has pointed to a growing standardization (i.e., regularity) of life experiences (Burkhauser, 2009; Hogan, 1981; Modell, 1989; Settersten et al., 2005), which is consistent with the growing homogenization of life stages more generally, from 'childhood' and 'youth' through 'old age' (e,g., Gillis, 1974; Kett, 1977; Laslett, 1991).

Age norms and the rise of age consciousness in modern societies

These trends are also consistent with the historical emergence of age norms, which have been a significant reality-defining component in late modern societies (Chudacoff, 1989): that is, lives are socially structured – organized and regulated by the institutional apparatuses of government policy, professional expertise, and culturally imposed definitions of reality – and age is a central part of how life is structured. Yet precisely how age matters, and in what spheres of life it may matter more or less, is a matter of debate among psychologists, sociologists, and demographers who have different definitions and theoretical starting points (for a review, see Settersten, 2003).

In essence, age norms are social prescriptions for, or proscriptions against, involvement in 'inappropriate' activities or roles at particular ages (e.g., the age by which one should leave home, or get married). To carry the force of a norm, there must be a high degree of consensus about the rules. Moreover, the rules are enforced through overt sanctions and other mechanisms of social control. If an age-normative system is operating, individuals will be aware of the sanctions for violating norms.

Age norms often have a very general plausibility, shared at the societal level (e.g., Settersten and Hagestad, 1996). As is true for norms generally, their regulatory power is realized in the course of everyday interaction in families, schools, the workplace, or other local settings among people who know and interact with one another often (e.g, Lawrence, 1996; Settersten, 2003). Evidence also suggests that the degree of formal age structuring (via institutions and policies) may be stronger in spheres such as education and work, whereas the degree of informal age structuring (though social expectations) may be stronger in private spheres such as family (Settersten, 2003).

As John Meyer (1986) has put it, norms become a way to 'construct appropriate individuals.' By providing a definition of what is 'normal,' age norms can, from a functionalist or constructivist perspective, provide a subtle sense of security to individuals. At the same time, they may operate as an effective source of personal constriction and social oppression across the spheres of schooling, work, and family. Many of these norms relate closely to ageist assumptions. Elders may fear sanctions for becoming romantically involved with or marrying a much younger person or for returning to school and taking a seat among a classroom full of twentysomethings. Lawrence has shown that norms about age-appropriateness of ranks and positions in a work organization exist, but workers actually estimate the age-in-rank to be younger than it actually is, thereby possibly contributing to ageism (Lawrence, 1984).

Especially if they are experienced as constrictive, why should such norms retain their plausibility and power, and why should individuals 'believe in' them? The key to the answer lies in the concept of naturalization, introduced earlier. Because age norms are legitimated by the pronouncements of pop psychology and supported by some serious clinicians and scholars, they are widely believed and followed, and in some cases defined and sanctioned by the state, which makes them plausible and compelling. Yet historical, sociological, and anthropological analyses have demonstrated that what is considered 'age-appropriate behavior' is historically and socially variable. Indeed, as Chudacoff, Rogoff, and others have clearly demonstrated, the very awareness of 'age-appropriateness' as a behavioral issue is socially and culturally constructed. Age-appropriateness, thus, is not a characteristic of the individual, but of social structure. To attribute these structurally generated norms to individual ageing or development constitutes a form of naturalization.

Age consciousness, chronologization, and the institutionalization of the life course

The ascendance of age norms and age consciousness through the 20th century offers a good illustration of the thesis of *chronologization* (Kohli, 1986b), which asserts that age and time are, and have increasingly become, salient dimensions of life. Among the prominent manifestations of chronologization were the development of age-graded compulsory schooling and the emergence of retirement, which together had the effect of partitioning off the front and back ends of the life course, thereby creating the 'three-box' model

noted earlier with education up front, work in the middle, and leisure and disengagement at the end (Riley and Riley, 1994). This model reinforces the distinctiveness of life periods and the allocation of roles and responsibilities on this basis.

The three-box model is also a good example of *institutionalization*, which refers to the ways in which the laws and policies of the state (e.g., compulsory schooling or mandatory retirement) as well as organizations, such as schools (with age-graded classes) and work organizations (with age-graded promotion ranks), define and structure the life course. European scholarship, especially, has emphasized the ways in which modern nation-states shape the life course via structural arrangements and the regulation of how resources are distributed (Kohli, 2007; Mayer, 2004). The mobility and urbanization that accompanied industrialization and its aftermath removed individuals from traditional community settings and attendant forms of informal social control, thereby creating new challenges for managing large and dense human populations. With this shift, the state began to regulate individuals formally and in far-reaching ways. Indeed, the very word *statistics,* which was originally defined as 'matters pertaining to the state' (Hacking, 1990), derived from the political and administrative challenges that were increasingly faced by governments. As part of the response to this challenge, age became a basis of social organization, with objectified depictions of the 'reality' of normal life at each of these stages.

De-institutionalization of the life course?

More recently, a debate has begun over the possible existence of counter-trends, as some scholars have begun to emphasize evidence of *de-chronologization, de-institutionalization, and de-standardization*. These tendencies are reflected in several parallel trends of increasing variability in life experience and transition behavior, which include evidence of increasing heterogeneity in experiences associated with the transitions to adulthood and to with retirement. This new evidence is especially apparent in the final decades of the 20th century and the beginning of the 21st century. For example, at the macro level, the globalization of labor leading to the collapse of manufacturing and the rise of service economies in advanced capitalist societies has led to declines both in secure, long-term jobs and retirement security that such work provided to large segments of the population through the 20th century. With the globalization of labor and concomitant corporate practices such as 'flexibilization' (e.g., Huiskamp and Vos, 2007; Stone, 2005), employers in advanced industrial societies no longer invest in their employees as they once did and seek to reduce further their commitments to them. These changes have created greater variability in work patterns throughout adult life, not only at entry and exit points but also in between.

These and other structural changes may force or create conditions that create instability in the organization and experience of the life course. This instability is often presented to workers as 'opportunity' or 'flexibility' and in some cases is so experienced (for an extended discussion, see Settersten, 1999). It appears that more often, however, it reflects precariousness and unpredictability, especially for those who are more vulnerably positioned in the labor force (Dannefer and Patterson, 2007; Hughes and Waite, 2007). More generally, such developments contribute to the increasing heterogeneity of retirement age, and to the movement of older people in and out of the labor force (Burkauser et al. 2009; O'Rand and Henretta, 1999).

Indeed, there is substantial evidence that life-course patterns that were once relatively standard are now crumbling. There is a strong trend in these directions with respect to work and retirement, but it is especially with respect to the bundle of experiences traditionally associated with the transition to adulthood – leaving the parental home, completing school, finding full-time work, getting married, and having children. As a set, these transitions in many countries now occur in a far more prolonged and variable sequence than just a half century ago (e.g., Furstenberg, 2002; Gauthier, 2007; Settersten et al., 2005). For reasons ranging from structural to personal, these transitions are often not completed until young people are in their late 20s and early 30s, though the story for privileged and disadvantaged youth is dramatically different (for further discussion, see Settersten, 2007).

Trends toward the individualization (or de-standardization) of the life course have implications for old age both in the present and in the future. In the present, the effects are to delay retirement and to increase the diversity of the older population in terms of economic status, labor force participation, and possibly lifestyle characteristics. Looking toward the future, there is speculation that the changes in labor force stability and economic security going forward are likely to reduce family stability (while creating more diversity of family structures) and increase inequality in midlife, both of which can be expected to contribute to heightened inequality and economic vulnerability when those who are currently in midlife reach old age.

Several theoretical assessments have been made of the prospect that trends toward the individualization of the life course may expand to the magnitude of a *Second Demographic Transition* (Hughes and Waite, 2007; Lesthaeghe and Neels, 2002). One of these, which remains close to the economic drivers of globalization and flexibilization emphasized above, can be called an *Inequality and Adversity* perspective. A second perspective, which might be called the *Third Age* perspective, focuses on the possibilities that may be enjoyed in later life when the constraints of institutionalized life course are loosened and when individuals are free of responsibilities in work and child care, in good health, have adequate resources and time left to live, and can realize new forms or a greater degree of self-fulfillment (e.g., Gilleard and Higgs, 2005).

A third perspective, which may be called the *Existential Risk* perspective, is articulate those who have expressed worry that current trends may put at risk those individuals whose lives no longer follow older models (e.g., Beck, 2001; Levy, 1996; Weymann and Heinz, 1996). These shifts may free individuals from institutionally defined life circumstances, but they also mean that individuals must shoulder the new risks associated with taking or being on paths that go 'against the grain.' Especially in the context of eroding welfare state supports, the more experimental nature of 'do-it-yourself' biographies makes them prone to 'biological slippage and collapse' (Beck, 2001). That is, when individuals take or find themselves on life pathways that are highly individualized and not reinforced in organizations, institutions, and social policies, they may lose yet other sources of informal and formal support. In this scenario, 'personal failures' that are actually traceable to changes in social structure are mistakenly understood as being one's own fault.

This tendency to generate a sense of social or existential security may well operate in tandem with economic adversity, thus serving to exacerbate the risks already faced by those who are in precarious positions to begin with. The individualization of transition patterns means that people are increasingly left to their own devices, with widely varying degrees of economic and social capital to confront demands, decision points, and challenges that will determine the directions their lives will take. As a result, the psychological capacities and social skills and resources of individuals may become even more important in determining life outcomes, even as such resources tend to covary with other forms of economic and social capital (Settersten, 2007).

In the above sections, we have attempted to demonstrate two broad approaches to the study of the life course, each of which has direct relevance to gerontology. The personological approach provides powerful evidence that 'how one ages' cannot be separated from one's earlier life experiences at both the individual and collective-cohort levels. The institutional approach demonstrates that the meanings of age are social constructs through which long-term historical trends of institutionalization, chronologization, and standardization come to be widely accepted and taken-for-granted aspects of human nature, despite their sociopolitical origins. These trends have led to an increasing amount of social regulation based on age, and an emergence of 'age consciousness' in the populations of late modernity. Seen from the vantage point of sociological analysis, these trends comprise a *naturalization* of age.

IMPLICATIONS OF LIFE-COURSE THEORIZING FOR SOCIAL GERONTOLOGY

We turn now to a more specific consideration of the implications of life-course theorizing for social gerontology. We propose four ways that the life course is useful in sensitizing gerontology to the empirical realities of the process of ageing.

The life-course perspective sensitizes social gerontology to the impact of social change on human ageing

Virtually all of the scientific research on human ageing is based on cohorts born early in the first few decades of the 20th century. The last century saw the bureaucratization of the major institutions of education, work, unionization, retirement, and health care through which people's lives and opportunities are organized, and it was also punctuated by remarkable events and changes related to war, economic calamity, health epidemics, social movements for civil and workers rights, and technological change in medicine, communication, and transportation. In many societies, the Great Depression and military service during World War II, in particular, heavily marked the lives of men and women who are now old (see Settersten, 2006), and postwar economic and technological developments shaped them in profound but often subtle ways.

The magnitude and rapidity of change in the 20th century meant that those who were born in the first few decades of the 1900s were quite different from those born even a decade or two before or after. As a cohort, they have had 'distinctive experience' with social change, to use Rosow's (1978) term, which brought 'differential effects'

for them relative to adjacent cohorts. For example, in the United States and parts of Europe, successive cohorts had better cognitive test performance because of gains in educational attainment; they had better physical health because of improvements in nutrition and health care; marriage and family formation was promoted because of dynamics related to war and military service; postwar economic growth and the growth of industry opened new opportunities for work.

We saw earlier, in discussing the research of Elder and colleagues on the Great Depression and World War II, that the same historical events and changes can have very different effects on the lives of adjacent cohorts. Their different cohort position means that they are at different ages when those historical events and changes occur. Even a few years can create a meaningful difference. For example, those born in advanced industrial societies in the late 1970s will recall at least part of their early childhood without personal computers, while most of those born in the mid-1980s and later will not be able to imagine life without them. Children today are immersed in and take for granted an expansive digital world that saturates their everyday lives and has dramatically altered how they think, learn, and interact with others.

Although we now know much about how ageing and life-course patterns have been influenced by the circumstances, events, and structural conditions of the 20th century, the scope and magnitude of forces involved may well mean that some still are not well known. One thing that the experience of 20th century ageing has made abundantly clear is that ageing is a variable and mutable process, not a universal and unchanging one. This is consistent with the foundational principles set forth at the beginning of the chapter. Thus, for scholarship on age, the 20th century served as something of a laboratory of change effects – illustrating both the potentials for change and the uncertainty endemic to human circumstances, as well as the consequences they have had for individual ageing in terms of changes in longevity (Riley, 2001), the postponement or elimination of what were assumed to be late-life disabilities (Langa et al., 2008; see also Chapter 7), and the institutionalization and then de-institutionalization of the life course (Dannefer and Patterson, 2007; Hogan, 1981; Settersten and Gannon, 2005). What the 20th century has made clear to us is that there is no such thing as 'normal ageing' or ageing in a general sense, apart from the definitions of normality imposed by socially constructed notions of what counts as normal. These considerations require gerontologists to acknowledge that we do not know to what extent current knowledge of ageing can be extended to members of future cohorts whose life experiences have been very different from those who are now old.

In some respects, we do not need to wait to see how they are different. In every society, the septuagenarians of 2075 and the nonagenarians of the year 2100 have been born, and the paths of their individual and collective lives have begun. Thus, we can already begin to discern some aspects of the future of global ageing. Of course, more is known about the cohorts currently in young and middle age (for illustrations, see Settersten, 2007). These cohorts have different physical, psychological, and social statuses relative to cohorts past and are themselves very different from one another. As their members age, these cohorts may challenge additional taken-for-granted assumptions about ageing.

The life-course perspective sensitizes social gerontology to variability in patterns and experiences of age

As noted earlier, the diversity of the aged is often emphasized to counter stereotypic or overly 'normalized' versions of ageing, but it also raises the significant question concerning the sources of diversity and inequality among older people. What are the processes or events responsible for this phenomenon? Available evidence suggests that this phenomenon results neither from sudden late-life changes in individuals, nor from cohort differences. Rather, it appears to develop biographically, as a *life-course* process.

As anticipated earlier in our discussion, the consistency of this pattern has significant implications for the study of age. If increasing diversity and inequality are regular features of cohort ageing that regularly recur in each succeeding cohort, it is misleading to describe ageing in terms of central tendencies or 'normative' patterns, and it is especially misleading to describe older people in homogenized ways (Dannefer, 1987, 2003a).

Describing trajectories of variability is not the endpoint but the beginning of understanding the factors underlying old age. Trajectories themselves reveal nothing about the underlying processes that bring the variability about as members of a cohort age. Few would contend that it can be explained by a single set of causal variables. In part, the diversity of the aged reflects the accumulation of particular experiences over many decades that create individual life courses that are in some ways as unique as fingerprints. Some scholars have emphasized the role of personality factors and processes of psychosocial 'accentuation' in which the characteristics and experiences of individuals become more pronounced with the passage of time, creating greater distinction and differentiation (Clausen, 1993; Feldman and Weiler, 1976; Neugarten, 1979b). Such enduring individual explanations, which emphasize factors such as biographical uniqueness, personal choice, and personality characteristics, are well established and familiar – and they are, understandably, a natural starting point in psychology and in societies characterized by a strong ethos of individualism.

Yet it is clear that trajectories of diversity and inequality develop as individuals encounter stratified social institutions as their lives unfold, starting with early experiences in the family and educational systems, including preschool (Kanter, 1972; Rogoff, 2002). These are early points of entry into the institutionalized and lifelong process of cumulative dis/advantage described earlier. Schools, work organizations, and healthcare institutions inevitably generate inequality because they are naturally structured to regulate access to scarce and desirable resources – whether effective teachers, safe working conditions, and intellectually and socially satisfying work, or access to needed medical technology.

A considerable and growing body of evidence supports the power of these social processes, which also operate in ways that are subtle, hard to detect, or intended to be invisible (Crystal and Shea, 2003; Dannefer, 2003b, 2009). This is a conceptually significant development because it makes clear the fact that patterns of ageing over the life course cannot merely be understood at the individual level but also must include analysis of generic properties of cohorts. It is therefore misleading to think of age as something that mainly happens *within* individuals, rather than as something that occurs *between* people and can only be grasped in the context of cohort processes and as a central feature of social structure (Dannefer, 1987; Rosenbaum, 1976).

In view of these developments, a life-course perspective should sensitize gerontologists to variability and to socially structured processes of inequality that produce it. Indeed, to the extent that major economic strains continue, social class seems likely to become an even more powerful factor determining ageing and in creating serious divisions within societies (see also Kohli 2007; Settersten and Trauten, 2009). Given the great degree of variability among old people, it seems likely that subgroups of people *within* the aged population have great competing needs – especially in terms of wealth and health – which fractures the potential for political solidarity that is often assumed to be true of older age groups (see also Binstock, 2004).

*The life-course perspective sensitizes
social gerontology to 'linked lives' and
their expanding significance in the
context of global ageing*

The general principle of 'linked lives' is an
explicit part of life-course frameworks (e.g., Elder
and Johnson, 2003; Settersten, 2003a). This principle simply states that the course of an individual's life is intimately shaped by the needs,
circumstances, and choices of others. Despite the
recognition that individual lives simply cannot be
understood in isolation from others, the irony is
that we analyze lives as if they are somehow
purely individual. Yet most of the things people
struggle with, hope and plan for, and feel pain
around are tied to relations with others.

At a micro level, there is a voluminous body of
research exploring how the linked nature of lives
creates unexpected changes and circumstances.
When lives are 'out of synch,' relationships are
often strained. This principle applies throughout
the life course. Common examples of such interdependence are found within the domain of
family, and include many direct applications to
later life. Widowhood, for instance, destroys what
is typically assumed to be the most central 'linked
life' – the partner relationship – and usually brings
profound effects. The linked nature of lives may
also constrain or foreclose opportunities, or drain
individuals of important resources. One example
of this is offered by the often-discussed 'sandwich
generation,' in which middle-aged adults must
simultaneously deal with the demands of raising
children and caring for ageing parents, creating a
'life-cycle squeeze' (Oppenheimer, 1982) that
constrains time, energy, finances, and choices.

The emphasis on 'linked lives' has focused
almost exclusively on familial or other face-
to-face relations, prompting a charge of 'microfication' in scholarship on the life course (Hagestad
and Dannefer, 2001). Yet there is a largely undeveloped potential and increasing need to explore
linked lives at meso and macro levels of analysis –
such as the linkages across generations in a society, or across nations.

The global linkage of lives is often unnoticed,
yet powerful. With the increasing global organization of late modernity, the lives of both young and
old, and indeed the lives of age peers who live far
apart and will never meet, are linked through sets
of political and economic processes, notably those
involving production and consumption: for example, with the lives of child laborers in the Global
South and in East Asia, who work long hours to
make low-priced consumer goods ranging from
toys to T-shirts, which are consumed far away
(Bales, 2002; Dannefer, 2003).

In some cases, such global linkages become
intensely personal: some nursing homes in countries like Singapore are built with dormitory space
to house migrant workers from India and other
nearby countries who staff frontline care positions. In the United States, immigrants from the
Philippines, Ghana, and the Caribbean fill the
demanding, low-paid positions of nursing assistants (Foner, 1994). In a study in the United States
of nursing home reform, the staff-hiring committee included resident members. Among a diverse
pool of applicants, the residents selected candidates from Ghana because they demonstrated a
palpable spirit of caring respect for elders that was
not evident in native North American applicants
(Dannefer and Daub, 2009). At the same time,
such laborers are also spouses and parents, and the
migrant work experience imposes strains on and
changes power dynamics for linked lives within
the family (Burawoy, 2000; Dannefer and Siders,
2009; Smith, 2005). Here, the focus is upon how
care may be spread across continents, part of the
'globalization' of family life affecting migrants
moving from the Global South to the Global
North. This process generates new forms of transnational care-giving, with supportive and financial ties maintained between 'first' and 'second'
homelands (Phillipson et al., 2003)

*The life-course perspective sensitizes
social gerontology to the existence
of age as a variable and alterable
property of social systems*

The articulation of age as a property of social
systems – i.e., as an integral part of cultural and
symbolic systems that define and organize social
life within a society – was given its most precise
and elegant theoretical formulation in Riley's
original formulation of the age stratification
framework (Riley et al., 1972; see also Dannefer
et al., 2005). This framework recognizes that societies differ in how they recognize and deal with
age, and that in modern societies, all ages exist at
once within a matrix of age-graded institutions
that direct human behavior and very often segment age groups. These institutions exist independently of the individuals who constantly pass
through them as they age, a process that Riley and
her associates termed 'cohort flow.' Along with
Cain's earlier paper, Riley's idea laid a firm foundation from which social science scholars could
conceptualize the formal segmentation of age
groups into institutionally differentiated spheres
as a major, long-term process of social change, a
process life-course scholars now refer to as the

institutionalization of the life course, described earlier.

In conceptualizing age as a property of social systems and not just of individuals, another potentially radical implication emerges for social gerontology: if age is a property of social systems, then it is possible to counterpose the social definitions of age with the experiences and interests of individuals who are ageing. Thus, Riley and her associates argued, a socially imposed age-segregated life course – one which dictated 'normal' behavior and excluded elders from full participation in society – ill-serves the potentials and interests of both members of a rapidly graying population and of a society as a whole, and needs to be changed. Yet age segregation continues to be a defining aspect of late modernity (e.g., Hagestad and Uhlenberg, 2006; Uhlenberg, 2009). The significance of this point is that these arrangements are not inevitable because they are socially created; they are not based on human nature and, in fact, are at odds with the interests of human well-being and quality of life. Social policies and cultural definitions that represent the human interests, and especially the interests of older people, will reject the forcing of individuals into outdated role structures based on age. The recognition that age is often a taken-for-granted 'fact' within a social system does not mean that it can or should be used in ways that are constraining or oppressive. Indeed, the wide interests, capacities, and resources of older people would seem to offer a liberating new vision for rethinking and inhabiting old age, or any period of life for that matter, in ways that would welcome at least some of the impulses to de-institutionalize the life course.

CONCLUDING COMMENT

We have sought to explain the necessity of the life-course perspective for social gerontology. Increasingly, leading gerontologists have issued a call to bring the life-course perspective to ageing research, policy, and practice. The life-course perspective recognizes the great degree and types of diversity among older people, and that this diversity must be understood as a function of earlier life experiences. It also recognizes that dynamics of ageing are a collective process characterized by the accumulation of inequality over the life course. A second paradigmatic approach to the life course is based on the recognition that, although age is important in every society, societies vary dramatically in how they define age and the meanings they attach to it. The meaning of age can also vary and change within societies. A familiar example

of such change has been the late 19th century and 20th century process of the institutionalization of the life course, and the concomitant rise in 'age consciousness.' The extent to which a counter-trend of de-institutionalization in the life course is occurring, and the implications of such a trend for ageing, are questions of ongoing and vigorous debate that will likely last for some time. However this debate plays out, one positive result is that it demonstrates the arbitrariness and often destructiveness of taken-for-granted notions of ageing – as well as the potentials of older people, and of people at any age, to rethink the possibilities of their lives in terms that are less defined by restrictive social roles that reify age and ignore human potentials.

NOTE

1 For a critical and comparative analyses of the perspectives of life-course sociology and life-span psychology, see Dannefer, 1984; Diewald and Mayer, 2009; and Settersten, 2009.

REFERENCES

Bales, K. (2002) *Disposable People: New Slavery in the Global Economy.* Berkeley, CA: University of California Press.

Baltes, P.B (1968) 'Longitudinal and cross-sectional sequences in the study of age and generation effects', *Human Development*, 11: 145–17.

Beck, U. (2001) 'Living your own life in a runaway world: individualization, globalization, and politics', in W. Hutton and A. Giddens (eds), *Global Capitalism.* New York: The New Press.

Ben-Shlomo, Y. and Kuh, D. (2002) 'A life course approach to chronic disease epidemiology: conceptual models, empirical challenges and interdisciplinary perspectives', *International Journal of Epidemiology*, 31: 285–93.

Berger, P. and Luckmann, T. (1967) *The Social Construction of Reality: A Treatise in the Sociology of Knowledge.* New York: Anchor.

Binstock, R.H. (2004) 'Anti-aging medicine and research: a realm of conflict and profound societal implications', *Journal of Gerontology: Biological Sciences*, 59A: 523–33.

Birren, J.E. (1959) 'Principles of research on aging', in J. Birren (ed.), *Handbook of Aging and the Individual.* Chicago, IL: University of Chicago Press.

Bromhall, C. (2003) *The Eternal Child: How Evolution Has Made Children of Us All.* London: Ebury Press.

Burawoy, M. (2000) *Global Ethnography: Forces, Connections, and Imaginations in a Postmodern World.* Berkeley, CA: University of California Press.

Burkhauser, R.V. and Rovba, L. (2009) 'Institutional responses to structural lag: the changing patterns of work at older ages', S.J. Czaja and J. Sharíteds (eds), *Aging and Work*. Baltimore, MD: Johns Hopkins University Press.

Butler, R., Miller, R.A., Perry, D., et al. (2008) '"New" model of health promotion and diseases prevention for the 21st century', *BMJ*, 337: 399.

Cain, L.D., Jr. (1964) 'Life course and social structure', in R.E. L. Faris (ed.), *Handbook of Modern Sociology*. Chicago, IL: Rand-McNally.

Chudacoff, H. (1989) *How Old Are You? Age Consciousness in American Culture*. Princeton, NJ: Princeton University Press.

Clausen, J.A. (1972) 'The life course of individuals', in M. Riley, M. Johnson, and A. Foner (eds), *Aging and Society: A Sociology of Age Stratification,* Vol. 3. New York: Russell Sage Foundation.

Clausen, J.A. (1993) *American Lives: Looking Back at the Children of the Great Depression*. Berkeley, CA: University of California Press.

Crystal, S. (1982) *America's Old Age Crisis: Public Policy and the Two Worlds of Aging*. New York: Basic Books.

Crystal, S. and Shea, D. (2003) 'Prospects for retirement resources in an aging society', in S. Crystal and D. Shea (eds), *Economic Outcomes in Later Life: Public Policy, Health, and Cumulative Advantage*. New York: Springer.

Crystal, S. and Waehrer, K. (1996) 'Later-life economic inequality in longitudinal perspective', *Journal of Gerontology: Social Sciences*, 51B(6): S307–18.

Dannefer, D. (1984) 'The role of the social in life-span developmental psychology, past and future: rejoinder to Baltes and Nesselroade', *American Sociological Review*, 49: 847–50.

Dannefer, D. (1987) 'Aging as intracohort differentiation: accentuation, the Matthew effect, and the life course', *Sociological Forum*, 2: 211–36.

Dannefer, D. (1988) 'Differential gerontology and the stratified life course', in G.L. Maddox and M.P. Lawton (eds), *Annual Review of Gerontology*, Vol. 8. New York: Springer.

Dannefer, D. (1996) 'The social organization of diversity, and the normative organization of age', *Gerontologist*, 36(2): 174–8.

Dannefer, D. (1999) 'Freedom isn't free: power, alienation and the consequences of action', in J. Brandtstadter and R.M. Lerner (eds), *Action and Development: Origins and Functions of Intentional Self Development*. New York: Springer.

Dannefer, D. (1999) 'Neoteny, naturalization and other constituents of human development', in C. Ryff and B. Marshall (eds), *Self and Society of Aging Processes*. New York: Springer.

Dannefer, D. (2003a) 'Cumulative advantage and the life course: cross-fertilizing age and social science knowledge', *Journal of Gerontology*, 58b: S327–37.

Dannefer, D. (2003b) 'Toward a global geography of the life course: challenges of late modernity to the life course perspective', in J.T. Mortimer and M. Shanahan (eds), *Handbook of the Life Course*. New York: Kluwer.

Dannefer, D. (2009) 'Stability, homogeneity, agency: cumulative dis/advantage and problems of theory', *Swiss Journal of Sociology*, 35: 193–210.

Dannefer, D. and Daub, A. (2009) 'Extending the interrogation: life span, life course, and the constitution of human aging', *Advances in Life Course Research*, 14(1–2): 5–27.

Dannefer, D. and Kelley-Moore, J.A. (2009) 'Theorizing the life course: new twists in the paths', in V. Bengtson, D. Gans, N.M. Putney, and M. Silverstein (eds), *Handbook of Theories of Aging*. New York: Springer.

Dannefer, D. and Patterson, R.S. (2007) 'The second demographic transition, aging families, and the aging of the institutionalized life course (commentary)', in K.W. Schaie and P. Uhlenberg (eds), *Demographic Changes and the Well-Being of Older Persons*. New York: Springer.

Dannefer, D. and Perlmutter, M. (1990) 'Development as a multidimensional process: individual and social constituents', *Human Development*, 33: 108–37.

Dannefer, D. and Sell, R. (1988) 'Age structure, the life course and 'aged heterogeneity': prospects for research and theory', *Comprehensive Gerontology B*, 2: 1–10.

Dannefer, D. and Siders, R.A. (2009) 'Social structure, social change, and the cycle of induced solidarity', in M. Silverstein and R. Giarusso (eds), *From Generation to Generation: Continuity and Change in Aging Families*. New York: Springer.

Dannefer, D. and Uhlenberg, P. (1999) 'Paths of the life course: a typology', in V. Bengston and K.W. Schaie (eds), *Handbook of Theories of Aging*. New York: Springer.

Dannefer, D., Uhlenberg, P., Foner, A., and Abeles, R.P. (2005) 'On the shoulder of a giant: the legacy of Matilda White Riley for gerontology', *Journal of Gerontology: Social Sciences*, 60B: S296–304.

Diewald, M. and Mayer, K.U. (2009) 'The sociology of the life course and life span psychology: integrated paradigm or complementing pathways?', *Advances in Life Course Research*, 14(1–2): 5–14.

Easterlin, R.A., Macunovich, D.J., and Crimmins, E.M. (1993) 'Economic status of the young and the old in the working-age population, 1964 and 1987', in V.L. Bengtson and W.A. Achenbaum (eds), *The Changing Contract Across Generations*. Newbury Park, CA: Sage.

Elder, G.H., Jr. (1974) *Children of the Great Depression: Social Change and Life Experience*. Chicago, IL: University of Chicago Press.

Elder, G.H., Jr. (1975) 'Age differentiation and the life course', *Annual Review of Sociology*, 1: 165–90.

Elder, G.H., Jr. (1999) *Children of the Great Depression: Social Change in Life Experience*, 25th anniversary edition. Boulder, CO: Westview Press. (Originally published in 1974 by University of Chicago Press.)

Elder, G.H., Jr. and Caspi, A. (1990) 'Studying lives in a changing society: sociological and personological explorations', in A.I. Rabin (ed.), *Studying Persons and Lives: The Henry A. Murray Lectures in Personality*. New York: Springer.

Elder, G.H., Jr. and Chan, C. (1999) 'War's legacy in men's lives', in P. Moen, D. Dempster-McClain, and H.A. Walker (eds), *A Nation Divided: Diversity, Inequality, and*

Community in American Society. Ithaca, NY: Cornell University Press.

Elder, G.H., Jr. and Johnson, M.K. (2003) 'The life course and aging: challenges, lessons, and new directions', in R.A. Settersten, Jr. (ed.), *Invitation to the Life Course: Toward New Understandings of Later Life.* Amityville, NY: Baywood Publishing Company.

Elder, G.H., Jr. and Liker, J.K. (1982) 'Hard times in women's lives: historical influences across 40 years', *American Journal of Sociology*, 88: 241–69.

Ewen, S. (1977) *Captains of Consciousness.* New York: McGraw-Hill.

Ewen, S. and Ewen, E. (1992) *Channels of Desire: Mass Images and the Shaping of American Consciousness.* Minnesota: University of Minnesota Press.

Feldman, K.A. and Weiler, J. (1976) 'Changes in initial differences among major-field groups: an exploration of the 'accentuation effect'', in W.H. Sewell, R. Hauser, and D.L. Featherman (eds), *Schooling and Achievement in American Society.* New York: Academic Press.

Ferraro, K.F. and Shippee, T.P. (2009) 'Black and white chains of risk for hospitalization over 20 years', *Journal of Health and Social Behavior*, 49(2): 193–207.

Foner, N. (1994) *The Caregiving Dilemma.* Berkeley, CA: University of California Press.

Furstenberg, F. (2002) 'Reflections on the future of the life course', in J.T. Mortimer and M.J. Shanahan (eds), *Handbook of the Life Course.* New York: Springer.

Gauthier, A.H. (2007) 'Becoming a young adult: an international perspective on the transitions to adulthood', *European Journal of Population/Revue Europ*, 23(3–4): 217–23.

Gilleard, C.J. and Higgs, P. (2005) *Cultures of Ageing: Self, Citizen, and the Body.* Harlow: Prentice Hall.

Gillis, J. R. (1974) *Youth and History: Tradition and Change in European Age Relations, 1770–present.* New York: Academic Press.

Gluckman, P.D. and Hanson, M.A. (2006a) *The Developmental Origins of Health and Disease: The Breadth and Importance of the Concept.* New York: Springer.

Gluckman, P.D. and Hanson, M.A. (2006b) *Mismatch: The Lifestyle Diseases Timbomb.* New York: Oxford University Press.

Gould, S.J. (1977) *Ontogeny and Phylogeny.* Cambridge, MA: Belknap Press of Harvard University.

Gutmann, D. (1987) *Reclaimed Powers: Toward A New Psychology of Men and Women in Later Life.* New York: Basic Books.

Hacking, I. (1990) *The Taming of Chance.* Cambridge, England: Cambridge University Press.

Hagestad, G.O. and Dannefer, D. (2001) 'Concepts and theories of aging: beyond microfication in social science approaches', in R.H. Binstock and L.K. George (eds), *Handbook of Aging and the Social Sciences.* New York: Academic Press.

Hagestad, G.O. and Neugarten, B.L. (1985) 'Age and the life course', in E. Shanas and R. Binstock (eds), *Handbook of Aging and the Social Sciences*, 2nd edn. New York: Van Nostrand Reinhold.

Hagestad, G.O. and Uhlenberg, P. (2006) 'Should we be concerned about age segregation? some theoretical and empirical explorations', *Research on Aging*, 28(6): 638–53.

Hitlin, S. and Elder, G.H. Jr. (2007) 'Time, self, and the curiously abstract concept of agency', *Sociological Theory*, 25(2): 170–91.

Hogan, D.P. (1981) *Transitions and Social Change: The Early Lives of American Men.* New York: Academic Press.

Hughes, M.E. and Waite, L.J. (2007) *The Aging of the Second Demographic Transition.* New York: Springer.

Huiskamp, R. and Vos, K.J. (2007) 'Flexibiliazation, modernization and the Lisbon strategy', *International Journal of Comparative Labour Law and Industrial Relations*, 23(4): 587–99.

Kanter, R. (1972) 'The organization child: experience management in a nursery school', *Sociology of Education*, 45(Spring): 186–212.

Kett, J.F. (1977) *Rites of Passage: Adolescence in America 1790 to the Present.* New York: Basic Books.

Kohli, M. (1986a) 'Social organization and subjective construction of the life course', in A. Sorensen, F.E. Weinert, and L.R. Sherrod (eds), *Human Development and the Life Course: Multidisciplinary Perspectives.* Hillsdale, NJ: Lawrence Erlbaum.

Kohli, M. (1986b) 'The world we forgot: a historical review of the life course', in V.W. Marshall (ed.), *Later Life: The Social Psychology of Aging.* Beverly Hills, CA: SAGE.

Kohli, M. (1999) 'Private and public transfers between generations: linking the family and the state', *European Societies*, 40: 81–122.

Kohli, M. (2007) 'The institutionalization of the life course: looking back to look ahead', *Research in Human Development*, 4(3): 253–71.

Kohli, M. and Meyer, J.W. (1986) 'Social structure and the social construction of life stages', *Human Development*, 29: 145–9.

Langa, L.M., Larson, E.B., Karlawish, J.H., et al. (2008) 'Trends in the prevalence and mortality of cognitive impairment in the United States: Is there evidence of a compression of cognitive morbidity?', *Alzheimers and Dementia*, 4(2): 134–44.

Laslett, P. (1991) *A Fresh Map of Life: The Emergence of the Third Age.* Cambridge, MA: Harvard.

Lawrence, B.S. (1984) 'Age-grading: the implicit organization time table', *Journal of Occupational Behavior*, 5: 23–35.

Lawrence, B.S. (1996). Interest and indifference: the role of age in the organizational sciences, *Research in Personnel and Human Resources Management*, 14: 1–60 .

Lerner, R.M. and Walls, T. (1999) 'Revisiting Individuals as producers of their development: from dynamic interactionism to developmental systems', in J. Brandstadter and R.M. Lerner (eds), *Action and Self-Development: Theory and Research Through the Life Span.* Thousand Oaks, CA: Sage.

Lesthaeghe, R. and Neels, K. (2002) 'From the first to the second demographic transition – an interpretation of the spatial continuity of demographic innovation in France, Belgium and Switzerland', *European Journal of Population*, 18(4): 225–60.

Levinson, D.J. (1997) *Season's of a Woman's Life*. New York: Knopf.

Levy, R. (1996) 'Toward a theory of life course institutionalization', in A. Weymann and W. Heinz (eds), *Society and Biography: Interrelationships Between Social Structure, Institutions, and the Life Course*. Weinheim, Germany: Deutscher Studien Verlag.

Link, B.G. and Phelan, J. (1995) 'Social conditions as fundamental causes of disease', *Journal of Health and Social Behavior*, 35: 80–94.

Loehlin, J.C. (2007) 'The strange case of $c^2 = 0$: What does it imply for views of human development?' *Research in Human Development*, 4(3): 151–62.

Maddox, G. and Douglass, E.R. (1974) 'Aging and individual differences: a longitudinal analysis of social, psychological and physiological indicators', *Journal of Gerontology*, 29: 555–63.

Marmot, M. (2004) *The Status Syndrome: How Social Standing Affects Our Health And Longevity*. New York: Time Books.

Mascolo, M.F., Fischer, K.W., and Neimeyer, R.A. (1999) 'The dynamics of codevelopment of intentionality, self and social relations', in J. Brandstadter and R.M. Lerner (eds), *Action and Self-Development: theory and Research Through the Life Span*. Thousand Oaks, CA: Sage.

Mayer, K.U. (1986) 'Structural constraints in the life course', *Human Development*, 29: 163–70.

Mayer, K.U. (2004) 'Whose lives? How history, societies, and institutions define and shape life courses', *Research in Human Development*, 1(3): 161–87.

Merton, R. (1968) 'The Matthew effect in science: the reward and communications systems of science', *Science*, 199: 55–63.

Meyer, J.W. (1986) 'The self and the life course: institutionalization and its effects', in A.B. Sørensen, F.E. Weinert, and L.R. Sherrod (eds), *Human Development and the Life Course: Multidisciplinary Perspectives*. Hillsdale, NJ: Lawrence Erlbaum Associates.

Modell, J. (1989) *Into One's Own: From Youth to Adulthood in the United States, 1920–1975*. Berkeley, CA: University of California Press.

Montagu, A. (1989) *Growing Young*. New York: McGraw-Hill.

Nelson, E.A. and Dannefer, D. (1992) 'Aged heterogeneity: fact or fiction? The fate of diversity in gerontological research', *The Gerontologist*, 32: 17–23.

Neugarten, B.L. (1979a) 'The young-old and the age-irrelevant society', in D. Neugarten (ed.), *The Meanings Of Age: Selected Papers of Bernice L. Neugarten*. Chicago, IL: University of Chicago Press.

Neugarten, B.L. (1979b) 'Time age, and the life cycle', *American Journal of Psychiatry*, 136(7): 887–94.

Oppenheimer, Valerie K. (1982) *Work and the Family: A Study in Social Demography*. New York: Academic Press.

O'Rand, A.M. and Henretta, J.C. (1999) *Age and Inequality*. Boulder, CO: Westview Press.

Perry, B. and Svalavitz, M. (2006) *The Boy Who Was Raised As A Dog: And Other Stories From A Child Psychiatrist's Notebook: What Traumatized Children Can Teach Us About Loss, Love and Healing*. New York: Basic Books.

Phillipson, C., Ahmed, N., and Latimer, J. (2003) *Women in Transition: A Study of The Experiences of Bangladeshi Women Living in Tower Hamlets*. Bristol: Policy Press.

Riegel, K.F. (1976) 'The dialectics of human development', *American Psychologist*, 16: 346–70.

Riley, J.C. (2001) *Rising Life Expectancy: A Global History*. New York: Cambridge University Press.

Riley, M. (1980) 'Age and aging: from theory generation to theory testing', in H.M. Blalock, Jr. (ed.), *Sociological Theory and Social Research*. New York: Free Press.

Riley, M.W. (1973) 'Aging and cohort succession: interpretations and misinterpretations', *Public Opinion Quarterly*, 37(1): 35–50.

Riley, M.W. and Riley, J.W., Jr. (1994) 'Structural lag: past and future. in M.W. Riley, R.L. Kahn, and A. Foner (eds), *Age and Structural Lag: Society's Failure To Provide Meaningful Opportunities In Work, Family, and Leisure*. New York: John Wiley and Sons.

Riley, M.W., Johnson, M., and Foner, A. (1972) *Aging and Society, Volume 3: A Sociology of Age Stratification*. New York: Russell Sage Foundation.

Rogoff, B. (2002) 'How can we study cultural aspects of human development?', *Human Development*, 45: 209–10.

Rosenbaum, J. (1976) *Making Inequality: The Hidden Curriculum of High School Tracking*. New York: Wiley.

Rosow, I. (1978) 'What is a cohort and why?', *Human Development*, 21: 65–75.

Rother, J. (2009) 'Presented commentary', MacArthur Conference on Intergenerational Issues in an Aging Society, Coral Gables, Florida, January.

Rowe, J. and Kahn, R.L. (1987) 'Human aging: usual and successful', *Science*, 237(4811): 143–9.

Rowe, J. and Kahn, R.L. (1997) 'Successful aging', *The Gerontologist*, 37(4): 433–40.

Ryder, N. (1965) 'The cohort as a concept in the study of social change', *American Sociological Review*, 30: 843–61.

Schaie, K.W. (1965) 'A general model for the study of developmental problems', *Psychological Bulletin*, 64: 92–107.

Schor, J. (2004) *Born to Buy*. New York: Scribner.

Settersten, R.A., Jr. (1999) *Lives in Time and Place: The Problems and Promises of Developmental Science*. Amityville, NY: Baywood Publishing Company.

Settersten, R.A., Jr. (2003a) 'Propositions and controversies in life-course scholarship', in R.A. Settersten, Jr. (ed.), *Invitation to the Life Course: Toward New Understanding of Later Life*. Amityville, NY: Baywood Publishing Company.

Settersten, R.A., Jr. (2003b) 'Age structuring and the rhythm of the life course', in J. Mortimer and M. Shanahan (eds.), *Handbook of the Life Course*. New York: Kluwer Academic/ Plenum Publishers.

Settersten, R.A., Jr. (2005) Toward a Stronger partnership between life-course sociology and life-span psychology. *Research in Human Development*, 2(1–2): 25–41.

Settersten, R.A., Jr. (2006) When nations call: How wartime military service matters for aging and the life course. *Research on Aging*, 28(1): 12–34.

Settersten, R.A., Jr. (2007) 'Ten reasons why shake-ups in the life course should change approaches to old-age policies', *Aging and Public Policy Report*, 17(3): 21–7.

Settersten, R.A., Jr. (2009) 'It takes two to tango: the (un)easy dance between life-course sociology and life-span psychology', *Advances in Life Course Research*, 14(1–2): 74–81.

Settersten, R.A., Jr. and Gannon, L. (2005) 'Structure, agency, and the space between: on the challenges and contradictions of a blended view of the life course', in R. Levy, P. Ghisletta, J.M. Legoff, and D. Spini (eds), *Towards an Interdisciplinary Perspective on the Life Course*. London: Elsevier.

Settersten, R.A., Jr. and Hagestad, G.O. (1996a) 'What's the latest? Cultural age deadlines for family transitions', *The Gerontologist*, 36(2): 178–88.

Settersten, R.A., Jr. and Hagestad, G.O. (1996b) 'What's the latest? II. Cultural age deadlines for educational and work transitions', *The Gerontologist*, 36(5): 602–13.

Settersten, R.A., Jr. and Trauten, M. (2009) 'Theorizing the new terrain of old age: hallmarks, freedoms, and risks', in V. Bengtson, M. Silverstein, D. Putney, and S. Gans (eds), *Handbook of Theories of Aging*. New York: Springer.

Settersten, R.A., Jr., Furstenberg, F.F. Jr., and Rumbaut, R.G. (eds). (2005) *On the Frontier of Adulthood: Theory, Research, and Public Policy*. Chicago, IL: University of Chicago Press.

Smith, R. (2005) *Mexican New York: Transnational Lives of New Immigrants*. Berkeley, CA: University of California Press.

Snowdon, D.N. (2002) *Aging With Grace: What the Nun Study Teaches Us About Leading Longer, Healthier, and More Meaningful Lives*. New York: Bantam.

Uhlenberg, P. (2009) 'Children in an aging society', *Journals of Gerontology Social Sciences*, 64B, pp. 489–496.

Weymann, A. and Heinz, W.R. (1996) *Society and Biography: Interrelationships Between Social Structure, Institutions, and the Life Course*. Weinheim, Germany: Deutscher Studien Verlag.

Wilson, A.E., Shuey, K.M., and Elder, G.H., Jr. (2007) 'Cumulative advantage processes as mechanisms of inequality in life course health', *American Journal of Sociology*, 112: 1886–924.

2

Past as Prologue: Toward a Global History of Ageing

W. Andrew Achenbaum

INTRODUCTION

To write a history of ageing in a global context is a daunting challenge. On the one hand, we must learn more about temporal shifts in the meanings ascribed to old age and about the historical experiences of old men and women. On the other hand, there are huge gaps geographically. While scholars have surveyed the terrain, much deemed historical gerontology remains *terra incognita*.

For three decades professional historians, experts in the humanities, and social scientists have been systematically reconstructing the lives of older people in disparate times and different places. Spaces remain in our knowledge base. We lack paradigms to describe and explain individual cultural and structural forces that shape late-life circumstances. Crucial details are missing about adult life expectancies, family dynamics, social relations, work patterns, civic engagement, beliefs, dependency, frailty, and abuse in times past.

That the canons guiding historiography differ from how other researchers of (old) age proceed impedes progress. Narrative matters to historians who write books; theoretical articles count more in other disciplines. Interests converge, to be sure. Social and behavioral investigators write more international comparisons than Clio's heirs, though some historians are making the world their stage. They emulate such early 20th-century authors as Oswald Spengler, Arnold Toynbee, and H.G. Wells; and latter-day students Alfred Crosby, Robert Fogel, William McNeill, and Peter Stearns.

The first wave of historians of ageing in the 1970s and 1980s amplified and/or criticized modernization theory then in vogue in social gerontology (Cowgill and Holmes, 1972). This approach largely was abandoned as researchers of ageing embraced other analytic frameworks. Since then, social scientists and experts in the humanities have offered two different methodological strategies for doing historical gerontology. Some borrow constructs from economics, epidemiology, the behavioral sciences as well as sociology and anthropology to bolster their narrative. Other scholars incorporate tropes from the humanities, an approach that yields felicitous discourse but does little for theory-building.

A middle ground exists – to compare and contrast across time and space how developments in urbanization, migration, technology, disease, secularization, and the arts affected continuities and changes in the meanings of age and the variegated situations of the aged over time. The environment, natural and made by humans, influence(d) how elders were perceived and treated, as well as how they acclimated and adapted to changes in their environs. Global histories generally omit cross-cultural similarities and variations over the life course. Consequently, they yield little about the paradoxical, ambiguous, and contingent features of maturity and senescence. Data come from national, regional, and local case studies.

This overview of historical patterns and developments in global ageing begins by analyzing the enduring impact of archetypes characterizing older men and women. Insofar as archetypes define the original pattern from which subsequent perceptions and concepts spring, such images are both descriptive and explanatory. Unpacking the clusters of how people viewed themes within archetypes helps to unravel the complexities of older persons' characteristics and conditions.

The aged historically have always been recognized as an identifiable, yet heterogeneous group. But images alone do not reflect late-life diversity. Alternations in social institutions and structural networks create distinctive contexts for all age groups. Developments in childhood and adulthood now and in the past influence the late-life experiences of successive cohorts. Wars, plagues, financial booms and bubbles over the centuries have caused profound transformations in the expectations and experiences of ordinary persons as they advance in years. Organizational changes typically have evolved more gradually than societal dislocations, but their cumulative impact on processes of senescence have been no less decisive. Institutional changes have been more gradual, but their cumulative impact no less real.

Institutions and inventions are central in any historical narrative of global ageing. Social networks, political systems, economic organizations, and cultural resources affect life courses and, in the process, have transformed institutions and networks themselves. Cultural values lagged sometimes behind structural conditions, and vice versa.

The history of global ageing rests so far mainly on information gleaned from North American and Western European sources (Thane, 2005). Premodern historical data about old age in the southern hemisphere – Africa, the Middle East, South America, Southeast Asia, the Subcontinent – lie buried in modern accounts (Makoni and Stroeken, 2002; Phillips, 1992). There are lacunae in information about the condition of the old north of the Equator: little is known, for instance, about the history of old age in Imperial Russia, Byzantian, or the Ottoman Empire (Minois, 1989).

This historical overview of global ageing has four parts. First, I deconstruct archetypes ascribed to late life. The chapter devotes more space to archetypes than I have elsewhere (Achenbaum, 2005a), because these foundational icons capture so many divergent trajectories of ageing. Secondly, to the extent possible, I trace similarities and differences in individual and collective journeys of life over time and space. I pay particular attention to commonalities and variations in the circumstances of the aged by region, period, cohort, class, gender, ethnicity, and race. Thirdly, the chapter illustrates how successive increments of institutional configurations have created age-based norms and caused anomalies and alliances in intergenerational relations. Finally, I turn briefly to 20th-century developments, wherein the most radical transformations in the histories of ageing everywhere on the globe have occurred.

Historical perspectives are essential to gerontology. Reconstructing past conditions serves as a prologue for understanding how current opportunities and future challenges impact individual and societal ageing. Textured histories of global ageing – at the individual, institutional, and (inter)national levels – remind us both of the universal qualities of senescence and of its distinctive manifestations in particular times and places.

ARCHETYPES OF AGE

Three archetypal characteristics of old age are easily recognizable. First are the physical features of late life. Older people often have thin or scraggly white or gray hair. Wrinkles line their faces and extremities. Elders are missing teeth. Dental care is a low priority even in the postmodern era. Physical variations among the old are also visible: some have shrunk in body size and height, others are sickly, while still others are robust. Virtually none retains a youthful appearance.

Secondly are the physical and other differences that distance facets of youth from old age. Variations in status and experiences count. Those with wealth and power historically have been respected. Having few assets in late life generally diminished a person's social status in the community (Demos, 1978: S 277). Those who must depend on others for shelter and sustenance were deemed pitiable, pitiful. Some got support because of their neighborliness or rectitude. The plight of others was ignored; they were subject to cruelty and abuse.

Third is gender's relevance in constructing imagery. In many historical epochs men and women lived in parallel (but not identical) separate spheres. Older women, on balance, have suffered greater indignities and deprivations than older men because of what is culturally defined as diminished beauty and their lack of independent control over resources. Some postmenopausal women were perceived to have greater access than men to the Divine. Such powers inspired awe and fear. Etymologically, these three archetypal features of senescence ultimately trace back to meanings associated with a cluster of words used to define 'old.'

The old ones, etymologically

Classical languages had specific terms with which people contrasted old humans (*geraios* and *senex* in Greek and Latin, respectively) from old inanimate objects (*palaios* and *vetus*). When Greeks used *palaios* to refer to the aged, the connotation was derogatory. According to the *Oxford English Dictionary*, 'old' built on Classical roots to form cognates in Early Middle English, Old High German, and Gothic. Greek and Latin words also had parallels in Etruscan, Sanskrit, and Armenian (*Omniglot*, 2007).

In the Classical era and subsequent centuries 'old' did not always refer to elderly men and women. The word 'old,' for example, could apply to the Devil, or it was used as a term of familiarity ('ol' buddy') in everyday encounters. Occasionally 'old' was affixed to a nation, especially to refer to inhabitants' experiences in ancient history.

Still, many definitions in English and other languages clearly applied to an advanced stage of human existence. The first verifiable use of the expression 'old age,' according to the *Oxford English Dictionary*, occurred in 1205, signifying an advanced phase period of life. Within decades, 'old man' had come into common parlance. So had the expression 'old woman,' which was deployed as a disparaging phrase in 1288. The phrase 'ripe old age' dates from the second half of the 1300s. 'Aged,' the condition of having lived or existed long, entered the English lexicon around 1440. Symbols represented letters in the Orient. Primitive Cantonese, Taiwanese, and ShuoWen had similar characters for an old man with long hair, leaning on a cane (Dictionary.com, 2007; Etymology, 2007).

Positive and a few negative connotations were associated with 'old age' in the 15th through 17th centuries. When features of late life were deemed praiseworthy, the adjective 'great' tagged with 'old age.' In the 16th century, wisdom (then defined as that capacity of knowing through lived experience) was associated with old age. During the same period, however, there were written instances of disrespect toward both older men and women; 'old age' was a term of jest directed toward both sexes a century later. Other combinations arose over time, such as 'old maid,' 'old woman,' 'old wife,' and 'old bachelor.' Twentieth-century American English incorporates 'old' and 'age' to identify public policies and age-based social organizations (Harris, 1988).

Not all such combinations referred to older humans (despite the likely presumption that they did). 'Old boy,' for instance, referred in the Middle Ages to a kind of strong ale. Botanists used human features of age to describe plants. In the 13th century, they named a certain type of cactus with the Latin cognate for 'old man's beard.' Some allusions to age in the botanists' taxonomy, such as the origin of the elderberry tree, are questionable.

Other words referred to the last stages of human existence. 'Alder' in Old English became 'elder' in Middle English. 'Elder' referred to a parent or ancestor as well as an older person.

In some African societies, 'elder' referred to a senior member of the tribe, usually someone invested with authority (www.Allwords.com, 2007). 'Eldership' was first used in 16th-century English texts to describe positively a senior position in ecclesiastical hierarchies. (The term was also employed negatively as a mock title of honor.) 'Elderly' entered the English language in the 17th century. Not necessarily referring to someone advanced in years, 'elderly' meant somewhat old, 'verging toward old age' (Achenbaum et al., 1996: 59–61).

The Latin term for old man, *senex*, was the basis for a variety of meanings in Indo European languages. The Old Persian term *hanata* meant 'old age, lapse of time.' *Sina* in Old Nordic referred to 'dry standing grass from the previous year.' The Old Welsh cognate meant 'weak or infirm from age' (Online Etymology Dictionary, 2007). Families placed 'senior' after a man's name to distinguish a father from his son. As early as 1380, 'senior' was an honorific title referring to an 'elderly person, worthy of deference by reason of age.' In English, the word 'senile' did not acquire pathological connotations until the 19th century; originally, it was simply a synonym for 'old.'

The realm of matriarchs and patriarchs

The differentiation of characteristics of older men and women dates back to the Classical era. *Senex* applied to old men; *anus*, which meant 'many years old,' referred only to old women. The Aberdeen Bestiary, which scholars date to the 13th century, abounds in distinctions between young and old, male and female, rich and poor. Asserting that older women were more lustful and passionate than men, the text refers to *virago*, a strong woman who does not perform offices assigned to a man though she does masculine things (Aberdeen Bestiary, 2007). Beginning in the 15th century a new set of late-life, gender-specific terms entered the English language. 'Grandfather' appeared in the mid-15th century. 'Patriarchy' was in the ecclesiastical vocabulary in 1561; the first recorded use of the term meant a 'system of society or government by fathers or elder males of the community' and occurred in 1632. 'Matriarch' was abstracted from 'patriarch' in 1606. 'Grandmother' like 'grandfather' found a place in the English lexicon around 1440. 'Beldam,' a flattering term to describe an aged woman, appeared in 1580. Use of the term 'matriarchy,' in contrast, cannot be verified before 1885 (Online Etymology Dictionary, 2007).

Patriarchies originated in the ancient era. Romulus founded Rome, Erectheus established

Athens, and Lacedaemon built Sparta. The Torah declares that Jews were descended from Abraham through Isaac; the Qur'an traces Arabic lineage to Abraham through Ishmael. These founders, great influences on their families and community, were accorded higher status than women as long as they fulfilled their proper roles. Men were not necessarily old when they established their patriarchies, but myth and history indicates that most founding fathers ruled for decades and lived to a ripe old age.

Wealth secured high status for men, but it did not necessarily qualify them as patriarchs. The Latin equivalent for an affluent Attic landowner in Greece was *paterfamilias*. They used their fortunes to secure sinecures for offspring, a practice extending at least into the Middle Ages (Herlihy, 1985). Wealth, conversely, gave elders a measure of control over adult children, to induce them to care for aged relatives in return for deferred compensation.

Gerontocracies were old men's institutions, dating back to the Spartan *gerusia*, which admitted 28 men over 60 years old to their council, and to the Roman Senate, which gave its eldest member the privilege of speaking first in a debate. A gerontocracy flourished in Renaissance Venice (Finlay, 1980). There are instances of more contemporary political gerontocracies. Old men ruled in Nigeria and wielded power in the Edo tribe. Especially after World War II, septuagenarians and octogenarians held key positions in the Soviet Politburo and in the Chinese Communist party (Davis-Friedman, 1991). Democracies mimic gerontocracies insofar as their leaders gain seniority in high positions by ageing in place. In the United States, key congressional committee chairs go to men who live long enough to benefit from incumbency (Achenbaum, 1985). Healthful age plus wealth generally assured high social status in premodern times; lacking wealth or power lowered old men's standing.

Old men were far more likely than older women to preside over religious institutions; in certain circumstances their rule may be considered gerontocratic. Joseph Smith was in his 20s when he founded the Church of the Latter Day Saints and led believers to Utah to escape persecution in antebellum America. Men well advanced in years control the polity and finances of the Mormon Church worldwide. Older clergy dominate affairs in Iran and Iraq, though they typically delegate day-to-day politics to younger men. The Roman Catholic hierarchy since the election of Gregory VII to the papacy in 1073 resembles a gerontocracy. There have been secular increases both in the average age of cardinals appointed to the Curia and in the ages at which successive popes die. Yet these geriatric indicators are counterbalanced by other historical developments. Paul VI restricted papal ballots in 1965 to cardinals under the age of 80. And the church bureaucracy in most countries depends in part on the energy of priests and lay people (including women) under the age of 65 to support ageing priests and prelates (Achenbaum, 1993).

It is difficult to verify ethnographic and etymological data that intimate that polities some places were governed by older women. Myths exist about matriarchal tribes, such as the Amazons in the Aegean and women ruling in certain South American tribes. I found two matriarchies. Based on a study of 68 African Bantu dialects, old females apparently dominated in prehistoric times until cattle ownership altered gender politics. Men were better able to defend cattle from marauders; they used cattle herds to acquire wives (Bhattacharya, 2003). Secondly, elderly clan mothers ruled the Chamorro people of the Mariana Islands in Micronesia when Magellan first sailed to Guam in 1521. After the Jesuits began subduing and converting Chamorro compounds roughly 150 years later, older women preserved the indigenous language and perpetuated traditional culture (Shimodate, 2007). There is no incontrovertible evidence that any contemporary matriarchal state exists.

That said, anthropologists among other investigators have studied many communities south of the Equator sustained through matrilineal lines. Women control the household wealth. Lineage is traced through the mother's side of the family. Some matrilocal societies are matrifocal: the Nair community in Kerala, South India (until 1975); the Mosuo people, who live on Lugu Lake between the borders of the Yunnan and Sichuan provinces in China; natives of the Bolma archipelago in Guinea; and the Guajiro tribes in Colombia. Scholars disagree over definitions and the full extent to which women (especially older ones) truly possess socioeconomic control in these places (Mosuo, 2007; Stearns, 2000). Yet the historical record proffers ample proof that older women had certain forms of gender-specific power.

Wise elders

Although older women seldom predominated in secular affairs, contacts with the Sacred empowered them with wisdom. Aged women in ancient times were respectfully called 'hags.' Derived from the Greek term for 'holy woman,' *hagia* was related to the ancient Egyptian word *heq*. Wise Goddesses reigned in many ancient civilizations: Athene possessed the Wisdom of Zeus, Minerva the Wisdom of Jupiter. Lesser male gods deferred to these women and sought their guidance. Pre-Islamic Arabs worshipped the Old Woman. Shakti was the Great Wisdom Goddess in India; mortal females were recognized to be shaktis on earth. Hebrew scripture (Prov. 9: 1–6; Job 38), such as the Book of Job, claims that Wisdom in the shape of a woman was present at Creation. Sophia and the Holy Spirit are portrayed as aged, feminine sources of Wisdom in the New Testament, Gnostic Gospels, and Syrian texts (Walker, 1985: 38, 55–59; Matthews, 2001). Even after male gods supplanted female gods in ancient cultures, people still considered the wisdom of older women divinely inspired. In the Middle East and Egypt, older women provided medical and social services through ecclesiastical auspices. They transcribed scripture and taught religious and secular subjects (Walker, 1985: 31). In the Confucian world, older women prevailed over their sons and daughters (Thang, 2000: 196). Despite the fact that by the 16th century the Roman Catholic and Orthodox churches banned women from sacerdotal roles, the Wise Goddess was called *Sapientia*, the essence, light, and life of all creation. This threefold characterization resembles the Oriental concept of a female goddess with the power (over men) to create, preserve, and destroy. Oriental cosmology in turn migrated back to the Renaissance: Jewish Cabalists sought to reunite God with his lost spouse (said to emanate from primordial Great Wisdom) in their mystic visions. Tradition dictated that men needed spouses who would direct them in matters sacred and profane (Walker, 1985: 61–2).

Years of experience, more than their connection to deities, ripened older men's wisdom. Hebrew Scripture ascribes extraordinary longevity to the Patriarchs. Methuselah supposedly died at the age of 969. Moses survived to 120, which Genesis 6:3 claimed to be the maximum human life span. Byzantine iconography venerated age as a source of moral worth; some Orthodox artists even portrayed Jesus as an old man (Dagron, 1991: 28). Ancient texts from the East make an analogous connection between male longevity and wisdom. 'May we, living, reach a happy old age,' read a Sanskrit text no later than the 9th century, BCE. 'Always with good minds, with good sight' (Linguistics Research Center, 2007). Confucius (551–479 BCE) in his *Analects* sketched the path to late-life wisdom:

> At fifteen, I set my heart on learning.
> At thirty, I became firm.
> At forty, I had no more doubts.
> At fifty, I understood Heaven's will.
> At sixty, my ears were attuned to this Will.
> At seventy, I could follow my heart's desires, and know they were right.

A millennium later the Indian poet and grammarian Bhartrihari (450–510) opined that wisdom in the last quarter of a 100-year life span came from the experiences of 'lamenting and grieving over a series of bereavements' (Bhartrihari, 2007). Paul's words in Acts and his Letter to the Romans three centuries earlier made a similar observation about suffering being a source of wisdom, although Paul did not live a long life.

Elders as strangers, crones, and conjurers

Aged men and women, in short, differed historically from the rest of the population because of (1) their relatively small numbers, (2) their appearances, and (3) their gifts of wisdom. No wonder older people over the centuries personified 'The Other,' an image from which less positive archetypal patterns derived. The aged could potentially deploy their distinctive assets to harm younger people. Indeed, the strengths of age paradoxically put elders at risk of being viewed less with deference and awe than with fear and trepidation. Youth often treated the old with indifference or contempt, particularly if the old lacked the strength and resources to exact revenge.

Psychologist David Gutmann (1987) has hypothesized, based on cross-cultural studies, that older people were 'strangers' in the land of the young – and to their own sense of selves. With few guides and precedents, the path in late life has been shrouded in mystery. 'Old age is the most unexpected of all things that happen to a man,' declared 56-year-old Lev Trotsky in 1935.

Social norms in most places and times required strangers to be hospitably welcomed as guests. But, like immigrants who do not speak with a proper accent and do not understand the customs and traditions in a foreign land, older people have felt lonely. They sought comfort in reminiscences of the past. Similarly, young ones who do not understand the assets and liabilities of age were likely to project their suspicions and anxiety unto senescence. Under the most dire scenario, older strangers have historically been physically abused, mocked, or killed (Brandes, 1996). Like conjurers whose strangely efficacious magic potions made them useful in times of crisis, old people wisely kept their distance until their services were required.

Women's role as strangers offers a vivid account of the historical transformation of an archetype. As we have seen, people in ancient times in the West revered the powers of 'crones,' earthly vessels of divine wisdom. Then something happened. Debates over women's changing place in ancient cults and religions have radicalized theological studies. Feminist scholars have been investigating 'that part of pre-Christian religion that was most obliterated because men found it most intimidating: the negative aspect of the all-powerful Mother, who embodied the fearful potential for rejection, abandonment, death' (Schaberg, 2004; Walker, 1985: 12). So 'hagia,' the holy one, over time became hags, in the pejorative sense of being witches, wicked stepmothers. Muslims dreaded the evil eye of postmenopausal women.

Shifts in religious practice did not always affect the aged in negative ways. Shamans and conjurers in pre-Islamic Turkey, rare in number, were usually elders. People valued old ones who not only ensured the presence of the Spirit in households and communities but also served a healing function. Oguz legends deprecated those who did not kneel before the old and kiss their hands. The Qur'an commanded respect for age, an injunction honored for centuries in this predominantly Muslim country. In secular, contemporary Turkey, traditional norms such as caring for the vulnerable old in children's homes remain in place (Altun and Ersoy, 1998).

Like Shamans, old conjurers played a role as healers – and not just in Turkey. Native American conjurers, relying little on visions and incantations, claimed to draw from the bodies of patients objects alleged to cause diseases (Berthrong, 2007). Conjurers were important in antebellum US slave quarters; elders were respected for their ability to ward off evil spirits or occult illnesses attributed to supernatural forces. In Eastern cultures, such as among the Hmong people, conjurers intervened with the spirits that promoted health or illness by attempting to align a sick person's soul and energy (Kleinman, 1980). Conjurers, in short, were a distinctive group of (generally) old men and women whose mystical powers served earthly purposes. Possessing such powers, however, did not protect the old from misery and illnesses of their own.

The vulnerable and superannuated

The cumulative losses and physical vicissitudes of growing old(er) have always made aspects of late life unattractive. Older people felt vulnerable, as Hebrew Scripture attests. Hence the Psalmist (71:9) gives voice to elders' fear of rejection: 'Do not cast me off in the time of old age; forsake me not when my strength is gone.' This universal sentiment underscores the fact that age suffers in comparison with the beauty and strength of youth. In his *Aphorisms* (430 BCE), Hippocrates documented such maladies of old age as nephritis, apoplexy, cachexia, defluxions of the bowels,

cataracts, joint pain, vertigo, and coughs. Seneca (4 BCE to 65 AD) succinctly observed that *senectus morbidus est*, 'old age is a disease.' Nobel Laureate Elie Metchnikoff (1905: 48) reiterated this pathological model of ageing 1900 years later: 'Old age … is an infectious, chronic disease which is manifested by a degeneration, or an enfeebling of the noble elements.'

Hebrew Scripture acknowledged that physical decline was progressive: 'The span of our life is seventy years, perhaps in strength even eighty; yet the sum of them is but labor and sorrow, for they pass away quickly and we are gone' (Psalm 90: 10). Ecclesiastes counterpoints the sorrows of age with the vanities of youth, while underscoring the transitory nature of all human existence from womb to tomb. Roman satirists, like Juvenal (AD 60–130) went further in visualizing the fate that awaited those who lived (too) long:

> What a train of woes – and such woes – come with a prolonged age. To begin with, this deformed, hideous, unrecognizable face; this vile leather instead of skin; these pendulous cheeks; these wrinkles like those around the mouth of an old she-ape as she sits scratching … . Old men are all the same; their voices tremble, so do their limbs; no hair left on their shining scalps; they run at the nose like little children. To chew his bread, the poor ancient has nothing but toothless gums … . A perpetual train of losses, incessant mourning and old age dressed in black, surrounded by everlasting sadness – that is the price of a long life.
> (quoted in de Beauvoir, 1972: 121–2)

When Bernice Neugarten in the 1970s differentiated the 'young old' from the 'old-old,' her scheme resembled the age-old distinction made between a 'green old age' and 'decrepitude.' Contemporary gerontologists recognize that octogenarians nowadays have greater vitality than even two generations ago. But with gains in adult longevity, the risk of co-morbidity increases. Everyone desires to live, noted Jonathan Swift, 'but no man would be old.'

For this reason, scientists, alchemists, and adventurers since ancient times have sought ways to prolong healthful longevity – indefinitely, if possible. Myths of rejuvenation existed from Icelandic sagas to Subcontinent legends. The promise of a Foundation of Youth, which cost Ponce de Leon his life, originated in the Orient (Hopkins, 1905: 15). In the West, some of gerontology's forebears – Aristotle, Francis Bacon, Luigi Cornaro, Cicero, William Godwin, Wilhelm Christhof Hufeland, and C.A. Stephens – 'were so optimistic that they foresaw a decisive solution to the problems of death and old age; they aimed at the attainment of virtual immortality and eternal youth' (Gruman, 1966: 5). Yet, unless the current anti-ageing movement succeeds where earlier experiments have failed spectacularly, there will be no reversal of the ravages of age. Even the most vital among the growing population of old-old ultimately confront the vicissitudes of living far too long.

Loss of strength eventually diminished men's capacity to gain a livelihood. Archeological evidence from Africa between 7000 and 3500 BCE indicates that the formation of agricultural communities affected all age groups. Older men could not keep up with younger tribal members on hunts. Aged women found it increasingly difficult to gather plants to eat. (The pattern obtained in northern climes where food supplies were limited; the harsh physical environment weakened persons past their prime.) Prehistoric African elders became *superannuated*, marginalized economically on account of advanced age. The word, which entered the English language in 1633, was associated with exemption from performing military service and with phasing out home-based manufacturing. That the definition was ageist – 'retired on account of age ... obsolete, out of date' – had obvious consequences. A man who could not support himself, much less his household, was dependent on kin and neighbors for essentials. In times of scarcity, inactive older men were at the mercy of others, who themselves lived precariously.

The situation was far grimmer for aged women, usually lacking assets in their own right. Widowhood made older women quite vulnerable. Remarriage was unlikely. Older women depended on compassion, traditional norms, and whatever legal rules protected their rights. Thus Hebrew Scripture and the New Testament entreated readers to remember to care for the widow. Revealingly, 'widow' in Sanskrit meant 'empty.' They were non-entities. The English Reformation, which closed many Roman Catholic charitable societies, forced widows to seek new sources of alms. Parliament thwarted the efforts of those deemed unworthy of support (Botelho and Thane, 2001: 25–6). Widows, even more than their younger peers, had to behave properly, lest they be subject to witch hunts and derision (Stearns, 1982: 10).

Along with pain, dependency, and vulnerability came varying degrees of rejection in late life. Aristotle in *Politics* contended that older men were too petty and inflexible to serve in public office. Aristophanes agreed, adding a list of sexual foibles to his indictment of old age. A Roman expression, *sexagenarius ex ponte*, indicates that drowning senior citizens in the Tiber was one way to eliminate their presence – a custom practiced by aboriginal people who set their decrepit elders afloat on chunks of ice. Islam, in contrast, affirmed virtue in suffering. The frailties of age were harbingers of disease and death, but the Qur'an taught that the vicissitudes of life provided an edifying opportunity to surrender to God (Thursby, 2000: 159).

Ageing and death

For most of recorded history, death struck at all ages, notably in infancy and childhood. Plagues, natural disasters, and wars killed people in their prime. To reach 40 historically raised chances of attaining a 'ripe old age.' In the contemporary era, people increasingly die in old age. Advances in public health, preventive medicine, diet, and technology enabled successive cohorts (initially those in industrializing nations) to survive until middle age. In addition to links between death and late life, older people served key roles in the rituals associated with death and burial at certain places and times.

Perhaps the most vivid image of age and death portrays Father Time as an old man. Around 1400, folk artists began to depict Father Time's sickle, an agricultural tool associated with fecundity, as an instrument of death. Father Time remains the Grim Reaper. Mexicans feature the image prominently in observances of the Day of the Dead.

Hinduism infuses its caste systems and cosmologies by connecting ageing and death from a life-course perspective. Most teachings link images of the birth canal and the burial ground. Believers hope to elude suffering through a series of rebirths. Some prayers honor the elders on their paths. Others allude to 'toothless and driveling' old age. Over time, people renounce familial bonds and social obligations. The aged in this context have been described as homeless sojourners who seek spiritual embodiment (Tilak, 1989).

Buddhist traditions treat old age and death differently from Hinduism. The founder, Gautama, had been shielded in his early years from sickness, poverty, ageing, and death. Confronting the ravages of age for the first time, Gautama shrunk from its ugliness as he awakened to the reality of suffering. Buddha sought several ways to achieve Enlightenment before he came upon his true nature, which meant giving up possessions and acknowledging the impermanence of mortal life. Over time, Buddha came to embody the compassionate wisdom that he so desired and taught. As a Cambodian aphorism puts it, 'Young people make rice, old people make merit.' The Buddha lived a long life; he was nearly 80 when poisoned by his cook.

Death and dying afford(ed) older women an unpaid but essential role to fulfill. The ancient Crone served as a Death Mother and funerary priestess.

Whereas old men performed the sacramental rites essential for the passage of the soul, older women cared for the dying and prepared the body for burial (Walker, 1985: 32–4). A gendered division of labor persists in modern-day rural Japan. Men oversee public festivals and ceremonies. Women console the survivors, by transmitting ancestral concern to kin. Performing such tasks makes the old ones 'rojin,' good individuals engaged in activities that promote social comity amidst a time of grief (Traphagan, 2004).

Many Archetypes, in sum, shadow the cultural history of global ageing. Far from conveying a monochromatic image, archetypes from different cultures and historical epochs reveal positive and negative, stereotypical and mythical, accurate and ambiguous characteristics of late-life physicality, wisdom, sexuality, roles, family relations, religiosity, and morbidity (among other things) in all its diversity, temporally and geographically. Some gender-specific meanings and circumstances have changed over time. Exceptions and anomalies exist. Ancient tropes resonate with modernity. Sometimes the words used to describe elders migrate from one extreme to another. At other times, transformations have been nuanced, fraught with ambivalence. How closely do continuities and shifts in archetypes of old age correspond to the lived experiences of older people in different times and different places?

THE JOURNEY OF LIFE

Demographic patterns over time

The limits of human longevity have fascinated people for millennia. Archeologists, anthropologists, and ethnographers have gathered reports from South America in the pre-colonial and modern era, in the state of Georgia in the former Soviet Union, and a few other places that boast that some residents have lived roughly 150 years. Cases of US men and women living 130 years and beyond are in Civil War pension records and Social Security beneficiary files. None can be authenticated. Respondents did not know when they were really born. Or, the claims of super-longevity served a societal purpose, such as promoting tourism.

The best scientific estimate of the maximum human life span is about 120 years, a span that has not changed greatly over historical time. That there are exceptions does not invalidate this historical generalization, although there have been dramatic changes in life expectancy. The average length of life in the Bronze Age was under 18, and in the Classical era was under 30, in medieval Britain 33. Currently, the worldwide average has doubled.

Some men and women reached remarkably advanced ages in societies past and present – an Egyptian papyrus claimed that the span between 40 and 100 were the best years of a person's life (Parsons, 2007) – but in prehistoric settlements the proportion of humans over 65 rarely exceeded 2% (Hauser, 1976). Infant and childhood mortality devastated younger populations. Millennia later, a child born in the United States in 1790 had as much chance of reaching his or her first year as a child born in 1970 had of attaining 65 years. Only one in three children survived their first birthday in Bombay in 1900 (Robinson, 1989: 119). If a person in past times were extraordinarily fortunate to live until 50 – Peruvians, that age on the eve of the Spanish conquest were called 'half old' (Collier et al., 1992: 83) – she or he had nearly as much chance of reaching old age as someone in that region in the contemporary era.

The onset of 'old age' throughout recorded history has been considered to occur at age 65 – give or take 15 years either way (Achenbaum, 1978). That is a span larger than any other period of life. And that demographic range helps to explain the tremendous variance in older people's physical, mental, economic, and social status. Gender differences matter: older women now on average live longer than older men; in past times, however, many died in childbirth. Ethnic differences persist. On average, chronic and accident-related disabilities disproportionately strike people of color.

Falling birth rates in North America and Western Europe since 1700 have resulted in increases in the percentage of older people in the population. Declining fertility rates and advances in life expectancy at birth (on average in the United States from 47 to 78 in the 20th century) have resulted in societal as well as individual ageing. There are striking global variations. Only 5 per cent of Japan's population was over 65 in 1950; it now boasts increases in life expectancy from 50 to 78 for men and from 55 to 83 for women between 1947 and 1995, making Japan an 'older' population than Sweden (Thang, 2000: 193). South of the Equator, unlike northern countries, fertility rates remain high. Simultaneously, however, the percentage of older people in the Caribbean, Chile, Costa Rica, and Mexico is expected to double between 2000 and 2025 (Dickerson, 2007). Thus, policymakers must allocate resources to dependents at both ends of the life course.

Economic patterns over time

For most of world history, humans have engaged in agricultural pursuits. Despite the hard work often performed in inhospitable settings, this activity has offered generally favorable economic conditions for the old. Even when their capacity diminished, the aged could help younger family members with necessary tasks and keeping track of the calendar and records. The elders knew how to interpret weather patterns and which parts of the land flooded. Years of experience made them useful managers, truly veterans of productivity. And the old almost invariably owned the household's land.

Maintaining possession of the family farm gave the old a measure of security in late life. Adult children had to work if they eventually were to inherit the land. Thus, wise aged men willingly gave their offspring parcels, on the condition that their heirs would care for them in their declining years and provide for widows when they were gone. While this pattern probably obtained in most places, the history of inheritance, especially in agrarian settings below the Equator, has not yet been written.

The Industrial Revolution transformed the economic status of the older persons at first in Europe and North America, in good and bad ways. New modes of production made improved goods accessible. New technologies made it easier for older people to perform daily tasks. Material progress contributed to overall prosperity, affording the old a higher standard of living (Haber and Gratton, 1994). Some elders profited mightily from industrialization. John D. Rockefeller, nearly 60 when he became the world's first billionaire, gave away $500 million by the time he died on the eve of his 100th birthday. Managers who owned railroads, steel mills, and other profitable corporations enjoyed a disproportionate share of the nation's wealth.

That said, with the declining importance of agriculture and the diminished demand for handmade products, the Industrial Revolution contributed to obsolescence in old age. Many elders found it difficult to adapt to the demands of mechanized production: they lacked the stamina and efficiency to keep up with the pace set by the clock. Titans of industry valued the agile youth and speedy machines more than the skills of the older craftsperson (Lynd and Lynd, 1929: 42–3). While historians debate the direction and magnitude of changes in employment rates during the initial phases of industrialization, according to official documents, labor force participation declined. By the 20th century the downward trend in old-age employment was unmistakable (Schaie and Achenbaum, 1993; Achenbaum, 1978). Among the unskilled, superannuation was treated as a form of disability. Older workers begged for money in saloons and at the factory gates as their middle-aged sons (prematurely old) risked life and limb performing hazardous tasks. Wives supplemented household incomes by taking in boarders, running saloons, and working as shopkeepers (Bell, 1944). Industrialization provided jobs for young women in mills and other factories; such positions rarely went to older women.

During the second half of the 19th century, British and US banks and transportation companies began to offer pensions based on a worker's age and years of experience. Besides being rewards for good service, corporate pensions were incentives to maintain the loyalty of middle-aged workers. Corporations, under no obligation to honor pension commitments, extended gratuities to a relatively small proportion of the labor force. Those who did not receive pensions had to find odd jobs, supplement income with modest savings, or rely on union-sponsored subsidies, which were limited in scope (Hannah, 1985). The advent of retirement plans for government employees and social insurance schemes for workers offered the old a measure of old-age security, which in turn inspired innovations by private insurance firms and businesses (Graebner, 1981).

Political patterns over time

The State has historically been the key political actor deciding the rights and entitlements of older people. The Senate exempted Romans from military service at age 60; centuries later British and French rulers followed suit, retiring military personnel at prescribed ages. Twelfth-century Chinese emperors were the first to give pensions to loyal bureaucrats. Suleiman the Magnificent, who ruled from 1520 to 1566, exempted elders, priests, women, and children from paying taxes (Embree, 2004).

In the Middle Ages, public institutions increasingly became an important source of old-age relief, taking over larger shares of healthcare services traditionally performed by monasteries and church-related hospitals (Thane, 2005). In addition, local institutions allocated resources, providing food and fuel to elders in their homes, in other people's residences, or in public almshouses. In the United States, thanks to the nation's first gray lobby, the Grand Army of the Republic, veterans' pensions became the most important source of old-age financial assistance for Union soldiers at the turn of the 20th century. Outlays to claimants over 62 were the largest item in the Federal budget in 1914. Adding to the burden of losing the Civil War, Southern states went further in debt to assist Confederate veterans who received nothing from the victors (Skocpol, 1992).

Institutions come and go, giving rise to circumstances that alter relations across and within age groups. It is worth noting that older people, by dint of their numbers and power as a voting bloc, gained unprecedented power in the 20th century as a political voice. The Townsend Movement, for instance, spurred age consciousness and political awareness and resulted in the political empowerment of the older population. Sexagenarian Frances Townsend filled stadiums with supporters convinced of his plan to give men and women over 60 years old $200 per month on the condition that they do not work and that they spend the sum in 30 days. Supporters formed Townsend Clubs coast to coast, mobilizing support for a plan that would prime the economy by making elders consumers of goods produced by younger workers back on the job (Putnam, 1970). But Townsend's panacea was never viable. Twentieth-century fund economists demolished its logic. Key congressional committees listened politely to advocates, but few were swayed. The Townsend Movement fizzled before the first Social Security check was issued.

National governments spearheaded social insurance programs, covering the risks of illness, disability, and senescence. Old-age assistance schemes typically preceded old-age insurance plans and health-insurance programs. Initially, measures sought to reduce poverty among the old rather than assure income security (Beland, 2005). European countries (starting with Bismarck's Germany in 1889) and New Zealand took the lead; the United States was a relative late comer. Now, virtually every nation in the world makes provisions for its older population. Population size, ideology, the state of the economy, and availability of funds determined the timing and extent of coverage. The growth of old-age interest groups spurred expansion and prevented serious contraction of entitlements (Binstock and Day, 1995). Population ageing and anticipated limits to economic growth have dampened popular confidence in the fiscal and political robustness of publicly funded social-insurance schemes. Yet relying primarily on individuals or the private sector presents its own risks in a global economy.

Social patterns over time

Families traditionally have been the first line of emotional and economic support for older people. Household structures and generational dynamics have varied over time and place. Older men in Western Europe remained heads of household as long as physically possible. Nuclear families since pre-industrial times have been the ideal and norm (Laslett and Wall, 1972), though death, divorce, and harsh circumstances have necessitated temporary 'stem' families or extended residency in households by kin. The Elizabethan Poor Law of 1601 required

grandparents to assist grandchildren and cousins to care for any kin in need. In the modern era, greater emphasis in Europe and North America has been placed on 'autonomy' over 'independence.'

Matrifocal or matrilocal patterns have prevailed south of the Equator in Asia and Africa (Humphrey and Oron, 1996: 96). Daughters-in-law often co-resided with their mothers-in-law, with the expectation that the youngest daughter would care for elders in due course. Sometimes aunts and cousins helped with cooking, cleaning, and caring. Deference to elders, with males taking precedence over females, continues to shape Japanese customs (Bowring and Kornecki, 1993: 236). Aborigines tended to prefer more 'open' arrangements: 'fathers' and 'elders' were sometimes fictive kin who control household affairs.

Yet families have always been fragile safety nets. Divorce, estrangement, and death broke bonds. Poverty strained resources. In such situations, elders historically had to rely on friends and neighbors on an informal basis. Faith-based communities have always cared for elders. In the West older people could also turn to voluntary associations, such as unions and fraternal lodges, charities, and civic groups. Such organizations have existed globally, but nowhere have they lasted permanently. Consequently, the major source of assistance in most countries historically came with the rise of public social services. In addition, new modes of transportation and communication compensated for the geographic mobility that distanced kin.

Cultural patterns over time

Although old age has always been a distinct (if oftimes marginalized) phase of life, throughout history everywhere elderhood has been interpreted in the context of other age groups. People move through time with other cohorts. An imaginative portrayal of this journey through life was rendered by European folk artists between the 14th and 18th centuries. In presenting 'the steps of ages,' male and female, artists traced the connection among biological age, chronological age, and social function upwards from birth to the prime of life (typically 40 or 50) and then depicted the descent to death.

Artists portrayed elders as vital beyond the prime of life. Roles changed: men in their 60s were businessmen or lawyers, no longer soldiers. They usually had beards, a mark of their learning and experience. In literature and historical accounts from the period, old men were mentors, willing and able to transmit life's practical and existential lessons to younger people wise enough to seek advice. Women, who did not look as healthful as men their age, nonetheless remained busy in the home, surrounded by adoring (grand) children. By 80, the gloomy aspects of late life were manifest. Stooped, the aged were content to remain near the hearth. A decade later they were depicted as bedridden, as helpless as infants as they entered second childhood.

Jainism, an offshoot of Hinduism, offers an Eastern religious counterpart to medieval renditions of the stages of life. Childhood, youth, adulthood, and old age are considered modifications of transient forms of a living being. Only the soul has permanent substance. According to Jainism, when we die, we are born into another body, with the same soul (JCNC, 2007).

Intergenerational relations have not always been happy. The aged could be victims and perpetrators in strife, as Hesiod recounts. Cronus got rid of his father, Uranus, by castrating him at his mother's request. Fearing a similar fate, Cronus swallowed his five children alive. Alas, he did not succeed in eliminating his competition. Again at his mother's contrivance, one child (Zeus) managed to live; Zeus thereupon killed Cronos.

Contemporary rivalries are rarely so violent, but they can be nasty. Money, control, and esteem have long been the source of discord. But the cultural roots of modern-day intergenerational conflict go beyond family politics. Robert Butler (1975) coined the term 'ageism,' to describe the cultural animus against people on the basis of their years. Butler considered ageism comparable to sexism and racism. Ageism affects not only personal relations but also is endemic in most contemporary institutions, ranging from health-care centers to faith-based communities (Achenbaum, 2005b).

Lately, institutional ageism has been particularly virulent in the media, which has made much of a so-called generation gap. Magazine covers graphically show narcissistic elders enjoying the good life in posh settings, unmindful of accusations that they are squandering their children's inheritance. Critics deride members of the 'Greatest Generation,' men and women who survived the Great Depression and won World War II, as 'greedy geezers.' Sometimes columnists take cues from organizations like the Association for Generational Equity, which pitted the interests of white elders against the needs of poor children of color. The charge had little basis: in fact, there has been greater economic transfer from old to young in terms of paying tuitions and covering mortgages than from young to old. But in a culture of consumption where advertisers and drug companies exalt beauty and sensuality, allusions to aged sexuality and elders' vain efforts to look young draw laughs. AARP, which claims that '60 is now 30,' has not yet convinced people.

Thus, it is important to examine age-relevant institutions, to assess whether they promote age-appropriate sensibilities.

PAST AS PROLOGUE

The historical watershed in global ageing occurred in the 20th century. Two-thirds of all gains in life expectancy have taken place since 1900. Retirement has become widespread. Lifelong learning opportunities proliferate after centuries of being the stepchild of adult-education plans. Out of desire or necessity, older workers seek part-time jobs or volunteer their talents in unprecedented ways. The State's age-specific policies determine the scope of old-age income security and health care. Gerontologists document that chronological age is a poor predictor of old-age characteristics, yet bureaucratic criteria paradoxically become increasingly age-based. Experts are beginning to differentiate between individual and societal ageing. As the challenges and opportunities of societal ageing slowly become part of policymakers' agendas, there is an urgent need to examine structural and cultural lags confronting men and women with extra years to live.

Ironically, taking the historical record seriously complicates contemporary assessments of global ageing. 'Age' in modern times has become a critical determinant of access to work, wealth, and power, resulting from seniority. But older people as a group have not been the prime movers who altered fertility rates, industrialization, urbanization, democratization, globalization, secularization, or commercialization. Women and minorities around the world have become key agents of intergenerational change. Ethnicity and class are important signifiers. So should we begin with the needs and gifts of older people because of their recent ascendancy in modern sensibilities, or should we deconstruct 'age' by gender, race, ethnicity, and class?

Finally, the diversity of global ageing over time raises the issue of whether scholars should emphasize universal trends over localized features, or vice versa. Will historical vectors converge with globalization? Or, will age-old customs and traditions persist, affording us a window on the fragile, complex, nuanced, contradictory, ever-changing aspects of the meanings and experiences of growing old(er)?

REFERENCES

Aberdeen Bestiary. http://www.abdn.ac.uk/bestiary/translat/ 92v.hti. Accessed June 4, 2007.

Achenbaum, W.A. (1978) *Old Age in the New Land*. Baltimore: Johns Hopkins University Press.

Achenbaum, W.A. (1985) 'Societal perceptions of old age and aging', in R.H. Binstock and E. Shanas (eds), *Handbook of Aging and the Social Sciences*, 2nd edn. New York: Van Nostrand Reinhold.

Achenbaum, W.A. (1993) '(When) did the papacy become a gerontocracy?', in K.W. Schaie and W.A. Achenbaum (eds), *Societal Impact on Aging: Historical Perspectives*. New York: Springer.

Achenbaum, W.A. (2005a) 'Ageing and changing: international perspectives on ageing', in M.L. Johnson (ed.), *The Cambridge Handbook of Age and Ageing*. Cambridge: Cambridge University Press.

Achenbaum, W.A. (2005b) *Older Americans, Vital Communities*. Baltimore: Johns Hopkins University Press.

Achenbaum, W.A., Weiland, S., and Haber, C. (1996) *Key Words in Socio-Cultural Gerontology*. New York: Springer.

Altun, I and Ersoy, N. (1998) 'Perspectives on old age in Turkey', *Eubios Journal of Asian and International Bioethics*, 8: 43–5. *AllWords.com*. http://www.allwords.com/query.php? Accessed June 4, 2007.

Beland, D. (2005) *Social Security*. Manhattan: University Press of Kansas.

Bell, T. (1944) *Out of This Furnace*. Pittsburgh: University of Pittsburgh Press.

Berthrong, D. (2007) Arapho. *Columbia Encyclopedia*, 7th edn. New York: Columbia University Press.

Berthrong, D. 'White dove's Native American Indian site elders', http://users.multipro.com/whitedover/encyclopedia/elders.html. Accessed June 8, 2007.

Bhartrihari. http://www.textetc.com/workshop/wt-bhartrihari-l.html. Accessed April 28, 2007.

Bhattacharya, S. (2003) 'Cattle ownership makes it a man's world', http://www.newscientist.com/article.ns?id=dn4220. Accessed April 24, 2007.

Binstock, R.H. and Day, C.L. (1995) 'Aging and politics', in R.H. Binstock and L. George (eds), *Handbook of Aging and the Social Sciences*, 4th edn. San Diego: Academic Press.

Botelho, L. and Thane, P. (2001) *Women and Ageing in British Society since 1500*. London: Longman.

Bowring, R. and Kornecki, P. (eds) (1993) *The Cambridge Encyclopedia of Japan*. Cambridge, MA: Cambridge University Press.

Brandes, S. (1996) 'Kinship and care for the aged in Rural Iberia', in T.K. Hareven, (ed.), *Aging and Generational Relations over the Life Course*. New York: Walter de Gruyter.

Butler, R.N. (1975) *Why Survive?* New York: Harper and Row.

Collier, S., Skidmore, T., and Blakemore, H. (eds) (1992) *Cambridge Encyclopedia of Latin America and the Caribbean*. Cambridge, MA: Cambridge University Press.

Cowgill, D. and Holmes, L. (1972) *Aging and Modernization*. New York: Appleton-Century Crofts.

Dagron, G. (1991) 'Holy images and likeness', *Dumbarton Oaks Papers*, 45: 23–33.

Davis-Friedman, D. (1991) *Long Lives: Chinese Elderly and the Communist Revolution*. Stanford, CT: Stanford University Press.

de Beauvoir, S. (1972) *The Coming of Age*. New York: G.P. Putnam and Sons.

Demos, J. (1978) 'Old age in early New England', in J. Demos and S.S. Boocock (eds), *Turning Points*. Supplement to the *American Journal of Sociology*, 84: S248–87.

Dickerson, M. (2007) 'Mexico, rest of Latin America get grayer', http://www.seattletimes.nwsource.com/html/nationworld/2002085643oldlatin03.html. Accessed April 23, 2007.

Dictionary.com http://dictionary.reference.com/browse/ripe%20old%20age. Accessed April 28, 2007.

Embree, M. (2004) 'Sulieman the Magnificant', http://www.ccds.charlotte.nc/History/MidEast/04/embree/embree.html. Accessed April 23, 2007.

Etymology. http://www.internationalscientific.org/CharacterASP/CharacterEtymology.aspx? Accessed June 4, 2007.

Finlay, R. (1980) *Politics in Renaissance Venice*. New Brunswick: Rutgers University Press.

Graebner, W. (1981) *A History of Retirement*. New Haven: Yale University Press.

Gruman, G.J. (1966) *A History of Ideas about the Prolongation of Life*. Philadelphia: The American Philosophical Society.

Gutmann, D. (1987) *Powers Reclaimed*. New York: Basic Books.

Haber, C. and Gratton, B. (1994) *Old Age and the Search for Security*. Bloomington, IN: Indiana University Press.

Hannah, L. (1985) *The Invention of Retirement*. Cambridge, MA: Cambridge University Press.

Harris, D.K. (1988) *Dictionary of Gerontology*. Westport, CT: Greenwood Press.

Hauser, P. (1976) 'Social statistics in use', *Social Science Review*, December

Herlihy, D. (1985) *Medieval Households*. Cambridge, MA: Harvard University Press.

Hopkins, E.W. (1905) 'Fountain of youth', *Journal of the American Oriental Society*, 45: 2–57.

Humphrey C. and Oron, U. (1996) *Shamans and Elders*. Oxford: Clarendon Press.

JCNC (2007) 'Tripadi – the three pronouncements', http://www.jcnc.org/jainism/PPOJ/7.htm. Accessed April 23, 2007.

Kleinman, A. (1980) *Patients and Healers in the Context of Culture*. Berkeley, CA: University of California Press.

Laslett, P. and Wall, R. (eds) (1972) *Household and Family in Past Time*. Cambridge, MA: Cambridge University Press.

Linguistics Research Center. http://www.utexas.edu/cola/centers/lrc/. Accessed April 28, 2007.

Lynd, R.S. and Lynd, H.M. (1929) *Middletown*. New York: Harcourt Brace.

Mahoni, S. and Stroeken, K. (eds) (2002) *Ageing in Africa*. Hampshire: Ashgate.

Matthews, C. (2001) *Sophia*. Wheaton, IL: Quest Books.

Metchnikoff, E. (1905) 'Old age', *Smithsonian Annual Report, 1904–05*. Washington, DC: Government Printing Office.

Minois, G. (1989) *History of Old Age*. Chicago: University of Chicago Press.

Mosuo. http://www.matriarchy.info/index.php?option=com_content&task=viewandid=5&itemid=26. Accessed April 24, 2007.

Omniglot. http://www.omniglot.com/writing/etruscan.htm. Accessed April 28, 2007.

Online Etymology Dictionary. http://www.etymonlinee.com/index.php? Accessed 6/4/2007.

Oxford English Dictionary (1971) Compact Edition. Oxford: Oxford University Press.

Parsons, M. (2007) 'Old age in Ancient Egypt', httpl//www.touregypt.net/featurerstories/oldage.htm. Accessed April 23, 2007.

Phillips, D.R. (2002) *Ageing in East and South-East Asia.* London: Edward Arnold.

Putnam, J. K. (1970) *Old-Age Politics in California.* Stanford, CT: Stanford University Press.

Robinson, F., ed. (1989) The Cambridge Encyclopedia of India, Pakistan, Bangladesh, Sri Lanka, Nepal, Bhuton and the Maldives. Cambridge, MA: Cambridge University Press.

Schaberg, J. (2004) *The Resurrection of Mary Magdalene.* New York: Continuum.

Schaie, K.W. and Achenbaum, (eds.) W.A. (1993) *Social Import on Aging: Historical Perspectives.* New York: Springer.

Shimodate, T. Chamorro. http://www.mnsu.edu/emuseum/oldworld/asia/chamorrow.html. Accessed April 24, 2007.

Skocpol, T. (1992) *Protecting Mothers and Soldiers.* Cambridge, MA: Harvard University Press.

Stearns, P.N. (ed.) (1982) *Old Age in Preindustrial Society.* New York: Holmes and Meier.

Stearns, P.N. (2000) *Gender in World History.* New York: Routledge.

Thane, P. (2005) *A History of Old Age.* Los Angeles, CA: The J. Paul Getty Museum.

Thang, L.L. (2000) 'Aging in the East: comparative and historical reflections', in T.R. Cole, R. Kastenbaum, and R.E. Ray (eds), *Handbook of Aging and the Humanities,* 2nd edn. New York: Springer.

Thursby, L. (2000) Buddhism, in T.R. Cole, R. Kastenbaum, and R. Ray (eds), *Handbook in Humanities and Aging,* 2nd edn. New York: Springer.

Tilak, S. (1989) *Religion and Aging in the Indian Tradition.* Albany, NY: State University Press of New York.

Traphagan, J.W. (2004) *The Practice of Concern: Well-Being and Aging in Rural Japan.* Durham, NC: Carolina Academic Press.

Walker, B.G. (1985) *The Crone: Woman of Age, Wisdom, and Power.* New York: Harper and Row.

3

The Economics of Ageing

James H. Schulz

INTRODUCTION

The economic situation of the aged has improved greatly over the years around the world. Schulz (2001: 2), for example, characterized the situation in the United States at the turn of the 21st century as follows:

> From a statistical point of view, the older population in this country is beginning to look a lot like the rest of the population: some very rich, lots with adequate income, lots more with very modest income (often near poverty), and a significant minority still destitute.

However, as Smeeding (2005) points out, while great strides have been made in reducing poverty among older people, the poverty rates in the United States (and the United Kingdom) are still higher than in other industrialized countries.

EARLY SOCIAL WELFARE IN THE UNITED STATES

From a historical perspective, the economic situation of the majority of older people before the mid-20th century was not good. The predominant situation was one of *dependence* and, as hard as it is to believe, one of *punishment*. Older persons in the 18th and 19th centuries who were landless in the United States found themselves at the mercy of a harsh market-oriented economy (Schulz and Binstock, 2006). Individuals were rewarded or punished, depending on their usefulness to the production of economic goods and services. As industrialization progressed in the United States during the 19th century, older workers found that they were increasingly unable to compete for new jobs paying living wages. Usually without savings, they were forced to survive on what was often erratic help from their families. Those without families able to help them were forced to turn to charities or the government for aid. In any event, the result, more often than not, was that individuals in old age often faced economic deprivation.

In colonial times, older persons with inadequate economic resources were actually taken from their homes and 'boarded out'. Towns would take their land and other assets (if they had any) and then auction off the older person to the lowest bidder (Trattner, 1989). These impoverished older persons would then receive food and shelter in return for work – a system very similar to that of indentured servitude. Starting in the middle of the 19th century, the system of support changed, though it remained equally harsh. The needy were sent to what became known as 'workhouses', the main function of which, according to officials of the time, was to punish, reform, and 'cure' the poor of their bad habits and character defects. Later, almshouses and asylums replaced the workhouse system. Some of these provided a reasonable level of support but many were places of degradation, disease, starvation, violence, and corruption.

Finally, in the Progressive Era of the early 20th century, the situation began to change for the better. Control of welfare agencies gradually shifted from (often corrupt) local officials to state agencies, which were often less dishonest. But living conditions for older people in the United States continued to vary considerably from state to state. As Quadagno (1988: 179) summarizes:

> Three crucial factors affected the structure of the American welfare state: first, the power of private sector initiatives; second, differences in the material interests and relative access to power of the two segments of the labor movement, mass-production and craft workers; and finally, the impact of the existence of two economic formations – the North and the South – within the boundaries of a single nation-state ... . Welfare programmes are not unique features of advanced capitalist societies but have served a dual function in most Western nations since at least the sixteenth century – *sustaining the vulnerable and allocating labor.* [emphasis added]

Over the years, there were many proposals for helping the poor through federal assistance. Unlike in Europe, however, the United States was slow to institute a public, collective insurance programme. Despite great need, there was a huge ideological obstacle – what has been called 'the gospel of thrift'. Quoting historian David Hackett Fischer, Quadagno (1988: 21) points out that self-reliance based on saving has been 'central to the system of secular morality in America since the Puritans'.

It took the Great Depression of the 1930s to galvanize the country into collective action. As economic conditions worsened, an unemployed doctor who was a political unknown, Frances E. Townsend, proposed a plan to help older people by giving a universal, flat pension of $200 per month to every retired citizen age 60 and older. It was a seemingly simple plan whose appeal, even to the surprise of Townsend, swept across the country. Within a year of its initial proposal, there were over a thousand Townsend Clubs urging enactment of the proposal. As a result, pension politics became a major issue. 'For many of its aged adherents, the Townsend Plan became a matter of faith, a new version of the millennium' (Holtzman, 1963: 28).

President Roosevelt strongly opposed the Townsend Plan. He was determined to create a programme where people had an opportunity to 'earn' their benefits through work and contributions of money into a collective fund. For Roosevelt, the Townsend Plan was a handout that undermined people's dignity, their desire to be self-reliant, and their incentive to work. The Townsend Plan proposal, however, 'clearly helped to marshal political support among voters for federal pension legislation to help older people, and it strongly encouraged President Roosevelt to act sooner rather than later in taking action to deal with the problems of older adults' (Schulz and Binstock, 2006: 52, based on information in

Brown, 1972). In 1935, Democratic leaders in the House of Representatives, urged on by Roosevelt, pressed the Congress to oppose the Townsend Plan, which was eventually voted down by a vote of 206 to 56. Following this, the Roosevelt plan, Social Security, passed the House by an overwhelming vote of 371 to 33 and then passed the Senate by a vote of 76 to 6.

BASIC PRINCIPLES AND SOCIAL SECURITY IN EUROPE

Social Security legislation initiated a dramatic change in the way that the United States managed economic support in old age. It was not, however, an American invention. By the time Social Security was adopted, it was already operating in most countries of Europe. Starting with Germany in 1889, under the leadership of Chancellor Otto von Bismarck, Social Security programmes were instituted to cover large segments of workers in Europe – not just military and government elites. Over a 25-year period, the Bismarck approach was adopted in a variety of forms in various countries – such as Denmark (1891), Belgium (1894), France (1903), Britain (1908), and Sweden (1913).

Many factors were important historically in stimulating the creation of Social Security programmes in Europe. Scholars generally agree that Bismarck, for example, was genuinely eager to help the masses but that other motives were also apparent. Bismarck, some other political leaders, and even a few large business owners, were concerned about the social problems that were a part of the industrial revolution and the new economic system built on competition. Bismarck was worried about the political consequences of ignoring these problems. Historian Hermann Beck (1995: 45) writes: 'Warnings that social misery was the precursor of revolution lay in the air'. Both political officials and economic producers feared a revolt, and, as a consequence, supported the idea of creating worker pensions run by the government. And as observed by Ooms et al. (2005), the early promoters of social insurance (from Otto von Bismarck to Franklin Roosevelt) understood that guarantees of income security were needed in market economies if social harmony and productivity were to be preserved. This was especially true because industrialization brought with it economic insecurity arising out of job loss, illness, disability, premature death, and old age.

As far as benefit levels were concerned: 'in most countries public old age benefits were initially designed as benefits for the 'poor'. They were social assistance (by another name) – providing low, subsistence-level benefits' (Schulz and Myles, 1990: 401). That is, the first plans focused on basic survival needs. After World War II, very different public pension programmes developed. Starting with Sweden in 1959, Social Security programmes were based on the principles of (1) universal eligibility (no means testing) and (2) measuring adequacy by the amount of wage replacement provided by pensions.

The first universal benefits, however, were typically low, flat rate payments that did not result in significant income security. Countries ultimately saw the need for earnings-related pensions on top of the flat rate benefit. According to Schulz and Myles (1990: 403):

> In the United States, coverage under Social Security expanded to most of the labor force through a series of amendments between 1950 and 1965. Income replacement levels were also raised in a series of changes between 1968 and 1972 to levels that approximated what were thought to be reasonable 'income security' standards.

The result was Social Security benefits that gave many people, for the first time, a meaningful option either to retire or to continue working.

At the present time, Social Security benefits are received by about 90 per cent of older persons. The *average* benefit paid in 2007 was about $12,530 a year for retired workers and about $20,560 a year for retired couples with both partners receiving benefits (Reno and Lavery, 2007). The Census Bureau (2006) reports that in the year 2004, 60 per cent of older persons received half or more of their income from Social Security, including about three in ten who got almost all their income from it.[1]

While there is now near-universal Social Security coverage in the United States and other industrialized countries, coverage in most other countries of the world is low. For example, in those with very low per capita incomes, 'statutory social security schemes, i.e. contributory and tax-finances programmes, do not cover more than 5 to 10 per cent of the labour force and/or population' (van Ginneken, 2007: 39). The biggest problems relate to the coverage of workers in the informal economy – finding the workers, financing the benefits, and dealing with administrative problems. In India, for example, these uncovered workers comprise about 93 per cent of the labor force (van Ginneken, 2007). However, promising developments have occurred in some developing countries, especially those with higher income per capita. The International Labour Organization (ILO) (2003) has reported, for example, significant progress in the *coverage of workers* under

Social Security programmes, citing improvements in Brazil, Chile, Columbia, Costa Rica, Korea, the Philippines, Thailand, and Tunisia.

WHAT ROLE FOR THE FAMILY?

While public and private pensions are very important, one should not ignore the economic role of the family. First and foremost, the key to the income security of older people is dependent on what individuals and families do. That is true for people in all nations – both more developed and developing. Governments can and should assist, but the economics of old age should always be viewed as a joint process – involving individuals, the family, often employers, and government (Schulz, 1999). Today, as economic development proceeds around the world, countries must deal with the fact that the government's activities 'are interlocked with the market's and the family's role in social provision' (Esping-Anderson, 1990: 21). Industrialization continues to place strains on family support systems. It also changes the basic nature of work and creates new ways for people to achieve income. The shift away from farming and other self-employment occupations complements the rise in labor markets. Increasing numbers of people face a new kind of insecurity as a result of no longer being able to directly exchange their labor for shelter and food. Individuals who enter these labor markets are subject to a new kind of coercion, given that their jobs can be terminated at any time. 'People must move, leave their homes, change their occupations – and any of a number of possible major changes, none of their choosing. In addition, the mere threat of termination can be as constraining, as coercive, as menacing as an authoritative governmental command' (Lindblom, 1977: 48).

At the same time, the nature of the family has been changing: smaller size, more females in the paid labor force, rising numbers of old people not working, and large numbers of the very old requiring extensive health and social supports. In addition, in many countries there have been growing divorce rates, increased geographic mobility, limited economic capacity for many, and changing attitudes about family obligations. Fortunately, despite all the problems, evidence indicates that many families continue to function well, providing economic and social support to various family members at appropriate time of need (Haber, 2006; see also Chapters 14 and 15). Yet, as indicated above, it would be a mistake to view 'successful families' as operating in isolation from the support of key community and governmental institutions.

In fact, over time, formal institutions have been given additional responsibilities for assisting families and, in some cases, have taken over some of their traditional responsibilities. This trend, however, should be viewed more as an effort *to supplement and support* the family and its traditional roles – not as a deliberate policy to supplant the family. One important example that illustrates this point is what happens at home during health crises requiring substantial care. In the United States and most other countries, families, not government, generally take on the bulk of caregiving responsibilities and do so quite willingly in most cases. However, crises at some point can overwhelm family resources – both personal caregiving and financial resources. 'With even the most conservative assumptions and estimates, the value of family care [in the United States] is huge, dwarfing the value of paid home health care and nearly matching the total national spending on home health care and nursing home care' (American Association of Retired Persons [AARP]/Public Policy Institute, 2007: 2). In November 2006, 30–38 million adults (mostly family members) gave care to other adults, care that was estimated to have a market value of $350 billion (AARP/Public Policy Institute, 2007).

Increasing numbers of countries recognize, however, that these family caregivers need help. They need assistance with services and care provided at home, but they especially need help financially when the sick person's state of illness and function requires institutionalization. To help meet this need, a number of countries have developed government-funded long-term care programmes to assist families in dealing with the financial burdens that arise (Cuellar and Weiner, 2000) (see Section Five).

MEASURING ECONOMIC WELFARE IN OLD AGE

The World Bank (Easterly and Sewadeh, 2001) estimated that in 2001 there were about 1.2 billion people (about one-fifth of the world's population) living in 'absolute poverty'. Aged poverty mirrors the general poverty of nations as a whole, with its rural character and a disproportionate number of women being affected. In many parts of the world, poverty in old age is the last phase in a *lifetime* of deprivation. Caution is in order, however, in generalizing from available statistics on income and assets (Schulz, 2001). Both underreporting and the lack of disaggregation cause serious problems for assessing the economic status of older people.

Money income is the most common measure for assessing economic well-being among older people. Using this measure, the official poverty rate in the United States for people 65+ in 2007 was 10 per cent, somewhat lower than the 12.5 per cent rate for all individuals; the rate for children below the age of 18 was 18 per cent. The major source of income in industrialized countries for older people remains that of Social Security, with earnings an important element for the minority of older people still working. For those no longer working, employer-sponsored pensions are the next most important source of income.

Expanding the analysis of economic status to include such factors as in-kind income, special tax provisions, and household size narrows considerably the measured differences between the economic well-being of the middle-aged versus the old. As the rates just cited indicate, many researchers and policymakers now say there are no significant differences between the two groups in the United States. Some even argue that older people are better-off. For example, Holden and Hatcher (2006) examined data on the percentage of households with incomes below the official government poverty threshold. They pointed out (using 2003 data) that:

> Older individuals are less likely to be in poverty than are younger individuals. The difference is striking when comparing the older population to children, who are more than 70 per cent more likely to live in poverty. This gap is quite different from 30 years ago, when the poverty rates for older and younger Americans were quite close ... . As is the case for the total population, among African Americans and Hispanics older individuals are less likely to be poor than are children in their racial categories (Holden and Hatcher, 2006: 222).

One major qualification to the 'better-off' conclusion (in terms of the prevailing poverty measure) is that Social Security benefit levels have been set by Congress in the United States at a level that barely keeps many elderly households out of poverty but results in a big reduction in the official poverty statistics reported annually. That is, large numbers of older people whose incomes are *above* the poverty index have incomes that are *clustered not far above it* – incomes that make them extremely vulnerable, for example, to the rising costs of healthcare and out-of-pocket healthcare payments.

One area where older people clearly do better than other groups is in managing inflation. Contrary to popular belief, they have a large measure of protection from inflation – given that Social Security, the Supplemental Security

Income (SSI) programme, civil service retirement pensions, and military pensions provide automatic adjustments for price increases. Those heavily dependent on financial assets and private pensions are the most vulnerable, since most financial assets and pensions do not automatically adjust.

Three decades ago, research by Moon (1977) described the limitations of the current official measure of poverty in the United States and called for a complete revision in concept and calculation methodology. Moon argued that a measure of potential consumption is superior to the current annual money income measure of economic status. In her proposed measure of poverty, Moon argued for including (1) imputations (i.e., researcher-generated estimates) for net worth; (2) imputations for the cash value of Medicare, Medicaid, and public housing; (3) the inclusion of intra-family transfers; and (4) deductions for income and payroll taxes paid. A later study by the National Academy of Sciences Study Panel on Poverty Measurement (Citro and Michael, 1995) also called for a new income measure, one that included changes in the poverty 'thresholds' and the use of different types of data.

One alternative approach to measuring welfare in old age is to compare the income received in retirement with the amount received before retirement, using what is called the 'replacement income approach'. The Center for Retirement Research at Boston College has developed a 'National Retirement Risk Index' using the replacement rate approach (Munnell et al., 2006). The index is based on measuring the proportion that an aged unit's retirement income represents of the unit's pre-retirement income. This amount is then compared to a 'target' replacement rate that, if achieved, would be sufficient to allow a retired household to maintain its *pre-retirement standard of living*. Based on this statistic, 'at-risk households' are defined as those where the projected replacement rates fall more than 10 per cent below the target replacement rate. That is, households with low replacements rates are designated to be at risk of not being able to maintain their standard of living into retirement as a result of declines in Social Security replacement rates.

INTERNATIONAL COMPARISONS

Smeeding (2005) points out that the preponderance of comparative international studies on poverty use a different measure of welfare and income adequacy from the ones discussed above.

The most common is a relative measure that defines poverty as falling below a certain percentage of the median income for all households in a country. However, the percentage used by various researchers differs. The European Statistical Office (Eurostat), for example, recommends a '60-per cent-of-median standard', while the majority of research studies, according to Smeeding, use a 50 per cent standard. Based on analysis using the relative measure, Smeeding (2005: 117–18) argues that

> Poverty among younger pensioners is no longer a major policy problem. Rather, poverty in old age is almost exclusively an older women's problem. Poverty rates among older women ... rise with both age and changes in living arrangements. Three-quarters of the poor elders, age 75 or older, in each rich nation are women

(See Chapters 9 and 37 for further international comparisons of poverty and inequality in old age.)

The future, however, may be very different. The impact of the stock market decline and the more general economic contraction in 2008–09 on economic well-being in retirement will not be known for many years, especially with regard to the role played by defined contribution (DC) pension plans. At the same time, more information is needed about poverty among older people in developing countries. Over the years, however, there have been a number of country studies and some studies of particular regions of the world, especially Asia.[2] Three regional studies encompass, in two cases, much of South and Central America (Bourguignon et al., 2004; del Popolo, 2001) and, in another, the African continent (Kakwani and Subbarao, 2005; see also Chapter 30). Barrientos (2006: 371) has reviewed the effectiveness of pension provision (mostly employment-based) in Latin America, highlighting variations in old-age poverty across countries in Latin America:

> Old age poverty ranges from 7.9 per cent in Chile to 38.4 per cent in Ecuador. In four countries, Chile, Uruguay, Argentina and Brazil, roughly one in ten older people are poor. In the next four countries, Peru, Nicaragua, Venezuela and Panama, around one in five older people are poor. In Honduras and Paraguay one in four older people are poor. For the remaining seven countries, roughly one in three older people are poor.

From this evidence, Barrientos (2006) concludes that old-age poverty remains a significant issue in the region, with new approaches needed

Table 3.1   Aged poverty in South America[a]

Country	In poverty[b] (age 60+)	Total population (age 60+)	Receiving pension (age 65+)
Chile	7.8%	11.0%	64%
Uruguay	8.4%	20.5%	87%
Argentina	9.3%	13.5%	68%
Brazil	10.1%	9.1%	86%
Peru	18.3%	9.1%	24%
Venezuela	20.8%	6.6%	24%
Paraguay	22.9%	7.6%	20%
Columbia	29.5%	8.9%	19%
Bolivia	37.1%	6.4%	15%
Ecuador	39.0%	7.6%	15%

[a] National household survey data for years 1999–2003.
[b] Poverty is defined as adult equivalent units with household income below half of median income for the country.
Source: Barrientos (2006)

for raising the incomes of older people living in poverty (Table 3.1).

NEW PENSIONS MODELS

After almost a century of Social Security programme development around the world – programmes that became the main pillar of income support in old age – a significant change has taken place. From the 1990s onwards there has been growing interest in pension programmes that embody *individual* retirement accounts that are *privately managed*. These plans are called defined contribution (DC) plans and contrast with others that are called defined benefit (DB) plans. Defined benefit plans are a promise to pay a benefit of a *specific amount*. That is, the pension provisions state before retirement how much the plans will pay in benefits at retirement – benefits whose amount usually varies by years of service and/or earnings. In contrast, DC plans promise only that certain *specific contributions* (payments) will be made into an employee's pension account. With DC plans, the ultimate benefit amount is determined at retirement on the basis of the total amount available at retirement (accumulated payments plus any asset earnings and any appreciation of assets).

Simultaneous with the rising interest in DC plans, there has been a rise in questions regarding the future viability of Social Security programmes. Concern has been especially strong regarding these programmes' future financial situation in light of population ageing around the world and rising revenue needs to pay promised benefits. Many argue that DB Social Security plans should in whole or part be replaced by DC plans.

Public pension privatization: the cases of Chile and the United Kingdom

Historically, and globally, one of the first important developments in Social Security was the switch in Chile in 1981 to a new nationwide defined contribution approach to managing pensions. In 1973, a *coup d'état* resulted in General Augusto Pinochet heading a military government in Chile. Facing an extremely serious shortfall in pension revenues relative to promised Social Security benefits, Pinochet implemented radical pension reform. The Social Security programme was replaced with a public pension system that the world had never seen before – a national mandatory savings scheme administered primarily by the private sector. All Chilean wage and salary workers were (are) required by law to participate (except for the military and a few other exceptions).[3]

In the years that followed, diverse countries have introduced the defined contribution approach into their public pension system. It is now found in the public pension systems of countries such as Argentina, Bolivia, Columbia, Hungary, Kazakhstan, Latvia, Peru, Poland, Sweden, the United Kingdom, and Uruguay (Orszag and Stiglitz, 2001).

It is over two decades since Chile privatized its public old-age pension system and its success can now be evaluated. And the assessment, according to Chilean political leaders themselves, is very negative. In the debates leading up to the 2006 presidential election in Chile, both candidates, Michelle Bachelet and Sebastian Pinera, agreed that their country's pension system had very serious problems and needed immediate repair. Ms. Bachelet, who eventually won the election, characterized the system as being 'in crisis' (Rohter, 2006). The problems in Chile are many and serious (Gill, et al., 2005; Kay and Sinha, 2008; Soto, 2005), and include the following:

- despite a legal requirement to participate, more than a third of the labor force remains out of the system;
- commissions and administrative costs have declined from the super-high amounts at the beginning but are still very high, dramatically reducing ultimate benefits;
- in the early years rates of return were very good, but the Chilean economy has been highly volatile, resulting in wide swings in investment returns;
- understanding financial matters (financial literacy) and the mechanics of the retirement programme are very low among participants;
- the hoped for competition among companies managing the retirement funds has never materialized;
- finally, while the aggregate impact of privatization on women is unclear and still very controversial, women have gained least benefit from the reforms.

In 1986, the Conservative government of Margaret Thatcher undertook a major reform of the UK's pension system. A defined contribution pension called the 'Personal Pension Plan' (PPP) was introduced with workers given the option, but also encouraged, to leave the old public and employer-sponsored plans in favor of this new alternative. In 2001, another defined contribution option called 'Stakeholder Pensions' was added, this time by a Labor government. The failings of these approaches were extensively discussed in reports of the UK Pensions Commission. The 2005 Report (Pensions Commission, 2005) concluded that the existing UK pension system was overly complex; not cost-efficient in many areas; not providing appropriate incentives to save; a contributing factor toward a highly unequal distribution of income; and, finally, likely to leave many individuals with inadequate pensions.

The Chilean and British experiences illustrate many of the serious problems that can arise with defined contribution plans. Yet many advocates of pension privatization in the United States have pointed to Chile and the United Kingdom as successful models to be followed. The final Report of the Pensions Commission (2005) discouraged such thinking, recommending that the United Kingdom rely *less* on Personal Pensions and *more* on the existing collective public and private pension programmes (Pensions Commission, 2005). The result has been major pieces of legislation passed in 2007 and 2008 that combine modifications to the Basic State Pension (BSP) with attempts to encourage new forms of pension savings. The former includes indexing the Basic State Pension to average earnings, and reducing the number of years required to work for receipt of a full BSP. The latter includes introducing a new pension saving scheme of portable individualized savings accounts (from 2012), automatic enrolment into a qualifying workplace pension, and a national minimum contribution from employers (Phillipson, 2009; see also Chapter 37).

Employer-sponsored pensions: the United States

Similar efforts toward more 'personal pensions' have occurred in the American *private* sector, especially among plans set up by employers for their workers. There has been a dramatic shift by employers to DC plans, away from the DB pensions that once dominated the private pension scene. The shift to DC plans was in part encouraged by government action. The Revenue Act of 1978, section 401(k), permitted employees to make tax-deferred contributions to an employer-sponsored plan. The new section 401(k) was designed to encourage employers to create special personal plans for their workers. Judged by their proliferation, these employer incentives were seen as quite successful. At the end of 2003, there were 438,000 401(k) plans and 42.4 million active participants (EBRI, 2005).[4] By the end of 2006, the value of assets in 401(k) plans had reached $2.7 trillion (Investment Company Institute, 2007).

The Employee Benefit Research Institute (EBRI, 2007) reports that in 2004, 56 per cent of heads of families who participated in an employment-based retirement plan had only a DC plan. This compares in the same year with DB coverage of only 26 per cent. (18 per cent of household heads had both types of plan.) According to EBRI (2007: 1), 'this was a significant change from 1992, when 42 per cent of heads of families had only a defined benefit plan and 41 per cent had only a defined contribution plan'. EBRI (2009b) reports that in 2006, 67 per cent of workers participating in employer-sponsored plans considered their primary type of retirement plan to be a DC plan; DB plans were primary for 31 per cent.

As various kinds of DC plans have proliferated, there has been a substantial rise in the concerns and criticism regarding their adequacy, viability, and equity (Schulz and Binstock, 2006). One of the biggest concerns is informed choice. Holders of DC accounts typically must make decisions about the nature (asset mix) of their investment portfolio and who will be entrusted to manage it.

The hope is that individual workers, as good investor 'managers', will achieve investment returns over time that will produce adequate retirement income. However, in 2008 the world was shocked to learn that a highly respected (until then) investment manager by the name of Bernard Madoff had swindled governments, investment organizations, charities, pension plans, movie stars and producers, hedge funds, and individuals (rich and not so rich) out of billions. The biggest Ponzi scheme in the history of the world had defrauded them of close to $100 billion. Unfortunately, many of the financial decisions that individuals and groups must make are very complex. The Madoff scandal demonstrated how unprepared people are in taking on that responsibility. So, for example, a survey of 1000 Dutch citizens found that the average respondent considers her/ himself financially unsophisticated and 'is not very eager to take control of retirement savings investment when offered the possibility to increase expertise' (van Rooij et al., 2007: 701). Lusardi and Mitchell (2007: 3) argue that such financial illiteracy is widespread: 'the young and older people in the United States and other countries appear woefully under-informed about basic financial concepts, with serious implications for saving, retirement planning, mortgages, and other decisions.'

One of the decisions DC pension holders have to make, for example, is deciding the proportion of their money to be placed in various types of investments. The most common general choice individuals must make is how much to invest in *bonds* as compared with *equities*. Bonds are viewed as safer in terms of fluctuating market value but typically have lower returns in the long run than equities. The investment decision with regard to the portfolio mix of these two types of investments is absolutely critical to determining the ultimate amount of benefits. Notwithstanding this, according to the Securities and Exchange Commission, *over 50 per cent of Americans do not even know the difference between a bond and an equity* (reported in Orszag and Stiglitz, 2001).

Another indication of problems is pension coverage for workers when changing jobs. Job changers in the United States typically have three options in dealing with any pension rights accumulated from a former employer: (1) leave it with the old employer, if permitted; (2) roll the funds over to another tax-qualified plan; or (3) take the money in a lump sum, pay taxes on it, and then spend what is left. Options 1 and 2 shelter the money from taxes and allow it all to grow until retirement; option 3 does not and undermines retirement income adequacy. What do job changers do? A study by the AARP Public Policy Institute (2006), using data for 2003, found that more than half (54 per cent) of job changers did not roll over any of their lump-sum distribution into another retirement plan, annuity, or IRA. Instead, 30 per cent spent the money on vacations, other consumption, or gifts; 55 per cent used it to pay off debt; and 15 per cent invested it. Given this financial knowledge and behavior, it is not surprising to find in one survey that 37 per cent of people saving for retirement said they were doing only a fair job of managing their retirement portfolios, and 7 per cent said they were doing a poor job (Dugar, 2002).

The common response to issues of informed choice is to call for educating investors. But the practical problems with this remedy are enormous: Who will do the teaching? How will quality be assured? Who will pay for it? Some see the problem as overwhelming. Behavioral economist Richard Thaler told *The Economist* magazine: 'The depressing truth is that financial literacy is impossible, at least for many of the big financial decisions all of us have to take ... . Financial literacy is not the right road to go down' (*The Economist*, 2008: 74).

In the United States, millions of citizens have lost substantial sums of money as a result of incompetent or illegal behavior by purveyors of investment and retirement products (Schulz and Binstock, 2006). The 2008 Madoff swindle, exposed by the strains produced by the broader financial crisis, is a more recent example of the results of financial illiteracy in the United States.

In 2008, the financial network in the United States ground almost to a halt as a result of the worst financial collapse since the Great Depression of the 1930s. Triggered by the deflation of a huge mortgage/housing bubble, it wiped out the value of many financial institutions stocks and bonds – leaving shareholders with huge losses. Again, the problem was predominantly unscrupulous individuals and unregulated businesses making huge profits by manipulation and using the financial system to entice people into risky investments that they did not understand. Millions of people were harmed.

Individuals are also faced with a variety of risks related to the honesty and competence of employers. These risks include companies going out of business or 'dumping' their retirement plans; companies inadequately funding plans and/or manipulating actuarial/accounting reports to hide problems; individuals and organizations promoting 'get rich quick' schemes; incompetent brokers and financial planners; and companies undertaking illegal acts of investment and trading (such as 'late trading' and 'market timing'). Another serious issue is the high costs associated with some of the defined contribution plans (Fioravante, 2007). Financial management costs can result in a reduction of 21–30 per cent in the assets available to pay benefits at retirement.

Employer-sponsored plans: the Netherlands

Recent pension developments in the Netherlands are of special interest. Like the United States, private pension plans in the Netherlands were until recently mostly defined benefit plans. However, in an attempt to deal with the problems arising from employer-sponsored pensions a new type of plan has been developed (Ponds and van Riel, 2007). For much of the period up to the 1990s, DB plans were in the mainstay of provision in the Netherlands, with benefits determined by a formula based on earnings and years of service. Typically, these plans were designed (in conjunction with the public pension) to provide 70 per cent of final earnings. The dramatic financial turmoil in the early years of the 21st century, with its sharp drop in stock values and historically low levels of interest rates, caused employers to re-evaluate their pension obligations. The predominant reaction that followed was for employers to switch to new hybrid pensions based on *indexed average* earnings instead of final earnings. According to Ponds and van Riel (2007: 2):

> An important feature of an average-wage plan is that the level of indexation in any given year depends on the financial position of the pension fund ... . A typical characteristic of these schemes is that indexation of *all* accrued liabilities is dependent on the solvency position of the pension fund through a so-called 'pension ladder'. A policy ladder explicitly relates the contribution and indexation policies to the financial position of the pension fund.

The operation of this pension ladder allows amelioration of pension costs in any particular year. When, because of economic conditions and the financial market, the actuarial funding situation of the pension fund is deteriorating, there is a specific provision in the plan that permits a pension fund's governing board (composed of employer and employee representatives) to reduce the indexed benefit accrual in any particular year. In contrast, when the pension plan is 'well funded' (in terms of the value of pension reserves relative to fund liabilities), there can be an 'over-indexation' of retirement benefits as a partial catch-up for prior years of less than full indexation. According to Ponds and van Riel (2007: 5): 'the hybrid pension plans that have evolved in the Netherlands offer a promising way to balance risk

between employers, active workers, and retirees'. But it is important to see that this 'balancing of risk' is achieved by changing from defined benefit plans where employers assumed *most of the risk* to plans where *much* of the risk is shifted to employees and retirees.

Certainly, for Dutch employers this new option makes the pension burden they face more manageable. Employers know that their pension obligations will not fluctuate wildly (as happened historically with the old DB plans). This makes funding requirements in the Netherlands more predictable. The major hope is that the risk-sharing that now occurs between employers and employees will result (given indexation flexibility) in a *more reliable* provision of private pension benefits, together with the prospect for *relatively high pension levels* (but, of course, with more risk exposure for employees).

Hybrid pension plans in the United States

Attempts have also been made, in both the private and public sectors of the United States, to create pensions that are variants of the older types of plans but are designed to minimize some of the serious drawbacks from earlier approaches. Such plans, like in the Netherlands, are generally referred to as 'hybrid plans'. There are many different forms for these hybrid pensions, the six most common being cash balance, pension equity, floor-offset, age-weighted profit-sharing, new comparability profit-sharing, and target benefit plans. (See EBRI, 2009a for descriptions of the various types.) These hybrid plans typically combine features of both DB and DC plans. For example, in the very popular (among employers) cash balance plans, the ultimate benefit is determined (as in DC plans) by applying a formula specified by the plan and results in a predictable level of benefits for any individual in retirement.

Unlike earlier DB plans, cash balance plans allow companies to spread pension benefits more evenly over a participant's career by granting 'pay credits' based on each year's compensation, not just the highest salary levels prior to retirement. In recent years, however, serious concerns have been raised about many of these plans. Most employers argue that the new approach is a response to the pension needs of young and mobile employees. Critics argue, however, that they have been designed primarily as a way for employers to save on pension costs. It is argued that workers with long years of service have been losing benefits when companies change to the hybrid plan. With most cash balance plans the per cent of pay set aside for workers' pensions basically stays the same each year. Traditional defined benefit plans, in contrast, increase a worker's pension accrual during the last years on the job when wages and salaries are usually higher than earlier in her or his working careers.

In fact, older workers in many companies have found the pensions they could expect upon retirement under the new cash balance plans to be lower. The argument over whether these new plans constitute age discrimination against older employees was taken to court, was ruled 'discriminatory' by a lower court, and then ruled 'not discriminatory' on appeal. The appeals court agreed with the lower court that older workers were financially worse off under the new plan. But the court then went on to argue that the plans were not discriminatory because workers with equal earnings and service got the same pension, regardless of age.

In view of the criticism and the legal arguments made about past practices, many American employers have modified their plans to avoid penalizing older workers with regard to benefits originally promised. Most companies that have switched from DB to cash balance plans have decided to give employees 40 and older a choice of either staying with the old plan or switching to the new one. As a further protection for these workers, some employers have decided to slightly increase the pension accrual each year as employees' age and seniority goes up (Hawthorne, 2007).

Notional plans

In some countries in Europe a new national pension type has emerged known as a notional defined contribution (NDC) plans. Again, as in the Netherlands, this new plan is a blend of the DC and DB plans. The major characteristics of the NDC plans are:

1 As the name implies, notional plans are pensions that in general appearance seem to be like one type of pension plan but in reality are actually another. Like DC plans in general, NDC benefits are tied to contributions, with employee and/ or employer contributions 'credited' to a special account set up for each participant. *However, unlike DC plans, none of the contributions are actually deposited in these accounts.*
2 Instead, retirement benefits are paid primarily using pay-as-you-go financing.
3 An indexing procedure is used to periodically increase the balances in the personal accounts (similar to the monetary returns that originate when private funds are invested in financial markets).

4 At retirement, an annuity-type benefit is calculated based on an individual's account balance.
5 Benefits in general are adjusted for changes that occur in national average life expectancy over time.
6 Unlike most Social Security programmes, NDC programmes do not have an income redistribution component and are likely, therefore, to result in greater retirement income inequality.

Sweden, from 1998, was the first government to adopt an NDC type of plan. The main stimulus was to lower projected high national pension costs, given that (1) benefits in Sweden had been set very high, (2) the Swedish population was living much longer (raising pension costs), and (3) economic conditions (i.e., productivity, wages, and price changes) were difficult to predict and, of course, constantly in flux. 'Swedish officials wanted to stabilize pension funding and insure pension sustainability'.[6]

Other reasons given for the reform were the need to improve inter- and intra-generational fairness, the desire to increase the amount of personal saving, and a policy goal to keep pensions a neutral factor in worker retirement decisions (Rix, 2007). At the national level, the new Swedish pension system combines a national notional pension plan with mandatory defined contribution plans. Similar financial reasons were given when notional plans were adopted in Italy, Poland, Latvia, Kyrgystan, and Mongolia. As Williamson (2004: 6) points out about the notional approach: '[It] offers a way to shift from the DB model to a less DC one without the diversion of payroll tax revenues into funded individual accounts.'

However, as we have commented (Schulz and Borowski, 2006: 375):

> Politically, the [notional] approach assists countries in the benefit retrenchment process – cloaking cutbacks with mechanistic programme provisions related to notional credits, indexing procedures, life expectancy adjustments, and transitional costs relating to prior programmes. At the same time, governments paradoxically hope that notional accounts will increase political support as a result of (1) what appears to be a more transparent benefit determination process, (2) personal accounts that foster a sense of ownership, and (3) a greater emphasis on individual equity.

THE ECONOMIC IMPACT OF POPULATION AGEING

Many argue that population ageing, as detailed by Victor in Chapter 5, seriously threatens the economic welfare of nations (e.g., Kotlikoff and Burns, 2005; Peterson, 1999). A frequently cited statistic is the changing 'aged dependency ratio': the number of individuals who are age 65 or older divided by the number of people of working age (assumed to be 20–64) – that result multiplied by 100. This ratio is a crude measure of the number of workers potentially available to support a growing older population. That is, it is a ratio that measures the number of older persons in the society that are assumed not to be producing output, relative to those assumed to be doing the producing. Almost every prediction of the negative impact of demographic ageing trends on economic growth starts with this basic statistic and the fact that the ratio is rising. In 2000, the aged dependency ratio was 20 (i.e., 20 older persons for every 100 people of working age). It is projected that the ratio will rise in 80 years to a little over 40 (Social Security Advisory Board, 2005).

Although policymakers have placed considerable emphasis on dependency ratios, a large literature has emerged that discusses the *limitations* of the dependency ratio approach and related demographic measures when they are used to predict the *economic* impacts of population ageing (see, for example, Disney, 1996; Easterlin, 1995; Schulz, 2001). Instead of just a demographic analysis, an *economic* analysis of the impact of population change is crucial. However, it is technically a far bigger challenge to estimate the population ageing impact in economic terms rather than simply presenting demographic dependency ratios. Economists, for example, have given a lot of attention to the role played by saving in the economic growth process (Buchanan, 1993). If saving is reduced by population ageing, then economic growth might be negatively affected as a result of lower capital investment. Thus, the potential impact of demographic ageing on saving and growth has for decades been a major question but has resulted in a relatively inconclusive debate over the economic impact of Social Security on saving and growth (see the discussion in Bosworth and Chodorow-Reich, 2007; Disney, 1996; Schulz, 2001).

Some have argued that population ageing – with its (1) dampening impact on the size of countries' labor forces and (2) an accompanying rise in governments' budgets to pay for entitlements – will result in lower rates of economic growth. One major study, for example, projects that the aggregate labor force of countries in the European Union will contract by almost 30 million between 2018 and 2050 (Carone and Costello, 2006). These labor force projections, together with other factors, have been used by economists working for the European Union to model the economic effects of population ageing. 'Econometric models' in economics are

mathematical abstractions of the much more complicated social/political/economic real world. These models permit economists – through the use of logic, mathematics, available statistics, and various assumptions about individual and institutional behavior – to gain insights and predictive power with regard to how the real economic world operates.

In the case of the 2006 European modeling effort, the focus was on ageing and economic growth. The results were based on assumptions (among others) about population change, labor inputs, investment rates, interest and wage rates, and changing technology. Using a 'productive function approach', a modeling approach used extensively in economics since Robert Solow's (1957) growth model was introduced in the 1950s, the European modelers made estimates of the impact of population ageing on economic growth. The study projected that the annual average potential GDP growth rate will decline from 2.4 per cent during the 2004–10 period to only 1.2 between 2031 and 2050. Based on this projection, the modelers concluded that the 'ageing populations will have a significant [negative] impact on Europe's economies' (Economic Policy Committee and European Commission, 2006).

However, once again, this type of modeling has been criticized as too simplistic (e.g., Mokyr, 2002; Nelson, 1996). For example, little or no role is given in such models to changing education and knowledge. One of the giants of economics, Alfred Marshall (1948: 159), wrote many years ago in his *Principles of Economics*: 'Knowledge is the most powerful engine of production; it enables us to subdue nations and satisfy our wants'. His statement reminds us that the job of dealing with any economic strain arising from population ageing does not rest solely on increasing the size of the labor force or on saving and investment. Solow (1957) found in his path-breaking research that when he applied his model to data measuring the gross national product (GNP) in the United States, only about 12 per cent of the increase was explained by the additions of physical capital (a product of saving and investment). Fully 85 per cent of the increase in growth was unexplained by the model, That is, a huge proportion of the growth was not statistically explained and remained in the 'residual' of his equation.

In the years that followed there was much research and debate over using neoclassical growth models and the sources of economic growth (see, for example, Warsh, 2006). While still controversial, there now seems to be a consensus. Many economists now point to a variety of factors (other than investment) that determine the rate of growth. These are factors such as institution building, changing knowledge, the education of potential workers, technological change, entrepreneurship, and culture. These factors together have had a powerful impact on the rate of economic growth. One group of economists emphasizes the importance of 'institutional' factors in the growth process (for example, North, 1990, 2005). Landes (1999) argues that growth is primarily about culture: i.e., some countries succeed because of hard-working and enterprising workers (as opposed to countries where workers are not). Paul Romer (1994) focuses on a broad concept of the economics of knowledge and, through it, innovation.

Certainly the more traditional factors featured in the earlier models – demography/labor force, saving, profits, and investment – are not ignored in the recent literature but are now seen as having less importance than originally portrayed in the economic literature. Thus, when highly regarded economist Edward Lazear argued: 'profits provide the incentive for physical capital investment, and physical capital growth contributes to productivity growth,' the equally regarded economist, Paul Krugman, replied in the *New York Times* that this was not necessarily true: 'today's record profits aren't being invested [to promote economic growth]. Instead, they're being used to enrich executives and a few lucky stock owners' (Krugman, 2007).

In summary, modeling the interactions of population and economic growth is a complex task and one still not well understood. Schulz and Binstock (2006) warn that most of the modeling and predictions of 'doom' arising from demographic ageing are wrong. Focusing solely on the size of the labor force and savings rates is bad economics that leads to bad policy recommendations. Today, as ever, the most important determinants of the future economic welfare of people (of all ages) are those many other factors listed above, which means the debate over changing economic growth and how best to run an economic system is concerned with far more than issues of ageing (or issues of financing Social Security). In fact, the ageing of populations has relatively little to do with the outcome (Schulz and Binstock, 2006).

CONCLUSION

With the institution of Social Security retirement programmes around the world during the 20th century, the challenges and risks associated with old age have been greatly moderated (Schulz, 1993, 2001). In addition, various types of health insurance programmes have dramatically increased the availability of quality health care as individuals enter a period of life with rising chronic and life-threatening illnesses. Statistically, the economic status of the older persons as a group in the United States, for example, is now very similar to the rest of the population at other ages – which is a dramatic change from their disadvantages position in the past. And expanding the analysis of economic status to include such factors as in-kind income, special tax provisions, and household size narrows the statistical differences considerably between the old and younger adult cohorts of the population.

Measures of poverty vary from country to country. In the United States the official poverty index that is reported by the government is considered by most experts to be out of date, resulting in a serious understatement of the number of poor people, regardless of age. Other measures, such as the recently developed 'National Retirement Risk Index', indicate that there are still many serious economic problems confronting older persons.

How will the draconian events of 2008–09 affect pension policy? Before the economic upheaval, the policy trend (especially among private employers) was to shift to individuals more responsibility for dealing with these problems and future economic security in old age. However, recent events and the lessons discussed by scholars of social welfare history (e.g., Bengston and Achenbaum, 1993; Berkowitz, 1997; Myles, 1984; Quadagno, 1988) support the expectation that the calls to rely heavily on non-government options will find acceptance more difficult. There is likely to be public pension reform based on old principles but modified mechanisms – with an overall return to heavy reliance on collective mechanisms of 'solidarity' (Diamond and Orszag, 2004; Thompson, 1998). No public or private programmes for older people have been static. Rather, they have continually changed as knowledge and conditions change. This will continue to be true in the future. The many reforms of public and private pensions that must by necessity occur in the future will provide the challenge and the opportunity to deal with past and future problems.

NOTES

1 US Census Bureau (2006). *Income of the Population 5 and Older, 2004*. Retrieved on June 6, 2007 from http//www.socialsecurity.gov.policy

2 Barrientos, A. (2006) 'Ageing, poverty and public policy in developing countries: new survey evidence.' Retrieved on April 4, 2007 from http://www.ids.ac.uk/ids/news/ageing-barrientos.pdf

3 The details of the Chilean approach can be found in Williamson (2005) and Kay and Sinha (2008).

4 EBRI (Employee Benefit Research Institute) (2005). *History of 401(k) Plans – An Update*. Retrieved on March 16, 2006 from http://www.ebra.org/pdf/publications/facts/0205fact.a.pdf

5 See Bogle (2005) for a discussion of this issue.

6 Mattoo, R (2006). 'Notional pensions: Does Sweden have the answer?' *Federal Reserve Bank of Chicago Pension Conference*. Retrieved on April 16, 2008, at http//pensionconference.chicagofedblogs.org/

REFERENCES

AARP Public Policy Institute (2006) *Pension Lump-Sum Distributions: Do Boomers Take Them or Save Them?* Washington, DC: AARP.

AARP Public Policy Institute (2007) *Valuing the Invaluable: A New Look at the Economic Value of Family Caregiving*. Washington, DC: AARP.

Barrientos, A. (2006) 'Poverty reduction: the missing piece of pension reform in Latin America', *Social Policy and Administration*, 40: 369–84.

Beck, H. (1995) *The Origins of the Authoritarian Welfare State in Prussia*. Ann Arbor, MI: University of Michigan Press.

Bengtson, V.L. and Achenbaum, W.A. (eds) (1993) *The Changing Contract Across Generations*. New York: Aldine de Gruyter.

Berkowitz, E.D. (1997) 'The historical development of social security in the United States', in E.R. Kingson and J.H. Schulz (eds), *Social Security in the 21st Century*. New York: Oxford University Press. pp. 22–38.

Bogle, J.C. (2005) *The Battle for the Soul of Capitalism*. New Haven, CT: Yale University Press.

Bosworth, B. and Chodorow-Reich, G. (2007) 'Saving and demographic change: the global dimension', *Working Paper*, No. 2007–2. Chestnut Hill, MA: Center for Retirement Research at Boston College.

Bourguignon, F., Cicowiez, M., Dethier, J., Gasparini, L., and Pestieau, P. (2004) *Alleviating Old Age Poverty in Latin America*. Washington, DC: The World Bank.

Brown, J.D. (1972) *An American Philosophy of Social Security*. Princeton, NJ: Princeton University Press.

Buchanan, J.M. (1993) 'We should save more in our own economic interest', in L.M. Cohen, (ed.), *Justice Across Generations: What Does It Mean?* Washington, DC: AARP, pp. 269–82.

Carone, G. and Costello, D. (2006) 'Can Europe afford to grow old?' *Finance and Development*, 43(3): 8–31.

Citro, C.F. and Michael, R.T. (eds) (1995) *Measuring Poverty: A New Approach*. Washington, DC: National Academy Press.

Cuellar, A.E. and Weiner, J.M. (2000) 'Can social insurance for long-term care work? The experience of Germany', *Health Affairs*, 29(3): 8–25.

del Popolo, F. (2001) 'Características sociodemográficas y socioeconómicas de las personas de edad en América Latina', *Serie Población y Desarrollo 16*. Santiago: CELADE.

Diamond, P.A. and Orszag, P.R. (2004) *Saving Social Security: A Balanced Approach*. Washington, DC: Brookings Institution Press.

Disney, R. (1996) *Can We Afford to Grow Older?* Cambridge, MA: MIT Press.

Dugar, C. (2002) 'Retirement crisis looms as many come up short', *USA Today*, July 19: 4.

Easterlin, R.A. (1995) 'Economic and social implications of demographic pattern', in R.H. Binstock and George, L.K. (eds), *Handbook of Aging and the Social Sciences*, 4th edn. San Diego, CA: Academic Press, pp. 73–93.

Easterly, W.R. and Sewadeh, M. (2001) *Global Development Network Growth Database*. Washington, DC: World Bank Group.

EBRI (Employee Benefit Research Institute) (2007) 'Retirement plan participation falls by 2 percentage points', *EBRI News*, February 13: 1.

EBRI (Employee Benefit Research Institute) (2009a) *Fundamentals of Employee Benefit Programs*. Washington, DC: EBRI.

EBRI (Employee Benefit Research Institute) (2009b) 'Workers' Primary Retirement Plan Type', EBRI Fast Facts, April 2.

Economic Policy Committee and European Commission (2006) 'The impact of aging on public expenditure: projections for the EU25 member states on pensions, health care, long-term care, education and unemployment transfer (2004–2050)', *European Economy*, Special Report No. 1. Brussels: European Commission.

The Economist (2008) 'Getting it right on the money', April 5: 73–5.

Esping-Andersen, G. (1990) *The Three Worlds of Welfare Capitalism*. Princeton, NJ: Princeton University Press.

Fioravante, J. (2007) 'Retirement plan fees receive increased scrutiny,' *Christian Science Monitor*, October 29: 13–4.

Gill, I.S., Packard, T., and Yermo, J. (2005) *Keeping the Promise of Social Security in Latin America*. Washington, DC: Stanford University Press.

Haber, C. (2006). 'Old age through the lens of family history'. in R.H. Binstock and L.K. George (eds), *Handbook of Aging and the Social Sciences*, 6th edn. Burlington, MA: Academic Press, pp. 59–75.

Hawthorne, F. (2007) 'New look for the nest egg', *New York Times*, April 10: H1, H4.

Holden, K. and Hatcher, C. (2006) 'Economic status of the aged', in R.H. Binstock and George, L.K. (eds), *Handbook of Aging and the Social Sciences*, 6th edn. Burlington, MA: Academic Press, pp. 219–37.

Holtzman, A. (1963) *The Townsend Movement: A Political Study*. New York: Bookman Associates.

ILO (International Labour Organization) (2003) *Extending Social Security: Policies for Developing Countries* (ESS Paper No. 13). Geneva: ILO.

Investment Company Institute (2007) *2007 Investment Fact Book*. Retrieved on October 29, 2007 at http://www.icifactbook.org/index.html

Kakwani, N. and Subbarao, K. (2005) 'Ageing and poverty in Africa and the role of social pensions', *Working Paper*, No. 8. Brasilia: International Poverty Centre – UNDP.

Kay, S.J. and Sinha, T. (2008) *Lessons from Pension Reform in the Americas*. Oxford: Oxford University Press.

Kotlikoff, L.J. and Burns, S. (2005) *The Coming Generational Storm*. Cambridge, MA: MIT Press.

Krugman, P. (2007) 'Another economic disconnect', *New York Times*, April 30: OP-ED.

Landes, S. (1999) *The Wealth and Poverty of Nations*. New York: W.W. Norton.

Lindblom, C.E. (1977) *Politics and Markets: The World's Political-Economic Systems*. New York: Basic Books.

Lusardi, A. and Mitchell, O.S. (2007) 'Financial literacy and planning: implications for retirement wellbeing', *Working Paper* WP 2005–108. Ann Arbor, MI: University of Michigan Retirement Research Center.

Marshall, A. (1948) *Principles of Economics*. New York: Macmillan.

Mokyr, J. (2002) *The Gifts of Athena: Historical Origins of the Knowledge Economy*. Princeton, NJ: Princeton University Press.

Moon, M. (1977) *The Measurement of Economic Welfare: Its Application to the Aged Poor*. New York: Academic Press.

Munnell, A.H., Sunden, A., and Lidstone, E. (2002) 'How important are private pensions?', *Center Issue Brief*, No. 8. Newton, MA: Center for Retirement Research at Boston College.

Munnell, A.H., Webb, A., and Delorme, L. (2006) 'A new national retirement risk index', *Center Issue Brief*, No. 48. Newton, MA: Center for Retirement Research at Boston College.

Myles, J. (1984) *Old Age in the Welfare State*. Boston, MA: Little, Brown.

Nelson, R. (1996) *The Sources of Economic Growth*. Cambridge, MA: Harvard University Press.

North, D.C. (1990). *Institutions, Institutional Change, and Economic Performance*. Cambridge, MA: Cambridge University Press.

North, D.C. (2005) *Understanding the Process of Economic Change*. Princeton, NJ: Princeton University Press.

Ooms, V.D., Macguiness, M.C., Mashaw, J.L., Niskanen, W., and Langbein, J.H. (2005) 'Perspectives on individual responsibility and social insurance', in T. Ghilarduici, V.D. Ooms, J.L. Palmer, and Hills, C. (eds), *In Search of Retirement Security*. New York: Century Fund Publications. pp. 82–113.

Orszag, P.R. and Stiglitz, J.E. (2001) 'Rethinking pension reform: ten myths about Social Security systems', in R. Holzmann and J.E. Stiglitz (eds), *New Ideas about Old Age Security*. Washington, DC: World Bank, pp.17–56.

Pensions Commission (2005) *A New Pension Settlement for the Twenty-first Century*. London: The Commission.

Peterson, P.G. (1999) *Gray Dawn: How the Coming Age Wave Will Transform America – and the World*. New York: Times Book.

Phillipson, C.R. 2009 'Pensions in crisis: aging and inequality in a global age', in L. Rogne, C. Estes, B. Grossman, B. Hollister, and E. Solway (eds), *Social Insurance and Social Justice: Social Security, Medicare, and the Campaign Against Entitlements*. New York: Springer, pp. 319–40.

Ponds, E.H.M. and van Riel, B. (2007) 'Sharing risk: the Netherlands' new approach to pensions', *Center Issue Brief*, No. 7–5. Newton, MA: Center for Retirement Research at Boston College.

Quadagno, J. (1988) *The Transformation of Old Age Security: Class and Politics in the American Welfare State*. Chicago, IL: University of Chicago Press.

Reno, V. and Lavery, J. (2007) 'Social Security and retirement income adequacy', *Social Security Brief*, No. 25. Washington, DC: National Academy of Social Insurance.

Rix, S.E. (2007) *Sweden's Move to Defined Contribution Pensions*. Washington, DC: AARP Public Policy Institute.

Rohter, L. (2006) 'Chile's candidates agree to agree on pension woes', *New York Times*, January 10: A3.

Romer, P.M. (1994) 'The origins of endogenous growth,' *Journal of Economic Perspectives* 8(1) (winter): 3–22.

Schulz, J. (1993) 'Economic support in old age: the role of social insurance in developing countries', in *The Implications for Social Security of Structural Adjustment Policies*. Geneva: International Social Security Association, pp. 17–82.

Schulz, J.H. (1999) 'Economic security in old age: a family–government partnership', in HelpAge International, *The Ageing and Development Report: Poverty, Independence and the World's Older People*. London: Earthscan Publications. pp. 82–97.

Schulz, J.H. (2001) *The Economics of Aging*, 7th edn. Westport, CT: Auburn House.

Schulz, J.H. and Binstock, R.H. (2006) *Aging Nation: The Economics and Politics of Growing Older in America*. Westport, CT: Praeger.

Schulz, J.H. and Borowski, A. (2006) 'Economic security in retirement: reshaping the public–private mix', in R.H. Binstock and L.K. George (eds), *Handbook of Aging and the Social Sciences*, 6th edn. Burlington, MA: Academic Press, pp. 360–79.

Schulz, J.H. and Myles, J. (1990) 'Old age pensions: a comparative perspective', in R.H. Binstock and L.K. George (eds), *Handbook of Aging and the Social Sciences*, 3rd edn. San Diego, CA: Academic Press.

Smeeding, T. (2005) 'Government programs and social outcomes,' *Working Paper*, No. 426. Luxembourg: Luxembourg Income Study.

Social Security Advisory Board (2005) *Social Security: Why Action Should Be Taken Now*. Washington, DC: Social Security Advisory Board.

Solow, R. (1957) 'Technical change and the aggregate production function', *Review of Economics and Statistics*, 39(3): 312–320.

Soto, M. (2005) *Chilean Pension Reform: The Good, the Bad, and the In Between*. Issue Brief. Newton, MA: Center for Retirement Research at Boston College.

Thompson, L. (1998) *Older and Wiser: The Economics of Public Pensions*. Washington, DC: The Urban Institute Press.

Trattner, W. I. (1989) *From Poor Law to Welfare State*, 4th edn. New York: Free press.

United Nations (1997) *Human Development Report*. New York: Oxford University Press.

van Ginneken, W. (2007) 'Extending Social Security coverage: Concepts, global trends and policy issues', *International Social Security Review*, 60(2–3): 39–57.

van Rooij, M.C.J., Kool, C.J.M. Prast H.M. (2007) 'Risk-return preferences in the pension domain: Are people able to choose?', *Journal of Public Economics*, 91: 701–22.

Warsh, D. (2006) *Knowledge and the Wealth of Nations: A Story of Economic Discovery*. New York: Norton.

Weir, F. (2003) 'Russia begins to reconsider wide use of abortion', *Christian Science Monitor*, September 28: 1.

Williamson, J. (2004) 'Assessing the notional defined contribution model', *Issues in Brief*, No. 24. Newton, MA: Center for Retirement Research at Boston College.

Williamson, J. (2005) 'An update on Chile's experience with partial privatization and individual accounts', *Publication No. 2005–19*. Washington, DC: AARP Public Policy Institute.

4

Social Anthropology and Ageing

Christine L. Fry

INTRODUCTION

Of all the social sciences, social anthropology is arguably among the best suited to address questions arising from global change and its impact on the lives of individuals and the communities in which they live. As a child of the mercantile expansion of Europe, anthropology invented itself to explore the worlds of very different and alien native cultures. The intentions of this enterprise were many. A central concern, however, was to document the enormous diversity discovered in the 3000 cultures identified across the world. To begin to make sense of this variation, a theoretical framework was needed. Initially this involved models of history involving progressive change, including social evolution and diffusion. As the field emerged, however, attention shifted to understanding these cultures from the native point of view.

Ironically, the conditions that created anthropology also appeared to destroy the alien worlds that are at the heart of anthropological data. When Bronislaw Malinowski first set foot on that isolated beach in the Trobriand Islands in 1915, the world he saw seemed to be one that was melting before his eyes. The villages on this seemingly isolated Melanesian island had been engulfed in the British Empire, with commercial enterprises, wage labor on plantations, pearl traders, colonial administration, and missionaries. However, Malinowski's lament over the creation of a field of study with trained researchers just in time for the data to disappear was overly pessimistic. Over half a century later, Annette Weiner (1976)

returned to see many of the same features in social life as Malinowski had witnessed. Like Malinowski, she saw ranked chiefs, yam houses displaying wealth, matrilineal descent, garden magic, *sagalis*, and the famed Kula network of exchange.

Our initial vision of anthropology has changed because the world has changed. The world is always changing, but since the 1970s all of the social sciences have documented a shift not only in the intensity of change but also in the all-encompassing nature of economic and cultural transformations. Globalization has created a world that is more homogeneous in some respects, and yet markedly stratified in others. Globalization is simply the most recent phase of change that was set in motion thousands of years ago. Rather than becoming a casualty of dramatic change, anthropologists have adapted their methods of participant observation to understand how people in local communities and specific contexts have responded to the changed circumstances triggered by global forces. Applied anthropologists attempt to use their ethnographic skills to help communities resolve problems created by the introduction of new technology or organizational change created by economic development.

The tendency in the nations of the industrialized part of the globalized world has been to see old age mostly as a 'social problem', with concerns raised over the increasing number of older adults. Yet, from the perspective of anthropology, old age has not generally been viewed as a problem for the majority of the world's cultures. That is not to say that being an older person did not have its difficulties. For better or worse, problems of disability and security were managed within the families of older people. This was not, in fact, always accomplished in an especially supportive way. It was only with the invention of industry, capitalism, and the reorganization of work, along with the familiar demographic transition, that old age became defined as a problem. At the same time, associated with capitalism was a vast increase in wealth and material comforts, as well as improvements in public health and sanitation – these developments promoting greater longevity. At the same time, this wealth is not evenly distributed, which exacerbates the problems of old age for those individuals disadvantaged across their life course.

This chapter focuses on five aspects of social anthropological research in gerontology: first, it reviews the legacy of British social anthropology to the study of age; secondly, there is an assessment of the expansion of American sociocultural anthropology into studies of ageing; thirdly, the chapter examines insights into ageing resulting from cross-cultural research and anthropological work in Western countries; fourthly, the chapter examines, from an anthropological perspective, issues relating to social structure and risks in old age; finally, a concluding section deals with the benefits of social anthropology for work in social gerontology.

AGE AND THE LEGACY OF SOCIAL ANTHROPOLOGY

Social anthropology has its origins in 19th century England, arising in response to a globalism created by the rise of international trade. In the aftermath of imperialism and colonialism, not only was it evident that peoples of vastly different cultures were brought into interaction with Europeans, but also that, with this contact, traditional ways of life were threatened. Intellectually, the anthropological effort endeavored to reconstruct the social processes to account for change in the world prior to European expansion. The first was the social evolution of Edward Tylor (1871), proposing evolutionary laws documenting the universal history of humans from a stage of 'savagery' to 'civilization'. The second was the diffusion theory of William Rivers (1914), explaining change through processes of historical contact and exchange of social forms. Reactions to these speculative reconstructions of histories led to the birth of functionalist anthropology – a distinctive school within social anthropology (Goody, 1995). The invention of fieldwork involving extended periods of living

with native peoples not only improved anthropological data but also changed the way anthropologists understood those alien worlds. Social anthropologists were soon moving in and studying people in all parts of the globe.

In their constructing a science of society, functional models represented simpler societies as integrated wholes. Although we now view this approach as an oversimplification, social anthropology left a legacy of considerable importance for research into ageing. This inheritance provided anthropology and gerontology with a vocabulary and a framework to investigate age structuring and the social uses of age. In the pastoral societies of Eastern Africa, ethnographers encountered a somewhat rare phenomenon. Males were socially stratified on the basis of generation and maturity, which in European eyes translates into age. As early as 1929, Radcliffe-Brown made a distinction between *age sets* and *age grades* with the intent to clarify quite different phenomena. Age sets are corporate groups, usually of males, that politically organize the more public life of a society. Group formation is roughly based on age, which, in the absence of chronology, may be operationalized as generational position in a kinship system. Other criteria may include initiation after a set interval, social maturity, or the purchase of the ritual paraphernalia of the next senior group. Age grades, on the other hand, are the broad categories used to recognize the passage through the life course as individuals move from childhood to old age. Age grades are common to most societies, although their specific features may vary.

The distinction between age sets and age grades helped to organize a growing ethnographic literature on societies in East Africa, Australia, Lowland South America, and the Great Plains of North America. One of the challenges was to explain why age stratification in these societies became explicitly defined with rules nearly as complicated as kinship (Stewart, 1977). A number of hypotheses have been offered regarding the functions of age homogeneous groups. These include factors such as socialization (Eisenstadt, 1956), conflict reduction (Wilson, 1951), population regulation (Legesse, 1973), and incorporation of young males into the adult-ordered political world. The variety and multifunctional nature of what we now identify as age class systems was to be systematically explored by Bernardi (1985).

This ethnographic literature influenced the work of Leonard Cain (1964) in his sociological formulation of the life course. Later, Bernice Neugarten (Neugarten and Datan, 1973) and Matilda Riley (1972; Foner and Kertzer, 1978; Riley et al., 1973) were influenced by age class systems[1] in their respective formulations of age norms and age stratification. Although the types of societies and age classes have no parallel to the use of age in industrialized societies, these ideas have created the foundation upon which we understand age structuring in the nation states of the 20th and 21st centuries.

Social anthropology has by and large been concerned with age and social organization. The literature is focused on what we now know as age class societies and is just as likely to look at youth as to focus on old age (Baxter and Almagore, 1978; La Fontaine, 1978; Spencer, 1990). Although social anthropology has expanded our knowledge of age, it has not embraced old age to the extent of sociocultural anthropology in the United States.

SOCIOCULTURAL ANTHROPOLOGY AND GERONTOLOGY

American anthropology discovered gerontology during its invention as a major disciplinary endeavor following World War II. Unlike social anthropologists in Europe, American anthropologists faced issues relating to the loss of native peoples and attempted to salvage what they could from the experiences and memories of older informants. Age itself remained a minor topic of social organization (Linton, 1942; Parsons, 1942) or a question in the study of kinship terminology. This shifted in 1945 when a Yale sociologist, Leo Simmons, embraced a new technological database developed by George Peter Murdock (Simmons, 1945). The Human Relations Area Files (HRAF)[2] created ethnographic files organized around a broad code book (*Outline of Cultural Materials*, Murdock, 2000). This database was innovative for its times in that it literally photographed each section of an ethnographic monograph and organized the relevant parts on microfiche cards. The topic Simmons researched was the status of the aged in primitive society. From 1945 to 1967, Simmons was the cross-cultural spokesperson for gerontology. Although a sociologist, Simmons had done considerable ethnographic work among the Hopi of Northern Arizona. In 1967, Margaret Clark brought a different anthropological perspective to gerontology, developing a culture and personality framework combined with cultural values. Her work with Barbara Anderson, *Culture and Aging* (1967), is a study of cultural values and mental health in relation to old age. By the early 1970s, Donald Cowgill and Lowell Holmes proposed a theory of modernization and ageing, which placed problematic issues of ageing in a comparative perspective (Cowgill and Holmes, 1972).

In the 1970s, the activities of American anthropologists were reflected in the formation

in 1978 of the Association for Anthropology and Gerontology. This formalized a group of around 300 researchers with a core of anthropologists as an independent organization that promoted anthropological and qualitative research on ageing and provided resources for teaching. The cross-fertilization between anthropology and gerontology proved to be highly rewarding. Gerontology had always welcomed the cross-cultural perspective of anthropology, and now, anthropologists brought with them a cultural perspective that looked at basic issues in ageing in a new light. For instance, ethnographic studies of retirement communities revealed new lifestyles that were far from the suspected 'geriatric ghettos' that should have been a product of the segregation of older people (see further below). Before long, anthropologists were investigating age structuring, well-being, personhood, ethnicity, senior centers, assisted living arrangements, and medical issues to name a few, both cross-culturally and at home.

AGE IN CROSS-CULTURAL PERSPECTIVE

Initially, social gerontologists explored the lives of older people and their well-being to ascertain issues around adjustment to daily life. Comparative anthropological work sought to discover the same thing, but through related variables of roles, status, and treatment. The early work by Leo Simmons (1945, 1960) challenged our folk wisdom that paradise was lost in the move from smaller-scaled societies. In fact, he suggested that it is well possible that paradise is to some extent gained, since the mistreatment and actual killing of older people is not unusual in simpler societies. Later research (Glascock, 1982, 1997) found that 'death-hastening' behavior toward older people occurred in 51 per cent of the societies in the Probability Sample of the HRAF. Also, older people are often scolded, teased, and sometimes beaten in the societies in the HRAF sample (Maxwell, 1986; Maxwell and Maxwell, 1980; Maxwell et al., 1982; Silverman and Maxwell, 1978, 1987). Why can old age be difficult in smaller-scaled societies? As long as one is intact and contributing, support and high prestige are often accorded. However, if one becomes disabled and is classified as decrepit, then in spite of high status, an older person may be abandoned, or possibly killed. What works *against* disabled older people in these societies? Mainly it is primarily the mobility required in foraging societies, combined with harsh seasonality and bilateral kinship. What works *for* older people in simpler societies? In general, it is the control of resources that comes with agriculture and a more sedentary life that grants more prolonged support. This not only involves land but also information (Press and McKool, 1972). Also, unilineal kinship (matrilineal or patrilineal) increases the number of junior kin involved in support simply by extending a part of the kin network (Fry, 2004).

The now much-revised modernization thesis of Cowgill and Holmes (1972) argued that these generalizations were reversed in industrialized societies, that modern health technology, education, economics, and urbanization, segregated the old and lowered their status. The sample of societies employed, however, did not include the simplest and therefore excluded some of the negative practices often found in the non-industrialized world. Further research concluded that as societies become more industrialized, the status of older people actually increased. Overall, combining findings from multiple studies has suggested an image of a zigzag curve with high status, but high risk for the disabled old in the simplest societies, but with the development of agriculture increasing support for this group. There then appears a decline in the situation of older people in the early stages of industrialization but then a rise in status with economic development. Thus, it can be readily claimed that paradise is more gained than lost, in spite of the problems that industrialization and capitalism has created for older people.

Well-being, quality of life, and successful ageing implicitly call for evaluations because they are anchored in cultural values. These are guides to what constitutes a good old age, but they are modified by context and circumstance. Thus, one should expect a plurality of features promoting or detracting from a successful old age. Researchers working in diverse cultures have had to deal with the problem of measuring well-being (Blandford and Chappell, 1990; Diener, 1984; Liang et al., 1987; Thomas and Chambers, 1989). Hadley Cantril (1965) was among the first to use the comparative method to investigate well-being in his study of 11 nations. Anthropologists have adapted his approach in smaller-scaled communities around the world (Keith et al., 1994; Nydegger, 1980). Although culture shapes the meaning of the reasons for well-being in locally specific ways, the broader themes show remarkable parallelism with the research on well-being in industrialized nations. Certainly, one major axis of well-being is health and functionality. In nation-states this means being free of disease and able to move around. In smaller cultures such as the Kung of the Kalahari, health and functionality mean being able to work. Another foundation of good well-being is material security. In industrialized nations this means having financial resources, while in non-industrial contexts the same theme means access to a good supply of food. Other factors in promoting well-being are social issues, especially family and the welfare of children and parents, as well as character issues.

Some criteria for a good old age, on the other hand, are expressed quite differently, depending on context and associated circumstances. In the study of seven communities carried out by Project AGE (Fry et al., 1997), 'sociality' emerged as a distinctive issue, especially in North America (Illinois and Pennsylvania) and in Hong Kong. Successful older people in America were seen as being 'active', while their counterparts in Hong Kong were seen as not being a 'nag' or 'busybody'. In the African sites, this theme was absent and in Ireland, rarely mentioned. Anthropologists continue to explore the cultural meanings and diversity in what constitutes a good old age in specific contexts (Shenk and Sokolovsky, 2001), with substantial research undertaken in countries such as Japan (Traphagan, 2004; Weiss et al., 2005; Wilcox et al., 2007) and China (Zhang and Liu, 2007). Immigration and well-being have received increased attention as older people make forced moves to be near kin in a new host country (Ajrouch, 2007; Detzner, 2004; Torres, 2006). Likewise, as younger people leave rural areas for urban jobs and new opportunities overseas, older parents can and often do experience increased vulnerability by being left behind (Kraeger, 2006). On the other hand, immigrant children are recognized as major supporters of families left behind, most likely including the senior generations. Migration can take a different form as retirees voluntarily leave for a less developed country in search of a new home and higher quality of life (Sunil et al., 2007).

Anthropology also joined into the gerontological debate over the use of chronology to define age. On a comparative basis there was the discovery of diverse, culturally specific metaphors to depict the passage of time and to describe ageing. How is age reckoned in cultures without the Gregorian calendar and without written records? Ageing does occur and it is recognized, but people do not know their ages or indeed need to know them, since, really, there is nothing to be gained by such knowledge. Physical characteristics and abilities are noted as rough indicators of functionality. Generational differences mark a temporal sequence down a line of descent from grandparents to parents to grandchildren (Kertzer, 1982). However, generations are not a good proxy for age since with long periods of reproduction one can have children who are younger than grandchildren. In asking people about age in these smaller-scaled societies, we did discover that they know relative age. They know who is senior and who is junior, and they act accordingly. They may also relate their age to notable events: for instance, being born before or after a great flood.

If people can get on quite well without knowing their age, why should some people be required to know the date and year of birth? For peoples of Europe and North America, it would be odd not to know your age. Age is essential in these societies simply because the nation-state has used age to structure a range of attachments and activities. The labor market and education are structured by age, entitlements are allocated by age, and the privileges of adulthood (driving, drinking, voting, and marriage) are determined by age. In essence, citizenship is defined by age. There are times at which one actually has to present a birth certificate to prove age and citizenship. The State uses chronological age as a convenient proxy based on cultural assumptions about what should be happening at those ages. This has two effects. First, chronology masks considerable heterogeneity within and across age groups (Dannefer, 1988). Secondly, the reliance on chronology has created a distinctive life course, one staged into a period of preparation (adolescence), a period of work and marriage (adulthood), and a period of retirement and leisure (old age). This contrasts with a generational life course, which is not staged, but is ordered by maturation, abilities, and kinship (Fry, 2002).

As anthropologists studied the phenomena of age, some surprises emerged. First, three separate populations reported superlongevity, with individuals living upwards of 130 years. These were the people in Vilcabamba, Ecuador (Davies, 1975), the Abkhazians of the Caucasus in the former Soviet Union (Benet, 1974), and the Hunzakut of Pakistan. Identifying those societies led to the hope of discovering what promotes longevity, such as life ways, diet, environment, or fortunate genetics. In documenting the ages of these long-living individuals using a combination of church records, birth orders, and known historical dates, we discovered that these seniors exaggerated their ages (Mazess and Foreman, 1979). The motivation was variable, but included such things as prestige, attention, and assuming a parent's identity to avoid the draft. We are familiar with age-defying strategies of Americans and Europeans with anti-wrinkle cream and plastic surgery and with the rapid growth of interest in the anti-ageing movement (see Chapter 35). Either way, by defying or escalating age, it turns out that age is not as ascriptive and immutable as we suspected.

Secondly, how is old age culturally evaluated? Is it a positive life stage to enjoy and prolong as our very long-living Abkhazians aspired to? Or is it a life stage full of dread? Certainly, in societies where one must have the functional abilities to

contribute to the food quest, old age is not positive. One is reduced to complaining (Rosenberg, 1997), and support can be withdrawn. When people were asked to evaluate life stages (Ikels, 1989), they most positively evaluated their present stage in life. Surprisingly, in America and Europe, youth was not all that positive and was a stage not to be repeated. At issue, were the decisions to be made and difficulties in getting started in the life course.

SOCIAL ANTHROPOLOGY AND AGEING AT HOME

With globalization, anthropologists have increasingly worked within the boundaries of their own societies. At home, our questions shift from the bigger picture of cross-cultural issues to more focused questions about specific contexts and problematic populations. Perspectives and methods that were worked out to understand the diversity of cultures around the world were adapted to comprehend issues in one's own culture. These include fieldwork involving participant observation, an appreciation of the native's point of view and knowledge of a context, and an ethnographic holism. In investigating ageing in these societies, anthropologists first went to where concentrations of old people could be found, since that is where ethnographic methods work best.

Among the earliest targets in research in the United States were age-homogeneous communities, ranging from luxurious suburban retirement communities in the Sunbelt to public housing for older people. Because of the homogeneity reinforced by local housing authorities or recruitment by developers, some urban planners feared the formation of geriatric ghettos once the newness and novelty wore off. Quite to the contrary, ethnographic research revealed social worlds of older adults who negotiated with each other in forming a future (Francis, 1984; Hochschild, 1973; Johnson, 1971; Keith, 1979, 1982; Fry, 1977).

Likewise, social anthropologists investigated the experience of growing old in contexts that were not especially friendly to the old, notably the inner city and rural contexts. Even in decaying inner cities where the old sought refuge in single room occupancy (SRO) hotels, we find social networks (based for example on friendship) that are not visible to a casual observer (Eckert, 1980; Sokolovsky and Cohen, 1987). In public housing estates for older people, social networks of support significantly improved relationships with adult children who could focus on quality rather than instrumental tasks (Jonas and Wellen, 1980).

Non-kin are found to be a significant source of support for some urban elders (Barker, 2002). Rural communities present challenges for older people, especially because of transportation issues and difficulties and service delivery to a dispersed population. Yet, here we find natural support networks (Shenk, 1998), although there is evidence that globalization is transforming the nature of rural communities (van Willigen, 1989). Likewise, nursing homes have become a target of anthropological research, revealing strengths as well as difficulties that these settings present for their residents (Foner, 1994, Henderson and Vesperi, 1995; Kayser-Jones, 1981; Safford, 2003; Savishinsky, 1991; Shield, 1988).

With the discovery of ageing as an ethnographic field of enquiry, anthropologists diversified. Sources of meaning in late life were documented (Kaufman, 1986; Luborsky, 1993). Gender and ageing is an issue of major importance with studies of older and middle-aged women (Kerns and Brown, 1992) and of older men living alone (Rubenstein, 1986). Comparative studies of menopause raise serious questions about its universality and its medicalization (Du Toit, 1990; Lock, 1993). The cessation of menses is universal, but the symptoms are by no means the same across different cultures.

Retirement as a phase of life and its meanings have also been ethnographically explored (Luborsky, 1994, Savishinsky, 2000.) Once retired and no longer locked into a schedule dictated by the clock, time becomes more multidimensional and complex (Tsuji, 2005). Isolated settings such as a day care center create conditions where time is reconstituted (Hazan, 1980) and in nursing homes it is highly regimented. At home, the ethnographic and comparative method extended research into the experience of ageing in ethnic and minority groups (Barker et al., 1998: Becker and Beyene, 1999; Groger and Kunkel, 1995).

Medical anthropologists have also turned their attention to ageing. Complementary and alternative medical therapies based on folk knowledge have been investigated for chronic conditions among diabetes sufferers in rural North Carolina (Arcury et al., 2006). Also, ageing differently and with disabilities such as deafness has yielded insights into alternative communities and in dealing with major disruptions such as the aftermath of a stroke (Becker, 1980, 1997). Bifurcated pathways to death through either high-tech medicine or the revolving door have been created by American hospitals through their policies and funding. Either way, the gap between life and death is an unpleasant 'grey area' (Kaufman, 2006).

Social anthropological research has increasingly been applied to countries such as the United States, in part because of globalization. First, research in foreign countries raises increasingly difficult issues and problems (Ikels and Beall, 2001). Many nations put restrictions on foreign researchers to protect their citizens and also because they have homegrown scientists with the necessary expertise to do the research. Secondly, with globalization there has been a cultural homogenization, with markets incorporating more and more people. Ever since the early 20th century, the truly exotic small-scaled cultures have been overwhelmed, incorporated into nations, and educated to become productive citizens. Although this is the state of the world, as scientists, we run the danger of losing the advantage of comparative research, i.e., awareness of cultural and social differences (Fry, 2006).

When entering foreign contexts, ethnographers often encounter a phenomenon known as 'cultural shock'. In negotiating an alien world, one's own world is turned 90 degrees. By looking at the world through native eyes and understandings, one's own cultural assumptions are challenged. A part of cultural shock results in an emotional and intellectual distancing from what one usually takes for granted. Domestic research engages one in familiar ideology. We use that common sense to ask questions. We also are likely to respond to the culture of funding and governmental agencies that have their own view of the way the world should work and the problems with it. The net effect is that we lose culture by not seeing it and questioning it.

What can we do about this state of affairs? We actually can benefit from the work of the social anthropologists from the 1920s to the 1960s. In trying to gain a holistic understanding of smaller, exotic cultures, they were not afraid to ask questions drawn from a wide range of disciplinary perspectives (Wolf 1982). To regain a holistic view of specific contexts, communities, or even nations, it was necessary to reclaim culture and its economic and political constitutents. This was essential to avoid researching ever smaller and smaller questions and phenomena, a research practice known as microfication (Bass, 2006; Hagestad and Dannefer, 2001).

SOCIAL STRUCTURE AND RISKS IN OLD AGE

Although much of anthropology has pursued questions of an individuated nature, social anthropology endures with enquiries into social structure. Social institutions organize the social relationships and interdependencies that comprise social life. The public life of a society is shaped by arrangements associated with the creation of wealth and related power structures. Humans use these economic and political institutions not only to organize daily lives but also to develop lifelong strategies to shape their old age. In the course of sociocultural evolution, humans have devised three basic modes of production: domestic, tribute, and capitalist. Diversity within each mode of production is a remarkable feature across cultures. In comparing these modes of production we see major differences in the organization of work, the use of technology, the organization of exchange, the intensification of production, and the amount of wealth created. From a social anthropological perspective on old age, a useful approach is to examine the consequences of the social units that organize work. Do these arrangements offer protection for older people or do they create risks in old age?

To provide security for either younger or older members of a society, there must be a combination of resources and rewards. For instance, we know that in a *domestic mode of production* based on foraging the lives of older people can be difficult. Disability combined with high mobility and scarcity can result in older members being provisioned at a base camp and possibly abandoned. Foragers simply cannot accumulate wealth. With sedentism associated with domestication, older adults and the very young do not face the rigors of frequent movement. With domestication (pastoralism, horticulture and agriculture) and increased wealth based on *tribute* (i.e., economies based on the removal of wealth from producers to finance the operations of a centralized political system), the issue of having sufficient resources is more adequate and predictable. Against this, wealth is not evenly distributed. A political hierarchy stimulates production through systems of taxation. Consequently, some families and some older people will have more wealth than others. Wealth also has to be managed and attention given to who will receive it once a person dies or becomes so disabled. Some protection is provided to older people in explicit rules for co-residence and inheritance of family wealth. In spite of diversity within societies organized by a domestic mode or a tribute mode of production, family units provide security. In these contexts, family units are also units of production. Rarely are older people excluded from the division of labor, because they are needed for their knowledge, work, connections, and sometimes wealth.

All modes of production provide security in food and material comfort to reduce the risks of environmental insults. But risk never vanishes. In the three modes of production with which humans have experimented, we find significant differences in intensification (energy used), social stability, amount of wealth produced, mechanisms for the distribution of that wealth, and the risks that are either diminished or amplified.

Domestic modes of production, with or without domestication, are by far the most stable. Foraging has endured for at least two and a half million years, first in Africa and then around the globe. Small-scale horticulture and pastoralism have been practiced for nearly 9000 years. Contributing to stability is the fact that comparatively little energy is used and environmental impacts are minimal. Of course, populations are small and little wealth is generated beyond subsistence. Risks to individuals come from the extremes of seasonality or from bad years and crop failure and self-managed conflicts. Entire bands or villages may disappear. Risk is not shared evenly – and the very young and the old are those most affected.

Tribute-based modes of production would appear to reduce risks through more centralized management, stockpiling of resources for use in lean years, and the increase of wealth. However, the centrality of a hierarchy makes instability a cultural feature of these societies. Any hierarchy is unstable because of divisiveness from within, the difficulties of communicating across levels to manage the system, and from predation from without. Instability can result in a societal collapse, which can range from a redistribution of population to abandonment of cities, or even to the annihilation of a population. Archaeologically, we see ruined cities on every continent with the exception of Antarctica. Instability constitutes a risk and the occasional crop failure and famine remains a threat. Some of this is self-inflicted because of environmental impacts associated with the intensification of agriculture. Again, it is very young and the old who are the most affected.

A *capitalistic mode of production* is by far the most intensive and unstable. Environmental impacts are enormous as raw material is removed to create commodities. Fossil fuels often mask the inefficiencies of production. For instance, when considering the petrochemicals involved in industrial agriculture, the energy inputs usually exceed energy outputs. Instabilities in this mode of production come from more than hierarchy and from the energetic disequilibrium in production. One example of creating wealth in capitalism involves not only the manufacture of products but also speculation in the future values of virtually anything produced. This may involve things such as railroads, canals, tulips, dot.com companies, or creative mortgages to finance a housing boom. Exchange value is used to grow capital (buy low, sell high). This is inherently unstable, as witnessed by the boom and bust cycles of capitalist economies. Markets involve speculative bubbles. When they burst, the results are spectacularly negative as wealth simply vanishes.

Global markets do have innumerable local effects, often unanticipated, yet complex. For instance, in Zambia, the construction of a dam in the Gwembe Valley transformed the economic base from subsistence hoe horticulture to cattle pastoralism oriented toward markets. Matrilineal kinship shifted to patrilineal, which altered gender-specific life strategies. Men herd cattle that bring wealth through the livestock market while women continue subsistence gardening that is not marketed for cash. As a result, older women were disadvantaged to the point of a very real possibility of being reduced to a diet of grass seeds (Cliggett, 2005). When urban neighborhoods benefit positively through entrepreneurial activity in global markets and become targets for regentrification, older residents may find housing is no longer affordable because of rising taxes. Younger, more affluent families displace them into less desirable housing. Mortgage companies who require no down payment for loans on new construction depress the value of older homes, which may mean that older homeowners may not get the value anticipated when they sell. These proceeds may have been targeted to finance long-term care.

GLOBALIZATION AND COMMUNITY CHANGE

Ethnography offers one highly fertile way to examine the indirect effects of global economic forces and the influence of globalization on communities (Phillipson and Scharf, 2005). In order to discern such changes, communities may need to be studied ethnographically over several decades. Momence, Illinois, a small community south of Chicago that the author studied in conjunction with Project AGE, has been studied for over 30 years. The changes are dramatic and attributable to: (1) globalization of the local labor market; (2) a change of scale in retail marketing; and (3) the effects of international migration.

In the 1970s, when Momence first came to my anthropological attention, it was a stable small town of about 3400 people and another 3000 individuals who identified with the town from the surrounding countryside. There was a definite feeling of stepping back into earlier decades of the 20th century, when people knew each other on a face-to-face basis and were somehow connected to the key players in the community and their institutions. The resource base was fairly strong, anchored in agriculture, light industry, a healthy commercial district, and unionized jobs in nearby Kankakee and the south side of Chicago. By the time Momence

came under systematic scrutiny in the 1980s, something was going wrong. Our informants told us that the biggest issue facing the community was unemployment. At the time, the Northern Midwest was experiencing de-industrialization as major industries closed their factories and moved south to states with a cheaper labor force. Consequently, Momence saw a decline in its resource base, and families experienced change as children moved away while those that stayed encountered higher rates of divorce and single parenthood. People were hopeful that the period was just another economic down cycle.

By the late 1980s, the regional economy saw the expansion of discount retail merchandizing as national chains such as Wal-Mart and K-Mart, among others, moved into Kankakee. By the 1990s, a mall was developed. A prominent Momence businessman told me that a Wal-Mart will destroy the downtowns of small communities within a radius of 50 miles simply because smaller businesses cannot compete with the larger scale. In fact, he set business goals for his store over a 2-year period. When the store did not meet his goals, he closed it and took a service job with the local bank. His wife continued the same line of retail work, but with a regional discount retailer. Fifteen years later, all one sees in the commercial district are primarily firms that are in the service industry – lawyers, insurance, banking, restaurants, hair care, and physical fitness. In the 1970s it was possible to buy furniture, appliances, antiques, gifts, clothing, and shoes, and even to get shoes repaired. A town that once had three grocery stores now has only one and this has moved about a mile north of the commercial district. To do the marketing for basic commodities, one now has to drive, which may be problematic for the very old.

In the late 1990s and early 2000s, the racial composition of Momence began to change. Momence has always had a presence of Blacks in the schools and in public places because of a sizable Black community to the south in Pembroke Township who do their marketing in Momence. Then, largely undocumented immigrants began to move into rental housing. Initially, these were younger males who crowded into small apartments to save money while they worked in low-paying agricultural jobs or factory jobs. By the early 2000s, immigrant families became more apparent and Momence has become increasingly Hispanic. Most people notice the cultural change, especially in public spaces such as the park, where immigrant families picnic and Mexican music fills the air. The effect of immigration on older people is not direct. The influx of immigrant families, however, further depresses the resource base of Momence since their income is based on low-paying jobs and any disposable income is sent to kin in Mexico. Also, an undercount in the 2000 Federal Census has affected the distribution of tax revenue on the county level. Older people see the changes and feel confused. One older man, a former mayor now approaching his 90s, commented in 2006 that he no longer knows very many people in Momence when 20 and even 10 years earlier he knew almost everybody. This comment is both about population replacement and about the fact he has out-survived his cohort.

The experience of Momence, and many smaller towns across the Midwest and the Great Plains, illustrates how subtle and how profound the impact of globalization can be at the local level. In the 1980s Momence, when compared with all the Project AGE communities, was seen as having a configuration of features that favored positive ageing. Slow growth and population stability favored availability of kin and continuity in social networks. Older adults gained seniority and leadership in voluntary association; they were visible in the downtown with businesses, either catering to them or serving as a public hangout spot. For instance, one restaurant reserved a table for the five men in their 80s who showed up every morning for sociality and coffee.

Epitomizing the reverence for seniority was the Momence Women's Club (a local affiliate of the Federated Women's Clubs of America). As an observer of the May luncheon meeting, I found the meeting itself predictable and ordinary. However, the spatial arrangements and costumes of the participants were quite remarkable. Most participants sat eating their lunch in smaller groups at tables in the hall of the restaurant. However, on a stage at what clearly was the top table sat eight women facing their audience. All of these 'ladies of the Club' were over 70 and dressed formally with hats and white gloves. These were the former presidents and the present president, who also was in her 70s. Their leadership and accomplishments were a part of the celebration.

Another celebration of the Women's Club took place in May of 2008, this time at the large home of a former president (the home is now a bed and breakfast). During lunch, 100 years of the Club's community activities and service to Momence were celebrated. In the business meeting that followed, in the first item of business, the club disbanded. They had failed to assemble a slate of officers for the 2008 season. One key informant stated that they had aged in place and failed to recruit younger members. Younger women, being stretched to the limit with children and work until their 40s and even into their 50s, were left with little time and energy for service organizations.

With a declining pool of women from which to recruit and increased competition from other organizations, the Club was no longer viable. One final gesture to seniority was that each past president was given a carnation. Increased competition within the global labor market means children leave for better jobs and those that stay work longer in lower-paid service sector jobs. The voluntary work that creates a positive sense of community goes undone, as the organizations that harness the energy fail because their members have become too senior.

Globalization has altered those features. The influx of immigrants has culturally altered the community. Parts of the community have responded to their presence by offering church services in Spanish and the grocery stocks more food products for a Hispanic market. As more families move in (in comparison to single males) the hope of native Momence dwellers is that these immigrants will become good citizens and neighbors. The downtown, however, is mostly deserted except for patrons to the restaurants and immigrant males and families who live in apartments above the shops. The depressed economy has altered the fortune and future of the community. Older residents have to maintain their ability to drive to do basic tasks such as shop or go to the doctor. Organizations creating the public culture of a community through the leadership of senior members have to compete with a changing labor market, and if they are not successful they disband and leave a diminished legacy. The story continues as the people of Momence respond and work with a vision of what lies ahead. From the perspective of lifelong residents, the social world in which they matured and planned for a good old age has been altered in threatening ways.

Markets are social inventions and as such are subject to manipulation. With globalized markets, events and decisions that are made on the other side of the globe have consequences at the local level. For the people of the Gwembe Valley, decisions about livestock markets changed their social structure to the disadvantage of older women. For the people of Momence, decisions about marketing strategies resulted in the near abandonment of the commercial district with increased transportation problems for older people. Legislation to convert food into fuel leaves many of the world's poor without food. Markets are volatile and unstable, although with consumer confidence they appear otherwise. As we have learned, especially in the downturn of the 1930s, older people are the most dramatically affected since they lack the access to jobs, resources, and time to recover.

SOCIAL ANTHROPOLOGY AND SOCIAL GERONTOLOGY

Gerontology, from its inception, is a discipline that is practical and pragmatic in understanding and resolving the difficulties of older people, especially in societies having capitalistic and industrial economies. Social anthropology brings to this endeavor a much broader and holistic perspective. It is quite clear that ageing is far more complicated than growing old. Individuals do grow old, but they do so in a social and cultural context. Cross-culturally, we see that the needs and support of older people are shaped by political and economic considerations. Social anthropology, as an intellectual tradition, provides a perspective and methods to understand how and why interdependent social units integrate older adults into or exclude them from their workings. For modes of production organized by domestic units or tribute, older adults are a part of a division of labor, contributing knowledge, skills, labor, or wealth. In capitalism, the young and the old are excluded from the division of labor and old age becomes a problem in terms of financial (both private and state-subsidized) issues, and disability and health care (with both private and state-subsidized insurance). The problem of old age is only intensified by globalization. The global assembly line leaves less desirable jobs at home and exports jobs to workers who work for very low wages. In a sense, the problem of old age is also exported.

As we realize the complexities of a hyper-connected and interdependent global world, the holism of social anthropology is essential to make that world work for all people. Scientifically, we are just beginning to figure out the complexities of the global environment and the longer-term impacts of human activities. Likewise, since the invention of social anthropology, we have seen the simpler and more exotic cultures of the world engulfed in a global social and economic order. Throughout the 20th century, the international world has become increasing complex, stratified, and rapidly changing. Because complexity and hierarchy are inherently unstable, we can see rapid expansion in markets such as that experienced since the 1970s. Similarly, we can see rapid contraction of markets as energy costs raise the costs of food and other commodities. It is a world that in its complexity is difficult to model, but social anthropology has the intellectual tools to make it comprehensible. As dependent members (young and old) of a population who participate in a division of labor, we need to expand our gerontological knowledge beyond the issues of dependency: namely, care-giving, social support, and well-being. Undue focus on the individual level obscures social and economic structure. We may think we are solving problematic issues, but we are leaving the core of the problem unaddressed. Social anthropology studies social structure and has a legacy that encourages an examination of the economic and political structures shaping lives at all ages.

NOTES

1 Age classes are corporate groups into which males (young boys) are recruited on the basis of age. As these males mature, the entire group advances to the next older group, thus advancing all age groups. Because all participating males are stratified into age sets, these societies are described as age class societies.

2 Today, the files use an expanded set of codes based on Murdock's original and are searchable electronically at the HRAF website or through subscribing libraries. The ethnographic database is much stronger, with contemporary monographs constantly being added.

REFERENCES

Ajrouch, K.J. (2007) 'Resources and well-being among Arab-American Elders', *Journal of Cross Cultural Gerontology*, 22: 167–82.

Arcury, T.A., Bell, R.A., Snively, B.A., et al. (2006) 'Complementary and alternative medicine use as health self-management: rural older adults with diabetes', *Journal of Gerontology: Social Sciences*, 61B: S62–71.

Barker, J., Morrow, J., and Mitteness, L.S. (1998) 'Gender and informal support networks, and elderly urban African Americans', *Journal of Aging Studies*, 12: 199–222.

Barker, J.C. (2002) 'Neighbors, friends and other non-kin caregivers of community-living dependent elders', *Journal of Gerontology: Social Sciences*, 57b: 158–67.

Bass, S. (2006) 'Gerontological theory: the search for the Holy Grail', *The Gerontologist*, 46: 139–44.

Baxter, P.T.W. and Almagor, U. (eds) (1978) *Age, Generation and Time: Some Features of East African Age Organizations*. New York: St. Martin's Press.

Becker, G. (1980) *Growing Old in Silence*. Berkeley, CA: University of California Press.

Becker, G. (1997) *Disrupted lives: How People Create Meaning in a Chaotic World*. Berkeley, CA: University of California Press.

Becker, G. and Beyene, Y. (1999) 'Narratives of age and uprootedness among older Cambodian refugees', *Journal of Aging Studies*, 13: 295–314.

Benet, S. (1974) *Abkhasians: The Long-lived People of the Caucasus.* New York: Holt, Reinhart and Winston.

Bernardi, B. (1985) *Age Class Systems.* London: Cambridge University Press.

Blandford, A.A. and Chappell, N.L. (1990) 'Subjective well-being among native and non-native elderly persons: Do differences exist?' *Canadian Journal on Aging,* 9 (4): 386–99.

Cain, L. D. (1964) 'Life course and social structure', in R.L. Faris (ed.), *Handbook of Modern Sociology.* Chicago: Rand McNally, pp. 272–309.

Cantril, H. (1965) *The Pattern of Human Concerns.* New Brunswick, NJ: Rutgers University Press.

Clark, M.M. and Anderson, B.G. (1967) *Culture and Aging: An Anthropological Study of Older Americans.* Springfield, IL: Charles Thomas.

Cliggett, L. (2005) *Grains from Grass: Aging, Gender and Famine in Rural Africa.* Ithaca, NY: Cornell University Press.

Cowgill, D.O. and Holmes, L.D. (eds) (1972) *Aging and Modernization.* New York: Appleton-Century-Crofts.

Dannefer, D. (1988) 'What's in a name: an account of the neglect of variability in the study of aging. In J.E. Birren and V.L. Bengtson (eds), *Emergent Theories of Aging.* New York: Springer, pp. 354–84.

Davies, D. (1975) *The C of the Andes.* London: Barne and Jenkins.

Detzner, D.F. (2004) *Elder Voices: South East Asian Families in the United States,* Walnut Creek, CA: Altimira Press.

Diener, E. (1984) 'Subjective well-being', *Psychological Bulletin,* 95(3): 542–75.

Du Toit, B. M. (1990) *Aging and Menopause Among Indian South African Women.* Albany, NY: State University of New York.

Eckert, K. (1980) *The Unseen Elderly: A Study of Marginally Subsistent Hotel Dwellers.* San Diego, CA: Campanile Press.

Eisenstadt, S.N. (1956) *From Generation to Generation.* New York: Free Press.

Foner, A. and Kertzer, D.I. (1978) 'Transitions over the life course: lessons from age set societies', *American Journal of Sociology,* 83: 1081–104.

Foner, N. (1994) *The Caregiving Dilemma: Work in an American Nursing Home.* Berkeley, CA: University of California Press.

Francis, D. (1984) *Will you Still Need Me, Will You Still Feed Me, when I'm 64.* Bloomington, IN; Indiana University Press.

Fry, C.L. (1977) 'The community as a commodity: the age graded case', *Human Organization,* 36: 115–23.

Fry, C.L. (2002) 'The life course as a cultural construct', in R.A. Settersten (ed.), *Invitation to the Life Course.* Amityville, NY: Baywood Publishing, pp. 269–94.

Fry, C.L. (2004) 'Kinship and supportive environments of aging', in. H.W. Wahl, R.J. Scheidt, and P.G. Windley (eds), *Aging in Context: Socio-physical Environments. Annual Review of Gerontology and Geriatrics.* Vol. 23. New York: Springer, pp. 313–33.

Fry, C.L. (2006) 'Whatever happened to culture?', in D. Sheets, D.B. Bradley, and J. Hendricks (eds), *Enduring Questions in Gerontology.* New York: Springer, pp. 159–76.

Fry, C.L., Dickerson-Putman, J., Draper, P., et al. (1997) 'Culture and the meaning of a good old age', in, J. Sokolovsky (ed.), *The Cultural Context of Aging: Worldwide Perspectives.* Westport, CT: Bergin and Garvey, pp. 99–124.

Glascock, A.P. (1982) 'Decrepitude and death-hastening: the nature of old age in third world societies', in J. Sokolovosky (ed.), *Aging and the Aged in the Third World: Part I. Studies in Third World Societies.* Williamsburg, VA: College of William and Mary, pp. 43–66.

Glascock, A.P. (1997) 'When is killing acceptable: the moral dilemma surrounding assisted suicide in America and other societies', in J. Sokolovsky (ed.), *The Cultural Context of Aging: Worldwide Perspectives.* Westport, CT: Bergin and Garvey, pp. 56–70.

Goody, J. (1995) *The Expansive Moment: The Rise of Social Anthropology in Britain and Africa, 1918–1970.* New York: Cambridge University Press.

Groger, L. and Kunkel, S. (1995) 'Aging and exchange: differences between black and white elders', *Journal of Cross-Cultural Gerontology,* 10: 269–87.

Hagestad, G.O. and Dannefer, D. (2001) 'Concepts and theories of aging: beyond microfication in social science approaches', in R.H. Binstock and L.K. George (eds), *Handbook of Aging and the Social Sciences,* 5th edn. San Diego, CA: Academic Press, pp. 3–21.

Hazan, H. (1980) *The Limbo People: A Study of the Constitution of the Time Universe among the Aged.* London: Routledge and Kegan Paul.

Henderson, J.N. and Vesperi, M. (eds) (1995) *The Culture of Long-term Care: Nursing Home Ethnography.* Westport, CT: Greenwood.

Hochschild, A.R. (1973) *The Unexpected Community.* Englewood Cliffs, NJ: Prentice Hall.

Ikels, C. (1989) 'Becoming a human being in theory and practice: Chinese views of human development', in D.I. Kertzer and K.W. Schaie (eds), *Age Structuring in Comparative Perspective.* Hillsdale, NJ: Lawrence Erlbaum Associates, pp. 109–34.

Ikels, C. and Beall, C.M. (2001) 'Age, aging and anthropology', in R.H. Binstock and L.K. George (eds), *Handbook of Aging and the Social Sciences.* 5th edn. San Diego, CA: Academic Press, pp. 125–40.

Johnson, S. (1971) *Idle Haven: Community Building among the Working Class Retired.* Berkeley, CA: University of California Press.

Jonas, K. and Wellen, E. (1980) 'Dependency and reciprocity: home health aid in an elderly population', in C.L. Fry (ed.), *Aging in Culture and Society: Comparative Viewpoints and Strategies.* Brooklyn, NY: Bergin and Garvey, pp. 217–38.

Kaufman, S.R. (1986) *The Ageless Self: Sources of Meaning in Late Life.* Madison, WI: University of Wisconsin Press.

Kaufman, S.R. (2006) *And a Time to Die: How American Hospitals Shape the End of Life.* Chicago: University of Chicago Press.

Kayser-Jones, J.S. (1981) *Old, Alone, and Neglected: Care of the Aged in Scotland and the United States.* Berkeley, CA: University of California Press.

Keith, J. (1979) 'The ethnography of old age', *Anthropological Quarterly*, 52: 1–76.

Keith, J. (1982) *Old People, New Lives: Community Creation in a Retirement Residence*. Chicago: University of Chicago Press.

Keith, J., Fry, C.L., Glascock, A.P., et al. (1994). *The Aging Experience: Diversity and Commonality across Cultures*. Thousand Acres, CA: Sage.

Kerns, V. and Brown, J.K. (1992) *In Her Prime: New Views of Middle-aged Women*. Urbana, IL: University of Illinois Press.

Kertzer, D.I. (1982) 'Generation and age in cross-cultural perspective', in M.W. Riley, R.P. Ables, and M.S. Teltelbaum (eds), *Aging from Birth to Death: Sociotemporal Perspectives*. Boulder, CO: Westview Press, pp. 27–50.

La Fontaine, J.S. (ed.) (1978). *Sex and Age as Principles of Social Differentiation*. New York: Academic Press.

Legesse, A. (1973) *Gada*. New York: Free Press.

Liang, J., Asano, H., Bollen, K.A., Kahana, E.F., and Maeda, D. (1987) 'Cross-cultural comparability of the Philadelphia Geriatric Center Morale Scale: An American–Japanese comparison', *Journal of Gerontology*, 42(1): 37–43.

Linton, R. (1942) 'Age and sex categories', *American Sociological Review*, 7: 589–603.

Lock, M. (1993) *Encounters with Aging: Mythologies of Menopause in Japan and North America*. Berkeley, CA: University of California Press.

Luborsky, M. (1993) 'The romance with personal meaning in gerontology: cultural aspects of life themes', *The Gerontologist*, 33: 440–54.

Luborsky, M. (1994) 'The retirement process: making the person and cultural meanings malleable', *Medical Anthropology Quarterly*, 8: 411–29.

Maxwell, E. (1986) 'Fading out: resource control and cross-cultural patterns of deference', *Journal of Cross-Cultural Gerontology*, 1: 73–89.

Maxwell, E., and Maxwell, R.J. (1980) 'Contempt for the elderly: a cross-cultural analysis', *Current Anthropology*, 24: 569–70.

Maxwell, R.J., Silverman, P., and Maxwell, E.K. (1982) 'The motive for gerontocide', in J. Sokolovosky (ed.), *Aging and the Aged in the Third World: Part I. Studies in Third World Societies*. Williamsburg, VA: College of William and Mary, pp. 67–84.

Mazess, R.B. and Foreman, S.H. (1979) 'Longevity and age exaggeration in Vilcabamba, Ecuador', *Journal of Gerontology*, 34: 97–8.

Murdock, G.P. (2000) *Outline of Cultural Materials*. New Haven, CT: Yale University Press.

Neugarten, B.L. and Datan, N. (1973) 'Sociological perspectives on the life cycle', in P.B. Baltes and K.W. Schaie (eds), *Life-span Developmental Psychology: Personality and Socialization*. New York: Academic Press, pp. 53–71.

Nydegger, C. (1980) 'Measuring morale', in C.L. Fry and J. Keith (eds), *New Methods for Old Age Research*, Chicago: Loyola University, Center for Urban Policy, pp. 177–203.

Parsons, T. (1942) 'Age and sex in the social structure of the United States', *American Sociological Review*, 7: 604–16.

Phillipson, C. and Scharf, T. (2005) 'Rural and urban perspectives on growing old: developing a new research agenda', *European Journal of Ageing*, 2(1): 67–75.

Press, I. and McKool, M. (1972) 'Social structure and status of the aged: toward some valid cross-cultural generalizations', *Aging and Human Development*, 3: 297–306.

Radcliffe-Brown, A.R. (1929) 'Age organization terminology', *Man*, 29: 21.

Riley, M.W., Johnson, M.E., and Foner, A. (eds) (1973) *Aging and Society, Vol. 3. A Sociology of Age Stratification*. New York: Russell Sage Foundation.

Rivers, W.H.R. (1914) *The History of Melanesian Society*. Cambridge: Cambridge University Press.

Rosenberg, H.G. (1997) 'Complaint discourse: aging and caregiving among the Juhoansi of Botswana', in J. Sokolovsky (ed.), *The Cultural Context of Aging: Worldwide Perspectives*. Westport, CT: Bergin and Garvey, pp. 33–55.

Rubinstein, R.L. (1986) *Singular Paths: Old Men Living Alone*. New York: Columbia University Press.

Safford, P.B. (ed.) (2003) *Gray Areas: Ethnographic Encounters with Nursing Home Culture*. Santa Fe, NM: School of American Research Press.

Savishinsky, J. (1991) *The Ends of Time: Live and Work in a Nursing Home*. Westport, CT: Bergin and Garvey.

Savishinsky, J. (2000) *Breaking the Watch: The Meanings of Retirement in America*. Ithaca, NY: Cornell University Press.

Shenk, D. (1998) *Someone to Lend a Helping Hand: Women Growing Old in Rural America*. Amsterdam: Gordon and Breach.

Shenk, D. and Sokolovsky, J. (eds) (2001) 'Positive adaptations to aging in cultural contexts', *Journal of Cross-Cultural Gerontology*, Special Issue, 16: 1–109.

Shield, R.R. (1988) *Uneasy Endings: Daily Life in an American Nursing Home*. Ithaca, NY: Cornell University Press.

Silverman, P. and Maxwell, R.J. (1978) 'How do I respect thee? Let me count the ways: deference toward elderly men and women, *Behavioral Science Research*, 13: 91–108.

Silverman, P. and Maxwell, R.J. (1987) 'The significance of information and power in the comparative study of the aged', in J. Sokolovsky (ed.), *Growing Old in Different Societies: Cross-Cultural Perspectives*. Acton, MA: Copley, 43–55.

Simmons, L.W. (1945) *The Role of the Aged in Primitive Society*. New Haven, CT: Yale University Press.

Simmons, L.W. (1960) 'Aging in preindustrial societies', in C. Tibbits (ed.), *Handbook of Social Gerontology: Societal Aspects of Aging*. Chicago: University of Chicago Press, pp. 62–91.

Sokolovsky, J. and Cohen, C. (1987) 'Networks as adaptation: the cultural meaning of being a "loner" among inner city elderly', in J. Sokolovsky (ed.), *Growing Old in Different Societies: Cross-Cultural Perspectives*. Acton, MA: Copley, pp. 189–201.

Spencer, P. (1990) *Anthropology and the Riddle of the Sphinx: Paradoxes of Change in the Life Course*. London: Routledge.

Stewart, F.H. (1977) *Fundamentals of Age Group Systems*. New York: Academic Press.

Sunil, T.S., Rojas, V., and Bradley, D.E. (2007) 'United States' international retirement migration: the reasons for retiring to the environs of Lake Chapala, Mexico', *Ageing and Society*, 27: 489–510.

Thomas, L.E. and Chambers, K.O. (1989) '"Successful aging" among elderly men in England and India: a phenomenological comparison', in L.E. Thomas (ed.), *Research on Adulthood and Aging: The Human Science Approach*. Albany: State University of New York Press, pp. 183–203.

Torres, S. (2006) 'Different ways of understanding the construct of successful aging: Iranian immigrants speak about what aging well means to them', *Journal of Cross-Cultural Gerontology*, 21: 1–23.

Traphagan, J.W. (2004) *The Practice of Concern: Ritual, Well-being, and Aging in Rural Japan*. Durham, NC: Carolina Academic Press.

Tsuji, Y. (2005) 'Time is not up: temporal complexity of older Americans' lives', *Journal of Cross-Cultural Gerontology*, 20: 3–26.

Tylor, E.B. (1871) *Primitive Culture*. London: John Murray.

van Willigen, J. (1989) *Getting' Some Age on Me: Social Organization of Older People in a Rural American Community*. Lexington: University of Kentucky Press.

Weiner, A.B. (1976) *Women of Value, Men of Renown: New Perspectives in Trobriand Exchange*. Austin, TX: University of Texas Press.

Weiss, R.S., Bass, S.A., Heimovits, H.K., and Oka, M. (2005) 'Japan's silver human resource centers and participant well-being', *Journal of Cross-Cultural Gerontology*, 20: 47–66.

Wilcox, D.C., Wilcox, B.J., Sokolovsky, J., and Sakihara, S. (2007) 'The cultural context of "successful aging" among older women weavers in a Northern Okinawan village: the role of productive activity', *Journal of Cross-Cultural Gerontology*, 22: 137–65.

Wilson, M, (1951) *Good Company: A Study of Nayakyusa Age Villages*. London: Oxford University Press.

Wolf, E.R., (1982) *Europe and the People without History*. Berkeley, CA: University of California Press.

Zhang, W. and Liu, G. (2007) 'Childlessness, psychological well-being and life satisfaction among the elderly in China', *Journal of Cross-Cultural Gerontology*, 22: 185–203.

5

The Demography of Ageing

Christina Victor

INTRODUCTION

The phenomena of population ageing is a recent one in terms of the sum of human experience but is a term with which most of us are familiar. According to Bloom and Canning (2005) the world population was (relatively) stable in terms of both size and broad age composition until the 18th century. Since that point, the world's population has increased significantly and has undergone a fundamental change in terms of age structure. We have experienced both a substantial absolute increase in the number of people living on the planet and a relative (and absolute) change in the age characteristics of those people. The key trend is the significant increase both in the number of older people within the population and in the contribution they represent to the total population. In 2007 there were 704,817,000 citizens of the world aged 60 years or older, representing 11 per cent of the total global family (United Nations, 2007), with the percentage expected to double to 22 per cent by 2050. In addition, there were 188,348,000 aged 80 and older, representing 1.4 per cent of the total world population. We can contrast this with the situation in 1950 when there was only a third of this number of people in the world aged 60 and older – approximately 210 million. So, over the space of 50 years, the population of the world has 'aged' significantly in both absolute and relative terms.

This chapter reviews the demographic processes that underpin the ageing of the world's population and which frame the issues discussed throughout this book. The discussion around population ageing is usually confined to debates concerning the challenges and burdens posed by an ageing population, with particular emphasis upon the need to provide health, social care, and provision for pensions. Yet population ageing, as this volume shows, has implications in many other spheres of life such as household composition, family relationships, labor supply, and social relationships. Demographic change affects virtually every sphere of our daily lives and is manifest at the micro level, in family structures and sizes, as well as at macro-level considerations, such as policy debates. This chapter provides an overview of the demography of ageing. First, we examine the definition of population ageing and review the distribution of demographic trends across the globe. Secondly, the chapter considers the reasons behind population ageing. Finally, we consider key trends and issues within population ageing.

THE DEVELOPMENT OF POPULATION AGEING

The broad distribution of the world's older citizens is summarized in Table 5.1 and suggests that, at first sight, this is an issue that is most pertinent to the developed nations of the world, especially Western Europe. This chapter, however, will emphasize the globalized nature of population ageing and the substantial variability between and within countries in the same regions.

Initially, demographic ageing was closely identified with the countries of the Western industrial world. France was the first country to demonstrate this trend and nine of the 'top 10' oldest countries,

Table 5.1   Distribution of the population aged 60+ by major region of the world

Major area/region	Total population 60+ (000s)	Total population 80+ (000s)	Per cent total population aged 60+	Per cent total population aged 80+
WORLD	704,817	188,384	10.7	1.4
More developed	252,026	95,745	20.7	3.9
Less developed	452,791	92,603	8.4	0.9
Least developed	40,774	6,036	5.3	0.4
Africa	50,056	7,667	5.3	0.4
Asia	385,379	83,906	9.6	1.0
Europe	153,476	55,699	21.1	3.8
Latin America & Caribbean	52,696	14,761	9.1	1.3
North America	58,294	24,494	17.3	3.6
Oceania	4,886	1,821	14.4	2.7

Source: United Nations (2007), Tables A.111.1 and A.111.2

in terms of population structure, are European (Table 5.2). However, it is an Asian country, Japan, that is the 'oldest' country in terms of the United Nations (UN) 'ageing' index – the ratio of people aged 65 and over per 1000 aged 0–14 (see Box 5.1 for key definitions) – with the highest percentage of the total population in the 60+ age group (at 28 per cent) and the highest median age at nearly 43 years (42.9, to be exact) (Table 5.2). At the opposite end of the scale, the 'youngest' countries of the world are located in the Middle East and Africa (Table 5.3). The United Arab Emirates (UAE) has 1.7 per cent of its total population in the 60+ age category and three African countries, Uganda, Niger and Mali, have median population ages of 16 or younger – less than a third of that of Japan.

There is now ample evidence that population ageing is a feature of both the developed and less developed world and especially of Asia, where countries such as Japan and China have experienced a fundamental change in the age structure

of their population. Tables 5.2 and 5.3 provide information about the size of the older population relative to other groups and facilitate direct comparisons between countries with the youngest and oldest populations. However, we also need to consider the distribution of older people across the world in terms of both relative and absolute terms. In absolute terms, China has the greatest number of older citizens, with 143 million people aged 60 and over, which is approximately 11 per cent of the total Chinese population and 19 per cent of the world population of elders. In absolute terms, other countries with very large numbers of people aged 60 and over are India (91 million), the United States (51 million), Japan (36 million) and Russia (27 million) (United Nations, 2007). These countries account for 45 per cent of those aged 60 and over worldwide, whereas the European countries account for 9 per cent of the globe's total. Thus, in absolute terms, the older population poses a major challenge for the countries of both the developed and developing world, and it is

Table 5.2   The world's oldest countries

Country	Per cent population aged 60+	Country	UN ageing index	Country	Median age (years)
Japan	27.9	Japan	201.0	Japan	42.9
Italy	26.4	Italy	189.8	Italy	42.3
Germany	25.3	Germany	182.3	Germany	42.1
Sweden	24.1	Bulgaria	172.5	Finland	40.9
Greece	23.4	Greece	166.0	Switzerland	40.8
Austria	23.3	Latvia	164.4	Belgium	40.6
Bulgaria	22.9	Austria	156.1	Croatia	40.6
Belgium	22.9	Slovenia	155.9	Austria	40.6
Latvia	22.8	Czech Republic	150.7	Bulgaria	40.6
Portugal	22.8	Croatia	150.0	Slovenia	40.2
Switzerland	22.7	Ukraine	149.5	Sweden	40.1

Source: United Nations (2007), Tables A.111.4, A.111.5, and A.111

Box 5.1 Definition of key demographic terms

Crude death rate	Deaths per 1000 total population
Infant mortality rate	Deaths in the first year of life per 1000 live births
Birth rate	Births (live or still) per 1000 total population
Total fertility rare (TFR)	The TFR is not a real measure of actual births. It is a measure of the fertility of an *imaginary* woman who passes through her reproductive life subject to *all* the age-specific fertility rates for ages 15–49 that were recorded for a given population in a given year. The TFR represents the average number of children a woman *would* have were she to fastforward through all her childbearing years in a single year, assuming all the age-specific fertility rates for that year. This is the number of children a woman would have if she was subject to prevailing fertility rates at all ages from a single given year, and survives throughout all her childbearing years
Ageing index	Total population aged 60/65+ per 1000 population aged 0–14/15

inappropriate to consider this as an issue confined solely to the developed world.

What is population ageing?

Given the extent of population change as identified above, it is relevant to ask, *what exactly do we mean by 'population ageing'?* This can be defined as the shift in the composition of any given population in favour of those of 'older ages'. Gavrilov and Heuveline (2003) observe that 'population ageing', also referred to as 'demographic ageing', is a portmanteau term used to describe changes in the internal age structure or a distribution of a population towards the older age groups. By convention, the threshold ages used to categorize the 'older age' group are usually 60 or 65 years. However, this is a rather arbitrary age cut-off that relates more to social welfare entitlements in Western industrialized countries rather than any more rational or theoretical criteria or relationship

to the sociocultural context of the less developed/developing world. Furthermore, the ages 60+ and 65+ are not consistently employed, making interpreting and comparing data over time and between countries challenging.

How do we define population ageing?

The indicator generally used to summarize population or demographic ageing is the relative size (percentage) of the group aged 60/65 years and over within a given population. The second way of summarizing the composition of populations is via the use of statistical measures of central tendency – calculating the median, mean, and modal ages of the population. The age at which exactly half the population is older and the other half is younger is known as the 'median age' and is the most widely used of these three statistical measures. A population is characterized as 'ageing' when this subgroup of the population is increasing,

Table 5.3 The world's 'youngest' countries

Country	Per cent population aged 60+	Country	UN ageing index	Country	Median age (years)
UAE	1.7	Niger	6.6	Uganda	14.8
Qatar	2.7	Uganda	7.4	Niger	15.5
Niger	3.2	Liberia	7.7	Mali	15.8
Kuwait	3.4	UAE	7.9	Guinea-Bissau	16.2
Liberia	3.6	Yemen	8.0	Burkina Faso	16.2
Yemen	3.7	Angola	8.5	Dem. Rep. of Congo	16.3
Uganda	3.8	Mali	8.6	Malawi	16.3
Angola	3.9	Burkina Faso	8.6	Chad	16.3
Rwanda	4.0	Dem. Rep. Congo	8.9	Congo - Kinshasa	16.3
Eritrea	4.0	Eritrea	9.0	Liberia	16.3
Papua New Guinea	4.0	Burundi	9.2	Yemen	16.5

Source: United Nations (2007), Tables A.111.4, A.111.5, and A.111.6

when there is a decline in the population of those aged 15 years and under, or when there is an increase in the mean or median age of the population under review (or indeed some combination of these indicators). What percentage of the population must be aged 60/65 or over for a population to be considered ageing? What median age constitutes an ageing population? Gavrilov and Heuveline (2003) suggest that, by convention, an ageing population is defined as one having 8–10 per cent (or more) of the total population aged 60 years or older. Using this criteria, in 2007 there were 66 countries in the world that had 10 per cent or more of their population aged 60 years and over, with a further 16 in the 8–10 per cent banding (United Nations, 2007). The 10 'oldest' countries have at least 20 per cent of their population in this age group (Table 5.2). In 2007 the world median age was 28 years, compared with 24 in 1950 and a projected 38 in 2050 (United Nations, 2007). Eleven countries had a median age of more than 40 years, with Japan (42.9) and Italy (42.3) recording the highest median ages (Table 5.2). Three countries had a median age of less than 16 years: Mali (15.8), Niger (15.5) and Uganda (14.8) (United Nations, 2007) (see Table 5.3).

These summary indicators do not reveal anything about the nature and composition of the older population, nor explain the factors responsible for the age distribution of a given population. In particular, the use of a simple index, such as the percentage aged 60 and over, does not indicate anything about the age distribution within this category, encompassing as it does an age range of 40+ years (from 60 to 100 or over). Indeed, simple indicators such as the overall percentage of older people conceal the heterogeneity in terms of age, gender, and other important socio-demographic factors within this group. In terms of age, the key distinction typically drawn by demographers is between those under 80/85 years and those above this age. As we see in Chapter 6, this reflects the age-related increases in chronic disease prevalence, mortality with age, and the relative use of health and social care resources by this subgroup of the population. Currently it is estimated that there are 188 million people aged 80 years and over worldwide, representing about 25 per cent of the total aged 60 and over.

What causes population ageing?

As the starting point from which to explore the factors that have brought about population ageing, demographers use the concept of the stable population (Preston et al., 2001). This is a theoretical model of the population that assumes that age-specific fertility and mortality rates are constant over time, resulting in a population with both a stable age distribution and size. Death rates and birth rates are in a symbiotic, stable relationship and changes to the age structure are the result of changes in these two factors and their inter-relationship. This model presumes that population size and/or composition is not influenced by migration, although this is now a key feature of population change in both developed and less developed countries. Reductions in fertility produce population ageing by reducing the size of the most recent birth cohorts relative to previous cohorts, thereby reducing the size of the youngest age groups relative to that of the older ones. Reductions in mortality contribute to population ageing because of the increased survival of those who previously would have died, thereby increasing the absolute size of the older cohorts. The current (and historic) pattern of population ageing is the result of the demographic transition that has been experienced by different countries at varying time points. Despite the unevenness of the transition's timing, the underlying principles are universal. Key to the demographic transition is the inter-relationship between mortality rate and fertility rate within any given population. In the pre-transition phase, populations are characterized by very high death (mortality) rates and very high birth (fertility) rates. The combination of high death and birth rates, which are in a type of balance, results in an approximately stable overall population size. The population is renewing itself but growing very little if at all in absolute terms and the age distribution is roughly constant. The demographic transition describes the process whereby a population moves from the 'high fertility–high mortality' situation to one characterized by low fertility and low mortality.

The demographic transition involves the disruption or destabilizing of the relationship between high birth and death rates and has two inter-related elements. In the first phase, mortality rates decrease in response to changes in economic development, material well-being, medical advances, and the development of public health measures to control infectious diseases. At the same time, fertility rates remain high during this first phase. Consequently, there is a rapid increase in the overall size of the population and the reverse of population ageing occurs because of the much larger size of the birth cohorts that now survive infancy and childhood. This trend is identifiable in several European countries in the early 19th century. This rapid (relative) increase in the size of populations formed the context for the theory of population advanced by Thomas Malthus. Essentially, Malthus argued that the growth in the population of Britain (and other

European countries) was unsustainable because of the finite limitations of food production and would be checked by famine and epidemics. Following the initial reductions in infant and childhood mortality, death rates in mid and later life declined, improving survival at older ages and resulting in a situation where more babies survive to adulthood and more adults live long enough to reach 'old age'. This, combined with the second element of the demographic transition (the decrease in fertility rates or the number of babies being born within particular societies), results in the increasing prominence of the older age groups. As fertility rates decline and birth and death rates converge again, as in the pre-transition situation, the rates of population growth decrease such that there is again a stable or very slowly growing overall population. However, as the case of Japan indicates, continuous declines in fertility combined with death rates influenced by an ageing population can lead to population decline. Deaths in Japan exceeded births by 51,000 in 2008, resulting in natural population decline. The estimated number of births for 2008 stood at 1.092 million – about 2000 more than the number of births confirmed the previous year. This was possibly because of the 'leap year' effect, but the estimated number of deaths increased by 35,000 people to reach 1.143 million. This was the second consecutive year that Japan's population declined, and the third year overall.

We can illustrate this theoretical model of the demographic transition by reference to specific examples. However, in doing this, especially historically, we are reliant upon the availability of complete and accurate data about births, deaths, and total population. We cannot calculate birth and death rates without both numerators (births, deaths) and denominators (total population, total number of women of childbearing age, etc.). Furthermore, only limited inferences can be drawn from data based on highly specific geographical localities, such as villages, rather than for larger areas, such as regions or nation-states. This model of demographic change is exemplified by the changes observable in Western European countries from the mid 18th century onwards. Bloom and Canning (2005) demonstrate these using the example of Sweden, one of the countries for which there is fairly complete and relatively accurate national time-series demographic data dating from about 1730. These authors demonstrate that prior to around 1800 death rates were high in Sweden, approximately 30 per 1000 population with occasional 'spikes' resultant from epidemics of infectious diseases, such as that in 1770 where the death rate peaked at over 50 per 1000 population. Whereas we can still observe isolated peaks in mortality after this period, such

as that resultant from the post- World War I flu epidemic, mortality rates in Sweden show a consistent trajectory of decline to approximately 20 per 1000 in 1900 and 10 per 1000 by 2000. These declines in crude mortality rate are noteworthy because they took place at the same time as the population was ageing. The changing age composition of the population towards older people, with the increasing focus of mortality into later life as a result of the reduction in childhood mortality, makes the decline in overall mortality more impressive. The pattern for fertility is also one of decline from a peak of about 40 births per 1000 pre-1800 to about 10 per 1000 in 2000. Bloom and Canning (2005) show that by about the turn of the millennium the two rates were approximately equal at about 8 per 1000, but there were still fluctuations in birth rates. However, there is a lag in the relationship between mortality and fertility decline, with the latter starting approximately 70–80 years after the decline in mortality and demonstrating more 'spikes' and fluctuations within an overall downward trend than mortality. Indeed, fertility rates worldwide demonstrate considerably more volatility than mortality rates. As a result of the initial fall in mortality rates, concentrated mostly in infancy and childhood, there are 'baby booms' or 'birth bulges' because of the increased survival rates relative to previous generations. These bulges are then visible in the age structure of the population as they 'age'. Within Europe and the United States the most obvious examples of baby booms are those following the ending of the World War I and World War II.

Bloom and Canning (2005) provide an overview of the process of demographic transition with their focus on overall mortality rates. These relate to deaths expressed as a ratio per 1000 total population but do not tell us about deaths within specific population subgroups. However, it is well established that the key driver for the onset of the demographic transition is the decline in deaths during infancy and childhood and specifically infant mortality (i.e. deaths in the first year of life). We can illustrate this with data from Great Britain. In 1850 the infant mortality rate was 150 per 1000 live births. This means that 150 of every 1000 live-born children died within the first year of life. In addition, another 20 per cent of babies died before the age of 5 (Victor, 2005a). Thus, overall, 35 per cent of live-born children died before the age of 5 years. Infant mortality rates in Britain decreased from 140 per 1000 in 1900 to 80 per 1000 after 20 years and, with the exception of small blips in the depression years and the 1940s, have steadily declined overall such that in 2005 it was approximately 5 per 1000 population: insufficient to reach the 'top 10' international

Table 5.4 'Top 10' countries with the lowest mortality rates

Country	Infant mortality	Country	Crude mortality	Country	Life expectancy at birth (years)
Singapore	2.3	UAE	2.1	Macau	84.3
Sweden	2.8	Kuwait	2.4	Andorra	82.6
Japan	2.8	Qatar	2.5	Japan	82.2
Hong Kong	2.9	Saudi Arabia	2.5	Singapore	81.9
Iceland	3.2	Jordan	2.7	Hong Kong	81.7
Macau	3.2	Brunei	3.2	Australia	81.5
Finland	3.3	Macau	3.4	Canada	81.1
France	3.3	Libya	3.4	France	80.8
Andorra	3.6	Gaza Strip	3.5	Sweden	80.7
Norway	3.6	Maldives	3.6	Switzerland	80.7

Source: CIA World Factbook 2008

infant mortality rates (Table 5.4). The infant mortality rates of Singapore, Sweden, and Hong Kong (at 3 per 1000 live births) are impressive, especially when contextualized by the larger number of multiple and low birth-weight babies (both groups vulnerable to infant death). However, national statistics presented at a macro level clearly conceal the heterogeneity underlying them. Again, we must be aware of the variability within these overall rates in terms of place and class and other important socio-demographic factors.

HISTORICAL RATES OF BIRTH AND DEATH

When dealing with numerical data such as birth and death rates, it is easy to lose sight of what these indicators mean in terms of the real experience of families. We cannot in this chapter dwell upon the social meaning of the loss of a child, either historically or across different cultural contexts. However, we can demonstrate the scale of the changes that have taken place and which we now take largely for granted. If we translate these historical rates of childhood death to contemporary Britain we can see the stark impact of these reductions. In 2006 there were 669,601 live births in England and Wales (Office of National Statistics, 2007). Infant mortality data are available for 2005 when 3118 of 645,881 babies born died within the first year of life, a rate of 4.9 per 1000. If the 1850 rates applied, 96,000 babies would have died in the first year of life and along with a further 130,000 in the subsequent 4 years. We can immediately see how such simple statistics conceal the very real impact upon individuals and families.

The reduction in death rates in infancy and childhood has served to change the epidemiology of death within Western developed countries.

The massive decrease in childhood deaths, in both absolute and relative terms, combined with substantial reductions in mortality in mid-life, has served to concentrate mortality into the last years of life. In England and Wales in 2006, 82 per cent of the 502,000 deaths were of those aged 65 years and older; 'premature deaths' of those before the age of 65 represented only 17 per cent of the total. This compression of mortality almost exclusively into the later years of life within the developed world has had substantial social implications. Old age and death are (virtually) synonymous in a way that was just not evident at earlier points in our history and is not the case in some developing countries. This trend has also spawned hypotheses about the health of older people and our ability to cope with an ageing population. The evident 'rectangularization' of the mortality curve noted by Fries (1980) has developed into ideas about morbidity, with ill health either being 'compressed' into the final years of life or expanding because of the survival into old age of those who would previously have died. We shall return to the issues of birth and death rates in the next section and Chapter 6 returns to issues concerned with the compression of mortality and morbidity.

THE DRIVERS OF POPULATION AGEING: CONTEMPORARY PATTERNS OF MORTALITY AND FERTILITY

Mortality rates and longevity

A significant component of the impetus towards demographic ageing has been reductions across the various measures of mortality: crude mortality rates, infant mortality, and late-age mortality rates (deaths per 1000 population aged 85 and over for example). Globally, these indicators have all shown substantial reductions but there are still substantial variations across (and within) countries. Focusing upon the extremes of the distribution, the lowest rates of infant mortality are, as observed previously, in parts of Asia and Northern Europe. Here, rates are exceedingly low: 2 per 1000 live births (or 0.2 per cent) (see Table 5.4). However, at the opposite end of the spectrum there are 10 countries in the world where 10 per cent of live-born children will die within the first year of life. In some places these rates are higher than those reported in mid-19th century Britain (Table 5.5). In Angola infant mortality rates were 18 per cent, with Sierra Leone, Afghanistan, and Liberia all recording infant mortality rates of approximately 15 per cent per annum. Such profound global inequalities in infant survival illustrate how much improvement is required for the developing countries to attain levels of childhood survival we take for granted in the developed world (see Marmot, 2008).

A number of different measures of mortality can be identified in the research literature. However, problems with the accuracy of numerators for many parts of the world mean that here we focus upon overall (crude) mortality rates. We can also see similar variability in terms of overall mortality rates as we did with infant mortality. There is a 15-fold difference in rates between the highest crude deaths rates, Swaziland at 30 per 1000 population, and lowest countries, United Arab Emirates at 2 per 1000 (see Tables 5.4 and 5.5). However, this measure is sensitive to the age structure of the population because of the increasing focus of deaths into later life. Those countries with a high proportion of very young people and few older people such as the Arab states of Qatar, Kuwait, Jordan, and Saudi Arabia, where those aged 60+ represent less than 5 per cent of the total population, illustrate low mortality (see Table 5.4). At the same time, the possession of a young population is not in itself a protection against high death rates, as the examples of the African countries of Swaziland and the others listed in Table 5.5 indicate. These countries all demonstrate overall mortality rates that are comparable with Britain in 1900, crude death rates of 20 per 1000 plus, yet they have 6 per cent or less of their population aged 60+.

We cannot cover all of the drivers of demographic change across the world. Hence we have focused upon the key indicators that are widely available so that we can concentrate on a global perspective and make explicit comparisons between populations. Inevitably this means we can give less attention to other factors such as late-life mortality rates where there are less comparable data available globally. However, we should not underestimate the importance of these changes. Victor (2005b) and Gjonca and Marmot (2005) draw our attention to the halving of the mortality rate for those aged 85+ in England and Wales during the 20th century. Such trends are evident across Europe, Scandinavia, and Japan (see Cheung and Robine, 2007). It remains a matter of lively debate as to the existence of a 'floor' below which late-life (or indeed infant) mortality rates cannot go. To date, while the rates of decrease may be slowing, the evidence suggests that a plateau has yet to be reached.

In combination, reductions in overall and infant mortality rates have brought about marked increases in overall life expectancy at birth: this is often described as 'living longer'. Life expectancy describes the statistically average age that an individual can expect to attain. We can calculate this from a variety of starting points, but the one most widely used is that of expectation of life at birth. We can also distinguish between cohort-based predictions based upon the use of anticipated changes in age-specific mortality rates and period-based predictions of life expectancy, which apply current age-sex specific rates and do not include anticipated changes. In 2007 the global average

Table 5.5 'Top 10' countries with the highest mortality rates

Country	Infant mortality	Country	Crude mortality	Country	Life expectancy at birth (years)
Angola	182.3	Swaziland	30.7	Swaziland	31.9
Sierra Leone	156.4	Angola	24.4	Angola	37.9
Afghanistan	154.6	Sierra Leone	22.2	Zambia	38.5
Liberia	143.8	Lesotho	22.3	Lesotho	40.1
Niger	115.3	Liberia	21.4	Liberia	41.1
Somalia	110.9	Zambia	21.3	Sierra Leone	40.9
Mozambique	107.8	Niger	20.2	Mozambique	41.0
Mali	103.8	Mozambique	20.3	Djibouti	43.3
Guinea-Bissau	101.6	Afghanistan	19.5	Malawi	43.4
Zambia	100.9	Djibouti	19.1	Afghanistan	44.2

Source: CIA World Factbook (2008)

period life expectancy at birth was 65.8 years (United Nations, 2007). However, this overall global average masks profound inequalities in the age to which the 'average' citizen of different parts of the world can expect to live. There are 10 countries where life expectancy at birth is over 80 years, including countries from Asia (Singapore, Hong Kong, and Japan), Europe (Sweden, Switzerland, and France), and Australia (Table 5.4). Lesotho, Zambia, Angola, and Swaziland all have a life expectancy at birth of 40 or under, with Swaziland recording the lowest expectation of life at birth of 32 years (Table 5.5). All of the countries with a life expectancy of less than 50 years are concentrated in Africa and we can see that five countries – Angola, Sierra Leone, Liberia, Zambia, and Mozambique – are in the world's top 10 for lowest life expectancy, and highest mortality and infant mortality.

Providing an historical context for these contemporary life expectancies at birth is problematic because of the requirement for accurate birth and death data. However, data from Great Britain illustrate the magnitude of the change. In 1900 the average Briton could expect to live to the age of 50, compared with 78 years in 2005 (76.6 years for men and 80.9 for women) (see Riley, 2001). Again, it is important not to ignore variability within populations. Kensington and Chelsea (England) had the highest life expectancy of 86.6 years compared with 76.6 years in Glasgow (Scotland) (Office of National Statistics, 2006). Undoubtedly, such variability exists within most countries and is based upon factors such as class, race, and place. It seems likely, therefore, that within very low life expectancy countries such as those in Africa this average masks variations, so that whereas some areas/groups may have longer life expectancies there will be those where it is substantially less than the 40 years average.

'Living longer', as measured by expectation of life at birth, is a central theme of most commentaries on demographic change and population ageing. Examining the data for most developed countries there is a pattern of increasing life expectancy similar to the case illustrated by Britain. It is important, though, to remain alert to the point that such increases are neither 'natural' nor inevitable, but result from human interventions such as improved living standards, basic public health measures controlling infections, improved housing, and the development of health and social care services and infrastructure. Where such social structures break down or there are other societal changes such as the arrival of new diseases such as HIV/AIDS, then life expectancy can decrease. In Zimbabwe in 1980, for instance, life expectancy was around 63 years; by 2008 this had reduced to around 40 years as a result of AIDS

and the profound economic and social problems affecting the country. The key point to stress here is that, like stocks and shares, expectation of life can go down as well as up. Hence we should not expect that the continuous and seemingly 'natural' and inevitable improvements in life expectancy at birth will continue or that they are immune to social and economic drivers.

Fertility rates

The other major influence of population ageing and the demographic transition is the fertility of a given population. Clearly the number of children being born is crucial to the structure and size of a population. However, understanding (and predicting) patterns of fertility is, perhaps, the most problematic element of demographic analysis. There are a number of different ways we can consider fertility: births per 1000 population and the expected numbers of children born per woman (presuming the continuation of 2006 fertility rates). For this latter indicator, the world average was 2.6 or slightly above the replacement level of 2.33. Replacement fertility level ranges from 2.1 children per woman in developed countries (2 children to replace the parents, with one-tenth of a child extra to make up for the different sex ratio at birth and early mortality prior to the end of their fertile life) to 2.5 to 3.3 in less developed areas (this is higher because of elevated childhood mortality rates). African countries, including the sub-Saharan countries, have the highest levels of fertility. For example, the 'average' woman in Mali or Niger will have 7 children (Table 5.6). There are 90 countries in the world where the total fertility rate is below the 2.1 replacement level threshold and these include Hong Kong, Italy, Germany, Austria, Singapore, Japan, and several countries from the 'old' Soviet bloc states (Table 5.7). The longer list of sub-replacement level fertility countries includes most of Western Europe, Scandinavia, the United States, Asian countries (Thailand, Sri Lanka), North Africa (Algeria), and Latin America. It remains to be seen if the governments of those countries with very low fertility rates will introduce 'family friendly' policies to encourage childbearing and if these will be successful.

Explaining these trends is both complex and contentious. Standard transition theory would explain reduced fertility as a response to the improvements in childhood survival, i.e., it is no longer necessary to have three children to ensure that one or two survive. Alternative explanations might focus upon, first, the 'cost' of child rearing in sophisticated education-based knowledge economies, with parents investing in fewer, 'high-quality' offspring. Secondly, there are culturally

Table 5.6   'Top 10' countries with the highest fertility rates

Country	Births per 1000 population	Country	Total fertility rate – average children per woman
Niger	49.6	Mali	7.3
Mali	49.3	Niger	7.3
Uganda	48.1	Uganda	6.8
Afghanistan	45.8	Somalia	6.6
Sierra Leone	45.0	Afghanistan	6.6
Burkina Faso	44.6	Yemen	6.4
Somalia	44.1	Burundi	6.4
Angola	44.0	Burkina Faso	6.4
Ethiopia	43.9	Demo. Rep. Congo.	6.3
Demo. Rep. Congo.	43.0	Angola	6.2

Source: CIA World Factbook 2008

based explanations that focus upon the role of women in society, their employment, the importance of consumption, and other social factors. Inevitably, the explanation is almost certainly multifactorial. What is important for our purposes is to note that many of the predictions about what will happen to the global population are based upon the forward projection of current trends and that both mortality and fertility rates are dynamic. In particular, predicting how many children people will have, and at what ages, is challenging, mainly because people remain capricious about both the number of children they have and the ages at which they have them.

DEMOGRAPHIC ISSUES: FUTURE CHALLENGES

The use of a single figure to summarize the age structure of a population provides only a superficial insight into the composition of this subgroup of the population. In later chapters, other aspects of this complexity associated with the role of class, gender, and health are examined. Here, we confine our attention to the 'traditional' details of the composition of the ageing population characteristic of demographic investigation and analysis: age, gender, location (i.e., urban or rural), and household composition (Harper, 2006). Before considering these issues we consider the worldwide distribution of the older population.

Ageing populations: the global distribution and future trends

Overall, the developed world demonstrates the highest relative percentage of their population in the older age groups. The United Nations (2007) report that in the developed world nearly one-third of the population is aged 60 years or over whereas in the less developed world only 8 per cent have

Table 5.7   'Top 10' countries with the lowest levels of fertility

Country	Births per 1000 population	Country	Total fertility rate – average children per woman
Hong Kong	7.3	Macau	0.9
Japan	7.8	Hong Kong	1.0
Germany	8.1	Taiwan	1.1
Italy	8.3	South Korea	1.2
Austria	8.6	Lithuania	1.2
Bosnia	8.8	Japan	1.2
Czech Republic	8.8	Czech Republic	1.2
Singapore	8.9	Belarus	1.2
Taiwan	8.9	Bosnia	1.2
Slovenia	8.9	Ukraine	1.2

Source: CIA World Factbook 2008

reached this age. However, we again need to consider absolute as well as relative indicators. In absolute terms, the majority of older people live in the developing nations (see Table 5.1). The older population is growing at a rate of 2.6 per annum, compared with 1.1 per cent for the overall population, a trend expected to continue for the next 50 years. Consequently, the UN estimate that the developing countries of the world will experience rapid population ageing and display a similar percentage of people aged 60+ as today's developed societies. Population ageing is taking place more rapidly in the developing world but from a basis of much lower levels of economic development. This is part of the continuing shift of the distribution of the global population from Europe and Asia to Africa. It is estimated that in 1800 Europe accounted for 20 per cent of the world population, Asia 26 per cent, and Africa 11 per cent. By 2050 these percentages will have changed such that Europe will account for 7 per cent of the world population, Asia 59 per cent, and Africa 22 per cent. Thus, the changing distribution of the world's older citizens forms part of a larger demographic realignment. Clearly, predicting the size and composition of the world population in the future is an exercise that requires a number of assumptions to be made about issues of fertility and mortality. On the presumption that these are accurate, the next 50 years will see the continuation and accentuation of existing trends of reductions in infant and adult mortality and the transition from high to low fertility. Continuation of these trends will see the global median age increase from 28 years to 38 years (United Nations, 2007) and with China and the Republic of Korea projected to record median ages of 54 years. Life expectancy globally will increase to 76 years by 2050. Again, presuming continued improvements in mortality and reductions in fertility, the very low life expectancy countries listed in Table 5.5 are all projected to increase their life expectancy at birth by about 20 years to about 60–62 years. If we focus upon absolute rather than relative population sizes, a similar pattern emerges. In 1950 there were three countries in the world with an absolute number of people aged 60+ of 10 million or more. These were China (42 million), India (20 million), and the United States (20 million). By the turn of the millennium this had increased to 12 countries and in 2050 it is predicted that there will 33 countries in this category, including 5 countries with a 60+ population over 50 million. These are China (437 million), India (324 million), the United States (107 million), Indonesia (70 million), and Brazil (58 million) (United Nations, 2002).

However, Harper (2006) draws our attention to the importance of the assumptions used in these predictions. For example, she notes that the projections about fertility that underpin these assumptions are challenging for both developed and developing countries. For the developing world, these presume a halving of fertility across two generations, or about 40 years. This is the magnitude of change in birth rates recorded in Japan between 1950 and 2000. For the developed world, the presumption is for increased fertility. Both of these may prove to be unrealistic and either overly optimistic or pessimistic. Less volatile, but still subject to assumptions of no change in mortality rates, are projections of the absolute numbers of elders in the world population in 2050. By this point there will be 2 billion people aged 60 years and over and 75 per cent will live in the countries of the developing world (Harper, 2006). However, this concentration of the absolute number of older people within the developing world is not a new phenomenon. As early as 1950, the United Nations (2002) noted that 54 per cent of the total world population was in developing countries. Hence, our preoccupation with relative methods of presenting data, and perhaps a preoccupation with the effect of population ageing upon Western health and social care systems, has served to obscure the numerical, if not relative, concentration of older people within the developing nations.

The pace of demographic change

The demographic transition from high to low mortality and fertility rates was first observed in Western Europe and took place over a fairly lengthy historical time frame. If we use the time it took a country to increase the percentage population aged 60 and over from 7 per cent to 14 per cent as our indicator, then this process, according to Kinsella and Gist (1995), took 115 years in France, 85 years in Germany, and over 60 years in countries such as Sweden, the United States, and Great Britain. We see a similar pattern if we use the increase from 10 per cent to 20 per cent of the total population accounted for by those aged 60 and over. This process took 61 years in Germany (1951–2012), 64 years in Sweden (1947–2011), and 57 years in the United States (1971–2028).

However, these transformations have been experienced much more rapidly in selected Asian countries. Japan took 23 years to experience a doubling of the population aged 60+, from 10 per cent to 20 per cent, and 26 years for the percentage aged 65+ to increase from 7 per cent to 14 per cent. China illustrates a very similar pattern to Japan; it is estimated that it will take about 20 years for the 60+ population to increase from 10 per cent to 20 per cent (2017–2037) and 26 years to move from 7 per cent of the population aged

65+ to 14 per cent. Kinsella and Gist (1995) report that a range of countries, including Chile, Brazil, Colombia, Jamaica, Sri Lanka, and Thailand, will also achieve this transition in 20–25 years and that Singapore will do so in 19 years (from 2000 to 2019). Although we should be wary of being overly precise about the exact timing of these changes, the rapidity with which they are being achieved and the variety of differing countries within which this is being experienced are unique, as is the nature of the challenges posed by such profound and rapid demographic change.

The 'ageing' of the ageing population

In addition to the growth in both absolute and relative terms of the world's older population we can also see that this population is itself ageing. According to Harper (2006), the population aged 80 years and over is the fastest growing segment of the world population, demonstrating an annual growth rate of 3.9 per cent. Although this is expected to decrease to 3 per cent per annum by 2050, it will still remain double that of the general rate for the 60+ population (United Nations, 2002). We can explain this observation by the intersections of two related trends: the reduction in late-age mortality rates and the increased absolute size of this birth cohort in the post-World War I 'baby boom'. However, we again need to consider this issue in both absolute and relative terms. The population aged 80+ represents approximately 1 per cent of the world population and consists of approximately 86 million people. The rates of increase noted above mean, however, that there will be a fivefold increase in the size of this group to nearly 400 million in 2050. Currently, six countries account for 54 per cent of the global family of the very old: China (12 million), United States (9 million), India (6 million), Japan (5 million), and Germany and the Russian Federation (3 million each). With the current distribution, 53 per cent of those aged 80+ are resident in the developed world; in contrast, by 2050, 70 per cent of this group will be residents of developing nations.

The group that, perhaps, best symbolizes the concept of the mature world are the centenarians and super centenarians (those aged 100 years and over). Before the complete and accurate registration of births and deaths it is difficult to produce accurate estimates of either the age composition of populations or to determine accurately individual ages. There have always been people within pre-industrial populations who lived longer than their peers or the average expectation of life at birth; yet, did any achieve the status of centenarian? Certainly there are reports of people living to this age and beyond, but they are difficult to

verify and such individuals would have been exceedingly rare or non-existent in the pre-industrial period (see Haycock, 2008). As of 2007/08, the United States has the largest number of centenarians within any country (at 55,000 in 2008); this is about 20,000 more than the second ranking country, Japan, where there are currently about 37,000 centenarians. There are 20,000 in France, 17,500 in China, and about 9000 in the United Kingdom. Worldwide, the United Nations estimated that there were 180,000 verifiable centenarians in 2001 (United Nations, 2002), although the number rises to about 450,000 if those whose age cannot be unquestionably validated are included. Again, over the next 50 years we will see an increase of about 18-fold in the total number of centenarians to 3.2 million, still predominantly located in the developed world (68 per cent) (United Nations, 2002). Japan is, perhaps, the country most associated with the growing band of the very old. The 37,000 people aged 100+ in Japan are predicted to increase to a million by 2050 and will account for 1 per cent of the total population. We can see the growth of the 100 population manifest in several ways: greeting card shops routinely sell age 100 cards, balloons, and badges and many countries formally mark the accomplishment of the 100th birthday by cards from the monarch (United Kingdom) or President (Ireland and the United States).

Gender

Within Western Europe, in particular, we are accustomed to the notion that old age and later life are predominantly female experiences – a notion influenced by substantial mortality differentials between men and women and the residual effects of the mortality resultant from war. Europe has the largest male:female differentials in terms of the composition of the older age groups. So, for those aged 60 and over in Europe, there are 67 men for every 100 women, and 41 per 100 for those aged 80 and over. These ratios reflect the social and health context for this particular region of the world. Yet we must be wary of drawing the inference that such large differentials are both 'natural' and universal. For example, the ratio in Asia for those 60+ is 87 and in Africa the 80+ ratio is 69. Over the next half century there will be a reduction in the differential survival rates of men and women into old age resultant from improved male mortality rates. In addition, there are some countries where the ratio is over 100, i.e. there are more men than women. For example, Pakistan, Qatar, and UAE report more men than women at age 60+ with ratios of 100, 245, and 264, respectively. The ratios for the

Table 5.8   Living arrangements of population aged 60+ by major world region

Major area/ region	Lives alone (%)	Lives with spouse (%)	Lives with children/ grand children (%)	Lives with others (%)
Africa	8	9	74	8
Asia	7	16	74	4
Europe	26	43	26	4
Latin America & Caribbean	9	16	62	14
North America	25	47	19	8
Oceania	25			

Source: United Nations (2005), Table 11.5

80+ population in these countries were 112, 151, and 126, respectively. These gendered ratios, which are counter-intuitive to gerontologists from European backgrounds, serve to remind us of the sociocultural specificity of much of our scholarship. What we take for granted as being a 'natural' and 'normal' part of the experience of later life – that it is a predominantly female experience – is much less generalized than we think. By 2050 the male:female ratios will be 78 for those aged 60+ and 56 for those aged 80+ in the developed world, (United Nations, 2002) and 87 and 63 for the less developed world, respectively. This, of course, is a global average and it is likely that substantial variations between countries in terms of gender ratios will be maintained.

Household and living arrangements

The living arrangements of older people is a topic that provokes considerable interest on the part of social commentators and policymakers. Historically, within Europe, the majority of older people lived in multi-generational households and such arrangements are thought to be a feature of the developing countries. However, there is a very well documented trend within developed countries of older people adopting independent households – living alone or with their spouse – while such trends are also evident across the developing world. Here we document the key demographic trends; the implications for social support and social engagement are covered elsewhere in the book. Again, the availability of robust data encourages us to be cautious about the inferences that we draw and in the areas that can be included in our analysis.

The United Nations (2005) reports that approximately 13 per cent of those people aged 60 years and over 'live alone'. This is a simple description of household size and does not imply anything about their level of social support, contact with family members, or general levels of social engagement. This global statistic masks a pattern of variability in this type of living arrangement across the world (Table 5.8). In Africa, approximately 8 per cent of this age group live alone, with approximately 7 per cent in Asia, and 25 per cent in Europe, Oceania, and North America. However, individual variability between countries is perhaps more extreme in the household composition variable than any other demographic factor: Bahrain had 1 per cent of those aged 60 and over living alone, compared with nearly 40 per cent in Denmark (Table 5.9). Similarly, within Africa, a continent with low levels of solo living for older people, some 22 per cent live alone in Ghana (United Nations, 2005). Of the Asian countries, only Japan demonstrates relatively high levels of living alone (at 12 per cent). Yet, it is difficult to accurately establish global trends in living alone because of data availability issues. However, the United Nations (2005) does suggest that there is evidence that solo living in later life is a global phenomenon. They report that over the period 1970–2000, all major regions of the world illustrated an increase in living alone (Table 5.10), although the starting points were very different. However, there is now some suggestion that the

Table 5.9   Countries with highest/lowest rates of those aged 60+ living alone

Country	Per cent living alone	Country	Per cent living alone
Denmark	39.1	Bahrain	0.7
Finland	35.4	Senegal	1.3
Netherlands	34.5	Comoros	1.5
UK	34.7	Bangladesh	1.8
Czech Republic	33.6	Guinea	2.2
Germany	33.6	Korea	2.1
Estonia	29.6	Burkina Faso	2.3
Belgium	29.3	Tunisia	2.7
France	28.7	Pakistan	2.7
Ireland	26.4	India	3.3

Source: United Nations (2005), Table 11.1

Table 5.10   Trends in living alone population aged 60+ (%)

Major Area/Region	1970/1980s	1990/200s
Africa	6.9	8.0
Asia	5.6	6.8
Europe	26.6	28.3
Latin America & Caribbean	7.8	8.3
North America	24.3	25.2

Source: United Nations (2005), Table 11.7

prevalence of solo living in the developed countries is levelling off or even declining, most notably Canada, Italy, and the United States. This reflects increased male survival rates, the decline in the size of the 'never married' segment of the population, and an increase in the age at which children leave home.

In tandem with the rise of solo living in later life we have seen an increase in older people living with their spouse. Meanwhile, the distribution of older people living as independent 'couples' reflects the same patterns as solo living. In the developed world, almost one-half (43 per cent) of those aged 60+ live with their spouse, compared with 13 per cent in the developing world. For this category of living arrangements we can also observe huge variability between countries, with couple-only households representing 1 per cent of elders in Senegal, 56 per cent in Denmark, 3 per cent in Sri Lanka, and 34 per cent in Japan.

In both Asia and Africa, approximately three-quarters of older people live with children or grandchildren; in Europe this proportion is approximately a quarter (see Table 5.8). Again, there are vast differences between individual countries within this general trend. In Denmark some 4 per cent of elders live with their children or grandchildren, compared with 85 per cent in Guinea and 90 per cent in Bangladesh. However, although Europe generally has low rates of co-residence with children and grandchildren, in Spain some 40 per cent of older people live in this type of household arrangement. Table 5.8 conceals an important subgroup within the 'living with children' category: older people living with grandchildren but not their children. These 'skipped-generation households' are found predominantly in sub-Saharan African countries or other locations with high levels of HIV/AIDS (see Chapter 30). In Malawi, Rwanda, Zambia, and Zimbabwe, for instance, 25 per cent of those aged 60+ live in skipped-generation households where the older person has responsibility for the welfare of their grandchildren (Zimmer and Dayton, 2005).

Worldwide, the majority of older people live in various types of 'private' households. However, within developed countries there is an acceptance that those who are frail and vulnerable may live in various forms of institutional or supported living arrangements. Given that such institutions vary enormously across the world, establishing global trends is challenging. Whereas rates of institutional living are higher in the developing world, they are clearly not universal. Approximately 1 per cent of elders in Africa live in some form of supported care, along with 2 per cent in Asia, 4 per cent in Europe, and 5 per cent in North America/Oceania.

CONCLUSION

Demographic data clearly demonstrate that the population of the world is ageing. Although the pace of change varies across countries, ageing is now a globalized phenomenon and one not confined to the developed world. Indeed, in absolute terms, the concentration of the world's older citizens is in the developing countries. This is not a new phenomenon. As early as 1950, the absolute number of older people (aged 60+) tended to be located in the less developed parts of the world. However, it is only recently that we have identified this feature of the worldwide population. It is in China and Asia that we find the largest absolute numbers of elders, along with the consequent implications for the numbers of people experiencing the health problems associated with old age such as dementia and impaired mobility (see Chapter 32). Population ageing affects the lives of older people across the globe both individually and in terms of social and political institutions. That ageing is now seen as a global phenomenon is reflected in the activities of the United Nations' activities, such as the World Assembly on Ageing (held in Madrid in 2002). As this chapter has indicated, the experience of old age and later life is not uniform across the globe. We have also indicated the existence of gender inequalities in terms of survival into old age. However, as other chapters in this book discuss, there are profound inequalities in the experience of old age across and between different countries of the world. This chapter has established the backdrop for the discussion of these issues in later chapters. We have demonstrated that the ageing of the worlds' population reflects a major triumph of public health in reducing mortality rates, especially those in infancy and childhood. However, we conclude with a note of caution; it is easy to become complacent about apparently inexorable and 'natural' improvements in life expectancy, death rates, and survival into old age. Two issues should challenge this complacency – the AIDS epidemic in Africa and, to a lesser degree, the creation in Latin America and the Caribbean of 'skipped-generation' households where older people live with grandchildren as a result of the mortality of the middle generation and work-related migration to urban areas. In addition to these issues, countries such as those in the former Eastern European block and countries like Zimbabwe demonstrate the fragility of the mortality improvement basis for population ageing – new diseases such as AIDS, along with social turmoil, can very easily reverse improvements in survival. We must always remember that predictions of future population structures are just that – the forward prediction of existing trends. As AIDS demonstrates, these can be challenged and are subject to the vagaries of human behaviour.

REFERENCES

Bloom, D. and Canning, D. (2005) 'Global demographic change: dimensions and economic significance', *Harvard Institute for Global Health Working Paper Series*. Working Paper No. 1. http://www.hsph.harvard.edu/pgda/working/working_paper1.pdf

Cheung, S. and Robine, J-M. (2007) 'Increase in common longevity and the compression of mortality: the case of Japan', *Population Studies*, 61: 85–97.

CIA World Factbook 2008 – available at: https://www.cia.gov/library/publications/the-world-factbook http://www.informaworld.com/smpp/title~content=t713689546~db=all~tab=issueslist~branches=61 - v61

Fries, J.F. (1980) 'Aging, natural death and the compression of morbidity', *New England Journal of Medicine*, 303: 130–5.

Gavrilov, L.A. and Heuveline, P. (2003) 'Aging of population', in P. Demeny and G. McNicoll (eds), *The Encyclopedia of Population*. New York: Macmillan Reference, pp. 32–7.

Gjonca, E. and Marmot, M. (2005) 'Patterns of illness and mortality across the adult lifespan', in M.L. Johnson (ed.), *The Cambridge Handbook of Age and Ageing*. Cambridge: Cambridge University Press, pp. 106–20.

Harper, S. (2006) *Ageing Societies*. London: Hodder Arnold.

Haycock, D.B. (2008) *Mortal Coil: A Short History of Living Longer*. New Haven, CT: Yale University Press.

Kinsella, K. and Gist, Y. (1995) *Older Workers, Retirement, and Pensions: A Comparative International Chart Book*. Washington, DC: US Census Bureau and US National Institute on Aging, International Data Base. http://www.census.gov/ipc/www/idbnew.html

Marmot, M. (Chair) (2008) 'Closing the gap in a generation', report of the WHO Commission on Social Determinants of Health, World Health Organisation, Geneva. http://www.who.int/social_determinants/en/

Office of National Statistics (2006) *Life Expectancy 2006*. http://www.statistics.gov.uk/downloads/theme_population/LE_Report_Nov06.pdf

Office of National Statistics (2007) *Live Births: England and Wales Factsheet*. http://www.statistics.gov.uk/cci/nugget.asp?id=369

Preston, S.H., Heuveline, P., and Guillot, M. (2001) *Demography: Measuring and Modelling Population Processes*. Oxford: Blackwell Publishers.

Riley, J.C. (2001) Rising Life Expectancy: A Global History. Cambridge: Cambridge University Press.

United Nations (2002) *World Population Ageing 1950–2050*. Department of Economic and Social Affairs/Population Division. New York: United Nations. http://www.un.org/esa/population/publications/worldageing19502050/

United Nations (2005) *The Living Arrangements of Older People around the World*. Department of Economic and Social Affairs/Population Division. New York: United Nations. http://www.un.org/esa/population/publications/livingarrangement/covernote.pdf

United Nations (2007) *World Population Ageing 2007*. Department of Economic and Social Affairs/Population Division. New York: United Nations.

Victor, C.R. (2005a) *The Social Context of Ageing*. London: Routledge.

Victor, C.R. (2005b) 'The epidemiology of ageing', in M.L. Johnson (ed.), *The Cambridge Handbook of Age and Ageing*. Cambridge: Cambridge University Press, pp. 95–105.

Zimmer, Z. and Dayton, J. (2005) 'Older adults in Sub-Saharan Africa living with children and grandchildren', *Population Studies*, 59(3): 295–312.

6

Epidemiology of Ageing

Dawn Alley and Eileen Crimmins

INTRODUCTION

Epidemiology is the study of the population distribution of health states and the factors that influence their distribution. Epidemiology is based on the underlying premise that health outcomes are not randomly distributed, but rather that the incidence, prevalence, and duration of health states follow identifiable patterns; its purpose is to describe and explain these patterns. This chapter provides a brief overview of major topics in the epidemiology of ageing, including an introduction to population ageing and the epidemiology of ageing, a review of theoretical frameworks for understanding health changes with age, a summary of major health outcomes associated with age, a review of major factors affecting health at older ages, and a summary of emerging research areas.

Demographic and epidemiological transitions

The demographic and epidemiological transitions have acted together to accelerate population ageing and increases in the burden of chronic disease and disability. The demographic transition refers to a combination of fertility and mortality decline. Fertility decline reduces family size and produces smaller cohorts at younger ages, while mortality decline increases life expectancy. This combination of smaller young cohorts and larger, more long-lived older cohorts results in population ageing.

The epidemiological transition refers to a decline in deaths from infectious diseases, especially in children, resulting in increased life expectancy and a shift to mortality from chronic diseases at older ages (Omran, 1971; Satariano, 2006). Historically, infectious diseases and injury and infections associated with childbirth resulted in high mortality among children and young women. Improving living standards, public sanitation, housing, and nutrition led to declines in infectious disease and increases in life expectancy. Advances in medical and public health interventions, including antibiotics and vaccines, further reduced morbidity and mortality from infectious diseases. As the burden of infectious diseases declined at younger ages and survival to older ages increased, the burden of late-onset, chronic adult diseases grew.

The epidemiology of ageing has emerged in this context of the demographic and epidemiological transitions, in response to the ageing of population and an increasing need for understanding the chronic conditions that affect older persons. The speed and timing of both transitions have varied dramatically across countries. The demographic transition was completed in most developed nations after the middle of the last century, about the time it began in many developing nations. In many developing countries, such as China and India, ageing of the population is currently proceeding at unprecedented rates because of very rapid declines in fertility. In these countries, people entering old age today were born and lived their early lives before the beginning of the epidemiologic transition, exposing them to the late-life consequences of a lifetime burden of infectious conditions. The emergence of new infectious diseases (e.g., HIV, drug-resistant tuberculosis) has challenged the framework of the epidemiological transition. Nonetheless, the historical perspective provided by the demographic and epidemiological transitions is helpful in understanding the growth of the field of epidemiology of ageing.

Epidemiology of ageing

Clearly, age is one of the most important factors representing risk of poor health outcomes. Biological ageing is associated with changes in the physical structures and physiological functioning of the body that affect viability. Figure 6.1 shows the per cent of the US population surviving to different ages based on 2003 US death rates. About 85 per cent of the population survives to age 60, but exponentially increasing mortality risk leads to fewer and fewer survivors at older ages. As the population ages, larger proportions of birth cohorts live to be old, and older people survive to increasingly higher ages.

The same physiological changes that lead to increased mortality risk with age also increase the risk of disease and disability. Thus, the epidemiology of ageing seeks not only to understand disease but also to understand the ways in which age, individual characteristics, the physical and social environment, and disease contribute to functioning and quality of life in old age. The issues of old age are unique, in that disability and loss of physical and cognitive functioning are centrally important; disease represents only one part of the beginning of a process of health change. In the older population, frailty, disability, and mortality represent the end of the process and are often the health outcomes of interest. Thus, the goal of the epidemiology of ageing is to generate knowledge that leads to minimizing the burden of illness, allowing people who are living longer to be in better health (Fried, 2000). This orientation is both theoretical and practical, reflecting the fact that the epidemiology of ageing has grown as a multidisciplinary field, incorporating the concerns of clinicians and others who seek to better both individual and population health, as well as those of policymakers interested in the health implications of an ageing society. In this context, the epidemiology of ageing asks questions about why the incidence of disease and mortality increases with age, why functional and cognitive abilities change with age, and why some groups are more at risk of poor health in old age than others. A major goal of this research is to reduce the period of disease and disability experienced by older persons, leading to a 'compression of morbidity.' This would occur if the age at onset of health problems increases faster than life expectancy, leading to a reduced period of disease and disability prior to death. There is significant debate about potential limits to human life expectancy (Oeppen and Vaupel, 2002; Olshansky et al., 1990), and the potential for compression of morbidity versus dynamic equilibrium, in which changes between morbidity and mortality occur together (Fries, 1980; Manton et al., 1991).

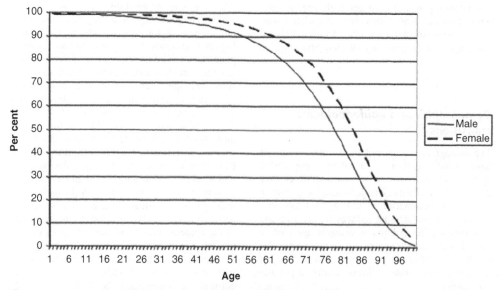

Figure 6.1   Percent surviving by age and sex: United States 2003

Source: Arias, E. (2006) 'United States Life Tables, 2003', *National Vital Statistics Reports,* 54(14): 10–14.

FRAMEWORKS FOR UNDERSTANDING HEALTH IN OLD AGE

The disablement process

Figure 6.2 provides a schematic of the disablement process derived from Verbrugge and Jette (1994) (Crimmins, 2004). This model was developed to describe the process of health change in an ageing population. As individuals develop a greater burden of chronic disease with age, the focus shifts from preventing and curing disease to managing chronic diseases, preventing disability, and increasing quality of life.

To begin, at the left of the figure, risk factors or biological markers such as cholesterol and other lipids, weight, and indicators of insulin regulation are markers of underlying health and disease risk. At the population level, the age of onset of these risk factors generally precedes the onset of related diseases like cardiovascular disease and diabetes. The second box comprises diseases, conditions, and impairments. Some conditions, such as frailty, may not reflect a specific disease process but may place older persons at increased risk of impairment. The third box, functioning loss, is the inability to perform certain physical or mental tasks, such as stooping, lifting, walking, balancing, reading, counting, and using fingers and hands to grasp objects. Functioning loss typically occurs at a later age than disease onset. The next box, disability, is the inability to perform an expected social role. In older people, disability is generally defined by an inability to live independently or provide self-care (see also Chapter 7). For middle-aged people, disability is often defined in terms of ability to work or do housework.

Recent updates to this conception of disability have emphasized activity more generally and focused more explicitly on social and environmental factors that affect an individual's ability to participate in desired activities (Jette, 2006). The distinction between functioning and disability is important: functional limitations are intrinsic to the individual, such as ability to stoop or kneel, while disabilities refer to an interaction with the physical and social environment, such as bathing and dressing, to accomplish a task. For instance, moving to a house without stairs or a home with a walk-in shower might alleviate disability and allow someone to live independently who could

not do so with different housing characteristics. The level of disability associated with a given level of functioning would be greater in a place where preparing meals involves carrying water and finding firewood than in a place with home-delivered meals and microwaves.

All of these dimensions of health may be affected by changes in underlying risk factors, and all can be influenced by different types of interventions. For instance, exercise and diet interventions may reduce the risk of diabetes for someone with impaired glucose tolerance. Interventions to reduce fall risk among those with balance problems may reduce the risk of a functional impairment progressing to a disability. Figure 6.2 is oversimplified; not all individuals pass through all phases of health deterioration. Some people may have a heart attack and die from heart disease before they ever know they have the condition or become disabled. In addition, individuals can move in and out of these states. Disability and functioning loss may be temporary, and people may return to full functioning and ability. Furthermore, there is a stronger link between disease and morbidity and mortality for some conditions, such as heart disease, than for others, such as arthritis, which are strongly related to morbidity but not to mortality.

The biopsychosocial model of health and ageing

The disablement model was designed largely to focus on the process of health change, rather than to identify external factors that affect that process. The biopsychosocial model seeks to integrate evidence linking social, psychological, and behavioral characteristics to biological changes and health outcomes. Figure 6.3 presents a simplified version of this model (Crimmins and Seeman, 2001; Seeman and Crimmins, 2001). This model emphasizes the ways in which background variables, including demographic characteristics and genetic background, influence social, psychological, and behavioral predictors of health outcomes. Health behaviors, social and psychological characteristics such as stress, feelings of control, and available social support, life circumstances such as job, family, and neighborhood characteristics, and access to and use of health care all have

Figure 6.2 The disablement process

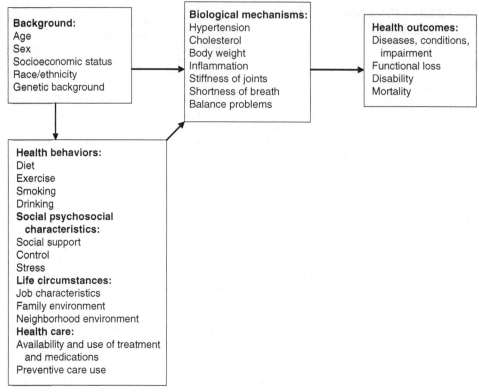

Figure 6.3   Biopsychosocial model of health and ageing

important effects on health that will be discussed more fully later in this chapter. In the context of the disablement model, these characteristics may influence biological risk factors and physiological state and in turn influence health outcomes.

DESCRIPTIVE EPIDEMIOLOGY OF HEALTH ISSUES IN OLD AGE

Mortality

As discussed above and shown in Figure 6.1, survival decreases with age and is lower in men than in women. Life expectancy for women now exceeds that for men in almost all countries of the world (Barford et al., 2006). In 2003, life expectancy in the United States at birth was 5 years higher for women than for men (80 vs 75) (Arias, 2006). However, the gap between men and women has been narrowing in recent years in many countries.

Figure 6.4 provides mortality rates for the most common causes of death in the US population aged 65 and over. Heart disease, including ischemic heart disease and heart failure, is the number one cause of death, responsible for 30 per cent of all deaths among older people. Cancer is

the second, accounting for another 22 per cent of all deaths, followed by cerebrovascular disease (stroke), respiratory disease, Alzheimer's disease, diabetes, pneumonia, infectious diseases including septicemia and HIV, renal failure, and essential hypertension. While some of these diseases are responsible for significant mortality at all ages (heart disease, cancer), others are primarily observed as a cause of death in older age groups (Alzheimer's disease, septicemia). The cause of death structure is roughly similar in most countries with low mortality; however, in Japan, the country with the highest life expectancy in the world, stroke is the most common cause of death. Mortality from stroke between ages 60 and 80 is twice as high in Japan as in the United States (National Center for Health Statistics, 1999; National Institute of Population and Social Security Research, 2000). Causes of these national differences are not well understood, but differences in diet and obesity are likely to play a role.

Chronic diseases

Chronic conditions are not only important causes of mortality but also are related to physical function,

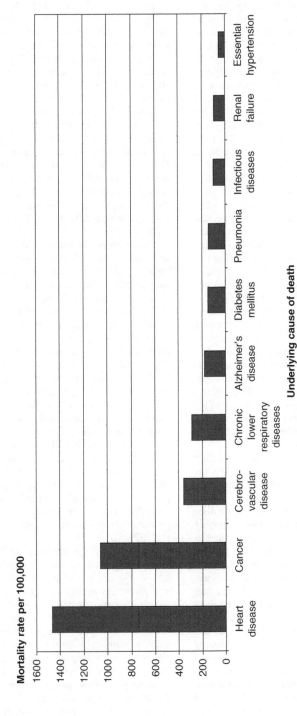

Figure 6.4 Mortality rates for the top 10 causes of death in the US population aged 65+, 2004

Source: Vital Statistics. National Center for Health Statistics, Trends in Health and Aging, http://www.cdc.gov/nchs/agingact.htm. Accessed on May 25, 2007.

disability, quality of life, and healthcare costs in old age. Figure 6.5 provides the age-adjusted prevalence of selected chronic diseases in adults 65 and over as self-reported in the US National Health Interview Survey. About half of all older persons (46 per cent of men and 51 per cent of women) reported having hypertension (high blood pressure). Arthritis affects more than a third (more prevalent among women); coronary heart disease affects approximately one quarter (more prevalent among men). Twenty-three per cent of men and 18 per cent of women report having had cancer, but the most common types of cancer vary by sex. Prostate cancer affects 9 per cent of older men, while breast cancer affects 6 per cent of women, and 2 per cent of women have a history of cervical or uterine cancers. The prevalence of most other cancers is slightly higher among men. Diabetes, stroke, asthma, emphysema, and chronic bronchitis are also major health issues in the older population. It is critical to note that self-reported data typically underestimate the prevalence of a disease in the population. Approximately 20 per cent of measured hypertension and 27 per cent of measured diabetes in older persons goes undiagnosed (Cowie et al., 2006; Crimmins et al., 2005).

While the most prevalent chronic conditions are similar in countries with low levels of mortality (Spiers et al., 2005), the United States appears to have a higher prevalence of many conditions than other countries with low mortality. For instance, cardiovascular disease, hypertension, and diabetes are higher in the United States than in England and Wales (Banks et al., 2006). This may be one of the reasons that the United States has a relatively poor ranking in life expectancy relative to other developed nations (Starfield, 2000).

Chronic diseases are important because of their impact on overall health. Figure 6.6 provides the rate of chronic conditions as a cause of disability (per 1000 in the population). Arthritis is not a primary cause of mortality, but it is the most disabling condition, which is particularly important because of its high prevalence. Sensory impairments, including vision and hearing loss, are also important predictors of disability that are not primary causes of mortality. Heart disease, diabetes, lung disease, and dementia are all important predictors of both disability and mortality. The links between disease and disability appear similar in England and the United States (Spiers et al., 2005), and the prevalence of some diseases appears to be increasing over time in both countries (Crimmins and Saito, 2000; Spiers et al., 2005). This has resulted in an increase in the proportion of older people with specific diseases, as well as an increase in the average number of conditions present in older people.

Functional impairment, disability, and active life expectancy

A number of studies based on US data have found declines in physical functioning difficulties throughout the 1980s and 1990s, as summarized in Freedman et al., (2002). Improvements in functioning and reductions in disability have also been reported in other countries (Bone et al., 1995; Robine et al., 1998; Schoeni et al., 2006). As an example, Figure 6.7 shows the prevalence of five indicators of physical functioning over time in the US Medicare Current Beneficiary Survey, which includes both community-dwelling and institutionalized Medicare beneficiaries 65 and older. Difficulty stooping is the most prevalent functional impairment. The prevalence of stooping and walking difficulty did not change markedly over this period, but the prevalence of reaching, grasping, and lifting difficulties all declined between 3 and 7 per cent.

Disability is often measured using two sets of tasks. The first, activities of daily living (ADLs), includes activities such as bathing, dressing, eating, transferring (into and out of bed or a chair), and toileting. These activities correspond closely with self-care levels required to live independently and are often used as a component of eligibility criteria for nursing home admission in the United States. The second, instrumental activities of daily living (IADLs), often include housework, shopping, preparing meals, using the telephone, managing medications, managing money, or using transportation. These activities require both cognitive and physical capacity to manage daily tasks both inside and outside the home. Risk of both ADLs and IADLs increases with age and in the United States is higher in women, Blacks, and those with fewer years of education. However, research suggests that the prevalence of both ADL and IADL limitations has been decreasing in the United States and in other countries (Freedman et al., 2002, 2004a; Schoeni et al., 2006).

One way of summarizing age-specific data on disability is to examine the number of years of life people can expect to live without disability, also known as healthy or active life expectancy. Active life expectancy measures integrate data on disability and mortality to develop estimates of total life expectancy disaggregated into periods with and without disability. Active life expectancy also provides a helpful way to examine differences in disability and mortality burden across different groups and geographic areas. Figure 6.8 shows active and disabled life expectancy at age 70 by sex, race, and education based on the US Longitudinal Study of Aging, 1984–1990

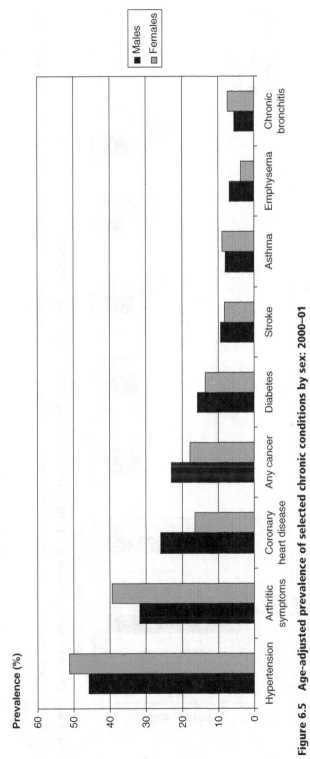

Prevalence (%)

■ Males
▨ Females

Figure 6.5 Age-adjusted prevalence of selected chronic conditions by sex: 2000–01

Source: National Health Interview Survey. National Center for Health Statistics, Trends in Health and Aging, http://www.cdc.gov/nchs/agingact.htm. Accessed on June 5, 2007.

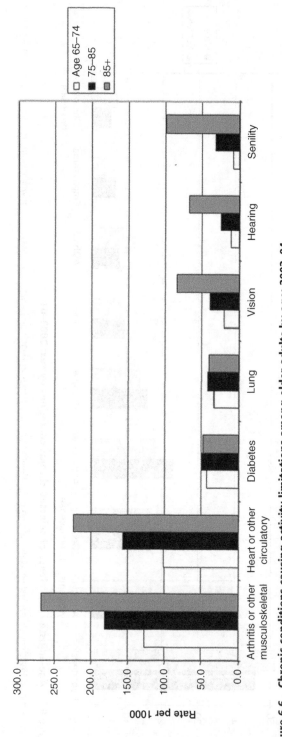

Figure 6.6   Chronic conditions causing activity limitations among older adults by age: 2003–04

Source: National Health Interview Survey. *Health, United States 2006.* Federal Interagency Forum on Aging-Related Statistics. http://www.cdc.gov/nchs/hus.htm. Accessed on June 12, 2007.

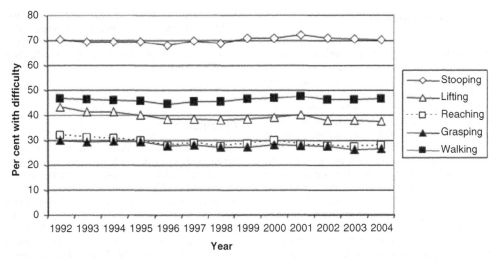

Figure 6.7   Age-adjusted percentage with difficulty in physical functioning, Medicare beneficiaries, 65+, 1992–2004

Source: Medicare Current Beneficiary Survey. National Center for Health Statistics, Trends in Health and Aging, http://www.cdc.gov/nchs/agingact.htm. Accessed on June 5, 2007.

(Crimmins et al., 1996). Total life expectancy (the sum of active and disabled) is higher for women and for those with higher levels of education. However, women also spend more years disabled, from 2.6–3.6, compared to men, who spend an average of 1.3–1.9 years disabled. This analysis also indicated that longer disability among women is due to longer life, rather than a higher incidence of disability. This type of disaggregation is a value of the healthy life expectancy approach. At age 70, Black men and women have similar total life expectancies to other groups, but live a greater proportion of their lives disabled. Depending on education level, black women spend 3.3–3.6 years disabled, compared to only 2.6–2.8 years for white women.

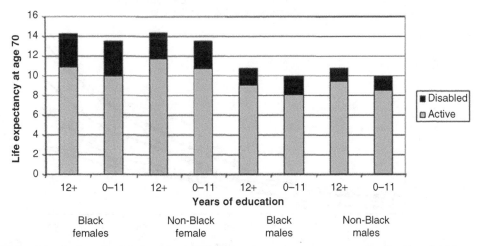

Figure 6.8   Active, disabled, and total life expectancy by race, sex, and education: LOSA, 1984–90

Source: Crimmins, E.M., Hayward, M.D., and Saito, Y. (1996) 'Differentials in active life expectancy ub the older population of the United States', Journal of Gerontology: Social Sciences, 51B:S111–120.

Cognitive impairment

Cognitive impairment is also a major quality of life issue for older persons. Although many cognitive abilities in tasks related to memory and processing speed begin to decline in early adulthood, most age-related cognitive changes do not interfere with the ability to engage in activities and live independently. However, serious cognitive impairments related to Alzheimer's disease, depression, subclinical vascular disease, and other health problems increase with age (see Chapter 26). In the United States the estimated prevalence of cognitive impairment in the community increases from less than 4 per cent in those 65–74 to 20 per cent in those aged 85 and over (Bernstein and Rembsburg, 2007). On average, Americans 70 and over can expect to live 1.5 years with cognitive impairment, and this period is longer for women than men (Suthers et al., 2003).

The prevalence of cognitive impairment has been shown to increase rapidly with age in a number of countries. Age-specific prevalence estimates from five countries [USA (Suthers et al., 2003), Belgium (Roelands et al., 1994), Canada (Graham et al., 1997), France (Ritchie et al., 1994), and three communities in England (Ritchie et al., 1993) are illustrated in Figure 6.9. Prevalence estimates vary across populations; they are highest for Melton Mowbray, England, and lowest for France.

There are a variety of potential sources of variability in the prevalence estimates between countries, including both behavioral and biological causes, as well as the difficulty of assessing cognitive function.

Depression

Mental health is a critical issue in population health, and depression is a leading contributor to the global burden of disease (WHO, 2008). Depression in older persons is uniquely problematic because of the interaction of depression and other health problems (including chronic conditions and cognitive impairment), the high prevalence of depressive symptoms in older persons, and the risk for suicide. Depression manifests itself in many forms, and includes a heterogeneous group of disorders with different symptoms and severity. Major depression occurs in about 1 per cent of the community-dwelling older population, but 8–15 per cent have clinically significant depressive symptomatology (Apfeldorf and Alexopoulos, 2003). Insomnia, bereavement, and cognitive impairment are important risk factors for depression in older persons, and depression is higher in medical settings and in those with chronic disease. Depression appears to increase

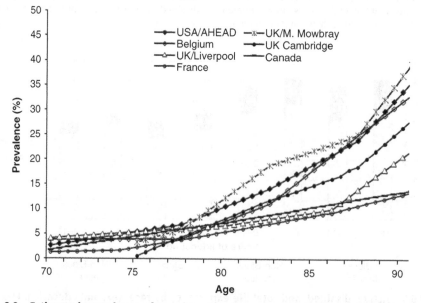

Figure 6.9 **Estimated prevalence of cognitive impairment: cross-national comparisons**

Sources: USA, Suthers et al., 2003; Belgium, Roelands et al., 1994; Canada, Graham et al., 1997; England/ Liverpool, Ritchie et al., 1993; France, Ritchie et al., 1994.

risk of comorbid illness, cognitive impairment, functional impairment, and mortality, and suicide rates are higher at older ages, particularly in men.

Geriatric syndromes

Geriatric syndromes are not diseases, per se, but conditions such as falls, frailty, and delirium and dementia that are highly associated with age and have important consequences in terms of health and quality of life for older people. Comorbidity, the presence of multiple chronic conditions, is also a critical issue for older people. We will briefly discuss some of the most important issues related to the epidemiology of each of these conditions.

Falls

Falls are common in the older population; approximately 35–40 per cent of persons aged 65 and older fall each year. Serious fall injuries such as fractures and head trauma occur in 5–15 per cent of falls in the community, and both fall incidence and fall-associated injuries are higher in institutional settings (King, 2003). Risk factors for falls include muscle weakness, a history of falls, gait and balance deficits, use of assistive devices, visual deficits, arthritis, disability, depression, cognitive impairment, and being aged 80 and over (Tinetti et al., 1988). Use of multiple medications and walking obstacles in the home may also contribute to risk of falling. Intervention research suggests that multifactorial interventions are the most effective way to reduce fall risk, including an emphasis on exercise and strength, correction of sensory deficits, medication review, and environmental modification.

Frailty

Both researchers and clinicians have been interested in identifying older adults at highest risk for poor health outcomes, including disability, cognitive impairment, hospitalization and nursing home placement, and mortality. Whereas many diseases are clearly risk factors for these outcomes, disease alone does not adequately identify the population at risk. A variety of theories and definitions of frailty have been put forth; we will briefly describe two of them. The first conceptualizes frailty as biologic dysregulation across multiple physiological systems (Ferrucci et al., 2005), eventually leading to a constellation of subclinical and clinically detectable diseases that inhibit an individual's ability to recover from health events.

A related definition defines frailty based on clinical symptoms, including weight loss, weakness, fatigue, slow walking speed, and inactivity (Bandeen-Roche et al., 2006; Fried et al., 2001). The presence of three or more of these symptoms increases risk of disability, hospitalization, and death.

Delirium and dementia

Delirium is defined as an acute disorder of attention and global cognitive function. Dementia is an irreversible syndrome of progressive, global cognitive impairment. In practice, it may be difficult to distinguish between cognitive impairment, dementia, and delirium, and they are often related (Insel and Badger, 2002). The distinguishing characteristics of delirium are its rapid onset and fluctuation, occurring more frequency in hospitalized and institutionalized older persons (Agostini and Inouye, 2003). Precipitating factors include medication use, immobilization, use of physical restraints, dehydration, malnutrition, iatrogenic events, medical illnesses, infections, metabolic disturbances, and emotional stress. Delirium is generally thought to be a reversible condition, although as few as 20 per cent of patients experience complete symptom resolution within 6 months. In contrast, true dementia is irreversible. The prevalence of dementia increases with age and is a major risk factor for nursing home placement. Overall, 42 per cent of nursing home residents 65 and over have a dementia diagnosis (Bernstein and Remsburg, 2007). A large number of disorders can cause dementia, but Alzheimer's disease is the most common, accounting for approximately 60–80 per cent of observed dementia (Knopman, 1998). (See Chapters 20 and 26).

Comorbidity

Comorbidity, or the existence of multiple conditions within an individual, has been called the ultimate geriatric syndrome (Yancik et al., 2007). Because disease incidence increases with ageing, any new diagnosis in an older person is likely to be made in the context of preexisting health problems. Among Medicare beneficiaries aged 65 and over, 65 per cent have multiple chronic conditions (Wolff et al., 2002). Although debate continues about the most appropriate ways to measure comorbidity, as well as which diseases and conditions should be included (Boyd et al., 2007; Karlamangla et al., 2007; Lash et al., 2007), it is clear that the presence of multiple chronic conditions affects the progression of disease, decreases quality of life, and increases the risk and severity of disability (Boyd et al., 2007).

WHAT FACTORS AFFECT HEALTH IN OLD AGE?

This section will draw on the biopsychosocial model of health and ageing presented in Figure 6.3 to discuss factors affecting health in old age.

Background: social and demographic characteristics

We have already discussed the association between age and chronic disease, loss of physical and cognitive function, and mortality. However, other demographic characteristics, notably sex, socioeconomic status, and race, also importantly predict health outcomes in older populations. Women live longer, as shown in Figure 6.1, but also have higher numbers of chronic conditions and higher levels of disability and cognitive impairment. Although some of these differences may result from differences in reporting, women have higher levels of functional impairment even when measured with observed performance, suggesting that these differences cannot be entirely accounted for by gender-based reporting differences (Merrill et al., 1997; Oman et al., 1999). As noted above, women's lower mortality rates may contribute to sex differences in the prevalence of functional impairment and disability.

Socioeconomic status (SES) may be measured by a variety of indicators, most frequently including education, income, occupation, or wealth. Based on any of these indicators, lower social class is significantly related to lower self-rated health, an increased prevalence of chronic conditions, and higher mortality (Adler and Ostrove, 1999). On average, low SES persons are likely to experience more years disabled and cognitively impaired (Crimmins et al., 1996; Lievre et al., 2008). Moreover, evidence suggests that the effects of social class on health are not confined to threshold effects of poverty, but occur across the entire socioeconomic gradient (Adler and Ostrove, 1999; Marmot, 2004). Research increasingly suggests that education may be the most important socioeconomic predictor of health, particularly in late life (Smith, 2005; Winkleby et al., 1992).

Socioeconomic differences in health are virtually universal throughout life, although they differ in size by country. They are relatively large in the United States and small in Japan, although they have been increasing in Japan in recent years (Marmot and Smith, 1989; Wilkinson, 1994). Socioeconomic differences also tend to be smaller in old age than at younger ages, partly reflecting the fact that people of lower SES are less likely to reach old age because of higher mortality. These factors may explain the different patterns of socioeconomic variability by age and disease prevalence in the four countries shown in Figure 6.10. Diabetes and hypertension are linked to higher mortality and are more common among older persons with lower education in the United States However, they are associated with higher education in Mexico – a reversal of the expected socioeconomic differential. This difference in pattern of the socioeconomic differential in old-age health may reflect differences in onset of disease, diagnosis and treatment, or mortality. It is also possible that there are differences in reporting of disease presence by education in these national surveys, particularly in Mexico and Korea. Persons with lower education have consistently higher disability in all four countries. Disability is less likely to be linked to mortality, and thus less likely to be affected by differentials in survival with the condition.

In the United States, large racial gaps are evident in health status measured by a variety of health indicators. The life expectancy gap between the group with the longest life expectancy, Asian Americans, and the group with the shortest, urban Blacks, is more than 20 years (Murray et al., 2006). On average, Asians have longer life expectancies accompanied by fewer years in poor health relative to Whites, while Hispanics live fewer years, but live a smaller portion of them disabled. Blacks appear to be the most disadvantaged group, because they average both shorter life expectancies and greater years of disability than other racial and ethnic groups (Hayward and Heron, 1999). These disparities may be explained in part by differences in SES across groups; they may also reflect past history of migration in populations that have high foreign-born proportions. In an analysis of the racial gap in chronic health conditions in midlife, Hayward and colleagues (2000) found that Black–White racial differences were present across a range of chronic conditions, including cardiovascular diseases, diabetes, asthma, pain, vision problems, depression, and disability measures. Disparities were largely explained by differences in SES, rather than health risk behaviors or other mechanisms. Racism and discrimination also contribute to the associations between race, SES, and health (Williams, 1999). Discrimination may affect health by restricting socioeconomic opportunities, by increasing stress, and by contributing to residential segregation and differential access to health services.

Background: genetics

Genes affect an individual's risk of both fatal (e.g., heart attack, Alzheimer's disease, cancer) and

Diabetes prevalence 65+ by education

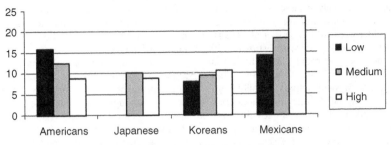

Hypertension prevalence 65+ by education

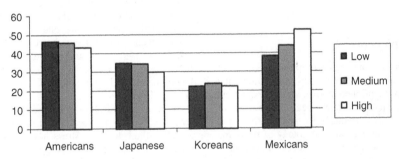

Physical difficulty prevalence 65+ by education

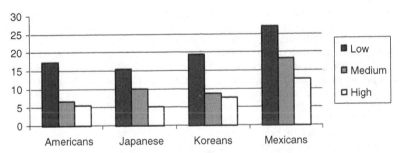

Figure 6.10 Diseases and disability by education level in four countries: 65+ population

Sources: Microdata from surveys: USA (National Health and Nutrition Examination Survey, 1999–2002); Japan (Nihon University Japanese Longitudinal Study on Aging, 1999); Korea (The Survey of Living Conditions and Needs for Social Welfare of the Elderly, 1998); Mexico (Mexican Health and Aging Study, 2003).

non-fatal (e.g., sarcopenia, osteoporosis) conditions associated with ageing. Between one-quarter and one-third of differences in life expectancy in humans appear to be due to heritability (Melzer et al., 2007), and exceptional longevity in centenarians may have an even stronger genetic basis (Perls et al., 2002). In general, we expect genetic risks to play a larger role in early-onset disease, whereas we expect environmental exposures or stochastic changes to be more important in late-onset disease. For example, genetic risk appears to

play a larger role in early-onset Alzheimer's disease (AD) occurring before age 60 than in late-onset AD (Tanzi and Bertram, 2001). Yet, there is also significant heritability of late-onset AD (Pedersen et al., 2004), and the apolipoprotein E gene associated with risk of late-onset AD has become one of the most widely studied genes associated with ageing processes. This research has uncovered a variety of interactions between the *ApoE-4* allele and gender, estrogen use, diabetes, and cardiovascular disease risk factors

(Haan et al., 1999; Hu et al., 2006; Seeman et al., 2005; Yaffe et al., 2000). Similarly, genetic susceptibility appears to play a larger role in heart disease at younger ages, and the genetic effect decreases at older ages (Marenberg et al., 1994). However, even at younger ages, an estimated 79 per cent of the risk of coronary heart disease is attributable to behavioral risk factors, including smoking, weight, physical activity, alcohol consumption, and diet, rather than to genetic risk (Chiuve et al., 2006). These examples illustrate the importance of genes, the environment, and their interactions in predicting disease risk in late life.

Health behaviors

Health behaviors are important predictors of most diseases of ageing and of cognitive and functional decline. As mentioned above, health behaviors importantly predict coronary heart disease, one of the major causes of disability and death in the older population. Remarkably, many of the same health behaviors that are associated with coronary heart disease are important predictors of nearly every major health outcome in old age. Smoking, being overweight, and lacking physical activity are also risk factors for dementia (Haan and Wallace, 2004) and disability (Vita et al., 1998). Because these health behaviors affect physiology across multiple systems, including cardiovascular, pulmonary, and endocrine systems, promoting positive health behaviors and modifying negative behaviors may be one of the most effective ways to simultaneously reduce the burden of disease and disability. Moreover, there is considerable evidence that it is never too late for health behaviors to have positive effects on health; smoking cessation and physical activity are beneficial even if they occur late in life (Appel and Aldrich, 2003; LIFE Study Investigators, 2006).

Social psychological characteristics

Higher social integration is associated with decreased risk of cardiovascular disease and mortality (Seeman and Crimmins, 2001). The strongest links between social support and health have been observed in studies examining recovery from cardiovascular events such as heart attack and stroke. Numerous studies have found that socially isolated individuals have greater mortality following cardiovascular events and that socially integrated individuals are more likely to recover. Social ties may affect health directly,

through physiological effects of decreased stress and improved effect. Alternately, social ties may affect health indirectly, by buffering individuals from stressful life events, leveraging instrumental assistance, and encouraging positive health behaviors.

A variety of control-related constructs, such as sense of control, locus of control, self-efficacy, fatalism, and personal agency, have been related to health. Although these concepts differ in their specifics, control or efficacy generally represents the extent to which an individual perceives having power and direction over personal and social outcomes, while fatalism represents a lack of control or a feeling that external factors control individual outcomes (Schieman, 2001). A higher sense of control and self-efficacy are related to better health behaviors and positive health outcomes (Mirowsky and Ross, 1998), although self-efficacy may be more closely related to an individual's perceived health than to underlying physical ability (Seeman et al., 1999).

Both acute and chronic stress can have long-term health consequences. Under stress, the brain activates the release of stress hormones into the bloodstream, mobilizing energy and increasing physiological readiness for a fight-or-flight action. Although such adaptive responses are essential during a stressful situation, repeated physiological overstimulation can cause dysregulation. Long-term exposure to stress has been associated with hypertension, impaired glucose tolerance, and impaired immune function (McEwen, 1998; Segerstrom and Miller, 2004). Stress in general, and activation of the hypothalamic–pituitary–adrenal (HPA) axis and secretion of stress hormones in particular, is hypothesized to be a critical mechanism through which social experiences affect physiology and ultimately affect health.

Life circumstances, including family, work, and neighborhood environments

Work, family, and neighborhood environments may positively influence health by providing social support and opportunities for positive health behaviors or may negatively influence health by increasing stress and decreasing personal control. An extensive literature links many aspects of work to late-life health, including occupational status, job control, and job complexity. Occupations may directly influence health through physical hazards associated with particular work environments, including occupational injury and exposure to chemicals or loud noise. However, work environment may also affect health psychologically; increased job control is associated with lower health risks, and job control appears to be particularly associated with coronary heart disease (Karasek, 1990; Marmot et al., 1997), presumably because greater control decreases stress or allows people to respond more effectively to stress. Employment may also be a resource by providing health insurance and health information.

The family environment is also an important contributor to health. Two family roles have received particular attention in the health literature: spouse and caregiver. Marriage is a primary social role in adulthood that structures behavior and interaction, creating a shared social environment that may impact health in a variety of ways. For most health outcomes, marital status appears protective, resulting in better health and lower mortality (Hu and Goldman, 1990; Waite, 2006). The marital relationship may supply social support and social control over health behaviors, especially for men (Umberson, 1992), reducing harmful behaviors like smoking. While marriage is generally viewed as a resource that provides support and protects spouses from stress, family caregiving is typically associated with poorer health and can be a major source of stress (Schulz and Martire, 2004). Caregivers who experience mental and emotional strain as a result of caregiving have higher mortality than non-caregivers (Schulz and Beach, 1999), and caregiver strain is associated with poorer self-rated health, anxiety, and depression (Beach et al., 2000). These examples illustrate the complex associations between family relationships and health, in which the family can act as both a source of stress and support for ageing persons.

Like the work and family environments, the neighborhood environment can be a resource or a risk to health. Research has documented independent effects of neighborhood-level socioeconomic status on health after controlling for individual-level characteristics (Pickett and Pearl, 2001; Robert, 1999). These findings suggest that neighborhood-level associations with health are not due entirely to the compositional effects of neighborhood residents, but that neighborhood context itself may influence health. Excessive noise, inadequate lighting, and heavy traffic are related to loss of physical function in older persons (Balfour and Kaplan, 2002). Both individual perceptions of neighborhood disorder (Ross and Mirowsky, 2001) and objective observations of neighborhood conditions (Schootman et al., 2005) are related to poorer health. In contrast, affluence and neighborhood social resources are related to better health (Wen et al., 2003). The specific mechanisms through which neighborhood conditions affect health are still under debate.

Health care

Access to health care is an important predictor of health at all ages because of its relationship to both preventive care and treatment. In the United States, a substantial proportion of the population less than 65 years of age does not have health insurance. Uninsured adults are less likely to be able to see a physician when needed and are less likely to have access to preventive services, including routine cancer, cardiovascular, and diabetes screening (Ayanian et al., 2000; Sudano and Baker, 2003). These differences in access to health services have important consequences for health; uninsured middle-aged adults are more likely to develop disability than those with insurance (Baker et al., 2001).

After age 65, more than 97 per cent of older adults receive healthcare coverage through Medicare, which is associated with increased use of preventive services (McWilliams et al., 2003). Despite Medicare coverage, many older adults continue to experience high out-of-pocket health costs that rise with age and that may interfere with their ability to access appropriate care. Until 2006, Medicare did not cover the cost of most prescription drugs. Restricted medication use due to cost is associated with greater health declines and increased risk of cardiovascular disease complications associated with cardiovascular disease among middle-aged and older persons (Heisler et al., 2004). Medicare Part D, implemented in 2006, may help to address this problem.

Biological mechanisms

A great deal of research has attempted to understand how social background, psychosocial, and behavioral factors 'get under the skin' to affect health outcomes (Seeman and Crimmins, 2001). Some of these mechanisms, particularly related to the role of health behaviors, are relatively straightforward: lack of exercise contributes to decreased strength and balance problems; smoking results in decreased lung capacity and shortness of breath. However, the mechanisms through which other factors affect health are more difficult to identify. Higher levels of social support from close friends and family are associated with better physiological profiles, including lower systolic blood pressure, lower serum cholesterol, and lower cortisol levels (Seeman and McEwen, 1996), while inadequate levels of social support are related to a higher risk of the metabolic syndrome, a cluster of risk factors including high waist circumference, low high-density lipoprotein (HDL) cholesterol, and high glucose that is known to confer additional risk of cardiovascular disease and diabetes (Vogelzangs et al., 2007). Lower socioeconomic status is associated with greater physiological dysregulation across a range of indicators, including cardiovascular risk factors, stress hormones, inflammatory markers, lung function, and glucose tolerance (Koster et al., 2005; Seeman et al., 2004).

EMERGING ISSUES AND DIRECTIONS FOR FUTURE RESEARCH

This is an exciting time in the epidemiology of ageing. There has been an extraordinary growth in multidisciplinary research that attempts to bring together social, psychological, behavioral, and biological characteristics to better understand the ageing process and the health of older persons and populations. These complex perspectives are necessary in order to accurately reflect the dynamic nature of the ageing process, which occurs in a constant interaction between the individual and the physical and social environment. Many of the emerging issues in the epidemiology of ageing (e.g., understanding the role of genetics and gene–environment interactions in ageing, the search for biological pathways through which social experiences 'get under the skin') have already been presented in this chapter. Here, we will highlight several other frontiers in the epidemiology of ageing.

The whole person: relationships across health outcomes

Until recently, many health outcomes were considered individually. Researchers typically studied predictors of disability, cognitive impairment, and mortality separately, or simply controlled for other health problems without explicitly considering interactions between them. Increasingly, research has moved toward a more integrated model that clearly recognizes the interdependence of these domains. Models of active life expectancy and life expectancy without cognitive impairment acknowledge the complex relationships between functional status and mortality, and some definitions of active life expectancy have incorporated cognitive impairment as a cause of physical disability (Jagger et al., 2007b; Manton and Land, 2000). Research has also begun to address the relationships between physical and cognitive function (Blaum et al., 2002; Covinsky et al., 2003; Fultz et al., 2003; Moody-Ayers et al., 2005) and the predictors of combined cognitive and physical decline (Atkinson et al., 2005). Although it is

difficult to untangle the causal associations between physical and cognitive decline, it is clear that they predict each other and often occur simultaneously. Furthermore, they share many risk factors, including age, IADL impairment, current smoking, and biological risk factors (Atkinson et al., 2005).

A life-course perspective: the influence of early-life exposures

The epidemiology of ageing has increasingly drawn on the life-course approach from the sociology of ageing and life-course epidemiological perspectives emphasizing the effects of timing of life events on human development (Elder et al., 2003; Lynch and Davey Smith, 2005). Low socioeconomic status in childhood appears to be a particularly important influence on adult health, both through its association with adult socioeconomic status and through more direct effects on development (Kaplan et al., 2001; Kittleson et al., 2006; Lawlor et al., 2006). Health problems in childhood also increase risk of chronic disease in adulthood (Blackwell et al., 2001; Hayward and Gorman, 2004). More research is needed to examine the mechanisms through which early life experiences affect health in later life and transmission of health across generations.

Beyond old age as a time of decline: understanding maintenance and recovery

Although the major emphasis in the epidemiology of ageing has been on old age as a time health decline, there is an increasing awareness that health trajectories are heterogeneous, even in late life. Some declines previously thought to be direct consequences of ageing are now believed to be the result of disease or behavior change. For instance, much of the association between age and losses in strength may be a result of age-related declines in physical activity. Furthermore, significant functional recovery occurs, even for older persons in poor health. In a 2-year follow-up of non-institutionalized participants aged 70 and over, 23–60 per cent of individuals impaired on ADL and IADL tasks at baseline were no longer impaired 2 years later (Crimmins and Saito, 1993). These results illustrate the diverse health trajectories of older persons. Disease and disability are the normative outcomes of ageing, but are not inevitable. Whereas predictors of physical and cognitive decline in old age are extensively documented, research has just begun to identify predictors of maintenance and recovery of function.

Understanding and influencing population disability levels

Although it is clear that disability in the older population declined in the 1980s and 1990s, it is much less clear why disability has declined. Some researchers have emphasized technology and medical care as possible explanations (Cutler, 2001), while others have emphasized improvements in education of the elderly (Freedman and Aykan, 2003). Understanding why disability decline has occurred is important in predicting whether or not it will continue and forecasting the future healthcare needs of the ageing population. It is also important in determining how best to promote disability decline. It is clear that the most effective interventions to reduce disability are likely to be multifactorial. In a review of intervention strategies, Freedman and colleagues identified physical activity promotion, depression screening and treatment, and fall prevention as potentially high-impact interventions and suggest that fall prevention may be the most promising (Freedman et al., 2006).

CONCLUSION

The epidemiology of ageing seeks to understand and explain health patterns in the older population, generating knowledge to improve the health of the older population. With increasing age, the risks of mortality, chronic disease, and physical and cognitive impairment increase. However, these risks vary over time and across groups. Women average longer life expectancies than men, but also have a higher average burden of chronic disease and disability. Life expectancy and the burden of chronic disease vary substantially across racial and ethnic groups in the United States, with Blacks emerging as the most disadvantaged group. Health by most metrics is also poorer among those of lower socioeconomic status, with education emerging as a particularly powerful predictor of health. However, despite persistent health inequities, disability and mortality have continued to decline.

Health in any age group is produced through complex interactions between individual characteristics and the physical and social environment. At older ages, it is not only the current characteristics of the individual and environment that may affect health but also an individual's life history. Health behaviors, social psychological characteristics, life circumstances, and health care all importantly contribute to health in later life.

REFERENCES

Adler, N.E. and Ostrove, J.M. (1999) 'Socioeconomic status and health: What we know and what we don't.' *Annals of the New York Academy of Sciences*, 896: 3–15.

Agostini, J.V. and Inouye, S.K. (2003) 'Delirium', in W.R. Hazzard, J.P. Blass, J.B. Halter, J.G. Ouslander and M.E. Tinetti, (eds), Principles of Geriatric Medicine & Gerontology 5th edn. New York: McGraw Hill, pp. 1503–15

Apfeldorf, W.J. and Alexopoulos, G.S. (2003) 'Late-life mood disorders', in W.R. Hazzard, J.P. Blass, J.B. Halter, et al. (eds), *Principles of Geriatric Medicine and Gerontology*, 5th edn. New York: McGraw-Hill.

Appel, D.W. and Aldrich, T.K. (2003) 'Smoking cessation in the elderly', *Clinical Geriatic Medicine*, 19: 77–100.

Arias, E. (2006) 'United States Life Tables, 2003', *National Vital Statistics Reports*, 54(14): 10–4.

Atkinson, H., Cesari, M., Kritchevsky, S., et al. (2005) 'Predictors of combined cognitive and physical decline', *Journal of the American Geriatrics Society*, 53: 1197–202.

Ayanian, J.Z., Weissmann, J.S., Schneider, E.C., Ginsburg, J.A., and Zaslavsky, A.M. (2000) 'Unmet health needs of uninsured adults in the United States', *The Journal of American Medicine*, 284: 2061–9.

Baker, D.W., Sudano, J.J., Albert, J.M., Borawski, E.A., and Dor, A. (2001) 'Lack of health insurance and decline in overall health in late middle age', *New England Journal of Medicine*, 345: 1106–112.

Balfour, J.L. and Kaplan, G.A. (2002) 'Neighborhood environment and loss of physical function in older adults: evidence from the Alameda County Study', *American Journal of Epidemiology*, 155: 507–15.

Bandeen-Roche, K., Xue, Q., Ferrucci, L., et al. (2006) 'Phenotype of frailty: characterization in the women's health and aging studies', *Journal of Gerontology, Medical Sciences*, 61A: 262–6.

Banks, J., Marmot, M., Oldfield, Z., and Smith, J.P. (2006) 'Disease and disadvantage in the United States and in England', *Journal of the American Medical Association*, 295(17): 2037–45.

Barford, A., Dorling, D., Davey Smith, G., and Shaw, M. (2006) 'Life expectancy: women now on top everywhere', *British Medical Journal*, 332: 808.

Beach, S.R., Schulz, R., Yee, J.L., and Jackson, S. (2000) 'Negative and positive health effects of caring for a disabled spouse: longitudinal findings from the caregiver health effects study', *Psychological Aging*, 15: 259–71.

Bernstein, A.B. and Remsburg, R.E. (2007) 'Estimated prevalence of people with cognitive impairment: results from nationally representative community and institutional surveys', *The Gerontologist*, 47: 350–4.

Blackwell, D.L., Hayward, M.D., and Crimmins, E.M. (2001) 'Does childhood health affect chronic morbidity in later life?', *Social Science and Medicine*, 52: 1269–84.

Blaum, C., Ofstedal M.B., and Liang, J. (2002) 'Low cognitive performance, comorbid disease, and task-specific disability: findings from a nationally representative survey', *Journal of Gerontology, Medical Sciences*, 57A: M523–31.

Bone, M.R., Bebbington, A.C., Jagger, C., Morgan, K., and Nicolaas, G. (1995) *Health Expectancy and Its Uses.* London: HMSO.

Boyd, C.M., Weiss, C.O., Halter, J., et al. (2007) 'Framework for evaluating disease severity measures in older adults with comorbidity', *Journal of Gerontology: Medical Sciences*, 62A: 275–80.

Chiuve, S., McCullough, M., Sacks, F., and Rimm, E. (2006) 'Healthy lifestyle factors in the primary prevention of coronary heart disease among men', *Circulation*, 114: 160–7.

Covinsky, K.E., Eng, C., Lui, L., Sands, L., and Yaffe, K. (2003) 'The last 2 years of life: functional trajectories of frail older people', *Journal of American Geriatrics Society*, 51: 492–98.

Cowie, C.C., Englelgau, M.M., Rust, K.F., et al. (2006) 'Prevalence of diabetes and impaired fasting glucose in adults in the U.S. population', *Diabetes Care*, 29: 1263–8.

Crimmins, E.M. (2004) 'Trends in the health of the elderly', *Annual Review of Public Health*, 25: 79–98.

Crimmins, E.M., Alley, D., Reynolds, S., et al. (2005) 'Changes in biological markers of health: older Americans in the 1990s', *Journal of Gerontology: Medical Sciences*, 60: 1409–13.

Crimmins, E.M., Hayward, M.D., and Saito, Y. (1996) 'Differentials in active life expectancy in the older population of the United States', *Journal of Gerontology: Social Sciences*, 51B: S111–20.

Crimmins, E.M. and Saito, Y. (1993) 'Getting better and getting worse: transitions in functional status among older Americans.' *Journal of Aging and Health*, 5: 3–36.

Crimmins, E.M. and Saito, Y. (2000) 'Change in the prevalence of diseases among older Americans: 1984–1994', *Demographic Research* [online] 3, November 2000.

Crimmins, E.M. and Seeman, T.E. (2001) 'Integrating biology into demographic research on health and aging (with a focus on the MacArthur Study of Successful Aging)', in C.E., Finch, J.W., Vaupel, and K. Kinsella, (eds), *Cells and Surveys.* Washington, DC: National Academy Press.

Cutler, D. (2001) 'Declining disability among the elderly', *Health Affairs*, 20: 11–27.

Elder, G.H., Johnson, M.K., and Crosnoe R. (2003) 'The emergence and development of life course theory', in J.T. Mortimer and M.J. Shanahan (eds), *Handbook of the Life Course.* New York: Kluwer/Plenum.

Ferrucci, L., Windham, B.G., and Fried, L.P. (2005) 'Frailty in older persons', *Genus*, 56: 39–53.

Freedman, V.A. and Aykan, H. (2003) 'Trends in medication use and functioning before retirement age: are they linked?', *Health Affairs*, 22: 154–62.

Freedman, V.A., Crimmins, E., Schoeni, R.F., et al. (2004) 'Resolving inconsistencies in trends in old-age disability: report from a technical working group', *Demography*, 41: 417–41.

Freedman, V.A., Hodgson, N., Lynn, J., et al. (2006) 'Promoting declines in the prevalence of late-life disability: comparisons of three potentially high-impact interventions', *The Milbank Quarterly*, 84: 493–520.

Freedman, V.A., Martin, L.G., and Schoeni, R.F. (2002) 'Recent trends in disability and functioning among older adults in the United States: a systematic review of the evidence', *Journal of the American Medical Association*, 288: 3137–46.

Fried, L.P. (2000) 'Epidemiology of aging', *Epidemiologic Reviews*, 22: 95–106.

Fried, L.P., Tangen, C.M., Walston, J., et al. (2001) 'Frailty in older adults: evidence for a phenotype', *Journal of Gerontology: Medical Sciences*, 56A: M146–56.

Fries, J.F. (1980) 'Aging, natural death, and the compression of morbidity', *The New England Journal of Medicine*, 303: 130–5.

Fultz, N.H., Ofstedal, M.B., Herzog, A.R., and Wallace, R.B. (2003) 'Additive and interactive effects of comorbid physical and mental conditions of functional health', *Journal of Aging and Health*, 15: 465–81.

Graham, J.E., Rockwood, K., Beattie, B.L., et al. (1997) 'Prevalence and severity of cognitive impairment with and without dementia in an elderly population', *Lancet*, 349, 1793–6.

Haan, M. and Wallace, R. (2004) 'Can dementia be prevented? Brain aging in a population-based context', *Annual Review of Public Health*, 25: 1–24.

Haan, M., Shemanski, L., Jagust, W.J., Manolio, T., and Kuller, L. (1999) 'The role of APOE e4 in modulating effects of other risk factors for cognitive decline in elderly persons', *Journal of American Medical Association*, 282: 40–6.

Hayward, M. and Heron, M. (1999) 'Racial inequality in active life among adult Americans', *Demography*, 36: 77–91.

Hayward, M.D. and Gorman, B.K. (2004) 'The long arm of childhood: the influence of early-life social conditions on men's mortality', *Demography*, 41: 87–107.

Hayward, M.D., Crimmins, E.M., Miles, T.P., and Yang, Y. (2000) 'The significance of socioeconomic status in explaining the racial gap in chronic health conditions', *American Sociological Review*, 65: 910–30.

Heisler, M., Langa, K.M., Eby, E.L., et al. (2004) 'The health effects of restricting prescription medication use because of cost', *Medical Care*, 42: 626–34.

Hu, P., Bretsky, P., Crimmins, E.M., et al. (2006) 'Association between serum beta-carotene levels and decline of cognitive function in high-functioning older persons with or without apolipoprotein E 4 alleles: macArthur studies of successful aging', *Journal of Gerontology: Medical Sciences*, 61: 616–20.

Hu, Y. and Goldman, N. (1990) 'Mortality differentials by marital status: an international comparison', *Demography*, 27: 233–50.

Insel, K. and Badger, K. (2002) 'Deciphering the 4 D's: Cognitve decline, delirium, depression and dementia – a review', *Journal of Advanced Nursing.* 360–368.

Jagger, C., Matthews, R., Matthews, F., et al. (2007a) 'The burden of diseases on disability-free life expectancy in later life', *Journal of Gerontology. Medical Sciences,* 62A: 408–14.

Jagger, C., Matthews, R.J., Matthews, F.E., et al. (2007b) 'Cohort differences in disease and disability in the young-old: findings from the MRC Cognitive Function and Ageing Study (MRC-CFAS)', *BMC Public Health,* 13(7): 156. doi:10.1186/1471-2458-7-156.

Jette, A.M. (2006) 'Toward a common language for function, disability, and health', *Physical Therapy,* 86: 726–34.

Kaplan, G.A., Turrell, G., Lynch, J.W., et al. (2001) 'Childhood socioeconomic position and cognitive function in adulthood', *International Journal of Epidemiology,* 30: 256–63.

Karasek, R. (1990) 'Lower health risk with increased job control among white collar workers', *Journal of Organizational Behaviour,* 11: 171–85.

Karlamangla, A., Tinetti, M., Guralink, J., Studenski, S., Wetle, T., and Reuben, D. (2007). 'Comorbidity in older adults: nosology of impairment, diseases, and conditions.' *Journals of Gerontology Series A: Medical Sciences,* 62: 296–300.

King, M.B. (2003) 'Falls', in W.R., Hazzard, J.P., Blass, J.B., Halter, et al. (eds), *Principles of Geriatric Medicine and Gerontology,* 5th edn. New York: McGraw-Hill.

Kittleson, M., Meoni, L., Wang, N., Chu, A., Ford, D., and Klag, M. (2006), 'Association of childhood socioeconomic status with subsequent coronary heart disease in physicians', *Archives of Internal Medicine,* 166: 2356–61.

Knopman, D.S. (1998) 'The initial recognition and diagnosis of dementia', *American Journal of Medicine,* 104: 2S–12S.

Koster, A., Penninx, BW., Bosma, H., et al. (2005) 'Is there a biomedical explanation for socioeconomic differences in incident mobility limitation', *Journal of Gerontology. Medical Sciences,* 60A: 1022–7.

Lash, T.L., Mor, V., Wieland, D., Ferrucci, L., Satariano, W., and Silliman, R.A. (2007). 'Methodology, design, and analytic techniques to address measurement of comorbid disease', *Journals of Gerontology Series A: Medical Sciences,* 62: 281–5.

Lawlor, D.A., Ronalds, G., Macintyre, S., Clark, H., and Leon, D.A. (2006) 'Family socioeconomic position at birth and future cardiovascular disease risk: findings from the Aberdeen Children of the 1950s cohort study', *American Journal of Public Health,* 96, 1271–7.

Lievre, A., Alley, D., and Crimmins, E.M. (2008) 'Educational differentials in life expectancy with cognitive impairment among the elderly in the United States', *Journal of Aging and Health,* 20: 456–77.

LIFE Study Investigators (2006) 'Effects of a physical activity intervention on measures of physical performance: results of the lifestyle interventions and independence for elders pilot (LIFE-P) study', *Journal of Gerontology. Medical Sciences,* 61A: 1157–65.

Lynch, J.L. and Davey Smith, G. (2005) 'A life course approach to chronic disease epidemiology', *Annual Review of Public Health,* 26: 1–35.

McEwen, B.S. (1998) 'Stress, adaptation, and disease: allostasis and allostatic load', *Annals of the New York Academy of Sciences,* 840: 33–44.

McWilliams, J.M., Zaslavsky, A.M., Meara, E., and Ayanian, J.Z. (2003) 'Impact of Medicare coverage on basic clinical services for previously uninsured adults', *Journal of the American Medical Association,* 290: 757–64.

Manton, K.G. and Land, K.C. (2000) 'Active life expectancy estimates for the U.S. elderly population: a multidimensional continuous-mixture model of functional change applied to complete cohorts, 1982–1996', *Demography,* 37: 253–65.

Manton, K.G., Stallard, E., and Tolley, H.D. (1991). 'Limits to human life expectancy: evidence, prospects, and implications', *Population and Development Review,* 17: 603–37.

Marenberg, M.E., Risch, N., Berkman, L.F., Floderus, B., and de Faire, U. (1994) 'Genetic susceptibility to death from coronary heart disease in a study of twins', *The New England Journal of Medicine,* 330: 1041–6.

Marmot, M. (2004) *The Status Syndrome: How Social Standing Affects our Health and Longevity.* New York: Times Books.

Marmot, M., Bosma, H., Hemingway, H., Brunner, E., and Stansfeld, S. (1997). 'Contribution of job control and other risk factors to social variations in coronary heart disease incidence.' *Lancet,* 350: 235–9.

Marmot, M.G. and Smith, G.D. (1989) 'Why are the Japanese living longer?', *British Medical Journal,* 299: 1547–51.

Marmot, M.G., Smith, G.D., Stansfeld, S., et al. (1991) 'Health inequalities among British civil servants: the Whitehall II study', *Lancet,* 337: 1387–93.

Melzer, D., Hurst, A.J., and Frayling, T. (2007) 'Genetic variation and human aging: progress and prospects', *Journal of Gerontology. Medical Sciences,* 62A: 301–7.

Merrill, S.S., Seeman, T.E., Kasl, S.V., and Berkman, L.F. (1997) 'Gender differences in the comparison of self-reported disability and performance measures', *Journal of Gerontology. Medical Sciences,* 52: M19–26.

Mirowsky, J. and Ross, C.E. (1998) 'Education, personal control, lifestyle and health: a human capital hypothesis', *Research on Aging,* 20: 415–49.

Moody-Ayers, S.Y., Mehta, K.M., Lindquist, K., Sands, L., and Covinsky, K. (2005) 'Black–White disparities in functional decline in older persons: the role of cognitive function', *Journal of Gerontology. Medical Sciences,* 60A: 933–9.

Murray, C., Kulkarni, S., Michaud C., et al. (2006) 'Eight Americas: investigating mortality disparities across races, counties, and race-counties in the united states', *PLOS Medicine,* 3: e545.

National Center for Health Statistics (1999) 'Total deaths for each cause by 5-year age groups, United States, 1999', Available online at: http://www.cdc.gov/nchs/data/vs00199wktbli.pdf

National Institute of Population and Social Security Research, (Japan) (2000) 'Vital Statistics of the Japanese Population.

Table 5–26', Available online at: http://www1.ipss.go.jp/tohkei/Popular/Popular

Oeppen, J. and Vaupel, J.W. (2002) 'Broken limits to life expectancy', *Science*, 296: 1029–31.

Olshansky, S.J., Carnes, B.A., and Cassel, C. (1990) 'In search of Methuselah: estimating the limits to human longevity', *Science*, 250: 634–40.

Oman, D., Reed, D., and Ferrara, A. (1999) 'Do elderly women have more physical disability than men do?' *American Journal of Epidemiology*, 150: 834–42.

Omran, A.R. (1971) 'The epidemiologic transition: a theory of population change', *The Milbank Memorial Fund Quarterly*, 49: 509–38.

Pederson, N.L., Gatz, M., Berg, S., and Johansson, B. (2004) 'How heritable is Alzheimer's disease late in life? Findings from Swedish twins', *Annals of Neurology*, 55: 180–5.

Perls, T.T., Wilmoth, J., Levenson, R., et al. (2002) 'Life-long sustained mortality advantage of siblings of centenarians', *Proceedings of the National Academy of Sciences*, 99: 8442–7.

Pickett, K.E. and Pearl, M. (2001) 'Multilevel analyses of neighborhood socioeconomic context and health outcomes: a critical review', *Journal of Epidemiology and Community Health*, 55: 111–22.

Ritchie, K., Jagger, C., Brayne, C., and Letenneur, L. (1993) 'Dementia-free life expectancy: preliminary calculations for France and the United Kingdom', in J.M. Robine, C.D. Mathers, M.R. Bone, and I. Romieu, (eds). *Calculation of Health Expectancies: Harmonization, Consensus Achieved and Future Perspectives*. Montepellier: Colloque INSERM.

Ritchie, K., Robine, J.M., Letenneur, L., and Dartigues, J.F. (1994) 'Dementia-free life expectancy in France', *American Journal of Public Health*, 84: 232–6.

Robert, S. (1999) 'Socioeconomic position and health: the independent contribution of community socioeconomic status', *Annual Review of Sociology*, 25: 489–516.

Robine, J-M., Mormiche, P. and Sermet, C. (1998) 'Examination of the causes and mechanisms of the increase in disability-free life expectancy', *Journal of Aging and Health* 10(2): 171–91.

Roelands, M., Van Oyen, H., and Baro, F. (1994) 'Dementia-free life expectancy in Belgium', *European Journal of Public Health*, 4: 33–7.

Ross, C.E. and Mirowsky, J. (2001) 'Neighborhood disadvantage, disorder, and health', *Journal of Health and Social Behavior*, 42: 258–76.

Satariano, W.A. (2006) *Epidemiology of Aging: An Ecological Approach*. Sudbury, MA: Jones and Bartlett.

Schieman, S. (2001) 'Age, education, and the sense of control: a test of the cumulative advantage hypothesis', *Research on Aging*, 23: 153–78.

Schoeni, R.F., Liang, J., Bennett, J., et al. (2006) 'Trends in old-age functioning and disability in Japan, 1993–2002', *Population Studies*, 60(1): 39–53.

Schootman, M., Andresen, E.M., Wolinsky, F.D., et al. (2005) 'Neighborhood conditions and risk of incident lower-body functional limitations among middle-aged African Americans', *American Journal of Epidemiology*, 163: 450–8.

Schulz, R. and Beach, S.R. (1999) 'Caregiving as a risk factor for mortalitiy: the Caregiver Health Effects Study', *The Journal of the American Medical Association*, 282: 2215–19.

Schulz, R. and Martire, L.M. (2004) 'Family caregiving of persons with dementia', *American Journal of Geriatric Psychiatry*, 12: 240–9.

Seeman, T.E. and Crimmins, E. (2001) 'Social environment effects on health and aging: integrating epidemiologic and demographic approaches and perspectives', *Annals of the New York Academy of Sciences*, 954: 88–117.

Seeman, T.E., Crimmins, E., Huang, M., et al. (2004) 'Cumulative biological risk and socio-economic differences in mortality: MacArthur studies of successful aging', *Social Science and Medicine*, 58: 1985–97.

Seeman, T.E., Huang, M., Bretsky, P., et al. (2005) 'Education and APOE-e4 in longitudinal cognitive decline: MacArthur studies of successful aging', *Journal of Gerontology: Psychological Sciences*, 60B: P74–83.

Seeman, T.E. and McEwen, B.S. (1996) 'Social environment characteristics and neuroendocrine function: the impact of social ties and support on neuroendocrine regulation', *Psychosomatic Medicine*, 58: 459–71.

Seeman, T.E., Unger, J.B., McAvay, G., and Mendes de Leon, C.F. (1999) 'Self-efficacy beliefs and perceived declines in functional ability: MacArthur studies of successful aging', *The Journals of Gerontology*, 54: P214–22.

Segerstrom, S.C. and Miller, G.E. (2004) 'Psychological stress and the human immune system: a meta-analytic study of 30 years of inquiry', *Psychological Bulletin*, 130: 601–30.

Smith, J.P. (2005) 'Unraveling the SES–health connection', *Population and Development Review*, 30: 108–32.

Spiers, N.A., Matthews, R.J., Jagger, C., et al. (2005) 'Diseases and impairments as risk factors for onset of disability in the older population in England and Wales: findings from the Medical Research Council Cognitive Function and Ageing Study', *Journal of Gerontology: Medical Sciences*, 60(2): 248–54.

Starfield, B. (2000) 'Is US health really the best in the world?', *Journal of the American Medical Association*, 284: 483–5.

Sudano, J.J. and Baker, D.W. (2003) 'Intermittent lack of health insurance coverage and use of preventive services', *American Journal of Public Health*, 93: 130–7.

Suthers, K., Kim, J.K., and Crimmins, E. (2003) 'Life expectancy with cognitive impairment in the older population of the United States', *Journals of Gerontology: Social Sciences*, 58B: S179–86.

Tanzi, R.E. and Bertram, L. (2001) New frontiers in Alzheimer's disease genetics', *Neurons*, 32: 181–4.

Tinetti, M.E., Speechley, M., and Ginter, S.F. (1988) 'Risk factors for falls among elderly persons living in the community', *New England Journal of Medicine*, 319: 1701–7.

Umberson, D. (1992) 'Gender, marital status and the social control of health behavior', *Social Science and Medicine*, 34: 907–17.

Verbrugge, L.M., and Jette, A.M. (1994) 'The disablement process', *Social Science and Medicine*, 38: 1–14.

Vita, A.J., Terry, R.B., Hubert, H.B., and Fries, J.F. (1998) 'Aging, health risks, and cumulative disability', *New England Journal of Medicine*, 338: 1035–41.

Vogelzangs, N., Beekman, A.T.F., Kritchevsky, S.B., et al. (2007). 'Psychosocial risk factors and the metabolic syndrome in elderly persons: Findings from the Health, Aging, and Body Composition Study.' *Journal of Gerontology Medical Sciences*, 62A: 563–9.

Waite, L.J. (2006) 'Marriage and family', in *Handbook of Population*, D.L. Poston and M. Micklin (eds). New York: Springer.

Wen, M., Browning, C.R., and Cagney, K.A. (2003) 'Poverty, affluence, and income inequality: neighborhood economic structure and its implications for health', *Social Science and Medicine*, 57: 843–60.

Wilkinson, R.G. (1994) 'The epidemiological transition: from material scarcity to social disadvantage?', *Daedalus*, 123: 61–77.

Williams, D.R. (1999) 'Race, socioeconomic status, and health: the added effects of race and discrimination', *Annals of the New York Academy of Sciences*, 896: 173–88.

Winkleby, M.A., Jatulis, D.E., Frank, E., and Fortmann, S.P. (1992) 'Socioeconomic status and health: how education, income, and occupation contribute to risk factors for cardiovascular disease', *American Journal of Public Health*, 82: 816–20.

World Health Organization. (2008) 'The global burden of disease: 2004 update.' Switzerland, World Health Organization.

Wolff, J.L., Starfield, B., and Anderson, G. (2002) 'Prevalence, expenditures, and complications of multiple chronic conditions in the elderly', *Archives of Internal Medicine*, 162: 2269–76.

Yaffe, K., Haan, M., Byers, A., Tangen, C., and Kuller, L. (2000) 'Estrogen use, APOE, and cognitive decline', *Neurology*, 54: 1949–53.

Yancik, R., Ershler, W., Satariano, W., et al. (2007) 'Report of the national institute on aging task force on comorbidity', *Journal of Gerontology. Medical Sciences*, 62A: 275–80.

Web resources in the epidemiology of ageing

National Center for Health Statistics Trends in Health and Aging: http://www.cdc.gov/nchs/agingact.htm

National Institute on Aging Demography Centers: http://agingcenters.org

National Institute on Aging Publications: http://www.nia.nih.gov/HealthInformation/Publications

Federal Interagency Forum on Aging-Related Statistics http://www.agingstats.gov

7

Disability and Ageing: The Social Construction of Causality

Jessica Kelley-Moore

INTRODUCTION

The discourse about ageing and disability is dominated by the perspective that functional decline is a normative part of the human ageing process leading inevitably and irreversibly to disability. Such an understanding is so pervasive in social, medical, and policy domains that it is considered to be axiomatic. Scholars have argued that such a perspective exemplifies ageism because it treats chronological age as a necessary and sometimes even sufficient causal factor in the disablement process, creating a pessimistic and ultimately flawed view of ageing (Riley and Bond, 1983). Others argue that such apologetics which attempt to de-link ageing and disability deny the corporeal constraints that many older adults endure, which can include substantially limited mental and physical function (Hughes and Paterson, 1997). The controversy lies, not in the extent of prevalent disability at advanced ages, but the degree to which organismic-level ageing processes *cause* disablement to the exclusion of social structural influences.

Despite the significant attention that 'ageing' receives in discussions of health and disability, little consideration is given to the impact of social constructions of age and the life course on functional decline. Epidemiological literature has focused extensively on the physiological aspects of the disablement process with only cursory attention to the social environment in which the disability develops (Verbrugge and Jette, 1994). Yet when the course of disability is overlaid on the life course, we have an opportunity to observe potential causes and consequences of disablement that are influenced by extra-individual factors. De-linking the physiological

processes of ageing from disability allows us to examine the social structural and environmental factors that serve to contextualize age and the life course and how those factors influence the timing, meaning, and experience of disability. Accounting for these social and environmental influences reduces the remaining variation that could be accounted for by chronological age or organismic ageing processes.

Even though scholars have long called for such an examination of extra-individual influences on disability over the life course (e.g., Riley and Bond, 1983; Priestley, 2001), little systematic attention has been given to this topic. Among those who have considered these questions, the body of work stops short of conceptually separating ageing from disability, as evidenced by the 'ghettoization' of age groups in disability research. Disability among younger persons, mid-life adults, and older adults is frequently considered independently, with little cross-fertilization of ideas or acknowledgement of life-course processes (e.g., Kane, et al., 2005; Walsh and LeRoy, 2004). Even work that does consider disability in a life-course context is frequently placed in outlets that reach only targeted audiences. For example, Kennedy and Minkler's (1999) chapter on the sociopolitical construction of disability and age, such as their common status as a state-defined dependency, appeared in an edited volume called *Critical Gerontology*. Priestley's work on disability over the life course appears almost exclusively in outlets marketed to disability scholars (e.g., Priestley, 2001, 2003).

This chapter addresses this gap by synthesizing the bodies of work in social gerontology and disability studies to demonstrate how the socially constructed life course influences the experience of both ageing and disability. Implicitly (or explicitly) considering physiological ageing as a dominant causal agent for disability means that we lose the opportunity to understand culture-bound processes of disablement as distinct from physiological processes of ageing, and how assumptions of 'normal' organismic ageing and other aspects of the social context tend to conflate older adults and disabled persons. The chapter has three sections. First, I describe the age distribution of disability in the population and address two misconceptions that frequently appear when explaining the concentration of disability at the oldest ages: (1) this is due to the aggregation of organismic ageing processes; and (2) it is a static or fixed characteristic of the population. These misconceptions have contributed to the demographic imperative, which is the argument that population ageing inevitably leads to a meteoric rise in the number of functionally limited elders, and has shaped the discourse about old-age policy, resource allocation, and health interventions in an ageing society.

The second section addresses the ambiguity in definitions of ageing and disability, which have contributed to the confounding of these processes in both scientific and lay interpretations. I use two illustrative examples to demonstrate the genesis and consequences of this definitional problem: (1) epidemiological studies of frailty in older adulthood; (2) labor force exits among middle-aged adults with chronic health problems. In both cases, social constructions of age and life course are bound up within the enacted or operationalized definition of disability. The final section of the chapter explores the intersectionality of ageing, life course, and disability. De-linking organismic ageing and disablement processes allows us to consider how and in what ways social constructions of age and life course intersect with and potentially influence the experience of disability. Although the causal direction is presumed to be from ageing to disability, there is evidence that the ways in which we socially construct disability likewise frame the meaning and experience of ageing. The chapter proposes new directions for research on disability across the life course, identifying the unique and common experiences of those who age with disabilities; those who acquire them at older ages; young disabled persons; and older non-disabled persons.

CONSTRUCTION OF THE DEMOGRAPIC IMPERATIVE

Scientific and popular media frequently cite a demographic imperative where in the coming decades we will observe a tidal wave of older, disabled persons managing multiple chronic conditions, which could potentially drain economic, healthcare, and social resources. The conclusion in a 1990 White Paper from the American Medical Association stated that '... one of the most important tasks that the medical community faces today is to *prepare for the problems in caring for the elderly* in the 1990s and the early 21st century' (Council on Scientific Affairs, 1990; emphasis added). The National Academy on an Ageing Society, the policy institute of the Gerontological Society of America, introduces its resources on chronic and disabling conditions with the preamble, 'Chronic conditions are the major cause of illness, disability, and death in the United States. Almost 100 million Americans have chronic conditions, and *millions will develop them as America ages*'[1] [emphasis added]. This perspective, which confounds population ageing and individual-level disablement processes, also sometimes called 'apocalyptic demography' (Robertson, 1999), can be observed frequently in discussions of Medicare, long-term care, and Social Security, citing the impending burden and cost that the growing number of older disabled persons will place on these systems (e.g., Friedland and Summer, 1999; LaPlante, 1991).

This supposed demographic imperative, that an inevitable consequence of population ageing is greater proportions of disabled persons, is born out of improperly linking two widely observed and concurrent population patterns: population ageing and the age distribution of disability. In this section, I describe these patterns and identify two misconceptions deriving from their linkage, which have fueled the development of the demographic imperative, and consider the implications of relying on this imperative in policy and healthcare resource debates.

The first pattern is that there is a rapid worldwide increase in the total population who are age 65 or older. In the United States alone, the per cent of persons age 65 or older is projected to increase from 13 per cent in 2010 to 20 per cent in 2050, while the per cent of children under the age of 18 will remain steady around 23 per cent in the same time period (US Census Bureau, 2008). Globally, this has sparked increased high-level attention to the implications of an 'ageing society,' evident in the *International Year of the Older Person* sponsored by the United Nations to highlight the unique issues to be faced in the coming decades. While there is no debate that the population is ageing, this trend is typically coupled with a second demographic distribution, which is that disability prevalence is heavily concentrated among older adults. Figure 7.1 shows the most recent estimates of disability in the US population by age group. Prevalence of limitations in the domains of communication, mental, and physical

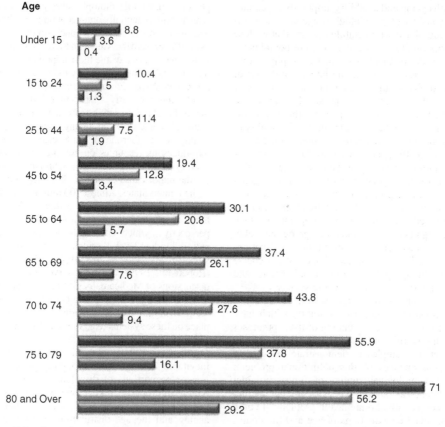

Figure 7.1   Prevelance and the need for assistance by age: 2005 (per cent)

Note: The need for assistance with activities of daily living was not asked of children under 6 years.
Source: US Census Bureau, Survery of Income and Program Participation. June–September 2005.
Originally Published in Brault (2008). US Census Bureau Report, *Americans with Disabilities*: 2005, US Census Bureau.

health increase exponentially across age groups. While only about 9 per cent of children under the age of 15 are classified as disabled, prevalence is greater in older age groups. Nearly 20 per cent of adults ages 45 to 54 are disabled and the prevalence is double that by ages 70 to 74. By these estimates, as many as 71 per cent of adults over the age of 80 have some form of disability (Brault, 2008).

As evidenced by the quotes at the beginning of this section, two key misconceptions about the relationship between population ageing and the age distribution of disability have lent support to the claims of the demographic imperative. First, the age distribution of disability prevalence is frequently interpreted as trend data, leading to conclusions that population ageing will definitively lead to a higher proportion of disabled persons and, more erroneously, that the ageing process itself leads inevitably to disability. Secondly, the currently observed age distribution of disability is a fixed or static characteristic in the

population. In other words, an inevitable consequence of population ageing is a rapidly increasing segment of the population who will drain resources by requiring substantial care. These are premised on the assumption that organismic ageing is a primary cause of disablement, and support a conclusion that, as a society, our best defense is to brace for the unavoidable impact of millions of functionally limited elders. In order to understand how the demographic imperative was constructed, we need to focus on the broader social environment that serves to create, classify, and perpetuate assumptions about impairment and disability.

Limits of organismic ageing for explaining age distribution of disability

The concentration of disability at advanced ages in a population is presumed to be simply the aggregated effects of organismic ageing. There are three premises of this argument: (1) ageing is an organismic process that leads inevitably and irreversibly to disability; (2) a global upward shift in the population that survives to older adulthood is occurring; (3) these older adults, who are ageing 'normally,' will cause a significant increase in prevalent disability in the population, concentrated at these advanced ages. Without doubt, risk of disability is highest in the older-age stratum, and certain ageing-related physiological processes increase that risk. However, the dominant explanatory framework – that rising rates of disability are an inevitable consequence of an ageing population due to the effects of organismic ageing – confounds macro-level associations and micro-level interpretations. Furthermore, it subverts consideration of the substantial variability in opportunities and experiences over the life course that may influence physical and mental functioning among older adults. Given the documented tendency for cohorts to become more heterogeneous as they age (Dannefer, 1987), we must consider the limits of organismic ageing as the primary explanatory factor in individual disablement processes *and* the growing concentration of disability prevalence among older adults in a population.

In this section, I present three examples that challenge the reliance on organismic ageing as a cause of disability: (1) social and medical advances that have simultaneously led to the delay of morbidity and functional limitations until late life *and* allowed more persons to age with disabilities; (2) over-reliance on prevalence estimates in disability counts to the neglect of incidence and duration; (3) standard classification of disability that confounds disease diagnoses, non-disease functional limitations, and age-correlated conditions (e.g., congenital, Alzheimer's disease), often leading to clinical and epidemiological reliance on chronological age in risk assessment, with little consideration of life-course influences on that risk.

First, the relationship between population ageing and the concentration of disability at the oldest ages is frequently assumed to be causal (population ageing leads to more disability), neglecting the possibility that these two phenomena may share an underlying etiology that causes both simultaneously. Increases in longevity have been spurred by improvements in living conditions, reduction of infectious disease, and medical advances (Olshansky and Ault, 1986; Omran, 1971). Humans are living longer and healthier lives, and a greater proportion survive to older ages. The social, medical, and historical processes that have facilitated population ageing have concomitantly allowed for greater numbers to survive with potentially disabling conditions and for more persons to live long enough to develop such conditions. A correlate of

the demographic imperative is that the age distribution of disability in a population will continue to concentrate disability at the highest ages due to 'normal' ageing processes. Elimination of infectious disease and other causes of premature mortality frees the human organism to age 'normally,' which includes late-life disability, an idea that is consistent with the 'compression of morbidity' thesis (Fries, 1980). Even so, this is not to deny an organismic basis for the risk of disability at advanced ages, but considering structural (non-organismic) influences that simultaneously influence both phenomena reduces the amount that can be attributed to biological processes on this observed population-level association.

Secondly, while Figure 7.1 shows the high concentration of disability at upper ages, it is important to note that these are prevalence estimates. We can draw no conclusions from this about age-based trends in disability because there is no information about incidence and duration. How many persons are ageing with disabilities versus how many develop such conditions in older adulthood is a compelling question, but one that has been rarely explored due to the over-reliance on prevalent estimates of disability. Given the extraordinary advances that have been made in population health and medicine, particularly disease management and trauma care, more individuals are surviving to middle and older ages with physical and mental limitations that would have previously been fatal. Social structural factors that increase the likelihood of survival are also producing more persons *ageing with disabilities* than at any other time in history (Shapiro, 1994). Furthermore, data on *severity* of disability are scant, so we do not know the degree to which individuals classified as disabled are limited functionally and in what domains. In prevalence estimates, all forms of disability are treated as equivalent and static, but such an approach obscures the dynamic nature of functional status at all ages.

Thirdly, the definition of disability is extremely broad and captures a range of functional limitations and diseases, many of which are correlated with chronological age but not necessarily caused by it. The question of who 'counts' as disabled has been an ongoing debate for many decades and has resulted in a substantial broadening of the definition of disability (Zola, 1993). The resulting definition of disability confounds disease diagnoses, injuries, sensory impairments, and congenital conditions, making it difficult if not impossible to identify specific age-related patterns of disablement in the population. Box 7.1 shows the standard definition of disability used by the US Census Bureau, a broad classification that includes a number of medical diagnoses that are

Box 7.1   Definitions of a disability in a communication, mental, or physical domain

For people 15 years and older, types of disability were categorized into domains (communication, mental, or physical), according to the following criteria:

Communication
1. Difficulty seeing, hearing, or having their speech understood.
2. Being blind or deaf.
3. Blindness or a vision problem, deafness or a hearing problem, or a speech disorder as a condition contributing to a reported activity limitation.

Mental
1. A learning disability, mental retardation or another developmental disability, Alzheimer's disease, or some other type of mental or emotional condition.
2. Some other mental or emotional condition that seriously interfered with everyday activities.
3. Difficulty managing money/bills.
4. Attention deficit hyperactivity disorder, autism, a learning disability, mental retardation, mental or emotional problems, senility, dementia, or Alzheimer's disease as a condition contributing to a reported activity limitation.

Physical
1. Use of a wheelchair, cane, crutches, or walker.
2. Difficulty walking a quarter of a mile, climbing a flight of stairs, lifting something as heavy as a 10-pound bag of groceries, grasping objects, or getting in or out of bed.
3. Arthritis or rheumatism, back or spine problems, broken bones or fractures, cancer, cerebral palsy, diabetes, epilepsy, head or spinal cord injury, heart trouble or atherosclerosis, hernia or rupture, high blood pressure, kidney problems, lung or respiratory problems, missing limbs, paralysis, stiffness or deformity of limbs, stomach/digestive problems, stroke, thyroid problems, or tumor/cyst/growth as a condition contributing to a reported activity limitation.

Source: Brault 2008. US Census Bureau Report, *Americans with Disabilities*: 2005, US Census Bureau.

correlated with ageing but not necessarily *caused by ageing*. Simply reporting one or more of these conditions is sufficient to be considered disabled. Persons who report an activity limitation due to a range of diseases, including arthritis/rheumatism, diabetes, high blood pressure, or thyroid problems, count as physically disabled. The ambiguity in the relationship between age/ageing and disablement is because many conditions that 'count' as disability are diagnosed in the second half of the life course, producing a robust correlation between risk of onset and chronological age. Yet many of these conditions are due to the accumulation of risk factors over the entire life course, including health behaviors, economic opportunity structures, access to health care, and geographic location. This lends further credence to the argument that disability as a category must be disaggregated so that the risk factors, disease process, and associated functional limitations can be considered in the context of social structure and over the entire life course.

Turning specifically to disability prevalence in the oldest age stratum, physiological ageing processes that may contribute to disablement among older adults are frequently not separated from

other types of physiological processes, specifically end of life. Disability prevalence rates are calculated on survivors in a specific age range. So while the rapidly increasing prevalence of disability in successively older age groups can seem to support the conclusion that disablement is the inevitable outcome of ageing, such figures are misleading because they confuse patterns of mortality with patterns of functional health (Diehr and Patrick, 2003). Those who invoke the demographic imperative rarely acknowledge the link between disability and end-of-life processes, rather presuming that disability is a static and permanent state. The spike of disability at the oldest ages is because risk of mortality is high and many older adults are experiencing terminal declines in function. Empirical studies show that the median duration between onset of severe disability and death is less than 3 months and the median duration between any type of disability transition and death is less than 1 year (Hardy et al., 2005). End of life, and terminal decline more generally, is related to disease or injury processes, independent of chronological age (Yancik et al., 1998). In other words, a dying 60-year-old individual and a dying 80-year-old individual are more alike functionally than their same-age counterparts who are healthy. Given this unique physiological period in a human life span, it calls into question whether end-of-life processes are truly the same as disablement, even when functional impairments are equivalent.

In sum, the demographic imperative is premised on the assumption that population ageing leads inevitably to the concentration of disability prevalence at advanced ages. There is no debate that certain aspects of physiological ageing increase exponentially the risk of disablement at older ages. Yet these processes are frequently treated as the *only* explanatory factor for functional decrements with age. This section has sought to demonstrate that recognizing social structural influences over the life course calls into question the significance of organismic ageing as the dominant causal influence on disablement. Social structural forces are often observed as the *barriers* to 'normal' ageing by contributing to premature mortality and morbidity. Yet it is the social structure that serves to classify and define disability and provides *opportunities* for persons with early, mid- and even late-life disabilities to survive and continue to age despite functional limitations. Disaggregating the types of disabilities and recognizing other concurrent processes such as end of life shows the dynamic pattern of physical function over the entire life course. To date, in both life-course and disability scholarship, this has received little attention.

Dynamic shifts in the age distribution of disability

The second misconception that frequently appears in discussions of population ageing is that the age distribution of disability, particularly the concentration of disability at the oldest ages (as shown in Fig. 7.1), is a fixed or static characteristic of a population. Prevalence rates of disability across age groups provide only a static picture and, as noted above, can lead to erroneous causal explanations linking ageing to disability processes. Considering such a distribution to be static precludes social structural explanations for both population ageing and disability rates. In order to examine trends in disability, we need to disaggregate the types of disability and then compare age differences in prevalence and incidence between birth cohorts. Once we begin to examine specific conditions or diseases that could lead to functional limitations, we are able to see the differences in functional health across and within cohorts, perhaps showing a 'phasing in' or a 'phasing out' of a particular condition as cohorts age, due to

contextual differences. Taking into account such complex cohort-based patterns may significantly weaken the explanatory power of chronological age for disability in a population.

First, we observe a 'phasing out' of certain types of disability as cohorts advance. When prevention and intervention efforts are effective enough, younger cohorts have better prognoses and fewer functional limitations throughout the collective life course. A compelling illustration of this phenomenon is polio vaccination. Following the successful field trials of Salk's polio vaccine in children in 1955, the United States launched a nationwide immunization campaign. The number of new reported cases of polio dropped from nearly 20,000 annual cases in the late 1940s to just 161 new cases in 1961 (Himman, 1984). The last confirmed case of poliovirus in North and South America was located in Peru in 1991 (World Health Organization, 2008). In first-world nations, survivors with residual complications from polio are in earlier birth cohorts and will eventually be replaced by cohorts that have a prevalence rate of zero. Indeed, in the United States, the youngest polio survivors are in their 50s, and have lived 40 years or more since their bout with childhood polio (Mitka, 2006). Currently, persons with post polio syndrome are concentrated in the second half of the life course and will eventually disappear as new cohorts replace them. There are ongoing efforts to eliminate polio from developing nations and, with their success, we will observe a similar 'phasing out' of residual complications from polio in these parts of the world.

Alternatively, we could observe a 'phasing in' of particular types of disability as more recent birth cohorts have a higher prevalence of other disabling conditions. This can occur because of a more effective medical treatment that increases the likelihood of survival for conditions once considered to be fatal. For example, survival rates following spinal cord injuries (SCI) have improved exponentially in the past 80 years. Vast improvements in both first-response trauma care and management of secondary complications (e.g., decubitus ulcers or 'bed sores') have reduced adverse risks. As a result, the number of persons living with spinal cord injuries has increased with successive cohorts. To illustrate, the number of US soldiers who sustained and survived SCI resulting from combat increased from fewer than 400 in World War I to more than 2000 in World War II (Shapiro, 1994). Today, even though spinal cord and column injuries are one of the three most common injuries sustained in combat, 5-year survival rates are nearly equivalent to non-injured peers (Rish et al., 1997). Veterans Affairs currently manages the health care of nearly 26,000 veterans with SCI and is beginning to address the needs that arise as they age.[2] Since spinal cord injuries occur overwhelmingly among adolescents and young adults, with improvement in long-term survival, this is one way we could potentially observe increasing disability with successive cohorts, replacing less disabled cohorts.

The third type of potential shift in the age distribution of disability is simultaneously an increase in the entire population *and* a 'phasing in' with successive cohorts. Social and cultural shifts in food consumption and physical activity have led to a 'fattening' of the entire nation, which has increased the disease burden associated with excess body weight (Ogden et al., 2006). In the past two decades, rates of diabetes, hypertension, and other complications of obesity have substantially increased across all age groups (Flegal, 2005). While such consequences of long-term excess body weight are generally observed in the second half of the life course, children and teenagers are developing Type II diabetes and/or hypertension at an alarming rate. Since there is compelling evidence that secular increases in the proportion of obese persons will affect morbidity rates but only negligibly affect mortality rates, we expect to observe higher disease and disability prevalence at all ages as current cohorts replace previous cohorts (Flegal, 2005). We have already observed a significant increase in diabetes-related work disability in the past 20 years (Stoddard et al., 1998).

The two misconceptions presented here – that the age distribution of disability in a population is both organismically bound and a fixed characteristic – presume that ageing temporally precedes disability. Although risk of functional limitations is undoubtedly highest at advanced ages, the demographic imperative relies unduly on the ageing process, framing disablement as an inevitable consequence of growing old. This perspective further underscores the stereotypes of socially unproductive elders who drain economic and health care resources and is used as justification for limiting resources for older adults such as preventive screenings for cancer (Maheshwari et al., 2008). An ageing population provides opportunities for more vertical integration of age in social institutions, but much of this has not been considered because of the presumption that these new waves of elders will be too functionally limited to participate in such activities.

Viewing functional decline as part of normative age-related changes in the body implies that disablement is immune to prevention, so intervention efforts should focus on delaying (inevitable) impairment or preventing secondary conditions (Fried et al., 2004). As a consequence, much less attention has been paid to the onset of potentially disabling conditions (which frequently occur in early and mid-life), predictors and unequal distribution of risk for these conditions over the entire life course, and the growing number of adults who are ageing with disabilities. Relying on the demographic imperative as an explanatory framework thus obscures the diversity of disability and disablement processes across the entire life course, and may deflect attention from policy initiatives to reduce them. Although one pathway is to develop disabilities in old age, other pathways include ageing with chronic conditions that are potentially disabling; ageing with a stable impairment such as deafness; recovering from acute health events, including stroke and hip fracture; and having congenital or early-life disabilities that could lead to premature mortality.

Since changes in the human genome that may affect ageing and/or disability are exceedingly slow to occur (operating only through natural selection), these do not explain the relatively rapid changes in the age distribution of disability that has occurred over the past century. The examples in this section illustrate the importance of considering social structural influences on disability, dynamics that are only detectable by comparing differences in the age distribution of disability across cohorts. Once we begin looking beyond ageing, and old age in particular, as the dominant explanation for the high concentration of mental, physical, and sensory decrements in older adulthood, the disablement process no longer seems inevitable and immune to intervention.

Definitions of ageing and disability: genesis and consequences of the ambiguity

The tendency to confound ageing with disability extends beyond demographic distributions in a population. There are significant definitional ambiguities in epidemiology, medicine, and policy stemming largely from efforts to classify individuals based on criteria such as working status that are conflated with social constructions of the life course. In this section, I present two illustrative examples that demonstrate these definitional ambiguities, and discuss the potential consequences of such an approach. The over-reliance on chronological age in determining whether or not someone is disabled is based on the assumption that age represents a set of homogeneous risks of disablement. Although ageing is presumed to contribute to disablement, and indeed the social constructions of age, ageing, and life course contextualize and influence the disablement process, both of these illustrations demonstrate that disability or functional limitations can conversely influence the social experience of age and the life course. Failing to consider these reciprocal influences denies researchers of opportunities to consider the complex and dynamic social forces at work on the experience of both.

Frailty among older adults

In an attempt to decompose the disablement process in old age, epidemiologists have concentrated efforts on identifying indicators of frailty, which is a physiological state entailing reduced stamina and strength. This 'phenotype,' as coined by Fried et al. (2001), is defined as a 'pathologic condition that results in a constellation of signs and symptoms and is characterized by high susceptibility, impending decline in physical function and high risk of death' (Ferrucci et al., 2003: 132). Frailty and disability, it is argued, are separate states that can reciprocally influence each other. Ferrucci et al. (2003) argue that the etiology of frailty is '… that disease, disuse, and ageing 'per se' trigger a mechanism that exhausts the redundancy of muscular and nervous backup systems and, when the damage goes beyond the threshold of possible compensation, leads to a measurable decline in physical performance' (emphasis added). Reflecting this definitional ambiguity, in a review of 34 studies measuring frailty conducted by Fried et al. (2001), 9 of them used chronological age as a specific indicator of frailty.

This conceptualization of frailty confounds social constructions of age, age-correlated physiological changes, end-of-life processes, and disability. Common indicators of frailty, which include weight loss, exhaustion, amount of physical activity, walking speed, and grip strength (Fried et al., 2001), could potentially indicate one or more of these processes simultaneously. For example, exhaustion calls into question the overlap between mental health and somatic complaints in older adults (Mirowsky and Ross, 1992). Furthermore, physical activity, walking speed, and grip strength share the problem of being both causes and effects of disablement. Intervention studies have demonstrated that 'practice' of these activities helps retain strength and even regain muscle strength. Yet if older adults are too ill or have too much pain to continue activities that use those muscle groups, there can be a precipitous decline in functional capacity.

While researchers acknowledge that the triggers for the frailty process could include '… inadequate nutrition, poor cognitive function, lack of social support, immobilization and other,' there is little consideration of the social structural context in which persons age that may lead to these physiological declines (Ferrucci et al., 2003: 133). Although it is acknowledged that the social and physical environment could precipitate frailty (Markle-Reid and Browne, 2003; Raphael et al., 1995) these social origins are rarely considered. Frailty is classified as a physiological syndrome even though much of its etiology is grounded in the enacted social constructions of age. It may be fruitful for gerontologists to follow the approach of disability scholars, who employ a social constructionist perspective to describe the 'disabling environment' as the social, economic, political, and physical features of our worlds that create and perpetuate dependency for individuals (Oliver, 1995; Siebers, 2008). Focusing on the social construction of the environment does not deny the corporeality of functional limitations, decrements, or even pain. Rather, these are bound up within diminished social expectations for seniors, social structures that exclude or isolate older adults, and other features of our constructed world that homogenize and de-stimulate the lives of older adults (Riley and Bond, 1983).

Thus, inadequate attention has been paid to the degree that the socially constructed environment of older adults is disabling or frailty-inducing. Living a culturally consonant lifestyle in the 'third age' could lead to a decline in mental acuity or lean muscle mass, which are identified risk factors for frailty (Fried et al., 2001). For example, there are fewer social roles available to older adults, commonly associated with more time spent in or near the home, less exposure to age-heterogeneous contexts, and in many cases, less overall activity (Riley and Foner, 1968). These older adults may experience atrophy in mental and physical function because they no longer participate in the types of complex and multidimensional activities as they had earlier in the life course. Indeed, empirical evidence indicates higher rates of frailty among those seniors who are socially isolated, participate in fewer social activities, and have smaller circumscribed life space (Satariano, 2006; Strawbridge et al., 1998). Reducing the challenges that the body or mind must accomplish can lead to a decrease in compensatory mechanisms and may trigger a cascade of functional decline (Ferrucci et al., 2003).

Frailty is one illustration of the broader problem of failing to put disease processes, functional decline, and even disablement in the broader social context. As a result, chronological age becomes a useful marker of likely characteristics in the social environment that influence physical and mental health. Ironically, if social constructions of age, including social roles, level of engagement in the community and family, and expected levels of activity, were not so overwhelmingly homogenized for older adults, it is possible that 'syndromes' such as frailty would not even exist but would rather be one of a diverse array of functional outcomes in late life. Disability scholars and social gerontologists do not deny that health decrements and functional limitations can and do occur, particularly among older adults. Rather, social constructions of both age and disability frame our expectations for 'normal' ageing and can also directly influence behavior, social engagement, and aggressiveness of medical care, all of which can influence functional outcomes.

LABOR FORCE EXITS AMONG MID-LIFE ADULTS WITH CHRONIC HEALTH PROBLEMS

In the United States and other industrialized nations, policymakers have used employment status and the ability to work as the defining state for both disability and old age (see Kennedy and Minkler, 1999 for a review). Employment disability, measured only for adults age 16–64, is defined as difficulties finding a job or remaining employed due to a health-related condition (Brault, 2008). Once adults reach the State-defined normal retirement age (e.g., age 65 in the United States), disability status is no longer relevant because subsequent benefits are entitlements based on chronological age. In other words, from a policy perspective, a person who is disabled at age 64 is simply 'old' at age 65. This is a compelling example of the way that chronological age supplants functional status in defining an individual's relationship to the State. A consequence of an age-determined benefit structure is that there are currently no provisions for those who age into Social Security eligibility with severe disabilities. All benefits are based solely on chronological age, not on functional need, in part because we presume functional dependency among *all* older adults.

There are a number of pathways through which one can cease work and enter the 'third age,' yet not all carry the same social affirmation or reward. Transitioning from the labor force to disability benefits creates a moral hazard for middle-aged adults with chronic health conditions. In order to qualify for the benefits the worker has to enter into a structurally dependent relationship with the State, which is accompanied by substantial social costs. The worker's health status becomes a public matter that is subject to medical, occupational, and political scrutiny. Given the substantial difficulty in establishing and maintaining one's disability status in order to qualify, individuals must embrace the label of disability internally and externally. Since disability benefits to working-age adults is not an entitlement, the question of 'deservedness' surfaces. Fraudulent claims of disability are investigated aggressively, so individuals frequently must curtail social and physical activities to ensure that their lifestyle is consonant with the diminished social expectations of a disabled or chronically ill person (Genton, 2003).

Adults who leave the labor force via working-age disability benefits lose the opportunity to achieve the normative life-course transition of retirement. In late modernity, retirement has come to represent a valued life stage characterized by the pursuit of personal interests that contribute to the fulfillment of personhood (Costa, 1998; Phillipson, 1999). Retirement is a celebrated rite of passage and carries a socially affirmed label. Early retirement (defined here as leaving the labor force prior to the State-defined normal retirement age) is a type of 'off-time' life-course transition that can be socially desirable because the period of 'leisure' and self-directed activity can begin sooner than is normatively expected. It signals that an individual has sufficient assets to maintain a comfortable lifestyle without at least the immediate help of old-age entitlements such as Social Security retirement benefits and Medicare.

Demonstrating systematic differences in wealth accumulation and anticipated retirement income, Black and Hispanic workers are more likely to leave paid employment through disability insurance whereas White workers are more likely to retire (Brown and Warner, 2008). Additionally, the 'risk' of seeking disability insurance peaks when adults are in their 50s and then precipitously declines as their age approaches Social Security eligibility (Hayward et al., 1996). Although retirement and labor force exit more generally are elements of the socially constructed life course, chronological age is frequently the determining factor for which type of employment transitions an individual makes.

Thus, the type of transition out of the workforce is bound up in actual health status, State definitions of disability, socioeconomic stratification, timing in the life course, and chronological age. Early retirement, for those who can afford it, creates a socially rewarded identity that can allow mounting functional declines or debilitating chronic conditions to remain privatized rather than thrust into the public sphere. Furthermore, those who voluntarily leave the labor force and do not pursue disability benefits do not have to justify their decision based on health and functional status. It is likely that early retirees could actually cease paid work *earlier* in the disablement process than is structurally allowed for those who rely on disability benefits. There has been little systematic attention paid to the ways in which the social constructions of age, disability, and retirement interact.

INTERSECTIONALITY OF AGE, LIFE COURSE, AND DISABILITY

De-linking organismic ageing from disability as a causal explanatory framework actually provides an opportunity to consider how the socially constructed life course and disability experience intersect. The timing of onset, severity, and progression of disabling conditions affects the way in which an individual interacts with the larger social environment, including family, work, and the healthcare system. Persons who age with disabilities and those who acquire them in older ages share some common challenges, but these groups are quite different in many aspects (Brietenbach, 2001). Furthermore, confounding organismic ageing and disability means a missed opportunity to consider the social experience of those who do not fit the presumed 'normative' categories: (1) non-disabled older adults; (2) young disabled persons.

Although gerontologists have long emphasized that older-age strata are diverse and we should resist homogenized characterizations of ageing (Dannefer, 1988; Maddox, 1986), disabled persons have not enjoyed the same focus on diversity and heterogeneity. Society's treatment of disability, particularly for young disabled persons, has resulted in a 'collective biographical pattern' marked by limited life choices, marginalization from mainstream activities, and dominant paternalism (Evans and Furlong, 1997; Tisdall, 2001). Given the diversity of mental and physical conditions that can lead to impairment and widely variable experiences of these conditions, we cannot (but frequently do) make generalized statements about the 'disabled life course' or 'disability experience' (Priestley, 2001). For example, some chronic conditions such as multiple sclerosis can be episodic and require intense disease management, whereas others such as deafness may be stable and require few or no healthcare resources.

Comparing younger and older disabled persons is an illustrative way to demonstrate how the socially constructed life course can be such a powerful influence on individuals. Older adulthood, stereotypically associated with declining health and greater dependency, can actually buffer one's self-concept as disablement occurs. Persons who experience impairments later in life are less likely to develop a 'disability-rooted' identity (Turnbull and Turnbull, 1999; Zink, 1992). This is because the experience and meaning of disability is bound within the socially constructed life course with its meaningful roles, transitions, and normative expectations. Those who have already experienced many life domains such as education

and employment as able-bodied persons may be less likely to orient their sense of self around the ability (or inability) to fulfill these social roles, reducing the perception of biographical disruption (Breitenbach, 2001; Williams, 2000; Zink, 1992). Many older adults who acquire limitation in one or more activities of daily living do not even consider themselves disabled although traditional medical and policy definitions would define them as such (Kelley-Moore et al., 2006; Langlois et al., 1996). Even older adults themselves frequently accept the diminished social expectations and 'normative' decrements in health (Priestley, 2003; Riley and Foner, 1968). Since social constructions of the life course place significant emphasis on early- and mid-life roles in determining achievement and value in society, becoming disabled early in life can have a substantial impact on the ageing experience, as disability can be the 'filter through which life flows,' affecting employment, spousal and parental roles, healthcare experiences, and even identity (Zink, 1992).

Even social networks can vary substantially between young and older disabled persons, further perpetuating the social constructions of both disability and life course. Young people who cannot participate in the types of normative activities where friendships spontaneously develop often must rely on siblings and parents for primary friendships (Rowlands, 2001). In this way, the family becomes the 'scaffolding' for the young disabled person's social world. Unwittingly, families can also be a significant agent for the stereotypes about disabled persons, informally discouraging particular life choices such as marriage or parenthood, independent living arrangements, or educational opportunities (Johnson et al., 2001). The inability to achieve normatively expected roles such as these can greatly influence perceptions of social worth. Conversely, family and non-family networks for older adults with functional limitations are frequently framed as buffers or moderators that keep the elder socially engaged (Shanas, 1986).

Although we predominantly concentrate on the ways in which constructions of age and the life course affect disability, there is evidence that the social construction of disability frames the meaning and experience of ageing as well. Persons with developmental disabilities, for example, are considered to be 'old before their time' and are perceived to age faster than their non-disabled peers (Bogdan and Biklin, 1993). More generally, younger persons with severe physical disabilities or degenerating chronic conditions tend to view getting older differently from those who do not experience disability until an advanced age. There can be apprehension about future mental or physical decrements and the ability to continue compensating for current limitations (Siebers, 2003; Zola, 1982). For some conditions, anticipated life expectancy can even be truncated (Murphy, 1990). On a positive note, persons who are ageing with disabilities or disabling conditions tend to be more proactive in the planning and management of potential long-term care needs relative to those who do not have current health problems (Iezzoni, 2003). This is often sparked by concern that family or friends have to provide substantial care.

The meaning of health, illness, and disability is bound up in the social construction of the life course such that there are perceptions of 'on time' and 'off time' periods to be functionally limited by health problems. Bury (1982)'s conceptualization of chronic illness as biographical disruption demonstrates the ways in which young and midlife adults can perceive disabling conditions as interrupting life and even thwarting future goals. Young, severely disabled persons can feel that life never even got started since they may fail to achieve markers of the normative life course such as living independently or being employed (Tisdall, 2001). At the other end of the life course, non-disabled older adults are frequently considered to be extraordinary, even rare specimens to be studied (e.g., Clark, 1995). This reveals the power of socially constructed disability in shaping life-course outcomes, particularly in determining identity, social value of individuals, and barriers to achieving full human potential.

'You Are Just Getting Older'

Narratives of medical encounters for older adults and persons ageing with disabilities have frequently included a similar frustrating scene where a physician dismisses specific health concerns as part of normal ageing. Persons with disabling chronic conditions at any age have to battle dismissive health diagnoses that attribute all symptoms to the disability itself (Scheer et al., 2003). An as-yet unaddressed question is the ways that these gestalt explanations for physical or mental health problems intersect for older adults with disabilities. Whether the disability was acquired in late life or earlier, many medical personnel fail to consider reported symptoms as potentially new health problems but rather symptoms of the existing disabling condition, normal ageing, or both. Such negligence can lead to delayed diagnoses, fewer preventive screenings, and limited access to rehabilitative services (Iezzoni, 2003; Neri and Kroll, 2003). As a consequence, older

persons with disabilities typically have to be more proactive in seeking care. As an older woman with multiple sclerosis recounted in an interview:

> My joints started getting sore – probably twenty years ago. The doctor that I went to then passed it off for a few years: 'Oh, it's just a little arthritis. You're getting older, and everybody has that. You just have to live with it.' But after a few years, I thought there might be some more comfortable way to live with the arthritis. A friend at a Boston hospital gave me a recommendation for a doctor over there. I went, and he sent me to a physical therapist and gave me exercises and things that really helped me. He did as much as he needed to do in two visits. Doctors really need to listen to the patients in the beginning. They shouldn't say, 'Oh, that's nothing.' (Quoted from Iezzoni, 2003: 138)

The ageing experience, in myriad ways, does influence the disability experience, both through physiological changes that are correlated with age and through the social experience of age. For example, there can be age-associated declines in the ability to compensate for functional limitations which require more intensive intervention for disabilities over time (Ferrucci et al., 2003). Among persons ageing with degenerative chronic conditions, rehabilitation goals frequently focus not on recovery of function, but on strategies to maintain current levels of function or compensating for recent declines (Zola, 1982). Even though increasing impairment may be solely symptomatic of the condition itself, 'ageing' has been given a tremendous amount of credit for declines in physical and mental function among those who acquire disabilities throughout the life course. Persons ageing with disabilities, even those who have had intensive care and therapy previously, must confront ageism in health care, such as the dominant pessimistic view that older adults can receive few long-term benefits from rehabilitation and are therefore not worth the resource investment (Becker, 1994; Scott and Couzens, 1996). Reduction or elimination of aggressive rehabilitation may hasten physiological decline, leading to greater impairment and more dependency.

Whereas early conceptions of successful ageing focused on the avoidance of disease and disability (Rowe and Kahn, 1987), researchers increasingly recognize that successful agers may also include those who effectively manage chronic conditions, adapt to limitations, and continue to maintain desired levels of activities (Walsh and LeRoy, 2004). Disability scholars, in part spurred by the independent living movement, have emphasized alternative definitions of independence, which include the ability to make decisions and have desires respectfully fulfilled, even when the individual cannot perform the actions themselves (Shapiro, 1994; Siebers, 2003). Persons who are older *and* disabled are at the greatest risk of losing their voice in directing their own care as significant others such as family and medical personnel subscribe to the ageist and 'ableist' assumptions of dependency and helplessness. Yet as more people age with disabilities we are likely to observe changes in the social expectations of older adults, even those who are functionally limited. These seniors may have greater levels of advocacy, expectation for services, and more self-directed care in older adulthood, which are tools for successful ageing.

CONCLUSIONS

Social constructions of age, ageing, and the life course play particularly important roles in the experience and meaning of disability, yet scant attention has been paid to the cultural meaning (and its implications) of disablement at all ages. In demographic, epidemiological, and policy domains, there has been an over-reliance on organismic ageing processes as the explanatory framework to the exclusion of social structural influences. This chapter set out to demonstrate that presumptions about 'normal' ageing leading inevitably and irreversibly to disability in older adulthood stems from these constructions of ageing. Additionally, it is invoked to justify use of chronological age as a marker of disability risk independent of actual health status. The assumption is that the natural course of functional decline and impairment with increasing age legitimizes allocation of benefits or rationing of medical treatment in older adulthood. Yet, current estimates indicate that the onset of severe disability is occurring at increasingly older ages (Schoeni et al., 2008), calling into question the utility of chronological age as a marker of disability risk. If old age and disability are presumed to be synonymous, does the delayed onset of disability mean that old age itself is being delayed?

There is no question that age-associated physiological changes increase risk of disablement at older ages. Rather, the challenge is in the degree to which we over-attribute causality to organismic processes in functional decline and under-consider the influence of the ways we characterize age and the process of ageing in society. The implications for social integration and identity among those who are disabled hinge on the age of onset and its timing in the life course. For example, becoming disabled prior to old age is framed as non-normative and disruptive to the life course. In effect, the negative meanings of disability and the perceived 'off time' experience of the impairment shapes subsequent life chances and available social roles for these younger disabled persons. Alternatively, becoming functionally limited in older adulthood is framed as normative, and this confounding of ageing and disability fuels lowered expectations for independence and self-directed care. Baltes and Wahl (1996) demonstrated this with their work on nursing home scripts where dependencies take institutional priority and independent behaviors are largely ignored.

Furthermore, disability is frequently defined and constructed as a homogeneous category that is both permanent and stable. This classification of disability obscures the diverse pathways through which an individual may become – and may or may not remain – functionally limited and its implications for adjustment and identity. Illness-based disabilities are frequently associated with older adults, whereas injury-based disabilities are associated with younger persons. Although some work has differentiated between progressive and catastrophic disabilities for older adults (Ferrucci et al., 1996), there has been little comparative work considering the social experience among those of the same age with different types of disabilities and those of different ages with the same disabilities. Once again, the ghettoization of disability research into age categories perpetuates assumptions about normative pathways to disablement and timing in the life course.

To date, the social constructions of age, ageing, and life course have received only cursory attention in the disablement process. Social constructions of disability can and do shape the ageing experience and opportunities across the life course, but this relationship has received even less attention. Failure to examine the social structural context in which persons age *and* in which persons become disabled risks over-reliance on explanations linked to organismic ageing processes. The cumulative life course, which includes health behaviors, availability of and access to medical treatment, and even normative expectations for health problems, can and does influence the types of disabilities, duration of time spent functionally limited, and even the severity of conditions. Heterogeneity in life-course pathways, which are culturally, socioeconomically, and geographically bound, most certainly leads to heterogeneity in functional outcomes at all ages. Systematic consideration of these social structural influences will help us consider the potential limits of organismic ageing in the disablement process.

NOTES

1 National Academy on an Ageing Society (2008). Retrieved on March 19, 2009 from http://www. agingsociety.org/agingsociety/publications/chronic/index.html

2 Veterans Affairs (2009) 'VA and Spinal Cord Injury.' Office of Public Affairs Media Relations Fact Sheet. Retrieved on March 3, 2009 from http://www1.va.gov/opa/fact/spinalcfs.asp

REFERENCES

Baltes, M.M. and Wahl, H-W. (1996) 'Patterns of communication in old age: the dependence-support and independence-ignore script', *Health Communication*, 8: 217.

Becker, G. (1994) 'Age bias in stroke rehabilitation – effects on adult status', *Journal of Aging Studies*, 8: 271–90.

Bogdan, R. and Biklen, D. (1993) 'Handicapism', in Mark Nagler (ed.), *Perspectives of Disability*. Palo Alto, CA: Health Markets Research. pp. 69–76.

Brault, M. (2008) 'Americans with disabilities: 2005', *Current Population Reports*, P70–117, Washington, DC.: US Census Bureau.

Breitenbach, N. (2001) 'Ageing with intellectual disabilities: discovering disability with old age: same or different?', in M. Priestley (ed.), *Disability and the Life Course: Global Perspectives*. Cambridge, MA: Cambridge University Press, pp. 231–9.

Brown, T.H. and Warner, D.F. (2008) 'Divergent pathways? Racial/ethnic differences in women's labor force withdrawal', *Journal of Gerontology: Social Sciences*, 63B: S122–34.

Bury, M. (1982) 'Chronic illness as biographical disruption', *Sociology of Health and Illness*, 4: 167–82.

Clark, E. (1995) *Growing Old is Not For Sissies II*. San Francisco, CA: Pomegranate Books.

Costa, D.L. (1998) *The Evolution of Retirement*. Oxford: Oxford University Press.

Council on Scientific Affairs (1990) 'Elderly health', American Medical Association White Paper. *Archives of Internal Medicine*, 150: 2459–72.

Dannefer, D. (1987) 'Aging as intracohort differentiation: accentuation, the Matthew effect, and the life course', *Sociological Forum*, 2: 211–36.

Dannefer, D. (1988) 'Differential gerontology and the stratified life course: conceptual and methodological issues', *Annual Review of Gerontology and Geriatrics*, 8: 3–36.

Diehr, P. and Patrick, D.L. (2003) 'Trajectories of health for older adults over time: accounting fully for death', *Annals of Internal Medicine*, 139: 416–20.

Evans, K. and Furlong, A. (1997) 'Metaphors of youth transitions: niches, pathways, trajectories or navigations', in J. Bynner, L. Chisholm, and A. Furlong (eds), *Youth, Citizenship and Social Change in a European Context*. Aldershot: Avebury.

Ferrucci, L., Guralnik, J.M., Simonsick, E., et al. (1996) 'Progressive versus catastrophic disability: a longitudinal view of the disablement process', *Journal of Gerontology: Medical Sciences*, 51: M123–30.

Ferrucci, L., Guralnik, J.M., Cavazzini, C., et al. (2003) 'The frailty syndrome: a critical issue in geriatric oncology', *Critical Reviews in Oncology/Hematology*, 46: 127–37.

Flegal, K.M. (2005) 'Epidemiologic aspects of overweight and obesity in the United States', *Physiology and Behavior*, 86: 599–602.

Fried, L.P., Tangen, C.M., Walston, J., et al. (2001) Frailty in older adults: evidence for a phenotype', *Journal of Gerontology: Medical Sciences*, 56A: M146–56.

Fried, L.P., Ferrucci, L., Darer, J., Williamson, J.D., and Anderson, G. (2004) 'Untangling the concepts of disability, frailty, and comorbidity: implications for improved targeting and care', *Journal of Gerontology: Medical Sciences*, 59: 255–63.

Friedland, R.B. and Summer, L. (1999) *Demography is Not Destiny*. Washington, DC: National Academy on an Aging Society.

Fries, J.F. (1980) Aging, natural death, and the compression of morbidity', *Annals of Internal Medicine*, 139: 455–9.

Genton, C. (2003) 'Chronic back pain sufferers – striving for the sick role.' *Social Science and Medicine*, 57: 2243–52.

Hardy, S.E., Dubin, J.A., Holford, T.R. and Gill, T.M. (2005) 'Transitions between states of disability and independence among older persons', *American Journal of Epidemiology*, 161: 575–84.

Hayward, M.D., Friedman, S., and Chen, H. (1996) 'Race inequities in men's retirement', *Journal of Gerontology: Social Sciences*, 51: S1–10.

Himman, A.R. (1984) 'Landmark perspective: mass vaccination against polio', *JAMA*, 251(22): 2994–6.

Hughes, B. and Paterson, K. (1997) 'The social model of disability and the disappearing body: towards a sociology of impairment', *Disability and Society*, 12: 325–40.

Iezzoni, L. (2003) *When Walking Fails: Mobility Problems of Adults with Chronic Conditions*. Berkeley, CA: University of California Press.

Johnson, K., Traustadottir, R., Harrison, L., Hillier, L., and Sigurjonsdottir, H.B. (2001) 'The possibility of choice: women with intellectual disabilities talk about having children', in M. Priestley (ed.), *Disability and the Life Course: Global Perspectives*. Cambridge, MA: Cambridge University Press, pp. 206–18.

Kane, R.L., Prister, R., and Totten, A.M. (2005) *Meeting the Challenge of Chronic Illness*. Baltimore, MD: Johns Hopkins University Press.

Kelley-Moore, J., Schumacher, J., Kahana, E., and Kahana, B. (2006) 'When do older adults become "disabled"? Social and health antecedents of perceived disability in a panel study of the oldest old', *Journal of Health and Social Behavior*, 47(2): 126–41.

Kennedy, J. and Minkler, M. (1999) 'Disability theory and public policy: implications for critical gerontology', in M. Minkler and C.L. Estes (eds), *Critical Gerontology*. Amityville, NY: Baywood Publishing, pp. 91–108.

Langlois, J.A., Maggi, S., Harris, T., et al. (1996) 'Self-report of difficulty in performing functional activities indentifies a broad range of disability in old age', *Journal of American Geriatrics Society*, 44: 1421–8.

LaPlante, M.P. (1991) 'The demographics of disability', *Milbank Quarterly*, 2: 55–77.

Maddox, G. (1986) 'Aging differently', Robert W. Kleemeier Award Lecture, 39th annual meeting of the Gerontological Society of America, Chicago.

Maheshwari, S., Patel, T., and Patel, P. (2008) 'Screening for colorectal cancer in elderly persons: Who should we screen and when can we stop?', *Journal of Aging and Health*, 20: 126–39.

Markle-Reid, M. and Browne, G. (2003) 'Conceptualizations of frailty in relation to older adults', *Journal of Advanced Nursing*, 44: 58–68.

Mirowsky, J. and Ross, C.E. (1992) 'Age and depression', *Journal of Health and Social Behavior*, 33: 187–205.

Mitka, M. (2006) 'Aging brings new challenges for polio survivors', *JAMA*, 296: 1718–19.

Murphy, R.F. (1990) *The Body Silent*. New York: W.W. Norton.

Neri, M.T. and Kroll, T. (2003) 'Understanding the consequences of access barriers to health care: experiences of adults with disabilities', *Disability and Rehabilitation*, 25: 85–96.

Ogden, C.L., Carroll, M.D., Curtin, L.R., et al. (2006) 'Prevalence of overweight and obesity in the United States, 1999–2004', *JAMA*, 295: 1549–55.

Oliver, M. (1995) 'Rehabilitating society', in *Understanding Disability from Theory to Practice*. New York: St. Martin's Press, pp. 95–109.

Olshansky, S.J. and Ault, A.B. (1986) 'The fourth stage of the epidemiologic transition: the age of delayed degenerative diseases', *Milbank Quarterly*, 64: 335–91.

Omran, A.R. (1971) 'The epidemiologic transition: a theory of population change', *The Milbank Memorial Fund Quarterly*, 49: 509–38.

Phillipson, C. (1999) 'The social construction of retirement: perspectives from critical theory and political economy', in M. Minkler and C.L. Estes (eds), *Critical Gerontology*. Amityville, NY: Baywood Publishing Company, pp. 315–28.

Priestley, M. (2001) *Disability and the Life Course: Global Perspectives*. Cambridge, MA: Cambridge University Press.

Priestley, M. (2003) 'It's like your hair going grey or is it?: impairment, disability, and the habitus of old age', in S. Riddell and N. Watson (eds), *Disability, Culture, and Identity*. Harlow, England: Pearson Prentice Hall, pp. 53–64.

Raphael, D., Cava, M., Brown, I., et al. (1995) 'Frailty: a public health perspective', *Canadian Journal of Public Health*, 86: 224–7.

Riley, M.W. and Bond, K. (1983) 'Beyond ageism: postponing the onset of disability', in M.W. Riley, B.B. Hess, and K. Bond (eds), *Aging in Society: Selected Reviews of Recent Research*. Hillsdale, NJ: Lawrence Erlbaum Associates, pp. 243–52.

Riley, M.W. and Foner, A. (1968) *Aging and Society: An Inventory of Research Findings*, Volume One. New York: Russell Sage Foundation.

Rish, B.L., Dilustro, J.F., Salazar, A.M., Schwab, K.A., and Brown, H.R. (1997) 'Spinal cord injury: a 25-year morbidity and mortality study', *Military Medicine*, 162: 141–8.

Robertson, A. (1999) 'Beyond apocalyptic demography: toward a moral economy of interdependence', in M. Minkler and C.L. Estes (eds), *Critical Gerontology*. Amityville, NY: Baywood Publishing, pp. 75–90.

Rowe, J.W. and Kahn, R.L. (1987) 'Human aging – usual and successful', *Science*, 237: 143–9.

Rowlands, A. (2001) 'Breaking my head in the prime of my life: acquired disability in young adulthood', in M. Priestley (ed.), *Disability and the Life Course: Global Perspectives*. Cambridge, MA: Cambridge University Press, pp. 179–91.

Satariano, W.A. (2006) *Epidemiology of Aging*. Sudbury, MA: Jones and Bartlett Publishers.

Scheer, J., Kroll, T., Neri, M.T., and Beatty, P. (2003) 'Access barriers for persons with disabilities', *Journal of Disability Policy Studies*, 13: 221–30.

Schoeni, R.F., Freedman, V.A. and Martin, L.G. (2008) 'Why is late-life disability declining?', *Milbank Quarterly*, 86(1): 47–89.

Scott, W.A. and Couzens, G.S. (1996) 'Treating injuries in active seniors', *Physician and Sports Medicine*, 24: 63–8.

Shanas, E. (1986) 'The family as a social support system in old age', in L.E. Troll (ed.), *Family Issues in Current Gerontology*. New York: Springer, pp. 85–96.

Shapiro, J.P. (1994) *No Pity: People With Disabilities Forging A New Civil Rights Movement*. New York: Three Rivers Press.

Siebers, T.A. (2003) 'My withered limb', in S. Crutchfield and M. Epstein (eds), *Points of Contact: Disability, Art, and Culture*. Ann Arbor: The University of Michigan Press, pp. 21–30.

Siebers, T.A. (2008) *Disability Theory*. Ann Arbor, MI: University of Michigan Press.

Stoddard, S., Jans, L., Ripple, J., and Kraus, L. (1998) *Chartbook on Work and Disability in the United States, 1998*. An InfoUse Report. Washington, DC: US National Institute on Disability and Rehabilitation Research.

Strawbridge, W., Shema, S.J., Balfour, J.L., Higby, H.R., and Kaplan, G.A. (1998) 'Antecedents of frailty over three decades in an older cohort', *Journals of Gerontology: Social Sciences*, 53: S9–16.

Tisdall, K. (2001) 'Failing to make the transition? Theorising the "transition to adulthood" for young disabled people', in M. Priestley (ed.), *Disability and the Life Course: Global Perspectives*. Cambridge, MA: Cambridge University Press, pp. 167–78.

Turnbull, H.R. and Turnbull, A.P. (1999) 'Family support: retrospective and prospective', in M. Wehmeyer and J. Patton (eds), *Mental Retardation in the Year 2000 and Beyond*. Austin, TX: ProEd, pp. 413–30.

United States Bureau of the Census (2008) 'Population projections of the United States by age, sex, race, and Hispanic origin: 1995 to 2050', *Current Population Reports*, P25–1130.

Verbrugge, L.M. and Jette, A.M. (1994) 'The disablement process', *Social Science and Medicine*, 38: 1–14.

Walsh, P.N. and LeRoy, B. (2004) *Women with Disability Aging Well*. Baltimore, MD: Brookes Publishing.

Williams, S.J. (2000) 'Chronic illness as biographical disruption or biographical disruption as chronic illness? Reflections on a core concept', *Sociology of Health and Illness*, 22: 40–67.

World Health Organization (2008) 'Polio weekly bulletin', *Pan American Health Organization*, 23(51).

Yancik, R., Wesley, M.N., Ries, L.A., et al., (1998) 'Comorbidity and age as predictors of risk for early mortality of male and female colon carcinoma patients: a population-based study', *Cancer*, 82: 2123–34.

Zink, J. (1992) 'Adjusting to early- and late-onset disability', *Generations*, 16: 59–60.

Zola, I. (1982) *Missing Pieces: A Chronicle of Living with a Disability*. Philadelphia: Temple University Press.

Zola, I. (1993) 'Disability statistics, what we count and what it tells us: a personal and political analysis', *Journal of Disability Policy Studies*, 4(2): 10–39.

8

Environmental Perspectives on Ageing

Hans-Werner Wahl and Frank Oswald

INTRODUCTION

According to Dannefer, context, broadly defined,[1] 'refers to the totality of the diverse range of phenomena, events and forces that exist outside the developing individual' (1992: 84). The assumption that ageing occurs in context has meanwhile become, implicitly or explicitly, a core feature of models of ageing in biology, as well as those in the social and behavioural sciences. How such context is defined more concretely and what kind of impact is attributed to context strongly depends on the meta-theoretical perspective on ageing behind each of these disciplinary approaches.

First, in current *biogerontological* theories, ageing is primarily viewed as an internal process of decline related to the flow of chronological age, ending in the event of death (Cristofalo et al., 1999). Environmental conditions are, however, expected to shape the survival time of ageing organisms, because it is generally acknowledged in models of longevity that genetic factors explain less than 30 per cent of variability in survival time in humans and in many other species (Vaupel et al., 2003). The understanding of context in biological models of ageing tends nevertheless to remain rather general, mostly referring to external physical properties such as temperature, kind and quantity of food, or environmental stress.

Secondly, the *social and behavioural sciences* have put major emphasis on the operation of historical, cultural, and societal contexts, and how these shape ageing processes. As has been convincingly argued, historical events along with societal expectations and norms play a critical role in the sequencing of the life course[2] from its very beginning to its very end (Baars et al., 2006; Dannefer, 1992; Elder, 1974). Hence, sociologists often focus on characteristics such as social class, cohort, and community-level variables to address the impact of contexts on older adults both today and in the future (e.g., see Phillipson, 2007).

Psychological models of human ageing have also argued that the contextual component of life-span and adult life development is critical to understanding development and ageing (Baltes et al., 1980, 1998). As compared to social science perspectives, the emphasis is more on *micro* rather than *macro* levels of person–environment (p–e) interfaces. That is, a fundamental psychological challenge for ageing individuals is continuously to adjust their relationship with the environment that they inhabit. Such adjustments may be required, for example, by loss in functional capacity (implying the need to relocate to a barrier-free environment), or by major life events related to ageing, such as the experience of retirement (occasioning, for instance, changes in the use of everyday living space at home with a partner). Accordingly, a major research task of psychological gerontology is to describe and explain stability and change of p–e dynamics as people age.

An additional approach to defining context, which has evolved within gerontology, places major emphasis on the physical environmental sphere. Social gerontology has always acknowledged the critical role of physical surroundings on older people. This was illustrated by the detailed treatment of the role of housing for older people in one of the first handbooks in the field, edited by Tibbitts (1960). Alongside the evolution of social gerontology, a subdiscipline emerged with strong nurturance from Kleemeier's work (1959), which has been called '*environmental gerontology*' (other terms include 'the ecology of ageing'). This research arena, founded on the basic principle that old age is a critical phase in the life course and can be characterized by the profound influence of the physical environment, was greatly expanded between the 1960s and 1980s by scholars such as Lawton (e.g. Lawton and Nahemow, 1973), Carp (1966), and Kahana (1982). Finally, the appearance of environmental psychology played a major role, with early contributions to ageing research illustrated in Barker and Barker's (1961) treatment of 'behaviour settings' in American and British towns. Partly inspired by Kurt Lewin's (1936) field theory, environmental psychology's emphasis on old people's physical environments also became instrumental in putting environmental gerontology high on the agenda of social and behavioural ageing research during the 1970s and 1980s (Wahl and Weisman, 2003).

This chapter focuses mainly on environmental gerontology as the preferred term in the field (Scheidt and Windley, 2006; Wahl and Gitlin, 2007). 'Environmental gerontology' indicates the necessarily interdisciplinary understanding of **person–environment (p–e)** interchange processes in ageing (Wahl, 2001; Wahl and Gitlin, 2007), involving disciplines such as psychology, sociology, architecture, social geography, occupational therapy, and urban planning. Furthermore, the term 'physical–social environment' may best acknowledge that there is no 'objective' environment 'out there' without social interpretation, cultural meaning, ongoing historical reassessment, and *Zeitgeist* influences. For example, the house is both a physical structure constructed through established cultural practices as well as a place infused with pronounced intimacy with one's partner, social interactions, and the symbolization of attachment, normalcy, and loss (Wahl and Gitlin, 2007). Moreover, new types of environmental change are being produced as the traditional view of 'ageing in place' has been challenged and we see an increasing proportion of older adults moving, for instance, to new places such as retirement communities or to southern European regions. It should finally be emphasized that, throughout the chapter, our focus will be on community-dwelling older people.

TASKS, SCOPE, AND FUNDAMENTAL RESEARCH QUESTIONS OF ENVIRONMENTAL GERONTOLOGY

Environmental gerontology emphasizes the development of an in-depth understanding of the interrelations between ageing persons and their physical–social environments and how these relationships influence a variety of outcomes for older people (Wahl and Gitlin, 2007; see also Wahl and Weisman, 2003). The overarching aim of environmental gerontology is thus to describe, explain, and modify/optimize the relationship between the ageing person and his/her physical–social environment.

With regard to sources of data and information, environmental gerontology places emphasis upon the day-to-day contexts of ageing individuals, reinforcing the importance of *natural settings* for gerontological research. The rationale is that older people spend most of their time (i.e. about three-quarters of their daytime) in the home and immediate home environment (Oswald and Wahl, 2005). As a consequence, housing has been a major focus of research in environmental gerontology (Oswald and Wahl, 2004). Moreover, older individuals tend to live a long time in the same place. For example, in the German Aging Survey, nearly one-third of those age 65 years and older have already lived for more than 40 years in the same home (Motel et al., 2000). Such long-term living and ageing at the same location often evokes rich cognitive and affective ties to the place one lives, known in German as *Heimat* (homeland). This is place identity and place attachment to the very specific genius loci of 'my place'. Seasonal changes occurring over the course of the year, such as those in lighting, temperature, weather conditions, smells, and noises, also contribute considerably to the environmental experience of the normal rhythm of life, and may be of particular importance for older people, as they provide orientation in space and time.

Explanation of behaviour (or development) has remained a major challenge of environmental gerontology. Theories have explored both the objective and subjective processes of ageing individuals interacting with their environments. Theories considering the objective dimension of p–e relations have primarily focused on level and type of competencies of ageing individuals in relation to design characteristics and the demands of physical environments (Lawton and Nahemow, 1973). Other approaches have posited a range of psychosocial processes by which ageing individuals form cognitive and effective connections, and have considered how these in turn impact on older individuals' lives. Yet, theoretical development has been uneven. In 1990, Parmelee and Lawton declared environmental gerontology to be languishing (1990: 483). Subsequently, European conceptual and empirical input from the field of environmental gerontology has been recognized as an increasingly important driver and innovator within the discipline (Phillipson, 2004, 2007; Scharf, 2000; Wahl and Iwarsson, 2007). Environmental gerontology's focus on *optimization* reflects an aspiration to contribute directly to the improvement of quality of life in old age through means of intervention. Prototypical is the involvement of environmental gerontology in advancing evidence-driven modifications to the home, adding to the development of new housing solutions for the diversity of ageing individuals, or designing public spaces. Seen on a more general level, optimization of the physical–social environment has created one of the strongest bridges to application in social and behavioural gerontology at large (Windley and Weisman, 2004).

Against these tasks, we see at least three inter-related research questions and challenges for environmental gerontology:

1 *Understanding how ageing individuals are managing the opportunities and constraints of their physical–social environmental conditions.* To achieve this, the following questions are relevant: How far and under what conditions are older people able to exert control and influence over their physical–social environments? What do we learn about ageing at large when we observe *proactive* use and change of physical–social environments, such as goal-directed and creative redesigning of existing home environments or even the active selection of new environments?

2 *Clarifying connections between the objective and the subjective dimensions to individuals and their world* is especially important for environmental gerontology. Relevant questions include: Why is the distinction between objective and subjective physical–social environments important, and why might it be particularly critical for ageing individuals to always consider both dimensions? Do older people, to take one illustration, compensate for loss of accessible housing through strong subjective bonds to the environment, or could processes of place attachment also be maladaptive?

3 *Examining the contribution of the p–e perspective to understanding the course and outcomes of ageing.* Such outcomes include well-being, autonomy, the preservation of self and identity, and somatic and mental health. It remains as yet unclear whether there is sufficient empirical evidence to drive interventions such as home modification or the reshaping of city, districts, or even the infrastructure of whole countries.

These are complex issues, and the available data is as yet incomplete. Unfortunately, the inclusion of variables targeting the physical–social environment (e.g., an intensive data protocol on objective and perceived housing characteristics) has remained the exception in major gerontological, particularly longitudinal, data sets. Thus, a commonly rich empirical research resource of primary and secondary data analysis for areas such as cognitive ageing, personality, social relations, or mental health is scarce when it comes to the understanding of the interface between ageing individuals and their physical–social context.

Given that persons with declining competencies are especially vulnerable to their physical–social environments, a particular focus of environmental gerontology has been on p–e attributes such as safety, accessibility, orientation, privacy, autonomy, and personal control among the very old and among individuals with a high prevalence of physical and cognitive impairments and chronic illnesses. Nevertheless, the scope of environmental gerontology reaches across the continuum of wellness, from the highly competent to the very frail. Furthermore, environmental gerontology considers the full scope of physical–social environments on the micro (e.g., traditional housing, the variation of purpose-built housing from assisted living to retirement care communities), meso (e.g., neighbourhoods, infrastructure, city districts), and macro level (e.g., urban versus rural, ageing in specific regions or countries, globalization).

From this review of the background to environmental gerontology, and some key questions for research, we turn to consider some of the main theoretical perspectives developed within the discipline.

MAJOR THEORETICAL PERSPECTIVES OF ENVIRONMENTAL GERONTOLOGY

Theorizing in environmental gerontology starts with the fundamental idea that human development over the life span, which includes old age, is driven by an ongoing interchange between individuals and their social and physical environment. According to Bronfenbrenner's (1999) bioecological model of lifelong coping with environmental conditions, different layers of p–e interchange must be considered, including:

- the *microsystem* (the interpersonal interactions within the immediate environment)
- the *mesosystem* (two or more microsystems directly affecting the developing individual)
- the *exosystem* (linkages between subsystems that indirectly influence the individual), and
- the *macrosystem* (values, norms, and legislation of a given society).

Furthermore, life-span development is seen as a never-ending sequence of ecological transitions in which new p–e territories are continuously conquered, while other p–e territories are left behind.

Prototypical examples include the transitions from school to the labour sphere, from the labour world to retirement, and from community-dwelling living to nursing home, assisted living, or retirement community.

Against this general ecological understanding of human development, the discussion moves to a more fine-tuned view of p–e interchange as people age. In order to address the complexity of p–e dynamics, Figure 8.1 outlines a conceptual framework that refers to two key processes of p–e interchange in later life, p–e belonging and p–e agency. These two constructs can be said to provide a useful basis for integrating the major theoretical approaches developed in environmental gerontology (Oswald and Wahl, 2005; Scheidt and Windley, 2006; Wahl, 2001; Wahl et al., 2004).

Processes of *belonging* account for the full range of p–e experiences; processes of *agency* emphasize the full range of goal-directed p–e cognitions, behaviours, and social practices. Processes of belonging entail mainly the cognitive and emotional evaluation and representation of physical environments, as well as processes of attachment to places over time, leading to patterns of place meaning. One aspect of p–e belonging is the individual's cognitive orientation towards her own environmental past, present, and future, verbalized as home-related reminiscence or housing plans. Processes of agency, in contrast, deal with the exertion of cognition, specifically physical environment-related cognitions such as the perceived controllability of one's physical environment. On the behavioural level, the interplay between being subdued by the demands of physical

environmental conditions ('docility') versus active use, compensation, adaptation, retrofitting, and creation of places ('proactivity') is particularly important. Moreover, the physical environment may or may not fit to the older individual's functional impairments and needs, echoing another facet of p–e agency with respect to enhancing or constraining conditions. Processes of p–e agency are considered to be especially important in old age due to the decrease in functional capacity and behavioural flexibility as people age. Furthermore, these two interrelated processes of p–e interchange are linked to major developmental outcomes as people age. These outcomes mainly echo what are often considered to be fundamental developmental tasks in later life – namely, to remain independent for as long as possible as well as to maintain one's integrity in terms of identity. To accomplish these developmental tasks, processes of p–e belonging and p–e agency are expected to play a major supporting role. Finally, it is assumed that both identity and autonomy are also globally related to well-being. We use this term in its widest sense to address cognitive and effective evaluations of one's life as well as healthy ageing outcomes in both the somatic and mental spheres.

The model under discussion simultaneously considers autonomy, identity, and well-being as major endpoints of p–e interchange as people age. This is significantly different from traditional approaches in environmental gerontology, which have concentrated on only *one* of well-being (e.g., Lawton and Nahemow, 1973), autonomy (e.g., Carp, 1987), or identity (e.g., Neisser, 1988).

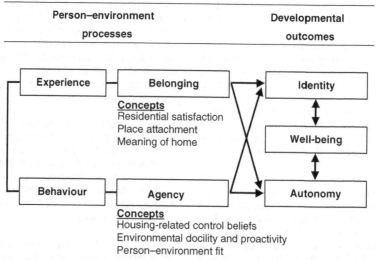

Figure 8.1   Overarching conceptual framework on person–environment relationships in later life

In order to illustrate the integrative potential of the constructs of p–e belonging and p–e agency, we discuss the classic approaches of environmental gerontology under these conceptual umbrellas, followed in the next section by a selection of respective empirical findings.

Processes of person–environment belonging

Processes of belonging have frequently been based on concepts and theories of residential satisfaction, including, to take one example, subjective evaluations of the environment based on age or geographic location, as well as the relationship between residential satisfaction and life satisfaction (Aragonés et al., 2002; Pinquart and Burmedi, 2004; Weideman and Anderson, 1985). Residential satisfaction is also considered as a manifestation of place evaluation processes. The potential of the construct of residential satisfaction in relation to p–e processes lies in its attempt to provide a broad attitudinal and cognitive evaluation of housing. Often, residential satisfaction is assessed by single-item self-evaluations (Oswald et al., 2003b; Pinquart and Burmedi, 2004). The criticism of this approach is reflected in the well-known residential satisfaction paradox, which is a special case of a general problem with measures of satisfaction. The problem is that evaluations are typically biased towards the positive and the correlation between subjective and objective ratings (in the case of residential satisfaction of the house, neighbourhood, or city district) tends to be low-to-medium at best, reflecting apparent satisfaction despite objective loss (Fernandez-Ballesteros, 2001; see further below).

Theories on place attachment and identity (Altman and Low, 1992; Neisser, 1988; Stedman, 2002) emphasize domains of belonging in a more process-oriented and differentiated way. Beyond residential satisfaction, place attachment both influences attitudes and encompasses the gamut of processes that operate when people form effective, cognitive, behavioural, and social bonds to the environment (Brown and Perkins, 1992), thereby transforming 'space' into 'place' (Altman, and Low, 1992; Rowles and Watkins, 2003). Often these aspects of physical, social, and personal bonding are assessed by global attachment evaluations, e.g., on indoor versus outdoor place attachment (Oswald et al., 2005). While most such studies are quantitative, a number of studies use a qualitative approach to explore the relation between place attachment and identity (Peace, 2005).

Furthermore, concepts of the meaning of home are directly related to place attachment, as they deal with the most frequent manifestation of attachment processes. Since older adults have often lived a long period of time in the same residence, cognitive and emotional aspects of the meaning of home are often strongly linked to biography. Such social, cognitive, and emotional links may become manifest through processes of reflecting on the past, symbolically represented in certain places and cherished objects within the home. Thus, belonging covers non-goal-oriented cognitive and emotional aspects of bonding. Moreover, it covers behavioural and physical bonding, because familiarity and routines have been developed over time. Most research on the meaning of home has relied on qualitative methodology (Rowles, 1983; Rubinstein, 1989; Sixsmith and Sixsmith, 1991), although some researchers have successfully developed quantitative measures of some aspects of meaning of home (Oswald et al., 2006; Rowles, 2006).

In terms of outcomes, a long-standing theoretical assumption is that a sense of belonging contributes to place-related identity (Born, 2002; Neisser, 1988). Rowles, using a social–geographical approach, argues that processes of place attachment and the allocation of meaning of place reflect physical, autobiographical, and social 'insideness' as a result of the long duration of living in the same place: 'Place becomes a landscape of memories, providing a sense of identity' (Rowles, 1983: 114; see also Rowles and Watkins, 2003). One observation here is that in discussions regarding the ageing self, the management of the relationship between interior and external worlds in later life is often reduced to the social environment, neglecting the role of physical aspects of the home (Biggs, 2005; Peace, 2005). Substantial links between processes of self and identity and well-being, as stated in our model (see again Figure 8.1), have been assumed in major psychological theories of life-span development, such as Erikson's psychosocial crisis approach (Erikson, 1950), Levinson's conception of adult development (Levinson, 1986), as well as in theories on successful ageing (Ryff, 1989). However, neither these scholars nor other life-span developmental scholars have paid attention to environmental determinants of ageing.

Processes of person–environment agency

Processes of p–e agency mainly cover cognitions and evaluations, which precede adaptive behaviour aimed to regulate p–e dynamics as people age. A prominent framework in this vein is psychological control theory (Lachman, 1986; Lachman and Burack, 1993), which has recently been applied to the housing domain (Oswald et al., 2007a). Housing-related control beliefs explain events at home either as contingent upon one's own behaviour, or upon luck, chance, fate, or powerful others. The argument is that control beliefs related to the regulation of p–e exchange at home become increasingly important in old age. As has been revealed in a number of longitudinal studies, external control beliefs are especially sensitive to age-related changes, particularly due to health and functional ability losses, but also due to negative stereotyping. They thus become crucial in explaining autonomy and well-being (Baltes et al., 1999a; Clark-Plaskie and Lachman, 1999).

On the behavioural level, processes of agency mainly rely on the concepts of environmental docility and proactivity, derived from the ecological theory of ageing (ETA) (Lawton, 1982, 1989; Lawton and Nahemow, 1973; Scheidt and Norris-Baker, 2004). The basic assumption is that the capacity to adapt to existing environmental press (the demands and limitations of the environment) decrease as people age, due to an increasing number of functional limitations. The original model describes behaviour and affect primarily as functions of the levels of personal competence and environmental press (Lawton, 1982; Lawton and Nahemow, 1973). The p–e agency in that sense is reduced to docile reactions on existing circumstances. However, in an extension of the model, the environmental proactivity hypothesis assumes that older adults may strive proactively to change housing conditions according to their own wishes and needs in order to maintain independence. This enables them to cope with environmental press and to profit from the full scope of available environmental opportunities (Lawton, 1989), including moving to another location that can better fulfil their housing needs (Oswald and Rowles, 2007; Warnes and Williams, 2006). An important methodological implication of using the docility and proactivity model is that both objective person-related information (e.g., on functional limitations) as well as independently gathered physical–social environment-related information (e.g., a comprehensive assessment of all barriers in a home) is necessary. A surprising observation in this regard is that though the ETA has reached wide prominence in research and application, assessment methods still seem to be far from any gold standard and many unevaluated person and environmental checklists have entered the field (Wahl and Iwarsson, 2007).

Other theoretical concepts address the level of p–e fit and misfit on several domains of p–e exchange as a prerequisite or manifestation of p–e agency, e.g., in the congruence model of p–e fit suggested by Kahana (1982) and in the complementary/congruence model proposed by Carp and Carp (1984). A critical message inherent in p–e fit concepts is that the level of behavioural competence in a certain domain corresponds with the given level of environmental press (e.g., barriers at home), leading to adaptation (fit) versus maladaptation (misfit). Establishing p–e fit assessment can open a perspective on p–e agency for those who are especially at risk in later life, in terms of the congruence of individual competence or needs and environmental demands or conditions. Again, however, assessment instruments have seldom surpassed the status of research devices, with some rare exceptions, particularly the concept of accessibility and respective measurement approach suggested by Iwarsson (2004).

As far as the relationship of p–e agency and autonomy is concerned, a common argument in environmental gerontology is that the physical–social environment may either constrain autonomy or compensate for reduced functional capacity (Carp, 1987; Wahl and Gitlin, 2007). As convincing as the argument may seem at first glance, it deserves differentiation in its understanding of ongoing p–e dynamics. For example, it could well be that nothing remains in terms of explanatory potential for the physical–social environment if a comprehensive assessment of functional limitations and other factors is introduced. Thus, this part of our model (see again Figure 8.1) is subject to further empirical evaluation, while the linkages between autonomy and well-being as proposed in our model have been demonstrated as quite robust (George, 2006).

Interaction of person–environment belonging, agency, and developmental change

Within environmental gerontology theorizing, the domains of p–e belonging and agency are typically addressed separately. However, it makes considerable sense to assume that both p–e interchange processes are closely intertwined and work hand in hand as people age. For example, older people living at home and suffering from severe competence loss can adapt to environmental challenges behaviourally, cognitively, and emotionally (Oswald and Wahl, 2005). They may objectively reduce their action range *and* subjectively re-evaluate their interior spaces as more valuable in contrast to the outdoor environment, which is no longer accessible to them. Thus, p–e adaptation in later life does not refer to either behaviour *or* experience; rather, it refers to both (Rowles et al., 2004). The methodological consequence of this insight is that a balanced set of behavioural (objective) as well as experiential (subjective) data related to the physical–social environment is needed in empirical research.

A SELECTION OF EMPIRICAL INSIGHTS FROM ENVIRONMENTAL GERONTOLOGY

This section examines a range of empirical work from environmental gerontology relevant to the conceptual framework suggested earlier. The dominant approach in the literature, as noted earlier, has tended to come from North American researchers. However, this review also includes coverage from European contributions.

Findings related to processes of person–environment belonging

As can be expected from our conceptual reasoning (see again Figure 8.1), processes of p–e belonging have been treated in the empirical environmental gerontology literature from a diversity of perspectives. Here, there has been a strong tradition of work focused on residential satisfaction. This is an important construct because it adds to the explanation of well-being and mental health (Oswald et al., 2003b; Windley and Scheidt, 1982), although its use in statistical analysis is limited by its usually low variance. As noted earlier, the majority of older persons are satisfied with their housing situation when asked in this general way, and responses are weakly correlated with objective conditions. For instance, Fernandez-Ballesteros (2001) observed in a study with Spanish elders that perceived (subjective) home environment quality correlated only moderately ($r = -0.36$) with objective need of repair. Pinquart and Burmedi (2004) have provided a meta-analytic integration of the available evidence on residential as well as neighbourhood satisfaction. Among their findings is that residential satisfaction increased with age, a finding reflected in longitudinal as well as cross-sectional studies. This is in accordance with the general assumption that motivations related to environmental belonging increase as people age.

Further support for the age-related increase of belonging comes from studies on place attachment and identity such that conducted by Zingmark et al. (1995) in North America, which considered a wide age range. Similarly, the work of Burholt and colleagues (e.g., Burholt and Naylor, 2005), Peace (2005), and Sixsmith and Sixsmith (1991) in England provided evidence confirming that attachment to place is an important feature of old age, particularly in old and very old individuals, underpinning core elements of the ageing person such as self, identity, and quality of life.

Investigations into the meaning of home have been explored in North American qualitative work, with Rowles (1983) and Rubinstein (1989) being among the landmark studies. Rubinstein and De Medeiros (2004) reported linkages between the physical–social environment and the ageing self, which accords with the argument of this chapter that processes of belonging are strongly connected to self and identity. The relation between meaning of home and competence loss in later life has been examined in a German study, with data drawn from qualitative in-depth semi-structured interviews with 126 elders (Oswald and Wahl, 2005). One-third of the participants were in good health, one-third suffered from severe mobility impairment, and one-third were blind. The meanings attached to home derived from this study were: (1) 'Physical', focusing on the experience of housing conditions such as experience of the residential area and furnishing; (2) 'Behavioural', related to the everyday behaviour of the person at home and to ways of rearranging items in the home; (3) 'Cognitive', representing biographical bonding to the home, such as the experience of familiarity and insideness; (4) 'Emotional', expressing the experience of privacy, safety, pleasure, and stimulation; and (5) 'Social', expressing relationships with fellow-lodgers, neighbours, or visitors. Healthy participants were more appreciative of the physical location, access, and amenity aspects of the home. Impaired participants emphasized the cognitive and biographical significance of the home. This is, at least indirectly, also in line with our conceptual expectation of a link between ageing and belonging. With respect to behavioural and social aspects, blind participants concentrated more on their social and cognitive sphere and less on behavioural and physical aspects of the home, while the meaning patterns for the mobility-impaired participants included behavioural aspects to a greater extent. About the same share of statements were made with regard to emotional themes in all three groups.

Findings related to person–environment agency

Research on perceptions regarding the older person's ability to control crucial aspects of their environment, such as housing, has been feature of work carried out by Oswald et al. (2003a). Perceptions that this aspect of the environment is beyond the individual's control contribute substantially to explanations of variance in outcomes related to autonomy (i.e., a measure of activities of daily living). This has been observed for different data sets from a selection of European countries; these indicate the expected negative relationship, with a belief that control over housing is beyond the individual's responsibility, linked to lower autonomy and higher depression in the range of countries covered in the study (Oswald, 2007b).

Going further, assumptions of the ETA concerning processes related to environmental docility and proactivity and p–e fit have also found considerable though not consistent empirical support. Iwarsson (2005) found that accessibility, a construct considering the fit between functional limitations *and* objectively observed barriers in the home environment, is more important for functional ability than the number of barriers as such, which was unrelated to functional ability. Wahl et al. (1999) found additional support for this assumption in a group of visually impaired elders, but also added some complexity to p–e dynamics in the home environment. The p–e fit was particularly important for those activities which assist independent living in the community, but less important for achieving the basic task of daily living. The explanation given for this was that the objective environment becomes particularly important in more complex activities, while basic activities are so critical for day-to-day autonomy that older adults strive to exert these even when experiencing adverse environmental conditions. Wahl et al. (2009) provide a literature analysis of all studies published between 1997 and 2006 in peer-reviewed journals, which addressed relations between the physical home environment and endpoints such as activities of daily living, amount of help and support needed, and falls. A total of 21 studies found supportive or at least partially supportive evidence for substantial linkages between environmental barriers and hazards in the home and disability-related outcomes, while only four did not. Again, the subset of studies also considering the fit or lack of fit between a person's functional limitations and physical barriers revealed the relative strongest linkages with disability-related outcomes.

Despite the critical mass of research, the absence of longitudinal studies remains a problem, as does the quality of many of the available studies. The latter particularly applies to the reliability and validity of home environment measurement devices. It is also disappointing that not a single study is available investigating the impact of the physical home environment on dementia-related disorders. Another limitation of the literature is the underuse of proactivity and the overuse of docility as a conceptual driver of empirical research, thus providing a somewhat one-sided

image of older people as being the pawns of 'bad' environments. Wahl et al. (1999) were able to underline, drawing from the sample case of elders with irreversible low vision, that even in the situation of severe loss of competence a rich set of 'palliative' compensations and adjustments on the p–e level can be found. For example, reducing one's outside and even inside available space seems a developmental loss at first glance, but is highly efficient in enhancing the feeling of being in control in a now 'smaller world'. Such 'gaining by losing' strategies may possibly provide a fundamental p–e mechanism to 'survive' in the situation of chronic functional loss that becomes more common in very old age.

In a wider understanding of p–e fit or misfit as suggested in our theoretical section, research on the role of neighbourhoods comes into play. Research into this aspect was conducted by Scharf et al. (2005) in urban communities in England. The major concept driving this research was the multidimensional phenomenon of social exclusion, composed of neighbourhood exclusion, exclusion from material resources, social relations, civic activities, and basic services. Among 600 persons aged 60+ living in deprived neighbourhoods, Scharf et al. found that a threefold differentiation existed: 33 per cent were not excluded on any of the five dimensions, whereas 31 per cent experienced exclusion in one dimension and 36 per cent exclusion in a cumulative manner. In Germany, Oswald et al. (2005) found that type of neighbourhood correlated with p–e fit in the expected direction: i.e., higher fit was observed in more pleasant city districts, particularly in the domain of higher-order needs such as privacy, comfort, familiarity, and favoured activities.

Simultaneous consideration of person–environment belonging and agency processes

As we have argued, processes of p–e belonging and p–e agency go hand in hand as people age. To address this conceptual need on the empirical level, selected findings from the European ENABLE-AGE Project are presented (Iwarsson et al., 2007).[3] The overarching aim of this study was to explore the home environment as a determinant for healthy ageing in very old age in Germany, Sweden, the UK, Hungary, and Latvia. Among the core components of healthy ageing considered in the ENABLE-AGE study were independence in daily activities and subjective well-being. Regarding processes of belonging, the ENABLE-AGE Project considered meaning of home, the perceived usability of one's home, and residential satisfaction. In terms of agency, p–e fit processes were considered via matching existing functional limitations with existing environmental barriers resulting in a total accessibility score (Iwarsson, 2004). In addition, housing-related control beliefs and meaning of home aspects (Oswald et al., 2003a) were assessed. The final ENABLE-AGE Survey Study sample at baseline comprised 1918 community-dwelling participants aged 75–89 years, living alone in urban regions in the five included countries. More details of the national samples and of the methods used are provided in Nygren et al. (2007) and Oswald et al. (2007b).

The findings (reported in detail in Oswald et al., 2007b) underscore that participants living in more accessible homes, who perceive their home as meaningful and useful, and who think that external influences are not responsible for their housing situation, were more independent in daily activities and had a better sense of well-being. In particular, it was not the number of environmental barriers in the home environment, but the magnitude of accessibility problems that was substantially related to different aspects of healthy ageing. Moreover, these results applied rather consistently to all five national samples. Taken together, the findings of the ENABLE-AGE Project can widen the perspective when striving for barrier-free building standards to encompass a holistic approach that takes both processes of p–e agency and p–e belonging into account.

NEW CHALLENGES FOR ENVIRONMENTAL GERONTOLOGY

As previously mentioned, most theories and concepts in environmental gerontology stem from the 1970s and 1980s and are predominantly North American in origin. Meanwhile, the argument has been made that the so-called 'new' ageing can be understood better when change over time in p–e relations find particular attention (Wahl et al., 2007). Prototypical examples include:

- transitions in the social environment (e.g., family, social exclusion, new contexts of care)
- the home environment (e.g., new housing solutions, smart home technology the continuing care retirement community movement, new relocation behaviours, temporary and/or secondary residences)
- the outdoor environment (e.g., new mobility behaviour, including new mobility means, as well as new lifestyle and leisure activity patterns), in the technology domain (e.g., internet, high-tech assistive devices)

- and in the societal and policy arena (e.g., globalization and urbanization issues, new understanding of the potential of ageing in politics, health care and in the labour force).

Two examples can be used to illustrate these trends in more detail – urbanization and increasing use of technology and their relation to ageing in the future. Gerontology research has been predominantly based in urban contexts, although this point and its implications are seldom made explicit (Phillipson, 2004). Urban environments raise a number of tensions and pressures for older residents. One such is the need for hypermobility, on the one hand (particularly for the young, well-educated, elite population), and a 'nomadic' lifestyle as well as for place attachment, 'cocooning', and *Heimat*, on the other hand (particularly for older people). Furthermore, there is reason to assume that urban settings, under the influence of globalization, economic pressure, and mega diversity of their populations, launch social exclusion and inequalities in day-to-day quality of life and in the use of resources, which traditionally have been among the fundamental motivations to live in the city (e.g., cultural and recreational facilities, health and care facilities, participation in the modernization of societies at large). The ETA or p–e fit approaches may be helpful to better understand why older adults have a high likelihood of becoming the targets of such social exclusion processes. There is, however, a clear need to bring such micro- to meso-level environmental gerontology theorizing together with macro perspectives, such as those offered in urban sociology and the political science of ageing, under conditions of modernity. Linking, for example, theoretical ideas of place attachment and identity with the social exclusion concept (Scharf et al., 2007) may be a promising conceptual avenue to understand why social exclusion produces depression and other adverse health conditions in a considerable portion of elders, while others (possibly those with high place identity) remain rather untouched by it. Similarly, current p–e fit approaches predominantly applied to the housing domain (e.g., Iwarsson, 2004; Wahl et al., 1999) deserve extension to liveable communities or even countries, and they may add to the better understanding of the role of ambiguities of ageing in the city. In other words, environmental gerontological theorizing and the theoretical approaches of a 're-vitalized' (Phillipson, 2004: 963) urban sociology and political science concerned with ageing should merge their conceptual strengths, also leading to new empirical research arenas, which could aim towards better understanding of modern ageing in challenging new environments.

Both the increasing availability of technology and the decreasing possibilities for avoiding new technologies (e.g., ticket machines, automatic teller machines, menu-driven services on all levels, mobile phones, information only available on the web) have become another challenging new environment for ageing individuals (see Chapter 47). It is obvious that technology cannot be excluded when it comes to the analysis of p–e dynamics. Technological solutions such as smart home appliances (e.g., Melenhorst et al., 2007) reshape the 'environmental press' and 'richness' of the traditional household and compensate for possible p–e mismatches. This also applies for many increasingly smart assistive devices, which now offer a full new potential of maintaining autonomy and participation. Examples here include the latest generation of powered wheelchairs, GPS-based orientation systems for those with low vision or blindness, or computerized devices to assist those with cognitive impairment (Mann and Helal, 2007). In conclusion, it no longer makes sense to reduce the semantics of environmental gerontology theorizing to the 'built' or 'physical' environment, because these concepts (and realities) are no longer separable from technological equipment.

CONCLUSION

Intervention research has become a major feature of environmental gerontology, particularly with the aim of reducing disability and loss of autonomy as people age. The argument is that improving the physical–social environment via means of home modification or the ecological optimizations of neighbourhoods or even communities at large should have a positive impact on quality of life in old age. Research findings, as described above, suggest that this omnibus argument is valid, but, as noted, most research has been cross-sectional. The real test will come only with controlled intervention research (Gitlin, 1998).

A recent literature review on the available evidence regarding the impact of home modification[4] revealed 29 original investigations, a considerable portion of which were randomized controlled trials, and 10 review papers in the period between 1997 and 2006 (Wahl et al., 2009). Typical outcomes included variations of activities of daily living assessment and falls and injuries in the home. A major finding of the review is that, taken as a whole, there is strong evidence for the hypothesis that home modification is able to reduce ADL–IADL-related outcomes, with the majority of studies reporting at least partially supportive evidence. In the array of falls and injuries,

the evidence of positive benefit is less clear. However, a number of studies clearly indicate that the elimination of home environment hazards is able to reduce the rate of falls in older adults (Wahl et al., 2009) and this evidence is in line with earlier compilations of the literature (Gillespie et al., 2003). There is also supportive evidence of the view that home modification is able to substantially help caregivers of demented elders (Gitlin et al., 2001), reflecting the need for a much broader scope of study than just emphasizing the link between p–e agency and autonomy.

Evidence for the crucial role of home modification also comes from a large body of documented best practice efforts and qualitative and case-oriented research (e.g., Connell and Sanford, 1997; Pynoos et al., 2003). From the vantage point of the dynamic interplay between belonging and agency, another issue is that a sense of belonging can play a major role in motivating home modification, but may also hinder the unfolding of its full potential. For instance, being too strongly attached to the current shape of one's house or apartment may question the readiness to go for profound changes in the physical outlet. Such strong or even rigid place attachment may also hinder a needed relocation, particularly in cases of limited capacity of the built environment to undergo substantial redesign (Oswald and Rowles, 2007). We still need to learn much more about the simultaneous 'work' of agency and belonging to understand which kind of interventions are best fitting to which kind of older adults, a challenge that asks for combinations of quantitative and qualitative research efforts. Moreover, we need to consider that older people are not oblivious to the forces at work on their situation. They often know very well about these simultaneously working processes of, for instance, decreasing agency and increasing belonging as they age in place without any retrofitting. Thus, in many cases they would gain from external help to negotiate and talk about pros and cons of belonging and agency instead of just getting a list of home modifications. This is particularly important, considering the insight that the potential of home modification is currently much underused and thus a likely efficient means to reduce (or even prevent) the burden of disability is much neglected in the practical sphere (e.g., Wahl and Gitlin, 2007).

The prominent issue of home modification should not, however, override other important application potentials of work in environmental gerontology. Critical are interventions on the level of the public space, with aims such as reducing 'anxiety areas', enhancing safety and participation at large through means of barrier-free design, and counteracting the tendency, particularly in big cities, for increasing separation of the generations in the public domain (e.g., Ståhl and Iwarsson, 2004). In conclusion, we urge for a still stronger development of what may be called a *p–e culture for ageing societies* in the future. Such a p–e culture of course should target all ages and the full diversity of our societies, including, besides the most heterogeneous population of older adults themselves, migrants and disabled people. Different measures, ranging from home modification and the profound reshaping of neighbourhoods to creative and innovative housing solutions and still hard to imagine technological potential, will shape our ageing societies in the years to come.

NOTES

1 We are using the terms 'context' and 'environment' interchangeably in this work.

2 We use the terms 'life course', preferred by sociologists, and 'life span', preferred by psychologists interchangeably throughout the chapter.

3 See also http//:www.enableage.arb.lu.se

4 This has been the second goal of the review already cited earlier in the chapter.

REFERENCES

Altman, I. and Low, S.M. (eds) (1992) *Human Behavior and Environment, Vol. 12: Place Attachment*. New York: Plenum.

Aragonés, J.I., Francescano, G., and Gärling, T. (2002) *Residential Environments. Choice, Satisfaction, and Behaviour*. Westport, CT: Bergin and Garvey.

Baars, J., Dannefer, D., Phillipson, C., and Walker, A. (eds) (2006) *Aging, Globalization and Inequality*. New York: Baywood Publishers.

Baltes, P.B., Reese, H.W., and Lipsitt, L.P. (1980) 'Life-span developmental psychology', *Annual Review of Psychology*, 31: 65–110.

Baltes, P.B., Lindenberger, U., and Staudinger, U.M. (1998) 'Life-span theory in developmental psychology', in W. Damon and R.M. Lerner (eds), *Handbook of Child Psychology: Theoretical Models of Human Development*, Vol. 1. New York: Wiley, pp. 1029–143.

Baltes, M.M., Freund, A.M., and Horgas, A.L. (1999a) 'Men and women in the Berlin Aging Study', in P.B. Baltes and K.U. Mayer (eds), *The Berlin Aging Study*. Cambridge: Cambridge University Press, pp. 259–81.

Baltes, M.M., Maas, I., Wilms, H.-U., Borchelt, M.F., and Little, T. (1999) 'Everyday competence in old and very old age: theoretical considerations and empirical findings', in P.B. Baltes and K.U. Mayer (eds), *The Berlin Aging Study*. Cambridge, UK: Cambridge University Press, pp. 384–402.

Barker, R.G. and Barker, L.S. (1961) 'The psychological ecology of old people in Midwest, Kansas, and Yordale, Yorkshire', *Journal of Gerontology*, 16: 144–9.

Biggs, S. (2005) 'Beyond appearances: perspectives on identity in later life and some implications for method', *Journal of Gerontology: Social Sciences*, 60B(3): S118–28.

Born, A. (2002) *Regulation persönlicher Identität im Rahmen gesellschaftlicher Transformationsbewältigung. [Regulation of Personal Identity in the Face of Societal Transformation]*. Münster: Wasmann.

Bronfenbrenner, U. (1999) 'Environments in developmental perspective: theoretical and operational models', in S.L. Friedman and T.D. Wachs (eds), *Measuring Environment Across the Life Span*. Washington, DC: American Psychological Association, pp. 3–28.

Brown, B. and Perkins, D. (1992) 'Disruptions in place attachment', in I. Altman and S.M. Low (eds), *Human Behaviour and Environment, Vol. 12: Place Attachment*. New York: Plenum Press, pp. 279–304.

Burholt, V. and Naylor, D. (2005) 'The relationship between rural community type and attachment to place for older people living in North Wales, UK', *European Journal of Ageing*, 2(2): 109–19.

Carp, F.M. (1966) *A Future for the Aged*. Austin: University of Texas Press.

Carp, F.M. (1987) 'Environment and aging', in D. Stokols and I. Altman (eds), *Handbook of Environmental Psychology*. Vol. 1. New York: Wiley, pp. 330–60.

Carp, F.M. and Carp, A. (1984) 'A complementary/congruence model of well-being or mental health for the community elderly', in I. Altman, M.P. Lawton, and J.F. Wohlwill (eds), *Human Behavior and Environment: Elderly People and the Environment*, Vol. 7. New York: Plenum Press, pp. 279–336.

Clark-Plaskie, M. and Lachman, M.E. (1999) 'The sense of control in midlife', in S.L. Willis and J.D. Reid (eds), *Life in the Middle: Psychological and Social Development in Middle Age*. San Diego, CA: Academic Press, pp. 181–208.

Connell, B.R. and Sanford, J.A. (1997). 'Individualizing home modification recommendations to facilitate performance of routine activities', in S. Lanspery and J. Hyde (eds), *Staying Put. Adapting the Places instead of the People*. Amityville, NY: Baywood, pp. 113–47.

Cristofalo, V.J., Tresini, M., Francis, M.K., and Volker, C. (1999) 'Biological theories of senescence', in V.L. Bengtson and K.W. Schaie (eds), *Handbook of Theories of Aging*. New York: Springer, pp. 98–112.

Dannefer, D. (1992) 'On the conceptualization of context in developmental discourse: four meanings of context and their implications', in D.L. Featherman, R.M. Lerner, and M. Perlmutter (eds), *Life-Span Development and Behavior*, Vol. 11. Hillsdale: Erlbaum, pp. 83–110.

Elder, G.H. (1974) *Children of the Great Depression: Social Change in Life Experience*. Chicago: University of Chicago Press.

Erikson, E.H. (1950) *Childhood and Society*. New York: Norton and Company.

Fernandez-Ballesteros, R. (2001) 'Environmental conditions, health and satisfaction among the elderly: some empirical results', *Psicithema*, 13(1): 40–9.

George, L.K. (2006) 'Perceived quality of life', in R.H. Binstock and L.K. George (eds), *Handbook of Aging and the Social Sciences*, 6th edn. San Diego, CA: Academic Press, pp. 320–66.

Gilleard, C., Hyde, M., and Higgs, P. (2007) 'Community and communication in the third age: the impact of internet and cell phone use on attachment to place in later life in England', *Journal of Gerontology, Social Sciences*, 62(4): S276–83.

Gillespie, L.D., Gillespie, W.J., Robertson, M.C., et al. (2003) 'Interventions for preventing falls in elderly people (Cochran Review)', *The Cochran Library*, 3, 2001.

Gitlin, L.N. (1998) Testing home modification interventions: issues of theory, measurement, design, and implementation', in R. Schulz, G. Maddox, and M.P. Lawton (eds), *Annual Review of Gerontology and Geriatrics*. New York: Springer, pp. 190–246.

Gitlin, L.N., Corcoran, M., Winter, L., Boyce, A., and Marcus, S. (2001) 'A randomized controlled trial of a home environmental intervention: effect on efficacy and upset in caregivers and on daily function of persons with dementia', *The Gerontologist*, 41(1): 4–22.

Iwarsson, S. (2004) 'Assessing the fit between older people and their home environments – an occupational therapy research perspective', in H.-W. Wahl, R. Scheidt, and P. Windley (eds), *Annual Review of Gerontology and Geriatrics*. New York: Springer, pp. 85–109.

Iwarsson, S. (2005) 'A long-term perspective on p–e fit and ADL dependence among older Swedish adults', *The Gerontologist*, 45(3): 327–36.

Iwarsson, S., Wahl, H.-W., Nygren, C., et al. (2007) 'Importance of the home environment for healthy aging: conceptual and methodological background of the ENABLE-AGE Project', *The Gerontologist*, 47: 78–84.

Kahana, E. (1982) 'A congruence model of person–environment interaction', in M.P. Lawton, P.G. Windley, and T.O. Byerts (eds), *Aging and the Environment: Theoretical Approaches*. New York: Springer, pp. 97–121.

Kleemeier, R.W. (1959) 'Behavior and the organization of the bodily and external environment', in J.E. Birren (ed.), *Handbook of Aging and the Individual*. Chicago: University of Chicago Press, pp. 400–51.

Lachman, M.E. (1986) 'Locus of control in aging research: a case for multidimensional and domain-specific assessment', *Journal of Psychology and Aging*, 1: 34–40.

Lachman, M.E. and Burack, O.R. (eds) (1993) 'Planning and control processes across the life span: an overview', *International Journal of Behavioral Development*, 16: 131–43.

Lawton, M.P. (1982) 'Competence, environmental press, and the adaptation of older people', in M.P. Lawton, P.G. Windley, and T.O. Byerts (eds), *Aging and the Environment*. New York: Springer, pp. 33–59.

Lawton, M.P. (1989) 'Environmental proactivity in older people', in V.L. Bengtson and K.W. Schaie (eds), *The Course of Later Life*. New York: Springer, pp. 15–23.

Lawton, M.P. and Nahemow, L. (1973) 'Ecology and the aging process', in C. Eisdorfer and M.P. Lawton (eds), *Psychology of Adult Development and Aging*. Washington, DC: American Psychological Association, pp. 619–74.

Levinson, D.J. (1986) 'A conception of adult development', *American Psychologist*, 41: 3–13.

Lewin, K. (1936) *Principles of Topological Psychology*. New York: McGraw-Hill.

Mann, W.C. and Helal, S. (2007) 'Technology and chronic conditions in later years: reasons for new hope', in H.-W. Wahl, C. Tesch-Römer, and A. Hoff (eds), *New Dynamics in Old Age: Individual, Environmental and Societal Perspectives*. Amityville, NY: Baywood Publishers, pp. 271–90.

Melenhorst, A.-S., Rogers, W.A., and Fisk, A.D. (2007) 'When will technology in the home improve the quality of life for older adults?', in H.-W. Wahl, C. Tesch-Römer, and A. Hoff (eds), *New Dynamics in Old Age: Individual, Environmental and Societal Perspectives*. Amityville, NY: Baywood Publishers, pp. 253–70.

Mollenkopf, H. and Fozard, J.L. (2004) 'Technology and the good life: challenges for current and future generations of aging people', in H.-W. Wahl, R. Scheidt, and P.G. Windley (eds), *Annual Review of Gerontology and Geriatrics*, Vol. 22. New York: Springer, pp. 250–79.

Motel, A., Künemund, H., and Bode, C. (2000) 'Wohnen und Wohnumfeld älterer Menschen' [Housing and neighbourhood of older adults], in M. Kohli and H. Künemund (eds), *Die zweite Lebenshälfte – Gesellschaftliche Lage und Partizipation im Spiegel des Alters–Survey*. Opladen: Leske and Budrich, pp. 124–75.

Neisser, U. (1988) 'Five kinds of self-knowledge', *Philosophical Psychology*, 1: 35–59.

Nygren, C., Oswald, F., Iwarsson, S., et al. (2007) 'Relationships between objective and subjective housing in very old age: results from the ENABLE-AGE Project', *The Gerontologist*, 47: 85–95.

Oswald, F., Hieber, A., Wahl, H.-W., and Mollenkopf, H. (2005) 'Ageing and person–environment fit in different urban neighbourhoods', *European Journal of Ageing*, 2(2): DOI 10.1007/s10433-005-0026-5

Oswald, F. and Rowles, G.D. (2007) 'Beyond the relocation trauma in old age: new trends in today's elders' residential decisions', in H.-W. Wahl, C. Tesch-Römer, and A. Hoff (eds), *New Dynamics in Old Age: Environmental and Societal Perspectives*. Amityville, NY: Baywood Publishers, pp. 127–52.

Oswald, F. and Wahl, H.-W. (2004) 'Housing and health in later life', *Reviews on Environmental Health*, 19 (Special issue: review on housing and health – guest editor: R.J. Lawrence), 223–52.

Oswald, F. and Wahl, H.-W. (2005) 'Dimensions of the meaning of home in later life', in G.D. Rowles and H. Chaudhury (eds), *Home and Identity in Later Life. International Perspectives*. New York: Springer, pp. 21–46.

Oswald, F., Wahl, H.-W., Martin, M., and Mollenkopf, H. (2003a) 'Toward measuring proactivity in person–environment transactions in late adulthood: the Housing-related Control Beliefs Questionnaire', *Journal of Housing for the Elderly*, 17(1/2): 135–52.

Oswald, F., Wahl, H.-W., Mollenkopf, H., and Schilling, O. (2003b) 'Housing and life-satisfaction of older adults in two rural regions in Germany', *Research on Aging*, 25(2): 122–43.

Oswald, F., Schilling, O., Wahl, H.-W., et al. (2006) 'Homeward bound: introducing a four domain model of perceived housing in very old age', *Journal of Environmental Psychology*, 26: 187–201.

Oswald, F., Wahl, H.-W., Schilling, O., and Iwarsson, S. (2007a) 'Housing-related control beliefs and independence in activities of daily living in very old age', *Scandinavian Journal of Occupational Therapy*, 14: 33–43.

Oswald, F., Wahl, H.-W., Schilling, O., et al. (2007b) 'Relationships between housing and healthy aging in very old age', *The Gerontologist*, 47: 96–1007.

Parmelee, P.A. and Lawton, M.P. (1990) 'The design of special environment for the aged', in J.E. Birren and K.W. Schaie (eds), *Handbook of the Psychology of Aging*, 3rd edn. New York: Academic Press, pp. 465–89.

Peace, S.M. (2005) *Environment and Identity in Later Life*. Berkshire: Open University Press.

Phillipson, C. (2004) 'Urbanisation and ageing: towards a new environmental gerontology', *Ageing and Society*, 24: 963–72.

Phillipson, C. (2007) 'The "elected" and the "excluded": sociological perspectives on the experience of place and community in old age', *Ageing and Society*, 27: 321–42.

Pinquart, M. and Burmedi, D. (2004) 'Correlates of residential satisfaction in adulthood and old age: a meta-analysis', in H.-W. Wahl, R. Scheidt, and P.G. Windley (eds), *Annual Review of Gerontology and Geriatrics*. New York: Springer, pp. 195–222.

Pynoos, J., Nishita, C., and Perelman, L. (2003) 'Advancements in the home modification field: a tribute to M. Powell Lawton', *Journal of Housing for the Elderly*, 17(1/2): 105–16.

Rowles, G.D. (1983) 'Geographical dimensions of social support in rural Appalachia', in G.D. Rowles and R.J. Ohta (eds), *Aging and Milieu. Environmental Perspectives on Growing Old*. New York: Academic Press. pp. 111–29.

Rowles, G.D. and Watkins, J.F. (2003) 'History, habit, heart and hearth: on making spaces into places', in K.W. Schaie, H.-W. Wahl, H. Mollenkopf, and F. Oswald (eds), *Aging Independently: Living Arrangements and Mobility*. New York: Springer, pp. 77–96.

Rowles, G.D., Oswald, F., and Hunter, E.G. (2004) 'Interior living environments in old age', in H.-W. Wahl, R. Scheidt, and P.G. Windley (eds), *Annual Review of Gerontology and Geriatrics*, Vol. 22. New York: Springer, pp. 167–93.

Rubinstein, R.L. (1989) 'The home environments of older people: a description of the psychological process linking person to place', *Journal of Gerontology*, 44(2): 45–53.

Rubinstein, R.L. and De Medeiros, K. (2004) 'Ecology and the aging self', in H.-W. Wahl, R.J. Scheidt, and P.G. Windley (eds), *Annual Review of Gerontology and Geriatrics*. New York: Springer, pp. 59–84.

Ryff, C.D. (1989) 'Beyond Ponce de Leon and life satisfaction: new directions in quest of successful ageing', *International Journal of Behavioral Development*, 12(1): 35–55.

Scharf, T. (2000) 'Social gerontology in Germany', *Ageing and Society*, 21: 489–505.

Scharf, T., Phillipson, C., and Smith, A.E. (2005) 'Social exclusion of older people in deprived urban communities of England', *European Journal of Ageing*, 2(2): 76–87.

Scharf, T., Phillipson, C., and Smith, A. (2007) 'Aging in a difficult place: assessing the impact of urban deprivation on older people', in H.-W. Wahl, C. Tesch-Römer, and A. Hoff (eds), *New Dynamics in Old Age: Individual, Environmental and Societal Perspectives*. Amityville, NY: Baywood Publishers, pp. 153–74.

Scheidt, R.J. and Norris-Baker, C. (2004) 'The general ecological model revisited: evolution, current status, and continuing challenges', in H.-W. Wahl, R.J. Scheidt, and P.G. Windley (eds), *Annual Review of Gerontology and Geriatrics* (Issue on Aging in Context: Socio-physical Environments). New York: Springer, pp. 35–48.

Scheidt, R.J. and Windley, P.G. (2006) 'Environmental gerontology: progress in the post-Lawton era', in J.E. Birren and K.W. Schaie (eds), *Handbook of the Psychology of Aging*, 6th edn. Amsterdam: Elsevier, pp. 105–28.

Sixsmith, A.J. and Sixsmith, J.A. (1991) 'Transition in home experience in later life', *Journal of Architectural and Planning Research*, 8(3): 181–91.

Ståhl, A. and Iwarsson, S. (2004) '"Let's go for a walk" – a project focusing on accessibility, safety and security for older people in the outdoor environment', *The Gerontologist*, 44 (Special Issue I): 151.

Stedman, R.S. (2002) 'Toward a social psychology of place. Predicting behaviour from place-based cognitions, attitude and identity', *Environment and Behavior*, 34(5): 561–81.

Tibbitts, C. (ed.) (1960) *Handbook of Social Gerontology: Societal Aspects of Aging*. Chicago: University of Chicago Press.

Vaupel, J.W., Carey, J.R., and Christensen, K. (2003) 'It's never too late', *Science*, 301: 1679–81.

Wahl, H.-W. (2001) 'Environmental influences on aging and behavior', in J.E. Birren and K.W. Schaie (eds), *Handbook of the Psychology of Aging*, 5th edn. San Diego: Academic Press, pp. 215–37.

Wahl, H.-W. and Gitlin, L.N. (2007) 'Environmental gerontology', in J.E. Birren (ed.), *Encyclopedia of Gerontology. Age, Aging, and the Aged*, 2nd edn. Oxford: Elsevier, pp. 494–501.

Wahl, H.-W. and Iwarsson, S. (2007) 'Person–environment relations in old age', in R. Fernandez-Ballesteros (ed.), *Geropsychology. European Perspectives for an Ageing World*. Göttingen: Hogrefe, pp. 49–66.

Wahl, H.-W. and Weisman, J. (2003) 'Environmental gerontology at the beginning of the new millennium: reflections on its historical, empirical, and theoretical development', *The Gerontologist* ('The Forum'), 43: 616–27.

Wahl, H.-W., Oswald, F., and Zimprich, D. (1999) 'Everyday competence in visually impaired older adults: a case for person–environment perspectives', *The Gerontologist*, 39(2): 140–9.

Wahl, H.-W., Scheidt, R., and Windley, P. (eds) (2004) *Annual Review of Gerontology and Geriatrics*, 23 (Issue on 'Aging in Context: Socio-physical Environments'). New York: Springer.

Wahl, H.-W., Tesch-Römer, C., and Hoff, A. (2007) 'Searching for the new dynamics in old age: a book opener', in H.-W. Wahl, C. Tesch-Römer, and A. Hoff (eds), *New Dynamics in Old Age: Individual, Environmental and Societal Perspectives*. Amityville, NY: Baywood Publishers, pp. 1–10.

Wahl, H.-W., Fänge, A., Oswald, F., Gitlin, L.N., and Iwarsson, S. (2009) 'The home environment and disability-related outcomes in aging individuals: What is the empirical evidence?' *The Gerontologist*. 49(3): 355–67.

Warnes, A.M. and Williams, A. (2006) 'Older migrants in Europe: a new focus for migration studies', *Journal of Ethnic and Migration Studies*, 32(8): 1257–81.

Weideman, S. and Anderson, J.R. (1985) 'A conceptual framework for residential satisfaction' in I. Altman and C.M. Werner (eds), *Human Behavior and Environment. Vol. 8: Home Environments*. New York: Plenum Press, pp. 153–82.

Windley, P.G. and Scheidt, R.J. (1982) 'An ecological model of mental health among small-town rural elderly', *Journal of Gerontology*, 37(2): 235–42.

Windley, P.G. and Weisman, G.D. (2004) 'Environmental gerontology research and practice: the challenge of application', in H.-W. Wahl, R.J. Scheidt, and P.G. Windley (eds), *Annual Review of Gerontology and Geriatrics*. New York: Springer, pp. 334–65.

Zingmark, K., Norberg, A., and Sandman, P.-O. (1995) 'The experience of being at home throughout the life span. Investigation of persons aged from 2 to 102', *International Journal of Aging and Human Development*, 41(1): 47–62.

Ageing and Social Structure

9

Age and Inequality in Global Context

Angela M. O'Rand, Katelin Isaacs,
and Leslie Roth

INTRODUCTION

Population ageing and the economic well-being of nations have been closely linked over recent centuries across phases of the demographic transition, which began in Europe around 1800 and spread to the rest of the developing world. The phases of the transition have proceeded from early declines in mortality to declines in fertility and then increased life expectancy. Since 1800 the population of the globe has increased by a factor of six and is projected to increase by a factor of 10 by 2100, when there will be 50 times as many older people but only five times as many children (Lee, 2003).

The major correlate of population ageing over phases of the demographic transition has been the general rise in average economic well-being. However, significant inequalities in economic well-being persist between nations at different levels of development and within nations with highly variable institutional structures intended to equalize economic opportunities for subgroups of the population, including age groups (children, workers, and the aged), classes (including the poor), and gender and minority groups.

This chapter will focus on age and inequality in a global context by reviewing the recent literature within a framework that examines (1) common trends (and variations in trends) in age-based and gender-based inequality over recent decades, (2) the interdependence of demographic, public policy, and market forces underlying variations in these trends, and (3) the theoretical challenges posed by these trends and changes for explaining

inequality and age. Two different analytical frames will be summarized: one that focuses on between-age group inequality and one that focuses on within-age group inequality over time. Also, data collected from selected countries will be examined to provide quantitative illustrations of these patterns. The substantial work on these issues completed by the ongoing Luxembourg Income Study (LIS)[1] will be highlighted in conjunction with data from several other sources, including the Comparative Welfare States Dataset,[2] the World Bank,[3] and national statistics bureaus of selected countries. Key concepts and their measurement of inequality will be defined and discussed: 'disposable personal income' (DPI), income inequality measures (Gini coefficients and cut-point ratios), poverty, and social exclusion. Wealth data are not readily comparable or available across countries and thus will not be examined here (although the Luxembourg Wealth Study is on its way to establishing a multi-country database that will facilitate further work in this area in the future).[4] These indicators of inequality will be considered within a framework that links macro-level processes with patterns of inequality by age. At the macro level are demographic (i.e., population ageing), public policy (i.e., the retrenchments of social welfare or equalizing institutions), and market (i.e., the fragmentation of compensation systems) trends that operate interdependently to produce cumulative patterns of inequality over the life course (i.e., processes of stratification within cohorts from birth to death) (Dannefer, 2003; DiPrete and Eirich, 2006).

SOCIAL CONTRACTS: POPULATION AGEING AND INEQUALITY

As defined here, social contracts are diverse national systems of interconnected State, market, and civic institutions that have developed since the 19th century to maintain economic and political stability. In the modern era, the idea of social contract is traceable to the British philosopher R.G. Collingwood who, in the midst of World War II, proposed that the post-war period should combine Enlightenment ideas of popular sovereignty and freedom with equality in order to reduce economic and political disparities (Zunz et al., 2002). These contracts are based on varying levels of risk pooling and risk sharing between and within age cohorts in national populations to protect against individual life-course risks related to educational attainment, income maintenance, health declines, and family stability. One principle of these contracts defines the obligations between cohorts (or generations) through tax and insurance institutions that oblige cohorts to care for the cohorts preceding them, i.e., for working cohorts to support older non-working cohorts (Leisering and Leibfried, 1999) and/or succeeding them, i.e., for adult cohorts to care for their children and for future cohorts (Anand and Sen, 2000). A second principle defines the obligations within cohorts to share risks and pool resources through taxation and redistribution. Both between- and within-cohort principles are implemented through the taxing and borrowing authority of the state.

Larger historical forces related to economic development, political change, and cultural legacies have shaped the forms that these contracts have taken across countries. Diverse national systems of public education, child and maternal support, national health insurance, and social retirement across countries have emerged and developed. These institutional arrangements have, in turn, contributed to the development and protection of large middle classes in advanced societies (Zunz et al., 2002), whose security is now being challenged by globalizing forces and the retrenchment of some elements of these contracts (Pressman, 2001; Wolff, 2004). The extraordinary increase of income inequality within advanced nations (Gottschalk and Smeeding, 1997), driven primarily by increases at the top of distributions, is arguably eroding their middle classes. The growth of poverty within some nations is also a product of mismatches between social and private welfare policies and the disadvantaged conditions of subgroups of the population, leaving these populations excluded from protections against life-course risks.

The diverse social contracts associated with economically developed countries have been identified for several decades as representing distinctive models of welfare policies (Esping-Andersen, 1999; Korpi, 2000). In the *liberal model*, associated with Anglo-American democracies, market institutions and private mechanisms for individual or family security are central. Employment is the basis of access to forms of social protection ranging from health insurance to retirement pensions. Social programmes serve only a residual role as means-tested safety nets. In these countries income inequality is highest and growing. And, those with marginal employment statuses (especially women, minorities, and part-time workers) are systematically excluded from some social protections.

Successive policy amendments over the past two to three decades have retrenched earlier more generous programmes, as in the case of welfare-to-work in the United States, which has redefined child welfare as mothers' obligations to work, and in the case of the introduction of stakeholder pensions in the United Kingdom, which is intended to replace most traditional social pensions with occupational pensions. The recent (defeated) proposal to privatize a portion of the American Social Security system with private defined contribution plans is another indicator of the tendency toward retrenching social welfare programmes – even the most successful ones – in order to stem the financial impact of population ageing.

The *social rights* model appears on the European continent in two forms. The social democratic form found in the Nordic countries is based on social rights and entitlements of citizenship, not employment, and the goal is universal solidarity. Social democratic institutions intervene in the market through wage controls and recognize marginal (part-time) employment as a basis of entitlement. The second form, referred to as the conservative corporatist model, allocates social rights across subgroup boundaries in ways to protect their distinctive interests and life circumstances. Specific institutional arrangements exist for different public and private occupational groups and industries. Similarly, families (and women) and the aged are protected through policies that are predicated on a breadwinner model of gender roles. The emphasis is on cash transfers rather than wage controls and social services. Southern European countries appear to subscribe to an extreme model of the conservative corporatist form. They emphasize cash transfers over services and tend to overprotect the aged population and underprotect families (women and children) and workers (Zunz et al., 2002).

However, it is important to note that under the pressures of population ageing, changes in family structure and globalization in all of these countries are leading to policy revisions in the direction of more individualized protection of life-course risks, especially retirement saving, although these revisions do not approach the liberal characteristics of the Anglo-American model (Esping-Andersen, 2007; O'Rand et al., 2009). These models are decreasingly accurate representations of current policies and serve more as legacies that moderate the degree of liberalization of social welfare policies occurring globally (O'Rand et al., 2009).

The newly industrializing 'welfare' states are establishing hybrid models anchored in the legacies of their cultural heritages. The Pacific Rim states integrate State, family, and market development through direct support of national industries with subsidization and tariff protection and the implementation of authoritarian educational and familial systems. Socialist states (now in post-Soviet Eastern Europe and Asia) are moving in the direction of liberal reforms adopting selected privatized and individualized insurance policies that follow the guidelines of the World Bank and the International Monetary Fund (Bonoli, 2003). Finally, other parts of the developing world are adopting liberal reforms following World Bank guidelines as well (World Bank, 1994). In Latin America, beginning with Chile in 1980, liberal policies in the form of mandatory individual retirement accounts have taken hold. The so-called Chilean model has spread throughout Latin America, where nearly a dozen countries have implemented mandatory private savings (Sinha, 2000). These programmes vary considerably in their details and are having uneven success in their management.

These factors contribute to considerable heterogeneity and change in social policies across countries, all of whom are experiencing increasing rates of population ageing related to decreased mortality and fertility and increased longevity (Bongaarts, 2004). The increased immigration of non-natives from Eastern Europe, Asia, and Africa to European countries has also complicated the politics of welfare reform. While temporary and permanent immigration have mitigating effects on the ageing structures of native-born European populations, they present new challenges to traditional premises on which welfare states were predicated. Citizenship rights, children's rights, and other traditional domains of European welfare state policy are confronted with new exigencies. Social exclusion as a basis of inequality has ascended as a new concern of European policies (Walker, 1995).

Common and variable trends in inequality

Common, but not universal, trends across countries include several master patterns. Demographic trends in population ageing (i.e., in the growing ratio of older to younger persons in a population)

and in the shift toward higher rates of women's participation in the labor force with implications for family size and structure and family welfare are evident across many, but not all, developed and developing countries. Table 9.1 provides demographic, inequality, and policy trends between 1990 and 2000 among eight countries selected to represent major welfare models and newly developing states. The last column of the table, which reports social security transfers as a per cent of GDP (Gross Domestic Product), strongly indicates the relative generosity of welfare state programmes. The liberal model is represented by the United States and the United Kingdom; the conservative corporatist model by France and Germany; the social democratic model by Sweden; southern Europe by Italy; and newly developing states by Mexico and Taiwan. Liberal states have remained relatively stable in their distributions and lower than all other states except the newly emerging industrial states. Continental European states have increased their proportional funding levels in response to costs related to population ageing. Sweden, on the other hand, has reduced its level between 1990 and 2000 – a response to population ageing with a notable shift toward a new pension system based on employee contributions to their 'notional contribution scheme' to anticipate rapid population ageing in the next decade (O'Rand et al., 2009).

By 2000, the Anglo-American and continental European countries (except Italy) reached relatively stable population structures, although nearly all have projected shifts toward significantly older populations within the next two decades as a result of declining fertility rates and increased longevity (Bongaarts, 2004; Kinsella and Phillips, 2005; World Bank, 1994). Italy, Mexico, and Taiwan represent more dramatic transitions to older populations as a result of significant declines in fertility and increases in the older population. Taiwan, in particular, mimics continental Europe's below population replacement levels with a total fertility rate of 1.1 in 2000, well below the 2.1 replacement threshold.

All countries, except Sweden and Italy, exhibit increases in women's labor force participation, a trend highly correlated with declining fertility and other family structure changes such as non-marriage, single-parenthood, cohabitation, and delayed fertility – this complement of trends is often referred to as the second demographic transition (Lesthaeghe, 1995; McLanahan, 2004). The second demographic transition highlights these changes in family structure above and beyond declines in fertility, all of which accelerate population ageing but also stratify populations into single-parent families versus traditional families with unequal access to resources and long-term

Table 9.1. Demographic characteristics of selected countries between 1990 and 2000

	Total population[a]			Total fertility rate[a]	Female labor force participation[c]	Inequality measures[b]			*Social security transfers[c]
	Per cent 0–14 years of age	Per cent 15–64 years of age	Per cent 65+ years of age			Gini	90/10	90/50	
USA									
1990	22.0	66.0	12.0	2.1	41.8	0.338	5.65	2.04	12.16
2000	22.0	66.0	12.0	2.1	44.4	0.370	5.68	2.12	12.65
UK									
1990	19.0	65.0	16.0	1.8	39.2	0.336	4.67	2.06	13.95
2000	19.0	65.0	16.0	1.7	40.9	0.343	4.57	2.14	13.17
France									
1990	20.0	66.0	14.0	1.8	32.4	0.287	3.46	1.82	16.73
2000	19.0	65.0	16.0	1.9	35.8	0.278	3.45	1.88	18.00
Germany									
1990	16.0	69.0	15.0	1.5	34.5	0.257	2.99	1.73	15.72
2000	16.0	68.0	16.0	1.4	38.0	0.275	3.37	1.80	18.97
Sweden									
1990	18.0	64.0	18.0	2.1	45.7	0.229	2.78	1.59	23.40
2000	18.0	64.0	17.0	1.5	44.4	0.252	2.96	1.68	18.31
Italy									
1990	16.0	69.0	15.0	1.3	24.8	0.303	3.91	1.97	15.42
2000	14.0	67.0	18.0	1.2	24.8	0.346	4.68	2.01	16.95
Mexico									
1990	39.0	57.0	4.0	3.3	31.0	0.485	10.72	3.12	Not available
2000	34.0	62.0	5.0	2.4	34.0	0.491	10.39	3.31	3.7[+++]
Taiwan									
1990	26.9[+]	67.0[+]	6.1[+]	1.8[++]	35.6[+]	0.271	3.35	1.89	4.00[++++]
2000	21.2[+]	70.2[+]	8.6[+]	1.1[++]	48.4[+]	0.296	3.81	1.96	5.84[++++]

[a]Data from the World Bank – available www.worldbank.org/data.

[b]Luxembourg Income Study (LIS) Micro Database, (2007); harmonization of original surveys conducted by the Luxembourg Income Study, Asbl. Luxembourg, periodic updating.

[c]Data from Huber et al. (2004). Comparative Welfare States Dataset. Northwestern University, University of North Carolina, Duke University, Indiana University.

*Social Security transfers as per cent of GDP, includes benefits for sickness, old age, family allowances, social assistance grants, and welfare.

[+]Data from Taiwan's National Statistics Bureau.

[++]Data from Taiwan's National Statistics Bureau for 1995 and 2005.

[+++]Data from Usami (2004).

[++++]Data from Ramesh (2003). Data from 1990 and 1997, respectively.

mobility opportunities for children. The Swedish case is distinct because it has had among the highest female labor force participation rates for decades, supported by social democratic institutions that provide health and child care as well as support for part-time work with wage solidarity and social benefits. The Italian case reflects the persistence of gender inequality in that country, with fewer opportunities for women in the marketplace and few if any welfare benefits and services available to help families.

Income inequality measured by the Gini coefficient has increased across the board following earlier studies (Gottschalk and Smeeding, 1997), except in France where it has remained unchanged. The Gini coefficient is a summary measure of the total income distribution which describes the proportion of the population that would have to change in order for disposable household income to be equal in the population. Disposable income is gross household income, including social insurance and cash transfers, minus direct taxes and social security contributions. The lowest levels of overall inequality are found in the social rights states of Europe, which have lower fertility rates, older populations, and higher levels of social security transfers. The Anglo-American liberal welfare countries (United States, United Kingdom) have higher levels of income inequality associated with younger populations (although the United Kingdom is older than the United States) and lower levels of social security transfers. The developing countries (Mexico and Taiwan) also have higher levels of income inequality than the European states and the lowest social security transfer rates.

However, these measures do not reveal where in the distributions the inequalities are increasing or decreasing. Cut-point ratios that compare the extremes (90th to 10th percentile), the top versus the median (90th to 50th percentile), or the median versus the bottom (50th to 10th percentile) of the distribution are more helpful in answering the latter question. A common trend across advanced and developing countries is for the top to be pulling away from the median. However, in Germany and Italy the ratios between top and bottom have also increased: i.e., they may vary to the extent that the inequality observed is being driven at the top or bottom or both top and bottom of the distributions. The least-developed country (Mexico) exhibits the highest dispersion between top and bottom, but also shows the globalized pattern of the highest income group pulling away from the middle. The Anglo-American countries have higher dispersions between top and bottom and top and middle than the European states.

In general, the demographic characteristics of these countries provide illustrations of how levels of economic development and cultural legacies are related to different levels of inequality. The most unequal countries have higher proportions of their populations aged 14 or less. And, the older adults in these countries are afforded lower levels of social security transfers. Hence, general inequality places the youngest and the oldest age groups at risk of impoverishment.

Age, gender, and risks for poverty

One key aspect of inequality is the bottom of the distribution, where people are actually impoverished. Women, children, and older populations are among the most vulnerable to poverty in all societies. Their statuses outside of the employment sector, a form of social exclusion discussed below, and dependency on transfers or other derived incomes largely account for their vulnerability. In societies where women have greater access to employment their fortunes improve. At the same time, the basis of their relatively greater vulnerability when compared to men shifts from non-work to lower wages, lower pension and health insurance coverage, and limited access to child care support (Gornick, 2004; Gornick and Meyers, 2003; Shuey and O'Rand, 2004). In effect, employment improves women's status, but in the absence of other social protections women and their children are at higher risk of poverty and other social hazards across their lives (Gauthier, 1996).

Table 9.2 examines trends in poverty rates in the same countries represented in Table 9.1. The poverty rates are calculated as the per cent of population subgroups that live in households with DPI that is 40 per cent below the median household DPI for the total population, for households with children under age 18, and for all, male-headed and female-headed households in three age groups (working ages 18–64, ages 65 and older, and ages 75 and older, respectively). Following recommended methods, LIS country-level data are bottom-coded at 1 per cent of equivalized mean income and top-coded at 10 times the median non-equivalized income. All missing values and values with zero income are excluded. Additional details on LIS methods regarding the construction of poverty rates and other key figures are available.[5] LIS also provides a Key Figure Search Engine[6] that compiles data on income inequality, income distribution, and relative poverty rates for LIS countries. Finally, statistical package coding of LIS key figures is also available).[7] The use of rates at 40 per cent below the median as the measure of poverty is intended to capture the 'depth' of relative poverty and may produce figures lower than those based on other measures (Brady, 2005; Smeeding, 2004).

Generally, the highest risks for poverty in advanced countries with diverse welfare legacies occur in female-headed households across age groups and in the liberal welfare regimes of the United States and the United Kingdom, although these risks generally declined between the early 1990s and 2000s. Women's increased labor force participation across most countries probably accounts for these declines. Women's employment appears to have had equalizing effects on all types of households and on those with children under the age of 18 (Esping-Andersen, 2007).

In Italy, Mexico, and Taiwan, which represent different legacies, the relative poverty rates of female-headed households and those with children under 18 have generally increased, except in the oldest age group. Fewer supports are offered to working families and children in these countries.

Among older populations, general poverty rates declined in advanced countries, except in the United States. This is a remarkable reversal in the United States after almost three decades of decline

Table 9.2 Per cent of population below 40% of median disposable income in selected countries

	Total population households			Children under 18	Individuals 18–64 households			Aged 65+ households			Aged 75+ households		
	All	Male-headed	Female-headed	All households	All	Male-headed	Female-headed	All	Male-headed	Female-headed	All	Male-headed	Female-headed
USA													
1991	12.1	7.4	30.8	18.2	9.3	6.5	23.4	12.6	7.3	23.6	15.3	8.1	24.6
2000	10.8	7.5	15.4	14.1	8.9	6.7	12.1	15.1	10.4	20.5	17.8	11.9	23.4
UK													
1991	6.7	5.1	14.9	8.6	5.6	4.9	11.1	8.2	4.5	15.9	12.0	6.6	18.4
1999	5.3	4.5	8.9	6.0	4.7	4.4	6.6	6.7	4.5	11.7	8.4	5.4	12.7
France													
1989	4.8	4.3	8.1	3.9	4.7	4.3	7.3	7.2	6.7	8.3	8.3	8.2	8.4
2000	2.8	2.1	7.2	2.6	2.8	2.1	7.4	3.0	2.1	5.6	3.9	2.2	7.4
Germany													
1989	3.2	1.6	10.9	1.6	2.9	1.8	10.7	6.2	2.9	10.8	8.7	3.8	12.9
2000	4.5	3.1	7.5	5.5	4.5	3.4	6.9	4.0	2.3	6.3	4.3	1.7	6.3
Sweden													
1992	4.1	3.1	8.5	1.6	5.9	4.2	14.2	1.5	0.6	3.1	1.7	0.4	3.1
2000	3.8	2.6	6.2	1.8	4.7	3.4	7.6	2.1	1.0	3.5	2.7	1.5	4.0
Italy													
1989	4.4	3.9	8.9	5.1	3.8	3.5	7.2	6.0	3.9	11.5	7.1	2.7	14.4
1998	8.4	7.1	13.4	12.3	8.0	6.8	13.4	7.0	5.2	10.5	5.7	2.9	9.4
Mexico													
1992	14.9	15.2	12.3	18.1	11.7	12.1	7.6	20.0	19.7	21.5	23.5	23.3	24.2
2000	15.4	15.7	14.0	19.7	12.2	12.4	10.8	21.9	21.3	23.6	28.3	28.8	27.3
Taiwan													
1991	2.3	2.0	6.8	2.0	1.6	1.5	3.7	9.7	9.0	17.6	11.2	9.5	29.1
2000	4.5	3.7	9.2	3.0	3.1	2.5	6.1	16.1	14.2	23.7	17.3	15.1	26.5

All data from Waves 3 and 4 of the Luxembourg Income Study (LIS) – available www.lisproject.org.

in poverty among the oldest populations that followed in the wake of Medicare legislation in the 1960s and a series of amendments to the Social Security over the 1970s and 1980s that extended benefits to the poor with the Supplemental Security Income programme, cost-of-living adjustments, and divorced spouse benefits. The oldest populations fare worse than other groups in Italy, Mexico, and Taiwan where families are still expected to bear the burden of supporting ageing parents.

Finally, households with children under 18 exhibit increased risks for poverty in five of the eight countries observed. The specific causes by country vary, but they are drawn from a list of factors that include the non-employment or underemployment of fathers and mothers, divorce, single-parenthood, illness, disability and other related factors (Esping-Andersen, 2007), and social policies that exclude women and children as directly entitled to social protections outside of employment or traditional family arrangements (Rainwater and Smeeding, 2003).

Intergenerational equity across countries?

A debate that emerged in the 1980s in the United States centered on whether welfare systems inevitably face competing choices between abating the risks for poverty among children or the aged (Preston, 1984). The question was motivated by US trends since the 1960s, which showed declines in poverty among the aged and increases in poverty among children. These trends had not occurred to the same extent elsewhere in the Anglo-European world. What is apparent in our descriptive statistics and other analyses is that the aged were indeed more likely to be poor before the 1970s and after 2000, whereas children were more likely to be poor in the period in between (Brady, 2004). However, systematic cross-national analyses challenge the divergence hypothesis that pits policies favoring children against those favoring older people. More generally, researchers find that overall poverty levels are highly associated with childhood and older people and that welfare and labor market policies targeting both groups and facilitating women's employment reduce all three forms of poverty (Brady, 2004, 2005; Brady and Kall, 2008).

Social exclusion, age, and inequality

Social exclusion refers to policies and practices that deprive persons and groups of (or disqualify them from) the resources and social protections provided for the general population. The concept

was adopted as part of the language of the European Union's social charter advocating the 'spirit of solidarity' and has generated policy debates in Europe. However, its measurement has proved problematic. Deprivation and disqualification implicate complex processes of the denial of (or incapacities for) participation in social institutions; social isolation and social distance from mainstream institutions; and cumulative disadvantage based on the sequentially contingent consequences of the deprivation of basic necessities in physical well-being, economic security, and education that result in marginalization and social exclusion.

Using data from the European Community Household Panel (ECHP), the statistical arm of the European Union (Eurostat) reports on patterns of deprivation of basic needs related to nutrition, health, income, indebtedness, etc., and their implications for risks for poverty[8] (Eurostat, 2002) and recommends policies for 'active inclusion.' Concerns over the heritability of poverty and the cumulative processes of adversity and disadvantage associated with it have generated considerable concern about childhood poverty and its eradication. In effect, social exclusion is treated in Europe as a syndrome (a latent construct with multiple indicators) with multiple causes and consequences over time. Proposed interventions to actively include children focus on nutrition, housing, health, and education.

The idea of social exclusion has not been as prominent in the United States, except in studies of race/ethnic stratification (Wilson, 1987). But recent interest has emerged around the topic of childhood deprivation and its long-term effects. The consequences of poor health in childhood are well documented to increase mid- and late-life risks for disease and mortality (Palloni, 2007). New longitudinal datasets are collecting information on the health trajectories of children and their correlates in response to rising social concerns about health over the life course and the cumulative effects of cascading social inequalities (see especially the National Longitudinal Study of Adolescent Health, aka Add Health).[9] Health disparities in the United States are anchored, in part, in unequal social origins embedded in a healthcare system that disproportionately excludes children from coverage.

Economic disadvantage also reproduces itself in patterns of intergenerational inequality associated with exclusion from mainstream educational, employment, and familial institutions. McLanahan (2004) has identified two divergent streams of families whose fortunes are stringently conditioned by the relative advantages/disadvantages of educational attainment, occupational location, and family structure. She uses the Fragile Families Study.[10] The first stream consists of mothers who attain higher levels of education and initiate their families later, bringing more resources to their children for early achievement. The second group begins families before attaining competitive educational credentials. They struggle over their lifetimes to attain economic security and promote the mobility of their children. This latter stream experiences social exclusion along several dimensions defined by Eurostat.

These US patterns of divergence and exclusion, based in part on the fortunes of families of origin, are also evident in other countries due to three common and spreading trends (Esping-Andersen, 2007). The first is the increase in single-mother households, most evident in Nordic and North American populations where upwards of one in five children live in these conditions. The second is the rise in educational homogamy, in which marital selection is driven by couple similarities in educational achievement that amplify and accentuate inequalities in income across households over time. The third is the increased growth of average women's earnings relative to men's (in part caused by men's stagnating or decline wages) and women's inequality in earnings among themselves that are culminating in greater household income inequalities. The consequences of these marital and household dynamics include the divergence of opportunities for children and what Charles Tilly (1998) has referred to as 'opportunity hoarding' among privileged households, who do not seek to explicitly exclude the more disadvantaged but systematically accumulate advantages for their own children by support of existing educational, childcare and health policies that advantage them and disadvantage others.

While earlier discussion in this chapter has emphasized patterns of inequality between age groups, social exclusion also points to the cumulative processes of inequality within age groups. Government, labor market, and civic institutions reinforce and even amplify family inequalities leading to divergent fortunes. Social class origins have enduring formative effects within cohorts that lead to increasing inequality as cohorts age. Children growing up in adverse conditions have fewer chances for social mobility and higher risks for lifelong vulnerability and impoverishment. The risks for lower educational attainment, employment insecurity, and poor health follow. Cumulative disadvantage thus increases the risks for poverty and poor health in old age and for early mortality.

CHALLENGES TO STRATIFICATION THEORY

The relationship of age and inequality in a global context poses challenges for comparative theory

and for stratification theory. Comparative theory has depended on ideal type approaches reflected in the influential works of Esping-Andersen (1999) and others. These approaches face challenges that emerge as country variations and deviations increase and non-European-Anglo-American contexts are included for comparison. Some call for 'unpacking' these models to consider specific aspects of country variations, preferring a variable-based as opposed to country- or type-based approach (Brady et al., 2005). Ideal types mask the effects of specific policies that may change in their relative importance over time. For example, population ageing may amplify the importance of labor market policies that encourage and support longer attachment to the labor force. Similarly, child-centered policies that encourage and support childbearing and/or support mothers' employment through leave policies that protect jobs may have greater effect on the well-being of families and children in some countries.

New concepts have also emerged that attempt to capture the complexities of age and inequality. The idea of social exclusion has gained prominence in the European Union as it has sought to integrate economies and to achieve social solidarity. But it is a multidimensional concept that implicates long-term processes of social deprivation, segregation, and cumulative disadvantage that are not easily captured. It requires that the policies and practices of societies are linked to the behaviors and responses of 'excluded' groups who contribute to patterns of social isolation, social distance, and cumulative divergence.

Stratification theory must attend to life-course processes. Cross-sectional age stratification approaches cannot account for the selection and allocation processes that lead to cumulative inequality over the life span. Cumulative inequality is a product of sequential selection based on status assignments (race, class, gender) driven by institutional mechanisms that socially construct these assignments and differentially support, reward or exclude status groups over time. Educational, workplace, and governmental institutions are linked by design *and* default to successively stratify the fortunes of status groups, leading to cumulative patterns of advantage or disadvantage over time.

CONCLUSIONS

Age and inequality are related in at least two ways. Inequality between age groups occurs as a result of unequal access to resources that emanates from institutional arrangements that link the market, the State, and the family for the provision of life-course needs. Children and older people have historically been disadvantaged by their positions relative to the market, especially within countries with weaker social contracts to transfer resources across cohorts. They have depended on the family to provide the principal safety net. Inequality within age groups emerges as the life courses of individuals with unequal family social origins and structural opportunities over their lives diverge and their positions in old age reflect cumulative economic and health disparities.

Patterns of social exclusion that are defined and reinforced by market and State institutions have become targets of social policy in European countries because they underlie both kinds of age inequality. These patterns vary by country, based on citizenship rights and/or market and family status. However, the mechanism is the same. Exclusion from access to resources that enhance human development from childhood to old age and that enrich lives at different ages is the major basis of inequality and poverty across countries.

NOTES

1 http://www.lisproject.org
2 http://www.lisproject.org/publications/welfaredata/welfareaccess.htm
3 http://www.worldbank.org/data
4 http://www.lisproject.org/wstechdoc.htm
5 http://www.lisproject.org/keyfigures/methods htm
6 http://www.lisproject.org/php/kf/kf.php
7 http://www.lisproject.org/keyfigures/programs.htm
8 http://ec.europa.eu/employment_social/spsi/child_poverty_en.htm
9 http://www.cpc.unc.edu/projects/addhealth
10 http//:www.fragilefamilies.princeton.edu/

REFERENCES

Anand, S. and Sen, A. (2000) 'Human development and economic sustainability', *World Development*, 28(12): 2029–49.

Bongaarts, J. (2004) 'Population aging and the rising cost of public pensions', *Population and Development Review*, 30(1): 1–23.

Bonoli, G. (2003) 'Two worlds of pension reform in Western Europe', *Comparative Politics*, 35(4): 399–416.

Brady, D. (2004) 'Reconsidering the divergence between elderly, child and overall poverty', *Research on Aging*, 26(5): 487–510.

Brady, D. (2005) 'The welfare state and relative poverty in rich western democracies', 1967–1997. *Social Forces*, 83(4): 1329–64.

Brady, D. and Kall, D. (2008) 'Nearly universal, but somewhat distinct: the feminization of poverty in affluent western democracies', 1969–2000. *Social Science Research*, 37: 976–1007.

Brady, D., Beckfield, J., and Seeleib-Kaiser, M. (2005) 'Economic globalization and the welfare state in affluent democracies', 1975–1998. *American Sociological Review*, 70: 921–48.

Dannefer, D. (2003) 'Cumulative advantage/disadvantage and the life course: cross fertilizing age and social science theory', *Journal of Gerontology – Social Sciences*, 58B: S327–38.

DiPrete, T.A. and Eirich, G.M. (2006) 'Cumulative advantage as a mechanism for inequality: a review of theoretical and empirical developments', *Annual Review of Sociology*, 32: 271–97.

Esping-Andersen, G. (1999) *Social Foundations of Postindustrial Economies*. New York: Oxford University Press.

Esping-Andersen, G. (2007) 'Sociological explanations of changing income distributions', *American Behavioral Scientist*, 50: 639–58.

Eurostat (2002) *European Social Statistics – Income, Poverty and Social Exclusion, 2nd Report*. Luxembourg: Eurostat.

Gauthier, A.H. (1996) *The State and the Family: A Comparative Analysis of Family Policies in Industrialized Countries*. Oxford: Oxford University Press.

Gornick, J.C. (2004) 'Women's economic outcomes, gender inequality, and public policy: findings from the Luxembourg Income Study', *Socio-Economic Review*, 2(2): 213–38.

Gornick, J.C. and Meyers, M.K. (2003) *Families That Work: Policies for Reconciling Parenthood and Employment*. New York: Russell Sage Foundation.

Gottschalk, P. and Smeeding, T.M. (1997) 'Cross-national comparisons of earnings and income inequality', *Journal of Economic Literature*, 35: 633–87.

Huber, E., Stephens, J.D., Ragin, C., Brady, D., and Beckfield, J. (2004) *Comparative Welfare States Data Set*. University of Carolina, Northwestern University, Duke University, and Indiana University.

Kinsella, K. and Phillips, D. (2005) 'The demographic drivers of aging', *Population Bulletin*, March: 8–11.

Korpi, W. (2000) 'Faces of inequality: gender, class and patterns of inequalities in different types of welfare states', *Social Politics*, 7(20): 127–91.

Lee, R. (2003) 'The demographic transition: three centuries of fundamental change', *The Journal of Economic Perspectives*, 17: 167–90.

Leisering, L. and Leibfried, S. (1999) *Time and Poverty in Western Welfare States*. Cambridge: Cambridge University Press.

Lesthaeghe, R. (1995) 'The second demographic transition in western countries: an interpretation', in K.O. Mason and A-M Jensen (eds), *Gender and Family Change in Industrialized Societies*. Oxford, UK: Clarendon.

Luxembourg Income Study (LIS) Database, http://www.lisproject.org/techdoc.htm (multiple countries; 2008)

McLanahan, S. (2004) 'Diverging destinies: how children are faring under the second demographic transition', *Demography* 41: 607–27.

O'Rand, A.M., Ebel, D., and Isaacs, K. (2009) 'Private pensions in international perspective', in P. Uhlenberg (ed.),

The International Handbook of the Demography of Aging. New York: Springer.

Palloni, A. (2006) 'Reproducing inequalities: luck, wallets and the enduring effects of childhood health', *Demography,* 43: 587–616.

Pressman, S. (2001) *The Decline of the Middle Class: An International Perspective. LIS Working Paper 280.* Luxembourg Income Study, Syracuse University, Maxwell School of Citizenship and Public Affairs.

Preston, S.H. (1984) 'Children and the elderly: divergent paths for Americas,' dependents', *Demography,* 21: 435–57.

Rainwater, L. and Smeeding, T.M. (2003) *Poor Kids in a Rich Country.* New York: Russell Sage.

Ramesh, M. (2003) 'Globalization and social security expansion in East Asia', in L. Weiss (ed.), *States in the Global Economy: Bringing Domestic Institutions Back In.* New York: Cambridge University Press.

Shuey, K. and O'Rand, A.M. (2004) 'New risks for workers: gender, labor markets and pensions', *Annual Review of Sociology,* 30: 453–77.

Sinha, T. (2000) *Pension Reforms in Latin America and its Lessons for International Policymakers.* Boston: Kluwer Academic Publishers.

Smeeding, T.M. (2004) 'Twenty years of research on income inequality, poverty and redistribution in the developed world: introduction and overview', *Socio-Economic Review,* 22: 149–63.

Tilly, C. (1998) *Durable Inequality.* Berkeley, CA: University of California Press.

Usami, K. (2004) 'Introduction: comparative study of social security systems in Asia and Latin America – a contribution to the study of emerging welfare states', *The Developing Economies,* 52: 125–45.

Walker, R. (1995) 'The dynamics of poverty and exclusion', in G. Broom (ed.), *Social Exclusion in European Welfare States.* Cheltenham, UK: Edward Edgar.

Wilson, W.J. (1987) *The Truly Disadvantaged: The Inner City, the Underclass and Public Policy.* Chicago: University Chicago Press.

Wolff, E.N. (2004) 'The unraveling of the American pension system, 1983–2001', in N. Ganesan and T. Ghilarducci (eds), *In Search of Retirement Security: The Changing Mix of Social Insurance, Employee Benefits and Personal Responsibility.* Washington, DC: National Academy of Social Insurance.

World Bank (1994) *Averting the Old Age Crisis.* New York: Oxford University Press.

Zunz, O., Schoppa, L., and Hiwatari, N. (2002) *Social Contracts Under Stress.* New York: SAGE.

10

Gender and Ageing in the Context of Globalization

Toni Calasanti

INTRODUCTION

This chapter develops a framework sensitive to power relations to explore the ways in which the globalization of economic trade affects older women and men. Gender inequalities in the context of global and local power relations structure family life, public and private pension policies, and paid labour markets in ways that constrict opportunities for old people as well as amplifying gender through the life course.

The chapter begins by reviewing demographic trends among old men and women, such as life expectancy, living arrangements, and poverty. Gender relations themselves are defined in a global context in order to provide a framework for understanding population trends. The chapter then considers labour force participation, pensions, and care work, to illustrate how the qualities of life experienced by old people worldwide are structured by gender (as well as class and other hierarchies) in a global context. I show how gender and global relations influence paid work over the life course such that old women are more likely to be poor, despite the fact that women's labour force participation (and unpaid work) is central to globalization in both the global South and North. Most workers across the globe do not have access to pensions, which are based on formal, paid labour and are often tied to wages. On this basis alone, old women receive less income in old age than old men do. Care work and other forms of unpaid labour go mostly unrewarded by pensions, again disadvantaging women, who tend to be the

ones engaged in such activities. By the same token, old women in the global North often fare better than most old men in the South – in part because they are tied to men in their locations, but also because they can take advantage of the low-waged work performed by women and men in the global South.

Because the resulting remittances aid the survival of their own families, some women in the global South migrate to care for those in the global North (where women are more likely to be employed and have 'careers'), and often leave their own families either in the hands of other female family members or even lower-paid women. Scholars have referred to this interrelation as the 'nanny chain' – a term that tends to ignore the importance of age and what in this context might be called the 'granny chain'. The chapter examines not only women's predominance in care work but also the reality that international migration has influenced both who provides care and to whom the care is provided. That is, while women typically provide care, their ability to do so is influenced by global location. The term 'granny chain' is meant to convey the ways in which care work is shaped by ageing, gender, and globalization. On the one hand, some of women's migration is spurred by the need for care workers for old people in the global North. On the other hand, although most discussions of care work assume a dependent older person, in both the global North and South many older persons, particularly women, are giving care to their spouses, children, and/or grandchildren. Forms and frequency of such care varies by gender and global context in ways that reveal the manner in which globalization shapes and is shaped by gender relations. Finally, the concluding section summarizes the ways in which gender relations have structured globalization and old-age experiences and speculates on the outcomes of trends associated with migration.

GENDER AND AGEING: A DEMOGRAPHIC OVERVIEW

In most countries of the world, women have higher life expectancies than men. In the global North, the gender gap in life expectancy is both larger than in the global South (both sexes live longer and hence their life expectancies diverge more over time), and has increased over the past several decades (Kinsella and Phillips, 2005). Data from the World Health Organization (WHO) show that, at birth, females in the United States have a life expectancy 5 years greater than males (80.4 vs 75.3 years); at age 65, women can expect to live an additional 19.9 years, and men, 17.1 (WHO, 2007). Women in Japan have the highest life expectancy at birth worldwide, at 85.5 years (they can expect to live an additional 23.2 years at age 65), compared to 78.7 (an additional 13.7 at age 65) years for Japanese men (see Chapter 5).

The growing disparity between North and South has much to do with differences in such factors as poverty, working conditions, access to health care, and the HIV/AIDS pandemic in many of the less developed countries (see Chapter 3). In the global South, where overall life expectancy is much lower, the gender gap is smaller. For instance, life expectancy at birth in Botswana is 41.7 years for men and 41.3 years for women; and in Somalia, 45.1 years for both sexes. For many of these countries, which have been heavily affected by HIV/AIDS, these mortality rates reflect a disease epidemic that has little to do with processes of ageing. Among those less affected by HIV/AIDS, we find higher numbers. Two examples are China (69 and 73 years, for men and women, respectively) and Egypt (67 years for men, 71 years for women) (Kinsella and Phillips, 2005).

As a result of their better life expectancy, old women outnumber old men, especially at higher ages, and in most nations, widows far outnumber widowers (Kinsella and Phillips, 2005). In 2005, worldwide, women over age 60 outnumbered men of the same age by 67 million, and there were almost twice as many women over age 80 years than men of that age (United Nations, 2007). Paradoxically, despite overall lower life expectancy, more old people (in absolute numbers) live in the global South. In terms of gender, this means that, in 2025, at least 7 out of 10 women 60 and over will live in this region (International Labour Organization, 2001). Although some scholars refer to the larger number of older women in terms of the 'feminization of ageing' and see the 'problems of ageing' as problems for women, a more gender-sensitive approach emphasizes not the number of old women (or men), but how gender shapes old age (including the likelihood of experiencing it). Such an approach focuses on how men and women face similar but also contrasting experiences of ageing, and how global location shapes these.

GENDER, POWER, AND GLOBALIZATION

Gender, global, and local power relations constrain the choices that people make, and thereby shape both their life courses and old age. Across macro and micro levels, gender repeatedly emerges as a basis for power differentials. As a concept, *gender relations* emphasizes that gender serves as a dynamic, *social organizing principle*, and that women's and men's *identities and power* are gained in relation to one another. That is, gender is embedded in social relationships at all levels, from individual interactions and identities to institutional processes. Societies are typically organized on the basis of gender, such that what people take to be masculine and feminine both influences and reflects a division of labour (paid and unpaid, productive and reproductive, and occupations within each of these), and also devalues what women do. Thus, the gender identities maintained in social interaction also serve to privilege men – give them an unearned advantage – while they usually disadvantage women, even as people resist and reformulate seemingly 'natural' gender differences and meanings. Because men's privileges are intimately tied to women's disadvantages, the situation of one group cannot be understood without at least implicit reference to the position of the other.

The impact of gender relations on old age is most easily documented in relation to paid and unpaid labour. People engage in activities that have economic value, whether or not they are paid; which group is assigned which activities shapes both the composition and amount of resources available to them. For example, in more developed countries like the United States, most women work for pay yet still bear responsibility for most domestic labour (Coltrane and Adams, 2008). Men rely upon that labour, which enables them to pursue their roles as breadwinners with greater ease. Men's often invisible privilege within families justifies their economic privileges in retirement (based on the belief that one should be rewarded in old age for one's history of paid labour).

Gender is linked with other hierarchies – such as race, ethnicity, sexuality, and class – in which the privilege of one group is tied, intentionally or not, to the oppression of others. Age relations also constitute an axis of inequality, and thus old age disadvantages both men and women. Even the most privileged men will be disadvantaged relative to their younger counterparts. For instance, though old men can occupy positions of political power, the point at which they should cede office remains a point of public debate that hinges on such intangibles as trust and competence. Here, we see age relations at work. The equation of mental and physical incapacity with old age often 'undermines even the most powerful, respected, or beloved of politicians' (Bytheway, 1995: 45).

These power relations are shaped by global location. Walker observes that with the 'interdependence between the global North and South: the fate of older people in developing countries is tied increasingly to the operation of world markets and to the preferences exercised by (ageing) consumers in the developed ones' (Walker, 2005: 820). At the same time, the experiences of many old people in the global North are predicated upon the gendered labour provided by those in the global South. To demonstrate this interplay of global and gender relations, following a demographic overview, I briefly explore paid labour (and financial security in later life) and unpaid labour – especially care work. Along the way, the chapter will indicate the ways in which gender (and other social locations) influences the likelihood and experiences of each type of work.

While the 'global North and South' divide remains a widely used heuristic, it also oversimplifies. For instance, while the global North is generally taken to include all of Europe, the collapse of the Soviet Union reduced the standard of living in many nations in Central and Eastern Europe. Some scholars prefer a continuum and write of countries as being more or less developed or advantaged;[1] others refer to developed, developing, and least developed countries (e.g., United Nations, 2006). The Human Development Index[2] is often used as an indicator of a country's level of development, differentiating among nations as containing high, medium, and low human development. For purposes of this chapter, I use the terms 'global South' and 'less developed' or 'less advantaged' interchangeably, acknowledging their vagueness and the complexity that underlies these.

Gender and later life: Global Demographics

Gender relations are themselves a major contributor to the growing gender gap in life expectancy. Scholars suggest that in the United States, masculinity often involves physical risk in competition with other men that leads to both higher rates of accidents and violence as causes of death, neglect of social networks and medical care, and avoidance of any self-report of emotional strain (Calasanti, 2004).

Such gender relations can intersect within a global context to shape health and life expectancy for both men and women. In terms of more developed countries, Eastern Europe is a case in point. The collapse of communism and the former Soviet Union 'undermined public health and led to severe declines in life expectancy', particularly for Russian men, whose life expectancy decreased by 7.3 years between 1987 and 1994 (Kinsella and Phillips, 2005: 17). While improvements in Eastern Europe have occurred, men's life expectancy at birth is still 11 years lower than women's for the region (63 vs 74 years), particularly in Russia, where, in 2006, men's life expectancy stood at only 59 years of age compared with women's at 72 (Population Reference Bureau, 2006: 10). Comparable figures for Poland were 70.8 (men) and 79.3 (women); and for Belarus, 63.1 and 74.7 (WHO, 2007). Public health changes alone cannot account for these gender-differentiated trends. Rather, men's risky health behaviours, such as high alcohol consumption and violence, increased as workplace hazards, availability of health care and other environmental conditions deteriorated. Furthermore, such conditions can strain men's support systems more than women's (Kinsella and Phillips, 2005).

Other power relations within countries, such as class, also intersect with gender and global context to influence health. For example, in the United States, class intersects with gender such that mortality rates are negatively related to class for both men and women, but the gender differences do not disappear; as a result, lower-class men are especially vulnerable to poor health (Williams, 2003). How class and gender differences matter is influenced by global context. For instance, research by the Population Reference Bureau (2004) shows that, within the 53 countries of the global South studied, class differences between women accrue in relation to their health. Based on a wealth index relative to each country, they found that the wealthiest women are far less likely to suffer malnutrition, and are more likely to use modern contraception and have medically assisted births than poorer women.

Thus, such demographics acquire meaning when placed in a social context of (global) gender inequality. Older men and especially older women who live alone have a greater likelihood of being poor than those who live with others. This circumstance is exacerbated by the fact that, worldwide, women are more likely than men to be unmarried, live alone, and thus face economic insecurity. Even in Africa, where most old people live with others, of the 10 per cent that live alone, the vast majority are women (Oppong, 2006).

Worldwide, the number of widows is higher than widowers, and is rising rapidly (as is the number of never-married older women). For instance, the number of widows in Guatemala has risen 116 per cent from 1973 to 1990. Over the same period, this number increased by 71 per cent in Canada (Kinsella and Gist, 1998). In addition, the lower life expectancy in the global South means that, generally, women enter widowhood at younger ages there than in the global North (Gist and Velkoff, 1997), although their generally lower life expectancies mean that they do not necessarily spend more years as widows. The spousal age gap is even greater in Africa, as men remarry younger and younger wives over their life course (some of which are polygamous unions). As a result, African men tend to be married throughout their lives, while African women are widowed at even younger ages (approximately 40 per cent are under age 60) than in the global North (where the vast majority are over age 60) (Oppong, 2006). In the global South, support for widows has been provided informally, through family networks; formal support mechanisms tend to be non-existent. However, trends toward lower fertility rates and increasing migration – from rural to urban areas, or to different countries – have rendered widows in these nations more vulnerable (Kinsella and Gist, 1998). In addition, violent conflict, displacement, economic hardship, famine, and women's lower education make old women even more subject to neglect and abuse than older men (Cliggett, 2005; HelpAge International, 2006a).

That living alone is especially likely to lead to poverty for women is due in great measure to gender relations. Worldwide, women have less education, less formal labour-force experience, and more caregiving responsibilities than do men, but this is even more the case in less advantaged countries (Gist and Velkoff, 1997; United Nations, 2007). Given gender differences in income and wealth, old single women are likely to be poor and widows often experience large declines in standard of living, due to the losses of their husbands' incomes or pensions. While men can certainly lose income if their wives die, they lose far less than women do when their husbands' relatively large earnings vanish. In the global South, older women's financial security is further influenced by threats to their ability to inherit land and property (United Nations, 2007). As a result, worldwide, old women have a greater likelihood of being poor than do men. This is magnified in the global South where, in less developed countries, poverty is 'especially prevalent and severe among women' and as many as 100 million older people live on less than 1 (US) dollar a day (Walker, 2005: 821–2).

The economic position of old women can be illuminated by examining specific aspects of the gender division of labour – paid as well as unpaid, taking local as well as global perspectives.

GENDER, PAID LABOUR, AND PENSIONS IN A GLOBAL CONTEXT: ECONOMIC IN/SECURITY

Labour force participation

Both gender and global position shape work over the life course. Worldwide, men do more paid work than do women, though labour force participation rates decline with age for both. Still, in 2000, women made up a larger share (31 per cent) of the worldwide labour force aged 65 and over than they did in 1950, as their rates have declined only slightly, while men's have decreased more precipitously (United Nations, 2002). However, important differences in these commonalities emerge across regions and countries, pointing to the stratification of nations within the globalized world (Kinsella and Velkoff, 2001).

Labour force participation rates for both old men and women are higher in the global South. Indeed, UN data for 2006 finds that among those aged 60 and over, 22 per cent of men and 11 per cent of women in more developed countries are economically active; 50 per cent and 19 per cent of same-aged men and women, respectively, in less developed countries are in the labour force (United Nations, 2006). In such contrasting countries as Mexico, Pakistan, and Bangladesh, more than 50 per cent of old men work for pay (Kinsella and Velkoff, 2001). As a continent, Africa has the highest proportion of economically active older people, with 40 per cent participating in the formal labour market (Oppong, 2006; United Nations, 2002).

In some African nations, both men and women over 65 have extremely high labour force participation rates. In Mozambique, for example, more than 80 per cent of men are employed, compared to more than 60 per cent of women (United Nations, 2002). In Malawi, 85 per cent of men and 72 per cent of women work for pay. Similarly, in Rwanda in the late-1990s rates for both men and women were quite high, only dropping below 50 per cent at age 75 and over. Thus, we see 87 per cent of men aged 60–64, and 82 per cent of those aged 65–69, are involved in economic activity; 78 per cent and 73 per cent of women, respectively, are similarly engaged (Kinsella and Velkoff, 2001).

By contrast, labour force participation among older people in the global North is much lower overall. For example, in New Zealand, only 4 per cent of women and 10 per cent of men 65 and over are engaged in economic activity. Similar numbers hold for Canada and Australia (Kinsella and Velkoff, 2001). Rates in Europe were markedly lower: about 5 per cent overall, but as low as 2 per cent among men in some countries (Austria, Belgium, Hungary, and Luxembourg); among women, less than 0.5 per cent worked in Belgium, Hungary, and the Netherlands (United Nations, 2002).

Despite their more privileged status overall, not all women and men of the global North have been touched similarly by globalization trends since the 1970s; class differences accrue. This is apparent in data from the United States, where we see widening disparities in wealth among old people (Kahn and Fazio, 2005; O'Rand and Henretta, 1999) and a reversal in the trend towards men's early retirement, while older women's labour force participation continues to inch upward. The roots of such findings lie in globalization's impacts on the depression of wages and benefits for most people, particularly those disadvantaged by class, race, and gender (e.g., African-American working class women, Bound and Dresser, 1999). While profits are increasingly concentrated among a select few, a financially dis/advantageous situation accumulates over time. This is also apparent in the fact that not only employment rates in general but also *full-time* employment of both men and women aged 60 and over have increased since the mid-1990s (Gendell, 2006).[3] The increased inequality in household incomes over the past two decades (Hughes and O'Rand, 2004) likely plays the larger role in this trend, as workers are motivated to work full-time, and for longer, to maintain their standards of living.

Mills notes that, although gender inequalities in relation to work are not new, today 'the gendered and ethnically segmented labour pool upon which capital accumulation depends encompasses every corner of the globe' (Mills, 2003: 42). Women workers are central to globalization in several respects (Sassen, 2002). Gender hierarchies allow women's labour to be defined as less valuable – socially and economically – and thus cheaper. Such devaluation is crucial to global capital accumulation; the feminization of global labour undergirds export-oriented industries and agriculture in less

developed countries, and low-waged sectors – both industrial and service work – in the global North (Mills, 2003). The migration of women from the global South to the global North into low-paying jobs (including service and domestic work) allows for and supports the higher-paying jobs in global cities that some members of the indigenous workforce are able to acquire (Sassen, 2002).

Similarly, women's migration from the global South to households in the global North allows women in the latter region more autonomy and the ability to challenge the gender order in paid work within their own societies. That is, hiring the low-waged labour of other women to perform domestic labour has allowed women of higher classes in the global North to spend more time in paid work and compete with men in this arena. At the same time, such migration and employment patterns do not challenge the gendering of unpaid, domestic labour. In their employment of immigrant women as domestic labourers, women in the global North simply pass on the 'women's work' to women from the global South (Parreñas, 2000), resulting in a 'feminized and racialized support structure for more privileged households' (Mills, 2003: 45). At the same time, remittances from women's migrant labour play a significant role in alleviating poverty and in economic development in their countries of origin (United Nations Population Fund, 2006). The importance of such migrant labour to economies and families in the country of origin can be seen in the estimate that between one-third and one-half of Filipinos rely on monies sent by migrant workers (Parreñas, 2002: 39). Furthermore, although migrant women usually receive lower wages than migrant men, research suggests that women consistently send a higher proportion of their pay home. For instance, Sri Lankan women were responsible for 62 per cent of remittances sent home, while on average, Bangladeshi women send home 72 per cent of their earnings (United Nations Population Fund, 2006).

Remittances are just one way in which women contribute to the revenues of less developed countries (Sassen, 2002). Furthermore, the structural adjustment policies promoted by such financial institutions as the International Monetary Fund or the World Bank are believed by many analysts to result in state withdrawal from many social programmes – a situation which assumes households, i.e., women, will absorb the repercussions by taking on additional paid and unpaid labour, while diminishing their ability to do so:

> In effect, structural adjustment plans mobilize women's unpaid labour as domestic nurturers and economizers to subsidize costs for international capitalism and to guarantee the debts incurred by poor states. At the same time, the tightened

economic conditions ... diminish the security of formal wage employment and increase dependence on informal means of income generation ... [which are themselves feminized activities]

(Mills, 2003: 47)

In the global South, a majority of older workers are employed in agricultural work (Kinsella and Phillips, 2005), which is often the main occupation for women. In the 1990s, among those aged 65 and over, agriculture accounted for the employment of 88 per cent of Chinese men and 93 per cent of Chinese women; 76 per cent of men and 32 per cent of women in the Philippines; and 76 per cent of men and 96 per cent of women in Turkey (Kinsella and Velkoff, 2001). In Africa, the agricultural labour force is both ageing and increasingly female; in some places, more than half of those producing food are women. Such areas lack technological development, and thus rely heavily on physical labour (Oppong, 2006: 661).

Still, labour force participation rates reflect only those persons employed for pay in the formal economy. Although most old people are economically productive, this work is often unpaid or occurs in the informal sector. In the global South, much of the work that women do, including subsistence agriculture and household industries, goes unnoticed by standard economic measures (Kinsella and Phillips, 2005; Oppong, 2006). Given this, women's labour force activity tends to be underestimated, so reports of older women's relatively high labour force activity rates in many of these countries are all the more striking, as they doubtlessly fall far short of the actual figures.

More than half (estimates are as high as more than 70 per cent) of all old men and half of older women remain economically active in many parts of the global South, mainly in the informal sector (HelpAge International, 2007; Kinsella and Phillips, 2005). Even in this sector, work (and pay) is gendered. One study of older people in Bolivia found 41 per cent worked in paid labour; older women received the lowest status (and lowest-paid) jobs, including domestic chores – washing clothes, cooking, and cleaning – and recycling rubbish or street vending. Older men resisted such work as beneath them. An additional 21 per cent of men and 38 per cent of women engaged in unpaid work for their families (HelpAge International, 2006a: 9). Even when they become unable to leave their homes, old women in Ghana engage in economic activities, such as petty trade, to survive; comparable men are less likely to do so (International Labour Organization, 2001). Employment rates and occupations among older people are both gendered and reflect their global positions, and do not necessarily tell us who is economically active.

Thus, the likelihood of working in old age is shaped by globalization in conjunction with gender. That is, employment rates are more similar within global regions than without; larger numbers of both older men and women are compelled to work longer in less developed countries, whether in the formal (United Nations, 2002) or informal sector, or in subsistence agriculture. At the same time, gender influences paid employment worldwide in that women are less likely than men to work for pay, and to earn less than comparable men when they do.

Age discrimination in the labour market plagues older workers in all countries, even where, as in the European Union, it is prohibited in employment legislation (Macnicol, 2006). At the same time, age discrimination in the labour market is also influenced by gender and global position. Research in Canada (McMullin and Berger, 2006) and Australia (Encel, 1999) finds that older women, who are more likely to have had disrupted careers, face a devaluation of their skills; their age, presumed lack of up-to-date qualifications, and gendered ideologies concerning why they are working results in mainly low-paid work. By contrast, unemployed men were able to equate their age with experience and thus turn it into an asset.

The number of older people in the global South who want to work far exceeds their paid employment. So many people want to work because, according to HelpAge International, 'two-thirds of older people in developing countries have no regular income' (2005/2006: 6). For example, old people in Moldova not only exhibit high poverty rates – their average income is only one-fifth of the minimum daily subsistence level – but also the majority (77 per cent) of those surveyed report that employers will not hire them (HelpAge International, 2006a: 3). Gender intersects such that women are taken to be too old to work at earlier ages than are men. In some less advantaged countries, such as China, Estonia, Latvia, and Lithuania, women are pushed out of the labour force 'as young as 35 ... on the grounds that they are "too old" to work' (International Labour Organization, 2001: 9).

Pension provision

Differences in labour force participation rates across countries in the global North and South are directly attributable to national wealth. Persons in the global North, where countries have higher gross national products, are more likely to have pensions available to them, and will thus have the option to cease engaging in paid work. Labour force participation rates are higher in the global

South, where older people work out of necessity (Kinsella and Phillips, 2005).

While benefit amounts and precise rules vary, more than 90 per cent of workers in more advantaged countries are presently covered by government pension plans (Kinsella and Phillips, 2005), and select workers also have access to private pensions. Gender inequalities in earnings in the global North lead to pension inequalities. This means that labour force participation may help but does not guarantee women's financial security in old age. This is a situation that can be further influenced by other social inequalities such as class or race (Calasanti and Slevin, 2001). Thus, evidence shows that pension receipt and amounts vary by gender (as well as race and ethnicity) in such countries as Great Britain, Italy, Germany, the United States, and Eastern Europe (Ginn and Arber, 1999; Naegele and Walker, 2007). Globalization has exacerbated these gender differences in pensions, as it has allowed for a dramatic change from defined benefit to defined contribution plans – programmes that further disadvantage women, (Calasanti and Slevin, 2001; Rogne et al., 2009; see also Ch. 3 of this volume).

Worldwide, pension receipt remains rare for most workers. Although three-fourths of countries report having some sort of old age/disability/survivor's pension, only 3 in 10 workers are actually covered (Kinsella and Velkoff, 2001). A particular feature in the global South is that pensions tend to be limited to higher class and male workers in urban areas (Kinsella and Phillips, 2005), such as civil servants, military personnel, and workers in the formal economy. In Bolivia, for instance, 26 per cent of old people in urban areas in comparison with 4 per cent in rural regions receive a pension (HelpAge International, 2006b). Help Age International (2004/2005) reported that fewer than one in five older people in developing countries receives a pension. Recent data show that only 40 per cent of those aged 70 and over receive *any* kind of pension income in the Caribbean and Latin America (HelpAge International, 2006b: 5). Even nations such as Thailand and Malaysia offer no comprehensive government pensions. Furthermore, the agricultural sector, in which most old workers are found, receives little or no pension coverage (Kinsella and Phillips, 2005). Those who work in agriculture must rely on families for support (Oppong, 2006), a precarious situation made all the more difficult in the context of globalization and migration.

It is important to recognize that most pensions assume formal labour force participation. Those whose labour is not recognized as pension-deserving are more likely to be women and poor people, and to be living in the global South. Yet, women's paid and unpaid reproductive labour, together with the informal economic activity of poor people and people in less developed countries, enable other, more privileged, workers in the global North to work for pay and to collect a pension. This reality, and the great poverty faced by many old people in less developed countries, has prompted a call for social (non-contributory) pensions (United Nations, 2007). Evidence suggests that even very small social pensions can have a large effect on poverty, as poor old people in developing countries tend to use these monies to enable other family members to attend school and acquire health care (HelpAge International, 2006b).

However, most countries do not have such pensions, reinforcing gender as well as class inequalities. Of the 44 African countries reported, only seven have pensions that are not earnings based. Only two countries, Botswana and Mauritius, have flat-rate, universal social (non-contributory) pensions, which would cover older residents, regardless of earnings (Social Security Administration, 2007). As a result, only 1 per cent of the Nigerian labour force is covered by pensions; in Zambia, 10 per cent are covered, while in Morocco, 21 per cent are covered (Kinsella and Velkoff, 2001: 117).

Recognizing that much of women's reproductive work is important to economic well-being, some countries – in both more and less developed regions – have allowed women to count some of their years out of the labour force towards pensions, allowing them to collect as 'dependents' of workers, albeit at a much lower rate (e.g. in the United States, the amount is half of the worker's pension), or to become eligible for benefits at earlier ages than men (Social Security Administration, 2007). Despite the fact that women are still more likely to be poor even with these provisions, concerns that the burden public pensions could place on some countries has led to a call (by the World Bank and others) for an end to some of this 'preferential treatment' for women (Zajicek et al., 2007). However, the International Labour Organization (2001) warns that 'reforms' or changes in social security programmes that treat women the same as men ignore the inequities in the gendered division of labour, women's lower wages in paid work, and the ways that globalization shapes the kinds of work available, to whom, and at what compensation. Implementing policies based on legal concepts of equality in terms of pensions in the global South would thus have similar impacts as in the North in terms of 'equality' – women face an even greater likelihood of poverty (Ginn, 1998; Zajicek et al., 2007).

Care work

Mention of care work and ageing can evoke images of old people as dependent recipients, aided by daughters, daughters-in-law, and other younger, female family (in both the global North and South), or paid female caregivers (in the global North). However, old people not only receive but also give care: to their spouses, their children, and their grandchildren. Furthermore, although gender relations around the world consign women to care work, men – usually spouses – also provide it (Velkoff and Lawson, 1998). Finally, the globalization of women's labour supply through intensive migration has played an important role in formal and informal care, such that the provision of care to old people in the global North may be occurring in ways that strain the care networks in the global South (Zimmerman et al., 2006).

Caregiving for old people poses major challenges for all countries, but with variations according to global location. In most cases, families provide informal care, assigning such reproductive labour to women, especially daughters or daughters-in-law (Calasanti and Slevin, 2001; Kinsella and Phillips, 2005). However, the trend towards joint survivorship into old ages (particularly in the global North) means that, worldwide, and although they still provide a minority of care, spouses are increasingly the primary caregiver. In the United States, spouses provide about one-fourth of informal care (Kinsella and Phillips, 2005; Shirey and Summer, 2000). Because women outlive men, they have done the most of this; but husbands also do a growing share (Fine and Glendinning, 2005).

As noted earlier, well-to-do women in the global North increasingly are turning to cheap domestic labour provided by women from the global South. Such labourers find themselves driven from their homelands to seek incomes when, for example, structural adjustment policies take the land that they farm and transform them into urbanized wage workers; or when middle-class wages in developing countries fall below those of the poor in the global North; or simply in response to the lure of jobs and good wages not available in home countries (Chang, 2004; DeParle, 2007; Hochschild, 2002a). Such migrant women often leave their own children or older family members behind, sometimes in the care of other female family members but also in the care of even poorer local women whom they hire in turn.

This commodification of gendered and racialized reproductive labour into the global arena has been referred to as the '*international transfer of caretaking*' (Parreñas, 2000: 561; italics, in original) and a *global care chain* – 'a series of personal links between people across the globe based on the paid or unpaid work of caring' (Hochschild, 2002b: 1) that is stratified by class and often ethnicity as well (United Nations Population Fund, 2006: 5). For instance, in her study of

Filipina migrants, Parreñas (2000) documents a three-tier transfer of reproductive labour: 'class-privileged women [in the global North] purchase the low-wage services of migrant Filipina domestic workers, migrant Filipina domestic workers simultaneously purchase the even lower-wage services of poorer women left behind in the Philippines' (Parreñas, 2000: 561). In this way, Filipina care workers not only help women in the host countries but they also contribute to the economic growth of these countries, while their remittances home aid the economy as well as their families there. At the same time, gender inequalities in both regions are reinforced, as women do not 'negotiate directly with male counterparts for a fairer division of household work but instead … rely on their race and/or class privileges' to transfer care work to women with even less privilege (Parreñas, 2000: 577).

The opportunities provided by globalization have spurred many women to migrate, departing from the male-dominated nature of previous movements (Castles and Miller, 1998). For example, the vast majority of Filipino migrants are now women, in contrast to only 12 per cent in 1975 (Parreñas, 2002). Such migration results in part from the increasing income gap between the global North and South, wherein the poor in the former earn more than the middle class in the latter. Thus, many of these women migrate to work, rather than for reasons of family reunification (Hochschild, 2002a).

Such migrants are employed to provide care in the formal sector as well as in family homes. Parreñas reveals that 'Between 1992 and 1999, the [Filipino] government deployed more than thirty-five thousand nurses' to 'help alleviate the care crisis plaguing hospitals and hospices in more developed nations' (2002: 288). Indeed, the United Nations Population Fund (2006) reports that about 85 per cent of employed Filipino nurses are labouring outside of their country. The Fund also notes that foreign workers comprise more than one-fourth of nurses and nurse's aides in major US cities. A similar proportion of nurses in New Zealand are foreign-born.

Despite the increased attention given to these care chains, and the acknowledgement that women perform some of this care work for older populations, scholars have focused almost exclusively on the care of children, and the implications of women's migration for their own children. The 'global care chain' has been virtually synonymous with the 'nanny chain' and domestic work, including maids. However, women's primary responsibility for reproductive labour – which has often translated into their performance of paid care work as well – also results in what we might call 'granny chains'. That is, women migrate to take jobs as care workers for old people (mainly old women). In addition, increasing numbers of old people – predominantly grandmothers – are caring for grandchildren (discussed below).

The global chain of care has critical implications for old people in the global South, particularly in Africa and South Asia, where family members provide most of the care that old people receive (Kaneda, 2006; Kinsella and Phillips, 2005; Oppong, 2006). Often, such informal care is also all that is available. Many developing countries lack adequate facilities and resources for older populations, and formal long-term care facilities are vastly underdeveloped. In terms of healthcare training alone, Chile has only 25 medical doctors with training in geriatrics (Benderly, 2007; Kaneda, 2006). Declines in fertility or the loss of adult children to AIDS results in fewer children to give care. In addition, women's migration to more developed nations exacerbates the 'care crisis' already noted in the global South (Parreñas, 2002). Some scholars argue that support for old unmarried women or childless widows is of particular concern, as they can only rely on extended kin (Kinsella and Phillips, 2005).

Gender and care work by older people: Raising Grandchildren

The granny chain also links women worldwide in their care for grandchildren. In the global North, grandparents often provide extensive (30 hours or more per week) child care while parents work or on an as-needed basis (Fuller-Thomson and Minkler, 2001). And, in the United States, 'skipped generation families', headed by grandparents, are on the rise. In other instances, parents are also present in grandparent-headed households (Minkler, 1999). More than three-fourths of grandparents raising grandchildren are women; 43 per cent are doing so without spouses. Furthermore, such households tend to be disproportionately poor and headed by women of colour (Fuller-Thomson et al., 1997; Bryson and Casper, 1999).

Grandparenting in the global South tends to occur at earlier ages than in the global North; thus we cannot equate grandparenting with old age in this region (Chazan, 2008), though certainly many are over age 60. Further, care for grandchildren while parents work assumes a different meaning in the global South, where parents migrate for work and leave grandmothers and aunts to care for their children for long periods (Oppong, 2006; Velkoff and Lawson, 1998). In such places as South Africa, decades of such migration means that grandmothers have long played such roles (Chazan, 2008). The prevalence of such situations has led to

the recognition of 'transnational families': 'those whose members belong to two households, two cultures and two economies simultaneously' (United Nations Population Fund, 2006: 12).

The need for such care – and the pressure on grandmothers (Chazan, 2008) – has been increased by health issues. In addition to continued high levels of maternal mortality in sub-Saharan Africa, the HIV/AIDS pandemic has decimated the young adult population in parts of Africa, leaving many orphans in the permanent care of grandparents (Oppong, 2006; Velkoff and Lawson, 1998; see also Chapter 30). As many as 95 per cent of children orphaned by AIDS worldwide live in Africa. In terms of solutions to the numerous children orphaned by the HIV/AIDS pandemic, Oppong writes that:

> Kin fostering (in effect, grandmaternal caretaking) is viewed by governments, as well as nongovernmental associations, as the most culturally appropriate, sustainable, and cost-effective solution. Assumptions that it is the 'African extended family' that is coping are, however, of limited validity. For it is particular individuals (i.e., grandmothers) who are doing the bulk of the caring. ...
> (Oppong, 2006: 662)

Studies in Ethiopia, Kenya, South Africa, Sudan, Tanzania, Uganda, and Zimbabwe find that, while grandparents care for an average of 2–4 orphans and vulnerable children, many care for more, as many as 7–10 (HelpAge International, 2007: 5). In five villages in Mozambique, more than half of all older people care for orphans (HelpAge International, 2004/2005). In Zambia, a study of older caregivers finds that almost two-thirds were responsible for five or more dependents, and more than half were caring for three or more orphans (HelpAge International, 2006b: 12). Older people are giving similar care in parts of Asia as well, including Cambodia and Vietnam (HelpAge International, 2006b). Research by HelpAge International demonstrates the stark plight of older people caring for children with HIV/AIDS or grandchildren suffering from or orphaned by the disease. Already poor themselves, they 'face the challenge of finding enough money to pay for medication, home-based care, food and water, burials, and school fees and uniforms' (HelpAge International, 2006a: 4). Nguina, a 58-year-old woman in Mozambique, cares not only for her son and daughter-in-law, who are both sick, but their three children as well. It is estimated that the monthly cost of caring for a child in this country is US$21; care for someone with HIV/AIDS is another US$30. Meanwhile, the monthly income for someone like Nguina is US$12 (HelpAge International, 2006a: 4).

Thus, while older people are not as frequently victims of the virus, they are deeply affected, socially and economically. They lose time in waged work as their domestic burden grows, and often sell assets or possessions to help pay for care expenses. When their children die, they are left with both fewer economic resources and greater obligations (caring for orphaned grandchildren) (Oppong, 2006; Population Reference Bureau, 2007).

Grandmothers – of all ages – are giving care as they have in the past, but are increasingly stretched as their resources are called upon to support larger numbers (Chazan, 2008). And their caregiving burdens come not just from disease but from violent conflict as well. In Darfur, Sudan, two-thirds of the older women interviewed by HelpAge International were looking after at least two children each (HelpAge International, 2004/2005).

Research on the economic value of childcare performed by grandmothers in South Africa finds that care of orphans only contributes US$625 million (or 0.27 per cent of GDP); all childcare for grandchildren totals US$1365 million a year (equal to 0.58 per cent of GDP). If figures are based on the cost of raising children in formal care settings, the contribution is even greater, between US$1513 million and 4732 million a year (between 0.64 and 2.01 per cent of GDP) (HelpAge International, 2006b: 12).

Given the vast amount of care grandmothers provide in the global South, scholars have begun to characterize old people in these countries as: 'an unrecognized resource in sustaining the national, sub-national, community, farm-household and individual levels… . Far from being a burden, they will be an indispensable resource and many will not be able to "rest" after working all their lives' (du Guerny, 2002: 6). Rest is one issue; perhaps more pressing is the extent to which grandmothers and their grandchildren can survive in a context in which poverty is exacerbated by not just disease but also by structural adjustment policies that assume that 'families' can absorb the costs.

CONCLUSION

Most analyses of globalization focus on class, ignoring the gender dimensions that are integral to these class relations. Not only do women work the low-paid jobs in many parts of the world that allow for increased consumption among higher classes and larger profits but their reproductive labour – both paid and unpaid – also enables globalization. In the global South, women bear the brunt of increased workloads resulting from structural adjustment policies; the commodification of

their reproductive labour enables women in more developed countries to work for (relatively) high pay and reap the greater benefits of globalization. An understanding of the ways that gender influences ageing in this global context is thus critical.

The experiences of old age vary widely with gender, global location, and local power relations, and are also intimately connected. Most workers in the global North collect pensions, but most in the global South do not and thus remain poor; the ability of the former to enjoy 'good jobs' and retirement rests on the labour performed by the latter. Likewise, the poverty rates of old women are tied to the privileges that many men enjoy, particularly in more developed countries.

Migration shapes the global and gendered experiences of old age. The movement of people, both from rural to urban areas and from the global South to the North, leaves old people in rural areas and in less developed countries – and especially women – even more vulnerable than before. Migration leaves many rural areas without their traditional labour forces, both paid and unpaid. Family structures come under strain, and old people, especially old women, become more vulnerable. Accusations of witchcraft, typically enacted in times of high social and economic uncertainty, are on the rise, and tend to target old women with often devastating consequences (Cliggett, 2005; Oppong, 2006). While old women may still play an important role in caring for children, traditional sources of respect and support, including the family structures that command them, are waning. The migration of women from the global South to the North also means that a care crisis is emerging in less developed countries (Parreñas, 2002). Not only do these countries lack facilities but also the women who provide informal care are leaving.

What the growth of 'transnational families' bodes for future ageing experiences is unclear. Whether migrants return to their countries of origin or not, they may face difficulty in garnering support in old age. Homeland families stressed by the effects of globalization and structural adjustment may have little to offer, and migrants who stay in host countries may face old age with no support at all. Their generally low wages and lack of benefits sharply constrain their quality of life, made worse if they lack documentation. Stuck in jobs with low pay, even in nations with pension plans, these old people (and especially widows among them) face old age with few if any economic resources (United Nations Population Fund, 2006).

Poverty in old age is not confined to migrants or people in the global South; in more developed countries, the gender division of labour and pension policies ensure that women face greater economic uncertainty in old age. To be sure, some old people can opt to retire into high-priced consumption in posh communities. For most old women, their ability to do so requires that they be attached to men privileged by race and class.

The overall structure of this regime of gendered mobility and stratification will not change simply because more women are employed. In the United States, initial changes in the gender gap in pay resulted from decreases in men's wages. More recently, the narrowing of the gender gap in pay has stalled, with working class and women of colour earning very low wages. Even for those women with more assets, the gender division of labour in homes has not balanced. And while both men and women may engage in spousal care work, old women, often lacking resources, are asked increasingly to take on grandparenting duties. Without challenging policies (such as those relating to welfare, pensions, families, and migration) that emanate from the interests and experiences of those with power in more developed countries, the gendering of old-age experiences we see in the present global context may not change to any great extent.

NOTES

1 Based on UN classifications, Ashford and Clifton (2005) designate all of Europe and North America, as well as Australia, Japan, and New Zealand as 'more developed countries'; the remainder are considered 'less developed'.

2 As used by the United Nations, and developed by Mahbub ul Haq and Amartya Kumar Sen, the Human Development Index (HDI) is a comparative measure of well-being, based on a country's life expectancy, literacy and education levels, and standard of living.

3 Although some economists believe that the 1983 amendment to the Social Security Act, which mandated a gradual increase in age at retirement for full benefits, may have contributed to this increase (Gendell, 2006). If so, it is likely to be slight. For example, for the 66–69 age group, in 2005, one could retire at 65 years and 6 months and be eligible for full benefits; so there is little reason for this group to show such a large gain.

REFERENCES

Ashford, L. and Clifton, D. (2005) 'Women of our world', Population Reference Bureau. http://www.prb.org/2005women. Accessed December 30, 2007.

Benderly, B.L. (2007) 'Grow old along with me – and 690 million other people by 2030', http://www.dcp2.org/features/56. Accessed November 12, 2007.

Bound, J. and Dresser, L. (1999) 'Losing ground: the erosion of the relative earnings of African American women during the 1980s', in I. Browne (ed.), *Latinas and African American Women at Work: Race, Gender, and Economic Inequality.* New York: Russell Sage Foundation, pp. 61–104.

Bryson, K. and Casper, L. (1999) 'Co-resident grandparents and grandchildren', P23-198. US Bureau of the Census: Washington, DC.

Bytheway, B. (1995) *Ageism.* Buckingham, UK: Open University Press.

Calasanti, T.M. (2004) 'Feminist gerontology and old men', *Journal of Gerontology. Social Sciences*, 59B(6): S305–14.

Calasanti, T.M. and Slevin, K.F. (2001) *Gender, Social Inequalities, and Aging.* Berkeley, CA: AltaMira Press.

Castles, S. and Miller, M. (1998) *The Age of Migration: International Population Movements in the Modern World.* New York: Guilford Press.

Chang, G. (2004) 'From the third world to "The third world within"', in G.G. Gonzalez, R. Fernandez, V. Price, D. Smith, and L.T Vo (eds), *Labor Versus Empire: Race, Gender, and Migration.* New York: Routledge, pp. 217–45.

Chazan, M. (2008) 'Seven "deadly" assumptions: unravelling the implications of HIV/AIDS among grandmothers in South Africa and beyond', *Ageing and Society*, 28: 935–58.

Cliggett, L. (2005) *Grains from Grass: Aging, Gender, and Famine in Rural Africa.* New York: Cornell University Press.

DeParle, J. (2007) 'A good provider is one who leaves', *The New York Times Magazine*, April 22: 50–7.

du Guerny, J. (2002) 'The elderly, HIV/AIDS and sustainable rural development', United Nations, Food and Agricultural Organization. http://www.fao.org/sd/2002/PE0101a_en.htm. Accessed July 15, 2007.

Encel, S. (1999) 'Age discrimination in employment in Australia', *Ageing International*, 25(2): 69–84.

Fine, M. and Glendinning, C. (2005) 'Dependence, independence, or inter-dependence? Revisting the concepts of "care" and "dependency"', *Ageing and Society*, 25(4): 601–21.

Fuller-Thomson, E. and Minkler, M. (2001) 'American grandparents providing extensive child care to their grandchildren: prevalence and profile,' *The Gerontologist*, 41(2): 201–9.

Fuller-Thomson, E., Minkler, M., and Driver, D. (1997) 'A profile of grandparents raising grandchildren in the United States,' *The Gerontologist*, 37(3): 406–11.

Gendell, Murray (2006) 'Full-time work among elderly increases', *Population Reference Bureau*. http://www.prb.org/Articles/2006/FullTimeWorkAmongElderlyIncreases.aspx. Accessed July 13, 2007.

Ginn, J. (1998) 'Older women in Europe: East follows West in the feminization of poverty?', *Ageing International*, 24(4): 101–22.

Ginn, J. and Arber, S. (1999) 'Changing patterns of pension inequality: the shift from state to private sources', *Ageing and Society*, 19(3): 319–42.

Gist, Y.J. and Velkoff, V.A. (1997) 'International brief: gender and aging: demographic dimensions', US Bureau of the Census. http://www.census.gov/ipc/prod/ib-9703.pdf. Accessed July 14, 2007.

HelpAge International (2004/2005) *Annual Review*, London: UK.

HelpAge International (2005/2006) *Annual Review*, London: UK.

HelpAge International (2006a) *Ageing and Development*, Issue 19 (February). London: UK.

HelpAge International (2006b) *Ageing and Development*, Issue 20 (August). London: UK.

HelpAge International (2007) *Ageing and Development*, Issue 21 (May). London: UK.

Hochschild, A.R. (2002a) 'The nanny chain', *The American Prospect*, November 30. http://www.prospect.org/cs/articles?article=the_nanny_chain. Accessed July 2, 2007.

Hochschild, A.R. (2002b) 'Love and gold' in B. Ehrenreich and A.R. Hochschild (eds), *Global Woman: Nannies, Maid, and Sex Workers in the New Economy*. Henry Holt and Company, pp. 15–30.

Hughes, M.E. and O'Rand, A.M. (2004) 'The lives and times of the baby boomers', *Population Reference Bureau*. http://www.prb.org/Articles/2004/TheLivesandTimesofthe BabyBoomers.aspx. Accessed July 13, 2007.

International Labour Organization (2001) *Realizing Decent Work for Older Women Workers*. http://www.ilo.org/public/english/employment/skills/older/download/olderwomen.pdf. Accessed July 15, 2007.

Kahn, J. and Fazio, E. (2005) 'Economic status over the life course and racial disparities in health', *Journals of Gerontology Series B: Social Sciences*, 60B (Special Issue II): S76–84.

Kaneda, T. (2006) 'Health care challenges for developing countries with aging populations', *Population Reference Bureau*. http://www.prb.org/Articles/2006/HealthCare ChallengesforDevelopingCountrieswith Aging Populations. aspx. Accessed July 13, 2007.

Kinsella, K. and Gist, Y.J. (1998) *Gender and Aging Mortality and Health*. US Centres Bureau. http://www.census.gov/ipc/prod/ib-9803.pdf. Accessed July 1, 2007.

Kinsella, K. and Phillips, D. (2005) 'Global aging: the challenge of success,' *Population Bulletin*, 60(1): 1–44.

Kinsella, K. and Velkoff, V. (2001) *An Aging World: 2001*. US Census Bureau, Series P95/01–1. Washington, DC: US Government Printing Office.

McMullin, J.A. and Berger, E.D. (2006) 'Gendered ageism/age(ed) sexism: the case of unemployed older workers,' in T.M. Calasanti and K.F. Slevin (eds), *Age Matters: Re-Aligning Feminist Thinking*. New York: Routledge, pp. 201–33.

Macnicol, J. (2006) *Age Discrimination: An Historical and Contemporary Analysis*. Cambridge: Cambridge University Press.

Mills, M.B. (2003) 'Gender and inequality in the global labour force', *Annual Review of Anthropology*, 32: 41–62.

Minkler, M. (1999) 'Intergenerational households headed by grandparents: context, realities, and implications for policy', *Journal of Aging Studies*, 13(2): 199–218.

Naegele, G. and Walker, A. (2007) 'Social protection: incomes, poverty and the reform of pension systems', in J. Bond, S. Peace, F. Dittmann-Kohli, and G. Westerhof (eds). *Ageing in Society*. London: Sage Books, pp. 142–66.

Oppong, C. (2006) 'Familial roles and social transformations: older men and women in Sub-Saharan Africa,' *Research on Aging*, 28(6): 654–67.

O'Rand, A.M. and Henretta, J.C. (1999) *Age and Inequality: Diverse Pathways Through Later Life*. Boulder, CO: Westview Press.

Parreñas, R.S. (2000) 'Migrant Filipina domestic workers and the international division of reproductive labour', *Gender and Society*, 14(4): 560–81.

Parreñas, R.S. (2002) 'The care crisis in the Philippines: children and transnational families in the new global economy', in B. Ehrenreich, and A.R. Hochschild (eds). *Global Woman: Nannies, Maids, and Sex Workers in the New Economy*. New York: Henry Holt and Company, pp. 39–54.

Population Reference Bureau (2004) *The Wealth Gap in Health: Data on Women and Children in 53 Developing Countries*. http://www.prb.org/Source/ACFAC29.pdf. Accessed December 30, 2006.

Population Reference Bureau (2006) *2006 World Population Data Sheet*. http://www.prb.org/pdf06/06WorldDataSheet.pdf. Accessed December 30, 2006.

Population Reference Bureau (2007) *Today's Research on Aging*, Issue 6, August. http://www.prb.org/pdf07/TodaysResearchAging6.pdf. Accessed November 7, 2007.

Rogne, L., Estes, C., Grossman, B., Hollister, B., and Solway, E. (2009) (eds) *Social Insurance and Social Justice: Social Security, Medicare and the Campaign Against Entitlements*. New York: Springer.

Sassen, S. (2002) 'Global cities and survival circuits', in B. Ehrenreich and A.R. Hochschild (eds), *Global Woman: Nannies, Maids, and Sex Workers in the New Economy*, New York: Henry Holt, pp. 254–74.

Shirey, L. and Summer, L. (2000) 'Caregiving: helping the elderly with activity limitations', *Challenges for the 21st Century: Chronic and Disabling Conditions, No. 7*. Washington, DC: National Academy on an Aging Society.

Social Security Administration (2007) *Social Security Programs Throughout the World: Africa, 2007*. http://www.socialsecurity.gov/policy/docs/progdesc/ssptw/2006-2007/africa/ssptw07africa.pdf. Accessed November 1, 2007.

United Nations (2002) *World Population Ageing: 1950–2050*. http://www.un.org/esa/population/publications/worldageing19502050/. Accessed July 17, 2007.

United Nations (2006) *Population Ageing, 2006*. http://www.un.org/esa/population/publications/ageing/ageing2006.htm. Accessed July 17, 2007.

United Nations (2007) *Major Developments in the Area of Ageing since the Second World Assembly on Ageing*. Commission for Social Development. http://daccessdds.un.org/doc/UNDOC/GEN/N06/625/90/PDF/N0662590.pdf?OpenElement. Accessed March 4, 2007.

United Nations Population Fund (2006) *A Passage to Hope: Women and International Migration*. http://www.unfpa.org/swp/2006/english/chapter_2. Accessed July 2, 2007.

Velkoff, V.A. and Lawson, V.A. (1988) 'International brief: gender and aging: caregiving', US Bureau of the Census.

http:/www.census.gov/ipc/prod/ib-9803.pdf. Accessed July 13, 2007.

Walker, A. (2005) 'Towards an international political economy of aging', *Ageing and Society*, 25: 815–39.

Williams, D. (2003) 'The health of men: structured inequalities and opportunities', *American Journal of Public Health*, 93(5): 724–31.

World Health Organization (2007) 'World Health Statistics 2007', http://www.who.int/whosis/database/life_tables/life_tables.cfm. Accessed July 15, 2007.

Zajicek, A.M., Calasanti, T., and Zajicek, E.K. (2007) 'Pension reforms and old people in Poland: an age, class, and gender lens', *Journal of Aging Studies*, 21(1): 55–68.

Zimmerman, M.K., Litt, J.S., and Bose, C.E. (2006) 'Globalization and multiple crises of care', in M.K. Zimmerman, J.S. Litt, and C.E. Bose (eds), *Global Dimensions of Gender and Carework*. Stanford, CA: Stanford University Press, pp. 9–27.

11

Ageing and Health Among Hispanics/Latinos in the Americas

Kyriakos Markides, Jennifer Salinas, and Rebeca Wong

AGEING AND HEALTH AMONG HISPANICS/LATINOS IN THE AMERICAS

The purpose of this chapter is to provide an overview of ageing and health in the Hispanic/Latino population in the United States and Latin America. The Hispanic/Latino population in the United States is growing rapidly through both high fertility and high rates of immigration. Although it is still relatively young, this population is projected to experience rapid rates of ageing in the decades ahead. The population of Latin America is also growing and ageing rapidly. The implications of these rapid rates of population ageing are not well understood, especially with respect to Latin America. Latin America's demographic transition and population ageing are occurring in a fraction of the time that was the case in developed countries in Europe and North America, making it paramount for most Latin American countries to put ageing in the forefront of policy.

Below we elaborate on the nature of the demographic changes affecting the Latin-origin populations in the United States and Latin America; we examine the health characteristics of these populations with a special focus on the health of older people; we subsequently discuss health care and health policy implications. In this task we rely on a variety of sources of information, including population censuses and projections, national health surveys, and specific studies. Special attention is given to a number of large studies. In the United States we rely heavily on selected findings from the Hispanic Established Population for the Epidemiologic Study of the Elderly (Hispanic EPESE), a longitudinal study of older Mexican Americans living in the Southwestern United States. Since large scale studies of other US Hispanic/Latino older populations are not currently available, we examine estimates of disability rates for these populations using data from the 2000 United States Census. For Mexico, we give special attention to the Mexican Health and Aging Study (MHAS), a large national survey of Mexicans aged 50 and over. In addition, special attention is given to the SABE (Salud y Bienestar en el Envejecimiento) studies of seven Latin American and Caribbean cities. Below we provide a brief description of the above studies. Other studies and data sources are also referred to and described briefly in the sections that follow.

DESCRIPTION OF STUDIES

The Hispanic EPESE is an ongoing epidemiologic study of older Mexican Americans living in the Southwestern states – Texas, New Mexico, Colorado, Arizona, and California. Funded in 1992 by the United States' National Institute on Aging to provide basic data on the health and healthcare needs of older Mexican Americans. A sample of 3050 community-dwelling Mexican Americans aged 65 and over residing in the five southwestern states was interviewed during 1993–94. Approximately 85 per cent of older Mexican Americans reside in the Southwestern United States and the baseline data were generalizable to approximately 500,000 people. Subjects were re-interviewed four times between 1995 and 2005, at which time 1167 of the original sample were re-interviewed. Another 902 Mexican Americans of the same age (75+) from the same area were randomly selected by using area probability sampling and interviewed in 2004–05. The combined sample of 1167 survivors and the 902 new subjects were re-interviewed in 2007 approximately 2.5 years later (see Ray and Markides, 2007; Tovar et al., 2007).

The MHAS is a two-wave study of health and ageing in Mexico. The baseline survey was conducted during 2001 with a representative sample of approximately 15,000 people aged 50 and over. In 2003, follow-up interviews were conducted with approximately 12,000 subjects. MHAS was funded by the United States' National Institute on Aging, modeled after the US Health and Retirement Study.

SABE is a multicenter survey of people age 60+ from seven urban centers in Latin America and the Caribbean conducted in 1999 and 2000 (total n = 10,898). SABE was initially funded by the Pan American Health Organization (PAHO). The National Institute on Aging later partially supported data preparation and analysis.

THE HISPANIC POPULATION OF THE UNITED STATES

The Hispanic population of the United States has grown rapidly in recent years. It is estimated to be over 47 million, considerably larger than the African American population at approximately 39 million. US Census Bureau projections estimate that by the year 2050, the US Hispanic population will be as high as 120 million and will constitute approximately 30 per cent of the population. Currently about 60 per cent of the Hispanic population is of Mexican origin, 14 per cent is of Central and South American origin, 8 per cent are Puerto Rican, 4 per cent are Cuban, with about 7 per cent from other countries. With the exception of Cuban Americans, the Hispanic population is relatively young and growing rapidly, fueled by high immigration and fertility rates. The older Hispanic population is projected to grow rapidly in the next few decades and is expected to represent an increasing proportion of the United States' older population.

POPULATION AGEING IN MEXICO

The population of Mexico grew rapidly during the 20th Century, from 16 million in 1921 to 100 million in 2000. Population growth was fueled by rapid mortality declines and high fertility rates. Life expectancy at birth increased from 33 years in 1921 to 74 years in 2000 (Partida, 2006). The population aged 60+ is expected to increase from 6 per cent in 2000 to 15 per cent by 2027, representing a rate of population ageing that has taken a considerably longer period of time in developed countries (CONAPO, 2005; see also Ham-Chande, 2003; Wong and Palloni, 2009).

Population ageing in other Latin American countries and the Caribbean

A similar situation with respect to population ageing can also be observed in most Latin American countries. The total population of Latin America and the Caribbean increased from around 60 million in 1900 to 520 million in 2000, and is expected to increase to 800 million in 2050 (CELADE, 2002). While the rates of growth have declined in recent years due to declining fertility rates, Latin America's population is still quite young and has the potential for rapid growth in the future (Brea, 2003).

Cuba, Argentina, Chile, and Uruguay are in the more advanced stages of the demographic transition. Argentina and Uruguay exhibited declining birth rates earlier than the rest of Latin America, while Cuba's and Chile's transition has been more recent. Life expectancies at birth in these countries have reached relatively high figures, ranging from 74 years in Argentina to 77 years in Chile and Cuba in 2002 (Brea, 2003).

Current trends indicate rapid ageing of Latin America's population over the next three decades. In 2000 only 5 per cent of the population was aged 65 and over, a figure that is projected to grow to 17 per cent in 2050. While there is substantial variation among countries, the sheer numbers of people aged 65 and over in the region are projected to increase from 27 million in 2000 to 66 million in 2025, and to 136 million in 2050. Such rapid rates of ageing are likely to put a great strain on societal and governmental resources given persisting high rates of poverty and expectation for public sectors to assume more responsibility for the welfare of their older citizens (Brea, 2003; Palloni et al., 2006).

GROWTH OF RESEARCH ON AGEING

Since the establishment of gerontology as a field in the 1940s, researchers have been interested in the challenges posed by the growing populations in Western societies. Much of the early research ignored the ethnic diversity within-national populations. In the United States, it was not until the 1960s and 1970s that a special focus on ageing in the African American population was developed, and not until the 1970s and 1980s that significant studies of the Hispanic/Latino population were conducted. These were primarily focused on the Mexican American population in the Southwestern United States (Markides and Black, 1995).

Attention to research on ageing in Latin America and other developing regions has been much more recent. The systematic attention given to ageing in South Asia (Hermalin, 2002) encouraged others to give attention to Latin America, and a number of significant studies have been conducted since 2000, including the SABE and MHAS studies described above. These studies are giving attention to health and economic aspects of ageing at a time of rapid rates of ageing. They provide a first important portrait of the health of older people in some Latin American countries and are likely to generate interest in additional research in these and other countries. They are also increasing interest in comparative research on ageing in Latin America and the United States (see e.g., Palloni et al., 2006; see also the special issue of *Journal of Aging and Health*, April 2006). This is an important development, given that Latin America, especially Mexico, is by far the largest source of immigrants to the United States (Wong et al., 2006).

AGEING AND HEALTH AMONG HISPANICS/LATINOS IN THE UNITED STATES

As noted earlier, Hispanics constitute the largest minority population in the United States. Economically, politically, and culturally this is an important component of the United States and is likely to become even more important in the future. Understanding the population's health, healthcare needs, as well as the health status of older Hispanics is of paramount importance.

Although Hispanics as a group are generally disadvantaged socioeconomically, they appear to have a relatively favorable health profile, which is often referred to in the literature as the Hispanic paradox (Crimmins et al., 2007; Eschbach et al., 2007; Franzini et al., 2001; Hummer et al., 2007; Markides and Coreil, 1986; Markides and

Eschbach, 2005; Palloni and Morenoff, 2001). The existence of the Hispanic paradox (also called the 'epidemiologic paradox') with respect to the overall health status of the US Hispanic population was first identified over two decades ago by Markides and Coreil (1986), who focused on Southwestern Hispanics who were mostly of Mexican origin. They found that the health status of Southwestern Hispanics was more comparable to the health status of non-Hispanic Whites than the health status of African Americans, with whom they are similar socioeconomically. The epidemiologic paradox applied to infant mortality, life expectancy, mortality from cardiovascular diseases, and mortality from certain major cancers, but not to diabetes or infectious and parasitic disease (see also Hayes-Bautista, 1992; Vega and Amaro, 1994). Possible reasons for this epidemiologic paradox discussed were strong family support and other cultural practices, ranging from diet to resisting placement of elders in nursing homes, and selective migration.

Initially, the existence of a paradox was based on relatively similar health profiles of Hispanics and non-Hispanic Whites. However, beginning in the 1990s evidence began to suggest the existence of a mortality advantage among Mexican Americans as well as among other Hispanic populations. The mortality advantage was present among both men and women and was greatest at old age. There is some evidence that the mortality advantage might be the result of selective migration back to Mexico and thus bias mortality statistics downwards among Mexican Americans (Abraido-Lanza et al., 1999; Palloni and Arias, 2004). Yet such a 'salmon bias' is unlikely to account for the overall mortality advantage including old age (Hummer et al., 2007; Markides and Eschbach, 2005) because few older people of Mexican origin appear to return to Mexico to die (Turra and Elo 2008, see discussion of MHAS below.)

The Hispanic paradox has become the leading theme in Hispanic health. Most available evidence suggests a mortality advantage among Mexican Americans and other Hispanics, or at a minimum equal mortality rates to those of the non-Hispanic population. As noted, the Hispanic advantage has been attributed primarily to selection of healthy migrants and to better health practices.

Advantages have been found mostly among immigrants, with the overall health status advantage declining with time in the United States and disappearing by the second generation (Crimmins et al., 2007; Eschbach, et al., 2007). With respect to mortality rates among older people, evidence of an advantage remains regardless of sources of data employed. The Social Security Administration's Medicare – NUDIMENT data, which have the fewest data quality issues, continue to show an advantage in mortality (Elo et al., 2004; Turra and Elo, 2008).

Despite lower rates of overall mortality and of both cancer and cardiovascular disease, Mexican Americans and other Hispanics do not appear to fare as well on other health indicators. For example, rates of diabetes and obesity are very high among Mexican Americans and Puerto Ricans (Haan et al., 2003; Markides, et al., 1997), and these problems, combined with sedentary lifestyles, contribute to high disability rates for these groups (Markides et al., 1997). Below we outline selected findings on the health of older Mexican Americans using data from the Hispanic EPESE, a large, longitudinal study.

THE HEALTH OF OLDER MEXICAN AMERICANS: SELECTED FINDINGS FROM THE HISPANIC EPESE

As indicated above, the Hispanic EPESE is a large ongoing study of Mexican Americans 65+ residing in the Southwestern United States. It is by far the most important source of information on the population's health status. Below, we rely on cross-sectional as well as longitudinal data to create a health profile of this population.

Baseline data collected during 1993–94 provided basic information on the socioeconomic situation as well as the healthcare needs of older Mexican Americans. This is a socioeconomically disadvantaged population, with limited education, income, and assets. Almost half were born in Mexico. In view of perceptions of high rates of intergenerational living arrangements, it is worth noting that one in five (21 per cent) of older Mexican Americans live alone and two in five (41 per cent) live in two-person households. At the same time, a pattern of quasi-extended family living arrangements has been observed in the Southwestern United States where children and other relatives of older Mexican Americans live in close proximity, often in the same block (Markides et al., 1999).

Older Mexican Americans are primarily Spanish speaking, even though many are US-born or have lived in the United States most of their lives. Well over 90 per cent are covered by Medicare, an insurance coverage rate that is considerably higher than the coverage rates of younger and middle-aged Mexican Americans (Angel et al., 2002).

Diabetes and depressive symptoms

With respect to prevalence of major chronic conditions, older Mexican Americans generally have rates comparable to those of older non-Hispanic Whites. One major exception is diabetes. We estimated that nearly 25 per cent of older Mexican Americans self-report diabetes, which is at least double the rate reported by older non-Hispanic Whites (Black, 1999; Black et al., 1999). The true prevalence rate among older Mexican Americans is likely to be considerably higher.

Diabetes is a significant source of comorbidity in the older Mexican American population. Of the 690 self-reported diabetics in the Hispanic EPESE at baseline, approximately 60 per cent reported complications (eye, kidney or circulation problems, or amputations), and 40 per cent died within a 7-year period (Otiniano et al., 2003).

Relatively high rates of depressive symptoms and possible depression were also found in older Mexican Americans (Black et al., 1998), and high depressive symptomatology appears to exacerbate the impact of diabetes on mortality as well as the development of complications and disability over time (Black and Markides, 1999; Black et al., 2003). We speculate that depressed diabetics are less likely to engage in physical activity or in appropriate self-care, leading to problems down the road. It appears that depression often goes untreated, leading to serious consequences (Black et al., 2003).

Disability

As suggested earlier, despite relatively high longevity, older Mexican Americans appear to be more disabled than older non-Hispanic Whites (Rudkin et al., 1997). It appears that the Mexican American population may be experiencing what the general population was experiencing during the 1970s and early 1980s when increasing longevity was accompanied by more disability (Freedman et al., 2002; Manton and Gu, 2001). The Hispanic EPESE has identified numerous predictors of activities of daily living (ADL) and instrumental activities of daily living (IADL) disability, including pain (Al Snih et al., 2001), visual impairment (DiNuzzo et al., 2001), diabetes (Black et al., 1999), emotional well-being (Ostir et al., 2000), and obesity (Al Snih et al., 2007). Our cross-sectional and longitudinal analyses over 2, 5, 7, and 10 years of follow-up suggest the special importance of diabetes, obesity, and sedentary lifestyle, as well as high rates of depressive symptoms, cognitive impairment, and poverty.

Obesity

While obesity at younger years is a significant predictor of health outcomes in old age, obesity in older people is not a major risk factor, at least for mortality. In one analysis of all EPESE data sets (including the Hispanic EPESE), subjects with a body mass index (BMI) of 25–35 (traditionally considered overweight and obese) had the lowest mortality rates of all weight categories (Al Snih et al., 2007). It appears that obesity in older people affords some protection from disease. At the same time, subjects who are obese in old age are survivors who may be genetically predisposed to longevity more so than obese subjects who have died before they became old. While obesity may be protective against mortality among older Mexican Americans (and others), it appears to be a risk factor for the development of disability over time (Al Snih et al., 2007). Interestingly, unintentional weight loss and weight gain of at least 5 per cent of one's weight are both associated with the development of disability in older Mexican Americans (Al Snih et al., 2005).

Neighborhood cohesion

There has been a lively interest shown in the influence of community context on health outcomes. Much research has focused on the influence of socioeconomic characteristics of neighborhoods on health over and above individual socioeconomic characteristics. There has been suggestion that despite poor socioeconomic conditions, Mexican American neighborhoods might be characterized by high degrees of cohesion and provide greater support to Mexican Americans than do neighborhoods with low density of Mexican Americans. Several analyses of EPESE data have suggested that higher per cent Hispanic in the neighborhood was indeed associated with better self-ratings of health (Patel et al., 2003), lower incidence of disability (Patel, 2004), lower depressive symptomatology (Ostir et al., 2003), and lower prevalence of stroke, cancer and hip fracture as well as lower mortality over a seven year period (Eschbach et al., 2004).

CENSUS DISABILITY RATES BY RACE/ ETHNICITY AND TYPE OF HISPANIC ORIGIN

To extend beyond Mexican Americans and the Southwestern United States, we employ the US Census' 5 per cent public use sample (PUMS) file, which includes data on approximately 1.8 million Americans aged 65 and over to investigate health differences by race/ethnicity and by type of

Hispanic origin. Disability rates, based on an index consisting of five items from the PUMS, are standardized to the structure of the 65+ population of the United States in the year 2000 for ages 65–69, 70–74, 75–79, 80–84, 85–89, and 90+.

Figure 11.1 presents disability rates by race/ ethnicity and gender for people aged 65+. As suspected, overall rates for both male and female older Hispanics higher than for non-Hispanic Whites and slightly lower than those of African Americans. As also expected, Asian Americans had rates comparable to those of non-Hispanic Whites while Native Americans had the highest rates and Pacific Islanders had rates (not shown) very similar to those of African Americans. In brief, these rates are consistent with what we would expect based on the literature.

Figure 11.2 presents rates by type of Hispanic origin. To facilitate the comparison we also repeat here the rates for non-Hispanic Whites as well as all Hispanics. The similarity of rates for Mexican-origin persons to those of all Hispanics reflects the fact that the majority of Hispanics are of Mexican origin. As expected from the few small studies available, Puerto Ricans have the highest disability rates among the major Hispanic groups (see also Tucker et al., 2000) while older Cubans have rates almost as low as those of non-Hispanic Whites. This is hypothesized to be related to their generally higher level of socioeconomic status and generally better health profiles (Markides et al., 1997).

The most interesting and original findings in Figure 11.2 relate to the rates for Central- and South American-origin persons. These groups have been neglected in the literature because of their small numbers in available studies. Perhaps because these are almost exclusively immigrant groups and therefore positively selected for good health they appear to have quite favorable disability rates, which are lower than the rates for the Mexican- and Puerto Rican-origin populations.

THE HEALTH OF OLDER MEXICANS: SELECTED FINDINGS FROM THE MEXICAN HEALTH AND AGEING STUDY (MHAS)

As noted earlier, the MHAS is a large-scale study of the health of Mexicans aged 50+. Baseline data were collected in 2001 on a sample that is representative of approximately 14 million older adults. These are cohorts who were born roughly between 1900 and 1950, who had relatively low education, and who survived periods of high infectious diseases and high mortality in Mexico. They lived their reproductive years over periods of relatively

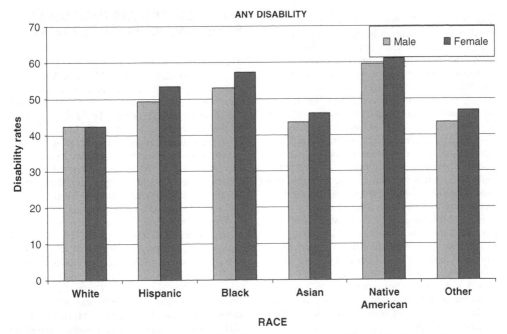

Figure 11.1   Age-standardized Census disability rates (per cent) by race/ethnicity for persons aged 65 and over: United States Census, 2000
Note: Directly standardized to age 65+ population, US all racial/ethnic groups in 2000, for ages 65–69, 70–74, 75–79, 80–84, 85–89, 90+

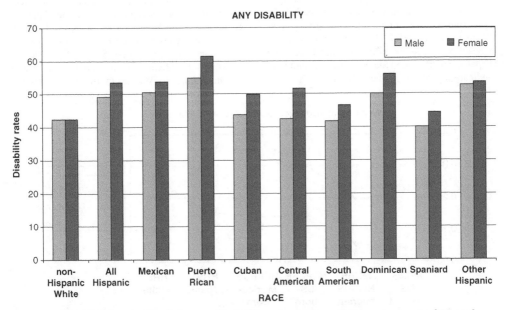

Figure 11.2   Age-standardized Census disability rates (per cent) for persons aged 65 and over by type of Hispanic origin: United States Census, 2000
Note: Directly standardized to age 65+ population, US all racial/ethnic groups in 2000, for ages 65–69, 70–74, 75–79, 80–84, 85–89, 90+. The Hispanic origin persons are recorded based on ancestry or country of birth, if they report general Hispanic. 'All Other' includes US-born Hispanics, who report non-specific identity, and who live in a Southwestern state

high fertility, and, men in particular, had long working careers. Currently, almost half (45 per cent) live in urban areas (population 100,000+), and 9 per cent of the men and one-quarter of the women are widowed. About two-thirds of the respondents had four or more children-ever-born; only 6 per cent had none. About one-half of the respondents have health insurance, although this represents 73 per cent in urban areas and 38 per cent in rural areas. About 40 per cent reported that they have never lived anywhere outside of their current community of residence. Eight per cent reported that at some point they had lived or worked in the United States. Among men, 14 per cent are former US migrants.

In this Mexican sample, the prevalence of self-reported diabetes is 15 per cent, and hypertension, 37 per cent. Undernourishment is a greater problem than obesity (30 vs 14 per cent) (Wong et al., 2007). While older Mexicans thus appear to be at less risk for cardiovascular disease, we are reminded of Mexico's underdeveloped status by the high proportion of subjects that do not have adequate nutrition.

The urban–rural divide is the basis for marked differences in the socioeconomic conditions of older Mexican adults. In general, those in urban areas have better access to health care and are more likely to have insurance than those in rural areas (73 per cent compared to 38 per cent). The unequal access to health care is associated with higher use of preventive care among those in urban areas (Wong and Díaz, 2007). This urban–rural disparity in healthcare coverage is not as salient for older Hispanics in the United States, most of whom have Medicare regardless of where they live.

THE HEALTH OF OLDER MEXICANS IN MEXICO AND IN THE UNITED STATES

The observed health advantage (at least with respect to mortality) among Mexican Americans points to a possible 'healthy immigrant' selection effect. By comparing data from the MHAS and the Hispanic EPESE, we can begin to understand if these processes are playing a role in the observed patterns. If the health advantage among Mexican Americans can be explained by a healthy immigrant effect, Mexican immigrants in the United States should be healthier than either US-born Mexican Americans and Mexicans that reside in Mexico who never migrated.

These comparisons suggest that a different picture emerges, depending on the specific health indicator used. Figure 11. 3 presents the adjusted prevalence of chronic conditions among persons aged 70 or older (adjusted by age, sex, and education). The data for the United States come from the Hispanic EPESE and Health and Retirement Study (HRS), and for Mexico from the MHAS. The rates shown are for women, and illustrate that for heart disease, the three Hispanic groups in the United States show similar prevalence, but lower than that of non-Hispanic Whites. On the other hand, the rates for Mexico are consistently lower than in the United States, not only for heart but also for stroke and cancer. As mentioned above, one exception to this general pattern is diabetes. The figure shows that prevalence of diabetes is highest among Mexicans and Mexican Americans in the United States, followed by Mexicans in Mexico, while the lowest rate is for non-Hispanic Whites in the United States.

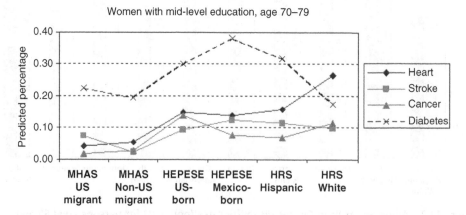

Figure 11.3   Adjusted chronic conditions for women aged 70–79 with mid-level education, Mexico and the United States
Source: **Mexican Health and Aging Study (MHAS), 2001; Hispanic Established Population for the Epidemiologic Study of the Elderly (EPESE), 1998; Health and Retirement Study (HRS), 1998**

Men with mid-level education, age 70–79

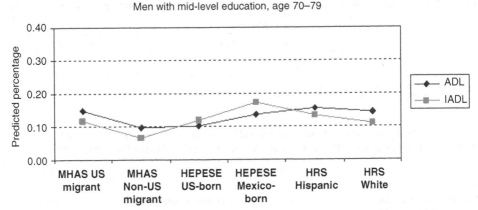

Figure 11.4   Adjusted prevalence of Functionality Problems for Men Aged 70–79 with mid-level education, Mexico and the United States
Source: **Mexican Health and Aging Study (MHAS), 2001; Hispanic Established Population for the Epidemiologic Study of the Elderly (EPESE), 1998; Health and Retirement Study (HRS), 1998**

A notable finding from these analyses is that, with the exception of diabetes and despite subgroup variations, persons of Mexican origin have favorable health profiles, regardless of country of residence. This suggests that the health advantage of this population may be influenced by ethnicity or culture.

Turning to functional health problems, Figure 11.4 presents adjusted prevalence data for activities of daily living (ADL) for men. Highest disability rates are for Mexicans who were born in Mexico and are now in the United States, and for former US migrants who have returned to Mexico. It is notable that the relative health standing of the subgroups is different with this indicator than with the chronic conditions reported in Figure 11.3. These comparative results, and those shown for Mexico alone using the MHAS, suggest that research seeking to compare health status of subgroups of the population by migration status should take into account the rural–urban differences in Mexico, as well as the sensitivity of the comparisons to the indicators used.

One of the reasons for reports of differential health, in particular for chronic conditions, is the lack of access to health care among the population in Mexico. Indeed, it is possible that the population under-reports chronic conditions because the very limited contact that individuals have with the healthcare system may preclude diagnosis. It appears that among older adults, healthcare coverage is vastly higher in the United States than in Mexico. Among persons aged 70+, the Hispanic EPESE data show that almost all (over 97 per cent) of Mexican-origin older persons in the United States, regardless of country of birth, have coverage.

In contrast, in Mexico only around 50 per cent have healthcare coverage, regardless of their former migration status.

As mentioned above, diabetes is an important health issue for Mexicans in both Mexico and the United States (Rull et al., 2005); another source of differences between Mexicans in Mexico and the United States is the treatment of this disease. Table 11.1 shows diabetes management by low-, medium-, and high-income levels, comparing older Mexican Americans (using Wave 3 of the Hispanic EPESE) to older Mexicans (using the MHAS). Diabetics in Mexico have a higher propensity to take oral glucose medications than older Mexican Americans in the United States. However (not shown), persons of low and middle income in the United States are prescribed a combination of oral glucose medication and insulin, whereas in Mexico and for the high income group in the United States, they are more likely to use either insulin or oral glucose to control medication. These results suggest that there may be differences between Mexico and the United States in clinical approaches to treating diabetes that may ultimately contribute to variation in disease courses over the long term.

Table 11.2 presents the odds of 2-year follow-up mortality comparing Mexicans and Mexican Americans. Results convey differences between the two countries in the risk of mortality for those who have diabetes in the association of economic resources with overall mortality. Older adults in Mexico who have diabetes are at significantly greater odds of 2-year mortality than their counterparts without the disease. Conversely, for Mexicans in the United States, diabetes does not

Table 11.1   Distributions (in percentages) for diabetes management by economic indicators

	United States			Mexico		
	Low	Middle	High	Low	Middle	High
Diabetes management						
Taking insulin	19.6	23.5	16.9	9.26	13.0	14.4
Taking oral glucose – control medication	69.0	64.9	81.9	87.0	95.1	82.7

Table 11.2   Weighted odds of mortality at follow-up for older Mexicans in Mexico (MHAS-bottom) and older Mexican Americans in the United States (Hispanic EPESE)††

Mexico	Odds ratios	United States	Odds ratios
Diabetes	1.822***	Diabetes	1.334
Currently employed (Yes)	0.448***	Currently employed (Yes)	0.908
Income (half the minimum wage)		Income ($20,000)	
One time the minimum wage	0.387**	0–$4999	2.790**
Twice the minimum wage	1.292	$5000–$9999	1.949*
Three times the minimum wage	0.457	$10,000–$14,999	1.886*
Four or more times the minimum wage	0.849	$15,000–$19,999	1.202
Type of living arrangement (House)		Type of living arrangement (House)	
Apartment	1.493	Apartment	0.744
Other	0.638	Other	0.741
n	2858	n	1876
−2 log likelihood	2121.50	−2 log likelihood	1156.91
Intercept	0.1129***	Intercept	0.0168***

$*p < 0.05$; $**\ p < 0.01$; $***\ p < 0.001$.

increase the risk of 2-year mortality. Income mediates the effect of diabetes on mortality in both countries. However, the effect of other resource-related factors is not so general. Being actively employed is associated with lower mortality in Mexico but not in the United States. On the other hand, having lower income is associated with a higher risk of 2-year mortality in the United States but not in Mexico. Thus, socioeconomic factors associate differently with mortality among Mexicans in the two countries. It is possible to speculate about the societal differences underlying these patterns. Since Mexico has a large informal labor market without generalized retirement benefits, remaining active in the labor market for older adults may be a necessity, and the inability to work may be associated with declining health. In the United States, higher mortality risk among the low-income groups may be a reflection of the current social welfare system's inability to counteract the negative health consequences of living in poverty.

Table 11.3 presents the effect of family support and migration on the relationship between diabetes and 2-year mortality risk using the Hispanic EPESE and the MHAS data. As previously observed, diabetes is a significant predictor of

2-year mortality in Mexico, but not among older Mexican Americans in the United States. Family resources and migration do not explain away this relationship. The effect of family factors on overall mortality varies between the two countries. For example, having never been married increases the odds of mortality in Mexico substantially, but marital status has no effect on mortality for older Mexican Americans. Interestingly, receiving family assistance has the opposite effect in Mexico as it does in the United States. Older Mexicans who receive family assistance are at an increased risk of mortality, whereas in the United States the effects are protective. This may be suggestive of country-specific familial distributions of labor. In Mexico, people work, often into old age, so that if older Mexicans require assistance from family it may be their health has declined so much that they themselves are unable to work and having to ask family for help may be as a last resort (Salinas et al., 2008).

Table 11.3 shows that migration experience, whether it is measured in years in the United States, country of birth, or years since returning to Mexico, is not a significant predictor of 2-year mortality in older Mexicans and Mexican Americans in these

Table 11.3 Weighted odds ratios of mortality by family support and migration history at 2-year follow-up for older Mexicans in Mexico (MHAS) and older Mexican Americans in the United States (Hispanic EPESE) aged 70, 2001–2003 in MHAS; 1998–1999 to 2000–2001 in Hispanic EPESE

Mexico	Odds ratios	United States	Odds ratios
Diabetes	1.798***	Diabetes	1.397
Marital status *(married)*		Marital status *(married)*	
Divorced/separated/widowed	1.007	Divorced/separated/widowed	1.038
Never married	1.898***	Never married	1.432
Receives assistance from family members (Yes)	1.994***	Receives assistance from family members (Yes)	0.514***
Years since returned to Mexico (Never been to United States)		Years in United States (US-born)	
More than 20 years ago	0.572	20 years or less	0.912
20 years or less	0.455	21–40 years	0.857
Years in United States (Never been to United States)		41–60 years	0.707
Less than 10	1.429	61 or more years	1.475
10 or more	1.267		
n	2858	*n*	1876
−2 log likelihood	2087.63	−2 log likelihood	1150.27
Intercept	0.0576***	Intercept	0.0470***

*** $p < 0.001$.

data sets. Although there may be variation in cause-specific mortality, these statistics imply that immigrant health and mortality advantages may only be beneficial early in the life course in these populations and that in later life the force of age-related factors on the body becomes more important.

In sum, we observe differences between older Mexican Americans and older Mexicans in the prevalence of diabetes, disease management, mortality, and the effect of socioeconomic resources on mortality. Even though the prevalence of diabetes is not as high in Mexico as it is in the United States for Mexican Americans, the impact of the disease appears to be more substantial with lower survival in Mexico. This result may be due to additional co-morbidities associated with diabetes in Mexico, to weaker healthcare systems, or to poorer access by the population. Nevertheless, the results point to implications for policy in both the United States and Mexico, since the overall picture suggests that country context is important in differentiating the manner in which health declines and is treated. In the United States, public health efforts that promote diabetes *prevention* may help avert new cases of the disease. In Mexico, perhaps focus should be placed more on *controlling* diabetes in order to prevent exacerbation into other conditions leading to premature death. If policy efforts are not properly targeted, significant devastation from diabetes may be experienced in the Mexican-origin populations living in Mexico and the United States.

AGEING AND HEALTH IN LATIN AMERICA AND THE CARIBBEAN: SELECTED FINDINGS FROM THE SABE STUDIES

As indicated earlier, most Latin American countries are expected to experience unprecedented rates of demographic ageing during the next several decades. This section reviews findings based on a relatively new data set on people aged 60 and over residing in seven large urban centers. These cities provide a good representation of the various stages of demographic ageing in the region. Buenos Aires (Argentina), Montevideo (Uruguay), Havana (Cuba), and Bridgetown (Barbados) are in advanced stages of the demographic transition and population ageing. Santiago (Chile), Mexico City (Mexico), and Sao Paulo (Brazil) are somewhat behind in the speed of ageing, with Santiago ahead of Mexico City, and Mexico City ahead of Sao Paulo. Poorer countries at the beginning of their demographic transition are not represented in the study. These include Peru, Bolivia, Ecuador, and Guatemala (Wong et al., 2006).

The speed of ageing experienced in Latin America and the Caribbean is taking place at a time of rapid change in traditional living arrangements that historically provided a safety net for older people. While the same change was observed in Western Europe and North America the process of change took place gradually and occurred mostly before rapid changes in ageing. In Latin America and the Caribbean it is happening concurrently with rapid ageing and in a climate of institutional volality. As Palloni and McEniry (2007: 265) suggest:

> ... no country in the Latin American and Caribbean region is blessed with institutional contexts designed to cope with changed demands from a growing elderly population. In almost all cases a highly compressed ageing process will take place in the midst of weak economic performance, tense intergenerational relations, fragile institutional contexts, and shrinking access to medical and health care services.

This unique situation makes it paramount to examine closely the health status and healthcare needs of older people. The SABE data set is a rich source of much-needed information. The data were collected between June 1999 and December 2000.

Palloni and McEniry (2007) provide an overview of findings on key health indicators. One such frequently employed indicator is self-rated health. As might have been expected, self-rated health varies considerably from country to country. Proportions rating their health as 'bad' ('mala') ranged from 21 per cent in Santiago and 20 per cent in Mexico City to only 5–7 per cent in Bridgetown, Buenos Aires, and Montevideo. The latter are in countries that had achieved relatively high standards of living before the beginning of the 21st century, which may partially accounting for better self-reported health. In all countries women were more likely to report bad health, a finding that has been observed generally. Rates reported in the Health and Retirement Study (HRS) in the United States are intermediate between the high rates in Santiago and Mexico City and the lower rates in Buenos Aires, Bridgetown, and Montevideo (Palloni and McEniry, 2007). Across the seven cities, the average rate of poor health is somewhat higher than for the United States using the HRS data.

When ADL and IADL disabilities are examined, there are significant age and gender differences but virtually no differences across countries. US data from the HRS indicate a slightly higher proportion of Americans reporting at least one ADL but a significantly lower proportion reporting an IADL disability than is the case in the pooled sample of the seven cities. The chronic conditions of old age observed in more developed countries

are also observed in the Latin American and Caribbean region: heart disease, cancer, arthritis, obesity, and diabetes. High rates of obesity and diabetes in the region are thought to result from the increasing adoption of Western diets and increasingly more sedentary lifestyles. Only Havana displays low rates of self-reported diabetes, especially among men, which likely can be explained by a low adoption of Western lifestyles.

Palloni and McEniry (2007) also examined the existence of health inequalities in the SABE countries. As expected, inequalities were found especially with respect to self-reported health and ADLs and IADLs. They were the least pronounced for obesity, which is unlike what we find in the United States (Al Snih et al., 2007). Not surprisingly, education and income inequalities were lowest in Havana. Based on HRS data, inequalities are considerably higher in the United States than in the SABE countries.

CONCLUSION

We have provided a brief overview of ageing and health issues in the Hispanic population of the United States as well as in Latin America and the Caribbean. The Hispanic population of the United States is growing at unprecedented rates and is expected to be approximately 30 percent by mid-century, or about 120 million people. Although still relatively young, the population is projected to experience rapid rates of ageing. In Mexico and the rest of the Latin American region rapid population ageing is being compressed into a considerably shorter period than has been the case in the United States and other developed countries, causing unprecedented challenges for the region.

An interesting and intriguing feature of the US Hispanic population is its relatively good health despite generally low living standards. This is especially the case with the Mexican-origin population, which, according to most estimates, has lower mortality rates than the general population. The so-called 'epidemiologic paradox' (or Hispanic paradox) has become the leading theme in Hispanic health and is partly the result of selective migration and better health behaviors of immigrants.

Perhaps another paradox is that despite the population's low mortality rates, especially in the older years, the health status of older Mexican Americans appears to be relatively poor. Data from the Hispanic EPESE and other sources indicate high disability rates, for example, which are related to high rates of obesity and diabetes, lower access to care than the general population, and sedentary lifestyles especially in old age. It appears that the

Mexican-origin population may be experiencing what the general population experienced in the 1970s and early 1980s when we were living longer with more disability.

Interest in comparisons of health and ageing between the US Hispanic populations and the populations of Mexico and the Latin American region is likely to increase in the future. An important reason for this interest is that the Latin American region is by far the largest source of immigrants to the United States. Data on ageing in Mexico from the MHAS study is particularly revealing with respect to their relevance for the Mexican American population. For example, migration histories of the MHAS subjects suggest that very few Mexican immigrants return to Mexico in their older years, challenging the notion of a 'salmon bias' for explaining the favorable mortality rates of Mexican Americans. We also learn that even though older Mexicans have relatively poor access to health care their health status is not too different than that of older Mexican Americans. They actually are less likely to report chronic conditions, but that may result from lower contact with the formal medical care system. Their physical disability rates are similar to those of Mexican Americans. This relatively good health status may very well be partly the product of mortality selection. Yet, rates of obesity and diabetes, while lower than in Mexican Americans, have been rising especially in the middle years, signaling the possibility that the older years may be afflicted with higher disability rates in the near future.

The situation in the rest of Latin America and the Caribbean is quite varied. Overall, people report better health in Bridgetown, Buenos Aires, and Montevideo than in Santiago and Mexico City. The former are in countries that until recently had achieved relatively high standards of living compared to the rest of the region, which may be a factor partly explaining good self-reports of health.

Little variability across countries in the region was observed in reports of disability in the form of ADLs. Also, common chronic conditions afflicting more developed societies are similarly prevalent in most of the SABE countries, perhaps reflecting adoption of Western diets and lifestyles. This is especially so with respect to obesity and diabetes. Cuba is an exception, reflecting perhaps the fact that a Western diet has not been an option there.

The ageing of the population of much of the Latin American region is being compressed into a much shorter period than in the more developed countries of North America and Western Europe. Unlike the more developed countries, Latin American countries have considerably fewer economic resources to adequately address the challenges of ageing. Declining intergenerational supports and volatile institutional environments provide additional challenges. Clearly, researchers and policymakers in the region must make ageing a top priority, as has become the case in more developed parts of the world.

REFERENCES

Abraido-Lanza, A.F., Dohrenwend, B.P., Ng-Mak, D.S., and Turner, J.B. (1999) 'The Latino mortality paradox: a test of the "salmon bias" and health migrant hypothesis', *American Journal of Public Health*, 89: 1543–8.

Al Snih, S., Markides, K.S., Ray, L., and Goodwin, J.S. (2001) 'Impact of pain on disability among older Mexican Americans', *Journal of Gerontology. Medical Sciences*, 56(7): M400–4.

Al Snih, S., Raji, M., Markides, K., Ottenbacher, K., and Goodwin, J. (2005) 'Weight change and lower body disability among older Mexican Americans', *Journal of the American Geriatrics Society*, 53(10): 1730–7.

Al Snih S., Ottenbacher, K.J., Markides, K.S., et al. (2007) 'The effect of obesity on disability versus mortality in Older Americans', *Archives of Internal Medicine*, 167: 774–80.

Angel, R.J., Angel, J.L., and Markides, K.S. (2002) 'Stability and change in health insurance among older Mexican Americans: longitudinal evidence from the Hispanic – EPESE', *American Journal of Public Health*, 92(8): 1264–71.

Black, S.A. (1999) 'Increased health burden associated with co-morbid depression in older diabetic Mexican Americans: results of the Hispanic EPESE', *Diabetes Care*, 22: 56–64.

Black, S.A and Markides, K.S. (1999) 'Depressive symptoms and mortality in older Mexican Americans', *Annals of Epidemiology*, 9(1): 45–52.

Black, S.A., Markides, K.S., and Miller, T.Q. (1998) 'Correlates of depressive symptomatology among older community dwelling Mexican Americans: the Hispanic EPESE', *The Journals of Gerontology Psychological Sciences and Social Sciences*, 53(4): 198–208.

Black, S.A., Ray L.A., and Markides K.S. (1999) 'The prevalence and health burden of self-reported diabetes in the older Mexican Americans: findings from the Hispanic EPESE of the elderly', *American Journal of Public Health*, 89(4): 546–52.

Black, S.A., Markides, K.S., and Ray, L.A. (2003) 'Depression predicts increased incidence of adverse health outcomes in older Mexican Americans with type 2 diabetes', *Diabetes Care*, 26(10): 2822–8.

Brea, J.A. (2003) 'Population dynamics in Latin America', *Population Bulletin*, 58(1). Washington, DC: Population Reference Bureau.

CELADE (2002) 'América Latina y el Caribe: estimaciones y proyecciones de población 1950–2050', *Boletin demográfico 69: parte A*.

CONAPO (2005) *Envejecimiento de la Población de México: Reto del Siglo XXI*. México: Consejo Nacional de Población.

Crimmins, E.M., Kim, J.K., Alley, D.M., Karlamanga, A., and Freeman, T. (2007) 'Hispanic paradox in biological risk profiles', *American Journal of Public Health*, 97(7): 1302–10.

DiNuzzo, A.R., Black, S.A., Lichtenstein, M.J., and Markides, K.S. (2001) 'Prevalence of functional blindness, visual impairment and related functional deficits among elderly Mexican Americans', *Journal of Gerontology: Medical Sciences*, 56(9): M548–51.

Elo, I.T., Turra, C.M., Kestenbaum, B., and Ferguson, R.F. (2004) 'Mortality among elderly Hispanics in the United States: past evidence and new results', *Demography*, 41: 109–28.

Eschbach, K., Ostir, G.V., Patel, K.V., Markides, K.S., and Goodwin, J.S. (2004) 'Neighborhood context and mortality among older Mexican Americans: Is there a barrio advantage?', *American Journal of Public Health*, 94(10): 1807–12.

Eschbach, K., Simpson, J.P., Kuo, Y-F., and Goodwin, J.S. (2007) 'Mortality of foreign-born and US-born Hispanic adults at younger ages', *American Journal of Public Health*, 97(7): 1397–404.

Franzini, L, Ribble, J.C., and Keddie, A.M. (2001) 'Understanding the Hispanic paradox', *Ethnicity and Disease*, 11: 4496–518.

Freedman, V.A., Martin, L.G., and Schoeni, R.F. (2002) 'Recent trends in disability and functioning among older adults in the United States', *Journal of the American Medical Association*, 288: 3137–46.

Haan, M.N., Mungas, D.M., and Gonzalez, H.M. (2003) 'Prevalence of dementia in older Latinos: the influence of Type 2 diabetes mellitus, stroke and genetic factors', *Journal of the American Geriatrics Society*, 51: 160–77.

Ham-Chande, R. (2003) *El Envejecimiento en México: El Siguiente Reto de la Transición Demográphica*. Mexico: El Collegio de la Frontera Norte.

Hayes-Bautista, D. (1992) 'Latino health indicators and the underclass model: from paradox to new policy models', in: A. Furino (ed.), *Health Policy and the Hispanic*. Boulder, Co: Westview Press.

Hermalin, A.I. (ed.), (2002) *The Well-being of the Elderly in Asia: A Four-Country Comparative Study*. Ann Arbor: University of Michigan Press.

Hummer, R.A., Powers, D.A., Pullum, S.G., Grossman, G.L., and Frisbie, W.P. (2007) 'Infant mortality in the Mexican-origin population in the United States', *Demography*, 44(3): 441–57.

Manton, K.G. and Gu, X. (2001) 'Changes in the prevalence of chronic disability in the United States black and non-black population above age 65 from 1982 to 1999', *Proceedings of the National Academies of Sciences USA*, 98: 6354–9.

Markides, K.S. and Black, S.A. (1995) 'Race, ethnicity, and aging: the impact of inequality', in: R.H. Binstock and L.K. George (eds), *Handbook of Aging and the Social Sciences*. San Diego: Academic Press.

Markides, K.S. and Coreil, J. (1986) 'The health of Southwestern Hispanics: an epidemiologic paradox', *Public Health Reports*, 101: 253–65.

Markides, K.S. and Eschbach, K. (2005) 'Aging, migration, and mortality: current status of research on the Hispanic Paradox', *Journal of Gerontolojy. Social Sciences*, GOB (Special Issue II): 68–75.

Markides, K.S., Eschbach, K., Ray, L.A., and Peek, M.K. (2007) 'Census disability rates among older people by race/ethnicity and type of Hispanic origin', in J.L. Angel and K.E.

Whitfield (eds), *The Health of Aging Hispanics: The Mexican-Origin Population*. New York: Springer.

Markides, K.S., Rudkin, L., Angel, R.J., and Espino, D.V. (1997) 'Health status of Hispanic elderly in the United States', in L.G. Martin and B. Soldo (eds) *Racial and Ethnic Differences in the Health of Older Americans*. Washington, DC: National Academy Press.

Markides, K.S., Stroup-Benhan, C.A., Black, S.A., et al. (1999) 'The health of Mexican American elderly: selected findings from the Hispanic EPESE', in M.L. Wykle, and A.B. Ford (eds), *Serving Minority Elders in the 21st Century*. New York: Springer.

Ostir, G.V., Markides, K.S., Black, S.A., and Goodwin, J.S. (2000) 'Emotional well-being predicts subsequent functional independence and survival', *Journal of the American Geriatric Society*, 48(5): 473–8.

Ostir, G.V., Eschbach, K., Markides, K.S., and Goodwin, J.S. (2003) 'Neighborhood composition and depressive symptoms among older Mexican Americans', *Journal of Epidemiology and Community Health*, 57: 987–92.

Otiniano, M.E., Markides, K.S., Ottenbacher, K., Ray, L.A., and Du, X. (2003) 'Self-reported diabetic complications and 7-year mortality in Mexican American elders: findings from a community-based study of five Southwestern states', *Journal of Diabetes and its Complications*, 17(5): 243–8.

Palloni, A. and Arias, E. (2004) 'Paradox lost: explaining the Hispanic adult mortality advantage', *Demography*, 41: 385–415.

Palloni, A. and McEniry, M. (2007) 'Aging and health status of elderly in Latin America and the Caribbean: preliminary findings', *Journal of Cross Cultural Gerontology*, 22(3): 263–85.

Palloni, A. and Morenoff, J. (2001) 'Interpreting the paradoxical in the 'Hispanic Paradox'. Demographic and epidemiological approaches', in A. Weinstein, A. Hermalin, and M. Soto (eds), *Population Health and Aging*. New York: New York Academy of Sciences.

Palloni, A., Peláez, M., and Wong, R. (2006) 'Aging and health among Latin American and Caribbean populations', *Journal of Aging and Health*, 18(2): 149–56.

Partida, V. (2006) 'Demographic transition, demographic bonus and ageing in Mexico', *Proceedings of the United Nations Expert Group Meeting on Social and Economic Implications of Changing Population Age Structures*. Mexico: National Population Council.

Patel, K.V. (2004) *Neighborhood Environment and the Disablement Process in Older Mexican Americans*. PhD dissertation, University of Texas Medical Branch.

Patel, K.V, Eschbach, K., Rudkin, L.L., Peek, M.K., and Markides, K.S. (2003) 'Neighborhood context of self-rated health in older Mexican Americans', *Annals of Epidemiology*, 13(9): 620–8.

Ray, L.A. and Markides, K.S. (2007) 'Hispanic established population for the epidemiological study of the elderly', in K.S. Markides (ed.), *The Encyclopedia of Health and Aging*. Thousand Oaks, CA: Sage Publications.

Rudkin, L., Markides, K.S., and Espino, D.V. (1997) 'Functional disability in older Mexican Americans', *Topics in Geriatric Rehabilitation*, 12: 38–46.

Rull, J.A., Aguilar-Salinas, C.A., Rojas, R., et al. (2005) 'Epidemiology of type 2 diabetes in Mexico', *Archives of Medical Research*, 36(3): 188–96.

Salinas, J., Eschbach, K., and Markides, K.S. (2008) 'The prevalence of hypertension in older Mexicans and Mexican Americans', *Ethnicity and Disease*, 18(3): 294–8.

Tovar, J.J., Angel. R.J., Espino, D.V., and Markides, K.S. (2007) 'Hispanic population for the epidemiologic studies of the elderly: selected longitudinal findings', in K.S. Markides (ed.), *The Encyclopedia of Health and Aging*. Thousand Oaks, CA: Sage Publications.

Tucker, K.L., Falcon, L.M., Bianchi, L.A., Cacho, E., and Bermudez, O.I. (2000) 'Self-reported prevalence and health correlates of functional limitation among Massachusetts's elderly Puerto Ricans, Dominicans, and a non-Hispanic neighborhood comparison group', *Journal of Gerontology: Medical Sciences*, 55A: M90–7.

Turra, C.M. and Elo, I.T. (2008) 'The impact of salmon bias on the Hispanic mortality advantage: new evidence from social security data', *Population Research and Policy Review*, 27(5): 515–30.

Vega, W.A. and Amaro, H.L. (1994) 'Latino outlook: good health, uncertain prognosis', *Annual Review of Public Health*, 15: 39–67.

Wong, R. and Díaz, J. J. (2007) 'Health care utilization among older Mexicans: health and socioeconomic inequalities', *Salud Pública de México*, 49 (Supplement 4): S505–14.

Wong, R. and Palloni, A. (2009) 'Aging in Mexico and Latin America', in P. Uhlenberg (ed.), *International Handbook of Population Aging*. New York: Springer.

Wong, R., Espinoza, M., and Palloni, A. (2007) 'Adultos mayoes mexicanos en contexto socioecónimico amplio: salud y envejecimiento', *Salud Pública de Méxcio*, 49 (Suppl 4): S436–47.

Wong, R., Peláez, M., Palloni, A., and Markides, K. (2006) 'Survey data for the study of aging in Latin America and the Caribbean – selected studies', *Journal of Aging and Health*, 18(2): 157–79.

12

Religion and Age

Peter G. Coleman

INTRODUCTION

Religion has played a relatively small part in social gerontological studies, a fact which itself requires explanation in the light of the strong associations between religious involvement and age observed in many cultures. For a large part of the 20th century, religion was viewed with disdain as an uninteresting phenomenon with limited implications for furthering study of the individual and society. In fact, research on religion was considered damaging for career prospects in the social sciences (Levin, 1994). As Baumeister (2002) has noted, academics, and social scientists in particular, tend to be less religious than the general population. As a consequence, many feel inexpert and ill at ease studying religion. Concerns have recently been raised at this deficiency as Western societies face increasing threat from religious-based terrorism.

However, the last 10–20 years have seen a marked growth of interest in the social scientific study of religion and the related concept of spirituality. This is not only because of the greater role of religion in politics and society but also because of the increased recognition of the role religious and spiritual beliefs can play in maintaining personal well-being and even physical and mental health. The latter focus has been particularly evident in gerontological research. However, one consequence of this has been an imbalanced view of religion, focusing on extrinsic benefits rather than on the central functions of religion in later life. The definition of what counts as religion is itself not a straightforward matter (Hill and Pargament, 2003), but in this chapter will be taken to refer to a shared system of beliefs and associated practices based on a transcendent view of life, arising usually as the result of revelation from a perceived sacred source.

Some secular humanists would like to separate the concept of spirituality from its religious origins, and to be able to refer to 'spiritual' or 'inspiring' experiences without reference to God or a religion, for example in contemplation of nature, in appreciation of fine music and art, and in valuing interpersonal relationships. This is not a problem if spirituality is defined as the affective basis of motivation to meaning (McFadden, 1996b), but it becomes one if both spirituality and religion are seen to converge on a transcendent realm of the sacred and/or divine (Pargament, 1997). Definition of the concept of spirituality is likely to remain problematic, which has led some commentators and researchers to eschew the term and to prefer the term existential meaning, i.e., that which gives meaning to existence.

Across the life course, religion provides a sense of significance, belonging, and rootedness to both individuals and societies, with one argument being that these functions become more salient in the second half of life (Marcoen, 2005). The social and psychological processes of ageing encourage greater reflection on the meaning of life and death, and traditional cultures have typically required older people to be the guardians of their spiritual values and beliefs (Gutmann, 1997). But the criticisms directed against religion, particularly within Europe, for limiting human exploration and explanation, has undermined the meaning-giving role of religion in society over the last 300 years. Such critique of structures of authority and interpretation has extended to many other features of modern society. Indeed, even the meaning of living to be old has been called into question, despite – or perhaps because of – the huge growth in numbers of older people in the world (Polivka, 2000). Some of the most interesting contemporary writing about ageing addresses these issues of meaning (Biggs, 1999; Gullette, 2004). Whereas religions once provided most answers to the human search for meaning, there are doubts whether it can provide acceptable and credible answers in the future.

The USA has consistently been in the vanguard in research on religion and ageing. The sociologist David Moberg was one of the earliest in the field, writing his doctoral dissertation in 1951 on the subject of 'Religion and Personal Adjustment in Old Age'. He also helped introduce discussion of religion and spirituality into the 1971 White House Conference on Aging. But despite its presence almost at the beginning of modern gerontology, research on religion did not expand along with other fields. A fresh wave of interest came with developments at Duke University (Blazer and Palmore, 1976) where the first substantial research began to be conducted examining the relevance of religion in the field of health studies (Koenig, 1993). The subject of religion gradually became incorporated within graduate gerontology courses. A journal of religious gerontology, now the *Journal of Religion, Spirituality and Aging*, was established in the 1980s, and by the 1990s, entries on religion and ageing were appearing in key publications such as major handbooks on ageing (e.g., McFadden, 1996a, 1996b). In the same period, federal agencies at the National Institute on Aging, as well as private organizations like the Fetzer Institute and the Templeton Foundation, began to fund research in this area.

While we must be grateful for input from the United States into this field, it is also necessary to acknowledge the limitations resulting from US-centrism in the study of religion and ageing. Although there is growing interest in religion and age in Europe, Canada, Australia (see especially MacKinlay, 2006) and elsewhere, the output remains relatively small. As a result there is a danger that a review such as this would rely heavily on US studies and findings. Such a bias needs to be counteracted in an international handbook. A more theoretically grounded basis for this decision is the importance of studying diversity in religion. Much of the research activity to date has only studied a narrow spectrum of Christianity. A focus on particular forms of religious expression may be appropriate if the intention is to review the study of the functions, benefits, and trends with age of religion conceived in its most generalized terms. But such a limitation is not appropriate if the goal is to understand the range of functions, antecedents, and consequences of the very great variety of religious systems that exist, as well as the huge differences in practice observable even within one religion such as Christianity. Although at a deeper level commonalities may be found across very different religions, these should not be presumed a priori.

Therefore, it seems appropriate to begin this chapter with a brief overview of features relevant to the study of ageing to be found among some of the world's major religions. That the teachings of most religions are favourable to age is an important fact in itself, and would justify discussion of religion in any social gerontology text. But even in this respect there are important variations to be found. Although the major religions convey respect for all stages of life, their depiction of the precise significance of ageing within the human life cycle and the consequent expectations on older people as well as the duties owed them by their families and the wider society vary considerably. These differences relate to variations in attitudes to self and identity, life and death, and have palpable consequences on the experience of ageing.

As already mentioned, much of the growing scientific interest in religion within gerontology is centred on associations between religious belief and practice and indices of health and quality of life. Therefore a significant part of this chapter must necessarily consider this evidence and its implications for health and welfare policy. This raises a variety of questions, from the nature of human health and well-being to the biomedical correlates of having a faith. Most of these questions can be grouped together by viewing religion as one of the most important resources people can call on in coping with life's stresses, losses, and crises.

However, the more fundamental questions about religion and ageing are different from these. People in general do not seek a religion in order consciously to further their health and well-being. Rather, a religious faith is the result of a search for what is of supreme importance and the need to relate and connect to it (Kirkpatrick, 2004). This need is often cultivated early in life as a result of parenting influences and general socialization, but grows and changes over time in accord with experience, education, and intellectual and moral challenges. Some of the most intriguing questions about religion are age-related. Do issues of belief and existential meaning become more salient with age? And if so, what are the implications for religious and other organizations for providing access to spiritual counselling in later life? An equally large part of the chapter therefore considers religious and/or spiritual belief as a developmental phenomenon in later life. What do we know about the spiritual developments and crises that older people experience? What are the consequences for older people living in religious and non-religious societies? Does the state have a responsibility in ensuring that this aspect of older people's lives receives attention?

The chapter closes with a consideration of research issues for the future. At present we only have a very superficial understanding of the role of religion and alternatives to religion in the processes of ageing. To make further advances we need to broaden consideration of religion and to connect with more fundamental theorizing in social gerontology.

THE WORLD'S FAITHS AND CONCEPTIONS OF AGEING

Investigators of the role of religion in people's lives need to be well-informed about the history, key concepts, and practices of the religions held by the people they study. In the case of gerontologists, it is also important to understand the influence that religious beliefs may have on attitudes to ageing. Not all religions view ageing in the same way. Therefore, one can expect differences in age-related behaviour, expectations, and self-conceptions to be related to a person's religion and depth of identification with it. For reasons of space, it is necessary to limit consideration of the great variety of faiths present in the world to the so-called 'Abrahamic' faiths of Judaism, Christianity, and Islam, which share a common root, and the inter-related faiths of Hinduism and Buddhism, which have influenced much of Indian, Chinese, and other Asian cultures. A fuller account of the world's religions would necessarily include some of the other early religions of the world such as Zoroastrianism, Confucianism, Shintoism, and Shamanism, as well as historically newer forms such as Sikhism and Baha'i. Much could certainly be written about how each of these major faiths influences the experience of ageing, and what follows is inevitably a personal selection.

Judaism, Christianity, and Islam

The monotheistic religions of Judaism, Christianity, and Islam emerged in succession in the Middle East, but expanded to influence the development especially of European, African, and American civilizations. They largely replaced the earlier systems of beliefs in these continents, including the characteristically polytheistic Indo-European religions. Their similarities and differences, both within and between one another, need careful study.

Judaism, like Hinduism (but unlike Christianity, Islam, and Buddhism) is closely associated with ethnicity. Its scriptures tell of the emergence of a people's loyalty to their belief in one God and to God's commandments, and their subsequent

history through various failures, disasters, and triumphs. The Hebrew scriptures provide some of the most powerful images of old age in Western culture (Dulin, 1988). They contain a variety of themes: historical accounts, realistic in their depiction of power and frailty, which demonstrate the importance of family life for all age groups; calls within the prophetic and psalmist writings for greater sensitivity to the needs of elderly people; and within the so-called 'wisdom' writings, such as 'Ecclesiastes', a focus on the personal dimensions of ageing, especially physical deterioration. Taken as a whole, they provide a strong moral teaching to society not to neglect the old, and it is probably not coincidental that Jewish homes and care organizations have long had a high reputation both in Europe and the US American and European social services. At the same time, perhaps partly because of these strong injunctions, absence or loss of family care can be a cause of great psychological pain in Jewish communities. This is evident from some key early studies in the social gerontological literature (e.g., Francis, 1984).

Christianity emerged out of Judaism during the period of Roman dominion of Palestine. As a result of its openness to different ethnic groups and the universality of its message, Christianity spread rapidly through the Greek and Roman world, and, despite the persecutions it encountered from the authorities, by the 4th century after Christ, had been adopted as the official religion of the Roman Empire. However, Christianity was characterized by controversy from its earliest days, occasioned by the subtlety and complexity of its beliefs about the relationship between God and humanity, as well as by difficulties in reconciling the exercise of authority across different communities (churches) of believers, along with the rights of individual conscience. As it grew, unity became increasingly difficult to maintain. Successive schisms took place, the most significant being the division of the Western (Catholic) church from the Eastern (Orthodox) churches by the early part of the second millennium after Christ, and the separation of Protestant sects from the Western Catholic church in the 16th and 17th centuries. The first North American colonies were established by Protestant émigrés from Western Europe, and Protestantism in its initially Calvinistic and later Evangelical forms has given a distinct character to American religion (Noll, 2002). This point is of special relevance to this chapter, as much of the US literature on religion and ageing reflects a Protestant emphasis on the individual's direct access to God rather than on mediation through the corporate body of believers (the Church), the latter being more characteristic not only of Catholicism but also of Judaism and Islam.

Although the early Christian Scriptures repeat Jewish prescriptions not to neglect the elderly, and particularly show concern for widows, the much stronger emphasis within Christianity on ongoing life with God beyond death diminished any special importance attributed to reaching old age *per se.* Disregard of ageing may also have been encouraged by the medieval characterization of Jesus' age of death as 'the perfect age' (Burrow, 1986). As a consequence, middle age came to be depicted as the high point of life. While a number of other powerful factors were involved (see, e.g., Fischer, 1977; Achenbaum, 1979, Chapter 2), this may also have contributed to the fading of the social significance of ageing in Europe and America (Cole, 1992). More recently, attempts have been made by Christian theologians to correct this historical neglect and embrace ageing, while combatting the contemporary culture of worship of youth and of autonomy, and to call older people to witness to moral commitments and to their hope in Christ (e.g., Hauerwas et al., 2003).

Islam emerged from the desert of the Arabian peninsula on the edge of the Christian world in the 7th century after Christ. To its early Christian opponents it appeared at first as yet another internal heresy. But, with surprising rapidity, Islam took over much of the Middle East as well as North Africa, and spread eventually into Asia as well. The Koran also offered a message of universal brotherhood, and belief in an almighty and merciful God who will judge humankind at the end of time. But at the same time it taught a simpler relationship of man as servant to God and cultivated in practice a stronger sense of social responsibility. Religious precepts were understood as determining all aspects of life, including care of older people (Abdul-Rauf, 1982). Ethical teachings about respect and honour due to older people have been taken more seriously than in Christianity.

Relatively little research has yet been conducted on religion and age within Muslim samples. Nevertheless, interview studies with older Muslims living both inside and outside Muslim countries testify to the huge importance of religion within their lives, its contribution to their quality of life, and development with ageing (Aflakseir and Coleman, 2009; Ahmadi and Thomas, 2000; Imamoglu, 1999).

Hinduism and Buddhism

Whereas Judaism, Christianity, and Islam, despite their history of reciprocal conflict and persecution, are closely interrelated religions, Hinduism together with Buddhism form a quite distinct way of approaching the transcendent. Hinduism is one of the oldest surviving belief systems in the world and remains vibrant in its homeland of the Indian subcontinent.

Fundamental to Hinduism is its teaching on the stages of life from student to householder to retired person to ascetic (Tilak, 1989). This makes it a very age-friendly religion. For despite the loss of physical vigour that accompanies ageing, the important aim of life is a state of stability and changelessness beyond death. It is old age that stands for maturity, not young adulthood or even middle age. In fact, Hinduism is remarkably unconcerned about ageing and death. Its most ancient texts – the Rig Veda – speak of death as a passing over to joy. The suffering and losses are key to the liberation experience. They waken people to reality. The resultant virtues of confrontation with finitude, the wise use of declining powers and abilities, and the creative response to limits are increasingly appreciated by Western thinkers (Ram-Prasad, 1995). There are therefore positive expectations on the behaviour of people as they become older. Like the Jewish prophets, old Hindu sages provide immensely attractive images and models of ageing.

Buddhism is also of particular interest from a gerontological perspective because its founding story of the Buddha gaining insight is based on confrontation with old age, disease, and death, from which he had been protected as young man. Although the Buddhist influence can be felt within later developments in Hinduism, Buddhism dealt with these problems quite differently by means of an ascetic renunciation of the world throughout life. It teaches in similar terms about the importance of karma, a key concept in both Hinduism and Buddhism about the automatic consequences of good and bad deeds, and reincarnation through further lives dependent on karma. Ageing itself is viewed as a product of good karma, providing the opportunity for further enlightenment. However, Buddhism puts more emphasis on eventual release from the cycle of rebirth through cultivation of high levels of spirituality.

From its origins in India, Buddhism spread to Tibet, and subsequently to China and Japan, developing somewhat different characteristics in each culture. Buddhism, unlike other Asian religions, has proved more exportable to other ethnic groups, including Westerners. It is popular also in intellectual circles because of its practical emphasis on developing ways of coping, principally through meditation, in facing the stresses of life, and consequently has strong links with contemporary popular psychology (e.g., Goleman, 1997). Similarly to Hinduism, Buddhism has created an attractive image and expectation of age, as a stage of life when a person's concerns should be primarily spiritual, concerned with the path of emancipation from reincarnation. At the same time it could be criticized as reinforcing passivity in the face of older people's diminished economic and political status. There is some research on older groups of Buddhists in Asian societies with strong social gerontological traditions, such as that of Singapore, whose mixed population also provides an excellent multi-religious and multi-ethnic context for studying religion and ageing (Jianbin and Mehta, 2003; Mehta, 1997).

Contemporary attitudes to religion

However, as a result of globalization, religion is no longer a predictable attribute of location or ethnic grouping. Increasing numbers of younger people in the West feel empowered to develop their own individual choices and mixtures of religious and spiritual teaching, independently of their religion of origin (Heelas, 1998). Spirituality, rather than religion, has also become the favoured term of the baby-boom generation, whereas older people still tend to see themselves as religious (Voas and Crockett, 2005). This contrast creates yet another form of generation gap, precisely in an area of life where older and younger people were traditionally bound together in common beliefs and practice.

Present Western society is also marked by a rise in expression of militant atheistic humanism. As the subject of religion has risen in the media and in public consciousness, opposing secular attitudes have also hardened and become more strident. The popularity in the United Kingdom of Richard Dawkins' 'The God Delusion' (2006), and in the United States of Christopher Hitchens' 'God is not Great' (2007), reflects the threat felt by many about the resurgence of religious authority, especially in the educational realm. From a theoretical point of view, consideration of atheism helps to put into relief the nature and functions of religion and religious belief. For example, in the field of coping with ageing, it is not possible to assess accurately the influence of religious belief without examining how people manage without it, and whether humanism or other principled approaches to life can provide similar benefits.

RELIGION AS A RESOURCE IN LIFE

The study of the physical, social, and psychological benefits of religious membership, belief, and practice have become growth areas in research in the last 10–15 years (Miller and Thoresen, 2003). Within this literature one might expect there to have been an even greater emphasis on ageing than in fact has been the case. For, as government and welfare interest groups consider the challenge of reducing the health problems arising from an ageing population, including high rates of depression and suicide (Pearson and Brown, 2000), religion offers a well-known source of solutions. But it is only relatively recently that gerontologists have argued for more attention to spiritual needs in assessment of older people's quality of life (Bond and Corner, 2004; Crowther et al., 2002).

Historically, the neglect of the benefits of religion can be attributed to the legacy of disparaging attitudes conveyed by leading thinkers of the 19th and 20th century from Marx to Freud. Despite the view of religion expressed by Jung as 'the great treasure' (Jung, 1938: 113), religion has generally been seen by social scientists and psychologists as an inferior form of response to life's problems, escapist and defensive. Yet, as Pargament and Park have illustrated (1995), religion is much more than a defence. It provides meaning to situations, sources of social support for managing problems, and opportunities for personal growth. Religious rites serve the purpose of marking difficult life transitions such as death rather than denying their reality. Religious coping contains as many active as passive elements; for example, calling on God's help in the search for the right solution, a sharing but not an abnegation of responsibility. This is not to deny that religion can sometimes be exploited for political or economic purposes, that it can have negative effects on psychological well-being, and that its misuses need to be studied as well as its uses.

Early work demonstrated the salience of religion, including the use of religious forms of coping, for older people (Blazer and Palmore, 1976; Koenig et al., 1988a, 1988b). The subsequent empirical evidence has suggested that the health associations of religion, from quicker recovery from physical and mental illness to lowered mortality rates, are stronger in older age groups, suggesting an age-related benefit to continued belief (McFadden and Levin, 1996). There are a number of theoretical considerations that would explain these findings. Traditional religious cultures in particular ascribe important roles to older people, and in this way also promote their mental health (Gutmann, 1997). Religious beliefs help to address issues surrounding limitation and finitude as well as questions of loss and suffering, which appear to figure more highly in people's consciousness as they age (Black and Rubinstein, 2004). Religion also provides resources in responding to questions about survival in states of growing dependency. Stronger beneficial associations of strength of spiritual belief with well-being have been found in older people of greater degrees of frailty compared with those less frail but also living in supported housing in the United Kingdom (Kirby et al., 2004).

However, what seems to be lacking in the literature is any systematic survey of the ways in which older people respond religiously to the challenges of later life. As Pargament et al. comment:

Many of the greatest religious dramas are played out by those in the later years of life. These are pivotal times, when people of greatest maturity meet situations of greatest challenge. It is in these moments that people move from the abstractions of a religion in theory to the concreteness of a religion in action (1995: 47).

But there is as yet little literature that specifically examines subjects of such crucial relevance to both ageing and religion as bereavement and death. Although religious affiliation is commonly included as a variable in studies of bereavement outcome, few studies have examined in-depth religious responses to bereavement (Becker et al., 2007). Yet it is only by such close attention to religion in action that its function and value can be appreciated (Coleman et al., 2007; Fry, 2001). Most studies of health and ageing have been of relatively simple design and able to demonstrate little more than associations. More longitudinal and other forms of study (e.g. intervention-based) are needed to take the subject further. It also needs repeating that most of the research in this field has been carried out in the USA, investigating the influence of evangelical Christianity within USA society; this is a rather narrow database upon which to make generalizations on ageing, health, and religion.

Mental health

The weight of empirical evidence indicates that religious belief and practice has, in general, a positive influence on mental health at every age, although this influence in itself appears not to be very large (Smith et al., 2003). The social support provided by religious communities clearly plays an important role in this association, but there is also increasing support for the importance of more intrinsic factors such as a subjective feeling of closeness to the divine, which Miller and Kelley (2005) and others conceptualize as 'personal devotion'.

The interaction between religion and mental health remains complex, and researchers have begun to examine the effects of belief in more sophisticated ways. In certain circumstances, religion can appear to have negative effects, heightening feelings of guilt and anxiety, for example, and colouring delusional and obsessional symptoms. Spiritual conflict itself can be a risk factor for decline in mental as well as physical health. It is also likely that certain aspects of religious behaviour could have both positive and negative effects, depending on the circumstances. Religious faith can add to the distress of especially difficult situations. For example, Strawbridge et al. (1998) found that elders of strong religious commitment coped worse with family stressors such as marital breakdowns, perhaps because of greater conflicts with the religious values involved. Moreover, there is also growing evidence of *curvilinear* rather than *linear* relationships between religious variables and mental health outcomes: those of *weak belief* and *moderate practice* fared *worse* than *strong believers* and *non-believers* when having a clear belief system was most adaptive, but then fared *better* when it was more beneficial to be of moderate view and practice (Krause, 1995; Miller and Kelley, 2005). This indicates that the character and context of belief in later life need careful analysis.

A further complexity in the study of mental health and religion is the direction of causality. It is not clear whether happier people are more likely to become and stay religious or whether misfortune also leads people to religion. In the absence of longitudinal studies, conclusions are difficult to draw. What evidence there suggests that religious involvement tends to precede positive well-being rather than vice versa (Levin and Taylor, 1998).

Hope is a major virtue within religions and there is much evidence that religious faith prevents depression by both promoting positive mood and counteracting despair (McCullough and Larson, 1999; Smith et al., 2003). By contrast, the evidence suggests that symptoms of anxiety are more closely related to religious activity. This does not necessarily mean that religion makes people anxious, but a curvilinear relationship may be at work with those with uncertain or insecure beliefs demonstrating most anxiety (Miller and Kelley, 2005). The same applies to anxiety about death (Pressman et al., 1992).

Together with depression, dementia is the major mental health issue of later life. The spiritual behaviour and needs of people with dementia are still greatly neglected topics. Nevertheless, there is much anecdotal evidence suggesting that people with dementia retain aspects of their previous religious behaviour and feelings even into advanced stages of the illness and that it is in fact one of the aspects of their identity and personality that can be longest protected and preserved (Allen and Coleman, 2006; Shamy, 2003).

Physical health

In recent years the benefits of religion for physical health have attracted if anything even more interest and research study than mental health. This is true across medicine, psychology, and social sciences (Koenig et al., 2001; Miller and Thoresen, 2003; Schaie et al., 2004). Associations have been identified with illness reduction, speed of recovery, and many other health indices. The field has sufficiently advanced for there to be clearly developed hypotheses about mediating factors, pathways, and causal mechanisms. A number of these are well set out by Oman and Thoresen (2005) and include encouragement of beneficial health behaviours, positive psychological states, effective ways of coping with stress, and provision of social support. Further discussion of these follows in the next section. There has also been considerable recent interest in applications from psychoneuroimmunology, the study of mental influences on the body's natural defence against disease (Koenig and Cohen, 2002).

Perhaps the most striking findings relevant to physical health and ageing come in studies of longevity. For example, an extensive cross-state study in the United States found a life expectancy difference of more than 7 years between those never attending religious services and those attending more than once weekly (Hummer et al., 1999). As the authors point out, this is a similar degree of difference to that commonly found and expected as a result of gender and racial differences in the United States. It is interesting that similar differences have been found – at least among women – in a European society such as Finland's (Teinonen et al., 2005), despite the very great differences in average levels of religious attendance between the two societies (only 1.1 per cent of the over 65-year-olds studied in Finland attending religious services at least weekly, compared with approximately a half in the United States). It may be that in both contexts religious attendance is acting as a marker of general physical activity, beneficial to health in itself. This is supported by associations between church attendance and protection against circulatory and respiratory disease, but not cancer mortality (Powell et al., 2003).

How does religion benefit health?

The most evident reasons for the association between religion and health are behavioural and social. In general, religion encourages healthy behaviour, cultivating an attitude of respect to the body and counteracting attitudes of despair. Membership of a religious organization both encourages activity and provides a potential support network able to rally round in times of difficulty.

However, there are additional benefits more intrinsically associated with religious belief and practice – benefits that seem to be more pronounced in later life – including a sense of coherence and meaning in life (George et al., 2000). At the same time, meaning in life can be provided by other sources than religion. Pargament and colleagues (2005b) go further in arguing that religion, or more properly, spiritual belief, provides persons with a unique source of meaning in making contact with the 'sacred', and therefore cannot readily be compared with more secular sources.

Certainly there are limitations to studying religion and spirituality primarily as health and welfare benefits or even as coping resources (Sloan and Bagiella, 2002). Religions may be intended to make people live better or more fully, but this evaluation is made in the context of religious faith, not of secular society. Religions themselves generally assess quality in eternal rather than temporal terms. As Rick Moody has commented: 'For the earliest Christians ... faith was not a ticket to health and longevity but a risk factor for early martyrdom' (2006: 148). In many parts of the world, being religious has often been associated with risks to one's life, health, and worldly success.

RELIGIOUS AND SPIRITUAL DEVELOPMENT WITH AGE

Age differences in religiosity

Much more significant than religion–health associations are religion–age associations. Cross-sectional evidence from North America and Europe on religious practice, especially attendance at communal worship, demonstrates higher levels of religiosity in older age groups. The only exception to rising levels of attendance with ageing is among the very old, which is explainable in terms of their reduced health and mobility, but this is often compensated by increased rates of other forms of religious and spiritual activity. In the USA, these differences have been found consistently over the last half-century during a period of considerable secular change. As Moberg (2001) has argued, this suggests the need for a genuine developmental rather than only historical explanation of these differences. Discussion of this subject in the social science literature dates back at least as far as William James (1902). Most commentators since then have attributed the association between religion and age to the way religion answers questions about the meaning of life, which become more salient as people age (McFadden, 2005). It is also significant that longitudinal studies in the United States of the dying process have shown that older people's religious beliefs and practices such as prayer held up in the face of death, despite declines in religious participation (Idler et al., 2001).

However, it cannot be assumed that results elsewhere would be similar to the United States. In most Western European countries there is, compared with the United States, a much larger difference between older and younger people in terms of church attendance, and the age at which the change occurs is rising. For example, Anglican censuses in the United Kingdom show a large over-representation of the over 55s and a large under-representation of the under 45s at Sunday worship. Most concern within the Christian churches in the United Kingdom is understandably focused on younger people's reluctance to commit to church, but, as Merchant (2003) has pointed out, it will not be very long before the churches face the challenge of evangelizing the newly retired 'baby boom' generation born after World War II, who in large part rejected religion when they were young but could be offered opportunities to re-engage. Indeed, there is some longitudinal evidence from the United Kingdom which suggests that decline of religious affiliation has already occurred among the older cohorts (Coleman et al., 2004).

Moreover, it is important to acknowledge that variation in religiosity exists also among older people in the United States, especially between urban and rural areas. One study showed that less than half of persons aged 85 years and older living in San Francisco stated that religion was important in their lives (cited in McFadden, 1996b). Another unique longitudinal study of a cohort, also from North California, describes a segment of the US population more prepared to break the norms of conventional religiosity, and to embrace the new language of 'spirituality' (Dillon and Wink, 2007).

Research on other types of religious differences – such as those related to gender and race as well as age – may give more insight into the everyday function of religion and the reason interest in religion might increase with age. One of the most well-established facts about religion, at least in Western societies, is the greater religiosity of women (e.g., WHOQOL, 2006). It has often been attributed to women's greater acceptance of dependency, and need for community. There is some suggestive evidence that in late life this trend may be reversed, consistent with theories of gender crossover effects in acceptance of dependency (Coleman et al., 2004; Gutmann, 1997;

Henry, 1988). Similarly, the greater benefit found for religion among Blacks than Whites in the USA may also relate to their more dependent position in society (Cicirelli, 2002).

Ageing and societal change in the religious sphere

Societal change in religion has fundamental importance for older people because it affects their role as transmitters of tradition (Gutmann, 1997). This is a subject that has attracted most attention in those parts of Europe which have shown exceptional levels of declining religiosity (Davie, 2002). This rejection of religious authority needs to be set in the context of a troubled history of conflict between rival Christian churches, between Church and State, and European wars in which the churches provided ineffective moral leadership. However, North America, even without this history, is showing evidence of religious decline. Indeed, Altemeyer (2004) has demonstrated that abandonment of religion is the most common religious category among middle-aged Manitoba parents (most commonly associated with observed hypocrisy in fellow believers), and suggests that, as their children have largely been raised without religious training, religious decline will continue.

Brown (2001) argues that British rejection of traditional Christian culture, despite its earlier origins, gained pace only in the 1960s. Certainly, even indigenous older people in Britain were brought up in a much more religious society than they now inhabit. The vast majority of Christians, whether Protestant or Catholic, attended Sunday school right up to the 1950s, an institution which, according to Davies (2004), has been of great importance in shaping the British character. Older people, as a consequence, tend to define themselves in relation to their religious education, whether influenced by it positively or negatively, or whether grateful for or hostile towards it. For most younger, people this is no longer the case.

Various evidence highlights the importance of religious generativity for older people. The impact can be seen most strongly perhaps in immigrant communities. For example, in a study of Hindu families in London, the mental health of the grandmothers was found to be related to whether their granddaughters expressed a Hindu identity (Guglani et al., 2000). Meanwhile, elders in immigrant communities have been found to flourish when their religious contributions are needed and valued (Grewal et al., 2004). Older persons' religious generativity is also evident in communities with a history of persecution. Although the current generation of older people who attend church in Russia did not do so when they were younger adults because it was not allowed, they do have the memory of their mothers' and especially grandmothers' examples, and therefore are able to continue where they left off (Coleman and Mills, 2004).

However, where culture has become hostile to the idea of tradition and learning from the old, as in many parts of Western Europe (Sheldrake, 2005), older people can seem to face an awkward choice: whether to maintain loyalty to their own religious tradition or to seek common ground with the younger generation. The latter often no longer accept that their first choice of spiritual discipline should be the religion of their parents, and may well feel that the language of spirituality matches better than any one religion onto a complex, pluralistic, and fragmented world. As a result, the old may feel that loyalty and witness to their own religious faith is no longer relevant to or appreciated by the young. But if spirituality is understood as essentially about the task of affirmation and integration of what is of ultimate meaning in life, older people should have much to contribute to the young from their life experience. Authenticity is the key to successful intergenerational communication.

Although it is usual to attribute religious conservatism to older people, it is important to recognize that they can also be radical in their thinking in the religious and spiritual arena. Faithfulness to a tradition is compatible with, and may also require readiness to accept, new insights into that tradition's meaning. It is often older people who have the necessary maturity of mind to integrate the tension between tradition and change (Sinnott, 1998). But where, for example, religious changes have been imposed with insufficient consultation, as can be argued has been the case with much Catholic liturgical and other reforms in the latter part of the 20th century, the resulting alienation benefits neither old nor young.

Religious/spiritual conflict in later life

The subject of religious/spiritual conflict is a significant growth area in the study of religion. One of the limitations of previous analyses using religious or spiritual indices is that they tend to be based on the assumption that being 'religious' or 'spiritual' is a relatively fixed and stable characteristic, similar to race, gender, and social class. But the processes of becoming religious or spiritual, or of a change in character or intensity of faith, are interesting in themselves. There is a growing realization that later life, far from being a period

of stability or consolidation, can be a time of questioning and turmoil. Although agnosticism can be argued to be more rational than either religious faith or atheism (Kenny, 2006), it also appears to be a more uncomfortable and insecure state of being.

As already mentioned, a number of studies in the USA suggest a curvilinear relationship between strength of religious involvement and measures of well-being and adjustment, including feelings of self-worth, and death anxiety, with those of uncertain belief doing worse (Kalish and Reynolds, 1976; Krause, 1995, 2006; Wink and Scott, 2005). However, questioning and doubt may be inherent to the ageing process. Indeed, the findings of one study (Krause et al., 1999) supported an Eriksonian view that older people would be more able to tolerate religious doubt with less loss of well-being than younger people because they were actively involved in questioning many aspects of their lives. UK studies, on the other hand, suggest that these findings might not be repeated in a less religious society. Rising rates of uncertain, unsupported, and troubled belief have been observed among older people, related to disappointment with lack of interest displayed by clergy, particularly in situations of loss and frailty (Coleman et al., 2004). Moreover, subsequent longitudinal studies of bereaved spouses have shown depressive symptoms to be concentrated in those of a weak to moderate faith in a transcendent power operating in their lives (Coleman et al., 2007).

ISSUES FOR FUTURE RESEARCH

Although religion has an increased presence within social gerontology, our actual knowledge base on religion/spirituality and ageing is extremely lopsided. Despite the title William James (1902) gave to his book (*The Varieties of Religious Experience*) more than a century ago, the 'varieties' of religious and spiritual attitudes held by older as well as younger people have been little addressed. Only a limited range of religious thinking and feeling have been studied intensively, mainly among Protestant Christians in North America. This bias is evident from systematic reviews that have recently been conducted on areas such as religion and bereavement (Becker et al., 2007).

A major priority, therefore, must be more comparative study both within and beyond the boundaries of the United States. However, such research is sensitive because of the risk of drawing invidious comparisons between rival religions and denominations. Some comparisons have been made between Catholic and Protestant Christians, for example, in regard to religious coping (Pargament et al., 2005a), but very little empirical work has been done on differences been religions in later life (the work of Mehta, already cited, in Singapore is an important exception). In order to carry out a comparative study of religion, it becomes even more necessary to investigate religious cultures in their entirety. Williams' classic study of older Scottish Protestants is a good example of such in-depth scholarship on the influence of religious faith in later life (Williams, 1990). Such research requires a greater variety of methods, particularly more longitudinal and case studies, and the employment of diary methods and autobiographical enquiry.

Comparative studies can also profitably be conducted on different types of religious practice. Research has been conducted examining the effects of religious and secular meditation (Pargament et al., 2005a). Other possible topics, especially relevant to ageing and closeness to death, are the practice of confession, and the use of ritual, for example, in relation to bereavement. In designing and evaluating appropriate scales of measurement, it is essential to involve experts in religious ministry. Education in comparative religion needs to be made more widely available. In multi-faith cities such as London, for example, it is crucial for mental health professionals to learn more about other faiths in order to collaborate with, or at least understand, the perspectives on mental illness held by a variety of diverse religious groups, some of whom may be overtly hostile to the practice of psychiatry (Leavey and King, 2007; Leavey et al., 2007).

It is also important to be sensitive to cohort differences and historical change. As indicated earlier, the present older generations of European Christians may receive less support from religious bodies than their predecessors, and at the same time be less secure than younger people about engaging with the new spiritual choices offered by globalization. Future cohorts of older people no doubt will be different. In fact many features of contemporary spiritual movements are ones with which older people no less than younger people can identify: for example, the growing emphasis on the interdependency of the human species with all that exists, and on the human person not as a self-contained entity but as constituted by his or her relationships.

Older people can also draw on some of the new possibilities being offered by spiritual direction, such as the rediscovery of the transformative character of sacred reading (Schneiders, 2005). It is important that older people are not neglected in these new developments in ministry, as they have been in the recent past. Studies that have invited older people's views on these matters show that they want to be needed and consulted by others within their religious communities, and not always to be seen as dependent and in need of care themselves (Coleman et al., 2006). Clearly, new forms of ministry to older people are required (MacKinlay, 2006).

Now that access to spiritual support is recognized as an aspect of quality of life, welfare policy itself needs to be concerned with the provision of religion and its alternatives. The London-based 'Centre for Policy on Ageing' has asked precisely this question in its report on religion and ageing (Howse, 1999). Such concerns may appear unnecessary in a strongly religious society such as the United States, but in the context of the secular and welfare states of modern Europe, religious decline has palpable consequences on the well-being of individuals and communities.

The study of religion and ageing has also to engage more with existing research across the whole spectrum of the social and psychological gerontology. The communal component of belief, for example, is clearly of great importance (Ramsey and Blieszner, 1999), but the types and functions of communities offered by religious organizations and groupings have been little subjected to sociological analysis. Similarly, change in religious cognitions and practice with age are likely to relate to more general cognitive, emotional, and personality changes, yet relatively few attempts have been made to apply concepts from these areas of psychology to the study of religion and ageing. Attachment is one concept that has been fruitfully applied (Brown et al., 2004; Kirkpatrick, 2004), but there are many other theories, for example on adaptation to ageing (e.g. socio-emotional selectivity, assimilation, and accommodation), which seem not yet to have been considered. It is important that religious gerontology does not continue as a separate speciality, divorced from mainstream social science and social gerontology. Rather, religion and spirituality need to be brought into the mainstream of gerontological interests and activity, in a manner comparable to their importance to human functioning in the later stages of life.

REFERENCES

Abdul-Rauf, M. (1982) 'The ageing in Islam', in F. Tiso (ed.), *Aging: Spiritual Perspectives*. Lake Worth, FL: Sunday Publications, pp. 171–82.

Achenbaum, W.A. (1979) *Old Age in the New Land*. Baltimore, MD: John Hopkins University Press.

Aflakseir, A. and Coleman, P.G. (2009) 'The influence of religious coping and personal meaning on the mental health of disabled Iranian war veterans', *Mental Health, Religion and Culture*, 12 (2): 175–90.

Ahmadi, F. and Thomas, L.E. (2000) 'Gerotranscendence and life satisfaction: studies of religious and secular Iranians and Turks', *Journal of Religious Gerontology*, 12: 17–41.

Allen, F.B. and Coleman, P.G. (2006) 'Spiritual perspectives on the person with dementia: identity and personhood', in J. Hughes, S. Louw, and S. Sabat (eds), *Dementia: Mind, Meaning and the Person*. Oxford: Oxford University Press, pp. 205–21.

Altemeyer, B. (2004) 'The decline of organized religion in Western civilization', *International Journal for the Psychology of Religion*, 14: 77–89.

Baumeister, R.F. (2002) 'Religion and psychology: introduction to the special issue', *Psychological Inquiry*, 13: 165–67.

Becker, G., Xander, C.J., Blum, H.E., et al., (2007) 'Do religious or spiritual beliefs influence bereavement? A systematic review', *Palliative Medicine*, 21: 207–17.

Biggs, S. (1999) *The Mature Imagination. Dynamics of Identity in Midlife and Beyond*. Buckingham: Open University Press.

Black, H.K. and Rubinstein, R.L. (2004) 'Themes of suffering in later life', *Journal of Gerontology: Social Sciences*, 59B: S17–24.

Blazer, D. and Palmore, E. (1976) 'Religion and aging in a longitudinal panel', *The Gerontologist*, 16: 82–5.

Bond, J. and Corner, L. (2004) *Quality of Life and Older People*. Buckingham: Open University Press.

Brown, C.G. (2001) *The Death of Christian Britain*. London: Routledge.

Brown, S.L., Nesse, R.M., House, J.S., and Utz, R.L. (2004) 'Religion and emotional compensation: results from a prospective study of widowhood', *Personality and Social Psychology Bulletin*, 30: 1165–74.

Burrow, J.A. (1986) *The Ages of Man: A Study in Medieval Writing and Thought*. Oxford: Clarendon Press.

Cicirelli, V.G. (2002) *Older Adults' Views on Death*. New York: Springer.

Cole, T. (1992) *The Journey of Life. A Cultural History of Aging in America*. Cambridge: Cambridge University Press.

Coleman, P.G. and Mills, M.A. (2004) 'Memory and preservation of religious faith in an atheistic society: accounts of the practice of religion in the former Soviet Union', in A. Portelli (ed.), *Proceedings of the 13th International Oral History Association Conference*. Rome: International Oral History Association.

Coleman, P.G., Ivani-Chalian, C., and Robinson, M. (2004) 'Religious attitudes among British older people: stability and change in a 20 year longitudinal study', *Ageing and Society*, 24: 167–88.

Coleman, P.G., Mills, M.A., and Speck, P. (2006) 'Ageing and belief – between tradition and change', in J. Vincent, C. Phillipson, and M. Downs (eds), *The Future of Old Age*. London: Sage, pp. 131–40.

Coleman, P.G., McKiernan, F, Mills, M., and Speck, P. (2007) 'In sure and uncertain faith: belief and coping with loss of spouse in later life', *Ageing and Society*, 27: 869–90.

Crowther, M.R., Parker, M.W., Achenbaum, W.A., Larimore, W.L., and Koenig, H.G. (2002) 'Rowe and Kahn's model of successful aging revisited: positive spirituality – the forgotten factor', *The Gerontologist*, 42: 613–20.

Davie, G. (2002) *Europe: The Exceptional Case. Parameters of Faith in the Modern World*. London: Darton, Longman and Todd.

Davies, C. (2004) *The Strange Death of Moral Britain*. New Brunswick, NJ: Transaction.

Dawkins, R. (2006) *The God Delusion*. London: Bantam Books.

Dillon, M. and Wink, P. (2007) *In the Course of a Lifetime. Tracing Religious Belief, Practice, and Change*. Berkeley, CA: University of California Press.

Dulin, R.Z. (1988) *A Crown of Glory. A Biblical View of Aging*. New York: Paulist Press.

Fischer, D.H. (1977) *Growing Old in America*. Oxford: Oxford University Press.

Francis, D. (1984) *Will You Still Need Me, Will You Still Feed Me, When I'm 84?* Bloomington: Indiana University Press.

Fry, P.S. (2001) 'The unique contribution of key existential factors to the prediction of psychological well-being of older adults following spousal loss', *The Gerontologist*, 41: 69–81.

George, L.K., Larson, D.B., Koenig, H.G., and McCullough, M.E. (2000) 'Spirituality and health: what we know, what we need to know', *Journal of Social and Clinical Psychology*, 19:102–16.

Goleman, D. (1997) *Healing Emotions. Conversations with the Dalai Lama on Mindfulness, Emotions and Health*. Boston: Shambhala.

Grewal, I., Nazroo, J., Bajekal, M., Blane, D., and Lewis, J. (2004) 'Influences on quality of life: a qualitative investigation of ethnic differences among older people in England', *Journal of Ethnic and Migration Studies*, 30: 737–61.

Guglani, S., Coleman, P.G., and Sonuga-Barke, E.J.S. (2000) 'Mental health of elderly Asians in Britain: a comparison of Hindus from nuclear and extended families of differing cultural identities', *International Journal of Geriatric Psychiatry*, 15: 1046–53.

Gullette, M.M. (2004) *Aged by Culture*. Chicago: University of Chicago Press.

Gutmann, D.L. (1997) *The Human Elder in Nature, Culture and Society*. Boulder, CO: Westview Press.

Hauerwas, S., Stoneking, C.B., Meador, K.G., and Cloutier, D. (eds) (2003) *Growing Old in Christ*. Grand Rapids, MI: William B. Eerdmans.

Heelas, P. (1998) *Religion, Modernity and Postmodernity*. Oxford: Blackwell.

Henry, J.P. (1988) 'The archetypes of power and intimacy', in J.E. Birren and V.L. Bengtson (eds), *Emergent Theories of Aging*. New York: Springer. pp. 269–98.

Hill, P.C. and Pargament, K.I. (2003) 'Advances in the conceptualization and measurement of religion and spirituality: implications for physical and mental health research', *American Psychologist*, 58:64–74.

Hitchens, C.E. (2007) *God is not Great. How Religion Poisons Everything*. New York: Warner Books.

Howse, K. (1999) *Religion and Spirituality in Later Life: A Review*. London: Centre for Policy on Ageing.

Hummer, R.A., Rogers, R.G., Nam, C.B., and Ellison, C.G. (1999) 'Religious involvement and U.S. adult mortality', *Demography*, 36: 273–85.

Idler, E.L., Kasl, S.V., and Hays, J.C. (2001) 'Patterns of religious practice and belief in the last year of life', *Journal of Gerontology. Social Sciences*, 56B: S326–34.

Imamoglu, E.O. (1999) 'Some correlates of religiosity among Turkish adults and elderly within a cross-cultural perspective', in L.E. Thomas and S.A. Eisenhandler (eds), *Religion, Belief, and Spirituality in Late Life*. New York: Springer, pp. 93–110.

James, W. (1902) *The Varieties of Religious Experience*. Cambridge, MA: Harvard University Press.

Jianbin, X. and Mehta, K.K. (2003) 'The effects of religion on subjective aging in Singapore: an interreligious comparison', *Journal of Aging Studies*, 17: 485–502.

Jung, C.G. (1938) *Psychology and Religion*. New Haven, CT: Yale University Press.

Kalish, R.A. and Reynolds, D.K. (1976) *Death and Ethnicity: A Psychocultural Study*. Los Angeles, CA: University of Southern California Press.

Kenny, A. (2006) *What I Believe*. London: Continuum.

Kirby, S.E., Coleman, P.G., and Daley, D. (2004) 'Spirituality and well-being in frail and non-frail older adults', *Journal of Gerontology. Psychological Sciences*, 59B: 123–9.

Kirkpatrick, L.A. (2004) *Attachment, Evolution and the Psychology of Religion*. New York: Guilford Press.

Koenig, H.G. (1993) 'Religion and aging', *Reviews in Clinical Gerontology*, 3: 195–203.

Koenig, H.G. and Cohen, H.J. (eds) (2002) *The Link between Religion and Health: Psychoneuroimmunology and the Faith Factor*. New York: Oxford University Press.

Koenig, H.G., George, L.K., and Siegler, I.C. (1988a) 'The use of religion and other emotion-regulating coping strategies among older adults', *The Gerontologist*, 28: 303–10.

Koenig, H.G., Kvale, J.N., and Ferrel, C. (1988b) 'Religion and well-being in later life', *The Gerontologist*, 28: 18–28.

Koenig, H.G., McCullough, M.E., and Larson, D.B. (2001) *Handbook of Religion and Health*. New York: Oxford University Press.

Krause, N. (1995) 'Religiosity and self-esteem among older adults', *Journal of Gerontology. Psychological Sciences*, 50B: 236–46.

Krause, N. (2006) 'Religious doubts and psychological well-being: a longitudinal investigation', *Review of Religious Research*, 47: 287–302.

Krause, N., Ingersoll-Dayton, B., Ellison, C.G., and Wulff, K.M. (1999) 'Aging, religious doubt, and psychological well-being', *The Gerontologist*, 39: 525–33.

Leavey, G. and King, M. (2007) 'The devil is in the detail: partnership between psychiatry and faith-based organisations', *British Journal of Psychiatry*, 191: 97–8.

Leavey, G., Loewenthal, K., and King, M. (2007) 'Challenges to sanctuary: the clergy as a resource for mental health care in the community', *Social Science and Medicine*, 65: 548–59.

Levin, J.S. (ed.) (1994) *Religion in Aging and Health*. Thousand Oaks, CA: Sage.

Levin, J.S. and Taylor, R.J. (1998) 'Panel analyses of religious involvement and well-being in African Americans: contemporaneous vs. longitudinal', *Journal for the Scientific Study of Religion*, 37: 695–709.

MacKinlay, E. (2006) *Spiritual Growth and Care in the Fourth Age of Life*. London: Jessica Kingsley.

Marcoen, A. (2005) 'Religion, spirituality and older people', in M.L. Johnson, V.L. Bengtson, P.G. Coleman, and T.B.L. Kirkwood (eds), *The Cambridge Handbook of Age and Ageing*. Cambridge: Cambridge University Press, pp. 363–70.

McCullough, M.E. and Larson, D.B. (1999) 'Religion and depression: A review of the literature', *Twin Research*, 2: 126–36.

McFadden, S.H. (1996a) 'Religion and spirituality', in J.E. Birren (ed.) *Encyclopedia of Gerontology*, Vol. 2. San Diego, CA: Academic Press, pp. 387–97.

McFadden, S.H. (1996b) 'Religion, spirituality and aging', in J.E. Birren and K.W. Schaie (eds), *Handbook of the Psychology of Aging*, (4th edn.) San Diego, CA: Academic Press, pp. 162–77.

McFadden, S.H. (2005) 'Points of connection: Gerontology and the Psychology of Religion', in R.F. Paloutzian and C.L. Park (eds), *Handbook of the Psychology of Religion and Spirituality*. New York: Guilford Press, pp. 162–76.

McFadden, S.H. and Levin, J.S. (1996) 'Religion, emotions and health' in C. Magai and S.H. McFadden (eds), *Handbook of Emotion, Adult Development and Aging*. San Diego, CA: Academic Press, pp. 349–65.

Mehta, K.K. (1997) 'The impact of religious beliefs and practices on aging: a cross-cultural comparison', *Journal of Aging Studies*, 11: 102–14.

Merchant, R. (2003) *Pioneering the Third Age. The Church in an Ageing Population*. Carlisle: Paternoster Press.

Miller, L. and Kelley, B.S. (2005) 'Relationships of religiosity and spirituality with mental health and psychopathology', in R.F. Paloutzian and C.L. Park (eds), *Handbook of the Psychology of Religion and Spirituality*. New York: Guilford Press, pp. 460–78.

Miller, W.R. and Thoresen, C.E. (2003) 'Spirituality, religion, and health. An emerging research field', *American Psychologist*, 58: 24–35.

Moberg, D.O. (2001) 'Research on spirituality', in D.O. Moberg (ed.), *Aging and Spirituality. Spiritual Dimensions of Aging Theory, Research, Practice and Policy*. Binghampton, NY: The Haworth Press, pp. 55–69.

Moody, H.R. (2006) 'Is religion good for your health?', *The Gerontologist*, 46: 147–9.

Noll, M.A. (2002) *America's God. From Jonathan Edwards to Abraham Lincoln*. New York: Oxford University Press.

Oman, D. and Thoresen, C.E. (2005) 'Do religion and spirituality influence health?', in R.F. Paloutzian and C.L. Park (eds), *Handbook of the Psychology of Religion and Spirituality*. New York: Guilford Press, pp. 435–59.

Pargament, K.I. (1997) *The Psychology of Religion and Coping. Theory, Research, Practice*. New York: Guilford Press.

Pargament, K.I. and Park, C.L. (1995) 'Merely a defense?: the variety of religious means and ends', *Journal of Social Issues*, 51: 13–32.

Pargament, K.I., Van Haitsma, K., and Ensing, D.S. (1995) 'When age meets adversity: religion and coping in the later years', in M.A. Kimble, S.H. McFadden, J.W. Ellor, and J.J. Seeber (eds), *Aging, Spirituality and Religion: A Handbook*. Minneapolis, MN: Fortress Press, pp. 47–67.

Pargament, K.I., Ano, G.G., and Wachholtz, A.B. (2005a) 'The religious dimension of coping. Advances in theory, research and practice', in R.F. Paloutzian and C.L. Park (eds), *Handbook of the Psychology of Religion and Spirituality*. New York: Guilford Press, pp. 479–95.

Pargament, K.I., Magyar-Russell, G.M., and Murray-Swank, N.A. (2005b) 'The sacred and the search for significance: religion as a unique process', *Journal of Social Issues*, 61: 665–87.

Pearson, J.L. and Brown, G.K. (2000) 'Suicide prevention in late life. Directions for science and practice', *Clinical Psychology Review*, 20: 685–705.

Polivka, L. (2000) 'Postmodern aging and the loss of meaning', *Journal of Aging and Identity*, 5: 225–35.

Powell, L.H., Shahabi, L., and Thoresen, C.E. (2003) 'Religion and spirituality: linkages to physical health', *American Psychologist*, 58: 36–52.

Pressman, P., Lyons, J.S., Larson, D.B., and Gartner, J. (1992) 'Religion, anxiety and fear of death', in J.F. Schumaker (ed.), *Religion and Mental Health*. New York: Oxford University Press, pp. 98–109.

Ram-Prasad, C. (1995) 'A classical Indian philosophical perspective on ageing and the meaning of life', *Ageing and Society*, 15: 1–36.

Ramsey, J.L. and Blieszner, R. (1999) *Spiritual Resiliency in Older Women: Models of Strength for Challenges through the Life Span*. Thousand Oaks, CA: Sage.

Schaie, K.W., Krause, N., and Booth, A. (eds.) (2004) *Religious Influences on Health and Well-Being in the Elderly*. New York: Springer.

Schneiders, S.M. (2005) 'Spirituality and scripture', in P. Sheldrake (ed.), *The New SCM Dictionary of Christian Spirituality*. London: SCM Press, pp. 62–7.

Shamy, E. (2003) *A Guide to the Spiritual Dimension of Care for People with Alzheimer's Disease and Related Dementia: More than Body, Brain and Breath*. London: Jessica Kingsley Publishers.

Sheldrake, P. (2005) 'Spirituality and history', in P. Sheldrake (ed.), *The New SCM Dictionary of Christian Spirituality*. London: SCM Press, pp. 38–43.

Sinnott, J.D. (1998) *The Development of Logic in Adulthood: Postformal Thought and Its Operations*. New York: Plenum Press.

Sloan, R.P. and Bagiella, E. (2002) 'Claims about religious involvement and health outcomes', *Annals of Behavioral Medicine*, 24: 14–21.

Smith, T.B., McCullough, M.E., and Poll, J. (2003) 'Religiousness and depression: evidence for a main effect and the moderating influence of stressful life events', *Psychological Bulletin*, 129: 614–36.

Strawbridge, W.J., Shema, S.J., Cohen, R.D., Roberts, R.E., and Kaplan, G.A. (1998) 'Religiosity buffers effects of some stressors on depression but exacerbates others', *Journal of Gerontology: Social Sciences*, 53B: S118–26.

Teinonen, T., Vahlberg, T., Isoaho, R., and Kivela, S-L. (2005) 'Religious attendance and 12-year survival in older persons', *Age and Ageing*, 34: 406–9.

Tilak, S. (1989) *Religion and Aging in the Indian Tradition*. Albany, NY: State University of New York Press.

Voas, D. and Crockett, A. (2005) 'Religion in Britain: neither believing nor belonging', *Sociology*, 39: 11–28.

WHOQOL SPRB Group (2006) 'A cross-cultural study of spirituality, religion and personal beliefs as components of quality of life', *Social Science and Medicine*, 62: 1486–97.

Williams, R. (1990) *A Protestant Legacy. Attitudes to Death and Illness among Older Aberdonians*. Oxford: Clarendon Press.

Wink, P. and Scott, J. (2005) 'Does religiousness buffer against the fear of death and dying in late adulthood?', *Journal of Gerontology: Psychological Sciences*, 60B: 207–14.

13

Intergenerational Relationships of International Migrants in Developed Nations: The United States and France

Merril Silverstein and
Claudine Attias-Donfut

INTRODUCTION

Intergenerational relationships are among the most durable and enduring of human bonds, and serve as important conduits through which tangible and symbolic resources are exchanged across the life course. Evidence is plentiful that older parents and their adult children derive mutual benefits from having close and mutually supportive relations with each other, often over far distances (Hogan et al.,1993; Silverstein et al., 1997). While these attributes of intergenerational relations hold almost universally, their stakes are higher for individuals living closer to the margins of society, as are many immigrants from developing nations for whom intergenerational relationships are virtual lifelines. While studies of international migration to Western Europe and North America have focused to a large degree on working-age migrants and their dependent children (e.g., see Massey, 1987), less is known about mature immigrants – those who have migrated in their later years or have aged within their host societies.

In this chapter we explore aspects of adult intergenerational family ties of international migrants living in the United States and in France. Although most Western nations will soon complete their demographic transition to becoming stable aged societies, they will remain dynamic with respect to

global forces that have shifted the social contexts in which ageing families find themselves. Despite the homogenizing influence of globalization, more fluid entry and egress of immigrant workers across national boundaries has variegated national populations where migration is most prolific. We specifically focus on immigrants residing in the United States and France, two nations that have long been destinations for those from abroad seeking economic opportunities and a better standard of life for themselves and their families.

We examine structural, cultural, and contextual aspects of ageing immigrant families and their intergenerational relations. Structural aspects include financial transfers, shared living arrangements, as well as the emergence of global families whose members are separated by national borders. Ideational aspects include how values and norms of origin and destination societies are reconciled through acculturation processes in multigenerational immigrant families. Contextual aspects include societal conditions and policies that shape immigrant flows and the types of intergenerational transactions that result.

In the 1980s and 1990s, the United States and Europe emerged as main destinations for migrants from low GDP (Gross Domestic Product) nations, abetted by advances in communication technology, the relatively free circulation of labor and capital across national borders, the emergence of transnational migrant networks, and, in the case of Europe, greater economic integration of the continent (Fargues, 2004). Multigenerational families generally operate in distinct ways in developed and developing parts of the world. A familiar discourse in much of the scholarship focusing on the aged of Western Europe and North America is that the state (and to some degree the market) has supplanted many of the supportive roles formerly occupied by adult children and other relatives. Conversely, older parents and their adult children in predominantly low-skilled, semi-subsistence rural economies are noted for their mutual interdependence as an adaptation to scarcity in the absence of formal support alternatives. In this chapter we consider multigenerational families where these worlds meet – in the form of immigrant groups from the less developed world living in developed countries. Global migrants link the society of origin with the society of settlement (Schiller et al., 1995), as will be evident both economically and culturally through the prism of cross-generational relationships.

IMMIGRANTS IN THE UNITED STATES AND FRANCE

The United States and France both offer examples of historically migrant-receiving nations where the acceptance of immigrants has been a national ideal as well as a national controversy (the immigrant connection of the two nations commemorated in France's gift of the Statue of Liberty to the United States in 1886). We concentrate our discussion primarily on the dominant émigrés to each nation, namely those from Latin American nations, predominantly Mexico, to the United States, and those from North African nations to France. Since both groups of immigrants tend to arrive with lower education and fewer skills than most other immigrants, their intergenerational ties are key to their ability to adapt and thrive in their respective destinations.

We begin by reviewing some of the basic characteristics of immigrants to the United States and France. We note that most statistics regarding immigrants represent individuals only, and typically do not consider native-born children and grandchildren living in immigrant households. Consequently, accounts of individuals living in immigrant households are likely to be underestimated.

We first discuss the situation in the United States. In 2003, more than 12 per cent of the total US population were foreign-born, a figure that has more than doubled since 1970; the percentage of foreign-born in the United States is currently close to what it was during the immigration surge of the early 20th century. Among the foreign-born, slightly more than half (53 per cent) were from Latin America, and about one in three (30 per cent) originated in Mexico, by far the largest sending nation (Larsen, 2004). Immigration from Latin America tends to be fluid, with multiple border crossings, driven by the availability of low wage, sometimes seasonal, labor and facilitated by the long shared border between the United States and Mexico. An estimated 11–12 million individuals are living in the United States as unauthorized (often called undocumented) migrants, the large majority from Latin American countries.[1] Gelbard and Carter (1997) estimate that 40% of unauthorized migrants originated in Mexico. Immigrants in the United States represent a diverse set of statuses; where 29 per cent are unauthorized, 42 per cent are naturalized American citizens (Passel et al., 2004).

Overall, the representation of migrants in France is comparable to that in the United States, with the foreign-born comprising about 10 per cent of the French population in 2006.[2] Among immigrants, slightly more than one-third (35 per cent) originated from North African nations (the largest sending nations being Algeria and Morocco), and slightly less than one-third (30 per cent) derived from southern European countries (Borrell and Durr, 2005). Almost half of foreign-born individuals living in France are French citizens.[3]

International emigration to France is part of a long history of constitution of the French population during the last two centuries (Noiriel, 1988). It has been greatly enhanced as the result of several converging trends that include greater international economic integration of Europe, the worldwide diffusion of new information and communication technologies, and the demand for younger workers created by population ageing (Fargues, 2004). As a consequence, the past decade has seen a sharp increase in the volume of international migration to and within Europe, reaching its highest level since World War II. To what extent France should be open to immigrants from its former colonies has been a politically charged question for some time (Weil, 2004).

While it is beyond the scope of this chapter to review specific public policies and socio-historical forces that have guided immigration flows over the last century, it is useful to comment briefly on the ways that immigrants differ between these two nations. Where a plurality of immigrants in France are from Muslim nations of North Africa, the largest immigrant groups in the United States are from Spanish-speaking, mostly Catholic nations of Mexico and those of Central America. Thus, the religious orientation of Hispanic immigrants is more likely than that of North African immigrants to be compatible with the overall Christian religious orientation of the destination countries.

The concept of race with regard to immigration is a complex one, and space does not permit us to fully elaborate on its importance to immigrant incorporation. However, we note that while the discourse about immigration in France tends to revolve around issues of citizenship, social class, and religious differences, distinctions based on race loom large in the United States and serve as one explanation for the economic exclusion of Hispanic immigrants and their descendants (Telles and Ortiz, 2008)). Fluency in the host country's language represents a form of cultural capital that may advantage immigrants. Given that former colonies of France are French-speaking, it is likely that that such fluency will be greater among North African immigrants in France than among Hispanic immigrants in the United States. Finally, while the economic development of immigrant-sending nations is less than that of immigrant-receiving nations, the gap in development between France and North Africa is greater than the gap in development between the United States and Latin America (particularly Mexico). Thus, North African immigrants in France are less likely than Hispanic immigrants in the United States to have marketable skills and receive economic assistance from abroad.

In spite of these aforementioned differences, we suggest that labor migrants to each nation share similar experiences and have adapted to their circumstances in similar ways. Immigrants in both nations were principally motivated to emigrate by the limited economic opportunities in their countries of origin and the expectation of more plentiful such opportunities in their destinations. Both groups face comparable challenges to full economic, linguistic, and cultural incorporation into their respective host societies. Differences between immigrant and native populations are consistent in the United States and France, with immigrants being more likely to live in multigenerational households, having larger family sizes, and tending to live in segregated ethnic enclaves. Finally, we suggest that both groups attempt to overcome barriers to full incorporation by virtue of resources embedded in their intergenerational relationships.

CROSS-NATIONAL STUDIES OF INTERGENERATIONAL RELATIONSHIPS

We begin by examining several studies that have used a common instrument to compare adult intergenerational relationships across nations with different political economies and cultures. Although these studies are primarily pan-European, their results reveal trends that are telling about the importance of national context in shaping intergenerational styles as measured by proximity, frequency

of contact, and provisions of support. Intergenerational relationships tended to be weakest in nations with generous public sectors and individualistic cultures (welfare states of Norway and Sweden), strongest in nations with residualist public sectors and coercive family cultures (Mediterranean nations of Greece, Spain, and Italy), and moderate in nations that fall in between on both dimensions (liberal-market states of Great Britain and Germany), and the centralized welfare state of France (Attias-Donfut et al., 2005; Hank, 2007; Lowenstein et al., 2005; Tomassini et al., 2004). For the most part, these differences follow a north–south divide and reflect fundamental differences in whether intergenerational responsibility for older people is chiefly considered a private family concern, or a collective public responsibility.

Older people in less developed nations tend to rely predominantly or exclusively on family to satisfy their basic needs. For instance, many less developed Asian nations have few public provisions for their older populations, and mandate that adult children provide eldercare and financial support for their elders as both a duty and a legal responsibility (see Chapter 15). In these contexts, cultural values emphasizing filial duty are in alignment with the absence of public resources; responsibility for support is by necessity put squarely on the family because there are few alternatives for older adults (Sun, 2002). Evidence in the developed nations of France and the United States suggests that intergenerational transfers remain important – but mostly in a *downward* direction, from older to younger generations (Attias-Donfut, 2003; Attias-Donfut and Wolff, 2008; McGarry, 1999).

As we have described, intergenerational support insures against risk and unmet need in both less developed and more developed nations, albeit with different strategic imperatives. It is likely that low-skilled immigrants will face demands from multiple generations in their origin and destination countries that are difficult to fulfill given barriers to their own achievement (e.g., insufficient human and economic capital, limited linguistic skills, and discriminatory employment practices). However, little systematic attention has been devoted to studying intergenerational relationships of immigrants and how they differ from those of their native-born counterparts.

INTERGENERATIONAL THEORIES APPLIED TO IMMIGRANT FAMILIES

In this section we address several theoretical orientations and paradigms that have guided scholarship on intergenerational relationships, and then ask whether they are more or less relevant to immigrant families. These orientations and paradigms are represented by two broad intellectual streams: *descriptive* theories that identify the building blocks of intergenerational cohesion and its manifestations, and *explanatory* theories that identify motivations for maintaining intergenerational cohesion in its various forms.

Intergenerational Solidarity

We begin by presenting an intergenerational solidarity paradigm, a codification of the sentiments, behaviors, attitudes, values, and structural arrangements that socially bind the generations and arguably the most widely used descriptive theory in research on cross-generational relationships (Mangen et al., 1988). As a meta-construct, solidarity is manifest by six principal dimensions: affection (emotional intimacy), consensus (agreement in opinions, values, and beliefs), filial norms (obligation), association (frequency of contact), structure (geographic propinquity), and function (help and support).

With the possible exception of affection, expressions of solidarity are likely to be different in the families of international migrants than in the families of the native-born. Contact and geographic propinquity take on more salience within families that are separated across national boundaries and continents. As we will discuss later in this chapter, many migrants maintain transnational contact with their families abroad, some of whom may be scattered across different international locations, as was common among the children of mature south Asian immigrants living in the United Kingdom (Burholt, 2004). However, larger geographic distances between family members increase the cost of interaction and limit the amount of direct contact between generations. In particular, providing instrumental support, such as caregiving, requires proximity and may be severely limited by physical separation. Government policies toward immigration also affect the return flow of migrants to the country of origin and family reunification in the destination country. In the instance of undocumented immigrants in the United States, intense border protection activity inhibits temporary visits to see family members in Mexico.

Immigrant families also face challenges to maintaining consensual and normative solidarity across generations by virtue of their binational positions – simultaneously influenced by their national origins and destinations. The process of immigrant acculturation has been viewed both as the erosion of traditional values, customs, and language, and as

the process of adopting the values, customs, and language of the host society (Caetano and Clark, 2003; Skinner, 2002). Thus, the cultural and linguistic orientations of immigrants will take hybridized forms, different than those of both their native-born and their native-land counterparts. Generation gaps are likely to emerge as successive generations drift toward the mainstream culture and away from their ancestral culture.

An important aspect of acculturation, with consequences for family functioning, is the degree to which norms of familism – the centrality of family life – is maintained in immigrant families (Baca Zinn and Wells, 2000). Intergenerational bonds are typically viewed as stronger and more durable in Hispanic families than they are in White non-Hispanic families (Strom et al., 1997). Research demonstrates that strong intergenerational norms of filial obligation – as well as intergenerational support and interaction – persist among immigrants and their descendants, though in a somewhat weakened form (Aranda and Miranda, 1997; John et al., 1997; Sabogal et al., 1987).

The study of grandparents raising their grandchildren represents a growing area of research that sheds light on the familistic values of immigrants (see also Chapter 34). Not only is the prevalence of caregiving grandparents greater in Hispanic than in White, non-Hispanic families, Hispanic caregivers are more likely to provide care in conjunction with other relatives (Goodman and Silverstein, 2005). In one study, Hispanic grandmothers caring for a grandchild (more than two-thirds of whom were immigrants) tended to be less depressed when the mother of the grandchild lived in the same household as the grandmother than when she lived in a different household (Goodman and Silverstein, 2002). That the same pattern was not found among non-Hispanic grandmothers suggests that Hispanic grandmothers benefit from co-parenting because they experience it as the fulfillment of underlying cultural values that emphasize familism (Burnette, 1999).

In addition, many immigrants from less developed countries maintain values adopted in their home countries that reinforce particular gender patterns within their extended families. For instance among middle-aged and older Muslim immigrants in France, sons receive financial transfers more often than daughters, whereas among non-migrants, daughters receive transfers more often, or at the same rate, as sons. This difference may be due to a culturally traditional gender division of roles where economic succession follows the male line in the family, and where daughters are presumed to be in their husbands' charge. Hispanic immigrants in the United States favor a more traditional gender division of labor and harbor the expectation that women perform care work in the family (Pyke, 2004).

Social distance between generations in immigrant families may grow due to economic mobility across successive generations. Attias-Donfut et al. (2006), in their national study of French immigrants ≥45 years old, found that the large majority in the workforce – more than three-quarters – felt on the whole that they had been more successful than their parents. The perception of intergenerational social mobility was particularly common among immigrants from poorer countries of North Africa. In the United States, Hispanic immigrants are rapidly closing the gap in home ownership, a defining characteristic of both economic and social success (Myers and Liu, 2005).

Much has been written about the nature of cultural blending among immigrants. Portes et al. (1999: p. 229) note that 'for immigrants involved in transnational activities and their home country counterparts, success does not so much depend on abandoning their culture and language to embrace those of another society as on preserving their original cultural endowment, while adapting instrumentally to a second'. Multiculturalism may not only be embodied within individual immigrants but also within the family system itself. Intergenerational relations in immigrant families represent a prime arena within which conflict between cultural orientations of older and younger family members may play out.

A culture gap in immigrant families may produce invidious effects on the quality of intergenerational relationships. This can be best seen in relationships between grandchildren and their immigrant grandparents, where the gap tends to be wider than it is between adjacent generations. Silverstein and Chen (1999) in a study of Mexican-American immigrant families found that young adult grandchildren who were more acculturated to American society in their language use and cultural practices tended to be less emotionally close to their traditional grandparents when compared to less acculturated grandchildren.

In summary, immigrant families face two types of dualism. First, immigrants culturally and linguistically adapt to their new environments while maintaining close relationships with more traditionally oriented family members back home. This form of biculturalism represents a form of *segmented assimilation*, the partial incorporation of immigrants into the host country (Portes and Rumbaut, 2001). Secondly, the acculturation of immigrants – whose identities are firmly anchored in their countries of origin – typically proceeds at a rate slower to that of their offspring (Silverstein and Chen, 1999). These dualisms potentially produce wide differences in cultural orientations across family generations, causing tensions that may prove difficult to resolve in familistic cultures.

Altruistic and Reciprocity as Motivations for Intergenerational Support

Theories from the fields of family economics and social psychology posit several reasons why individuals provide resources to family members across generations. While there are many variants of these theories, they can be classified into two major groups: altruism and reciprocity. It is beyond dispute that families are inherently altruistic social organizations. Many studies have shown that time and money resources are targeted at the most needy members of the family, and that these flows are redistributive across generations (Altonji et al., 1992; Stark, 1995), Private transfers of time and money flow up and down generational lines as an insurance mechanism that protects family members against unforeseen difficulties and risks.

In Western Europe and the United States, pension systems and the income security and relative affluence of the older populations have reduced the upward flows of financial support to a relative trickle, and has provided older adults the means to make downward transfers to their children. In the United States and Western Europe, downward transfers tend to be targeted at adult children in need, such as the divorced, the unemployed, and single mothers, supporting an altruistic model of giving (Attias-Donfut and Wolff, 2000; Fritzell and Lennartsson, 2005; Kohli, 1999; Künemund et al., 2005; McGarry and Schoeni, 1997).

A family of theories deriving from the principle of reciprocity) – the expectation that a social debt should be repaid (Gouldner, 1960) – provides a competing perspective on support provided within intergenerational relationships. In this formulation, family members transfer valued resources to others in order to attract resources of equal or greater value, a perspective rooted in rational choice theory (Becker, 1975) as well as theories of small-group cohesion (Homans, 1950; Whitbeck et al., 1991). Research examining long-term serial patterns of intergenerational exchange in the United States has found that parents who provided financial assistance to their young-adult children tended to receive more social support from them in old age (Henretta et al., 1997; Silverstein et al., 2002). A study of intergenerational reciprocity in the Netherlands found that children who provided social support to their older parents were motivated by their perception that they were repaying a debt to their parents (Ikkink et al., 1999).

Formal comparisons of altruism and reciprocity as motives for intergenerational transactions in immigrant families are rare. However, Wolff et al. (2007) found in their study of intergenerational economic transfers made by immigrants ≥45 years old living in France that both Muslim and non-Muslim parents transferred money disproportionately to their poorest adult children regardless of their geographic distance. That parents did not provide more often to their more proximate children – those best situated to be caregivers – was taken as evidence that altruism more than reciprocity drove their downward transfers. Additional research of this issue with regard to time transfers among immigrants in France found that grandmothers devoted time in the service of grandchild care unequally to their adult children, privileging mothers with *greater* labor market potential (Dimova and Wolff, 2008). This result argues against altruism as a motivation, and points to the strategic allocation of time to the daughter most likely to optimize her family's resources – a perspective not inconsistent with exchange theory should some of those resources flow back to the grandmother (Becker, 1991).

Since altruism and reciprocity are often found together in families with high levels of transactions, it is particularly difficult to distinguish these motives in familistic cultures or societies. Intergenerational patterns in the developing world – and by extension those of immigrants from the developing world – are often subsumed under the mutual aid model of family functioning. The mutual aid model specifies that transfers are made as needs in each generation arise, such that the family functions as an insurance policy against unmet need in the absence of public alternatives (Lee et al., 1994; Sun, 2002). In this respect, the willingness of family members to provide aid to others is consistent with altruistic motivations.

On the other hand, many, if not most, transfers are reciprocal. A common observation in developing countries is a 'time-for-money' exchange, where parents provide household labor and/or childcare services to the families of their adult children, and adult children provide money to their parents (Frankenberg et al., 2002). As such, the mutual aid model of intergenerational support rests on principles of both altruism and reciprocity, but does not privilege one over the other. The difficulty in distinguishing motivations is highlighted by Sloan et al. (2002) who suggest that double-sided altruism may guide intergenerational relationships. In their formulation, adult children's feelings of gratitude for having earlier been supported by their parents motivate them to later provide support to their ageing parents: empathetic and transactional are made of the same cloth and are virtually inseparable. To the extent that

immigrant family members are frequently engaged with each other under a pact of mutual aid, the altruism/exchange dichotomy may be a false one in this population.

Another challenge in specifying the underlying motives of transfer motives of immigrants is that support provided to other generations is isomorphic with familistic cultural orientations as well as the lack of social protection programmes, such as retirement pensions, unemployment insurance, income maintenance for indigent families, and childcare. Although immigrants may be eligible for some social benefits in their new countries, various personal and institutional barriers block their full availability and use, essentially 'crowding in' family support. The question of whether normative structures or lack of alternatives promotes hyperexchange activity in immigrant communities has yet to be resolved.

In summary, immigration brings into sharp relief the adaptive potential of intergenerational families. As a result of their lower than average access to public benefits and concentration in peripheral low-wage labor markets, international migrants often engage in mutual cross-generational exchanges of support, both as a survival strategy and as an expression of cultural traditions.

TRANSNATIONAL AND TRANSACTIONAL ASPECTS OF IMMIGRANT FAMILIES

Immigrant families that maintain relationships across national borders are characterized as *transnational*. Transnationalism is 'the process by which immigrants forge and sustain multistranded social relations that link together their societies of origin and settlement' (Schiller et al., 1995: 48). Transnational family networks are made possible by 'space and time compressing technology' that renders national borders more permeable and allow 'regular and sustained social contact' in the service of occupational activities (Portes et al., 2002). Some scholars criticize this definition as overemphasizing economic production at the expense of the domestic sphere, particularly in circumstances where older family members are concerned (e.g., social visits; caregiving; correspondence; remittances). In general, focusing solely on immigrant labor obscures the explicit involvement of multiple generations in the immigrant enterprise. Rarely have family systems been used as the unit of investigation despite the fact that migration is a family decision with consequences for older generations. Tellingly, a recent college textbook titled *Global Families* (Karraker, 2008) has no entries in its index for 'ageing', 'elderly', or 'generation'.

Transmigrants usually retain close ties and maintain contact with family members left behind. Indeed, the intergenerational axis is an important conduit of resources prior to and after emigration. Resources provided by family members in the country of origin may have helped pay the cost of emigrating, and may continue to provide material and informational support as well as care for dependent family members (children and ageing parents) of the migrant (Cong and Silverstein, 2008; Massey and Goldring, 1994).

Transnational families have complex filial ties balanced on a cross-national fulcrum that may tilt in later life toward the country of origin as the pull of family reunification intensifies. Attias-Donfut et al. (2006) found that the intention of immigrants to return to their homelands strengthened after their retirement, particularly among those who had children living abroad. Conversely, those retirees having children and other relatives in France expressed less willingness to return.

Immigration policy also affects transmigration in dramatic ways. In the United States there is evidence that transmigration from Mexico may have slowed in recent years. Mexican migrants appear to be settling more permanently in the United States due to 1986 legislation that provided a means for immigrants to petition for family reunification (Roberts et al., 1999). More recently, the intensification of border patrols has made it more perilous to leave and return to the United States. As a consequence, the decline in transnational border crossings may be compelling domestic immigrant families to rely on each other to a greater extent than before.

Much of the literature on support exchanged between family members of immigrant families has focused on flows of financial support or remittances sent back to relatives in the country of origin. According to the International Fund for Agriculture Development, about 150 million migrant workers across the world sent remittances of approximately US $300 billion in 2006. Money sent by migrants to a great extent improves the standard of living of older and younger family members left behind. Despite the large size of these aggregate transfers and their global consequences (particularly for sending and receiving nations), there are relatively few micro-level studies regarding how transfers are directed within migrant families (Rapoport and Docquier, 2006).

A study of intergenerational financial transfers made by mature immigrants in France that partially remedies this deficiency found that immigrants gave more cash gifts than they received, both up and down the generational line (Attias-Donfut and Wolff, 2009). The tendency was to provide money back home to compensate for wage differentials and standard of living differences between origin and destination counties (altruism) and to honor a debt for money received from family members prior to emigrating (reciprocity). Immigrants also provided more often to older parents than to adult children, and this was particularly obvious among migrants from Morocco, Tunisia, and sub-Saharan African nations, among the poorest regions sending migrants. Rates of giving to parents were higher than in the native-born French population. That remittances sent by migrants went to older parents living in countries with weak pension systems suggests the continued importance of children for old-age support in those sending nations and the family's strategic use of migration as a means to generate resources for that purpose.

Remittances sent by Hispanic immigrants in the United States follow a pattern similar to African immigrants in France. One study used the *Health and Retirement Study* to investigate intergenerational financial transfers among Hispanics based on their nativity and language acculturation (Silverstein, 2008). Foreign-born Hispanics were more likely to provide transfers than native-born Americans, and this was driven primarily by their elevated propensity to provide to ageing parents. Those with stronger preferences to speak Spanish were more likely to provide transfers to parents and relative children, paralleling similar results among French immigrants with respect to French proficiency. Immigrants in both nations – because they must balance the demands of older and younger generations – face challenges to investing sufficiently in their own well-being.

MULTIGENERATIONAL LIVING ARRANGEMENTS

Older immigrants are more likely than their native-born counterparts to live in multigenerational households (Kritz et al., 2000), a pattern that appears to hold among immigrants worldwide (e.g., see Lowenstein, 2002 concerning older Russian immigrants in Israel). Migration in later life for the purpose of family reunification is often motivated by the need of older adults for assistance from their migrant children, or the need of migrant children for assistance with childcare and domestic labor (reviewed by Longino and Bradley, 2006).

Older Hispanics in the United States are more likely than non-Hispanic Whites to reside in multigenerational households (Himes et al., 1996), and are welcomed into the homes of their children for both practical and symbolic reasons (Treas and Torrecilha, 1995). In France, immigrants from

North Africa, as well as those from sub-Saharian Africa and Turkey, have among the highest rates of cohabitation with ageing parents (Attias-Donfut and Wolff, 2009).

Intergenerational co-residence mitigates some of the socioeconomic challenges faced by Hispanic immigrants in the United States and North African immigrants in France. Sharing a household confers mutual benefits for older parents and their adult children in terms of the availability of on-site, trustworthy, and cost-free childcare labor, the ability to pool economic and space resources, and the potential of the older adults to receive care from children when needed (Treas and Chen, 2000). Whether multigenerational living arrangements among immigrants are simply an adaptation to poverty and lack of societal benefits, or fulfillment of cultural expectation, has not been resolved, yet it is likely that both factors are relevant.

However, multigenerational co-residence may come at a cost to older individuals. In the United States immigrant parents who live with their children and are more likely to be financially dependent on them, particularly Latin American immigrants (Angel et al., 1996; Burr and Mutchler, 1999; Glick and Van Hook, 2002; Wilmoth, 2001). Dependence of older immigrants on younger family members was found to be greater when the English-language ability of the former was more limited (Angel et al., 2000). Such dependence may socially isolate older migrants from the wider social environment, particularly among those who don't live in ethnic enclaves. Thus, it is not surprising that late middle-aged immigrants, especially those with the most limited English proficiency, tended to have more depressive symptoms than their native counterparts (Wilmoth and Chen, 2003). Angel et al., (2001) similarly found that Spanish language use was associated with worse physical and emotional health among older foreign-born Hispanics, concluding from this that their segregation from mainstream society produced deleterious effects. Contrary to expectations, the quality of family relations did little to improve the well-being of Spanish-speaking immigrants.

Interpersonal strains and conflict may emerge within migrant families who live in multigenerational households when adult children make household decisions independently of their co-residing parents (Detzner, 1996; Treas and Mazumdar, 2002). Treas and Mazumdar (2002) point out several family challenges unique to older immigrants who live in multigenerational households. First, older immigrants are at elevated risk of social isolation as a result of their limited English proficiency and tendency to subordinate their own needs to those of their families. Secondly, older immigrants are expected to care for their grandchildren at an age when they are also likely to experience the need for care themselves. Thirdly, they are often called upon to sustain the cultural integrity of their native land at the same time as their adult children are acculturating into the host society.

Thus, the literature suggests that the view of older immigrants as contentedly embedded in family-based support networks is probably an oversimplified, idealized image demanding more nuanced accounts of the experiences of older people in culturally diverse migrant families (see Chapter 15). Along these lines, we note that it would be erroneous to generalize about household arrangements across all immigrant groups. In a study of Korean immigrants to the United States, Sung and Kim (2002) found that normative prescriptions of the native land find different expressions in a new environment. Older Korean immigrants were *less* likely than their age peers in Korea to live with their children, reflecting a preference for the independent lifestyles of their new land and the availability of community programmes that allowed them to live independently. Similar findings are reported by Pang et al. (2003) with respect to older Chinese immigrants.

CONCLUSION

Discussions of globalization related to issues of ageing have focused on the weakening of institutions that serve older people and the increased exposure of older individuals and their families to risk (Dannefer, 2003; Phillipson, 2003). Institutional retrenchment of state benefits has compelled individuals to adapt by relying more on traditional social obligations of family and community and less on public forms of support (Giddens, 2000). As we have discussed, immigrants adapt to their peripheral positions by relying on intergenerational ties for material and sociocultural support within the context of mutual-exchange networks. In short, multigenerational families are vital economic and social safety nets for immigrants. Immigrant adaptation may be an exaggerated version of how native-born citizens will adapt to welfare state retrenchment, and a weakening economy, with all the perils that this may bring.

It is clear that international migration does not purely rest on the decisions of individuals. More often than not, the decision to migrate across national borders is a family decision and has family consequences. When young adults move to take advantage of emerging labor markets they do so with intergenerational family members in mind. As Phillipson (2005) notes, global migration is producing 'a new kind of ageing in which the dynamics of family and social life may be stretched across different continents and across different types of societies' (2005: 507), but producing something of a 'crisis' for communities supporting older adults.

Evidence shows that older adults who migrate to new international locations with, or following, their adult children, often lack the linguistic and cultural capital to integrate fully into their new surroundings and consequently suffer from loneliness and depression (particularly when they are not so subtly pressed into service providing labor for the households of adult children). However, the question of whether the lives of older migrants are materially or emotionally better off than they would have been in their native country remains unanswered. Migration may produce a net benefit for older adults. Older adults in migrant families benefit from resource-sharing in the family and feel as valued providers to the family good, from which they share in the returns, and remittances from migrant children may offset the strains faced by older adults who are left behind. By focusing solely on ageing individuals, we are apt to ignore the intergenerational complexities that moderate the more onerous trends anticipated by the literature.

Ease of communication and transportation has made it possible for migrant families to fluidly reconstitute and adapt to changing international labor market conditions in ways they could not before. Whether this results in greater opportunities for younger family members at the expense of older adults or whether 'a rising tide raises all boats' in the family will await future research. As we have seen in the United States and France, middle-aged and pre-retirement immigrants face strong intergenerational demands on their economic resources. Western researchers should not let the cultural biases of their societies blind them to considering the multigenerational family as the unit of analysis when studying how immigrants adapt to their new circumstances through mutual exchanges and altruistic transfers within and across generations. We suggest that scholars studying both immigrant and native families focus on *family* well-being as well as individual well-being in their conceptualizations and investigations.

Immigrants serve an important economic purpose of providing a labor pool for Western nations with ageing populations. But most immigrants do not return to their native countries and grow old in their host nations. The fastest growing segment of the 65+ population in the United States are Hispanic, whose proportionate representation of the nation's population above age 65 will almost triple over the first half of the 21st century.[4] Over the next several decades the working-age populations of the United States and France will shrink relative to their older populations, but they will shrink less than in other Western nations due to the *younging* effects of immigration. But this should not blind us to the fact that an increasing proportion of the older populations of both nations will be composed of ageing immigrants and their descendants.

Does growth in the immigrant population portend a period of strengthened intergenerational relationships? From a cultural perspective we are tempted to conclude in the affirmative. However, immigrants face structural disadvantages, such as economic insufficiency, that may suppress their ability to help family members in spite of strong intentions to do so (e.g., Angel and Angel, 2006). The unique complexities in immigrant families require that models and theories of intergenerational relations be sensitive to the types of solidarity and motivations that are most apt to vary between them and their native-born counterparts. In conclusion, we suggest five issues that deserve further investigation for understanding intergenerational relationships in ageing immigrant families in developed Western European nations and the United States:

1 Immigrant families are dynamic with respect to their acculturation and economic integration into the dominant society. As such, their values and orientations may vary substantially across generations within the same families. How this influences the distribution of resources and the availability of support to and from elders in multigenerational immigrant families is not well understood.

2 Migrants are not representative of their origin populations. Research has identified advantages in the resilience and health of immigrants relative to the native-born as a consequence of selective processes that favor general robustness among those who successfully migrate and remain in their destination countries. Intergenerational relationships of migrants may have similar characteristics in their capacity to allocate strategically and target resources that optimize family success.

3 The ability of immigrants to provide and receive economic and social support across generations is shaped by the availability and generosity of public benefits and the opportunity structure of the labor market. Older immigrants who are not pension-eligible and their adult children who face higher than average unemployment rates and tend to work in low-wage occupations will be highly constrained in their ability to make money and time transfers to other generations – even those from strongly familistic cultures. Social benefits available to immigrants shape the interplay between filial duty, norms of reciprocity, and exigent need. Comparisons of immigrants between the United States and Europe, as well as among European nations,

require that both immigrant culture and the public policies of sending and receiving nations be considered.

4   Immigrants, particularly recent immigrants, tend to have complex transnational family networks and maintain relationships with relatives in their adopted country as well as in their country of origin. Thus, intergenerational relationships of migrants are maintained within common households as well as over vast geographic distances. Immigrants from developing nations also tend to have larger families than the native-born, enhancing opportunities to receive and provide assistance, but also increasing competition for scarce resources. How the various demands of family members are negotiated and whose needs are privileged – for instance, older parents in the origin nation or young children in the host nation – is a prime area for further research.

5   Finally, current theories and concepts developed to guide our understanding of intergenerational relationships – solidarity, exchange, and altruism – are well suited for studying the intergenerational relationships of immigrants. By using these existing paradigmatic tools, the organization and goals of immigrant families can be better clarified, particularly if the analytic lens is widened beyond intergenerational dyads to the multigenerational, multinational system of relationships that immigrants maintain.

NOTES

1   Passel, J.S. (2005) *Unauthorized Migrants: Numbers and Characteristics*. Pew Hispanic Center. http://pewhispanic.org/reports/report.php?ReportID=46

2   Dumont, J.C. and Lemaître, G. *Counting Immigrants and Expatriates: A New Perspective*. OECD, Social, Employment and Migration Working papers. http://www.oecd.org/dataoecd/27/5/33868740.pdf

3   Regnard, C. (2004) 'Immigration and the presence of foreign population in France in 2004', *Ministry of Employment and Social Cohesion*. (Retrieved, May 30, 2008, www.social.gouv.fr)

4   US Bureau of the Census. (2002) *Race and Hispanic or Latino Origin by Age and Sex for the United States: 2000* (Census 2000 PHC-T-8). Release date: 2/25/02. http://www.census.gov/population/cen2000/phc-to8/phc-t-08.pdf (Retrieved May 25, 2008)

REFERENCES

Altonji, J.G., Hayashi, F., and L.J. Kotlikoff, (1992) 'Is the extended family altruistically linked? Direct tests using micro data', *The American Economic Review*, 82: 1177–1198.

Angel, J.L. and R.J. Angel, (2006) 'Minority group status and healthful aging: social structure still matters', *American Journal of Public Health*, 96: 1152–9.

Angel, J.L. Angel, R.J., and Markides, K.S. (2000) 'Late life immigration, changes in living arrangements and headship status among older Mexican-origin individuals', *Social Science Quarterly*, 81: 389–403.

Angel, J.L., Angel, R.J., McClellan, J.L., and Markides, K.S., (1996) 'Nativity, declining health, and preferences in living arrangements among elderly Mexican Americans: implications for long-term care', *Gerontologist*, 36: 464–73.

Angel, J.L., Buckley, C.J., and Finch, B. K. (2001) 'Nativity and self-assessed health among pre-retirement age Hispanics and non-Hispanic whites', *International Migration Review*, 35: 784–804.

Aranda, M.P. and Miranda, M.R. (1997) 'Hispanic aging, social support and health: does acculturation make a difference?', in K.S. Markides and M.R. Miranda (eds), *Minorities, Aging and Health*. Thousand Oaks, CA: Sage, pp. 271–94.

Attias-Donfut C. (2003) 'Family transfers and cultural transmissions between three generations in France', in V.L. Bengtson and A. Lowenstein (eds), *Global Aging and Challenges to Families*. New York: Aldine de Gruyter, pp. 214–50.

Attias-Donfut, C. and Wolff, F.C. (2000) 'Complementarity between private and public transfers', in S. Arber and C. Attias-Donfut (eds), *The Myth of Generational Conflict: The Family and State in Aging Societies*. London: Routledge, pp. 47–68.

Attias-Donfut, C. and Wolff, F. C. (2008) 'Patterns of intergenerational transfers of immigrants in France', in C. Saraceno (ed), *Families, Ageing and Social Policy: Intergenerational Solidarity in European Welfare States*. Cheltenham: Edward Elgar, pp. 259–84.

Attias-Donfut, C. and Wolff, F.C. (2009) Le destin des enfants d'immigrés. Un désenchaînement des générations. Paris: Stock.

Attias-Donfut, C., Ogg, J., and Wolff, F. C. (2005) 'European patterns of intergenerational transfers', *European Journal of Ageing*, 2: 161–73.

Attias-Donfut, C., Daveau, P., Gallou, R., Rozenkier, A., and Wolff, F.C. (2006) *L'Enracinement. Enquête sur le Vieillissement des Immigrés en France*. Paris: Armand Colin.

Baca Zinn, M. and Wells, B. (2000) 'Diversity within Latino families: new lessons for family social science', in D.H. Demo, K.R. Allen, and M.A. Fine (eds), *Handbook of Family Diversity*. New York: Oxford University Press, pp. 293–315.

Becker, G.S. (1975) *Human Capital*. New York: Columbia University Press.

Becker, G.S. (1991) *A Treatise on the Family*. Cambridge: Harvard University Press.

Borrel, C. and Durr, J.M. (2005) 'Enquêtes annuelles de recensement: premiers résultats de la collecte 2004. Principales caractéristiques de la population et des logements', *Insee Première*, 1001.

Burholt, V. (2004) 'Transnationalism, economic transfers and families' ties: intercontinental contacts of older Gujaratis, Punjabis and Sylhetis in Birmingham with families abroad', *Ethnic and Racial Studies*, 27: 800–29.

Burnette, D. (1999) 'Social relationships of Latino grandparent caregivers: a role theory perspective', *The Gerontologist*, 39: 49–58.

Burr, J.A. and Mutchler, J.E. (1999) 'Race and ethnic variation in norms of filial responsibility among older persons', *Journal of Marriage and the Family*, 61: 674–87.

Caetano, R. and Clark, C.L. (2003) 'Acculturation, alcohol consumption, smoking, and drug use among Hispanics', in K.M. Chun, P. Balls Organista, G. Marin (eds), *Acculturation: Advances in Theory, Measurement, and Applied Research*. Washington, DC: American Psychological Association, pp. 223–39.

Cong, Z. and Silverstein, M. (2008) 'Intergenerational time-for-money exchanges in rural China: Does reciprocity reduce depressive symptoms of older grandparents?', *Research in Human Development*, 5: 6–25.

Dannefer, D. (2003) 'Toward a global geography of the life course', in J. Mortimer and M. Shanahan (eds), *Handbook of the Life Course*. New York: Kluwer Academic/Plenum Press, pp. 647–59.

Detzner, D.F. (1996) 'No place without a home: Southeast Asian grandparents in refugee families', *Generations*, 20: 45–8.

Dimova, R. and Wolff, F.C. (2008) 'Grandchild care transfers by ageing immigrants in France: intra-household allocation and labour market implications', *European Journal of Population*, 24: 315–40.

Fargues, P. (2004) 'Arab migration to Europe: trends and policies', *International Migration Review*, 38: 1348–71.

Frankenberg, E., Lillard, L., and Willis, R. J. (2002) 'Patterns of intergenerational transfers in Southeast Asia', *Journal of Marriage and the Family*, 64: 627–41.

Fritzell, J. and Lennartsson, C. (2005) 'Financial transfers between generations in Sweden', *Ageing and Society*, 25: 1–18.

Gelbard, A.H. and Carter, M. (1997) 'Mexican immigration and the U.S. population', in F.D. Bean, R.O. de la Garza, B.R. Roberts, and S. Weintraub (eds), *At the Crossroads: Mexico and U.S. Immigration Policy*. Lanham, MD: Rowman and Littlefield, pp. 116–43.

Giddens, A. (2000) *The Third Way and Its Critics*. Cambridge: Polity Press.

Glick, J.E. and Van Hook, J. (2002) 'Parents' coresidence with adult children: Can immigration explain race and ethnic variation?', *Journal of Marriage and the Family*, 64: 240–53.

Goodman, C. and Silverstein, M. (2002) 'Grandmothers raising grandchildren: family structure and well-being in culturally diverse families', *The Gerontologist*, 42: 676–89.

Goodman, C. and Silverstein, M. (2005) 'Latina grandmothers raising grandchildren: Acculturation and psychological well-being', *International Journal of Aging and Human Development*, 60: 305–16.

Gouldner, A.W. (1960) 'The norm of reciprocity: a preliminary statement', *American Sociological Review*, 25: 161–78.

Hank, K. (2007) 'Proximity and contacts between older parents and their children: a European comparison', *Journal of Marriage and Family*, 69: 157–73.

Henretta, J., Hill, M., Li, W., Soldo, B., and Wolf D. (1997) 'Selection of children to provide care: the effect of earlier parental transfers', *Journal of Gerontology: Social Sciences*, 52: 110–19.

Himes, C.L., Hogan, D.P., and Eggebeen, D.J. (1996) 'Living arrangements of minority elders', *Journal of Gerontology: Social Sciences*, 51B: S42–8.

Hogan, D.P., Eggebeen, D.J., and Clogg, C.C. (1993) 'The structure of intergenerational exchanges in American families', *American Journal of Sociology*, 98: 1428–58.

Homans, G.C. (1950) *The Human Group*. New York: Harcourt, Brace and World.

Ikkink, K.K., Van Tilburg, T., and Knipscheer, K. (1999) 'Perceived instrumental support exchanges in relationships between elderly parents and their adult children: normative and structural explanations', *Journal of Marriage and the Family*, 61(4): 831–44.

John, R., Resendiz, R., and De Vargas, L.W. (1997) 'Beyond familism? Familism as explicit motive for eldercare among Mexican American caregivers', *Journal of Cross-Cultural Gerontology*, 12: 145–62.

Karraker, M. (2008) *Global Families*. Boston: Pearson.

Kohli, M. (1999) 'Private and public transfers between generations: linking the family and the state', *European Societies*, 1: 81–104.

Kritz, M., Gurak, D. T., and Chen, L. (2000) 'Elderly immigrants: their composition and living arrangements', *Journal of Sociology and Social Welfare*, 27: 85–114.

Künemund, H., Motel-Klingebiel, A., and Kohli, M. (2005) 'Do intergenerational transfers from elderly parents increase social inequality among their middle-aged children? Evidence from the German Aging Survey', *Journal of Gerontology: Social Sciences*, 60b(1): S30–6.

Larsen, L. J. (2004) *The Foreign-Born Population in the United States: 2003*. Current Population Reports, P20-551. Washington, DC: US Census Bureau.

Lee, Y.J., Parish, W.L. and Willis, R.J. (1994) 'Sons, daughters, and intergenerational support in Taiwan', *American Journal of Sociology*, 99: 1010–41.

Longino, C.F., Jr. and Bradley, D.E. (2006) 'Internal and international migration', in R.H. Binstock and L.K. George (eds), *Handbook of Aging and the Social Sciences*, (6th edn.). San Diego, CA: Elsevier, pp. 76–93.

Lowenstein, A. (2002) 'Solidarity and conflicts of three-generational immigrant families from the former Soviet Union', *Journal of Aging Studies*, 16: 221–41.

Lowenstein, A., Katz, R., and Daatland, S.O. (2005) 'Filial norms and intergenerational support in Europe and Israel: a comparative perspective', in M. Silverstein (ed.), *Annual Review of Gerontology and Geriatrics: Intergenerational Relations Across Time and Place*, Vol. 24. New York: Springer, pp. 200–23.

Mangen, D.J., Bengtson, V.L. and Landry, P.H., Jr. (eds) (1988) *The Measurement of Intergenerational Relations*. Beverly Hills, CA: Sage Publications.

Massey, D. (1987) 'Understanding Mexican migration to the United States', *American Journal of Sociology*, 92: 1372–403.

Massey, D. and Goldring, L. (1994) 'Continuities in transnational migration: an analysis of nineteen Mexican communities', *American Journal of Sociology*, 99: 1492–533.

McGarry, K. (1999) 'Inter vivos transfers and intended bequests', *Journal of Public Economics*, 73: 321–51.

McGarry, K. and Schoeni, R.F. (1997) 'Transfer behavior within the family: results from the Asset and Health Dynamics study', *Journal of Gerontology, Series B: Psychological Sciences and Social Sciences*, 52: 82–92.

Myers, D. and Liu, C.Y (2005). 'The emerging dominance of immigrants in the US housing market 1970–2000', *Urban Policy and Research*, 23: 347–65.

Noiriel, G. (1988) *Le Creuset Français. Histoire de l'Immigration aux XIX è et XXè siècles*. Paris: Le Seuil.

Pang, E.C., Jordan-Marsh, M., Silverstein, M., and Cody M. (2003) 'Health-seeking behaviors of elderly Chinese Americans: shifts in expectations', *The Gerontologist*, 43: 864–74.

Passel, J.S., Van Hook, J., and Bean, F.D. (2004) *Estimates of the Legal and Unauthorized Foreign-born Population for the United States and Selected States, Based on Census 2000*. Washington, DC: US Bureau of the Census.

Phillipson, C. (2003) 'Globalization and the reconstruction of old age: new challenges for critical gerontology', in S. Biggs, A. Lowenstein, and J. Hendricks (eds), *The Need for Theory: Critical Approaches to Social Gerontology*. Amityville, NY: Baywood Publishing, pp. 163–79.

Phillipson, C. (2005) 'The political economy of old age', in M. Johnson, (ed.), *The Cambridge Handbook of Age and Ageing*. Cambridge: Cambridge University Press, pp. 502–10.

Portes, A. and Rumbaut, R. (2001) *Legacies: The Story of the Immigrant Second Generation*. Berkeley, CA: University of California Press and Russell Sage Foundation.

Portes, A., Guarnizo, L.E., and Haller, W. J. (2002) 'Transnational entrepreneurs: an alternative form of immigrant economic adaptation', *American Sociological Review*, 67: 278–98.

Portes, A., Guarnizo, L.E., and Landolt, P. (1999) 'The study of transnationalism: pitfalls and promise of an emergent research field', *Ethnic and Racial Studies*, 22: 217–37.

Pyke, K. (2004) 'Immigrant families in the U.S.', in J. Scott, J. Treas, and M. Richards (eds), *The Blackwell Companion to the Sociology of Families*. Oxford: Blackwell, pp. 253–69.

Rapoport, H. and Docquier, F. (2006) 'The economics of migrants' remittances', in S.C. Kolm and J. Mercier-Ythier (eds), *Handbook of the Economics of Giving, Reciprocity and Altruism*. Amsterdam: North-Holland, pp. 1135–98.

Roberts, B.R., Frank, R., and Lozano-Ascencio, F. (1999) 'Transnational migrant communities and Mexican migration to the U.S.', *Ethnic and Racial Studies*, 22: 238–66.

Sabogal, F., Marín, G., Otero-Sabogal, R., Marín, B.V., and Pérez-Stable E.J. (1987) 'Hispanic familism and acculturation: What changes and what doesn't?', *Hispanic Journal of Behavioral Sciences*, 9: 397–412.

Schiller, N.G., Basch, L., and Blanc, C.S. (1995) 'From immigrant to transmigrant: theorizing transnational migration', *Anthropological Quarterly*, 68: 48–63.

Silverstein, M. (2008) 'Intergenerational resource allocation in Hispanic families: immigration, acculturation, and family structure', Paper presented at the Gerontological Society of America, National Harbor, Maryland.

Silverstein, M. and Chen, X. (1999) 'The impact of acculturation in Mexican-American families on the quality of adult grandchild–grandparent relationships', *Journal of Marriage and the Family*, 61: 188–98.

Silverstein, M., Bengtson, V.L., and Lawton, L. (1997) 'Intergenerational solidarity and the structure of adult child–parent relationships in American families', *American Journal of Sociology*, 103: 429–60.

Silverstein, M., Conroy, S., Wang, H., Giarrusso, R., and Bengtson, V. (2002) 'Reciprocity in parent – child relations over the adult life course', *Journal of Gerontology: Social Sciences*, 57B: S3–13.

Skinner, J.H. (2002) 'Acculturation: measures of ethnic accommodation to the dominant American culture', in J.H. Skinner, J.A. Teresi, H. Douglas, S.M. Stahl, and A.L. Stewart (eds), *Multicultural Measurement in Older Populations*. New York: Springer, pp. 37–51.

Sloan, F.A., Zhang, H.H., and Wang J. (2002) 'Upstream intergenerational transfers', *Southern Economic Journal*, 69: 363–80.

Stark, O. (1995) *Altruism and Beyond: An Economic Analysis of Transfers and Exchanges within Families and Groups*. Cambridge, MA: Cambridge University Press.

Strom, R.D., Buki, L.P., and Strom, S.K. (1997) 'Intergenerational perceptions of English speaking and Spanish speaking Mexican-American grandparents', *International Journal of Aging and Human Development*, 45:1–21.

Sun, R. (2002) 'Old age support in contemporary urban China from both parents' and children's perspectives', *Research on Aging*, 24: 337–59.

Sung, K. and Kim, M.H. (2002) 'The effects of the U.S. welfare system upon elderly Korean immigrants' independent living arrangements', *Journal of Poverty*, 6: 83–94.

Telles, E.E. and Ortiz, V. (2008) *Generations of Exclusion: Mexican Americans, Assimilation, and Race*. New York: Russell Sage Foundation.

Tomassini, C., Kalogirou, S., Grundy, E., et al. (2004) 'Contacts between elderly parents and their children in four European countries: current patterns and future prospects', *European Journal of Ageing*, 1: 54–63.

Treas, J. and Chen, J. (2000) 'Living arrangements, income pooling, and the life course in urban Chinese families', *Research on Aging*, 22: 238–61.

Treas, J. and Mazumdar, S., (2002) 'Older people in America's immigrant families: dilemmas of dependence, integration, and isolation', *Journal of Aging Studies*, 16: 243–58.

Treas, J. and Torrecilha, R. (1995) 'The older population', in R. Farley, (ed.), *State of the Union: America in the 1990s*. New York: Russell Sage, pp. 47–92.

Weil, P. (2004) *La France et ses Étrangers*. Paris: Gallimard Folio.

Whitbeck, L.B., Simons, R.L., and Conger, R.D. (1991) 'The effects of early family relationships on contemporary relationships and assistance patterns between adult children and their parents', *Journal of Gerontology: Social Sciences*, 46: S301–37.

Wilmoth, J. (2001) 'Living arrangements among immigrants in the United States', *The Gerontologist*, 41: 228–38.

Wilmoth, J. and Chen, P.C. (2003) 'Immigrant status, living arrangements, and depressive symptoms among middle-aged and older adults', *Journal of Gerontology. Social Sciences.* 53: S303–15.

Wolff, F.C., Spilerman, S., and Attias-Donfut, C. (2007) 'Transfers from migrants to their children: Evidence that altruism and cultural factors matter', *Review of Income and Wealth*, 53: 619–44.

14

Family and Age in a Global Perspective

Ariela Lowenstein and Ruth Katz

INTRODUCTION

Population ageing is a global phenomenon, with a decreasing share of younger people and a corresponding increase in the proportion of older people. This process alters the age structures of nations with similar numbers in each age category in most developed countries, starting from children and adolescents, moving through to those over age 60 (Bengtson et al., 2003). Such changes have major implications for the organization of society. Fewer younger people mean fewer children and grandchildren, resulting in fewer family members and caregivers available for older people in need of care. Population ageing is not necessarily apocalyptic for individuals, families, and their social systems. It does, though, entail a changing balance between older and younger people in society and the challenge of finding new ways of communicating between generations, as well as understanding the balance between families and the state in the provision of care: ageing itself can become a risk factor, or an opportunity for realizing new possibilities.

Demographic shifts represent an ever-present structural change in modern society. Increased life expectancy implies that an individual will be a member of a three- and/or four-generation family for longer periods of time, while declining fertility rates and delayed parenthood suggest that others will never become members of such families. Sociologists have long recognized that forms of social organization influence well-being. The family constitutes perhaps the most basic social institution, representing the first group into which one enters at birth: ties that remain primary over the life course (Hoff and Tesch-Römer, 2007). The structural organization of the family is particularly critical for those in middle age, a phase in life when individuals are likely to play multiple roles.

Parallel to the ageing of populations have been changes in family structures. There has been a substantial decline in fertility, together with changes in the timing of transitions associated with marriage, parenthood, and grandparenthood. This has resulted in contrasting family structures based on the timing of fertility: *age-condensed* (small age distances between generations arising from early fertility) and *age-gapped* (large age distances between age groups because of late fertility) (Bengtson et al., 1995). Another feature in developed countries has been the move from a *'pyramid'* of family relations to what has been described as a *'beanpole'*: i.e., a structure which is 'long and thin' with more family generations alive but with few members within each generation (Bengston et al., 2003). Additionally, changes in patterns of family formation and dissolution and the resulting diversification of families lead to more complex household structures. Such diversity creates uncertainty in intergenerational relations and expectations and has specific effects on transitions associated with retirement and grandparenthood.

Added to the above are trends such as changing employment patterns, with the increased labour force participation of women having a major influence on care within the family. Other structural changes affecting the lives of older persons include the growing number of older people in single households, an increase in the proportion of childless women, and the increased mobility of adult children; all of which contribute to a shrinking pool of family support (Wolf and Ballal, 2006). Along with transformations in family structure and family life, there is the impact of broader societal changes associated with internal and external migration. Additionally, shifts in social policies, arising from a changing global political and economic climate, seem to suggest less government responsibility to be expected in the future for elder care, with associated pressures on families.

Given these trends, intergenerational bonds among adult family members may be more important today than in earlier decades because individuals live longer and thus can share more years and experiences with other generations (Lowenstein et al., 2007). However, some important cross-cultural questions must be addressed regarding family relationships in modern and post-modern societies: (1) What is the relevance of different theoretical perspectives for current social realities? (2) How strong are the bonds of obligations and expectations between generations? (3) Is there potential for intergenerational family conflict and/or ambivalence? (4) What is the interplay between the informal support network of the family and the formal support service system, regarding the enhancement of family relations? (5) What is the role of family policy in addressing the above issues?

The need to understand family relationships and their diverse processes across time and place was noted by Bengtson et al. (2002), who indicated that we must look outside national borders to construct global conceptualizations of families and age. This is especially important because most family studies may have an unacknowledged ethnocentric bias, given that they are conducted in a single country. Conducting a cross-national study means that one can demonstrate cross-national similarities as well as differences and national idiosyncrasies that must be understood and interpreted in the appropriate historical and political contexts (Katz et al., 2005).

Following this last point, this chapter will: first, address the relevant theoretical paradigms and their associated discourses; secondly, review results from cross-national and cross-cultural European studies, linking these to various theoretical perspectives and controversies; thirdly, assess the implications of research for public policy and family care; and, finally, consider future perspectives for research on intergenerational issues.

THEORETICAL PERSPECTIVES AND EMPIRICAL EVIDENCE

Macro level

Modernization theory

Among the most general concepts dealing with time is that of modernity and its attendant concept of post-modernity (Cheal, 2005). Modernization theory was put forward in the 1970s as an explanation for what was viewed as the long-term decline in the social status of older people. The theory suggested that the more advanced the economy of a society, the lower the status accorded its older citizens (Cowgill, 1986). In an economy characterized by rapid increases in knowledge, especially technical knowledge, and high levels of specialization, adult children were viewed as compelled to move from their families of origin to maximize educational and occupational opportunities. This was reinforced by political and economic ideologies that emphasized individual achievement, with personal development based on merit and superiority. The nuclear family was viewed as better suited to this setting than the larger intergenerational one, and its dominance over the extended household coincided with the emphasis placed upon economic growth (Sussman, 1991).

In the 1950s and 1960s, issues relating to family solidarity were related to concerns about the rise of the so-called 'nuclear family'. More recently, however, it has been connected to the debate on the expanding individualism of late modernity. The 'isolated nuclear family thesis' assumed that horizontal and vertical lines outside the nuclear family had diminished in importance (Parsons, 1955). At the same time, the assumed threat from individualism led to another view: this maintained that individualism's emphasis on concern for oneself over concern for others was likely to weaken social bonds. Wolfe (1989) relates this argument specifically to the expansion of the welfare state as a potential 'moral risk' that might impact upon societal and family solidarity.

A number of challenges to the normative basis of modernization theory have been identified. The theory suggests that as societies develop there will be a concomitant weakening of filial responsibility for older people and a reduction in their status. Here, discussion has focused on the issue of the impact of modernization on intergenerational family relations. Will, for example, adult children continue to be sources of support for their older parents in the wake of economic development and associated changes in social values? Concerns have been raised that the decline in intergenerational co-residence, and the rise of the welfare state, have compromised the capacity and willingness of the contemporary family to care for its older members. This is taken by some as evidence that the importance of the intergenerational family is declining, and that older parents tend to be isolated from their children and other family relationships (Parsons, 1944; Popenoe, 1993).

Empirical evidence, however, suggests that although intergenerational relationships are affected by modernization, the changes are not uniformly in the direction of weaker ties. For example, the OASIS study, cross-national research covering Norway, England, Germany, Spain, and Israel,[1] confirms that family solidarity is still strong, but may be expressed in other ways when circumstances change (Katz et al., 2005). Filial responsibility, for example, represents the extent to which adult children feel obligated to meet the basic needs of their ageing parents. Findings on this issue from the OASIS study are presented in Table 14.1.

The data indicate that the majority of people in all five countries acknowledge some degree of filial obligation, but more so in Spain and Israel than in Germany, England, and Norway. Differences among countries are though moderate. If the assumed family-oriented Spain is taken as our criterion, it may be concluded that filial obligation norms remain strong in northern European countries. This is also found in rapidly developing Asian nations such as the Philippines (Domingo and Asis, 1995) and Thailand (Knodel, 1995; see also Chapter 15). A United Nations study of seven developing countries (India, Singapore, Thailand, South Korea, Egypt, Brazil, and Zimbabwe) concluded that older people's expectations were likely to favour co-residing with their children, despite rapid urbanization and economic growth. Indeed, beliefs may supersede the influence of economic development and urbanization on family structure and function, as is evidenced in Japan, where the idea of familial piety is still recognised

(Koyano 2003; see also Chapters 15 and 32 of this volume). Pervasive cultural beliefs about families may overwhelm other population distinctions: for instance, in Spain, where older people in both urban and rural areas expect similarly high levels of contact with and help from their children (Katz and Lowenstein, 2003).

Based on empirical findings such as the above, Silverstein et al. (2003) criticize modernization theory, suggesting task-specific theory and the intergenerational solidarity-conflict paradigm as more relevant to changing family structures and norms in the modern and post-modern industrialized world.

Task-specific theory

All welfare states probably share a common concern about how to build supportive relationships between families and the state. Relevant questions here include: (1) What is the balance between families and formal care? (2) Are families and services substituting or complementing each other? Task-specific theory focuses on the complementary roles played by families and the formal care system, postulating that families and formal organizations seek unique but complementary goals (Silverstein et al., 2003). Moreover, the theory suggests that while the structures of the family and the service system may be in conflict, they are mutually dependent for achieving common goals (Litwak, 1985). How does the task-specific theory address the problems of modernization and family change? Data confirm the centrality of family support and the importance of economic transfers within the family. On the other hand, families and formal organizations fulfil complementary tasks unique to each (Attias-Donfut and Arber, 2000; Spilerman, 2000). Thus, task-specific theory suggests that 'modernization does not herald the demise of the family, but signals a redistribution

Table 14.1   Per cent in agreement (agree or strongly agree) with filial obligations,* by item and country (n)[a]

Item	Norway	England	Germany	Spain	Israel
Item 1 (should live close)	29	31	40	57	55
Item 2 (should sacrifice)	41	47	36	44	37
Item 3 (able to depend on)	58	41	55	60	51
Item 4 (entitled to returns)	38	48	26	55	64
Agree with at least one item	76	74	68	83	83
(n)	(1,195)	(1,172)	(1,255)	(1,173)	(1,183)

* All differences are significant at the 0.001 level.
[a] Weighted samples, age 25+ living at home in large urban settings (100,000+), $n \approx 1200$ for each country. The scale is adopted from Lee, Peek, and Coward (1998).
Source: Lowenstein and Daatland (2006). Per cent in agreement (agree or strongly agree) with each item and the total scale (agree with at least one item).

of efforts between families and organizations' (Silverstein et al., 2003: 188).

Two approaches are derived from this perspective – the *substitution approach* and the *complementary approach* (Lingsom, 1997). The former suggests an inverse relationship between service provision and family care. The Scandinavian social democratic model typifies this approach, which favours more direct governmental involvement in the supply of services that are predominantly public. The substitution question is often raised when the introduction of new services is discussed. Among the arguments against services is that they allow families to reduce their efforts, and discourage civic responsibility. According to this perspective, solidarity is seen as forced by necessity, whereas moral obligations will be corrupted if alternative sources of support are available. To some, this argument sums up the 'moral risk' of the welfare state in the post-modern era (Wolfe, 1989). Substitution theory tends to assume that some form of decline in family care initiates the process of providing formal services and makes it necessary to develop additional services. Increasing the provision of these services, in turn, further threatens family solidarity.

A contrasting view is the '*complementary*' *approach*, which postulates that informal and formal care networks complement each other, both having certain kinds of caregiving responsibilities and abilities best suited to each (Litwak, 1985; Edelman and Hughes, 1990). According to this model, the highly specialized nature of each network has the potential to cause friction and precipitate conflict. Therefore, formal and informal networks work best when the amount of contact or level of involvement between them is minimized. A criticism of this approach, however, is that it is difficult to differentiate between formal and informal responsibilities in contemporary caregiving situations (Soldo et al., 1990).

The 'complementary thesis' takes two slightly different forms: *family support theory* and *family specialization theory*. The former is based on exchange theory, and suggests that families will be more willing to provide help – and older people more willing to accept it – when the burden of care is not too heavy. Services may then strengthen family solidarity by sharing the pressures associated with caregiving. Chappell and Blandford (1991) support this thesis on the basis of a Canadian study; Attias-Donfut and Wolff (2000) do likewise in a French study, while Lingsom (1997) finds mixed support for this position in Norway. Kohli (1999) and Künemund and Rein (1999) suggest pension provision allows the older generation to reciprocate support from the younger generation. Older people's position in the family is thus strengthened and more balanced, which in turn strengthens intergenerational solidarity. Similar data were reported when studying exchange patterns in the OASIS study. More than 40 per cent in all countries, and in Spain and Israel more than half of older parents, provided as much help and support (including emotional, instrumental, and financial assistance) as they received from their adult children. This fact points to the salience and the norm of reciprocity between the generations (Lowenstein et al., 2007).

An alternative form of complementary support is represented by *family specialization theory*, where access to services is seen to allow families to concentrate on emotional support rather than instrumental help. Thus, families are not deprived of their function by the welfare state, but have changed their focus (Litwak et al., 2003). Most research finds that services complement family care (Daatland, 1990). Some researchers argue for an even stronger case of complementary assistance, suggesting that a generous welfare state is a stimulant to family solidarity and exchange (Künemund and Rein, 1999; Lowenstein and Daatland, 2006).

Data from the OASIS project show that more generous welfare state services have not 'crowded out' the family but have contributed to a change in how families relate, and have helped generations establish more independent relationships. Formal services seem to encourage family support, providing empirical backing for the notion of a form of 'crowding-in' (Motel-Klingebiel et al., 2005). The findings also suggest that family solidarity is not easily lost, considering the fundamental and often existential character of these relationships (Daatland and Lowenstein, 2005).

Judged on these data, it may be concluded that respondents in the OASIS study do not have a clear-cut preference for family care, nor do they reluctantly make use of services as a secondary option, as implied in the substitution argument. The attitudinal aspects follow more or less the same pattern as general societal attitudes, but seem to favour welfare state arrangements. It seems reasonable, then, to say policies aimed at containing welfare provision, where government is restricting its expenditures for family and elder care, partly as a result of the ideology of privatizing public services, find little support in any of the five countries (Daatland and Lowenstein, 2005).

Data from the EUROFAMCARE project, drawing on national surveys in Germany, Greece, Italy, Poland, Sweden, and the United Kingdom,[2] indicate that the majority of family caregivers (over 80 per cent) felt caring was worthwhile and that they coped well even under difficult circumstances. The positive value attached to family caregiving is probably the most critical element in ensuring good-quality care for older people with high levels of dependency. However, family caregivers need support from integrated formal care services both to aid in the provision of good care to older people as well as for the protection of the family caregivers' own health and well-being.

Another cross-national study, the SOCCARE project (a qualitative study of care arrangements in Finland, France, Italy, Portugal, and the United Kingdom),[3] identified two main types of care networks supporting older people. The first type was those composed of '*weak ties*,' where the network is minimal or even absent and caregiving falls mainly to one person. The second type, in contrast, has relatively *rich and polycentric networks* that share care responsibilities. Both networks have connections with professional and non-professional services. The range of professionally provided services is vast, ranging from less intensive health-related services and home services to 'total assistance,' such as nursing homes or assisted living centres. Families in Finland, France, and England most often use combinations of informal care and publicly provided formal care. Only Portuguese and Italian families use mostly third sector and private care facilities. On the other hand, the informal non-professional paid sector is broad and varied in Italy, France, and Portugal. There are marked differences, however, between Italy, Portugal, and France in the relationship between families and paid services. In the former two countries, private assistance, especially for the elderly, is used to substitute for public services. In France, it is used only to complement public services. Concerning the general organization of care arrangements, the family, and particularly the main caregiver, remains the most important resource. It is s/he who, even in the richer and more cooperative networks, assures the coordination of the various activities. However, if too little help – or none at all – is available to her/him from the outside, this fundamental resource tends to become quickly exhausted. From this point of view, formal and informal services need to be combined in a complementary way, in terms of an integrated system or network of care.

Micro level

Exchange theory, intergenerational solidarity-conflict, and intergenerational ambivalence

Although concerns about the weakening of intergenerational ties were commonly expressed in the 1960s, empirical evidence since that time has demonstrated the continued importance of these linkages. Furthermore, most parents and adult children report that their relationships are meaningful and supportive (Bengtson and Roberts, 1991; Chambers et al., 2009; Katz et al., 2005).

However, troubled relationships do exist and are a significant source of psychological distress for parents and children alike. Reflecting this reality, family scholars have called for the development of theoretical frameworks that can interpret seemingly contradictory findings by capturing the complexity of intergenerational relations (Fingerman, 2001; Luescher and Pillemer 1988). To that end, several theories have been developed which are reviewed below.

Exchange theory

The basic tenet of social exchange theory, which is based on the economic principles of costs and rewards, is that individuals wish to maximize rewards (both material and non-material) and minimize costs in relationships with significant others (Blau, 1964; Homans, 1961). Participants in an exchange relationship will continue only so long at it is perceived as being more rewarding than it is costly. If both parties in the exchange relationship are equally dependent upon each other, the relationship is balanced. When the exchange relation is unbalanced, the more dependent partner will attempt to rebalance the relationship, and reduce the costs incurred from the exchange.

The exchange framework has been applied as a starting point for the perception of parent – adult child relationships as characterized by multidimensional resources, costs and benefits, and emotional and financial exchanges (Dowd, 1980; Silverstein et al., 2002). The exchange perspective posits that older parents who receive more support than they provide experience higher levels of well-being. Empirical evidence, however, shows that in such a situation, older people may feel inadequate and dependent, leading to a decline in their sense of well-being. Data from the OASIS study revealed that the ability to be an active provider in exchange relations enhances older people's satisfaction with life. When exchange patterns are balanced, satisfaction with life is quite high. In contrast, being largely the recipient of help from adult children is related to a lower level of satisfaction with life (Lowenstein et al., 2007).

Findings from The Survey of Health, Ageing and Retirement in Europe (SHARE)[4] found that a majority of respondents were involved in the exchange of resources, both as givers and receivers. The data show that being very old and in poor health predicted the receipt of support (time transfers), whereas having a high income and position during the course of one's life predicted the giving of monetary resources (Litwin, 2005). The exchange theory perspective contributes both to our understanding of intergenerational support, as well as those factors contributing to the psychological well-being of older people.

Intergenerational family solidarity-conflict paradigm vs. intergenerational ambivalence

Demographic transitions and changes in family structures have prompted a rethinking of family relations. One of the most common organizing conceptual frameworks for understanding family relations in later life is the Intergenerational Solidarity Model (Bengtson and Mangen, 1988; Bengtson and Roberts, 1991). Family solidarity has been considered an important component of family relations, particularly in successful coping and social integration in old age (McChesney and Bengtson, 1988). Intergenerational relationships are found to be one of the most important elements that influence quality of life in the family context (Lowenstein, 2007; Silverstein and Bengtson, 1991). Research in this tradition has tended to emphasize shared values across generations, normative obligations to provide care, and enduring ties between parents and children.

The model conceptualizes intergenerational family solidarity as a multidimensional phenomenon with six components, expressing the behavioural, emotional, cognitive, and structural aspects of family relations (Bengtson and Schrader, 1982). These components reflect exchange relations and include structural solidarity, contact, affect, consensus, functional transfers/help, and normative solidarity. The solidarity model has proven adaptable to innovations in methods and resilient to challenges to its dominance and universality. The paradigm was modified in the 1980s to become the 'family solidarity-conflict' model, which incorporates conflict and considers the possible negative effects of too much solidarity (Silverstein et al., 1996).

In developing the intergenerational conflict model, Bengtson and others (Clarke et al., 1999; Parrott and Bengtson, 1999) argued that conflict is a normal aspect of family relations, affecting how family members perceive one another and, consequently, their willingness to assist one another. Solidarity and conflict do not represent a single continuum ranging from high solidarity to high conflict; rather, family relations can exhibit both high solidarity and high conflict, or low solidarity and low conflict, depending on family dynamics and situations (Lowenstein, 2007).

In 1998, Lüscher and Pillemer proposed that the experience of intergenerational relations in adulthood is characteristically ambivalent (Lüscher and Pillemer, 1998; Pillemer and Lüscher, 2004). Rather than operating on a basis of affection, assistance, and solidarity, or being under threat of conflict or dissolution, the dynamics of intergenerational relations among adults revolve around sociological and psychological contradictions or dilemmas and the management of these in day-to-day family life. Indeed, scholars from a variety of orientations have argued that to understand the quality of parent–child relations, studies must begin to incorporate both positive and negative elements in a single study (Bengtson et al., 2002; Clarke et al., 1999; Connidis and McMullin, 2002a, 2002b).

Bengtson et al. (2002) questioned the utility of the ambivalence construct and suggested that it *complemented* rather than *competed* with the solidarity-conflict framework, which is conceptually adequate for exploring mixed feelings: '...from the intersection of solidarity and conflict comes ambivalence, both psychological and structural' (2002: 575). They argue that both solidarity-conflict and ambivalence models can be regarded as lenses 'through which one can look at family relationships – complementary instead of competing' (2002: 575). Empirical support for ambivalence, though, has been provided by Fingerman and Hay (2004); Pillemer and Suitor (2002, 2005); and Wilson et al., (2003).

The OASIS study tested the two conceptual frameworks across different nations. Table 14.2 presents the means and standard deviations of these different dimensions, compared across the five societies. ANOVA and Duncan Multiple Range tests were conducted to test the differences (Lowenstein, 2007).

A general conclusion is that family intergenerational solidarity appears to be very strong in all five countries in the OASIS study. This indicates that older people are firmly embedded within their families across these societies, although there are variations in the strength of the various dimensions in the different countries. The data indicate that the strength of the structural – behavioural dimension (proximity and contact) was very similar in four of the countries, while significantly higher in Spain. The affective – cognitive dimension (affection and consensus) was high in all countries, though there were differences – Israel had the highest score, while Germany and Spain the lowest. The functional dimension of solidarity regarding receipt of help from adult children was relatively low, but again with differences between countries. Germany was the highest, with Norway and Israel being the lowest. Regarding help provided, however, no differences between the countries were found. Levels of conflict and ambivalence appeared to be low in all countries. The impact of the different dimensions on quality of life was also studied, revealing that the affective – cognitive dimension and the exchange of support predicted a positive quality of life and ambivalence predicted a negative quality of life. Conflict and ambivalence were mainly reflected during periods of transitions in the life course, when older parents move towards dependency, challenging older parents and their children to renegotiate roles (Katz et al., 2005).

Table 14.2   Means[a] and standard deviations (SD) of the family relationship dimensions[b]

| Intergenerational family relations | Country | | | | | | | | | |
| | Norway | | England | | Germany | | Spain | | Israel | |
	Mean	SD	Mean	SD	Mean	SD	Mean	SD	Mean	SD
Solidarity S (proximity + contact)	3.6	1.4	3.8	1.4	3.7	1.4	4.5	1.3	3.8	1.2
Solidarity A (affect + consensus)	4.4	0.9	4.5	1.0	4.2	0.9	4.2	0.8	4.7	0.9
Solidarity H-1 (help received)[c]	1.4	1.3	2.0	1.7	2.1	1.6	1.9	1.7	1.4	1.4
Solidarity H-2 (help provided)[c]	1.0	1.1	0.9	1.2	0.9	1.2	0.8	1.2	0.8	1.0
Conflict	1.4	0.7	1.3	0.6	1.6	0.7	1.4	0.7	1.7	0.8
Ambivalence	1.7	0.0	1.6	0.8	1.7	0.8	1.7	0.8	1.7	0.9
Base	378		368		390		370		356	

[a]Mean scores on a scale of 1–6, with 6 indicating high feelings of solidarity and conflict. For ambivalence the scale is 1–5, a higher score indicating higher feelings.
[b]Based only on observations with no missing data.
[c]Receiving or providing help from/to at least one child, in at least one of the following areas: shopping, transportation, household chores, house repair and gardening, and personal care.

PUBLIC DISCOURSE AND FAMILY POLICY

Laws and policies affect the life situation of families as well as the opportunities of individuals inside and outside their family context. Moreover, families operate in the context of larger social institutions that shape how adult children function in the support systems of their older parents. Indeed, families and state institutions intersect to jointly produce portfolios of care and support for older people (Minkler and Estes, 1998).

Policy changes should be promoted because people and societies are changing. Policies and programmes that might have been appropriate when they were introduced may eventually become unusable, unfair, and remote from new realities. All countries need to revise their services for older people in a direction that will accommodate the requirements of modern life, including equal opportunities for women. We therefore need more information about how services and families may complement and support each other, and when they do, we need to learn how to convince policymakers that these models should be replicated.

In the new millennium, a child might have any number of parents, grandparents, and great or even great-great grandparents. Technological developments should thus be sought to help healthcare and welfare organizations deliver services more efficiently and to foster independence among the frail elderly. As new generations of older people will be better educated and will have higher incomes, and as most families will be composed of four and five generations, care demands in the 21st century and the balance between informal and formal care will be different, tending more towards the complimentary. Rising levels of affluence and the introduction of state welfare

provision will allow the operation of choice in family relationships. Thus, sentiment rather than obligation might increasingly govern the ties between elderly parents and younger generations.

It is well established that in ageing societies, quality of life rests on the relationship between intergenerational family solidarity and the responses of the formal service systems. In addition, data suggest that as a result of the increased availability and social acceptability of public services, there is more willingness by older people and their families to use public services when dependency begins (Daatland, 1997). Thus, the care of the aged is a public/private mix, with the exact proportions of this mix varying according to country. The specific mix is related to two factors: (a) the family culture that guides the level of readiness to use public services; and (b) the availability, accessibility, quality, and cost of those services.

All welfare states have expanded into what had previously been a totally familial responsibility, but some have done so earlier and more than others. And, consequently, what is considered a reasonable balance between public and private services and families will also vary. In conservative, liberalist, and residual welfare states, the state is more reluctant to introduce services that have traditionally been within the purview of the family than in universalistic and social democratic welfare regimes. The latter have removed the legal responsibility of adult family members, and based their social policies on the needs of the individual, not the family. They have consequently developed higher levels of social services in general, and higher levels of home care services in particular (Daatland, 1997). The more familistic welfare states operate under the principle of subsidiarity. They still place the primary responsibility with the family, while government responsibility is activated only when family care is missing or professional competencies are needed.

Yet another line of inquiry is through family values and preferences for care. If a preference for services over family care is related to low family solidarity, this might be seen as support for the substitution theory. If, on the other hand, the preference for services is not – or even positively – related to family solidarity, complementary support may be the case.

In light of the rising costs of welfare and health services, it seems that a balance should be found between these conflicting perspectives. In a study in Israel, where children are legally obliged to support their parents financially, data about the impact of the Long-Term Care Insurance Law on care relations have shown that the involvement and care of families was not reduced, but in some cases the nature of care might have changed to providing more emotional support (Lowenstein and Katan, 1999). Thus, it seems that more emphasis should be placed on services that strengthen and complement family care and increase 'cooperation' between caregiving families and the available service systems. Furthermore, we must find ways to assess what is considered good-quality care, both from the familial perspective and from that of the formal service systems. Finally, we must also study the relationships between family networks and the policy-related outcomes described above.

It has been pointed out that the needs and interests of family caregivers must be incorporated into public policy debates. Programmes supporting older people are often confusing and poorly coordinated. This was the conclusion of an OECD study that covered several European and some non-European countries. In evaluating these programmes, Sundstrom et al. (2008) conclude that 'programs seem rarely to be the outcome of rational considerations, but rather reflect more profound distinctions, and many European countries strive to establish an ideal relation between state and family in elder care' (2008: 262).

A sizable 'overlap' between family care and public services seems to be a workable method for safeguarding care, both formal and informal, and also implies support to carers. International studies demonstrate that both the elderly and their families often prefer a solution in which there is shared responsibility between the family and the public services. This may be especially true when the need for care is high (Sundstrom et al., 2008).

Based on the above discussion, the following policy issues should be addressed:

• *First, it is important to examine the significance of the 'retreat' of the welfare state for the balance* among the three systems – the welfare system, the labour market, and the family system. Thus, it is important to strengthen intergenerational relationships and obligations and to try to achieve a balance among the three systems. Policies should not build on families as the primary foundation for elder care, but should be aimed towards increasing autonomy and independence. There should be a redefinition of the roles of families in care provision. When families are involved they have to be supported with for example the development of services in the workplace and those that free families to provide different forms of care based on the wishes and needs of adult children and their older parents.

• *A second issue is the importance of encouraging productive activities, employment, and involvement in the community for older people as well as intergenerational programmes.* Younger generations should be encouraged to make arrangements for their old age, to invest more in private pensions and saving schemes, and, at the same time, to strengthen intergenerational ties on the basis of the concept of generational mutuality and mutual dependence – what has been termed the interdependence of generations (Attias-Donfut, 2003; Attias-Donfut et al., 2005).

CONCLUSIONS AND IMPLICATIONS – GAPS IN UNDERSTANDING PERSPECTIVES FOR FUTURE RESEARCH

This chapter has addressed issues relating to the globalization of ageing and the impact on the family. A variety of theoretical perspectives have been presented both on the macro and micro levels of analysis. Usually, theories vary in scope and focus, both of which are determined by the dependent variables the theory is intended to explain and the assumptions it lays out. For example, on the macro level, modernization theory attempts to explain the low status of the aged in modern society and the move from the extended to the nuclear family. However, empirical evidence does not necessarily corroborate these assumptions. Post-modern approaches point to the importance of studying the status and role of the aged further because age roles are becoming more fluid. Furthermore, we must address age heterogeneity as well as the impact of various family formats on family relationships and intergenerational solidarity. Regarding the micro level of theoretical analysis, this chapter has explored insights from exchange theory that focus on the internal processes of the individual such as motivation and attitudes in family relations. The chapter also demonstrated the salience of the relationship levels of analysis regarding intergenerational solidarity-conflict complemented by intergenerational ambivalence. We suggested that the combination of both the macro level, using models such as the task-specific theory, and the micro level, using models such as the solidarity theory, creates 'viable frameworks for understanding the consequences of modernization and social change for intergenerational relations of the aged' (Silverstein et al., 2003: 194).

Comparative studies are driven by contrasting goals. One is the search for generalities – (the structuralist approach) and the other is the search for distinctiveness (the culturalist position). Uncovering cross-national similarities is an avenue to more general knowledge, yet any cross-national differences and national idiosyncrasies found must be understood and interpreted in the appropriate historical and political contexts. The European studies discussed adopted both approaches. Europe is in the forefront of the demographic transitions of decreasing fertility, increased life expectancy, and postponement of childbearing (e.g., Kaufmann et al., 2002). Therefore, it is possible to learn from the European experience and use this knowledge to inform policy development in other countries. Secondly, and perhaps more importantly, variations in policy environment across various European countries promote a better understanding of the interplay between factors at the societal, familial, and individual levels (Wolf and Ballal, 2006), potentially informing family policy development. In response to the call by Glaser et al. (2004) for incorporating more comparative cross-national data on family support in research, we feel that the data from the various European projects enabled us to examine the various complexities of the variations throughout Europe. However, one has to bear in mind that more data and theoretical developments based on such data should be encouraged in other cultures such as those in East Asia or Africa, because such data can provide indications about the fit or lack of fit of existing theories in other areas of the world and suggest hypotheses for testing in a broader context (see Chapter 31).

Regarding policy, the division of responsibility between the family and the public sector is a standing controversy in all welfare states. What should be the boundaries for government intervention? Should the areas of responsibility for families and service systems overlap? What is the rational – and reasonable – way of sharing the responsibility between the welfare state and the family? Additionally, we should see older people not only as receivers but also as active agents. Hence, we have a triangle of interacting actors, families (family carers), services, and elderly

people, not just a dyad of families and services, which has been the model for most other studies. Issues like these will be even more important in the years to come, in particular with reference to elder care. Needs are growing exponentially in this sector, while changes in female roles and family norms, on the one hand, and the need to contain public expenditures, on the other, will tend to pull in different directions and consequently sharpen the controversy.

The issue of the preferred balance between family care and (formal) services is crucial and is important to understand from the viewpoint of potential caregivers and care receivers. To assess the future demands for family care, it is important to look at family values and attitudes towards family care. These values will have an interacting and moderating effect on demographic changes. What older people receive in terms of family support or services affects, and is affected by, popular and governmental notions of what families 'should' provide and to what extent they should be responsible for caring for elderly relatives. Clearly, there is a complex interaction between intergenerational behaviours, expectations, political ideology, and level of formal care provision (Blieszner and Bedford, 1995).

The empirical data analysed in this chapter demonstrate that intergenerational solidarity and conflict were manifested at two different levels, as suggested by Bengtson and Murray (1993), who differentiate between the macro-public arena level and the micro-intergenerational family level. On the macro level, attention should be given to the larger social context, where social norms are created and activated, and where state policies and responses of various welfare regimes to the needs of the growing elderly populations are shaped. On the micro-family level, attention should be given to issues of filial obligations, expectations of different generations in the family, and the actual flow of help and support between the generations.

NOTES

1 The OASIS (Old Age and Autonomy: The Role of Service Systems and Intergenerational Family Solidarity) project was designed to enhance cross-cultural knowledge about the interplay between personal, familial, and social service factors as they impact the quality of life of ageing Europeans in diverse family cultures and welfare state regimes. In the study, data were collected from a stratified random sample of 1200 urban dwellers aged 25 and over in each of the five countries, a total of 6000 individuals.

2 EUROFAMCARE (Services for Supporting Family Carers of Elderly People in Europe) surveyed Germany,

Greece, Italy, Poland, Sweden, and the United Kingdom, where data were collected based on personal interviews with about 6000 European family carers, who provided at least 4 hours of care a week to a dependent older person of at least 65 years.

3 The SOCCARE project focused on four key family types affected by demographic, socioeconomic, and structural changes within European societies: single-parent families, dual-career families, immigrant families, and 'double front carer' families (those that have young children and, at the same time, elderly family members in need of care). Almost 400 European families were interviewed in detail about their opportunities for and difficulties in making flexible and responsive care arrangements and their ability to combine these arrangements with participation in paid employment.

4 The countries in the SHARE project range from Scandinavia (Denmark and Sweden) through Central Europe (Austria, France, Germany, Switzerland, Belgium, and the Netherlands) to the Mediterranean (Spain, Italy, and Greece). Further data were collected in 2005 and 2006 in Israel. Two new EU member states – the Czech Republic and Poland – as well as Ireland joined SHARE in 2006. SHARE is funded through the 5th framework programme of the European Commission.

REFERENCES

Attias-Donfut, C. (2003) 'Cultural and economic transfers between generations: one aspect of age integration', *The Gerontologist*, 40(3): 270–1.

Attias-Donfut, C. and Arber, S. (2000) 'Equity and solidarity across the generations', in S. Arber and C. Attias-Donfut (eds), *The Myth of Generational Conflict: The Family and State in Aging Societies*. New York: Routledge, pp. 1–21.

Attias-Donfut, C. and Wolff, F.C. (2000) 'Complementarity between private and public transfers', in S. Arber and C. Attias-Donfut (eds), *The Myth of Generational Conflict: The Family and State in Aging Societies*. New York: Routledge, pp. 47–68.

Attias-Donfut, C., Ogg, J., and Wolff, F.C. (2005) 'European patterns of intergenerational financial and time transfers', *European Journal of Ageing*, 2: 161–73.

Bengtson, V.L. (2001) 'Beyond the nuclear family: the increasing importance of multi-generational bonds', *Journal of Marriage and the Family*, 63: 1–15.

Bengtson, V.L. and Mangen, D.J. (1988) 'Family intergenerational solidarity revised: suggestions for future management', in D.J. Mangen, V.L. Bengtson, and P.H. Landry, Jr. (eds), *Measurement of Intergenerational Relations*. Beverly Hills: SAGE, pp. 222–38.

Bengston, V.L. and Murray, T.M. (1993) '"Justice" across generations (and cohorts): sociological perspectives on the life course and reciprocity over time', in L. Cohen, (ed.) *Justice across Generations: What Does It Mean?*

Washington, DC: American Association of Retired Persons, pp. 111–38.

Bengtson, V.L. and Roberts, R.E.L. (1991) 'Intergenerational solidarity in aging families: an example of formal theory construction', *Journal of Marriage and the Family*, 856–70.

Bengtson, V.L. and Schrader, S. (1982) 'Parent – child relations', in D. Mangen and W.A. Peterson (eds), *Research Instruments in Social Gerontology*, Vol. 2. Minneapolis: University of Minnesota Press, pp. 115–86.

Bengtson, V.L., Rosenthal, C.J., and Burton, L.M. (1995) 'Paradoxes of families and aging', in R.H. Binstock and L.K. George (eds), *Handbook of Aging and the Social Sciences*, 4th edn. San Diego, CA: Academic Press, pp. 253–82.

Bengtson, V.L., Giarrusso, R., Mabry, B., and Silverstein, M. (2002) 'Solidarity, conflict and ambivalence: complementary or competing perspectives on intergenerational relationships?', *Journal of Marriage and the Family*, 64: 568–76.

Bengtson, V.L., Giarrusso, R., Silverstein, M., and Wang, H. (2000) 'Families and intergenerational relationships in aging societies', *Hallym International Journal of Aging*, 2: 3–10.

Bengtson, V.L., Lowenstein, A., Putney, N.M., and Gans, D. (2003) 'Global aging and the challenge to families', in V.L. Bengtson and A. Lowenstein (eds), *Global Aging and the Challenge to Families*. Hawthorne, NY: Aldine de Gruyter, pp. 1–26.

Blau, P. (1964) *Exchange and Power in Social Life*. New York: Wiley.

Blieszner, R. and Bedford, V.H. (1995) *Handbook of Aging and the Family*. Westport, CT: Greenwood Press.

Chambers, P., Allen, G., Phillipson, C., and Ray, M. (2009) *Family Practices and Later Life*. Bristol: Policy Press.

Chappell, N. and Blandford, A. (1991) 'Informal and formal care: exploring the complementarity', *Ageing and Society*, 11: 299–317.

Cheal, D. (2005) 'Theorizing family: from the particular to the general', in V.L. Bengtson, A.C. Acock, K.R. Allen, P. Dilworth-Andersen, and D.M. Klein (eds) *Sourcebook on Family Theory and Research*. Thousand Oaks, CA: SAGE, pp. 29–33.

Clarke, E.J., Preston, M., Raskin, J., and Bengtson, V.L. (1999) 'Types of conflicts and tensions between older parents and adult children', *The Gerontologist*, 39: 261–70.

Connidis, I.A. and McMullin J. (2002a) 'Sociological ambivalence and family ties: a critical perspective', *Journal of Marriage and the Family*, 64: 558–67.

Connidis, I.A. and McMullin J. (2002b) 'Ambivalence, family ties, and doing sociology', *Journal of Marriage and the Family*, 64: 594–601.

Cowgill, D. (1986) *Aging around the World*. Belmont, CA: Wadsworth.

Daatland, S.O. (1990) 'What are families for? On family solidarity and preferences for help', *Ageing and Society*, 10: 1–15.

Daatland, S.O. (1997) 'Welfare policies for older people in transition: emerging trends and comparative perspectives', *Scandinavian Journal of Social Welfare*, 6: 153–61.

Daatland, S.O. and Lowenstein, A. (2005) 'Intergenerational solidarity and the family–welfare state balance', *European Journal of Ageing*, 2: 174–82.

Domingo, L.J. and Asis, M.M.B. (1995) 'Living arrangements and the flow of support between generations in the Philippines', *Journal of Cross-Cultural Gerontology*, 10(1–2): 21–51.

Dowd, J.J. (1980) 'Exchange rates and old people', *Journal of Gerontology*, 35: 596–602.

Edelman, P. and Hughes, S. (1990) 'The impact of community care on provision of informal care to homebound elderly persons', *Journal of Gerontology*, 45(2): S74–84.

Fingerman, K.L. (2001) *Aging Mothers and Their Adult Daughters: A Study in Mixed Emotions*. New York: Springer.

Fingerman, K.L. and Hay, E. (2004) 'Intergenerational ambivalence in the context of the larger social network', in K. Pillemer and K. Luescher (eds), *Intergenerational Ambivalences: New Perspectives on Parent–Child Relations in Later Life*. Oxford: Elsevier Science, pp. 133–52.

Glaser, K., Tomassini, C., and Grundy, E. (2004) 'Revisiting convergence and divergence: support for elderly people in Europe', *European Journal of Ageing*, 1, 64–72.

Hoff, A. and Tesch-Römer, C. (2007) 'Family relations and aging: substantial changes since the middle of last century?', in: H.-W. Wahl, C. Tesch-Römer, and A. Hoff (eds), *New Dynamics in Old Age: Individual, Environmental and Societal Perspectives*. Amityville, NY: Baywood, pp. 65–83.

Homans, G.C. (1961) *Social Behavior: Its Elementary Forms*. New York: Harcourt.

Katz, R. and Lowenstein, A. (2003) 'Elders quality of life and intergenerational relations: a cross-national comparison', *Hallym International Journal of Aging*, 5(2): 131–58.

Katz, R. Lowenstein, A., Phillips, J., and Daatland, S.O. (2005) 'Theorizing intergenerational solidarity, conflict and ambivalence in a comparative cross-national perspective', in V.L. Bengtson, A.C. Acock, K.R. Allen, P. Dilworth-Andersen, and D.M. Klein (eds), *Sourcebook on Family Theory and Research*. Thousand Oaks, CA: Sage, pp. 393–407.

Kaufmann, F.X., Kuijsten, A., Schulze, H.J., and Strohmeier, K.P. (2002) *Family Life and Family Policies in Europe*, Vol. 2. Oxford: Oxford University Press.

Knodel, J. (guest editor) (1995) 'Focus group research on the living arrangements of elderly in Asia', *Journal of Cross-Cultural Gerontology (special issue)*, 10:1–2.

Kohli, M. (1999) 'Private and public transfers between generations: linking the family and the state', *European Societies*, 1: 81–104.

Koyano, W. (2003) 'Intergenerational relationships of Japanese seniors', in V.L. Bengtson and A. Lowenstein (eds), *Global Aging and the Challenge to Families*. Hawthorne, New York: Aldine de Gruyter, pp. 272–83.

Künemund, H. and Rein, M. (1999) 'There is more to receiving than needing: theoretical arguments and empirical explorations of crowding-in and crowding-out', *Ageing and Society*, 19: 93–121.

Lingsom, S. (1997) *The Substitution Issue. Care Policies and their Consequences for Family Care*. NOVA Rapport 6/97. Oslo: NOVA.

Litwak, E. (1985) *Helping the Elderly: The Complementary Roles of Informal Networks and Formal Systems*. New York: Guilford Press.

Litwak, E., Silverstein, M., Bengtson, V.L., and Hirst, Y.W. (2003) 'Theories about families, organizations, and social supports', in V.L. Bengtson and A. Lowenstein (eds), *Global Aging and Challenges to Families*. New York: Aldine de Gruyter, pp. 54–74.

Litwin, H. (2005) 'Intergenerational relations in an aging world', *European Journal of Ageing*, 2: 213–15.

Lowenstein, A. (2007) 'Solidarity-conflict and ambivalence: testing two conceptual frameworks and their impact on quality of life for older family members', *Journal of Gerontology Social Sciences*, 62B: S100–7.

Lowenstein, A. and Daatland, S.O. (2006) 'Filial norms and family support in a comparative cross-national context: evidence from the OASIS study', *Ageing and Society*, 26: 203–23.

Lowenstein, A. and Katan, Y. (1999) *Evaluation of the Long-Term-Care Insurance Law – A Decade of Operation*. Jerusalem, Israel: The Center for Social Policy in Israel (Hebrew).

Lowenstein, A., Katz, R., and Gur-Yaish, N. (2007) 'Reciprocity in parent–child exchange and life satisfaction among the elderly: a cross-national perspective', *Journal of Social Issues* 63(4): 865–83.

Luescher, K. and Pillemer, K. (1998) 'Intergenerational ambivalence: a new approach to the study of parent–child relations in later life', *Journal of Marriage and the Family*, 60: 413–25.

McChesney, K.Y. and Bengston, V.L. (1988) 'Solidarity, integration and cohesion in families: concepts and theories', in D.J. Mangen, V.L. Bengtson, and P.H. Landry, Jr. (eds), *Measurement of Intergenerational Relations*. Beverly Hills: Sage, pp. 15–30.

Minkler, M. and Estes, C.L. (1998) *Critical Gerontology: Perspectives from Political and Moral Economy*. Amityville, NY: Baywood.

Motel-Klingebiel, A., Tesch-Romer, C., and Kondratowitz, H.J. (2005) 'Welfare states do not crowd out the family: evidence for mixed responsibility from comparative analysis', *Ageing and Society*, 25: 863–82.

Parrott, T.M. and Bengtson, V.L. (1999) 'The effects of earlier intergenerational affection, normative expectations and family conflict on contemporary exchanges of help and support', *Research on Aging*, 21: 73–105.

Parsons, T. (1944) 'The social structure of the family', in R.N. Anshen (ed.), *The Family: Its Function and Destiny*. New York: Harper, pp. 173–201.

Parsons, T. (1955) 'The American family: its relations to personality and the social structure', in T. Parsons and R.F. Bales (eds), *Family, Socialization and Interaction Process*. Glencoe: The Free Press, pp. 140–50.

Pillemer, K. and Luescher, K. (2004) *Intergenerational ambivalences: New Perspectives on Parent–Child Relations in Later Life*. London: Elsevier.

Pillemer, K. and Suitor, J.J. (2002) 'Explaining mothers' ambivalence toward their adult children', *Journal of Marriage and Family*, 64: 602–13.

Pillemer, K. and Suitor, J.J. (2005) 'Ambivalence and the study of intergenerational relations', in M. Silverstein (ed.), *Annual Review of Gerontology and Geriatrics, Volume 2: Intergenerational Relations across Time and Place*. New York: Springer, pp. 3–28.

Popenoe, D. (1993) 'American family decline, 1960–1990: a review and appraisal', *Journal of Marriage and the Family*, 55: 527–41.

Silverstein, M. and Bengtson, V.L. (1991) 'Do close parent–child relations reduce the mortality risk of older parents?', *Journal of Health and Social Behavior*, 32: 382–95.

Silverstein, M., Bengtson, V.L., and Litwak, E. (2003) 'Theoretical approaches to problems of families, aging and social support in the context of modernization', in S. Biggs, A. Lowenstein, and J. Hendricks (eds), *The Need for Theory: Critical Approaches to Social Gerontology*. Amityville, NY: Baywood, pp. 181–98.

Silverstein, M., Chen, X., and Heller, K. (1996) 'Too much of a good thing? Intergenerational social support and the psychological well-being of older parents', *Journal of Marriage and the Family*, 58: 970–82.

Silverstein, M., Conroy, S.J., Wang, H.T., Giarrusso, R., and Bengtson, V.L. (2002) 'Reciprocity in parent–child relations over the adult life course', *Journal of Gerontology: Social Sciences*, 57B: S3–13.

Soldo, B.J., Agree, E.M., and Wold, D.A. (1990) 'Family, households and care arrangements of frail older women: a structural analysis', *Journal of Gerontology, Social Sciences*, 45: 238–49.

Spilerman, S. (2000) 'A wealth and stratification process', *Annual Reviews of Sociology*, 16: 497–524.

Sundstrom, G., Malmberg, B., Sancho Castiello, M., et al. (2008) 'In family care for elders in Europe: policies and practices', in M.E. Szinovacz, and A. Davey (eds), *Caregiving Contexts*. New York: Springer, pp. 235–68.

Sussman, M.B. (1991) 'Reflections on intergenerational and kin connections', in S.P. Pfeifer and M.B. Sussman (eds), *Families, Intergenerational and Generational Connections*. New York: Haworth Press, pp. 2–9.

Wilson, A.E., Shuey, K.M., and Elder, G.H., Jr. (2003) 'Ambivalence in the relationship of adult children to aging parents and in-laws', *Journal of Marriage and Family*, 65(4): 1055–72.

Wolf, D. A. and Ballal, S.S. (2006) 'Family support for older people in an era of demographic change and policy constraints', *Ageing and Society*, 26: 693–706.

Wolfe, A. (1989). *Whose Keeper? Social Science and Moral Obligations*. Berkeley, CA: University of California Press.

15

Intergenerational Relations: Asian Perspectives

Leng Leng Thang

INTRODUCTION

The study of intergenerational relations is predominantly situated within the familial realm. For older persons, intergenerational relationships are focused primarily around parent–child and grandparent–grandchild relations. In both relationships, caregiving is the most studied aspect of intergenerational relations. Caregiving includes both adult children caring for older parents, and the care of grandchildren by grandparents. In the earlier sections of this chapter, both dimensions are considered in relation to living arrangements, and the concepts of filial piety and reciprocity that have underpinned intergenerational relations. In the latter sections, other domains of intergenerational relations are examined, including relationships in the non-familial as well as familial realm. Intergenerational relations beyond the familial warrant attention, since longer life expectancy provides opportunity and necessity for older persons to connect across the generations in alternate ways to give meanings to later life, and also to contribute towards shaping the community and society with intergenerational involvement. There are also intricate interrelations between the familial and non-familial realms.

RAPID AGEING IN ASIA

One of the most dramatic changes in Asia since the 1950s is the rapid ageing of the population,

attributed to the rise in life expectancy and a sharp fall in total fertility rate (Tables 15.1 and 15.2). This pan-continent trend reflects the impact of economic development, urbanization, industrialization, and globalization on Asian societies. While medical advances and improvements in public health and hygiene led to the fall in mortality rate and rising life expectancy, the fall in fertility rate is attributed to social and attitudinal changes such as later age of marriages, increase in the number of singles in the population, the availability of contraception, and a conscious choice by couples to have fewer children – especially as more women remain in the workforce.

The ageing of Asia is characterized by the increase in the proportion of the old-old (age 80+) and the feminization of ageing. The proportion of people aged 80+ will roughly double in all regions of Asia from 2000 to 2025 (Table 15.1). Moreover, it is projected that by 2020 nearly half (48 per cent) of the world's people age 80+ will reside in Asia (UNESCAP, 2002: 2). As elsewhere, in Asia the elder population is disproportionately female, especially among the old-old. Compared to older men, older women are more likely to be poor, widowed, and unemployed; they also tend to be burdened with the caregiving of both the older and younger generations (Chan, 2005). Together with lower birth rates, gains in longevity create a vertical extension of family structure referred to as the *beanpole family* by Bengtson et al. (1990). This structure, already common in Europe and North America, looks set to become a norm among the more developed societies in Asia as well. It increases the likelihood that children will have

Table 15.1 Demographic comparisons in Asia I

Region	Proportion 65+ (% of population)			Proportion 80+			Aging index*			Median age (years)			Total fertility rate (per woman)		
	1975	2000	2025	1975	2000	2025	1975	2000	2025	1975	2000	2025	1975	2000	2025
Asia (general)	4.2	5.9	10.1	0.5	0.8	1.7	16.8	29.0	64.3	20.3	26.2	33.1	4.2	2.5	2.1
East Asia	4.7	7.7	14.5	0.6	1.2	2.7	19.5	47.3	116.5	21.5	30.8	39.8	3.1	1.8	1.9
SouthCentral Asia	3.8	4.6	7.4	0.3	0.6	1.1	15.0	20.1	43.3	19.5	22.6	29.4	5.1	3.2	2.2
Southeast Asia	3.6	4.7	8.4	0.3	0.6	1.2	13.5	22.1	54.1	18.7	23.9	32.1	4.9	2.5	2.1
West Asia	4.3	4.7	6.9	0.5	0.6	1.1	15.7	19.8	34.3	18.9	22.1	26.6	5.2	3.6	2.8

Source: United Nations (2002)
* Number of persons aged 60 years or over per 100 persons under age 15.

Table 15.2   Demographic comparisons in Asia II

Region	Life expectancy (at birth)			Life expectancy (at 65)			Sex ratio (per women) (65+)			Sex ratio (80+)		
	1975	2000	2025	1975	2000	2025	1975	2000	2025	1975	2000	2025
Asia (general)	58.4	67.4	73.9	–	14.6	16.7	85.1	84.3	84.2	76.4	61.2	60.9
Male	57.6	65.8	71.8	–	13.3	15.1						
Female	59.2	69.2	76.2	–	15.9	18.2						
East Asia	66.4	72.3	77.3	–	15.4	17.7	75.6	81.6	81.4	69.5	51.6	55.0
Male	65.2	69.9	74.8+	–	13.6	15.5						
Female	67.6	74.9	80.0	–	17.3	19.7						
South Central Asia	52.5	63.3	70.9	–	13.6	15.5	103.0	90.2	89.2	99.7	81.4	72.5
Male	52.7	62.7	69.4	–	12.9	14.5						
Female	52.3	64.1	72.6	–	14.2	16.5						
Southeast Asia	54.6	67.0	74.0	–	14.0	15.9	83.6	81.8	81.2	67.9	69.9	63.3
Male	52.9	64.8	71.6	–	13.2	14.6						
Female	56.5	69.2	76.4	–	14.7	17.1						
West Asia	60.5	70.0	75.5	–	15.1	16.7	82.6	82.8	90.4	67.6	62.5	66.9
Male	58.6	68.0	73.6	–	14.0	15.3						
Female	62.4	72.1	78.0	–	16.1	18.0						

Source: United Nations (2002)

living grandparents and even great-grandparents, especially grandmothers.

The extent and pace of the trend toward population graying differs among Asian societies, as does its impact on families and intergenerational relations. Asia is highly diverse in its population and socioeconomic development. It claims the country with the world's highest life expectancy (Japan) as well as the country with the biggest absolute number of older persons (China). The more developed countries in East and Southeast Asia (South Korea, Singapore, Hong Kong, and Taiwan) are experiencing rapid growth in the proportions of population aged 65+. A two- or three-fold jump in the pace of ageing is also being experienced by developing countries in Southeast Asia and South Asia, including India, Indonesia, Brunei, Malaysia, Vietnam, the Philippines, and Thailand. Urban–rural differences are especially important: the pace of ageing in urban areas is expected to occur about a decade ahead of the rural areas (Heller, 2006). In comparison, countries such as Laos and Cambodia, and most countries in South Central and West Asia, are estimated to have a youthful population for some time to come, with only 5–8 per cent of their populations aged 65+ by 2025. Although this proportion is expected to double by 2050, these countries will still be relatively young. Thus, although the highly developed countries of East Asia resemble Europe in respect of population ageing, Asia as a whole is projected to remain relatively youthful, with less than 20 per cent of the total population age 65+ in 2050 (Table 15.3). Phillips

(2000) notes that predominantly Catholic and Islamic countries have higher fertility rates and therefore a more gradual rate of ageing. In the East Asian countries, successful family planning policies such as the one-child policy in China have contributed much to the rapid demographic transformation. In China, the imbalance in the generations is frequently depicted through visual images of the *little emperor* syndrome, where six adults – parents and two pairs of grandparents – are doting over one (preferably male) child.

So far, the dominant framework among policy-makers in Asia has been to take an *ageing-as-problem* approach (see, e.g., Phillips and Chan (2002); see also Chapter 33). As changing social conditions threaten the traditional mode of elder care, governments are being forced to reconsider the adequacy of current patterns of intergenerational support and policies for older persons (Croll, 2008; UNESCAP, 2002). To what extent the state should step in and assume the responsibilities to care and support for older persons remains a tension between the state and the citizens in most Asian societies (Chan, 2005; Kaplan and Chadha, 2004; Teo et al., 2006).

More recently, faced with increasing longevity, and hence with concerns similar to those of Western societies regarding the economic and social burden of old-age dependency, advanced Asian countries have also moved toward an 'active ageing' discourse. Together with the adoption of the concept of 'social capital' to describe the older population (Quah, 2005: 80), such an *ageing-as-resource* frame of approach argues that older

Table 15.3   Aging indicators for selected Asian countries

Region and country	Proportion 65+ (% of population)			Proportion 80+			Old age dependency ratio		
	2000	2025	2050	2000	2025	2050	2000	2025	2050
East Asia									
China	6.9	13.2	22.7	0.9	2.1	6.8	10	19.4	37.2
China (HK)	10.6	20	29.2	2	3.8	11	14.5	30.1	51.3
Japan	17.2	28.9	36.4	3.8	10.4	15.4	25.2	49	71.3
Rep. Korea	7.1	16.9	27.4	1	3.3	9.1	9.8	25.1	48.8
Southeast Asia									
Cambodia	2.8	4.2	7.4	0.3	0.5	1.2	5.2	6.9	10.9
Vietnam	5.3	8.1	17.1	0.8	1.2	3.9	8.7	11.9	27.1
Indonesia	4.8	8.4	16.4	0.5	1.2	3.2	7.5	12.2	25.8
Laos	3.5	4.5	8.8	0.5	0.6	1.4	6.5	7.2	13
Malaysia	4.1	9	15.4	0.6	1.3	3.7	6.7	13.4	23.8
Myanmar	4.6	8.1	15.8	0.7	1.2	3.3	7.4	11.8	24.5
Philippines	3.5	6.8	13.9	0.4	0.9	2.7	5.5	10.9	19.5
Singapore	7.2	21.5	28.6	1.4	3.8	12.6	10.2	33.4	49.8
Thailand	5.2	11.4	21.1	0.6	1.7	5.5	7.7	16.4	34.1
South Central Asia									
India	5.0	8.3	14.8	0.6	1.3	3.1	8.1	12.1	22.6
Pakistan	3.7	4.8	8.3	0.4	0.7	1.4	6.7	7.9	12.1
Nepal	3.7	4.6	8.3	0.4	0.6	1.2	5.9	7.1	12.4
Bangladesh	3.1	5.2	10.9	0.3	0.6	1.6	5.4	7.8	16.2
West Asia									
Oman	2.5	4.5	6.9	0.3	0.6	1.2	4.2	6.6	10.5
Qatar	1.5	13.7	15.1	0.1	0.7	4.7	2.1	21.1	23.1
Saudi Arabia	3.0	5.7	8.7	0.3	0.7	1.5	5.5	9.6	12.8
United Arab Emirates	2.7	17.6	19.8	0.4	2.2	6.4	3.8	28	32.1

Source: United Nations (2002)

people today are ageing with better health and more financial resources, and contribute to society in multiple ways – as volunteers, as they continue to work in the workforce, and as caregivers to their families. In Japan, where older persons enjoy the highest level of health as well as life expectancy, older persons increasingly refer to retirement as the beginning of a new stage of life where they are free to do what they like. Many have taken on volunteering and other meaningful activities to remain socially engaged (Nakano, 2005; Thang, 2006). In Singapore, a government-sponsored non-profit sector called the Council for Third Age (C3A) was set up in 2007 to focus on active ageing.

Active ageing, especially in the form of connecting with younger generations through volunteering and other activities, also contributes to age integration (Hagestad and Uhlenberg, 2006; Riley and Riley, 2000). In Japan, opportunities for cross-generational interaction outside the family context appear as indications of age integration. For example, older persons who actively interact with the young are referred to as 'grandpa' or 'grandma' by the non-kin children in what is termed the 'big

family' setting within an age-integrated institution or community setting within an elementary school. Some such schools offer space for elders to spend time within the school (Thang, 2008). Hagestad and Uhlenberg highlight the family as 'the only truly age integrated social institution' which they suggest is central to combating ageism, reducing the risk for isolation in later life, and fostering societal generativity. Yet they are concerned that rapid changes will limit the family's capability to promote intergenerational connection. Such forms of emergent non-family ties thus have the potential to compensate for the limitations of the family in creating the desired cross-age relationships.

LIVING ARRANGEMENTS, INTERGENERATIONAL SUPPORT, AND RELATIONSHIPS

Older persons' co-residence with their children is regarded as a common practice that provides family support and intergenerational interaction in traditional Asian families. However, especially among the more developed Asian societies such as Japan, Taiwan, and South Korea, the trend toward single-older person households observed in developed countries is similarly evident, with changing household structures characterized by a fall in household size and a trend toward the nuclear family (Kinsella, 1995; Palloni, 2005).

Another common form of living arrangement for older persons is living only with one's spouse. This arrangement indicates the impact of rural–urban migration and a preference for nuclear family structure among the children. It also reflects increased longevity and an increasing practice of independent living among older persons.

Despite such trends, living with at least one adult child still constitutes the most common form of living arrangement in Asia (Chan, 2005; Martin, 1988, 1989). A panel analysis of changes in living arrangements for Indonesia, Singapore, and Taiwan reveals very high (about 85 per cent) rates of co-residence (Frankenberg et al., 2002). Even in a developed Asian country like Japan, where the proportion of three-generational households fell from 32 per cent in 1991 to 22 per cent in 2001, the figure is still high compared with other developed countries such as the United States (2 per cent) and Germany (1 per cent) (Ogawa, et al., 2006).

The gender of the co-resident children differs with regard to the prevailing family system. In East Asian societies (China, Japan, Korea) and India, the preference according to the patrilineal/patriarchal family system is for co-residence with a son, particularly the eldest son in the stem family system. However, studies of Southeast Asian societies and Sri Lanka find little preference for sons over daughters, and in Malaysia the preference is for co-residence with daughters (Chan, 2005; DaVanzo and Chan, 1994; Knodel and Chayovan, 1997; Martin, 1989; Ofstedal et al., 1999; Lee et al., 1994).

Classic modernization theory (Cowgill and Holmes, 1972) would view living arrangements as one determinant of well-being, since elders who live with adult children or grandchildren are assumed to be better provided for and hence enjoy higher status. However, this assumption is being questioned as researchers called for a re-conceptualization of the relationship between living arrangement, well-being, and status of older persons (Chan, 2005; Hermalin, 1997, 2002; Martin, 1989). Intergenerational relations within the same household involve both solidarity and conflict, and can often be quite tenuous. Just as multigenerational living arrangements in the preindustrial United States were romanticized, (e.g., Achenbaum, 1978; Fischer, 1978), so may be filial piety. Contemporary literature and mass media featuring intergenerational conflicts (especially between

mother-in-law and daughter-in-law) and issues such as elder abuse and suicide are all indicators of the stresses facing individuals in multigenerational households (Hu, 1995; Jamuna, 2003; Yamanoi, 1995).

In arguing for a distinction of 'form versus function', Hermalin (1997) highlights the flaw of expecting co-residence in Asia to mean a one-way support of the young to the old. Instead, co-residence may indicate the younger generations' dependence on the old. For example, in Singapore, where housing policy limits the availability of public housing for single under age 35, it is not uncommon for single adult children to continue to live with their parents due to the trend toward later age of marriage and high cost of private housing. While such a phenomenon is readily accepted in some societies, in Japan, adult children who still 'live off' their parents are often viewed in a somewhat negative light, reflected in the term 'parasite singles'. When older persons are healthy and well, it is common for them to assume the role of caring for their grandchildren within the same household, thereby providing caregiving relief and emotional and social security to the younger generation (Chan, 2005).

It also needs to be recognized that a lack of co-residence does not necessarily imply a lack of intergenerational support or a distancing of relationships. There is ample evidence suggesting an active exchange of monetary and non-monetary support between older persons and their non-co-resident children in Asian societies (Chan, 2005; Croll, 2008; Knodel et al., 2000; Natividad and Cruz, 1997; Sorensen and Kim, 2004; Wang, 2004). One place this flow of support is evident is in child care, since grandparents often continue to play an active role, caring for grandchildren during the day and returning them to their parents in the evenings. In Singapore and Malaysia, 'weekends' parents – whose children are cared for by grandparents during the week and only return to live with their own dual-working parents on weekends – have become a convenient caregiving option.

In attempting to balance between the traditional ideal of multigenerational living and the desire of many young people for independent households, one preferred strategy seems increasingly to be living close by, to maintain 'intimacy at a distance' – 'where the soup is still hot', as they say in Japan. Such arrangements of subdividing the property so that the younger family lives in a separate house next door to the older parents helps reduce conflicts, as daughter-in-law and mother-in-law each care for a separate household, yet embody the extended family unit through intergenerational contacts and mutual reliance (Brown, 2003; Janelli and Yim, 2004; Wang, 2004). It is important for such variations in living arrangements to be captured with more precision by social researchers in order to have an accurate picture of intergenerational support and connections (Rebick and Takenaka, 2006).

FILIAL PIETY AND RECIPROCITY IN INTERGENERATIONAL RELATIONS

Behind the desire for multigenerational living arrangements among Asian elders is the expectation that children should continue the intergenerational social contract that has traditionally provided support for parents' later years. Such reliance on the family instead of the state to care for older persons is often regarded as the essence of Asian values, which lays the foundation of not only the family but also state policies on aged care (Croll, 2008).

Across multiple Asian societies, the practice of filial obligation has its roots in cultural and religious references. In Indian culture, explicit laws govern parent–son relationships. The Vedas, the older Hindu scriptures, stipulate that sons must respect and obey their parents, and the ideal son is one who lives with his parents (Salva and Davey, 2004: 511). In Islamic States of Asia, religious doctrines condemn children who fail in the duty of providing for their elders financially and socially (Cleary and Alimaricar, 2000: 327). In East Asian culture, the Confucian concept of filial piety, which demands children's selfless devotion and respect to one's parents (Liu and Kendig, 2000: 13) is widely regarded as a normative factor regulating intergenerational solidarity, although subtle differences can be found among its Chinese, Korean, and Japanese versions (Koyano, 2000; Thang, 2000).

Despite these long and multiple cultural legacies, the actual practice of such ideas must be viewed in a more nuanced light. Ethnographic data across Asia consistently show that elders perceive a decline in respect and authority toward the senior generation (Croll, 2008: 104). Moreover, class and social economic status have an impact on the experiences of older persons in the family (see, e.g., Yin and Lai [1983] on China, Soh [1997] on Korea, Vincentnathan and Vincentnathan [1994] on India). As Goransson observes in a study of filial piety and family dynamics among Chinese families in Singapore '…the prevalence of filial piety, seniority, and solid intergenerational ties in notions of Chinese culture suggest that familial support and care of elders would be somehow in-built in the minds of Chinese people. In practice however, the image proves to be problematic' (2004: 20). Conflicting expectations between elders and their children in rural China has inspired a new mode of short-term intergenerational co-residence

known as 'ritualistic co-residence', in which newlyweds move in temporarily to the paternal household for a few days to a month for the purpose of displaying their 'filial piety' (Wang, 2004). In Japan, both the older persons and their children would prefer a more affection-based, convenience-oriented living arrangement pattern and type of care that is free from the norm of filial piety when possible (Koyano, 2000).

However, the culture of filial piety is not disappearing. Instead, new interpretations and modifications to the meanings and practice of filial piety are being developed, showing the influence of 'local circumstances of history, economics, social organization and demography, and personal circumstances of wealth, gender, and family configuration' (Ikels, 2004: 2). For example, for some affluent Koreans, the performance of filial piety has become strongly linked with material consumption where purchases of services for old-age care 'make co-residence and other forms of personal care old-fashioned and unnecessary' (Sorensen and Kim, 2004: 181). In China, placement in a long-term care institution has shifted from involving a stigma, to becoming an interpretation of filial piety – when affluent and busy children substitute quality and costly professional care institutions for personal filial care (Zhan et al., 2008). This resonates with Croll's review of ethnographic studies on ageing in Asia, which depicts younger generations' reinterpretation of filial support as modified to relate more to 'support, service and care based on need, volunteerism and mutual appreciation, gratitude and affection', instead of 'piety, obedience or duty' (2008: 109).

The modification and reinterpretation of filial piety suggests the need to look beyond mere cultural tenacity to understand family care and intergenerational relationships in the Asian context. Critical perspectives on ageing draw from political economy, critical theory, and macro-structural approaches, for example, examining the structural inequalities that create dependency in intergenerational relationships (Estes et al., 2003; Teo et al., 2006).

From the interactionist and exchange perspectives, the concept of reciprocity has been used frequently to explain intergenerational care in Asian families. The concept assumes a balance in relationships through repaying the benefits received, frequently with the understanding that repayment needs not be immediate (Burger et al., 1997). In analyzing such relationships, Wentowski's (1981) three types of reciprocity – 'immediate', 'deferred' (over time), and 'generalized' (over life course) – remain relevant. While the first two are based on reciprocity between individuals, the third, generalized reciprocity is based on the general assumption that one who contributes to the well-being of another person will eventually be compensated by others. In Japan, Lebra's (1974) analysis of 'compensative transference' in family care offered one example of generalized reciprocity, where through generational succession, parents are seen as entitled to demand care from their children as compensation for their care of their own parents. A similar dynamic of reciprocity is described by Hashimoto in the notion of 'reward', as in the case of a Japanese older woman living in a four-generation household who can designate her children and grandchildren to be caregivers, 'because she has earned this reward through past sacrifices and hardships' (1996: 177).

Caring for grandchildren by the grandparents can also help to balance the intergenerational equation. In Japan, thus, reciprocity maintained as childcare by grandparents is seen as 'repaying to the grandchildren for the kindness of their daughters-in-law' (Akiyama et al., 1990: 133). In Hong Kong, family caregivers of older persons who are in relatively good physical health may actually receive help from the elders they are to care for, since the latter may provide care to grandchildren (Wong, 2000). Based on another Hong Kong study revealing a similar pattern, Lee (2004) suggests that reciprocity, not filial piety, is the basis of the relationship between adult children and their parents. Earlier experiences of caring for the grandchildren gives justification for older persons to receive care from the younger generations at the time when they turn frail (Mehta and Thang, 2008). Such generalized reciprocity promotes intergenerational interdependence throughout the life course and provides an important role and agency to older persons. In this and other ways, grandparents contribute significantly toward the well-being of grandchildren (see Chapter 34).

GRANDPARENT–GRANDCHILD RELATIONSHIPS IN ASIA

Across Asia, the ideal image of grandparent–grandchild interaction is often that of a smiling grandparent surrounded by grandchildren in a multigenerational household. However, recent developments in family dynamics and intergenerational support and relations in contemporary Asia have contested such an ideal image and given rise to inquiries regarding the place and meaning of grandparenthood in the nexus of family relations and regarding perceptions and attitudes of the young toward grandparents and older persons generally. The literature on Asia focuses on three main areas of inquiry – intergenerational solidarity, attitudes toward older persons, and roles and functions of grandparents.

Intergenerational solidarity

Studies of intergenerational solidarity, inspired by Western approaches such as the model developed by Bengtson and associates, report generally positive intergenerational ties (see Chapter 13). In a qualitative study of families in Northeast Thailand, Kamnuansilpa et al. (2005) found that positive relationships sustain the family solidarity. Mehta and Thang's (2006) exploration of affectual solidarity in intergenerational relationships among grandparents and grandchildren in Singapore found mutual desire for emotional closeness.

Various factors interact to affect and shape intergenerational solidarity. At least some of these appear to be similar to the differentiated pattern of solidarities observed in the Western literature. For example, Lin (2005) analyzed Taiwanese middle school students' relationships with their grandparents in terms of three dimensions of solidarity: affectual (degree of emotional attachment), associational (frequency of contact), and functional (extent of help and exchanges) (Bengtson and Roberts, 1991). Consistent with others (Hagestad, 1985; Roberto and Stroes, 1992), she found that affection and associational solidarity are important with grandmothers, especially maternal grandmothers who provide care to grandchildren. She also reports that the patrilineal pattern of co-residence has resulted in greater interaction with paternal grandparents, but greater affection with maternal grandparents. Moreover, the study suggests closer intergenerational bonds with grandparents who possess more resources, such as those who are younger, healthy, and have higher educational level. These findings suggest that cultural as well as economic capital may be under-researched factors that influence the quality of intergenerational relations.

Attitudes toward older persons

A second area of literature on Asia comprises inquiries into young people's attitudes and perceptions toward older persons, an area of interest which has developed in the Western literature since the 1970s, especially relating to concerns about ageism. Contrary to expectations that older persons are held in high regard, with the traditional norms of revering the old in Eastern culture, a number of studies have reported negative attitudes toward older generations to be prevalent among younger generations in Japan (Koyano, 1989), China and Hong Kong (Harwood et al., 2001), and India (Singh, 2004, cited in Kaplan and Chadha, 2004). Again, this appears to imply a decline in the norms of filial piety and respect for the older generations among Asian youths.

In both Japan and Singapore, positive images of older persons have been found to decline as children mature, suggesting a diminishing in mutual engagement with the declining health of grandparents (Nakano, 1991; Nakano et al., 1994; Thang and Mehta, 2004). In these countries and Taiwan, attitudes toward older people in general appear to be correlated with attitudes toward grandparents: students (including college) who report greater affection toward and positive interaction with grandparents are more likely to express positive attitudes toward older persons generally (Lin and Su, 2004; Thang and Tsuji, 2003; Thang et al., 2006).

In contrast with the ideal image of multigenerational living, co-habitation with older persons is not necessarily associated with positive images toward old age on the part of youth (Nakano, 1991; Nakano et al., 1994). This finding is similar to US findings indicating stereotyping and negative attitudes toward older people among youths who interact frequently with grandparents (Braren, 1989; Wiles, 1987). The discrepancy between these findings and the generally positive attitudes reported earlier suggests the need to understand further the nature of intergenerational interaction. In Asia, the common functions of grandparents in providing care and companionship to grandchildren may have instilled in youths a sense of appreciation and nostalgia toward their grandparents. On the other hand, youths co-living with their grandparents are also likely to experience multigenerational family stresses such as mother-in-law/daughter-in-law conflicts, a sense of a lack of freedom with the presence of the older generation at home, as well as caregiving stresses when the senior generation's health declines. Such realities could lead to negative perceptions of youths toward older persons in general.

Roles and functions of grandparents

The third area of inquiry explores the roles and functions of grandparents in the family.

Grandparents have the potential to serve as important resources in childcare and other aspects of family life (see Chapter 34). Research in the Philippines, Taiwan, and Thailand has shown that grandparents are heavily involved both in caring for grandchildren and in performing household chores (Hermalin et al., 1998). Grandparents act as surrogate parents in 'skipped generation' households when parents are absent, whether due to work migration or AIDS. A study of such a phenomenon in Northeast Thailand found this pattern to be more prevalent among rural families, and that grandparents who serve as replacement parents

tend to be worse off in economic and physical well-being (Kamnuansilpa and Wongthanavasu, 2005). By providing such care, grandparents contribute significantly to economic development, as Silverstein (2005) found in rural China and others have reported elsewhere.

Although caring for grandchildren can nurture valued family relationships and is often idealized in this way, research utilizing in-depth interviews reveals a different picture: grandparents, especially grandmothers, often experience this work as involving considerable sacrifice and burden. For Chinese grandparents, it may entail geographic relocation by the grandmother, and even separation from her husband and giving up retirement plans, such as traveling, pursuing hobbies, and lifelong learning opportunities. Physical exhaustion is also a common theme articulated by grandparents (Goh, 2007). In Singapore, grandparents express a desire to stop or do less. Although they often continue to help because of a normatively imposed sense of duty, they also complain about the insensitivity of the parent generation in understanding their needs (Teo et al., 2006). These tensions suggest the relevance of the concept of 'ambivalence', which recognizes the coexistence of solidarity and conflict in intergenerational ties (Connidis, 2001). In identifying the approach with feminist, critical and symbolic interactionist theory, Connidis and McMullin (2000, cited in Connidis, 2001: 119) assert that

> Because intergenerational ties are ambivalent, they must be negotiated in an ongoing process of family relations. Therefore, the study of intergenerational relations must address the tensions and contradictions between social structural forces and individual interests that family members must work out in their encounters with one another.

The study of intergenerational relations in Asia will similarly benefit from incorporating the complementarity of ambivalence with the concepts of solidarity and conflict (Bengtson et al., 2002).

STRENGTHENING INTERGENERATIONAL RELATIONSHIPS THROUGH GENERATIONAL REENGAGEMENT

Since Mead's (1970) call for the need of generations to learn from each other and later scholars' critiques of age segregation, there has been little doubt about the general desirability of intergenerational interaction (Hagestad and Uhlenberg, 2005, 2006; Newman, 1997; Riley and Riley, 2000). In contrast to the emphasis on caregiving in the study of intergenerational relationships generally, studies of efforts to strengthen intergenerational family connections tend to address the basic need for interpersonal connection.

In Asia, intergenerational activities (such as children's visits to old-age institutions) are well established at the community level. In several countries, including Korea, Philippines, Japan, India, and Singapore, such activities receive substantial state support (Kaplan and Chadha, 2004; Thang et al., 2003). These initiatives are usually classified into one of several broad categories:

1) Services initiated by the young (e.g., HelpAge India's 'Adopt a grandparent' scheme).
2) Services initiated by seniors (e.g., RSVP [Retired Seniors Volunteer Program] mentorship programme in Singapore where senior volunteers serve as mentors to the young).
3) Community initiatives (e.g., intergenerational activity day).
4) Initiatives in shared sites (e.g., age-integrated facilities combining old-age home with childcare centers or schools).

The last category is the least common, partly because of the inevitable complications when two or more separate organizations are involved (such as Ministry of Education and Ministry of Welfare).

Across these kinds of programmes, three characteristics can be identified: (1) a strong idealization of the family; (2) the transmission of cultural values and traditions through intergenerational activities; and (3) the opportunity for elders to make positive contributions to community life.

First, the primacy of family – especially the ideal of mutual support in a multigenerational family – is found in the conceptualization of intergenerational programmes. This represents an important difference from intergenerational programmes in the West, which typically emphasize developing relationships between non-related individuals. Programmes in Asia tend to focus on developing intergenerational familial relationships. In Singapore, intergenerational programming is explicitly framed as a strategy to strengthen the 'family' (Thang, 2002). Even in Japan, where rapid decline in the rate of intergenerational co-residence has prompted a hope that intergenerational programming can compensate for what the family can no longer provide, it is common to publicize intergenerational programmes by invoking metaphorical allusions to 'family', with concepts like *daikazoku* (big family, multigenerational family) and phrases such as *kazoku danran* ('family harmonic atmosphere') and *honto no kazoku no yona atatakasa* ('warmth like a real family') (Kaplan et al., 1998).

Not surprisingly, one of the success measures of an intergenerational programme across Asia seems to be the achievement of family-like feeling, including the way participants perceive each other as surrogate grandchildren and grandparents (e.g., Kaplan and Chadha, 2004).

The second characteristic of programmatic efforts to nurture intergenerational engagement is the focus on transmitting traditional culture and values. The cultural regeneration function is a common objective in intergenerational programmes (Kaplan et al., 1998). Having older persons teach the young about traditional arts and crafts and local languages, traditions, and festivities represents a common form of programming. Such activities position seniors as a knowledge reservoir and a useful resource for children. For example, in Western Australia a 'playgroup assistance programme' was initiated by a group of retired volunteers who teach playgroups about traditional Japanese games and crafts, such as paper and bamboo crafts. The programme was created in response to requests from young Japanese migrant mothers (including those in mixed marriages) who felt an urgent need for their children to be connected with Japanese tradition, which they themselves were not able to provide. The programme has been shown to benefit not only the children but also mothers, who often develop close bonds with the older volunteers. Being geographically distant from Japan, young mothers missed support from their own parents, which the senior volunteers sometimes provided, offering emotional and instrumental support such as advice on child rearing and other family matters (Sone, 2007). In this and other cases, the middle generation's support for such activities also reflects the limitations faced by parents as transmitters of traditional knowledge in nuclear families.

Finally, from a social capital perspective, intergenerational programming offers opportunities for the older person to contribute and to be seen as an asset instead of a burden. Volunteering among older persons is most evident in the more developed Asian countries with rapid rise in life and health expectancy. A survey in Japan shows that those age 50 and above made up 79 per cent of the number of people who volunteer, among which those age 60 and above comprised 52 per cent. Although for senior volunteers, engaging with the younger generation is only one among a variety of volunteering options, those who have chosen it report benefits such as satisfaction from achieving a sense of generativity (Thang, 2006). Moreover, when older persons are active in engaging the young, they contribute toward balancing the 'reciprocity equation'.

CONCLUSION

Changing demography and social and cultural transformations are challenging the dynamics of intergenerational relationships in Asia. On the one hand, generational interdependence is increasingly desired to provide intergenerational care not only from the young to the old but also from the old to the young. On the other hand, social structural forces and individual interests continue to widen the generation gap, catalyzing shifts in core values epitomized by the decline of filial piety. Such tensions have implications for intergenerational solidarity and family resilience.

Policymakers awake to the impending implications have begun to formulate responses. In the past decade, especially among the developed East Asian and Southeast Asian countries facing a rapid rate of ageing, budgets for ageing welfare have increased, and more public facilities such as community day care and nursing homes have been built (Lee, 2004). However, with the fear that the family's declining capacity to care for their aged will further burden public expenditure, the strategy among the Asian governments has increasingly been to expand family-based intergenerational care through policies which support the family to care for elders. Policies promoting the traditional intergenerational contract reflect governments' efforts to adapt to changing sociocultural contexts. For example, besides the more common array of policies to encourage multigenerational families (e.g., tax incentives and subsidies for live-in caregivers; preference for multigenerational families in the queue of applicants for public housing), Singapore, Taiwan, Hong Kong, and Malaysian governments are also allowing families to employ foreign domestic workers (from fellow Asian countries such as Indonesia, Philippines, Myanmar, Sir Lanka, or Nepal) as live-in caregivers. This is a direct response to the problem of a lack of family caregivers, since more families are composed of two working spouses. This enables families to meet care needs without having the care necessarily performed by family members (Mehta and Thang, 2008). Beyond such innovations, efforts to promote the responsibility of family care are supplemented by a re-emphasis on filial obligations, including 'moral education' modules in schools, and legislation to compel adult children to provide for their aged parents. One example of such legislation is the Parental Maintenance Act introduced in Singapore in 1996 (Teo et al., 2006: 31).

However, as Croll argues, legislation or rhetoric alone is unlikely enough to encourage and maintain resilient reciprocal flows between the generations '… if it was not based on mutual need and dependence' (2008: 115). This signals the need to recognize the flow of resources from old to young, as well as the reverse. Not only do grandparents contribute significantly to the well-being of their grandchildren and the family but also they contribute toward enriching the lives of the younger generations as community volunteers and in other ways, thereby enhancing mutual need and dependence between generations. But the older generation is equally affected by larger structural and socioeconomic-cultural changes. Similar to policy responses in the Western societies toward demographic challenges, Asian governments are also extending retirement age and encouraging healthy older workers to remain in the workforce. To what extent will this affect grandparents' availability for their children and grandchildren? How will this upset the reciprocity equation between the generations?

To assess the continuing impact of modernization and globalization on intergenerational relationships in Asia, studies taking into consideration national and rural–urban, gender, class, and cultural differences are needed to provide understanding of how various emerging phenomena – e.g., transnational mobility, modern technology, and changing lifestyle among new cohorts of seniors – are impacting intergenerational relationships and the intergenerational contract in specific Asian contexts. Asia in transition is certainly a fertile ground for further inquiries on the complex challenges facing the future of intergenerational relationships for the individuals, families, communities, and the states.

REFERENCES

Achenbaum, W.A. (1978) *Old Age in the New Land: The American Experiences Since 1790*. Baltimore: Johns Hopkins University Press.

Akiyama, H., Antonucci, T.C., and Campbell, R. (1990) 'Exchange and reciprocity among two generations of Japanese and American women', in J. Sokolovsky (ed.), *The Cultural Context of Aging: Worldwide Perspectives*. New York: Bergin & Garvey Publishers.

Bengtson, V.C. and Roberts, R.E. (1991) 'Intergenerational solidarity and aging families: an example of formal theory construction', *Journal of Marriage and the Family*, 53: 856–70.

Bengtson, V.C., Rosenthal, C.J., and Burton, C. (1990) 'Families and aging: diversity and heterogeneity', in R.H. Binstock and L.K. George (eds), *Handbook of Aging and the Social Sciences*, 3rd edn. New York: Academic Press.

Bengtson, V.C., Giarrusso, R., Mabry, J.B., and Silverstein, M. (2002) 'Solidarity, conflict and ambivalence: complementary or competing perspectives on intergenerational relationships?', *Journal of Marriage and the Family*, 64(3): 568–76.

Braren, K.H. (1989) *Adolescent's Knowledge and Attitudes about Elderly*. MSW dissertation, Southern Connecticut State University.

Brown, N.C. (2003) 'Under one roof: the evolving story of three-generation housing in Japan', in T. Traphagan and J. Knight (eds), *Demography Change and the Family in Japan's Aging Society*. Albany, NY: SUNY Press.

Burger, J.M., Horita, M., Kinoshita, L., Roberts, K., and Vera, C. (1997) 'Effects of time on the norm of reciprocity', *Basic and Applied Social Psychology*, 19(1): 91–100.

Chan, A. (2005) 'Aging in Southeast and East Asia: issues and policy directions', *Journal of Cross-Cultural Gerontology*, 20(4): 269–84.

Cleary, M. and Alimaricar, H. (2000) 'Ageing, Islam and care for older persons in Brunei Darussalam', in D.R. Phillips (ed.), *Ageing in the Asia-Pacific Region: Issues, Policies and Future Trends*. New York: Routledge.

Connidis, I.A. (2001) *Family Ties and Aging*. Thousand Oaks, CA: Sage.

Cowgill, D.O. and Holmes L.D. (1972) *Aging and Modernization*. New York: Appleton-Century-Crofts.

Croll, E. (2008) 'The intergenerational contract in the changing Asian family', in R. Goodman and Harper, S. (eds), *Ageing in Asia*. London: Routledge.

DaVanzo, J. and Chan, A. (1994) 'Living arrangements of older Malaysians: Who coresides with their adult children?', *Demography*, 31(1): 95–114.

Estes, C.L., Biggs, S., and Phillipson, C. (2003) *Social Theory, Social Policy and Ageing: A Critical Introduction*. London: Open University Press.

Fischer, D.H. (1978) *Growing Old in America*. New York: Oxford University Press.

Frankenberg, E., Chan, A., and Ofstedal, M.B. (2002) 'Stability and change in living arrangements in Indonesia, Singapore, and Taiwan, 1993–1999', *Population Studies*, 56: 201–13.

Goh, E.C.L. (2007) 'Beyond tangible rewards: grandparents' motivation for providing child care in three-tier families in urban Xiamen, China', *International Conference on Contemporary China Studies*. Hong Kong: The University of Hong Kong.

Goransson, K. (2004) *Filial Children and Ageing Parents: Intergenerational Family Ties as Politics and Practice Among Chinese Singaporeans*. Working paper in Social Anthropology, Lund University.

Hagestad, G.O. (1985) 'Continuity and connectedness', in V.L. Bengtson and J.F. Robertson (eds), *Grandparenthood*. Beverly Hills, CA: Sage.

Hagestad, G.O. and Uhlenberg, P. (2005) 'The social separation of old and young: a root of ageism', *Journal of Social Issues*, 61: 3–21.

Hagestad, G.O. and Uhlenberg, P. (2006) 'Should we be concerned about age segregation? Some theoretical and empirical explorations', *Research on Aging*, 28(6): 638–53.

Harwood, J., Giles, H., McCann, R.M., et al., (2001) 'Older adults trial rating of three age-groups around the Pacific Rim', *Journal of Cross-Cultural Gerontology*, 16: 157–71.

Hashimoto, A. (1996) *The Gift of Generations: Japanese and American Perspectives on Aging and the Social Contract*. Cambridge, MA: Cambridge University Press.

Heller, P.S. (2006) *Is Asia Prepared for an Aging Population?* IMF Working paper, Fiscal Affairs Department. http://www.imf.org/external/pubs/ft/wp/2006/wp06272.pdf

Hermalin, A.I. (1997) 'Drawing policy lessons for Asia from research on ageing', *Asia Pacific Population Journal*, 12 (4): 89–102.

Hermalin, A.I. (ed.) (2002) *The Well-Being of the Elderly in Asia: A Four-Country Comparative Study*. Ann Arbor, MI: University of Michigan Press.

Hermalin A.I., Roan, C., and Perez, A. (1998) *The Emerging Role of Grandparents in Asia*. Comparative Study of the Elderly in Asia Research Report No. 98–52. Population Studies Center, University of Michigan.

Hu, Y-H. (1995) 'Elderly suicide risk in family contexts: a critique of the Asian family care model', *Journal of Cross-Cultural Gerontology*, 10(3): 199–217.

Ikels, C. (ed.) (2004) *Filial Piety: Practice and Discourse in Contemporary East Asia*. Stanford: Stanford University Press.

Jamuna, D. (2003) 'Issues of elder care and elder abuse in the Indian conflict', in P.S. Liebig and S.I. Rajan (eds), *An Aging India: Perceptions, Prospects, and Policies*. Amityville, NY: Haworth Press.

Janelli, R.L. and Yim, D. (2004) 'The transformation of filial piety in contemporary South Korea', in C. Ikels (ed.), *Filial Piety: Practice and Discourse in Contemporary East Asia*. Stanford: Stanford University Press.

Japan Aging Research Center (JARC) (2004) *Statistical Abstracts of Aging in Japan*. Japan: Aging Research Center.

Kamnuansilpa, P. and Wongthananvasu, S. (2005) 'Grandparents' relationships with grandchildren in Thailand', *Journal of Intergenerational Relationships*, 3(1): 49–66.

Kamnuansilpa, P, Promjit, H., and Supawatanakorn, W. (2005) 'Intergenerational relationship in Thailand', Paper presented at 'Alternate Generations in the Family: the Asian Perspective', National University of Singapore.

Kaplan, M. and Chadha, N.K. (2004) 'Intergenerational programs and practices: a conceptual framework and an Indian context', *Indian Journal of Gerontology*, 18(3/4): 301–17.

Kaplan, M., Kusano, A., Tsuji, I., and Hisamichi, S. (1998) *Intergenerational Programs: Support for Children, Youth and Elders in Japan*. New York: SUNY Press.

Kinsella, K. (1995) 'Aging and the family: present and future demographic issues', in B. Rosemary and V.H. Bedford (eds), *Handbook of Aging and the Family*. Westport, CT: Greenwood Press.

Knodel, J. and Chayovan, N. (1997) 'Family support and living arrangements of Thai older persons', *Asia-Pacific Population Journal*, 12(4): 51–68.

Knodel, J., Chayovan, N., Graisurapong, S., and Suraratdecha, C. (2000) 'Ageing in Thailand: an overview of formal and informal support', in D.R. Phillips (ed.), *Ageing in the Asia Pacific Region: Issues, Policies and Future Trends*. London: Routledge Advances in Asia-Pacific Studies.

Koyano, W. (1989) 'Japanese attitudes toward the elderly: a review of research findings', *Journal of Cross-Cultural Gerontology*, 4: 335–45.

Koyano, W. (2000) 'Filial piety: co-residence, and integenerational solidarity in Japan', in W.T. Liu, and H. Kendig (eds),

Who Should Care for the Elderly? An East–West Value Divide. Singapore: Singapore University Press and World Scientific.

Lebra, T.S. (1974) 'Reciprocity and the asymmetric principle: an analytical appraisal of the Japanese concept of On', in T.S. Lebra and W. Lebra (eds), *Japanese Culture and Behavior: Selected Readings*. Honolulu: University of Hawaii Press.

Lee, W.K.M. (2004) 'Living arrangements and informal support for the elderly: alteration to intergenerational relationships in Hong Kong', *Journal of Intergenerational Relationships*, 2(2): 27–49.

Lee, Y.J., Parish, B., and Willis, R. (1994) 'Sons, daughters and intergenerational support in Taiwan', *American Journal of Sociology*, 99(4): 1010–41.

Lin, J. (2005) 'Relationship between adolescents and grandparents in Taiwan: intergenerational solidarity and types of grandparent–grandchildren relations', Paper presented at 'Alternate Generations in the Family: the Asian Perspective', National University of Singapore.

Lin, J. and Su, M. (2004) 'The relationship between adolescents and grandparents: Does it affect their attitudes toward the elderly?', *Journal of Taiwan Home Economics*, 35: 75–90.

Liu, W.T. and Kendig, H. (eds) (2000) *Who Should Care for the Elderly? An East–West Value Divide*. Singapore: Singapore University Press and World Scientific.

Martin, L. (1988) 'The aging of Asia', *Journal of Gerontology*, 43: S93–113.

Martin, L. (1989) 'Living arrangements of the older persons in Fiji, Korea, Malaysia and the Philippines', *Demography*, 26(4): 627–43.

Mead, M. (1970) *Culture and Commitment: the New Relations between the Generations in the 1970s*. New York: Columbia University Press.

Mehta, K. and Thang, L.L. (2006) 'Interdependence in Asian families: the Singapore case', *Journal of Intergenerational Relationships*, 4(1): 117–26.

Mehta, K. and Thang, L.L. (2008) 'Visible and blurred boundaries in familial care: the dynamics of multigenerational care in Singapore', in A. Martin-Matthews (ed.), *Aging at the Intersection of Work and Family Life: Blurring the Boundaries*. Florence, KY: Lawrence Erlbaum Associations.

Nakano, I. (1991) 'Children's images of elderly', *Social Gerontology* (in Japanese), 34: 24–36.

Nakano, L. (2005) *Community Volunteers in Japan: Everyday Stories and Social Change*. London: Routledge.

Nakano, I., Shimizu, Y., Nakantani, Y., and Baba, J., (1994) 'Primary school students and middle school students' images of elderly', *Social Gerontology* (in Japanese) 39: 11–22.

Natividad, J. and Cruz, G.T., (1997) 'Patterns in living arrangements and familial support for the older persons in the Philippines', *Asia-Pacific Population Journal* 12(4): 17–34.

Newman, S. (1997) 'History and evolution of intergenerational programs', in S. Newman, C.R. Ward, T.B. Smith, and J. Wilson (eds), *Intergenerational Programs: Past, Present and Future*. Bristol, PA: Taylor and Francis.

Ofstedal, M.B., Knodel, J., and Chayovan, N., (1999) 'Intergenerational support and gender: a comparison of four Asian countries', *Journal of Southeast Asian Studies* 27(2): 21–42.

Ogawa, N., Retherford, R.D., and Matsukura, R. (2006) 'Demographics of the Japanese family', in M. Rebick, and Takenaka A. (eds), *The Changing Japanese Family*. London: Routledge.

Palloni, A. (2005) *Living Arrangements of Older Persons*. UN Population bulletin 42-43. http://www.un.org/ese/population/publications/bulletin42-43/palloni.pdf

Phillips, D.R. and Chan, A.C.M. (2002) *Ageing and Long Term Care: National Policies in the Asia-Pacific*. Singapore and Canada: ISEAS (Institute of Southeast Asian Studies) and International Development Research Centre.

Quah, S.R. (2005) *Home and Kin: Families in Asia*. Singapore: Marshall Cavendish Academic.

Rebick, M. and Takenaka, A. (eds) (2006) *The Changing Japanese Family*. London: Routledge.

Riley, M.W. and Riley, J.W., Jr. (2000) 'Age integration: historical and conceptual background', *The Gerontologist*, 40: 266–72.

Roberto, K.A. and Stroes, J. (1992) 'Grandchildren and grandparents: roles, influences and relationships', *International Journal of Aging and Human Development*, 34: 227–39.

Salva, J. and Davey, A. (2004) 'From distance: experiences of long-distance Indian caregivers', *Indian Journal of Gerontology*, 18(3/4): 509–21.

Silverstein, M. (2005) 'Beyond the nuclear family: grandparents as social resources', paper presented at 'Alternate Generations in the Family: the Asian Perspective', National University of Singapore.

Soh, C.S. (1997) 'The status of the elderly in Korean society', in S. Formanek and S. Linhart (eds), *Aging: Asian Concepts and Experiences Past and Present*. Vienna: Verlag der Osterreichischen Akademie der Wissenschaften.

Sone, S. (2007) 'Recent developments within the Japanese Community in Western Australia', Paper presented at Asian Studies Seminar, University of Western Australia.

Sorensen, C. and Kim, S-C. (2004) 'Filial piety in contemporary urban Southeast Korea: practices and discourses', in C. Ikels (ed.), *Filial Piety: Practice and Discourse in Contemporary East Asia*. Stanford: Stanford University Press.

Teo, P., Metha, K., Thang, L.L., and Chan, A. (2006) *Ageing in Singapore: Service Needs and the State*. London: Routledge.

Thang, L.L. (2000) 'Aging in the East: comparative and historical reflections', in T.R. Cole, R. Kastenbaum, and R.E. Ray (eds), *Handbook of the Humanities and Aging*, 2nd edn. New York: Springer.

Thang, L.L. (2002) 'Intergenerational initiatives in Singapore: commitments to community and family building', in M. Kaplan, N. Henkin, and A. Kusano (eds), *Linking Lifetimes: A Global View of Intergenerational Exchange*. Lanham, MD: University Press of America.

Thang, L.L. (2006) 'Defining a second career: volunteering among seniors in Japan', in P. Matanle and W. Linsing (eds), *Perspectives on Work, Employment, and Society in Contemporary Japan: Sociological and Anthropological Perspectives*. Basingstoke: Palgrave Macmillan.

Thang, L.L. (2008) 'Engaging the generations: age-integrated facilities', in F. Coulmas, H. Conrad, A. Schad-Seifert, and G. Vogt (eds), *The Demographic Challenge: A Handbook About Japan*. Leiden: The Netherlands Brill.

Thang, L.L. and Mehta, K. (2004) 'Grandparents, How do I view thee? A study of grandparenting in Singapore', *Indian Journal of Gerontology*, 18(3/4): 375–90.

Thang, L.L. and Tsuji, A. (2003) 'Gaps between generations: young adults' perceptions of intergenerational relationships with grandparents in Japan and Singapore', Paper presented at Seventh Asia/Oceania Regional Congress of Gerontology.

Thang, L.L., Kaplan, M., and Henkin, N. (2003) 'Intergenerational programming in Asia: converging diversities toward a common goal', *Journal of Intergenerational Relationships* 1(1): 49–70.

Thang, L.L., Lim, W.L., and Yeo, S. (2006) 'Grandchildren's perception of grandparents in Singapore', Paper presented in Third International Consortium for Intergenerational Programs Conference, Melbourne.

UNESCAP (United Nations Economic and Social Commission for Asia and the Pacific) (2002) Report on the Regional Survey on Ageing.

Vincentnathan, S.G. and Vincentnathan, L. (1994) 'Equality and hierarchy in untouchable intergenerational relations and conflict resolutions', *Journal of Cross-Cultural Gerontology*, 9: 1–9.

Wang, D. (2004) 'Ritualistic co-residence and the weakening of filial practice', in C. Ikels (ed.), *Filial Piety: Practice and Discourse in Contemporary East Asia*. Stanford: Stanford University Press.

Wentowski, G.J. (1981) 'Reciprocity and the coping strategies of older people: cultural dimensions of network building', *The Gerontologist*, 21: 600–9.

Wiles, W. (1987) *Seventh Grade Children's Attitudes Towards Older People and the Aging Process: Implications for Guidance Curriculum Development*. PhD dissertation. University of Florida.

Wong, O.M.H. (2000) 'Children and children-in-law as primary caregivers: issues and perspectives', in W.T. Liu and H. Kendig (eds), *Who Should Care for the Elderly? An East–West Value Divide*. Singapore: Singapore University Press and World Scientific.

Yamanoi, K. (1995) *Ways to Have a Happy Family*. Tokyo: Kodansha.

Yin, P. and Lai, K.H. (1983) 'A reconceptualization of age stratification in China', *Journal of Gerontology*, 38: 609–13.

Zhan, H.J., Feng, X.T., and Luo, B.Z. (2008) 'Placing elderly parents in institutions in urban China: a reinterpretation of filial piety', *Research on Aging*, 30(5): 543–71.

16

Societal Dynamics in Personal Networks

Theo van Tilburg and Fleur Thomése

INTRODUCTION

In studying ageing and personal networks, the dominant focus has been towards a presumed reduction in social ties over the later stages of the life course. Life events such as retirement and widowhood, death or incapacity of network members result in the loss of personal ties; limitations arising from health problems may further reduce possibilities for maintaining relationships. However, not all older people are confronted with a shrinking network. This chapter examines the variations characteristic of personal networks in later life. It begins by reviewing the concept of the social network with subsequent sections focusing on the interrelationship between societal dynamics and personal networks. Recent advances in the study of network change have enabled a stronger focus on societal influences on personal networks beyond individual characteristics (Thomése et al., 2005). Personal networks are embedded in a dynamic social context. The argument presented in this chapter is that the nature of personal relationships is subject to societal change, and that recent changes will affect the characteristics of social networks in the future, including the networks of older people. We introduce societal dynamics by describing three societal shifts that are pertinent to networks and network change in late life. Following this, it is argued that theoretical concerns are embedded in a societal context and the main theoretical perspectives in this area are examined in respect of their approach to network change. The chapter then revisits the analysis of network change in late life and concludes with an overview of possible developments affecting future generations.

INTRODUCTION TO PERSONAL NETWORKS

There is a long-standing tradition in the field of gerontology devoted to studying the personal networks of older people (Phillipson, 2004). Networks are regarded as a source of support, contributing to older people's functioning and well-being. A personal network is generally defined as all persons (network members) with whom a focal individual has a direct relationship. The network approach starts with the proposition that social actors are interdependent and that their relationships channel information, affection, support, and other resources. The structure of those relationships both restricts and creates opportunities for behavior. The personal networks of individuals reflect their social opportunities and personal choices to maintain a specific set of relationships with relatives, neighbors, friends, acquaintances, and so on (Adams and Allan, 1998; Hall and Wellman, 1985). This means, first, that relationships are tied to larger social structures, creating opportunities and restraints in the formation and meaning of personal relationships (Entwisle et al., 2007). It also means that personal relationships are not isolated from each other (Thomése et al., 2003). Researchers have too often studied the personal relationships of individuals without taking the linkages between various network members into account. However, network members do not function independently of each other. It is crucial to regard the interaction between the focal individual and one network member in relation to the interaction with other network members. For example, which of the adult children is to provide support for an elderly parent might be the outcome of a family meeting at which they decide to rotate caregiving tasks. If linkages between these relationships and between network members are also taken into account, the scope is extended to broader social structures around the focal person.

Network research in gerontology expanded in the 1980s, in the wake of findings showing the importance of social support for several measures of physical and mental health (Berkman and Syme, 1979; Caplan, 1974). The term 'social networks' had previously been used in gerontology to describe groups of people interacting in face-to-face situations (Lowenthal and Robinson, 1976), focusing on the older adults' ties to society through participation in networks and social roles (Rosow, 1967). The central issues and concepts in subsequent gerontological network research increasingly reflect the social support approach, which links personal relationships to health and well-being. Networks are considered a source of social support, with the focus on disentangling the ways in which networks, relationships, and support are beneficial to ageing individuals. House and Kahn (1985) were among the first to distinguish the *structural* properties of networks and relationships from their *existence* and *functions*. These three conceptualizations – existence, structure, and function – each map different parts of the personal network (Broese van Groenou and van Tilburg, 2007) and will now be discussed in turn.

The existence of (formal) relationships is the focus within the *social integration approach*. Networks consist of more or less institutionalized relationships: for example, those with relatives, co-workers, fellow members of organizations, and neighbors. Researchers who use these relationships as their point of departure take living arrangements, household composition, marital status, or employment status as criteria for network membership (e.g., Berkman and Syme, 1979). Others include relationships that are to some degree close or important to the focal person (Kahn and Antonucci, 1980).

In the *structural approach* it is recognized that people are embedded in various interlocking structures. The network is one of these structures, in which supportive and non-supportive interactions both occur (Knipscheer et al., 1995). The focus is on a multiplex system of partly overlapping sets of relationships in which interactions take place on a regular basis. This indicates to what degree older people are socially involved and the number of relatives, friends, co-workers, and so on, with whom contact is maintained.

The *functional approach* typically addresses the network as a source of support to the individual, such as the older person in need of assistance. Studies define a social network as a set of persons with whom specific types of support are exchanged (Fischer et al., 1977). This exchange might pertain both to support receiving and support giving. This approach is biased against the many relationships in which very little if any support is exchanged.

NETWORK DYNAMICS IN LATE LIFE – THEORETICAL PERSPECTIVES

There is great diversity and change in personal networks in later life (van Tilburg, 1998). Networks are currently understood from three different perspectives: (1) social and personal transitions in later life; (2) changes in the expected returns from relationships within the network; and (3) individual proactive management of personal relationships.

The first perspective offers a life-course view (see Chapter 1). This view conceptualizes an individual as surrounded by what has been termed a '*convoy*' of persons with whom he or she develops relationships from early childhood to old age (Kahn and Antonucci, 1980). During the life course, some relationships end due to (role) transitions (e.g., divorce, death of the spouse, changing jobs), while other relationships may last a lifetime. New members may enter the network as a result of (re) marriage (including relatives, friends, and acquaintances of the new partner), a new job (co-workers and the people they are associated with), or becoming a parent or grandparent (the next generation, but also relationships that emerge in the new role as parent or grandparent). Thus, people enter old age with a personal network that reflects earlier transitions affecting their opportunities and individual choices to maintain and develop relationships. Unfettered by employment obligations and the responsibility for children at home, older people have greater opportunities to organize and structure their social lives. On the other hand, a decline in health may impose restrictions upon older adults' capacities to engage in interaction with others. Hearing problems can limit conversational exchanges, reduced physical mobility can limit participation in shared activities, and cognitive impairment may limit exchange of ideas with others. Role changes and restricted capacities in later life are expected to reduce non-kin relationships and emphasize the importance of family relationships in the network.

The second perspective, based on exchange theory, explains network change in later life from changes within specific relationships. People constantly evaluate their relationships and prefer balanced support, i.e., they give support with the expectation of receiving something in return at some point in time (Blau, 1964; Gouldner, 1960).

If the receiving party is not able to return the support and it is clear that this will not change in the future, the exchange of support may decline. Older adults may become more dependent on others, lacking the ability to perform certain tasks themselves. The existing balance in their relationships may be disrupted, introducing strain and discomfort; imbalance results in the decline of supportive exchanges with older adults, particularly within less close relationships. The deterioration of balance within relationships could be prevalent among older adults, especially when restricted capacities in later life prevent older adults from investing in other people by providing them with instrumental support. Imbalance does not always end in the termination of a relationship, however, as disparity in support to needy older adults can be normatively accepted and even viewed as desirable.

From the third perspective, network change results from alterations in an individual's motivation. This perspective has been developed, for example, by socio-emotional selectivity theory (Carstensen, 1992). With increasing age, the time horizon for the individual becomes more limited, and emotional regulation becomes the most important drive for social interaction. As a result, older people disengage from peripheral and role-guided relationships because the emotional engagement with core network relationships is viewed as more rewarding. This predicts selective shrinking in network size with age. People feeling near to death deliberately discontinue their less close relationships, reduce the emotional closeness with many others, and increase the emotional closeness with core network members such as kin and friends.

It can be concluded that dynamics in the personal networks of older people are related to changes in situational and personal characteristics. A network reflects individual transitions, relationship norms, structural constraints on contact with others, and personal characteristics. In studying networks in later life, it is recommended to relate changes in network features to changes in situational, as well as personal, characteristics of older people. However, changes in personal networks cannot be studied in isolation from macro-social trends that create individual opportunities to design and maintain a personal network. The way macro-social structures are related to network dynamics will be addressed in the remaining sections of this chapter.

NETWORK DYNAMICS IN SOCIETAL CONTEXT

People's behavior and the network structures around them are related to a variety of characteristics of the macro-social environment. This is particularly recognizable when the environment changes. One can think of specific periods in history that affect personal networks, like the former communist regimes creating neighborhoods of mixed social composition aimed at creating friendship between classes (Völker and Flap, 1997) or the occurrence of a natural disaster such as a flood that affected the help exchanged within networks (Tyler, 2006). Societal conditions and changes also play an influential role in determining the structure and function of personal networks. In the following, we will discuss three important changes influencing the structure of social networks.

Before doing so, it is important to acknowledge that the theoretical description of society is itself subject to wider societal changes. Theories are not just abstract statements on empirical facts and associations between phenomena, but may be viewed as a discourse (Marshall, 1999). The value of theory is that it allows us to generalize about particular cases of issues and problems that we want to understand. However, not only might the events themselves and their causes and consequences be affected by changes in the social context in which they appear but also our understanding of them is bounded by historical conditions. Theories themselves reflect the society at the time of origin and initial development (Hagestad and Dannefer, 2001).

Two theories continue to transmit powerful messages to periods that no longer correspond to their original context of Western society half a century ago: the disengagement paradigm formulated by Cumming and Henry (1961) and the modernization thesis of Cowgill and Holmes (1972). The disengagement paradigm described society withdrawing from the older person; investments in a person's human capital are discontinued because of their diminished productivity. The withdrawal is presented as mutual: people withdraw from active involvement in society just as society withdraws or 'disengages' from the individual. The disengageing process starts with a shift in self-perception, results in less contact and interaction with others, and aims to prepare the individual for the end of life. The theory reflects the societal view of old people at the time as passive, uninteresting, and uninterested in the world around them (Achenbaum, 2009; Ajrouch et al., 2007). The dominant view on late life as a phase of withdrawal has hampered a thorough analysis of the opportunities and specific characteristics of old age as it has been developing in the past decades. For example, a new third life phase has emerged between working life and late old age (Gilleard and Higgs, 2005; Laslett, 1996). In this period, good health and much free time could stimulate the extension and deepening of one's personal relationships in various ways. For example, grandparents can play a more active role in the lives of their grandchildren. Such an increased role for grandparents may be optional in some cases, but in others it may be asked for by dual-earner children or even necessitated by their problems. This is not to say that the third age is only a period full of options. As employment is one of the pillars of the welfare state, jobless people – whether they are young or old – experience a degree of exclusion from society (Offe, 2000). Furthermore, old non-working people lose contact with younger generations, and, for many, such contact is only maintained within the family context (Hagestad and Uhlenberg, 2006). The disengagement paradigm fits with a shrinking social world of older people. However, it does not allow for viewing late life in terms of an expansion in social networks or new opportunities.

The modernization thesis also predicts society withdrawing from older people, but presents this as arising purely from societal dynamics. Systemic changes associated with modernization, such as urbanization, the increased rate of social change, and cultural changes, appear to make older people redundant, forcing them back into the realm of family life, where they also experience a degree of isolation. This thesis of exclusion matches the general concern with the effects of social change on the family in postwar societies. Although the theory has been challenged by empirical findings, the idea of older people being 'abandoned' continues to inform the study of family life (Aboderin, 2004). The perception that older people suffer from a lack of meaningful contacts remains widespread in research and public debate (Tornstam, 2007).

In terms of network dynamics, both theories depict older adults as increasingly isolated from their direct personal environment and broader social structures. Both see societal requirements as a cause of this isolation, with the disengagement paradigm stressing the voluntary side, and the modernization thesis focusing on the unintended and undesirable aspects. This socially induced change puts older people in a dependent exchange position in their relationships, and is accompanied by active withdrawal from a broad range of personal relationships. In the following we will point to some recent societal developments relevant to the size, composition, and content of personal networks. Three areas of societal developments can be distinguished that have continued relevance for network dynamics: changing family structures, the emergence of welfare states, and the weakening of the geographical foundation of networks. Based on empirical data, we counter the biased interpretation of changes in these areas as contributing to detachment from social relationships in late life.

Changing family structures

As highlighted in Chapter 6, one of the most profound and dramatic demographic changes that Western societies has witnessed during the 20th century has been the ageing of the population. It has resulted in both longer years of linked lives between generations and longer lives as grandparents, parents, and children than ever before in human history (see Chapter 14). At the same time, birth rates have decreased in many Western countries, lowering the number of siblings, children, and extended kin such as aunts, uncles, nieces, and nephews. Developments such as increasing divorce rates in the final decades of the 20th century have also affected family structures in many Western countries (Chambers et al., 2009).

In many countries, however, these developments have not yet led to a dramatic decrease in the number of kin available to current generations of older people compared to some decades ago. The rate of decline in birth rates has varied considerably across Western countries with, for example, an early start in Italy and a late start in Ireland and the Netherlands where birth rates are still relatively high. Childlessness has decreased from the generations born in the beginning of the 20th century up to generations born in 1950 in many countries – a change which will be visible among later generations (Rowland, 2007). Divorce primarily affects intergenerational relationships of fathers, but they remarry more often than divorced mothers and relationships with stepchildren might begin to replace those with biological children (Lye, 1996; van der Pas and van Tilburg, 2010).

Moreover, at least within the limits of Western family structures, family life may not be all that susceptible to social change. Silverstein et al. (1998) contrasted parent–child relationships among very old parents in rural Wales to those of parents in the urbanized United States; these were taken to represent two stages of modernization. Contrary to expectations, relatively few differences were observed. There were more geographically close relationships among the Welsh parents and the contact frequency was higher, but there were no differences observed in the amount of support exchanged. A British study comparing networks of older people across a period of around 50 years concluded that children still represented a major part of the social networks of older people (Phillipson et al., 2001). Vollenwyder et al. (2002) compared changes in contact frequency between older people and their families in two Swiss surveys carried out in 1979 and 1994. Despite a decrease in proximity of children, they observed an increase in contact across cohorts, which can partly be explained by structural factors, such as a decline in family size and improvements in means of communication. Van der Pas et al. (2007) examined relationships of young-old parents and their adult children over two successive cohorts in the Netherlands. Parents of the later cohort had more contact and support exchanges with their children than the earlier cohort, revealing that families have not declined in importance.

The results of these studies revealed that, as concluded earlier by Troll (1971), the level of intergenerational contact has not substantially declined in the second half of the previous century. If intergenerational contact has changed at all, it appears to be toward an improvement in the quality of contact. The intergenerational relationship remains at the heart of the family and is an important source of contact and support (see Chapters 13 and 14).

The emergence of welfare states

Beside the impact of demographic changes on current generations of older people, the emergence of welfare systems has affected families' traditional functions, shifting responsibility from the family and personal network to a public solidarity system. One of the core issues in mid-20th century sociology (e.g., Litwak and Szelenyi, 1969) has been concern about the possible detrimental effects of modern welfare states on informal solidarity. The so-called 'crowding out' hypothesis states that within welfare states increased levels of services provided to citizens lead to substitution effects: citizens will decrease their own efforts to provide services (Abrams and Schitz, 1978). Alternative interpretations of the relation between government action and actions by citizens have been put forward. First, the 'crowding in' effect assumes that if the state donates more, the citizen will also increase his donation. For example, Künemund and Rein (1999) used a central concept from social exchange theory to understand the relation between the actions of a government and the actions of an individual. Exchange relationships assume reciprocity between giving and receiving. If the state gives to an individual, his position will be strengthened and he, for his part, will have the possibility to give to other citizens. According to the reciprocity concept, a citizen who receives will want to give back. The individual in need will thus be supported in two ways: namely, by the state and by the citizen. Secondly, there is the possibility that donations by the citizen and donations by the state are entirely unrelated. The literature about intergenerational relationships assumes that there are personal motives, such as affection, intimacy, and love, as well as normative motives, such as filial responsibility expectations,

which induce children to provide care to their parents independent of other sources of aid (Künemund and Rein, 1999). Finally, Kohli (1999) observed that the emergence of state welfare ruled out financial support from adult children to their parents, but he disputed the idea that this damaged intergenerational support. In contrast, the intergenerational flow of resources continues, but by means of monetary transfers and bequests from older people to their children. Kohli suggests in fact that public old-age security has enabled new links between family generations.

Various types of welfare states have been compared according to the degree to which citizens give to individuals in need. Motel-Klingebiel et al. (2005), in one such study, used cross-national data to examine differences in the informal help and formal help given to old persons in various countries having different types of welfare states. After elimination of a number of personal characteristics, there appeared to be substantial differences in the degree to which elderly people receive formal help. Compared to Germany, a conservative-corporatist regime, much more formal help is given in social-democratic Norway, while far less formal help is given in Mediterranean Spain. The researchers did not find such differences for help given by the family. The researchers concluded that 'crowding out' does not occur. We have to add that this evidence pertains to a period in which welfare states were expanding. In such a situation, assistance from family members does not appear to come under direct pressure.

We conclude that the emergence of welfare states, in particular those within Europe with a high level of help provided by the state, did not directly affect informal support systems. Both systems appear to have their own dynamics, while care provided by the state supplements rather than replaces help given by family or other personal network members. At the end of the 20th century, welfare state provisions in Europe and the United States were reduced in accordance with the assumption that this would lead to increased private and informal help. In these more individualized societies, people with few material and social resources are under high pressure to ensure that their needs are met. We return to this issue in the next section of this chapter.

Geographical disembedding of networks

There is a continuous debate within the social sciences regarding the apparent decline of local communities in urbanized society – aptly called the 'community question' (Wellman, 1979).

'*Community lost*' arguments point to the disintegration of local communities due to increased residential mobility, leading to instability in local relationships. Rather than focus on relationships in the neighborhood, people have geographically dispersed networks and they exchange support mainly with non-local network members. According to '*community saved*' arguments, close local communities continue to exist in urban settings, especially in lower-class neighborhoods where relatives and friends live at close distance and where there is intense exchange of support between all people involved. Wellman (1979) showed that in metropolitan Toronto the most common type of community could be termed 'liberated': people do have local ties, but these ties are of limited importance because people focus more on relationships outside the neighborhood for support and socializing. Moreover, Wellman argued that neighborhood or shared location could no longer be seen as a priori context for community. In his view, communities are personalized, consisting of individuals' personal networks. The members of these 'personal communities' can be located anywhere, as their common denominator is not the neighborhood, but their tie to the focal person, or anchor, in the network. In this sense, local communities have been lost for many people.

The geographical dispersion of personal networks is recognized in various studies, although empirical tests of the assumed network loss for older adults are scarce. We have already pointed to research that reported on the dispersion of families. McPherson et al. (2006) analyzed the size of discussion networks, i.e., the number of people who have someone to talk to about matters that are important to them, in 1985 and 2004. Among adults of various age categories there was a relatively large loss of discussion partners, and the largest losses were observed among network members from the community and neighborhood. Instability of neighbor relationships has also been demonstrated among older adults (Martire et al., 1999). However, this does not imply a general decay of local communities, or a special vulnerability of older adults to neighborhood change. Krause (2006) found no direct effect of neighborhood deterioration on support received by older adults. More generally, Ajrouch et al. (2007) analyzed cohort changes on the basis of three nationally representative samples in the United States. Based on data from 1957, 1976, and 1992 there was no evidence for a decrease in contact among people aged 65 or older. Middle-aged people, however, had low levels of contact. The decrease in contact among this age category over successive cohorts might be explained by the increase in multiple roles and the amount of time middle-aged people spent in each role.

In sum, it appears that the geographic disembedding of networks has had some impact upon personal networks. Many local communities disappeared and the immediate environment acquired less significance as a foundation of personalties. However, social life within a local context remains alive for many older people and personal relationships are initiated and maintained within this context.

SOCIETAL CHANGES IN RELATIONSHIPS: A REASSESSMENT

Available empirical evidence does not point to an unequivocal loss of network availability for older adults in contemporary developed societies, nor to any other straightforward social loss in later life. This may be seen as a refutation of the modernization and disengagement interpretations of relationships in later life. At the same time, we have observed societal-induced changes in personal relationships. In order to understand the social processes that are currently affecting networks in late life, and to gain insight in the direction these networks will be taking in the near future, we propose to look at network dynamics from the perspective of 'accentuated modernization', a perspective developed for personal relationships by Allan (2001) and for later life by Phillipson and Biggs (1998), Gilleard and Higgs (2005), and Leach et al. (2008).

Rather than discard the significance of the three processes described in the previous section for personal networks in late life, or reject the relevance of modernization, we argue that these are major manifestations of what Giddens (1990) termed 'de-traditionalization', and Beck (1992) called 'individualization'. Although not identical (Beck et al., 1994), both point to the loss of constraining power from traditional social structures and communities. Traditional forms of bonding, including postwar welfare states, both protected and constrained people. They protected people because social relationships were naturally available from occupying more specific roles such as family member, employee, or neighbor. For example, being a family member consequentially resulted in social relationships with family members. These relationships were structured and constrained by familial norms and prescribed behaviors. Deviation could lead to eviction from the family. As an example, one might consider the situation of a gay person. Coming out could be evaluated as contrary to usual family life, resulting in losing kin relationships. The same would probably occur in his or her community-based network (church, neighborhood). In a de-traditionalized situation, the gay person might develop a network fitting with his or her own preferences, and not be bound to the dominant norms of a traditional community.

However, this leaves an individual somewhat alone in the management of his or her life. The implied liberation from traditional bonds has a downside in the potential shortage of resources to accomplish this task. Bauman (2000) describes this new phase of modernity as 'liquid', pointing especially to the disconnection between macro-social and structural constraints on the one hand, and individual experience on the other. The social constraints governing behavior escape individual control, as with health hazards or economic prospects. A traditional situation where constraining agencies were generally nearby and visible has been replaced by constraining agencies on a higher level such as ethnic diversity in a neighborhood, or, as in our earlier example, covert discrimination by employers or insurance companies. Protection from surrounding structures, such as family, church, or associations, is no longer given. This fluidity of the social context leaves individuals with a fundamental incapability to realize their own autonomy.

This type of modernization continues to affect personal networks. Indeed, personal relationships increasingly become the focal point of these developments, as other more structurally embedded social bonds become fluid. According to Allan (2001), the significance of friendship and other informal relationships has increased rather than decreased because of the more fragmented and less predictable social life people are leading in modern societies. The more individualized identities and biographies, giving individuals a greater scope beyond traditional social structures, increase the complexity of subjectivities and lifestyles (Giddens, 1991).

Whereas in the past personal relationships may have been perceived as both obligatory and rigid, they have transformed over time so that while personal relationships are still perceived as critically important, they are now likely to be thought of as both more flexible and voluntary. Close ties involve more options and a flexibility of roles that may be perceived as less binding. Network structures are now more diffuse and less certain. Structural constraints on the formation of networks persist; work and income, for example, condition the opportunities to find and maintain relationships. But the association between social positions and network structure becomes more complex, and many personalized contradictions are also articulated in personal relationships. The latter is the most obvious in women's responsibilities in informal care for younger and older relatives: the systemic, and often contradictory,

demands for caregivers and employees appear in the lives of women as personal choice between work and family.

From this viewpoint of accentuated modernization we can now return to the three developments discussed in the previous section (i.e., changes in families, welfare states, and geographical disembedding), and re-evaluate their impact on network dynamics for current and future older adults.

Changing family structures revisited

We concluded that the changed family structures had not created a decline in the importance of the family. However, the loosening of the structural basis of the personal network will almost certainly affect family networks. More complex family structures are becoming visible, and are less reliant upon traditional rules of belonging. Higher rates of re-partnering after a first union create a variety of stepfamilies. Riley (1983) referred to this new family structure as a 'matrix of latent relationships,' a network potential that can be activated when appropriate. An increasing proportion of older adults have experienced diverse marital transitions, which have affected the availability and structure of their kinship networks. Remarriage or re-partnering, particularly when parents have both biological and stepchildren, creates a new family structure where family norms and obligations are less clearly defined and understood than in first-marriage families. Intergenerational relationships are increasingly diverse and are embedded in changed family structures (Bengtson et al., 2003). These new structures have predominantly been created since the 1970s among middle-aged people – people who will become the next generation of older people.

The changing demographics of families resulted in increasing insecurity about the content of these relationships. The smaller number of children, the disappearance of co-residence, and the emergence of stepfamilies contribute to increasing uncertainty as to whether a child is available for frequent contact and the exchange of support. For example, it will not be obvious that the stepchild takes the role of biological children when the step-parent becomes more dependent and needs care (van der Pas, and van Tilburg, 2010). Whether stepchildren will provide help and care will not specifically depend on their role as child, but on the shared history, the personal investments made within the relationship, and the contact that was built it will be shaped in the context of normative expectations within the peer group or within society in general. Our thesis is that it will be increasingly unpredictable from the existence of specific family relationships whether essential functions in the daily lives of older people will be fulfilled. People who have material, personal, and social resources are well equipped to cope with this uncertainty. However, new and complex family structures prevail more among economically, personally, or socially vulnerable people like divorced people and single parents.

Changes in the welfare state revisited

We discussed whether the emergence of welfare states has eroded primary functions of personal networks in the exchange of support. The personal responsibility in the context of welfare state arrangements has been a feature of research (Beck et al., 1994). The reshuffling of public and private responsibilities may have two major consequences for personal networks.

First, there will be a stronger emphasis on personal responsibility to initiate and maintain personal networks as a form of social capital. This emphasis on the utility of personal relationships may be at odds with the increasing emotional expectations of personal relationships. Personal relationships are increasingly directed toward intimacy, personal fulfillment, and support. Receiving help, and also providing help, is not obvious; rather, reciprocity of help is maintained as part of the relationship's history. With the weakening of traditional institutions it will be less certain that the needs of the individual will be met within the broader personal network. The traditional social structure directed to mutual instrumental help, which has disappeared, did fit better with a reduced level of governmental welfare provision than does the contemporary and foreseen individualized behavior directed on intimacy, personal fulfillment, and emotional support. People who are vulnerable in any respect might fall victim under the new social conditions in contemporary welfare states.

Secondly, the increasing reliance on individual responsibility may lead to a decrease of welfare state support to older adults as a category (Gilleard and Higgs, 2005; Walker, 2000). Instead, individual life-course management may come at the basis of welfare policy, making individuals responsible for providing for their needs in late life, through insurances, prophylaxis, and, again, personal network management. At the same time, basic social economic and health inequalities continue to persist throughout the life course and even increase with age (Chappell and Penning, 2005; Dannefer, 2003). The basic capacities needed to manage one's own life and deal with an increasingly complex environment are unequally distributed, often along social class distinctions, which again puts

older adults at risk of becoming victims of modernization – not because of their advanced age, but because of the invisibility of structural inequalities among age peers. Thus, withdrawal of the welfare state may amplify basic social class differences over the life course, by boosting the process of cumulative advantage–disadvantage (Dannefer, 2003; Polivka, 2000).

Geographical disembedding of networks revisited

Strongly related to the loosening of the role-based character of personal relationships is the loosening of the geographical basis of relationships. With increasing mobility, networks have transformed from being part of local communities to virtual communities. In a globalizing world many relationships are not maintained on a local but on a personal basis. However, there are also signs of localization. Some studies on embeddedness of people, in particular from the working class, have revealed stable patterns of social life rooted in place. Wellman (2002) distinguishes between the more traditional networks consisting of fellow members of the few groups to which people belong, networked individualism with permeable boundaries, and 'glocalized' networks based upon shared interests, with clusters of individuals rooted in shared kinship and locality. Among future older generations, not all traditional networks will disappear. Across individual time, people's lives will often be a mixture of both types of networks. Phillipson (2007) points to inequalities that are involved in these network types as a consequence of globalization: whereas some older adults (the 'elected') profit from new means for occupying an ever larger world, others (the 'excluded') become prisoners of their local communities, often bereft of resources to influence their direct environment.

CONCLUSIONS

For the study of network dynamics in later life we identified three different perspectives: changes in roles and transitions in later life; the changes in the expected returns from relationships within the network; and individual proactive management of personal relationships. The first perspective embraces the idea that transitions in life trigger changes in the personal network. Many of these transitions were role-based. The perspective emphasizes that networks in old age on the one hand reflect the transitions in previous life stages and on the other hand are guided to a lesser extent by role expectations. In this context we discussed a number of developments. Since networks are decreasingly guided and constrained by roles, our expectation is that there will be more variety and less predictability in responses to life transitions.

The emergence of a third life phase in which older people continue to have strong physical and cognitive capacities has consequences for the exchange perspective. Gerontology has already changed from a view of older people as predominantly dependent on the support received from other people to a view in which the giving of support is important as well. However, in current and future times many older people will be able to be predominantly providers of support up to high ages. Investments in personal relationships increase in order to enjoy life and to increase the meaning of old age. Older people will start new activities and initiate new social relationships. Moreover, they will have the intention and capacities to develop these relationships into members of the personal network. When these people arrive at the fourth phase of life they may profit from these investments, which may temper the deterioration of network relationships due to increasing incapacities.

The guiding idea within the third perspective is that individuals are motivated to develop and maintain emotional engagement within personal relationships. A selective shrinking in network size with age is predicted because older people disengage from peripheral and role-guided relationships. In this chapter we argued that people in any phase of their life will stress the importance of emotional engagement and that personal networks will move away from being derived from someone's position in society. It is no longer the limited time horizon of older adults that causes this development. Thereby, the structure and functions of older adults' personal network will be increasingly similar to that of people of younger ages.

The developments we described only partially touch the contemporary cohorts of older people. Role- and locally-based networks will continue to be important in the lives of many older people. One reason for this might be that not all members of these cohorts were and will be equipped by socialization or training to develop and maintain networks separate from roles and locality. A more important reason, however, is that many personal relationships were initiated within the context of roles and locality and may fulfill the needs of people in old age.

Cohorts of older adults born around World War II will be markers of a transformation to late modernity. In a sociological sense, a new generation emerged that set a new and distinct course through adult life (Gilleard and Higgs, 2005; Leach et al., 2008). Raised in a historical period characterized by traditional patterns, they matured in the 1960s and 1970s when modern patterns were not yet common and developed. In many respects, these cohorts were increasingly expected, amongst others urged by the following generation of their children, to transform personal networks into a modern fashion. These generations will enter old age in the decades to come.

Our expectations signify a change in structural embeddedness of people's network. Where popular and also scientific descriptions often emphasize the loss of embeddedness, we have stressed the changed character of embeddedness. Our main thesis is a weakening of role guidance in networks and an increase in the personalization of networks, contributing to greater diversity among older adults. Empirically, we have recognized a number of developments that fit with this perspective. However, it is less easy to predict the persistence or the speed of such developments among future generations of older people. Empirical evidence on developments in earlier phases of life among adults current in midlife is missing; we therefore do not know how these generations will enter old age. Moreover, the entrance into old age might disrupt or strengthen the proposed developments among these generations. A second source of uncertainty about persistence or speed of the indicated developments among older adults is the lack of guidance from the perspective of accentuated modernization. Central in this perspective is the loss of constraining power from traditional social structures. The increased personalization of networks, however, is not at all a sign of the absence of structural constraints, leading to a situation where a person is fully free to develop a network that fits with his or her needs. Rather, it will be a situation in which a specific configuration of socially structured situations produces specific boundaries of choices with respect to someone's personal network. Which configurations are important is an important topic for future research.

REFERENCES

Aboderin, I. (2004) 'Modernisation and ageing theory revisited: current explanations of recent developing world and historical Western shifts in material family support for older people', *Ageing and Society*, 24: 29–50.

Abrams, B.A. and Schitz, M.D. (1978) 'The "crowding-out" effect of governmental transfers on private charitable contributions', *Public Choice*, 33: 29–39.

Achenbaum, A. (2009) 'A metahistorical perspective on theories of aging', in V.L. Bengston, D. Gans, N. Putney and M. Silverstein (eds), *Handbook of Theories of Aging*, 2nd edn. New York: Springer, pp. 25–38.

Adams, R.G. and Allan, G. (1998) *Placing Friendship in Context*. Cambridge, MA: Cambridge University Press.

Ajrouch, K.J., Akiyama, H., and Antonucci, T.C. (2007) 'Cohort differences in social relations among the elderly', in H.-W. Wahl, C. Tesch-Römer, and A. Hoff (eds), *New Dynamics in Old Age: Individual, Environmental, and Societal Perspectives*. Amityville, NY: Baywood, pp. 43–63.

Allan, G. (2001) 'Personal relationships in late modernity', *Personal Relationships*, 8: 325–39.

Bauman, Z. (2000) *Liquid Modernity*. Cambridge: Polity.

Beck, U. (1992) *Risk Society: Towards a New Modernity*. London: SAGE.

Beck, U., Giddens, A., and Lash, S. (1994) *Reflexive Modernization: Politics, Tradition and Aesthetics in the Modern Social Order*. Cambridge: Polity.

Bengtson, V.L., Lowenstein, A., Putney, N.M., and Gans, D. (2003) 'Global aging and the challenge to families', in V.L. Bengtson and A. Lowenstein (eds), *Global Aging and Challenges to Families*. Hawthorne, NY: Aldine de Gruyter, pp. 143–58.

Berkman, L.F. and Syme, S.L. (1979) 'Social networks, host resistance, and mortality: a nine-year follow-up study of Alameda County residents', *American Journal of Epidemiology*, 109: 186–204.

Blau, P.M. (1964) *Exchange and Power in Social Life*. New York: Wiley.

Broese van Groenou, M.I. and van Tilburg, T.G. (2007) 'Network analysis', in J.E. Birren (ed.), *Encyclopedia of Gerontology, Vol. 2, Age, Aging, and the Aged*. San Diego, CA: Elsevier, pp. 242–50.

Caplan, G. (1974) *Support Systems and Community Mental Health*. New York: Behavioral Publications.

Carstensen, L.L. (1992) 'Social and emotional patterns in adulthood: support for socioemotional selectivity theory', *Psychology and Aging*, 7: 331–8.

Chambers, P., Allen, G., Phillipson, C., and Ray, M. (2009) *Family Practices and Later Life*. Bristol: Policy Press.

Chappell, N.L. and Penning, M.J. (2005) 'Family caregivers: increasing demands in the context of 21st-century globalization?', in M.L. Johnson and V.L. Bengtson (eds), *The Cambridge Handbook of Age and Ageing*. Cambridge, UK: Cambridge University Press, pp. 455–62.

Cowgill, D.O. and Holmes, L.D. (1972) *Aging and Modernization*. New York: Appleton-Century-Crofts.

Cumming, E. and Henry, W.E. (1961) *Growing Old: The Process of Disengagement*. New York: Basic Books.

Dannefer, D. (2003) 'Cumulative advantage/disadvantage and the life course: cross-fertilizing age and social science theory', *Journal of Gerontology*, 58: 327–37.

Entwisle, B., Faust, K., Rindfuss, R.R., and Kaneda, T. (2007) 'Networks and contexts: variation in the structure of social ties', *American Journal of Sociology*, 112: 1495–533.

Fischer, C.S., Jackson, R.M., Stueve, C.A., et al. (1977) *Networks and Places: Social Relations in the Urban Setting*. New York: Free Press.

Giddens, A. (1990) *The Consequences of Modernity*. Cambridge: Polity.

Giddens, A. (1991) *Modernity and Self-identity*. Cambridge: Polity.

Gilleard, C. and Higgs, P. (2005) *Contexts of Aging: Class, Cohort, and Community*. Cambridge: Polity.

Gouldner, A.W. (1960) 'The norm of reciprocity: a preliminary statement', *American Sociological Review*, 25: 161–79.

Hagestad, G.O. and Dannefer, D. (2001) 'Concepts and theories of aging: beyond microfication in social science approaches', in R. Binstock and L. George (eds), *Handbook of Aging and the Social Sciences*. San Diego, CA: Academic Press, pp. 3–21.

Hagestad, G.O. and Uhlenberg, P. (2006) 'Should we be concerned about age segregation? Some theoretical and empirical explorations', *Research on Aging*, 28: 638–53.

Hall, A. and Wellman, B. (1985) 'Social networks and social support', in S. Cohen and S.L. Syme (eds), *Social Support and Health*. Orlando, FL: Academic Press, pp. 23–41.

House, J.S. and Kahn, R.C. (1985) 'Measures and concepts of social support', in S. Cohen and S.L. Syme (eds), *Social Support and Health*. Orlando, FL: Academic Press, pp. 83–108.

Kahn, R.L. and Antonucci, T.C. (1980) 'Convoys over the life course: attachment, roles, and social support', *Life Span Development*, 3: 235–86.

Knipscheer, C.P.M., Dykstra, P.A., de Jong Gierveld, J., and van Tilburg, T.G. (1995) 'Living arrangements and social networks as interlocking mediating structures', in C.P.M. Knipscheer, J. de Jong Gierveld, T.G. van Tilburg, and P.A. Dykstra (eds), *Living Arrangements and Social Networks of Older Adults*. Amsterdam: VU University Press, pp. 1–14.

Kohli, M. (1999) 'Private and public transfers between generations: linking the family and the state', *European Societies*, 1: 81–104.

Krause, N. (2006) 'Neighborhood deterioration, social skills, and social relationships in late life', *International Journal of Aging and Human Development*, 62: 185–207.

Künemund, H. and Rein, M. (1999) 'There is more to receiving than needing: theoretical arguments and empirical explorations of crowding in and crowding out', *Ageing and Society*, 19: 93–121.

Laslett, P. (1996) *A Fresh Map of Life: The Emergence of the Third Age*. London: Macmillan.

Leach, R., Phillipson, C., Biggs, S., and Money, A-M. (2008) 'Sociological perspectives on the baby boomers: an exploration of social change'. *Quality in Ageing*, 9(4): 19–26.

Litwak, E. and Szelenyi, I. (1969) 'Primary groups structures and their functions: kin, neighbours, and friends', *American Sociological Review*, 34: 465–81.

Lowenthal, M.F. and Robinson, B. (1976) 'Social networks and isolation', in R.H. Binstock and E. Shanas (eds), *Handbook of Aging and the Social Sciences*. New York: Van Nostrand Reinhold, pp. 432–56.

Lye, D.N. (1996) 'Adult child–parent relationships', *Annual Review of Sociology*, 22: 79–102.

Marshall, V.W. (1999) 'Analyzing social theories of aging', in V.L. Bengtson and K.W. Schaie (eds), *Handbook of Theories of Aging*. New York: Springer, pp. 434–55.

Martire, L.M., Schulz, R., Mittelmark, M.B., and Newsom, J.T. (1999) 'Stability and change in older adults' social contact and social support: the Cardiovascular Health Study', *Journal of Gerontology*, 54B: S302–11.

McPherson, M., Smith-Lovin, L., and Brashears, M.E. (2006) 'Social isolation in America: changes in core discussion networks over two decades', *American Sociological Review*, 71: 353–75.

Motel-Klingebiel, A., Tesch-Roemer, C., and von Kondratowitz, H.J. (2005) 'Welfare states do not crowd out the family: evidence for mixed responsibility from comparative analyses', *Ageing and Society*, 25: 863–82.

Offe, C. (2000) 'The German welfare state: principles, performance and prospects after unification', *Thesis Eleven*, 63: 11–37.

Phillipson, C. (2004) 'Social networks and social support in later life', in C. Phillipson, G. Allan, and D. Morgan (eds), *Social Networks and Social Exclusion: Sociological and Policy Perspectives*. Aldershot: Ashgate.

Phillipson, C. (2007) 'The "elected" and the "excluded": sociological perspectives on the experience of place and community in old age', *Ageing and Society*, 27: 321–42.

Phillipson, C. and Biggs, S. (1998) 'Modernity and identity: themes and perspectives in the study of older adults', *Journal of Aging and Identity*, 3: 11–23.

Phillipson, C., Bernard, M., Phillips, J., and Ogg, J. (2001) *The Family and Community Life of Older People: Household Composition and Social Networks in Three Urban Areas*. London: Routledge.

Polivka, L. (2000) 'Postmodern aging and the loss of meaning', *Journal of Aging and Identity*, 5: 225–35.

Riley, M.W. (1983) 'The family in an aging society: a matrix of latent relationships', *Journal of Family Issues*, 4: 439–454.

Rosow, I. (1967) *Social Integration of the Aged*. New York: Free Press.

Rowland, D.T. (2007) 'Historical trends in childlessness', *Journal of Family Issues*, 28: 1311–37.

Silverstein, M., Burholt, V., Wenger, G.C., and Bengtson, V.L. (1998) 'Parent–child relations among very old parents in Wales and the United States: a test of modernization theory', *Journal of Aging Studies*, 12: 387–409.

Thomése, G.C.F., van Tilburg, T.G., and Knipscheer, C.P.M. (2003) 'Continuation of exchange with neighbors in later life: the importance of the neighborhood context', *Personal Relationships*, 10: 535–50.

Thomése, G.C.F., van Tilburg, T.G., Broese van Groenou, M.I., and Knipscheer, C.P.M. (2005) 'Network dynamics in later life', in M.L. Johnson and V.L. Bengtson (eds), *The Cambridge Handbook of Age and Ageing*. Cambridge, UK: Cambridge University Press, pp. 463–8.

Tornstam, L. (2007) 'Stereotypes of old people persist: a Swedish "facts on aging quiz" in a 23-year comparative perspective', *International Journal of Ageing and Later Life*, 2: 33–59.

Troll, L.E. (1971) 'The family of later life: a decade review', *Journal of Marriage and the Family*, 33: 263–90.

Tyler, K.A. (2006) 'The impact of support received and support provision on changes in perceived social support among older adults', *International Journal of Aging and Human Development*, 62: 21–38.

van der Pas, S. and van Tilburg, T.G. (2010) 'The influence of family structure on the contact between older parents and their adult biological children and stepchildren in the Netherlands', *Journal of Gerontology. Social Sciences* (in press)

van der Pas, S., van Tilburg, T.G., and Knipscheer, C.P.M. (2007) 'Changes in contact and support within intergenerational relationships in the Netherlands: a cohort and time-sequential perspective', in T. Owens and J.J. Suitor (eds), *Advances in Life Course Research, Vol. 12, Interpersonal Relations across the Life Course*. London: Elsevier, pp. 243–74.

van Tilburg, T.G. (1998) 'Losing and gaining in old age: changes in personal network size and social support in a four-year longitudinal study', *Journal of Gerontology*, 53B: S313–23.

Völker, B. and Flap, H. (1997) 'The comrades' belief: intended and unintended consequences of communism for neighbourhood relations in the former GDR', *European Sociological Review*, 13: 241–65.

Vollenwyder, N., Bickel, J.F., Lalive d'Epinay, C.J.L., and Maystre, C. (2002) 'The elderly and their families, 1979–94: changing networks and relationships', *Current Sociology*, 50: 263–80.

Walker, A. (2000) 'Public policy and the construction of old age in Europe', *The Gerontologist*, 40: 304–8.

Wellman, B. (1979) 'The community question: the intimate networks of East Yorkers', *American Journal of Sociology*, 84: 1201–31.

Wellman, B. (2002) 'Little boxes, glocalization, and networked individualism', in M. Tanabe, P. van den Besselaar, and T. Ishida (eds), *Digital Cities*. Berlin: Springer, pp. 10–25.

17

Lesbian, Gay, Bisexual, and Transgender Ageing: Shattering Myths, Capturing Lives

Dana Rosenfeld

INTRODUCTION

Lesbian, gay, bisexual, and transgender (LGBT) ageing is a new area of investigation and a new phenomenon. Over the last century, same-sex relations were constructed, regulated, and experienced in vastly different ways. From the 'invention' of the modern homosexual (Foucault, 1990; Plummer, 1981) to the criminalization, medicalization, and demedicalization[1] (Conrad and Schneider, 1992) of homosexuality, to the creation of the 'liberated gay man and lesbian' in the 1960s and 1970s and of 'queers' in the 1990s, sexual and gender minorities have come of age in vastly different cultures with distinctive, historically specific discourses of the sexual self. Same-sex relations also operate in different socio-political contexts that make possible, constrain, and, often, sanction sexual expression and relations. Consequently, 'being gay' – and being 'an old gay' – in one era has very different implications for self, identity, social networks, financial status, and the like, than doing so in another.

The same, of course, can be said of any group: race, gender, class, and parenthood are historically as well as situationally shaped, and the lessons learned and actions taken at any point in the life course, corresponding to a particular era, have consequences that dynamically unfold throughout that life course and into old age. But LGB elders underwent perhaps the most radical reformulation of self during their lifetime of any group of people

over the last century, coming of age during, or directly after, the rise of a postwar homosexual subculture that reinvented itself into a politicized community in response to repressive actions from the medical and state enterprises (D'Emilio, 1983; Johnson, 2003). Galvanized by the Stonewall uprising of 1969[2] and by the gay liberation and lesbian-feminist movements that followed (Duberman, 1994), the homosexual subculture was claimed, and reshaped, by an identity-politics movement that rejected the stigmatization of homosexuality and constructed disclosure of homosexuality, or 'coming out', as politically authentic, morally mandated, and mentally healthy (Bernstein, 1997; Valocchi, 1999). In their middle and later years, LGB elders experienced the ravages of HIV/AIDS, and the rise of an AIDS movement that introduced a new radical queer politics, visibility, and identity (Seidman, 1988). Finally, they saw a strong and well-funded LGBT community work to revoke anti-sodomy legislation and to secure legal recognition for same-sex civil partnerships. Homosexuality is now a political, as well as a 'purely' sexual, concept, entwined in identity politics, 'sexual citizenship' (Bell and Binnie, 2000), and debates over entitlements, marriage, and health and nursing care. LGBT ageing, then, is less an ahistorical instance of sexuality in later life than it is a complex field in which the historically, culturally, and socially contingent nature of homosexual identity and life is a central feature. This makes LGBT ageing both an important topic in its own right and a window onto the impact of social change on later life, particularly in the areas of self and identity, social relations and networks, and, given the uncertain legal status of same-sex relationships, citizenship entitlements and their impact on care provision.

Indeed, as de Vries and Blando (2004) argue, studies of LGB ageing provide an opportunity to expand the conceptual remit of social gerontology beyond its traditional, if tacit, reliance upon a heterosexual vision of social arrangements, identities, and concerns that are not only inapplicable to homosexuals but are becoming less applicable to heterosexuals as well. Examples cited by de Vries and Blando (2004) are how communities mourn the loss of large numbers of their members, political action as generative moves, and friendship networks functioning as alternative families, and/ or providing sociality, support, and care (see also Dorfman et al., 1995; Muraco et al., 2008).

Scholarship on LGBT ageing is just as historically situated as is the phenomenon itself. The former began in the early 1970s, when gerontology had been established for a generation and, significantly, when the gay-liberationist discourse of homosexuality was ascending. This research argues that LGB elders experience ageing in a unique way, due to the challenges to self of having come of age in a particularly oppressive environment; the reaction of heterosexuals to their homosexuality, both over the course of their own lives (affecting self-concept and mental well-being) and in the context of medicine and care; the systematic denial to homosexuals of such entitlements as legal marriage and survivor benefits; and ageism within the LGB community. Thus, the literature is driven by a concern with distinctive needs, and/or universal needs (e.g., for financial security in old age) that are filtered through distinctive circumstances.

This has been explored through two broad frames. The first is a more 'sociological' concern with the lived experience of homosexuality in later life (e.g., support networks, and stigma and its management). Less common, but more theoretically informed, sociological research considers generational and cohort effects on homosexual self, identity, and everyday life in old age. The second is a more policy-oriented concern with the heterosexism embedded in the provision of services and resources for elders (e.g., biases in nursing homes and in partner and survivor benefits, pensions, and social security).

This chapter will first identify some methodological difficulties associated with studying LGB populations in general and LGB elders in particular. The chapter then critically reviews the social-gerontological research into LGB ageing. It traces this scholarship's evolution from an early concern with successful ageing, life satisfaction, and social networks to an exploration of social worlds and of generational and life-course influences on later life, on the one hand, and a more policy-oriented concern with political economies and the provision of citizenship-based resources in later life, on the other. The chapter then reviews research into social arrangements among LGB elders. This research empirically questioned the distinction between friends and biological family, recognizing that homosexuals are increasingly treating friends *as* family. It also uncovered a more complex picture of social and family relations across the homosexual life course than had originally been imagined, with many self-identified homosexuals having been heterosexually married earlier in their lives, and parenting throughout their middle and later years.

The chapter then considers the focus by policy-oriented research on the failure by government and related agencies (taking the example of the United States) to grant homosexual partnerships the same status, and thus the same financial and legal benefits, as they grant heterosexual marriage. The impacts of this failure on financial security (e.g., through pensions, social security, and tax relief) and on the provision of health and nursing care in later life are explored by this strain of research, which is also concerned with discriminatory attitudes and practices within nursing and healthcare settings. Finally, after briefly summarizing the relatively sparse literature into transgendered elders and their distinctive life histories and needs, the chapter concludes with a summation of key points, a deeper consideration of the strengths and limitations of the literature into LGBT ageing (e.g., its generally Western focus and its limiting reliance on self-identified lesbians and gay men, small samples, and interviewing rather than observational methods), and a linking of research into LGBT ageing with research into the ageing of other groups.

'IDENTIFYING' AND 'MEASURING' 'HOMOSEXUAL ELDERS'

Studies of LGB ageing often criticize the failure of national surveys to include a question on sexual orientation (census data-collection instruments used in Australia, the United States, New Zealand, and Canada have recently included a measure for 'same-sex household'). But this critique assumes a stable, essential, and measurable distinction between homosexuality and heterosexuality. This distinction is problematic, as it tacitly assumes that thoughts or fantasies about homosexuality necessarily translate to homosexual relations, and that those who engage in them inevitably identify as homosexual. In fact, long-standing empirical studies (Weinberg, 1978) have shown, and theoretical scholarship (see, e.g., Butler, 1990; Sedgwick, 1990) has demonstrated, that sexual identity is much more complex than this distinction assumes, as the category 'homosexual' is the product of reifying diverse sexual desires and practices according to a homo/heterosexual binary that is more of a heuristic device than a 'true' representation of the actual practices and identifications in which actors engage. As Weston (1997) notes, it is difficult to secure a representative sample of a population whose criteria for inclusion are unclear. Thus, LGB ageing scholarship invariably studies those who are willing to identify themselves as homosexual to researchers as well as to self. Indeed, most LGB research focuses on self-identified informants gathered from gay community centers or places where LGB persons gather openly, and this has resulted in samples that over-represent White, urban, and middle-class informants (Barker, 2004). This may obscure the very process of sexual identification, exclude those engaging in same-sex ideations and practices without identifying as lesbian or gay, elide the existence of same-sex practices among the 'heterosexual' elderly, and construct certain social arrangements and self-concepts as unique to self-identified homosexuals. Ironically, LGB ageing research may limit the recognition of diversity while trumpeting its celebration.

This becomes even more complex when we consider the bisexual population, which is notoriously difficult to study because once a bisexual person 'falls in love he or she sometimes begins to identify ... as lesbian, gay, or heterosexual and thus becomes invisible as a bisexual person' (Dworkin, 2006: 36). From a data-collection perspective, this problem is exacerbated by the fact that there are limited community settings in which bisexuals can socialize *as* bisexuals, and by the fact that fellowship with lesbian or gay organizations may (a) shift, depending upon the relationship the person is in at the time, and (b) be discouraged by the LG community's own 'bi-phobia'. Perhaps as a result, 'Despite the politically correct addition of a B for bisexuality to most LG writing, there [is little scholarship on] bisexual elders' (Dworkin 2006: 36); indeed, some of the statements in Dworkin's chapter, devoted to filling the gaps in the literature on bisexual ageing, are based upon extrapolations from findings on lesbian elders.

That said, the presumed demographics of LGB ageing are worthy of note. Recent estimates of the number of LGB elders in the United States, for example, range from one to three million, depending upon whether one accepts 3 or 8 as the percentage of homosexuals in the population, the latter representing Fischer's (1972) heavily

relied-upon interpretation of Kinsey et al.'s seminal findings 'that 37 per cent of men and 20 per cent of women had at least one sexual experience with someone of the same sex since puberty, while 13 per cent of men and 7 per cent of women had more homosexual than heterosexual experiences' (Cahill et al., 2000: 7). Given the provisos noted above, that the percentage of the population found to 'be' homosexual varies widely – from 1 to over 10 per cent – is not surprising; nonetheless, it is clear that as the elder population grows, and barring any significant change in whether, and how, humans identify as LGB across the life course, so too will the LGB elder population. However, given our changing sexual culture, and historical shifts in the social and psychological consequences of identifying as homosexual, it is likely that these percentages will wax and wane over time. Moreover, it is still unclear how likely a person is to identify as homosexual or bisexual at different points in the life course, so that predicting the future number, and proportion, of LGB elders becomes problematic. Finally, as research in this area is increasingly emphasizing, counting LGB elders does little, in and of itself, to capture their lived experiences, as sexuality, sexual identity, and the lifelong consequences of decisions made around these are filtered through the same range of factors that affect heterosexual ageing: family structure and relations, socioeconomic status, health, gender, ethnicity, housing, caring arrangements, and the like.

THE LIVES OF LGB ELDERS: NEEDS, WORLDS, AND PROBLEMS

The first wave: myth-shattering, life satisfaction, and the closet

The first wave of LGB ageing research, almost exclusively US-based, combined the gay liberationist approach to lesbian and gay identity with social gerontology's concern with 'successful ageing', social networks and integration, and the 'crisis of role loss'. These early studies had limited theoretical perspectives, small sample sizes, and a primarily psychosocial and network-driven focus on the young-old, even middle-aged, while failing to recognize 'the influence of economic, material, physical, social and cultural factors' (Heaphy et al., 2004: 884) on the LGB ageing experience. But they also laid the foundation for a later, more considered use of generational and life-course theory, and for an appreciation of the complex social worlds and needs of LGB elders.

Prior to the 1970s, homosexuality was consistently portrayed as dangerous and unhealthy, particularly for older people. Kelly (1977) was the first to empirically question the assumption that homosexuals would age badly, isolated from gay culture on the one hand and from family support on the other, showing that gay men were less isolated, and had higher life satisfaction, than had been assumed. This seminal work was followed by that of such scholars as Kimmel (1978), Friend (1980), and Berger (1980, 1982a, 1982b) who studied gay men, Minnigerode and Adleman (1978), who studied LG elders, and Kehoe (1986, 1988) and Raphael and Robinson (1981), who studied older lesbians (for a review of this early literature, see Cruikshank, 1991; Lee, 1987) to find that these elders, who had entered later life before, or on the heels of, gay liberation, were functioning well, many were in long-term relationships, and, as Berger showed in 1982, their mental health was no worse than that of their heterosexual counterparts (see also Dorfman et al., 1995).

Given the prevailing assumption that a closeted existence was a dispiriting one, this was both surprising and welcome news. The gay liberationist and lesbian-feminist movements of the early 1970s had radically changed the lives of gay men and women, particularly in the United States. But they also grounded the division by gay liberationist and feminist scholarship of the homosexual 'population' into 'in' or 'out' of the closet, and its assumption of isolation and 'internalized homophobia' among the 'closeted'. Indeed, much of this literature assumes that the decision by many lesbian and gay elders to keep their sexuality private was rooted in fear of reprisal rather than a moral stance regarding privacy and sexuality (see Rosenfeld, 1999, 2003a, 2003b), and this produced a tacit equation of disclosure of homosexuality with positive LGB ageing that was only explicitly challenged by Lee in the late 1980s.

Berger (1982a) had found that those who disclosed their homosexuality to others had higher life satisfaction. But Lee (1987) found that his 47 gay male subjects, aged 50 and above, whom he interviewed between 1980–84, experienced 'the closet' as a source of security rather than shame, and that they were contented in later life not because they had developed what Kimmel (1978: 117) had termed 'crisis competence'.[3] Rather, they were contented because they had managed to avoid stressful events in the first place, including that of disclosing their homosexuality or of having had it discovered. Passing as heterosexual was thus not a source of shame, as claimed by gay liberationist ideologies (and scholarship), but of pride – moreover, the security these informants attributed to the closet was, they felt, threatened by younger gay liberationist men (see also Vacha, 1985). Gay liberation,

then, created generational tensions within the gay male community of the late 1960s and early 1970s (these tensions continue in later life, and among lesbians as well – see Rosenfeld, 2003a, 2003b), rather than providing an escape from a purportedly oppressive 'closet' existence. However, the younger generation of gay liberationist men (which Grube [1990] termed 'the settlers') that was calling upon Grube's (1990) older 'natives' to live a more public gay life had not come of age in an era in which disclosing one's homosexuality invariably incurred penalties, and in which being closeted offered protection from them. As a result, to this younger generation, the closet was oppressive and would provide fewer benefits in old age.

Thus, the differences between Berger's and Lee's findings centered on the age and generation of their samples, a point made by Adelman (1991), who wrote that Lee's sample included more men aged 60 and over (who were born, therefore, before 1927) than did Berger's 1982 study. Since those whom Lee interviewed constituted the last generation of gay elders to have lived most of their lives before the Stonewall uprising, they would have experienced, and witnessed, the disclosure of homosexuality to others as traumatic in a historical context that negatively sanctioned homosexuality. Berger's informants, however, would have experienced or witnessed this disclosure as a more benign, even positive, experience. Adelman went on to historicize her own findings – that among her sample of LG elders aged 60 and above in the year 1980, those who engaged in same-sex erotic encounters before they identified as gay displayed higher life satisfaction scores, lower self-criticism, and fewer psychosomatic complaints than did those who identified before they engaged in these encounters. Rather than an ahistorical developmental phenomenon, this suggested that for this generation of gay men, postponing self-identification as gay until they had developed the effective and social skills to cope with the stigma that cohered around homosexuality in their youth was beneficial to mental health, whereas identifying as gay in such a hostile environment before they had amassed these skills was damaging to it. Here, then, we have the seeds for subsequent sociological research into LGB ageing that was sensitive to history, life course, and generation.

Generational and cohort effects

The generation gap between liberationists and those who came of age and/or identified as lesbian or gay in the pre-liberation era, however, is more complex than the above-mentioned argument suggests. First, as Adelman (1986) and Lee (1989) noted, this gap was less pronounced among lesbians than it was among gay men, with lesbians benefiting from a feminist and, later, lesbian-feminist movement that provided a cross-generational ideology through which to construct a lesbian identity, and brought previously self-identified heterosexual women into a movement offering lesbianism as a political solution to patriarchal oppression. The implications of these politicized lesbian identities for community involvement were noted by Raphael and Robinson as early as 1980, when they found that feminist lesbian elders were more active in organizations, more likely to be single, and more interested in collective living than were their non-feminist counterparts. In 1988, they built on Mina Meyers' 1979 research that distinguished between those who began living as lesbians early in life and those 'late-blooming' lesbians who often did so through feminism and lesbian-feminism. The latter group had formed relationships with kin and friends before they identified as lesbian – indeed, many had been heterosexually married and entered lesbian life with children – whereas the 'long-timers' had formed their adult relationships as lesbians, and thus entered later life with vastly different friendship and family networks than did the 'late bloomers'.

Secondly, the shifting discursive context inspired by gay liberation and lesbian-feminism intersects with the agentic process of homosexual identification, which can occur at virtually any point in the life course, to produce a field in which the type of homosexual identity one adopts can be relatively independent of birth cohort and generation – indeed, can create intra- rather than intergenerational tensions. This makes a strict reliance upon birth cohort or generation when gauging homosexual identities, and their impact on later life, somewhat limiting. Consider Stein's 1997 book that explored the identities and social worlds of two 'lesbian cohorts' (the baby-boom, feminist one born between 1945 and 1961 and who identified as lesbian between the late 1960s and the late 1970s, and the 1990s generation, born 1961–71), to uncover markedly different understandings of sexual identity (the older cohort held a more stable, traditionally feminist understanding, while the younger one championed a more fluid, 'queer' identity). This demonstrated the importance of the historical era in which her informants came of age for sexual identity and sexual politics, but did so by embracing the static division between birth cohorts, which relies on year of birth as the primary influence, typical of most life-course and generational studies. Similarly, Robinson (2008) interviewed 80 gay men evenly spread across three age cohorts (aged 60+, 40–59, and 22–39), conforming to three periods of gay history (the 'camp' era of 1940 to the late 1960s, the 'gay period'

of the late 1960s to mid 1980s, and the 'post-liberation period' of the mid 1980s to the early 2000s). Robinson chose these periods to 'outline the context in which the men grew up, reached social maturity and came out (or did not come out) so as to understand what if any variations existed within and between the cohorts and if these affected the members' lives as gay men' (Robinson 2008: 12). This approach was similar to Stein (1997) in treating the birth cohort as a proxy for a range of practices surrounding identifying as a homosexual and for the experience of living as a homosexual during key periods of personal development.

Compare this with Rosenfeld's (1999, 2003a, 2009) research, which documented a more complex intersection between historical period, generation, and sexual identity. Her 35 informants (self-identified gay men and women born before 1930) had all come of age before the advent of gay liberation and lesbian-feminism, and most had identified as homosexual before 1969 (the historical dividing line between pre- and post-gay liberationist society), but a small minority had identified as such after 1969, and thus through the parameters of the gay liberationist, or 'accrediting', discourse of homosexuality. Most, then, had adopted stigmatized ('discreditable') identities, while the smaller group adopted liberationist ('accredited') ones. The discourses that provided these identities defined the nature of homosexuality (a stigmatizing aspect of self, or an accrediting essential self), its consequences for self (stigmatizing or accrediting), and standards for appropriate action (pass as heterosexual when in the company of heterosexuals in the interests of self-preservation and sexual decorum, or disclose one's homosexuality to heterosexual and homosexual others in the interests of social reform and personal pride). These definitions and prescriptions continued to shape social relations and self-concept in later life. Rosenfeld terms those who identified in an historical era with its own distinctive discourse of identity 'identity cohorts', thus complicating generational and life-course approaches to LGB ageing. While Stein, Robinson, and Rosenfeld demonstrate the historicity of homosexual and/or lesbian identity, and thus the significance of cohort effects for LGB ageing, Rosenfeld highlights the historical era in which actors identify as homosexual as a potentially stronger influence on sexual identity and everyday life than is birth cohort or generation.

Social arrangements

The social and relational contexts in which LGB people age were explored early on, with the LGB community discovered to host a stark youth orientation (an apparently enduring feature, at least among gay men – see Robinson, 2008), hence an abiding concern in the literature with 'accelerated ageing' (the subjective sense of being older than one actually is, or that one's counterparts consider themselves to be) among gay men. This, however, appears to be affected by gender, with Sharp (1997) linking her lesbian informants' acceptance of their ageing with their acceptance of their lesbianism. Bennett and Thompson (1991) question the validity of the concept of accelerated ageing and Quam and Whitford (1992) found that of their 80 LG informants aged 50–73, men were almost twice as likely as were women to be very accepting of the ageing process. Nonetheless, this research highlights both the distinctiveness (and gendered nature) of the gay subculture and its possible implications for self-concept in later life, and points to the importance of situating LGB ageing in its social context – here, the LGB community itself.

Mindful that LGB people would age without recourse to socially or legally legitimated marriage, LGB ageing scholars have tended to focus on relations with family and friends, particularly the question of how, if at all, LGB elders access family support and/or manage their lack of it (due to strains within the family rooted in biases against homosexuality and/or to the lack of traditional marriage and family forms, particularly children).[4] As early as 1980, Friend, along with Raphael and Robinson, found that LGB elders replaced weak or strained family ties with friendship networks. As Kimmel wrote, LGB elders live in 'self-created networks of friends, significant others, and selected biological family members that provide mutual support of various kinds, as a family system might do' (1992: 38). Indeed, Lipman (1986) suggests that homosexuals have more friends than do heterosexuals, and Robinson found that among his sample of gay men, including elders, 'friendship is their most valued effective relationship' (2008: 14). Interestingly, while family acceptance of homosexuality appears to be increasing, the significance of friendship networks as 'families of choice' (Weston, 1997) for LGB elders has endured. Grossman et al. (2000) found that 9 out of 10 of their LGB elder respondents listed friends as a primary support group, and 'that these created support networks provide 64 per cent of the emotional support for elderly gays and lesbians, 54 per cent of the practical support, 13 per cent of the financial support, and 72 per cent of the social support' (Schmitz-Bechteler, 2006: 33). There are, of course, variations among LGB elders. Dorfman et al. found that while 'lesbians receive more family support than gay men, but less than heterosexual[s]' (1995: 37), lesbians received more friend support than did gay males, but gay males received more

support did heterosexuals. Moreover, 'whereas younger couples in which the husband is bisexual tend to socialize more with other lesbian or gay couples, older couples socialize with heterosexual couples' (1995: 37), but it is difficult to know if this is due to age or to cohort effects.

That is not to say that LGB elders necessarily function entirely outside of the 'traditional' biological family, or that they do so in equal measure. While we lack statistics on LGB elders' parental status, gay parenthood appears to be increasing. Perrin et al. (2002) estimate that 1–9 million children are being raised by gay parents, but this is based upon the assumption that a certain percentage of the US parent population is LG, rather than on concrete data, and does not consider the parent's age or even generation. Relations with one's family of origin vary, and much depends upon decisions made across the life course, particularly as regards heterosexual marriage and childbearing, in which many LGB elders had engaged in their young and middle years. This was often due to a declination to identify as lesbian or gay in the pre-gay liberationist era. Moreover, as mentioned above, the feminist movement and its lesbian-feminist offshoot inspired many women to disavow their heterosexuality in pursuit of a lesbian-feminist politics, but Herdt et al.'s (1997) research suggests that women identify as lesbian after heterosexually married life more often than men regardless of the draw of feminist politics. Of their sample of 160 LGB elders, 4 per cent had been heterosexually married; the same proportion of women, and 24 per cent of the men, had had children. Although the women of both cohorts (age 45–50 and ≥51 years) had similar marriage rates, the same cohorts of men varied, with 29 per cent of the younger and 40 per cent of the older men having been married. This suggests that the rates at which gay men, but not gay women, had been heterosexually married in their earlier years are dropping over time, and this might produce a larger proportion of lesbian elders with children in the future.

These patterns implicate LGB elders' family relations, support systems, and caregiving obligations (see Cantor et al., 2004; Fredriksen, 1999), as they enter later life with varying degrees of connections, resources, and responsibilities shaped by the 'traditional' biological family (the homosexual 'baby boom' of the 1990s, during which self-identified lesbians and gay men bore within, or adopted children into, gay family networks, also has clear implications for future LGB elders). The AIDS epidemic decimated the generation of gay men about to enter later life, depleted its caregiving resources (the reader is reminded of LG persons' heavy reliance on friends-as-family noted above), and took a heavy toll on gay men, including elders and those now entering later life, who cared for them (see Brown et al. 2001).

Another crucial influence on LGB ageing is the refusal of most governments to recognize long-term same-sex relationships. Because of the dearth of large-scale data on LGB elders, we lack statistics on partnerships. We do know that, in the case of the United States, between 41 and 75 per cent live alone (Cahill et al., 2000: 96) and that 'more than one in 10 same-sex couples include a partner aged 65 years or older, and nearly one in 10 couples are comprised of two people aged 65 or older'[5] (Bennett and Gates, 2004: 1). Very few countries afford same-sex partnerships the legal and financial benefits that heterosexual couples enjoy. This grounds the current move within the United States and elsewhere to legalize gay marriage (similarly, 'next of kin' refers to blood relations or heterosexually married spouses, which means that same-sex partners are often denied hospital visitation rights or end-of-life decision-making – see Langley, 2001: 922). The hetero-normative equation of marriage with heterosexuality has policy implications for LGB ageing, as state-recognized (heterosexual) partnerships afford distinctive financial and health benefits in later life. This equation also has consequences for family structure, as states in the United States forbidding 'unmarried' couples to adopt children effectively bar homosexual couples, whose relationships are not thus recognized, from adopting (see Nasaw, 2008), and so they may face a childless old age.

POLICY ISSUES: HEALTH, ENTITLEMENTS, AND CARE

For policy-centered LGB ageing research, especially that being conducted in the United States, the most pressing issues are financial security and short- and long-term health and nursing care. This area is shaped by government policies that discriminate against same-sex couples and survivors of same-sex relationships (the United States has no federal regulation mandating that private firms grant same-sex partners the same health insurance entitlements as they grant heterosexual married couples). Surviving same-sex partners cannot receive survivor benefits from Social Security, despite they and/or their partners having paid into it during their working lives; moreover, as Cahill et al. explain:

Married spouses are eligible for Social Security spousal benefits, which can allow them to earn half their spouse's Social Security benefit if it is larger than their own ... . Unmarried partners in life-long relationships are not eligible for spousal benefits ... [and] Medicaid regulations protect the assets and homes of married spouses when the other spouse enters a nursing home or long-term care facility; no such protections are offered to same-sex partners (2000: 2).

Nor do US tax laws and pension policies recognize same-sex marriages, 'costing the surviving partner in a same-sex relationships tens of thousands of dollars a year, and possibly over $1 million during the course of a lifetime' (2000: 2; see also Knauer, 1998). To Bennett and Grant (2004: 1–3), this has implications for income (same-sex couples earn, on average, 34.7 per cent less in retirement income than do heterosexual couples (2004: 1–3), and since same-sex couples are considered strangers under the tax code, survivors of these relationships must pay taxes when they inherit a partner's retirement income). It also has consequences for housing in later life: the surviving partner of a same-sex couple is more likely to be making mortgage payments, and is at greater risk of losing his or her home, than is a heterosexual widow or widower. Moreover, 'Medicaid regulations protect the assets and homes of married spouses when the other spouse enters a nursing home or long-term care facility; no such protections are offered to same-sex partners' (Cahill and South, 2002: 2). Clearly, LGB elders' finances and housing are filtered through governmental policies, which vary across countries and states,[6] but these US examples point to the centrality of legal marriage to many entitlements that are key to physical and financial well-being in old age.

Equally significant are the attitudes, practices, and arrangements within care settings themselves, which are shaped by, not reducible to, the policies detailed above. The scant research that exists documents clear biases against LGB elders among nursing home staff and discriminatory treatment that may affect quality of care: for example, 'moving gay residents to placate others' (Gross, 2007) is apparently a common practice in nursing homes, including moves to parts of the home dedicated to 'patients with severe disabilities or dementia' (Gross, 2007). These biases and practices are often due to staff's unfamiliarity with homosexuality (Cahill and South, 2002; Cahill et al., 2000: 2). Indeed, Phillips and Marks (2006) note that hetero-normativity is built into nursing homes' intake documentation. With no empirical studies of LGB people in nursing homes (a limitation exacerbated by the failure of these settings' agents to ask about sexual identity, and by residents' fear of identifying as LGB), research in this area is hypothesized or extrapolated from data on heterosexual elders; focused on the attitudes of nursing home staff (Tolley and Ranzjin, 2006); or empirical but prospective, such as asking middle-aged and young-old LGB people about their feelings toward nursing home care (Langley, 2001) – not surprisingly, this yielded concerns about, *inter alia*, issues of disclosure (Hughes, 2004), discrimination by nursing home staff, and the marginalization of partners and friends. While, again, we know little about LGB life within aged-care settings, we can envision cohort effects shaping it in the future: as Tolley and Ranzjin note, the 'current cohort' of middle-aged homosexuals will bring their disinclination to pass as heterosexual into nursing homes when they reach old age, and this will challenge the 'heterosexism and heteronormativity in residential aged care facilities' (2006: 79). Despite this optimistic prediction, the LGB community has begun to secure nursing home care specifically for LGB seniors and to educate long-term providers in LGB issues (see Gross, 2007).

Concerns about heterosexism in nursing home settings find their counterpart in medical settings. Disclosure to healthcare providers is a core concern to gay men and women of all ages – indeed, 'the disclosure of sexual orientation has been identified as the most problematic component in consulting a health care professional or gaining access to treatment' (Brotman et al., 2002: 58). There is also some evidence that this has led LGB people, particularly seniors, to delay or avoid seeking medical advice and treatment. Perceived or imagined bias on the part of the healthcare community (which may be more distressing than the health problem in question – see Harrison, 2002: 1–2) may be a significant obstacle to good health in later life, especially given the continued risk of HIV infection and the incidence of HIV/AIDS among gay elders. Elford et al. (2008) found that HIV-positive gay men aged 50 and above reported the same incidence of engaging in unprotected sex with men as did younger HIV-positive gay men and, in 1997, Linsk wrote that gay men aged 60 and over have more multiple partners, are less likely to have a primary relationship, and find it more difficult to adopt safer sex practices than do their younger counterparts (for older gay men's experience of HIV/AIDS, see Emlet, 2006). In short, the institutionalized discrimination faced by LGB elders deprives this group of key protections and resources, highlighting the importance of sexual citizenship to well-being in later life.

TRANSGENDERED ELDERS

If there is little research into LGB ageing, there is even less on transgendered (TG) ageing, as sexual realignment surgery has only recently become relatively easily available (although it remains very costly), and most of those who underwent it in their younger years are only now beginning to enter later life. It is important to note that transgender status centers not on sexual practices or identifications (although the sexual orientation of TG persons varies), as in the case of LGB persons, but on the gender with which one identifies, and which conflicts with one's natal sex and with the ascribed gender identity that 'matches' it. TG persons, then, have an uneasy relationship with the LGB community, many of whose members do not see the former as 'truly belonging' to it. Nonetheless, TG and LG elders alike face stigma, the perceived need to 'pass', and disruptions to family and social life that take on a distinctive resonance in later life. TG persons are, like LGB elders, likely to have spent a lifetime experiencing or fearing discrimination or abuse (Balsam and D'Augelli, 2006), and face issues of disclosure or discovery similar to those voiced by them: specifically, that nursing home staff will discover their natal sex and that their quality of care will deteriorate as a result.

For TG persons, the very process of transitioning, particularly in later life, can be extremely stressful – for the reasons listed above, and for reasons revolving around medical needs and interactions. In addition to medical complications (health conditions more common in later life, i.e., cardiac or pulmonary problems, pose surgical dangers, and long-term exposure to hormones taken to transition in youth or middle age pose their own health risks as well – Witten and Eyler, 2006), TG elders face tense, even frightening, medical encounters. As Cook-Daniels (2006) details, while homosexuality has been demedicalized, transgendered persons are still subject to medical definition and control, not only because their transition requires medical interventions (hormone treatments and/or surgery) but also because they must convince medical professionals that they have a 'gender identity disorder', a process that can cause resentment, especially since the hormones that may or may not be prescribed to them are, to their minds, readily available to non-TG persons. Thus, TG persons must undergo often tense and degrading encounters with the very professionals whose help they most need; moreover, many medical professionals remain uneducated about, and/or biased toward, TG persons and their psychosocial and medical needs.

As Cook-Daniels explains, to avoid uncomfortable responses from their children and/or work colleagues, many TG persons begin to transition in later life, once they have left work or their children have left home. This may also be a cohort effect, as information about TG issues and resources are becoming increasingly available, and web-based and other support networks are growing. But for those who lived through the medical and psychiatric regulation of sexual minorities in their younger years, placing themselves in the hands of medical agents can be traumatic as well. If surgery is conducted, medical control continues afterward, since hormones must continuously be taken to sustain the transition from one sex/gender to the next. Health coverage becomes all the more important in later life, then, as, in the United States, Medicare does not cover these medications, and it becomes more difficult for TG elders to afford them, especially post-retirement. Finally, even 'routine' medical consultations raise the specter of discovery that one's natal sex does not conform to one's surface gender appearances.

CONCLUSION

The vast majority of LGB ageing research has focused on and has been conducted by scholars in North America, Great Britain, and Australia, after earlier research in the United States having laid the conceptual and theoretical foundations for developments elsewhere. This is probably because the United States witnessed a sharp break with old, stigmatized discourses of homosexuality via the rise of gay liberation and lesbian-feminism, on the heels of the Stonewall uprising of 1969, which inspired an awareness of generational tensions within the gay world and thus encouraged a sensitivity to LGB ageing. This sensitivity may also have been encouraged by the fact that the feminist movement in the United States influenced other groups more quickly than it did in other countries, thus introducing a concern with sexuality, caregiving, and intimate relations to political groups that may not have otherwise considered them as pressing social issues. While Europe's gay community was galvanized by the social movements that emerged from the Stonewall uprising of 1969, it experienced no similar demarcation between the old gay world and the new, gay-liberationist one. Studying cohort differences between LGB elders outside of the United States is thus, arguably, a murkier proposition, and this makes us mindful of how applicable, if at all, are the insights and findings of LGB ageing research. It also forces the question of how we can legitimately study LGB ageing in non-Western worlds in which the very concept of homosexuality may not (or is just beginning to) conform to the Western construction of homosexuality as a stable, unitary master status. Indeed, by examining sexual practices and identities outside of the Anglo-West, we can and, should,

appreciate the socio-historical distinctiveness of Western sexual typologies and the thought systems and actions that are built upon them.

This is not to say that research into LGB ageing in the West is sufficiently extensive or robust to ground international research in the first place. As this chapter has shown, this scholarship is, while no less inventive than other research areas in social gerontology, built on relatively thin ground. Very little research into LGB ageing is observational or ethnographic – with few exceptions (e.g., Cohler, 2004), this research relies on interviews, questionnaires, and focus groups. Clearly, observational data needs to be gathered on the experience and negotiation of age in LGB settings. More generally, samples are notoriously small (for some exceptions, see Dorfman et al., 1995; Heaphy et al., 2004; Herdt et al., 1997); tend to rely on LGB elders who are 'out', White, middle-class, and the like; often include the young-old without adequately distinguishing them from older informants; and tend to be too young overall (a weakness that we must correct before 'the old order passeth' altogether). I suggest that more insidious still is the tendency (which this chapter has, ironically, reproduced) to accept the hetero/homosexual binary (the inclusion of bisexuals notwithstanding), and thus to elide the range of sexual and social identities and relations across the life course. The emergence of more explicitly fluid sexual identities under the umbrella term 'queer' is thus not merely a phenomenon to be studied, as new generations reject or renegotiate traditional sexual taxonomies, but may be an opportunity to abandon terminologies that restrict our ability to recognize and appreciate the rich overlap between sexuality, identity, interaction, social and family forms, history, and generations.[7]

It is difficult to escape the overall question of how, if at all, LGB ageing is relevant to social gerontology other than by capturing the experiences and challenges of a relatively small population of elders. How much insight can LGB ageing provide into, for example, intergenerational relations among heterosexuals, or the provision of care in later life? Here, I point the reader to the potential, cited above, for LGB ageing research to highlight gerontology's unconscious use of heterosexist constructs of family, social support, sexuality, caregiving arrangements, and entitlements in later life. LGB ageing research, and policy moves within the LGB community itself, also underscore the increasing centrality of sexual citizenship and its link to the political economy of health and long-term care, on the one hand, and financial security in old age, on the other, not only to sexual minorities but also to elders as a whole. Finally, concerns over privacy in nursing homes – in the case of LGB elders, regarding biography, sexuality, and intimate relations – point to the perhaps growing significance of these issues to elders of all sexual preferences, although the increased move toward ageing in place may make this a less pressing issue than it is at present.

This chapter began with a brief description of the historical changes in homosexual identity and social position in the postwar era, focusing on those changes that most directly impacted the generation of LGB elders born before the war. But the next cohort of LGB elders – the baby boomers – differs from preceding ones in that it generally lacks a personal history of state oppression, or medical control, of homosexuality, and has come of age having reaped some of the benefits of gay liberation and (lesbian) feminism: the partial destigmatization, and the demedicalization and decriminalization, of homosexuality, and of sexuality in general; the reconfiguration of gender roles; and the emergence of a public, international LGB community with vast social, political, and cultural resources. LGB elders are more visible and connected, both inter- and intragenerationally, than ever before, and, along with their younger counterparts, comprise a small but recognizable voting bloc (at least, again, in the West). They also comprise the generation that has been most affected by the AIDS epidemic, and how this, along with the features mentioned above, will affect their negotiation of social, political care, and financial challenges in later life remains an open question, and one which we would do well to examine.

Finally, of course, there is the question of how younger generations of LGB persons will age in the more distant future. Western LGB youth are maturing in a world in which blended families, gay parents, and same-sex households and civil partnerships are, if not the norm, generally visible, as are 'a plethora of websites aimed specifically at LGBT youth' (Russell and Bohan 2005: 3). They are also tied into an increasingly global network of LGB persons, organizations, and communities, and more likely to come out at a young age and thus to live their lives as openly LGB (or queer) persons for the longest period of time (enjoying a level of support from friends and family almost unimaginable in previous years) than have any others before. The potential consequences of this for self, identity, and social relations in later life are immense, especially given the rapid changes in how we structure, understand, and experience sexuality, on the one hand, and in ageing and the life course, on the other. This will be reinforced by the greater complexity of intergenerational relations within the LGBT community, as differences in its generations' experiences, resources, and identities increase (Russell and Bohan, 2005). Such changes make LGB ageing at all phases of the life course a fruitful area of research for social gerontology.

NOTES

1 Homosexuality was only removed from the American Psychiatric Association's *Diagnostic and Statistical Manual of Mental Disorders* in 1973.

2 The Stonewall uprising occurred in late June of 1969, during which gay men and women resisted a police raid on a homosexual club (the Stonewall Inn) in New York's Greenwich Village. Considered the first instance of organized resistance to police harassment that had become increasingly frequent throughout the 1950s–1960s, the uprising, which spiralled into violent rioting lasting 3 days, galvanized an incipient gay rights movement, and quickly became a symbol of homosexual resistance and, later, of gay liberation itself. (See Carter, 2004; Duberman, 1994)

3 According to the crisis competence thesis, homosexuals arrived at old age with a lifelong history of handling threats to self, stigma, and the fluidity of gender that would serve them well in old age, for example, in the face of the death of a partner, whereas heterosexuals would face old age without this history and would thus find it more of a shock to self. See Friend (1991) for the related argument that the gender flexibility of gay culture affords better coping mechanisms in later life.

4 For bisexuals who 'come out' to their heterosexual spouses, family relations, including those with children, may become strained, and their marriages may end entirely.

5 'Nearly one in four same-sex couples [in the USA] include a partner 55 years or older, and nearly one in five couples are comprised of two people aged 55 or older' (Bennet and Gates 2004: 2). Heaphy et al. (2004: 886) found that of the 266 LGB elders aged 50–80 and above in their sample, 60 per cent of the women and 40 per cent of the men were in couple relationships (9 of the 61 men were in 'cross-sex relationships').

6 The United Kingdom's 2004 Civil Partnership Act grants same-sex couples the same rights as heterosexual ones, and other legal recognitions such as Denmark's 'civil unions' and The Netherlands' 'registered partnerships' bridge much, if not the entire, gap between same-sex and heterosexual couples as regards the marital rights and entitlements that exists in the United States. That said, the US social and political landscape is a fast-changing one. In December 2009, the Washington DC council legalized gay marriage in the US capital, New Hampshire legalized gay marriage in the state, following the passage of similar laws in Iowa, Vermont, Massachussets, Connecticut, and Vermont. These marriages are recognized only at the state level, given the federal Defiense of Marriage Act passed in 1996. Some other states recognize same-sex civil unions, with others (Illinois, Washington State, Maryland, and Rhode Island) 'laying the groundwork for bills in favor of same-sex marriages' (MacAskill, 2009).

7 That said, 'queer' identities are historically specific social constructions, as are the essentialized gay liberationist homosexual identities that drive current LGB policy discourse, and should no more be quickly adopted as analytic resources than other constructions.

REFERENCES

Adelman, M. (1986) *Long Time Passing: Lives of Older Lesbians*. Boston: Alyson Press.

Adelman, M. (1991) 'Stigma, gay lifestyles, and adjustment to aging: a study of later-life gay men and lesbians', *Journal of Homosexuality*, 20: 7–32.

Balsam, K.F. and D'Augelli, A.R. (2006) 'The victimization of older LGBT adults: patterns, impact, and implications for intervention', in D. Kimmel, T. Rose, and S. David (eds), *Lesbian, Gay, Bisexual and Transgender Aging: Research and Clinical Perspectives*. New York: Columbia University Press, pp. 110–30.

Barker, J.C. (2004) 'Lesbian aging', in G. Herdt and B. de Vries (eds), *Gay and Lesbian Aging: Research and Future Directions*. New York: Springer, pp. 29–72.

Bell, D. and Binnie, J. (2000) *The Sexual Citizen: Queer Politics and Beyond*. Cambridge, UK: Polity Press.

Bennett, K.C. and Thompson, N.L. (1991) 'Accelerated aging and male homosexuality', *Journal of Homosexuality*, 20(3–4): 65–75.

Bennett, L. and Gates, G.J. (2004) 'The cost of marriage inequality to gay, lesbian, and bisexual seniors: a Human Rights Campaign Foundation report', Washington, DC: Human Rights Campaign.

Berger, R.M. (1980) 'Psychological adaptation of the older homosexual male', *Journal of Homosexuality*, 5(3): 161–74.

Berger, R. (1982a) *Gay and Gray: The Older Homosexual Man*. Urbana-Champaign, IL: University of Illinois Press.

Berger, R.M. (1982b) 'The unseen minority: older gays and lesbians', *Social Work*, 29: 236–42.

Bernstein, M. (1997) 'Celebration and suppression: the strategic uses of identity by the lesbian and gay movement', *American Journal of Sociology*, 103(3): 531–65.

Brotman, S., Ryan, B., and Cormier, R. (2002) 'Mental health issues of particular groups: gay and lesbian seniors', *Writings in Gerontology: Mental Health and Aging* 2. Ottawa, ON: National Advisory Council on Aging, 55–65.

Brown, L., Alley, G., Sarosy, S., Quarto, G., and Cook, T. (2001) 'Gay men: aging well!', *Journal of Gay and Lesbian Social Services*, 13(4): 41–54.

Butler, J. (1990) *Gender Trouble: Feminism and the Subversion of Identity*. London: Routledge.

Cahill, S. and South, K. (2002) 'Policy issues affecting lesbian, gay, bisexual and transgender people in retirement', *Generations*, 26(2): 49–54.

Cahill, S., South, K., and Spade, J. (2000) *Outing Age: Public Policy Issues Affecting Gay, Lesbian, Bisexual and Transgender Elders*. Washington, DC: The Policy Institute of the National Gay and Lesbian Task Force Foundation.

Cantor, M.H., Brenna, M., and Shippy, R.A. (2004) *Caregiving Among Older Lesbian, Gay, Bisexual and Transgender New Yorkers*. Washington, DC: NGLTF Policy Institute. http://www.thetaskforce.org/downloads/Caregiving.pdf

Carter, D. (2004). *Stonewall: The Riots that Sparked the Gay Revolution*. New York: St. Martin's Press.

Cohler, B.J. (2004) 'Saturday night at the tubs: age cohort and social life at the urban gay bath', in G. Herdt and B. de Vries (eds), *Gay and Lesbian Aging: Research and Future Directions*. New York: Springer, pp. 211–34.

Conrad, P. and Schneider, J.W. (1992) *Deviance and Medicalization: From Badness to Sickness*. Philadelphia, PA: Temple University Press.

Cook-Daniels, L. (2006) 'Trans aging', in D. Kimmel, T. Rose, and S. David (eds), *Lesbian, Gay, Bisexual and Transgender Aging: Research and Clinical Perspectives*. New York: Columbia University Press, pp. 20–35.

Cruikshank, M. (1991) 'Lavender and gray: a brief survey of lesbian and gay aging studies', in J.A. Lee (ed.), *Gay Midlife and Maturity*. New York, NY: Haworth Press, pp. 77–97.

D'Emilio, J. (1983) *Sexual Politics, Sexual Communities: The Making of a Homosexual Minority in the United States*. Chicago: University of Chicago Press.

De Vries, B. and Blando, J.A. (2004) 'The study of gay and lesbian aging: lessons for social gerontology', in G. Herdt and B. de Vries (eds), *Gay and Lesbian Aging: Research and Future Directions*. New York: Springer, pp. 3–28.

Dorfman, R., Walters, K., Burke, P., et al. (1995) 'Old, sad, and alone: the myth of the aging homosexual', *Journal of Gerontological Social Work*, 24: 29–44.

Duberman, M.B. (1994) *Stonewall*. New York: Plume Books.

Dworkin, S.H. (2006) 'The aging bisexual: the invisible of the invisible minority', in D. Kimmel, T. Rose, and S. David (eds), *Lesbian, Gay, Bisexual, and Transgender Aging: Research and Clinical Perspectives*. New York: Columbia University Press, pp. 36–52.

Elford, J., Ibrahim, F., Bukutu, C., and Anderson, J. (2008) 'Over 50 and living with HIV in London', *Sexually Transmitted Infections*, 84: 468–72.

Emlet, C.A. (2006) '"You're awfully old to have *this* disease": experiences of stigma and ageism in adults 50 years and older living with HIV/AIDS', *The Gerontologist*, 46: 781–90.

Fischer, P. (1972) *The Gay Mystique: The Myth and Reality of Male Homosexuality*. New York: Stein and Day.

Foucault, M. (1990) *The History of Sexuality: An Introduction*. Toronto: Random House.

Fredriksen, K.I. (1999) 'Family caregiving responsibilities among lesbians and gay men', *Social Work*, 44(2): 142–55.

Friend, R.A. (1980) 'GAYging: adjustment and the older gay male', *Alternative Lifestyles*, 3(2): 231–48.

Friend, R.A. (1991) 'Older lesbian and gay people: a theory of successful aging', *Journal of Homosexuality*, 20: 99–118.

Gross, J. (2007) 'Aging and gay, and facing prejudice in twilight', *The New York Times*, October 9 http://www.nytimes.com/2007/10/09/us/09aged.html

Grossman, A.H., D'Augelli, A.R., and Herschberger, S.L. (2000) 'Social support networks of lesbian, gay and bisexual adults 60 years of age and older', *Journal of Gerontology: Psychological Sciences*, 55B(3): 171–9.

Grube, J. (1990) 'Natives and settlers: an ethnographic note on early interaction of older homosexual men with younger gay liberationists', *Journal of Homosexuality*, 20(3/4): 119–35.

Harrison, J. (2002) 'What are you really afraid of? Gay, lesbian, bisexual, transgender and intersex ageing, ageism, and activism', *Word is Out*, 2: 1–11.

Heaphy, B., Yip, A.K.T., and Thompson, D. (2004) 'Ageing in a non-heterosexual context', *Ageing and Society*, 24: 881–902.

Herdt, G., Beeler, J., and Rawls, T.W. (1997) 'Life course diversity among older lesbians and gay men: a study in Chicago', *Journal of Gay, Lesbian, and Bisexual Identity*, 2(3–4): 231–46.

Hughes, M. (2004) 'Privacy, sexual identity and aged care', *Australian Journal of Social Issues*, 39(4): 381–92.

Johnson, D.K. (2003) *The Lavender Scare: The Cold War Persecution of Gays and Lesbians in the Federal Government*. Chicago: University of Chicago Press.

Kehoe, M. (1986) 'Lesbians over 65: a triply invisible minority', *Journal of Homosexuality*, 12(3/4): 1139–52.

Kehoe, M. (1988) *Lesbians Over 60 Speak for Themselves*. New York: Harrington Press.

Kelly, J. (1977) 'The aging male homosexual: myth and reality', *The Gerontologist*, 17: 328–32.

Kimmel, D.C. (1978) 'Adult development and aging: a gay perspective', *Journal of Social Issues*, 34: 113–30.

Kimmel, D. (1992) 'The families of older gay men and lesbians', *Generations*, 17(3): 37–8.

Knauer, N.J. (1998) 'Heteronormativity and federal tax policy', *West Virginia Law Review*, (101): 130.

Langley, J. (2001) 'Developing anti-oppressive empowering social work practice with older lesbian women and gay men', *British Journal of Social Work*, 31: 917–32.

Lee, J.A. (1987) 'What can homosexual aging studies contribute to theories of aging?' *Journal of Homosexuality*, 13(4): 49–78.

Lee, J.A. (1989) 'Invisible men: Canada's aging homosexuals. Can they be assimilated into Canada's liberated gay communities?' *Canadian Journal of Aging*, 8(1): 79–97.

Linsk, N.L. (1997) 'Experience of old gay and bisexual men living with HIV/AIDS', *Journal of Gay, Lesbian, and Bisexual Identity*, 2: 289–90.

Lipman, A.(1986) 'Homosexual relationships', *Generations*, 10(4): 51–4.

MacAskill, E. (2009) 'Moves to legalise gay marriage in Vermont and Iowa signal cultural shift', The Guardian, April 8. http://www.guardian.co.uk/world/2009/apr/08/gay-marriage-usa

Minnigerode, F.A. and Adelman, M. (1978) 'Elderly homosexual women and men: Report on a pilot study', *The Family Coordinator*, 27(4): 451–6.

Muraco, A., LeBlanc, A.J., and Russell, S.T. (2008) 'Conceptualizations of family by older gay men', Journal of Gay and Lesbian Social Services 20(1 and 2): 69 –90.

Nasaw, D. (2008) 'US election: California narrowly approves ban on same-sex marriage', The Guardian, November 5. guardian.co.uk

Perrin, E.C. and Committee on Psychosocial Aspects of Child and Family Health (2002) 'Technical report: co-parent or second-parent adoption by same-sex parents', *Pediatrics*, 109(2): 341–4.

Phillips, J. and Marks, G. (2006) 'Coming out, coming in: How do dominant discourses around aged care facilities take into account the identities and needs of ageing lesbians?', *Gay and Lesbian Issues and Psychology Review*, 2(2): 67–77.

Plummer, K. (ed.) (1981) *The Making of the Modern Homosexual*. London: Hutchinson.

Quam, J. and Whitford, G.S. (1992) 'Adaptation and age-related expectations of older gay and lesbian adults', *The Gerontologist*, 32: 367–74.

Raphael, S.M. and Robinson, M.K. (1980) 'The older lesbian: love relationships and friendship patterns', *Alternative Lifestyles*, 3(2): 207–29.

Raphael, S.M. and Robinson, M.K. (1981) 'Lesbians and gay men in later life', *Generations*, 6(7):16–18.

Robinson, P. (2008). *The Changing World of Gay Men*. Basingtoke, UK: Palgrave Macmillan.

Rosenfeld, D. (1999) 'Identity work among lesbian and gay elderly', *Journal of Aging Studies*, 13(2): 121–44.

Rosenfeld, D. (2003a) *The Changing of the Guard: Lesbian and Gay Elders, Identity, and Social Change*. Philadelphia, PA: Temple University Press.

Rosenfeld, D. (2003b) 'Homosexual bodies in time and space: the homosexual body as a sexual signifier in lesbian and gay elders' narratives', in C. Faircloth (ed.), *Aging Bodies: Meanings and Perspectives*. Walnut Creek, CA: Alta Mira Press, pp. 171–203

Rosenfeld, D. (2009) 'Heteronormativity and homonormativity as practical and moral resources: The case of lesbian and gay elders'. *Gender & Society*, 23: 617–638.

Russell, G.M. and Bohan, J.S. (2005) 'The gay generation gap: communicating across the LGBT generational divide', *Angles: The Policy Journal of the Institute for Gay and Lesbian Strategic Studies*, 8(1): 1–8.

Schmitz-Bechteler, S. (2006) 'Those of a queer age: insights into aging in the gay and lesbian community', *Advocates Forum*. Chicago, IL: SSA/University of Chicago, pp. 26–36.

Sedgwick, E. (1990) *Epistemology of the Closet*. Berkeley, CA: University of California Press.

Seidman, S. (1988) 'Transfiguring sexual identity: AIDS and the contemporary construction of homosexuality', *Social Text*, 19/20: 187–205.

Sharp, E. (1997) 'Lesbianism and later life in an Australian sample: How does development of one affect anticipation of the other?' *Journal of Gay, Lesbian, and Bisexual Identity*, 2(3–4): 247–63.

Stein, A. (1997) *Sex and Sensibility: Stories of a Lesbian Generation*. Berkeley, CA: University of California Press.

Tolley, C. and Ranzijn, R. (2006) 'Heteronormativity amongst staff of residential aged care facilities', *Gay and Lesbian Issues and Psychology Review*, 2(2): 78–86.

Vacha, K. (1985) *Quiet Fire: Memoirs of Old Gay Men*. Trumanburg, NY: The Crossing Press.

Valocchi, S. (1999) 'Riding the crest of a protest wave? Collective action frames in the gay liberation movement, 1969–1973', *Mobilization: An International Quarterly*, 4(1): 59–73.

Weinberg, T.S. (1978) 'On "doing" and "being" gay: sexual behavior and homosexual male self-identity', *Journal of Homosexuality*, 4(2): 143–56.

Weston, K. (1997) *Families We Choose: Lesbians, Gays, Kinship*. New York: Columbia University Press.

Witten, T.M. and Eyler, A.E. (2006) 'Transgender aging: the graying of transgender', *American Public Health Association Gerontological Health Section Newsletter Winter*. http://www.apha.org/membergroups/newsletters/sectionnewsletters/geron/winter06/2560.htm

18

Friendship and Ageing

Graham Allan

INTRODUCTION

In recent years the topic of friendship has received an increasing amount of attention from social researchers. Various developments within different disciplines have fostered this, along with a renewed interest from policymakers on issues of social integration. For example, the development of social network research over the last 30 years (Scott, 2002; Wellman et al., 1988), interest in ideas about social capital (Putnam, 2000), and a growing focus on the increased fluidity of personal relationships with late modernity (Giddens, 1992; Spencer and Pahl, 2006) have all resulted in friendship ties being given greater prominence within social analysis. Similarly, from a policy perspective, increased interest in issues of social inclusion and exclusion has led to a focus on the role played by different types of informal relationships in people's lives (Phillipson et al., 2003). Within this general framework, friendships are now seen as having relevance to diverse policy matters such as informal support, physical and mental health, and neighbourhood renewal.

Interestingly, social gerontology has a longer history of involvement in friendship research than most other fields of social research. Perhaps this is not surprising given the dominant perspectives that initially helped frame the discipline. In particular, much mid-20th century research on the social conditions of older people was concerned with investigating loneliness and social isolation. Taking its lead from popular theories about family restructuring and community decline, as well as from ideas that later life inherently entailed a decline in role activity and social participation, research focused on older people's informal relationships with family, neighbours, and friends. Such classic studies as Litwak and Szelenyi (1969) and Townsend (1957)

(see also Phillipson et al., 2001) were concerned with exploring the forms of support and solidarity that existed across these different types of personal relationship. More specifically, Litwak (Litwak and Szelenyi, 1969; see also Litwak, 1985, 1989), along with Beth Hess (1972), was particularly influential in raising interest in the role that friendship played in older people's lives. Later research built on these pioneering studies in investigating older people's friendship circles, particularly with respect to later-life transitions such as widowhood, retirement, geographical mobility, and ill-health and infirmity.

This chapter will be concerned with understanding the role that friendship plays in later life. Its main argument is that friendship patterns in old age are shaped by the same set of factors that shape friendship participation in earlier life phases, with the consequence that simple models of friendship declining in later life are inappropriate. To do this it will focus first on issues concerned with the definition of friendship, including a discussion of the different elements that comprise cultural understandings of friendship. It then considers the ways in which people's sets of friendship are patterned by the circumstances of their lives and the consequences for their friendships of the changes in these circumstances over the life course. The final section considers the diversity there is in people's friendship participation in later life, paying attention particularly to the impact of gender.

THIS THING CALLED FRIENDSHIP

Numerous writers have discussed the difficulties of knowing the boundaries of friendship (e.g., Allan, 1989; Bell and Coleman, 1999; Pahl, 2000).

Most forms of relationships, such as those with family, neighbours, or colleagues, are defined on the basis of criteria that are independent of the actual quality of the relationships involved. A sibling, for example, remains a sibling whether or not the relationship is particularly active or close. The fact that someone is in one of these relationships infers almost nothing about the relationship's content. Friendship, on the other hand, is defined principally, if not wholly, in terms of the quality of the relationship those involved maintain. Though this raises few issues in everyday practice, in research terms it does generate issues around how friendship is defined. In particular, different people may have different ideas about who to include within the category 'friend'. People will have more or less extensive – narrower or broader – notions of what the relationship needs to be like to be placed in the friendship category. More importantly, the notion of friend also varies depending on the context of its use, with the boundary of friendship becoming particularly problematic in situations, such as interviews, where people are required to reflect explicitly on whether others can be categorized in this way.

As a result, it is difficult to provide a clear-cut and unambiguous definition of friendship, particularly one that would apply across different societies and subgroupings. As will be argued more fully below, the construction of friendship is inevitably influenced by a range of contextual factors that shape the organization of people's social and leisure lives. Indeed, the fact that people hold divergent views of what friendship actually comprises makes it extremely unlikely that any single definition of friendship is going to apply generally. Moreover, while it is possible for a researcher to construct a definition that he or she applies in a particular study, the general utility of such an approach is limited by the inherently subjective criteria intrinsic in the meaning of friendship. One person's idea of friendship is not necessarily mirrored in the notions others hold.

There are a number of responses social researchers have made to this definitional difficulty. One response is to focus on a narrow set of friendships, typically those with whom an individual is particularly close. Indeed, respondents in friendship research often have a notion of 'best' (or 'true' or 'real') friends that they draw on to distinguish different levels of commitment and solidarity within their friendship circles. Researchers sometimes make use of this in order to render the category 'friend' more specific, typically through asking people questions about a fixed number – usually three, four, or five – of their closest friends (Kalmijn, 2003; Pahl and Pevalin, 2005). A second response is to access friendship circles by asking questions around specific dimensions of friendship.

Researchers may, for example, ask about those non-family others that their respondents see most frequently, or those they rely on for different support, or those in whom they are most likely to confide.

A third response is for researchers to take a more global approach, asking respondents about all those others in their personal networks who are important in their lives, and then comparing the properties of the different relationships involved, including those which are categorized as friendships. An advantage of this approach is that it effectively bypasses issues of friendship definition, instead relying on the respondents' judgements of the importance of others in their networks. Once a list of relevant others has been generated, respondents can be interrogated about the properties of each tie, with the properties of concern being defined by the focus of the study. Thus, in some studies the core issue might be extent of social integration and forms of contact; in others, it might concern the relationships' exchange content; and in still others, the focus could be on change over time. A number of important gerontological studies have used this type of personal network approach, including Antonucci and Akiyama (1987); Wenger (1995); and Phillipson et al. (2001).

This chapter will take a wide perspective on friendship, as its purpose is to examine the significance of these relationships in later life rather than be concerned with particular constructions of friendship. In this regard, the focus is on what anthropologists have termed 'ties of amity' (Bell and Coleman 1999) – that is, the set of relationships that involve elements of friendship irrespective of whether the label 'friend' (or 'buddy', 'pal', 'mate', etc.) is actually applied to them (Allan, 1989). In what follows, the term 'friendship' will be used in this broad sense unless specified otherwise. While in this way not seeking to be tied to a specific definition of friendship, it is nonetheless useful to consider some of the key components or dimensions that are commonly associated with friendships. These components are not necessarily found in all ties of amity to the same degree, but they represent important elements within common understandings of friendship within Western culture, broadly defined.

DIMENSIONS OF FRIENDSHIP

The first dimension to note concerns the voluntary character of friendships. The ties are understood to be developed freely by the individuals concerned rather than being imposed by others or being consequent on particular positions within the social structure. For example, a colleague may be a friend but being a colleague does not of itself entail friendship. In this regard, friendship represents a personal rather than a social solidarity; whatever commitment exists between those who are friends is a matter of their own choosing and determination. Secondly, friendship is generally seen as a tie marked by equality: that is, within the relationship itself there is no structured hierarchy or perception of differential. Even if friends differ in terms of their social or economic location, in theory, such difference should not impinge on their personal tie of friendship. In practice, external inequalities often do create tensions within a friendship, with the result that friendship ties tend to be socially and economically homogeneous (Kalmijn and Vermunt, 2007; Smith, 2002; Ueno and Adams, 2006). Thirdly, in line with understandings of friendship being a relationship between equals, reciprocity and a balance of exchange are important elements within these ties. In other words, friendship is routinely constructed on an assumption that what one side gives or receives will be repaid in some appropriate form by the other at some future time. Normally this is implicit in the relationship, rather than involving any formal calculation. Indeed, what counts as appropriate exchange is a matter for those involved. Generally though, when there is a perceived lack of reciprocity in the relationship, the friendship will be increasingly questioned. Fourthly, and linked to this point, friendship is commonly defined as a non-instrumental relationship. This does not mean that friends do not help each other out in a range of ways depending on their circumstances. Such mutual assistance is an integral part of friendship. But friendships are non-instrumental in the sense that the solidarity between the friends is the reason for help being offered, rather than the relationship itself being sustained for any advantages that might accrue from it. If people begin to feel they are being 'used' by a friend in this way, as above the friendship is likely to fade.

Finally, because friendship is culturally understood to be a structurally 'free-floating' relationship based upon a personal solidarity, its core rationale is concerned with the enjoyment that being in the relationship generates. Typically this is manifested through sociability and sharing leisure activities. Indeed, it is through such joint sociable activities that most friendships are routinely enacted and, in the process, consolidated. In turn, too, when sociable activities cease, there is a tendency for more 'run-of-the-mill' friendships to wane. In contrast, though, some friendships are sustained despite a relative absence of explicit sociable interaction. These friendships are usually perceived as being especially strong – often they are ones people characterize as 'real' or 'true'

friendships on the grounds that a committed solidarity has continued even though there are limited opportunities for socializing.

In this, they encapsulate a rather different component of friendship, one based around ideas of intimacy and understanding rather than sociability per se. Generally, knowledge of the friend develops over time through the process of sharing a variety of personal experiences together, with different forms of sociability often acting as a vehicle for this. However, while both intimacy and sociability are key elements within friendship, the extent to which they overlap in practice varies. As mentioned, some friendships defined as highly significant continue even though there is (now) little sociable interaction, but with the relationship characterized by high degrees of perceived intimacy and knowledge of the other's 'real' self. Others are built upon more active sociability but are nonetheless seen as less personally significant because they lack this degree of intimacy and self-revelation.

While all the elements discussed above are constitutive of common understandings of friendship, it is important to emphasize that they do not represent a defining set of 'rules' of friendship as such. Rather, they provide a framework for constructing friendships, one on which people also commonly draw when deciding whether a particular relationship does or does not meet their criteria of friendship. While it is likely that any relationship that meets these criteria would be seen as falling within the realm of friendship, ties of amity can exist even when these elements are not fully in place. At this level, the only people who can determine a friendship are those directly involved. However, in examining people's patterns of friendship and understanding the role that friendship plays in their lives, these elements are of consequence. Not only do they allow us to consider differences in the ways that friendship ties are patterned but also, as importantly, they can help us interpret the impact of people's changing circumstances on the friendship networks they sustain.

THE CONTEXTS OF FRIENDSHIP

Because friendship is understood to be a personal and voluntary relationship, there is a strong tendency to view it as simply a matter of individual choice. Thus, friends not only exercise agency over who their friends are but also, as importantly, they have control over the activities and 'content' of these relationships. In this, friendship cannot be forced by others; it is a relationship over which the individual has discretion. At the same time though, it is important to recognize that friendship is not a form of relationship isolated from the broader organization of social life. Although agency plays a more evident part in friendships than in many other forms of relationship, these ties are nonetheless socially structured. Friendships do not just arise haphazardly; nor are they organized in a random way. Instead, they are embedded in social contexts that frame their performance (Allan and Adams, 2007).

Adams and Allan (1998) identified four different levels at which context influences patterns of friendship: the *personal environment* level, the *network* level, the *community* level, and the *societal* level. It is not necessary to review the details of these different levels here. What is important though is to recognize that friendships are not structurally 'free-floating' in the way contemporary friendship ideology suggests. Instead, the possibilities people have for developing and sustaining friendships are consequent upon the structural characteristics of their everyday lives. For the purposes of this chapter, this can best be seen by considering the personal environment level of context. Adams and Allan (1998: 6) define this as those 'immediate features of a person's life that affect the character and pattern of friendships that they develop and sustain [including], *inter alia*, their economic circumstances, their domestic responsibilities, their work commitments, their leisure preferences, and the like'.

There are two key issues here, both highly relevant to a consideration of friendship in later life. The first is that friendships need to be developed. Self-evidently, they do not just somehow arise independently of the activities in which individuals are involved. People need to be met and known before friendship emerges. Consequently, the opportunities people have to engage with others in settings that directly or indirectly facilitate sociability and other friendship-relevant activities are of importance. Secondly, friendships need servicing. While, as discussed above, some special friendships can be sustained despite a lack of activities, most friendship ties require some level of continuing involvement if they are to remain of consequence. Frequently such involvement is based around participation in specific organizational settings that foster interaction. In some cases, the friendship is incidental to the setting, at least formally. For example, friends who are colleagues are often able to service their friendship through informal interaction in the workplace, even though their sociability is largely supplemental to work activities. In other cases though, the rationale for participation in the setting is more evidently sociable, as for example when friends routinely organize their relationship around involvement in particular sports, hobbies, or social clubs.

As a consequence, the patterns of friendship that people sustain will be shaped in part by the ways in which their personal circumstances facilitate or discourage participation in different friendship arenas. In some instances, their personal environment will be such as to encourage the servicing of friendships; in others, it will constrain their opportunities for doing this. Most relevantly, as people's personal circumstances change across the life course so too the possibilities open to them for servicing existing friendships and developing new ones will alter. Classically of course this was recognized in disengagement theory (Cumming and Henry, 1961), which emphasized how people's social integration depended on their institutional involvement. While simpler versions of disengagement theory were rightly discredited for uncritically assuming that disengagement was intrinsic and universal as people aged, the notion that social participation is linked to structural context and not just individual agency still carries force.

We can also refer here to Antonucci and Akiyama's (1987) analysis of social convoys. The idea of this model is that it illustrates how relationships alter across time, with some becoming more significant to the core individual and others less so over the life course. In part, these shifts in the relative importance of different relationships as individuals age reflect both changes in their personal environment and the differential opportunities available to them to engage sociably with others. Importantly, with this model, there is no assumption that friendships necessarily decline in later life. For some individuals they will; for others though, later life will offer opportunities for equivalent or even fuller sociable engagement with others. New opportunities for developing and servicing friendships will emerge as ageing alters constraints that characterized their earlier personal environments.

CHANGE IN FRIENDSHIP

Thus it is likely, as the above would suggest, that people's patterns of friendship will change as they age, both in terms of the personnel of friendship and the interactions that occur. However, how they will change is not consequent on ageing alone. Rather, it is the result of the situational changes that arise across the life course – and these situational changes are not uniform across the ageing population. Rather, with the increased flexibility of late modernity in general, the experience of ageing has become more diverse than in previous eras. Of course there are still many structural constraints influencing the life chances of older people, in particularly (lifelong) class location, gender, and ethnicity. Equally though, current cohorts are experiencing greater freedom in the construction of their life course as compared with previous cohorts. Given this, friendship patterns are also likely to be somewhat more diverse, both as a consequence of the different experiences people have in their earlier lives and because later life itself will offer different opportunities for friendship participation.

It is important to recognize here that change in friendship is routine and normal. As we move through the life course, the set of people who are our friends alters. In particular, when an aspect of our status changes significantly, then it is likely that this will have an impact on our friendship networks (Kalmijn and Vermunt, 2007). This applies to a wide range of features that position us socially and economically. For example, when our familial and relational status alters – when we marry or divorce or have children, for example – this is likely to have a consequence for our friendships. Similarly, if we change job or move location, then again our friendship interactions are likely to be affected by the change. So too, if we are widowed or suffer longer-term infirmity, there is likely to be some impact on the patterns of friendship we sustain. In this regard, friendships are inherently fragile. While some – usually those regarded as 'real' or 'true' – friendships survive significant status movements on the part of one or both friends, many tend not to survive, especially over the long-run. In this regard, friendships are not characterized by the type of enduring solidarity commonly found in family relationships.

It is important to recognize the processes at play here, not least because their impact on later life phases can be significant. As noted earlier, friendship is a non-hierarchical tie. It is also a relationship in which reciprocity and balance of exchange are important. When someone's personal and social location changes, it often becomes more difficult to sustain the sense of equality and balance within their existing friendships (Allan, 1989). For example, where disparities of income arise, the individual with the fewer resources can begin to feel that he or she can no longer engage so readily on an equal basis with the other because the latter's activities now assume greater levels of consumption expenditure. Similarly, it becomes more difficult to sustain a balance to a relationship if there is significant difference in family status. Those with young children, for example, tend to socialize more with others who also have young children rather than with those who have no such responsibilities. Similarly, those who experience a separation, divorce, or widowhood often find it more difficult to sustain friendships with those still in couples. Over the time their friendship

circles come to contain more others in similar partnership/ familial circumstances to themselves.

None of this is inevitable – some friendships are unaffected by such changes. The issue is simply that the greater the difference in the individuals' structural locations, the more difficult it becomes to sustain the equality that lies at the root of friendship. Birds of a feather flock together; but, to develop this aphorism further, those with different feathers tend not to. This point has been argued well by both Hess (1972) and Jerrome (1984) who, in examining the role of that friends play in identity construction, highlight the importance of similar social and economic positions (Allan, 2001). Identifying with friends who are like you provides continuing confirmation of who you are. However, when interaction makes social distinction and difference more apparent, this can often foster social distance and a sense of not fully belonging. As a consequence, the friendship gradually becomes more problematic and over time more prone to fracture.

Furthermore, when people's social and economic status changes in significant ways, frequently their patterns of activities also tend to alter. Participation in those activities that fitted readily into their lifestyle previously, and in part helped constitute that lifestyle, may now become more problematic, or indeed may simply be replaced by somewhat different pursuits that reflect their new circumstances. As this happens, so it becomes more difficult to service those existing friendships that were based around the old activities, especially those that were structured in a way that bounded them to particular social and/or leisure settings. In these circumstances, the existing friendships are likely to become that much less active in people's timescapes, and much less central in their friendship networks. Gradually these ties are liable to ebb, as new lifestyles become established.

In this regard, it is no coincidence that in later life people are often perceived as losing friends and becoming more isolated. In particular, when the focus is on elderly people who are becoming increasingly infirm and finding it difficult to maintain previous lifestyles, a concern for friendship loss is generally appropriate (though, see Adams; 1987; Jerrome and Wenger, 1999). In addition to friendship networks shrinking through the death of others, the more difficult routine interaction becomes, the harder it is to service friendships. As already mentioned, this is less so with friendships that are particularly close, as the shared history and commitment of the relationship keeps the friendship alive despite relative lack of contact. It is those more 'run of the mill' friendships that depend on shared activities that tend to fade when interaction becomes more problematic. How this impacts on feelings of isolation and loneliness varies, though until recently friendship itself received relatively little attention from loneliness scholars. (See the special edition of the *Canadian Journal on Aging* [2004] for research on this topic.)

However, most people in later life are not in this position. They do not need additional support or find it difficult to engage with others sociably. Over time, some friendships will become less active as those involved withdraw from the contexts that facilitated, or even defined, the friendships. Retirement from employment is the classic example of this. But equally, new friendships can be developed in later life as new activities and involvements replace previous ones. Of course, the ability to develop new informal solidarities in later life depends in part on the skills and personalities of those involved. Over their lifetime some individuals become adept at engaging with others and making new friendships; others find this more difficult. Equally though, the creation of new friendships generally requires participation in social arenas that facilitate this. Accessing such arenas generally remains more difficult for older people than for those who are younger. There are more institutional supports for sociable connection – at college, in work, through parenting activities – in early adulthood than there are in later life. Nonetheless, with the growth of 'grey power', the balance here has been changing somewhat. There are now increased levels of commercial and other provision facilitating social participation in later life, especially for those with greater affluence (Leach et al., 2008).

FRIENDSHIP PARTICIPATION IN LATER LIFE

There have been a number of studies that have been concerned with the size of older adults' friendship networks, though the results are somewhat inconclusive. Perhaps such variation is to be expected given the difficulties there are in defining and measuring friendship and the diversity there is in people's social circumstances and personal experiences. However, it is evident from these different studies that friendship remains a significant relationship in older adults' lives (Dugan and Kivett, 1998; Jerrome and Wenger, 1999; Kalmijn, 2003). There are fewer studies that examine change in the numbers of friendships across the life course. Some research, like Kalmijn's (2003) study of friendship in the Netherlands, indicates that the number of friends people have alters systematically as they age: 'The older the people are, the fewer friends and the fewer friendship contacts they report.' (Kalmijn, 2003: 247). Other research,

however, suggests that it is only in very late life that friendship numbers decline, emphasizing instead the extent to which new friendships replace ties that have become less active (Adams, 1987; Jerrome and Wenger, 1999).

Jerrome and Wenger's (1999) study is particularly interesting. This research reports findings from the Bangor Longitudinal Study of Ageing, data for which was first collected in 1979 from people then aged over 65. Further data was collected from surviving respondents in 1983, 1987, 1991, and 1995. The focus of the research was on people's support networks as they aged. At each stage, respondents were asked about their (self-defined) real friends and the part they played within their support networks. This provided rich material on the way that the respondents' friendship networks altered as they aged. A key finding from this study is that while respondents certainly lost a number of their friends over the 16 years of the study, many also developed new friendships across the period. The authors provide numerous case examples to illustrate this, emphasizing a pattern of change and replacement rather than simple decline in friendship networks with increasing age.

Many of the losses in the friendship networks on which Jerrome and Wenger (1999) report were consequent on factors that lay outside their respondents' control. They stemmed, for example, from increasing levels of infirmity and reduced mobility, from one or other party's geographical mobility (including in some cases relocation to care homes), from the need to provide increased care for a spouse, and of course from their friends' passing away. But equally, many of the respondents demonstrated agency in the construction of their later-life friendship networks. This was evident in the strategies of friendship replacement that they developed in response to the circumstantial demise of existing friendships. Significantly, for these elderly respondents, the processes through which new friendships emerged as existing ones waned frequently mirrored the unexceptional ebb and flow of friendship ties in earlier phases of the life course (Allan, 1989; Allan and Adams, 2007). As among younger cohorts, some friendships develop from new contacts that people have made, perhaps through participation in new social settings. But other friendships emerge from the strengthening of pre-existing ties (with, for example, neighbours, fellow Church worshippers, or old school friends) that had previously not been framed within the realm of friendship (Jerrome and Wenger, 1999: 671).

Other research has examined gender differences in later-life friendship networks, though again there is a good deal of variation in their findings. Hatch and Bulcroft's (1992) research on retired people in the United States found that older men in their sample had more friends than older women. Other research has reached quite different conclusions. Field and Minkler (1988), for example, found that men aged 65 had fewer friends than women of this age, a differential that widened as people aged further. On the basis of a longitudinal study over a 14-year period, Field (1999) also reports that, as they age, older women were more successful than older men at making new friendships. However, any generalization over these issues is problematic, even if there could be agreement over what constituted friendship. As argued above, patterns of friendship are not wholly shaped by such variables as age or gender in themselves. What matters is how such factors as these differentially structure the opportunities open to people to engage sociably with others, thereby facilitating the servicing of existing friendships and the generation of new ones.

Inevitably these opportunities will vary depending on people's individual circumstances and personality characteristics. Adams and Ueno (2006) discuss how, over time, people establish different modes of relating – what Adams and Ueno term different 'interactive motifs' – which shape their friendship (and other) interactions (see also Adams and Blieszner, 1994). Gender is of consequence within these interactive motifs. The ways in which people's masculinities and femininities have been developed over the life course will continue to have an impact in later life. For example, Wright's (Wright, 1982; Wright and Scanlon, 1991) broad argument that men's friendships tend to be 'side-by-side' while women's are more 'face-to-face' continues to apply to the ways in which people construct and manage their friendships in later life. What Wright is indicating here is the tendency for men's friendships to involve a greater focus on activities of different types, whereas women's friendships tend to be built more around expressivity and self-disclosure. In later life, these same tendencies are apparent, with women drawing more on their (female) friends for emotional and social support than men do with their (male) friends.

This is not meant to indicate a complete gender divergence in later-life friendships; the differences that exist are tendencies rather than absolutes. Both men and women draw on their friends in a variety of ways: for sociability, shared activities, and different forms of support. Similarly, both women and men, in later life as well as earlier in the life course, use their friends to discuss issues of personal consequence to them. The point though is that women do seem more ready than men to confide in their friends and discuss more personal issues. Such disclosure is clearly linked to the dominant gender division of labour inside and outside the home. In particular, women's common positioning as 'relational experts' within the family sphere across all life phases fosters higher levels of discussion of relational issues. In this regard, women often draw on their friends as a ready resource for talking about and working through the contingencies, whether mundane or exceptional, of their everyday lives. These tendencies in the willingness to talk with and confide in friends are found across the life course. As in earlier phases, in later life men are less likely than women to frame their friendships in a manner that embraces such personal disclosure. (For discussions of friendship and confiding in later life, see Ha, 2008; Wenger and Jerrome, 1999).

While many aspects of friendship behaviour in later life represent continuities of earlier patterns, there is some evidence to suggest that friendships between men and women become more common, especially in widowhood. Jerrome and Wenger (1999: 671), for example, report that 'a striking feature of late-life friendship is the tendency to cross gender boundaries'. Akiyama et al. (1996) found that this was particularly the case for older men. Some of these cross-gender friendships stem from couple relationships where both individuals have been widowed. Others are new friendships or relationships developed from previous ties that had not been defined as friendships. It would appear that in late old age, gender homophily matters less than in earlier life phases, perhaps because issues of sexual boundaries become of reduced consequence or perhaps simply because the pool of potential friends is significantly reduced through death and infirmity. Somewhat similarly, it appears that age homophily in friendship also becomes less marked in later old age, with people reporting some friendships with others who are significantly younger than they are (Adams, 1987; Jerrome and Wenger, 1999).

CONCLUSION

This chapter has been concerned with understandings of friendship in later life. Its aim has been to provide a broad discussion of some of the ways in which friendship patterns are structured by the circumstances of people's lives. It has argued that though friendship is often perceived culturally as a matter of personal choice, the opportunities there are for developing and sustaining friendships are shaped at least in part by the circumstances and personal environments of people's lives. This applies in old age just as much as it does in earlier life phases.

As a consequence, there is diversity in the friend-ships people sustain as they age and in their ability to develop new ties as existing friendships become less active for whatever reason. It is important to recognize that change in friendship circles is a rou-tine feature of these relationships. Some friendships are of course sustained over many years, sometimes despite there being little face-to-face interaction. Other friendships are less enduring. They are active for a while, then gradually become less significant in people's lives as their personal environments alter and make sociable interaction between the friends more difficult. This does not indicate that these relationships were unimportant. It is simply a consequence of the way in which friendship is patterned and socially constructed.

The importance of this for this chapter is that these processes occur in later life. Some friend-ships are sustained as people age; others are not. As people's circumstances alter in the later phases of the life course, the informal ties they maintain with others will also alter. This is not a simple process of friendship decline, as some everyday under-standings of ageing suggest. Later life may also offer opportunities for increased involvement with others, especially when there is more time avail-able for leisure and sufficient material resources for participation in different forms of sociable activity. Of course, individuals also have different friend-ship 'motifs', and, in particular, different skills and abilities for making friends – skills and abilities that have been developed and honed in different ways over their life-course experiences.

The consequence is that friendship patterns in later life are quite diverse. Further diversity is added as a result of the uncertainties of the life course itself. Although these have not been discussed in this chapter, such events as retirement, widowhood, and one's own or one's partner's/spouse's incapac-ity through illness or infirmity all carry potential consequences for patterns of social participation and friendship. Moreover, as Antonucci's convoy model (Antonucci and Akiyama, 1987) captures so well, patterns of friendship need to be understood within the context of the set of informal relation-ships in which people are involved. In particular, different family relationships, obligations, and responsibilities can, in diverse ways, influence the resources individuals choose to make available for friendship. (See for example Wenger's [1995] typology of personal networks.)

REFERENCES

Adams, R.G. (1987) 'Patterns of network change: a longitudinal study of friendships of elderly women', *The Gerontologist*, 27: 222–7.

Adams, R.G. and Allan, G. (1998) 'Contextualising friendship', in R.G. Adams and G. Allan (eds), *Placing Friendship in Context*. Cambridge: Cambridge University Press, pp. 1–17.

Adams, R.G. and Blieszner, R. (1994) 'An integrative concep-tual framework for friendship research', *Journal of Social and Personal Relationships*, 11: 163–84.

Adams, R.G. and Ueno, K. (2006) 'Middle-aged and older adult men's friendships', in V.H. Bedford and B.F. Turner (eds), *Men in Relationships: A New Look From a Life Course Perspective*. New York: Springer, pp. 103–24.

Akiyama, H., Elliott, K., and Antonucci, T.C. (1996) 'Same-sex and cross-sex relationships', *Journals of Gerontology Series B: Psychological Sciences and Social Sciences*, 51: 374–82.

Allan, G. (1989) *Friendship: Developing a Sociological Perspective*. Hemel Hempstead: Harvester Wheatsheaf.

Allan, G. (2001) 'Personal relationships in late modernity', *Personal Relationships*, 8: 325–39.

Allan, G. and Adams, R.G. (2007) 'The sociology of friend-ship', in C. Bryant and D. Peck (eds), *21st Century Sociology: A Reference Handbook*. Thousand Oaks, CA: SAGE, pp. 123–31.

Antonucci, T.C. and Akiyama, H. (1987) 'Social networks in adult life: a preliminary examination of the convoy model', *Journal of Gerontology*, 4: 519–27.

Bell, S. and Coleman, S. (1999) *The Anthropology of Friendship*. Oxford: Berg.

Canadian Journal on Aging (2004) Special issue on social isolation and loneliness, 23(2): 107–88.

Cumming, E. and Henry, W. (1961) *Growing Old: The Process of Disengagement*. New York: Basic Books.

Dugan, E. and Kivett, V.R. (1998) 'Implementing the Adams and Blieszner conceptual model: predicting interactive friendship processes of older adults', *Journal of Social and Personal Relationships*, 15: 607–22.

Field, D. (1999) 'Continuity and change in friendships in advanced old age: findings from the Berkeley Older Generation Study', *International Journal of Aging and Human Development*, 48: 325–46.

Field, D. and Minkler, M. (1988) 'Continuity and change in social support between young-old and old-old or very-old age', *Journals of Gerontology Series B: Psychological Sciences and Social Sciences*, 100–6.

Giddens, A. (1992) *The Transformation of Intimacy*. Cambridge, UK: Polity Press.

Ha, J.-H. (2008) 'Changes in support from confidants, children, and friends following widowhood', *Journal of Marriage and Family*, 70: 306–18.

Hatch, L.R. and Bulcroft, K. (1992) 'Contact with friends in later life: disentangling the effects of gender and marital status', *Journal of Marriage and the Family*, 54: 222–32.

Hess, B. (1972) 'Friendship', in M.W. Riley and A. Foner (eds), *Aging and Society*. New York: Russell Sage, pp. 357–93.

Jerrome, D. (1984) 'Good company: the sociological implica-tions of friendship', *Sociological Review*, 32: 696–718.

Jerrome, D. and Wenger, G.C. (1999) 'Stability and change in late-life friendships', *Ageing and Society*, 19: 661–76.

Kalmijn, M. (2003) 'Shared friendship networks and the life course: an analysis of survey data on married and cohabit-ing couples', *Social Networks*, 25: 231–49.

Kalmijn, M. and Vermunt, J. (2007) 'Homogeneity of social networks by age and marital status: a multilevel analysis of ego-centered networks', *Social Networks*, 29: 25–43.

Leach, R., Phillipson, C., Biggs, S., and Money, A-M (2008) 'Sociological perspectives on the baby boomers: an exploration of social change', *Quality in Ageing*, 9(4): 19–26.

Litwak, E. (1985) *Helping the Elderly: The Complementary Roles of Informal Networks and Formal Systems*. New York: Guilford Press.

Litwak, E. (1989) 'Forms of friendship among older people in an industrial society', in R.G. Adams and R. Blieszner (eds), *Older Adult Friendship: Structure and Process*. Newbury Park, CA: SAGE, pp. 65–88.

Litwak, E. and Szelenyi, I. (1969) 'Primary group structures and their functions', *American Sociological Review*, 34: 465–81.

Pahl, R. (2000) *On Friendship*. Cambridge, UK: Polity.

Pahl, R. and Pevalin, D. (2005) 'Between family and friends: a longitudinal study of friendship choice', *British Journal of Sociology*, 56: 433–50.

Phillipson, C., Bernard, M., Phillips, J., and Ogg, J. (2001) *The Family and Community Life of Older People*. London: Routledge.

Phillipson, C., Morgan, D., and Allan, G. (2003) *Social Networks and Social Exclusion: Sociological and Policy Perspectives*. Aldershot, UK: Ashgate.

Putnam, R. (2000) *Bowling Alone: The Collapse and Revival of American Community*. New York: Simon and Schuster.

Scott, J. (2002) *Social Networks: Critical Concepts in Sociology*, Vol.1. London: Taylor and Francis.

Smith, T.W. (2002) 'Measuring inter-racial friendships', *Social Science Research*, 31: 576–93.

Spencer, L. and Pahl, R. (2006) *Rethinking Friendship: Hidden Solidarities Today*. Princeton: Princeton University Press.

Townsend, P. (1957) *The Family Life of Old People*. London: Routledge and Kegan Paul.

Ueno, K. and Adams, R.G. (2006) 'Adult friendship: a decade review', in P. Noller and J. Feeney (eds), *Close Relationships: Functions, Forms and Processes*. New York: Psychology Press, pp. 151–69.

Wellman, B., Carrington, P., and Hall, A. (1988) 'Networks as personal communities', in B. Wellman and S.D. Berkowitz (eds), *Social Structures: A Network Analysis*. Cambridge: Cambridge University Press.

Wenger, G.C. (1995) 'As comparison of urban with rural support networks: Liverpool and North Wales', *Ageing and Society*, 15: 59–81.

Wenger, G.C. and Jerrome, D. (1999) 'Change and stability in confidant relationships: findings from the Bangor Longitudinal Study of Ageing', *Journal of Aging Studies*, 13: 269–94.

Wright, P.H. (1982) 'Men's friendships, women's friendships and the alleged inferiority of the latter', *Sex Roles*, 8: 1–20.

Wright, P.H. and Scanlon, M.B. (1991) 'Gender role orientations and friendship: some attenuation, but gender differences abound', *Sex Roles*, 24: 551–66.

Ageing and Individual Change

19

Age, Self, and Identity in the Global Century

Jon Hendricks

INTRODUCTION: DIMENSION OF SELF AND SOCIAL IDENTITY

The shifting sands of social change can be enough to make anyone lose their footing. Adapting to changes in one's world and in one's life portend transformations in an individual's worldview, sense of self, and social identity. Change itself has a kind of duality, coming from within or from without. It is self-evident to say that the greater the displacement imposed by change, the more taxing it is to maintain a viable and accommodating sense of self or social identity. At the same time, as change envelops an actor, perceptions of that actor will be anchored by the terms of transformations in the broader social context and portends associated challenges. Needless to say, change comes in many guises, yet a common theme is that it is accompanied by the need for adapting to new circumstances, be they internal or external, and brings forth new metrics for judging lives – our own and others. Of course, life itself is about change; by definition, the life course implies transitions, transformations, and fluidity.

Discussions of ageing, self, and social identity can be found throughout social gerontology. In many discussions an accentuation of individual characteristics, personal experience, and personal agency has predominated, with prominence ceded to proximal circumstances. By and large, facets of self-concept and social identity have been examined within the context of personality development, and via associative social relationships of daily practice sometimes cast in a broader framework of production, reproduction, and consumption. Changes over time in how an individual thinks of him or herself, and how they are perceived by others, are said to reflect transformations in personal traits, characteristics, competencies, and social relationships. In the past decades, the influence of socioeconomic status, policies, and other decisions in the public sphere, and social change more broadly conceived, have entered into discussions of life experiences and been recognized as causes channeling many aspects of identity and imputed changes accompanying age (Cockerham, 2005; Dittmann-Kohli, 2007; Hendricks, 2004).

The goal of this chapter is to review some fundamental tenets of investigations of self and social identity, to provide a more inclusive template linking self, identity, and social context, and to cast the elements in terms of life-course change and experiences affecting older actors. In so doing, the key literature will inform the discussion and, to the extent possible, issues of dynamic global changes early in the 21st century will be melded with discussions of selfhood and social identity. As will be apparent, the similarity or dissimilarity of an actor to those around him and the affinity that actor feels with the social environment will not only affect experience but also the nature of the self (Rosenberg, 1986: 99). The self is inherently intentional, and is, therefore, the lens through which meaningfulness is created; it is a crucial component of psychological well-being. Whitbourne and Primus (1996) suggest self-concept is akin to a predicate, providing the schema by which the lifeworld is organized. One thing is certain, the self emerges from social processes in a life-world that furnishes the social capital underlying shared understandings as well as the seeming stability of the life course (Dannefer, 1996; Hendricks, 1999, 2003).

SELF, IDENTITY, AND PERSONAL CIRCUMSTANCES

Gecas and Burke (1995) suggest that sense of self and social identity arise from the reflexivity that is vital to the human condition. Cognition and connections between frontal lobes and limbic systems aside (they are beyond the scope of this discussion), actors formulate their consciousness within a web of relationships that provide essential categorizations and help define who they are. Some factors influencing sense of self are endogenous, evolving over the course of life from earliest infancy to time of death. From the outset, developmental models within psychology cast evolution in sense of self as one of the characteristic 'tasks' of development, part and parcel of the process of becoming that is ongoing as actors move through life and that are coupled to maintaining optimal functioning and well-being (Erikson, 1968; George, 2003b). Part of an actor's sense of self includes anticipations of events and changes yet to come, their projected life stories, that serve as lenses through which experience is filtered (Hendricks, 1999; Markus and Nurius, 1986).

Gecas and Burke (1995) characterize sense of self as the 'sum total of the individual's thoughts and feelings about him/herself as an object'. It is via that sense of self that life is imbued with an essence of continuity, both temporal and subjective. Gecas and Burke provide a number of important parameters and are of the opinion that subjectivity is a creation of both immediate and structural circumstances that provide the arena in which self-relevant processes play out. Attention to structural issues stresses situational factors within an actor's direct realm of experience; structural conditions grounded in lifestyles and membership groups; biographical–historical aspects of life, including temporality and relational bonds arising from time and place; and intrapersonal processes, including bodily and psychological functioning such as cognitive and emotional facets that affect the social construction of selfhood (Biggs, 2001).

Rosenberg (1986) summarizes ways in which self and social identities are constituted via three interconnected processes. First is a process of *attribution*, by which judgments about entire personalities are constructed from observations of a limited range of behaviours. Secondly, in going about daily routines, actors adhere to or infringe upon *normative expectations*. All actors are embedded within relational networks, and it is from negotiations within these 'webs of significance' (Geertz, 1973) that they gain a sense of themselves. Via *reflected appraisals* perceived in reactions of interaction partners, starting in the family, actors monitor how they match-up to expectations (Felson, 2000: 2507; Rosenberg, 1986). Analyzed from the outside, such appraisals provide a mirror for an actor's identity as perceived by others; and those reactions are integral to how actors think of themselves. As noted below, the external dimensions of identity are coloured by myriad factors grounded in the ongoing flow of events, including social change. In a meta-analysis of over 60 empirical studies of changes in self-concept, Bengtson et al. (1985) conclude that self-concepts are relatively stable over time, yet people adapt to changes in their environment and when change in sense of self occurs, it does so due to changes in social circumstances and not for developmental reasons. Others, Breytspraak (1984) being a case in point, focus on reflected appraisals contained in increasingly negative 'ageing messages' encountered by middle-aged actors. The research suggests that, for good or ill, self-concept inevitably takes account of perceived feedback anchored in societal attitudes communicated via normative expectations (Biggs, 2001; Gergen and Semin, 1990; Heidrich and Ryff, 1993).

Thirdly normative expectations also affect actors via *social comparisons* with others perceived to be in comparable circumstances. Master status characteristics (e.g., age, education, gender, ethnicity, social status groupings, and other salient attributes) are categories by which others are selected for comparative purposes (Felson, 2000; Rosenberg, 1986). These allusive role models are part of an actor's self-referential frame throughout life, especially for those actors prone to 'self-in-relation-to-other' comparisons (Heidrich and Ryff, 1993; Markus and Kitayama, 1991). Wood (1989) points to three purposes served by social comparisons: self-evaluation, self-improvement, and self-enhancement. Comparisons with others may have salutary effects for those who perceive themselves as doing well and negative effects for those who see themselves doing less well (Heidrich and Ryff, 1993; Hendricks, 1992). Either way, these comparisons supply touchstones for self-appraisal and differentiation (Breytspraak, 1984; Markus and Cross, 1990).

People do not grow old in isolation; they are enmeshed in ongoing relationships. Social circumstances, labour markets, public policies, and other aspects of daily life are germane to what happens to actors as they age. Socially communicated expectations arise from every realm and are integral to actors' mindsets and behaviours. As the societal backdrop against which ageing unfolds undergoes change, so, too, will sense of self and perceptions of ageing actors. Research suggests that disapproving situational signals have adverse affects on an actor's performance. Steele et al. (2002) use the phrase 'stereotype threats' to describe how, to the extent actors are perceived, negative perceptions of individuals have adverse effects on their performance. Ryff (1991) examines how actors conceive of themselves and concludes they carry self-referential expectations brought into play as they appraise themselves. Actors inevitably have anticipated scripts, future life histories, and trajectories in mind, based on societal norms, social resources, and collective ideologies. Projected scripts exert influence over current thinking, though they have yet to be realized (Hendricks and Peters, 1986; Markus and Ruvolo, 1989). These possible future states and selves function like incentives, paving the way for future recourse, providing license while simultaneously supplying interpretative beacons (Markus and Cross, 1990; Ryff, 1991). To the extent expectations incorporate an actor's perception of events relative to his present status, these *self-appraisals* are integral to self-concept. Felson asserts that 'specific self-appraisals of ability affect performance' (Felson, 2000: 2508). Ryff (1991) frames the issue in terms of actors harbouring expectations based on *self-assessments* of improvement, maintenance, or declining abilities and competencies.

It may be that with advancing age, self-comparisons exert a greater influence over self-concept than social comparisons (Giddens, 1991; Suls and Mullen, 1992). Yet, there is fluidity in self and social comparisons affecting how actors construe themselves because of age or situational changes (Kohli and Meyer, 1986). In formulating self-assessments, actors may monitor their physical and psychological capacity vis-à-vis anticipations of what they thought they would be like (Markus and Cross, 1990; Whitbourne and Primus, 1996). In the face of impairments in later life, declining functions may foreshadow spoiled identities and exacerbate the need for adaptation. Some investigators suggest certain personality types rely more extensively on interpersonal relationships while others rest on independence self-definitions (Markus and Kitayama, 1991). Of course, encountering certain events in old age may mean that self-assessments and reflected appraisals become all the more significant.

As George (2003a) notes, the self is established, modified, and sustained within 'webs of significance' and there are predictable, strong links between social context and self-concept. Actors' experiences, ways of thinking, and interpretations of diverse dimensions of their lives are mediated by their relational life space with attendant norms, commitments, relations, and entitlements. Whether narrowly defined, as in role theory, or more broadly conceived as in social capital, a central tenant of discussions of self and social identity is that social status and accompanying lifestyles provide the impetus for behavioural repertoires and for expectations by self and others about self-concept and social identity. Even in the more narrowly focused perspective of role theory, it is reasonable to assume a corollary: changes in the nature of available roles and social relationships will lead to changes in status and, consequently, self-perception, social identity, and relative social power.

As the circumstances of an actor's life offer opportunity or constraint they facilitate or impede expressions of long-standing identity and related facets of psychological functioning, including cognitive performance (Biggs, 2001; Hess, 2006; Kohn and Slomczynski, 1990). Commenting on the formulation of stress in an actor's life, Dohrenwend (1973) points out that taxing consequences may follow any form of 'status loss'. Psychologists generally assert that an actor's sense of efficacy or mastery is compromised when previously functional behaviours or attitudes cease to yield comparable effects. Even absent dramatic disjuncture, the age-normative expectations actors carry with them, employed in assessing their own performance and that of others, may become ambiguous as they are separated from long-term roles providing pace, pattern, and sequence to their lives (Pavalko, 1997). Being deprived of consensually valued characteristics evokes 'distressful self-feelings' that subvert or destabilize sense of well-being (Hess, 2006; Kaplan, 1996). In the face of social change, it may feel as though the ground is eroding out from under an actor as skills once valued are deprecated. The results are not only stressful, as in something to be managed, but also corrosive in terms of how people evaluate themselves or are judged by others.

THE ECOLOGY OF SELF AND IDENTITY

Bronfenbrenner's (1979) phrase, the 'ecology of human development', expresses the view that lives are embedded in social milieux, be they immediate, more extensive but in which actors still participate, or societal and structural arrangements that shape opportunities and experience.

Throughout life, actors are enmeshed in and move with a 'convoy of social relations' (Antonucci and Akiyama, 1987) from one age-related identity to another, sharing certain characteristics with cohort members – some of which are derived from master status characteristics, some from being in the penumbra of structural conditions, relational processes, and lifestyles – while others are based on personal attributes – age, stage, or phase of life (Brandstadter and Greve, 1994; Dannefer, 1999; Gergen and Semin, 1990; Hockey and James, 2002). It is these compositional characteristics that distinguish one cohort from another and underpin what Rosenberg (1986) labels 'contextual dissonance', situations wherein actors receive neither validation nor indications they are functioning successfully. At each step, subjectivity and interpersonal relationships embody contextual strictures, the array of experiences, and statuses through which an individual passes. Sense of self and imputed social identities are dynamic, shifting, and responsive to changes in both social and physical environments, including bodily changes and constraints or opportunities accompanying master status and unremitting social change. Lawton and Nahemow (1973) refer to 'environmental press', or the notion that dissonant person–environment fits affect individuals' ability to cope and their sense of self.

As they go about their lives, actors call on their personal attributes, competencies, and mental and physical capabilities or skill sets – what is generally considered their stock of human capital. To the extent that a subset of these reveals age-related decrements, it is reasonable to assume that alterations in self-concept and social identity will occur and that physical or social contexts will become more challenging. The way those characteristics are perceived, evaluated by others, and reflected back to actors is part of the picture and is grounded in larger societal surrounds. Contextual competence is likely to have salutatory effects, while the converse accompanies contextual dissonance. To counter possible negative effects, it is likely that with age, and to the extent they have discretion, actors will optimize involvement in certain realms and minimize involvements in others where they receive less reinforcement or perceive their competence to be compromised (Carstensen et al., 2006; Hendricks and Cutler, 2004).

Actors also possess an internalized stock of social capital, social conventions, and social relationships that are reproduced in the course of life and that are also a component of self and social identity (Giddens, 1991: 35). This social capital includes language, metaphors, shared knowledge, networks, lifestyles, and so on, undergirding what Gadamer (1976) referred to as the 'forestructure'

of an actor's understanding, those principles presumed without question and utilized to make sense of their lives. They also constitute resources upon which actors draw as they negotiate their way in the world. The same social contexts are also the source of relationships, lifestyles, or status that mitigates how life unfolds (Bourdieu, 1989; Hendricks and Hatch, 2006; Lin, 2000). Actors' supply of social capital stems from their master status characteristics, their formal and informal relationships, and those resources they accrue by virtue of their social niches. These are part of the ecology of selfhood, as well as the opportunities and constraints underpinning how actors perceive themselves and others. The templates actors utilize as they interpret, represent, perform, and interact with consociates are part of their social capital (Hendricks, 2003). Continuing interaction and membership sustains those interpretative frameworks, providing a sense of 'we-ness' essential to an actor's anchorage for self-validation, personal meaning, and social identity. A corollary is that with interrupted or non-functional network support, the accessibility of social capital is attenuated with reverberations reaching to self-concepts and social identity.

Ambient social milieux supply vital resources that are the font of values, expectations, and worldviews that actors internalize as their own and incorporate into sense of self. A consequence is that as actors are involved in diverse spheres of activity, they manifest disparate facets of themselves based on what is called for within a particular sphere. It is fair to say that no facet of personal agency is isolated from social practices, membership groups, or structural conditions. One of the reasons this is so is that the social and cultural capital that translates into those resources available to actors derives from exactly those sources. Interacting with others for any length of time creates communal interpretative templates, negotiated meanings, and shared definitions (Hendricks, 1999). This is the point Weber (1921) was making about lifestyles emerging from the relational bonds of associative status groups playing out in daily practice and enveloping all those who share that lifestyle. Lifestyles are interactive and relational, resulting in a self-structure dialectic wherein each shapes the other (Hendricks and Hatch, 2006).

LIFE COURSE, SELF, AND OPPORTUNITY STRUCTURES

Implicit in the above is that many of life's chances are influenced by variables acknowledged as factors structuring the life course. From prenatal health to late-life satisfaction and well-being, the accoutrements accompanying those variables affect how life unfolds. In stable circumstances a modicum of expectability is the norm, with life unfolding reasonably predictably: i.e., stable family, work life, health, and social circumstances promote probable life courses (Gecas and Burke, 1995: 42).

Settersten (2006; see also Hagestad and Dannefer, 2001), however, notes a number of threats to stability. In the face of broad-reaching social change, stability is easier to suppose than to validate. A number of investigators note that there is an increasing fluidity, even fracturing of the life course, as society becomes progressively pluralistic so that ageing itself follows multiple trajectories as it is affected by social change (George, 2003b; Gilleard and Higgs, 2005). As Kohli (1986) comments, the social transformations associated with industrialization resulted in a kind of rationalization of the life course. He highlights the synchronization bringing 'temporalization' and 'chronologization' of life as a result of industrial production. He also speaks of the standardized reckoning, along with a kind of 'individualization', wherein actors are no longer tied to traditions that control their lives, and of the advent of labour markets with their career paths that impose sequencing on life. With the types of social changes occurring early in the 21st century, some of the patterns thought to characterize the life course over the last 150 years may become less stable than previously assumed. A case in point concerns the rapid changes in labour market opportunities. If labour-force participation becomes less predictable, less career-like, both self-concepts and life-course structures will be affected as the structure as well as the rewards derived from work become less salient (Kohn and Slomczynski, 1990). That is not to say that replacement benchmarks may not emerge, but merely to say that benchmarks of one sort or another provide normative structures and serve as a basis for sense of self.

Life is about change. The occurrence of key events that are either intrinsic or extrinsic in nature provide essential gauges and denote passage along the way. The focus in this discussion will consider how social participation intermingles with the way life unfolds and what that portends for sense of self. There is little doubt that the dynamic interrelatedness of the developing individual and changing sociocultural contexts affects sense of self and social identity. If actors experience being estranged from a particular cultural orientation, such feelings will affect the ways in which they view themselves as well as their sense of well-being (Diehl, 1999; Rosenberg, 1986).

Life-course adaptation occurs in the face of both normative and non-normative events. Some argue the latter have more significant consequences and require greater readjustments than do changes affecting most members of a cohort. In either instance, however, actors are potentially proactive and agentic, able to affect the nature of the changes and the reintegration required within the confines of the boundaries imposed by opportunities and constraints within which they operate (Brandtstadter, 1983; Diehl, 1999). The complexity is that social changes do not affect all age cohorts or even all members of the same cohort in the same fashion. In the case of older cohorts, transformations associated with social change may be antithetical to the mechanisms by which they had had previously garnered social standing or demonstrated competencies. It may also be the case that one group of actors may be acting under one set of suppositions while other actors have another. Imagine the discontinuity, even the stress, felt by a generation anticipating a life script revolving around one set of definitions of self (or even selflessness), productivity, filial responsibility, community, individualism (selfishness), and temporality, then becoming old under the auspices of a different script formulated by a different generation in the face of an influx of new ideas or new modes of interaction (Liu, 2002).

Regardless of whether they are predictable or unpredictable, life-course transformations are dynamic, unrelenting, and requiring of re-stabilization efforts following successive transitions. With each transition and in the face of all manner of social change there is a possibility that ill-matched competencies will result in what Rosenberg (1986) refers to as contextual dissonance and a marginalization of affected actors. As Diehl (1999) remarks, re-establishing person–environment fit in the face of change depends on antecedent status, anticipatory socialization, personal resources, relational ties, contextual conditions, the nature of the event, and characteristics of the change itself. Countless commentaries contend that encountering offsetting changes from a position of relative strength or advantage generally portends having the resources necessary for greater success in re-synchronizing and adapting to changes in a self-protective fashion (Diehl, 1999; Hendricks and Hatch, 2006; Kohn and Slomczyski, 1990). Optimal adaptation will result in a new goodness of fit; suboptimal adaptation will be evident in an asymmetrical fit, creating a sense of contextual dissonance affecting sense of self. The appropriateness of the adaptation will be apparent in the reflected appraisals of others and in an actor's ability to weave a coherent and meaningful narrative supportive of his self-concept (Brandtstadter and Greve, 1994).

The ability to exert control, to manage change and outcomes, validates an actor's sense of self, while the converse is corrosive of perceived mastery and sense of self. As Ross and Mirowsky (1989) assert, if as an outgrowth of circumstances actors experience feelings of powerlessness, linked to feeling unable to affect things going on around them, depression, stress, and other undesirable emotional consequences follow. Certainly, in the face of social changes that undervalue characteristics core to actors' sense of themselves, the outcome can only be injurious, threatening interpersonal validity. There is any number of intervening variables affecting outcomes but those changes that are identity-relevant pose challenges that must be managed if sense of self is not to be adversely effected (Diehl, 1999).

It is important to note that actors are not entirely passive or reactive to changes eddying around them. As suggested earlier, one strategy is to selectively optimize one's sense of competence by attending to those realms in which one can maximize feelings of mastery and sidestep areas less likely to yield positive outcomes. The goal of selective optimization is to capitalize on a sense of continuity and efficacy but also to invest time and energy in those valued areas where returns may be maximized (Carstensen et al., 2006; Hendricks and Cutler, 2004; Riediger et al., 2006). Of course, contextual competence has its own limitations in that areas such as public policies, the structure of opportunities, and ability to exercise control are not just of an actor's making. It is not an overstatement to say that life's choices are determined by life's chances or opportunity structures, any numbers of which are beyond actors' control. When societal conditions are in flux, an actor's contextual competencies may be eroded by unfamiliar demands or by virtue of the fact that attributes that have long served well may be devalued under the aegis of the new situation.

Insofar as social factors differentiate among actors, one may assume they also affect self and social identity. So, for example, lifestyles associated with social class enter into ability to exert control or mastery and thereby also affect subjectivity. Lifestyles, derived from membership groups, provide an integrated set of perspectives and practices that serve as guides for action, the creation of meaning, and as factors in exerting mastery. As familiar groundings, lifestyles are a source of security, surety, direction, and anticipated futures. When lifestyles are disrupted, the converse is the likely result (Giddens, 1991; Hendricks and Hatch, 2006).

It is important to note that hierarchical statuses are endemic to life in industrialized societies. Social class and income levels are the most obvious facets of status rankings, accompanied by occupational categories and education, but they are not the sole bestowers of status. Gender, ethnicity, even bodily type may enter the picture. Not only do each of the categorical memberships provide essential resources for making one's way in the world, thereby affecting actors' ability to exert themselves, but also they are integral to how actors perceive themselves and how they are perceived by others (Hendricks, 1999; Ryff, 1991). As sense of self is an outgrowth of social participation, experience, and social resources, it makes a difference whether one's status provides enablements or constraints, access or denial, inclusion or exclusion.

PUBLIC MARKERS, LIFE'S SCRIPT, AND EVOLUTION OF SELF

Quadagno (1982) has challenged social gerontologists to move beyond individual-level explanations to address economics, the polity, and the societal structure as an integral aspect of their efforts to explicate the experience of ageing. As should be clear, social participation includes interpersonal interaction but also another set of factors represented by the policy environment that establishes parameters of meaning-making and the shaping of membership categories affecting identity. As Fraser (1997) avers, whether public policies are age-based or age-related, their 'deep grammar' is among the factors influencing nominal aspects of identity, including master status, self-concepts, and how actors are categorized. This is true of young and old or anyone whose life is subject to statutory regulations. For a portion of the population, especially those from disadvantaged circumstances covered by social assistance programmes, policy definitions carry greater salience than for actors less dependent on social welfare. Not only is structural milieu and communal circumstances worthy of considered attention – no one grows old insulated from their influence – but also public policies are principles apportioning options, relational life space, and key aspects of subjectivity.

Public policy permeates life via stipulations about the nature of family life, education, welfare, work, retirement, and other facets of interpersonal relationships. Policies frame many aspects of life from age categorizations, personal identity, and transitions in the life course. As Townsend (1981) notes, the created conditions of life shape the experience of ageing, of dependency, of selfhood and public policy provisions, and their attendant normative expectations are integral. Most industrial societies have implemented provisos ranging from foreign trade to the distribution of resources and the furnishing of old-age benefits. The statutory rationalities incorporated into the wide array of policies are instrumental in defining the life course, as their specifications assume taken-for-granted status inflecting essential facets of experience and identity. As a way of illustrating the point, work life is central to how life unfolds, and to an actor's sense of self. Work is one arena where public policies are thoroughly intertwined. Entering the work-a-day world is an early life marker, and age at entry into full-time employment is generally indicative of subsequent work-life trajectory. It may also be predictive of certain aspects of autonomy within the world of work, control over retirement years, and self-concepts and personal meaning systems (Kohn and Slomczynski, 1990; Westerhof and Dittmann-Kohli, 2000).

TEMPORAL GROUNDING AND SENSE OF SELF

Time and temporality are constructs grounded in societal conditions and closely linked with sense of self and social identity. As actors experience life's myriad transitions, their sense of temporal rootedness must be brought into alignment in order to maintain well-being. Various disciplines tend to analyze temporality in terms of their substantive focus. Psychologists, for example, routinely assert that psychological time is composed of nuances based on succession, duration, and perspective, all of which are anchored by memory processing, hippocampal functioning, and other neurophysiological processing (Schroots, 1996; van der Meer, 2007). Biologists maintain that innate biological processes impose a temporal patterning that may also shape consciousness. Both are valid perspectives but this discussion will confine itself to societal influences on things that are temporal.

Age grading, age norms, and socially prescribed transitions are virtually universal in all societies and provide fundamental temporal reckoning. Although they are familiar concepts, their relevance to identity and temporality merits closer attention, as life's transitions are typically normative, when they are not catastrophic. The implications are apparent: as social conditions affect personal development and the way life unfolds, they also affect temporal orientation. The causal linkage seems to run through shifting socio-historical conditions, socialization experiences, and temporal patterning. Seemingly, societal and individual

times are interwoven, with the former providing normative integration through recurrent rhythms and periodicities embedded in social activities, lifestyles, and forms of engagement. It is widely believed that social roles and social class are factors influencing individuals' temporal reckoning. So, for example, future orientation is more characteristic of individuals in advantaged circumstances than it is among those from disadvantaged social positions or with jobs that do not portend career-like trajectories. In terms of ageing, as individual consciousness is altered, as in life-course transitions, subjective temporality is affected (Hendricks, 2001).

Temporal aspects of selfhood pose interesting questions since a great many aspects of sense of self are anchored by the reciprocal influence of time, the structuring of experience, and social change. To begin with, the past is present in an actor's sense of self in that elements of previous experience are incorporated into how actors think of themselves. Simultaneously, sense of futurity is also a factor in the present and one that is important for action and decision-making since actors' aspirational sense of who they may become is part of their current sense of themselves. In a nutshell, actors carry proleptic images, assumptions that certain future developments may have occurred as they contemplate their 'possible selves', or anticipated representations of what the future will hold (Hendricks, 1992; Markus and Nurius, 1986). A positive sense of self is contingent, at least in part, on an actor's sense that he impose his will on time rather than the other way around, and in the face of social change an actor's ability to manage may be put into question. According to Dittmann-Kohli (2007), the salience of temporal frameworks increases in later life due to the piling-up of myriad cues coming from body, psyche, and society. Schaie (2007) speaks of event time, those occurrences which have significant meaning to individuals that denote transitions and turning points. Actors attend to these events in terms of intentional mindsets, cataloguing events relevant for their frame of meaning, while letting others slide by (Hendricks, 1999). Normative expectations are also constitutive of event times. Through social comparisons with others believed to be in comparable circumstances, actors make judgments about whether they are 'on time' or 'off time' in terms of their own projected life courses (Settersten and Hagestad, 1996).

To appreciate the role of temporality in subjectivity in the face of rapid social change, it is important to consider that existing normative structures, benchmarks, and transitions are subject to revision. One influence of globalization is that parochial selections are being undermined as people around the world become more closely interconnected and time keeping is standardized. Furthermore, technological innovation occurring elsewhere quickly comes to roost in new locales, resulting in a compression and reorganization of temporal markers and social timekeeping (Steger, 1997). Any attenuation of earlier reckoning requires a recalibration and reintegration as new templates are incorporated into mental models of what life is about. Even in stable situations, transitions and transformations over the life course necessitate reorientation if actors are to retain their sense of efficacy or control.

Discussions of globalization refer to the fragmentation and acceleration of the sense of time accompanying global flows (Lestienne, 2000). For those who live along the margins of such change, feelings of being in control may be challenged as the tempo and pace of life are altered. As cultural representations of the shape of life are reformulated and/or personal functionality wanes, the prospect that older people will lose track of their reference guidelines increases. It should also be underscored that social locations are manifestly relational, defined through interpersonal interaction and reactions of others. As a result, older people may feel detached from succeeding generations that are more immersed with those aspects of global flows and social life shaping chronological time and temporality.

AGE AND IDENTITY IN THE GLOBAL CENTURY

Discussions about self and social identity need to take cognizance of how globalization reaches into many aspects of life, regardless of where actors live. Simply put: globalization encompasses the spread of free-market economies, standardization, commoditization, and changes in the nature of labour or public policies, as well as the hegemony of new modes of being over traditional cultural templates. Global economic change portends more than alterations in per capita income, financial products, or the rapid circulation of goods and technologies; it is precursor to broad cultural shifts, including interpersonal changes as well as social and political changes that exert dominance over pre-contact modes of being. It would be a mistake to assume globalization replaces one surety with another; instead, we find pervasive uncertainty, in which time and place may be amorphous and discontinuous vis-à-vis what had gone before (Giddens, 1991). Despite avowals about the secularity of modern life, economic thinking is

accorded near theological status – its canons are seen as universally applicable, providing appropriate tenants for what is fair and just, as well as normative prescriptions, values and moralities, attitudes, and worldviews. In the face of globalization, it is assumed that technological and economic changes will benefit all and, accordingly, social and market systems become closely aligned (Geertz, 1973; Hendricks, 2005).

Ironically, under globalization, economic development and transnational corporate intensification take place without any palpable concern for nation-building, national interests, or public sector regulatory control (McMichael, 2000). As industrializing countries encounter global influences, it is as if the warrant of accumulated experience relied on as a guide to action is displaced by new modes and new norms, fraught with risk, and the surge of the new that leads to a reconfiguration of daily life. Under such circumstances, a growing proportion of the reflected appraisals may not provide consensual validation of an older actor's abilities or achievements as negativity is attributed to difference. If contextual competence wanes, a cycle of disconcerting results may follow (Rosenberg, 1986). Self-attributions go hand-in-hand with these reflected appraisals and so can further harsh self-evaluations. Not all such attributions derive from locally defined priorities, however. For individuals anticipating their life script, by which a course of action is selected, the basis of their deliberations is subject to processes which may be non-proximate but which play out locally. Liu's (2002) ethnographic study of selfhood in the coastal city of Beihai, in south China, provides insight into the impact of a high-tech industry locating in a previously and markedly un-modern place. Liu provides a glimpse at how notions of self and temporality shifted dramatically between cohorts on either side of the importation of technology and the modes of production associated with rapid industrialization.

In many considerations of global change, commentators assert the world is becoming compressed, that intersocietal integration is increasing, that knowledge is being defined globally not locally, and that globalization results in an 'intensification of worldwide social relations which link distant localities in such a way that local happenings are shaped by events occurring many miles away and vice versa' (Giddens, 1990: 64; Robertson, 1997). There is an exponential 'widening, deepening and speeding up of worldwide interconnectedness in all aspects of social life, from the cultural to the criminal, the financial to the spiritual' (Held et al., 1999: 2). In terms of interpersonal exchange, these globalizing flows may not banish pre-contact patterns of interaction but they can elide their significance. Going along with the above is a shift in the lodging and apportionment of knowledge-power equations, status hierarchies, types of family relationships, and so on, as new criteria are implemented and written into laws circumscribing an actor's identity. At the same time, jurisdictions as arbiters of one question or another may be increasingly limited as goods, services, and influences are defined globally. As knowledge becomes standardized, commodified, and keyed, if you will, to transportable patterns, prior modes of knowing fall into disregard, along with those who embody them (Hendricks, 2004).

Globalization brings transformational changes in the nature of experience as the distinction between local and global relationships is resignified by global flows (Dallmayer, 2005). A reality of the 21st century is that the availability of keystroke technologies has undercut local coherence – just about anyone at least has the potential for instantaneous interaction across vast reaches and the incursion of external ideas has become a constant torrent. Specter (2007) recently noted that junk email is an example of globalization's successes as untold numbers make their way around the world minute by minute. What was once stable becomes unpredictable. For example, career paths may no longer stretch over a lifetime and futures become uncertain. Of course, once a new pattern stabilizes, new normative models will emerge. It is during the transition, when new perspectives are not yet inculcated into all actors that those on the trailing edge find themselves on the outside looking in. As Gilleard and Higgs (2005) assert, societal segmentation follows, and generations are cleaved from one another via distinctive experiences and attributions. The social reproduction that traditionally took place between generations that fostered coherence no longer occurs, as successive generations no longer share common contextual symbolism (Cole and Durham, 2007). In the face of globalization, age is no longer a continuum but becomes a series of disconnected categories defined by participation in new modes of production and interaction. For the young, it means fewer role models for what life portends; for older people, it means identification with their own children or grandchildren is attenuated.

Whereas life was once integrated in a place and across generations, globalization tends to destabilize the solidarity sustaining generational transitions (Gilleard and Higgs, 2005). Two cultural forms may coexist, and it is not as though the one is totally submerged with the advance of the other, but the one that is not constantly reinforced is depreciated in an increasingly co-opting way (Appadurai, 1996). As traditional codes, creeds, and ideologies are challenged by the incursion of new models of exchange that alter the quality of life and sources of validation, identities lodged in local, long-standing practices can be destabilized, as frames of reference upon which identity had rested no longer receive consensual validation (King, 1997). It is as if the coordinates by which the life course is charted are thrown into a state of flux and beset with an array of side effects. Such a dissonant environment sends adverse messages to those not central to its focus. As Rosenberg (1986) observes, actors see themselves as others see them, notwithstanding penchants for optimizing reflected appraisals.

For newly industrializing countries that have historically been agricultural and rural in nature, utile symbols and beliefs rooted in long-standing traditions are assailed by dynamic and disjunctive forces forged in the cauldron of a global marketplace that implies differential social relations, institutional changes, market transactions, and temporal frames hinged to economic and technological activities rather than localized circumstances. Dynamic changes confront traditional arrangements and affect fundamental aspects of life and the most personal aspects of experience, including sense of self and social identity. There is one side effect, however, that bears emphasizing. By definition, generations are marked by diverging worldviews, yet in the face of globalizing change, the disjuncture between those schooled in the old ways and those schooled in the new may be amplified by structural changes. For example, socialization into lifestyles based on consumption will separate younger generations from older ones, as ability to participate in that world of consumption is going to carry social attributions of relevance and worth (Gilleard and Higgs, 2005). One might predict that with additional affluence there will be a rapid increase in consumer growth as people attempt to identify with the new.

As consumerism spreads and experience is commodified, there is a likelihood that one's sense of self will incorporate material goods, much like Ozymandius in Percy Bysshe Shelley's well-known poem by the same name. In it, the pharaoh who built the Great Pyramids invites all travellers to look on his material possessions and thereby to know him. Meaning, you will know the kind of ruler he was when you see the monuments he built for himself. It is among those who live on either edge of rapid social change that the effects are most visible or perhaps most displacing as the values of one era career into the values of another. Living with any form of insecurity cannot help but take a toll on sense of self, and the insecurities may become insufferable. Globalization stresses rationality, efficiency, and other economically derived principles, while earlier ideologies were more communal and cooperatively based.

For societies that experienced industrialization 100 or more years ago, the advent of globalization means that complexities increase and nation-states are no longer able to control local policies without consideration of broader economic forces. Consequently, nation-state sovereignty has become a matter to be asserted rather than taken for granted, as state policies are no longer paramount in influencing daily life (Dallmayer, 2005; Fraser, 2005). For example, nations that had previously been able to negotiate with local business interests based on labour pools and tax structures must learn to deal with transnational corporations able to relocate key functions depending upon policies and costs of doing business. As several commentators point out, from the 1980s, public welfare provisions in industrialized societies have become increasingly contentious as national economies have come to be less autonomous and more subject to the 'internationalization of labour markets' and global capital flow (Biggs, 2001; Gilleard and Higgs, 2005: 50). There has also been a global labour market bifurcation, with those who participate in the global economy being relatively more advantaged than those who remain focused on local markets (McMichael, 2000). Among other ramifications of the latter is the far greater prospect of labour-force redundancy, marginalization, and structural unemployment, with but dim prospects for re-employment.

THE MOVEMENT OF VENERABLE TO VULNERABLE

The constructs of daily life are rooted in social interaction, embedded in categorical memberships and relationships, and internalized by actors at every stage of the life course. Yet, as globalizing social change occurs, the underpinning of these relationships is altered, with potentially corrosive consequences as the building blocks upon which sense of self and autonomy are erected are assaulted and actors face increased uncertainty, being less able to regulate or effect what goes on around them. Of course, it matters where an actor is in the life course when change occurs, but it may be that the problems are amplified by structural factors and with age. As psychologists maintain, age-related losses can produce socio-emotional vulnerability, a decrease in sense of control, a decline in sense of self-sufficiency, and a sense of helplessness, all of which may accelerate ageing (Fry, 1989: 2).

In the face of globalization, some actors experience social transformations that create uncertainties about their futures, positions, and the basis of their social relationships since they are less able to exert themselves in social transactions. In effect, previous status rankings are reconfigured by new circumstances and modes of engagement incompatible with long-standing bases of identity. If identity cannot be sustained in terms of the status quo ante, a sense of apprehension and attenuation ensues, with all that portends for an actor's emotional state. One effect of globalizing change for older actors is a range of induced outcomes, resulting in structured or created dependencies that mirror societal change rather than biological destinies (Biggs, 2001; Townsend, 1981).

With the advent of global markets there is an increasing partition between advantaged and disadvantaged, accompanied by a rationalizing ideology justifying benefits and entitlements. Social locations are inescapably relational, defined through interpersonal interaction and reactions of others. As a consequence, it is as though older people and other disadvantaged populations lose their cultural fluency and have precious little presence in the new regime. With little positive feedback, feelings of alienation may result, and feeling alienated has consequences in terms of social exclusion or subjectivity. The way in which an actor's abilities are encapsulated by social-referents contained in unflattering reflected appraisals or social comparisons can have a profound effect on subjective well-being. Paradoxically, another facet of such situations is a heightened sensitivity to the reactions of others, accompanied by a proliferation of 'failure scenarios' (Bandura and Jourdan, 1991). Dasgupta cast the impact of global flows in sharp relief:

> Globalization has thus created an identity crisis, since many are neither local nor global and are overloaded with changing stimuli ... resulting in a 'don't care' attitude, commercial interactions among family members, rise of individualism, break down of family ties, domination of individual identity and spatial disequilibrium come to the fore. All clash with values of older people and traditionalists and the latter feel alienated (2006: 159).

CONCLUSION

No aspect of subjectivity is stationary – each evolves as actors move through life, through status passages, past various turning points, and find themselves in diverse contexts (Hazelrigg, 2000; Hendricks, 1999). Generally speaking, efforts to adapt and feedback received take place within the proximate life space of individual actors – with work, interpersonal and familial contacts, as well as other contiguous conditions commonly assumed to have primacy. In all instances, the interactional space of ongoing associations is believed to provide social capital that configures cultural and behavioural repertoires and normative expectations, engendering taken-for-granted worldviews and the tacit knowledge actors utilize to make sense of their situations. Regardless of how well actors do in becoming accustomed to one transition, there is no rest after success, as another adjustment is over the horizon.

As actors move through life, their human and social capital co-mingle with historical and structural circumstances to shape opportunities, worldviews, and perceptions they have of themselves and others. The consequences play out in sense of self, social identity, and subjective well-being. Much of the literature suggests that an important aspect of life events is whether they are controllable or not and that a portion of whatever controllability an individual may have relates to their relative social position and the personal or social resources they bring to bear as required. The interpretative templates formulated via the practical consciousness of daily life reflect the recursive sweep of social roles and membership groups that supply archetypal representations or that characteristic lens of interpretation (Bourdieu, 1989).

As though driven by a kind of instinctual self-preservation, actors inevitably attempt to differentiate among events and realms of engagement, thereby maximizing their investment of emotion and self. The more identity-relevant an event or situation is, the more actors attempt to optimize engagement with that event or situation while paying less heed to more distal events or situations (Carstensen et al., 2006; Diehl, 1999). Certain events, be they familiar or unexpected, as well as the subjective reactions and reflected appraisals of others, affect the ways actors think of themselves and how they are perceived by others. Life's transformations may be tantamount to successive starting points for subsequent developmental phases as they require adjustments in order to maintain subjective well-being. In addition to personal and social resources, adjustments are affected by the duration of previous states, by the timing and age at which a transition occurs, and by the magnitude of change to the new state.

In fashioning their anticipated futures, actors are reflexive, creating narrative lines incorporating temporal orientation, including future goals that are both participatory and intentional. As actors deal with the ongoing flow of events, they continuously monitor and select for self-relevance and formulate meanings via their individualized

'interpretative practices' of daily life (Markus and Cross, 1990, Whitbourne and Primus, 1996). This practical consciousness, as I have termed it elsewhere, creates meaning and corroborates the logic of ways of knowing, yielding precedents and principles that are incorporated into worldviews insofar as perception itself is concept-laden, reflecting the purpose-at-hand of the perceiving actor. The results stand as presumptively real, enabling action while becoming the reference point for new experiences and for grounding of self-concepts (Giddens, 1991:76; Hendricks, 1999).

There is any number of non-proximate factors that colour subjective aspects of an actor's world. To begin with, public policy provisions of modern societies impose a structure and institutions that are powerful definers of ages and stages. Echoing a theme enunciated by Quadagno (1982), Estes (2001), and others, Schulz and Binstock phrase it succinctly, '... politics and government play a major and growing role in determining the outcome of what life will be like ... in old age' (2006: 20). Beyond the realm of social policy, there is a raft of global changes afoot that have a profound effect on individual actors, regardless of whether they are aware of their influences.

Late in the 20th century, global economic integration imposed an extensive blueprint for social change. Global flows wrest experience from the situatedness of local circumstance, undermining the basis of trust and solidarity that comes of provenance, taken-for-granted practice and tradition, that long served as the basis for interaction, perception, and anticipation of the future. Few aspects of social life are immune from the reach of globalization (Held et al., 1999). Moving into the global century, Beck et al. (2003) aver that globalization not only subverts local economic autonomy but also shifts frames of reference in such a way that long-standing boundaries become less salient. As Dasgupta puts it, globalizing forces are 'running fast towards a goal where traditions, sense of localism, and community feelings have no room' (2006: 159). It is as if the metric of meaningfulness is altered so that formerly taken-for-granted covenants no longer hold sway. Such shifts matter insofar as habitual ways of knowing provide essential cognitive maps that guide action as well as provide evaluative frameworks for judging action; any disruption cannot help but affect subjectivity (Cockerham, 2005).

As labour markets shift from rural and agricultural to urban and industrial, definitions of appropriate gendered divisions of labour shift as well. And, as labour markets swing from production to service and export functions, these same gender roles evolve yet again, rewriting anticipated scripts as they do so and causing a type of discontinuity in the lifetimes of adjacent generations. Constructs that were once taken as foundational for identity are called into question to such an extent they no longer serve as lodestars by which actors can chart their own course. What was once certain becomes contingent and issues of agency, subjectivity, and perception are thrown into flux. As global change occurs, and new ways of knowing or new sets of skills become more highly valued than previous ways of knowing, individuals who represent traditional knowledge may find themselves moving from venerated to vulnerable. Even if there is not an active degradation of old ways and thereby old people, those with new skill sets and knowledge bases tend to look externally for navigational cues for their own lives.

In the face of globalization, regardless of the economic stage of a nation-state when the movement occurs, meanings change. Beck et al. (2003) point out that globalization continues to transform itself even after it has taken root. As meanings change, so, too, does the significance of individuals and the social construction of ageing. One thing is sure: global flows sweeping round the world and back again mean that although processes take place locally, they are no longer grounded entirely by indigenous circumstances and cannot be understood in isolation from global flows (Kearney, 1995). In practical terms it means that policies, programmes, and life experiences occurring in any one country are not shaped solely by events in that county but are influenced by events originating half a world away. Globalization brings a metric that may not be an outgrowth of what had gone before but includes ideas, values, and policies brought from without, from beyond. Ideas migrate as surely as do people and they settle much the same way. In so doing, they inevitably reconfigure relational dynamics, life scripts, and subjectivities (Appadurai, 1996). As one generation gains experiences not known among its predecessors, it is reasonable to assume the existence of a disconnect between their collective worldviews will occur and intergenerational interaction will reflect those shifts. The ways in which actors anticipate their life course will also reflect those same shifts and result in separation between those who hew to one scenario and those who adopt a new perspective on what the future holds (Cole and Durham, 2007).

REFERENCES

Antonucci, T. and Akiyama, H. (1987) 'Social networks in adult life and a preliminary examination of the convoy model', *Journal of Gerontology*, 42: 519–27.

Appadurai, A. (1996) *Modernity at Large: Cultural Dimensions of Globalization*. Minneapolis, MN: University of Minnesota Press.

Bandura, A. and Jourdan, F. (1991) 'Self-regulation mechanisms governing the impact of social comparisons on complex decision-making', *Journal of Personality and Social Psychology*, 60: 941–51.

Beck, U., Bonss, W., and Lau, C. (2003) 'The theory of reflexive modernization: problematic, hypotheses and research programme', *Theory, Culture and Society*, 20: 1–33.

Bengtson, V., Reedy, M., and Gordon, C. (1985) 'Aging and self-conceptions: personality processes and social contexts', in J. Birren and K.W. Schaie (eds), *Handbook of the Psychology of Aging*, 2nd edn. New York: Van Nostrand Reinhold, pp. 544–93.

Biggs, S. (2001) 'Toward critical narrativity: stories of aging in contemporary social policy', *Journal of Aging Studies*, 15: 303–16.

Bourdieu, P. (1989) 'Social space and symbolic power', *Social Theory*, 7: 14–25.

Brandtstadter, J. (1983) 'Personal and social control over development: some implications of an action perspective in life-span developmental psychology', in P. Baltes and O. Brim, Jr. (eds), *Life-Span Development and Behavior*, Vol. 6. New York: Academic Press, pp. 1–32.

Brandtstadter, J. and Greve, W. (1994) 'The aging self: stabilizing and protective processes', *Developmental Review*, 14: 52–80.

Breytspraak, L. (1984) *The Development of Self in Later Life*. Boston: Little, Brown.

Bronfenbrenner, U. (1979) *The Ecology of Human Development: Experiments by Nature and Design*. Cambridge, MA: Harvard University Press.

Carstensen, L., Mikels, J., and Mather, M. (2006) 'Aging and the intersection of cognition, motivation, and emotion', in J.E. Birren and K.W. Schaie (eds), *Handbook of the Psychology of Aging*. San Diego, CA: Academic Press, pp. 362–73.

Cockerham, W. (2005) 'Health lifestyle theory and the convergence of agency and structure', *Journal of Health and Social Behavior*, 46: 51–67.

Cole, J. and Durham, D. (2007) 'Introduction: age, regeneration, and the intimate politics of globalization', in J. Cole and D. Durham (eds), *Generations and Globalization: Youth, Age, and Family in the New World Economy*. Bloomington, IN: Indiana University Press, pp. 1–28.

Dallmayer, F. (2005) *Small Wonder: Global Power and Its Discontents*. Lanham, MD: Rowan and Littlefield.

Dannefer, D. (1996) 'The social organization of diversity and the normative organization of age', *The Gerontologist*, 36: 174–7.

Dannefer, D. (1999) 'Freedom isn't free: power, alienation, and the consequences of action', in J. Brandstadter and R. Lerner (eds). *Action and Self-Development*. Thousand Oaks, CA: SAGE, pp. 105–31.

Dasgupta, S. (2006) 'Globalization and its future shock', in S. Dasgupta and R. Kiely (eds), *Globalization and After*. Thousand Oaks, CA: SAGE, pp. 143–83.

Diehl, M. (1999) 'Self-development in adulthood and aging: the role of critical life events', in C.D. Ryff and V.W. Marshall (eds), *The Self and Society in Aging Processes*. New York: Springer, pp. 150–83.

Dittmann-Kohli, F. (2007) 'Temporal references in the construction of self-identity: a life-span approach', in J. Baars and H. Visser (eds), *Aging and Time: Multidisciplinary Perspectives*. Amityville, NY: Baywood, pp. 83–119.

Dohrenwend, B. (1973) 'Life events as stressors: a methodological inquiry', *Journal of Health and Social Behavior*, 14: 167–75.

Erikson, E. (1968) *Identity: Youth and Crisis*. New York: Norton.

Estes and Associates (2001) *Social Policy and Aging*. Thousand Oaks, CA: SAGE.

Felson, R. (2000) 'Self-concept', in E. Borgatta and R. Montgomery (eds), *Encyclopedia of Sociology*, 2nd edn. New York: Macmillan, pp. 2505–10.

Fraser, N. (1997) 'The force of law: metaphysical or political?', in N.J. Holland (ed.), *Feminist Interpretations of Jacques Derrida*. University Park, PA: Pennsylvania State University Press, pp. 157–63.

Fraser, N. (2005) 'Transnationalizing the public sphere', in M. Pensky (ed.), *Globalizing Critical Theory*. Lanham, MD: Rowman and Littlefield, pp. 37–47.

Fry, P. (1989) 'Preconceptions of vulnerability and controls in old age: a critical reconstruction', in P.S. Fry (ed.), *Psychological Perspectives of Helplessness and Control in the Elderly*. Amsterdam: North-Holland, pp. 1–39.

Gadamer, H.G. (1976) *Philosophical Hermeneutics*. Berkeley, CA: University of California Press.

Gecas, V. and Burke, P.J. (1995) 'Self and identity', in K.S. Cook, G.A. Fine, and J.S. House (eds), *Sociological Perspectives in Social Psychology*. Boston: Allyn and Bacon, pp. 41–67.

Geertz, C. (1973) *The Interpretation of Cultures*. New York: Basic Books.

George, L.K. (2003a) 'Well-being and sense of self: what we know and what we need to know', in K.W. Schaie and J. Hendricks (eds), *The Evolution of the Aging Self: The Societal Impact on the Aging Process*. New York: Springer, pp. 1–35.

George, L.K. (2003b) 'Life course research: achievements and potential', in J. Mortimer and M. Shanahan (eds), *Handbook of the Life Course*. New York: Kluwer Academic, pp. 671–80.

Gergen, K. and Semin, G. (1990) 'Everyday understanding in science and daily life', in G. Semin and K. Gergen (eds), *Everyday Understanding: Social and Scientific Implications*. Newbury Park, CA: SAGE, pp. 1–18.

Giddens A. (1990) *The Consequences of Modernity*. Cambridge: Polity Press.

Giddens, A. (1991) *Modernity and Self-identity: Self and Society in the Late Modern Age*. Cambridge: Polity Press.

Gilleard, C. and Higgs, P. (2005) *Contexts of Ageing: Class, Cohort and Community*. Cambridge: Polity Press.

Hagestad, G. and Dannefer, D. (2001) 'Concepts and theories of aging: beyond microfication in social science approaches', in R. Binstock and L. George (eds), *Handbook of Aging and the Social Sciences, 5th edn*. San Diego, CA: Academic Press, pp. 3–21.

Hazelrigg, L. (2000) 'Individualism', in E. Borgatta and R. Montgomery (eds), *Encyclopedia of Sociology*. New York: Macmillan, pp. 901–7.

Heidrich, S. and Ryff, C. (1993) 'The role of social comparisons processes in the psychological adaptation of elderly adults', *Journal of Gerontology: Social Science*, 48: 127–36.

Held, D., McGrew, A., Goldblatt, D., and Perraton, J. (1999) *Global Transformations: Politics, Economics and Culture*. Stanford, CA: Stanford University Press.

Hendricks, J. (1992) 'Learning to act old: heroes, villains, or old fools', *Journal of Aging Studies*, 6: 1–12.

Hendricks, J. (1999) 'Practical consciousness, social class, and self-concept: a view from sociology', in C.D. Ryff and V.W. Marshall (eds), *The Self and Society in Aging Processes*. New York: Springer, pp. 187–222.

Hendricks, J. (2001) 'It's about time', in S.H. McFadden and R.C. Atchley (eds), *Aging and the Meaning of Time*. New York: Springer, pp. 21–50.

Hendricks, J. (2003) 'Structure and identity – mind the gap: toward a personal resource model of successful aging', in S. Biggs, A. Lowenstein, and J. Hendricks (eds), *The Need for Theory: Critical Approaches to Social Gerontology*. Amityville, NY: Baywood, pp. 63–87.

Hendricks, J. (2004) 'Public policies and identity', *Journal of Aging Studies* 18: 245–60.

Hendricks, J. (2005) 'Moral economy and aging', in M.L. Johnson (ed.), *Cambridge Handbook of Age and Ageing*. Cambridge: Cambridge University Press, pp. 510–17.

Hendricks J. and Cutler, S. (2004) 'Volunteerism and socioemotional selectivity in later life', *Journal of Gerontology: Social Science*, 59B: S251–257.

Hendricks, J. and Hatch, L. (2006) 'Lifestyle and aging', in R. Binstock and L. George (eds), *Handbook of Aging and the Social Sciences*, 6th edn. San Diego, CA: Academic Press, pp. 301–19.

Hendricks, J. and Peters, C.B. (1986) 'The times of our lives: an integrative framework', *American Behavioral Scientist*, 29: 662–76.

Hess, T.M. (2006) 'Attitudes toward aging and their effects on behavior', in J.E. Birren and K.W. Schaie (eds), *Handbook of the Psychology of Aging*. San Diego, CA: Academic Press, pp. 379–406.

Hockey, J. and James, A. (2002) *Social Identities Across the Life Course*. Basingstoke, UK: Palgrave Macmillan.

Kaplan, H. (1996) 'Perspectives on psychosocial stress', in H.B. Kaplan (ed.), *Psychosocial Stress: Perspectives on Structure, Theory, Life-course, and Methods*. San Diego, CA: Academic Press, pp. 3–24.

Kearney, M. (1995) 'The local and the global: the anthropology of globalization and transnationalism', *Annual Review of Anthropology*, 24: 547–65.

King, A. (1997) 'Introduction: spaces of culture, spaces of knowledge', in A. King (ed.), *Culture, Globalization and the World-System*. Minneapolis: University of Minnesota Press, pp. 1–18.

Kohli, M. (1986) 'Social organization and subjective construction of the life course', in A. Sorensen, F. Weinert, and L. Sherrod (eds), *Human Development and the Life Course: Multidisciplinary Perspectives*. Hillsdale, NJ: Erlbaum, pp. 271–92.

Kohli, M. and Meyer, J. (1986) 'Social structure and the social construction of the life stages', *Human Development*, 29: 145–56.

Kohn, M. and Slomczynski, K. (1990) *Social Structure and Self Direction*. Oxford: Basil Blackwell.

Lawton, M.P. and Nahemow, L. (1973) 'Ecology and the aging process', in C. Eisdorfer and M.P. Lawton (eds), *The Psychology of Adult Development and Aging*. Washington, DC: American Psychological Association, pp. 619–74.

Lestienne, R. (2000) 'Time and globalization: does the emergence of a global identity entail a loss of individualities?' *Time and Society*, 9: 289–91.

Lin, N. (2000) 'Inequality in social capital', *Contemporary Sociology*, 29: 785–95.

Liu, X. (2002) *The Otherness of Self: A Genealogy of the Self in Contemporary China*. Ann Arbor, MI: University of Michigan Press.

Markus, H. and Cross, S. (1990) 'The interpersonal self', in L. Pervin (ed.), *Handbook of Personality: Theory and Research*. New York: Guilford Press, pp. 576–608.

Markus, H. and Kitayama, S. (1991) 'Culture and the self: implications for cognition, emotion, and motivation', *Psychological Review*, 98: 224–53.

Markus, H. and Nurius, P. (1986) 'Possible selves', *American Psychologist*, 41: 954–69.

Markus, H. and Ruvolo, A. (1989) 'Possible selves: personalized representations of goals', in L. Pervin (ed.), *Goal Concepts in Personality and Social Psychology*. Hillsdale, NJ: Erlbaum, pp. 211–41.

McMichael, P. (2000) *Development and Social Change*. Thousand Oaks, CA: Pine Forge Press.

Pavalko, E. (1997) 'Beyond trajectories: multiple concepts for analyzing long-term process', in M.A. Hardy (ed.), *Studying Aging and Social Change: Conceptual and Methodological Issues*. Thousand Oaks, CA: SAGE, pp. 129–47.

Quadagno, J. (1982) *Aging in Early Industrial Society: Work, Family and Social Policy in Nineteenth Century England*. New York: Academic Press.

Riediger, M., Li, S.-C., and Lindenberger, U. (2006) 'Selection, optimization, and compensation as developmental mechanisms of adaptive resource allocation: review and previews', in J. Birren and K.W. Schaie (eds), *Handbook of the Psychology of Aging*. San Diego, CA: Academic Press, pp. 289–313.

Robertson, R. (1997) 'Social theory, cultural relativity and the problem of globality' in A.D. King (ed.), *Culture, Globalization and the World-System*. Minneapolis: University of Minnesota Press, pp. 69–90.

Rosenberg, M. (1986) *Conceiving the Self*, 2nd edn. New York: Basic Books.

Ross, C. and Mirowsky, J. (1989) 'Explaining the social patterns of depression: control and problem solving – or support and talking?', *Journal of Health and Social Behavior*, 30: 206–19.

Ryff, C. (1991) 'Possible selves in adulthood and old age: a tale of shifting horizons', *Psychology and Aging*, 6: 286–95.

Schaie, K.W. (2007) 'The concept of event time in the study of adult development', in J. Baars and H. Visser (eds), *Aging and Time: Multidisciplinary Perspectives*. Amityville, NY: Baywood, pp. 121–35.

Schroots, J. (1996) 'Time: concepts and perceptions', in J.E. Birren (ed.), *Encyclopedia of Gerontology*, Vol. 2. San Diego, CA: Academic Press, pp. 585–90.

Schulz, J.H. and Binstock, R.H. (2006) *Aging Nation: The Economics and Politics of Growing Older in America*. Westport, CT: Praeger.

Settersten, R. (2006) 'Aging and the life course', in R. Binstock and L. George (eds), *Handbook of Aging and the Social Science*, 6th edn. San Diego, CA: Academic Press, pp. 3–19.

Settersten, R. and Hagestad, G. (1996) 'What's the latest? II. Cultural age deadlines for educational and work transitions', *The Gerontologist*, 36: 602–13.

Specter, M. (2007) 'Damn spam: the losing war on junk e-mail', *The New Yorker*, August.

Steele, C.M., Spencer, S.J., and Aronson, J. (2002) 'Contending with group image: the psychology of stereotype and social identity threat', in M.P. Zanna (ed.), *Advances in Experimental Social Psychology*, Vol. 34. San Diego, CA: Academic Press. pp. 379–440.

Steger, M.B. (1997) 'The future of globalization', in A.D. King (ed.), *Culture, Globalization and the World-System*. Minneapolis: University of Minnesota Press, pp. 116–29.

Suls, J. and Mullen, B. (1992) 'From the cradle to the grave: comparison and self-evaluation across the life-span', in J. Suls (ed.), *Psychological Perspectives on the Self*, Vol. 1. Hillsdale, NJ: Erlbaum, pp. 97–128.

Townsend, P. (1981) 'The structured dependency of the elderly: a creation of social policy in the twentieth century', *Ageing and Society*, 1: 5–28.

van der Meer, E. (2007) 'Psychological time: empirical evidence, theories and aging-related effects', in J. Baars and H. Visser (eds), *Aging and Time: Multidisciplinary Perspectives*. Amityville, NY: Baywood, pp. 43–82.

Weber, M. (1921) *Economy and Society*. New York: Bedmister Press (1968).

Westerhof, G. and Dittmann-Kohli, F. (2000) 'Work status and the construction of work-related selves', in K.W. Schaie and J. Hendricks (eds), *The Evolution of the Aging Self: The Societal Impact on the Aging Process*. New York: Springer, pp. 123–57.

Whitbourne, S. and Primus, L. (1996) 'Physical identity in later adulthood', in J. Birren (ed.), *Encyclopedia of Gerontology*. San Diego, CA: Academic Press, pp. 733–42.

Wood, J. (1989) 'Theory and research concerning social comparisons of personal attributes', *Psychological Bulletin*, 106: 231–48.

20

Social Structure, Cognition, and Ageing

Duane F. Alwin

INTRODUCTION

The demographic reality of population ageing in both Western and non-Western societies (United Nations, 2002) raises a number of important social policy issues linked to the cognitive ageing of the population. Within that context, many observers have stated that the 'ageing mind' is one of *the* most burning questions for researchers, scholars, and policymakers concerned with the future of ageing (see, e.g., Alwin and Hofer, 2008). How does population ageing affect the nature and prevalence of cognitive ageing? As the population ages, what will be the consequences for the overall level of cognitive impairment in the population? If the technological advances that increase longevity do not also reduce cognitive ageing, greater numbers of persons aged 85+ in future years will bring about the greater prevalence of lower cognitive functioning, including the dementias associated with an ageing population (Alwin et al., 2008a; Brookmeyer et al., 1998; Kawas and Brookmeyer, 2001).

And, how does the structure of society, specifically the structure of inequality in cognitively relevant resources, enter the picture? First, do resources linked to socially structured opportunities and constraints help or hinder the nature of the process of 'typical' or 'normative' ageing, whereby people experience a progressive loss of cognitive functional capacity as they age? Secondly, do differences in access to resources linked to social structure contribute to differential risks of susceptibility to dementia (as well as to non-disease processes linked to cognitive change in older age)?

If structurally rooted inequalities affect the nature and extent of cognitive ageing, the level of anticipated social inequality should be an important consideration in gauging the impact of population ageing on levels of cognitive functioning in a future world.

This chapter conceptualizes the link between socio-environmental factors thought to be tied to social structures and the nature of age-related cognitive change. I rely on the concepts of 'cognitive functioning,' 'cognitive ageing,' and 'social structure' developed elsewhere (see Alwin, 2008) and place them within a life-span developmental framework. In addition, I review the relevant literature on specific environmental factors that are known to be related to levels of cognitive functioning and which can potentially also relate to processes that are associated with sustaining or changing cognitive factors.

COGNITION, AGEING, AND SOCIAL STRUCTURE

In this section, I briefly introduce the nature of the three main phenomena of concern – *cognitive functioning*, *cognitive ageing*, and *social structures*. Ultimately, the chapter places these concepts within a life-span developmental perspective (see, e.g., Alwin, 2009c; Alwin and Wray, 2005), in order to examine the life cycle changes inhering in human development and their relationship to cognitive function and cognitive ageing, as well as potential life-course events and transitions that may contribute to cognitive change. I ultimately consider what we know about the relationship between social structure and cognitive ageing.

It is common these days for people to refer to the 'ageing mind.' What is it? What 'mental' dimensions are being talked about? A range of human cognitive abilities, many of which decline in older age – attention, reaction time, processing speed, learning, memory, language use, sensation and sensory function, inductive reasoning, knowledge, and so forth – coordinate with one another to permit cognitive functioning (see Hofer and Alwin, 2008: 122–258). Thus, cognitive function is a broad concept reflecting a range of abilities that allow one to function effectively within society. By definition, then, cognitive functioning does not occur in a social vacuum – it happens within a configuration of opportunities and constraints linked to social roles, institutional arrangements, and interpersonal relationships. For the purposes of this chapter, *mind* is a central element in the relationship of the individual to society, and therefore the notion of the *ageing mind* is of great interest with respect to the changing status of the individual in society over biographical time. The *ageing mind* must be distinguished from the *ageing brain*, which refers to age-related physiological changes in brain function that occurs due to ageing processes. The 'ageing mind,' by contrast, refers to changes in the human ability to manipulate the environment in such ways as to solve problems posed by that (primarily external) environment. These processes condition the formation, maintenance, and expression of cognitive abilities across the entire life span. Linking the complexities of 'mind' and environmental structures is necessary if we are to understand the nature of cognitive ageing (see Alwin, 2008).

Historically, the concept of 'ageing' refers to change resulting from some combination of biological, psychological, and social mechanisms. The 'life-span developmental' perspective is a somewhat broader framework (e.g., Baltes, 1987, 1997; Featherman, 1983), as it considers 'ageing' to begin at birth and conceptualizes human development as multidimensional and multidirectional processes of growth involving both gains and losses. From this perspective, as noted above, human development and ageing are embedded in multiple contexts and are conceived of in terms of dynamic processes in which the ontogeny of development interacts with a multilayered social and cultural context (Bronfenbrenner, 1979).

In addition, the uniqueness of individual biographies – what is often referred to as the *life course* (Dannefer, 1984; Elder, 1985) – and the diversity of life patterns have encouraged a complementary

approach to human development within the social sciences. As defined here, the life course is primarily concerned with the social pathways experienced by individuals, defined by events and transitions and the sequences of roles they follow (see Alwin and Wray, 2005). Influences of development, maturation, and ageing are also contributors to within-person change. For simplicity, I refer to all of these types of 'within-person' change as potentially the effects of (or consequences of) ageing, and thus 'ageing' is often identified simply as 'age-related change' (Bengtson and Schaie, 1999; Hofer and Alwin, 2008).

Consistent with the life-span developmental perspective mentioned above, we consider 'cognitive ageing' to be any time-dependent changes that reflect systematic alterations of functional capacity after a point of maturity. It is important to clarify that age-related changes that reflect a progressive loss of function are not necessarily irreversible. Indeed, it is difficult to apportion the reversible from the irreversible. Baltes and Willis (1981), for example, showed that actual decline was a function of lack of practice, which may be taken as a surrogate for the lack of intellectual stimulation in everyday life. In this discussion, we consider cognitive ageing to refer to changes in the individual's functional relationship with society. Of course there is a great deal of heterogeneity in a population, but from this perspective an increase in frailty, including changes in respiratory function, hearing, vision, and cognitive function, are to some extent intrinsic to the organism rather than brought about by the environment; and they occur in a pattern that is characteristic of all members of a given species (see Weiss, 1990). The study of cognitive ageing focuses on the heterogeneity in trajectories of cognitive function and the environmental factors that contribute to variation in the nature and extent of age-related change (Hofer and Alwin, 2008).

Studies of cognitive ageing often treat ageing as a process that is empirically separable from disease. However, to study the causes of cognitive loss in ageing individuals, one must directly measure the influence of age-related diseases and risk processes. Because our designs do not usually permit fine-grained analyses of individuals over time, research on cognitive ageing has commonly examined the effects of dementia (and other diseases, like diabetes) mostly as a dichotomous between-person variable. A more sophisticated treatment would recognize that dementia (like other age-related diseases) is a progressive process that unfolds over time. The focus of contemporary perspectives on cognitive ageing emphasize the study of within-person change in functional components, including both behavioral and disease-related aspects of the process. Understanding how the progression of dementia and other diseases (in their pre-clinical stage) influences cognition is an essential step in formulating descriptive accounts of cognitive ageing effects.

The concept of structure is central to virtually all schools of social scientific thought (see Merton, 1949), as well as many of the theories that are important for understanding processes of ageing (Bengtson and Schaie, 1999). Although often misunderstood, the concept of social structure is 'one of the most important and most elusive terms in the vocabulary of current social sciences' (Sewell, 2005: 124). In this chapter, I use the concept of social structure to refer to *opportunities and constraints within networks of roles, relationships, and communication patterns, which are relatively patterned and persisting* (see Williams, 1960). In this sense, structure may refer, on the one hand, to large organic institutional structures, such as bureaucracies; or, at the other extreme, to a set of dyadic norms negotiated between two individuals for purposes of social exchange (Alwin, 1995: 219). The relevance of social structures, as defined here, is that the 'opportunities' and 'constraints' have implications for whether cognitive functioning is enhanced or inhibited in relation to the social environment.

Both the concepts of 'social structure' and 'cognitive ability' involve the foundational concept of *resources*, a concept that ties them together in the process of socialization. Cognitive function is considered to be a set of mental or 'within-person' resources, applied in the process of adapting to environmental demands, which are an essential component of social functioning across the life span. Similarly, the concept of social structure reflects a robust and persistent set of social arrangements that provide resources, opportunities, and constraints that impinge upon behavior and functioning of individuals across a wide range of domains. It is therefore useful to examine the linkage of cognitive resources to key elements of social structure, as well as the manner in which these linkages change over the life span.

This approach is consistent with the current literature, although there are some differences. At minimum, the concept of social structure is used to understand those 'opportunities and constraints' posed by social relationships, e.g., a set of organizational role relationships (see Kohn and Slomczynski, 1990). Social science theory suggests structural factors impinge on the ageing process and that their influence needs to be understood with respect to cognitive ageing (e.g., Barnes et al., 2008; Berg, 2008; Blanchard-Fields et al., 2008; Manly, 2008). Thus, the critical questions are not *whether*, or even *how much*, social structural

factors matter for the production of individual differences in cognitive function and change; rather, the over-riding questions are *when* (with respect to the part of the life span) *and in what manner* do social environmental factors matter?

Researchers often reify individual-level variables, e.g., educational level or occupational status, as aspects of social structure. However, these are not measures of social structure, per se, but instead individual-level resources that result from structural relations. Bronfenbrenner and Crouter (1983) considered such approaches to be limited in that they focus on the 'social address' of the individual and criticized their failure to undertake a thorough conceptualization of the linkage between structural elements at the societal or group level and the individual (see also Bronfenbrenner, 1986; Bronfenbrenner and Ceci, 1994; Dannefer, 1992). On the other hand, such individual-level properties, e.g., level of education, may be useful indicators of the resources deriving from a person's location in the network of positions that define social structure, which exist apart from the aggregation of individual attributes. Structural variables are defined at the group or social-system level. Such structural arrangements produce advantages (benefits) to some and disadvantages (or fewer benefits) to others. Many individual-level attributes (such as gender, race-ethnicity, and level of education) reflect the ways socially structured arrangements shape and organize the experiences of individuals, but they are not measures of social structure per se.

THE RELATIONSHIP BETWEEN SOCIAL STRUCTURE AND COGNITIVE AGEING

From a life-span developmental perspective, three elements define the relationship between social structure and individual differences: (1) the processes by which social structures produce differences among individuals; (2) the extent to which features of social structure help maintain individual differences over the life span; and (3) the extent to which differences in structurally organized exposure to resources continue to promote levels and rates of individual change in older age.

Social environment and cognitive development

The social organization of experience can influence cognitive development in two ways: via its influence on *levels of cognitive functioning* and its influence on *rates of within-person cognitive change*. Tracking levels of functioning through time creates a *trajectory* of within-person change. Most research on social structure and cognitive function has focused on levels rather than on rates of change (e.g., Kohn and Schooler, 1978, 1983; Schooler, 1984, 1987). However, in order to understand how social structure is related to life-span changes in cognitive function, it is important not only to consider the distinction between levels and rates of change but also to attend to the issues addressed by each component of trajectories. Paradoxically, the earliest influences of social structural factors on cognitive functioning may have effects that allow for powerful effects on levels of functioning, but less of a role for the influences of environmental differences on cognitive change later in life.

In the main, research has shown that environmental differences early in life, particularly socioeconomic differences, influence levels of intellectual functioning (Alwin and Thornton, 1984; Kohn and Schooler, 1983; Sewell and Hauser, 1975). Thus, social-structural effects in cognitive functioning are most potent during the period of rapid developmental change. In Bloom's (1964: vii) words, 'variations in the environment have greatest quantitative effect on a characteristic at its most rapid period of change and least effect on the characteristic during the least rapid period of change.' In Figure 20.1, I present Bloom's developmental curve and the limits of environmental variation (see Bloom, 1964: vii). The gradually rising curve of the level of development that changes as a function of age in this figure represents the average trajectory of the development of cognitive function. Clearly, there is between-person variation in the nature of this

trajectory, and this graph is intended to reflect the average or typical trajectory. This curve exhibits its highest rates of change at the youngest ages, and slows as age increases. The shaded area surrounding this curve represents the potential for differences in environments to affect the rate of change. When the band is wide, it means the environment is having an impact on developmental change, and when it is narrow, the influences of differential experiences with the environment are substantially less. The greater the potential for environmental effects, the more we would expect variation in individual trajectories, and the less stable we would expect are the individual differences in the attributes of individuals. On the other hand, where there is less potential for environmental change, the more highly stable are individual differences (see Alwin, 1994; Dannefer, 1993).

This picture of development in the early years is assumed in Bloom's scheme to be very general, applying to aspects of physical as well as mental development, and it is consistent with much theorizing in psychology of cognitive development. Cattell's (1963) distinction between *fluid* and *crystallized* intelligence, as inter-related components of cognitive abilities, is useful in the present context. Fluid intelligence is conceptualized as *'the capacity for insight into complex relations ... independent of the sensory or cultural area in which the tests are expressed'* (Cattell, 1971a: 13, emphasis in the original). [It is worth noting that this literature uses the term 'intelligence' where I prefer the term 'abilities.' As indicated in the above discussion, there are myriad abilities that combine to make up 'cognitive function,' which is a more general concept than 'intelligence,' although the latter is usually considered to be an important part of the former.] Crystallized abilities,

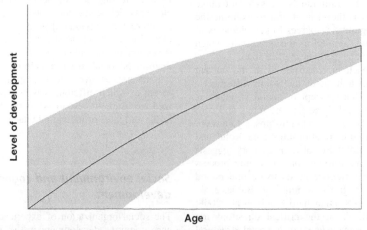

Figure 20.1 Bloom's developmental curve and the limits of environmental variation. Adapted from Bloom (1964).

on the other hand, have their origins in experience but are not expected to be independent of other capacities because they arise '... as the result of the investment of fluid intelligence, over the years, in whatever higher-level cultural skills the individual is exposed to' (Cattell, 1971a: 13; see also Cattell, 1971b; Denny, 1982; Horn, 1968, 1976, 1982a, 1982b, 1994; Horn and Cattell, 1967; Horn and Donaldson, 1980). Similarly, Salthouse (1991) distinguished 'process' from 'product' abilities, and Baltes (1987) between the 'mechanics' and the 'pragmatics' of intelligence. Contemporary taxonomies and models of intelligence include a much more complex array of domains (see Carroll, 1996, 1998; Horn, 1985, 1988, 1991; Woodcock, 1994), but the fluid–crystallized distinction continues to guide thinking about how to conceptualize intelligence (see Flanagan et al., 2000; McGrew, 1997; McGrew and Flanagan, 1998; see Hertzog, 2008 for an alternate view).

Although Cattell (1971a) argued that the development of these two aspects of cognitive functioning is collinear through adolescence, little is known about the relative role of environmental change in affecting each of these distinct sets of cognitive function. While Bloom (1964) speculated that 'intelligence remains constant after about age 20,' his empirical work does not go beyond age 18, and he conceded that at the time

he did his study there was very little available evidence on adult intelligence (Bloom, 1964: 80). He speculated that the environments in which people live after young adulthood would likely determine the nature of further intellectual development, and he implied that after the age of 20, intelligence is stable if the environment is stable. He suggested that further development is possible if the forces reflecting environmental change are powerful enough to produce cognitive change, although he surmised that during most of adult life, environments are decidedly static and that massive levels of intellectual stability is typical (Bloom, 1964: 80–90). Ultimately, this pattern is not necessarily normal, or inevitable, since the level of stability is a reflection of the relationship of the person and the environment, which is something that varies culturally and historically. Nevertheless, research on the person–environment relationship often suggests that individuals are stable over large portions of the life span (Alwin, 1994, 1995, 1997; Alwin et al., 1991; Ryder, 1965). Thus, it may be useful to consider the logical *extension* of Bloom's (1964) work concerning the role of the environment in producing cognitive change. Figure 20.2 depicts both Bloom's (1964) and Cattell's (1971a) models, projecting both the age-related levels and potential role of environmental variation throughout the life span – from birth to age 100. Early differences

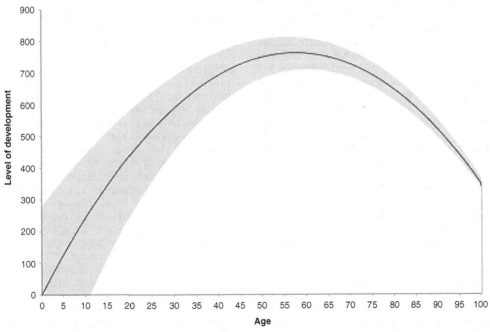

Figure 20.2 Developmental curve and declining limits of environmental influence across the entire life span

in experiences play a critical role in shaping individual differences, and a vast literature in behavioral science shows that such differences exist.

There are several things to notice about this model of human development with respect to levels and trajectories. First, the developmental curve depicted here is completely consistent with the ideas inherent in the conception of development and the declining role of environmental differences that is depicted earlier in Figure 20.1. Levels of functioning increase, while rates of increase decline with time. As the rate of increase slows, so does the potential of the environment to affect cognitive change. This is a theoretical curve and is not intended to necessarily reflect empirical evidence about levels and rates of change – at some point the growth in cognitive functioning levels off and an asymptote is reached; thereafter, there is a tendency toward decline at an increasing rate. There are several possible trajectories of the life-span development of abilities, especially with regard to when the development of abilities peaks and levels off, prior to any significant decline. Nevertheless, with some risk of oversimplification, this is probably the typical pattern.

According to Cattell (1971a, 1971b), the average trajectory of fluid abilities declines with age, while that of crystallized abilities increases slightly or remains relatively stable with respect to age (see Horn, 1982a; Horn and Cattell, 1967). The cognitive ageing literature generally supports Cattell's theory, although the bulk of available opinion is that substantial declines in fluid abilities are delayed into older age. For example, research shows that significant cognitive declines in fluid or process-based abilities (e.g., memory) do not occur until well past age 65 (Hertzog and Schaie, 1988) and tend not to show more rapid declines until after age 80 (Scherr et al., 1988). Measures of crystallized or education-based abilities (vocabulary recognition or verbal reasoning) decline later and less predictably (Park, 1999; Park et al., 1996; Schaie, 2005). Most scholars agree no pure measures exist for either component and that any given measure may constitute some combination of both. To the extent that available cognitive measures are dependent upon education, there may be a confounding of age-related trajectories with schooling, given the well-known pattern of inter-cohort differences in levels of schooling. Finally, unlike Bloom (1964), Cattell's (1971a, 1971b) classic prediction about the age-related patterns of fluid and crystallized abilities is about levels and trajectories of cognitive function alone; he does not address the relationship between environmental and individual change.

Stability of environments and individuals

Figure 20.2 depicts a relationship between the rate of change in the average trajectory of development and the limits of environmental influence, suggesting the declining potential for individual differences in environmental exposures to affect individual differences in development. Again, to the extent features of the social environment are stable, and thus, help maintain individual differences in cognitive and intellectual functioning produced early in the life span, then we expect for human lives to reflect that degree of stability. In Figure 20.2, when we extend the curve beyond early adulthood, the continuing decline of the shaded area reflects a diminished potential for environmental influence, despite the increasing rate of change in functioning in old age.

Some contend that cognitive decline is not inevitable, and that individuals can 'age successfully' by engaging in ameliorative behaviors and avoiding risk factors associated with deteriorative and chronic diseases (Rowe and Kahn, 1998). Nevertheless, the average trajectory is one of cognitive decline (Hofer and Alwin, 2008). The diminution of the range of environmental potential for cognitive change represented in Figure 20.2 corresponds loosely to the concept of the 'stability of individual differences,' in that we expect that the limits of environmental variation is a reflection of the complex relation between the individual and society that results from personological and environmental persistence, leading to the stability of individual differences (see Alwin, 1994; Dannefer, 1993). In this model of development, the potential for individual change arising from differences in environments occurs a great deal more in the early periods of the life span, i.e., prior to adulthood, than later on. This model is supported by the growing literature on the stability of individual differences in cognitive function, which shows high degrees of stability after early adulthood (see Alwin, 2008: 429–32). For example, the Seattle Longitudinal Study reflects the typical pattern – Hertzog and Schaie's (1986) estimate of the stability of the common factor underlying individual differences in a version of Thurstone's Primary Mental Abilities is found to be 0.92 over a 14-year period, and stability increases with age. Similarly, Kohn and Schooler (1978) find a normative stability value of 0.93 for their concept of 'ideational flexibility' assessed over a 10-year period. Across the entire range of available studies, results indicate that stability grows in magnitude from adolescence onward and from the age of 40 the typical 'molar stability' of intellectual ability is roughly 0.9 (see Alwin, 2008: 430). Preliminary results for the older population, those aged 65+, suggest that stability remains high but declines slightly with time, although it is not clear to what extent these differences are due to mortality selection (see Alwin, 2008: 432).

These results challenge claims that socialization or learning affecting basic cognitive abilities continues well into adulthood. Obviously, some openness to change is possible during adulthood, but if we understand that stability is a function of constancies of person–situation or person–structural linkages, then continuities over time may be viewed as reflections of the stability of socially structured experience (Ryder, 1965), and the proper adjudication of the issue of whether a socio-environmental interpretation exists for the stability of cognitive abilities would have to focus on the segment of the population that experiences change in social locations at different points in the life cycle. Schooler's (Schooler, 1987; see also Schooler and Mulatu, 2001; Schooler et al., 1999, 2004) analysis of the development of intellectual flexibility over the life span through exposure to changes in the complexity of the environment represents one creative attempt to apply theories of social structure and personality to human development (see also, e.g., Kohn and Schooler, 1978, 1983; Kohn and Slomczynski, 1990; Schooler, 1987). Again, greater change in cognitive function may be expected when environments are changing most rapidly, and those who remain in stable environments are least likely to change,

as found in other areas of research investigation (Alwin, 1994; Alwin et al., 1991; Musgrove, 1977).

Social environments and cognitive ageing

In contrast to the above model of declining environmental influence, Figure 20.3 presents a hypothetical pattern showing the result if resource or risk exposures change or increase in their influence or as inequalities increase. Under such conditions, individuals may continue to change as they age, after a period of midlife stability. As in Figure 20.2, this display represents an *extension* of Bloom's (1964) model, projecting both age-related levels and the potential role of environmental variation from birth to age 100. Figure 20.3 projects both absolute level of cognitive development and of the environmental potential for cognitive change into old age. Thus, this model more explicitly follows Bloom's (1964) line of argument: namely, that differences in the experience with the environment are most potent during rapid changes at the maturational level. To repeat Bloom's words, 'variations in the environment have greatest quantitative effect on a characteristic at its most rapid period of change and least effect on the characteristic during the least rapid period of change' (Bloom, 1964: vii).

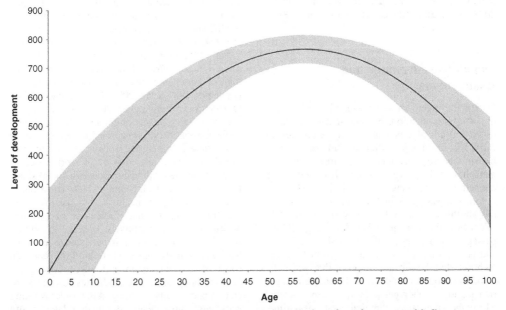

Figure 20.3 Developmental curve and changes in the limits of environmental influence across the entire life span

As discussed above, the midlife environment may promote stability rather than change, and if it is increasingly stable, it will encourage the persistence of individual differences (e.g., Alwin, 1994; Ryder, 1965). This is reflected in Figure 20.3, along with the possibility that, in older age, individual experience may again parallel that of childhood and youth – and environmental influences may regain their importance as factors linked to cognitive change. Although little research has addressed the changing influence of the social environment on cognitive function over the life span, there are several important contributions to the understanding of early influences on adult development. For example, the ideas advocated by the cognitive reserve perspective highlight the importance of initial environment on late-life cognitive changes (Richards and Deary, 2005; Stern, 2007). The work of Schooler (Schooler, 1987; see also Schooler and Mulatu, 2001; Schooler et al., 1999, 2004) on environmental complexity (see also Kohn and Slomcyznski, 1990), illustrates how environmental factors assessed across the life span help shape cognitive complexity. There is also evidence linking social resources and network ties with later-life cognitive functioning (Bassuk et al., 1999), including dementia (Fratiglioni et al., 2004). Virtually all of this literature has focused on levels of cognitive functioning, and there has been a relative neglect of the serious examination of issues related to the impact of variations in the social environment on levels, trajectories, and rates of change in cognitive function *over the entire life span* (but see Barnes et al., 2008; Berg, 2008; Blanchard-Fields et al., 2008).

Cumulative advantage and disadvantage

One of the timeworn hypotheses in the literature on social stratification, but one that is not often tested empirically, is that the consequences of early socioeconomic differences in the lives of individuals are accentuated over time. Using the metaphor of the *parable of the talents*, which he dubbed the 'Matthew Effect,' Robert Merton's (1968) famous paper in *Science*, about inequalities in the reward systems governing credit in scientific authorship, quoted the following Biblical passage: 'unto everyone that hath shall be given, and he shall have abundance; but from him that hath not shall be taken away even that which he hath.' In short, Merton suggested that 'the rich get richer and the poor get poorer,' in other words, advantage and disadvantage cumulate over time. One need not be a Biblical scholar to know that

however true the hypothesis of accumulation may be to the development of social inequality, it has absolutely nothing literally to do with what the gospel writer was trying to say about investments in *the kingdom of heaven* (see Matthew, chapter 25, verses 15–30). It is purely a metaphor.

Nevertheless, few would doubt Merton's observation, that the social environment is structured in such a way as to promote the accrual of greater resources to those who already have them – or, cumulative advantage – and the withholding of resources from those who begin with less – or cumulative disadvantage. The focus of the present chapter is on the development of cognitive resources, and whether the accrual of 'cognitive reserve' (see Stern, 2007) follows the same pattern, as Merton suggests it does in other realms. Few doubt that the socioeconomic environment is an important element in cognitive development: it is a well-accepted fact that cognitive function is shaped by differences in structural opportunities and other factors and, theoretically at least, greater opportunities promote the investment in activities that lead to greater cognitive development. In fact, one of the prevailing assumptions is that both the early and later environments contribute independently to the development of intellectual resources in childhood (see Alwin and Thornton, 1984).

The argument is typically extended to suggest there is a further compounding, or an accentuation, of the influences of the social environment over time, but this has not been closely examined in the realm of cognitive functioning. Not only do socio-environmental inequalities impact upon individual differences at multiple time points over the life span, there is considerable theory suggesting that the residues of these influences in individual differences cumulate over time. Hence, there is a literature that has developed under the topic of 'cumulative advantage/disadvantage theory' (Dannefer, 1987, 1988, 2003, 2008; O'Rand, 1996; O'Rand and Hamil-Luker, 2005), which may be applied to the outcome of cognitive functioning.

Few researchers have applied the *hypothesis of cumulative advantage/disadvantage* to cognitive functioning. One related body of work concerns research on the relationship between social status factors and physical health, which consistently finds inequalities in health across the life span. Cognitive function and indicators of physical health would presumptively operate in similar ways; however, despite this persistence and posited increasing strength of the relationship between social status and health with increasing age, a growing body of research indicates that the association is generally strongest at the 'older working ages,' and subsequently diminishes later in life (e.g., Crimmins, 2001, 2005; Crimmins et al., 2004;

Hayward et al., 2000; House et al., 1992, 1994, 2005; Kunst and Mackenbach, 1994; Lynch, 2003; Marmot and Shipley, 1996; Molla et al., 2004; Robert and House, 1996). These researches have consistently found a declining role of social status factors in older age, despite the parallel findings of the declining significance of genetic differences in affecting health outcomes in older age (see Rowe and Kahn, 1998). Moreover, unless one factors in the effects of selective mortality, such findings are hard to account for based on the premises of cumulative advantage/disadvantage theory, in that one would expect the socioeconomic gradient to become steeper with time – i.e., 'the rich get richer and the poor get poorer.' One would expect that those higher in status (i.e., more highly educated), who are also cognitively advantaged, would actually increase their advantage over time, although as far as we can tell, there is hardly any evidence for it, at least with respect to measures of health.

Rethinking the social status and cognition relationship

The findings cited above appear on the face of it to be at odds with the *hypothesis of cumulative advantage/disadvantage* (the CAD hypothesis). This hypothesis assumes (1) increasing heterogeneity in the older population with respect to

resources that matter for cognitive development, and (2) an increasingly strong relationship between social inequalities and cognitive function. Again, using the analog to the relationship between social status and health, we can rephrase the question of the relationship between the environment and cognitive functioning in terms of the following:

1 What is the nature of the relationship between social inequalities at time T and cognitive inequalities at time $T + j$ or $T - j$?
2 How does the relationship between social inequalities and cognitive inqualities vary *across the life span* for cohort i? Specifically, does this relationship increase, or decrease, or what?
3 What role do population processes (particularly mortality selection) play in producing the changing nature of that relationship?

Figure 20.4 depicts three different models of the relationships of social status and health status (assumed to include cognitive function) over the life span. The 'constant advantage/disadvantage' model (solid line) assumes the net impact of advantages and disadvantages between individuals in social status have an effect on health inequalities, but that the relationship does not differ across the life span. Note that the model underlying this case does not presume any influence of mortality selection in the status-specific prevalence rates for health status for a given cohort – they are essentially the same, regardless of the

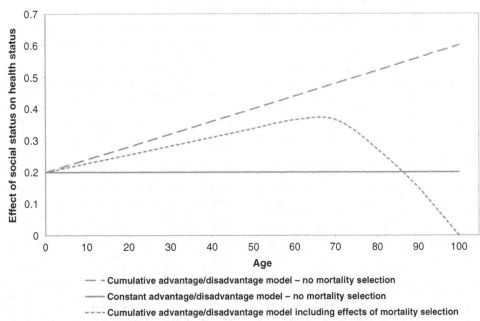

- - Cumulative advantage/disadvantage model – no mortality selection
—— Constant advantage/disadvantage model – no mortality selection
- - - - Cumulative advantage/disadvantage model including effects of mortality selection

Figure 20.4   The relationships of social status and health status over the life span

point in the life span they are assessed. The model represented by the broken line in Figure 20.4 is consistent with the hypothesis of cumulative advantage/disadvantage, which posits that the relationship between social status and health status increases over time. This model – the 'cumulative advantage/disadvantage model' – is by far the most popular way of thinking about the question of how the relationship between social inequalities and health vary across the life span for a given cohort. Again, this model does not presume any influence of mortality selection on status-specific prevalence rates: in fact, most proponents of this model either ignore, or deny, the influences of mortality selection processes.

Finally, a third model (the dotted line), one that like the previous one, posits cumulative advantage/disadvantage, adds the operation of mortality selection (e.g., Vaupel and Yashin, 1985). This is an important consideration, because mortality selection is a phenomenon that changes the composition of the population under consideration. We elaborate on these issues in the following few paragraphs, but suffice it to say at this point that mortality selection refers to a set of homogenizing influences, which create a more homogeneous cohort composition with time: i.e., these processes selectively reduce the heterogeneity by 'selecting out' those individuals who have both the lowest status and the lowest levels of health (or cognitive function). Beckett (Beckett, 2000; see also Beckett and Elliott, 2001) tested the hypothesis that the convergence in health inequalities in older age resulted from mortality selection, concluding that selection biases do not account for the declining levels of association between social status and health. If mortality selection cannot account for this pattern, then this may be seen as an even greater setback for cumulative advantage/disadvantage theory, in that it reflects a diminution in the accumulation of cognitive benefits over the life span. These results appear to conform to the developmental theory implied by the trajectory and pattern of environmental influence shown in Figure 20.2.

How does mortality selection work? What are its consequences for assessing the relationships between social statuses and health? I cannot fully answer these questions here, although it is possible to provide a brief sensitizing discussion. First, the problem requires that we think of the phenomenon within a cohort framework that highlights the differences in the experiences of different cohorts (see Dannefer and Uhlenberg, 1999: 311–12). A given birth cohort can be thought of as a collection of subpopulations defined by longevity (subpopulations surviving $0 + t$ years). At a given point in historical time, birth cohorts differ

substantially in their representation of these subpopulations. Membership in these subpopulations is not discernible prior to death; however, a person's current age serves as a lower bound. As a result, given stable (or at least proportional) age-specific mortality rates, heterogeneity in longevity decreases with age, meaning that *at a given time* later-born cohorts are more heterogeneous with respect to their expected age at death than are earlier-borns. If the longevity of a cohort declines in heterogeneity over the life span, we therefore also expect those factors related to longevity to decline in heterogeneity with time. Since the likelihood of relative longevity increases with age, we expect those social resources contributing to inequalities in health also to decline in heterogeneity, rather than increase, and the social status–health correlation to decline as a result, as illustrated by the dotted line in Figure 20.4.

To date, we have had neither the needed data nor the statistical models needed to understand the relationship between mortality processes and cohort differences. Recently, our research empirically examined several hypotheses found in theorizing about life–span development and cognitive performance, hypotheses gleaned from writings on ageing and social inequality, relevant to the above set of issues, and guided by the CAD framework (Alwin et al., 2008b). Using data from the Health and Retirement Study (HRS), hypotheses were tested regarding the role of schooling in cognitive performance and how the salutary effect of schooling changes with age. We examine two central questions:

1 Does the effect of schooling on cognitive performance vary across cohorts differing in age and historical experience?
2 How do individual differences in schooling influence the shape of the ageing trajectory of cognitive performance within and between cohorts.

Using latent curve models (see Alwin et al., 2006), we specifically ask whether higher levels of schooling diminish the rate of change in cognitive decline, acting to buffer the processes of normal cognitive ageing. Our findings do not support the major ideas drawn from the CAD perspective; we find that cognitive inequalities in returns to school decline in older age. Our results lead us to conclude that for some cognitive outcomes across cohorts there are indeed differences in educational 'rates of return' to cognitive functioning – the further one gets from the completion of schooling, the less overall benefit it has for cognitive performance. At the same time, analyses within cohorts from the early 1900s to 1947 indicate greater amounts of schooling contribute to higher levels of cognitive functioning, but little if any to rates of change in cognitive performance in adulthood over time. We concluded that, across cohorts, greater schooling does not in general appear to provide a protective influence on cognitive ageing (i.e., rates of cognitive change). On the other hand, regardless of cohort, higher levels of schooling produce higher levels of functioning: i.e., there is plenty of support for the *advantage hypothesis*. What we have not been able to detect is an accentuation or accumulation of the education-related advantages. If anything, the cognitive benefits accruing to higher levels of schooling decline (within cohorts) over time. What is not clear is whether these patterns result from life-span development, i.e., age-related changes, unique cohort experiences, or compositional differences due to mortality selection (see Alwin, 2009a, 2009b).

CONCLUSIONS

Understanding the relationship of ageing to cognitive function is a high priority in a number of national settings, not only because of its intrinsic relevance to the lives of ageing members of society but also because of the realities of population ageing. With increases in population ageing, cognitive ageing researchers are increasingly called upon to respond to the question of its consequences for the future of cognitive ageing. At the same time, the influence of social structural factors on the ageing process needs to be understood in order to grasp the relationship between population ageing and population cognitive ageing.

Projections about time trends in levels of cognitive ageing must come to terms with the relationship between the resources, opportunities, and constraints tied to social structure. I have argued that differences in patterns of cognitive ageing are linked theoretically and empirically to key elements of social structure, notably through the various types of resources tied to social status. This chapter reviewed the theoretical role of structural factors that contribute to levels and trajectories of change in cognitive function in older age, and we have argued that differences in social resources (defined broadly) linked to the social structure may contribute to the understanding of cognitive ageing in several ways.

Within this context, a principal focus of future research should be on the ways in which social status variables linked to social structural factors – specifically educational, occupational, socioeconomic, racial/ethnic, and gender factors – produce differences in levels and rates of change in cognitive function, not only in a static sense but also *at different points across the life span* (see Alwin, 2008). In addition research should continue to examine the role of environmental differences across the life span, and particularly the *timing* of the influence of the environment on cognitive development. For example, is the social environment equally important across the life span, or are there 'critical years' in which the bulk of the impact of differences in the environment matter? Are there ways in which old age replicates childhood with respect to increased levels of environmental influence (see Alwin, 2008)? Or, does the influence of the environment on individual differences in cognitive function primarily occur early in life? Future empirical research can best address the potentially changing role of socio-environmental influences across the life span by studying rates of within-person change over time using longitudinal data that assesses both changes in individual cognitive functioning as well as changes in the environment.

Lastly, the role of mortality selection must be included in the interpretation of empirical assessments of the relationship between social status factors and cognitive function (see Aldwin, 2009a). Until we can get a handle on the relative influences of the social environment on cognitive functioning at various phases (or stages) of the life cycle, using methods that take mortality selection into account, it may be risky to speculate about the implications of socio-environmental factors for levels of population cognitive ageing in future years.

ACKNOWLEDGEMENT

The research reported here was supported by a grant titled 'Latent Curve Models of Cognitive Aging' from the National Institute on Aging (R01-AG021203–06). The author acknowledges the collaboration of colleagues Scott Hofer, Linda Wray, and Dale Dannefer in the development of the ideas presented here – the author is solely responsible for the presentation made in this chapter.

REFERENCES

Alwin, D.F. (1994) 'Aging, personality and social change: the stability of individual differences over the adult life span', in D.L. Featherman, R.M. Lerner, and M. Perlman (eds),

Life Span Development and Behavior, Vol. 12. Hillsdale, NJ: Lawrence Erlbaum, pp. 135–85.

Alwin, D.F. (1995) 'Taking time seriously: studying social change, social structure and human lives', in P. Moen, G.H. Elder, Jr., and K. Lüscher (eds), *Examining Lives in Context: Perspectives on the Ecology of Human Development*. Washington, DC: American Psychological Association, pp. 211–62.

Alwin, D.F. (1997) 'Aging, social change and conservatism: the link between historical and biographical time in the study of political identities', in M.A. Hardy (ed.), *Studying Aging and Social Change: Conceptual and Methodological Issues*. Thousand Oaks, CA: SAGE, pp. 164–90.

Alwin, D.F. (2008) 'Social structure and cognitive change', in S.M. Hofer and D.F. Alwin (eds), *Handbook of Cognitive Aging: Interdisciplinary Perspectives*. Thousand Oaks, CA: SAGE, pp. 418–44.

Alwin, D.F. (2009a) 'History, cohorts and cognitive aging', in H. Bosworth and C. Hertzog (eds), *Aging and Cognition – Research Methodologies and Empirical Advances: Essays in Honor of Warner Schaie*. Washington, DC: American Psychological Association.

Alwin, D.F. (2009b) 'The aging mind in social and historical perspective', Center on Life Course, Health and Aging, Pennsylvania State University, University Park, PA. 16802. Unpublished manuscript.

Alwin, D.F. (2009c) 'Integrating varieties of the life course', Center on Life Course, Health and Aging, Pennsylvania State University, University Park, PA. 16802. Unpublished manuscript.

Alwin, D.F. and Hofer, S.M. (2008) 'Opportunities and challenges for interdisciplinary research', in S.M. Hofer and D.F. Alwin (eds.), *Handbook of Cognitive Aging: Interdisciplinary Perspectives*. Thousand Oaks, CA: SAGE, pp. 2–31.

Alwin, D.F. and Thornton, A. (1984) 'Family origins and the schooling process: early vs. late influence of parental characteristics', *American Sociological Review*, 43: 784–802.

Alwin, D.F. and Wray, L.A. (2005) 'A life-span developmental perspective on social status and health', *Journal of Gerontology*, 60B: S7–14.

Alwin, D.F., Cohen, R.L., and Newcomb, T.M. (1991) *Political Attitudes Over the Life Span: The Bennington Women After Fifty Years*. Madison, WI: University of Wisconsin Press.

Alwin, D.F., Hofer, S.M., and McCammon, R.J. (2006) 'Modeling the effects of time: Integrating demographic and developmental perspectives', in R.H. Binstock and L.K. George (eds), *Handbook of Aging and the Social Sciences*. New York: Academic Press, pp. 20–38.

Alwin, D.F., McCammon, R.J., Wray, L.A., and Rodgers, W.L. (2008a) 'Population processes and cognitive aging', in S.M. Hofer and D.F. Alwin (eds), *Handbook of Cognitive Aging: Interdisciplinary Perspectives*. Thousand Oaks, CA: SAGE, pp. 69–89.

Alwin, D.F., Wray, L.A., and Rodgers, W.L. (2008b) 'Cumulative advantage and cognitive change: Is aging kinder to the better educated?', Paper presented at the annual meetings of the American Sociological Association, Boston, MA, August.

Baltes, P.B. (1987) 'Theoretical propositions of life-span developmental psychology: on the dynamics between growth and decline', *Developmental Psychology*, 23: 611–26.

Baltes, P.B. (1997) 'On the incomplete architecture of human ontogeny: selection, optimization and compensation as the foundation of developmental theory', *American Psychologist*, 52: 366–80.

Baltes, P.B. and Willis, S.L. (1981) 'Plasticity and enhancement of intellectual functioning in old age', in F.M. Craik and E.E. Trehub (eds), *Aging and Cognitive Processes*. New York: Plenum, pp. 353–89.

Barnes, L.L., Cagney, K.A., and Mendes de Leon, C.F. (2008) 'Social resources and cognitive function in older persons', in S.M. Hofer and D.F. Alwin (eds), *Handbook of Cognitive Aging: Interdisciplinary Perspectives*. Thousand Oaks, CA: SAGE, pp. 603–13.

Bassuk, S.S., Glass, T.A., and Berkman, L.F. (1999) 'Social disengagement and incident cognitive decline in community-dwelling elderly persons', *Annals of Internal Medicine*, 131: 165–73.

Beckett, M. (2000) 'Converging health inequalities in later life – an artifact of mortality selection?', *Journal of Health and Social Behavior*, 41: 106–19.

Beckett, M. and Elliott, M.N. (2001) 'Mortality and sample selection', *Journal of Health and Social Behavior*, 41: 328–31.

Bengtson, V.L. and Schaie, K.W. (eds) (1999) *Handbook of Theories of Aging*. New York: Springer.

Berg, C.A. (2008) 'Everyday problem solving in context', in S.M. Hofer and D.F. Alwin (eds), *Handbook of Cognitive Aging: Interdisciplinary Perspectives*. Thousand Oaks, CA: SAGE, pp. 207–23.

Blanchard-Fields, F., Horhota, M., and Mienaltowski, A. (2008) 'Social context and cognition', in S.M. Hofer and D.F. Alwin (eds), *Handbook of Cognitive Aging: Interdisciplinary Perspectives*. Thousand Oaks, CA: SAGE, pp. 614–628.

Bloom, B.S. (1964) *Stability and Change in Human Characteristics*. New York: Wiley.

Bronfenbrenner, U. (1979) *The Ecology of Human Development: Experiments by Nature and Design*. Cambridge, MA: Harvard University Press.

Bronfenbrenner, U. (1986) 'Ecology of the family as a context for human development: research perspectives', *Developmental Psychology*, 22: 723–42.

Bronfenbrenner, U. and Ceci, S.J. (1994) 'Nature–nurture reconceptualized in developmental perspective: a bioecological model', *Psychological Review*, 101: 568–86.

Bronfenbrenner, U. and Crouter, A.C. (1983) 'The evolution of environmental models in developmental research', in P.H. Mussen (Series ed.) and W. Kessen (Vol. ed.), *Handbook of Child Psychology: History, Theory and Methods*, Vol. 1, 4th edn. New York: John Wiley and Sons, pp. 357–414.

Brookmeyer, R., Gray, S., and Kawas, C. (1998) 'Projections of Alzheimer's disease in the United States and the public health impact of delaying disease onset', *American Journal of Public Health*, 88: 1337–42.

Carroll, J.B. (1996) 'Mathematical abilities: some results from factor analysis', in R.J. Sternberg and R. Ben-Zeev (eds), *The Nature of Mathematical Thinking*. Mahwah, NJ: Erlbaum, pp. 3–25.

Carroll, J.B. (1998) 'Human cognitive abilities', in J.J. McArdle and R.W. Woodcock (eds), *Human Cognitive Abilities in Theory and Practice*. Mahwah, NJ: Erlbaum, pp. 5–24.

Cattell, R.B. (1963) 'Theory of fluid and crystallized intelligence: a critical experiment', *Journal of Educational Psychology*, 54: 1–22.

Cattell, R.B. (1971a) 'The structure of intelligence in relation to the nature–nurture controversy', in R. Cancro (ed.), *Intelligence: Genetic and Environmental Influences*. New York: Grune and Stratton, pp. 3–30.

Cattell, R.B. (1971b) *Abilities: Their Structure, Growth and Action*. Boston, MA: Houghton-Mifflin.

Crimmins, E.M. (2001) 'Mortality and health in human life spans', *Experimental Gerontology*, 36: 885–97.

Crimmins, E.M. (2005) 'Socioeconomic differentials in mortality and health at the older ages', *Genus*, 61: 163–76.

Crimmins, E.M., Hayward, M.D., and Seeman, T. (2004) 'Race/ethnicity, socioeconomic status, and health', in N. Anderson, R. Bulatao, and B. Cohen (eds), *Critical Perspectives on Race and Ethnic Differences in Health in Later Life*. Washington, DC: National Academies Press, pp. 310–52.

Dannefer, W.D. (1984) 'Adult development and social theory: a paradigmatic reappraisal', *American Sociological Review*, 49: 100–16.

Dannefer, W.D. (1987) 'Aging as intracohort differentiation: accentuation, the Matthew effect, and the life course', *Sociological Forum*, 2: 211–36.

Dannefer, W.D. (1988) 'What's in a name? An account of the neglect of variability in the study of aging', in J.E. Birren and V.L. Bengtson (eds), *Emergent Theories of Aging*. New York: Springer, pp. 356–84.

Dannefer, W.D. (1992) 'Four meanings of context and their implications', in D.L. Featherman, R.M. Lerner, and M. Perlmutter (eds), *Life-Span Development and Behavior*, Vol. 11. Hillsdale, NJ: Lawrence Erlbaum Associates.

Dannefer, W.D. (1993) 'When does society matter for individual differences? Implications of a counterpart paradox', *Psychological Inquiry*, 4: 4.

Dannefer, W.D. (2003) 'Cumulative advantage/disadvantage and the life course: cross-fertilizing age and social science theory', *Journal of Gerontology: Social Sciences*, 58B: S327–57.

Dannefer, W.D. (2008) 'Social forces, life course consequences', in J.M. Wilmoth and K.F. Ferraro (eds), *Gerontology: Perspectives and Issues*, 3rd edn. New York: Springer, pp. 223–43.

Dannefer, W.D. and Uhlenberg, P. (1999) 'Paths of the life course: a typology', in V.L. Bengtson and K.W. Schaie (eds), *Handbook of Theories of Aging*. New York: Springer, pp. 306–26.

Denny, N.W. (1982) 'Aging and cognitive change', in B.B. Wolman (ed.), *Handbook of Developmental Psychology: Research and Theory*. Englewood Cliffs, NJ: Prentice-Hall, pp. 807–27.

Elder, G.H., Jr. (1985) 'Perspectives on the life course', in G.H. Elder, Jr. (ed.), *Life Course Dynamics: Trajectories and Transitions, 1968–1980*. Ithaca: Cornell University Press, pp. 23–49.

Featherman, D.L. (1983) 'Life-span perspectives in social science research', in P.B. Baltes and O.G. Brim, Jr. (eds), *Life-Span Development and Behavior*, Vol. 5. New York: Academic Press, pp. 1–57.

Flanagan, D.P., McGrew, K.S., and Ortiz, S.O. (2000) *The Wechsler Intelligence Scales and Gf-Gc Theory: A Contemporary Approach to Interpretation*, Boston, MA: Allyn and Bacon.

Fratiglioni, L., Paillard-Borg, S., and Winblad, B. (2004) 'An active and socially integrated lifestyle in late life might protect against dementia', *Lancet Neurology*, 3: 343–53.

Hayward, M.D., Crimmins, E., Miles, T., and Yang, Y. (2000) 'The significance of socioeconomic status in explaining the race gap in chronic health', *American Sociological Review*, 65: 910–30.

Hertzog, C. (2008) 'Theoretical approaches to the study of cognitive aging: an individual-differences perspective', in S.M. Hofer and D.F. Alwin (eds), *Handbook of Cognitive Aging: Interdisciplinary Perspectives*. Thousand Oaks, CA: SAGE, pp. 34–49.

Hertzog, C. and Schaie, K.W. (1986) 'Stability and change in adult intelligence: I. analysis of longitudinal covariance structures', *Psychology and Aging*, 1: 159–71.

Hertzog, C. and Schaie, K.W. (1988) 'Stability and change in adult intelligence: 2. simultaneous analysis of longitudinal means and covariance structures', *Psychology and Aging*, 3: 122–30.

Hofer, S.M. and Alwin, D.F. (eds) (2008) *Handbook of Cognitive Aging: Interdisciplinary Perspectives*. Thousand Oaks, CA: SAGE.

Horn, J.L. (1968) 'Organization of abilities and the development of intelligence', *Psychological Review*, 75: 242–59.

Horn, J.L. (1976) 'Human abilities: a review of research and theory in the early 1970s', *Annual Review of Psychology*, 27: 437–85.

Horn, J.L. (1982a) 'The theory of fluid and crystallized intelligence in relation to concepts of cognitive psychology and aging in adulthood', in F.I.M. Craik and S.Trehub (eds), *Aging and Cognitive Processes*. New York: Plenum, pp. 237–78.

Horn, J.L. (1982b) 'The aging of human abilities', in B.B. Wolman (ed.), *Handbook of Developmental Psychology: Research and Theory*. Englewood Cliffs, NJ: Prentice-Hall, pp. 847–70.

Horn, J.L. (1985) 'Remodeling old theories of intelligence: Gf-Gc theory', in B.B. Wolman (ed.), *Handbook of Intelligence*. New York: Wiley, pp. 267–300.

Horn, J.L. (1988) 'Thinking about human abilities', in J.R. Nesselroade and R.B. Cattell (eds), *Handbook of Multivariate Psychology*, revised edn. New York: Academic Press, pp. 645–85.

Horn, J.L. (1991) 'Measurement of intellectual capabilities', in K.S. McGrew, J.K. Werder, and R.W. Woodcock (eds), *Woodcock–Johnson Technical Manual*. Chicago: Riverside, pp. 197–232.

Horn, J.L. (1994) 'Theory of fluid and crystallized intelligence', in R.J. Sternberg (ed.), *Encyclopedia of Human Intelligence*. New York: Macmillan, pp. 443–51.

Horn, J.L. and Cattell, R.B. (1967) 'Age differences in fluid and crystallized intelligence', *Acta Psychologica*, 26: 107–29.

Horn, J.L. and Donaldson, G. (1980) 'Cognitive development in adulthood', in O.G. Brim, Jr. and J. Kagan (eds), *Constancy and Change in Human Development*. Cambridge, MA: Harvard University Press, pp. 445–529.

House, J.S., Kessler, R.C., Herzog, A.R., et al. (1992) 'Social stratification, age, and health', in K.W. Schaie, D. Blazer, and J.S. House (eds), *Aging, Health Behaviors and Health Outcomes*. Hillsdale, NJ: Erlbaum, pp. 1–32.

House, J.S., Lepkowski, J.M., Kinney, A.M., et al. (1994) 'The social stratification of aging and health', *Journal of Health and Social Behavior*, 35: 213–34.

House, J.S., Lantz, P.M., and Herd, P. (2005) 'Continuity and change in the social stratification of aging and health over the life course: evidence from a nationally representative longitudinal study from 1986 to 2001/2002 (Americans' Changing Lives Study)', *Journal of Gerontology: Social Science*, 60B (special issue II): 15–26.

Kawas, C.H. and Brookmeyer, R. (2001) 'Editorial – aging and the public health: effects of dementia', *The New England Journal of Medicine*, 344: 1160–1.

Kohn, M.L. and Schooler, C. (1978) 'The reciprocal effects of the substantive complexity of work and intellectual flexibility: a longitudinal assessment', *American Journal of Sociology*, 84: 24–52.

Kohn, M.L. and Schooler, C. (1983) *Work and Personality: An Inquiry into the Impact of Social Stratification*. Norwood, NJ: Ablex.

Kohn, M.L. and Slomczynski, K.M. (1990) *Social Structure and Self-Direction: A Comparative Analysis of the United States and Poland*. Cambridge, MA: Basil Blackwell.

Kunst, A.E. and Mackenbach, J.P. (1994) 'The size of mortality differences associated with education level in nine industrialized countries', *American Journal of Public Health*, 84: 932–7.

Lynch, S.M. (2003) 'Cohort and life-course patterns in the relationship between education and health: a hierarchical approach', *Demography*, 40: 309–31.

Manly, J.J. (2008) 'Race, culture, education, and cognitive test performance among older adults', in S.M. Hofer and D.F. Alwin (eds), *Handbook of Cognitive Aging: Interdisciplinary Perspectives*. Thousand Oaks, CA: SAGE, pp. 398–417.

Marmot, M.G. and Shipley, M.J. (1996) 'Do socioeconomic differences in mortality persist after retirement? 25 year follow up of civil servants from the first Whitehall Study', *British Medical Journal*, 313: 1177–80.

McGrew, K.S. (1997) 'Analysis of the major intelligence batteries according to a proposed comprehensive Gf-Gc framework', in D.P. Flanagan, J.L. Genshaft, and P.L. Harrison (eds), *Contemporary Intellectual Assessment: Theories, Tests, and Issues*. New York: Guilford, pp. 151–80.

McGrew, K.S and Flanagan, D.P. (1998) *The Intelligence Test Desk Reference (ITDR): Gf-Gc Cross-Battery Assessment*. Boston, MA: Allyn and Bacon.

Merton, R.K. (1949) *Social Theory and Social Structure*. New York: The Free Press.

Merton, R.K. (1968) 'The Matthew Effect in science', *Science*, 159(3810): 56–63.

Molla, M.T., Madans, J.H., and Wagener, D.K. (2004) 'Differentials in adult mortality and activity limitation by years of education in the United States at the end of the 1990s', *Population and Development Review*, 30: 625–46.

Musgrove, F. (1977) *Margins of the Mind*. London: Methuen.

O'Rand, A.M. (1996) 'The precious and the precocious: understanding cumulative disadvantage and cumulative advantage over the life course', *The Gerontologist*, 36: 230–8.

O'Rand, A.M. and Hamil-Luker, J. (2005) 'Processes of cumulative adversity: childhood disadvantage and increased risk of heart attack across the life course', *Journal of Gerontology: Social Science*, 60B (special issue II): 117–24.

Park, D.C. (1999) 'Cognitive aging, processing resources, and self-report', in D.C. Park and N. Schwarz (eds), *Cognition, Aging, and Self-Reports*. Philadelphia, PA: Taylor and Francis, pp. 45–69.

Park, D.C., Smith, A.D., Lautenschlager, G., et al. (1996) 'Mediators of long-term memory performance across the life-span', *Psychology and Aging*, 11: 621–37.

Richards, M. and Deary, I.J. (2005) 'A life course approach to cognitive reserve: a model for cognitive aging and development?', *Annals of Neurology*, 58: 617–22.

Robert, S. and House, J.S. (1996) 'SES differentials in health by age and alternative indicators of SES', *Journal of Aging and Health*, 8: 359–88.

Rowe, J.W. and Kahn, R.L. (1998) *Successful Aging*. New York: Pantheon.

Ryder, N.B. (1965) 'The cohort as a concept in the study of social change', *American Sociological Review*, 30: 843–61.

Salthouse, T.A. (1991) *Theoretical Perspectives on Cognitive Aging*. Hillsdale, NJ: Lawrence Erlbaum.

Schaie, K.W. (2005) *Developmental Influences on Adult Intelligence: The Seattle Longitudinal Study*. Oxford: Oxford University Press.

Scherr, P.A., Albert, M.S., Funkenstein, H.H., et al. (1988) 'Correlates of cognitive function in an elderly community population', *American Journal of Epidemiology* 128: 1084-101.

Schooler, C. (1984) 'Psychological effects of complex environments during the life span: a review and theory', *Intelligence*, 8: 259–81.

Schooler, C. (1987) 'Psychological effects of complex environments during the life span: a review and theory', in C. Schooler and K.W. Schaie (eds), *Cognitive Functioning* and *Social Structure over the Life Course*. Norwood, NJ: Ablex.

Schooler, C. and Mulatu, M.S. (2001) 'The reciprocal effects of leisure time activities and intellectual functioning in older people: a longitudinal analysis', *Psychology and Aging*, 16: 466–82.

Schooler, C., Mulatu, M.S., and Oates, G. (1999) 'The continuing effects of substantively complex work on the intellectual functioning of older workers', *Psychology of Aging*, 14: 483–506.

Schooler, C., Mulatu, M.S., and Oates, G. (2004) 'Occupational self-direction, intellectual functioning, and self-directed orientation in older workers: findings and implications for individuals and societies', *American Journal of Sociology*, 110: 161–97.

Sewell, W.H. and Hauser, R.M. (1975) *Education, Occupation, and Earnings: Achievement in the Early Career*. New York: Academic Press.

Sewell, W.H., Jr. (2005) *Logics of History: Social Theory and Social Transformation*. Chicago, IL: University of Chicago Press.

Stern, Y. (ed.) (2007) *Cognitive Reserve: Theory and Applications*. New York: Taylor and Francis Group.

United Nations (2002) *World Population Aging: 1950–2050*. Population Division, Department of Economic and Social Affairs. New York: United Nations Publications.

Vaupel, J.W. and Yashin, A.I. (1985) 'Heterogeneity's ruses: some surprising effects of selection on population dynamics', *The American Statistician*, 39: 176–85.

Weiss, K.M. (1990) 'The biodemography of variation in human frailty', *Demography*, 27: 185–206.

Williams, R.M., Jr. (1960) *American Society: A Sociological Interpretation*, 2nd edn. New York: Knopf.

Woodcock, R.W. (1994) 'Measures of fluid and crystallized intelligence', in R.J. Sternberg (ed.), *The Encyclopedia of Intelligence*. New York: Macmillan, pp. 452–6.

21

Stress and Agentic Ageing: A Targeted Adaptation Model Focused on Cancer

Eva Kahana and Boaz Kahana

INTRODUCTION

Stress research is a highly interdisciplinary field of study, drawing on the works of psychologists, sociologists, medical researchers, and organizational analysts. The stress paradigm is recognized as a useful framework for understanding quality of life outcomes for older adults who face challenges ranging from physical illness and increasing frailty to social losses (Kahana and Kahana, 2003). This framework has offered constructs that can connect with broader theoretical formulations, and can also be empirically tested (Pearlin et al., 1981). Although stress research has been fraught with definitional problems and ambiguities in both conceptualization and measurement, the stress model has remained attractive to researchers due to its flexibility, face validity, and suitability for empirical research that is relevant to real-life problems (Kahana, 1992).

The stress paradigm has been described as a microcosm of the interface between individuals and society (McLeod and Lively, 2007). It allows for consideration of macro influences, which are reflected in stress exposure of different populations, and which may translate into effects on individuals who craft diverse strategies to counteract negative influences. Stress exposure may result from life transitions, environmental demands, and the social arrangements that differentially impinge on people's lives (Pearlin, 1989).

This chapter outlines prevailing approaches to conceptualizing and operationalizing key components of the stress paradigm, including stress exposure, and the resources that can help ameliorate adverse effects of stress exposure on quality of life outcomes. In the first section, we offer a critical assessment of research on stress and ageing. In the second, we address these limitations through the development of a refined, situation-specific stress model, the targeted *adaptation* (TAD) model.

INTERNATIONAL PERSPECTIVES ON STRESS AND AGEING: A BIRD'S EYE VIEW

Although a comprehensive review of research on age and stress is beyond the scope of this paper, we can nevertheless point to notable trends in the study of stress exposure or adaptations both within and outside the United States. Although much stress research to date has been conducted in North America, the recently initiated cross-national Survey of Health, Ageing and Retirement in Europe (SHARE) includes 14 countries from Scandinavia to Central Europe and the Mediterranean (Borsch-Supan et al., 2005). This study is broadly modeled on the US Health and Retirement Study (Juster and Suzman, 1995), and the English Longitudinal

Study of Ageing (Marmot et al., 2003). These longitudinal studies do not specifically focus on stress or adaptation. Nevertheless, they include variables that relate to key components of the stress paradigm, such as functional limitation and job flexibility (sources of stress exposure), central control beliefs (psychological resource), and informal assistance received (social resources). These studies hold great promise for a comparative understanding of the stress process and will offer long-term longitudinal data that can be accessed by stress researchers around the world.

In the rapidly growing field of traumatic stress studies, the impact on older adults of both natural and man-made disasters has been extensively researched across the globe. Studies on the impact of natural disasters on older people offer evidence of both vulnerability and resilience in later life. Although natural disasters often have less long-term impact than human-made ones (such as wars), they can nevertheless have strong proximal effects on well-being. For example, the Taiwan (Ji-Ji) earthquake was found to be a trigger for acute myocardial infarction among older persons (Tsai et al., 2004). In a comparative study of post-traumatic stress disorder (PTSD) after the 1988 earthquake in Armenia, proximity to the epicenter of the disaster proved to be a more important predictor than age in contributing to the development of PTSD (Goenjian et al., 1994).

Traumatic stress research has found evidence for long-term effects of earlier war trauma on older adults (Elder and Clipp, 1989; Shmotkin and Lomranz, 1998). Studies by Israeli social scientists have demonstrated how wounds from earlier trauma, such as the Holocaust, can be reopened by new stressors in late life (Solomon and Prager, 1992). These findings call attention to conditional vulnerability of older adults who were traumatized earlier in life. Older adults may also face individual trauma, as victims of elder abuse, crime, and other traumatic events, where age may contribute to stress exposure (McCabe and Gregory, 1998).

While trauma of natural disasters and war has been extensively studied around the world, international focus on stressful life events and normative stressors of ordinary life in old age is more limited (Busuttil, 2004). There is considerable international interest in the roles of social capital, social ties, and social integration as protective of health in the face of diverse stressors. Social ties have thus been linked to better health among elderly Taiwanese (Cornman et al., 2003). Social engagement has been linked to survival of *elderly* people in Sweden (Lennartsson and Silverstein, 2001). British researchers have been at the forefront of studying the role of social capital in the stress process (Kunitz, 2004).

Caregiving stress among older persons has also been explored in international research. In Australia, health risks and disability of both care receivers and caregivers were found to be risk factors for psychological morbidity (Draper et al., 1996). Coping with illness-related late-life stressors has also been extensively studied internationally, with many stress-relevant studies published in the medical literature. Typical of such attention is a recent review article by Italian researchers on the special impact of stress resulting from the treatment of breast cancer (Crivellari et al., 2007).

Comparative cross-national studies of stress have explored work-related stress in European Union (EU) countries. This area of stress research, while not targeting older persons, is notable for its concern with consequences of chronic work stressors that impinge on social policies in areas such as disability, workmen's compensation, and legal remedies (Cox et al., 2006). It also has implications for ageing, as the effects of midlife stressors may cumulate through the life course.

In tracing the lineage of social stress scholarship, there are notable patterns of geographic distribution. Outside the United States, Germany is a major center, particularly for psychological research. Baltes and Baltes (1990) and Brandtstadter and colleagues (1991) have done seminal work in proposing compensatory mechanisms as older adults deal with stress. They also emphasize special strengths of older persons, when a life history of effective coping translates into wisdom and resilience (Yates and Masten, 2004). This research tradition parallels recent interest in resilience and post-traumatic growth (PTG) whereby stress exposure can lead to positive sequelae, such as benefit-finding (Gross, 1998).

Canadian researchers have focused on biological mechanisms in the stress response in late life (Hawkley et al., 2005), as have British researchers, who report that stressful life events result in effects on blood pressure (a precursor to cardiovascular disease) (Waldstein et al., 2004). The authors suggest that the impact of serious events is likely to have hemodynamic effects in older cohorts.

We now turn to a more systematic review of age-related research on elements of the stress paradigm: stress exposure, appraisal, coping, and use of social resources in late life.

LATE-LIFE STRESS EXPOSURE

Stress models are predicated on the assumption that stressful life events, life crises, and chronic stressors threaten the equilibrium of the person, and may adversely affect quality of life. Thus, stress exposure may be viewed as a stimulus which, in the absence of ameliorative resources, threatens health and well-being (Aldwin and Yancura, 2004). Wheaton defines stressors as 'conditions of threat, demands, or structural constraints that by the very fact of their occurrence or existence, call into question the operating integrity of the organism' (1996: 32). Pearlin and colleagues (1997) have called attention to stress proliferation, whereby primary stressors can generate additional secondary stress exposure situations, such as illness-related-stressors producing caregiving burden.

It is notable that older adults generally report fewer negative life events than do their younger counterparts (Hughes et al., 1988). In a cross-sectional study of 754 community-dwelling older persons during the past 5 years, social losses (including death of or illness of a family member or friend) were identified as the most stressful events (Hardy et al., 2002). Only 18 per cent of this sample of older adults (age 70+) referred to their own physical illnesses as the most stressful events. While the majority of older adults reported negative consequences of stressful life events, a significant minority reported PTG. Stress exposure in late life has often been studied in terms of age-associated stressors of caregiving and bereavement (Aneshensel, 1993; Aneshensel et al., 2004).

Older persons disproportionately live in neighborhoods that pose chronic stressors by threatening safety. Housing in such neighborhoods may be substandard, and may tax adaptive abilities of frail or functionally impaired individuals (Taylor and Repetti, 1997). Neighborhood contexts that pose chronic stressors are even more common for older adults who are racial minorities and those who live in poverty. Both chronic stressors and negative life events are more frequently observed among persons of lower occupational status, and such structurally based differences in stress exposure are related to differences in depressive symptoms (Turner et al., 1995).

Ill health and physical impairment represent universal sources of stress for older adults, as illustrated in the well-known cascade of disability (Verbrugge and Jette, 1994). Functional declines that threaten the ability to live independently are common during the final years of life (Lunney et al., 2003). Across societies, negative sequelae of illness-related stressors are widely reported (Walter-Ginzburg et al., 2002). Nevertheless, moderators between illness and quality of life are considered only on the most general level. In the presence of social resources and 'good' coping strategies, the adverse effects of illness-related stress exposure may be minimized (Ferlander, 2007; Krause, 2006).

Moderators in the stress paradigm

A broad array of resources have been considered as factors that may reduce adverse effects of stress exposure. Among these, one broad category encompasses external resources, including availability of financial resources, social networks, access to health care, and access to technology. Such resources are primarily a function of an individual's social structural position (Turner and Avison, 2003). Nevertheless, it is now widely recognized that individuals regularly call upon proactive strategies to minimize stressors and their impact (Aspinwall and Taylor, 1997). In our prior formulation of preventive and corrective proactivity (Kahana and Kahana, 1996, 2003) we proposed that helping others can result in availability of social supports in late life. Similarly, planning ahead throughout the life course can contribute to the development of assets in late life.

Social support

The most widely studied external resources are social supports (Krause, 2006). The theoretical salience of social supports relates to the importance of social self and of the interactional basis of the stress process. Obtaining both instrumental and esteem support is related to quality of life among stress-exposed individuals (Turner and Turner, 1999). Availability of social resources is generally estimated from the size and density of social networks (Acock and Hurlbert, 1993). Social networks, in turn, can translate into specific assistance when activated. *Perceived* support has been found to be more closely linked to positive quality of life than *received* support (Wethington and Kessler, 1986). Thus, it is the older adult's perception of having support available that becomes particularly important. Recently, 'Care-Getting' which may involve ingenious proactivity in marshaling support, has been linked to quality of life, particularly close to the end of life (Kahana, Kahana, Wykle, and Kulle, in press).

The importance of strong ties and emotionally close interpersonal relationships in dealing with the late-life stressors has been well established (Carstensen, 1995). Yet, existing measures of social support and networks do not focus on the depth of relationships, and current conceptualization and measurement of social support are fraught with other major ambiguities (Krause, 2006). For example, receiving instrumental support to deal with stressful situations may imply a limitation in one's adaptive capacity. As we detail below, research has increasingly focused on social resourcefulness (Rapp et al., 1998) and on the importance of individual coping skills in marshaling social support (see Gottlieb, 1988).

Age, coping, appraisal, and attribution of meaning

To explore mechanisms by which stressors affect psychological well-being and identity, several lines of inquiry have been followed. The first one relates to attribution of meaning to adverse events, and is prevalent in sociological and social psychological literature (McLeod and Lively, 2007). A second approach focuses on appraisal of threat and stress (Lazarus and Folkman, 1984), and has been generally pursued in the field of psychology. Within this framework, problem-focused coping refers to active efforts to solve the problem, whereas emotion-focused coping aims at maintenance of psychological well-being in the face of problem situations. Both of these general approaches – meaning-making and appraisal – allow for consideration of the heterogeneity of human reactions` to stressful or traumatic situations. Accordingly, persons attributing more negative meaning to a stressful event are more likely to exhibit long-term signs of distress (Van der Kolk et al., 2005), and are less likely to undergo positive transformation such as PTG (Tedeschi et al., 1998). Appraisals of continuing threat of past trauma may also reflect the structural context of stress exposure. Accordingly, Holocaust survivors living in Hungary (where their trauma was perpetrated) portrayed greater beliefs in the possibility of another Holocaust, and showed much higher levels of depressive symptoms than did their counterparts, who emigrated to the United States or Israel (Kahana et al., 2005).

A second approach to the study of coping with stressors focuses on the type of cognitive, emotional, and behavioral adaptations individuals invoke as they encounter stressful life situations (Aldwin, 1992). Cognitive responses include positive comparison ('my health is better than my peers') and denial or reinterpretation of stress (Breznitz, 1983). Escapist or avoidant coping strategies may also reflect cognitive orientations (Aldwin, 1992). Emotional regulation and emotion-focused coping appear to have strong cultural components (Wong, 2002). Active, positive, or instrumental coping strategies are also referred to as problem-focused coping, which represents constructive responses to stress – e.g., taking action to solve the problem, seeking support or advice from others; or engaging in advocacy (Carver et al., 1989).

Longitudinal studies of coping are few, and findings regarding age differences are ambiguous. Data from the Normative Aging Study, based on men aged 45–90, suggest that older men appraise problems as less stressful and report fewer negative emotions than do younger men (Aldwin et al., 1993). Use of downward comparisons was found to benefit the quality of life of British community-dwelling older people (Beaumont and Kenealy, 2004).

Leading developmental theories have focused on accommodative or compensatory strategies of older persons, as they deal with limitations by reducing energy expenditures (Baltes and Baltes, 1990; Rothermund and Bradtstadter, 2003). Thus, older adults may select more highly valued activities and focus their resources on maintaining them. Such accommodative coping has been found to benefit older adults facing disability (Boerner, 2004). Older persons also engage in social 'selectivity', focusing on close family members and friends, and emphasizing strong over weak ties (Carstensen, 1995). This view, represented in socio-emotional selectivity theory, is consistent with propositions of early psychological theorists (Jung, 1933) and with views of later researchers in human development, who described a tendency by older adults to turn inward (Neugarten, 1979) and disengage from social interaction (Cumming and Henry, 1961).

Despite an upsurge in studies of coping and social resources (Aldwin and Yancura, 2004; Hawkley et al., 2005), few studies involve long-term longitudinal follow-ups that could elucidate either age-related changes or cohort effects. For example, it might be argued, that the formative experience of the Great Depression for today's old-old has made them an unusually self-reliant group in old age who may resist assistance from others (Ryff et al., 1999). However, such self-reliance might be less noticeable among future cohorts of older people who are accustomed to elements of support from the welfare state.

To the extent that cumulative stress increases with age, older adults are likely to have developed a broader array of coping skills and perspectives that help them regulate their responses. Recent interest by gerontologists (particularly in Germany) in the concept of wisdom (Ardelt, 2000, Chapter 23; Staudinger et al., 2006), explores its connection to successful coping efforts. Polish researchers have found wisdom to be related to adaptation to late-life bereavement (Starzomska, 2006). The development of coping skills with age may also increase wisdom, since some aspects of wisdom involve problem-solving (Hall, 2007). The ability of many older persons to retain composure and equilibrium in the face of impending death reflects a coping skill for anticipation of the ultimate uncertainty at the end of life. Gerontologists bringing sociological orientations to concepts of coping and wisdom call attention to the embeddedness of wisdom in relationships with significant others (Staudinger et al, 2006). This is a manifestation of the continuing self that is constantly evolving in interaction (Cooley, 1902).

Religious coping has many alternate definitions, including attendance, prayer, or trusting God. In the study of late-life stress, interest in religion has received growing attention (Idler, 2006; Pargament, 1997). Religious coping has been useful in dealing with negative late-life transitions, and has been associated with health among hospitalized older adults (Koenig et al., 1998). A broad array of studies in the United States report religious coping to be prevalent (especially among African Americans) and to play a protective role for a wide array of stressors (Boswell et al., 2006).

In the stress paradigm, mediators between stressors and adverse quality of life outcomes have been conceptualized primarily in terms of (1) social resources or support and (2) cognitive or behavioral coping resources. Although the literature is generally subdivided along these lines (Aldwin and Yancura, 2004; Krauss, 2006), it is apparent that these domains overlap, and that focusing on links between social and coping resources would further understanding of the stress paradigm.

Limitation in conceptualization and measurement of elements of the stress paradigm

Despite their dominance in the literature, the standard instruments used in stress research are often far removed from commonsense notions or personal narratives of coping. The narrow range of existing measures may constrain understanding of coping and social resources.

An important challenge in studying coping is the assumption of universal patterns of coping, or *essentialism* (Goldhaber, 2000). A universal orientation helps to simplify the discussion, but fails to recognize the possibility that age brings growing differentiation in coping as in other domains (Dannefer and Sell, 1988; Neugarten, 1979). In an effort to recognize systematic sources of such heterogeneity, we note how master statuses, such as race, class, and gender, influence proactive efforts and resource use among older adults who encounter major stressors (Dannefer, 2003). We have already seen, for example, how different race and ethnic groups use different styles of coping and mobilize different resources.

In the measurement of coping, similar problems abound. Typical coping scales ask for respondents' propensity to engage in diverse cognitive maneuvers when facing a hypothetical or real problem situation. There are problems of face validity in assuming that individuals can reflect on and report their cognitive maneuvers, and that such self-reports correspond to behavior (Aldwin, 1992).

Yet, few measures used in research on coping capture how older people actually behave as they encounter stressful situations.

Studies of coping typically aggregate diverse actions taken to address problem situations, alternatively referring to them as instrumental, active, or positive coping (Kahana et al., 2008). To enhance our understanding of effective coping efforts in late life, it is important to differentiate a broad array of actions that older adults pursue in order to deal with problem situations. In response to this problem, our prior work proposed the preventive and corrective proactivity (PCP) model (Kahana and Kahana, 1996, 2003). This model differentiates among preventive activities such as planning, helping others, and health promotion. These behaviors may diminish stress exposure, and enhance social supports. The PCP model also distinguishes diverse corrective adaptations, ranging from exercise of social skills (e.g., marshaling support in times of need). The value of proactive efforts in further articulating conceptualization of coping has also been recognized in the work of Thoits (1995). In addition, advances have been made in linking self-regulation, coping, adaptation, and health (Aspinwall, 2004). Future orientation and proactive coping have also been recognized as promoting psychological well-being among older adults (Aspinwall, 2005). The value of proactive coping efforts has also been articulated in recent work by Thoits (1995) and Aspinwall (2004). Additional positive formulations of coping and adaptation have been presented by proponents of resilience or PTG that may occur in response to traumatic stress exposure (Tedeschi et al., 1998).

There have been some encouraging advances in recognizing the complexity of the coping process, and the need to expand both conceptualization and measurement in this field (Folkman and Moskovitz, 2004); however, little conceptual development has occurred. To address this issue, we propose the TAD model, which aims to further our understanding of modes of coping with stress, presenting an ecological orientation (Kahana et al., 2008).

THE TARGETED ADAPTATION MODEL

The proposed TAD model shown in Figure 21.1 shares some commonalities with Suchman's (1965) stages of the illness experience, particularly in recognition of a temporal dimension. The model is focused on the periods following diagnosis and treatment, without endorsing assumptions of the sick role or the dependent patient role, which are central tenets of Suchman's model. A major assumption of

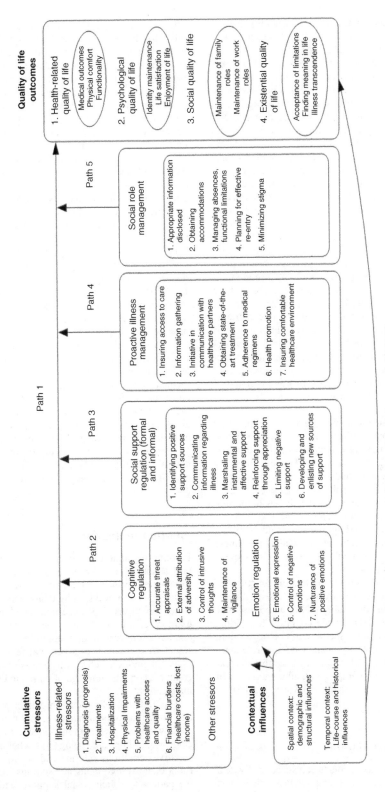

Figure 21.1   Stress and agentic ageing: a targeted illness adaptation model (TAD)

the TAD model is the value of patient initiative and assertiveness in dealing with illness adaptive tasks (Kahana and Kahana, 2003, 2007).

The most distinctive feature of the TAD model relates to unpacking the complex actions and efforts at self-regulation required of older persons, including those who face life-threatening illness. The model aims to specify the range of adaptive tasks faced by patients living with serious illness in an ecological framework. It outlines adaptations that are tailored to actively address each psychological and social domain where adaptation is needed. It provides a differentiated portrayal of task-specific coping in order to enhance explanatory power of research linking coping efforts to quality of patients' lives.

Targeted illness adaptation describes proactive efforts that patients tailor to adaptive tasks, involving regulation of thoughts, feelings, health care, social supports, and social roles. We use the term *regulation* to denote the purposive nature of these positive adaptations, and to emphasize the connotation of mastery within situational constraints that older patients may achieve. This concept is linked to more macro sociological frameworks that posit the importance of agency within structure (Settersten, 1999), in that it delineates proactive efforts within the constraints and demand of illness, and of healthcare environments such as hospitals.

In this discussion, we use the case of older cancer patients to illustrate the relevance of the TAD model. The full complexity of what an older cancer patient confronts can be illustrated by examining the post-diagnosis and early treatment-seeking phases of the illness experience. During this early period, the patient is still new to the sick role, and uncertainties abound as she aims to define the problem (Helgeson and Sheldon, 1996). Enduring cancer treatments, as well as the illness itself, represent a highly stressful set of experiences (Hewitt et al., 2006).

Figure 21.1 depicts the moderating functions of TAD in reducing the adverse effects of illness-related stressors on quality of life outcomes. Key dimensions of TAD include cognitive regulation, emotion regulation, social support regulation, proactive illness management, and social role management. Figure 21.1 also recognizes that contextual influences may impinge on all components of the model (see also Kahana and Kahana, 2003).

Cognitive regulation

Before older cancer patients can successfully deal with confronting illness adaptive tasks, they must find ways for cognitive regulation, to avoid immobilization by depression and anxiety. Challenges of this complex and often life-threatening illness also call for making wise choices in decision-making. Cognitive maneuvers to effect wise choices often involve social components of advice-seeking, collaboration, and negotiation that may reflect wisdom (Staudinger et al., 2006). Through these actions, an individual can retain salient role identities without embracing the sick role. Harpham (1994) suggests that one way of living with the 'Sword of Damocles' is by mentally creating distance between oneself and the treatment and uncertainty. Cognitive maneuvers to thwart despair may include external attributions of adversity as well as distancing (LeShan, 1994). Targeted efforts that sustain hopefulness have also been found to benefit cancer patients (Snyder, 1994).

Cognitive regulation typically involves distancing, denial, and cognitive restructuring (Breznitz, 1983), yet such actions cannot be at the expense of maintaining vigilance. Alertness and vigilance are needed for accurate threat appraisals and effective instrumental coping with the illness situation (Aspinwall and Taylor, 1997; Strauss et al., 1990). For the older patient, forgetfulness may pose an added challenge, as she strives to recall details of medical encounters (Brown, 2007). Societal influences on cognitive functioning in late life are now increasingly recognized (Dannefer and Patterson, 2008; Negash and Petersen, 2006). Accordingly, educational and occupational attainment, along with cognitive activity, is likely to facilitate successful cognitive regulation in dealing with difficult challenges effectively in late life.

Emotion regulation

Emotion regulation is viewed as a second important adaptive task for patients living with life-threatening illness. Emotion regulation has focused on the ways individuals can influence which emotions they experience and how they express emotions (Gross, 1998). Despite the emphasis on reason and cognitive maneuvers, some stress researchers argue that feelings serve as useful guides to action. Little research has been conducted on emotion regulation related to illness management.

The TAD model's focus on patient proactivity and conscious approaches to emotion regulation acknowledges the patient's need to express emotions, while not being overwhelmed with negative emotions (John and Gross, 2004). Emotional expression, in safe settings, can enable the patient to solicit social support, and to deal with adaptive tasks more effectively (Denollet et al., 2008). A special challenge to older patients is to avoid a relation of emotional dependency in relation to family members or healthcare professionals who may have a tendency to exclude older patients from decision-making. Such exclusion, a common form of ageism, can be a trigger for emotional distress that poses an additional challenge for older patients. On the other hand, the ability to exercise some measure of control over one's emotions may represent an important source of empowerment to patients (Cousins, 1983; O'Hanlon, 2004).

While emotion regulation serves adaptive functions, excessive suppression of emotions may result in adverse outcomes (Denollet et al., 2008). Beyond regulating negative emotions, fostering positive emotions (e.g., gratitude and appreciation) can also serve useful functions. Indeed, older cancer patients frequently note expression of such positive emotions in their advice to other cancer patients (Kahana et al., in press).

Social support regulation

Social support can buffer the adverse effects of illness (Helgeson and Cohen, 1996; Wortman, 1984). Yet there has been only limited explication of the processes by which social support exerts its salutary effects (Krauss, 2006). Most researchers focus on support as a function of kin networks, social ties, and availability of formal and informal support sources (Helgeson and Sheldon, 1996). Yet, for the patient, regulation of social supports represents a critical adaptive task. Decisions about disclosure of the diagnosis involve identification of positive support sources and communication of information about the illness (Gottlieb, 1988).

Soon after receiving the diagnosis, probably still in a state of confusion and shock, the patient must make refined judgments about disclosure. She may realize that, while disclosure is a foundation for obtaining social support, it also involves risks of stigma, and of receipt of unwanted and negative attention (Kahana, 1992). Even well-meaning friends and family may overwhelm the newly diagnosed patient with intrusive attention and inquiries that function as stressors rather than sources of comfort (Thornton and Perez, 2007). Accordingly, regulation of social support becomes a key adaptive task for the patient.

After surgery for breast cancer, patients report unwanted 'support' from friends and family, but inadequate support from physicians (Neuling and Winefield, 1988). While cancer patients are generally satisfied with short-term support, help from friends and family has been found to drop off significantly over time (Arora et al., 2007). Consequently, reinforcement of support through appreciation and communication represents an important adaptive function for cancer patients.

Even as patients endeavor to regulate interaction from their existing support network, they also need to consider developing new sources of support from among individuals knowledgeable about cancer, and about navigating the healthcare system. Accordingly, a salient aspect of support regulation involves identifying cancer support groups and/or other cancer patients as well as informational resources about cancer. An important new source of support for cancer patients is offered by the Internet (Seçkin and Kahana, 2005) where patients may find an added source of both informational and emotional support. Although older patients are less likely to use computer-based supports than younger counterparts, the Internet is becoming increasingly accessible and useful for new cohorts of older adults (Kahana et al., 2006).

Proactive illness management

Assuming a proactive role as a healthcare consumer has been consistently found to benefit the patient (Faller and Buelzbruck, 2002; Petticrew et al., 2002). Proactive patients aspire to be involved in treatment decision-making and take initiative in communicating with their physicians (Kahana and Kahana, 2003; Siebert, 1993). These active efforts by patients are usually aimed at obtaining state-of-the-art treatments. For the older patient, or for terminally ill patients, proactive illness management may at times relate to limiting debilitating treatments (even at the cost of a reduced life expectancy), information gathering, and marshaling social supports (Earle, 2007). By actively seeking healthcare information and enlisting healthcare advocates, the patient is better able to obtain timely access to health care and to negotiate with healthcare providers (Harpham, 1994; LeShan, 1994). Armed with good information, patients can play an active role in identification of providers who can offer quality and patient-centered care (Earle, 2007). Patients can also play effective roles to insure that their healthcare environments (at home, at work, and at healthcare facilities) are as comfortable as possible. Limited social resources, reflected in low levels of health literacy, have been found to diminish patient proactivity in seeking medical care (Kahana and Kahana, 2007).

In considering proactive illness management, healthcare consumers appear to benefit most if they positively partner with their healthcare providers, rather than assuming a conflict-oriented perspective (Haug and Lavin, 1981). Part of positive partnering involves adherence to potentially taxing treatments and medical regimens and undertaking active health promotion efforts, including diet and exercise (Kahana et al., 2002). For older patients, controlling fatigue and insuring adequate nutrition can pose special challenges (Ng et al., 2007; Uhley and Jen, 2007). As cancer survivors transition past the initial treatment plan, obtaining surveillance for cancer recurrence and maintaining awareness of potential late effects of treatment represent important adaptive tasks (Earle, 2007). Proactive initiatives are also valuable in maintaining physical and existential quality of life and a good death for those facing advanced cancer (Low et al., 2007).

Social role management

Older cancer patients confront day-to-day challenges of maintaining social roles within the family and possibly within the work environment (Main et al., 2005). Even while seeking social support from others, they also strive to remain an integrated and contributing family member (Verbeek and Spelten, 2007). Older cancer patients often have to find ways to continue family caregiving roles, even in the face of functional limitations. Among couples, there are special challenges in maintaining supportive and satisfying relationships (Manne et al., 1999).

Concerns about stigma have been found to hamper self-disclosure in work or social settings (Koller et al., 1996). At the same time, research confirms high levels of social role functioning among breast cancer survivors (Ganz et al., 1996). Couples must deal with potentially conflicting wishes while needing to make joint decisions (Koczwara and Clark, 2003). To the extent that the cancer patient can pursue meaningful activities despite the illness, social role performance may be facilitated. Thus, for example, cancer patients can make use of legal protections afforded to the disabled if they need accommodations in the workplace (Hoffman, 2005), and in the case of older patients, resist the pressure of forced retirement.

Maintenance of social roles in late life also may include participating in meaningful civic engagement, friendship networks, and leisure activities. Such engagement promotes self esteem through fulfilling interactions and through providing goals and meaning in life (Kahana and Kahana, 2003).

Continued role performance even with functional limitations, or in spite of pain or fatigue, contributes to maintaining a positive identity (Payne, 2007).

Maintenance of family roles can also be facilitated by proactive adaptations. Patient proactivity in maintaining positive interactions with spouses can reduce conflict and maintaining supportive relationships. There are also special challenges in maintaining parental roles, even with adult children (Visser et al., 2004). Direct communication about needs and issues in healthcare decision-making, initiated by older patients, can help in maintaining control and respect, and in obtaining responsive care. Maintenance of family roles is thus intertwined with successful care-getting (Kahana, Kahana, Wykle, and Kulle, in press).

Successful social role management also involves planning for necessary curtailment of social roles and negotiating changing abilities to deal with role demands. The patient can thus minimize stigma and burden of illness by discussing their changing needs and abilities, thereby paving the way for acceptance by family, friends, or coworkers throughout their illness trajectory. Developments in cancer treatment and life expectancy of cancer survivors underscore the importance of identifying how patient proactivity can facilitate social role performance and maintenance of valued activities and relationships.

CONCLUSION

Our goal in developing the TAD model has been to recognize the multifaceted adaptive tasks encountered by elders facing difficult circumstances, which we illustrate by focusing on cancer survivors. Our model is envisioned as an empowerment model that can facilitate identity maintenance, good quality of life, and even PTG among patients living with cancer and other life-threatening illnesses or chronic stressors (Tedeschi et al., 1998). There has been much emphasis in the stress literature on potential benefits of social supports and health care in facilitating patient outcomes. Our goal here has been to develop an understanding of behavioral coping efforts that may be undertaken to deal with specific adaptive challenges and tasks. We feel that the social stress field must move beyond exploration of trait-like coping dispositions and focus on transactional aspects of coping (Aldwin et al., 2006). Such coping efforts may be usefully targeted toward mastery of specific stressful life situations. This approach also helps us recognize the multidimensional nature of cognitive and affective, as well as active or behavioral coping. Additionally, we advocate moving beyond standardized coping scales and toward assessment of the lived experience of those coping with stressful life situations, such as chronic or life-threatening illness (Payne, 2007).

In the new conceptual model presented here, we call for disaggregating stressors of late life by removing their unidimensional characterization as single events and recognizing that experiences such as chronic illness or widowhood reflect a road, or process, along which older adults must journey. Throughout this journey they may be saddled with structural constraints or buoyed by personal resources. In confronting these stressors, they must address unique adaptive tasks by invoking the self as a protagonist, targeting each component of the stressful life situation (Kraaij et al., 2002; Moos et al., 2006).

REFERENCES

Acock, A.C. and Hurlbert, J.S. (1993) 'Social networks, marital status, and well-being', *Social Networks,* 15: 309–34.

Aldwin, C.M. (1992) 'Aging, coping, and efficacy: theoretical framework for examining coping in a lifespan developmental context', in M. Wykle, E. Kahana, and J. Kowal (eds), *Stress and Health Among the Elderly.* New York: Springer.

Aldwin, C.M. and Yancura, L. (2004) 'Coping and health: a comparison of the stress and trauma literatures', in P.P. Schnurr and B.L. Green (eds), *Physical Health Consequences of Exposure to Extreme Stress.* Washington, DC: American Psychological Association.

Aldwin, C.M., Chiara, G., and Sutton, K.J. (1993) 'Stress and coping in older men: findings from the normative aging study', *The Gerontologist,* 33: 248.

Aldwin, C.M., Spiro, A., and Park, C.L. (2006) 'Health, behavior, and optimal aging: a life span developmental perspective', in J.E. Birren and K.W. Schaire (eds), *Handbook of the Psychology of Aging,* 6th edn. Amsterdam, Netherlands: Elsevier.

Aneshensel, C.S. (1993) 'Stress, role captivity, and the cessation of caregiving', *Journal of Health and Social Behavior,* 34: 54–70.

Aneshensel, C.S., Botticelli, A.L., and Yamamoto-Mitani, N. (2004) 'When caregiving ends: the course of depressive symptoms after bereavement', *Journal of Health and Social Behavior,* 45: 422–40.

Ardelt, M. (2000) 'Antecedents and effects of wisdom in old age: a longitudinal perspective on aging well', *Research on Aging,* 22(4): 360–94.

Arora, N.K., Rutten, L.J.F., Gustafson, D.H., Moser, R., and Hawkins, R.P. (2007) 'Perceived helpfulness and impact of social support provided by family, friends, and health care providers to women newly diagnosed with breast cancer', *Psycho-Oncology,* 16(5): 474–86.

Aspinwall, L. (2004) 'Dealing with adversity: self-regulation, coping, adaptation, and health', in M. Brewer and M. Hewstone (eds), *Applied Social Psychology.* Malden, MA: Blackwell.

Aspinwall, L. (2005) 'The psychology of future-oriented thinking: from achievement to proactive coping, adaptation, and aging', *Motivation and Emotion,* 29(4): 203–35.

Aspinwall, L. and Taylor, S. (1997) 'A stitch in time: self-regulation and proactive coping', *Psychological Bulletin,* 121: 417–36.

Baltes, P.B. and Baltes, M.M. (1990), 'Psychological perspectives on successful aging: the model of selective optimization with compensation', in P.B. Baltes and M.M. Baltes (eds), *Successful Aging: Perspectives from the Behavioral Sciences.* New York: Cambridge University Press.

Beaumont, J.G. and Kenealy, P.M. (2004) 'Quality of life perceptions and social comparisons in healthy old age', *Ageing and Society,* 24: 755–69.

Boerner, K. (2004) 'Adaptation to disability among middle-aged and older adults: the role of assimilative and accommodative coping', *Journals of Gerontology Series B: Psychological Sciences and Social Sciences,* 59: P35–42.

Borsch-Supan, A., Hank, K., and Jurges, H. (2005) 'A new comprehensive and international view on ageing: introducing the Survey of Health, Ageing and Retirement in Europe', *European Journal of Ageing,* 2: 245–53.

Boswell, G., Kahana, E., and Dilworth-Anderson, P. (2006) 'Spirituality and healthy lifestyle behaviors: stress counterbalancing effects on the well-being of older adults', *Journal of Religion and Health,* 45(4): 587–602.

Brandtstadter, J., Baltes-Gotz, B., Kirschbaum, C., and Hellhammer, D. (1991) 'Developmental and personality correlates of adrenocortical activity as indexed by salivary cortisol: observations in the age range of 35 to 65 years', *Journal of Psychosomatic Research,* 35(2–3): 173–85.

Breznitz, S. (1983) *The Denial of Stress.* Madison, CT: International Universities Press.

Brody, D., Khaliq, A., and Thompson, T. (1997) 'Patients' perspective on the management of emotional distress in primary care settings', *Journal of General Internal Medicine,* 12(7): 403–6.

Brown, S.C. (2007) 'How older patients learn medical information', in D.C. Park and L.L. Liu (eds), *Medical Adherence and Aging: Social and Cognitive Perspectives.* Washington, DC: American Psychological Association.

Busuttil, W. (2004) 'Presentations and management of post traumatic stress disorder and the elderly: a need for investigation', *International Journal of Geriatric Psychiatry,* 19: 429–39.

Carstensen, L.L. (1995) 'Evidence for a life-span theory of socioemotional selectivity', *Current Directions in Psychological Science,* 4(5): 151–6.

Carver, C.S., Scheier, M.F., and Weintraub, J.K. (1989) 'Assessing coping strategies: a theoretically based approach', *Journal of Personality and Social Psychology*, 56(2): 267–83.

Charmaz, K. (1997) 'Speaking of sadness: depression, disconnection, and the meanings of illness', *Symbolic Interaction*, 20(3): 311–14.

Cooley, C.H. (1902) *Human Nature and the Social Order*. New York: Scribner's.

Cornman, J.C., Goldman, N., Glei, D.A., Weinstein, M., and Chang, M.C. (2003) 'Social ties and perceived support: two dimensions of social relationships and health among the elderly in Taiwan', *Journal of Aging and Health*, 15(4): 616–44.

Cousins, N. (1983) *The Healing Heart. Antidotes to Panic and Helplessness*. New York: Norton and Company.

Cox, T., Griffiths, A., and Houdmont, J. (2006) *Defining a Case of Work-Related Stress*. University of Nottingham, Nottingham: Institute of Work, Health, and Organizations.

Crivellari, D., Aapro, M., Leonard, R., et al. (2007) 'Breast cancer in the elderly', *Journal of Clinical Oncology*, 25(14): 1882–90.

Cumming, E. and Henry, W.E. (1961) *Growing Old: The Process of Disengagement*. New York: Basic Books.

Dannefer, D. (2003) 'Cumulative advantage/disadvantage and the life course: cross-fertilizing age and social science theory', *Journals of Gerontology Series B: Psychological Sciences and Social Sciences*, 58: S327–37.

Dannefer, D. and Patterson, R. (2008) 'The missing person: some problems in the study of cognitive aging', in D. Alwin and S. Hofer (eds), *International Handbook of Cognitive Aging*. Thousand Oaks, CA: SAGE.

Dannefer, D. and Sell, R.R. (1988) 'Age structure, the life course, and "aged heterogeneity": prospects for research and theory', *Comprehensive Gerontology. Section B, Behavioural, Social, and Applied Sciences*, 2(1): 1–10.

Denollet, J., Nyklicek, I., and Vingerhoets, J.J.M. (2008) 'Introduction: emotions, emotion regulation, and health', in A. Vingerhoets (ed.), *Emotion Regulation*. New York: Springer.

Doka, K.J. (1993) *Living with Life-Threatening Illness*. New York: Lexington Books.

Draper, B.M., Poulos, R.G., Poulos, C.J., and Ehrlich, F. (1996) 'Risk factors for stress in elderly caregivers', *International Journal of Geriatric Psychiatry*, 11(3): 227–31.

Earle, C.C. (2007) 'Quality of care', in M. Feuerstein (ed.), *Handbook of Cancer Survivorship*. New York: Springer.

Elder, G.H. and Clipp, E.C. (1989) 'Combat experience and emotional health: impairment and resilience in later life', *Journal of Personality*, 57: 311–41.

Faller, H. and Buelzbruck, H. (2002) 'Coping and survival in lung cancer', *American Journal of Psychiatry*, 159: 2105–7.

Ferlander, S. (2007) 'The importance of different forms of social capital for health', *Acta Sociologica*, 50(2): 115–28.

Folkman, S. and Moskowitz, J. T. (2004) 'Coping: pitfalls and promise', *Annual Review of Psychology*, 55: 745–74.

Ganz, P., Coscarelli, A., Fred, C., Kahn, B., and Polinsky, M. (1996) 'Breast cancer survivors: psychosocial concerns and quality of life', *Breast Cancer Research and Treatment*, 38(2): 183–99.

George, L.K. (1996) 'Social factors and illness', in L.K. George and R.H. Binstock (eds), *Handbook of Aging and the Social Sciences*, 4th edn. New York: Academic Press.

George, L.K. (2006) 'Perceived quality of life', in R.H. Binstock and L.K. George (eds), *Handbook of Aging and the Social Sciences*, 6th edn. Amsterdam, Netherlands: Elsevier.

Goenjian, A.K., Najarian, L.M., Pynoos, R.S., et al. (1994) 'Posttraumatic stress disorder in elderly and younger adults after the 1988 earthquake in Armenia', *American Journal of Psychiatry*, 151: 895–901.

Goldhaber, D.E. (2000) *Theories of Human Development: Integrative Perspectives*. Mountain View, CA: Mayfield Publishing Company.

Gottlieb, B. (ed.). (1988) '*Marshaling Social Support*'. Newbury Park, CA: SAGE.

Gross, J. (1998) 'The emerging field of emotion regulation: an integrative review', *Review of General Psychology*, 2(3): 271–99.

Hall, S.S. (2007) 'Wisdom, long a subject for philosophers, is now being scrutinized by a cadre of scientific researchers. The trick lies not just in measuring something so fuzzy, but also in defining it in the first place', *The New York Times*, May 6: 58–66.

Hardy, S.E., Concato, J., and Gill, T.M. (2002) 'Stressful life events among community-living older persons', *Journal of General Internal Medicine*, 17(11): 841–7.

Harpham, W. (1994) *After Cancer: A Guide to Your New Life*. New York: W.W. Norton.

Haug, M. and Lavin, B. (1981) 'Practitioner or patient – Who's in charge?', *Journal of Health and Social Behavior*, 22: 212–29.

Hawkley, L.C., Berntson, G.G., Engeland, C.G., et al., (2005) 'Stress, aging, and resilience: Can accrued wear and tear be slowed?', *Canadian Psychology*, 46(3): 115–25.

Helgeson, V. and Sheldon, C. (1996) 'Social support and adjustment to cancer: reconciling descriptive, correlational, and intervention research', *Health Psychology*, 15(2): 135–48.

Hewitt, P. and Flett, G. (1996) 'Personality traits and the coping process', in M. Zeidner and N.S. Endler (eds), *Handbook of Coping*. New York: John Wiley and Sons, Inc.

Hewitt, M., Greenfield, S., and Stovall, E. (eds) (2006) *From Cancer Patient to Cancer Survivor*. Washington, DC: The National Academic Press.

Hoffman, B. (2005) 'Cancer survivors at work: a generation of progress', *CA Cancer Journal for Clinicians*, 55: 271–80.

Holahan, C., Moos, R., and Schafer, J. (1996) 'Coping, stress resistance, and growth: conceptualizing adaptive functioning', in M. Zeidner and N.S. Endler (eds), *Handbook of Coping: Theory, Research, Applications*, New York: John Wiley and Sons.

Hughes, D.C., Blazer, D.G., and George, L.K. (1988) 'Age differences in life events: a multivariate controlled analysis', *International Journal of Aging and Human Development*, 27: 207–20.

Idler, E. (2006) 'Religion and aging', in R.H. Binstock and L.K. George (eds), *Handbook of Aging and the Social Sciences*, 6th edn. Amsterdam, Netherlands: Elsevier.

John, O.P. and Gross, J.J. (2004) 'Health and unhealthy emotion regulation: personality processes, individual differences, and life span development', *Journal of Personality*, 72: 1301–33.

Jung, C.G. (1933) *Modern Man in Search of a Soul*. Oxford: Harcourt Brace.

Juster, F.T. and Suzman, R. (1995) *The Health and Retirement Study: An Overview*. HRS Working Papers Series #94–1001; *Journal of Human Resources*, 1995 Supplement (JHR 30-S).

Kahana, E. (1992) 'Stress research, and aging: complexities, ambiguities, paradoxes, and promise', in M. Wykle, E. Kahana, and J. Kowal (eds), *Stress and Health Among the Elderly*, New York: Springer.

Kahana, E., and Kahana, B. (1996) 'Conceptual and empirical advances in understanding aging well through proactive adaptation', in V. Bengtson (ed.), *Adulthood and Aging: Research on Continuities and Discontinuities*. New York: Springer.

Kahana, E. and Kahana, B. (2003) 'Patient proactivity enhancing doctor–patient–family communication in cancer prevention and care among the aged', *Patient Education and Counseling*, 2075: 1–7.

Kahana, E., and Kahana, B. (2007) 'Patient proactivity enhancing doctor–patient–family communication in cancer prevention and care among the aged', in D.O'Hair, G. Kreps, and L. Sparks (eds), *Handbook of Communication and Cancer Care*. New York: Hampton Press.

Kahana, B., Harel, Z., and Kahana, E. (2005) *Holocaust Survivors and Immigrants: Late Life Adaptations*. New York: Springer.

Kahana, E., Kahana, B., and Hammel, R. (2008) 'Stress in later life', in D. Carr (ed.), *Encyclopedia of the Life Course and Human Development*. Farmington, MI: Macmillan Reference USA.

Kahana, E., Kahana, B., and Kercher, K. (2003) 'Emerging lifestyles and proactive options for successful aging', *Ageing International*, 28(2): 155–80.

Kahana, B., Kahana, E., Lovegreen, L., and Seçkin, G. (2006) 'Compensatory use of computers by disabled older adults', in K. Meisenberger et al. (eds), *ICCHP 2006, Lecture Notes in Computer Science*, 4061. Berlin: Springer, pp.766–9.

Kahana, B., Kahana, E., Sterns, S., and Deimling, G. (2007) 'Predictors of posttraumatic growth among elderly long-term cancer survivors'. Presented at the Gerontological Society of America annual meeting, San Francisco, CA, November.

Kahana, E., Kahana, B., Kelley-Moore, J., et al. (in press) 'Toward advocacy in cancer care among the old-old: cautionary personal actions and bold advice to others', *Journal of American Geriatric Society*.

Kahana, E., Kahana, B., Wykle, M., and Kulle, D. (in press) 'Marshalling social support: active roles in care-getting for cancer patients throughout the life course', in D. Biegel and

G. Singer (eds), *Journal of Family Social Work* (special issue).

Kahana, E., Lawrence, R., Kahana, B., et al. (2002) 'Long-term impact of preventive proactivity on quality of life of the old-old', *Psychosomatic Medicine*, 64(3): 382–94.

Koczwara, B. and Clark, M. (2003) 'A couple with cancer: conflicting wishes, joint decisions', *Journal of Clinical Oncology*, 21(1): 174–6.

Koenig, H.G., Pargament, K.I., and Nielsen, J. (1998) 'Religious coping and health status in medically ill hospitalized older adults', *Journal of Nervous and Mental Disease*, 186(9): 513–21.

Koller, M., Kussman, J., Lorenz, W., et al. (1996) 'Symptom reporting in cancer patients: the role of negative affect and experienced social stigma', *Cancer*, 77(5): 983–95.

Kraaij, V., Garnefski, N., and Maes, S. (2002) 'The joint effects of stress, coping, and coping resources on depressive symptoms in the elderly', *Anxiety, Stress, and Coping: An International Journal*, 15(2): 163–77.

Krauss, N. (2006) 'Social relationships in late life', in R.H. Binstock and L.K. George (eds), *Handbook of Aging and the Social Sciences*. San Diego, CA: Academic Press.

Kunitz, S.J. (2004) 'Social capital and health', *British Medical Bulletin*, 69(1): 61–73.

Lawton, M.P. (1999) 'Quality of life in chronic illness', *Gerontology*, 45(4): 181–3.

Lazarus, R., and Folkman, S. (1984) *Stress, Appraisal, and Coping*. New York: Springer.

Lennartsson, C. and Silverstein, M. (2001) 'Does engagement with life enhance survival of elderly people in Sweden? The role of social and leisure activities', *Journals of Gerontology: Series B: Psychological Sciences and Social Sciences*, 56(6): S335–42.

LeShan, L. (1994) *Cancer as a Turning Point*. New York: Plume.

Low, C.A., Beran, T., and Stanton, A.L. (2007) 'Adaptation in the face of advanced cancer', in M. Feuerstein (ed.), *Handbook of Cancer Survivorship*, New York: Springer.

Lunney, J.R., Lynn, J., Foley, D.J., Lipson, S., and Guralnik, J.M. (2003) 'Patterns of functional decline at the end of life', *Journal of the American Medical Association*, 289: 2387–92.

Main, D., Nowels, C., Cavender, T., Etschmaier, M., and Steiner, J. (2005) A qualitative study of work return in cancer survivors', *Pscyho-Oncology*, 14(11): 992–1004.

Manne, S.L., Alferi, T., Taylor, K.L., and Dougherty, J. (1999) 'Spousal negative responses to cancer patients: the role of social restriction, spouse mood, and relationship satisfaction', *Journal of Consulting and Clinical Psychology*, 67: 352–61.

Marmot, M., Banks J., Blundell R., Lessof C., and Nazroo J. (eds) (2003) *Health, Wealth and Lifestyles of the Older Population in England: the 2002 English Longitudinal Study of Ageing*. London: Institute for Fiscal Studies.

McCabe, K.A. and Gregory, S.S. (1998) 'Elderly victimization: an examination beyond the FBI's index crimes', *Research on Aging*, 20: 369–72.

McLeod, J.D. and Lively, J. (2007) 'Social psychology and stress research', in W.R. Avison, J.D. McLeod, and

B.A. Pescosolido (eds), *Mental Health, Mental Mirror.* New York: Springer.

Moos, R.H., Tsu, V.D., and Schaefer, J.A. (1989) *Coping with Physical Illness.* New York: Plenum.

Moos, R.H., Brennan, P.L., Schutte, K.K., and Moos, B.S. (2006) '"Older adults" coping with negative life events: common processes of managing health, interpersonal, and financial/work stressors', *International Journal of Aging and Human Development,* 62(1): 39–59.

Negash, S. and Petersen, R. (2006) 'Societal influences that affect cognitive functioning in old age', in K.W. Schaie and L.L. Carstensen (eds), *Social Structures, Aging, and Self-Regulation in the Elderly.* New York: Springer.

Neugarten, B.L. (1979) 'Time, age, and the life cycle', *American Journal of Psychiatry,* 136(7): 887–94.

Neuling, S. and Winefield, H. (1988) 'Social support and recovery after surgery for breast cancer: frequency and correlates of supportive behaviours by family, friends and surgeon', *Social Science Medicine,* 27(4): 385–92.

Ng, A.V., Alt, C.A., and Gore, E.M. (2007) 'Fatigue', in M. Feuerstein (ed.), *Handbook of Cancer Survivorship,* New York: Springer.

O'Hanlon, B. (2004) *Thriving through Crisis. Turn Tragedy and Trauma into Growth and Change.* New York: Berkeley Publishing.

Pargament, K.I. (1997) *The Psychology of Religion and Coping: Theory, Research, Practice.* New York: Guilford Press.

Parsons, T. (1975) 'The sick role and the role of the physician reconsidered', *Millbank Memorial Fund Quarterly,* 53(3): 257–78.

Payne, S. (2007) 'Living with advanced cancer', in M. Feuerstein (ed.), *Handbook of Cancer Survivorship,* New York: Springer Publishing Company.

Pearlin, L.I. (1989) 'The sociological study of stress', *Journal of Health and Social Behavior,* 30: 241–56.

Pearlin, L.I., Aneshensel, C.S., and LeBlane, A.J. (1997) 'The forms and mechanisms of stress proliferation: the case of AIDS caregivers', *Journal of Health and Social Behavior,* 38: 223–36.

Pearlin, L.I., Menaghan, E.G., Lieberman, M.A., and Mullan, J.T. (1981) 'The stress process', *Journal of Health and Social Behavior,* 22(4): 337–56.

Petticrew, M., Bell, R., and Hunter, D. (2002) 'Influence of psychological coping on survival and recurrence in people with cancer: systematic review', *BMJ,* 325: 1066.

Pierret, J. (2003) 'The illness experience: state of knowledge and perspectives for research', *Sociology of Health and Illness,* 25(silver anniversary issue): 4–22.

Rapp, S.R., Shumaker, S., Schmidt, S., Naughton, M., and Anderson. (1998) 'Social resourcefulness: its relationship to social support and wellbeing among caregivers of dementia victims', *Aging and Mental Health,* 2(1): 40–8.

Rothermund, K. and Brandtstadter, J. (2003) 'Coping with deficits and losses in later life: from compensatory action to accommodation', *Psychology and Aging,* 18(4): 896–905.

Ryff, C.D., Marshall, V.W., and Clarke, P.J. (1999) 'Linking the self and society in social gerontology: crossing new territory via old questions', in C.D. Ryff and V.W. Marshall (eds), *The Self and Society in Aging Processes.* New York: Springer.

Seçkin, G. and Kahana, E. (2005) 'Patient participation and decision making in the age of communication technology'. Presented at the International Conference on Communication in Health Care, Northwestern University, Chicago, Illinois., October.

Settersten, R.A. (1999) *Lives in Time and Place: The Problems and Promises of Developmental Science.* Amityville, NY: Baywood Publishing Company.

Sherman, A., Shumaker, S., Rejeski, W., et al. (2006) 'Social support, social integration, and health-related quality of life over time: results from the Fitness and Arthritis in Seniors Trial (FAST)', *Psychology and Health,* 21(4): 463–80.

Shmotkin, D. and Lomranz, J. (1998) 'Subjective well-being among Holocaust survivors: an examination of overlooked differentiations', *Journal of Personality and Social Psychology,* 75: 141–55.

Siebert, A. (1993) *The Survivor Personality.* Portland, OR: Practical Psychology Press.

Smith, G., Kohn, S., Savage-Stevens, S., et al. (2000) 'The effects of interpersonal and personal agency on perceived control and psychological well-being in adulthood', *The Gerontologist,* 40: 458–68.

Snyder, C. (1994) *The Psychology of Hope: You Can Get There from Here.* New York: Free Press.

Solomon, Z. and Prager, E. (1992) 'Elderly Israeli Holocaust survivors during the Persian Gulf War: a study of psychological distress', *American Journal of Psychiatry,* 149(12): 1707–10.

Starzomska, M. (2006) 'Coping with bereavement among old people and using such experiences in helping others bereaved in the light of wisdom theories', *Psychogeriatria Polska,* 3(1): 23–30.

Staudinger, U.M., Kessler, E.M., and Dorner, J. (2006) 'Wisdom in social context', in K.W. Schaie and L.L. Carstensen (eds), *Social Structures, Aging, and Self-Regulation in the Elderly.* New York: Springer.

Strauss, D., Spitzer, R., and Muskin, P. (1990) 'Maladaptive denial of physical illness: a proposal for DSM-IV.', *The American Journal of Psychiatry,* 147: 1168–72.

Suchman, E. (1965) 'Social patterns of illness and medical care', *Journal of Health and Human Behavior,* 6: 2–16.

Taylor, S.E. and Repetti, R.L. (1997) 'What is an unhealthy environment and how does it get under the skin?', *Annual Review of Psychology,* 48: 411–47.

Tedeschi, R.G., Park, C.L., and Calhoun, L.G. (1998) *Posttraumatic Growth: Positive Changes in the Aftermath of Crisis.* Mahwah, NJ: Lawrence Erlbaum Associates.

Thoits, P. (1995) 'Stress, coping and social support processes: Where are we? What next?', *Journal of Health and Social Behavior, Extra Issue: Forty Years of Medical Sociology: The State of the Art and Directions for the Future,* 35: 53–79.

Thornton, A.A. and Perez, M.A. (2007) 'Interpersonal relationships', in M. Feuerstein (ed.), *Handbook of Cancer Survivorship.* New York: Springer.

Tsai, C.H., Lung, F.W., and Wang, S.Y. (2004) 'The 1999 Ji-Ji (Taiwan) earthquake as a trigger for acute myocardial infarction', *Psychosomatics,* 45(6): 477–82.

Turner, R.J. and Avison, W.R. (2003) 'Status variations in stress exposure: implications for the interpretation of research on race, socioeconomic status, and gender', *Journal of Health and Social Behavior,* 44: 488–505.

Turner, R.J. and Turner, J.B. (1999) 'Social integration and support', in C.S. Aneshensel and J.C. Phelan (eds), *Handbook of the Sociology of Mental Health.* New York: Kluwer/Plenum.

Turner, R.J., Wheaton, B., and Lloyd, D.A. (1995) 'The epidemiology of social stress', *American Sociological Review,* 60: 104–25.

Uhley, V. and Catherine Jen, K.L. (2007) 'Nutrition and weight management in cancer survivors', in M. Feuerstein (ed.), *Handbook of Cancer Survivorship.* New York: Springer.

Van der Kolk, B.A., Roth, S., Pelcovitz, D., Sunday, S., and Spinazzola, J. (2005) 'Disorders of extreme stress: the empirical foundation of a complex adaptation to trauma', *Journal of Traumatic Stress,* 18(5): 389–99.

Verbeek, J. and Spelten, E. (2007) 'Work', in M. Feuerstein (ed.), *Handbook of Cancer Survivorship.* New York: Springer.

Verbrugge, L.M. and Jette, A.M. (1994) 'The disablement process', *Social Science and Medicine,* 38(1): 1–14.

Visser, A., Huizinga, G.A., van der Graaf, W.T., Hoekstra, H.J., and Hoekstra-Weebers, J.E. (2004) 'The impact of parental cancer on children and family: a review of the literature', *Cancer Treatment and Review,* 30: 683–94.

Waldstein, S., Siegel, E., Lefkowitz, D., et al. (2004) 'Stress-induced blood pressure reactivity and silent cerebrovascular disease', *Stroke,* 35: 1294–8.

Walter-Ginzburg, A., Blumstein, T., Chetrit, A., and Modan, B. (2002) 'Social factors and mortality in the old-old in Israel: the CALAS study', *Journals of Gerontology Series B: Psychological Sciences and Social Sciences,* 57(5): S308–18.

Wethington, E. and Kessler, R.C. (1986) 'Perceived support, received support, and adjustment to stressful life events', *Journal of Health and Social Behavior,* 27(1): 78–89.

Wheaton, B. (1996) 'The domains and boundaries of stress concepts', in H.B. Kaplan (ed.), *Psychosocial Stress: Perspectives on Structure, Theory, Life-Course, and Methods.* New York: Academic Press.

Wong, D.F.K. (2002) 'Stage-specific and culture-specific coping strategies used by Mainland Chinese immigrants during resettlement in Hong Kong: a qualitative analysis', *Social Work in Health Care,* 35(1–2): 479–99.

Wortman, C. (1984) 'Social support and the cancer patient: conceptual and methodological issues', *Cancer,* 15(53): 2339–62.

Yates, T.M. and Masten, A.S. (2004) 'Fostering the future: resilience theory and the practice of positive psychology', in P.A. Linley and S. Joseph (eds), *Positive Psychology in Practice.* Hoboken, NJ: John Wiley and Sons.

Zeidner, M. and Endler, N. (1996) *Handbook of Coping: Theory, Research, Applications.* New York: John Wiley and Sons.

22

Agency and Social Structure in Aging and Life-course Research

Victor W. Marshall and Philippa J. Clarke

INTRODUCTION

Understanding the relationship between agency and structure has always been a core theoretical preoccupation of sociologists and other social scientists. Many volumes and countless papers by social theorists and philosophers have argued radically different approaches to this general topic. Social gerontology has from its inception been concerned with aging individuals making their way in what are for the most part aging societies. Thus, it is no surprise that concerns with work in social gerontology have included a concern with agency. At the same time, it must be noted that explicit theoretical consideration of agency and structure is far more limited in life-course research than in general theoretical discussions.

The difficulty in theorizing agency, structure, and their relationship has several causes, including lack of agreement as to the definition of key terms such as micro/macro, self/society, and agency/structure; disputes as to whether the differences between levels of analysis focused on the individual in micro-level social interaction on the one hand, and on macro-level social structure on the other hand, are ontologically real; the fact that some prominent theorists see structure not only at the macro level but also at the micro level of social interaction; disagreements as to whether micro and macro levels can be analytically investigated as different; and disagreements as to how the linkages between the two levels can be analyzed. Additional disagreements are methodological – notably, the tendency of some researchers to identify uncritically a specific theoretical concept with a specific methodology (e.g., to assume that agency can be grasped only with qualitative methods).

To reduce our topic to manageable levels, this chapter can address only briefly conceptual controversies about agency and structure in the general social science literature, before turning to the ambiguities and debates as they appear in the research literature on aging and the life course. In this discussion, particular attention will be paid to the use of these two concepts in later life, where life-course transitions related to health and occupational change or retirement are generally considered to be important.

AGENCY AND STRUCTURE IN THE SOCIAL SCIENCE LITERATURE

The so-called agency–structure debate (sometimes framed as the micro–macro or self-society debate) has long been identified by scholars as the central problem for sociological theorizing (Alexander, 1988; Giddens, 1984; Layder, 2006; Marshall, 1996). Ritzer notes that 'the micro-macro link does not constitute something new, but rather a widespread rediscovery of a focal concern that lies at the heart of the work of most of the major thinkers in the history of sociology (Marx, Weber, Simmel, even Durkheim)' (Ritzer, 1988: 486). Although some notable thinkers (Blau, 1977, 1987a, 1987b; Foucault, as discussed in Layder, 2006; Goffman, 1983; Rawls, 1987; Turner, 1990) have questioned whether linking micro and macro levels in sociology is a worthwhile enterprise, there are strong reasons for the continuing recognition that it comprises the central theoretical problem and a topic of vigorous, ongoing debate in sociology (Marshall, 1995; Waitzkin, 1989: 221).[1]

We cannot here address these various theoretical debates in any detail (see Campbell, 1996; Layder, 2006; Marshall, 2005; Mouzelis, 1995; Sewell, 1992; Smelser, 1988; Stones, 2007).[2] Our own position is influenced by Berger and Luckmann (1967) and Giddens (1993), both of whom take a 'dualism' or 'duality of structure' approach to assert that social structures are constituted by social actions just as social actions are enabled and constrained by the very structures they create (McMullin and Marshall 1999).[3]

Sewell's approach to structure

Sewell (1992: 1) observes that: '"Structure" is one of the most important and most elusive terms in the vocabulary of current social science.' Indeed, the problems in linking agency and structure have much to do with the plethora of definitions of both concepts. Giddens sees social structure and agency as a 'dualism', with agency creating social structure and social structure both enabling and constraining agency. In Giddens' duality, structure consists of 'rules and resources', and it exists (is instantiated) only through social action (Giddens, 1984: 377). As Sewell (1992: 6) notes, Giddens' formulation is unsatisfactory in that structure has only '... a "virtual" existence ... . Structures do not exist concretely in time and space except as "memory traces" ... (... as ideas or schemas lodged in human brains) and as they are "instantiated in action" (i.e., put into practice)'.

In contrast, Sewell argues that '... publicly fixed codifications of rules are actual rather than virtual and should be regarded as *resources* rather than as rules in Giddens' sense' (Sewell 1992: 8). For example, when social arrangements allocate financial resources differentially based on age, the social structuring of age is more than virtual; it has legal, economic, and cultural dimensions of reality. This is a critical strength of Sewell's

approach, and a key point in distinguishing it from not only that of Giddens but also from other approaches such as structural-functionalism, which largely treat social structure as normative and cultural.

If this position on social structure is adopted, it is possible analytically to distinguish social structure, defined by patterned systems of rules *and resources*, from social action, and to see that while social action is shaped by these systems of rules and resources, social action also changes structure. Yet just how this link between individual action and social structure is formulated remains a matter of considerable disagreement (Layder, 2006; Marshall, 1995).

Approaches to agency in social theory

Parsonian structural-functionalism is 'the elephant in the room' when concerns turn to the concept of agency, because Parsons' development of a 'voluntaristic theory of action' (Parsons 1937/1949) dominated sociology in and beyond the United States for decades. Parsons attempted to incorporate into his functionalist framework a notion of an 'acting', choosing person. However, he also saw the stability of the social system as largely guaranteed by shared values and norms, internalized by the individual 'actor' through socialization (Marshall, 1986). Effective socialization, leading to the internalization of 'need-dispositions', greatly constrained choice. As Giddens (1976: 1) puts it: Parsons identifies '... voluntarism with the "internalization of values".... *There is no action in Parsons "action frame of reference"*' (italics in original). This charge, that Parsons' 'voluntarism' is based on behavior and does not really allow for action at all, has also been noted by others (see, e.g., Campbell, 1996; Marshall, 1986).

Despite the domination of structural-functionalist approaches in the early period of social gerontology, a minority of researchers drew on interpretive theory rooted in symbolic interactionism, phenomenology, and cultural anthropology. These approaches view individuals as creating and using symbols intentionally to fashion meaning in their lives. In this view, human behavior is constrained but not fully determined by social structures. Symbolic interactionism stresses constant change, novelty, and emergent behavior in response to problematic situations (Chappell and Orbach, 1986). The self is a process involving the 'I' and the 'Me', and the former is a necessary construct to move beyond stasis to process in the dialectic of the self and its engagement with society (Marshall, 2005).[4] More broadly conceived, an 'interpretive approach' views society as '... the creation of its members; the product of their construction of meaning, and of the action and relationships through which they attempt to impose meaning on their historical situations' (Dawe, 1970: 216). Weber, who defined sociology as 'a science concerning itself with the interpretive understanding of social action' (Weber, 1978: 4) is the exemplary figure. He said, 'We shall speak of "action" insofar as its subjective meaning takes account of the behavior of others and is therefore oriented in its course'.

Building on these interactionist and phenomenological traditions, Emirbayer and Mische turn to the American pragmatists, especially Dewey and Mead, and to the phenomenologist Schutz, to place agency within a temporal framework and contrast it with structural-functionalist and rational choice approaches. These figures 'insist that action not be perceived as the pursuit of pre-established ends, abstracted from concrete situations, but rather that ends and means develop coterminously within contexts that are themselves ever changing and thus always subject to reevaluation and reconstruction ...' (Emirbayer and Mische, 1998: 967–8). They also stress the creativity of agency, drawing on the European theorist Hans Joas (1996).

Emirbayer and Mische (1998: 970) define human agency as 'the temporally constructed engagement by actors of different structural environments – the temporal-relational contexts of action – which, through the interplay of habit, imagination, and judgment, both reproduces and transforms those structures in interactive response to the problems posed by changing historical situations.' They go on to break down agency into different temporal types, to examine actions more oriented to the past, the future, and the present. The most important aspects of their contribution to theorizing agency are:

- to root the construct in the interpretive perspective, in distinct contrast to approaches taken by structural-functionalists and rational choice theorists;
- to add explicitly a temporal dimension;
- and to develop a typology of different forms of agency in relation to temporality.

While Emerbayer and Mische contribute a provocative and nuanced understanding of agency, a limitation of their approach is the confounding of social action with the capacity to act, and they do not deal adequately with structure.

This problem is avoided by Sewell (1992: 17), who defines agency '... as entailing the capacity to transpose and extend schemas to new contexts'.

He maintains that agency '... is inherent in the knowledge of cultural schemas that characterize all minimally competent members of society'. Sewell thus views agency as a constituent of social structure but in a very special way:

'To be an agent means to be capable of exerting some degree of control over the social relations in which one is enmeshed, which in turn implies the ability to transform those social relations to some degree ... agency arises from the actor's control of resources, which means the capacity to reinterpret or mobilize an array of resources in terms of schemas other than those that constituted the array. Agency is implied by the existence of structures'.

(Sewell, 1992: 20)

Linking micro and macro

As C. Wright Mills argued over 40 years ago in *The Sociological Imagination*: 'Neither the life of an individual nor the history of a society can be understood without understanding both' (Mills 1959: 3). However, the incorporation of both the individual and social structural perspectives in one theory or explanation has not been easily accomplished. In other papers (Marshall, 1995, 1996; Ryff et al., 1999), we have noted that micro and macro perspectives on aging are rarely linked, and even then by using only weak or simplistic linking mechanisms. Marshall (1995) advocates a theoretical approach that explicitly specifies how macro-level social structures and the individual interact. This approach draws on interpretive social theory to postulate interactionist and dialectical mechanisms whereby the individual's lived experience is meaningfully constrained by social structure, but where the impact of that social structure can be modified through individual action and social interaction, to the point where social structures themselves may be altered. As Waitzkin argues: '... macrolevel structures profoundly influence interpersonal processes, but ... microlevel processes cumulatively reinforce social structures at the macro level as well' (Waitzkin, 1989: p. 221; see also Gecas, 2003). It is also critically important to build time into our theorizing. Archer (1995, 2007), Emirbayer and Mische (1998), and Sewell (1992) have all in effect argued that social action in 'temporal period one' creates structures, both through intended and unintended consequences, and these take on a reality that becomes the structural context that both enables and constrains social action in 'temporal period two'.

AGENCY AND STRUCTURE IN STUDIES OF AGING AND THE LIFE COURSE

Early approaches: normative structure and little agency

From its inception, social gerontology was concerned with the fit between the individual and society. This implied a social structure and a relationship of the individual to that social structure. One major early strand of research addressed the extent to which the modernization of society affected the social status of older people. Initiated by Burgess (1960) and developed by Cowgill (1974), there was no real social psychology in this work and individuals were viewed without any consideration of agency: i.e., their fates were seen as dependent solely on dimensions of modernization and not on their own action. However, the second major strand of early work, pursuing the question of social integration of the aging individual in society through the activity theory–disengagement theory debate, did deal with the individual in more detail.

Common to these early approaches, is their reliance on a Parsonian theoretical framework and on Linton's (1936) classic distinction between status and role. As Burgess (1960) had argued that modernization took away meaningful roles, creating the role-less role of older persons, the disengagement theorists saw a mutual severing of role ties that linked the individual to society, and the activity theorists saw a non-voluntary severing of such role ties. Activity theorists argued that activity (considered as role occupancy) was necessary for well-being in the later years. While little is to be found in the entire disengagement theory literature about mechanisms, it might be argued that the assertion that disengagement is voluntary is a bow to the principle of agency – although this was not a language used at that time. However, in a critical response to Cumming and Henry's (1961) work on disengagement theory, Havighurst, Neugarten and colleagues (Havighurst et al.,1963; Neugarten, 1966; Neugarten et al., 1964) presented evidence from the same Kansas City studies that psychological disengagement preceded sociological disengagement. Of course, 'social ties' hardly exhausts the range of social influences that were continuously present prior to psychological disengagement. They described a growing interiority of the self, a self-focusing and withdrawal of 'ego energy' from the external world that occurred prior to the severing of social ties. It would be difficult to characterize this as fully agentic, however, because these authors considered psychological disengagement to be developmental.

As a developmental principle, it is a 'naturally occurring' and hence irreversible age-related change, independent of volition (Dannefer, 1984; Hochschild, 1975)[5].

In essence, while the mechanisms were different, both camps in the great activity theory–disengagement theory debate (which captured the imagination of social gerontologists for almost two decades) saw aging as a progressive disengagement of the individual from social structure, defined in terms of roles defined in terms of norms, and with no consideration of the possibility that people might behave as agents in this process.

At one point, Bernice Neugarten advocated the activity theory position: that loss of roles with aging has adverse effects on people's well-being (Havighurst et al., 1963). Later, however, she moved from a developmental psychology approach to a structural-functionalist one that saw socialization as effectively preparing people for the occupancy of highly defined status positions with well-developed norms to guide appropriate behavior (Neugarten et al., 1965). In this, her theoretical approach could be characterized as very similar to that of Riley's Parsonian structural-functionalism. The individual was not the focus of attention and was simply conceptualized as a bundle of roles, not in terms of an agentic self. However, Neugarten later came to advocate an interpretive theoretical approach to aging and, in that context, she suggested the importance of studying people's goal-setting over their life course (Neugarten, 1985).

The age stratification perspective (Riley, 1971; Riley et al., 1972) can be considered an extension of the modernization, activity, and disengagement theories, with its structural-functionalist stance and emphasis on an age-based system of roles. As such, it gave little weight to agency, although Riley's later work attempted to incorporate individual action and its effect on social change (Riley, 1987). The main thrust of the perspective is the conceptualization of life course, like society as a whole, as an age-graded structure defined by the social organization of status positions and roles through which cohorts of individuals flow as they age. Each stratum in an age stratification system has its own sets of expectations for behavior, and rewards for fulfilling these expectations, 'channeled by the rules, linkages, and mechanisms governing role sequences within the social structure' (Riley, 1987: 4).

What is rarely recognized is that the age stratification perspective also postulated an explicit link between the individual and society through a dialectical process whereby structural change is instigated by the action of individuals (clearly described by Riley et al., 1972: Chapter 1). While this sounds very much like the duality of structure advocated by Giddens and Sewell, the actual link between action and structure in this perspective includes little of the actor's capacity to mobilize an array of resources for the purposes of transforming social structure. In fact, structural change is more a result of new and emergent age behaviors (e.g., early retirement) as successively different cohorts pass through the age structure: '... these behavior patterns then become defined as age-appropriate norms and rules, are reinforced by "authorities", and thereby become institutionalized in the structure of society' (Riley, 1987). Social change, therefore, is conceptualized as the changing characteristics of social structure and/or cohorts, rather than any concerted effort or capacity on the part of individual actors, or of actors engaged in collective action, to use their resources to effect social change. With respect to the retirement example (used by Riley, 1987), it could very well be that collective action brings about changes in state and corporate policies around social security and retirement benefits in response to the aging of the population, which are largely responsible for changing retirement patterns. To recognize social action in this situation it is necessary to focus on the joint production of collective action, not the purposeful actions of individuals per se.[6]

Leonard Cain, the first sociologist to explicitly identify the life course as an area of systematic study, viewed the life course as itself a social structure. His 1964 essay on the topic was titled, 'Life course and social structure' and, as he put it, 'A social structure may be viewed as a system of statuses, and among the universal criteria in the articulation of a status system is the age of its members' (Cain, 1964: 272). This position in itself is effectively identical to that Riley described for the age stratification system.

Increasing attention to agency

However, Cain also recognized the importance of what is now called 'agency'. Here he cites the symbolic interactionist Anselm Strauss to emphasize that institutions do not fully shape individual lives: 'Also important is "the open-ended, tentative, exploratory, hypothetical, problematical, devious, changeable, and only partly-unified character of human course of action."' (Cain 1964: 286, citing Strauss, 1959: 91; see Marshall and Mueller, 2003: 5).

Other theoretical work, not explicitly cast as a sociology of the life course, also drew on phenomenological (Gubrium, 1973; Holstein and Gubrium, 2000) and symbolic interactionist approaches. Everett Hughes' (1971) concept of career, also employed by Howard Becker (Becker and Strauss, 1956) and Victor Marshall (1978–79, 1980, 2005) morphed into the concept of status passage for Glaser and Strauss (1971), and both were antecedents of Elder's 'trajectory' concept. As noted below, much European and some North American research in the life course and aging area draws heavily on this tradition (Marshall and Mueller, 2003), and a greater rapprochement of these two approaches in indicated in the recent paper on agency by Hitlin and Elder (2007).

Critiques and recent developments

Glen Elder's prolific writings have established the concept of agency as an explicit aspect in contemporary aging and life-course scholarship. He considers agency to be one of five 'defining principles' of the life course: 'Individuals construct their own life course through the choices and actions they take within the opportunities and constraints of history and social circumstances' (Elder and Johnson, 2003). Settersten (2003: 39) calls agency an 'emerging proposition' of the life-course perspective, a perspective which 'promotes models of human agency within structure.' Yet, referring to the prominence of choice-making in studies of action, Dannefer and Uhlenberg (1999: 312) have claimed that the 'remarkably unproblematic appearance (of the concept of choice) in life course theory cannot be defended'.[7]

Elder sees the concept as having antecedents in early life-course works such as Thomas and Znaniecki's (1918–20) classic study of the *Polish Peasant in Europe and America*. But agency is also used by Elder to refer to overcoming resistance. That is, while Elder seems to argue that humans always manifest agency (from which we might infer he sees it as an aspect of human nature, much like Sewell or Giddens), his writings at times imply that agency is something manifested only at critical turning points in the life course, or in resistance to social norms. We pursue this idea below.

Marshall (2005) critically reviewed the many and confusing definitions and usages of the concept of agency, including those within Elder's work itself. These can be considered in three categories: developmental psychology, Elder's formulations, and a view of agency that is more faithful to traditional usage.

Developmental psychology usage

The *first* usage, prominent in psychological literature of life-span human development, is to view agency as production of a life – the concept that human beings create environments that in turn elicit responses from them. This view sees the human as dynamic and driven towards mastery of the world, both produced by and producing that world.

A *second* usage, sometimes seen in scholarship based on Erik Erikson's life-span developmental psychology, considers agency to be environmental proactivity or adaptation. For example, Lawton (1989: 140) introduced the hypothesis of 'environmental proactivity', to recognize 'action and agency – the person's competence as a determinant of environment'. A *third* but related usage by some personality researchers treat agency as a masculine trait related to 'ego strength' and contrasted with personality characteristics often attributed to females. These scholars view agency as a variable property of individuals (see Marshall, 2005).

Usages by Elder

Elder offers a *fourth* usage of agency, as one of the five basic defining principles of the life course: 'Individuals construct their own life course through the choices and actions they take within the opportunities and constraints of history and social circumstances' (Elder and Johnson, 2003: 60). In a *fifth* usage, again from Elder, agency refers to choices people make among available options (leaving a place for social structure). He relates such choices to his principle of 'loose coupling', which is his way of conceptually avoiding a stance of strict determinism.[4] Thus, 'Age grades and loose coupling exemplify two sides of the adult life course – its social regulation and the actor's behavior within conventional boundaries, and even outside of them' (Elder and O'Rand, 1995: 457). 'Loose coupling reflects the agency of people even in constrained situations as well as their accomplishments in rewriting their journeys in the course of aging' (Elder, 1997: 965). This principle is invoked by Elder when people's life transitions are seen as not fully determined by social constraints. In a sense, agency might be viewed as a basis to account for, or at least name, 'unexplained variance' in statistical modeling.

A *sixth* usage, also found in Elder, is to invoke agency as the cause of behavior that overcomes resistance. Thus, he maintains that the agency manifested in loose coupling exemplifies: 'the actor's initiatives and interpretations that press for individuality and deviations from convention'

(Elder, 1997: 965). In other work, he implies that agency is found only at transition points: what Giddens (1991) calls 'fateful moments'. While Elder sometimes seems to argue that humans *always* exercise agency (from which we might infer it is a property of human nature), in some descriptions Elder invokes the term specifically to describe behavior that does not follow convention, comply with social norms, or defer to social control mechanisms. In other words, behavior that is not conforming would be seen as agentic, whereas conforming behavior would not. These usages reflect a much narrower view of agency than found, for example, in Giddens (1984, 1993), Sewell (1992), Dannefer (1999), or the present authors.

A *seventh* way in which agency is used conceptually is when Elder situates it not in descriptions of the smooth routines or flows of everyday life, but rather sees it as operative in moments of transition rather than continuity, in life's more dramatic moments, even if resistance is not implied.

Agency as responsibility

Finally, an *eighth way* in which agency is used in the research literature is in the notion of 'being an agent' for someone or something. This is the most commonsensical, lay person's usage of agency, being rooted in everyday business practices, law, and diplomacy. This usage is little found in the life-course literature but quite widely used in other social science literature, including that of rational choice theory. Meyer and Jepperson (2000: 10) argue that the modern actor is a cultural construction who is '... an authorized agent for various interests (including those of the self)'. For them, agency is 'legitimated representation of some legitimated principal, which may be an individual, an actual or potential organization, a nation-state, or abstract principles ... the concept of agency draws attention to the devolution of external authority, and to the external legitimation and chartering of activity' (Meyer and Jepperson, 2000, Note 2). A person can act as their own agent or someone else can act as their agent, but people can be constructed as having authority to act on behalf of themselves. This can be formulated, as these authors recognize, in terms of the I–me distinction found in G.H. Mead. In life-course parlance, Elder and O'Rand (1995: 465) note that '... people function as agents of their own life course and development'. In largely European life-course theorizing, a move towards a 'risk society' may be characterized by a shift of authority for life-course management from society to the individual (Marshall, 2005).

In more recent work, Hitlin and Elder (2007) acknowledged the 'slippery' use of the concept of agency, as noted by Marshall (2005), and proposed a social behaviorist approach that distinguished four types of agency.[8] Drawing on Mead's emphasis on temporality in the self process, and on Emirbayer and Mische (1998), who stressed the importance of Mead for a proper understanding of agency, they argue that 'Agency is exerted differentially depending on the actor's salient time horizon' (Hitlin and Elder, 2007: 171). Their four types of agency are: *existential*, a capacity for exerting influence in our environment (a general 'anchor' for the other types); *pragmatic*, the ability to innovate when routines break down; *identity*, the capacity to act within socially prescribed role expectations; and *life course*, an umbrella term for retrospective analysis of decisions made at turning points and transitions.

These distinctions among different types of agency allow Hitlin and Elder to mitigate Marshall's charges about confusing and different usages of the agency term. This paper also provides a welcome explicit infusion of Meadian thinking into the work of Elder on the life course. Symbolic interactionist approaches rooted in Mead have been important in European life-course research (see Marshall and Mueller, 2003) and in a long-standing symbolic interactionist approach to the life course exemplified in the work of scholars such as Everett Hughes (1971), Anselm Strauss (1959), and Victor Marshall (1980, 2005).

Elder's approach has also been criticized for his treatment of social structure, most notably in a paper by Dannefer and Uhlenberg (1999). While they correctly classify most of his work at the individual level and with outcomes explained in 'personological terms', they recognize that 'no one can doubt that his explanations utilize context extensively' (1999: 315). However, they point out that for Elder, the social and historical context is considered:

> Primarily as a part of the prior experience of individuals, experiences that are carried forward through time within the personality or in some cases the physiology of the individual. For example, whether or not one was deprived during the Depression was certainly a contextual factor, but its 'effects' found in the 1980s are assumed to be carried forward in time largely through the effects of that early experience upon the person, whether through learning coping skills, personality change, or something else. There is no explicit conceptualization of present social structure as having an effect on individual outcomes.
>
> (Dannefer and Uhlenberg, 1999: 315)

Social structure, then, has a 'selection effect' that can affect people's subsequent life courses through mechanisms such as those Dannefer and Uhlenberg describe or through more complex processes of cumulative advantage and disadvantage. Dannefer and Uhlenberg's criticism is that the effects of current social structure are neglected in this approach. However, they also note the flip side of this, which is the neglect of serious research attention to history in life-course studies (despite it being a central principle of the approach as noted by both Elder and Riley).

The relative influence of agency and structural constraint

A few recent and suggestive studies explicitly deal with the relationship of agency to social structure in aging and life-course research in different domains, and address the question of the relative contribution of agency and structure to shaping the life course of individuals. One such study shows that macro-level social resources are influential for the successful implementation of micro-level interpretive processes of adaptation to illness and disability. Drawing on Atchley's (1989) theory of continuity in her research on adaptation to stroke, Clarke and Black (2005) found that adapting to one's physical and cognitive limitations, especially as they permitted the return to valued self-defining activities, was an important strategy for the maintenance of subjective well-being following a stroke. Economic resources (e.g., to purchase a car with leather seats to make it easier to get in and out) and social supports (e.g., a spouse's help to develop an extensive filing system designed to overcome memory problems) were some of the many structural resources that either facilitated or discouraged these micro-level adaptive strategies. Many micro-level theorists implicitly recognize the importance of these structural constraints and opportunities for successful adaptation to poor health and disability in later life (Atchley 1989). As acknowledged by Herzog and Markus (1999: 234):

> Whereas people can be quite inventive and selective in how they think about themselves – indeed, this is one key to health adaptations and adjustment – they are also responsive to the requirements of their various sociocultural environments and typically create selves in ways that resonate with what is valued in those environments.

In Clarke's (2003) research on stroke, an explicit theoretical examination of interactionist mechanisms in both the quantitative and qualitative data allows insight into the *processes* by which social structural forces and resources combine with micro-level factors and strategies to shape the experience of stroke in later life, as noted above. Structural forces can reduce the effects of poor health and disability at the micro level by functioning as a resource that moderates the impact of such sequelae on well-being. Structural resources can also enhance or impede micro-level adaptive strategies designed to overcome the effects of impairment and disability on well-being. Finally, structural forces can themselves be subtly altered by efforts and resistance at the micro level, where individuals act back upon structures in an attempt to alter their impact (Clarke, 2003).

Thoits emphasizes the importance of agency in understanding the stress process within a life-course framework. She takes personal agency to mean 'that people made choices or decisions, acted intentionally or deliberately, formulated and followed plans of action, or set goals and pursued them' (Thoits 2006: 309). However, she notes that coping resources are unequally distributed by social status, accounting for status differences in mental health that are amplified over time.

Smith-Lovin (2007: 107) wishes to modify Stryker's (1980) classic statement of structural symbolic interaction: that society shapes self, which then shapes social interaction. She notes that Stryker only allowed for identity to shape social interaction in cases where choices were available. Smith-Lovin, however, asserts 'that the glass of "choice" is more than half empty – that the majority of encounters in actor's lives are shaped not by self-structures, but by the social environments in which they are embedded.' We know, she argues, that choices are influenced by many factors other than identity structures. This is a highly structural perspective yet still rooted in notions of human agency as informed by the symbolic interactionist perspective. Hers is a critique (as was Stryker's) of those symbolic interactionists who emphasized agency or action to the neglect of structure and constraint.

Smith-Lovin's argument in many ways echo's that of Dannefer, who asserts that

> In sum, the force of an individual's intentional action in constituting and sustaining a system of social relations varies according to such features of the social system in question as size, structure, and the individual's position within that system. Although action is potent and perhaps necessary to the viability of the overall system, the magnitude of its effect on the social system is less than that of the system upon the actor.

(Dannefer 1999: 115)

CONCLUSIONS AND RECOMMENDATIONS

Our purpose in this review has been to provide greater clarity as to how the agency–structure issue might be more usefully conceptualized in relation to research on the life course and aging. By failing to tackle these theoretical issues head on, countless studies on aging and the life-course model social factors in relation to various forms of well-being over the life course, but with little theorizing about social structure itself or how aspects of social structure interact dynamically with individual-level action, let alone collective action.

We believe a version of the 'duality of structure' approach that combines agency with a view of structures as including resources (and therefore as durable) holds the most promise for capturing the complexities of aging. We recommend that future theoretical and methodological approaches in life course and aging research endeavor to incorporate the basic tenets of this approach in order to advance our understanding of the dynamics of aging and the life course.

Finally, we argue that to address adequately agency and social structure in life-course research, it is critical to distinguish between four constructs (Marshall 2005: 67–9):

1. The human *capacity* to make a choice: that is, to be intentional.
2. The *resources* within the individual or at the command of the individual that can be brought to bear in intentional or agentic behavior.
3. *Behavior* of individuals that reflects intention.
4. The social and physical *structuring* of choices.

Recognizing that many scholars take different views, we urge that the term agency be used for the first construct – capacity to choose, or to be intentional. Agency *can* be treated as a variable, rather than simply a statement about human nature, because humans develop the capacity to make choices over time. This capacity includes awareness, thus requiring cognitive abilities to give identity to objects and events in the world. Agency is thus the human *capacity* to act intentionally, planfully, and reflexively and in a temporal or biographical mode. However, once this capacity is acquired, it is unlikely to add much to any explanation of action to say that it is a demonstration of agency (because action is always, by definition, based on this characteristic).

The second construct, *resources*, refers to *additional* acquired capacities of the individual (for example, literacy, strength), and other possessions at his or her command (for example, fiscal or social capital, designated authority (or agency in the commonsense notion of the term discussed above). As an example, we would consider 'planful competence' (Clausen 1991), 'the ability to make informed, rational decisions and set realistic short- and long-term goals' to be a resource rather than a capacity (a resource that can be acquired or enhanced, for example, by education in strategic decision-making, or by gains in self-confidence and awareness of both strengths and opportunities).

The third construct, behavior that reflects intention, is of course action (or social action or voluntaristic action) in the traditional Weberian sense and many related derivatives: see Dannefer (1999: 106–8) for a clear discussion of what is and is not included in action.

The fourth construct, the social and physical structuring of activities, refers to the de facto structure of opportunities or life chances that is open within the range of action of the actor. It constitutes the field that constrains but also facilitates the choices made by all people, all of whom possess agency but who vary widely in the personal, social, and economic resources they can employ as they try to construct their biographies over the life course.

Needless to say, we have neither the ability nor the desire to legislate the adoption of the conceptual definitions we advance. However, at the least, an understanding of these distinctions should assist life-course and aging scholars to better understand the growing literature in this field.

NOTES

1 There is even contention about the distinction between 'action' and 'social action'. We will be content in this discussion to assert that virtually all action is social and that it is social action that is the interest of (most) sociologists. For a detailed examination of this issue see Campbell (1996).

2 Stones, R. (2007) 'Structure and agency', in G. Ritzer (ed.), *Blackwell Encyclopedia of Sociology*. Blackwell Publishing, Blackwell Reference Online. Retrieved April 28, 2007. http://www.blackwell publishing.com/pdf/Sociology_Catalogue.pdf

3 The term is not used by Berger and Luckmann but we consider it to be implied in their characterization of the dialectical relationship of three moments: externalization, objectivation, and internalization. For example, they assert that 'The social reality of everyday life is apprehended in a continuum of typifications, which are progressively anonymous as they are removed from the "here and now" of the face-to-face situation', but go on to say, 'Social structure

is the sum total of these typifications and of the recurrent patterns of interaction established by means of them' (Berger and Luckmann, 1967: 33).

4 Symbolic interactionist theory in relation to social action contrasts with Parsonian sociology. In his essay, 'The Social Self', Mead argues that, in interaction with others who have different interests, the growth of the self arises out of a partial disintegration, 'the appearance of the different interests in the forum of reflection , the reconstruction of the social world, and the consequent appearance of the new self that answers to the new object.' Thus, the self and the actor's social world are co-constituted through active reflection. (Mead, 1964: 149, as cited in Emirbayer and Mische, 1998: 1013).

5 Additional analyses from the same data by Neugarten and others (Neugarten et al., 1964; Reichard et al., 1962), however, advanced a stronger critique of disengagement theory that was also not based on principles of agency: namely, that there were many different styles of aging, and that successful aging reflected a continuation of earlier lifestyle patterns. This led some investigators to conclude that personality factors have a great influence on the matter of successful aging. In sociological language influenced by symbolic interactionism, this stimulated the 'continuity theory' of aging (Atchley, 1989, 1999). For a discussion of the common 'role theory' foundation of activity theory, disengagement theory, and continuity theory, see Marshall and Clarke (2007).

6 On social interaction as fitting lines of action together, see Blumer's (1966) classic essay, 'Sociological implications of the thought of George Herbert Mead' and for an extensive examination of these issues, Barnes (2000), especially Chapter 5.

7 In a wider discussion of sociological treatment of agency, Barnes (2000: 49) states, 'References to agency in sociology proliferated in a context where overblown and unsubstantiated deterministic accounts of human activities had flourished, and needed to be challenged. Assertion of individual agency was the rhetorical device employed for that essential task.'

8 These authors claim that 'only the field of life course studies explicitly engages agency from an empirical perspective' (Hitlin and Elder, 2007: 172). This is almost certainly not true except by eliminating all studies based on similar terms, such as action, production, and rational choice, and confining the generalization to those who use the term agency for these types of phenomena, or by adopting a narrow view of 'empirical' to exclude, for example, qualitative studies dealing with strategic interaction, the negotiated order, and so forth: e.g., Gubrium's concept of 'biographically active respondents (1993: 8) in his study of nursing home residents; Handel's (2000) life history, *Making a Life in Yorkville*; Heinz'

(2002) study of occupational self-socialization; Marshall's (1975) description of how retirement community residents collectively act to deal with death and dying; and McMullin and Marshall's (2001) explicit use of the agency concept to describe aging garment workers attempting to control their life courses. Hitlin and Elder also contradict themselves in noting several empirical studies of related concepts such as self-efficacy, planful competence, and free will. For *theoretical* consideration of like terms that refer to aspects of 'agency', see Barnes (2000), Dannefer (1999), and Joas (1996).

REFERENCES

Alexander, J.C. (1988) 'The new theoretical movement', in N.J. Smelser (ed.), *Handbook of Sociology*. Newbury Park, CA: SAGE, pp. 77–101.

Archer, M.S. (1995) *Realist Social Theory: The Morphogenetic Approach*. Cambridge, MA: Cambridge University Press.

Archer, M.S. (2007) *Making Our Way through the World: Human Reflexivity and Social Mobility*. Cambridge, MA: Cambridge University Press.

Atchley, R.C. (1989) 'A continuity theory of normal aging', *The Gerontologist*, 29: 183–90.

Atchley, R.C. (1999) 'Continuity, self, and social structure', in C.D. Ryff and V.W. Marshall (eds), *The Self and Society in Aging Processes*. New York: Springer, pp. 94–121.

Baars, J. (2006) 'Beyond neomodernism, antimodernism, and postmodernism: basic categories for contemporary critical gerontology', in J. Baars, D. Dannefer, C. Phillipson, and A. Walker (eds), *Aging, Globalization, and Inequality: The New Critical Gerontology*. Amityville, NY: Baywood Publishing, pp. 17–42.

Barnes, B. (2000) *Understanding Agency: Social Theory and Responsible Action*. London: SAGE.

Becker, H.S. and Strauss, A.L. (1956) 'Careers, personality and adult socialization', *American Journal of Sociology*, 62: 253–63.

Berger, P.L. and Luckmann, T. (1967) *The Social Construction of Reality*. Garden City, NY: Anchor Books (originally published by Doubleday and Company 1966).

Blau, P. (1977) 'A macro sociological theory of social structure', *American Journal of Sociology*, 83: 26–54.

Blau, P. (1987a) 'Micro process and macro structure', in K.S. Cook (ed.), *Social Exchange Theory*. Newbury Park, CA: SAGE, pp. 83–7.

Blau, P. (1987b) *Inequality and Heterogeneity: A Primitive Theory of Social Structure*. New York: The Free Press.

Blumer, H. (1966) 'Sociological implications of the thought of George Herbert Mead', *American Journal of Sociology*, 71: 535–44.

Burgess, E.W. (1960) 'Aging in western culture', in E.W. Burgess (ed.), *Aging in Western Societies*. Chicago: The University of Chicago Press, pp. 3–28.

Cain, L.D., Jr. (1964) 'Life course and social structure', in R.E.L. Faris (ed.) *Handbook of Modern Sociology*. Chicago: Rand McNally, pp. 273–309.

Campbell, C. (1996) *The Myth of Social Action*. Cambridge: Cambridge University Press.

Chappell, N.L. and Orbach, H.L. (1986) 'Socialization in old age: a Meadian perspective', in V.W. Marshall (ed.), *Later Life: The Social Psychology of Aging*. Beverley Hills, CA: SAGE, pp. 75–106.

Clarke, P. (2003) 'Towards a greater understanding of the experience of stroke: integrating quantitative and qualitative methods', *Journal of Aging Studies*, 17(2): 171–87.

Clarke, P. and Black, S.E. (2005) 'Quality of life following stroke: negotiating disability, identity, and resources', *Journal of Applied Gerontology*, 24(4): 319–36.

Clausen, J.S. (1991) 'Adolescent competence and the shaping of the life course', *American Journal of Sociology*, 96: 805–52.

Cowgill, D.O. (1974) 'Aging and modernization: a revision of the theory', in J.F. Gubrium (ed.), *Late Life: Communities and Environmental Policy*. Springfield, IL: Charles C. Thomas, pp. 123–45.

Cumming, E. and Henry, W. (1961) *Growing Old: The Process of Disengagement*. New York: Basic Books.

Dannefer, D. (1984) 'Adult development and social theory: A paradigmatic reappraisal', *American Sociological Review*, 49: 100–16.

Dannefer, D. (1999) 'Freedom isn't free: power, alienation, and the consequences of action', in J. Brandstadner and R.M. Lerner (eds), *Action and Development: Origins and Functions of Intentional Self Development*. New York: Springer, pp. 105–31.

Dannefer, D. and Uhlenberg, P. (1999) 'Paths of the life course: a typology', in V.L. Bengtson and K.W. Schaie (eds), *Handbook of Theories of Aging*. New York: Springer, pp. 306–26.

Dawe, A. (1970) 'The two sociologies', *British Journal of Sociology*, 21: 207–18.

Elder, G.H., Jr. (1997) 'The life course and human development', in R.M. Lerner (ed.), *Handbook of Child Psychology: Theoretical Models of Human Development*, Vol. 1. New York: John Wiley and Sons, pp. 939–91.

Elder, G.H., Jr. and Johnson, K.M. (2003) 'The life course and aging: challenges, lessons, and new direction', in R.A. Settersten, Jr. (ed.), *Invitation to the Life Course: Towards New Understandings of Later Life*. Amityville, NY: Baywood Publishing Company, pp. 49–81.

Elder, G.H., Jr. and O'Rand, A.A. (1995) 'Adult lives in a changing society', in K.S. Cook, G.A. Fine, and J.S. House (eds), *Sociological Perspectives on Social Psychology*. Boston, MA: Allyn and Bacon, pp. 452–75.

Emirbayer, M. and Mische, A. (1998) 'What is agency?', *American Journal of Sociology*, 103(4): 962–1023.

Gecas, V. (2003) 'Self-agency and the life course', in J.T. Mortimer and M.J. Shanahan (eds), *Handbook of the Life Course*. New York: Kluwer Academic/Plenum, pp. 369–88.

Giddens, A. (1974) *Positivism and Sociology*. London: Heinemann.

Giddens, A. (1984) *The Constitution of Society: Outline of the Theory of Structuration.* Berkeley, CA: University of California Press.

Giddens, A. (1991) *Modernity and Self-Identify: Self and Society in the Late Modern Age.* Stanford, CA: Stanford University Press.

Giddens, A. (1993) *New Rules of Sociological Method: A Positive Critique of Interpretative Sociologies,* 2nd edn. (1st edn. published 1976). New York: Basic Books.

Glaser, B.G. and Strauss, A.L. (1971) *Status Passage.* Chicago: Aldine-Atherton.

Goffman, E. (1983) 'The interaction order', *American Sociological Review,* 48: 1–17.

Gubrium, J.F. (1993) *Speaking of Life: Horizons of Meaning for Nursing Home Residents.* New York: Aldine De Gruyter.

Handel, G. (2000) *Making a Life in Yorkville: Experience and Meaning in the Life-Course Narrative of an Urban Working-Class Man.* Westport, CT: Greenwood Press (reprinted in paperback by Aldine de Gruyter, 2000).

Havighurst, R.J., Neugarten, B.L., and Tobin, S. (1963) 'Disengagement and patterns of aging', in B.L. Neugarten (ed.), *Middle Age and Aging.* Chicago: University of Chicago Press (abridged from a paper presented at the International Association of Gerontology, Copenhagen, August 1963), pp. 161–72.

Heinz, W.R. (2002) Transition discontinuities and the biographical shaping of early work careers. *Journal of Vocational Behavior,* 60: 220–40.

Herzog, A.R. and Markus, H.R. (1999) 'The self concept in life span and aging research', in V.L. Bengtson and K.W. Schaie (eds), *Handbook of Theories of Aging.* New York: Springer, pp. 227–52.

Hitlin, S. and Elder, G.H. Jr. (2007) 'Time, self, and the curiously abstract concept of agency', *Sociological Theory,* 25(2): 170–91.

Hochschild, A.R. (1975) 'Disengagement theory: A critique and proposal', *American Sociological Review,* 40: 553–69.

Holstein, J.A., and Gubrium, J.F. (2000) *The Self We Live by: Narrative Identity in a Postmodern World.* New York: Oxford University Press.

Huber, J. (ed.) (1991) *Macro-Micro Linkages in Sociology.* Newbury Park, CA: SAGE.

Hughes, E.C. (1971) 'Cycles, turning points, and careers', in E.C. Hughes (ed.), *The Sociological Eye: Selected Papers on Institutions and Race.* Chicago: University of Chicago Press, pp. 124–31.

Joas, H. (1996) *The Creativity of Action.* Chicago: University of Chicago Press.

Lawton, P. (1989) 'Environmental proactivity and affect in older people', in S. Spacapan and S. Askamp (eds), *The Social Psychology of Aging.* London: SAGE, pp. 135–63.

Layder, D. (2006) *Understanding Social Theory,* 2nd edn. London: SAGE.

Linton, R. (1936) *The Study of Man.* New York: Appleton-Century.

Linton, R. (1940) 'A neglected aspect of social organization', *American Journal of Sociology,* 45: 870–86.

Linton, R. (1942) 'Age and sex categories', *American Sociological Review,* 7: 589–603.

Marshall, V.W. (1975) 'Socialization for impending death in a retirement village', *American Journal of Sociology,* 81(5): 1122–44.

Marshall, V.W. (1978–79) 'No exit: a symbolic interactionist perspective on aging', *International Journal of Aging and Human Development,* 9(4): 345–58.

Marshall, V.W. (1980) *Last Chapters: A Sociology of Aging and Dying.* Monterey, CA: Brooks/Cole.

Marshall, V.W. (1986) 'Dominant and emerging paradigms in the social psychology of aging', in V.W. Marshall (ed.), *Later Life: The Social Psychology of Aging.* Beverly Hills, CA: SAGE, pp. 9–31.

Marshall, V.W. (1995) 'The micro–macro link in the sociology of aging', in C. Hummel and C.L. D'Epinay (eds), *Images of Aging in Western Societies.* Geneva: Center for Interdisciplinary Gerontology, pp. 337–71.

Marshall, V.W. (1996) 'The state of theory in aging and the social sciences', in R.H. Binstock and L.K. George (eds), *Handbook of Aging and the Social Sciences,* 4th edn. San Diego, CA: Academic Press, pp. 12–30.

Marshall, V.W. (2005) 'Agency, events, and structure at the end of the life course', *Advances in Life Course Research,* 10: 57–91.

Marshall, V.W., and Clarke, P.J. (2007) 'Theories of aging: social', in J. Birren (ed.), *Encyclopedia of Gerontology,* 2nd edn. San Diego, CA: Academic Press, pp. 621–30.

Marshall, V.W. and Mueller, M.M. (2003) 'Theoretical roots of the life-course perspective', in W.R. Heinz and V.W. Marshall (eds), *Social Dynamics of the Life Course: Transitions Institutions, and Interrelations.* New York: Aldine De Gruyter, pp. 3–32.

McMullin, J.A. and Marshall, V.W. (1999) 'Structure and agency in the retirement process: a case study of Montreal garment workers', in C.D. Ryff and V.W. Marshall (eds), *The Self and Society in Aging Processes.* New York: Springer, pp. 305–38.

McMullin, J.A. and Marshall, V.W. (2001) 'Ageism, age relations and garment industry workers in Montreal', *The Gerontologist,* 31(1): 111–22.

Mead, G.H. (1964) 'The social self', in A.J. Reck (ed.), *George Herbert Mead: Selected Writings.* Indianapolis: Bobbs-Merril, pp. 142–9.

Meyer, J.W. and Jepperson, R.L. (2000) 'The "actors" of modern society: the cultural construction of agency', *Sociological Theory,* 18(1): 100–20.

Mills, C.W. (1959) *The Sociological Imagination.* New York: Oxford University Press.

Morgan, L.A., Eckert, J.K., Piggee, T., and Frankowski, A.C. (2006) 'Two lives in transition: agency and context for assisted living residents', *Journal of Aging Studies,* 20: 123–32.

Mouzelis, N. (1995) *Sociological Theory: What Went Wrong?* New York: Routledge.

Neugarten, B.L. (1966) 'Adult personality: a developmental view', *Human Development,* 9: 61–73.

Neugarten, B.L. (1985) 'Interpretive social science and research on aging', in A.S. Rossi (ed.) *Gender and the Life Course.* New York: Aldine, pp. 291–300.

Neugarten, B.L., Crotty, W.S., and Tobin, S. (1964) 'Personality types in an aged population', in B.L. Neugarten (ed.), *Personality in Middle and Late Life: Empirical Studies.* New York: Atherton, pp. 159–87.

Neugarten, B.L., Moore, J.W., and Lowe, J.C. (1965) 'Age norms, age constraints, and adult socialization', *American Journal of Sociology*, 70: 710–17.

Parsons, T. (1949) *The Structure of Social Action.* New York: The Free Press (originally published 1937).

Pearlin, L.I., Lieberman, M.A., Menaghan, E.G., and Mullan, J.T. (1981) 'The stress process', *Journal of Health and Social Behavior*, 22: 337–56.

Rawls, A. (1987) 'The interaction order *sui generis*: Goffman's contribution to social theory', *Sociological Theory*, 5: 136–49.

Reichard, S., Livson, F., and Peterson, P.G. (1962) *Aging and Personality.* New York: John Wiley and Sons.

Riley, M.W. (1971) 'Social gerontology and the age stratification of society', *The Gerontologist*, 11: 79–87.

Riley, M.W. (1987) 'On the significance of age in sociology', *American Sociological Review* (American Sociological Association 1986 Presidential address), 52: 1–14.

Riley, M.W., Johnson, M., and Foner, A. (1972) *Aging and Society: A Sociology of Age Stratification*, Vol. 3. New York: Russell Sage Foundation.

Ritzer, G. (1988) 'The emergence of a central problem in sociological theory', in G. Ritzer (ed.), *Sociological Theory.* New York: Alfred Knopf, pp. 484–502.

Rosow, I. (1974) *Socialization to Old Age.* Berkeley, CA: University of California Press.

Rosow, I. (1976) 'Status and role change through the life span', in R.H. Binstock and E. Shanas (eds), *Handbook of Aging and the Social Sciences.* New York: Van Nostrand Reinhold, pp. 457–82.

Ryff, C.D., Marshall, V.W., and Clarke, P.J. (1999) 'Linking the self and society in social gerontology: crossing new territory via old questions', in C.D. Ryff and V.W. Marshall (eds), *The Self and Society in Aging Processes.* New York: Springer, pp. 3–41

Sampson, R.J. and Laub, J.H. (1993) *Crime in the Making: Pathways and Turning Points Through Life.* Cambridge, MA: Harvard University Press.

Schutz, A. (1967) *The Phenomenology of the Social World* (translated by Goerge Walsh and Frederick Lehnert). Evanston: Northwestern University Press (originally published in German in 1932).

Settersten, R.A., Jr. (2003) 'Propositions and controversies in life-course scholarship', in R.A. Settersten, Jr. (ed.), *Invitation to the Life Course: Towards New Understandings of Later Life.* Amityville, NY: Baywood Publishing Company, pp. 15–45.

Sewell, W.A. (1992) A theory of structure: duality, agency, and transformation, *American Journal of Sociology*, 98(1): 1–29.

Smelser, N. J. (1988) 'Social structure', in N.J. Smelser (ed.), *Handbook of Sociology.* Newbury Park, CA: SAGE, pp. 103–29.

Smith-Lovin, L. (2007) 'The strength of weak identities: social structural sources of self, situation and emotional experience', *Social Psychology Quarterly*, 70(2): 106–24.

Strauss, A. (1959) *Mirrors and Masks.* Glencoe, IL: The Free Press.

Stryker, S. (1980) *Symbolic Interactionism.* Menlo Park, CA: Benjamin/Cummings.

Thoits, P.A. (2006) 'Personal agency in the stress process', *Journal of Health and Social Behavior*, 47: 309–23.

Thomas, W.I. and Zaniecki, F. (1918–20) *The Polish Peasant in Europe and America*, Vols. 1 and 2. Boston, MA: Richard G. Badger.

Turner, J. (1990) *A Theory of Social Interaction.* Cambridge: Polity Press.

Waitzkin, H. (1989) *A Critical Theory of Medical Discourse: Ideology, Social Control and the Processing of Social Context in Medical Encounters.* Cambridge: Polity Press.

Weber, M. (1978) in G. Roth and C. Wittich (eds), *Economy and Society: An Outline of Interpretive Sociology*, 2 volumes. Berkeley, CA: University of California Press.

23

Age, Experience, and the Beginning of Wisdom

Monika Ardelt

To understand reality is not the same as to know about outward events. It is to perceive the essential nature of things. The best-informed man is not necessarily the wisest. Indeed there is a danger that precisely in the multiplicity of his knowledge he will lose sight of what is essential. But on the other hand, knowledge of an apparently trivial detail quite often makes it possible to see into the depth of things. And so the wise man will seek to acquire the best possible knowledge about events, but always without becoming dependent upon this knowledge. To recognize the significant in the factual is wisdom.

Dietrich Bonhoeffer

He who knows others is learned; he who knows himself wise.

Lao-Tzu

philosopher and theologian St. Augustine, and the French Renaissance statesman and scholar Montaigne (Birren and Svensson, 2005; Robinson, 1990). The discussion of whether wisdom consists of intellectual knowledge of the world and the human condition or is a quality that 'transcends the intellect' (Naranjo, 1972: 225) and whose characteristics are timeless and universal (Ardelt, 2000b) continues until this day. In this chapter, I first distinguish between Western and Eastern approaches to wisdom before I introduce culturally inclusive definitions of wisdom. I then discuss the hypothetical and empirical relation between wisdom and age and address the role of crises and hardships in the development of wisdom. The chapter concludes with speculations about the promotion of wisdom in everyday life and the benefits of wisdom, particularly for older adults.

INTRODUCTION

What wisdom is and what it contains has been variously defined across the ages, starting with the earliest 'wisdom literature' among the ancient Sumerians in 3000 BC (Birren and Svensson, 2005). Distinctions between wisdom as knowledge of the material and social world (*episteme* or *scientia*), as the pursuit of timeless, universal truths (*sophia* or *sapientia*), or as good and prudent behavior (*phronesis* or practical wisdom) can be found, for example, in the wisdom writings of the Ancient Greek philosophers, the 4th century

DEFINITIONS OF WISDOM

Contemporary wisdom researchers distinguish between explicit or 'expert' theories of wisdom and implicit or 'lay' theories of wisdom, which can be further divided into Western and Eastern approaches to wisdom (Sternberg and Jordan, 2005). In general, Western definitions of wisdom emphasize analytic abilities, such as increases in knowledge and information processing, whereas Eastern wisdom definitions tend to integrate analytic abilities with a compassionate concern for others (Takahashi, 2000; Takahashi and Bordia, 2000; Takahashi and Overton, 2005).

Western definitions of wisdom

Western explicit theories describe wisdom as expertise and knowledge in the fundamental pragmatics of life (which includes life planning, life management, and life review) and in the meaning and conduct of life (Baltes and Smith, 1990; Baltes and Staudinger, 2000; Baltes et al., 1995; Dittmann-Kohli and Baltes, 1990; Smith and Baltes, 1990; Smith et al., 1994), as 'the application of tacit knowledge as mediated by values toward the achievement of a common good through a balance among multiple (a) intrapersonal, (b) interpersonal, and (c) extrapersonal interests in order to achieve a balance among (a) adaptation to existing environments, (b) shaping of existing environments, and (c) selection of new environments' (Sternberg, 1998: 347), as the transformation of intrapersonal, interpersonal, and transpersonal experiences in the domains of personality, cognition, and conation (Achenbaum and Orwoll, 1991), as 'seeing through illusion' (McKee and Barber, 1999), as understanding the deeper (interpretative) meaning of (descriptive) knowledge (Kekes, 1983), as the art of questioning (Arlin, 1990), as the balance between knowing and doubting (Meacham, 1990), as expertise in handling the cognitive, emotional, and behavioral aspects of uncertainty (Brugman, 2000), as the balance between emotion and detachment, action and inaction, and knowledge and doubt in dealing with life's vicissitudes (Birren and Fisher, 1990), or as self-transcendence (Levenson et al., 2005).

In contrast, Western implicit theories describe how laypersons understand the concept of wisdom. Since modern scientific inquiries into wisdom are relatively new, the first step in the study of wisdom consisted of asking laypersons to define this elusive concept. Analysis of wisdom descriptors supplied by adults from a wide range of ages and backgrounds and rated by groups of laypersons or professors reveals that participants tend to perceive wisdom as a combination of cognitive (knowledgeable, experienced, intelligent, pragmatic, and observant), reflective (introspective and intuitive), and affective (understanding, empathic, peaceful, and gentle) dimensions (Clayton and Birren, 1980), as exceptional understanding, judgment and communication skills, general competencies, interpersonal skills, and social unobtrusiveness (Holliday and Chandler, 1986), and as reasoning ability, sagacity, learning from ideas and environment, judgment, expeditious use of information,

and perspicacity (Sternberg, 1990a). Bluck and Glück (2005) who reviewed five studies on implicit wisdom theories, including the three mentioned above, identified cognitive ability, insight, reflective attitude, concern for others, and real-world skills as essential aspects of wisdom that were mentioned in at least two of the five studies.

To summarize, although Western wisdom definitions vary considerably, most explicit definitions emphasize cognitive and analytic skills, whereas most implicit definitions contain a combination of cognitive, reflective, and affective elements.

Eastern definitions of wisdom

Eastern explicit theories of wisdom can be found in a number of venerated and influential ancient traditions. The Upanishads of ancient India are a collection of wisdom teachings that offer advice and explanations of the deeper meaning of life. Written between 800 and 500 BC, they are based on an even older oral tradition (Birren and Svensson, 2005). The Bhagavad-Gita, which provides an overview of Hindu philosophy, was probably written between 500 and 200 BC (Zaehner, 1969). Jeste and Vahia's (2008) analysis of the Bhagavad-Gita identifies 10 wisdom domains: knowledge of life, emotional regulation, control over desires, decisiveness, love of God, duty and work, self-contentedness, yoga or integration of personality, compassion/sacrifice, and insight/humility. Buddhism is another major source of explicit wisdom in the East. The teachings of the Buddha (563–483 BC) encourage people to acquire their own wisdom through meditative practices that strengthen their ability to engage in mindful self-observation, which leads to the development of equanimity, (self-)insight, compassion, and wisdom (Hart, 1987; Ñanamoli, 2001).

In ancient China, Lao-Tzu (earlier than 300 BC) also taught that self-observation and the ability to follow the *Tao* or *The Way* through the development of intuition and compassion would lead to wisdom (Birren and Svensson, 2005). In contrast, Confucius (551–479 BC) rejected intuition, instead emphasizing the importance of learning and reflection.

Yet both of these foundational Chinese thinkers considered compassion and personal morality the basis for the development of wisdom (Birren and Svensson, 2005). Hence, in contrast to the focus of Western explicit wisdom theories on cognitive and analytic abilities, Eastern explicit theories of wisdom emphasize the importance of right behavior, self-insight, and the development of compassion in the attainment of wisdom.

Research on Eastern implicit theories of wisdom is relatively rare. However, the few studies that have been conducted found that Eastern laypersons tend to emphasize the affective element of wisdom more than Western laypersons (Takahashi and Bordia, 2000; Takahashi and Overton, 2005). Yet, similar to Western laypersons, Taiwanese Chinese adults perceived wisdom as a combination of cognitive (competencies and knowledge), affective (benevolence and compassion), and reflective (openness and profundity) components (Yang, 2001). The major difference to Western implicit theories was that Taiwanese adults also considered modesty and unobtrusiveness as essential elements of wisdom.

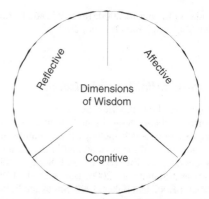

Figure 23.1   The three dimensions of wisdom based on Clayton and Birren (1980)

CULTURALLY INCLUSIVE DEFINITIONS OF WISDOM

Attempting to transcend what they term as 'cultural egocentrism', Takahashi and Overton (2005) define wisdom as a combination of two modes of thinking: the analytical (knowledge and abstract reasoning abilities), dominant in Western explicit theories, and the synthetic (reflective understanding, emotional empathy, and emotional regulation), which receives greater emphasis in Eastern explicit theories. Hence, it appears that, at a minimum, a culturally inclusive definition of wisdom should include cognitive, reflective, and affective elements. It is important to note that despite the differences in emphasis, both Western and Eastern implicit theories of wisdom contain all three of those components (Takahashi and Bordia, 2000), and some influential Western scholars deem the affective element of wisdom as centrally important as it is in Eastern explicit theories (Achenbaum and Orwoll, 1991; Csikszentmihalyi and Nakamura, 2005; Kramer, 1990; Manheimer, 1992; Pascual-Leone, 1990; Taranto, 1989; Vaillant, 1993).

With these considerations in mind, I have advanced a definition of wisdom that integrates cognitive, reflective, and affective qualities (e.g., Ardelt, 1997, 2003, 2004). The *cognitive wisdom dimension* in the three-dimensional model of wisdom (Figure 23.1) represents a deep understanding of life, particularly with regard to intrapersonal and interpersonal matters, and a desire to know the truth (Ardelt, 2000b; Blanchard-Fields and Norris, 1995; Chandler and Holliday, 1990; Kekes, 1983; Osbeck and Robinson, 2005; Sternberg, 1990a). To obtain such insight requires 'seeing through illusion' (McKee and Barber, 1999) and overcoming one's subjectivity and projections. The *reflective wisdom dimension* entails the ability to perceive phenomena and events from multiple perspectives through the practice of self-examination, self-awareness, and self-insight. Self-reflection and a transcendence of one's subjectivity and projections, in turn, tend to reduce one's self-centeredness and increase one's understanding of life in general and the human condition in particular (Csikszentmihalyi and Rathunde, 1990; Hart, 1987; Kekes, 1995; Levitt, 1999; Taranto, 1989). The whole process is likely to lead to a greater compassionate understanding of self and others, which describes the *affective wisdom dimension* (Achenbaum and Orwoll, 1991; Clayton and Birren, 1980; Csikszentmihalyi and Rathunde, 1990; Holliday and Chandler, 1986; Kramer, 1990; Levitt, 1999; Orwoll and Achenbaum, 1993; Pascual-Leone, 1990). This three-dimensional definition is designed to be parsimonious, while simultaneously containing the major characteristics of both implicit and explicit wisdom theories from the Western as well as the Eastern wisdom traditions (Blanchard-Fields and Norris, 1995; Curnow, 1999; Levitt, 1999; Manheimer, 1992; Sternberg, 1990b, 1998; Sternberg and Jordan, 2005; Takahashi and Bordia, 2000).

THE RELATION BETWEEN AGE, EXPERIENCE, AND THE DEVELOPMENT OF WISDOM

Do people grow wiser with age? To answer this question, I summarize hypothetical associations between wisdom and age and then present what is known from existing empirical evidence.

Hypothetical associations between wisdom and age

Sternberg (2005) introduces five hypothetical scenarios or views that might explain the association between wisdom and age. First, according to the 'received' view, wisdom might develop in old age due to a spiritual awakening or reawakening. This idea receives inspiration from Erikson's model of human development (Erikson, 1963, 1982; Erikson et al., 1986), which hypothesized that wisdom results from the successful resolution of the final developmental crisis, integrity versus despair, involving a reconciliation with one's past and acceptance of finitude. Secondly, similar to 'fluid intelligence' (information-processing and synthesizing efficiency), wisdom might increase until early adulthood and then remain stable until beginning to decline in late middle adulthood. Thirdly, wisdom might follow the path of 'crystallized intelligence' (accumulated knowledge and skills), steadily increasing with age until the end of life or until overtaken by disease processes. Fourthly, wisdom might follow a trajectory that is a combination of the fluid and crystallized pathways. Under this scenario, wisdom will increase until middle or late middle adulthood but decrease thereafter due to decreases in fluid intelligence that cannot be counterbalanced by increases in crystallized intelligence. Fifthly, wisdom might continually decline with age, starting at a relatively early age.

Almost all of these models assume that wisdom will increase during adolescence and young adulthood. Richardson and Pasupathi (2005) suggest that an increase in wisdom during the earlier years might reflect normal intellectual and personality development. Beyond adolescence and young adulthood, wisdom might increase with age if individuals actively pursue its development and learn from their life experiences (Ardelt, 2000b; Baltes, 1993; Kekes, 1983; Kramer, 1990; Taranto, 1989). However, models that posit either no change or a decrease in wisdom after young adulthood assume that the development of wisdom is unrelated to adult-life experiences or that life experiences might even cause a loss of wisdom. An extreme version of such a view is offered by Meacham (1990), who argued that all children are wise and life experiences in the form of personal tragedy, cultural uncertainty, and even personal success actually lead to the loss of wisdom. Personal tragedy and cultural uncertainty might decrease wisdom due to a loss of meaning and confidence in the world and increasing doubt. By contrast, educational, economic, occupational, and social success might cause the loss of wisdom if it results in unquestioned certainty, self-centeredness,

prejudice, and intolerance. According to Meacham (1990), people can at most hope to retain and preserve the wisdom of their youth. However, it should be mentioned that Meacham's view is not shared by the majority of wisdom researchers. Rather, most wisdom scholars believe that the opportunity and motivation to learn from life experiences is crucial in the development of wisdom (Ardelt, 2000b; Kramer, 1990; Moody, 1986; Sternberg, 2005; Taranto, 1989). As Kekes (1983: 286) stated, 'one can be old and foolish, but a wise man is likely to be old, simply because such growth takes time.'

Of course, those theoretical considerations of the hypothetical relation between wisdom and age ignore the variations in people's acquisition of wisdom across the life course (Sternberg, 2005). Contemporary wisdom researchers generally do not believe that wisdom automatically grows with age (Ardelt, 1997; Assmann, 1994; Baltes and Freund, 2003; Dittmann-Kohli and Baltes, 1990; Jordan, 2005; Staudinger, 1999; Sternberg, 1990b; Webster, 2003). Like other personal characteristics, it is more likely that wisdom increases with age for some people, remains stable for others, and even decreases at certain times. Age alone is unlikely to explain the development of wisdom across the life course. In fact, variation in degree of wisdom might increase with age, similar to the increasing within-age variation of many biological, cognitive, and personality characteristics (Baltes, 1979; Nelson and Dannefer, 1992), which might be explained by cumulative advantage and disadvantage across the life course (Dannefer, 2003; Hatch, 2005; O'Rand et al., 2006). For example, both cross-sectional and longitudinal studies have demonstrated increasing variability in health outcomes with advancing age due to educational attainment and socioeconomic status (Mirowsky and Ross, 2008; Ross and Wu, 1996; Willson et al., 2007). In a similar vein, social conditions and social processes might promote or thwart the attainment of wisdom. One can imagine, for example, that a supportive childhood environment with appropriate mentors, an education that encourages open-mindedness, tolerance, sincerity, equanimity, compassion, and the pursuit of a deeper knowledge, and a career path that is conducive to self-development and lifelong learning will foster the development of wisdom (Ardelt and Jacobs, 2008; Baltes and Staudinger, 2000). Although research on the long-term effects of social conditions on wisdom is rare, one longitudinal study of a small sample of women found that socioeconomic status in early adulthood was positively correlated with the women's cognitive, reflective, and affective personality qualities of wisdom over 40 years later. The socioeconomic status of the women's parents, the women's child-hood quality, and their personality characteristics in early adulthood, however, were unrelated to their wisdom in old age (Ardelt, 2000a). Yet, in a different longitudinal study of women, mature personality characteristics at the age of 21 (low repression, tolerance of ambiguity, achievement via independence, psychological mindedness, and tolerance) and a sense of meaning in life and benevolence toward others at the age of 43 were related to greater wisdom at the age of 61 (Helson and Srivastava, 2002).

Although it is unlikely that age alone will lead to wisdom, it might increase for those individuals who are motivated and have the necessary socio-economic resources and support to learn from their life experiences (Ardelt, 2000b; Birren and Fisher, 1990; Kramer, 1990; Moody, 1986; Sternberg, 2000). This assumption directly contra-dicts Meacham's (1990) hypothesis of the loss of wisdom with age. Hence, it is necessary to turn to empirical research to examine the association between age and wisdom.

The association between wisdom and age across the life course: empirical findings

Although variability in the development of wisdom across the life course may be expected, the ques-tion remains which of the above hypothetical scenarios is supported by empirical evidence and under which conditions. The answer to this ques-tion depends in part on the operationalization and measurement of wisdom.

The Berlin Wisdom Group approaches wisdom through a measure of 'wisdom-related knowl-edge,' which asks participants to 'think aloud' about ill-defined hypothetical life problems in the area of life review, life planning, or life manage-ment (Baltes and Staudinger, 2000; Smith and Baltes, 1990). Responses are rated on five wisdom criteria: factual knowledge, procedural knowledge, life-span contextualism, value relativism/tolerance, and recognition and management of uncertainty. Wisdom-related knowledge is calculated as the average of these five criteria (Kunzmann and Baltes, 2005).

The Berlin Group found that wisdom-related knowledge was positively related to age only up to the age of about 24 years, then remained relatively stable, but showed a possible decline after the age of 80 (Pasupathi et al., 2001; Staudinger, 1999). Moreover, younger and older adults were equally likely to receive a wisdom-related knowledge score

in the top 20 per cent of all responses (Baltes et al., 1995; Staudinger et al., 1992). However, a weak positive relationship between age and wisdom was found for the subgroup of partici-pants who scored above the median level on moral reasoning (Kohlberg and Puka, 1994; Pasupathi and Staudinger, 2001). Although cross-sectional, it appears that the development of wisdom-related knowledge follows Sternberg's (2005) 'fluid intel-ligence' view for the general population and the 'crystallized intelligence' view for people who might have a greater interest in the pursuit of wisdom as indicated by relatively strong perform-ances on moral reasoning tasks.

Webster's (2003, 2007) studies, based on the Self-Assessed Wisdom Scale (SAWS), suggest that age is also unrelated to non-cognitive compo-nents of wisdom (i.e., critical life experiences, reflectiveness/reminiscence, emotional regulation, openness to experience, and humor). Similarly, self-transcendent wisdom, as measured by Levenson et al., (2005) Adult Self-Transcendence Inventory (ASTI's), was unrelated to age.

Yet, positive trajectories of wisdom with age have been reported for other measures of wisdom. Takahashi and Overton (2002), who measure the analytic and synthetic modes of wisdom, as described above, report that older American and Japanese adults ($M = 70$ years) tended to score significantly higher on both wisdom modes than did middle-aged adults ($M = 45$ years). Using the Three-Dimensional Wisdom Scale (3D-WS), which measures the cognitive, reflective, and affective personality qualities of wisdom (Ardelt, 2003), Ardelt (in press) found that college-edu-cated older adults (aged 52–87) tended to score significantly higher on the 3D-WS than current college students. Those older respondents were also overrepresented among the top 20 per cent of wisdom scorers compared to the younger stu-dents. Yet, older adults without a college degree tended to score significantly lower on the 3D-WS than both college-educated older adults and cur-rent college students, suggesting that social proc-esses rather than age affect the development of wisdom. Those studies support the 'crystallized intelligence' view and even the 'received' view of wisdom and ageing, particularly for those indi-viduals who have the motivation, opportunity, resources, and support to grow wiser.

All of the results discussed above have been based on cross-sectional studies, which are ulti-mately not able to determine the association between wisdom and age, because they cannot distinguish between age, period, and cohort effects and risk a *life-course fallacy* (Riley, 1973). Unfor-tunately, longitudinal studies that track the devel-opment of wisdom over time are extremely rare.

However, a 6-year longitudinal study using the Reflective Judgment Interview (RJI), which assesses wisdom-related performance in regard to the recognition and understanding of the limits and uncertainty of human knowledge (Kitchener and Brenner, 1990; Kitchener and King, 1981), showed that scores on the RJI tended to increase over a 6-year period for participants who were on average 16 and 20 years old, respectively, at the beginning of the study. Moreover, increases in RJI scores were positively associated with number of years in higher education and highest obtained educational degree. Yet, increases in RJI scores occurred only for a minority of graduate students in their late 20s at the start of the study (Kitchener et al., 1989). This might, in part, reflect a ceiling effect, since the most highly educated participants scored already high at the beginning of the study (Kitchener and Brenner, 1990). In contrast, longitudinal research by Wink and Helson (1997) suggests that practical wisdom (measured by self-reported cognitive, reflective, and mature adjectives from the Adjective Check List) continues to increase in young and middle adulthood. In their study, participants tended to experience gains in practical wisdom between the ages of 27 and 52 years, and those gains tended to be even more pronounced for clinical psychologists, supporting the 'crystallized intelligence' view of wisdom and ageing.

None of the empirical findings reveals a loss of wisdom with age. Yet, keeping in mind the possibility of variation in individual trajectories, this is a distinct possibility. If some people lose wisdom with age, whereas others gain in wisdom, the observed association between wisdom and age might be misleading. For example, could personal tragedy result in the loss of wisdom, as Meacham (1990) claims, or might it actually be a source for stress-related growth (Park, 1998; Park and Fenster, 2004) and ultimately wisdom? The next section explores this question in detail.

THE ROLE OF CRISES AND HARDSHIPS IN THE DEVELOPMENT OF WISDOM

Linley (2003) proposes that wisdom might be both the process and outcome of positive adaptation to trauma in accordance with Hegel's dialectic. In this view, normal life *(thesis)* that is disrupted by trauma *(antithesis)* is transformed to a higher level of functioning through the development of wisdom *(synthesis),* which subsequently facilitates successful coping with future crises and hardships. According to Elder (1991: 14), crises

and hardships in life might function as a 'form of apprenticeship ... in learning to cope with the inevitable losses of old age.' The longer people live, the more crises and hardships they tend to encounter, which might provide opportunities for stress-related growth (Baltes and Smith, 1990; Kekes, 1983; Kramer, 1990; Taranto, 1989). Yet, it is certainly true that not all crises and hardships will result in greater wisdom. On the contrary and in support of Meacham's (1990) argument, some individuals feel easily defeated by crises and hardships, and sometimes a personal tragedy might be so devastating that it leads to hopelessness, despair, and a loss of wisdom. In general, however, the development of wisdom might not depend on *what* people experience but on *how* they deal with events (Holliday and Chandler, 1986), which might be facilitated by cultural, social, and personal resources and assets early in life, such as membership in a higher social class, a good education, supportive social relationships, and personal maturity (Ardelt, 2000a).

For example, the same 40-year longitudinal study that was mentioned above showed that both male and female participants who received relatively high ratings on the cognitive, reflective, and affective personality qualities of wisdom in old age (in 1968–69) were more likely to belong to the middle class rather than the working class in 1929 than participants who were rated as relatively low on wisdom 40 years later (Ardelt, 1998). Although both wisdom groups were equally likely to experience economic deprivation during the Great Depression, the relatively low wisdom group in old age tended to decline in psychological health after the Depression years, whereas the relatively high wisdom group tended to increase in psychological health between 1930 and 1944. The psychological health of participants who were spared from economic loss during the Depression years did not change significantly in the same time period. For the middle-class women in the sample, the experience of Depression-related economic deprivation was also related to greater emotional health and life satisfaction 40 years later, even after controlling for emotional health in 1930–31, whereas for the working-class women, Depression hardship failed to have any beneficial effects in old age (Caspi and Elder, 1986; Elder and Liker, 1982). This extends to wisdom the possibility that wisdom differentials can be understood as the result of a process of cumulative advantage and disadvantage, as has been found for other characteristics (Dannefer, 2003; Hatch, 2005; O'Rand et al., 2006).

The studies demonstrate that experiences of crises and hardships in life are not a sufficient condition for the acquisition of wisdom, although some hardship might be necessary to initiate a life-changing transformation and growth in wisdom (Linley, 2003; Martin and Kleiber, 2005; Staudinger and Kunzmann, 2005). For example, middle-aged and young-old adults who experience a life-threatening situation, such as a serious illness, accident, or medical intervention, often express a newfound appreciation of life, a deeper sense of spirituality, and greater love, caring, and compassion for others (Ardelt et al., 2008; Kinnier et al., 2001). Yet, without socioeconomic and personal resources, crises and hardships might lead to despair rather than psychosocial growth (Ardelt, 1998; Caspi and Elder, 1986; Elder and Liker, 1982).

How exactly do wise persons deal with crises and obstacles in their lives? In a qualitative study that investigated the coping processes of six older adults who were rated and scored either relatively high or relatively low on the cognitive, reflective, and affective personality qualities of wisdom, Ardelt (2005) found that the three relatively wise elders first mentally distanced themselves from a negative event to calm down, relax, and not get overwhelmed by the situation. Secondly, they mentally reframed the situation and actively coped with it by taking mental and/or physical control of the crisis. Thirdly, they learned from their experiences, became aware and accepted life's unpredictability and uncertainty, and applied the life lessons to current crises and hardships (Linley, 2003). Their successful mastery of earlier crises and hardships resulted in stress-related growth (Park, 1998; Park and Fenster, 2004), reduced self-centeredness (Kramer, 1990), and increased wisdom expressed through insight, understanding, and sympathy and compassion for others. This process prepared them to cope with the physical and social losses of old age and to accept death (Ardelt, 1998; Bianchi, 1994; Caspi and Elder, 1986; Giesen and Datan, 1980). By contrast, the three elders who scored and were rated as relatively low on wisdom used passive rather than active coping strategies, such as passive acceptance and/or a reliance on God, to deal with obstacles and hardships in their lives even if active coping strategies would have been more appropriate for the problems they faced. As a result, they did not learn from their experiences, did not obtain a greater understanding of life, and remained extremely vulnerable and defenseless when faced with trauma.

DISCUSSION

The theoretical considerations and empirical evidence suggest that wisdom does not 'automatically' increase with age, although as a generalization this statement must be considered tentative. A uniform definition and measurement of wisdom does not exist and cross-sectional studies are ultimately unsuitable to examine the association between wisdom and age. What is needed are carefully designed longitudinal studies that investigate quantitatively and qualitatively the concrete conditions under which wisdom develops, declines, and remains stable with age. Based on the available data, however, it appears that people who are willing and able to learn the lessons that life teaches them and are transformed in the process by becoming less self-centered and more compassionate toward others will gain greater insight into life and grow in wisdom over time. Crises and hardships in life can be triggers for this transformational process, although they might lead to a loss of wisdom if they overwhelm the individual. Yet, there might be other ways to foster the development of wisdom. If the intellectual and social environment, as indicated by education and socioeconomic status, has a positive effect on the acquisition of wisdom (Ardelt, 1998, 2000a, 2006; Kitchener et al., 1989), it might be possible to promote wisdom development in schools and universities (Brown, 2004; Reznitskaya and Sternberg, 2004; Sternberg, 2001). Past studies have also shown that meditation is positively related to wisdom (Hoffman, 2007; Levenson et al., 2005). Hence, it is encourageing that schools and universities increasingly include meditation in their curriculum (Holland, 2006; Leoni, 2006; Oman et al., 2007; Tloczynski and Tantriella, 1998; Wall, 2005).

Given the persistence of economic, social, and environmental injustices despite great technological and scientific advancements and access to a vast amount of information, it might not be surprising that wisdom as a topic of scientific and personal inquiry has received renewed importance and urgency. There is clearly a need for an approach to apprehend the world that transcends intellectual knowledge through a deep and thorough understanding of all interpersonal and intrapersonal aspects of life. Wisdom is believed to be beneficial at all stages of the life course, but might be especially valuable in old age to confront unique challenges and opportunities. Although it is true that old age is characterized by physical and social losses, freedom from social and societal obligations – such as raising a family and earning a living – can also provide extra time to pursue the acquisition of wisdom (Ardelt, 2000b). Far from being a consolation prize for older adults to keep quiet and abstain from social criticism (Woodward, 2003), wisdom is inherently concerned with ethical and moral conduct (Kupperman, 2005) and the pursuit of social justice for all (Edmondson, 2005). Hence, instead of being perceived as a burden to society and the financial health of the social security system, wise elders might become our most valuable asset to guide us on the path to a more ecologically balanced and socially just future.

REFERENCES

Achenbaum, A.W. and Orwoll, L. (1991) 'Becoming wise: a psycho-gerontological interpretation of the Book of Job', *International Journal of Aging and Human Development*, 32(1): 21–39.

Ardelt, M. (1997) 'Wisdom and life satisfaction in old age', *Journal of Gerontology: Psychological Sciences*, 52B(1): P15–27.

Ardelt, M. (1998) 'Social crisis and individual growth: the long-term effects of the Great Depression', *Journal of Aging Studies*, 12(3): 291–314.

Ardelt, M. (2000a) 'Antecedents and effects of wisdom in old age: a longitudinal perspective on aging well', *Research on Aging*, 22(4): 360–94.

Ardelt, M. (2000b) 'Intellectual versus wisdom-related knowledge: the case for a different kind of learning in the later years of life', *Educational Gerontology: An International Journal of Research and Practice*, 26(8): 771–89.

Ardelt, M. (2003) 'Development and empirical assessment of a three-dimensional wisdom scale', *Research on Aging*, 25(3): 275–324.

Ardelt, M. (2004) 'Wisdom as expert knowledge system: a critical review of a contemporary operationalization of an ancient concept', *Human Development*, 47(5): 257–85.

Ardelt, M. (2005) 'How wise people cope with crises and obstacles in life', *ReVision: A Journal of Consciousness and Transformation*, 28(1): 7–19.

Ardelt, M. (in press) 'Are older adults wiser than college students? A comparison of two age cohorts', *Journal of Adult Development*.

Ardelt, M. and Jacobs, S. (2008) 'Wisdom, integrity, and life satisfaction in very old age', in M. Cecil Smith (ed.), *Handbook of Research on Adult Learning and Development*. New York: Routledge, pp. 732–60.

Ardelt, M., Ai, A.L., and Eichenberger, S.E. (2008) 'In search for meaning: the differential role of religion for middle-aged and older persons diagnosed with a life-threatening illness', *Journal of Religion, Spirituality and Aging*, 20(4): 288–312.

Arlin, P.K. (1990) 'Wisdom: the art of problem finding', in R.J. Sternberg (ed.), *Wisdom: Its Nature, Origins, and Development*. Cambridge, UK: Cambridge University Press, pp. 230–43.

Assmann, A. (1994) 'Wholesome knowledge: concepts of wisdom in a historical and cross-cultural perspective', in D.L. Featherman, R.M. Lerner, and M. Perlmutter (eds),

Life-Span Development and Behavior, Vol. 12. Hillsdale, NJ: Lawrence Erlbaum, pp. 187–224.

Baltes, P.B. (1979) 'Life-span developmental psychology: some converging observations on history and theory', in P.B. Baltes and O.G. Brim (eds), *Life-Span Development and Behavior*, Vol. 2. New York: Academic Press.

Baltes, P.B. (1993) 'The aging mind: potential and limits', *The Gerontologist*, 33(5): 580–94.

Baltes, P.B. and Freund, A.M. (2003) 'The intermarriage of wisdom and selective optimization with compensation: two meta-heuristics guiding the conduct of life', in Corey L.M. Keyes and J. Haidt (eds), *Flourishing: Positive Psychology and the Life Well-Lived*. Washington, DC: American Psychological Association, pp. 249–73.

Baltes, P.B. and Smith, J. (1990) 'Towards a psychology of wisdom and its ontogenesis', in R.J. Sternberg (ed.), *Wisdom: Its Nature, Origins, and Development*. Cambridge, UK: Cambridge University Press, pp. 87–120.

Baltes, P.B. and Staudinger, U.M. (2000) 'Wisdom: a meta-heuristic (pragmatic) to orchestrate mind and virtue toward excellence', *American Psychologist*, 55(1): 122–36.

Baltes, P.B., Staudinger, U.M., Maercker, A., and Smith, J. (1995) 'People nominated as wise: a comparative study of wisdom-related knowledge', *Psychology and Aging*, 10(2): 155–66.

Bianchi, E.C. (1994) *Elder Wisdom. Crafting Your Own Elderhood*. New York: Crossroad.

Birren, J.E. and Fisher, L.M. (1990) 'The elements of wisdom: overview and integration', in R.J. Sternberg (ed.), *Wisdom: Its Nature, Origins, and Development*. Cambridge, UK: Cambridge University Press, pp. 317–32.

Birren, J.E. and Svensson, C.M. (2005) 'Wisdom in history', in R.J. Sternberg and J. Jordan (eds), *A Handbook of Wisdom: Psychological Perspectives*. New York: Cambridge University Press, pp. 3–31.

Blanchard-Fields, F. and Norris, L. (1995) 'The development of wisdom', in M.A. Kimble, S.H. McFadden, J.W. Ellor, and J.J. Seeber (eds), *Aging, Spirituality, and Religion: A Handbook*. Minneapolis, MN: Fortress Press, pp. 102–18.

Bluck, S. and Glück, J. (2005) 'From the inside out: people's implicit theories of wisdom', in R.J. Sternberg and J. Jordan (eds), *A Handbook of Wisdom: Psychological Perspectives*. New York: Cambridge University Press, pp. 84–109.

Brown, S.C. (2004) 'Learning across the campus: how college facilitates the development of wisdom', *Journal of College Student Development*, 45(2): 134–48.

Brugman, G.M. (2000) *Wisdom: Source of Narrative Coherence and Eudaimonia*. Delft: Eburon.

Caspi, A. and Elder, G.H., Jr. (1986) 'Life satisfaction in old age: linking social psychology and history', *Journal of Psychology and Aging*, 1(1): 18–26.

Chandler, M.J. and Holliday, S. (1990) 'Wisdom in a postapocalyptic age', in R.J. Sternberg (ed.), *Wisdom: Its Nature, Origins, and Development*. Cambridge, UK: Cambridge University Press, pp. 121–41.

Clayton, V.P. and Birren, J.E. (1980) 'The development of wisdom across the life-span: a reexamination of an ancient topic', in P.B. Baltes and O.G. Brim, Jr. (eds), *Life-Span*

Development and Behavior, Vol. 3. New York: Academic Press, pp. 103–35.

Csikszentmihalyi, M. and Nakamura, J. (2005) 'The role of emotions in the development of wisdom', in R.J. Sternberg and J. Jordan (eds), *A Handbook of Wisdom: Psychological Perspectives*. New York: Cambridge University Press, pp. 220–42.

Csikszentmihalyi, M. and Rathunde, K. (1990) 'The psychology of wisdom: an evolutionary interpretation', in R.J. Sternberg (ed.), *Wisdom: Its Nature, Origins, and Development*. Cambridge, UK: Cambridge University Press, pp. 25–51.

Curnow, T. (1999) *Wisdom, Intuition, and Ethics*. Brookfield, VT: Ashgate.

Dannefer, D. (2003) 'Cumulative advantage/disadvantage and the life course: cross-fertilizing age and social science theory', *Journal of Gerontology: Psychological Sciences*, 58B(6): P327–37.

Dittmann-Kohli, F. and Baltes, P.B. (1990) 'Toward a neofunctionalist conception of adult intellectual development: wisdom as a prototypical case of intellectual growth', in C.N. Alexander and E.J. Langer (eds), *Higher Stages of Human Development: Perspectives on Adult Growth*. New York: Oxford University Press, pp. 54–78.

Edmondson, R. (2005) 'Wisdom in later life: ethnographic approaches', *Ageing and Society*, 25(3): 339–56.

Elder, G.H., Jr. (1991) 'Making the best of life: perspectives on lives, times, and aging', *Generations*, 15(1): 12–17.

Elder, G.H., Jr. and Liker, J.K. (1982) 'Hard times in women's life: historical influences across forty years', *American Journal of Sociology*, 88: 241–69.

Erikson, E.H. (1963) *Childhood and Society*. New York: Norton.

Erikson, E.H. (1982) *The Life Cycle Completed: A Review*. New York: Norton.

Erikson, E.H., Erikson, J.M., and Kivnick, H.Q. (1986) *Vital Involvement in Old Age: The Experience of Old Age in Our Time*. New York: Norton.

Giesen, C.B. and Datan, N. (1980) 'The competent older woman', in N. Datan and N. Lohmann (eds), *Transitions of Aging*. New York: Academic Press, pp. 57–72.

Hart, W. (1987) *The Art of Living: Vipassana Meditation as Taught by S. N. Goenka*. San Francisco: Harper.

Hatch, S.L. (2005) 'Conceptualizing and identifying cumulative adversity and protective resources: implications for understanding health inequalities', *Journal of Gerontology: Social Sciences* 60B(2): S130–4.

Helson, R. and Srivastava, S. (2002) 'Creative and wise people: similarities, differences and how they develop', *Personality and Social Psychology Bulletin*, 28(10): 1430–40.

Hoffman, K.T. (2007) 'A scale development and construct validation study of the Buddhist construct of nonattachment', Unpublished PhD dissertation, Fielding Graduate University, Santa Barbara, CA.

Holland, D. (2006) 'Contemplative education in unexpected places: teaching mindfulness in Arkansas and Austria', *Teachers College Record*, 108(9): 1842–61.

Holliday, S.G. and Chandler, M.J. (1986) *Wisdom: Explorations in Adult Competence*. Basel: Karger.

Jeste, D.V. and Vahia, I. (2008) 'Comparison of the conceptualization of wisdom in ancient Indian literature with modern views: Focus on the Bhagvad Gita', *Psychiatry: Interpersonal and Biological Processes*, 71(3), 197–209.

Kekes, J. (1983) 'Wisdom', *American Philosophical Quarterly*, 20(3): 277–86.

Kekes, J. (1995) *Moral Wisdom and Good Lives*. Ithaca, NY: Cornell University Press.

Kinnier, R.T., Tribbensee, N.E., Rose, C.A., and Vaughan, S.M. (2001) 'In the final analysis: more wisdom from people who have faced death', *Journal of Counseling and Development*, 79(2): 171–7.

Kitchener, K.S. and Brenner, H.G. (1990) 'Wisdom and reflective judgment: knowing in the face of uncertainty', in R.J. Sternberg (ed.), *Wisdom: Its Nature, Origins, and Development*. Cambridge, UK: Cambridge University Press, pp. 212–29.

Kitchener, K.S. and King, P.M. (1981) 'Reflective judgment: concepts of justification and their relationship to age and education', *Journal of Applied Developmental Psychology*, 2(2): 89–116.

Kitchener, K.S., King, P.M., Wood, P.K., and Davison, M.L. (1989) 'Sequentiality and consistency in the development of reflective judgment: a six-year longitudinal study', *Journal of Applied Developmental Psychology*, 10(1): 73–95.

Kohlberg, L. and Puka, B. (1994) *Kohlberg's Original Study of Moral Development*. New York: Garland Publishing.

Kramer, D.A. (1990) 'Conceptualizing wisdom: the primacy of affect-cognition relations', in R.J. Sternberg (ed.), *Wisdom: Its Nature, Origins, and Development*. Cambridge, UK: Cambridge University Press, pp. 279–313.

Kunzmann, U. and Baltes, P.B. (2005) 'The psychology of wisdom: theoretical and empirical challenges', in R.J. Sternberg and J. Jordan (eds), *A Handbook of Wisdom: Psychological Perspectives*. New York: Cambridge University Press, pp. 110–35.

Kupperman, J.J. (2005) 'Morality, ethics, and wisdom', in R.J. Sternberg and J. Jordan (eds), *A Handbook of Wisdom: Psychological Perspectives*. New York: Cambridge University Press, pp. 245–71.

Leoni, J. (2006) 'Communicating quietly: supporting personal growth with meditation and listening in schools', *Support for Learning*, 21(3): 121–8.

Levenson, M.R., Jennings, P.A., Aldwin, C.M., and Shiraishi, R.W. (2005) 'Self-transcendence: conceptualization and measurement', *International Journal of Aging and Human Development*, 60(2): 127–43.

Levitt, H.M. (1999) 'The development of wisdom: an analysis of Tibetan Buddhist experience', *Journal of Humanistic Psychology*, 39(2): 86–105.

Linley, P.A. (2003) 'Positive adaptation to trauma: wisdom as both process and outcome', *Journal of Traumatic Stress*, 16(6): 601–10.

Manheimer, R.J. (1992) 'Wisdom and method: philosophical contributions to gerontology', in T.R. Cole, D.D. Van Tassel, and R. Kastenbaum (eds), *Handbook of the Humanities and Aging*. New York: Springer, pp. 426–40.

Martin, L.L. and Kleiber, D.A. (2005) 'Letting go of the negative: psychological growth from a close brush with death', *Traumatology*, 11(4): 221–32.

McKee, P. and Barber, C. (1999) 'On defining wisdom', *International Journal of Aging and Human Development*, 49(2): 149–64.

Meacham, J.A. (1990) 'The loss of wisdom', in R.J. Sternberg (ed.), *Wisdom: Its Nature, Origins, and Development*. Cambridge, UK: Cambridge University Press, pp. 181–211.

Mirowsky, J. and Ross, C.E. (2008) 'Education and self-rated health: cumulative advantage and its rising importance', *Research on Aging*, 30(1): 93–122.

Moody, H.R. (1986) 'Late life learning in the information society', in D.A. Peterson, J.E. Thornton, and J.E. Birren (eds), *Education and Aging*. Englewood Cliffs, NJ: Prentice-Hall, pp. 122–48.

Ñanamoli, B. (2001) *The Life of the Buddha: According to the Pali Canon*. Seattle, WA: BPS Pariyatti Editions.

Naranjo, C. (1972) *The One Quest*. New York: The Viking Press.

Nelson, E.A. and Dannefer, D. (1992) 'Aged heterogeneity: fact or fiction? The fate of diversity in gerontological research', *The Gerontologist*, 32(1): 17–23.

Oman, D., Shapiro, S.L., Thoresen, C.E., et al. (2007) 'Learning from spiritual models and meditation: a randomized evaluation of a college course', *Pastoral Psychology*, 55(4): 473–93.

O'Rand, A.M., Binstock, R.H., and George, L.K. (2006) 'Stratification and the life course: life course capital, life course risks, and social inequality', in *Handbook of Aging and the Social Sciences*, 6th edn. Elsevier: Amsterdam, pp. 145–62.

Orwoll, L. and Achenbaum, A.W. (1993) 'Gender and the development of wisdom', *Human Development*, 36: 274–96.

Osbeck, L.M. and Robinson, D.N. (2005) 'Philosophical theories of wisdom', in R.J. Sternberg and J. Jordan (eds), *A Handbook of Wisdom: Psychological Perspectives*. New York: Cambridge University Press, pp. 61–83.

Park, C.L. (1998) 'Stress-related growth and thriving through coping: the roles of personality and cognitive processes', *Journal of Social Issues*, 54(2): 267–77.

Park, C.L. and Fenster, J.R. (2004) 'Stress-related growth: predictors of occurrence and correlates with psychological adjustment', *Journal of Social and Clinical Psychology*, 23(2): 195–215.

Pascual-Leone, J. (1990) 'An essay on wisdom: toward organismic processes that make it possible', in R.J. Sternberg (ed.), *Wisdom: Its Nature, Origins, and Development*. Cambridge, UK: Cambridge University Press, pp. 244–78.

Pasupathi, M. and Staudinger, U.M. (2001) 'Do advanced moral reasoners also show wisdom? Linking moral reasoning and wisdom-related knowledge and judgement', *International Journal of Behavioral Development*, 25(5): 401–15.

Pasupathi, M., Staudinger, U.M., and Baltes, P.B. (2001) 'Seeds of wisdom: adolescents' knowledge and judgment about difficult life problems', *Developmental Psychology*, 37(3): 351–61.

Reznitskaya, A. and Sternberg, R.J. (2004) 'Teaching students to make wise judgments: the "teaching for Wisdom" program', in P.A. Linley and S. Joseph (eds), *Positive Psychology in Practice*. New York: Wiley., pp. 181–96.

Richardson, M.J. and M. Pasupathi (2005) 'Young and growing wiser: wisdom during adolescence and young adulthood', in R.J. Sternberg and J. Jordan (eds), *A Handbook of Wisdom. Psychological Perspectives*. New York: Cambridge University Press, pp.139–59.

Riley, M.W. (1973) 'Aging and cohort succession: Interpretations and misinterpretations', *Public Opinion Quarterly*, 37(1): 35–49.

Robinson, D.N. (1990) 'Wisdom through the ages', in R.J. Sternberg (ed.), *Wisdom: Its Nature, Origins, and Development*. Cambridge, UK: Cambridge University Press, pp. 13–24.

Ross, C.E. and Wu, C. (1996) 'Education, age and the cumulative advantage in health', *Journal of Health and Social Behavior*, 37(1): 104–20.

Smith, J. and Baltes, P.B. (1990) 'Wisdom-related knowledge: age/cohort differences in response to life-planning problems', *Developmental Psychology*, 26(3): 494–505.

Smith, J., Staudinger, U.M., and Baltes, P.B. (1994) 'Occupational settings facilitating wisdom-related knowledge: the sample case of clinical psychologists', *Journal of Consulting and Clinical Psychology*, 62(5): 989–99.

Staudinger, U.M. (1999) 'Older and wiser? Integrating results on the relationship between age and wisdom-related performance', *International Journal of Behavioral Development*, 23(3): 641–64.

Staudinger, U.M. and Kunzmann, U. (2005) 'Positive adult personality development: adjustment and/or growth?' *European Psychologist*, 10(4): 320–9.

Staudinger, U.M., Smith, J., and Baltes, P.B. (1992) 'Wisdom-related knowledge in a life review task: age differences and the role of professional specialization', *Psychology and Aging*, 7(2): 271–81.

Sternberg, R.J. (1990a) 'Wisdom and its relations to intelligence and creativity', in R.J. Sternberg (ed.), *Wisdom: Its Nature, Origins, and Development*. Cambridge, UK: Cambridge University Press, pp. 142–59.

Sternberg, R.J. (ed.) (1990b) *Wisdom: Its Nature, Origins, and Development*. Cambridge, UK: Cambridge University Press.

Sternberg, R.J. (1998) 'A balance theory of wisdom', *Review of General Psychology*, 2(4): 347–65.

Sternberg, R.J. (2000) 'Intelligence and wisdom', in R.J. Sternberg (ed.), *Handbook of Intelligence*. New York: Cambridge University Press, pp. 631–49.

Sternberg, R.J. (2001) 'Why schools should teach for wisdom: The balance theory of wisdom in educational settings', *Educational Psychology*, 36(4): 227–45.

Sternberg, R.J. (2005) 'Older but not wiser? The relationship between age and wisdom', *Ageing International*, 30(1): 5–26.

Sternberg, R.J. and Jordan, J. (eds.) (2005) *A Handbook of Wisdom: Psychological Perspectives*. New York: Cambridge University Press.

Takahashi, M. (2000) 'Toward a culturally inclusive understanding of wisdom: Historical roots in the East and West', *International Journal of Aging and Human Development*, 51(3): 217–30.

Takahashi, M. and Bordia, P. (2000) 'The concept of wisdom: A cross-cultural comparison', *International Journal of Psychology*, 35(1): 1–9.

Takahashi, M. and Overton, W.F. (2002) 'Wisdom: A culturally inclusive developmental perspective', *International Journal of Behavioral Development*, 26(3): 269–77.

Takahashi, M. and Overton, W.F. (2005) 'Cultural foundations of wisdom: An integrated developmental approach', in R.J. Sternberg and J. Jordan (eds.), *A Handbook of Wisdom: Psychological Perspectives*. New York: Cambridge University Press. pp. 32–60.

Taranto, M.A. (1989) 'Facets of wisdom: A theoretical synthesis', *International Journal of Aging and Human Development*, 29(1): 1–21.

Tloczynski, J. and Tantriella, M. (1998) 'A comparison of the effects of Zen breath meditation or relaxation on college adjustment', *Psychologia: An International Journal of Psychology in the Orient*, 41(1): 32–43.

Vaillant, G.E. (1993) *The Wisdom of the Ego*. Cambridge, MA: Harvard University Press.

Wall, R.B. (2005) 'Tai Chi and mindfulness-based stress reduction in a Boston public middle school', *Journal of Pediatric Health Care*, 19(4): 230–7.

Webster, J.D. (2003) 'An exploratory analysis of a self-assessed wisdom scale', *Journal of Adult Development*, 10(1): 13–22.

Webster, J.D. (2007) 'Measuring the character strength of wisdom', *International Journal of Aging and Human Development*, 65(2): 163–83.

Willson, A.E., Shuey, K.M., and Elder, G.H., Jr. (2007) 'Cumulative advantage processes as mechanisms of inequality in life course health', *American Journal of Sociology*, 112(6): 1886–1924.

Wink, P. and Helson, R. (1997) 'Practical and transcendent wisdom: their nature and some longitudinal findings', *Journal of Adult Development*, 4(1): 1–15.

Woodward, K. (2003) 'Against wisdom: the social politics of anger and aging', *Journal of Aging Studies*, 17(1): 55–67.

Yang, S. (2001) 'Conceptions of wisdom among Taiwanese Chinese', *Journal of Cross-Cultural Psychology*, 32(6): 662–80.

Zaehner, R.C. (1969) *The Bhagavad-Gita: With a Commentary Based on the Original Sources*. Oxford: Clarendon.

FURTHER READING

Bianchi, Eugene C. (1994) *Elder Wisdom. Crafting Your Own Elderhood*. New York: Crossroad.

Birren, James E. and Feldman, Linda (1997) *Where to Go from Here: Discovering Your Own Life's Wisdom in the Second Half of Your Life*. New York: Simon and Schuster.

Curnow, Trevor (1999) *Wisdom, Intuition, and Ethics*. Brookfield, VT.: Ashgate.

Dalai, Lama and Cutler, Howard C. (1998) *The Art of Happiness: A Handbook for Living*. New York: Riverhead Books.

Dass, Ram (2001) *Still Here: Embracing Aging, Changing, and Dying*. New York: Riverhead.

Erikson, Erik H. (1982) *The Life Cycle Completed: A Review*. New York: Norton.

Frankl, Viktor E. (1963) *Man's Search for Meaning: An Introduction to Logotherapy*. New York: Washington Square Press.

Fromm, Erich (1976) *To Have or to Be?* New York: Harper and Row.

Kekes, John (1995) *Moral Wisdom and Good Lives*. Ithaca, NY: Cornell University Press.

Macdonald, Copthorne (1993) *Toward Wisdom: Finding Our Way to Inner Peace, Love and Happiness*. Willowdale, Ontario, Canada: Haunslow.

Maslow, Abraham H. (1971) *The Farther Reaches of Human Nature*. New York: The Viking Press.

Schachter-Shalomi, Zalman and Miller, Ronald S. (1997) *From Age-ing to Sage-ing: A Profound New Vision of Growing Older*. New York: Warner Books.

Sternberg, Robert J. (ed.) (1990) *Wisdom: Its Nature, Origins, and Development*. Cambridge, UK: Cambridge University Press.

Sternberg, Robert J. and Jordan, Jennifer (eds) (2005) *A Handbook of Wisdom: Psychological Perspectives*. New York: Cambridge University Press.

Vaillant, George E. (2002) *Aging Well: Surprising Guideposts to a Happier Life from the Landmark Harvard Study of Adult Development*. Boston, MA: Little, Brown.

WEBSITES

The Wisdom Page: http://www.wisdompage.com/index.html

Collective Wisdom Initiative: http://www.collectivewisdom initiative.org/

Wisdom Factors International: http://www.wisdomfactors.com/

Age-ing to Sage-ing: http://www.allaboutaging.com/index.html

Metanexus Institute: http://www.metanexus.net/Institute/

The Institute for Research on Unlimited Love: http://www.unlimitedloveinstitute.org/

24

Loneliness and Ageing: Comparative Perspectives

Marja Jylhä and Marja Saarenheimo

INTRODUCTION

Social relationships, and their structures and meanings, comprise some of the major issues in social gerontology. This chapter discusses one dimension in this field, that of loneliness. The concept of loneliness is closely linked with themes such as family life, social integration, quality of life, and life satisfaction. This chapter examines the experience of loneliness, with particular attention given to issues of theory, measurement, and comparisons across different societies. The chapter reviews a number of important questions:

- To what extent does loneliness belong to old age?
- To what extent is loneliness similar for young and older people?
- To what degree do the conditions and forms of loneliness vary according to different cultural environments?

The chapter assesses a number of approaches to measuring loneliness, the main risk factors involved, and models of intervention to reduce the experience of loneliness in community settings.

Classic social research on loneliness has included studies such as those by Moustakas (1972), Weiss (1973), and Peplau and Perlman (1982a) on the nature and content of loneliness; Townsend (1968) on cross-national comparisons in old age; and Tunstall (1966), Lopata (1969), and Elias (1985) on the differential meanings and experience of loneliness. Since these earlier studies, theoretical models have been refined, research methods have

advanced, and research focusing on loneliness and ageing has increased (see, e.g., Victor et al., 2009). However, these seminal studies still constitute the basis for understanding the nature, causes, and consequences of loneliness.

WHAT IS LONELINESS? CONCEPTS AND THEORIES

Definitions of loneliness refer to negative or unpleasant feelings, arising from deficiencies – quantitative or qualitative – in social relationships (Peplau and Perlman, 1982b). Loneliness is best understood as a relational concept. First, the individual experience of loneliness requires, at minimum, an awareness of what it means to have meaningful relationships or contact with others, or to be a part of a community. Secondly, most theoretical models of loneliness rely on comparisons, where a current state of being is set against a person's past or anticipated future situation or the situation of others.

The literature on loneliness employs a wide spectrum of interrelated and partly overlapping concepts, including 'being alone', 'living alone', 'aloneness', 'solitude', and 'feeling lonely'. Being alone does not necessarily lead to loneliness, nor is it necessarily a negative experience. Temporary solitude can be seen as necessary for personal growth and creativity, and in contemplative religious traditions, withdrawal from social interaction has maintained its essential role through the centuries.

On the other hand, research confirms that one can 'feel lonely' even in the presence of others (de Jong Gierveld, 1998; Townsend, 1968; Victor et al., 2009). An important distinction lies between social isolation, operationalized as an objective measure, and the experience of loneliness, referring to a subjective state that is recognizable only by a person her/himself. The experience or 'feeling' of loneliness refers not to the amount of social relationships but to a discrepancy, either in quantity or quality, between the relationships one has and those one desires (de Jong Gierveld et al., 1987; Lopata, 1969; Perlman and Peplau, 1998). This discrepancy can arise in various ways. Lopata makes the point here that: 'A person may feel lonely when no one else is present, when a particular one is absent, when interaction partners treat him differently than he desires, or when aspects of the situation make him feel alienated from those with whom he could develop different relations' (1969: 250).

Another relevant distinction concerns *social* versus *emotional* loneliness (de Jong Gierveld et al., 1987; Van Baarsen et al., 2001; Weiss, 1973). Social loneliness is related to an absence of a broad social network and isolation from any accepting community (de Jong Gierveld and Havens, 2004; Weiss, 1973). Emotional loneliness comes from the absence of a reliable attachment figure and a lack of intimate relations (Weiss, 1973). In Lopata's (1969) study of widows, participants associated loneliness with a desire to carry on interaction with a particular other no longer available, to an experience of being no longer an object of love, to an absence of someone to care for, or to an absence of a person with whom to share experiences.

Depending on theoretical focus, loneliness in old age has been examined from individualistic, interpersonal, or societal perspectives. These different ways of understanding loneliness should not be seen as mutually exclusive but complementary. Social and demographic perspectives focus on the role of social and environmental factors, such as socio-demographic position, material circumstances, social inequality, health, and life events (Victor et al., 2005a) that may marginalize or isolate older people (see further below). Psychological perspectives often view loneliness as originating in earlier interpersonal experiences (Andersson, 1990) or as deficits in social skills. Psychologists have claimed that personal traits or characteristics such as neuroticism (Costa and McCrae, 1987), negative affectivity (Watson and Pennebaker, 1989), and tendency to adopt passive roles (Vitkus and Horowitz, 1987) would, through the individuals´ own behaviour and their sensitivity to unfavourable life circumstances, make them especially vulnerable to feelings of loneliness.

Sociological as well as psychological research has discussed selectivity in social interaction as an important element of late-old age. In psychology, Erikson (1959) suggested that old age represents a time of lessening social activity and a tendency to review one's life history. In social gerontology, disengagement theory (Cumming and Henry, 1961) linked reduced social interaction with life satisfaction and positive adjustment to retirement and widowhood. The concept of gero-transcendence, developed by Tornstam (2005), emphasized a decrease in superfluous interaction and increasing importance of symbolic rather that concrete communion with others as characteristics of old age. According to the socio-emotional selectivity theory (Carstensen et al., 1999), an awareness of the limited scope of time leads to a selective narrowing of the range of relationships to those that are most predictable and satisfying. These theories, notably disengagement theory, have been criticized for their underlying assumptions of more or less universal stages of life, for failing to recognize the social malleability of the human life course, and for neglecting the impact of social and economic inequalities (Dannefer, 1984; Hochschild, 1975). Nevertheless, the descriptions they offer contribute to understanding the complex mental landscape of loneliness and solitude in old age, and the importance attached to quality rather than quantity of social interaction.

DEPRESSION AND LONELINESS

Depression and loneliness are distinct but overlapping concepts (Stek et al., 2004; Tiikkainen and Heikkinen, 2005). The notion of depression refers to mood disturbance characterized by loss of pleasure and low mood. Transient depressive symptoms are not unusual and can be considered part of normal life. A major depressive disorder, however, often characterized also by sleeping problems and eating disorders, among others, is a severe clinical diagnosis. Empirical studies show that depression and loneliness often appear together, although loneliness is not included in standard diagnostic definitions of depression (see, e.g., DSM–IV). A combination of loneliness and depression often characterizes older people who attempt suicide (Lebret et al., 2006).

Some studies suggest that loneliness is a factor associated with depressive symptoms (Hawkley et al., 2006; Heikkinen and Kauppinen, 2004); others consider it as a risk factor (Adams et al., 2004). Older people may prefer to describe depressive mood in terms of loneliness, because it provides a more acceptable, less stigmatizing way to refer to psychological problems (Barg et al., 2006). When asked to elaborate their conceptions and experiences of depressive mood, the most salient terms that older people used to describe themselves with when depressed included 'lonely', 'sad', and 'tired'. Participants spoke about loneliness and depression in three different ways: first, as a natural and inevitable part of ageing; secondly, lonely people as being responsible for withdrawing from social life and thus causing their loneliness; third, as a gateway to depression (Barg et al., 2006).

In a study of older people living independently in the community (Cohen-Mansfield and Parpura-Gil, 2007), loneliness was the most important predictor of depressed affect, with the main predictors of loneliness consisting of self-efficacy (psychological barrier), insufficient financial resources and opportunities for social contacts (environmental barriers), and mobility difficulties (health barriers).

In general terms, research has considered loneliness as a contributing factor, as a characteristic, and as a consequence of depression. The interpretation also depends on the focus and theoretical perspective of a given study. Although loneliness and depression do not always appear together, their complex but close mutual relationship emphasizes the role of loneliness as a cause of pain and suffering in old age.

RESEARCH APPROACHES AND INDICATORS

The approaches and instruments used in empirical research on loneliness both reflect and influence the ways in which loneliness has been understood (Perlman, 2004). Quantitative studies focusing on the frequency and intensity of experienced loneliness usually collect data through structured questions in personal interviews or mailed surveys. Both single, global questions and lengthy, multi-item scales (most of them originally developed for young people) have been used (Russell, 1982). The measures most frequently used with older people include the UCLA Loneliness Scale (Russell 1982, 1996) and scales developed by de Jong Gierveld (de Jong Gierveld and Kamphuis, 1985) and Wenger (Wenger, 1983; Wenger and Burholt, 2004; Wenger et al., 1996). The third version of the UCLA Loneliness Scale consists of 20 questions, each starting with 'How often do you feel ...?', and continue, for example , '... that you are "in tune" with the people around you?' (item 1), '... alone?' (item 4), or '... that there are people who really understand you?' (item 16). Eleven of

the questions are worded negatively (reflecting loneliness) and 9 positively (reflecting non-loneliness). For each question the person is asked to select one of the options: 'often', 'sometimes', 'rarely', or 'never' (Russell, 1996).

Many of the multi-item scales recognize the two dimensions of loneliness based on the theory of Weiss (1973) – *emotional loneliness* related to intimate relationships and *social loneliness* related to the sufficiency and functions of broader social networks. The de Jong Gierveld scale (de Jong Gierveld and Kamphuis, 1985; van Tilburg et al., 2004) is specifically developed for older people. It includes 11 items, six negatively phrased (e.g., 'I experience a general sense of emptiness'), indicating emotional loneliness, and five positively phrased (e.g., 'There is always someone I can talk to about my day-to-day problems'), indicating the social side of loneliness. The items have three response categories: 'no', 'more or less', and 'yes'. A six-item version is also available (de Jong Gierveld and van Tilburg, 2006). The instrument developed by Wenger (1983) consists of two distinct groups of questions. Social isolation is measured by eight questions where the person is asked, for example, whether he or she lives alone, or whether he or she has a telephone. Loneliness is measured by eight questions focusing on social relations, such as having a confidant or spending the previous Christmas alone and lonely.

Most of the studies where older people are asked about their loneliness have used one single global question, usually worded 'Do you feel lonely?' or 'How often do you feel lonely?', with four or five alternative answers from 'never' to 'often' or 'always' (Russell, 1996; Victor et al., 2005a). In a few studies, the participants have been asked how serious a problem is loneliness to them personally (Mullins et al., 1988) or whether they suffer from loneliness, and how often (Savikko et al., 2005; Tilvis et al., 2000).

One issue of note is that the major multi-item loneliness scales often avoid mentioning the word 'loneliness' or 'lonely'. Avoidance of direct questions, the attempt to 'disguise what is being measured' (Russell, 1982: 85), has been typical in studies of mood or attitudes. The practice has been justified by the sensitivity of these questions; expressing feelings of loneliness may be socially more accepted in some situations, such as having recently been widowed, than in others (de Jong Gierveld and Van Tilburg, 1999), or for women more than for men (Perlman, 2004). Researchers have argued that only part of the loneliness experiences will be captured if socially less desirable direct questions are used.

On the other hand, given that most multi-item loneliness scales have been validated in comparison to the single global question suggests that there is no better standard to the experience of loneliness than the reports of the person her/himself. From this perspective, the ethical fairness of defining individual experiences indirectly might also be questioned. It has been argued that a direct single question presumes a common understanding of the concept of loneliness by the study participants. Yet the nature and meaning of 'loneliness' may differ between people and over time. The use of multi-item scales has been seen as a solution to this problem, with the different experiences associated with loneliness better understood by approaching the issue from different angles (de Jong Gierveld, 1998; Victor et al., 2005a). However, it can also be argued that by using preset, indirect questions, the researcher justifies his own definition of the phenomenon and its dimensions. The recognition of loneliness as a genuinely personal experience implies that there is neither a gold standard nor an exhaustive operational definition for loneliness. Seen this way, it may be difficult to cover the whole spectrum of loneliness by any restricted set of specific items (Rokach, 2000; Van Der Geest, 2004). A single-item global direct question, again, by definition accepts these multiple and contextual forms of loneliness. It reflects the 'loneliness' as understood by the respondent, not that defined by the researcher. Obviously, both global and multidimensional measures of loneliness have their own advantages and, in our view, neither can be in general preferred over another. It is worth noting, however, that notwithstanding similar results, the different measures may reflect somewhat different approaches and different understandings of the phenomenon of loneliness.

The limited qualitative research on loneliness in old age has drawn on methodological perspectives such as ethnography, in-depth and thematic interviews, and discourse analysis (Lopata, 1969; Palkeinen, 2007; van Der Geest, 2004). In his pioneering study, Tunstall (1966) combined both quantitative and qualitative approaches. Further qualitative research is needed to improve our understanding of the varying meanings, contents, and contexts of loneliness in different cultural environments.

FREQUENCY, ANTECEDENTS, AND CONSEQUENCES

Frequency of loneliness

The most accurate estimates of the frequency of loneliness come from surveys drawing upon representative samples of older populations. For countries in Northern Europe and the United States, the findings are similar, even if different questions or measures are used. In response to the single global question, 5–10 per cent of older people in different studies express feelings of loneliness 'often', and some 20–40 per cent 'at least sometimes'. The countries studied include: Sweden (Andersson, 1982; Holmen et al., 1992), Finland (Jylhä, 2004; Savikko et al., 2005), Denmark (Townsend, 1968), the United Kingdom (Townsend, 1968; Victor et al., 2009), the United States (Townsend, 1968), and the Netherlands (van Tilburg and de Jong Gierveld, 1999). Using the given cut-points of the de Jong Gierveld scale, 4 per cent of the Dutch sample was categorized as lonely or extremely lonely, and 28 per cent as moderately lonely (van Tilburg and de Jong Gierveld, 1999; de Jong Gierveld, 1999, in Peeters et al., 2005). In Southern Europe, the reported figures appear to be higher (Walker, 1993; Jylhä and Jokela, 1990, these findings are discussed below). The time trends of loneliness are hard to estimate since very few comparable data sets are available for different time points (Dykstra, 2009). In Finland, identical surveys suggest a decline in loneliness between 1994 and 2006 (Moisio and Rämö, 2007), but comparison of five UK studies since 1948 show fluctuations in the percentages of loneliness, and an increase rather than decrease in the proportion of those 'never lonely' (Victor et al., 2002, 2009).

Antecedents of loneliness

As a personal experience, loneliness cannot be completely determined by any external or internal factors. Nonetheless, it is possible to identify situations and life circumstances that reduce or jeopardize opportunities for significant social relationships and make people susceptible to feelings of loneliness. The list of conditions found to be associated with loneliness is presented in Box 24.1.

Understandably, loneliness is more common for those who spend a considerable proportion of time alone, but in a British study (Victor et al., 2005a), one-third of those who said they were alone often or always, reported never feeling lonely. Across a range of societies, older people living with a spouse report less loneliness than those living alone or with other people (Savikko et al., 2005; Tunstall, 1966). Non-married people, especially men, appear to be more lonely than those who are married (Andersson, 1998; Stack, 1998), as are widows and widowers (Savikko et al., 2005;

Box 24.1 Personal circumstances that are likely to increase vulnerability to lonelinesss

Older age

Living alone rather than with spouse

Living in an institution

Being non-marrierd: more important to men than women

Widowhood

Childlessness, or unsatisfying relationships with children

Spending much time alone, particularly if not voluntarily

No close friends or confidants

Low degree of social participation

No regular interests or hobbies

Lower social class

Poverty

Chronic disease, comorbidity

Functional disability

Problems with hearing or vision

Townsend, 1968). Older women report loneliness more than men, mainly because differential mortality between the genders produces different life situations. One study, specifically focusing on gender differences, found similar results for women and men, controlling for age, marital status, and household size (Victor et al., 2005b). Those with satisfying contacts with children seem to be less lonely than the childless (de Jong Gierveld and van Tilburg, 1999; Holmen et al., 1992; Townsend, 1968). The quantity of social contacts, as such, is less important than the extent to which they meet one's hopes and expectations (Pinquart and Sörensen, 2001; Wheeler et al., 1983). The presence of a close friend and confidante (Holmen et al., 1992; Routasalo et al., 2006), a reasonable degree of social participation, or at least some regular interest (Holmen et al., 1992; Jylhä, 2004) help to avoid loneliness. People living in institutions express more loneliness than those living in the community (Jylhä, 2004; Pinquart and Sörensen, 2001; Savikko et al., 2005). In part, this may be due to poorer health and fewer family members, compared to age peers in the community, but may also reflect breakage of long-time networks, radical change in social roles, and loss of a meaningful home environment.

Health, both mental and physical, is closely connected to loneliness in old age. The link between loneliness and depression has already been discussed. Chronic disease, poor functional

capacity, and poor self-rated health all contribute to the experience of loneliness (Jylhä, 2004; Russell, 1996; Savikko et al., 2005; Victor et al., 2005a). In a longitudinal study (Dykstra et al., 2005), increase in loneliness was concomitant with a decline in functional capacity, as was decrease in loneliness with improving functioning. In a Finnish study (Savikko et al., 2005), people who had problems with vision or hearing were three times as likely to feel lonely than people without these problems, but people who were using a hearing aid did not differ from the rest.

To a great extent, loneliness is related to societal factors such as poverty, neighbourhood deprivation, social exclusion, and degrading social welfare systems (Butterworth et al., 2006; Lauder et al., 2006; Murray et al., 2006; Scharf and de Jong Gierveld, 2008). Accumulating evidence shows that older people with poorer education, lower socio-economic group, and limited financial resources, who are also known to have poorer health, less stable families, smaller social networks, and poorer possibilities for social participation, are more likely to experience loneliness. Direct and indirect evidence indicates that increasing age segregation, negative images of old age, and the position of the 'other' given to old people in present societies create the conditions for loneliness (Hagestad and Uhlenberg, 2005). For many people, low social position and old age together lead to cumulative disadvantage and marginalization (Dannefer, 2003). This is characteristic of industrialized Western countries and developing countries (Pinquart and Sörensen, 2001; Savikko et al., 2005; Seabrook, 2003; Andrews et al., 1986). In a Finnish study, older people, when asked about loneliness, referred to factors such as insecurity, inadequate health and social services, and public images of old people as a burden to others rather than useful members of society (Palkeinen, 2007).

In real life, the factors described above do not influence older peoples' lives as distinct variables; they should not be interpreted as mechanical 'causes' of loneliness, nor are they independent from each other. All the 'risk factors' play their role as inseparable parts of a unique totality of a life course that has its own history and direction. They may modify the life circumstances of an individual, or the way in which he or she interprets these circumstances – in different lives and in different contexts, 'risk factors' can have different roles.

Does loneliness increase with ageing?

To gerontologists, the relation of age with loneliness is crucial. Do older people experience greater loneliness as compared with younger people at a given point of time? If the answer is yes, does it really mean that loneliness increases with advanced age? The results of studies on loneliness and age have varied. Tornstam (1988), for example, in a Swedish study found loneliness was more frequent in adolescence and young people as compared with older people. However, representative population studies from different countries have demonstrated that older people report more loneliness than the middle-aged, and the very old more than the young-old (Andrews et al., 1986; de Jong Gierveld and van Tilburg, 1999; Heikkinen et al., 1983; Jylhä and Jokela, 1990; Savikko et al., 2005). A few longitudinal studies have followed changes in loneliness with increasing age. One of these (Holmen and Furukawa, 2002) reported a decrease, but others (Dykstra et al., 2005; Jylhä, 2004; Wenger and Burholt, 2004) found increasing feelings of loneliness experienced over periods of between 10 and 20 years. This increase can largely be understood on the basis of the negative changes people experience in late-old age, such as decreasing functional capacity, increasing dependence, and death of a spouse. The studies also show that for many, feelings of loneliness are temporary, and may be reduced by improved health and expanding social networks (Dykstra et al., 2005; Jylhä, 2004).

Health consequences of loneliness

The association of weak social ties with poor health and mortality, and particularly with cardiovascular disease, has been demonstrated in numerous epidemiological studies (Andersson, 1998; Berkman and Syme, 1979; House et al., 1988; Sorkin et al., 2002). Only a few studies have focused on the consequences of loneliness, and many studies do not make a clear distinction between the quantity of social contacts and loneliness as a personal experience.

It is unclear why and how deficient social relationships, including experiences of loneliness (Penninx et al., 1997), increase the risk of death. Researchers have suggested that limited resources, problems coping with chronic disease, and less support by other people towards better health practices, as possible pathways to ill health. Moreover, it seems that loneliness, through psychobiological mediations, has adverse effects on neuroendocrine and immunological systems (Loucks et al., 2006; Steptoe et al., 2004). Factors such as inflammatory markers and biological response to stress may be particularly important mediators in the association of social networks

and cardiovascular disease (Loucks et al., 2006). Cacioppo et al. (2002) have demonstrated that stress causes a greater increase in resistance to blood flow in lonely people compared to the non-lonely.

Recent empirical studies suggest that weak social networks and experiences of loneliness are significant predictors of cognitive decline and Alzheimer's disease (Fratiglioni et al., 2000; Tilvis et al., 2004; Wilson et al., 2007). The interpretation of these results and the possible causal pathways are unclear, but a strong hypothesis is that an active and socially integrated lifestyle can protect against dementia (Fratiglioni et al., 2004).

There is some evidence to suggest that people who feel lonely may seek medical care more frequently than others at the same level of health. In a British sample (Ellaway et al., 1999), loneliness was associated with high rates of consultation with primary care doctors, and in a US study (Russell et al., 1997) it increased the likelihood of nursing home admission and decreased the time until admission.

AGEING AND LONELINESS IN DIFFERENT CULTURES

Although personal, loneliness is not a purely individual phenomenon but embedded in given forms of social organization and cultural fabrics. Therefore, cross-cultural comparisons are challenging. If the system of social organization varies between countries, does it not imply that the feelings associated with loneliness might also vary? To what extent do questions of loneliness and their multiple meanings translate from one language and culture to another? In fact, not all languages have an exact equivalent to the word 'loneliness' but use concepts that refer to the experience of being alone (Jylhä and Jokela, 1990; Van Der Geest, 2004). The researcher should be vigilant about possible qualitative differences in the meanings and contexts of loneliness between cultures.

Research on loneliness and ageing has been focused on Northern Europe, the United Kingdom, and the United States, with studies from other countries fewer in number and scope (examples are Chalise et al., 2007; Sheykhi, 2006; Stack, 1998; Steed et al., 2007; Wilson et al., 1992). However, loneliness is not a homogeneous phenomenon, even in Europe. The classic comparative study by Townsend (1968) found varying rates of prevalence, with the lowest in Denmark, the middle in the United Kingdom, and the highest in the United States, although the differences were rather small. Three major surveys have compared the frequency of loneliness across Europe and both found a clear and systematic increasing gradient in feelings of loneliness from North to South. In the Eurobarometer, a survey conducted by the EU, the per cent of those feeling lonely 'often' was lowest in Denmark (5 per cent), followed by Germany and the Netherlands (7–9 per cent), and highest in Portugal (23 per cent) and Greece (36 per cent) (Reif and Melich, 1992; see also Andersson, 1998; Walker, 1993). In the Eleven Countries Study, a European survey coordinated by the World Health Organization (WHO), the results varied by age and gender, but, in total, loneliness was least frequent in Finland, Belgium, and Berlin and most frequent in Yugoslavia, Italy, and Greece (Heikkinen et al., 1983). The geographic loneliness gradient was exactly opposite to the gradient of living alone; reported loneliness was lowest where living alone was most frequent, and highest where living alone was rare (Jylhä and Jokela, 1990). In every area, feelings of loneliness were more frequent for those who lived alone than those who lived with someone, but the North–South gradient in feelings of loneliness existed in both groups. The people living with others in Greece reported more loneliness than those living alone in Finland. None of living circumstances, marital status, or functional capacity explained the differences in loneliness between these two countries at the opposite ends of the loneliness gradient. A clear North-South gradient was observed also in the SHARE project (Sundström et al., 2009).

Similarly, de Jong Gierveld and van Tilburg (1999) found that older people in Italy generally reported more loneliness than older people in the Netherlands. Poor health contributed to loneliness in both countries, but other factors associated with loneliness differed between the countries: in the Netherlands, loneliness was also associated by the absence of a partner and small social networks, and, in Italy, with socioeconomic dependence and living alone.

In Asia, the percentage of older people who reported being lonely 'often' also appears to vary substantially across countries. Examples include: 7 per cent in the Philippines, 10 per cent in Malaysia, 22 per cent in the Republic of Korea, and 24 per cent in Fiji (Andrews et al., 1986: 46). In each of these countries, loneliness was associated with older age, being non-married, not working, insufficient contact with family and friends, having insufficient money, not being a professional or white-collar worker, having poor self-rated health, and having difficulty in activities of daily living. These factors did not, however, explain the differences between the countries. Cultural patterns of loneliness have been explained by variations in the predominant cultural values that shape both personalities and the forms of social relationships.

Johnson and Mullins (1987) use the concept of loneliness threshold to suggest that in different societies, different levels of social relationships are needed to avoid loneliness. Where more individualistic values prevail, old people might emphasize independence and be happy with less contact than in more collectivistic societies. In contrast, in a society with strong collectivistic or familistic values, the loneliness threshold would be lower, and older people would need more social contacts and interaction to avoid feelings of loneliness. Loneliness, of course, exists in both types of society. In a more individualistic society, pursuing individual goals may result in a deficiency of intimate relationships during earlier adulthood, and, thus, increase the risk of loneliness in old age when creating new relationships is more difficult. In the more collectivistic societies, again, older people may be more tightly knit into primary group networks, but the high expectations for social interaction still may not be met (Johnson and Mullins, 1987). Moreover, 'feeling lonely' is likely to have different implications, depending on the cultural environment. In a culture that demands independence and stigmatizes loneliness, old people may be less inclined to define themselves as 'lonely' than in a more familistic culture where expressions of loneliness may serve as an appeal to family and friends.

This framework may help us to understand the 'loneliness gradient' in Europe (de Jong Gierveld and van Tilburg, 1999; Jylhä and Jokela, 1990; Reif and Melich, 1992). In Northern Europe, independence is highly valued and is supported by the welfare state. Typically, old people prefer to live either with their spouse or alone, not with their children. Independent living in old age is considered as beneficial to good relations between the generations, not as a sign of tensions between them. In the European comparison by Jylhä and Jokela (1990), Finland was taken as representative of the North European system, while Greece represented a familistic society. In Greece, living alone was rare: 4 out of 10 older people in the study lived with their children, and mutual dependence was strong. However, eroding family systems and the movement of younger people from rural into urban areas made older people susceptible to feelings of loneliness because their situation no longer accorded with cultural expectations.

In recent decades, 'familistic' societies in Africa, Asia, and Latin America have experienced major transformations in the patterns of family life and social relations. The position of old people changes rapidly in societies where old age traditionally has been respected. With urbanization and migration accompanying globalization, families are dispersed to other continents, old values are eroded, and where they still remain, they are not actualized in real life (Van Der Geest, 2004). This often leads to extreme poverty and loss of social protection, in addition to social isolation and loss of meaningful roles for old people, both those who live their old age in a new land and those who are left behind (Seabrook, 2003). An experience of deprivation and emptiness results, particularly when, in official rhetoric, old people are still presented as a valuable source of wisdom and tradition, yet the younger generation is not interested in their advice. In rural Ghana, says Van Der Geest (2004), the problem is not so much the absence of 'someone I can talk to about my day to day problems', as goes the first statement in the de Jong Gierveld scale, but rather the absence of someone who comes *to me* to talk about his/her day-to-day problems.

INTERVENTIONS AND PREVENTION

A variety of interventions have been implemented to alleviate loneliness, but it remains questionable how and how well they work. It is not clear, either, whether this ambiguity reflects the multiple faces and aetiologies of loneliness more than the difficulties in designing and carrying out intervention studies in this field – for systematic reviews, see Findlay (2003) and Cattan et al. (2005).

Intervention research covers qualitative as well as quantitative studies, including some randomized controlled trials. One-to-one interventions have included cognitive-behavioural therapy sessions (Jones, 1982), home help (Clarke et al., 1992), and telephone contacts. Group interventions have used approaches such as peer discussions, group exercise (Hopman-Rock and Westhoff, 2002; McAuley et al., 2000), visual arts (Wikström, 2002), and pet therapy (Banks and Banks, 2002). Examples of randomized group interventions are provided by Andersson (1984), Pitkälä et al. (2009), and Routasalo et al. (2009). In Sweden, the intervention consisted of group discussions. The results were positive for those who continued the treatment, but there were many refusals and drop-outs during the programme (Andersson, 1984, 1985). In Finland, (Pitkälä et al., 2009; Routasalo et al., 2009) the participants could choose a group that focused on physical exercise, on arts and creative stimulation, or on psychotherapy and therapeutic writing. As a result, not only did the participants' health and quality of life improve but also they

used fewer health services than the control group. To prevent drop-outs, participants were offered transportation to the day centre and group facilitators were trained and supervised to pay attention to group dynamics. Consequently, the participants were highly committed, and 40 per cent of the groups continued their meetings several months after the intervention.

The most obvious conclusion from the existing research on interventions is that it is very difficult to reach reliable results. Many studies have not been evaluated in an appropriate way. The selection of outcomes may be problematic as there is no knowledge about the sensitivity of loneliness measures to change. A typical problem has been selection effects deriving from refusals and withdrawals (Andersson, 1984, 1985), and lack of comparability between study groups. In most studies, the follow-up times are short, and even if an effect has been reached, this disappears over time (McAuley et al., 2000). Thus, no single proven method of intervention against loneliness is generally preferred. Still, the most successful interventions seem to share some characteristics: they have made use of group methods and participatory orientation (Cattan et al., 2005; Findlay, 2003; Pitkälä et al., 2009; Routasalo et al., 2009). A combination of psychological, social, and environmental focus enables the creation of a 'toolbox' that allows individual tailoring of the intervention.

Instead of focusing on individuals directly, environments or even societal practices can also be targeted. Rook (1984) has suggested three types of environmental interventions: first, network building can help create new contacts when existing opportunities are limited; secondly, social settings can be restructured and designed in a way that facilitates contact; thirdly, measures such as offering transportation or giving practical help to informal caregivers can remove obstacles to social contacts. Even if it is not possible to totally eliminate loneliness, all the societal measures that support welfare, social protection, equality, and full social participation of older people are likely to reduce loneliness and the suffering it causes.

CONCLUSIONS

Loneliness as a personal, emotional experience is related to but not determined by deficient social relationships. In different periods of time and different cultures, loneliness is likely to have somewhat different causes and contents. The present Western culture includes elements that contribute to loneliness in old age, such as preference for nuclear families, individualism, and the tendency to discriminate against old people. Empirical research indicates that old people express loneliness more in societies where traditional familistic values are in conflict with individualistic life practices. In fact, a majority of older people do not report suffering from loneliness in any society.

However, for those who are lonely, it may be a painful and highly negative experience. The results of interventions vary, and are difficult to capture by using traditional experiments or randomized trials. On the societal level, it is likely that loneliness in old age could be diminished by preventing discrimination, promoting age integration and other opportunities for social engagement, and improving care for older people – especially those in late-old age. In terms of analyzing causes and solutions, again, insights from classical sociology are highly relevant. The anonymity and depersonalization, migration and transience typical of experience in modern life, and the rise of secondary relationships replacing primary ones, are important macro-level causes that need proper acknowledgement in developing affecting responses to the issue of loneliness across different societies.

REFERENCES

Adams, K.B., Sanders, S., and Auth, E.A. (2004) 'Loneliness and depression in independent living retirement communities: risk and resilience factors', *Aging and Mental Health*, 8(6): 475–85.

Andersson (1982) 'Inter-disciplinary study of loneliness – with evaluation of social contacts as a means towards improving competence in old age', *Acta Sociologica*, 25: 75–80.

Andersson, L. (1984) 'Intervention against loneliness in a group of elderly women: a process evaluation', *Human Relations*, 37(4): 295–310.

Andersson, L. (1985) 'Intervention against loneliness in a group of elderly women: an impact evaluation', *Social Science and Medicine*, 20(4): 355–64.

Andersson, L. (1990) 'Narcissism and loneliness', *International Journal of Aging and Human Development*, 30(2): 81–94.

Andersson, L. (1998) 'Loneliness research and interventions: a review of the literature', *Aging and Mental Health*, 2(4): 264–74.

Andrews, G.R., Esterman, A.J., Braunack-Mayer, A.J., and Rungie, C.M. (1986) *Ageing in the Western Pacific*. Manila: World Health Organization, Regional Office for Western Pacific.

Banks, M.R. and Banks, W.A. (2002) 'The effects of animal-assisted therapy on loneliness in an elderly population in long-term care facilities', *Journals of Gerontology Series A: Biological Sciences and Medical Sciences*, 57(7): M428–32.

Barg, F.K., Huss-Ashmore, R., Wittink, M.N., et al. (2006) 'A mixed-methods approach to understanding loneliness and depression in older adults', *Journals of Gerontology Series B: Psychological Sciences and Social Sciences*, 61(6): S329–39.

Berkman, L.F. and Syme, S.L. (1979) 'Social networks, host resistance, and mortality: a nine-year follow-up study of Alameda County residents', *American Journal of Epidemiology*, 109(2): 186–204.

Butterworth, P., Fairweather, A.K., Anstey, K.J., and Windsor, T.D. (2006) 'Hopelessness, demoralization and suicidal behaviour: the backdrop to welfare reform in Australia', *Australian and New Zealand Journal of Psychiatry*, 40(8): 648–56.

Cacioppo, J.T., Hawkley, L.C., Crawford, L.E., et al. (2002) 'Loneliness and health: potential mechanisms', *Psychosomatic Medicine*, 64(3): 407–17.

Carstensen, L.L., Isaacowitz, D.M., and Charles, S.T. (1999) 'Taking time seriously: a theory of socioemotional selectivity', *American Psychologist*, 54(3): 165–81.

Cattan, M., White, M., Bond, J., and Learmouth, A. (2005) 'Preventing social isolation and loneliness among older people: a systematic review of health promotion interventions', *Ageing and Society*, 25: 41–67.

Chalise, H., Saito, T., Takahashi, M., and Kai, I. (2007) 'Relationship specialization amongst sources and receivers of social support and its correlation with loneliness and subjective well-being: a cross-sectional study of Nepalese older adults. *Archives of Gerontology and Geriatrics*, 44: 299–314.

Clarke, M., Clarke, S.J., and Jagger, C. (1992) 'Social intervention and the elderly: a randomized controlled trial', *American Journal of Epidemiology*, 136(12): 1517–23.

Cohen-Mansfield, J. and Parpura-Gill, A. (2007) 'Loneliness in older persons: a theoretical model and empirical findings', *International Psychogeriatrics*, 19(2): 279–94.

Costa, P.T., Jr. and McCrae, R.R. (1987) 'Neuroticism, somatic complaints, and disease: Is the bark worse than the bite?', *Journal of Personality*, 55(2): 299–316.

Cumming, E. and Henry, W.E. (1961) *Growing Old: The Process of Disengagement*. New York: Basic Books.

Dannefer, D. (1984) 'Adult development and social theory: a paradigmatic reappraisal', *American Sociological Review*, 49: 100–16.

Dannefer, D. (2003) 'Cumulate advantage/disadvantage and the life course: cross-fertilizing age and social science theory', *Journal of Gerontology: Social Sciences*, 58: S327–37.

de Jong Gierveld, J. (1998) 'A review of loneliness: concept, definitions, determinants and consequences', *Reviews in Clinical Gerontology*, 8: 73–80.

de Jong Gierveld, J. and Havens, B. (2004) 'Cross-national comparisons of social isolation and loneliness: introduction and overview', *Canadian Journal on Aging (La Revue Canadienne du Vieillissement)*, 23(2): 109–13.

de Jong Gierveld, J. and Kamphuis, F. (1985) 'The development of a Rasch-type loneliness scale', *Applied Psychological Measurement*, 9(3): 289–99.

de Jong Gierveld, J. and van Tilburg, T. (1999) 'Living arrangements of older adults in the Netherlands and Italy: coresidence values and behaviour and their consequences for loneliness', *Journal of Cross-Cultural Gerontology*, 14(1): 1–24.

de Jong Gierveld, J. and van Tilburg, T. (2006) 'A 6-item scale for overall, emotional, and social loneliness – confirmatory tests on survey data', *Research on Aging*, 28(5): 582–98.

de Jong-Gierveld, J., Kamphuis, F., and Dykstra, P. (1987) 'Old and lonely?', *Comprehensive Gerontology. Section B, Behavioural, Social and Applied Sciences*, 1(1): 13–17.

Dykstra, P.A. (2009) 'Older adult loneliness: myths and realities', *European Journal of Ageing*, 6(2): 91–100.

Dykstra, P.A., van Tilburg, T.G., and Gierveld, J.D. (2005) 'Changes in older adult loneliness – results from a seven-year longitudinal study', *Research on Aging*, 27(6): 725–47.

Elias, N. (1985) *The Loneliness of the Dying*. Oxford: Blackwell.

Ellaway, A., Wood, S., and Macintyre, S. (1999) 'Someone to talk to? The role of loneliness as a factor in the frequency of GP consultations', *British Journal of General Practice*, 49(442): 363–7.

Erikson, E.H. (1959) *Identity and the Life Cycle*. New York: International Universities Press.

Findlay, R.A. (2003) 'Interventions to reduce social isolation amongst older people: where is the evidence?', *Ageing and Society*, 23: 647–58.

Fratiglioni, L., Paillard-Borg, S., and Winblad, B. (2004) 'An active and socially integrated lifestyle in late life might protect against dementia', *Lancet Neurology*, 3(6): 343–53.

Fratiglioni, L., Wang, H.X., Ericsson, K., Maytan, M., and Winblad, B. (2000) 'Influence of social network on occurrence of dementia: a community-based longitudinal study', *Lancet*, 355(9212): 1315–19.

Hagestad, G.O. and Uhlenberg, P. (2005) 'The social separation of old and young: a root of ageism', *Journal of Social Issues*, 61(2): 343–60.

Hawkley, L.C., Masi, C.M., Berry, J.D., and Cacioppo, J.T. (2006) 'Loneliness is a unique predictor of age-related differences in systolic blood pressure', *Psychology and Aging*, 21(1):152–64.

Heikkinen, R.L. and Kauppinen, M. (2004) 'Depressive symptoms in late life: a 10-year follow-up', *Archives of Gerontology and Geriatrics*, 38(3): 239–50.

Heikkinen, E., Waters, E., and Brzezinski, Z.J. (eds) (1983) *The Elderly in Eleven Countries: A Sociomedical Study*. Copenhagen: World Health Organization, Regional Office for Europe.

Hochschild, A. (1975) 'Disengagement theory: a critique and a proposal', *American Sociological Review*, 40: 553–69.

Holmen, K. and Furukawa, H. (2002) 'Loneliness, health and social networks among elderly people – a follow-up study', *Archives of Gerontology and Geriatrics*, 35(3): 261–74.

Holmen, K., Ericsson, K., Andersson, L., and Winblad, B. (1992) 'Loneliness among elderly people living in Stockholm: a population study', *Journal of Advanced Nursing*, 17(1): 43–51.

Hopman-Rock, M., and Westhoff, M.H. (2002) 'Gezondheidsvoorlichting en bewegingsstimulering voor ouderen: ontwikkeling en evaluatie van het programma "Gezond and Vitaal"' ['Health education and exercise stimulation for older people: development and evaluation of the program "healthy and vital"'], *Tijdschrift Voor Gerontologie En Geriatrie*, 33(2): 56–63.

House, J.S., Landis, K.R., and Umberson, D. (1988) 'Social relationships and health', *Science*, 241(4865): 540–5.

Johnson, D.P. and Mullins, L.C. (1987) 'Growing old and lonely in different societies: toward a comparative perspective', *Journal of Cross-Cultural Gerontology*, 2(3): 257–75.

Jones, W. (1982) 'Loneliness and social behaviour', In L.A. Peplau and D. Perlman (eds), *Loneliness: A Sourcebook of Current Theory, Research and Therapy*. New York: John Wiley, pp. 238–54.

Jylhä, M. (2004) 'Old age and loneliness: cross-sectional and longitudinal analyses in the Tampere Longitudinal Study on Aging', *Canadian Journal on Aging (La Revue Canadienne du Vieillissement)*, 23(2): 157–68.

Jylhä, M. and Jokela, J. (1990) 'Individual experiences as cultural – a cross-cultural study on loneliness among the elderly', *Ageing and Society*, 10(3): 295–315.

Lauder, W., Mummery, K., and Sharkey, S. (2006) 'Social capital, age and religiosity in people who are lonely', *Journal of Clinical Nursing*, 15(3): 334–40.

Lebret, S., Perret-Vaille, E., Mulliez, A., Gerbaud, L., and Jalenques, I. (2006) 'Elderly suicide attempters: characteristics and outcome', *International Journal of Geriatric Psychiatry*, 21(11): 1052–9.

Lopata, H. (1969) 'Loneliness: forms and components', *Social Problems*, 17(2): 248–61.

Loucks, E.B., Sullivan, L.M., D'Agostino R.B., et al. (2006) 'Social networks and inflammatory markers in the Framingham Heart Study', *Journal of Biosocial Science*, 38(6): 835–42.

McAuley, E., Blissmer, B., Marquez, D.X., et al. (2000) 'Social relations, physical activity, and well-being in older adults', *Preventive Medicine*, 31(5): 608–17.

Moisio, P. and Rämö, T. (2007) 'Koettu yksinäisyys demografisten ja sosioekonomisten taustatekijöiden mukaan Suomessa vuosina 1994 ja 2006', *Yhteiskuntapolitiikka*, 72(4): 392–401.

Moustakas, C.E. (1972) *Loneliness and Love*. Englewood-Cliffs, NJ: Prentice-Hall.

Mullins, L.C., Sheppard, H.L., and Andersson, L. (1988) 'A study of loneliness among a national sample of Swedish elderly', *Comprehensive Gerontology. Section B, Behavioural, Social, and Applied Sciences*, 2(1): 36–43.

Murray, J., Banerjee, S., Byng, R., et al. (2006) 'Primary care professionals' perceptions of depression in older people: a qualitative study', *Social Science and Medicine*, 63(5): 1363–73.

Palkeinen, H. (2007) 'Yksinäisyys ja vanhuus – erottamaton parivaljakko?', *Janus*, 15(2): 104–7.

Peeters, A., Bouwman, B., and Knipscheer, K. (2005) 'The Netherlands: quality of life in old age II', in A. Walker (ed.),

Growing older in Europe. Maidenhead: Open University Press, pp. 201–18.

Penninx, B.W., van Tilburg, T., Kriegsman, D.M., et al. (1997) 'Effects of social support and personal coping resources on mortality in older age: the Longitudinal Aging Study Amsterdam', *American Journal of Epidemiology*, 146(6): 510–19.

Peplau, L.A. and Perlman, D. (eds) (1982a) *Loneliness. A Sourcebook of Current Theory, Research and Therapy*. New York: John Wiley.

Peplau, L.A. and Perlman, D. (1982b) 'Perspectives on loneliness', in L.A. Peplau and D. Perlman (eds), *Loneliness: A Sourcebook of Current Theory, Research and Therapy*. New York: John Wiley, pp. 1–18.

Perlman, D. (2004) 'European and Canadian studies of loneliness among seniors', *Canadian Journal on Aging (La Revue canadienne du vieillissement)*, 23(2): 181–8.

Perlman, D. and Peplau, L.A. (1998) 'Loneliness', in H. Friedman (ed.), *Encyclopedia of Mental Health*. San Diego, CA: Academic Press. pp. 571–81.

Pinquart, M. and Sörensen, S. (2001) 'Influences on loneliness in older adults: a meta-analysis' *Basic and Applied Social Psychology*, 23(4): 245–66.

Pitkälä, K., Routasalo, P., Kautiainen, H., and Tilvis, R.S. (2009) 'Effects of psychosocial group rehabilitation on health, use of health care services, and mortality in older persons suffering from loneliness: a randomized, controlled trial', *Journal of Gerontology Medical Sciences*, 64(7): 792–800.

Reif, K. and Melich, A. (1992) *Eurobarometer 32:2: Elderly Europeans*, 2nd edn. Brussels: INRA.

Rokach, A. (2000) 'Loneliness and the life cycle', *Psychological Reports*, 86(2): 629–42.

Rook, K.S. (1984) 'Promoting social bonding: strategies for helping the lonely and socially isolated', *American Psychologist*, 39(12): 1389–407.

Routasalo, P.E., Savikko, N., Tilvis, R.S., Strandberg, T.E., and Pitkala, K.H. (2006) 'Social contacts and their relationship to loneliness among aged people – a population-based study', *Gerontology*, 52(3): 181–7.

Routasalo, P.E., Tilvis, R.S., Kautiainen, H., and Pitkälä, K.H. (2009) 'Effects of psychosocial group rehabilitation on social functioning, loneliness and well-being of lonely, older people; randomized controlled trial, *Journal of Advanced Nursing*, 65(2): 297–305.

Russell, D. (1982) 'The measurement of loneliness', in L.A. Peplau and D. Perlman (eds), *Loneliness: A Sourcebook of Current Theory, Research and Therapy*. New York: John Wiley, pp. 81–104.

Russell, D.W. (1996) 'UCLA loneliness scale (version 3): reliability, validity, and factor structure', *Journal of Personality Assessment*, 66(1): 20–40.

Russell, D.W., Cutrona, C.E., de la Mora, A., and Wallace, R.B. (1997) 'Loneliness and nursing home admission among rural older adults', *Psychology and Aging*, 12(4): 574–89.

Savikko, N., Routasalo, P., Tilvis, R.S., Strandberg, T.E., and Pitkala, K.H. (2005) 'Predictors and subjective causes of loneliness in an aged population', *Archives of Gerontology and Geriatrics*, 41(3): 223–33.

Scharf, T. and de Jong Gierveld, J. (2008) 'Loneliness in urban neighbourhoods: an Anglo-Dutch comparison', *European Journal of Gerontology*, 5: 103–15.

Seabrook, J. (2003) *A World Growing Old*. Sterling, VA: Pluto Press.

Sheykhi, M.T. (2006) 'The elderly and family change in Asia with a focus in Iran: a sociological assessment', *Journal of Comparative Family Studies*, 37(4), 583–8.

Sorkin, D., Rook, K.S., and Lu, J.L. (2002) 'Loneliness, lack of emotional support, lack of companionship, and the likelihood of having a heart condition in an elderly sample', *Annals of Behavioral Medicine*, 24(4): 290–8.

Stack, S. (1998) 'Marriage, family and loneliness: a cross-national study', *Sociological Perspectives*, 41(2): 415–32.

Steed, L., Boldy, D., Grenade, L., and Iredell, H. (2007) 'The demographics of loneliness among older people in Perth, Western Australia', *Australasian Journal on Ageing*, 26(2): 81–6.

Stek, M.L., Gussekloo, J., Beekman, A.T., van Tilburg, W., and Westendorp, R.G. (2004) 'Prevalence, correlates and recognition of depression in the oldest old: the Leiden 85-plus study', *Journal of Affective Disorders*, 78(3): 193–200.

Steptoe, A., Owen, N., Kunz-Ebrecht, S.R., and Brydon, L. (2004) 'Loneliness and neuroendocrine, cardiovascular, and inflammatory stress responses in middle-aged men and women', *Psychoneuroendocrinology*, 29(5): 593–611.

Sundström, G., Fransson, E., Malmberg, B., and Davey, A. (2009) 'Loneliness among older Europeans', *European Journal of Ageing*, 6(4): 267–75.

Tiikkainen, P. and Heikkinen, R.L. (2005) 'Associations between loneliness, depressive symptoms and perceived togetherness in older people', *Aging and Mental Health*, 9(6): 526–34.

Tilvis, R.S., Pitkala, K. H., Jolkkonen, J., and Strandberg, T. E. (2000) 'Social networks and dementia', *Lancet*, 356(9223): 77–8.

Tilvis, R.S., Kahonen-Vare, M.H., Jolkkonen, J., et al. (2004) 'Predictors of cognitive decline and mortality of aged people over a 10-year period', *Journals of Gerontology. Series A, Biological Sciences and Medical Sciences*, 59(3): 268–74.

Tornstam, L. (1988) *Ensamhetens ansikten. en studies av ensamhetsupplevelser hos svenskar 15–80 år. arbetsrapport 29*. Uppsala: Projektet Äldre i Samhället – förr, ny och i framtiden.

Tornstam, L. (2005) *Gerotranscendence: A Developmental Theory of Positive Aging*. New York: Springer.

Townsend, P. (1968) 'Isolation, desolation, and loneliness', in E. Shanas, P. Townsend, D. Wedderburn, et al. (eds), *Old People in Three Industrial Societies*. London: Routledge and Kegan Paul, pp. 258–87.

Tunstall, J. (1966) *Old and Alone. A Sociological Study of Old People*. London: Routledge and Kegan Paul.

Van Baarsen, B., Snijders, T., Smit, J.H., and Van Duijn, M. (2001) 'Lonely but not alone: emotional isolation and social isolation as two distinct dimensions of loneliness in older people', *Educational and Psychological Measurement*, 61(11): 119–35.

Van Der Geest, S. (2004) '"They don't come to listen": the experience of loneliness among older people in Kwahu, Ghana', *Journal of Cross-Cultural Gerontology*, 19(2): 77–96.

van Tilburg, T.G. and de Jong Gierveld, J. (1999) 'Cesuurbepaling van de eenzaamheidsschaal' ['Reference standards for the loneliness scale'], *Tijdschrift Voor Gerontologie En Geriatrie*, 30(4): 158–63.

van Tilburg, T., Havens, B., and de Jong Gierveld, J. (2004) 'Loneliness among older adults in the Netherlands, Italy, and Canada: a multifaceted comparison', *Canadian Journal on Aging (La Revue Canadienne du Vieillissement)*, 23(2): 169–80.

Victor, C.R., Scrambler, S., and Bond, J. (2009) *The Social World of Older People: Loneliness and Social Isolation in Later Life*. Buckingham: Open University Press.

Victor, C.R., Scambler, S., Bowling, A., and Bond, J. (2005a) 'The prevalence of and risk factors for, loneliness in later life: a survey of older people in Great Britain', *Ageing and Society*, 25: 357–75.

Victor, C.R., Scambler, S.J., Marston, L., Bond, J., and Bowling, A. (2005b) 'Older people's experiences of loneliness in the UK: Does gender matter?', *Social Policy and Society*, 5(1): 27–38.

Victor, C.R., Scambler, S.J., Shah, S., et al. (2002) 'Has loneliness amongst older people increased? An investigation into variations between cohorts', *Ageing and Society*, 22: 585–97.

Vitkus, J. and Horowitz, L.M. (1987) 'Poor social performance of lonely people: lacking a skill or adopting a role?', *Journal of Personality and Social Psychology*, 52(6): 1266–73.

Walker, A. (1993) *Age and Attitudes: Main Results from a Eurobarometer Survey*. Brussels: Commission of the European Communities.

Watson, D. and Pennebaker, J.W. (1989) 'Health complaints, stress, and distress: exploring the central role of negative affectivity', *Psychological Review*, 96(2): 234–54.

Weiss, R. R. (1973) *Loneliness: The Experience of Emotional and Social Isolation*. Cambridge, MA: MIT Press.

Wenger, G.C. (1983) 'Loneliness: a problem of measurement', in D. Jerrome (ed.), *Ageing in Modern Society*. London: Croom-Helm, pp. 388–94.

Wenger, G.C. and Burholt, V. (2004) 'Changes in levels of social isolation and loneliness among older people in a rural area: a twenty-year longitudinal study', *Canadian Journal on Aging (La Revue Canadienne du Vieillissement)*, 23(2): 115–27.

Wenger, G.C., Davies, R., Shahtahmasebi, S., and Scott, A. (1996) 'Social isolation and loneliness in old age: review and model refinement', *Ageing and Society*, 16(3): 333–58.

Wheeler, L., Reis, H., and Nezlek, J. (1983) 'Loneliness, social interaction and sex roles', *Journal of Personality and Social Psychology*, 45: 943–53.

Wikström, B. (2002) 'Social interaction associated with visual art discussions: a controlled intervention study', *Aging and Mental Health*, 6(1): 82–7.

Wilson, D., Cutts, J., Lees, I., Mapungwana, S., and Maunganidze, L. (1992) 'Psychometric properties of the revised UCLA loneliness scale and two short-form measures of loneliness in Zimbabwe', *Journal of Personality Assessment*, 59(1): 72–81.

Wilson, R.S., Krueger, K.R., Arnold, S.E., et al. (2007) 'Loneliness and risk of Alzheimer disease', *Archives of General Psychiatry*, 64(2): 234–40.

25

Biosocial Interactions in the Construction of Late-life Health Status

Kathryn Z. Douthit and Andre Marquis

POSITIONING BIOSOCIAL RESEARCH

In the last century, disciplinary boundaries separating the social and biomedical sciences have simultaneously been the purveyor of sweeping technological advances and an encumbrance and barrier to understanding the possibilities for inter-disciplinary knowledge exploration. This chapter attempts to help the reader dismantle persistent notions that compartmentalize knowledge in the social and biological sciences in order to highlight important advances in our understanding of how physical health is linked to the health of our local and global communities. Although a post-disciplinary lens bears relevance across the life course, the story it reveals in the study of ageing and old age is particularly compelling in that it underscores the cumulative impact of a lifetime of stratified experiences on human bodies, bringing into sharp focus issues of justice, compassion, and collective responsibility for segments of the population facing a lifetime of structurally mediated challenges.

Four central principles will guide our consideration of biosocial interactions. First, the human body and the social universe created by human activity are inextricably and reciprocally united in form and function. While Western imagination can easily grasp how humans work to weave the complexities of social fabric, to see how that social fabric in turn configures the molecular mechanisms of sickness and health is less accessible to the Western eye. In a stealthy process, occurring far beyond the realms of conscious awareness, the social order dictates neurophysiological, endocrinological, immunological, and cardiovascular health in addition to various other dimensions of human development.

Secondly, due to the interdependent nature of human biological and social functioning, the bodies of elders can be viewed metaphorically as living time capsules representing tangible lifelong accumulations of social and cultural artifacts. Unlike the often trivial and non-essential nature of time-capsule artifacts, the flesh and blood artifacts amassed through distributive social forces can directly impact human life in profound ways. 'Social physiology' can configure the workings of human physiology to create states of health or disease, sanity or 'insanity', ability or 'disability', and ultimately joy or sorrow. A sizable body of literature currently exists that describes the various social, psychological, and biological outcomes of what has been termed cumulative advantage and disadvantage (CAD) (Dannefer, 2003; Douthit and Dannefer, 2007). This literature underscores the notion that repetitive cycles exist over time in which social advantages set the stage for subsequent successes, which in turn create a substrate favoring an ever-expanding pattern of success, opportunity, and healthy human development. Likewise, social disadvantages are amplified over time such that conditions of poor health and other hardships accumulate through cyclical reproductive processes.

Thirdly, an ethical imperative emerges from a post-disciplinary understanding of the biosocial organism. Social advantages and disadvantages, both material and non-material, are precursors of life and death. Social environments, as sources of sustenance or harm, thus become legitimate targets for public health initiatives and a central focus of intervention informed by principles of justice and care. Particularly for those citizens who are among the most marginalized, notably including the poor and older people, disregard for noxious social arrangements often results in painful late-life battles with morbidity, mortality, and psychological pain (Newman, 2006).

Fourthly, biosocial phenomena are not exclusively biosocial (Bertalanffy, 1968; Dannefer, 1999; Parsons, 1978; Wilber, 1995). Just as disciplinary boundaries have impeded the study of biosocial phenomena, these same boundaries have veiled the complex ecology of mechanisms that mediate the imprint of social experience onto human physiology. While the range of physiological expression is constrained by the physical limitations of the human body, the ways in which social phenomena are processed is profoundly idiographic and involves a daunting interdependent network of variables ranging from the spiritual, cultural, and psychological to the genetic and neurodevelopmental. Understanding the complex ecology that translates social experience into physiological function is a centrally important aspect of the larger social justice imperative inherent in the study of biosocial phenomena. Although mediating factors (such as having positive familial relationships or social support from a faith community) often do not carry the potential for direct social transformation, they carry considerable liberatory potential at the individual level.

What follows is an attempt to describe some of the more widely recognized human biosocial phenomena. More specifically, we focus primarily on acute and chronic stress, including their neuroendocrinological and psychoneuroimmunological dimensions. In reality, the scope of known biosocial phenomena extends far beyond the examples that will be explored in this chapter. The topics considered here are, however, among those socially mediated biological mechanisms that impart a dramatic impact on life-course trajectory and quality of life in midlife and old age. As interest in interdisciplinarity intensifies within the walls of the academy and the persistent dichotomy distinguishing the biological self from the social self fades, other equally compelling biosocial phenomena will likely emerge.

INTEGRATING SOCIAL AND BIOMEDICAL RESEARCH

As is the case for most emerging bodies of cross-disciplinary knowledge, increased understanding of biosocial mechanisms depends largely on our ability to adapt methodologically and theoretically, a process that is wrought with logistical and conceptual complexities. In recognition of the centrality of research and theory innovation in advancement of biosocial ageing research, we begin with a brief overview of the challenges inherent in crafting and researching interdisciplinary conceptual models. We specifically address the difficulties inherent in blending levels of analysis and conceptualizing the intervening forces that link life-course social and biological phenomena and then give a brief history of theoretical constructs that have attempted to achieve disciplinary integration.

Levels of analysis and 'intervening' variables

The study of ageing attracts scholars from a diversity of disciplines, each bearing their own set of theoretical assumptions and each trained in research methodologies that allow them to explore knowledge frontiers forged by those with whom they share a language and research tradition. But what of scholars who choose to cross disciplinary lines? For those attempting to integrate diverse scholarship traditions, bold new research questions emerge that require innovative theoretical and methodological adaptations.

More specifically, researchers in social gerontology and life-course studies who are attempting to build a knowledge base in the emerging biosocial tradition encounter the problem of having to link independent and dependent variables from disciplines that have historically been compartmentalized. This compartmentalization into so-called disciplines is predicated on a wider Western ontology in which componentiality and atomization are central to the concept of disciplinary knowledge (Berger et al., 1973). Scholars with an integrative, interdisciplinary agenda generally acknowledge that deconstructive approaches to research aimed at decontextualized, localized phenomenon may have some justification (Bale, 1995; Bertalanffy, 1968; Wilber, 1995; Wilshire, 1990), but these same scholars agree that in order to grasp the rich ecology of dynamic human systems of activity, various levels of analysis (Anderson, 1998) and knowledge gained through a process of deconstruction need to be skillfully reconstructed and reintegrated.

The process of reintegration has become increasingly complex as disciplinary knowledge has developed. A century ago biosocial inquiry might have entailed linking a routinely recognizable social practice with a biological outcome observable at the gross level. In the present, integrating social and biological phenomena often requires eliding sophisticated, longitudinal social modeling data with biological research that unveils complex molecular mechanisms. In addition, as clearly articulated in the work of Ken Wilber, biosocial integration research cannot be considered complete unless there is a clear understanding of the translational processing that takes place at the mind–body interface. Much of this translation is idiographic in its nature and is understood as an intersection of modernist developmental constructs with more postmodern approaches to understanding individual experience (Wilber, 1995).

Thus, blending 'levels of analysis' in biosocial research is inherently epistemologically and ontologically quite complex with social and psychological methodologies ranging from structural and modern to post-structural and postmodern and biological research being embedded in a long-standing modern tradition that is quite positivist in its orientation. Thorny ontological questions emerge, particularly those that attempt to characterize the mechanisms that transform the social into the biological such as: What are the functions of mind and brain in perceiving, processing, and internalizing the conditions presented by the social world? What roles do culture, social identity, and spirituality play in mediating the anatomical and physiological imprints that reflect the internalization of social phenomena? In the context of this chapter, it is important to underscore that social, translational, and biological phenomena have had a lifetime to develop and that the interdependence and synergy among these three heuristically conceived areas of interest can attest to its own particular forms of cumulative advantage and disadvantage. Put more simply, social phenomena, translational/psychological phenomena, and biological phenomena all display powerful evidence of their own particular manifestations of CAD (Dannefer, 2003; Douthit and Dannefer, 2007; Ferraro and Shippee, 2009).

A short history of the biosocial tradition

Although biosocial inquiry has become increasingly sophisticated in recent history, the interdependent relationship between social and biological phenomena has been the focus of centuries of scholarly inquiry and curiosity. Plato's *Republic* (trans. 1991) portrays human constitution as a miniaturized iteration of the structure and dynamics of city-states, with the physical body being a reflection of the physical infrastructure of the city-state and aspects of the human soul being compartmentalized in a manner that reflects

ancient Greek social class structure (Gaarder, 1994). Sigmund Freud's original work utilized literary references (e.g., to Oedipus and his mother Jacosta) and other psychological terms in lieu of what he understood to be yet undiscovered neurophysiological imprints of social life on the human psyche (Solms, 2004). By the mid 20th century, many notable scholars were attempting to develop models of natural world activity that would account for the complex, interdependent, and dynamic systemic processes seen in nature and would act as a counterpoise to the increasingly atomized understanding of the natural world coming from the natural and social sciences (Bale, 1995). Systems-oriented theories coming from this new breed of scholar included: Systems Theory (Bertalanffy, 1950); cybernetics (Bateson, 1979; Wiener, 1950); Living Systems Theory (Miller, 1978); and social action theory (Parsons, 1978).

> Systems (-oriented) theorists acknowledged the impressive gains in scientific inquiry, and the subsequent technological advances, afforded by the classical scientific paradigm. Granted, highly sophisticated methods of dissecting and quantifiably analyzing natural phenomena have provided important insights into the construction of our world, ... (affording) a ... capacity to predict and control small pieces of reality at a given moment in time. Yet, these gains have been achieved at considerable costs, costs that notably include: overspecialization and narrow professionalism in scientific research; the fracturing and fragmentation of science's vision of nature; and a subsequent sense of alienation from the beauty of nature's underlying unity.
>
> (Bale, 1995: 29)

In the context of human activity, the aims of the new breed of 20th century systems-oriented theorists, can, with some notable exceptions, be generalized as follows:

1 To account for the negentropy in the natural world; i.e., the tendency of organisms and their social formations to contradict the second law of thermodynamics and to become increasingly complex in their interdependent self-sustaining, homeostatic, and self-organizing capacities.
2 To capture the *Gestalt* of human ecology that could not be understood through decontextualized and fragmented objects of study.
3 To understand how organisms as living systems are engaged in a dynamic exchange of matter, energy, and data with the substance of their larger ecology.

> (Bale, 1995)

As systems-oriented theories gained traction in the second half of the 20th century, various iterations and extensions of the theory emerged. Many of these theories spotlighted the notion of hierarchical, multilayered activity structures. Talcott Parsons (1978) worked over several decades to hone his General Theory of Action in which he conceived of social structure as being constituted at four levels, including the cultural system, the social system, the personality system, and the behavioral system. Alternatively, Miller's Living Systems Theory (Miller, 1978; Miller and Miller, 1992) proposed a system of human activity composed of eight nested levels of organization, including cells, organs, organisms, groups, organizations, communities, societies, and supranational systems, while Bronfenbrenner's (1979, 2004) Ecological Systems Theory involved five nested subsystems, and Integral Theory (Marquis, 2008; Wilber, 1995) presents a model of cross-disciplinary integration in which four Integral quadrants are formed by the intersection of two axes: interior-exterior and individual-collective. Integral Theory posits that a comprehensive description of any human phenomenon must account for these four irreducible perspectives:

- Experiential (micro-subjective) (upper left quadrant): as 'felt' by the individual from the inside
- Behavioral (micro-objective) (upper right quadrant): the individual as observable from the outside
- Cultural (macro-intersubjective) (lower left quadrant): the experience of sociocultural phenomena
- Social (macro-interobjective) (lower right quadrant): observable group behavior.

Wilber's theory is also seen as valuable in the study of biosocial phenomenon in that it attends to the complex dimensions of human ecology that mediate the relationship between individual biochemistry and social spheres of functioning: i.e., it attempts to capture the complexities that comprise the translational interface between the social world and the biology of the ageing body, and endeavors to reconcile competing epistemologies and capture and integrate the multiple levels of analysis.

EMERGING EVIDENCE OF BIOSOCIAL PHENOMENA

Although pockets of scholarship have long reflected elements of biosocial theory (Bateson, 1979; Marmot et al., 1991, 1997; Mead, 2001; Miller, 1978), more recent research initiatives involving both in vitro and in vivo designs have sought to answer increasingly complex questions related to biosocial mechanisms. Of the array of biosocial research agendas that have emerged in the last 20–30 years, this chapter will narrow its focus to the burgeoning literature on stress. More specifically, we consider the allostatic load wrought by chronic stress and its relationship to (1) psychoneuroimmunological sequelae and (2) endocrine dysfunction tied to metabolic syndrome and diabetes, and we identify ways in which chronic stress serves as a link between disabling physiological dysfunction in old age and the cumulative disadvantage embedded in institutionalized, inequitable distributive social phenomena.

Although many other examples of biosocial interaction exist, the social conditions that generate chronic stress, and the consequences of stress's sustained assault on multiple body systems, collectively exemplify a larger biosocial mechanism that statistically bears much relevance to disease and disability in old age. In fact, many socially mediated stress-related ailments have become synonymous with old age and include disorders such as heart disease, stroke, diabetes, cancer, arthritis, and dementia; including dementia of the Alzheimer's type (DAT).

Acute and chronic stress: physiological manifestations of social strain

In any discussion of stress that relates to issues of health, it is important to distinguish between short-term or acute stress and long-term or chronic stress. While an acute stress response represents a physiological mechanism that plays an essential role in human survival, the physiological changes that accompany chronic stress are a deterrent to long-term physical and mental health. Hence, we begin by considering the nature and consequences of acute stress and then segue into a discussion of the mechanisms and consequences of chronic or prolonged stress, in relation to ageing.

Upon encountering a stressful situation (e.g., a prescription needs to be refilled but the pharmacy is closed, a physician fails to return a call concerning a new cardiac symptom that has emerged, an adult child with three school-aged children is suddenly fired, an overdue credit card bill is discovered), a series of physiological mechanisms is set into motion that involves two primary pathways: namely, the sympathetic–adrenal–medullary (SAM) axis and the hypothalamic–pituitary–adrenal (HPA) axis. Together, the HPA, which is primarily endocrine in nature, and SAM, which is primarily neurological, constitute the foundation of the now well-known mammalian acute stress response apparatus, sometimes called the fight-or-flight response.

The fight-or-flight response to imminent life-threatening danger (Selye, 1936) can be described as follows (Charmandari et al., 2005; Tsigos and Chrousos, 2002): Any fight-or-flight response begins with the organism actually perceiving stress through a structure in the brain termed the amygdala. If the amygdala detects that there is an environmental threat, it 'sounds an alarm' by sending a neurological signal to two separate parts of the brain, the hypothalamus and the locus cereleus. The signal that is sent to the hypothalamus initiates a cascade of reactions that are the body's main biological defense against offending environmental stressors. The hypothalamus sends a hormonal signal, corticotropin-releasing hormone (CRH), to the brain's pituitary gland, which then makes contact with the adrenal glands by releasing another hormone into the bloodstream called adrenocorticotropic hormone (ACTH). When the ACTH reaches the adrenal glands, and more specifically the outer shell of the adrenal gland called the adrenal cortex, it induces the release of hormones called glucocorticoids (GCs), the best known of which is cortisol. The GCs provide an essential function for mammals whose survival is threatened. These hormones aid in the metabolism of glucose in a manner that raises the level of sugar in the blood, thus making energy available to the muscles used to either flee a threatening situation or to stay and fight a threatening foe. The increased blood sugar also ensures that the brain will have the energy it needs to think of clever ways of evading harm.

At the same time, the SAM arm of the acute stress response, also originating in the amygdala, signals the locus cereleus to initiate a sympathetic nervous system (SNS) activation, which triggers physiological changes that complement the release of GCs by preparing the organism to respond to potential threat. These SNS-related changes, which ensure the maximum delivery of oxygen and nutrients to the brain and muscles, include increased heart rate, a rise in blood pressure, acceleration in respiratory rate, and a release of opioids to decrease the experience of pain. At the same time, activity is directed away from nonessential functions such as digestion, elimination, excretion, and cellular repair.

Following abatement of the acute stress stimulus, the threatened organism sets into motion an adaptive response that counteracts the activating elements of the SAM and HPA cascades. The faster the individual is able to return to their prestressor neuroendocrine baseline, the smaller the overall burden that the stress response places on the body (Baum and Posluszny, 1999). Some of the burdens associated with an acute stress response are illustrated in now-classic studies of students taking final examinations. These studies show students in the examination condition with less effective antibody production in response to hepatitis B vaccination (Glaser et al., 1992) and slowed wound healing (Marucha et al., 1998) in comparison to controls.

Despite the adaptive and potentially life-saving value of these acute physiological changes, accumulating evidence suggests that chronic activation of such systems results in threats to overall physical and mental health (Baum and Posluszny, 1999). Hence, social arrangements that create sustained conditions of compromised safety, security, and well-being – particularly cases of threat or instability that are intractable and wrought with unpredictability – are the harbingers of morbidity and mortality stemming from a host of disorders, including cardiovascular disease, Alzheimer's disease, asthma, HIV-AIDS, cancer, gastrointestinal disturbance, viral illness, and depression (Logan and Barksdale, 2008; McEwen, 1998).

The injurious effects of chronic activation of the stress response can be traced to several key phenomena, including excessive adrenal and sympathetic stimulation that leads to immunosuppression; destructive inflammatory processes; pathological changes in glucose metabolism that favor the accumulation of toxic central abdominal fat and insulin resistance; hypertension; cardiovascular disease; and slowed wound repair (Kiecolt-Glaser et al., 2002). In the context of ageing, the chronic stress generated by long-term caregiving responsibilities for a spouse or parent with Alzheimer's disease has been given considerable attention (González-Salvador et al., 1999; Torti et al., 2004). Studies have shown that numerous health changes occur in the caregiver, such as slowed wound healing, decreased response to vaccination, and other indicators of endocrine and immune dysregulation (Kiecolt-Glaser, 1999; Kiecolt-Glaser et al., 2002).

The aspects of both acute and chronic stress that relate to dysregulation of immunological functioning have been studied for several decades as part of the larger field of psychoneuroimmunology (Kiecolt-Glaser, 1999). Likewise, chronic stress-related changes in metabolism that lead to the accumulation of toxic central abdominal fat, insulin resistance, hypertension, and atherosclerosis, i.e., the elements that comprise the so-called 'metabolic syndrome', have been given considerable attention (Chrousos, 2000). As technology and the knowledge base in molecular biology and cell physiology have become increasingly sophisticated, so too has our understanding of the relationships shared by chronic stress, immunity, glucose metabolism, and late-life morbidity and mortality. What follows is a brief overview of these complex areas of stress-related dysregulation and the disease-related sequelae linked to the dysregulation processes.

Psychoneuroimmunology

The field of psychoneuroimmunology (PNI) seeks to elucidate the interdependent relationship between aspects of the central nervous system responses to psychosocial experience and mechanisms involved in regulation of the immune response tied to experience (Ader and Cohen, 1975). As knowledge in PNI has progressed, the role of the sympathetic nervous system and the endocrine system in brain–immune system communication has become clearer and our understanding of the links between thoughts and emotions, particularly as they relate to stress and immune function, are increasingly refined.

PNI is of particular relevance for understanding biosocial dimensions of ageing. Researchers in this burgeoning field explore how psychological responses wrought by structural elements that determine life-course trajectory precipitate neurophysiological and hormonal processes that ultimately guide regulation of the immune system, and hence the health and well-being of elders. The PNI literature makes a clear case that social arrangements affecting chronic psychological distress can, over time, create modulations in immune function that result in disease, disability, and death. It will become evident as our discussion of PNI unfolds that connections between mind, body, and CAD have profound implications not only for how we think about medical and psychological intervention but also how we create larger ecological blueprints for universal healthy ageing.

Mechanisms of immune regulation and dysregulation

Immunoregulatory mechanisms play a centrally important role in allowing humans to live in relative comfort and safety amidst biological agents capable of wreaking havoc on virtually every part of the human body. Disease agents related to bacterial, viral, fungal, and parasitic infection, if left unchallenged by immunological mechanisms, use the human body as a medium or substrate to aid the invading organism's growth and/or reproduction. Additional threats come not from invading organisms, but from our own cells, whose DNA

has been modified by agents such as viruses and environmental toxins or by errors that occur in otherwise normal cellular reproduction, such that these now abnormal cells are no longer of use to us physiologically but are able to rapidly multiply and spread as a life-threatening form of cancer. In all of these cases of bodily invasion, be they infectious organisms from without or cancer cells from within, our ability to 'upregulate' or stimulate our immune response is essential to our viability as humans. Various components of the immune system, if properly mobilized, can detect and destroy harmful agents and protect body tissues against the myriad of invasive agents, thus preserving the health and integrity of the body's key functional and structural elements.

Ironically, immunological functions that are mobilized beyond what is needed for protection of invading substances can be as injurious to the human body as the diseases they keep in check. Excessive stimulation of the immune response is linked to inflammatory diseases such as atherosclerosis and Alzheimer's disease and a wide array of autoimmune disorders, including systemic lupus erythematosus (SLE) and rheumatoid arthritis. Whether we are speaking about unwanted inflammation or autoimmunity, the underlying principle to glean from these examples is that immune responses that are not properly attenuated or downregulated can cause disease and destruction of body tissue that is as formidable as the destruction wrought by diseases that result from a suppressed immune response (Kiecolt-Glaser et al., 2002). In fact, speculation regarding the pathology of the 2009 swine flu deaths suggests that mortality from this particular flu strain, which appears to be more common in those with healthy immune systems, may be associated in some way with a vigorous immune response known as cytokine storm (Clark, 2007) rather than a failure to mobilize immunity against the influenza virus (Lacey and McNeil, 2009; Osterholm, 2005).

Disease resulting from immunoregulatory impairment can have a number of underlying causes, including immunosuppressant drugs that prevent rejection of transplants, intake of steroids that prevent damage from inflammatory disease, illnesses such as HIV/AIDS that overwhelm the immune system, genetic predispositions to autoimmune disease, and ageing. In the context of biosocial interactions and ageing, a salient underlying mechanism of immune dysregulation is triggered by the neuroendocrinological response to stress. Because of the importance of the stress response in our understanding of the ageing immune system, the remainder of this section is devoted to an exploration of injurious up- and downregulations of immune function as they pertain to the potential immunological consequences, over time, of distress and hardship.

Let us now return to the biology of stress. As explained in detail above, an acute stress response, including the release of GCs from the adrenal glands, is an important aspect of a key survival mechanism. However chronic stress, and its associated sustained release of GCs, can have serious physiological consequences, including compromised immune function. Immunologists have elucidated increasingly detailed and nuanced models depicting the complex multimodal interaction between the cells of the immune system, GCs, and other aspects of the stress response (Elenkov and Chrousos, 2002; Segerstrom and Miller, 2004). Simply stated, chronic stress can result in one of two very general immunological outcomes: one can be understood as a form of immunosuppression, and the other as an injurious form of immune stimulation. It is important to note that these mechanisms are presented here in a somewhat skeletal and oversimplified way that circumvents the underlying and often non-linear complexity.

Turning first to immunosuppression, the stress response involves a feedback system that attempts to keep the immune system from overreacting to invading substances and injury by suppressing certain elements of immune response. This prevents immunological responses to body injury from being so robust that the immune response itself is the cause of tissue destruction (Elenkov and Chrousos, 2002). Glucocorticoids, for example, can inhibit the movement of key immunity-promoting cells to sites of infection or foreign substance invasion (Elenkov and Chrousos, 2002) and, over the short term, this inhibition serves a self-protective function. In the face of chronic stress, however, immunosuppressant effects such as these may compromise the body's ability to adequately fight infection. An example of an immunity-related cell that loses its mobility in the presence of GCs is the neutrophil (Nathan, 2006), whose long-term loss of mobility could be of considerable significance in chronic stress because these specialized white cells are normally among the first to arrive at a site of infection and invading organisms.

Other evidence of stress-related immune downregulation comes from work with so-called latent viruses, which are typically dormant in body tissue and tend to appear (as in the case of herpes cold sores) when they are unchecked by immune mechanisms that normally block their expression. Glaser and Kiecolt-Glaser (1997) assert that under conditions of chronic stress, as might be expected, latent viruses indeed become active, indicating a disruption in normal immune function.

Another important example of immunosuppression can be seen in the activity of natural killer cells. These cells are part of a surveillance system that works to detect and destroy newly formed abnormal and potentially cancerous cells. Under conditions of chronic stress, natural killer function is suppressed, thus disabling an important mechanism for cancer prevention from working effectively (Kiecolt-Glaser, 1999; Miller et al., 2002). This loss of natural killer cell surveillance may hold an important key to the link between stress and cancer (Kiecolt-Glaser and Glaser, 1999).

In contrast to the immunosuppression described above, other work in the field of PNI has shown that stress can also result in abnormal upregulation or apparent stimulation of particular cells in the immune system. For example, work by Miller et al. (2008) shows that individuals who have participated in caregiving responsibilities for a family member with cancer actually demonstrate genetic changes in cells that increase the risk of inflammation. More specifically, it appears that monocytes – cells that play a key role in inflammation – undergo a genetic transformation over time such that they become less responsive to the anti-inflammatory messages normally conveyed in the presence of GCs during an acute stress response, and more responsive to certain pro-inflammatory messages. This potential for increase in inflammation is particularly significant because there is considerable support for the notion that bolstering the inflammatory process may contribute to diseases such as depression, cardiovascular disease, cancer, and diabetes (Kiecolt-Glaser et al., 2002).

The heightened immune response reported by Miller et al. (2008) is one of many found in the PNI literature. In a review of apparent stress-related immune stimulation responses, both the increases in inflammation that occur in relation to stress conditions and other stress-related aspects of immune modulation that may play a role in triggering autoimmune disease are highlighted (Elenkov and Chrousos, 2002).

Stress and metabolic disease

While it is clear that the link between chronic stress and immune dysregulation can lead to serious illness and decreased vigor in old age, stress-related dysregulation related to glucose metabolism also presents a major threat to long-term health prospects (McEwen, 1998). Among the diseases related to dysregulation of glucose metabolism, and also to morbidity and mortality in old age, are hypertension, cardiovascular disease, stroke, diabetes, and dementia. What follows is a brief orientation to this form of chronic stress-related metabolic dysregulation and the metabolic challenges that are generated in its wake.

The sugar, glucose, is the major source of energy for fueling human cell function. As described above, a perceived threat triggers an acute stress response in which the body provides as much energy as possible, in the form of glucose, to those parts of the body (brain, heart, and skeletal muscles) most critical to confronting or fleeing from the threat. In non-stress situations, excess glucose is removed from the blood through the action of insulin. Insulin is a hormone produced by the pancreas that encourages storage of glucose in the form of glycogen. When glucose is needed (e.g., during an acute stress response), glycogen is broken down and the stored glucose is released into circulation. This release of glucose occurs with a decrease in insulin blood levels. In addition to glucose made available through glucose uptake inhibition and the breakdown of glycogen into glucose, even more glucose can be made available for the stress response through metabolic processes that allow the synthesis of new glucose from amino acids and lipids (gluconeogenesis). This means, more generally, that under conditions of stress the body favors catabolic functions, i.e., functions related to breakdown of body substances, in this case glycogen, lipids, and proteins, rather than anabolic functions that build body substance, i.e., storing glucose by building glycogen molecules.

Chronic stress, sustained action of GCs, and the persistent catabolic state that ensues can lead to a series of metabolic challenges that, over a prolonged period, present serious health risks. Included among these challenges are a number of conditions that are collectively called 'metabolic syndrome'. Included under the rubric of metabolic syndrome are:

1   Obesity, which is characterized by an increase in a particularly dangerous form of fat called central abdominal fat.
2   Insulin resistance, which is characterized by the body no longer being able to use insulin properly, hence causing blood sugar to rise and setting the stage for diabetes.
3   Loss of lean muscle mass and bone (a potential precursor to osteoporosis).
4   Increase in triglyceride and LDL (low-density lipoprotein) levels.
5   Hypertension.
6   Atherosclerosis.
7   Hypercoagulation (i.e., increased blood clot formation).
8   Exacerbation of the pro-inflammatory state described in the previous section on PNI.
(McEwen, 1998, 2004, 2008)

In regard to the latter pro-inflammatory state, it is now recognized that adipocytes (fat cells) secrete pro-inflammatory cytokines, and that body mass indices (BMIs) correlate with increased adipocyte pro-inflammatory cytokine secretion (Coppack, 2001). The link is clear between metabolic syndrome and many disorders that are the scourge of old age, including cardiovascular disease, cancer, Alzheimer's disease, stroke, and depression (McEwen, 1998, 2004, 2008; McEwen and Wingfield, 2003). Furthermore, the high rates of morbidity and premature mortality among economically and racially marginalized elders, related to diseases wrought by metabolic syndrome (Muntaner et al., 2004; Newman, 2006), provide powerful circumstantial evidence for the impact of chronic stress on health and vitality in old age.

BIOLOGICAL AND SOCIAL MODELS OF CHRONIC STRESS

Although much evidence in the literature supports the notion that social arrangements, mediated by psychological reactivity and resiliency, are correlated with various metabolically and immunologically related health outcomes, the methodological sophistication necessary to demonstrate causality is at best emergent. Still, the associations are powerful and epidemiological evidence certainly bolsters suspicions around issues of causality. In response to compelling stress data, an explanatory theoretical model for understanding the impact of stress on health has emerged. This model, known by the terms 'allostasis' and 'allostatic load', provides a transdisciplinary conceptual framework that underscores the biological significance of stress-related dysregulation and the ethical imperatives that pertain to the injurious social arrangements that form the backdrop for experiences of chronic stress. The allostasis/allostatic load construct marries well with the cumulative advantage/disadvantage (CAD) framework discussed earlier and expands CAD's interdisciplinary utility, thus providing more opportunities for effective long-term intervention.

Allostasis and allostatic load

When viewed through the lens of allostasis and allostatic load, the acute stress response can be understood as the body shifting away from its preferred homeostatic (balanced) state to an alternative homeostatic state that allows it to maintain some modicum of stability in the face of environmental challenge. This mechanism, whereby the body fosters a dynamic state of homeostasis relative to variations in the social ecology, is termed *allostasis*. Allostasis is thus an 'extension of the concept of homeostasis and represents the adaptation process of the complex physiological human system to physical, psychosocial, and environmental challenges or stress' (Logan and Barksdale, 2008: 201).

Under ideal conditions, the HPA, immune system, cardiovascular system, and SAM all work in the face of environmental fluctuations to maintain allostasis. Provided that these systems are not activated too frequently for this purpose, the body can effectively cope with challenges. However, when environmental challenges or stressors are sustained to the point where they place an excessive burden on these systems, they become either overactive or underactive, and are no longer able to maintain adaptive levels of response to the environment. This inability of the body to maintain adaptive levels of functioning is called *allostatic load*. In simple terms, allostatic load is the toll exacted on the body for adaptation to a set of ecological stressors or the physical manifestation of social, psychological, and physical erosion of body stability (McEwen, 1998, 2008). Allostatic load is a composite index that describes how the cumulative strain of the body's stress response can, across the life course, damage the body and accelerate disease processes, including a number of chronic maladies. The components that are reflected in the index actually represent a complex, non-linearly-related factor cluster that includes the action of GCs, inflammatory cytokines, anti-inflammatory cytokines, the sympathetic nervous system, the parasympathetic nervous system (i.e., that portion of the nervous system that acts in opposition to the sympathetic nervous system, thus imparting a calming effect rather than a stimulating effect), and oxidative stress (i.e., physiological stress placed on the body by its inability to maintain sufficient detoxification functions in relation to accumulated toxins that come from pollution, processed foods, smoking, and other sources) (McEwen, 2008).

Causes of allostatic load include:

1 Frequent and repeated provocation of allostatic systems by assaults from novel stressors (e.g., low-income, urban women of color encountering ongoing racism, sexism, crime, inadequate housing, financial burdens, and a general lack of essential community infrastructure).
2 Inability to adapt to chronic stressors that are similar in nature (e.g., repeatedly experiencing anxiety over an inability to provide one's children

with adequate health care or ongoing problems with neighborhood crime).
3 Failure to deactivate allostatic activity after the stressor abates, as in people who are chronically anxious and hyper-vigilant, even in the absence of 'objective' stressors (e.g., a resident of a high-crime area who, even in the absence of criminal activity, carries considerable anticipatory anxiety as well as residual trauma from past experiences).

The common theme underlying these causes of allostatic load is that the activation of the HPA and SNS occur on a repeated basis to such an extent that mechanisms that would normally return individuals to their preferred homeostatic state (i.e., allostasis) are no longer functional.

Allostatic load, CAD, and socioeconomic status

Considerable evidence has been amassed indicating that variations in allostatic load, and hence mortality and health, correlate strongly with socioeconomic status (SES) (McEwen and Wingfield, 2003; Marmot, 2004; Marmot and Wilkinson, 2005). Moreover, SES gradients remain even after adjusting for individual factors such as smoking or structural issues such as access to health care. This means 'the gradients of health across the range of socioeconomic status relate to a complex array of risk factors that are differentially distributed in human society and that have a cumulative impact on ... allostatic load' (McEwen and Wingfield, 2003: 11). In the context of allostatic load, as framed by McEwen and Wingfield, it is clear that cumulative disadvantage and allostatic load are actually different lenses on the same expanding net of disadvantage. The former focuses on social ecology and the latter attempts to capture biological ecology. For CAD, the dimensions of interest are typically types of social opportunities and distributive hierarchies, of which income is a relatively accessible and straightforward example (Dannefer, 2003). Alternatively, allostatic load identifies biological markers that are predictors of debilitating disease and disorder and serve as markers of overtaxed body systems pushed to unhealthy limits by the lived realities of cumulative disadvantage.

It is not surprising that epidemiologists and others have consistently found that social class, a powerful mediator of CAD and allostatic load, is a robust predictor of personal health (Marmot, 2004; Marmot and Wilkinson, 2005). Looking at behaviors associated with SES, studies have demonstrated links between allostatic load and work involving repetitive tasks (Schnorpfeil et al., 2003), smoking (McEwen, 2008), ingestion of high-fat, high-sugar foods (Patel et al., 2007), and lack of exercise (McEwen and Seeman, 1999), while others have posited links between stress and sexual and physical abuse (Seeman and McEwen, 1996). The inverse relationship between allostatic load and cumulative advantage is also well documented, particularly as it pertains to the relationship between biological markers of allostatic load and SES (Singer and Ryff, 1999; Steptoe et al., 2002). Furthermore, a number of scholars, including Turra and Goldman (2007) and Muntaner et al. (2004), have compellingly argued, based on mortality studies, that the intersection of race and poverty, more than either variable in isolation, exerts a deadly strain on the human body. Inquiry into allostatic load in poor communities confirms what is blatantly obvious – toxic environments are contributing to premature death and disease (Marmot, 2004; Newman, 2006).

Even after adjusting for one's current financial circumstances, a retrospective lens reveals that long-term financial hardship is associated with a host of health outcomes in later life (Kahn and Pearlin, 2006). According to Kahn and Pearlin, the findings are unequivocal:

> Financial hardship experienced prior to age 35 has an effect on late life health *only* when it is followed by additional hardship after age 35 ... (T)hese results strongly suggest that *the potency of strain is cumulative* ... (and) that a chain of successive periods of strain intensifies the cumulative sensitivity of health to the strains (p. 26, italics in original).

Hence it appears that the *persistence* of hardship matters in relation to health more than its timing or episodic occurrence, thus presenting a good example of the cumulative impact of environmental distress and the suggested relationship between cumulative disadvantage and allostatic load.

It should now be clear that health disorders can be linked to a sustained burden of allostatic load, and that this sustained burden is particularly prevalent among individuals experiencing unremitting SES-related hardships. While an exhaustive, detailed review of all of the disorders linked to allostatic load is not possible within the context of this chapter, a compelling example is subsequently presented that aptly illustrates biosocial interactions and disease process in old age. More specifically, the disabling symptoms of Alzheimer's disease are considered in the context of allostatic load and cumulative disadvantage.

Alzheimer's disease and allostatic load

Evidence suggests that the effects of poverty accumulating over the life course can increase individual risk of developing Alzheimer's-related dementia (Douthit, 2006; Douthit and Dannefer, 2007). By tracing various poverty-related life-course phenomena that correlate with factors known to increase the risk of being diagnosed with dementia of the Alzheimer's type (DAT), Douthit (2006) constructed a model that theorizes the destructive effect that a lifetime of cumulative disadvantage and related allostatic load can have on the cognitive capacity of the ageing body. The model, which borrows evidence from biomedicine, psychiatry, neuroscience, nutrition, and literacy education, suggests that the risk of manifesting the symptoms of DAT can be systematically shaped by cumulative disadvantage and related allostatic load that begins as early as the prenatal portion of the life course (Douthit, 2006; Douthit and Dannefer, 2007). A portion of the evidence used to build the model is presented below and includes three conditions that are related to allostatic load and are known to increase the intensity of DAT symptoms: namely, cardiovascular health, nutrition, and depression.

Cardiovascular health, DAT, and allostatic load

Healthy brain performance, including the cognitive functions typically lost in DAT, depends on the availability of oxygen and nutrients that are delivered by way of the circulatory system. It is not surprising then that poor cardiovascular health in later life, particularly in relation to the arterial blood supply to the brain, has been shown to intensify the cognitive deficits that characterize DAT (Bowler, 2004; Breteler, 2000; Iadecola and Gorelick, 2003; Tzourio et al., 2003). Seminal work by Marmot and Wilkinson (2005) shows that economic position has a significant bearing on the general health of the cardiovascular system. A number of independent variables are suspected in this well-documented relationship between wealth and vascular health, some of which have already been discussed at length. Included among them are chronic stress; lack of exercise; first- and second-hand smoke; and poor nutrition consisting of low-cost, high-fat, high-sodium, processed food (McEwen, 1998, 2008; McEwen and Seeman, 1999; Patel et al., 2007). Stress-related assaults on the cardiovascular system, many of which are related to distributive social forces, have been described in considerable detail above, but the subject of nutrition, which has not yet been considered in this chapter, is highly contingent on economic status, provides a compelling example of a biosocial phenomenon, and is subsequently discussed.

The DAT–nutrition link

For adults, adolescents, children, and developing fetuses living in conditions of poverty, geographical and economic barriers exist to obtaining high-quality whole-food sources rich in vitamins, phytochemicals, and fiber, and low in sodium and saturated fat. Particularly for those living in conditions of urban poverty, fresh produce and low-fat sources of protein are often unavailable in local neighborhood grocery stores (Marmot and Wilkinson, 2005; Shaffer, 2002). Inexpensive processed foods, high in saturated fat, refined carbohydrates, and sodium, become dietary staples, forming the foundation for epidemic levels of obesity, hypertension, and ultimately, poor cardiovascular health (Marmot and Elliot, 1992; Marmot and Wilkinson, 2005).

The inaccessibility of high-quality food products is exacerbated in low-income environments by the ready availability of 'fast food'. These foods are attractive for their ease of preparation and affordability, but are high in saturated fat, cholesterol, sodium, and refined carbohydrates; they are low in nutrient substances known to promote vascular health. In many urban neighborhoods, fast-food chains are the primary restaurant alternatives and contribute to epidemic levels of cardiovascular disease (Schlosser, 2002). The lack of high-quality food sources is particularly dangerous in children and adolescents who are increasingly plagued with obesity, metabolic syndrome, and diabetes (de Ferranti et al., 2004; Weiss et al., 2004).

The DAT–nutrition–allostatic load association is also germane to prenatal development. Pregnant women living in conditions of poverty whose dietary practices reflect the availability of the low-cost, high-calorie, nutrient-poor foods are more likely to give birth to children who will suffer from a subsequent weight problem (Kuzawa, 2004; McGill and McMahan, 2003). Likewise, the risk for childhood and ultimately adult obesity is increased if prenatal development is marked by the kind of calorie deficiency that is characteristic of extreme poverty or maternal mental illness or addiction. Likewise, maternal smoking during pregnancy is associated with subsequent obesity in the growing child (Huang et al., 2007).

Depression, DAT, and allostatic load

The factors that unite depression, allostatic load, and DAT also tell a compelling story of how biosocial interaction shapes the ageing process. Retrospective studies suggest that bouts of depression in middle and late adulthood increase the likelihood that individuals will eventually be diagnosed with DAT (Kennedy and Scalmati, 2001). Although the actual mechanism linking depression to Alzheimer's disease remains elusive, considerable speculation (spurred by brain imaging studies) points to the toxicity of the depressive state on the hippocampus (Bremner et al., 2000; Sapolsky, 2000), a brain structure that plays a major role in memory, learning, and emotion. Depression, particularly if untreated, causes shrinkage of this vital structure and may be a contributing factor in the manifestation of Alzheimer's disease symptoms. Whether or not this hypothesis turns out to be correct, several findings remain clear: (1) DAT is more likely to develop in men and women who earlier had symptoms of depression (anywhere between 1 and 25 years before onset) (Green et al., 2003), and (2) Alzheimer's disease subjects who develop depression have more severe dementia symptoms than those who do not (Lyketsos et al., 1997).

The relationship between DAT and depression is particularly germane in the context of allostatic load and cumulative disadvantage for at least two reasons. First, conditions of poverty are notoriously stress-inducing and are a factor in the high incidence of depression in populations experiencing financial hardship (Perl, 2004). Secondly, the likelihood of depression going untreated due to lack of financial resources or limited clinical services is a greater risk in less affluent populations than it is in populations having sufficient means. Failure to treat depressive symptoms prolongs the impact of allostatic load, imposes the possibility of more sustained damage to hippocampal function, and by virtue of the loss of social and occupational functioning (American Psychiatric Association, 2000), runs the risk of increasing the stress level within the immediate proximal ecology of the afflicted individual.

CONCLUSION

The Western view of the individual as a self-sustaining, autonomous, and unfettered agent is reflected in medicine's unwitting embrace of the notion of 'microfication', (Hagestad and Dannefer, 2001), i.e., the tendency to conceptualize health and other challenges as either issues of individuals, or as issues to be apprehended at the level of primary relations, thus highlighting themes such as family, micro-interaction, choice, and decision-making. At its core, microfication harbors a veiled misconception that the biological sphere of human functioning is somehow disconnected from the ecology of proximal and distal systems of human activity. As this chapter has illustrated, an interdisciplinary lens challenges trenchant Western assumptions about the seemingly limitless power of the individual and implores us to explore how the micro-interaction of everyday experience, and its imprint on biological function at the level of life and death, is in part regulated by larger social-structural arrangements imposing trajectories of cumulative advantage or disadvantage. Failure to interrogate the role of social and cultural processes along with continued misattribution of human disease processes to genetic, volitional, and other individual-level phenomena will perpetuate needless suffering across the life course and fatally disadvantage many of those who are ageing under the cloud of unjust social constraints.

REFERENCES

Ader, R. and Cohen, N. (1975) 'Behaviorally conditioned immunosuppression', *Psychosomatic Medicine*, 37: 333–40.

American Psychiatric Association (2000) *Diagnostic and Statistical Manual of Mental Disorders* (4th edn.). Washington, DC: American Psychiatric Association.

Anderson, N. (1998) 'Levels of analysis in health science: a framework for integrating sociobehavioral and biomedical research', *Annals of the New York Academy of Sciences*, 840: 563–76.

Bale, L.S. (1995) 'Gregory Bateson, cybernetics, and the social/behavioral sciences', *Cybernetics & Human Knowing*, 3: 27–45.

Bateson, G. (1979) *Mind and Nature: A Necessary Unity*. New York: E. P. Dutton.

Baum, A. and Posluszny, D.M. (1999) 'Mapping biobehavioral contributions to health and illness', *Annual Review of Psychology*, 50: 137–63.

Berger, P.L., Berger, B., and Kellner, H. (1973) *The Homeless Mind: Modernization and Consciousness*. New York: Random House.

Bertalanffy, L. von (1950) 'An outline of general systems theory', *British Journal for the Philosophy of Science*, 1: 134–65.

Bertalanffy, L. von (1968) *Organismic Psychology and Systems Theory*. Worcester, MA: Clark University Press.

Bowler, J.V. (ed.) (2004) *Vascular Cognitive Impairment: Preventable Dementia*. New York: Oxford University Press.

Bremner, J.D., Narayan, M., Anderson, E.R., et al. (2000) 'Hippocampal volume reduction in major depression', *American Journal of Psychiatry*, 157: 115–18.

Breteler, M.M.B. (2000) 'Vascular risk factors for Alzheimer's disease: an epidemiologic perspective', *Neurobiological Aging*, 21: 153–60.

Bronfenbrenner, U. (1979) *The Ecology of Human Development: Experiments by Nature and Design*. Cambridge, MA: Harvard University Press.

Bronfenbrenner, U. (2004) *Making Human Beings Human: Bioecological Perspectives on Human Development*. Thousand Oaks, CA: SAGE.

Charmandari, E., Tsigos, C., and Chrousos, G. (2005) 'Endocrinology of the stress response', *Annual Review of Physiology*, 67: 259–84.

Chrousos, G.P. (2000) 'The role of stress and the hypothalamic–pituitary–adrenal axis in the pathogenesis of the metabolic syndrome: neuro-endocrine and target tissue-related causes', *International Journal of Obesity and Related Metabolic Disorders*, 24: 550–5.

Clark, I.A. (2007) 'The advent of the cytokine storm', *Immunology and Cell Biology*, 85: 271–3.

Coppack, S.W. (2001) 'Proinflammatory cytokines and adipose tissue', *Proceedings of the Nutrition Society*, 60: 349–56.

Dannefer, D. (1999) 'Neoteny, naturalization, and other constituents of human development', in C.D. Ryff and V.W. Marshall (eds), *The Self and Society in the Aging Process*. New York: Springer, pp. 67–93.

Dannefer, D. (2003) 'Cumulative advantage/disadvantage and the life course: cross-fertilizing age and social science theory', *The Journals of Gerontology Series B: Psychological Sciences and Social Sciences*, 58: S327–37.

de Ferranti, S.D., Gauvreau, K., Ludwig, D.S., et al., (2004) 'Prevalence of the metabolic syndrome in American adolescents: findings from the Third National Health and Nutrition Examination Survey', *Circulation*, 110: 2494–7.

Douthit, K. (2006) 'Dementia in the iron cage: the biopsychiatric construction of Alzheimer's dementia', in C. Philipson, J. Barrs, and D. Dannefer (eds), *Aging, Globalisation, and Inequality: The New Critical Gerontology*. Amityville, NY: Baywood Publishers, pp. 159–81.

Douthit, K.Z. and Dannefer, D. (2007) 'Social forces, life course consequences: cumulative disadvantage and "getting Alzheimer's"', in J. Wilmoth and K. Ferraro (eds), *Gerontology: Perspectives and Issues*, 3rd edn, New York: Springer, pp. 223–42.

Elenkov, I.J. and Chrousos, G.P. (2002) 'Stress hormones, proinflammatory and anti-inflammatory cytokines, and autoimmunity', *Annals of the New York Academy of Science*, 966: 290–303.

Ferraro, K.F. and Shippee, T.P. (2009) 'Aging and cumulative inequality: how does inequality get under the skin?', *The Gerontologist*, 49: 333–43.

Gaarder, J. (1994) *Sophie's World: A Novel about the History of Philosophy* (P. Moller, Trans.). New York: Farrar, Straus and Giroux.

Glaser, R. and Kiecolt-Glaser, J.K. (1997) 'Chronic stress modulates the virus-specific immune response to latent herpes simplex virus type 1', *Annals of Behavioral Medicine*, 19(2), 78–82.

Glaser, R., Kiecolt-Glaser, J.K., Bonneau, R.H., et al., (1992) 'Stress-induced modulation of the immune response to recombinant hepatitis B vaccine', *Psychosomatic Medicine*, 54: 22–9.

González-Salvador, M.T., Arango, C., Lyketsos, C.G., Barba, A.C. (1999) 'The stress and psychological morbidity of the Alzheimer patient caregiver', *International Journal of Geriatric Psychiatry*, 14: 701–10.

Green, R.C., Cupples, L.A., Kurz, A., et al. (2003) 'Depression as a risk factor for Alzheimer's disease: the MIRAGE study', *Archives of Neurology*, 60, 753–9.

Hagestad, G.O. and Dannefer, D. (2001) 'Concepts and theories of aging: beyond microfication in social science approaches', in R.H. Binstock and L.K. George (eds), *Handbook of Aging and the Social Sciences*. New York: Academic Press, pp. 3–19.

Huang, J.S., Lee, T.A., and Lu, M.C. (2007) 'Prenatal programming of childhood overweight and obesity', *Maternal and Child Health Journal*, 11: 461–73.

Iadecola, C.P. and Gorelick, B. (2003) 'Converging pathogenic mechanisms in vascular and neurodegenerative dementia', *Stroke*, 34: 335–7.

Kahn, J.R. and Pearlin, L.I. (2006) 'Financial strain over the life course and health among older adults', *Journal of Health and Social Behavior*, 47: 17–31.

Kennedy, G.J. and Scalmati, A. (2001) 'The interface of depression and dementia', *Current Opinion in Psychiatry*, 14: 367–9.

Kiecolt-Glaser, J.K. (1999) 'Norman Cousins Memorial Lecture 1998. Stress, personal relationships, and immune function: health implications', *Brain, Behavior and Immunity*, 13: 61–72.

Kiecolt-Glaser, J.K. and Glaser, R. (1999) 'Psychoneuroimmunology and cancer: fact or fiction?', *European Journal of Cancer*, 35: 1603–7.

Kiecolt-Glaser, J.K., McGuire, L., Robles, T.F., and Glaser, R. (2002) 'Psychoneuroimmunology: psychological influences on immune function and health', *Journal of Consulting and Clinical Psychology*, 70: 537–47.

Kuzawa, C.W. (2004) 'Modeling fetal adaptation to nutrient restriction: testing the fetal origins hypothesis with a supply–demand model. *Journal of Nutrition*, 134: 194–200.

Lacey, M., and McNeil, D.G. (2009) 'Fighting deadly flu: Mexico shuts schools' [electronic version], *New York Times*, April 24, 2009. Retrieved June 1, 2009 from http://www.nytimes.com/2009/04/25/world/americas /25mexico.html?_r=1&bl&ex=1240891200&en=ce91d53e13153eed&ei=5087

Logan, J.G. and Barksdale, D.J. (2008) 'Allostasis and allostatic load: expanding the discourse on stress and cardiovascular disease', *Journal of Clinical Nursing*, 17: 201–8.

Lyketsos, C.G., Steele, C., Baker, L., et al. (1997) 'Major and minor depression in Alzheimer's disease: prevalence and impact', *Journal of Neuropsychiatry and Clinical Neuroscience*, 9: 556–61.

Marmot, M.G. (2004) *The Status Syndrome: How Social Standing Affects Our Health and Longevity*. New York: Times Books.

Marmot, M. and Elliot, P. (1992) *Coronary Heart Disease: From Etiology to Public Health*. New York: Oxford.

Marmot, M.G. and Wilkinson, R.G. (2005) *The Social Determinants of Health*. Oxford: Oxford University Press.

Marmot, M.G., Bosma, H., Hemingway, H., Brunner, E., and Stansfield, S. (1997) 'Contribution of job control and other risk factors to social variations in coronary heart disease incidence', *Lancet*, 350: 235–9.

Marmot, M.G., Smith, G.D. Stansfeld, S., et al. (1991) 'Health inequalities among British civil servants: the Whitehall II study', *Lancet*, 337: 1387–93.

Marquis, A. (2008) *The Integral Intake: A Guide to Comprehensive Idiographic Assessment in Integral Psychotherapy*. New York: Routledge.

Marucha, P.T., Kiecolt-Glaser, J.K., and Favagehi, M. (1998) 'Mucosal wound healing is impaired by examination stress', *Psychosomatic Medicine*, 60: 362–5.

McEwen, B.S. (1998) 'Stress, adaptation, and disease: allostasis and allostatic load', *Annals of the New York Academy of Sciences*, 896: 33–44.

McEwen, B.S. (2004) 'Protection and damage from acute and chronic stress: allostasis and allostatic overload and relevance to the pathophysiology of psychiatric disorders', *Annals of the New York Academy of Sciences*, 1032: 1–7.

McEwen, B.S. (2008) 'Central effects of stress hormones in health and disease: understanding the protective and damaging effects of stress and stress mediators', *European Journal of Pharmacology*, 583: 174–85.

McEwen, B.S. and Seeman, T. (1999) 'Protective and damaging effects of mediators of stress: elaborating and testing the concepts of allostasis and allostatic load', *Annals of the New York Academy of Sciences*, 896: 30–47.

McEwen, B.S. and Wingfield, J.C. (2003) 'The concept of allostasis in biology and biomedicine', *Hormones and Behavior*, 43: 2–15.

McGill, H.C. and McMahan, C.A. (2003) 'Starting earlier to prevent heart disease', *Journal of the American Medical Association*, 290: 2320–2.

Mead, M. (2001) *Sex and Temperament in Three Primitive Societies*. New York: Perennial.

Miller, J.L. and Miller, J.G. (1992) 'Greater than the sum of its parts: subsystems which process both matter-energy and information', *Behavioral Science*, 37: 1–38.

Miller, G.E., Cohen, S., and Ritchey, A.K. (2002) 'Chronic psychological stress and the regulation of pro-inflammatory cytokines: a glucocorticoid-resistance model', *Health Psychology*, 21, 531–41.

Miller, G.E., Chen, E., Sze, J., et al. (2008) 'A functional genomic fingerprint of chronic stress in humans: blunted glucocorticoid and increased NF-κB signaling', *Biological Psychiatry*, 64: 266–72.

Miller, J.G. (1978) *Living Systems*. New York: McGraw-Hill.

Muntaner, C., Hadden, W.C., and Kravets, N. (2004) 'Social class, race/ethnicity and all-cause mortality in the US: longitudinal results from the 1986–1994 National Health Interview Survey', *European Journal of Epidemiology*, 19: 777–84.

Nathan, C. (2006) 'Neutrophils and immunity: challenges and opportunities', *Nature Reviews Immunology*, 6: 173–82.

Newman, K.S. (2006) *A Different Shade of Gray: Midlife and Beyond in the Inner City*. New York: New Press.

Osterholm, M.T. (2005) 'Preparing for the next pandemic', *New England Journal of Medicine*, 352: 1839–42.

Parsons, T. (1978) *Action Theory and the Human Condition*. New York: Free Press.

Patel, C., Ghanim, H., Ravishankar, S., et al. (2007) 'Prolonged reactive oxygen species generation and nuclear factor-κB activation after a high-fat, high-carbohydrate meal in the obese', *The Journal of Clinical Endocrinology and Metabolism*, 92: 4476–9.

Perl, L. (2004) *Poverty, Depression, and Congressional Inaction*. Retrieved October 7, 2004 from The Century Foundation http://www.tcf.org/4L/4LMain.aspSubjectID=4&TopicID=0&ArticleID=720

Plato (trans. 1991) *The Republic of Plato* (A. Bloom, trans.). New York: Basic Books.

Sapolsky, R.M. (2000) 'The possibility of neurotoxicity in the hippocampus in major depression: a primer on neuron death', *Biological Psychiatry*, 48: 755–65.

Schlosser, E. (2002) *Fast Food Nation: The Dark Side of the American Meal*. New York: Perennial.

Schnorpfeil, P., Noll, A., Schulze, R., et al. (2003) Allostatic load and work conditions. *Social Science and Medicine, 57*, 647–56.

Seeman, T.E. and McEwen, B.C. (1996) 'Impact of social environment characteristics on neuroendocrine regulation', *Psychosomatic Medicine*, 58: 459–71.

Segerstrom, S.C. and Miller, G.E. (2004) 'Psychological stress and the human immune system: a meta-analytic study of 30 years of inquiry', *Psychological Bulletin*, 130: 601–30.

Selye, H. (1936) 'A syndrome produced by diverse noxious agents', *Nature*, 138: 2.

Shaffer, A. (2002) *The Persistence of L.A.'s Grocery Gap: The Need for a New Food Policy and Approach to Market Development*. Report from Center for Food and Justice, Urban and Environmental Policy Institute, Occidental College, May 2002.

Singer, B. and Ryff, C.D. (1999) 'Hierarchies of life histories and associated health risks', *Annals of the New York Academy of Sciences*, 896: 96–115.

Solms, M. (2004) 'Freud returns', *Scientific American*, 290: 82–90.

Steptoe, A., Feldman, P.J., Kunz, N., et al. (2002) 'Stress responsivity and socioeconomic status: a mechanism for increased cardiovascular disease risk?', *European Heart Journal*, 23: 1757–63.

Torti, F.M., Gwyther, L.P., Reed, S.D., Friedman, J.Y., and Schulman, K.A. (2004) 'A multinational review of recent trends and reports in dementia caregiver burden', *Alzheimer's Disease and Associated Disorders*, 18: 99–109.

Tsigos, C. and Chrousos, G.P. (2002) 'Hypothalamic–pituitary–adrenal axis, neuroendocrine factors, and stress', *Journal of Psychosomatic Research*, 53: 865–71.

Turra, C.M. and Goldman, N. (2007) 'Socioeconomic differences in mortality among U.S. adults: insights into the Hispanic paradox', *The Journals of Gerontology Series B: Psychological Sciences and Social Sciences*, 62: 184–92.

Tzourio, C., Anderson, C., Chapman, N., et al. (2003) Effects of blood pressure lowering with perindopril and indapamide therapy on dementia and cognitive decline in patients with cerebrovascular disease. *Archives of Internal Medicine*, 63: 1069–75.

Weiss, R., Dziura, J., Burgert, T.S., et al. (2004) 'Obesity and the metabolic syndrome in children and adolescents', *New England Journal of Medicine*, 350: 2362–74.

Wiener, N. (1950) *The Human Use of Human Beings: Cybernetics and Society*. Cambridge, MA: Riverside Press.

Wilber, K. (1995) *Sex, Ecology, Spirituality: The Spirit of Evolution*. Boston: Shambhala.

Wilshire, B. (1990) *The Moral Collapse of the University*. Albany, NY: SUNY Press.

26

Dementia and Mild Cognitive Impairment in Social and Cultural Context

Danny George and Peter Whitehouse

INTRODUCTION

Mark Twain once observed that life would be infinitely happier if we could only be born at the age of 80 and gradually approach 18, a concept that was later developed into a short story by F. Scott Fitzgerald, and more recently adapted into the major motion picture *The Curious Case of Benjamin Button*. Life, however, unfolds in rather the opposite direction, and anyone who lives long enough will experience the normal concomitants of aging: graying hair, wizened skin, and fading memory abilities. In a rapidly 'graying' Western culture that often satirizes but mostly laments the aging process, the benefits conferred by increasing years – knowledge, judgment, self-possession, experience, and even the opportunity for wisdom, just to name a few – are often buried beneath the perceived deficits.

Nowhere has our insecurity about aging been made more manifest than in Western culture's collective fear of Alzheimer's disease (AD), said to be the most common form of dementia, which afflicts 25 million people worldwide, and 5 million people in America alone (Ferri et al., 2005). Having inherited a worldview that values rationality and regards cognition as a requisite of selfhood ('I think, therefore I am'), 'losing one's mind' to dementia is, for many, the worst imaginable illness – a tragedy that, in eroding the brain, erodes the essence of one's personhood (DeBaggio, 2002; James, 1998).

The last half of the 20th century has witnessed the dominance of molecular-reductionist approaches in the dementia field, which tend to emphasize the negative aspects of growing older and treat brain aging as a disease to be overcome. Social scientists have often referred to such transitions as 'medicalization': a process by which more and more of everyday human behavior has been brought under medical dominion, influence, and supervision (Estes and Binney, 1989; Foucault, 1994; Illich, 1976; Zola, 1990). In dementia, the dominant reductionist model has framed senility as a neuropathological 'disease-to-be-cured,' effectively narrowing its focus to the organic basis of dementia, feeding a largely technical view of brain aging, subsuming day-to-day issues of care and prevention beneath the search for a cure, and enabling the cultural stigmatization of persons diagnosed with AD and other dementias – and even those who are merely aging and experiencing the statistically normal decrements associated with senescence. This view of aging has suffused Western culture, frequently serving to limit the potential of aging persons to contribute to society in the later stages of their lives by isolating them, and thus depriving them of the benefits of social participation and precluding the possibility that they might help build social capital through their efforts. Even in academic research, people with dementia have been perceived to be incapable of eliciting personal accounts of their experience because their cognitive and verbal deficits are perceived as insurmountable (Bond and Corner, 2001; Hubbard et al., 2003).

The purpose of this chapter is to place dementia, particularly AD and its supposed precursor, mild cognitive impairment (MCI), in a broad social and historical context so that we may better comprehend the framework that has prevailed in Western culture to shape our current notion of what brain aging is. Such an understanding, which has its roots in contemporary critical gerontology (Baars et al., 2006), can help modern society humanize our models of care and challenge the overwhelming dread and angst that surround brain aging with a sense of hope and potential. While we may not be able to miraculously age backwards as Twain proposed, we do have the power to change our backwards approach to aging.

HISTORY OF DEMENTIA

Although it is true that all diseases have biological substrates, it is equally accurate that any disease, in order to be understood, must be situated in a cultural context and endowed with a set of common meanings. Thus, throughout human history, the comprehension of all disease has been contingent upon culturally specific frameworks and narratives used to understand particular biological events. Before influenza was understood as being caused by a virus, for instance, persons in the Middle Ages attributed it to the 'influence of the stars'; and before a condition like schizophrenia became a documented mental illness in modern times, previous generations regarded such persons as being possessed of spiritual gifts and healing talents. In similar fashion, brain aging and its associated pathology of beta-amyloid plaques (BAP) and neurofibrillary tangles (NFTs) hasn't always been thought of as a disease called Alzheimer's-type dementia, for which we could expect a pharmacological solution.

Indeed, before our molecular-reductionist era, the story of brain aging has been told in many ways. Dementia, which has its origins in Latin and means 'away from one's mind,' was long ago used to identify various dissidents and deviants, especially older women, who were castigated as witches when they began to show signs of mental decline. Moral degeneration was seen as a cause before biological degenerative processes took the stage of etiological concerns. The story has evolved throughout history. Scientists in the 18th and 19th centuries believed that age-related changes in cognitive health were the result of a dissipation of vital energy from the brain (Katzman and

Bick, 2000). Suffering in old age was seen as inevitable and natural, a fact of existence that was to be ameliorated perhaps, but not eliminated (Ballenger, 2006).

However, in the late 19th century, brain aging came to be understood as a biological event, as scientists began noting changes in the brain tissues and blood vessels of the elderly and associating this pathology with the loss of cognitive functioning. 'Brain psychiatry' was legitimated as a field, as sectioning and staining techniques provided scientists with a visual window into brain pathology (Engstrom, 2007). As knowledge of this pathology widened, the cognitive changes in old age that previous generations had resigned themselves to or associated with external factors such as profligacy were now seen as something internal that could potentially be eliminated with greater biological understanding. Brain aging had gone from the normal to the pathological (Canguilhem, 1989). There appeared to be good reason to replace the vague concept of 'senility' with more scientifically rigorous disease categories. Medical treatments became dependent on accurate diagnosis and specific therapies. The excitement of the discovery of the causative agent for syphilis, a common cause of dementia at that time, and the emergence of the first crude therapies, created a sense of progress based on biological knowledge. It was within this context that Dr. Alois Alzheimer of Germany received his formal training as a researcher and developed a particular skill in histology (the study of tissue through the use of a microscope).

Dr. Alzheimer and Auguste D.

In November 1906, at the age of 42, Alois Alzheimer presented a lecture entitled 'On a Peculiar, Severe Disease Process of the Cerebral Cortex' to the 37th Assembly of Southwest German Alienists (institutionally based psychiatrists) in Tübingen, Germany (Maurer and Maurer, 2003: 4). In his talk, he detailed his observations of a 51-year-old woman named Auguste Deter (Auguste D.), a patient whom he first treated in 1901 while serving as the director of the *Irrensstalt* (asylum) in Frankfurt. Auguste D. had presented with a multitude of symptoms relating to progressive cognitive impairment – delusions and speech impairments – and, upon postmortem investigation in 1906, was found to have high concentrations of plaques and tangles on her brain and a paucity of cells in the cerebral cortex (Tollis, 1994: 49).

Alzheimer faced a crucial classificatory dilemma: did Auguste D.'s symptoms represent an atypical, early-onset form of 'senile dementia,' or could they possibly represent a separate disease entity altogether? Since Auguste D.'s range of behavioral symptoms (hallucinations, wandering, emotional lability, etc.) and pathological markers (BAP and NFTs) were also observed in a great number of older persons in their 60s and 70s who were diagnosed with senile dementia, Alzheimer was apprehensive about formally classifying her condition as a specific disease process separate from aging. His boss, Emil Kraepelin – a man nicknamed by his peers as the 'Linnaeus of Psychiatry' – was not so hesitant. In 1910, Kraepelin officially coined the term *'Alzheimer's krankheit'* (Alzheimer's disease), including it on page 627 of the 8th edn. of his authoritative *Textbook of Psychiatry* (Kraepelin, 1910: 627).

Although the description was a mere paragraph obscurely placed in the nether-regions of Kraepelin's massive textbook, Alzheimer's reaction to the promulgation of the eponymous disease was one of ambivalence. In an article he submitted to the *Zeitschrift fur die Gesamte Neurologie and Psychiatrie* in 1911, he wrote that: 'Kraepelin still considers that the position of these cases is unclear,' and later concluded that 'There is, then, *no tenable reason to consider these cases as caused by a specific disease process*. They are senile psychoses, atypical forms of senile dementia. Nevertheless, they do assume a certain separate position so that one has to know of their existence' (cited in Whitehouse et al., 2000: 41). In Alzheimer's writing, then, one observes a scientist who was not particularly keen to see his 'peculiar' form of dementia enshrined as a pathological disease category separate from aging, especially in the absence of clearly differentiating biomarkers. Tellingly, throughout most of the early and mid 20th century, the clinico-pathological boundaries described by Kraepelin were called into question, and clinicians often avoided using the label 'Alzheimer's disease'.

The Rothschild movement: from reductionism to humanism

The inability to correlate Alzheimer's-type dementia with a clear and differentiable pathological substrate enabled the paradigmatic emphasis, the dominant narrative, to gradually shift from understanding the underlying biology of dementia to developing psychosocial methods that would better help aging persons and families cope with the day-to-day challenges of caring for loved ones with cognitive decline. Pioneers such as the American psychiatrist David Rothschild, who began his career trying to resolve the anomalous

findings concerning the pathology of Alzheimer's disease, developed a psychodynamic model of dementia care that predominated in Euro-America in the 1940s and 1950s, challenging the dominant biomedical models that dealt with dementia as a pathological event (Kitwood, 1997:55). He and his colleagues argued that, since the pathological structures characteristic of Alzheimer's disease and senile dementia (BAP and NFTs) had been found in a variety of other conditions these structures were not an expression of any particular disease process and should not be construed as such.

So too did this paradigm contain a humanistic message that still resonates today: that the bleak neuro-pathologization of aging could be damaging to modern society. 'Too exclusive a preoccupation with the cerebral pathology,' Rothschild wrote, had 'led to a tendency to forget that the changes are occurring in living, mentally functioning persons' (Ballenger, 2006: 46). The perils of aging were hard enough without reductionist disease labels like AD further marginalizing the elderly within the culture and denying them the respect conferred by age, not to mention the benefits of inclusion and social capital-building, Rothschild seemed to be saying. Even persons with decrements in memory and functionality had something to give back to their society.

It was not that the pathological substrate of aging was unimportant to Rothschild and his colleagues, but rather that each individual case required 'individual scrutiny, and instead of focusing attention solely on the impersonal tissue process ... the main object should be to estimate the relative importance of these (bio cultural) forces as factors in the origin' of dementia (2006: 49). In many ways, Rothschild and his colleagues were forerunners to the person-centered, quality-of-life-oriented approach to dementia that has emerged as a powerful cultural narrative in the past two decades that countervails against the reductionist paradigm, thanks to the work of such advocates as Tom Kitwood.

Technology and the renaissance of reductionism

Several developments in the 20th century increased the life expectancy of people living in industrialized countries; namely, the advent of modern medicines, machines, surgical procedures, improved diets, and sanitation measures that prolonged and protected life. By the late 1960s, thanks to improvements in hygienic and social conditions, and the successes of public health efforts in controlling epidemics and improving nutrition, an increasing portion of Western populations began living to ≥85 years old. These so-called 'old-old' persons became the most rapidly growing segment of populations in the industrial world. By 1970, the proportion of persons aged ≥ 65 years old in the US population had grown to almost 10 per cent, up from only 4.3 per cent in 1910 (US Bureau of the Census, 1970).

As societies were becoming populated by men and women who could look forward to longer lives, technical developments in various aspects of neuropathological and biochemical research – electron microscopy studies that could zero in on plaques and tangles, neurological imaging devices that could peer into the brain, laboratory procedures that could measure neurotransmitter levels in aging brains, for example – had advanced our ability to study the biology of dementia. Furthermore, research began to show that neurogenesis was possible in adult brains, and neuroscience's century-old dogma that there could be no addition of new neurons in the adult mammalian brain has gradually been revised (Gross, 2000). Taken together, these developments have paved the way for a return to a more reductionist, disease-oriented approach to senility.

THE CONTEMPORARY STATE OF ALZHEIMER'S DISEASE

Epidemiology

While Alzheimer's disease may have started with one nebulous case in 1906, and remained obscure through most of the 20th century, at present, it is said to affect 25 million people around the world (Ferri et al., 2005). The World Health Organization (WHO) predicts that by the year 2020, there will be nearly 30 million demented people in both developed and developing countries. These numbers will rise exponentially as life expectancy continues to increase in countries worldwide (Haan and Wallace, 2003). By the year 2030, it is estimated that nearly one-fifth (70 million) of the American population will be ≥ 65 years old, with average life expectancy being approximately 77.5 years for men and 83 for women.[1] And in 2040, it is estimated that there will be 40 million people aged ≥ 85 years old (Valiant and Mukamal, 2001: 839); this will push the percentage of persons in their 80s in the 65+ category from 26 per cent in 2000 to nearly 40 per cent 2040. Projections are similar in Europe, where half the population is expected to be 50 or older by 2030 (Harper, 2006: xii).

The demography is even more profound in the developing world, which, broadly speaking, has large populations with increasing numbers of people who are living to an older age as modernization occurs. Between 2000 and 2030 the percentage of persons aged ≥65 years old in developing nations is expected to go from 14 per cent to 23 per cent, and particular regions will experience more rapid growth than others. For instance the Asian-Pacific region, currently home to 600 million older people, is the most quickly aging world region, with 20 per cent of its projected population over 60 by 2050, which will at that date account for two-thirds of the world's two billion elders (Goodman and Harper, 2006: 373–4). Longer lives and lower fertility rates will keep shifting this age distribution exponentially in this region and others.

As medicine continues to advance in its ability to treat such conditions as cardiovascular disease, people will live longer. And as people live longer, there will be unprecedented levels of persons in the later stages of brain aging. The number of Americans to be diagnosed with Alzheimer's disease is projected to reach 14 million by 2050, and the organization Alzheimer's Disease International (ADI) estimates the number of people worldwide will exceed 80 million in that timeframe (Ferri et al., 2005). India and China already constitute the largest-ever populations of persons with dementia, and the developing world as a whole will comprise two-thirds of the worldwide Alzheimer's population in the next 50 years.[2] It seems that in order to prepare for the 'demographic boom', especially in the absence of a pharmacological 'silver bullet', the human species will need to be creative in figuring out ways to integrate aging persons into our cultures and to engage older persons as valuable cultural resources rather than as 'burdens'.

Current usage

The *DSM-IV (Diagnostic and Statistical Manual of Mental Disorders,* 4th edn.), National Institutes of Health, the Alzheimer's Association, and indeed nearly all other current classification authorities refer to Alzheimer's disease as the most common worldwide cause of dementia (American Psychiatric Association, 1994: 139). Despite the prevalence of other processes that cause dementia (including strokes, Parkinson's disease, hemorrhages, tumors, traumatic brain injury) (Schneider et al., 2007), 'Alzheimer's' has become a shorthand term for any memory problem associated with dementia. Despite the pervasiveness of the

AD label in our culture and its universally recognized associations with memory loss and neurodegeneration, clinicians still cannot agree on what Alzheimer's is or how to diagnose it properly. Consequently, there is an ongoing debate as to when someone should be diagnosed, or whether we should even diagnose aging persons with a 'disease' at all, given the stigma associated with the AD label.

Indeed, biocultural research has long presumed that cognitive health in old age is at least partly reliant on cultural factors such as strong supportive relationships within the community (Marmot and Syme, 1976; Marmot et al., 1975; Nagamoto et al., 1995), and that the stigmatizing effects of AD and other mental illness labels can limit the potential for older persons to contribute, and encourage age-discrimination practices (Marmot, 2003: 574–75; 2006) while elevating levels of stress and psychological and social morbidity (Williams and Goffman, 1987). In addition to dehumanizing affected persons, this social response can exacerbate the progression of dementing conditions by marginalizing diagnosed individuals and depriving them of the benefits of inclusion and interaction, autonomy, self-respect, and self-esteem. Recent contributions to the literature have noted that human biology is affected across the life span (Douthit and Dannefer, 2007; Hagestad and Dannefer, 2001; Leatherman and Goodman, 1997), and that a number of social conditions are detrimental to brain health, and may specifically affect one's resistance to the characteristic pathologies of so-called Alzheimer's disease (Douthit, 2006; Snowdon et al., 1997).

In an interesting double-entendre, AD is sometimes called a 'diagnosis of exclusion,' since no direct clinical proof of its presence can be obtained, and 25 or more other diagnoses for cognitive deficits must first be ruled out (American Psychiatric Association, 1994: 138–40). These other kinds of dementia include conditions associated with inadequate metabolic support of brain functions (such as hypothyroidism, vitamin B_{12} deficiency or external toxins), structural problems of the brain (such as strokes or tumors), and infectious diseases (such as HIV/AIDS and syphilis), just to mention a few.

Because the disease diagnosis is the result of an attempt to eliminate all other causes of the presenting symptoms, patients with dementia for which no specific cause can be identified are often labeled with a 'presumptive' diagnosis of Alzheimer's disease. Based on commonly used research criteria, a diagnosis of AD can only formally be made after death when autopsy tissue is available (although this classification is still suspect because, as mentioned, the key pathological

features of AD – BAP and NFTs – are also the pathological corollaries of normal brain aging) (American Psychiatric Association, 1994: 141).

The limits of current understanding concerning the toxicity of BAP and NFTs in AD has been further reinforced by The Nun Study (Snowdon et al., 1996, 1997), a landmark longitudinal investigation of Alzheimer's disease and aging. The study was conducted with 678 American members of the School of Sisters of Notre Dame religious order. For decades, researchers traced the cognitive development and degeneration of these cloistered women, scrutinizing everything from their writings as 20 year olds to their memory retention in old age to their postmortem brains. These postmortem exams were especially revealing, as they provided significant evidence that individuals may still function normally with relatively high concentrations of plaques and tangles, while those with the cognitive and behavioral symptoms of Alzheimer's may often be found to have a relatively smaller plaque burden. This scientific uncertainty, combined with the recognition that AD is a potentially 'excluding' and stigmatizing label for persons and families, has served to problematize the dominant reductionist-biomedical framework of Alzheimer's on which the search for a pharmacological cure is based.

There are further problems with classifying the *stages* of AD, as progression varies on an individual basis and can range anywhere from 3 to 20 years. While there are commonly held to be three stages of AD (mild, moderate, and severe), some have posited eight stages (see Reisberg et al., 1982), while others like the Alzheimer's Association have posited seven[3] (*DSM-III*, 1987: 119). Adding to the diagnostic quandary is the fact that it is often difficult to differentiate psychiatric causes of cognitive impairment from the neurological. For example, depression in older persons can manifest as cognitive retardation and simulate the symptoms of dementia (American Psychiatric Association, 1994: 141). Patients may be slow to speak and so preoccupied with internal concerns that they do not attend to other people adequately; thus, they often appear to forget what they are told, and seem to be succumbing to the early stages of Alzheimer's. Moreover, there is considerable overlap between different diagnostic groups. Despite advances in neuroimaging, there is now more confusion amongst professionals about how to differentiate vascular dementia from degenerative causes. Moreover, we have no definitive test to identify those at risk for Alzheimer's, so called pre-Alzheimer's.

There has been a recent push by some academics and the pharmaceutical industry to classify such pre-dementia persons as having a pathological condition called mild cognitive impairment or MCI (Petersen et al., 2001). MCI is said to be characterized by a degree of memory and other cognitive deficits that are not of sufficient magnitude to cause a problem in activities of daily living (ADLs), and hence do not represent a full-blown dementia. However, it is unclear just how disrupted the ADLs must be to warrant a diagnosis of AD or some other dementia. The 'onset' of MCI is equally fuzzy; specifically, there are questions about how many standard deviations below the norms of a reference population (and which population using which test) a formerly 'normal' person must fall before the MCI label is applied. Furthermore, in MCI, different cognitive abilities may be affected (memory, language, attention, etc.), resulting in considerable clinical variability. Some people who are labeled MCI actually improve over time; no two trajectories are the same. Consequently, MCI has been assailed as an arbitrary and heterogeneous term that should not be used clinically and may need to be discarded in research settings as well (Whitehouse and Juengst, 2005). Despite this critique, the National Institute on Aging (NIA; see below) has listed the discovery of MCI first on the 10 most important contributions of the federally funded Alzheimer Center programmes.

SOCIAL FORCES AND ALZHEIMER'S DISEASE

Western countries are said by scientifically oriented physicians to be entering an era of 'molecular medicine,' based on reductionist thinking about human health and disease. This molecular paradigm has promised to spawn an era of personalized care in which information about one's genetic makeup may be used to tailor individual strategies for the detection, treatment, or prevention of disease. It is a movement predicated on three premises: (1) that we will be able to identify key genetic lesions associated with a particular disease or disease subgroup; (2) that we will have a variety of available treatments for particular diseases; and (3) that we will be able to identify those genetic markers in such a way that we personally match the treatment with the individual. This has led to the emergence of pharmacogenomics, which, as the word implies, combines genetics with pharmaceutical treatments.

According to this genetic form of personalized medicine, such conditions as AD are principally caused by alterations in DNA that lead to changes in proteins, and once we know the proper molecular markers, we can offer early diagnosis and prepare

personalized treatments. Just how helpful the molecular–genetic paradigm can be for a condition such as Alzheimer's disease, which is clearly influenced by a variety of environmental and lifestyle factors throughout the life course, remains to be seen. In general, this form of medicine is based on somewhat outdated concepts of the nature and function of genes – that they are single agents relating to single or a small set of proteins. Regulation of genes by other genes through time and in different microcellular and macro-external environments are not part of this simplistic formulation. Moreover, single deterministic autosomal dominant mutations (such as those on chromosomes 1, 14, and 21, which cause some rare cases of early-onset familial AD) are easier to understand than non-causative susceptibility genes such as apolipoprotein E (*ApoE*), which is on chromosome 19. Although many studies show that having one or two copies of the *ApoE-4* allele (one of the three common forms or 'alleles' of *ApoE*) increases risk for AD, possessing it does not mean someone will get AD, or that he/she will be cognitively vital without it. Moreover, *ApoE-4* is a risk factor for other neurological conditions and for heart disease, and it may actually be protective for macular degeneration (Lock et al., 2006).

Although our molecular genetic comprehension of Alzheimer's disease is still nebulous, what is clear is that powerful social forces such as government organizations and the pharmaceutical industry have promoted the molecular movement in Alzheimer's for the last several decades, and in doing so, endorsed a story that has misled the public with promises for a cure, while directing attention away from likely social causes and more fundamental issues of inclusion and community response (Douthit, 2006; Whitehouse and George, 2008).

Government organizations

In 1974, the National Institute on Aging (NIA) was born as a part of the National Institute of Health. Immediately, the NIA, under the leadership of Dr. Robert Butler, a practicing clinical psychiatrist and gerontologist, began promoting AD as its primary research area, allowing federal funding for the 'disease' to be channeled from federal coffers to individual researchers. Butler said, 'I decided that we had to make it (Alzheimer's disease) a household word. And the reason I felt that, is that's how the pieces get identified as a national priority. And I call it *the health politics of anguish*' (Fox, 1989, my italics). This strategic campaign was soon associated with predictions for the rapid development of effective therapies, and even cures. Butler's efforts were largely successful and, within years, dementia of the Alzheimer's type became a frequent talking point in Congress. On September 15, 1983, the US House of Representative proposed a resolution declaring November of that year to be National Alzheimer's Disease month. Congress passed the resolution in the hope that 'an increase in the national awareness of the problem of Alzheimer's disease may stimulate the interests and concern of the American people, which may lead, in turn, to increased research and eventually to the discovery of a cure' (Ballenger, 2006: 193). As Lawrence Cohen has pointed out in his ethnography *No Aging in India* (1998), while geriatricians such as Butler may have been driven by the well-intentioned motivation to transform senility into treatable, researchable categories that would absolve individuals of moral responsibility through the attribution of cognitive loss to subcellular disease processes, those who were relegated to Alzheimer's victimhood found themselves bearing the dehumanizing brunt of an unquestionable pathology that differentiated and isolated them. Butler has since acknowledged that Alzheimer's is not one condition, and certain scientific views concerning its nature have come to dominate excessively (personal communication).

Ongoing advocacy by high-profile celebrities – such as former US president Ronald Reagan and Princess Yasmin Aga Khan (daughter of film star Rita Hayworth) – brought even more attention to Alzheimer's, promoting hope that a cure would be possible with increased funding. Over time, the US government has responded to such appeals. In 1979, the NIA spent approximately $4 million on AD research; by 1991, it spent $155 million – a 37-fold increase (Ballenger, 2006). In 2007, federal research funding for the 'War on AD' swelled to $643 million.

The re-framing of senility as Alzheimer's disease and the large-scale financial commitments from the government over the past several decades has reified brain aging as a 'disease' to be defeated through intervention on the molecular level. The approach to finding a cure has been largely split between those who believe beta-amyloid plaques initiate neuronal death (referred to as BAPtists) and those who believe neurofibrillary tangles are the causal agent (referred to as TAUists, since tau proteins form the NFTs). Even though there remains a weak correlation between BAP plaques and cognitive dysfunction, no definitive proof exists to distinguish amyloid as the lone perpetrator of Alzheimer's disease, and evidence is that a variety of processes co-occur to produce dementia (Schneider et al., 2007; Wang et al., 2003).

The BAPtists have dominated the field for the past decade, monopolizing governmental funding and limiting research into other fruitful areas of biological and psychosocial research, including quality of life, caregiving, and prevention.

The somewhat simplistic promise of a molecular cure for AD has generated excitement among researchers that has trickled down to family members and caregivers of Alzheimer's victims, who speak passionately and publicly, and have helped shape the contemporary paradigm of AD. Not only has dementia come to be known as a discrete 'organic disease' (*DSM III*, 1987), but also a mainstream 'idiom of distress' (Nichter, 1981) has begun to emerge around the concept of AD. Alzheimer's has acquired dreadful monikers – as '*a loss of self*,' a '*slow death of the mind*,' a '*second childhood*,' a '*living death*' that creates a '*never-ending funeral*' for caregivers (Fox, 1986). AD is personified as a ravaging, marauding '*mind robber*,' a '*stealer of decades*' – in short, a microscopic antagonist against which science, with strong backing from the public and private sectors, is fighting a '*war*'. As Jaber Gubrium's work (1986) has shown, these metaphors are powerful in guiding cultural understandings of brain aging. Emily Martin's (1987, 1990, 1994) work on the metaphors and tropes used to describe immunological and physiological processes has elucidated the degree to which doctors and patients view health as a military-like battle and 'disease' as an enemy. Aggressive metaphors in Alzheimer's disease place aging persons and families on a medical battlefield against a dark, shadowy foe, promising impending victory and creating millions of 'victims' in the process. As Tom Kitwood has written, this 'highly defensive tactic … turn[s] those who have dementia into a different species, not persons in the full sense' (Kitwood, 1997: 14).

In the United States, the NIA continues to be a driving force in such cultural understandings. Most of the energy from the federal government focuses on improving diagnostic approaches through imaging, genetics, and biological research linked to attempts to find drug therapies. A neuroimaging initiative was designed to develop biological markers to track the progression of disease and develop diagnostic tests, and much hype has been associated with imaging of amyloid protein. However, these studies continue to demonstrate significant overlap amongst those variously labeled normal, MCI, and AD. In our opinion, AD will remain a clinical diagnosis and sociomarkers (i.e., clinically applied disease labels) will be more important than biological ones. Moreover, there are significant methodological problems with imaging that tend to get ignored. Other biomarkers such as measurements of amyloid protein in the cerebrospinal fluid have similar limitations due to overlap between different populations. It is possible that tracking a biological marker will allow us to understand the effects of new drugs. However, it will be necessary to demonstrate clinical benefit. If a correlation between reduced amyloid burden and disease modification with symptomatic relief cannot be established, then the benefits of imaging are seriously limited.

The field of dementia has moved from an emphasis on drug treatments to improve cognitive symptoms to treatments that might slow the biological progression of disease. Animal studies frequently provide evidence that particular substances prevent brain damage in rats and other species, and epidemiological studies in human populations also confirm that particular substances are associated with a lower risk of dementia. For example, hormone replacement therapy may ostensibly 'work' in animal models of AD and may be associated with less AD incidence in human populations. However, randomized controlled trials have not supported the protective effects of such agents. And even though such trials are considered the 'gold standard' in scientific research, their value is often exaggerated and results from multiple studies are often inconsistent. Generalizability from a carefully selected efficacy trial may not be possible, and approved drugs are often found to be less effective in actual practice. Most of the studies conducted by the NIA AD Cooperative Study (a national multicenter trials group of agents to treat AD) have not provided evidence of efficacy.

In essence, the problem with the NIA approach is the assumption that Alzheimer's is one condition that is unrelated to normal aging and hence will yield itself to single diagnostic tests or therapies. This linear, reductionist way of viewing the world, while common to Western biomedical theorizing, is not altogether helpful when considering a complex and variable condition such as brain aging. When one recognizes the variability in AD and the possibility that multiple diagnostic panels and multiple drug regimens might be necessary, there emerge major concerns about discovering singular profiles in the first place, monitoring for serious interaction effects, and paying for these multiple interventions.

The pharmaceutical industry

Ineluctably, capitalism and profit have also been forces that have defined the contours of public understanding of Alzheimer's. The pharmaceutical industry influences our very conceptions of health and disease. Through a combination of lobbying efforts at the levels of national and state governments, investments of resources in educating and entertaining physicians and other healthcare providers, and perhaps most concerning, direct marketing to patients and their families, the industry teaches us how to be sick and hence how to be consumers of their products (Angell, 2004). Health is considered to be the absence of disease, with pills and treatments serving to maintain and regain health. The industry even attempts to create disease labels – for example, most recently a probable failure in so-called involuntary emotional expression disorder (IEED) in AD (Whitehouse and Waller, 2007) – and also contributes to extending the boundaries of disease into normality by sponsoring conferences and enlisting respected physicians to promote concepts such as MCI. The sum effect of such actions serves to reify and legitimate such labels as MCI in medical circles. Without a doubt, big pharma is the prime force for the medicalization of aging, and the billions of dollars spent trying to influence politicians, physicians, and patients might be more wisely spent in better basic research (Kassirer, 2005).

Lay organizations

Alzheimer's Disease International (ADI) is an umbrella organization of associations around the world that aims to help establish and strengthen lay associations throughout the world, and to raise global awareness about AD and other causes of dementia. At present, there are Alzheimer's associations in nearly 80 different countries; in the United States, there are more than 200 Alzheimer's Association (AA) chapters and 2000 support groups. As their mission, these associations provide core services to families, including information and referral, support groups, care consultation and assessment, education, and safety services. Whereas ADI tends to emphasize care, advocacy, and education on an international scale, the American AA has led the search for a cure, and has thus promulgated the reductionist biological story of AD in its pursuit of visibility and funding. Tellingly, its mission statement explains that the organization has the 'Compassion to care, and the leadership to conquer.'

Person-centered care

Some lay organizations have been influenced by the person-centered care (PCC) movement which has emerged in the last several decades as a response to this reductionist, medicalized focus. PCC adherents believe that the emphasis on 'dementia as an organic condition' has framed brain aging as an aberrant pathophysiological event rather than as a normal life process, causing us to view aging persons, even loved ones, as 'diseased' and in doing so producing what Tom Kitwood has famously termed a 'malignant social psychology' that is rampant in our culture (Cohen, 1998; Kitwood, 1997). Kitwood's provocative term focuses on the tendencies to ignore the subjectivity and quality of life of those who are suffering dementia, and to stigmatize, devalue, disempower, banish, objectify, and invalidate them on account of their neuropathological condition. Those who emphasize a PCC approach hypothesize that such treatment has biocultural consequences. Rather than engaging those with dementia and viewing their condition empathetically, or drawing upon their remaining strengths to help build social capital and maintain their cognitive vitality, this malignant social psychology distances us from persons with dementia, emphasizes deficits, and precludes the empathetic engagement that persons who are aging deserve in a civil society.

A further problem with the dominant approach identified by the PCC perspective is its justification of a physical separation and social exclusion of 'Alzheimer's victims' or persons with MCI, which often entails placement in institutions where they are given ritualized care with minimal regard for their wishes, needs, and fears. Numerous researchers might agree with John Bond and colleagues (2002) that once the label of dementia has been applied, even normal behavior is interpreted in terms of disease stages. Thus, the PCC movement believes that the 'loss of self' is linked not to the neuropathology of a degenerative disease alone, but results from a 'neuro-pathic' ideology in society that positions people with dementia as hopeless and confused, and creates a 'loss of place' for demented persons (Sabat and Harré, 1992). Proponents of PCC believe that the effects of this marginalization can exacerbate dementia symptoms and, since the 1990s, researchers and lay organizations espousing PCC values have called for future research, care practice, and policy formulation to seek out the perspective of the individual and study the socio-environments in which individuals are embedded rather than merely settling for objective symptomatology (Nygard, 2006; Hubbard et al., 2003). Both professionals and ethnographic researchers who have worked closely with persons with dementia have argued that amidst the diminishing grasp of a historical self remains a yearning for a self-in-relation, and that this possibility must not be eclipsed by the hegemony of the medical model (Stein, 2002).

EFFORTS TO REFRAME DEMENTIA AND COGNITIVE AGING

The observations suggest that the current framework for defining Alzheimer's may prevent us from seeing the potential for vitality, fulfillment, and even wisdom that still exists during declining years. Elsewhere we and others (Ballenger, 2006; Cohen, 1998; Kitwood, 1997; Stein, 2002; Whitehouse and George, 2008; Whitehouse et al., 2005) have argued for the need to challenge the tyranny of the scientifically uncertain and socially stigmatizing Alzheimer's disease story to make both cultural understandings and social institutions more responsive, and so that persons with memory challenges and their families may tell their own stories about brain aging rather than succumbing to the generality of a vague, imprecise, and stigmatizing disease label that emphasizes only decline.

Thinking about dementia in terms of narrative is important because the stories we tell about brain aging can position people in a culture, affecting the way they are regarded, their modes of interaction, their self-perceptions, and our estimations of their capacity to be self-sufficient and give to others, with all of these psychosocial effects invariably impacting biologically upon individual brains. It is conceivable to think that by changing the story we tell about AD as a culture, we can improve the trajectory of persons who are aging, and can change the entire way we regard the process of growing older in Western culture. Such changes are already underway around the world.

The winds of change

Interventions influenced by the PCC movement have sought to bring the person into focus rather than the disease. For instance, a form of patient care called validation therapy (Feil, 1993) was developed to affirm the experiences of people with dementia rather than pathologize them. This approach was taken further by Goudie and Stokes (1989) whose resolution therapy approach emphasizes empathy and communication. Another major contribution has been the development of narrative therapies (Basting, 2001) that encourage expressions of creativity in persons with dementia.

Reminiscence therapies (Butler, 1963; Coleman, 1988) have emerged, using aids such as music, photographs, and household equipment (Ashida, 2000; Mills and Coleman, 1994; Woods et al., 2005; 1992) to help persons with dementia engage long-term memory and so retain a semblance of coherence to their personhood (Brooker and Duce, 2000). Alzheimer's units in some assisted living facilities have been renamed 'Memory Support Units'. Some clinical neurologists have empowered their patients with the ability to choose or reject the label 'Alzheimer's' and 'MCI,' explaining that, in addition to its potentially stigmatizing effects, AD and MCI are not singular conditions, but represent a variety of biological conditions intimately related to brain aging, and that these biomedical labels can have deleterious effects on one's late-life course (Whitehouse, 2001).

Additionally, some person-centered facilities have begun making efforts to collect life histories from each resident so that staff can incorporate biographical knowledge into care planning and practice and see residents as persons with meaningful histories rather than aging persons with decrepit brains (Gibson, 1991; Murphy, 1994). Some facilities have even recruited local schoolchildren to elicit these histories from residents; others have involved residents in 'work groups' where they generate ideas and offer input to the facility about how to change institutional practices, policies, and décor to make the place more liveable (Dannefer et al., 2008). Person-centered therapies as diverse as massage, relaxation, aromatherapy, pet therapy, and Reiki therapy have also grown in popularity in PCC facilities. Others reject such therapeutic approaches as 'add-ons', and have successfully incorporated comparably rich social and interactive experiences into the ordinary routines of everyday life (Barkan, 2005; Dannefer et al., 2007). Still others have called for persons with AD to be engaged as collaborators in research to help them construct a worthy valued social persona and mitigate against the 'learned helplessness' while offering useful insights about their environment (Patterson, 2007; Sabat, 2003; Siders et al., 2006). Such research can accrue other benefits as well, such as enhancing our knowledge about the effects of dementia and about how to provide a more supportive, humane, and enlivening environment. Ultimately, each of these developments in PCC shares in the belief that de-pathologizing and de-stigmatizing brain aging can create therapeutic, non-medicalized environments that may have neurophysiological benefits for persons with dementia and can, at very least, promote quality of life and not expedite cognitive decline (Karlsson et al., 1987).

Re-imagining the Alzheimer's narrative

In Japan, there are efforts underway to evolve the diagnostic terminology for persons labeled with mental illnesses associated with aging. The label traditionally given to persons with Alzheimer's-type dementia, *chihou*, is a compound word, meaning something akin to 'foolish' or 'stupid.' This connotation is commonly perceived as an insult, and many people given a *chihou* diagnosis are often, quite understandably, ashamed and deeply resentful (Miyamoto et al., 2007). The severe stigma has engendered a need for a new label, and laypersons, government agencies, and professionals in the field have proposed that the new label be *ninchishou*. *Ninchishou* is also a compound word, with *ninchi* meaning 'cognition', and *shou* meaning something akin to 'syndrome', creating an expression that means something akin to 'cognitive syndrome.'

In 2005, Japan's Ministry of Health, Labor, and Welfare (MHLW) posted the intent, purpose, and related information of changing the name for dementia on their website and invited opinions from the public, and *ninchishou* was eventually selected. Shortly thereafter, the MHLW distributed notice of the name change widely across official, professional, and academic bodies as well as the popular press. These social institutions began disseminating this new label through a variety of grassroots and mass-media strategies.

The intention of this semantic adaptation is to lessen the tendency to ostracism and to help communities see the person rather than the dementia. The logic behind the change went something like this: modify the label that is commonly used in clinics, change the story patients and their families find themselves a part of, emphasize the remaining capacity of those who are aging, and improve quality of life without compromising clinical care. Most importantly, this change was brought about democratically by the Japanese people rather than by the medical community.

Similarly, in Canada, the Alzheimer's Society hands out t-shirts that read 'The Story is Changing.' Leaders at the provincial chapter in Québec have developed a campaign to try to eradicate the word 'dementia' from the international psychiatric language, arguing that, in English, and particularly French, the word 'dementia' has connotations that are far too pejorative.

A narrative shift is also present in Alzheimer's caregiving literature. An American author, Ann Davidson has written two books about the experience of caregiving for her husband, Julian, who was affected by dementia. Whereas other books in the genre tend to emphasize the horror of succumbing to dementia, and the burdens of caregiving, the title of Davidson's first book, *Alzheimer's Disease: A Love Story* is significant. She argues that it is not necessary that tragedy be the lens through which we view cognitive decline. Instead of seeing her husband's condition as a loss of self that created a shell of a man and endless bereavement for her, she wanted to grow closer to him by embracing the interdependency caused by cognitive challenges, and actually battled with the publisher to include the words 'Alzheimer's' and 'love' in the book's title. In her second book, *A Curious Kind of Widow*, which focuses on caregiving, she writes:

> During that first year after the diagnosis, in a hypnosis session with a psychiatrist, an insight came. As I lay stiff with anxiety on the doctor's couch, that wise man asked me what I wanted. Suddenly, a flash appeared: I wanted to 'go down' in a spirit of love, not fear and anger, no matter what happened.

Ann's and Julian's journey was still a great struggle, but one that was defined by emotional connection and happy, joyful times. Even when her husband's decline necessitated that he be placed in assisted living, he and Anne would still share quality time together – walking outdoors, listening to music, holding hands – and Julian still managed to maintain a circle of friends and volunteer at a local food bank. Ann's choice to go down in a spirit of love never faltered and her narrative of love prevailed over the mainstream cultural narrative of AD.

Building in environmental challenges and social justice

While the changing framework of Alzheimer's can be observed on a micro level in the narratives of individuals, it will also have a bearing on our larger cultural approach to treating and preventing dementia. The current and controversial BAP and NFT models upon which most public and private research endeavors on AD are based are not only incomplete, but also they are limited in their scope. Specifically, their disproportionate focus on the pathology that appears late in life has the effect of obscuring the many insults to the brain that occur over the continuum of one's life. Since AD appears not to be one disease, but rather a variety of conditions related to aging, it is unlikely to expect a silver bullet for Alzheimer's, and incumbent on us to think more holistically about brain aging.

Rethinking current models will require us to change our conception of what brain aging means.

If we accept the mounting evidence that late-life dementia has correlates in early development, and indeed with environmental and dietary exposures across the continuum of one's life (Barker, 1996; Basha et al., 2005; Dosunmu et al., 2007; Stein et al., 2008), the 'fight' against 'Alzheimer's disease' must begin early in the life course (Douthit, 2006; Douthit and Dannefer, 2007). Younger brains are most vulnerable to the deleterious effects of polluted, malnourished, and stressful environments. Creating holistic strategies of intervention and prevention based on a life-course perspective and a richer understanding of social and cultural context is necessary. Although investments in basic biological research may provide some benefit and hope for the future, they will not likely be enough.

CONCLUSION

This chapter's purpose has been to place dementia in a historical context and to provide a perspective on contemporary frameworks for interpreting brain aging. We have discussed how standard biomedical approaches often fail to account for the origins of concepts, and thus lose the capacity for critical engagement, which can stifle progress. The last half of the 20th century has witnessed the dominance of molecular-reductionist approaches in the dementia field, which emphasize the negative aspects of growing older and militarize brain aging as a disease to be defeated. Medicalization has suffused our social and political institutions, narrowing Western culture's focus to the organic basis of dementia, at times feeding a largely technical view of brain aging, subsuming day-to-day issues of care and prevention beneath the search for a cure, and enabling the cultural stigmatization of persons diagnosed with AD and other dementias. This has perhaps limited the potential of aging persons to contribute to society and deprived them of the benefits of social participation. It seems reasonable to ask whether a more sociohistorically informed understanding of the current cultural 'narrative' of dementia can expand our horizons beyond conventional approaches, humanize those with aging brains, challenge the overwhelming dread and angst that surround brain aging with a sense of hope and potential, and make the importance of care and prevention commensurate with finding a cure.

As we move into the future, as a species, the world will be increasingly challenged by the environmental consequences of global warming and other human interventions in the biosphere.

Global population aging represents a major challenge to social institutions and cultural beliefs. Innovative ways of informing, educating, and adapting societies to the challenges ahead are required. The questions are manifold:

- How are age-related changes in mental processing to be understood?
- Can we more comprehensively understand the reality and experience that is called dementia?
- With other pressing health and environmental concerns, how much should we be investing in biological solutions to dementia?
- How can we use information technologies and other non-pharmacological therapies to address the cognitive challenges of aging?
- How can we protect and educate the minds of our younger generations and foster the kind of ethical discourse that can create individual and collective moral imaginations necessary to keep adapting to our changing world?
- What are our responsibilities to future generations?
- How can we take maximum advantage of the experience and remaining skills and talents of older citizens and enable opportunities to create wisdom?

Ultimately, if we can continue to increase our understanding of the social and cultural context in which our 'medicalized' conceptions of cognitive aging have emerged, it may allow us to imagine a wide range of possibilities – in sum, a new cultural narrative – that can be applied for the continuation of wellness and quality of life for citizens both now and in the future.

NOTES

1 Alzheimer's Association. http://www.alz.org/AboutAD/statistics.asp (accessed October 12, 2006).
2 Alzheimer's Association. http://www.alz.org/AboutAD/statistics.asp (accessed October 12, 2006).
3 http://www.alz.org/AboutAD/stages.asp (accessed October 26, 2006).

REFERENCES

American Psychiatric Association (1994) *DSM-IV: Diagnostic and Statistical Manual of Mental Disorders*, 4th edn. Washington, DC: American Psychiatric Association.

Angell, M. (2004) *The Truth About the Drug Companies*. New York: Random House.

Ashida, S. (2000) 'The effect of reminiscence music therapy sessions on changes in depressive symptoms in elderly persons with dementia', *Journal of Music Therapy*, 37(3): 170–82.

Baars, J., Dannefer, D., Phillipson, P., and Walker, A. (2006) *Aging, Globalization and Inequality: The New Critical Gerontology*. Amityville, NY: Baywood.

Ballenger, J. (2006) *Self, Senility, and Alzheimer's Disease in Modern America: A History*. Baltimore, MD: Johns Hopkins University Press.

Barkan, B. (2005) 'How elders can rebalance the world', *Tikkun*, 23: 54.

Barker, D.J.P. (1996) 'The origins of coronary heart disease in early life', in C.J.K. Henry and S. Ulijaszek (eds), *Long Term Consequences of Early Environment: Growth, Development and the Lifespan Developmental Perspective*. Cambridge: Cambridge University Press.

Basha, M.R., Wei, W., Bakheet, S.A., et al. (2005) 'The fetal basis of amyloidogenesis: exposure to lead and latent overexpression of amyloid precursor protein and beta-amyloid in the aging brain', *The Journal of Neuroscience*, 25(4): 823–9.

Basting, A.D. (2001) 'God is a talking horse: dementia and the performance of self', *The Drama Review*, 45(3): 78–94.

Bond, J. and Corner, L. (2001) 'Researching dementia: are there unique methodological challenges for health services research?', *Aging and Society*, 21: 95–116.

Bond, J., Corner, L., Liley, A., and Ellwood, C. (2002) 'Medicalization of insight and caregivers' responses to risk in dementia', *Dementia*, 1(3): 313–28.

Brooker, D. and Duce, L. (2000) 'Well-being and activity in dementia: a comparison of group reminiscence therapy, structured goal-directed group activity, and unstructured time', *Aging and Mental Health*, 4: 354–8.

Butler, R.N. (1963) 'The life review: an interpretation of reminiscence in the aged', *Psychiatry*, 26: 65–76.

Canguilhem, G. (1989) *The Normal and the Pathological*. New York: Zone Books.

Cohen, L. (1998) *No Aging in India: Alzheimer's, the Bad Family, and Other Modern Things*. Berkeley, CA: University of California Press.

Coleman, J.S. (1988) 'Social capital in the creation of human capital', *American Journal of Sociology*, 94(S1): S95–120.

Dannefer, D., Stein, P., Siders R., and Patterson, R.S. (2008) 'Is that all there is? The concept of care and the dialectic of critique', *Journal of Aging Studies*, 22: 101–8.

DeBaggio, T. (2002) *Losing My Mind: An Intimate Look at Life with Alzheimer's*. New York: The Free Press/Simon and Schuster.

Dosunmu, R., Wu, J., Basha, M.R., and Zawia, N.H. (2007) 'Environmental and dietary risk factors in Alzheimer's disease', *Expert Rev Neurother*, 7(7): 887–900.

Douthit, K.Z. (2006) 'Dementia in the Iron Cage: the biopsychiatric construction of Alzheimer's dementia', in J. Baars, D. Dannefer, C. Phillipson, and A. Walker (eds), *Aging, Globalization and Inequality: The New Critical Gerontology*. New York: Haywood Publishing Company.

Douthit, K.Z. and Dannefer, D. (2007) 'Social forces, life course consequences: cumulative disadvantage and "getting Alzheimer's", in J.M. Wilmouth and K.F. Ferraro (eds), *Gerontology: Perspectives and Issues*, 3rd edn. New York: Springer.

DSM-III. Diagnostic and Statistical Manual of Mental Disorders, 3rd edn. Washington: APA, 1987.

Engstrom, E.J. (2007) 'Researching dementia in imperial Germany: Alois Alzheimer and the economics of psychiatric practice', *Culture, Medicine, and Psychiatry*, 31: 405–13.

Estes, C.L. and Binney, E.A. (1989) 'The biomedicalization of aging: dangers and dilemmas', *The Gerontologist*, 29(5): 587–96.

Feil, N. (1993) *The Validation Breakthrough: Simple Techniques for Communicating with People with Alzheimer's Type Dementia*. Baltimore, MD: Health Professions.

Ferri, C., Prince, M., Brayne, C., et al. (2005) 'Global prevalence of dementia: a Delphi consensus study', *Lancet*, 366: 2112–17.

Foucault, M. (1994) 'The birth of social medicine', in J.D. Faubion (ed.), *Michael Foucault Power: Essential Works of Foucault: 1954–1984*, Vol. 3. London: Penguin.

Fox, P. (1989) 'Rise of the Alzheimer's disease movement', *The Milbank Quarterly*, 67(1): 82.

Fox, P.J. (1986) 'Alzheimer's disease: an historical overview', *The American Journal of Alzheimer's Care and Related Disorders and Research*, 1(4): 18–24.

Gibson, C. (1991) 'A concept of empowerment', *Journal of Advanced Nursing*, 16: 354–61.

Goodman, R. and Harper, S. (2006) 'Introduction: Asia's position in the new global demography', *Oxford Development Studies*, 34:4, 373–85.

Goudie, F. and Stokes, G. (1989) 'Understanding confusion', *Nursing Times*, 85(39): 35–7.

Gross, C.G. (2000) 'Neurogenesis in the adult brain: death of a dogma', *Nature Reviews*, 1: 67–73.

Gubrium, J. (1986) *Oldtimers and Alzheimer's: The Descriptive Organization of Senility*. Greenwich, CT: JAI Press.

Hagestad, G.O. and Dannefer, D. (2001) 'Concepts and theories of aging: beyond microfication in social science approaches', in R.H. Binstock and L.K. George (eds), *Handbook of Aging and the Social Sciences*, 5th edn. New York: Academic Press.

Hann, M.N. and Wallace, R. (2003) 'Can dementia be prevented? Brain aging in a population context', *Annual Review of Public Health*, 25: 1–24.

Harper, S. (2006) *Aging Societies: Myths, Challenges and Opportunities*. London: Hodder-Arnold.

Hubbard, G., Downs, M., and Tester, S. (2003) 'Including older people with dementia in research: challenges and strategies', *Aging Mental Health*, 7: 251–62.

Illich, I. (1976) *Medical Nemesis*. New York: Bantam Books.

James, A. (1998) 'Stigma of mental illness', *Lancet*, 352(26): 1048.

Karlsson, I., Brane, G., Melin, E., Nyth, A.L., and Rybo, E. (1987) 'Effects of environmental stimulation on biochemical and psychological variables in dementia', *Acta Psychiatrica Scandinavica*, 77(2): 207–13.

Kassirer, J. (2005) *On the Take: How America's Complicity with Big Business Can Endanger Your Health*. Oxford: Oxford University Press.

Katzman, R. and Bick, K. (2000) *Alzheimer Disease: The Changing View*. San Diego, CA: Academic Press.

Kitwood, T. (1997) *Dementia Reconsidered: The Person Comes First*. Philadelphia: Open University Press.

Kraepelin, E. (1910) *Psychiatrie: Ein Lehrbuch für Studierende und Ärzte*. Leipzig: Barth.

Leatherman T, and Goodman, A. (1997) 'Expanding the biocultural synthesis toward a biology of poverty', *American Journal of Physical Anthropology*, 102: 1–3.

Lock et al. (2006) *Genetics and Alzheimer Research: Thinking about Dementia*. New Jersey: Rutgers University Press.

Marmot, M. (2003) 'Self esteem and health', *BMJ*, 327: 574–5.

Marmot, M. (2006) Health in an unequal world, *Lancet*, 368: 2081–94.

Marmot, M.G. and Syme, S.L. (1976) 'Acculturation and coronary heart disease in Japanese Americans', *American Journal of Epidemiology*, 104: 225–47.

Marmot, M.G., Syme, S.L., and Kagan, A. (1975) 'Epidemiologic studies of coronary heart disease and stroke in Japanese men living in Japan, Hawaii, and California: prevalence of coronary and hypertensive heart disease and associated risk factors', *American Journal of Epidemiology*, 102(6): 514–25.

Martin, E. (1987) *The Woman in the Body*. Boston: Beacon Press.

Martin, E. (1990) 'Toward an anthropology of immunology: the body as nation state', *Medical Anthropology Quarterly*, 4(4): 410–26.

Martin, E. (1994) *Flexible Bodies: Tracking Immunity in American Culture from the Days of Polio to the Age of AIDS*. New York: Beacon Press.

Maurer, K. and Maurer, U. (2003) *Alzheimer: The Life of a Physician and the Career of a Disease*. New York: Columbia University Press.

Mills, M.A. and Coleman, P.G. (1994) 'Nostalgic memories in dementia – a case study', *International Journal of Aging and Human Development*, 38(3): 203–19.

Miyamoto, M., Asada, T., Whitehouse, P.J., and George, D.R. (in press) 'The coordinated government, professional and public effort to change the word for "dementia" in Japan'.

Murphy, F. (1994) 'A staff development programme to support the incorporation of the McGill model of nursing into an out-patient clinic department', *Journal of Advanced Nursing*, 20(4): 750–4.

Nagamoto, I., Nomaguchi, M., and Takigawa, M. (1995) 'Anxiety and quality of life in residents of a special nursing home', *International Journal of Geriatric Psychiatry*, 10(7): 541–5.

Nichter, M. (1981) 'Idioms of distress: alternatives in the expression of psychosocial distress: a case study from South India', *Culture, Medicine and Psychiatry*, 5(4): 379–408.

Nygard, L. (2006) 'How can we get access to the experiences of people with dementia? Suggestions and reflections',

Scandinavian Journal of Occupational Therapy, 13: 101–12.

Patterson, R.S. (2007) 'Learning from those who know: empowering elders to promote culture change in a skilled nursing facility', The 60th Annual Scientific Meeting of the Gerontological Society of America, San Francisco, CA.

Petersen, R., Doody, R., Kurz, A., et al. (2001) 'Current concepts in mild cognitive impairment', *Archives of Neurology*, 58(12): 1985–92.

Reisberg, B., Ferris, S., deLeon, M., and Crook, T. (1982) 'The global deterioration scale for the assessment of primary degenerative dementia', *American Journal of Psychiatry*, 139(9): 1136–9.

Sabat, S.R. (2003) 'Some potential benefits of creating research partnerships with people with Alzheimer's disease', *Research Policy and Planning*, 21(2): 5–12.

Sabat, S.R. and Harré, R. (1992) 'The construction and deconstruction of self in Alzheimer's disease', *Aging and Society*, 12: 443–61.

Schneider, J.A., Arvanitakis, Z., Bang, W., and Bennett, D.A. (2007) 'Mixed brain pathologies account for most dementia cases in community-dwelling older persons', *Neurology*, 69(24): 2197–204.

Siders, R.A., Patterson, R.S., and Dannefer, D. (2006) 'Students "do" culture change: Learning action research in long-term care settings', the 59th Annual Scientific Meeting of the Gerontological Society of America, Dallas, TX.

Snowdon, D.A., Kemper, S.J., Mortimer, J.A., et al. (1996) 'Linguistic ability in early life and cognitive function and Alzheimer's disease in late life: findings from the Nun Study', *JAMA*, 275(7): 528–32.

Snowdon D.A., Kemper, S.J., Mortimer, J.A., et al. (1997) 'Aging and Alzheimer's disease: lessons from the Nun Study', *Gerontologist*, 37(2): 150–6.

Stein, P. (2002) 'Beyond culture change: action research in long-term care', Paper presented at the meeting of the Gerontological Society of America, Boston, MA.

Tollis, D. (1994) 'Who was Alzheimer?', *Nursing Times*, 90(34): 24–30.

US Bureau of the Census (1970) *Statistical Abstract of the United States: 1970*, 91st edn. Washington, DC: US Government Printing Office.

Valliant, G. and Mukamal, K. (2001) 'Successful aging', *American Journal of Psychiatry*, 158(6): 839–47.

Wang, S.S., Kazantziw, V., and Good, T.A. (2003) 'A kinetic analysis of the mechanism of β-amyloid induced G protein activation', *Journal of Theoretical Biology*, 221(2): 269–78.

Whitehouse, P.J. (2001) 'The end of Alzheimer's disease', *Alzheimer Disease and Associated Disorders*, 15(2): 59–62.

Whitehouse, P.J. and George, D.R. (2008) *The Myth of Alzheimer's: What You Aren't Being Told About Today's Most Dreaded Disease*. New York: St. Martin's Press.

Whitehouse, P.J. and Juengst, E.T. (2005) 'Anti-aging medicine and mild cognitive impairment: practice and policy issues for geriatrics', *J American Geriatrics Society*, 53: 1417–22.

Whitehouse, P.J. and Waller, S. (2007) 'Involuntary emotional expressive disorder: a case for deeper neuroethics', *Neurotherapeutics*, 4(3): 560–7.

Whitehouse, P.J., Maurer, K., and Ballenger, J.F. (2000) *Concepts of Alzheimer's Disease: Biological, Clinical and Cultural Perspectives*, Baltimore, MD: Johns Hopkins University Press.

Whitehouse, P.J., Gaines, A.D., Lindstrom, H., and Graham, J.E. (2005) 'Anthropological contributions to the understanding of age related cognitive impairment', *Lancet Neurology*, 4: 320–6.

Williams, S. and Goffman, E. (1987) 'Interactionism, and the management of stigma in everyday life', in G. Scambler (ed.), *Sociological Theory and Medical Sociology*. London: Tavistock.

Woods, B., Portnoy, S., Head, D., and Jones, G. (1992) 'Reminiscence and life review with persons with dementia: which way forward?', in G. Jones and B. Miesen (eds), *Caregiving in Dementia: Research and Application*. London: Routledge.

Woods, B., Spector, A.E., Jones, C.A., Orrell, M., and Davies, S.P. (2005) 'Reminiscence therapy for dementia', *Cochrane Database of Systematic Reviews*, (2): 1–22.

Zola, I.K. (1990) 'Medicine as an institution of social control', in P. Conrad and R. Kern (eds), *The Sociology of Health and Illness: Critical Perspectives*, 3rd edn. New York: St Martin's Press.

27

Sociocultural Perspectives on Ageing Bodies

Stephen Katz

INTRODUCTION

All research in gerontology begins with the body. In both its physical and social aspects, the body is the foundational ground of gerontological knowledge and its associated health and service professions. As Mike Hepworth remarks, 'if the body did not age there would literally be no gerontological story to write or read' (2000: 9). Historically, the body became the material resource for scientific discovery about old age. In the late 19th and early 20th centuries, medical geriatricians such as Jean-Martin Charcot, Elie Metchnikoff, and Ignatz Nascher transformed the aged body into a separable senile form of life encompassing new scientific truths about ageing. As Charcot stated in the introduction to his seminal work, *Clinical Lectures on the Diseases of Old Age*, 'The new physiology absolutely refuses to look upon life as a mysterious and supernatural influence which acts as its caprice dictates', but rather, 'purposes to bring all the vital manifestations of a complex organism to workings of certain apparatuses, and the action of the latter to the properties of certain tissues of certain well-defined elements' (Charcot and Loomis, 1881: 12).

The social counterpart to the ageing body is the collective body of the elderly population. Its construction in the industrial era as a special demographic force problematized certain social and economic crises that still haunt us today. As I have argued elsewhere (Katz, 1996), the ageing body and elderly population were co-constituted in the wake of a biopolitical modernity that took life itself as a basis for the governance of society, while also providing older groups with collective identities amenable to establishing their own needs and rights. Today, the body and the population 'live' not only as objects of knowledge and government but also as political subjects mobilized as an emboldened senior citizenry to challenge the burdens of later life in a neoliberal era.

Despite the ubiquity of physical and social bodies in the sciences and politics of ageing, social gerontology has neglected to reflect critically on the historical and theoretical significance of bodies in research on ageing. Social gerontologists, in their campaign against narrowly biomedicalized and ageist characterizations of the ageing body as failing and dysfunctional, have pushed the boundaries of their field to include social, political, economic, geographical, spiritual, and global issues. However, the physical dimension of the body is often marginalized or abandoned to the very sciences and service professions targeted by gerontological criticism for their reductionism and objectification of the body. As Kathleen Woodward points out, 'we cannot detach the body in decline from the meanings we attach to old age' (1991: 19), and we cannot resolve the problem of the denigration of the aged body by ignoring its physical reality. Thus, gerontologists are faced with the question of how to acknowledge the experiences and meanings of physical difference, suffering, and decline that come with age, without at the same time reinforcing negative or positive ageist discourses that alienate the body.

This simultaneous presence and absence of the ageing body within gerontological culture – what Peter Öberg identifies as the paradox of the absent ageing body (1996, 2003) – also provides the point of departure for this chapter's elaboration of current sociocultural perspectives, organized into four basic themes: (1) the materiality of the absent ageing body; (2) the mask of ageing and the postmodern life course; (3) ageing identities and embodied performance; and (4) the ageing body in the biosocial order. In the course of explicating these themes and selected empirical illustrations, I delineate some of the ways whereby a more nuanced understanding of the ageing body can be achieved. To do so, I look to those sociocultural perspectives on the body that have enlivened gerontological theory by their borrowing from research in history, biography, sociology, feminism, performativity, ethics, and aesthetics. Together they enhance the interdisciplinary understanding of bodily life (and death) and intensify the critical scholarly flow between ageing studies, the sociology of the body, the history of medicine, disability studies, feminist theory, and gay/lesbian studies. Such perspectives create an imaginative thought space that counteracts our assumptions about both the cultural and the natural aspects of the ageing body. Throughout the chapter I refer to the 'ageing body' as mainly a conceptual entity related to its physicality. However, I recognize that there is no singular ageing body: rather, there are male and female ageing bodies further differentiated by race, (dis)ability, class, and region. As gerontological feminist (Calasanti and Slevin, 2006) and sexuality studies (Jones and Pugh, 2005) make clear, it is through the structuring of embodiment within systems of difference and inequality that ageing, gender, and sexuality come to be experienced together.

THE MATERIALITY OF THE ABSENT OF THE AGEING BODY

The sociology of the body is an influential subfield that has grown rapidly in the past three decades and generated key debates about the orientation of theoretical and empirical research on the body across disciplines (Crossley, 2001; Leder, 1990; Nettleton and Watson, 1998; Petersen, 2007; Shilling, 1993, 2005, 2008; Thomas and Ahmed, 2004; Turner, 1996, 2008). Inspired by the various structural, feminist, and phenomenological traditions developed by Bourdieu, Butler, Elias, Foucault, and Merleau-Ponty, sociologists have pursued the body as an intellectual route to a wider critique of consumer culture, social regulation,

medicalization, gender performativity, and the 'civilizing process' itself. While several of these debates have addressed the absence of the body and processes of embodiment in social research, the problem of the absent *ageing* body has not received the same attention and remains a lacuna in the field. Overly constructivist approaches in sociocultural research either treat the biological realities of ageing as outside the purview of social inquiry or theorize the biological sphere as a discursive or constructed creation of an anti-ageing culture. This leaves older individuals themselves in a paradoxical position, as Öberg (1996) defines it, because while the ageing body is absent from most gerontological and sociocultural conceptions of the ageing process, the body is everywhere in social representations of the ageing process, embedded in all the surfaces and identities of ageing individuals' cultural and moral worlds. This is the paradox at the heart of social gerontology, whereby the body becomes the target of the overlapping resistance to and denial of ageing.

The issue of the absent body is also related to the research areas common to most sociocultural studies of ageing, such as popular media images, film, fashion, and the cosmetics industry. Certainly these areas produce ample evidence that the youth-based idealization of appearance is largely responsible for our culture's life-course narratives that disparage ageing. Julia Twigg rightly notes that anti-ageing culture has made the body a technology of denial, because, after all, 'it is the bodily appearance of the old person that places them in the category of the old' (2006: 45). The imperative to grow older without the visible signs of ageing permeates our cultural industries and valorizes a new kind of public celebrity associated with anti-ageing heroes (Katz, 2005). However, the materiality and finitude of ageing remain rooted in physical change and to the extent that such change underlies systems of difference and social inequality, the understanding of the biological dimension cannot be left to reductionist biomedical science alone (see Calasanti, 2005). In other words, the approach to the ageing body in cultural research needs to reach beyond typical cultural representations of the body to probe their assumptions about biological materiality.[1] Work is one example, where those who do physical labor suffer more specific health and pain problems later in life compared to those who work at more sedentary jobs (LeMasters et al., 2006). Carework is another obvious example of the embodied interaction between the physical and social worlds, particularly in relation to falling and bathing.

In Canada, falls are a major cause of injury, a reason for entering care facilities, a factor in morbidity, and an expense to the healthcare system. According to Ward-Griffin et al., 'Falls are the second leading cause of hospitalization in Canada for women aged 65 years and older and the fifth leading cause of hospitalization for men of this age' (2004: 308). Falls also cause 90 per cent of all hip fractures for seniors, 20 per cent of whom die within a year of the fracture (The Council on Aging of Ottawa, 2006: 3). Other studies by Edwards et al. (2003, 2006) concur that the fear of falling creates tremendous anxiety for older people who can develop a resistance to physical activities because of it. Falling can mark a threshold between community living and hospitalization. Hence, fall prevention in Canada has become an important research and policy agenda, as it is in the United Kingdom as well (Bunn et al., 2008).

Edwards et al. also claim that 10–15 per cent of all non-syncopal falls (not due to sudden loss of consciousness) happen in bathrooms, with 5–7.5 per cent of such falls occurring because of bathtub transfer problems (2006: 296). Fortunately, there are inexpensive preventive solutions available, such as installing grab-bars, non-slip surfaces, and easy-to-reach faucets and towel racks. However, even such straightforward technical apparatuses imply embodied relations, because the phenomenon of falling is a microcosm of larger issues involving social support, gender differences, independent living, health policy, housing, and supportive environments. These points are evident where Edwards et al. find that bathtub grab-bars are more often installed in publicly than privately owned buildings. Since one-third of all Canadian seniors live in apartment buildings, this is an important area where risky home environments are considered (2006: 301). Where they are installed to facilitate bathtub transfer, grab-bars also range in quality and style. Those persons with and those persons without one or more high-quality grab-bars are not only environmentally but also physically separated in the very quotidian use of their bathrooms. Thus, the grab-bar, the bathtub, the bathroom, the apartment, and the resident, form a spatial assemblage of physical relationships through which anxieties about assistance and independence and types of social and self-carework in ageing converge.

The material conditions around bathing are also the subject of Julia Twigg's critical ethnography of carework in Britain, especially where bathing becomes the focus of intimate bodycare in the relationship between private and public spaces (Twigg, 2000, 2006). Twigg demonstrates how, in care environments, bathing requires scheduling, timing, and regulating; hence, the physical pleasures and comforts of bathing become invisible as older people 'experience their bodies in the contexts of a profound cultural silence' (2000: 46). In bathing as well as toileting, carework becomes bodywork for both careworkers and care recipients,

as feelings such as embarrassment and shame emerge in the process. Twigg's work suggests that bodies are not simply 'medicalized' or 'objectified', but through interactive touch and movement they enact class, race, and gender relations and identities. According to Twigg, carework of the ageing body is often considered dirty and demeaning; therefore, care recipients perceive and experience their own bodies as dirty and contaminating. However, carework can also provide an opportunity for equality and reciprocity that generates mutual respect, dignity, and friendship between people who learn to care for each other, whether they give or receive carework. In both their negative and positive aspects, the status, treatment, and experience of the ageing body in the caregiver–recipient relationship point to the ambivalence about ageing that structures our culture's attitudes. As in the case of bathtub grab-bars, bathing and carework are material examples of how sociocultural and gerontological approaches to ageing can afford neither to ignore the body nor to theorize the problems of ageing in its absence.

THE MASK OF AGEING AND THE POSTMODERN LIFE COURSE

The ageing body implies an ageing self. However, the relational dynamics between self and body are forged within contemporary culture's coercive asymmetry between the subjective experience and 'feeling' of age and the body's outward ageing appearance. For those who experience their middle and later lives as youthful and thus feel younger than they look, the tension between young and old identities becomes a critical motif in their life-course narratives. British cultural sociologists Mike Featherstone and Mike Hepworth first used the term 'mask of ageing' to characterize the growing gap between the experiences and the 'look' of ageing (Featherstone and Hepworth, 1991). Middle-aged and older people are encouraged to feel themselves as permanently young, but they are betrayed by their ageing faces and bodies. Furthermore, our postmodern society's obsession with eternal youthfulness and its powerful symbolic denigration of physical maturity in later life leave few opportunities to experience bodily ageing in a meaningfully biographical way throughout the time of the body. Thus, bodywork techniques and the fantastical allure of cosmetic, lifestyle, exercise, pharmaceutical, and 'life-extension' products aimed at enhancing agelessness become the primary means by which one can successfully grow older, paradoxically, by denying and resisting ageing.

Consumer culture exacerbates the masking of age through its relentless promotion of ageing as a lifelong discontinuity between an authentic, inner, youthful self and an outer, ageing, physical body that masks it. Ageing identities thus become further alienated and distanced from the opportunities of maturity. Those who refuse to work on their bodies and pay homage to the commercial rhetoric of the cosmetic, recreational, and nutritional industries risk becoming stigmatized as irresponsible or literally 'old-fashioned'. And for those who live through age-related poverty, disability, despair, and decline, their suffering is unfairly publicized as the result of an individual failure to participate in the so-called 'empowering' opportunities of responsible consumerism. These aspects of the masking process apply to women across a deeper personal and cultural horizon of experiences than men because of the inflated role that appearance and the construction of beauty are made to play in defining a successful femininity that triumphs over age (see Clarke and Griffin, 2007; Tseëlon, 1995).

Structurally, the dilemmas and masking of bodily ageing derive from the shift from a rigid, chronology-fixed, modern industrial life course to a fluid, chronology-blurred, postmodern life course (Blaikie, 1999; Danesi, 2003; Featherstone and Wernick, 1995; Gilleard and Higgs, 2000; Jones et al., 2008). The domestic and institutionalized boundaries that had set apart age groups and generations have become indeterminate because of new work, leisure, and consumer cultures, and the changing retirement arrangements of increasingly healthy and more numerous ageing populations. In TV shows children speak like adults and in Disneyland adults act like children, with both wearing the same kind of clothes. As middle age becomes extended farther into later life, mid-life technologies and lifestyles of bodycare become more prominent across the life course (Gullette, 2004). Gilleard and Higgs remark that 'only in the late 20th century has the idea emerged that human agency can be exercised over how ageing will be expressed and experienced' (2000: 3). However, critics who argue against the claims that postmodern choice, experimentation, and liberation have fashioned new avenues of self-expression and self-definition for older individuals also emphasize that such postmodern ideals diminish the genuinely ethical struggles to live successfully, diversely, and meaningfully in our society. If life in the postmodern world is, as Zygmunt Bauman says about it, 'a succession of self-cancelling determinations' where 'no loss is irretrievable' (1992: 169, 173), then the rewards and values that come from living in time become masked as well.

AGEING IDENTITIES AND EMBODIED PERFORMANCE

The mask of ageing motif suggests that postmodern cosmetic bodycare industries and the aestheticizing technologies of disguise have turned the conventional certainty of maturity into a negotiable contingency. The sociocultural approaches that take up this motif focus on how the masking of the ageing body links it to the lifestyles and life courses narrated by postmodern culture. However, two aspects of the masking process deserve greater attention than they have received within such approaches. The first is clothing, since clothing mediates between bodily representation and social identity. Julia Twigg asks why, if clothing is a realm of unrestricted choice and personal expression, is it so limited for older people (Twigg, 2007). One reason is that social pressure dictates age-appropriate dress. A resulting 'moral ordering of dress' (2007: 294) polices the ageing body through micro-codes of garment size, color, fit, style, comfort, seasonality, and conspicuousness. For instance, older women must wear looser fitting, longer, and more color-muted clothing if they are not to disrupt their identities. For older women who resist age-stereotyping rules of dress, or appear too youthful or sexual, the penalty is further abjection and ridicule, despite the fact that clothing fashion is rooted in youthful styles. Samantha Holland studied a group of women who experiment with non-traditional forms of appearance, such as bohemian, 'freaky', and 'girly' styles in order to break free of conventional age and gender role constraints (2004). In the process of negotiating their clothing choices, the women also discover colliding meanings about female ageing.

The question of the embodied self is a second issue that complements and extends the mask of ageing perspective and its focus on the body. Simon Biggs (1999, 2003), Efrat Tseëlon (1995), and Kathleen Woodward (1991) use the term 'masquerade' to develop a more flexible and psychodynamic model of the relationship between self and body. They do this with the goal of exploring how the tension between inner depth and physical appearance, and biographical continuity and disruption, creates meaningful maturation throughout the course of life. According to Biggs, masquerade is not simply a masking process, but, rather 'a bridge between the inner and outer logics of adult aging' (2003: 152–3) that 'creates a necessary inner space in which to build a stable identity and a stance from which to assess and connect with the social world' (2003: 154). Thus, both self and body are dynamic entities that change together as an individual grows through various age-identities as a 'mature imagination' (Biggs, 1999) takes hold. Research studies on performance cultures of sport and dance are good illustrations of how the relationship between the ageing self and body might be considered a form of dialogue, akin to Biggs' idea of masquerade that bridges inner and outer logics of ageing. In such cultures optimal physical prowess is essential; hence, the contradictions between ageless and age-limited bodily life are most starkly revealed within the careers of athletes or dancers that end at relatively young ages.[2]

The sport of long-distance running, which might be continued longer than say hockey or football, illuminates these contradictions poignantly. An example is Emmanuelle Tulle's creative research on veteran Masters long-distance runners, which portrays a complex athletic culture in which the body becomes the medium for expressing and understanding ageing (2003a, 2003b, 2008). Here, the body is the source of physical and social capital, and runners must maintain its status by managing their training, injuries, endurance, pain, and record-keeping. In this taxing regime, the body's age becomes a shared frame of reference; the runners work on their bodies *as* ageing bodies, adopting specific strategies to deal the loss of strength or the risk of injury, while being aware that their position as elite runners defies traditional images of ageing and retirement, even where such images drip with the workout sweat of repetitive exercise and endless activity. Some of Tulle's subjects even had heart conditions (2003b: 239). The runners also come to know ageing through their intimate interpretations of their bodies' performance, where pushing the limits comes to define who they are as older subjects:

> The body is emerging not simply as a tool that allows people to continue engaging in their regular activities but is itself acting as a field of possibilities. The constraints and opportunities presented by the body are perceptible to social actors through a close intermeshing of intimate bodily sensations and of age-based prescriptions of appropriate behaviours disseminated in the wider cultural and social context in which people are becoming older.
>
> (Tulle 2003b: 250)

Balletic dance is another example of how the struggle to negotiate physical capital generates a field of possibilities around identity, career, and embodied ageing. In their ethnographic research on dancers at the Royal Ballet of London, Wainwright and Turner explore the corporeal world that articulates ageing and performance in a culture dominated by the capacities and images of youth (2003, 2006). Here the dancers learn to embody and express the style, stamina, and competence of an elite physical capital that rewards them with status and self-definition, both offstage and onstage. In this case, the attainment of physical capital also involves constant discipline to manage the extreme physical demands of rehearsals, recovery from injuries, maintenance of strict diets, and exhaustion. However, physical capital is transient, and by early middle age most dancers must face the encroaching limitation of their physical abilities. For those who do not move forward from performance to become instructors or coaches, retirement from their short-lived careers is difficult because of the intense association of the dancer's identity with the dancer's body. As in Tulle's research, Wainwright and Turner emphasize the point that the self-fashioning of the performing body inevitably creates an internal dialogue about the capacity to adapt to ageing, as the wear and tear on their bodies eventually take its toll.

The physical cultures of elite runners and ballet dancers demonstrate three important aspects about the embodied ageing self. First, the embodiment of self is a material process whereby the vicissitudes of the body's symbolic meanings and social capital are shaped through grounded practices in physical cultures. Secondly, ageing binds self to body in interactive ways that both sustain and disrupt biographical identity – embodied life is continually interpreted and negotiated within reflexive, narrative practices. Thirdly, empirical and ethnographical studies are invaluable to understanding how, and identifying where, the ageing body is experienced and expressed in everyday language, rituals, and performance. Such studies of performing ageing bodies, along with the sociocultural approaches to the materiality of the (absent) ageing body discussed above, together provide a sense of the interdisciplinary terrain being explored by ageing body studies. The chapter now turns to an instructive example of how the ageing body in its physical materiality and relation to the embodied ageing self is being shaped through the gerontologic discourses and technologies of biosocial functionality.

THE AGEING BODY IN THE BIOSOCIAL ORDER

Today, several theorists observe that a growing set of reproductive, neurochemical, vascular, and cognitive crises, fostered by refined pharmaceutical interventions and an exponential growth in genetic knowledge, are remapping and even reversing the boundaries between the natural and the cultural, and the real and the artificial. Paul Rabinow has referred to this reversal as *biosociality*, where 'nature will become known and remade through technique and will finally become artificial, just as culture becomes natural' (1996: 99). Similarly, Mike Featherstone and Mike Hepworth suggest that we live in an era where a series of 'natures' overlap, the first three being the 'bio', the 'built', and the 'cyber', and the fourth nature based in 'a post-anthropogenetic domain' (1998: 65) – that is, a nature based on the technological mutability of human nature. There are also arguments by Nikolas Rose and other Foucauldian thinkers that biosocial technologies have become the blueprints of collective life in general, because of their resonance with political and commercial rationalities geared to new regimes of health and lifestyle (Franklin and Lock, 2003; Gibbon and Novas, 2008; Rose, 2007). Susan Squier has traced the literary and cultural genealogies of 'posthuman' bodies and modes of reproduction related to biosociality (2004).[3]

The idea of a biosocial order, based on a transformed and reversed relationship between culture and nature, has inspired my colleague Barbara Marshall and I to suggest that new standards of functionality and performance are restructuring the ageing body and its physical terms of reference. It is useful to recall that the late George Canguilhem had radicalized the field of medical history by arguing that the medical binary of the *normal and the pathological* extended beyond the clinic and laboratory to encompass social, legal, political, and moral values (1978, 1988). In Canguilhem's study of scientific worlds, the normal and the pathological are predicated on a body poised between culture and nature, with nature playing the role of ontological depth to culture's surfaces of structures and systems. We contend that the normal/pathological binary elaborated by Canguilhem has been absorbed and supplanted by a new binary: *the functional and the dysfunctional* (Katz and Marshall, 2004). Ideas about the functional body go back to Aristotle's treatises on natural science; however, it was Western biomedicine that transformed physical function into an universal calculus with which to measure all activities of living beings – all of life itself. In this sense, Foucault defines medical function as 'a constant middle term' that makes 'it possible to relate together totalities of elements without the slightest visible identity' (1973: 265). The concept of 'dysfunction' also made its appearance in early 20th-century medical literature, much of it in relation to brain functioning.

Furthermore, there are wider historical connections around functional bodies between the medical sciences, industrial economics, and national preparedness in war throughout the 20th century.

In our view, the functional and the dysfunctional binary acts as a potent articulation of biosocial values and standards. In turn, these have expanded the powers of expertise and the governance of everyday life to include a broader horizon of human problems, disorders, and syndromes, especially those related to neurological, cognitive, and behavioral issues. The functional–dysfunctional binary creates three important conditions applicable to the ageing body and professional gerontological research and practices.

First, functionality is primarily about measurement and performance because functional states are quantifiable; they are states relative to adjustment through technologies of enablement. Unlike normal states against which pathologies are seen to be 'deviations', functional states can coexist with pathologies, because they can be adjusted or enhanced via experiment, therapy, diet, lifestyle, and drugs. And if we think of major disorders such as depression, attention-deficit disorder, addictions, autism, sexual dysfunction, and Alzheimer's disease, each with their own variability, the approach to their management has been by means of technically adjusted function rather than 'cure' or 'recovery'. For example, in the normal–pathological discourse, the brain was a locked natural organ, an object of science (and science fiction) that was crudely mapped as a kind of neurological landscape within the skull. Today, the brain is an open biosocial laboratory into which human attributes are continually molecularized, functionalized, and compressed, including addictions, desire, creativity, memory, violence, and even love. As Nikolas Rose claims, 'when mind seems visible within the brain, the space between person and organ flattens out – mind is what brain does' (2007: 198).

Secondly, advanced informational technologies, such as scanning, screening, mapping, imaging, and coding, make visible and concretize functional and dysfunctional conditions.[4] For example, in a case study examining the effects of bone scans on Danish women's perceptions of their own bodies, Reventlow et al. (2006) discover how a purely preventive procedure for osteoporosis becomes the agent of personal change. Since the scanning technology renders the invisible body visible, the women physically 'felt' the results and began to interpret pain and weakness as signs of possible bone-density problems. As the authors conclude, 'the bone scan created a new view of the body' (2006: 2726). Thus, the veracity and elegance of functional measurement, and its ease of flow between bodies, individuals, and populations, are products of the informational technologies that shape it and make it transparent. In a larger sense, communication and medical technologies also create a data-sphere that connects scientific, insurance, and popular online communities with expert literature, research studies, population statistics, and commercial marketing.

Thirdly, the standardization of functional and dysfunctional states contributes to the development of bio-identities, where individual status becomes rooted in somatic experience and tied to ethical practices around key decisions related to physical well-being. In other words, people come to know themselves according to the ways in which their biosocial lives are judged as worthy. Rose and Novas have encapsulated the personal politics of bio-identities as 'biological citizenship', whereby 'individuals shape their relations with themselves in terms of knowledge of their somatic individuality' (2005: 441). In the hands of bio-citizens, biology itself becomes 'knowable, mutable, improvable, eminently manipulable' (2005: 442), and ultimately about hope. Again, in the case of the bone-scan study, it was through a biological discourse involving professional, technological, and lay perceptions that the women came to know themselves as being at risk for osteoporosis. The scan also articulated and naturalized the image of the ageing female body as vulnerable and delicate, but open to intervention. These imaged conditions, in turn, augmented the women's sense of self-care and bio-citizenry by encourageing them to be cautious and avoid challenging physical exercise. Thus, bio-citizenry involves a critical curiosity about quality-of-life choices and decisions, in addition to the larger mobilization of groups around issues of health, environment, reproductive rights, and access to pharmacological research.

These conditions surrounding the functional–dysfunctional binary in professional fields – measurability and performance, data and informational technologies, and bio-identities and bio-citizenry – have forged new relationships between functionality and bodily ageing. This can be seen most clearly in gerontology's historical recalibration of the meaning of physical age itself. As students of gerontology are aware, ageing research on the body has traditionally relied on a model of chronological age structured across developmental life-course transitions. In the later 20th century, however, the life sciences began to reconsider chronological age as an obstacle to research because the concept lacked predictive value and conceptual rigor.[5] As James Birren states, 'chronological age is only an index, and unrelated sets of data show correlations with chronological age that have no intrinsic or causal

relationship with each other' (1999: 460). Gerontologists such as I.M Murray (1951) and Heron and Chown (1967) had already begun to work on the new idea of *functional age* as an articulation point for a series of other 'ages' around and within the body. Hence, talk of a person having the heart of a 20-year-old, the bones of a 40-year-old, the lungs of a 60-year-old, etc. became common. The new research demonstrated that physiological and chronological ages vary relative to each other, producing in the end a measurable 'age' based on 'functions' (also advantageous to life insurance companies, according to Murray).

In 1963, *functional age* was a key concept in The Normative Aging Study (NAS) conducted at the American Veterans Administration Outpatient Clinic in Boston. Results of the longer-term study were gathered into a special issue of the journal *Aging and Human Development* in 1972. The journal's articles not only pose functional age as the alternative to chronological age but also praise functional age as an expansive concept to include psychological and social, as well as biological functions, thus extending functional health to an ageing person's whole life. While functional age has also been criticized, the professional enthusiasm for it remains because of its potential to measure, standardize, and open the ageing body and inventory its risks according to current governmental policy agendas such as health-promotion and independent-living programmes. Ironically, although it appears to transcend the limitations of chronological age, functional age firmly embodies age into everything that can be measured or performed *as* functional or dysfunctional. The ubiquity of functionality in ageing research is evident from a brief scan of *Abstracts in Social Gerontology* where, under the heading 'functional states', is listed an enormous group of topics that folds every activity of the ageing body, however disparate, into a function-oriented health model or one of its functional or dysfunctional correlates.

Functional states of the ageing body also imply functional states of the ageing-embodied self. The 1972 special issue of *Aging and Human Development* on functional age included a study by Robert Kastenbaum on how people feel about their age, or ages, since the interview project was called the 'ages of me' (Kastenbaum et al., 1972). Not surprisingly, most of the subjects viewed their personal age as younger than their chronological age, with their functional age providing a popular vocabulary with which to self-reflect upon the relation between self and body. What is interesting about this and later research is the question of how older individuals come to understand themselves in functional terms. In many qualitative studies of *self-reporting* we find that the subjects' self-reports are frequently inaccurate (Glass, 1998; Rodgers and Miller, 1997), or the self-assessment skills required to differentiate between the vocabularies of everyday health status and professionalized functional health status are lacking. As Gubrium and Holstein (1998) have argued, professional ideas are embodied and practiced in everyday contexts before subjects can reflect upon or evaluate their meanings in a shared vocabulary of expertise. As well, research subjects often attempt to fit subjective experiences of functional abilities and activities of daily living to the research design.

Hence, the work of older individuals to know themselves and their lifestyles in functional terms and ages is interpretive, despite the overarching professional discourse of biosocial functionality by which gerontological research on the ageing body and related health promotion campaigns are now established. Critical gerontology, therefore, faces the important task of questioning the role of functionality and its empire of human capacities as it not only constitutes new ways of knowing the ageing process in a biosocial order but also new ways of experiencing ageing and being old.

CONCLUSIONS

The paradox of the absent ageing body is that its presence is everywhere, despite its neglect in scholarly and professional discourses. Thus, the body challenges the very fields of knowledge to which it is tied. This chapter has outlined selected issues and theoretical orientations that bridge sociocultural approaches to the body with gerontological research. Specifically, I have chosen to discuss the materiality of the ageing body in everyday contexts, the ambivalence and dialogue between body, self, and masks of ageing within a postmodern life course, the subjective dimension of embodiment in fields of performance, and the body's recent disaggregation into functional and dysfunctional states within a biosocial order. On one level, these areas serve to organize the field, but the deeper purpose has been to ask how we can understand the ageing body as the central mediation point between the structured mandates by which we live our lives and the agential and experimental forms of identity we use to negotiate such mandates. Finally, for gerontology to continue with its humanistic goals to support successful ageing, independent living, mindful bodycare, intergenerational reciprocity, social equality, and dying with dignity, it needs to reclaim its bodies

from the margins of its vision and care for them in thought as well as in practice.

NOTES

1 Examples where such an approach is accomplished in different ways include Simon Williams' critical realist approach to health (2003), Myra Hird's 'non-linear' materialist critique of sexual reproduction (2002), and Pia Kontos' adoption of Margaret Lock's notion of 'local biology' to examine the gerontology of the body (1999). These and other innovative approaches remind us that biological materiality is a necessary component of any sociocultural research on the absent ageing body.

2 While this discussion focuses on the relationship between the presence of the ageing body in situations of physical performance, research on theatrical, symbolic, and musical performance is also relevant – for example, Anne Basting's work on theatrical groups (1998, 2000). Another important theoretical inspiration has been the work of Judith Butler (1990, 1993), whose writings elaborate how ritualistic bodily performances bind women to arbitrary and fictional feminine identities, which then become normalized. According to Butler, the deconstruction of such performances leads to a critical questioning of these identities and their eventual undermining. Schwaiger (2006) comments on the usefulness of Butler's performativity theory to ageing studies.

3 An area whose significance goes beyond the scope of this chapter concerns the relationship between the biosocial order and the commodification of the body. While speculative fiction (Vint, 2006) as well as medical science have entertained ideas about the potential of new technological, robotic, prosthetic, genetic, virtual, and cellular enhancements of the human condition, the disturbing global market in body organs seems to be the more realistic underside.

Sharon Kaufman et al. (2006) and Nancy Scheper-Hughes (2005) have considered the bioethical parameters of organ transplants. Lawrence Cohen uses the term 'bioavailability' to refer to those bodies which become 'available for the selective disaggregation of one's cells or tissues and their reincorporation into another body (or machine)' (2005: 83) – a reincorporation that usually involves a transfer from the poor to the rich.

4 Medical visual technologies have a history of their own that is far from straightforward. For example, the development of ultrasound involved several changes in application, design, and fields of expertise (Yoxen, 1987), while brain scanning has helped to reshape relationships amongst the life sciences (Cohn 2004).

5 See Katz (2006) for a lengthier discussion of the historical and theoretical shifts from chronological to functional age in gerontological research.

REFERENCES

Basting, A.D. (1998) *The Stages of Age: Performing Age in Contemporary American Culture.* Ann Arbor: University of Michigan Press.

Basting, A.D. (2000) 'Performance studies and age', in T.R. Cole, R. Kastenbaum, and R. Ray (eds), *Handbook of the Humanities and Aging*, 2nd edn. New York: Springer, pp. 258–71.

Bauman, Z. (1992) *Mortality, Immortality and Other Life Strategies.* Oxford, UK: Polity Press.

Biggs, S. (1999) *The Mature Imagination: Dynamics of Identity in Midlife and Beyond.* Buckingham: Open University Press.

Biggs, S. (2003) 'Negotiating aging identity: surface, depth, and masquerade', in S. Biggs, A. Lowenstein, and J. Hendricks (eds), *The Need for Theory: Critical Approaches to Social Gerontology.* Amityville, NY: Baywood, pp. 145–59.

Birren, J.E. (1999) 'Theories of aging: a personal perspective', in V.L. Bengtson and K. Warner Schaie (eds), *Handbook of Theories of Aging.* New York: Springer, pp. 459–71.

Blaikie, A. (1999) *Ageing and Popular Culture.* Cambridge, UK: Cambridge University Press.

Bunn, F., Dickinson, A., Barnett-Page, E., McInnes, E., and Horton, K. (2008) 'A systematic review of older people's perceptions of facilitators and barriers to participation in falls prevention interventions', *Ageing and Society*, 28(4): 449–72.

Butler, J. (1990) *Gender Trouble: Feminism and the Subversion of Identity.* New York: Routledge.

Butler, J. (1993) *Bodies That Matter: On the Discursive Limits of 'Sex'.* New York: Routledge.

Calasanti, T. (2005) 'Ageism, gravity, and gender: experiences of aging bodies', *Generations*, 29(3): 8–12.

Calasanti, T. and Slevin, K.F. (eds) (2006) *Age Matters: Realigning Feminist Thinking.* New York: Routledge.

Canguilhem, G. (1978) *On the Normal and the Pathological.* Dordrecht: D. Reidel Publishing.

Canguilhem, G. (1988) *Ideology and Rationality in the History of the Life Sciences.* Cambridge, MA: MIT Press.

Charcot, J.-M. and Loomis, A.L. (1881) *Clinical Lectures on the Diseases of Old Age.* Tr. L.H. Hunt. New York: William Wood.

Clarke, L.H. and Griffin, M. (2007) 'The body natural and the body unnatural: beauty work and aging', *Journal of Aging Studies*, 21(3): 187–201.

Cohen, L. (2005) 'Operability, bioavailability, and exception', in A. Ong and S.J. Collier (eds), *Global Assemblages: Technology, Politics and Ethics as Anthropological Problems.* Oxford, UK: Blackwell, pp. 79–90.

Cohn, S. (2004) 'Increasing resolution, intensifying ambiguity: an ethnographic account of seeing life in brain scans', *Economy and Society*, 33(1): 52–76.

Crossley, N. (2001) *The Social Body: Habit, Identity and Desire.* London: SAGE.

Danesi, M. (2003) *Forever Young: The 'Teen-Aging' of Modern Culture.* Toronto: University of Toronto Press.

Edwards, N., Lockett, D., Aminzadeh, F., and Nair, R.C. (2003) 'Predictors of bath grab-bar use among community-living older adults', *Canadian Journal on Aging*, 22(2): 217–27.

Edwards, N., Birkett, N., Nair, R., et al. (2006) 'Access to bathtub grab bars: evidence of a policy gap', *Canadian Journal on Aging*, 25(3): 295–304.

Featherstone, M. and Hepworth, M. (1991) 'The mask of ageing and the postmodern life course' in M. Featherstone, M. Hepworth, and B.S. Turner (eds), *The Body: Social Process and Cultural Theory.* London: SAGE, pp. 371–98.

Featherstone, M. and Hepworth, M. (1998) 'Aging, the life-course and the sociology of embodiment', in G. Scambler and P. Higgs (eds), *Community, Medicine and Health.* New York: Routledge, pp.147–75.

Featherstone, M. and Wernick, A. (eds) (1995) *Images of Aging: Cultural Representations of Later Life.* New York: Routledge.

Foucault, M. (1973) *The Order of Things: An Archaeology of the Human Sciences.* New York: Vintage Books.

Franklin, S. and Lock, M. (eds) (2003) *Remaking Life and Death: Toward an Anthropology of the Biosciences.* Sante Fe, NM: School of American Research Press.

Gibbon, S. and Novas, C. (eds) (2008) *Biosocialities, Genetics and the Social Sciences: Making Biologies and Identities.* London: Routledge.

Gilleard, C. and Higgs, P. (2000) *Cultures of Ageing: Self, Citizen and the Body.* London: Prentice-Hall.

Glass, T.A. (1998) 'Conjugating the "tenses" of function: discordance among hypothetical, experimental, and enacted function in older adults', *Gerontologist*, 38(1): 101–12.

Gubrium, J.F. and Holstein, J.A. (1998) 'Narrative practice and the coherence of personal stories', *Sociological Quarterly*, 39(1): 163–87.

Gullette, M.M. (2004) *Aged by Culture.* Chicago: University of Chicago Press.

Hepworth, M. (2000) *Stories of Ageing.* Buckingham: Open University Press.

Heron, A. and Chown, S. (1967) *Age and Function.* Boston: Little, Brown.

Hird, M.J. (2002) 'Re(pro)ducing sexual difference', *Parallax*, 8(4): 94–107.

Holland, S. (2004) *Alternative Femininities: Body, Age and Identity.* Oxford: Berg.

Jones, I.R., Hyde, M., Victor, C.R., et al. (2008) *Ageing in a Consumer Society.* Bristol: Policy Press.

Jones, J. and Pugh, S. (2005) 'Ageing gay men: lessons from the sociology of embodiment', *Men and Masculinities*, 7(3): 248–60.

Kastenbaum, R., Derbin, V., Sabatini, P., and Artt, S. (1972) '"The ages of me": toward personal and interpersonal definitions of functional aging', *Aging and Human Development*, 3(2): 197–211.

Katz, S. (1996) *Disciplining Old Age: The Formation of Gerontological Knowledge.* Charlottesville, VA: The University Press of Virginia.

Katz, S. (2005) *Cultural Aging: Life Course, Lifestyle, and Senior Worlds.* Peterborough: Broadview Press.

Katz, S. (2006) 'From chronology to functionality: critical reflections on the gerontology of the body', in J. Baars, D. Dannefer, C. Phillipson, and A. Walker (eds), *Aging, Globalization and Inequality: The New Critical Gerontology.* Amityville, NY: Baywood, pp. 123–37.

Katz, S. and Marshall, B. (2004) 'Is the functional "normal"? aging, sexuality and the bio-marking of successful living', *History of the Human Sciences*, 17(1): 53–75.

Kaufman, S., Russ, A.J., and Shim, J.K. (2006) 'Aged bodies and kinships matters: the ethical field of kidney transplant', *American Ethnologist*, 33(1): 81–99.

Kontos, P. (1999) 'Local biology: bodies of difference in ageing studies', *Ageing and Society*, 19(6): 677–90.

Leder, D. (1990) *The Absent Body.* Chicago: University of Chicago Press.

LeMasters, G., Bhattacharya, A., Borton, E., and Mayfield, L. (2006) 'Functional impairment and quality of life in retired workers of the construction trades', *Experimental Aging Research*, 32(2): 227–42.

Murray, I.M. (1951) 'Assessment of physiologic age by combination of several criteria – vision, hearing, blood pressure, and muscle force.' *Journal of Gerontology*, 6(1): 120–6.

Nettleton, S. and Watson, J. (eds) (1998) *The Body in Everyday Life.* New York: Routledge.

Öberg, P. (1996) 'The absent body – a social gerontological paradox', *Ageing and Society*, 16(6): 701–19.

Öberg, P. (2003) 'Images versus experience of the aging body', in C.A. Faircloth (ed), *Aging Bodies: Images and Everyday Experience.* Walnut Creek, CA: Altamira Press, pp. 103–39.

Petersen, A. (2007) *The Body in Question: A Socio-Cultural Approach.* London: Routledge.

Rabinow, P. (ed.) (1996) 'Artificiality and enlightenment: from sociobiology to biosociality', in *Essays on the Anthropology of Reason.* Princeton, NJ: Princeton University Press, pp. 91–111.

Reventlow, S. Dalsgaard, H.V., and Malterud, K. (2006) 'Making the invisible body visible: bone scans, osteoporosis and women's bodily experiences', *Social Science and Medicine*, 62(11): 2720–31.

Rodgers, W. and Miller, B. (1997) 'A comparative analysis of ADL questions in surveys of older people', *Journals of Gerontology: Psychological and Social Sciences*, 52B: 21–36.

Rose, N. (2007) *The Politics of Life Itself: Biomedicine, Power, and Subjectivity in the Twenty-First Century.* Princeton, NJ: Princeton University Press.

Rose, N. and Novas, C. (2005) 'Biological citizenship', in A. Ong and S.J. Collier (eds), *Global Assemblages: Technology, Politics and Ethics as Anthropological Problems.* Oxford, UK: Blackwell, pp. 439–63.

Scheper-Hughes, N. (2005) 'The last commodity: post-human ethics and the global traffic in "fresh" organs', in A. Ong and S.J. Collier (eds), *Global Assemblages: Technology, Politics and Ethics as Anthropological Problems.* Oxford, UK: Blackwell, pp. 145–67.

Schwaiger, L. (2006) 'To be forever young? Towards reframing corporeal subjectivity in maturity', *International Journal of Ageing and Later Life*, 1(1): 11–41.

Shilling, C. (1993) *The Body and Social Theory.* London: SAGE.

Shilling, C. (2005) *The Body in Culture, Technology and Society.* London: SAGE.

Shilling, C. (2008) *Changing Bodies: Habit, Crisis and Creativity.* London: SAGE.

Squier, S.M. (2004) *Liminal Lives: Imagining the Human at the Frontiers of Biomedicine.* Durham, NC: Duke University Press.

The Council on Aging of Ottawa Bulletin (March 2006). www.coaottawa.ca

Thomas, H. and Ahmed, J. (eds) (2004) *Cultural Bodies: Ethnography and Theory.* Malden, MA: Blackwell.

Tseëlon, E. (1995) *The Masque of Femininity.* London: SAGE.

Tulle, E. (2003a) 'Sense and structure: toward a sociology of old bodies', in S. Biggs, A. Lowenstein, and J. Hendricks (eds), *The Need for Theory: Critical Approaches to Social Gerontology.* Amityville, NY: Baywood, pp. 91–104.

Tulle, E. (2003b) 'The bodies of veteran elite runners', in C.A. Faircloth (ed.), *Aging Bodies: Images and Everyday Experience.* Walnut Creek, CA: Altamira Press, pp. 229–58.

Tulle, E. (2008) *Ageing, the Body and Social Change.* London: Palgrave Macmillan.

Turner, B.S. (1996) *The Body and Society: Explorations in Social Theory*, 2nd edn. London: SAGE.

Turner, B.S. (2008) *The Body and Society: Explorations in Social Theory*, 3rd edn. London: SAGE.

Twigg, J. (2000) *Bathing – The Body and Community Care.* New York: Routledge.

Twigg, J. (2006) *The Body in Health Social Care.* London: Palgrave Macmillan.

Twigg, J. (2007) 'Clothing, age and the body: a critical review', *Ageing and Society*, 27(2): 285–305.

Vint, S. (2006) *Bodies of Tomorrow: Technology, Subjectivity, Science Fiction.* Toronto: University of Toronto Press.

Wainwright, S. and Turner, B.S. (2003) 'Aging and the dancing body', in C.A. Faircloth (ed.), *Aging Bodies: Images and Everyday Experience.* Walnut Creek, CA: Altamira Press, pp. 259–92.

Wainwright, S. and Turner, B.S. (2006) '"Just crumbling to bits"? An exploration of the body, ageing, injury and career in classical ballet dancers', *Sociology*, 40(2): 237–55.

Ward-Griffin, C., Hobson, S., Melles, P., et al. (2004) 'Falls and fear of falling among community-dwelling seniors: the dynamic tension between exercising precaution and striving for independence', *Canadian Journal on Aging*, 23(4): 307–18.

Williams, S.J. (2003) 'Beyond meaning, discourse and the empirical world: critical realist reflections on health', *Social Theory and Health*, 1(1): 42–71.

Woodward, K. (1991) *Aging and Its Discontents.* Bloomington and Indianapolis: Indiana University Press.

Yoxen, E. (1987) 'Seeing with sound: a study of the development of medical images', in W.E. Bijker, T.P. Hughes, and T. Pinch (eds), *The Social Construction of Technological Systems.* Cambridge, MA: The MIT Press, pp. 281–303.

28

Time and Ageing: Enduring and Emerging Issues

Jan Baars

INTRODUCTION

Human beings are born, they grow up, age, and die just like other mammals, but these processes are interpreted and organized according to sociocultural contexts that are very diverse, both in historical and contemporary societies. These contexts are deeply formative as humans go through a relatively long period in which they are dependent on others. They begin to absorb the specific culture even before they are born, before they begin to drink the milk that feeds them. Some fundamental cultural assets, such as language, take a considerable time to acquire but then, eventually, are essential to participate competently and actively, and to develop the abilities that are usually associated with human autonomy.

In this short observation we can distinguish three dimensions – natural (physical and biological), sociocultural, and personal – which *co-constitute* human lives. As human ageing can be characterized as living for a relatively long time, it will typically be shaped through these three dimensions, which change and interact in time. The *temporal* characteristics of the three constitutive dimensions can, in a first approach, be described as follows:

1 The *natural* dimension involves the more or less regular physical and biological processes or rhythms that form and reproduce the materiality or corporeality of ageing. Especially in premodern times, natural rhythms have been seen as giving meaning to human ageing in the form of 'seasons', 'phases', or 'ages' of human lives (Burrow, 1986; Sears, 1986). With the rise of modern science, such traditionally meaningful natural rhythms have been stripped of their meaningful content and used as a foundation of chronological time. Characteristic of this form of time is that it contains only instrumental properties of measurement. In addition to the difference between precise or imprecise measurement, chronological time contains no meaning of itself; all meaning of chronological time has been ascribed to it from the other two dimensions.

2 The *sociocultural* dimension involves narratives that articulate when 'ageing' is supposed to begin; what its challenges, qualities and drawbacks are; how the 'aged' should be approached; whether they should be respected or not; what counts as 'young', 'normal', 'old', 'very old', 'innocent', 'experienced', 'wise', etc. All this depends on interpretations of what it means to 'age' and these interpretations are transmitted and renewed through sociocultural narratives. These narratives are not just 'stories': they carry structural weight in the way in which, for example, markets are organized, political power is exercised, and income and life chances are distributed.

3 The *personal* dimension involves experiences of living in time: persons are unique in the ways they undergo the influences from the other dimensions (such as genetic make-up or education), but they also actively form their own lives and actively interact with the other

two dimensions as they influence their bodies through their lifestyles, or contribute to the sociocultural narratives about ageing by communicating their experiences and perspectives.

I have called the complex interaction of these three constitutive dimensions of human life over time the '*triple temporality of ageing*' (Baars, 2007b), which will briefly be discussed in the final part of this chapter after having analyzed some of the key issues around the construction of time in relation to ageing.

The main purpose of this chapter will be to demonstrate the problems which arise when ageing is simply conceptualized as 'getting a higher chronological age', using merely the methodical perspective of chronological time, which is merely the abstract and instrumental form of one of the constitutive dimensions of ageing. This criticism does not imply that chronological *time* is not an important analytical tool for many purposes. Within gerontological discourse, however, the significance of chronological *age* is limited and its use too often serves to evade the question what ageing actually is supposed to be. That ageing is poorly indicated by higher chronological ages may often be admitted, but this does not appear to lead to much change in research practices. The vast majority of studies still use a chronological approach to define populations for research purposes (i.e., determine who the 'aged' are that should be studied) and try to establish how (social, economic, health, etc.) characteristics of people change as a function of their chronological age. This may lead to an accumulation of data, but in itself not to *explanatory* knowledge.

In this chapter I will discuss the overemphasis on chronological time in two forms, which presuppose and strengthen each other: as a chronologization of *ageing* and as a chronologization of the *life course*. In this chronologization, the three dimensions that were distinguished at the beginning of this chapter, as co-constituting human lives (natural, sociocultural, and personal) are reduced to an instrumentalized version of one domain. Chronological age, however, usually carries more meaning than could strictly be derived from chronological measurements and tends to reduce ageing to just one constitutive dimension. This tendency is one of the enduring issues in the study of ageing regarding its concepts of time. The emerging issue is to arrive at a better understanding of the 'triple temporality of ageing': the mutual presupposition and interconnection of the temporal characteristics that are typical of the three constitutive dimensions of human ageing.

THE CHRONOLOGIZATION OF AGEING

Ageing means basically living 'in time' and concepts of time shape the ways in which ageing is approached. A fundamental problem and enduring issue in the study of ageing is the assumption that chronological age forms the key to the understanding of ageing processes. A persistent emphasis on chronological age orients gerontological studies, although it is an emphasis that is not corroborated or justified by results of these studies. This overemphasis on chronological age does, however, have consequences for the way ageing processes are organized. An important problem with this '*chronologization*' of ageing is that this approach suggests that the exactness of measuring chronological time (since birth) gives exact outcomes in terms of age-related properties. As its main vehicle is the measurement of chronological time, which is necessarily abstract and carries no meaning of itself, chronologization often carries implicit narratives about ageing without being openly discussed. Moreover, it obstructs the acknowledgement of the importance of meaningful narratives of ageing stemming from diverse sociocultural sources and from personal experiences. Processes of ageing are meaningfully constituted in an interplay between natural rhythms and regularities, more generally guiding sociocultural narratives and personal experiences; if 'chronological age' has any meaning, it comes from this interplay, not from time measurements.

So, what exactly is chronological time? How can we measure it precisely? Throughout its history chronological time has been indicated by rudimentary or refined 'clocks' such as water clocks, sundials, hourglasses, mechanical clocks, and atomic clocks, in combination with calendars that count the years (Baars, 1997). In a sophisticated form they make it possible to measure the duration of a process or locate an event (the birth of a baby, a future appointment) on a time scale. We know that some clocks do not function well; that they are not precise. But how can we determine whether a clock really measures 'the' time precisely? Usually, we establish the accuracy of a clock by comparing it with the clock of an institution with 'more authority', such as the telephone company or television. But again, how can we determine the accuracy of such an authoritative clock? To what most 'authoritative clock' or most 'fundamental time' are these clocks attuned? To the movement of the earth around the sun? Is that time in an ultimate sense? Or something else entirely? Unfortunately, following this line of questioning does not lead to an ultimate time or an ultimate clock. In all chronological time concepts that we know of, a specific, more or less regular process has been selected as a standard to establish what 'time' is. In most traditions the movements of the celestial bodies have been taken to represent 'time': defining years, seasons, months, day and night, hours, and minutes.

In principle, there are many processes that might be used as the basis of a chronological time concept. In fact, all natural rhythms could be taken into consideration. However, a *general* time concept must be based on processes that cannot be influenced by the different processes it should measure. Therefore the movements of the earth and the moon were excellent candidates to form the basis of a general time concept, as their regular movements are clearly independent of anything happening on earth. But, eventually, this way of defining time resulted in many problems of measurement since these basic cosmological movements turned out to be too irregular. The elliptic form of the movement of the earth around the sun and the procession of the equinoxes caused, in the long run, a lack of precision, which led in 1582 to a change from the Julian to the Gregorian calendar (Richards, 1998).

After this repair, the calendar has more or less been left to itself, as human beings could live very well with small long-term irregularities. These were, however, increasingly regarded as intolerable to the degree that ever more precise measurements became of vital importance for several types of scientific research. Therefore the search has been intensified for still more delicate regular movements that could be used as a basis for a general standard to measure all other movements.

The technical criteria which must be met have become extremely demanding. To be able to establish a natural process as a standard for measuring time, we need a periodic process with extremely short phases, that can easily be reproduced and which has outcomes that are highly stable with respect to possible external disturbances. In searching for this time standard, the frequency of the periodical processes has risen to the level of the cesium atomic clock, which is based on a cycle of over 9 billion vibrations during one (old) astronomical second. This has become the basis of International Atomic Time, which is continuously broadcast from stations in Colorado (United States), Rugby (United Kingdom), and Braunschweig (Germany) and which is received by the authoritative clocks referred to above. On this atomic foundation it is, in principle, possible to make chronological measurements extending from the millions of years that astrophysicists work with, to the nanoseconds that are needed in other areas of physical research. This form of time is indicated precisely by the clock, but this is in no way 'time as such'. Its foundation is only a specific stable movement that has been selected to function as a standard for chronological measurement. It is only a very sophisticated convention that enables time to be measured by offering a precise instrument to be used for exact measurement and for the temporal coordination of actions or processes (Baars, 2007b).

Concepts of time are so important because we have no organ to perceive time like we can *see* objects in *space*. And although what we can see for ourselves may often seem self-evident but actually may be self-deceiving, grasping time is even more difficult. Therefore, spatial images and evenly distributed distances have often been used to represent time, as in an old-fashioned clock where the pointers tick away the time as they move over the face of the clock. Another example of a spatial projection of the passage of time is drawing a straight line, which visualizes the time which is passing even during the very act of drawing the line. This can easily be transformed into the 'arrow of time' or into one of the axes in the common diagrams which show changes in certain characteristics as a function of ageing. These visualizations tend to reduce time to spatial characteristics, as if time is something which moves with a regular pace from A to B – from birth to death – and would affect everybody equally. In that way somebody's chronological age would be the key to understanding a person and his or her situation.

MISTAKEN ASSOCIATIONS: TIME WORKING AS A REGULAR CAUSE

Generalizations about people with a certain calendar age actually presuppose a *causal* concept of time: because time has worked for a certain duration in ageing people, certain inevitable effects should be reckoned with. Moreover, the effects are assumed to develop steadily and universally according to the rhythm of the clock. However, such a causal concept of time can never generate knowledge that might explain something of the differences that exist between human beings of the same age, or allow us to understand that ageing is a generalizing concept that is actually composed of many specific processes. While it is true that all causal relations are *also* temporal relations, or relations working 'in time', it would be wrong to identify causality with time or to reduce the process of ageing to the causal effects of time.

However, the grand ambition of gerontology often seems to be to establish how the chronological or calendar age of persons determines the characteristics of ageing persons. This would eventually reduce gerontology to a straightforward set of simple formulas in which scientific precision and practical use would be united. In the early days of gerontology this option was stated with much self-assurance. Birren (1959: 8), for example, argued that: 'Chronological age is one of the most useful single items of information about an individual if not the *most* useful. From this knowledge alone an amazingly large number of general statements or predictions can be made about his anatomy, physiology, psychology and social behavior.'

Although such an explicit claim may be scarce, this articulates the presupposition of much research on ageing. Its author has been one of the few theorists who has dealt extensively and over a long period of time with temporal aspects of ageing. Forty years later he expressed serious reservations about these claims which, however, still appeared to be held as part of the 'data-rich' but 'theory-poor' character of gerontology:

> By itself, the collection of large amounts of data showing relationships with chronological age does not help, because chronological age is not the cause of anything. Chronological age is only an index, and unrelated sets of data show correlations with chronological age that have no intrinsic or causal relationship with each other.
>
> (Birren, 1999: 460)

Although *processes* (which can be measured in chronological time) will have their effects, time by itself does not have any effects. To assume this leads away from an understanding of ageing although it may produce neat distributions of characteristics of persons according to their ages. In spite of their importance, explicit analyses of the different concepts of time that are inevitably used in the study of ageing have still been scarce, although there have been some notable exceptions (cf. Baars and Visser, 2007).

To develop a more intrinsic measure of ageing than chronological age would, even in a mere functionalist perspective, require establishing clear indicators of 'normal' functioning. If we define ageing in terms of 'biological reliability theory' (Gravilov and Gravilova, 2006), as a phenomenon of increasing risk of failure with the passage of time, the question remains in what way the statistical notion of increasing risk can be supported by an understanding of ageing processes. Even if we would have reliable biomarkers to determine somebody's (biological or functional) *age*, this would not allow us to explain *ageing* as a regular process. If biological ageing would

develop in synchrony with chronological age, the differently marked *ages* would have to be included in a continuum, as subsequent *phases* which would demonstrate a structured development away from a state of adult 'health' or 'normality'. It is doubtful whether all biological processes of ageing can be adequately seen as *continuous* and *regular* functional deterioration; some processes may respond to training or treatment, others may suddenly collapse. Moreover, human ageing appears to imply many distinct but interrelated processes that are relatively independent, but also interact with other processes in the same body (Kirkwood et al., 2006). The many different processes of ageing may have their specific dynamical properties, but these usually include an openness to the environments inside and outside the human body, extending to ecological or social contexts and personal lifestyles. This explains their intrinsic malleability (Kirkwood, 2005; Westendorp and Kirkwood, 2007), which is demonstrated in the large differences in life expectancy and health that we can observe when we compare several historical and contemporary countries or regions with each other.

How important such contexts are can be gathered from the enormous change in life expectancies that has taken place in the countries of the Global North during the last 150 years; changes that cannot be explained by a major shift or mutation in the evolutionary substrate of human life. Seen from this perspective, our bodies have hardly changed since long before the ancient Greeks, let alone since the 19th century. Yet the chances to live longer have changed impressively. Social and cultural contexts with their still advancing technological possibilities appear to become increasingly important and may necessitate a rethinking of evolutionary theory (Promislov et al., 2006).

HUMAN AGEING AND ITS CONSTITUTIVE CONTEXTS

We cannot study processes of ageing as we would study other processes, because we cannot isolate 'ageing' in an experimental group and compare the results with a control group that does not age. Moreover, all human ageing takes place in specific contexts that co-constitute its outcomes. This fundamental human condition haunts even the most sophisticated research strategies. The notorious age–period–cohort problem (cf. Baars, 2007a; Schaie, 2007) confronts us with questions about what we have actually established when we have found, for instance, that a high percentage of a group of 70 year olds suffers from high blood pressure. Is this because of their age? Is it part of their specific 'cohort identity'? Is it because they grew up and older in a specific period in a specific society? Is it 'a little bit of all that'? Human ageing cannot be studied in a *pure* form: even a scientifically controlled life in a laboratory would be a life in a specific context that would co-constitute the processes that would take place.

The search for general ageing characteristics based on chronological age has produced much counterevidence, testifying to the many differences in ageing processes. This counterevidence comes hardly as a surprise when we try to imagine persons with the same chronological age but living in very different circumstances. Think, for instance, of 60 year olds: one would expect major differences in many important respects between, let us say, a contemporary poor Russian farmer, a wealthy Japanese, or a homeless American of that age; not to mention 60 year olds in ancient Egypt, in classical China, or among 19th century factory workers. The fact that in Western Europe the average life expectancy for males has practically doubled in the last 150 years (Oeppen and Vaupel, 2002) implies that chronological age cannot by itself give any precise reference to (a phase of) ageing processes. Statistics using chronological age should not be misused to *explain* ageing processes without further gerontological investigation.

Chronological calculations of life expectancy are prognostic estimates that presuppose specific *historical* contexts. And, as we can read in this handbook, this is just the beginning: in the *same* historical period different social backgrounds – in education, gender, labor markets, medical care, pension systems, housing, care arrangements, or medical technology – are likely to result in different ageing experiences. Even a 'cohort identity', established by contrast with other cohorts within the same historical context, remains to a high degree an abstract construction which has to tolerate a considerable amount of internal differentiation. Therefore, the analysis of inter-cohort differences has to be supplemented by analysis of intra-cohort differences (Dannefer, 1984; 2003).

THE CHRONOLOGIZATION OF THE LIFE COURSE

Just like societies organize ways to educate children to prepare them for active adult lives, they tend to organize ageing processes, especially when a relatively large part of the population counts as 'aged'. This social organization of ageing processes has many complicated aspects, as can be seen in other chapters of this volume. One of them is the way this organization is informed by statistical overviews, gerontological studies, or common prejudice which are based on calendar age or chronological age. In such cases, a specific concept of time, chronological time, is directly applied to represent ageing processes and their effects, resulting in the many statistical tables in which we find 'age' on one axis and on the other axis certain characteristics that are shown to change with 'age'.

The danger of an unreflected overemphasis on chronological time presents itself once more as this concept of time has been institutionalized to measure and coordinate processes and actions in modern societies, assuming that societal processes can be optimally organized on the basis of the ages of the people concerned. This can easily lead to self-fulfilling prophecies: if in a given society the dominant agents in the labor market are under the impression that productivity is declining after the age of 50, this will most likely become true; not because this is inherent in their ageing process, but as an artifact of the strategies that define these persons as 'older workers'.

According to Kohli (1986), a historical process of 'chronologization' has resulted in a 'chronologically standardized "normative life course"' (Kohli, 1986: 272). Although this proposition has encountered some historical criticism (cf. Grillis, 1987), it has been fruitful in many debates about the life course (Levy et al., 2005; Settersten, 1999, 2003; Vickerstaff, 2006). This section connects with these debates, but also introduces some further distinctions.

A first distinction concerning the chronologization of *ageing* in gerontological research has already been discussed above. This specific chronological approach to time has many important limitations but is nevertheless quite dominant, as its measurements and age-related generalizations seem to offer a superficial clarity that can be applied in policies regarding ageing and the life course. Through such applications, the inter-related complex of gerontological research and age-related policies further strengthens the chronologization of the *life course*. In this regard, it appears also to be fruitful to distinguish a chronologization of the life course from its possible *standardization*. This last aspect of Kohli's (1986) proposal has aroused much debate, as standardization does not harmonize well with processes of individualization (Baars, 2006; cf. Beck, 1992; Uhlenberg and Mueller, 2004) or, for example, the many effects of international migration (Vincent, 1995, 2005), which lead to deviations from the usual life-course patterns with regard to education, work, and pensions.

Furthermore, I propose that the concept of a 'chronologization of the life course' is not necessarily restricted to *ages* but can also imply that *durations* of participations of persons in institutions and organizations will be regulated and registered bureaucratically, with consequences for the persons concerned. The number of years that were (allowed to be) spent in education, in work, in paying for a mortgage or pension may have important effects over the life course. Chronological durations of education or employment may not only structure the way persons remember, evaluate, or plan their lives but can also have many consequences in later life – for instance, in terms of both access to and amount of pensions. Consequently, even if the life course were to be less organized or standardized in terms of age, it could still be organized chronologically in terms of duration. This interpretation of a chronologization of the life course can easily be connected to research of event time (cf. Schaie, 2007).

Although careers may tend to become less standardized, the idea of a 'late modern' or 'post modern' de-standardization of the life course appears to be more adequate for *personal* relationships, where traditional family patterns have become much less dominant in a few decades and lifestyles of many (early) retired older people are changing drastically (Gilleard and Higgs, 2000, 2005) than for careers in education or employment (cf. Henretta, 2003). The effects of these careers still remain important during later life as they are connected with the distribution of education and (pension) income (cf. Dannefer, 2003). As institutions and organizations in postmodern societies tend to use chronological time to control and coordinate actions and processes, ageing processes will not be able to evade the different 'chronological regimes' (Baars, 2007b) that combine chronological age and duration of participations in education, employment, social services, or care (cf. Leisering and Leibfried, 1999).

CHRONOLOGICAL REGIMES

In everyday life, chronological age is often, explicitly or implicitly, used to explain ageing processes or as an 'argument' to distinguish persons who have become 'older' (sic!), 'senior', 'elderly', or 'aged' from 'normal' adults. In many Western countries, persons who have lived for 50 years are invited to join organizations such as the US American Association of Retired Persons (AARP) or in the European Union (EU), one of the many national organizations which are active

in the member states, that will support their suddenly weakened existence with age-specific benefits that may partly compensate for the negative effects of the age segregation these organizations paradoxically emphasize. The media confront us with scientifically based reports about the things these seniors are doing, what they prefer, desire, what they are still capable of, or not any more, although this category of people represents often a third or even half of the adult population. It has even become customary to speak of 'older workers' for people over 40 years of age, not only in Europe but also in many other countries (Henretta, 2003; see also Chapter 41).

It does not take more than a few moments to realize the absurdity of this situation, which could be interpreted as typical of a culture that is so obsessed with youth that a distinction between 'normal' and 'older' adults is made as soon as possible, followed by indifference regarding the many possible differences between those who deviate from normality. This awkward status of being 'aged' may remain with individuals for several decades, much longer than their 'normal' adulthood, and they are likely to change and to 'fan out', becoming even more different from other members of their birth cohorts, because they tend to follow their specific interests without being tied down by the institutional regularities of education, work, or raising children.

The paradoxical *acceleration of chronologically ascribed ageing* in the labor markets of most Western countries stands in strong contrast with the risen and still rising life expectancy (Oeppen and Vaupel, 2002), which can be interpreted as a *slowing down* of ageing processes. Here also, chronological age serves as a pseudo-exact labeling device which has been programmed by cultural trends that are easily obfuscated by it. This paradoxical development may offer attractive perspectives of many 'golden years' to persons who can afford them, but also enforces age segregation and even excludes many ageing people from important possibilities of gaining a decent income (Macnicol, 2006). Women who want to return to the labor market after having raised their children are particularly disadvantaged as they are right from the start labeled as 'older workers' (Baars et al., 1997; Ginn et al., 2001). Finally, this acceleration of ascribed ageing has increased the pressure on the lives of 'normal adults' (25–45 years of age) to combine family life with a relatively short and intense career during which income and the assets to support a long life must be gathered. When such long-term overburdening eventually leads to health problems, these are too often 'explained' by referring to the *ages* of the persons concerned, offering another superficial argument to legitimate an early exit from the labor market.

Although age discrimination legislation has been introduced in the EU, the labor market position of older workers fluctuates with the general economic situation and investment in updating or retraining their capacities tends to slow down or stop as soon as they have reached the status of an 'older worker' (Baars, 2006). Even in the United States, where mandatory retirement does not exist, older workers have the lowest rates of re-employment, which will typically be in part-time positions or jobs with low skill and training requirements, resulting in large wage losses (Chan and Stevens, 1999; Hirsch et al., 2000). In spite of generally more positive views about aged workers, employers are still under the spell of negative prejudice. In her overview on this topic, Hardy (2006) concludes that research on the relationship between age and job performance fails to include contextual factors, thus resulting in little understanding of the multiple forces underlying the relationship (see also Avolio, 1992; Czaja, 1995). The main reason is again a narrow focus on chronological age, although age accounts for only a fraction of the inter-individual variability in performance (Avolio et al., 1990).

This situation leads to many unfortunate conflicts, as the abilities and needs of numerous people clash with implicit or explicit prejudice or regulations regarding their calendar age. As populations age in differentiated ways, these developments conflict with life-course structures that are not flexible enough, demonstrating the actuality of the theory of 'structural lag' that played a central role in the later work of Matilda Riley (cf. Riley et al., 1994).

Given these circumstances, knowing the chronological age of persons can be quite informative because ages can easily be related to certain characteristics. We can predict, for example, that the unemployment of older workers will tend to be longer than the unemployment of 'normal' workers. The point is, however, that this does not demonstrate that older workers are, as a result of 'a higher age', 'slower' or 'less flexible', than younger ones. Given the tendency to exclude older workers from the labor market and the importance of work for income, housing, health, social contacts, participation, and the articulation of personal identities, these important aspects of life may become increasingly at risk as people reach higher ages. Such increasing risks of loss and failure cannot be understood as being caused by ageing processes per se; they are to a large degree constituted by age-related processes in the labor market. For ageing studies, to focus on age without analyzing the processes which constitute many of the characteristics associated with these ages, merely because chronological age has been institutionalized in the societies in which people live, enforces the chronological regimes of these societies and does nothing to advance our understanding of human ageing.

Not only are contexts co-constitutive for ageing but also this holds for research on ageing (Baars, 2008). The identification of 'aged' research populations, for instance, presupposes an organization of the life course in which chronological time has become an important instrumental perspective (Kohli, 1986; Mayer and Müller, 1986). Concepts such as 'age groups', 'age norms', or 'age grading' presuppose chronological age which has become the typical instrument to regulate many transitions or entitlements. Concepts used in the discussions of 'ageing' societies, such as 'age-structure', 'birth cohorts', 'dependency-ratio', 'age-cost profile', and all kinds of tables in which ages are associated with particular characteristics, pretending to give a quick informative overview, have become so general that their gerontological meaning is rarely questioned. In all instances where age-related generalizations are presented without further questioning their suggested meanings, conventional generalizations about ageing and the aged are reproduced or new ones introduced. That such generalizations are unfounded does not imply that they are without any effect; even unfounded statements about categories of people with certain ages can be implemented in policies regarding, for instance, specific forms of care or housing for 'the aged' and thus contribute to a reality which forces ageing people to fit in, because they have no other options than those that were organized for them. Consequently, later research can affirm the earlier generalizations, not because they grasped the realities of ageing, but because gerontological expertise has again played its unreflected role in co-constituting the realities of ageing. In such cases the analytical apparatus of gerontology runs the danger of becoming an uncritical instrument catering to all kinds of organizational contexts, in which ageing people are mainly relevant as the subjects of planning procedures and average estimates, even if the objective is to help and support them.

That *personal* dimensions of ageing processes cannot always be acknowledged may be unavoidable, because social entities like institutions, communities, and societies want to assure their continuity while individuals fade away, sooner or later. Therefore, these entities tend to use perspectives that are detached from limited personal horizons, and the chronological perspective may be useful for such long-term planning as it can interrelate average chronological *duration of activities* with the chronological *ages* or average life expectancies of the actors involved. Practical as such age-related generalizations may seem, they should not guide and certainly not dominate the way ageing is approached or understood; for gerontological purposes this can hardly be satisfactory.

Nonetheless, chronological time plays an increasingly important role, as it is typically used to measure all kinds of events or processes to see whether they can be more efficiently ('better') organized: smoother or faster and less 'time-consuming'. Such a restructuring of processes and situations from the perspective of chronological measurements may have several important consequences for the aged. We can think of the phenomenon of *time budgets* in institutions for care. There is a crucial transition from measuring the times of particular conversations or acts of care, establishing that these activities take 5 or 9 minutes on the average, to regulations that a conversation or a specific act of care *may not exceed a precise amount of time*. Such tightly calculated chronological regimes may clash with the time perspectives that are inherent in situations of personal contact (cf. Baars, 2007b) as the need for contact may fluctuate with situations and persons.

TOWARDS A TRIPLE TEMPORALITY

As chronological *time* can easily be used in bureaucratic calculations it will tend to dominate other perspectives on time and ageing with its implicit pseudo-narrative that chronological *age* would present a reliable indicator of ageing. This all too simple model is defied by the constitutive complexity of the three interrelated dimensions that have been distinguished in the Introduction section.

(1) *Natural* (physical and biological) rhythms are constitutive of ageing as this remains a process that is 'bodily driven', but the complexity and variability of these rhythms cannot be grasped by establishing chronological age. Moreover, human ageing is always interpreted meaningfully through (2) *sociocultural narratives* that are not just interesting 'stories' but are connected to structural contexts which co-constitute ageing processes. Even within communities that are integrated by common narratives, there are structural arrangements and forms of social inequality leading to important differences in life chances that defy the idea of uniform ageing processes.

When ageing is only approached from a chronological perspective, the necessarily abstract character of chronological time discussed above will empty human ageing from its constitutive structural backgrounds and meaningful contents that are, however, essential to understand its variations.

Even years, the units of chronological measurement of human lives, are laden with meaning. Calendars are not only used to count the years, as we do when we speak of calendar age but also there are many different calendars around the world that meaningfully structure the years with religious holidays and the remembrance of historical events, ranging from a global to the most personal level. The yearly cycles and the rhythms of the natural environment are meaningfully structured with seasonal activities and festivities, markets, contests, and holidays (Zerubavel, 1981). Such sociocultural narratives also form an interpretative background of human life courses and articulate what it means to be born, to grow up, to become adults, to get older and to die. Meaningful temporal horizons belong to human ageing; chronological time can hardly be more than a tool to date and locate events on a time scale.

Because being born and dying are inherent to human life and everything in between – growing up and ageing – quite common, generalizations are easily developed. But, paradoxically, being born, growing up, ageing, and dying never take place 'in general'; only particular persons are born and they grow up, age, and die as specific persons in specific circumstances. Therefore, (3) *personal* experiences of ageing as *living in time* deserve a place in gerontology, as the third dimension from which ageing processes derive their meaning. That personal perspectives on ageing as living in time are relatively independent from the other two constitutive dimensions can be gained from everyday experiences we can make with time. The 'same' time (in terms of duration) is experienced very differently in waiting, sleeping, having a beer with friends, or in supporting our favorite football team as it tries to make up for its loss while 'time' is running out. From everyday life we also know that our memories do not work according to chronological time. Memories of something that happened 50 years ago can be much more vivid than memories of something that took place last week. Still, the realization that the remembered situation is not actual but lays 50 years behind us adds to the understanding of what it is to live in time, which comprises more than only personal experiences.

The three fundamental dimensions – natural (physical and biological), sociocultural narratives, and personal experiences – continually presuppose each other and are in that sense co-constitutive of ageing processes. To attain a better understanding of ageing processes it is necessary to understand more of this temporal interplay of these dimensions – what I have called the 'triple temporality of ageing' (Baars 2007b).

CONCLUSION

The scientific precision that is associated with chronological *time* (as it is expressed in numbers and used in calculations) can easily lead to an uncritical acceptance of certain constructions of chronological *age*. Chronological age, however, is only the amount of chronological time that has passed since somebody was born. We are getting older with every tick of the clock, but this 'older' only has a precise meaning in a chronological, not in a gerontological sense. Therefore, the 'aged' have no more in common than a certain minimal calendar age. As the life courses of postmodern societies tend to be chronologically organized, research on ageing should maintain a certain independence and question age-related generalizations rather than enforce them by failing to investigate actual ageing processes. To understand these processes more fully, three co-constitutive dimensions of ageing should be taken into account and their interrelated temporal properties analyzed as they contribute to ageing.

This 'triple temporality of ageing' implies a modest role for chronological time. It appears to be indispensable for research on ageing processes as it serves to measure durations, but this covers only a part of the complex realities of ageing. Chronological age would suffice if the same duration (age) would lead to the same result in all humans and this is only true of durations that exceed the maximum life span, namely death.

The arguments against a widespread overemphasis on chronological age are no denial of the finitude of human life, nor do they deny that 'ageing' can be observed in any human being, if we compare characteristics of the same person over a relatively long period of time. The question is how to approach these themes to get a better understanding. To achieve this it is essential to understand the specific significance and relativity of chronological time and its unfounded seductions in relation to ageing to open up ways to investigate the ways in which human ageing is constituted in time.

REFERENCES

Avolio, B.J. (1992) 'A levels of analysis perspective of aging and work research', in K.W. Schaie and M.P. Lawton (eds), *Annual Review of Gerontology and Geriatrics*. New York: Springer, pp. 239–60.

Avolio, B.J., Waldman, D.A., and McDaniel, M.A. (1990) 'Age and work performance in non-managerial jobs: the effects of experience and occupational type', *Academy of Management Journal*, 33: 407–22.

Baars, J. (1997) 'Concepts of time and narrative temporality in the study of aging', *Journal of Aging Studies*, 11: 283–96.

Baars, J. (2006a) *Het Nieuwe Ouder Worden: Paradoxen en Perspectieven van Leven in de Tijd*. Amsterdam: Humanistics University Press.

Baars, J. (2006b) 'Beyond neo-modernism, anti-modernism and post-modernism: basic categories for contemporary critical gerontology', in J. Baars, D. Dannefer, C. Phillipson, and Alan Walker (eds), *Aging, Globalization and Inequality: The New Critical Gerontology*. Amityville, NY: Baywood Publishing, pp. 17–42.

Baars, J. (2007a) 'Introduction chronological time and chronological age – problems of temporal diversity' in J. Baars, and H. Visser (eds), *Aging and Time. Multidisciplinary Perspectives*. Amityville, NY: Baywood Publishing, pp. 1–14.

Baars, J. (2007b) 'A triple temporality of aging: chronological measurement, personal experience and narrative articulation', in J. Baars and H. Visser (eds), *Aging and Time. Multidisciplinary Perspectives*. Amityville, NY: Baywood Publishing, pp. 15–42.

Baars, J. (2008) 'The challenge of a critical gerontology: The problem of social constitution', in S. McDaniel (ed.), *Ageing, Volume 4, Key Debates*. London: SAGE, pp. 227–62.

Baars, J. and Visser, H. (eds) (2007) *Aging and Time. Multidisciplinary Perspectives*. Amityville, NY: Baywood Publishing.

Baars, J., Beck, W., and Graveland, I. (1997) *De verjonging van de ouderdom in een vergrijzende samenleving: Een kritische beschouwing van de sociale gerontologie*. Amsterdam: SISWO.

Beck, U. (1992) *Risk Society: Towards a New Modernity*. London: SAGE.

Birren, J. (1959) 'Principles of research on aging', In J. Birren, (ed.), *Handbook of Aging and the Individual: Psychological and Biological Aspects*. Chicago: University of Chicago Press, pp. 2–42.

Birren, J. (1999) 'Theories of aging: a personal perspective', in V.L. Bengtson and K.W. Schaie (eds), *Handbook of Theories of Aging*. New York: Springer, pp. 459–72.

Burrow, J.A. (1986) *The Ages of Man: A Study in Medieval Writing and Thought*. Oxford: Oxford University Press.

Chan, S. and Stevens, A.H. (1999) 'Employment and retirement following a late-career job loss', *American Economic Review*, 70: 335–71.

Czaja, S.J. (1995) 'Aging and work performance', *Review of Public Personnel Administration*, 15(2): 46–61.

Dannefer, D. (1984) 'Adult development and social theory: a paradigmatic reappraisal', *American Sociological Review*, 49: 100–16.

Dannefer, D. (2003) 'Cumulative advantage/disadvantage and the life course: cross-fertilizing age and social science theory', *Journal of Gerontology*, 58b: S327–37.

Gilleard, C. and Higgs, P. (2000) *Cultures of Ageing: Self, Citizen and the Body*. Harlow: Pearson.

Gilleard, C. and Higgs, P. (2005) *Contexts of Aging: Class, Cohort and Community*. Malden, MA: Polity Press.

Ginn, J., Street, D., and Arber, S. (eds) (2001) *Women, Work and Pensions: International Issues and Prospects*. Buckingham: Open University Press.

Gravilov, L.A. and Gravilova, N.S. (2006) 'Reliability theory of aging and longevity', in E.J. Masoro and S.N. Austed (eds), *Handbook of the Biology of Aging*, 6th edn. San Diego: Academic Press, pp. 3–42.

Grillis, J.R. (1987) 'The case against chronologization: changes in the Anglo-American life cycle 1600 to the present', *Etnologia Europaea*, 17: 97–106.

Hardy, M. (2006) 'Older workers', in R.H. Binstock, and L.K. George, (eds), *Handbook of Aging and the Social Sciences*, 6th edn. Boston: Academic Press, pp. 201–18.

Henretta, J.C. (2003) 'The life course perspective on work and retirement', in R.A. Settersten (ed.), *Invitation to the Life Course: Toward New Understandings of Later Life*. Amityville, NY: Baywood, pp. 85–106.

Hirsch, B., MacPherson, D., and Hardy, M. (2000) 'Occupational age structure and access for older workers', *Industrial and Labor Relations Review*, 42: 401–18.

Kirkwood, T.B.L. (2005) 'Understanding the odd science of ageing', in *Cell*, 120: 437–47.

Kirkwood, T.B.L., Boys, R.J., Gillespie, C.S., et al. (2006) 'Computer modelling in the study of aging', in E.J. Masoro, and S.N. Austed (eds), *Handbook of the Biology of Aging*, 6th edn. San Diego: Academic Press, pp. 334–59.

Kohli, M. (1986) 'The world we forgot: a historical review of the life course', in V. Marshall (ed.), *Later Life: The Social Psychology of Aging*. London: SAGE, pp. 271–303.

Levy, R., Ghisletta, P., Le Goff, J.-M., Spimi, D., and Widmer, E. (eds) (2005) *Towards an Interdisciplinary Perspective on the Life Course, Volume 10: Advances in Life Course Research*, Amsterdam: Elsevier.

Macnicol, J. (2006) 'Age discrimination in history', in L. Bauld, K. Clarke, and T. Maltby (eds), *Social Policy Review 18*. Bristol: Policy Press, pp. 249–69.

Masoro, E.J. (2006) 'Are age-associated diseases an integral part of aging?' in E.J. Masora and S.N. Austed (eds), *Handbook of the Biology of Aging*, 6th edn., San Diego: Academic Press, pp. 43–62.

McCarter, R.J.M. (2006) 'Differential aging among skeletal muscles', in E.J. Masoroand S.N. Austed (eds), *Handbook of the Biology of Aging*, 6th edn. San Diego: Academic Press, pp. 470–97.

Oeppen, J. and Vaupel, J. (2002) 'Broken limits to life expectancy', *Science*, 296.

Promislov, D.E.L., Fedorka, K.M., and Burger, J.M.S. (2006) 'Evolutionary biology of aging: future directions', in E.J. Masoro and S.N. Austed (eds), *Handbook of the Biology of Aging*, 6th edn. San Diego: Academic Press, pp. 217–42.

Richards, E.G. (1998) *Mapping Time: The Calendar and its History*. Oxford: Oxford University Press.

Riley, M.W., Kahn, R.L., and Foner, A. (1994) *Age and Structural Lag*. New York: Wiley.

Schaie, K.W. (2007) 'The concept of event time in the study of adult development', in J. Baars and H. Visser (eds), *Aging and Time. Multidisciplinary Perspectives*, Amityville: NY: Baywood Publishing, pp. 121–36.

Sears, E. (1986) *The Ages of Man: Medieval Interpretations of the Life Cycle*. Princeton: Princeton University Press.

Settersten, R.A. (1999) *Living in Time and Place: The Problems and Promises of Developmental Science*. Amityville, NY: Baywood Publishing.

Settersten, R.A. (ed.) (2003) *Invitation to the Life Course: Toward New Understandings of Later Life*. Amityville, NY: Baywood Publishing.

Settersten, R.A. (2004) 'Age strucuring and the rhythm of the life course', in J.T. Mortimer and M.J. Shanhan (eds), *Handbook of the Life Course*. New York: Spinger, pp. 81–102.

Uhlenberg, P. and Mueller, M. (2004) 'Family context and individual well-being: patterns and mechanisms in life course perspective', in J.T. Mortimer and M.J. Shanhan (eds), *Handbook of the Life Course*. New York: Spinger, pp. 123–48.

Vickerstaff, S. (2006) 'Life course, youth and old age', in P. Taylor-Gooby and J.O. Zinn (eds), *Risk in Social Science*. Oxford: Oxford University Press, pp. 180–201.

Vincent, J.A. (1995) *Inequality and Old Age*. London: UCL Press.

Westendorp, R.G.J. and Kirkwood, T.B.L. (2007) 'The biology of aging', in J. Bond, S. Peace, F. Dittmann-Kohli, and G. Westerhof (eds), *Ageing in Society. European Perspectives on Gerontology*. London: SAGE, pp. 15–37.

Zerubavel, E. (1981) *Hidden Rhythms: Schedules and Calendars in Social Life*. Berkeley, CA: University of California Press.

Ageing, Culture, and Development

29

Ageing and International Development

Peter Lloyd-Sherlock

INTRODUCTION

This chapter begins by examining what is meant by 'international development'. It shows that this can be interpreted in different ways and that these interpretations have important consequences for how we identify and perceive ageing and development issues. The second part of the chapter provides an overview of how ageing and older people have remained a relatively marginal concern for global development agencies, and how this has been supplanted by a narrow focus on pension reform. This leads on to a discussion of the simplified and largely negative portrayal of older people in development thinking. The final part of the chapter makes a number of suggestions about how to move towards a more nuanced and helpful understanding of ageing and development issues.

DIFFERENT PERSPECTIVES ON INTERNATIONAL DEVELOPMENT

International development can be understood as a set of processes, such as globalization, modernization, migration, and cultural and institutional change. These processes influence richer countries just as much as poorer ones. The speed and abruptness with which they occur vary between and even within countries, making generalization dangerous. Broadly speaking, demographic transition has occurred much more rapidly in developing regions than it did in developed ones. Yet it should not be forgotten that in some of the world's poorest countries fertility levels remain very high and mortality decline has been reversed, due to factors such as HIV/AIDS and conflict. Some countries, notably India and China, are experiencing unprecedented transformations, against which Britain's own Industrial Revolution is a pale reflection. In others, especially in sub-Saharan Africa, changes such as urbanization, the spread of mobile phone technology, and unhealthy Western eating habits belie a life of continued hardship and poverty for the vast majority of their populations (see Chapter 31). For all countries, the consequences of rapid change for cultural norms, attitudes, and household dynamics remain unclear and deeply contested (DFID, 2000; Scholte, 2000). While development processes will inevitably have important effects on the lives of current and future generations of older people, these effects will be complex and context-specific. For gerontologists working in the field, striking a balance between generalized understandings and unique experiences represents a major challenge. As will be seen, there has been a strong tendency to produce overgeneralized claims, and this has contributed to simplistic policy responses.

A second interpretation of international development is a geographical focus on so-called developing regions. This would seem to be almost tautological, but it is an important distinction from the previous 'process' interpretation that has a global scope. In many ways, focusing on developing regions is highly problematic. First, the distinction between a less-developed region or country and a more-developed one is somewhat arbitrary, particularly at the margins. For example, it is unclear whether many formerly socialist countries belong in one camp or the other. Secondly, it implies a neat, polarized distinction between conditions prevailing in developing and developed countries, and this goes on to imply that it is safe to make generalizations about older people in one set of countries vis-à-vis the other set. In fact, the extent of socioeconomic, epidemiological, and demographic variation among developing countries is much greater than the variation between the developed and developing worlds (Table 29.1). For example, Brazil's per capita gross domestic product (GDP) may be only a third of that of the United Kingdom, but Ethiopia's is less than a tenth of Brazil's. In terms of the share of population aged ≥60, the gap between developed and developing countries is rather more obvious, at least for now. However, the other indicators in Table 29.1 show that generalizations about later-life experiences across developing countries are even less appropriate than they are for the developed world. This volume contains separate chapters on Africa and Australasia that provide further detail about the extent of diversity both between and within developing countries.

It is possible to identify a third distinct interpretation of international development. This refers to a set of targets, norms, and concerns about international issues held by influential global policy actors. They include large multilateral organizations, mostly linked to the United Nations, as well as bilateral agencies (such as the UK's Department For International Development, or DFID) and a plethora of non-governmental organizations (NGOs) and other groups. Until the 1980s, the priorities of most of these agencies were strongly focused on facilitating economic growth and reducing fertility in poorer countries, and they were substantially influenced by Cold War ideological and strategic concerns. Since then, the emphasis has shifted in a number of ways. Most obviously, there has been an apparent move away from the primacy of economic growth towards issues of sustainability, poverty reduction, and human development (Remenyi, 2004). On the surface, this has been a major shift; for example, all World Bank and DFID activities now have to be justified in terms of their poverty impacts. For the larger and more influential agencies, however, there are signs that while the language of development may have changed, the fundamental priorities have not. Among NGOs and academics, there is general recognition that recent poverty initiatives, such as the Poverty Reduction Strategy Papers, are little more than neoliberal macroeconomic policy frameworks, albeit dressed up in softer language (Marshall et al., 2001). Similarly, it is not accidental that the World Bank's most influential publication on pension reform (World Bank, 1994) is entitled 'Averting the old age crisis. Policies to protect the old and promote economic growth' – the underlining is the Bank's, not this author's. The shift in development language has been more meaningful in the growing advocacy role of international and local NGOs, especially in areas such as gender, human rights, and the environment. However, the overall effect of these activities on the underlying priorities of the most powerful development agencies should not be overstated.

As will be seen in this chapter, the implications of these various agendas for older people are not entirely clear. Linking older people's well-being to specific issues such as poverty eradication and AIDS mitigation may provide some opportunities, but may also risk skewing priorities and overlooking other

Table 29.1 Socioeconomic, epidemiological, and demographic data for selected regions and countries

Paramater	UK	Brazil	China	Ethiopia	Senegal
Total fertility rate, 1970–75	2.0	4.7	4.9	6.8	7.0
Total fertility rate, 2000–05	1.7	2.3	1.7	5.3	5.2
GDP/capita, US$ ppp*, 2003	27,147	7,790	5,003	711	1,648
Per cent of total mortality due to chronic disease, 2002	87	63	66	32	30
Per cent urban, 2005	89.2	84.2	40.5	16.2	51.0
Per cent population aged 60+, 1975	19.7	6.0	6.9	4.4	5.4
Per cent population aged 60+ 2005	21.2	7.8	10.1	4.7	6.2

*Purchasing power parity: this is a weighting for national variations in living costs
Sources: United Nations Population Division (2002); United Nations Population Division (2006); United Nations Development Programme (2005); World Health Organisation (2007)

key areas of concern. In particular, it raises the issue of whether gerontologists working in development should largely ignore older people from middle or upper socioeconomic strata. Since these may account for the majority of older people in some countries, this is a large group to exclude.

These three different takes on international development are not mutually exclusive, but it is important to recognize that they have different implications for research and policy on older people. HelpAge International is the only major NGO that is primarily concerned with ageing and development. It largely conforms to the third interpretation of development, paying particular attention to poverty and human development agendas. However, HelpAge International's activities are not exclusively focused on the world's poorest countries, and its remit refers to 'disadvantaged older people worldwide'. By contrast, the United Nations Department for Economic and Social Affairs, the lead agency in organizing the Second World Assembly on Ageing and the Madrid International Plan of Action on Ageing, has a broader and more global remit. As such, its concerns are just as focused on the European Union as they are on sub-Saharan Africa.

POPULATION AGEING AND DEVELOPMENT

Attempts to make explicit reference to older people's needs in global development agreements date back to 1948, when a draft 'Declaration of Old Age Rights' was proposed at the United Nations General Assembly (Gorman, 1999). The failure to ratify this proposal, and the long delay until the 1982 Vienna World Assembly on Ageing, reflect the limited attention ageing commanded as a global development issue. This was hardly surprising, since most developing countries had yet to reach the final stage of demographic transition, and fertility rates remained high (see Table 29.1). Consequently, international concern was focused on total rates of population growth and the implications of bottom-heavy population pyramids for poorer countries (Ehrlich, 1971).

During the early 1990s it was increasingly recognized that population ageing had become a global trend and this was expected to create substantial challenges for public policy in a number of areas. These concerns were fuelled by events in different parts of the world: recognition of the long-term demographic effects of one-child policies in China, the rising cost of health care and social services in OECD (Organization for Economic Co-operation and Development) countries, the multi-billion dollar bankruptcies of state pension funds across Latin America, and the collapse of state provision for older people in former socialist economies (Banister, 1987; Mesa-Lago, 1991; Moon, 1993; Rush and Welch, 1996). At the same time, fertility rates in most developing countries had started to fall rapidly. This gave demographers and policymakers time and space to consider new issues, and past worries about a 'population time-bomb' gave way to new fears about an 'old age crisis' (World Bank, 1994).

As such, population ageing might have been expected to feature relatively prominently in the 1994 Cairo International Conference on Population and Development. This did not happen, as the central thrust of that event became the replacement of a narrow approach to population control with a rights-based reproductive healthcare agenda (Lane, 1994). Instead of emerging as an integral part of wider population and health strategies, population ageing rapidly become associated with global pensions policy. This should be seen as a major turning point in the international response to population ageing, and it continues to frame debate and policy. Its contribution to a coherent and contextualized policy response to population ageing in developing countries has, however, been almost entirely negative.

In the same year as the 1994 Cairo Conference, the World Bank published its influential and controversial *Averting the Old Age Crisis*. The report begins apocalyptically:

> The world is approaching an old age crisis. As life expectancies increase and birth rates decline, the proportion of the population that is old is expanding rapidly, swelling the potential economic burden on the young. Meanwhile, existing systems of financial security for older people are headed toward collapse.
>
> (World Bank, 1994)

The World Bank's proposed solution to this impending 'crisis' was exclusively focused on the reform of public pension programmes, promoting private administration, and moving to more sustainable financing models. For those poorer countries where pension systems were less extensive, the World Bank cautioned against state provision for older people, arguing that this would crowd out support from extended families. These proposals provoked a strong response from those opposed to the World Bank's explicit neoliberal agenda, such as the International Labour Organization (Charlton and McKinnon, 2001). Discussion was dominated by the pros and cons of different models of pension management and largely overlooked the fact that pension pro-grammes had a minimal impact on the well-being of the majority of older people in most developing countries, especially the poorest.

This conflation of ageing and development with pension reform agendas continues to the present day, partly reflecting the World Bank's dominance across international development thinking. According to its own website, between 1984 and 2004, the World Bank gave over 200 loans and issued more than 350 papers on pension reform, but made no loans or publications for other projects specifically concerned with older people (Bretton Woods Project, 2006). Over this period, the Bank's position, and that of other key development agencies has shifted, with a cosmetic softening of the initial hard-line neoliberal approach, and increased emphasis on new 'social pension' schemes for the poor (Holzmann, 2000; Holzmann and Hinz, 2005). Yet the impres-sion remains that pension reform is essentially the be-all and end-all of ageing and development policy.

The extent to which the pension reform agenda has skewed attention away from potentially more significant aspects of ageing and development is highlighted by the relative lack of attention given to older people in global health initiatives. This can be seen in a number of ways. First, there remains a heavy emphasis on infectious 'killer diseases', such as AIDS, malaria, and tuberculosis. While these illnesses undoubtedly deserve the attention given to them, the fact that chronic dis-eases account for a much larger number of deaths in most developing countries goes largely unrec-ognized. The key tools and targets of international development – Poverty Reduction Strategy Papers and the Millennium Development Goals – make no specific references to chronic disease. When efforts are being made to raise the profile of chronic disease, there is a tendency to distance the issue from older people. According to one influen-tial paper, 'Chronic diseases in developing coun-tries are not just diseases of the elderly, since cardiovascular disease accounts for as many deaths in young and middle-aged adults as HIV/AIDS' (Yach et al., 2004).

Related to the continued focus on infectious disease, there is little indication that more general health priorities have responded to the changing demographic composition of developing coun-tries. The emphasis remains firmly on mother and child health services. For example, in 2001 the influential World Health Organization (WHO) Commission on Macroeconomics and Health identified 49 priority health interventions for low-income countries, none of which has specific rel-evance for older people (Hanson et al., 2003).

Older people scarcely figure in national plans for essential primary healthcare interventions (Ensor et al., 2002; Gómez-Dantés, 2000). There is no evidence that interventions for older people were carefully considered and then screened out of selective programmes; instead, it would seem that older peoples' health needs were ignored from the outset of policy design. Many developing coun-tries are heavily dependent upon NGOs for the provision of basic health services, and these NGOs may find that the plight of older people in poor countries is a less marketable issue for fund-raising than that of other groups.

The virtual exclusion of older people from key areas of global policy contrasts with the optimistic and ambitious tone of recent international meet-ings, the most notable being the Second World Assembly on Ageing, held in Madrid in 2002. The resulting International Plan of Action on Ageing includes no less than 239 recommenda-tions, all of them worthy, directed at rich and poor countries alike. Many of these Action Points are framed in very general terms, such as, 'Promote and strengthen solidarity among generations and mutual support as a key element for social devel-opment' (United Nations Department of Economic and Social Affairs, 2002) and, 'Ensure, as appro-priate, conditions that enable families and com-munities to provide care and protection for persons as they age'.

However, there are few, if any, indications that the Madrid Plan of Action has led on to significant new policy interventions for older people in devel-oping countries, and the general profile of ageing as a global development priority remains as mini-mal as ever. Arguably, a major barrier to the crea-tion of a clear and meaningful international policy agenda is the absence of an influential global policy community whose primary focus is on older people. Instead, ageing and development remains an esoteric and secondary concern for all the development agencies, and resources remain fragmented and ghettoized. For example, the United Nations Department of Economic and Social Affairs is required to juggle its responsibil-ity for the Madrid Plan of Action with a host of other development concerns, ranging from wom-en's health to international migration. The size and the resources devoted to the WHO Ageing and Life Course Programme are negligible compared to most of its other activities. As organizer of the 1994 Cairo Conference, the United Nations Population Fund is primarily concerned with promoting reproductive healthcare agendas. While establishing a separate UN agency exclusively concerned with older people could lead to further ghettoization of this issue, this may be the only way to raise its global profile. Sadly, the

United Nation's current funding crisis makes this a remote prospect.

DEPICTIONS OF OLDER PEOPLE AND THE CONSEQUENCES OF POPULATION AGEING

Debates about the implications of population ageing for international development are heavily influenced by very generalized and largely negative understandings of what it means to be old. These associate later life with dependency, vulnerability, an inherent lack of capability, and a poor quality of life. With reference to economic performance, it is claimed that older people use up savings, sell off assets, are unproductive, and have expensive needs whose cost reduces the resource base of the economy as a whole. These views are encapsulated in demographic dependency ratios, which are still widely used by development economists and typically assume that all people aged 15–64 are productive, and all those aged ≥65 are not. According to the United Nations Population Fund:

> A growing working age population compared with older and younger dependants opens up a window of opportunity for developing countries … .Wise use of the 'demographic bonus' can lighten the burden of a rising older population in later years.
> (UNFPA, 1998: 14)

These negative depictions of older people sometimes translate into specific policy agendas. For example, the main cost–benefit analysis instrument used by the World Bank to allocate healthcare resources in poor countries, the disability-adjusted life year, gives a lower value to health improvements for people aged ≥60 than it does for younger groups. The World Bank justifies this on the grounds that younger people are productive, but older people are not (Paalman et al., 1998).

In fact, the evidence about ageing, economic participation, and productivity in more general terms strongly contradicts these simplifications. Table 29.2 provides official data on estimated levels of economic participation for countries at different levels of development (see Chapter 10). It is likely that the data for India and Senegal understate real levels of old-age employment, due to the highly informalized nature of labour markets in these countries (Kaiser, 1994). Also, salaried work does not capture the full contributions made by older people, such as in the voluntary sector, where they are particularly prominent in many countries. More general contributions

Table 29.2 Estimated rates of economic activity (%), selected countries, 2005

Age (years)	Japan	India	Senegal
15+	61	59	69
65+	20	30	36
Women 15+	48	34	56
Women 65+	13	12	22

Source: ILO Laborsta Database: http://laborsta.ilo.org/. Accessed April 11, 2007

include childcare, sharing accommodation with younger relatives, and pension-pooling across households (Lloyd-Sherlock, 2006; Schröder-Butterfill, 2003). For those people who do remain in the workforce, evidence about any relationship between old age and productivity is ambiguous and context-specific (Disney, 1996).

The view that population ageing inevitably retards development, since investment is lost to the mounting costs of social provision, is also open to doubt. The effect will be strongly mediated by the ways in which people experience later life and the ways in which social provision is organized. The costs of supporting older generations with high levels of disability, chronic disease, and general dependence will be greater than if they are relatively healthy and active. While there is a link between ageing and health expenditure, the United States spends twice as much of its GDP on health services as the United Kingdom does, despite having a more youthful population. Rather than ageing, the gap is mainly due to inefficiencies in the US private health insurance market (Detmer, 2003). Similarly, Argentina's health fund for pensioners has generated a deficit of several billion US dollars, contributing to the country's economic crisis in 2001. Again, the deficit has been caused by mismanagement and corruption on a grand scale, and has no relationship to population ageing (Lloyd-Sherlock, 2003). In poorer countries the social sectors fail to meet the basic needs of many people, old and young. For example, between 1997 and 2000, annual per capita health spending is estimated to have been US$11 in Ghana, US$23 in India, and US$45 in China (World Bank, 2004). In these cases, it is meaningless to project the impact of population ageing on expenditure.

Some NGOs and academics have sought to challenge the prevailing negative paradigm. According to HelpAge International, 'The substantial productive contribution of older people … is largely unrecognized by policymakers. Too often older people are stereotyped as passive or helpless – the realities of their lives unobserved' (1999: xiii). These arguments resonate with the WHO's 'active ageing' agenda and the growing prominence of concepts such as successful ageing in Western gerontology. These alternative perspectives are an important counterweight to the more influential negative paradigm, but there are dangers that some development agencies may take this new approach to the other extreme, playing down the real needs and vulnerabilities of many older people. In some cases, organizations such as HelpAge International seek to portray older people in ways that will satisfy the different dictates of the development agenda (Tonteri, 2006): on the one hand, older people (especially women) are characterized as heroically altruistic and productive (addressing the human capital and productivist agendas); on the other hand, they are labelled as highly vulnerable and among the poorest of the poor (addressing the poverty reduction agenda). Two separate HelpAge International publications claim that '[Older people are] the poorest of the poor, [who] lack the financial and social support and resources to meet their own needs and those of the children under their care' (HelpAge International, 2004, cited in Tonteri, 2006) and that 'Despite the exclusion they face, older people provide a vast pool of social capital as knowledge bearers and educators, as well as taking on the triple roles of caregiver, homemaker and income earner in many households' (International HIV/AIDS Alliance/HelpAge International, 2003, cited in Tonteri, 2006).

These views are both generalized and, to some extent, contradictory. As such, they run the risk of damaging the credibility of challenges to equally problematic negative depictions of later life. Generalizing about what it means to be old, either from a positive or negative perspective, leads to generalizations about the consequences of population ageing, and to generalized policy responses. While it may be obvious to Western gerontologists, there is an urgent need to replace oversimplified and under-evidenced claims with a sense of old age as a fluid, heterogeneous, and contextualized experience.

One starting point for developing a more nuanced view would be to challenge the standard 'sixty plus' approach for measuring and understanding later life. Almost all international reports about population ageing exclusively define old age in simple chronological terms – usually as all those aged 60 or over. For example, the United Nations Population Division's various publications on ageing trends provide no information about those aged 59 or less. The implication is that all those aged 60 or more have important things in common, which clearly distinguish them from people at younger ages. This definitional simplification is particularly problematic when comparisons are made between richer and poorer countries. Table 29.3 shows that being 60 years old means rather different things for women in Japan, India, and Senegal, with wide variations in the number of years they may expect to survive and to remain healthy. Equally significantly, nearly half of Senegalese women born in 2002 will die before their 60th birthday, despite substantial falls in infant mortality and low rates of AIDS by sub-Saharan African standards.

Given these variations in experience, developing alternative, less rigid chronological markers of later life could reduce the artificiality of demographic presentation. It could also have valuable policy implications. A 60+ approach is in part linked to the dominance of pension reform concerns, and so presenting the numbers differently might help challenge the notion that old age equals retirement. One alternative, already used when calculating annuities, could be to use chronological markers based on estimated remaining years of life. If this were set, say, at 20 years, the proportion of women in Japan and Senegal classified as 'old' would become around 13 and 7 per cent, respectively. This suggests a much smaller 'ageing gap' between rich and poor countries.

As well as using simplistic thresholds, development policy still thinks in terms of simple life stages. The ageing and development agenda essentially means 'old age' and development. Rather than reflecting gerontologists' capture of a wider agenda linked to ageing through life, this has entailed a separation of old age from wider understandings of ageing. Life-course thinking has had little influence over development research, partly due to the limited availability of birth cohort data sets. Utilizing life-course frameworks and analysis might do much to break down the walls of the 'old age ghetto'. For example, where processes

Table 29.3 Indicators of ageing of female population, selected countries

Indicator	Japan	India	Senegal
Women aged 60+ (% total female population) (2000)	25.7	8.2	4.6
Female life expectancy at age 60 (years) (2002)	27.0	17.9	14.4
Female healthy life expectancy at age 60 (years) (2002)	21.7	11.4	10.7
Per cent of women who survive to age 60 from birth (2002)	95.3	74.6	60.7

Source: Calculated from United Nations Population Division (2002) and World Health Organization (2004)

of development have been especially rapid, it would be helpful to examine how changing cohort experiences of lifetime reproduction, migration, and employment go on to influence well-being in later life.

Linked to this, there must be greater appreciation of the rapidly changing circumstances of older people in many developing countries. In some settings, current cohorts lack literacy skills, have spent most or all of their lives in rural areas, and have relatively large numbers of children, but fewer grandchildren. As the experiences of developing countries diverge, this generalization has already become increasingly invalid. Over the next few decades, the majority of older people in countries such as China will be literate, have fewer children, and will have spent most of their lives working in the urban formal sector. Both the contexts older people will be living in and the nature of those older people themselves will be very different. To some extent, there is a tendency to assume that the experience of current cohorts of older people will foreshadow those of future ones: in other words that quantitative aspects of population ageing are more important than the qualitative ones. Given that our knowledge of current circumstances remains limited, our capacity to project the future is negligible.

At the same time, there is a need for more sophisticated understandings of old age and other cross-cutting identities. Discourse and policy still tend to take an additive approach to issues such as gender and development, emphasizing the double disadvantage of being both a woman and old. Unsurprisingly, the limited research from developing countries challenges these simplifications, revealing the complexities of gender relations in later life (Bledsoe, 1999; Knodel and Chayovan, 2008; Varley and Blasco, 2003). In many respects, an older women in Senegal may have more in common with her younger compatriots than with older women in India or Japan. While older women in all countries face a relatively high probability of widowhood, the consequences of this are much more severe in a country like India (where the social status of widows is strongly disadvantaged) than in Senegal (where the picture is complicated by widespread polygamy) or Japan (where widowhood is less socially sanctioned) (Chen, 1998; Iwao, 1993; Lardoux and Van de Walle, 2003). On a more practical level, understanding the nature of these interacting identities may provide new opportunities to link concerns about older people more effectively into more influential development agendas, such as gender and ethnicity.

Over the past decade, there has been a growing body of research on older people in some parts of the developing world. Yet our knowledge base is very limited when compared to research in richer countries, or to other development concerns such as gender and children's well-being. As the body of research grows, it throws up an increasingly complex and sometimes contradictory set of messages about how older people are affected by processes of development. These sometimes challenge the standard generalizations that international agencies still make. According to UNFPA,

> Although the family still constitutes the main support system for older people in most cultures, traditional family support mechanisms are being eroded due to: reduction in average family size; rural to urban migration of young adults; declining levels of co-residence; and, in some countries, because young-adult family members are dying of HIV/AIDS. Nevertheless, despite the numerous negative forces being exerted in most societies, there are still many cultural settings in which older people continue to be revered for their wisdom and treated with respect by their families and communities.... This is particularly true for older women who, in most societies, comprise the catalyst for the perpetuation of cultural beliefs, attitudes and values.
>
> (2002: 26)

These views resonate closely with Cowgill's modernization hypothesis and the largely debunked notion of a 'Golden Age' for older people (Cowgill, 1974; Laslett, 1985). For gerontologists working in other contexts, they are worryingly naive. Complex processes of development are leading to a plethora of scenarios that, more often than not, challenge the received wisdom in development circles. To take just one case, for older people in urban neighbourhoods characterized by insecurity, social exclusion, high levels of youth unemployment, and drug abuse, co-residence with younger relatives may be as much a source of vulnerability as a source of support (Lloyd-Sherlock and Locke, 2008). In this case, the standard notions about inter-generational dynamics and household processes are almost entirely misplaced.

More nuanced understandings of later life in developing countries will provide the basis for more informed policies. Here, the main challenge remains moving beyond the narrow focus on pension programmes, but there are few signs that this is happening. On a positive note, there is growing recognition that contributory pension schemes, be they publicly or privately run, are unable to include significant numbers of workers outside the urban formal sector. This has led to a shift in emphasis towards 'social pension' programmes, which theoretically operate as a non-contributory safety net for relatively poor older people. A small number of developing countries, notably Brazil and South Africa, have large, well-established social pension programmes, paying out around US$3 a day (Barrientos and Lloyd-Sherlock, 2002). In recent years, efforts have been made to establish similar programmes in other countries, including Bangladesh, Bolivia, Zambia, and parts of India, and there is considerable optimism that these schemes will benefit substantial numbers of very poor older people (Willmore, 2007). These developments are welcome, but their capacity to reach the majority of those in need should not be overstated. A key issue here is whether policy elites in poorer countries have the political will to establish schemes that may cost in the order of 1 per cent of GDP for a group which many continue to view as 'unproductive'. In the case of Bolivia, commitment to the social pension has ebbed and flowed from one political regime to another (Revollo, 2004). In the case of Zambia, a pilot programme is largely financed by external donors and the barriers, political and institutional, to scaling up are formidable (Shubert, 2004). In some cases, such as those of Thailand and India, social pension programmes only pay out a few dollars per month, which, though better than nothing, are unlikely to transform the lives of beneficiaries. In many countries, including China, the prospects of a social pension remain remote (Shi, 2006).

One consequence of the current interest in social pensions is that it maintains the focus on pension policies, crowding out opportunities for effective interventions in other areas. In particular, there is potential to develop effective primary healthcare interventions specifically concerned with chronic disease and older people, such as training, screening, and basic medication for hypertension and diabetes. The majority of developing countries already have at least a rudimentary infrastructure of primary health provision, which should be able to deliver these simple and relatively low-cost interventions (Lloyd-Sherlock, 2004). Reducing the risk of stroke or diabetes-related illness and disability could do much to further the reality of an active ageing agenda. Put simply, the number of older people in developing countries affected by stroke (either directly or via an immediate relative) is far higher than the number of those who currently receive a pension. Depressingly, there is no indication that any of the more influential global actors are prepared to champion this issue.

In summary, the current state of debate and thinking on ageing and international development provides few grounds for optimism or complacency.

Our understanding of the relationship between processes of development and experiences of later life remains sketchy (Lloyd-Sherlock, 2009). Consequently, discourse continues to be dominated by sweeping generalizations and exaggeratedly negative views of both later life and the consequences of population ageing. While the recent interest in social pensions is a welcome development, there are no signs that a more coherent and informed set of policy options is emerging at the level of global policy. This should be seen as a major failure, and one that will have lasting consequences.

NOTE

1 See Lloyd-Sherlock (2007) for a much more detailed discussion of this approach to measuring later life and its policy implications.

REFERENCES

Banister, J. (1987) *China's Changing Population*. Stanford: Stanford University Press.

Barrientos, A. and Lloyd-Sherlock, P. (2002) 'Non-contributory pensions and social protection', Discussion Paper 12, International Labour Office, Issues in Social Protection, Geneva.

Bledsoe, C. (1999) *Contingent Lives: Fertility, Time and Aging in West Africa*. Chicago: University of Chicago Press.

Bretton Woods Project (2006) 'The World Bank and ageing', http://www.brettonwoodsproject.org/art.shtml? x =538507. Accessed April 10, 2007.

Charlton, R. and McKinnon, R. (2001) *Pensions in Development*. Aldershot, UK: Ashgate.

Chen, M. (1998) 'Introduction', in M. Chen (ed.), *Widows in India: Social Neglect and Public Action*. London: SAGE.

Cowgill, D. (1974) 'Ageing and modernization: a revision of the theory', in J. Gubrium (ed.), *Late Life: Communities, and Environmental Policy*. Springfield, IL: Thomas, pp. 124–46.

Department For International Development (DFID) (2000) 'Eliminating world poverty: making globalisation work for the poor', DFID White Paper on International Development, London.

Detmer, D. (2003) 'Addressing the crisis in US health care: moving beyond denial', *Quality and Safety in Health Care*, 12: 1–2.

Disney, R. (1996) *Can We Afford to Grow Old?* London: MIT Press.

Ehrlich, P. (1971) *The Population Bomb*. New York: Ballantine Press.

Ensor, T., et al. (2002) 'Do essential services packages benefit the poor? Preliminary evidence from Bangladesh', *Health Policy and Planning*, 17(3): 247–56.

Gómez-Dantés, O. (2000) 'Health reform and policies for the poor in Mexico', in P. Lloyd-Sherlock (ed.), *Healthcare Reform and Poverty in Latin America*. London: Institute of Latin American Studies.

Gorman, M. (1999) 'Development and the rights of older people', in HelpAge International (ed.), *The Ageing and Development Report*. London: Earthscan.

Hanson, K., Ranson, K., Oliveira-Cruz, V., and Mills, A. (2003) 'Expanding access to priority health interventions: a framework for understanding the constraints to scaling up', *Journal of International Development*, (15)1: 1–14.

HelpAge International (1999) 'Ageing and development: the message', in HelpAge International (ed.), *The Ageing and Development Report. Poverty, Independence and the World's Older People*. London: Earthscan.

Holzmann, R. (2000) 'The World Bank approach to pension reform', *International Social Security Review*, 53(1): 11–34.

Holzmann, R. and Hinz, R. (2005) *Old Age Income-Support in the 21st Century: An International Perspective on Pension Systems and Reform*. Washington, D.C: World Bank.

Iwao, S. (1993) *The Japanese Woman: Traditional Image and Changing Reality*. London: Macmillan.

Kaiser, M. (1994) 'Economic activities of the elderly in developing countries: myths and realities', *UN Bulletin on Ageing*, Vol. 2/3.

Knodel, J. and Chayovan, N. (2008) 'Gender and ageing in Thailand: a situation analysis of older women and men', Population Studies Center, report 08–664, University of Michigan.

Lane, S.D. (1994) 'From population control to reproductive health: an emerging policy agenda', *Social Science and Medicine*, 39(9): 1303–14.

Lardoux, S. and Van de Walle, E. (2003) 'Polgyny and fertility in rural Senegal', *Population*, 58(6): 717–44.

Laslett, P. (1985) 'Societal development and aging', in R.H. Binstock and E. Shanas (eds), *Handbook of Aging and the Social Sciences*. New York: Van Nostrand.

Lloyd-Sherlock, P. (2003) 'Financing health services for pensioners in Argentina: a salutary tale', *International Journal of Social Welfare*, 12(1): 24–30.

Lloyd-Sherlock, P. (2004) 'Primary health care and older people in the South – a forgotten issue', *European Journal for Development Research*, 16(2): 283–90.

Lloyd-Sherlock, P. (2006) 'Simple transfers, complex outcomes: The impacts of pensions on poor households in Brazil', *Development and Change*, 37(5): 969–995.

Lloyd-Sherlock, P. (2007) 'Alternatives to "sixty plus": reconceptualising population ageing in developed and developing countries' mimeo.

Lloyd-Sherlock, P. (2009) *Population Ageing and International Development: From Generalisation to Evidence*. Bristol: Policy Press.

Lloyd-Sherlock, P. and Locke, C. (2008) 'Vulnerable relations: lifecourse, wellbeing and social exclusion in a neighbourhood of Buenos Aires, Argentina', *Ageing and Society*, 28(6): 779–803.

Marshall, A., Woodroffe, J., and Skell, P. (2001) 'Policies to roll-back the state and privatise? Poverty reduction strategy papers investigated', World Development Movement, London. http://www.id21.org/society/S7bam1g1.html. Accessed April 18, 2007.

Mesa-Lago, C. (1991) 'Social security: ripe for reform', in Inter-American Development Bank, *Economic and Social Progress in Latin America: The 1991 Annual Report*. Washington, DC: IADB.

Moon, M. (1993) *Medicare Now and in the Future*. Washington, DC: Urban Institute Press.

Paalman, M., Bekedam, H., Hawken, L., and Nyheim, D. (1998) 'A critical review of policy setting in the health sector: the methodology of the 1993 World Development Report', *Health Policy and Planning*, 13(1): 13–31.

Remenyi, J. (2004) 'What is development?', in Kingsbury (ed.), *Key Issues in Development*. Basingstoke: Palgrave, PP. 22–44.

Revollo, A. (2004) 'The pension reform in Bolivia: implementing a reform', Inter-American Development Bank Working Paper, http://www.iadb.org/sds/doc/IFM-Revollo-Pension-WP-2004-E.pdf

Rush, D. and Welch, K. (1996) 'The first year of hyperinflation in the former Soviet Union: nutritional deprivation among elderly pensioners, 1992', *Am J Public Health*, 86: 790.

Scholte, J. (2000) *Globalization: A Critical Introduction*. London: Macmillan.

Schröder-Butterfill, E. (2003) '"Pillars of the family": support provided by the elderly in Indonesia', Oxford Institute of Ageing Working Papers 303, Oxford.

Shi, S. (2006) 'Left to market and family – again? Ideas and the development of the rural pension policy in China', *Social Policy and Administration*, 40(7): 791–806.

Shubert, B. (2004) 'Test phase results of the Pilot Cash Transfer Scheme, Kalomo District. 4th Report', mimeo.

Tonteri, T. (2006) 'Protection of older people in the context of HIV/AIDS – the discourse of HelpAge International', MA Dissertation, University of East Anglia.

UNFPA (2002) *Population Ageing and Development: Operational Challenges in Developing Countries*. New York: UNFPA.

United Nations Department of Economic and Social Affairs (2002) 'Madrid International Plan on Ageing, 2002', http://www.un.org/esa/socdev/ageing/. Accessed April 11, 2007.

United Nations Development Programme (UNDP) (2005) *2005 Human Development Report*. New York: United Nations.

United Nations Population Division (2002) *World Population Ageing 1950–2050*. New York: United Nations.

United Nations Population Division (2006) *World Population Prospects. The 2006 Revision*. New York: United Nations.

United Nations Population Fund (UNFPA) (1998) *The State of World Population: The New Generations.* New York: UNFPA.

Varley, A. and Blasco, M. (2003) 'Older women's living arrangements and family relationships in urban Mexico', *Women's Studies International,* 26(5): 525–39.

Willmore, L. (2007) 'Universal age pensions: Strategies for the extension of social protection', International Labour Organisation, International Training Centre, Turin.

World Bank (1994) *Averting the Old Age Crisis: Policies to Protect the Old and Promote Growth.* Oxford: Oxford University Press.

World Bank (2004) *2004 World Development Report: Making Services Work for Poor People.* Oxford: Oxford University Press.

World Health Organization (2004) *World Health Report, 2004.* Geneva: WHO.

World Health Organization (2007) *Global Burden of Disease and Risk Factors.* Geneva: WHO.

Yach, D., Hawkes, C., Gould, C., and Hofman, K. (2004) 'The global burden of chronic diseases: Overcoming impediments to prevention and control', *Journal of the American Medical Association,* 291(21): 2616–22.

30

Migration and Age

Tony Warnes

INTRODUCTION

This chapter examines several connections between migration and older people's living circumstances, referring to both those who have been migrants themselves and those *whose* social situation and welfare have been radically affected by others' moves. The focus is then on the outcomes of migrations – individually and in aggregate – on older people's family positions and social welfare. Migrations are omnipresent. Myriad international migration flows shift people between countries and cultures. Less apparently, perhaps, nearly everyone migrates several times in their lives and, at least in affluent countries, a majority undertake at least one long-distance migration that radically alter the frequencies of their contacts with their closest family members and friends. Broad generalizations about migration are possible, but migrations are immensely varied and deep understanding requires knowledge of their many forms. The study of migration has a long history and the accumulated work is vast. The first systematic analyses and theories, expressed by Ravenstein (1985) as 'laws of migration', anticipated the first recorded use of the term 'gerontology' by 20 years. In Europe today, there are many more migration researchers and institutes than those dedicated to gerontology research, old-age medicine, or social policy.

The aims of this chapter are to provide an overview of the interests that bridge migration and social gerontology, to provide a guide to the most interesting recent research, and to comment on the newest migration forms that have impacts on old-age lives. The chapter begins with a close discussion of the definitions of migrations and migrants (for the terms are used in several senses). The chapter then moves to the rarely considered, but instructive, relationship between age and the likelihood of migration. The third substantive section reviews the exchange of ideas between gerontology and migration studies since the 1940s – the initial presumption was that all migrations (or transfers) are risky and ill-advised, but a more sophisticated understanding that moves can be stimulating as well as stressful was soon adopted. Then follows an outline of the diverse characteristics of two broad categories of older migrants: those who migrate early in adult life and reach old age in the new location, and those who make radical moves in old age. The heterogeneity of migrations and migrants is touched on through four summary case studies of older migrants, which reveal both the challenging adjustments that long-distance moves require and the widespread concern about the care and support that migrants can access should they become sick or frail in old age. The chapter concludes with a discussion of the relationships between migration, contemporary expressions of filial responsibility, and intergenerational relations.

MIGRATION, RESIDENTIAL MOBILITY, AND 'CIRCULATION'

An inclusive definition of a migration is 'a change in residence from one location to another', but it is not accepted by all social scientists and differs from common meanings. It includes local housing moves that demographers and sociologists call 'residential mobility', but because no single distance distinguishes a local residential adjustment from a 'total displacement' migration, many analysts of migration favour the inclusive definition. There are shared technical and colloquial meanings. In every large country, long-distance, permanent changes of address from one region to another are called migrations, and phrases such as 'rural–urban migration' and 'migration to the east, west, north or south' are widely understood. Journalists and researchers are drawn to the more visible and innovative forms, which are generally unrepresentative (Sriskandarajah and Drew, 2006). Although most migrations are short-distance, mundane moves that have little impact on the migrants' lives, nonetheless, in aggregate and over time, their accumulative effect can be radical changes in the composition and distribution of national, regional, and metropolitan populations (International Organization for Migration, 2005).

In tabloid journalism and policy discourse, 'migrants' are commonly identified with recently arrived foreigners (by birth and culture), about which attitudes are notably split. Those responsible for managing the economy and employers broadly welcome the free movement of labour, to increase the supply and lower its price, but established residents and employees object to the increased competition for jobs and housing, and, often, racist and xenophobic attitudes are invoked. There are claims such as, 'increased migration is one of the most visible and significant aspects of globalization, [and that] growing numbers of people move within countries and across borders, looking for better employment opportunities and better lifestyles' (Tacoli and Okali, 2001: 1; see also Joly, 2007). The reasoning is sound, but many commentaries are overstated and lack historical awareness. Mass, long-distance migrations have occurred in every era (Castles and Miller, 2003; Eltis, 2002). Two rarely remembered instances include the welcome of over 300,000 Sephardic Jews into the Ottoman Empire following their expulsion from Spain in 1492 (Marcus, 1938: 51–5), and the migration of people from China into Malaya during the 18th century. By 1911, Malaya's Chinese population had reached 269,854; by 1949, it was around one million; and by 2000, the census enumerated over five million Chinese speakers, just over one-quarter of the population (Kent, 2005). Moreover, the scale of two better-known migrations has not yet been surpassed – of Africans to the Caribbean and the southern United States during the 18th and 19th centuries, and of mainly impoverished Europeans to North America from the 1840s to 1910s.

There are other definitional difficulties. Some people change residence periodically, seasonally or temporarily, as with students who attend colleges distant from their parents' homes, as with retired 'snowbirds' who every winter move for a few weeks or months to warmer and drier climates, and as with convalescents who recuperate at spas or in nursing homes. Then again, in affluent countries more and more people own homes or have residence rights in two, three, or more locations, some in different countries and continents. The formerly serviceable concept of a single 'permanent place of residence' is on the way to obsolescence. In every society and era, some have followed peripatetic and multi-location residential lives, even if there is little doubt that international and intercontinental mobility – or as some say, 'circulation' – has increased rapidly since the 1960s.

AGE, LIFE-COURSE STAGES, AND MIGRATION

One strand of migration study with a close affinity to mainstream demography examines the migration component of regional and national population change and the age distribution of migrants. It is quite common for a city or region to have negligible *net* migration, but for there to be simultaneously a substantial loss of young people and a substantial gain of older people (or vice versa). Knowledge of the age composition of inward and outward migrations is required for population projections. The basic requirement is an age-migration schedule, a table of the age-specific rates of in- and out-migration that is similar to the 'life table' of mortality and survival. Schedules for international and internal migrants and for short-, intermediate-, and long-distance moves can be compiled. They are mostly used by actuaries and by those who produce population projections, who generally do not research the underlying social processes, but when gerontological understanding is deployed, much is learnt about the intricacies of migration behaviour and the welfare outcomes for older people.

In affluent, politically stable countries, the age-migration schedule reveals an interesting, non-linear relationship between age and the propensity to change address. Four identified inflections in the 'curve' are commonly observed (Figure 30.1). The most universal is a very strong peak in the propensity to migrate in adolescence or the first years of adulthood. This is manifestly the result of young people becoming independent of their parents, leaving full-time education, beginning their working lives, and forming new intimate partnerships and households. The age of this peak has risen considerably since the pre-industrial era, when many as young as 12–15 years moved away from their parents to be live-in farm or domestic servants. As recently as the mid-20th century in the United Kingdom, most children left school at

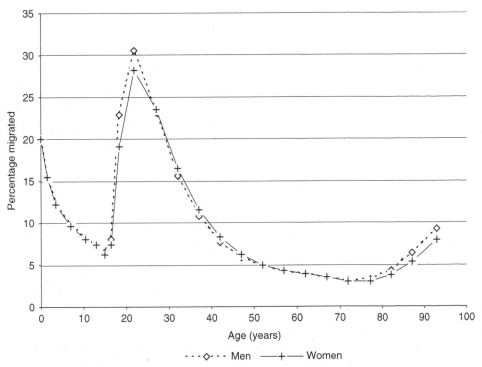

Figure 30.1   A characteristic age-migration schedule: rates of migration over 1 year between UK Government Office Regions, 2000–01

Source: UK Population Census 2001, Special Migration Statistics. Raw data downloaded from http://cider. census.ac.uk

14 or 15 years of age, and the average age of marriage for girls was in the late teens. In affluent countries today, by contrast, the majority of young people remain in full-time education until at least 18 years of age, and substantial percentages attend colleges until 21 years of age and are dependent upon their parents financially and for accommodation even longer. After the peri-adolescent peak, the age-specific rate of migration declines with increasing age, at first steeply and then at an exponentially declining rate.

The second universal feature is the declining rate of migration with increasing age among young children. The main explanation is an echo or mirror effect from the average age of the parents and the positive relationship between that average and the number of children already born. The effect is reinforced by factors particular to the children. As a child's age increases, it becomes more important to avoid disruption to his or her friendship networks and schooling. A secondary explanation for a minority of moves involving infant children is the motivation to live closer to grandparents so that they can help with parenting. It is unclear whether this motive for reducing the separation distance from older parents is less, as

or more common than the desire to provide the parents with support and care. A study of older couples who had two adult children and who migrated within England found that when an adult child made one long-distance move, it increased the separation distance from their parents, but among those who made a second long-distance move, on average the distance to the parent decreased (Warnes 1986; Warnes and Ford, 1995). A recent analysis of Swedish data has corroborated and elaborated such effects (Fors and Lennartsson, 2008).

The remaining two prominent inflections in the age-migration schedule refer to common transitions in later life. At the highest ages, from the early seventies upwards, with each additional year of age there is an exponential rise in the likelihood of migration. This is clearly an expression of the increasing probability with rising age of various losses, as of spouse, good health, mobility, functional abilities, and income. These losses reduce independence and increase the need for support, and they stimulate moves to smaller and more manageable homes, to live near or with relatives, and to move into specialist and supported accommodation, including nursing homes.

The fourth ubiquitous inflection is the most sensitive to the societal context and the least strongly associated with particular chronological ages. It is a rise in the migration rate at the ages of transition from work to retirement. An understanding of the 'structured dependency' of older people and of the contemporary 'third age' assists interpretation. Prominent 'retirement migration' peaks were found in the United Kingdom and the United States during the 1960s. They were brought about by the spread of occupational and public pensions since the 1940s, more affluence in old age, an unusually strong (and short-lived) tendency for men to retire at the stipulated 'state pension age' (SPA), and the strong gender differences in paid-work histories (Warnes, 1983, 1992). In more recent decades, with higher rates of divorce, remarriage, and women's participation in the labour force, a greater proportion of households reaching the SPA have had two earners and are second partnerships (with greater disparities of the partners' ages). From the 1970s to the 1990s, as Françoise Cribier (1981, 2005) demonstrated from her studies of successive cohorts of Parisian retirees, there was a decline in the association between a man retiring and the couple moving out of the city. The retirement peak is still evident in the age-migration schedules of moves away from metropolitan regions and capital cities, and among 'amenity-seeking' international retirement migrations, as from northern European countries to Spain. Among the latter, however, the modal age is now in the mid- to late-fifties rather than the mid-sixties (King et al., 2000).

AGE, MOBILITY, AND MIGRATION

There have been overlaps between migration studies and social gerontology for decades. The earliest actively researched topic was whether an older person's migration or residential move has negative or positive personal consequences for health and even for survival. From the late 1930s, clinicians asked whether moves into residential institutions – or between hospitals – had mortality risks. The interest spread to all between-institution moves and then to all moves. By the early 1980s, Pastalan (1983) identified 34 published US studies and reached 17 conclusions about the factors that influence the outcomes of older people's moves. Ever since, a major concern of acute hospitals in all developed countries has been to improve discharge arrangements, partly to minimize the harmful sequelae for the patients, but increasingly, as an element of the hospital management of acute beds, to minimize 'delayed discharge' and the average duration of hospital stays.

The conceptualization took hold among clinicians that any migration is a stressful life event, with a real risk for survival among frail older people. Abstract or theoretical formulations went further, setting the migration experience in a psychosocial framework of personal life-stage adjustment, which involves the acceptance of losses (as of the work role or physical agility), and the optimization of resources and abilities. This conceptualization recognized that migration brings stimulation as well as stress. As Kahana and Kahana put it,

> The total stimulation of anticipating a move, moving and environmental change can benefit those who are under-stimulated relative to their capacities and exhaust the lesser capacities of others ... [which] shows the value of interaction concepts in understanding the gamut of relocation phenomena from [hospital] transfer trauma to eager globetrotting by the 'adventurous aged'.
> (1983: 221)

This interest was elaborated by M. Powell Lawton (1971, 1976) and other psychologists and clinicians with a special interest in old age into one of applied gerontology's strongest achievements – the development of instruments for assessing the functional abilities and mental states of sick and impaired older people, and the application of these tools to care plans in different residential settings. This in turn was one foundation for 'environmental gerontology', which subsequently developed the complementary conceptual frameworks, such as Lawton's notion of environmental 'press' and 'fit' (Phillipson 2007; Wahl et al., 2007a, 2007b).

Another long-standing shared interest of gerontology and migration studies has been in the few distinctive international migrations that have involved many older people, most of which are 'impelled' or 'forced' migrations of refugees from natural disasters, famines, wars, political oppression, and racial enmity. Prominent recent manifestations have included the mass evacuations of Montserrat and New Orleans, 'ethnic cleansing' in the former Yugoslavia, and the substantial emigration of Russian Jews to North America and Israel since 1973, when some aspects of institutionalized Soviet anti-Semitism were relaxed, including punitive charges for exit visas. The main themes of the many published studies of the latter dispersal have been the experience and welfare ofthe migrants in the destination societies (e.g., Lowenstein and Katz, 2005), although there are accounts of the migration process and its selectivity (Petersen, 1975: 691–2).

A third long-established bridging research field has been retirement migration, but until the 1990s almost all studies were concerned with internal migrations in European countries, the United States, and Australia (for reviews and bibliographies see Longino, 1995; Longino and Warnes, 2005; Walters, 2002; Warnes, 1993, 2004). The attraction of retired people to coastal resorts and spas was evident even before the railway era, and slowly spread from the very rich down the socioeconomic spectrum until, by the 1920s, it was a mass phenomenon in Europe, particularly in France, England, Wales, and Belgium, and in the United States, particularly in California and Florida. By the 1970s, retirement migration was well established in research and undergraduate teaching on both sides of the Atlantic (e.g., Law and Warnes, 1973). Subsequently, research in the United States has diversified from the patterns, motivations, and personal welfare consequences of retirement migrations to the regional economic stimulation effects, to the consequences for migrants' identity and social inclusion, and to cultural studies critiques of the implicit illusions and denials in the marketing of retirement 'communities' and property (Bradley et al., 2008; Haas and Serow, 1993; Longino and Warnes, 2005; McHugh, 2003). For over a decade, a growing number of European researchers have studied those in mid and later life who move from northern to southern Europe for the 'third age' or retirement (see Warnes, 2009; Warnes and Williams, 2006).

Categories of older migrants

Having undertaken a migration plays an important part in shaping the experience and identity of three groups of older people:

- those who moved a long distance in early adulthood and have reached old age in the destination areas
- those who moved a long distance in old age
- those whose same-age peers and children all or mostly moved away.

International moves generally imply many more changes in a person's life than moves within a country. In contemporary Europe, the most numerous migrants who have aged-in-place are those who moved to northern Europe's cities and industrial areas for employment reasons during the 1950s and 1960s. Long-distance, rural–urban migrations were prominent, as within France and Italy, as also cross-border moves from southern Europe, North Africa, Turkey, and the Levant. Whatever their own or their employers' original

intentions, a high proportion have remained and aged at the destinations. Many came from depressed rural areas and had relatively little education and few formal or technical job skills. Aged labour migrants are very diverse, not just in their origins and cultural or ethnic characteristics but also in the extent to which they have raised children and formed social networks at the destination, which are important factors in their ability to develop satisfying roles when no longer in work and, should their abilities decline, to turn to informal family and community support (Silveira and Allebeck, 2001). There is also considerable diversity in their knowledge of, entitlements to, and the use that they make of state income, social housing, social services, and healthcare benefits and services (Chau, 2007). Aged labour migrants include some of the most disadvantaged and socially excluded of Western Europe's and North America's older people (Brockmann and Fisher, 2001; Burholt, 2004a, 2004b; Chau and Yu, 2000, 2001; Ng et al., 2007; Yu, 2000).

The second group, retirement migrants, are also diverse but generally more affluent and socially advantaged. Among them are some of the most resourceful and innovative of the 1940s and 1950s birth cohorts of Europe's older people (King et al., 2000). The cohorts have attracted the label 'baby boomers' and the assertion that they are less family-oriented and more concerned with 'quality of life' than their predecessors (Giddens, 1991). A recent British study found that baby boomers are 'more anti-establishment, more non-conformist, less deferential, less trusting of those in authority, and more hostile to organised religion' (Huber and Skidmore, 2003: 34–5). The term is from North American 'marketing demographics', however, and in Europe the variable histories of fertility and 'modernization' reduce its validity and have slowed its adoption. Moreover, a well-conducted recent US study found that, 'with the exception of cognitive age, there were no significant differences between younger and older baby boomers regarding a large number of salient behavioural variables' (Reisenwitz, 2007: 202). Certainly some international retirement migrants are fashioning new lifestyles, activities, roles, and patterns of social participation in what they themselves perceive as positive approaches to old age (Gustafson, 2001, 2008; Huber and O'Reilly, 2004; Oliver, 2008; O'Reilly, 2000, 2004, 2007). Like all international migrants, they are also taking risks, by moving to countries with different languages, customs, institutions, and social welfare and healthcare policies (Ackers and Dwyer, 2002, 2004; Migration Policy Institute, 2006; Sriskandarajah and Drew, 2006). One reason for giving close attention to their situation is that little is yet known about how the decrements of old age – in vigour, health, income, and social networks – interact with people's household and support arrangements when living in a foreign country.

Alongside the two core groups, there are others about which much less is known. The most apparent are 'return migrants', the labour migrants of long residence in Western European countries who return to their native countries and regions when they cease work. They are themselves diverse, and their migrations straddle internal and international moves. In all countries, some who moved to the capital or largest commercial cities of a country from rural provinces return to their native regions when they retire, and some make similar returns across an international boundary. Only a few of these moves have attracted systematic study and published accounts (Byron and Condon, 1996; Klinthall, 2006; Malcolm, 1996; Rodríguez and Egea, 2006).

There has recently, however, been informative research on return migrants to the Caribbean, particularly Jamaica (Dawson, 2007; Morris, 2008; Thomas-Hope, 2000). This shows that many of the migrants who return to Jamaica are retired (or do not take up work on the island), that they strongly over-represent higher status (white collar) occupations, and that the annual total from the United Kingdom has been falling, from around 600 in 2000 to 350 in 2006 (Dawson, 2007: 12). The recent studies of return migrations give less prominence to the attractions than to the deterrents, which include reduced social security benefit income, the limitations of social services (including the lack of social transport services for people with limited mobility), doubts about the stability of the island's financial institutions, and concerns about criminality, particularly house thefts and dishonest traders and builders.

Social security and insurance agencies in Germany, the United States, and the United Kingdom release statistics on the number of their clients receiving old-age benefits that are resident in other countries. The number of UK State Pensions paid to overseas addresses quadrupled from 252,000 in March 1981, through 679,800 in 1995, to 1,094,430 in March 2008, an average annual growth rate during 1981–1995 of 5.6 per cent, a very high rate of sustained growth for any socio-demographic change. The number of residents in foreign countries is a rising percentage of all UK retirement pensioners (RPs) (6.6 per cent in 1995 and 8.6 per cent in 2005). Their distribution is truly global but highly concentrated in a few countries. In 2008, nearly one-quarter of the recipients abroad were in Australia, over one-sixth in Canada, just under one-sixth in the United States, and one-tenth in the Republic of Ireland. Those four countries accounted for 59 per cent of

the total (this percentage has been declining: it was 66 per cent in 2005). There were more than 10,000 recipients in 12 countries, and more than 1,000 beneficiaries in 39 countries (and in Guernsey and in Jersey – separately distinguished).

Previous analyses of trends in the RP overseas statistics during the 1990s found differential growth rates in a number of country groups (Warnes, 2001). In particular, among the most popular destinations, the rates of growth have been high to Mediterranean countries and low to Australia, Canada, New Zealand, and South Africa. This was seen as a sign of the changing overseas connections of the population, and the rising enthusiasm for 'amenity-seeking' retirement migrations to warmer countries (especially in the winter). Very high rates of growth, albeit from very low bases, were also seen to several Nordic and to two South East Asian countries.

The analysis is updated in Table 30.1, which identifies five distinctive country groups and separately tabulates the United States and Ireland. Between 1995 and 2008, the number of UK RP recipients in seven southern European countries increased on average by 9.5 per cent a year, whereas the increase in the number in Australia, Canada, New Zealand, and South Africa was only 2.6 per cent. Even higher growth rates applied to Denmark, Norway, and Sweden (11.8 per cent), and to Thailand and the Philippines (16.6 per cent). Although several Caribbean islands have seen growing numbers, and in March 2008 there were 21,230 recipients in Jamaica, the growth rate (2.5 per cent) among six Caribbean countries has been below the rate for all overseas destinations. Moves to the Caribbean include both 'retirement returns' of 1950s and 1960s immigrants, and 'amenity-seeking' retirement migrations of the UK born.

Much lower percentages of German and US old-age social security beneficiaries reside abroad. In 2005, 115,768 German *citizens* who received a *Deutsche Rentenversicherung* (the new unified German social security agency) pension lived in foreign countries, just 0.7 per cent of the total. In addition, however, 848,529 *non-citizens* received these pensions and lived in other countries, 65.1 per cent of the non-citizen beneficiaries. Altogether, 964,297 German pensioners lived abroad, 5.7 per cent of the total, and 88 per cent of the total were non-citizens. This is clear evidence that the majority of German retirement migrants were labour migrants from Italy, Spain, the Balkans, and Turkey who went to Germany during the 1950s and 1960s and who until recently were unable to obtain citizenship, or, like many Turks, do not wish naturalization. Turning to US retirees abroad, among the old-age, survivor (widowed),

Table 30.1 Thousands of UK retirement pensioners in four country groups, the United States, and Ireland growth statistics, the sex ratio and rates of increase, 1995–2008

Measures	Country group						
	A	B	C	D	United States	Ireland	Thailand and the Philippines
1995							
Both sexes	1.7	67.8	23.8	357.9	85.6	71.2	0.4
Men	(0.5)	(27.2)	(10.3)	(139.6)	(29.5)	(26.4)	(0.2)
Women	(1.1)	(40.5)	(13.6)	(218.3)	(56.2)	(44.7)	(0.2)
2000							
Both sexes	2.9	95.6	30.2	419.6	107	84.1	0.9
Men	(0.9)	(38.5)	(13.1)	(166.3)	(36.1)	(31.2)	(0.6)
Women	(1.9)	(56.9)	(17)	(253.3)	(70.9)	(52.9)	(0.3)
2005							
Both sexes	4.8	153.8	31.5	471.1	123.9	97.7	1.7
Men	(1.9)	(62.2)	(14.1)	(190.4)	(43.0)	(36.2)	(1.2)
Women	(2.9)	(91.6)	(17.4)	(280.8)	(80.9)	(61.5)	(0.5)
2008							
Both sexes	6.5	201.0	32.0	489.4	132.2	109.9	2.9
Men	(2.7)	(82.2)	(14.3)	(199.2)	(45.0)	(42.7)	(2.1)
Women	(3.8)	(118.8)	(17.7)	(290.2)	(87.1)	(67.2)	(0.8)
Increase in 1995–2008 (%)	282.3	196.5	34.5	36.7	44.7	54.4	625.0
Mean annual per cent increase	11.8	9.5	2.5	2.6	3.7	3.7	16.6
Mean annual increase 2005–08	10.6	9.3	0.5	1.3	2.2	4.0	15.6
Female : male ratio							
1995	2.20	1.49	1.32	1.56	1.91	1.69	1.00
2000	2.11	1.48	1.30	1.52	1.96	1.70	0.50
2005	1.53	1.47	1.23	1.47	1.88	1.70	0.41
2008	1.41	1.45	1.24	1.46	1.94	1.57	0.38
Average age in 2008 (years)*	72.5	72.9	75.9	75.8	75.6	74.5	71.5

Notes: The country groups in the first four columns, respectively, are: (A) Denmark, Norway, and Sweden; (B) Cyprus, France, Greece, Italy, Malta, Portugal, and Spain (Southern Europe); (C) Barbados, Dominican Republic, Grenada, Jamaica, St Lucia, and Trinidad and Tobago (the Caribbean); (D) Australia, Canada, New Zealand, and South Africa. The tabulation includes only countries with at least 1000 customers in 2005, and the estimates are from a 5 per cent sample of the client roll. The female : male ratio among all overseas beneficiaries was 1.56 in 2005 and 1.50 in 2008.
*Men and women aged at least 65 years.
Source: UK Department for Work and Pensions, Overseas Division, personal communication

and disability (OASDI) social security beneficiaries aged ≥ 65 years in December 2005, 372,010 – or just 1.1 per cent – were resident in foreign countries. The 167,670 that received retirement benefits (RB) and were living in foreign countries were 1.2 per cent of the RB total (US Social Security Administration, 2006: Table 5J3). Nearly a quarter (22.8 per cent) were in Canada, one-sixth (12.4 per cent) were in Mexico, and exactly 10 per cent in Italy (Warnes, 2009).

The social security statistics make it apparent that other types of migration in later life are more voluminous than either amenity-led or return retirement migrations (Warnes, 2001, 2009). For both the Germans and the British, the largest overseas beneficiary populations are in the United States,

Canada, and Australia. There are many German recipients in Austria, Switzerland, and Brazil, and there are many British recipients in Ireland and Germany. The clear inference is that there are substantial flows of family-joining migrants who follow their children's earlier migrations, and that the dispersion is influenced by both long-established colonial and trading links and new commercial, educational, and social connections. While there are studies of the processes and consequences of the migration of older parents from Southeast Asian countries who join their migrant adult children in Australia and the United States (Ip et al., 2007; Min et al., 2005), the comparable flows of older migrants from northwest Europe to North America and Australasia have not been researched.

During the last decade in several European countries, many investigations of older migrants' welfare have been commissioned by healthcare and social service agencies, and several cities have responded to their distinctive problems and needs, usually in collaboration with community organizations. One leader has been the City of Frankfurt-am-Main, where 'inter-cultural day and inpatient care, home circumstances and the possibility to meet people of the same nationality are all issues that the City takes seriously and supports with dedicated measures' (Frankfurt, 2005). The Swiss Red Cross and Red Crescent have also given special attention to older migrants, and, with other sponsors, established the multilingual *Alter und Migration* website for older migrants (see http://www.alter-migration.ch). The sensitivity of local administrations to the needs of older migrants varies, of course, and in many places has not overcome the prevailing view that the needs of all older people are the same (Schopf and Naegele, 2005). Sandra Torres (2001, 2004) has lucidly criticized Sweden's health and social service agencies, which for a long time paid little attention to the needs of older foreign migrants, and when that was corrected, tended to overgeneralize and problematize a very heterogeneous population. In the next section, the great diversity of older migrants' experiences and circumstances is illustrated by reference to four particular groups that have been closely studied.

THE FAMILY AND WELFARE CIRCUMSTANCES OF OLDER MIGRANTS

Italian and Spanish older labour migrants in Switzerland

Bolzman et al. (1999, 2001, 2004) carried out research on the experience of the large numbers of Italian and Spanish migrants who entered Switzerland during the 1950s and 1960s and have remained in the country into old age. They were recruited as 'guest workers', not expected to stay permanently, worked mostly in unskilled jobs, and experienced restrictions on family reunification, geographical and professional mobility, and access to social security and public assistance. They also met hostility from the native Swiss. No integration policy was implemented to counteract the structured disadvantages of this 'first generation' of immigrants: the task was left to the immigrants' enterprise. Many initially wished to return to Italy or Spain, but by the time that they approached retirement, which for many was premature through redundancies and occupation-related incapacities,

they were aware that their villages of origin had radically changed, and that their children's best prospects were to remain in Switzerland. The preferred residential option had become to stay in Switzerland and to visit their native regions frequently.

Only recently have Switzerland's public welfare services 'discovered' older immigrants and their welfare problems. The Bolzman team's research found that the situation of Italians and Spaniards as they approached retirement was precarious: many were disadvantaged or in outright poverty. Since 1965, the cantons and communes have paid supplementary benefits to those whose old-age pensions are insufficient to cover basic needs, but for a foreigner to qualify for the supplementary benefits, they need to have had 10 years' unbroken residence in Switzerland, and for those from countries without a bilateral social security agreement, entitlement depends on already receiving a Swiss old age, survivors or invalidity pension (the last two terms are used in many countries to refer to widow(er)s pensions and to social security benefits paid to people with disabilities). Some migrants do not claim benefits to which they are entitled, because they fear that if and when they need long-term assistance, they will lose their residence permit.

Foreign migrants of Chinese origin

China's peoples have been involved in an extended and worldwide dispersal or diaspora from their East Asian heartland. During the 19th century, many became indentured labourers in other continents, some in association with the gold rushes in California and Australia, and through the 20th century in many parts of the world they have been associated successively with the laundry, fast-food, and restaurant trades. Until very recently, the majority of Chinese emigrants came from rural, peasant backgrounds and had little formal education and few job skills. Many of their overseas communities have been characterized by high proportions of never-married men. The least advantaged tended not to learn the local language or to engage fully in the formal economy, compromising their health, welfare, and social housing entitlements when they reached old age.

The majority of Chinese immigrants to the UK arrived in two waves. During the 1950s, many young men came from rural areas of Hong Kong. Characteristically, they worked long and unsocial hours in family catering businesses and for low wages. The family enterprises sanctioned poor working conditions and sustained attachments to their own community but hindered integration with the host society, particularly formal welfare services (Yu, 2000: 4). The heavy workloads and vulnerability to occupational hazards resulted in a high prevalence of health problems among middle-aged and older workers. Then from the late 1960s, many wives and relatives followed. Common causes of both groups' detachment from the mainstream community include language barriers, insufficient knowledge of social and public services, lack of a sense of social rights, low expectations of formal support, negative experiences of retirement, poor mental and physical health, and low self-image.

A study of older Chinese migrants in Brisbane, Australia is of great interest (Ip et al., 2007). Chinese immigration to Australia grew rapidly during the late 1980s, and after the Tiananmen Square protests in 1989, 'nearly 37,000 Chinese students were granted permanent residence and the right to be accompanied by immediate family members' (Ip et al., 2007: 721). Two other flows also grew. During the late 1980s, many Taiwan-born Chinese entrepreneurs moved to Australia when the Taiwan government eased restrictions on overseas travel and money transfers. A decade later, numerous professionals, managers, and technical workers from Hong Kong, concerned about their future when its sovereignty returned to China in 1997, were admitted as entrepreneurs or highly-skilled, independent migrants. Many older relatives were brought along, but have had little time to acculturate. Ip and colleagues found that:

> The older Chinese people, and particularly the women, experience significant restrictions in their activity patterns, social isolation and loneliness. Their lack of proficiency in the English language, and the difficulties they have in accessing language-support and interpretation services, limit their autonomous mobility and make them heavily dependent on their adult children, not least for transport. Their physical and psychological wellbeing is affected further by strained relations with their adult children, and these are compounded by financial concerns.
>
> (Ip et al., 2007: 721)

Levantine migrants in Detroit

Another long established intercontinental labour migration has been from the Levant to the United States, a major destination in the 1960s and 1970s being the car plants in Detroit, Michigan. Many of the earlier migrants have now reached old age. Kristine Ajrouch (2005) facilitated focus groups with English-speaking and Arabic-speaking samples on their attitudes to filial responsibility and

experiences of intergenerational support and care. The focus groups uncovered tensions 'between cultural ideals and pragmatic realities' in their attitudes to three aspects of personal care in old age: nursing-home placements, expectations that children would be providers, and formal or state-sponsored support. On children's support, 'there was a clear preference for independence alongside appreciation of children's help and not wishing to burden them' (Ajrouch, 2005: 655). State-sponsored support was seen as providing resources to support independence, but as blighted by discriminatory attitudes and practices.

Early socialization had instilled among the focus group participants strong adherence to the cultural ideal of filial responsibility for the care of frail parents, but their own life course, and their children's current circumstances, had led them to more realistic expectations of what their children could and should provide. Many had emigrated as young adults and left siblings or others to support their parents, and some recognized that if they asserted filial piety, there was an element of self-deceit. For many, their children had acculturated rapidly; both fathers and mothers were committed to work, to material success, and to maximizing the opportunities for their own children. The older migrants articulated the anxieties of having a foot in two cultures; they were concerned that their relationships with their children were inconsistent with the cultural ideal. In consequence, they were disparaged by ethnic peers, especially those back in the native country.

The focus groups enabled the migrants to share their experiences, helped them accommodate their ideals with their circumstances, and reduced the felt stigma of accepting help from beyond the family. Accordingly, 'this adjustment helped to empower the immigrant elders, because their various dependencies on their children as a first-generation immigrant', through their poor education, ability in English, and knowledge of US customs and institutions, 'were not compounded by adding instrumental care to the children's responsibilities' (Ajrouch, 2005: 669). The Levantine older migrants showed immense empathy for their children and had developed clear strategies to minimize the demands they made upon them.

Amenity-seeking, affluent long-distance retirement migrants

The older migrants that have been most extensively studied are those who move long distances for 'amenity-seeking' reasons shortly after they cease paid work. The first such international retirement flow to attract the attention of American researchers was of Canadians to Florida (Longino, 1995), and the first to attract the attention of European population geographers was the settlement of northern country retirees in various regions of southern Europe (King et al., 2000). These amenity-seeking moves increased rapidly from the 1960s for several reasons:

- the new democratic regimes in Spain, Portugal, and Greece and the admission of these countries to the European Union
- the development of large capacity jet planes and of the mass 'package' holiday trade and the associated services infrastructure
- the spread of occupational pensions, early retirement, and home ownership in the northern countries (which enabled more people to purchase a property abroad).

A warm climate and longer winter daylight hours are the main attractions. Most of the migrations are by couples in their late fifties and early sixties: some move to the popular holiday islands or 'costas' and their hinterlands, as in Spain; others disperse across rural areas of high landscape value, as in the south of France and in Tuscany and Umbria, Italy. The cultural, psychosocial, and behavioural transformations involved in retiring abroad are beginning to be documented (O'Reílly, 2000, 2007). Studies of the phenomenon are rapidly diversifying. There are now impressive contributions from many European countries (see Rodríguez et al., 2006; Warnes and Williams, 2006), empirical studies of retirement migration to foreign countries by citizens of the United States (Banks, 2004; Migration Policy Institute, 2006; Sunil et al., 2007), a study of the distinctive settlement of male Western retirees in Thailand (Howard, 2008), and the first signs of a research literature on the phenomenon in Turkey, South East Asia, and Australia (Görer et al., 2006; Ip et al., 2007; Shinozaki, 2006). There are useful reviews and recent contributions in two journal special issues, *Ageing and Society* (24[3], May 2004) and the *Journal of Ethnic and Migration Studies* (32[8], September 2006), and in the final report of a European Science Foundation scientific network (Warnes, 2004).

There is limited information about the medium- and long-term personal welfare consequences of international retirement migrations. Most published evidence is from local surveys of recently formed clusters, where the average age is relatively young. The strong consensus of the findings is that the migrants report high levels of satisfaction with their move and new domestic and social circumstances (Warnes, 2004; Warnes et al., 1999). As with all migration evaluations, however, the respondents in the destination areas exclude

the disenchanted movers that have returned. The majority of the respondents to such surveys are generally in early old age, and believe that they will return to their countries of origin in later life. Most probably do but no data show the flow, and many stay on and resolve never to return. The British retirees in advanced old age that have been interviewed in southern Europe give convincing accounts of their adjustment and positive evaluations of their move and expatriate lives, even when beset by illness and frailty (King et al., 2000). The well-serviced towns and villages of Malta and the Spanish islands and coasts are more supportive of single, frail older migrants than low population-density rural areas in France and Italy, which the migrants recognize. There are of course many cases of increasing difficulties, as brought about by interactions between diminishing resources (e.g., below-inflation pension increases), bereavement, increasing care needs, and compromised entitlements to social security income and state welfare support (Ackers and Dwyer, 2002, 2004). A few find themselves in impossible situations of unmet need, neglect, and abuse (Hardill et al., 2005). Those in desperate situations characteristically turn to formal welfare agencies or a national consul for help to 'get them home'. In the UK case, however, a citizen who has not been habitually resident in the country is not entitled to other than emergency treatment on the National Health Service, and for those without a 'local connection', no local government authority is required to offer social services support (a legacy of poor-law entitlement rules).

A comparative analysis of the health of British retirement migrants in Spain and their origin and host-country peers has been published (La Parra and Mateo, 2008). The authors carried out a survey of 155 British retirees resident on the Costa Blanca, Alicante, for more than 3 months a year. They asked questions about health and the utilization of healthcare services, some of which were identical to those asked in the *Health Survey for England 2003*, the *National Health Survey for Spain 2003*, the *British Household Panel Survey 2004*, and the *Spanish Household Panel Survey 2000*. The health-status distributions were then compared with those reported by the first two mentioned national surveys. It was found that British nationals aged ≥45 years resident on the Costa Blanca had a similar health profile to the Spanish and the British home populations of age-peers, but had fewer mobility or self-care problems, more personal autonomy, and more positive self-evaluated health. The British retired migrants' frequency of visits to a general practitioner was similar to that of their Spanish neighbours, but the frequency of admissions to hospital, while similar to that of their compatriots living in the UK, was higher than among the Spanish in Spain. Greater use was made of private healthcare by the migrants than by both home populations.

There are two competing hypotheses about the selectivity of older migrants who move from high latitudes to warmer climate regions. One is the 'healthy migrant' proposition, that long-distance migrants are selective of the more active and healthier – it is a variant of a general hypothesis about migrants of all ages, that they over-represent the better educated, more ambitious, and more resourceful. The converse hypothesis is that the southward flow over-represents those with respiratory and other chronic disorders for which moving to a drier and warmer climate is prescribed:

Among the British residents on the Costa Blanca, men aged 45–64 years seemed to have worse health than women in the same age group, or in relative terms, than older men. This suggests that a poor health condition could be a factor for an early retirement and for the move to Spain.

(La Parra and Mateo, 2008: 97)

Cigarette smoking and alcohol consumption were comparatively high among the British living in Alicante, and the consumption of both rose after they moved to Spain. This effect among British women in Alicante was the opposite of that among women of the same age living in the United Kingdom. Overall, the evidence available to date reveals no substantial or consistent differentials between the health of international 'amenity-seeking' retirement migrants and their age-peers in the home country, or indeed in the incidence of negative health events once they have moved.

MIGRATION, CARE-GIVING, AND CARE-RECEIVING

This final section takes the growing evidence of the social and particularly family situations of older migrants and attempts a general discussion of the impact of migrations – one's own, others', and those in society at large – on the nature, quality, and acceptability of care and support for older people. The issues are complex, but, too often, commentators present the trends as alarming. Building on the assumptions that migration over long distances is increasing and that they are inimical to family care in old age, it is commonly argued that older migrants and older parents left behind by migrants are unusually vulnerable to isolation and perceived neglect. As the preceding case synopses have shown, gerontological assessments of the outcomes for older people pay little attention to material achievement and focus on the migrants who find themselves in problematic circumstances at the destination (less-often studied are those whose material and family arrangements are not problematic and who do not come to the attention of welfare agencies, and those who return to the origin to rejoin multi-generational and extended family support networks, whether or not they are materially and emotionally supportive).

There is considerable evidence that certain forms of support-exchange and care between households are highly dependent on close proximity (sometimes called propinquity), particularly visits, hands-on personal care, and some types of instrumental help (e.g., daily cleaning). In Peter Townsend's influential 1950s study of older people's family support in a working-class district of London, *The Family Life of Old People*, he made explicit reference to the intricate *and two-way* influences between inter-personal closeness or dependency, migration, and residential proximity:

Migration was influenced by family structure. If there were brothers and sisters at home or in the district, a married child seemed more likely to move to a housing estate outside London. Youngest and only children (whether sons or daughters) tended to stay in Bethnal Green, and other children, particularly the eldest, to move out. Elder children did not have to worry about leaving their parents on their own, and anyway now depended less on their parents. ... Moreover, with two, three or more children of their own, they were allotted more points by the housing authorities and so qualified sooner [than their younger siblings] for a house on an outside housing estate. ... [Close kin who lived] in the same dwelling or nearby were seen regularly and frequently ... [they] did each others' shopping and household tasks and cared for each other in illness. They included the daughters who came to wash and polish the floors; the sons who came to a midday meal from work, brought gifts, and repaired broken chairs and hinges on doors; the grandchildren who came while their parents were at work, and the sisters who dropped in for an afternoon chat.

(Townsend, 1963: 47, 52)

The account alludes to a general rule, that emotional and geographical closeness are mutually reinforcing, and that a migration away is both a sign of relative separation and the social process that consolidates it. Townsend's reference to the bureaucratic reinforcement of the rule is worth noting: the children who were the first to have large families of their own were the first to be enabled by the public-housing system to move away. While British working-class lives have immensely changed since the 1950s – then few attended school beyond 15 years of age and few households had cars – today, the general processes and relationships still apply, but over vastly greater distances.

Today, if adult children migrate 1000 kilometres, they are unable to provide regular personal care to a parent left behind. The same applies to economic migrants who move from low-income societies to the rich world. The decision to migrate must not, however, be equated with a decision either callously to turn away from currently dependent parents or to disavow an underlying filial obligation norm (that will influence future actions and behaviour). To give an historical example, the uneducated and bereft Irish men and women who fled the 1840s famine and destitution of the 'Congested Districts' , and established footholds in, for example, Glasgow, Manchester, London, Boston, New York, and Melbourne, provided an escape and a means of financial support for many generations of their relatives to come. Taking a long-term view, they should be commended for inconveniencing themselves for the benefit of their descendants.

In today's affluent world, a migrant's decision to move a long distance follows an intricate assessment of the likely returns, to them personally, to their partner or spouse (e.g., of higher earnings), to their children now and in the future (e.g., access to better education, better prospects), and in many cases to their older parents and extended family (e.g., remittances, opening up a pathway for others to 'escape' restricted lives and destitution). Some will place more weight on a material evaluation than others (there may be differences by gender and by whether a child was the first, second or later born), but for the majority the material evaluation is tempered by awareness that the separation will literally distance their parents from themselves and their children. Most understand well that if they move away, their grandparents' involvement with their own children will be hindered. Both the senses of guilt and loss, and the implications of ending propinquity, are likely to be greatest among those who have been raised in societies, communities, and families in which ways of life are embedded in the extended family, and in which norms of inter/generational exchange and filial responsibility are strongest (or widely taken for granted).

The effects of international migration on family lives, the instrumental circumstances, and 'life satisfaction' of older people left behind have been vividly revealed by King and Vullnetari's (2006) studies of the Albanian experience (Vullnetari and King, 2008). During the era of Stalinist central planning under the dictator Enver Hoxha, when income per head was the lowest in Europe, legal emigration was impossible. Following his death in 1985, the state-managed economy collapsed, and emigration of 'epic proportions' began: 'According to the 2001 census, net emigration during 1989–2001 exceeded 600,000, and most emigrants were men aged 18–35 years ... more recent estimates raised the figure to one million, a quarter of Albania's population' (King and Vullnetari, 2006: 784). King and Vullnetari show that young Albanian migrants are concerned about their older parents, and those who are parents wish to facilitate the grandparents' role, but the immigration and visitor-visa rules in the main destination countries (Greece, Germany, the United Kingdom, and the United States) artificially restrict the amount of coming and going. It has been structural and policy restrictions on international travel since Albania's societal upheaval that have restricted intergenerational involvement and affinity, not the migrations themselves or the migrants' attitudes.

In France, a large dataset on the circumstances of aged labour migrants and their families has produced valuable evidence that transnational social and residential connections are now the norm among labour migrants, and that many sustain both material and instrumental support across international boundaries (e.g., Attias-Donfut and Wolff, 2005; Attias-Donfuta et al., 2005; Wolff and Dimova, 2006).[1] As Wolff and Dimova observed, 'Nearly one-third (28 per cent) of the older migrants' (surviving) parents lived in France, and most of the remainder in the country of origin' (2006: 126). One-in-ten migrants provided informal care to their parents, and one-in-five made cash gifts. Furthermore, 'As expected, [parents in France] attract the bulk of the upward transfers of time, while [those abroad] attract the bulk of the upward financial transfers' (Wolff and Dimova, 2006: 126). An analysis of the factors associated with providing the two forms of support proceeded from several assumptions and propositions about migrants' behaviour towards their parents. It was assumed, for example, that carers are aware of the opportunity costs of the time spent in providing care (namely lost earnings), that time and money transfers are substitutable and a function of the marginal product of labour, and that personal care can be substituted by paid care. Characteristic of econometrics, the attitudes, and motivations that led a person to be a carer were bundled together as 'altruism'. Despite these simplifications, the analysis generated interesting evidence about intergenerational contacts and support. Over time, a greater percentage of migrants provided care and a lower percentage provided money gifts. The tendency was explained by the increasing care needs of the parents, the rising percentage that joined the migrants in

France, and the increasing ability of the migrant to visit their parents in the country of origin (Wolff and Dimova, 2006: 127).

Baldassar and colleagues have recently published an interesting study of the ways in which migrants in Perth, Western Australiai, practise long-distance family relations and aged care with their parents in Afghanistan, Iran, Ireland, Italy, the Netherlands, New Zealand, and Singapore (Baldassar, 2007; Baldassar et al., 2007). Based on interviews with 95 migrants in Perth and 61 interviews with parents, mainly in the three European countries, the study distinguished different types of care and support, different modes of contact, and routine from emergency helping patterns. When these variables were combined with variations in the resources, abilities, and opportunities to provide care, and differences in culturally based expectations (as explored by Ajrouch (2005) among *older* migrants in Detroit), the complexity of influences on the nature and intensity of long-distance care and support is revealed.

CONCLUSIONS

Few of us never migrate, and most people during their lives engage in at least one long-distance move that radically changes the residential setting and social network, including the frequency and nature of interactions with close family members. There have been radical and mass migrations in every historical era, and claims that recent advances in airtravel and telecommunications have resulted in an *unprecedented* level of global migration should be treated sceptically. It is more likely that the new technologies have stimulated and facilitated new transnational activity patterns, and lifestyles. For many, they have made a migration less imperative (Baldassar, 2007; Baldassar et al., 2007).

Given the immense diversity of migrations, generalizations about migrants' characteristics and motivations and about the consequences of the moves are both difficult and prone to distortion, because both popular commentaries and academic studies focus on atypical forms and flows. Social gerontologists with an interest in the topic have been drawn, for example, to amenity-seeking international retirement migrations and to welfare-excluded aged labour migrants. While, in terms of their material resources (or human capital) on the threshold of old age, these two migrant groups represent polar extremes of older people in rich nations, neither group have much in common with the majority of family-joining migrants in either early or late old age.

Migrations and migrants tend to be problematized. It is sometimes asserted that migrants have less commitment to the welfare and care of aged parents, and that their behaviour is less motivated by filial responsibility than that of non-migrants. As Townsend's observations of adult children who moved out of London during the 1950s to peripheral housing estates suggested, there is truth in this but a nuanced understanding is required. Higher-income groups, and particularly those with above-average education, are more likely to migrate long distances than others. The average distance of residential separation between next-generation kin positively correlates with income and education. It would be a travesty, however, to suggest that the more educated are less concerned with their children's and their parents' well-being than those of average or less education. The types of kin interactions, the instrumental expressions of their mutual concern, and the types of support and care exchanged all vary by era, income, and socioeconomic group, and by the life-course stage of the participants. Today, northern European parents who retire to the Mediterranean coast, or Americans and Canadians who retire to Mexico or the Caribbean, can be in touch several times each day with their children who are raising infants, or with an increasingly frail parent living on their own – and, should there be a crisis, they can be back the same day. Several aspects of the 'social insurance' that extended working-class families provided in Europe until the 1940s have been made redundant by greater affluence, state social welfare, rapid travel, and instant communication.

The study of older migrants deserves a more prominent place in social gerontology. They include many deeply disadvantaged and excluded people, and understanding their situation tells us a great deal about social change and about the policy and administrative bases of their ills. Incidentally, in comparison to older people who are disadvantaged through physical and mental illnesses, the disadvantage that accrues from a migration history or cultural difference may be more tractable through community initiatives and service change. The other main category of older migrants includes many of the most enterprising and self-assertive practitioners of 'positive ageing' and 'personal development' in later life. Some visible groups have already provided rich anthropological case studies of life in the 'third age' and of the distinctiveness of the baby boomers (and in the process shown that generalizations of the attitudes and behaviour of entire birth cohorts are precarious). There is every chance that the pace of social, economic, and demographic change will be faster in the next few decades than in the last, and that an abiding element will be substantial international migration. As average living and welfare standards rise, partly through the contributions of international migrants, the case for a closer integration of migration and social policy is strong.

ACKNOWLEDGEMENTS

I thank Jim Rynn of the UK Department for Work and Pensions for assistance in obtaining the UK social security data, and Claudia Kaiser of the University of Halle-Wissenberg, Germany, for help with obtaining the equivalent German data.

NOTE

1 *The Passage à la Retraite des Immigrés* is a representative sample of 6211 immigrants aged 45–70 years compiled by the Caisse Nationale d'Assurance Vieillesse in Paris during 2002–03.

REFERENCES

Ackers, L. and Dwyer, P. (2002) *Senior Citizenship? Retirement, Migration and Welfare in the European Union.* Bristol: Policy.

Ackers, L and Dwyer, P. (2004) 'Fixed laws, fluid lives: the citizenship status of post-retirement migrants in the European Union', *Ageing and Society*, 24(3): 451–75.

Ajrouch, K.J. (2005) 'Arab-American immigrant elders' views about social support, *Ageing and Society'*, 25(5): 655–74.

Attias-Donfut, C. and Wolff, F.-C. (2005) ' Transmigration et choix de vie à la retraite [Transmigration and life choices in retirement]', *Retraite et Société*, 44(1): 79–105.

Attias-Donfut, C., Tessier, P., and Wolff, F.-C. (2005) 'Les immigrés au temps de la retraite [Immigrants at their retirement]', *Retraite et Société*, 44(1): 12–47.

Baldassar, L. (2007) 'Transnational families and aged care: the mobility of care and the migrancy of ageing', *Journal of Ethnic and Migration Studies*, 33(2): 275–97.

Baldassar, L., Baldock, C.V., and Wilding, R. (2007) *Families Caring Across Borders: Migration, Ageing and Transnational Caregiving.* Basingstoke, UK: Palgrave Macmillan.

Banks, S. (2004) 'Identity narratives by American and Canadian retirees in Mexico', *Journal of Cross-Cultural Gerontology*, 19(4): 361–81.

Bolzman, C., Fibbi, R., and Guillon, M. (eds) (2001) *Emigrés-Immigrés: Vieillir et Là-bas [Emigrants-Immigrants: Growing Old Here and Over There].* Special issue, *Revue Européenne des Migrations Internationales*, 17(1): 7–198.

Bolzman, C., Fibbi, R., and Vial, M. (1999) 'Les Italiens et les Espagnols proches de la retraite en Suisse: Situation et projets d'avenir [Italians and Spanish residents close to retirement: their situations and projects for the future]', *Gérontologie et Société*, 91: 137–51.

Bolzman, C., Poncioni-Derigo, R., Vial M., and Fibbi, R. (2004) 'Older labour migrants' well being in Europe: the case of Switzerland', *Ageing and Society*, 24(3): 411–29.

Bradley, D.E., Longino, C.F., Stoller, E.P., and Haas, W.H. (2008) 'Actuation of mobility intentions among the young-old: an event-history analysis', *The Gerontologist*, 48(2): 190–202.

Brockmann, M. and Fisher, M. (2001) 'Older migrants and social care in Austria', *Journal of European Social Policy*, 11(4): 353–62.

Burholt, V. (2004a) 'Transnationalism, economic transfers and families' ties: inter-continental contacts of older Gujaratis, Punjabis and Sylhetis in Birmingham with families abroad', *Ethnic and Racial Studies*, 27(5): 800–29.

Burholt, V. (2004b) 'The settlement patterns and residential histories of older Gujaratis, Punjabis and Sylhetis in Birmingham, England', *Ageing and Society*, 24(3): 383–410.

Byron, K. and Condon, S. (1996) 'A comparative study of Caribbean return migration from Britain and France: towards a context-dependent explanation', *Transactions, Institute of British Geographers*, 21(1): 91–104.

Castles, S. and Miller, M.J. (2003) *The Age of Migration.* New York: Guilford.

Chau, R. (2007) *The Involvement of Chinese Older People in Policy and Practice: Aspirations and Expectations.* York: Joseph Rowntree Foundation.

Chau, R. and Yu, W.K. (2000) 'Chinese older people in Brita: double attachment to double detachment', in A.M. Warnes, L. Warren, and M. Nolan, (eds), *Care Services for Later Life: Transformations and Critiques.* London: Jessica Kingsley, pp. 259–72.

Chau, R. and Yu, W.K. (2001) 'Social exclusion of Chinese older people in Britain', *Critical Social Policy*, 21(1): 103–25.

Cribier, F. (1981) 'Changing retirement patterns of the seventies: the example of a generation of Parisian salaried workers', *Ageing and Society*, 1(1): 51–71.

Cribier, F. (2005) 'Changes in the experiences of life between two cohorts of Parisian pensioners, born in *circa* 1907 and 1921', *Ageing and Society*, 25(5): 637–54.

Dawson, L.R. (2007) *Brain Drain, Brain Circulation, Remittances and Development: Prospects for the Caribbean.* Caribbean Paper 2, Center for International Governance Innovation, Waterloo, Ontario, Canada. Available online at http://www.cigionline.org

Eltis, D. (ed.) (2002) *Coerced and Free Migration: Global Perspectives.* Stanford, CA: Stanford University Press.

Fors, S. and Lennartsson, C. (2008) 'Social mobility, geographical proximity and intergenerational family contact in Sweden', *Ageing and Society*, 28(2): 253–70.

Frankfurt (2005) *Alter und Migration [Migration and Old Age].* City of Frankfurt website, Available online at http://www.

frankfurt.de/sixcms/detail.php?id=799469. Accessed August 2, 2007.

Giddens, A. (1991) *Modernity and Self-Identity: Self and Society in the Late Modern Age*. Cambridge: Polity.

Görer, N.T., Erdoğanaras, F., Güzey, Ö., and Yüksel, Ü. (2006) 'Effects of second home development by foreign retirement migration in Turkey', Paper presented at the 42nd Congress of the International Society of City and Regional Planners, Istanbul, Turkey. http://www.isocarp.net/projects/case_studies/cases/list01.asp?accepted=%27yes%27

Gustafson, P. (2001) 'Retirement migration and transnational lifestyles', *Ageing and Society*, 21(4): 371–94.

Gustafson P. (2008) 'Transnationalism in retirement migration: the case of North European retirees in Spain', *Ethnic and Racial Studies*, iFirst paper, 25 pp., DOI: 10.1080/01419870701492000.

Haas, W.H. and Serow, W.J. (1993) 'Amenity retirement migration process: a model and preliminary evidence', *The Gerontologist*, 33(2): 212–20.

Hardill, I., Spradbery, J., Arnold-Boakes. J., and Marrugat, M.L. (2005) 'Severe health and social care issues among British migrants who retire to Spain', *Ageing and Society*, 25(5): 769–84.

Howard, R.W. (2008) 'Western retirees in Thailand: motives, experiences, wellbeing, assimilation and future needs', *Ageing and Society*, 28(2): 147–66.

Huber, A. and O'Reilly, K. (2004) 'The construction of *Heimat* under conditions of individualised modernity: Swiss and British elderly migrants in Spain', *Ageing and Society*, 24(3): 327–52.

Huber, J. and Skidmore, P. (2003) *The New Old: Why the Baby Boomers Won't be Pensioned Off*. London: Demos.

International Organization for Migration (IoM) (2005) *Internal Migration and Development: A Global Perspective*. Report 19, Migration Research Series, IoM, Geneva, Switzerland.

Ip, D., Lui, C.W., and Chui, W.H. (2007) 'Veiled entrapment: a study of social isolation of older Chinese migrants in Brisbane, Queensland', *Ageing and Society*, 27(5): 721–40.

Joly, D. (2007) *International Migration in the New Millennium: Global Movement and Settlement*. London: Ashgate.

Kahana, E. and Kahana, B. (1983) 'Environmental continuity, futurity, and adptation of the aged', In G.D. Rowles and R.J. Ohta (eds), *Aging and Milieu: Environmental Perspectives on Growing Old*. New York: Academic, pp. 205–28.

Kent, J. (2005) *Chinese Diaspora: Malaysia*. BBC News, 3 March. http://news.bbc.co.uk/2/hi/asia-pacific/4308241.stm

King, R. and Vullnetari, J. (2006) 'Orphan pensioners and migrating grandparents: the impact of mass migration on older people in rural Albania', *Ageing and Society*, 26(5): 783–816.

King, R., Warnes, A.M., and Williams, A.M. (2000) *Sunset Lives: British Retirement Migration to the Mediterranean*. Oxford: Berg.

Klinthall, M. (2006) 'Retirement return migration from Sweden', *International Migration*, 44(2): 153–80.

La Parra, D. and Mateo, M.A. (2008) 'Health status and access to health care of British nationals living on the Costa Blanca, Spain', *Ageing and Society*, 28(1): 85–102.

Law, C.M. and Warnes, A.M. (1973) 'The movement of retired persons to seaside resorts: a study of Morecambe and Llandudno', *Town Planning Review*, 44(3): 373–90.

Lawton, M.P. (1971) 'The functional assessment of elderly people', *Journal of the American Geriatric Society*, 19: 465–81.

Lawton, M.P. (1976) 'The relative impact of congregate and traditional housing on elderly tenants', *The Gerontologist*, 16: 237–42.

Longino, C.F., Jr (1995) *Retirement Migration in America*. Houston, TX: Vacation.

Longino C.F., Jr and Warnes, A.M. (2005) 'Migration and older people', in M.L. Johnson, (ed.), *Cambridge Encyclopaedia of Ageing*. Cambridge: Cambridge University Press, pp. 538–45.

Lowenstein, A. and Katz, R. (2005) 'Living arrangements, family solidarity and life satisfaction of two generations of immigrants in Israel', *Ageing and Society*, 25(5): 749–67.

Malcolm, E. (1996) *Elderly Return Migration from Britain to Ireland: A Preliminary Study*. Dublin: National Council for the Elderly.

Marcus, J. (1938) *The Jew in the Medieval World: A Sourcebook, 315–1791*. New York: JPS.

McHugh, K.E. (2003) 'Three faces of ageism: society, image and place', *Ageing and Society*, 23(2): 165–86.

Migration Policy Institute (2006) *America's Emigrants: US Retirement Migration to Mexico and Panama*. Washington, DC: Migration Policy Institute.

Min, J.W., Moon, A., and Lubben, J.E. (2005) 'Determinants of psychological distress over time among older Korean immigrants and Non-Hispanic White elders: evidence from a two-wave panel study', *Aging and Mental Health*, 9(3): 210–22.

Morris, C. (2008) *Returning Nationals from the United Kingdom to the Caribbean*. Older People Residing Abroad Project, Age Concern England, London. Available online at http://www.ageconcern.org.uk. Accessed October 2008.

Ng, C.F., Northcott, H.C., and Abu-Laban, S.M. (2007) 'Housing and living arrangements of South Asian immigrant seniors in Edmonton, Alberta', *Canadian Journal on Aging*, 26(3): 185–94.

Oliver, C. (2008) *Retirement Migration: Paradoxes of Ageing*. New York: Routledge.

O'Reilly, K. (2000) *The British on the Costa del Sol: Trans-national Identities and Local Communities*. London: Routledge.

O'Reilly, K. (2004) *The Extent and Nature of Integration of European Migrants in Spanish Society*. School of Social Science, University of Aberdeen, Aberdeen, Scotland.

O'Reilly, K. (2007) 'Intra-European migration and the mobility-enclosure dialectic', *Sociology: Journal of the British Sociological Association*, 41(2): 277–93.

Pastalan, L. (1983) 'Environmental displacement: a literature reflecting old-person–environment transactions', in G. Rowles and R.J. Ohta (eds), *Aging and Milieu:*

Environmental Perspectives on Growing Old. New York: Academic Press, pp. 189–203.

Petersen, W. (1975) *Population*, 3rd edn. London: Macmillan.

Phillipson, C. (2007) 'The "elected" and the "excluded": sociological perspectives on the experience of place and community in old age', *Ageing and Society*, 27(3): 321–42.

Ravenstein, E.G. (1985) 'The laws of migration', *Journal of the Royal Statistical Society*, 48: 167–235.

Reisenwitz, T. (2007) 'A comparison of younger and older baby boomers: investigating the viability of cohort segmentation', *Journal of Consumer Marketing*, 24(4): 202–13.

Rodríguez, V.R., Casado-Díaz, M.A., and Huber, A. (eds) (2006) *La Migración de Europeos Retirados en España* [*The Migration of Retired Europeans to Spain*]. Estudios de Política y Sociedad 23, Consejo Superior de Investigaciones Científicas, Madrid.

Rodríguez, V.R. and Egea, C. (2006) 'Return and the social environment of Andalusian emigrants in Europe', *Journal of Ethnic and Migration Studies*, 32(8): 1377–93.

Schopf, C. and Naegele, G. (2005) 'Age and ethnicity: an overview', *Zeitschrift fur Gerontologie und Geriatrie*, 38(6): 384–95.

Shinozaki, M. (2006) 'Japanese international retirement migration: a case study of Japanese retired couples in New Zealand', Workshop Paper, Graduate School of Asia-Pacific Studies, Waseda University, 28 July. Available online at www.wiaps.waseda.ac.jp/initiative/2006/work/international_01/pdf/Group_02.pdf

Silveira, E. and Allebeck, P. (2001) 'Migration, ageing and mental health: an ethnographic study on perceptions of life satisfaction, anxiety and depression in older Somali men in east London', *International Journal of Social Welfare*, 10(4): 309–20.

Sriskandarajah, D. and Drew, C. (2006) *Brits Abroad: Mapping the Scale and Nature of British Emigration.* London: Institute for Public Policy Research.

Sunil, T. S., Rojas, V., and Bradley, D.E. (2007) 'United States' international migration: reasons for returning to the environs of Lake Chapala, Mexico', *Ageing and Society*, 27(4): 489–510.

Tacoli, C. and Okali, D. (2001) *The Links Between Migration, Globalisation and Sustainable Development.* London: International Institute for Environment and Development.

Thomas-Hope, E. (2000) *Trends and Patterns of Migration to and from Caribbean Countries.* http://www.eclac.org/celade/proyectos/migracion/ThomeasHope.doc

Torres, S. (2001) 'Understandings of successful ageing in the context of migration: the case of Iranian immigrants to Sweden', *Ageing and Society*, 21(3): 333–55.

Torres, S. (2004) 'Late-in-life immigrants in Sweden: who are they and what do they need?', in A.M. Warnes (ed.), *Older Migrants in Europe: Essays, Projects and Sources.* Sheffield: University of Sheffield, Institute for Studies on Ageing, pp. 59–62.

Townsend, M. (1963) *The Family Life of Old People.* Harmondsworth, UK: Penguin, Books.

UK Population Census (2001) Special Migration Statistics. http://cider.census.ac.uk/

US Social Security Administration (2006) *Social Security Bulletin: Annual Statistical Supplement 2005. Old-Age, Survivors, and Disability Insurance, Benefits in Current-Payment Status.* Washington, DC: Government Printing Office. Available online at www.socialsecurity.gov

Vullnetari, J. and King, R. (2008) 'Does your granny eat grass?" On mass migration, care drain and the fate of older people in rural Albania', *Global Networks*, 8(2): 139–71.

Wahl, H.-W., Mollenkopf, H., Oswald, F., and Claus, C. (2007a) 'Environmental aspects of quality of life in old age: conceptual and empirical issues', in H. Mollenkopf and A. Walker (eds), *Quality of Life in Old Age: International and Multi-Disciplinary Perspectives.* Vol. 31, Social Indicators Research Series. Netherlands: Springer, pp. 101–22.

Wahl, H.-W., Tesch-Roemer, C., and Hoff, A. (eds) (2007b) *New Dynamics in Old Age: Individual, Environmental and Societal Perspectives.* Amityville, NY: Baywood.

Walters, W.H. (2002) 'Later-life migration in the United States: a review of recent research', *Journal of Planning Literature*, 17(1): 37–66.

Warnes, A.M. (1983) 'Migration in late working age and early retirement', *Socio-Economic Planning Sciences*, 17 (5–6): 291–302.

Warnes, A.M. (1986) 'The residential mobility histories of parents and children and relationships to present proximity and social integration', *Environment and Planning A* 18: 1581–94.

Warnes, A.M. (1992) 'Temporal and spatial patterns of elderly migration', in J. Stillwell, P. Rees, and P. Boden (eds), *Migration Processes and Patterns: Volume II, Population Redistribution in the 1980s.* London: Belhaven, pp. 248–70.

Warnes, A.M. (1993) 'The development of retirement migration in Great Britain', *Espace Populations Sociétés*, 1993/3: 451–64.

Warnes, A.M. (2001) 'The international dispersal of pensioners from affluent countries', *International Journal of Population Geography* 7(6): 373–88.

Warnes, A.M. (2004) *Older Migrants in Europe: Essays, Projects and Sources.* Sheffield, UK: Sheffield Institute for Studies of Ageing, University of Sheffield.

Warnes, A.M. (2009) 'International retirement migration', in P. Uhlenberg (ed.), *International Handbook of the Demography of Aging.* New York: Springer-Verlag, pp. 341–63.

Warnes, A.M. and Ford, R. (1995) 'Migration and family care', in I. Allen and E. Perkins (eds), *The Future of Family Care.* London: Her Majesty's Stationery Office, pp. 65–92.

Warnes, A.M. and Williams, A. (2006) 'Older migrants in Europe: a new focus for migration studies', *Journal of Ethnic and Migration Studies*, 32(8): 1257–81.

Warnes, A.M., King, R., Williams, A., and Patterson, G. (1999) 'The well-being of British expatriate retirees in southern Europe', *Ageing and Society*, 19(6): 717–40.

Wolff, F.-C. and Dimova, R. (2006) 'How do migrants care for their elderly parents? Time, money and location', *Schweizerische Zeitschrift für Volkswirtschaft und Statistik*, Sondernummer, 123–30.

Yu, W.K. (2000) *Chinese Older People: A Need for Social Inclusion in Two Communities.* Bristol: Policy Press.

31

Global Ageing: Perspectives from Sub-Saharan Africa

Isabella Aboderin

INTRODUCTION

Contemporary social gerontology continues to be dominated by empirical and theoretical contributions focusing on Western industrialized societies, particularly Europe and the United States. However, recent years have seen growing attention paid to issues of old age in the Global South, including sub-Saharan Africa (SSA). This chapter – the first dedicated discussion on SSA to be included in a major gerontological textbook – is an expression of this interest. The increased consideration of ageing in SSA reflects two sources: first, mounting awareness of ageing as a global phenomenon that affects developed and developing societies alike and poses especially complex policy challenges in the latter (United Nations, 2002); and secondly, an emergent critical gerontological focus on globalization and ageing. Building on established sociological and political science debates, this chapter considers the influence of global actors or forces on dominant discourses, policy agendas, and local conditions of old age, including in the poor Global South (Baars et al., 2006; Phillipson, 2006). Critical gerontology's growing engagement with less developed regions marks an important departure. Yet, it might be argued that its analyses – as applied to policy discourses and realities of old age in SSA – remain circumscribed. African gerontology, meanwhile,

has barely begun to embrace either global or critical perspectives.

This chapter assesses the status of African policy and research debates on ageing as well as the present scope of Western gerontological perspectives on them. The first part of this chapter traces the trajectory of, and major influences on, the African gerontological endeavour and examines the dominant ideas and concerns that lie at its heart. Building on this, the second part critically appraises the state of current African and Western analysis of (1) the coherence of the dominant policy discourse on ageing in SSA and (2) the conditions and realities of old age in the region. A concluding section charts avenues for closer engagement between SSA and Western ageing research in pursuit of a 'global' gerontology.

TRAJECTORY AND DOMINANT CONCERNS IN AFRICAN GERONTOLOGY

Origins: a United Nations-led enterprise

African gerontology has thus far reflected little on the major influences that have shaped the debate on ageing on the continent. Yet, much of its origin was 'externally' driven by Western concerns and theoretical conjecture. International awareness of ageing in Africa effectively emerged in the early 1980s, as part of a UN-led drive to address perceived policy challenges of population ageing in less developed countries (LDCs). The drive was launched with the 1982 first UN World Assembly on Ageing (WAA I) in Vienna and the ensuing Vienna International Plan of Action on Ageing (Vienna Plan) (UN, 1982). Prior to this, international interest in issues of ageing in Africa was limited to a small body of US and British anthropological studies (e.g. Nahemov and Adams, 1974; Shelton, 1972) as well as holocultural ethnographic analyses, which compared existing ethnographic data on formal age relations or old age in different 'pre-industrial' societies (stored in databases such as the Human Relations Area Files) (Glascock and Feinman, 1981; Palmore and Manton, 1974; Simmons, 1945, see Chapter 4).

The Vienna Assembly's deliberations on LDCs built on previously compiled profiles of older populations in a number of selected countries (including Ghana and Uganda in SSA). Given the scant pre-existing empirical evidence, the profiles were based on simple pilot surveys on the socioeconomic circumstances of older persons. The surveys themselves were typically conducted by designated 'experts' who had little prior engagement with gerontological research or debate (Apt, 2005; Marshall, 1990). Perhaps for this reason, the generated findings were interpreted in accordance with dominant UN thought on ageing in LDCs at the time. The thinking focused on two 'transitions' in the status of older populations that were expected to occur in LDCs, just as they had ostensibly done earlier in Western societies. These expectations built directly on modernization theory (Goode, 1963; Rostow, 1960), which views development as a linear, uniform process of change from 'traditional' to 'modern'. Contemporary LDCs are thus equated with historical, pre-industrial societies in the West, and are presumed to undergo the same transformations – and to eventually resemble – today's 'advanced' industrialized nations (Neysmith and Edwardh, 1983). The two key ageing-related transformations that the UN anticipated in LDCs were a demographic transition and changes in traditional support arrangements for older persons.

Demographically, the UN forecast a sharp rise in the absolute number of older persons in LDCs and, eventually, a rise in their population share – echoing the process of population ageing that was already underway in Western societies. In line with neoclassical views forged in the West (Walker, 1990), the projections were seen as heralding a rising 'burden' of old-age support in LDCs as expressed in rising dependency ratios (UN, 1982). However, it was expected that some developing populations, especially those in SSA, would age much more slowly and retain small proportions of older persons for the foreseeable future. As regards support arrangements, the UN predicted a gradual erosion of traditional family systems that customarily provided support and security for the aged in LDCs. As a result, older persons would become increasingly dependent on state assistance – which most poor nations would be unable to provide, given resource limitations and the dearth of formal support structures such as pensions (UN, 1982).[1] The expectation of eroding family support in LDCs, interestingly, did not build on any supporting evidence (Marshall, 1990); rather, it was a theoretical conjecture based squarely on the tenets of modernization and ageing theory (Burgess, 1960; Cowgill, 1974). First advanced by US scholars in the 1960s and 1970s as an interpretation of observed developments in Western societies, the theory holds that family support and social status of older persons are high in 'traditional', pre-industrial societies, underpinned by norms of familism and filial obligation. However, these supporting mechanisms weaken and are replaced by values of individualism and secularism as societies become progressively industrialized and 'westernized'. As a result, older people are left without roles, abandoned, and dependent on the state (see Aboderin, 2004). Perplexingly, UN thinking embraced this 'prediction', despite the strong rebuttal modernization and ageing theory had received in the Western debate. Trenchant theoretical critiques had exposed the fallacy of assuming a uniform, linear mode of development and static traditional and 'modern' states (see Aboderin, 2004), while empirical evidence from historical, contemporary, and ethnographic research had shown the 'abandonment' notion to fit neither with 'history nor with contemporary arrangements' (O'Rand, 1990).

The UN's uncritical adoption of the modernization and ageing thesis shaped an official 'humanitarian' policy concern – expressed in the Vienna Plan – which assumed steadily rising unmet need among older persons in areas of health, housing, family support, social welfare, and income security. The plan consequently asserted a pressing need for policy responses to prevent or address such vulnerability and for research to inform policy development (UN, 1982).

Early research: 1982 to mid 1990s

Propelled by the Vienna Plan's recommendations and by associated initiatives, such as the 'Special UN Programme for Research on Aging', the decade following 1982 saw a small burst of investigations on older persons in SSA countries. Most studies – mainly single country, modestly sized quantitative surveys – focused on collecting basic descriptive data on older persons' health, economic, housing, family, and support statuses (e.g. Apt, 1987, 1996a; Brown, 1985; Dorjahn, 1989; Ekpenyong, et al., 1987; Ferreira et al., 1992; Nyanguru and Peil, 1993; Nyanguru et al., 1994; Peil et al., 1989), or on the degree to which customary norms of filial obligation continued to be endorsed in African societies (e.g. Ohuche and Littrell, 1989; Togonu-Bickersteth, 1989; Togonu-Bickersteth and Akinnawo, 1990). Parallel ethnographic and qualitative studies described conditions of old age and intergenerational support in various cultural contexts (e.g. Apt et al., 1995; Campbell, 1994; Cattell, 1997; Everatt and Orkin, 1994; Foner, 1993; Keith et al., 1994; Sangree, 1992). Employing modernization and ageing theory as a dominant framework for exploration and analysis (Shapiro and Kaufert, 1983), much of the research essentially sought to assess the extent to which modernization had already impacted on older persons' well-being. Little effort was made to critically examine the modernization thesis or the *actual* nature, causes, and implications of changes in older persons' situation (Aboderin, 2004; Ferreira, 1999).

Evidence accumulating from the early research showed, on the one hand, a high prevalence of intergenerational co-residence and support from the family for elderly people. On the other hand, and complemented by anecdotal or small-scale qualitative evidence of neglect of older persons, surveys found sizeable proportions of older people reporting inadequacies, especially in material support from family members. Some study findings, moreover, suggested subtle shifts in customary normative expectations. In keeping with the modernization framework, the generated findings were largely interpreted as signifying a broad continuity of 'traditional' modes, but also the beginnings of a decline in old-age family support, wrought by forces associated with modernization. Some authors additionally noted the effects of widespread economic strain (which took hold in SSA in the 1980s) as further negative impacts on family support (e.g. Apt, 1992, 1996a). However, unlike some concurrent Asian and Latin American research (e.g. DeLehr, 1992; Goldstein et al., 1983), no attempt was made to link such empirical insights to critiques of the modernization thesis or to other explanatory frameworks, such as political economy (Aboderin, 2004). This omission highlights a level of disconnect that existed between early African research and Western gerontological debate, including critical perspectives at the time (e.g. Fennell et al., 1988; Phillipson, 1982; Walker, 1981).

Contemporary research and debate: late 1990s to the present

A second phase of African gerontological research emerged in the late 1990s, fuelled by evidence of inadequacies in old-age support, updated demographic projections of dramatic rises in the numbers (though not proportions) of older persons in coming decades in SSA, and countries' minimal progress in forging policy responses (UN, 1999; UNPD, 2007, 2008a). Expanding on the scope of early work, the contemporary research debate comprises two distinct, though overlapping strands: a 'conventional' academic track and an increasingly dominant advocacy discourse. Both tracks, however, retain a core focus on older persons' vulnerability. Considerations of the societal and economic implications of changing population age structures – which are central to ageing debates in Western and rapidly maturing Asian countries – remain marginal in African debates (see Aboderin, 2009).

Academic research

Much contemporary academic research in Africa has taken the form of small-scale quantitative surveys and secondary analyses of population survey data. Such studies, like earlier research, have focused on describing the basic nature and patterns of older persons' demographic, health, economic, residential, or family support status. A few investigations, moreover, have examined prevailing attitudes towards old age and family support. Their descriptive findings have served to bring into relief a number of key features, namely:

- A majority of older persons live in rural areas (e.g. Mba, 2004, 2005, 2007; NPC, 2004).
- Most live with at least one child and only a small minority live alone or with a spouse only (e.g. Mba, 2005, 2007; UNPD, 2005, Zimmer and Dayton, 2005).
- A majority of older persons, especially in rural areas, continue to work, with only small proportions receiving pensions or income from formal assets or savings (e.g. Apt, 1996b; Baiyewu et al., 1997; Kuepie, 2007; NPC, 2004).
- Sizeable proportions (though not always the majority) suffer from various, mostly preventable or manageable, disease conditions (see Aboderin, 2009; Clausen et al., 2005; Ezeh et al., 2006; Kahn et al., 2006), although only a minority report poor health or functional limitations (e.g. see Aboderin, 2009; Kuate-Defo, 2006). Indications are that older people may receive less

health care than younger adults despite similar or higher incidence of disease (McIntyre, 2004) and that a considerable minority of those with functional limitations lack access to informal family care (Gureje et al., 2006).

- There may be a considerable prevalence of ostensibly 'non-traditional' attitudes among the young regarding the 'value' of old age and the provision of family support to older parents (Akinyemi et al., 2007).
- Older persons' health status and living arrangements vary (though not uniformly) by gender and/ or rural/urban residence, while employment and access to pension (or other private) income is consistently higher among older men than women. Evidence on differences by socioeconomic position (SEP) is more limited and conflicting. What exists (mainly in the area of health) suggests that the risk of some conditions (e.g. depression) may rise with SEP (Gureje et al., 2007) – a pattern that differs from the SEP-health gradient found in the Global North (Ferraro and Shippee, 2007; Marmot, 2006), while self-reported poor health and disability appears as 'expected' to fall with SEP (Kuate-Defo, 2006; see Aboderin, 2009).

More extensive insights on patterns of health in old age in SSA are expected to be generated by the ongoing World Health Organization (WHO) multi-country study on global ageing and adult health (SAGE), which, so far, has collected comprehensive data in South Africa and Ghana (WHO, 2008).

Adding to the quantitative findings, several qualitative investigations have offered more detailed descriptions of older persons' intergenerational relationships, support systems, and health practices. These studies have again highlighted older persons' unmet needs for family support and health care as well as their provision of support to younger generations (e.g. Cliggett, 2001; Ferreira, 2006a; Møller and Sotshongaye, 1996; Sagner and Mtati 1999; van der Geest, 1997a, 1997b, 2002, 2004).

Like earlier research many of the above studies have, implicitly or explicitly, continued to embrace modernization and ageing theory as an explanatory framework. In response to this, a few scholars have forged explicit critiques of the continued salience of modernization and ageing theory in African gerontology and the limited attention paid to micro-level, interpretive evidence[2] (Aboderin, 2004; Ferreira, 1999; Makoni and Stroeken, 2002). Building on such critiques, a few in-depth investigations have sought to examine and theorize the actual nature and causes of changes in material old-age family support, illuminating the role of complex interactions between individual motives and structural material and normative changes (Aboderin, 2006). Socio-linguistically oriented ethnographic studies, meanwhile, have explored

meanings and experiences of old age in various local contexts (Makoni and Stroeken, 2002), They suggest that many older individuals experience ageing in terms of crisis – a 'generation gap' between young 'trend seekers' and old 'tradition keepers' – and that their multiple concepts of self conflict with common, unidimensional categorizations of the 'elderly' (Devisch et al., 2002).

In addition to inquiries on the situation and well-being of older people in general, a focus on three specific issues has emerged over the last decade. First, a burgeoning number of studies have investigated the circumstances of older persons affected by HIV/AIDS – which affects SSA more than any other world region (UNAIDS, 2008). Most research has described older persons' roles as carers for ailing children and/or orphaned grandchildren, their loss of support from such younger kin and, to a limited degree, their own HIV/AIDS infection (see Cohen and Menken, 2006; Ferreira, 2006b). Additional analyses have explored impacts of HIV/AIDS-related mortality on residential arrangements, pointing to reductions in instances of older persons residing with adult children and increases in skipped-generation households in which grandparents live with orphaned grandchildren (Zimmer, 2007). Secondly, nascent research has focused on profiling the situation of older residents in urban slums as part of a broader concern with the conditions of slum dwellers in SSA (which comprise 62 per cent of the region's urban population) (UN HABITAT, 2008). Emerging findings indicate extensive unmet healthcare and economic needs among this population and a lack of ability to realize desired return migrations to rural homesteads (e.g. Chepngeno and Ezeh, 2007; Ezeh et al., 2006). However, scant understanding as yet exists of older slum dweller's own perspectives and the relative extent of their vulnerability compared to younger slum populations and older non-slum populations. Thirdly, growing attention is being paid to the implications of migration for older persons, focusing both on impacts of massive rural–urban or international out-migration of younger persons on the intergenerational old-age support (e.g. Aboderin, 2005a; Ferreira, 2008), as well as on migration strategies of older persons themselves (e.g. Nxusani, 2004).

Policy advocacy discourse

Much of the contemporary 'academic' research has fed into an increasingly dominant and explicitly advocacy-oriented discourse on ageing in Africa. Part of broader international efforts to promote ageing policy in developing regions, the discourse has been driven by UN and international non-governmental organizations (NGOs), specifically UNFPA, WHO, and, most prominently, HelpAge International (HAI). These bodies have marshalled selected evidence and directly commissioned or conducted research to forge an authoritative case on why national governments should introduce social pensions and other policies for the rising number of older citizens.

To strengthen its case, the advocacy discourse has, moreover, sought to directly connect its arguments to three dominant mainstream agendas for development in SSA.[3] First, neoliberal agendas, which focus on achievement of economic growth through free market mechanisms and curtailments in public spending and, consequently, discourage the introduction of comprehensive public pensions, advocating instead for private, 'voluntary', and/or family-based schemes (World Bank, 1994). Secondly, increasingly salient, UN-led paradigms of 'human and social development', which emphasize not economic growth, but the attainment of human rights, welfare, and social justice as core means and goals of development (see Jolly, 2003). The paradigms draw on tenets of the capability approach (Sen, 1993), which sees the goal of development as expanding the freedom of individuals to pursue the life 'they have reason to value' (Clark, 2006). Thirdly, the United Nations 'Millennium Development Goals' (MDGs), which, embedded in individual countries' poverty reduction strategies (PRS), lie at the heart of present development efforts in most SSA states (ADB, 2006).[4] Building on human and social development perspectives, the MDGs entail specific targets (to be achieved by 2015) on reduction of extreme income poverty and hunger, and improvements in primary education, infant, child, and maternal health, containment of HIV/AIDS and malaria, access to drinking water, and slum conditions (UN, 2000). To achieve the targets, PRS typically promote:

- infrastructure development, governance reform, and establishment of efficient markets to promote investment, private enterprise, and employment opportunities
- direct social sector spending on primary education, HIV/AIDS, child and maternal health, and a longer-term focus on addressing youth un- and underemployment and lack of training
- social protection measures to safeguard the most vulnerable groups in society (see Aboderin and Ferreira, 2009).

To connect to these mainstream agendas, the ageing advocacy discourse has presented two key types of evidence, often drawn from small-scale, participatory research (HAI, 2002a). The first is evidence documenting older persons' vulnerability

to poverty, ill-health, and limited family support. Such vulnerability is broadly ascribed to a combination of: (1) physical, mental, and social changes or attributes associated with chronological ageing; (2) the effects of rapid sociocultural change, economic stress, and acute crises, such as HIV/AIDS or armed conflict, which strain family support systems and place added care burdens on older persons (see Ferreira, 2006b); and (3) the dearth of appropriate health and social provision for older people in most SSA countries, including in emergency or conflict situations (e.g. Bramucci and Erb, 2007; McIntyre, 2004; WHO, 2006). Drawing on the above, advocacy arguments have posited an association between old age and the risk of poverty due to the 'reduced framework of capacity arising from the social and biological ageing process' (Barrientos, 2002; Gorman and Heslop, 2002; Heslop and Gorman, 2000). Older persons, in other words, are asserted as one, if not *the* most, vulnerable population group in SSA (and other developing regions) (HAI, 2006). The second type of evidence highlighted by the advocacy track are findings on the significant contributions that older persons, particularly older women, make to the welfare and capacity of younger generations in their families and in their communities more generally (Ahenkora, 1999; Mohatle and de Graft Agyarko, 1999). Specific emphasis is given to older people's care roles in the context of HIV/AIDS and to their sharing of pension incomes with children and grandchildren for the purposes of education and health care (Ferreira, 2006b; HAI, 2004, 2006; IDPM/HAI, 2003).

Building on the marshalled evidence, the advocacy discourse has forged three potentially persuasive arguments on why SSA countries need to introduce policies on ageing as part of their overall development endeavour. First, governments must address the needs of older persons as part of (1) their duty to honour older citizens' fundamental human rights and (2) their efforts to protect the most vulnerable in society. Secondly, governments need to acknowledge, encourage, and support the often critical contributions that older people make to enhancing the capacity of children, youth, and young adults. Older persons, in other words, should be seen as 'catalysts' for achieving major development goals (AU/HAI, 2003; HAI, 2002b, 2004; WHO, 2002). Thirdly, public non-contributory pensions are an optimal social protection measure, given that such schemes (where they exist)[5] are shown to be affordable, to effectively reduce old age poverty, and to have significant redistributive effects to younger age groups through older persons' pension sharing (Charlton and McKinnon, 2001; HAI, 2004, 2006, 2007).

Crucially, the advocacy arguments have been incorporated and thus legitimized in two key recent official policy frameworks: namely, the UN Madrid International Plan of Action on Ageing (MIPAA) and the African Union Policy Framework and Plan of Action on Ageing (AU Plan). The MIPAA, ratified at the second UN World Assembly on Ageing in Madrid in 2002, offers a fresh framework for the formulation of policies on ageing in developing (and developed) nations in a quest to forge 'societies for all ages' (Sidorenko and Walker, 2004; UN, 2002). The AU Plan provides a largely comparable blueprint specifically for African states (AU/HAI, 2003). Both plans tie their recommendations to key international human rights covenants, including the 1986 UN Declaration on the Right to Development and to the 1991 UN Principles for Older Persons, which emphasize the right to independence, participation, care, self-fulfilment, and dignity (as set out in the UN General Assembly Resolution 46/91). Both plans, moreover, adopt a quality of life (QoL) perspective, declaring improvements in the QoL of present and future cohorts of older persons as a central goal of policies on ageing.

Recent developments

All SSA member states are signatory to the UN MIPAA and the AU Plan and, as such, have expressed their readiness, at least rhetorically, to develop national policy responses. Yet, as Aboderin and Ferreira (2008) discuss, little comprehensive policy action has ensued. The policy impasse in conjunction with an intensifying international focus on African development, has, in recent years, provoked some reflective thought of the state of African gerontology as a policy-relevant and intellectual enterprise (Aboderin, 2005b, 2007; Aboderin and Ferreira, 2009; Ferreira, 2005). Building on these reflections, the remainder of this chapter appraises current African and Western understanding of (1) the coherence of the dominant policy discourse on ageing in SSA and (2) the conditions and realities of old age in the region.

APPRAISING THE DOMINANT POLICY DISCOURSE

The policy discourse on ageing in SSA (and the poor Global South more generally), as crystallized in the AU Plan and MIPAA, has in many senses become an orthodoxy. Contemporary African writing largely accepts the policy advocacy arguments with seemingly little reflection. Western analyses too, while critiquing the MIPAA on other

points, appear to find no fault with its principal case on policy for older persons in the poor Global South (Phillipson, 2006). Yet, scrutiny of the policy calls is warranted. Though outwardly powerful, closer inspection reveals problematic elements in their lines of reasoning, on two levels.

First is the policy calls' failure to sufficiently clarify the rationales for policy on older persons in the context of mainstream poverty reduction agendas and the severe resource constraints that oblige governments to set priorities among development needs. Specifically, the policy arguments omit four areas of ambiguity (Aboderin and Ferreira, 2009):

1   *Ambiguity over the term 'rights'.* Are rights something that must be provided actively? Or are human rights simply something that should not be removed?
2   *Ambiguity over priorities of age groups.* Both old and young citizens already do, or have the potential to, contribute to development. Both, moreover, are recognized as vulnerable and as having fundamental economic and social rights. Given resource constraints, whose needs and rights are to be met as a priority? The emphasis of mainstream agendas suggests it is likely to be those of the young. Moreover, the suggestion, implicit in policy calls, of a particularly pronounced vulnerability of older persons (compared to younger age groups) to detrimental health, economic, or social outcomes in fact remains unsubstantiated. Evidence of such age-related disparities is scanty, conflicting, and hampered by the use of aggregate household – rather than individually based – measures (Aboderin, 2009; Barrientos, 2002; Kakwani and Subbarao, 2005).
3   *Ambiguities over cohorts and time frames.* Policy frameworks assert a need to ensure the well-being of present and future cohorts of older persons. In practice, however, advocacy calls focus almost exclusively on present cohorts of older persons. In addition, policy frameworks assume implicitly that future cohorts will suffer the same vulnerability as those today. A likely expectation among policymakers, however, is that present youth and MDG-related investments in the young will avert such vulnerability in their old age.
4   *Ambiguities over policy priorities.* Where governments *are* prepared to realize policies for older persons, they are faced with the multifaceted nature of older persons' vulnerability and contributions amid an almost complete lack of understanding of the priorities that older persons themselves would set in pursuit of a better life. Which facets should policy therefore focus upon and why?

The second, perhaps more serious, weakness in the official policy calls are a number of questionable underlying assumptions that may contravene the very principles of independence and self-fulfilment for older persons that the calls claim to promote. The assumptions are most evident in the tendency to conflate calls for policy to support older people's contributions with calls to enhance their quality of life. The two, seemingly, are presumed to be congruent. This reflects a very problematic presumption that older persons' present contributions to family and community (the MIPAA specifically mentions 'financial support and the care and education of grandchildren and other kin' (para 34)) are (1) valued by older persons and young recipients alike, and (2), more importantly, are contributions that older persons, if given the choice, wish to continue to make (to this extent). It is inferred, in other words, that the *existing* patterns of intergenerational support from old to young are beneficial to, and desired by, both parties, and thus should be strengthened (e.g. Temple, 2007). Perplexingly, this assumption appears to hold even with respect to older persons' care burdens in the context of HIV/AIDS. Thus far, policy arguments have failed to consider whether (1) current types and levels of intergenerational support from old to young (which are often necessitated precisely by social and/or economic deprivation) are, in fact, *not* beneficial or desirable for old and/or young; and (2) there may be a consequent need or demand for formal mechanisms to assume these support functions. A similar lack of consideration of older persons' actual preferences underlies the advocacy call for non-contributory pensions as a key social protection tool. The argument assumes, without grounding in evidence, that cash transfers are the best way to address older persons vulnerability and enhance their quality of life. Similarly, there is an assumption that such transfers should be allocated to older persons to then be redistributed (i.e., 'shared') with children and grandchildren. Little thought has been given to whether a direction of flows from old to young (as opposed to cash allocations to strengthen customary support from young to old) is in fact desirable and commensurate with present African visions on intergenerational ties (see Aboderin and Ferreira, 2009).

That most African gerontological writing has thus far failed to note the drawbacks in the dominant policy discourse on ageing highlights, if nothing else, the absence of critical and associated self-reflexive perspectives (Moody, 1988) in most of the debate. Western critical gerontology, meanwhile, in overlooking the discourse's problematic nature and assumptions, risks being guilty of the same uncritical acceptance of 'orthodox' ideas that it so incisively censures in mainstream ageing studies (Baars et al., 2006). Indeed, several of critical gerontology's key assertions could serve to theoretically ground critiques of the official policy discourse. These include: (a) arguments on the need for greater consideration of older persons' autonomy and agency in forming policy on ageing (Phillipson, 1998; Polivka and Longino, 2006; Walker, 2006); (b) feminist critiques of discourses on a 'natural' family caregiving role of women (Binney et al., 1993, Qureshi and Walker, 1989; Walker, 1983); (c) critiques of a neoliberally inspired individualization of risks that ought possibly to be collectivized (Ferge, 1997; Phillipson, 2006); and (d) what King and Calasanti (2006) have termed the 'patron mentality' of gerontological endeavours of the Global North regarding 'solutions' for old age in the Global South.

UNDERSTANDING OF REALITIES AND CONDITIONS OF OLD AGE IN SSA

The weaknesses in current arguments on ageing policy in SSA betray major gaps in African gerontology's understanding of the realities and conditions of old age in the region. Most research has remained decidedly descriptive, with few attempts to generate grounded explanations and theoretical ideas, and even fewer efforts to connect empirical insights to theoretical gerontological debates. The limited analytical outlook has gone hand in hand with a neglect of certain conceptual and methodological 'bedrock elements' (Baars et al., 2006) that are vital to the study of ageing, irrespective of geographical or cultural location. These include: (1) the demarcation and comparative study of successive cohorts over time, in order to discern age and cohort effects (Riley et al., 1988); (2) consideration of life-course exposures and trajectories in order to understand circumstances in old age (Elder, 1992); and (3) illumination of the interrelationships between micro-level (individual), meso-level (family), and macro-level (structural) factors in shaping experiences and conditions of old age (see Baars et al., 2006; Giddens, 1991; Guba and Lincoln, 1994; Ryff and Marshall, 1999).

Two main reasons arguably exist for African gerontology's poor engagement with such relevant methodological, conceptual, and theoretical perspectives. First is the advocacy orientation of much contemporary SSA research. This likely militates against precise analyses of older persons' (relative) situation, and may consider 'theorizing' an unwarranted luxury, given the pressing problems and severely constrained research resources. Secondly, and more important, is a serious deficit in SSA research capacity on ageing (and other subject areas). This reflects a general crisis in tertiary education in the region and makes for major global inequalities in conditions for academic work (CfA, 2005). Today, many SSA universities are characterized by chronically underresourced library and research facilities and a deterioration of infrastructure and equipment – all of which impede the ability of scholars to access, absorb, and partake in methodological developments and debates in their disciplines (Aboderin, 2005b; Assie-Lumumba, 2006; Ferreira, 2005; World Bank, 2002). An unfortunate consequence for African gerontology is the persisting lacunae in our present understanding of core aspects of the ageing experience in SSA.

INEQUALITY IN OLD AGE

The accumulated findings of recent academic research on ageing in SSA underscore the basic fact that experiences and well-being in old age in SSA are not uniform, but differ between population groups. While sizeable proportions of older persons may be extremely vulnerable to ill-health or poverty, this is not the case for all – or even most. The evidence, in other words, points to clear inequalities in old age. Astonishingly, most African gerontological research has thus far neither emphasized the inequalities, nor made them a subject of inquiry. Instead, the focus has been almost exclusively on vulnerable groups. We know little about the precise nature of social disparities in old age in SSA and about the life course and contemporaneous factors that give rise to them. This is compounded by the questionable merit of currently available measures for capturing older individuals' social and economic position or health status (e.g., Aboderin and Ferreira, 2009; Cohen and Menken, 2006; Kuhn et al., 2006).

It is similarly perplexing to note that Western critical gerontological perspectives on the poor Global South seemingly embrace the selective focus on vulnerable elders. While the analyses rightly recognize global inequalities between the 'poor south' and 'rich north' (King and Calasanti, 2006; Phillipson, 2002, 2006), they omit the existence of differentials *within* older populations in the South, despite the fact that the study of such social inequalities in old age lies at the heart of critical gerontological theorizing and debate (Crystal, 2006; Dannefer, 2003; O'Rand, 2003; Walker, 2006).

AGE RELATIONS

Related to the scant understanding of inequalities in old age is African gerontology's dearth of insight on how relations between old and young operate and are shaped in contemporary SSA societies. While there are dispersed indications of intergenerational support flows and power dynamics within families (Aboderin, 2006; Møller, 1994; Sagner and Mtati, 1999; van der Geest, 2007), we have little grasp of age-related power and economic relations at the societal level. What dominates is an advocacy-oriented perspective that emphasizes old-age exclusion and disenfranchisement. Besides lacking firm evidence, the narrowness of such a perspective is perhaps intuitive considering, for example, that a majority of African national leaders are, in fact, older persons (see Aboderin, 2007). Western analyses, too, have thus far not queried the nature of age relations in SSA or the poor Global South generally, despite the centrality of this subject specifically to critical gerontology (Riley and Riley, 1994).

GLOBAL INFLUENCES

Most African ageing research, as indicated above, has thus far failed to explore the interactions of micro-, meso-, and macro-level influences on conditions of old age. A specific omission in this regard is the dearth of analyses of global impacts.

Advocacy-oriented contributions have certainly recognized – and sought to respond to – the fact that major global policy agendas can shape local public provision for older persons. Moreover, some SSA analyses have linked certain causes of shifts in old-age family support to effects of global charters on children's rights and World Bank/IMF administered Structural Adjustment Programmes (SAPs) implemented during the 1980s and 1990s (Aboderin, 2006). Beyond this, however, there has been little attempt to further explicate major global influences on the lives of older persons in the region.

Western critical gerontological analysis has usefully highlighted the need to theorize the effects of global actors and forces in interaction with nation-state and local contexts (Phillipson, 2006). The analysis moreover suggests two key opposing global influences on conditions of old age in the poor Global South. On the one hand, neoliberal agendas, purveyed by the World Bank, IMF (International Monetory Fund), WTO (World Trade Organization), and OECD (Organization for Economic Co-operation and Development), which militate against public sector spending and pensions and foster growing income inequalities between rich and poor countries. On the other hand, the UN-led agenda for policy on ageing in developing nations, as articulated in the MIPAA, which supports expansion of welfare provision for older persons as part of a 'new politics of global social responsibility' (Phillipson, 2006; Walker and Deacon, 2003). This juxtaposition is circumscribed in a number of ways. First, it overlooks the overriding influence of mainstream 'global social responsibility' agendas, encapsulated in the MDGs in constraining provision for the old trough its priority focus on younger age groups. In other words, critical analysis has, thus far, omitted the effects of *competing* social responsibility agendas in shaping conditions of old age. Secondly, the analysis overlooks a possible continued influence of neoliberal interests in social responsibility measures. Indeed, closer inspection of the MDG agenda – which, in fact, was derived from OECD International Development Goals – reveals such an influence. Its focus on improving health and education of the young is explicitly geared to raising labour productivity and, ultimately, economic growth and capital accumulation. This approach rests on assumptions about a greater productivity of the young compared to older age groups and coincides with current World Bank demographic 'dividend' agendas (Aboderin and Ferreira, 2009, World Bank, 2006).

IMPACTS OF MAJOR DEMOGRAPHIC TRENDS: URBANIZATION

A further gap in African gerontological understanding concerns the implications of urbanization for old age in the region. The unprecedented rate of growth in urban populations in SSA (the highest globally), and exceptionally high rates of urban poverty and inequality are regarded as one of the most critical demographic and development challenges for SSA today (UN HABITAT, 2008; UNPD, 2008b).

Some SSA research, as noted earlier, has (cross-sectionally) explored, and occasionally compared, aspects of older persons' situation in rural and urban areas. Yet, it has provided scant insight into how processes and circumstances of urbanization – at structural, family, and individual levels – are shaping experiences of old age in SSA.

Instead, two simple notions prevail. The first notion is that rural–urban or international migration of the young renders rural older people 'socially isolated', with reduced informal social and economic support (Mba, 2004; UN, 2002). The second notion holds that urban elders fare badly as infrastructural constraints and urban lifestyles impede the maintenance of 'traditional' family networks and support arrangements (UN, 2002). A more nuanced understanding is certainly needed.

As some evidence indicates, effects of kin out-migration and urban life are likely to be intricate and to vary (for instance, kin-migration may be predominantly positive due to remittances), depending on older individuals' social position, migration history, and family network characteristics, and on structural conditions in rural and urban areas (e.g., Aboderin, 2005a; Kreager, 2006). Therefore, research is required that couples exploration of urbanization impacts with an explicit analysis of inequalities and possible processes of social exclusion in old age (see also Scharf and Smith, 2003).

QUALITY OF LIFE IN OLD AGE

A final and critical lacuna in understanding concerns the question of how older persons' circumstances relate to their quality of life. Despite the fact that both the MIPAA and AU Plan advocate improvements in older people's QoL, we have little insight into what such QoL in fact entails in SSA (Aboderin and Ferreira, 2009). Salient Western and nascent Asian research underscores the importance of considering older persons' own conceptions and 'lay theories' for meaningfully assessing QoL in different cultural contexts (Bowling and Gabriel, 2007; Mollenkopf and Walker, 2007; Nilsson et al., 2005). Critical European contributions, moreover, emphasize the need to understand and pursue older people's well-being, or 'social quality', within the context of their communities (Walker, 2006). Yet, these areas remain virtually unexplored in the SSA debate, though initial conceptual and empirical explorations are emerging (Aboderin and Ferreira, 2009).

CONCLUDING REMARKS

Building on a review of the trajectory, central concerns, and foci of African gerontology, this chapter identifies important limitations in the coherence of the present dominant policy discourse on ageing in SSA. Similarly, the review highlights critical gaps in current African analysis and understanding of ageing and old age in SSA, including on core issues such as the nature of societal age relations and inequalities in old age, global influences, older persons' quality of life, and the impacts of urbanization upon them. The shortcomings betray a limited research capacity on ageing on the continent, which in turn reflects significant global inequalities in conditions for the academic endeavour. Scrutiny of Western, in particular critical, gerontological perspectives on ageing in the poor Global South underscores some valuable insights – for example, on approaches to examining the role of global impacts. Mostly, however, the analyses remain circumscribed, as critical gerontology has omitted to apply some of its core principles and approaches to considerations of ageing in the region. Yet, such critical perspectives (on old-age inequality, age relations, globalization, quality of life and social quality, and dominant neoliberal ideologies) may prove immensely valuable for sharpening our understanding of discourses on, and realities of, old age in SSA. It is a potential that SSA and Western scholars should harness as one step towards greater comparative and collaborative engagement between African and mainstream gerontology.

There is, perhaps, a second step to take. This is to move beyond conventional cross-cultural comparative analyses, which are ultimately confined to confirming that experiences of ageing and old age differ between countries, cultures, and regions (Fry, 1999; Hendrie et al., 2001; Keith et al., 1994). Instead, there may be a potential for 'global' analyses, which, simply put, would capture aspects of national or regional divergence in conditions of old-age and would account for these with reference to effects of global forces in interaction with domestic contexts. Of course, not all facets of the old-age experience will sensibly lend themselves to such an approach. However, aspects such as health, for example, that are significantly influenced by global agendas and resource flows may clearly benefit from such analysis. So, too, may exploration of connections that exist between (changing) circumstances of older persons in SSA and those in other parts of the globe, mediated, for example, through transnational processes such as international care labour migration (Aboderin, 2005a). With few exceptions (Robine and Michel, 2004), mainstream gerontology has so far given little consideration to such global analysis. Current attempts to develop overarching explanations emphasize integration across social, biological, and medical disciplines, but still remain geographically bounded (Bengtson et al., 2005; Ferraro and Shippee, 2007). A focus on integration across world regions is needed if a truly global gerontology is to be forged.

NOTES

1 At the time of the first World Assembly on Ageing, virtually no SSA country provided comprehensive pension schemes. Pensions were, if at all, only available to a small minority, namely: former public sector or military employees.

2 The lack of micro-analysis in African gerontological research contrasts with the tendency for microfication critiqued in Western research (Hagestad and Dannefer, 2001).

3 SSA is the world's poorest and least developed subregion. 22 of the world's 24 countries with low human development (UNDP, 2009) and three quarters of its low-income economies are in SSA (World Bank, 2010).

4 PRS stipulate a framework for macroeconomic, structural, and social policies that countries will pursue in order to reduce the pervasive poverty in their populations. PRS typically form the basis for national budgets and medium-term expenditures and have become the key vehicle for the coordination of major donor assistance – upon which most SSA states are heavily and increasingly reliant (see Aboderin and Ferreira, 2009)

5 Only a handful of wealthier SSA countries, South Africa, Namibia, Lesotho, and Botswana, currently provide public non-contributory old-age pension schemes

REFERENCES

Aboderin, I. (2004) 'Modernisation and ageing theory revisited: current explanations of recent developing world and historical western shifts in material family support for older people', *Ageing and Society,* 24: 29–50.

Aboderin, I. (2005a) 'Migration rationales and impacts among Nigerian nurses working in the UK eldercare sector: implications for old age and intergenerational support in their families: a preliminary analysis', paper presented at the 34th annual conference of the British Society of Gerontology, Keele.

Aboderin, I. (2005b) 'Understanding and responding to ageing, health, poverty and social change in sub-Saharan Africa: A strategic framework and plan for research'. Report, Oxford Institute of Ageing, University of Oxford, UK.

Aboderin, I. (2006) *Intergenerational Support and Old Age in Africa.* Piscataway, NJ: Transaction Publishers.

Aboderin, I. (2007) 'Development and ageing policy in sub-Saharan Africa: approaches for research and advocacy', *Global Ageing,* 4(3): 7–22.

Aboderin, I. (2009) 'West Africa', in P. Uhlenberg (ed.), *International Handbook of the Demography of Ageing.* New York: Springer, pp. 253–276.

Aboderin, I. and Ferreira, M. (2009) 'Linking ageing to development agendas in sub-Saharan Africa: challenges and approaches', *Journal of Population Ageing,* 1: 51–73.

African Development Bank (ADB) (2006) *African Development Report 2006: Aid, Debt Relief and Development in Africa.* Oxford: Oxford University Press.

African Union/HelpAgeInternational (AU/HAI) (2003) *The African Policy Framework and Plan of Action on Ageing.* HelpAge International Africa Regional Development Centre, Nairobi, Kenya.

Ahenkora, K. (1999) *The Contributions of Older People to Development: The Ghana Study.* HelpAge International, London.

Akinyemi, I.A., Adepoju, O.A., and Ogunbameru, A.O. (2007) 'Changing philosophy for care and support for the elderly in South-Western Nigeria', *BOLD,* 18(1): 18–23.

Apt, N.A. (1987) *Aging, Health, and Family Relations: A Study of Aging in the Central Region of Ghana.* Legon: University of Ghana.

Apt, N.A. (1992) 'Family support to elderly people in Ghana', in H.L. Kendig, L.C. Coppard, and A. Hashimoto (eds), *Family Support to the Elderly: The International Experience.* Oxford: Oxford University Press, pp. 203–12.

Apt, N.A. (1996a) *Coping With Old Age in a Changing Africa.* Aldershot, UK: Avebury.

Apt, N.A. (1996b) *Ageing in Ghana: Review Studies.* Legon: Centre for Social Policy Studies, University of Ghana.

Apt, N.A. (2005) '30 years of African research on ageing: history, achievements and challenges for the future', *Generations Review,* 15(2): 4–6.

Apt, N., Koomson, J., Williams, N., and Grieco, M. (1995) 'Family finance and doorstep trading: social and economic wellbeing of elderly Ghanaian female traders', *Southern African Journal of Gerontology,* 4: 17–24.

Assie-Lumumba, N. (2006) 'Higher education in Africa: crisis, reforms and transformation', CODESRIA Working Paper Series, CODESRIA, Dakar: Senegal.

Baars, J., Dannefer, D., Phillipson, C., and Walker, A. (2006) 'Introduction: critical perspectives in social gerontology', in J. Baars, D. Dannefer, C. Phillipson, and A. Walker (eds), *Aging, Globalization and Inequality: The New Critical Gerontology.* Amityville, NY: Baywood, pp. 1–14.

Baiyewu, O., Bella, A.F., Adeyemi, J.D., Bamgboye, E.A., and Jegede, R.O. (1997) 'Health problems and socio-demographic findings in elderly Nigerians', *African Journal of Medical Science,* 26: 13–17.

Barrientos, A. (2002) 'Old age, poverty and social investment', *Journal of International Development,* 14: 1133–41.

Bengtson, V.L., Putney, N.M., and Johnson, M.L. (2005) 'The problem of theory in gerontology today', in M.L. Johnson (ed.), *The Cambridge Handbook of Age and Ageing.* Cambridge: Cambridge University Press, pp. 3–20.

Binney, E.A., Estes, C.L., and Humphers, S.E. (1993) 'Informalization and community care', in C.L. Estes, J.H. Swan, and Associates (eds), *The Long Term Crisis: Elders Trapped Into the No Care Zone.* Newbury Park, CA: SAGE, pp. 155–70.

Bowling, A. and Gabriel, Z. (2007) 'Lay theories of quality of life in older age', *Ageing and Society,* 27: 827–48.

Bramucci, G. and Erb, S. (2007) 'An invisible population: displaced older people in West Darfur', *Global Ageing,* 4(3): 23–34.

Brown, C.K. (1985) 'Research findings in Ghana: a survey on the elderly in the Accra Region', *African Gerontology,* 4: 11–37.

Burgess, E.W. (ed.) (1960) *Ageing in Western Societies.* Chicago: University of Chicago Press.

Campbell, C. (1994) 'Intergenerational conflicts in township families: transforming notions of respect and changing power relations', *Southern African Journal of Gerontology,* 3: 37–42.

Cattell, M. (1997) 'The discourse of neglect: family support for elderly in Samia', in T.S. Weisner, C. Bradley, and P.L. Kilbride (eds), *African Families and the Crisis of Social Change.* Westport, CT: Bergin and Garvey, pp. 157–83.

Charlton, R. and McKinnon, R. (2001) *Pensions in Development.* Aldershot, UK: Ashgate.

Chepngeno, G. and Ezeh, A. (2007) '"Between a rock and a hard place": perception of older people living in Nairobi City on return-migration to rural areas', *Global Ageing,* 4(3): 67–78.

Clark, D. (2006) 'Capability approach', in D. Clark (ed.), *The Elgar Companion to Development Studies.* Cheltenham, UK: Edward Elgar, pp. 32–45.

Clausen, T., Romoren, T.I., Ferreira, M., and Kristensen, P. (2005) 'Chronic diseases and health inequalities in older persons in Botswana', *Journal of Nutrition, Health and Ageing,* 9: 455–61.

Cliggett, L. (2001) 'Survival strategies of the elderly in Gwembe Valley, Zambia: gender, residence and kin networks', *Journal of Cross Cultural Gerontology,* 16: 309–32.

Cohen, B. and Menken, J. (2006) 'Report', in B. Cohen and J. Menken (eds), *Aging in Sub-Saharan Africa: Recommendations for Furthering Research.* Washington, DC: The National Academies Press, pp. 7–45.

Commission for Africa (CfA) (2005) *Our Common Interest: Report of the Commission for Africa.* London: Commission for Africa Secretariat.

Cowgill, D.O. (1974) 'Aging and modernization: a revision of the theory', in J.F. Gubrium (ed.), *Late Life.* Springfield, IL: Thomas, pp. 123–45.

Crystal, S. (2006) 'Dynamics of late-life inequality: modeling the interplay of health disparities, economic resources and public policies', in J. Baars, D. Dannefer, C. Phillipson, and A. Walker (eds), *Aging, Globalization and Inequality: The New Critical Gerontology.* Amityville, NY: Baywood, pp. 205–14.

Dannefer, D. (2003) 'Cumulative advantage/disadvantage and the life course: cross-fertilizing age and social science theory', *Journal of Gerontology,* 58B: S327–37.

DeLehr, E.C. (1992) 'Aging and family support in Mexico', in H.L. Kendig, L.C. Coppard, and A. Hashimoto (eds), *Family Support to the Elderly: The International Experience.* Oxford: Oxford University Press, pp: 215–23.

Devisch, R., Makoni, S., and Stroeken, K. (2002) 'Epilogue: African gerontology: critical models, future directions', in S. Makoni and K. Stroeken (eds), *Ageing in Africa: Sociolinguistic and Anthropological Approaches.* Aldershot, UK: Ashgate, pp. 277–84.

Dorjahn, V.R. (1989) 'Where do the old folks live? The residence of the elderly among the Temne of Sierra Leone', *Journal of Cross-Cultural Gerontology,* 4: 257–78.

Ekpenyong, S., Oyeneye, O., and Peil, M. (1987) 'Health problems of elderly Nigerians', *Social Science Medicine,* 24: 885–8.

Elder, G.H.J, Jr (1992) 'Models of the lifecourse', *Contemporary Sociology: A Journal of Reviews,* 21: 632–5.

Everatt, D. and Orkin, M. (1994) 'Families should stay together: intergenerational attitudes among South African youth', *Southern African Journal of Gerontology,* 3: 43–8.

Ezeh, A., Chepngeno, G., Kasiira, A.Z., and Woubalem, Z. (2006) 'The situation of older people in poor urban settings: the case of Nairobi', in B. Cohen and J. Menken (eds), *Aging in Sub-Saharan Africa: Recommendations for Furthering Research.* Washington, DC: The National Academies Press, pp. 189–213.

Fennell, G., Phillipson, C., and Evers, H. (1988) *The Sociology of Old Age.* Milton Keynes: Open University Press.

Ferge, S. (1997) 'A Central European perspective on the social quality of Europe', in W. Beck, L. van der Maesen, and A. Walker (eds), *The Social Quality of Europe.* The Hague: Kluwer.

Ferraro, K. and Shippee, T.P. (2007) 'Aging and cumulative inequality: how does inequality get under the skin?', paper submitted to the GSA Social Gerontology Award sponsored by UMBC, Theoretical Developments in Social Gerontology.

Ferreira, M. (1999) 'Building and advancing African gerontology', *Southern African Journal of Gerontology,* 8: 1–3.

Ferreira, M. (2005) 'Research on ageing in Africa: What do we have, not have and should we have?', *Generations Review,* 15: 32–5.

Ferreira, M. (2006a) 'The differential impacts of social pension income on poverty alleviation in three South African ethnic groups', *Ageing and Society,* 26: 337–54.

Ferreira, M. (2006b) 'HIV/AIDS and older people in sub-Saharan Africa: towards a policy framework', *Global Ageing,* 4(2): 56–71.

Ferreira, M. (2008) 'Ageing policies in Africa', in United Nations Department of Economic and Social Affairs (UN/DESA), *Regional Dimensions of the Ageing Situation.* New York: United Nations, pp. 70–92.

Ferreira, M., Møller, V., Prinsloo, F.R., and Gillis, L.S. (1992) *Multidimensional Survey of Elderly South Africans 1990– 1991: Key Findings.* Cape Town: HSRC/UCT, Centre for Gerontology.

Foner, N. (1993) 'When the contract fails: care for the elderly in nonindustrial cultures', in V.L. Bengtson and W.A. Achenbaum (eds), *The Changing Contract Across Generations.* New York: Aldine de Gruyter, pp. 101–17.

Fry, C.L. (1999) 'Anthropological theories of age and ageing', in V.L. Bengtson and K.W. Schaie (eds), *Handbook of Theories on Aging.* New York: Springer, pp. 271–86.

Glascock, A.P. and Feinman, S.L. (1981) 'Social asset or social burden: treatment of the aged in non-industrial societies', in C. Fry (ed.), *Dimensions: Aging, Culture and Health.* South Hadley, MA: Bergin and Garvey, pp. 13–21.

Giddens, A. (1991) *Modernity and Self Identity.* Oxford: Polity Press.

Goldstein, M.C., Schuler, S., and Ross, J.L. (1983) 'Social and economic forces affecting intergenerational relations in a third world country: a cautionary tale from South Asia', *Journal of Gerontology,* 38: 716–24.

Goode, W.J. (1963) *World Revolution in Family Patterns.* New York: Free Press.

Gorman, M. and Heslop, M. (2002) 'Poverty, policy, reciprocity and older people in the south', *Journal of International Development,* 14: 1143–51.

Guba, E.G. and Lincoln, Y.S. (1994) 'Competing paradigms in Qualitative Research', in N.K. Denzin and Y.S. Lincoln (eds), *Handbook of Qualitative Research.* Thousand Oaks, CA: SAGE, pp. 105–17.

Gureje, O., Kola, L., and Afolabi, E. (2007) 'Epidemiology of major depressive disorder in elderly Nigerians in the Ibadan Study of Ageing: a community-based survey', *Lancet,* 370(9591): 957–64.

Gureje, O., Ogunniyi, A., Kola, L., and Afolabi, E. (2006) 'Functional disability in elderly Nigerians: results from the Ibadan Study of Ageing', *Journal of the American Geriatrics Society,* 54: 1784–9.

Hagestad, G and Dannefer, D. (2001) Concepts and Theories of Aging: Beyond Microfication in Social Science Approaches' in R. Binstock and L. George (eds) *Handbook of Aging and the Social Sciences* 5th ed. San Diego: Academic Press, pp 3–21.

HelpAge International (HAI) (2002a) *Participatory Research with Older People: A Sourcebook.* London: HelpAge International.

HelpAge International (HAI) (2002b) *State of the World's Older People 2002.* London: HelpAge International.

HelpAge International (HAI) (2004) *Age and Security: How Social Pensions Can Deliver Effective Aid to Poor Older People and Their Families.* London: HelpAge International.

HelpAge International (HAI) (2006) *Why Social Pensions Are Needed Now.* London: HelpAge International.

HelpAge International (HAI) (2007) *Social Cash Transfers for Africa. A Transformative Agenda for the 21st Century.* London: HelpAge International.

Hendrie, H.C., Ogunniyi, A., Hall, K.S., et al. (2001) 'Incidence of dementia and AD in two communities: Yoruba residing in Ibadan, Nigeria, and African Americans residing in Indianapolis, USA', *JAMA,* 285: 739–47.

Heslop, M. and Gorman, M. (2000) 'chronic poverty and older people in the developing world', IDPM, Manchester (mimeo).

Institute for Development Policy and Management /HelpAge International (IDPM/HAI) (2003) *Non-Contributory Pensions and Poverty Prevention: A Comparative Study of South Africa and Brazil.* London: HelpAge International.

Jolly, R. (2003) 'Human development and neo-liberalism: paradigms compared', in S. Fukuda-Parr and A.K. Shiva Kumar (eds), *Readings in Human Development.* Oxford, MA: Oxford University Press, pp. 82–92.

Kahn, S., Tollman, S., Thorogood, M., et al. (2006) 'Older adults and the health transition in Agincourt, Rural South Africa: new understanding, growing complexity', in B. Cohen and J. Menken (eds), *Aging in Sub-Saharan Africa: Recommendations for Furthering Research.* Washington, DC: The National Academies Press, pp. 166–88.

Kakwani, N. and Subbarao, K. (2005) 'Ageing and poverty in Africa and the role of social pensions', UNDP International Poverty Centre, Working Paper No. 8, UNDP, New York.

Keith, J., Fry, C.L., Glascock, A.P., et al. (1994) *The Aging Experience: Diversity and Commonality Across Cultures.* Thousand Oaks, CA: SAGE.

King, N. and Calasanti, T. (2006) 'Empowering the old: critical gerontology and anti-aging in a global context', in J. Baars, D. Dannefer, C. Phillipson, and A. Walker (eds), *Aging, Globalization and Inequality: The New Critical Gerontology.* Amityville, NY: Baywood, pp. 139–57.

Kreager, P. (2006) 'Migration, social structure and old age support networks: a comparison of three Indonesian communities', *Ageing and Society* 26: 37–60.

Kuate-Defo, B. (2006) 'Interactions between socioeconomic status and living arrangements in predicting gender-specific health status among the elderly in Cameroon', in B. Cohen and J. Menken (eds), *Aging in Sub-Saharan Africa: Recommendations for Furthering Research.* Washington, DC: The National Academies Press, pp. 276–313.

Kuepie, M. (2007) 'The socioeconomic implications of ageing in Africa: labour market participation and alternative sources of income', paper presented at the International Conference *'Population Ageing. Towards an Improvement of the Quality of Life?'*, Brussels, March 1, 2007.

Kuhn, R., Rahman, O., and Menken, J. (2006) 'Survey measures of health: how well do self-reported and observed indicators measure health and predict mortality', in B. Cohen and J. Menken (eds), *Aging in Sub-Saharan Africa: Recommendations for Furthering Research.* Washington, DC: The National Academies Press, pp. 314–42.

Makoni, S. and Stroeken, K. (2002) *Ageing in Africa: Sociolinguistic and Anthropological Approaches.* Aldershot, UK: Ashgate.

Marmot, M. (2006) 'Introduction', in M. Marmot and R.G. Wilkinson (eds), *Social Determinants of Health.* Oxford: Oxford University Press, pp. 1–5.

Marshall, V.W. (1990) 'WHO health policy and United Nations aging policy: an analysis', paper presented at International Sociological Association Meetings, XII, World Congress of Sociology, Madrid, Spain.

Mba, C.J. (2004) 'Population ageing and survival challenges in rural Ghana', *Journal of Social Development in Africa,* 19(2): 90–112.

Mba, C.J. (2005) 'Racial Differences in Marital Status and Living Arrangements of Older Persons in South Africa' *Generations Review,* 15(2) 23–31.

Mba, C.J. (2007) 'Population ageing in Ghana and correlates of support availability', *Gerontechnology,* 6(2): 102–11.

McIntyre, D. (2004) 'Health policy and older people in Africa', in P. Lloyd-Sherlock (ed.), *Living Longer: Ageing, Development and Social Protection.* London and New York: Zed Books, pp. 160–83.

Mohatle, T. and de Graft Agyarko, R. (1999) *The Contributions of Older People to Development: The South African Study.* London: HelpAge International.

Mollenkopf, H. and Walker, A. (2007) 'Quality of life in old age: synthesis and future perspectives', in H. Mollenkopf and A. Walker (eds), *Quality of Life in Old Age: International and Multidisciplinary Perspectives.* Dordrecht: Springer, pp. 235–52.

Møller, V. (1994) 'Intergenerational relations in a society in transition: a South African case study', *Ageing and Society,* 14: 155–89.

Møller, V. and Sotshongaye, A. (1996) 'My family eat this money too: pension sharing and self-respect among Zulu grandmothers', *Southern African Journal of Gerontology,* 5: 9–19.

Moody, H.R. (1988) 'Toward a critical gerontology: the contribution of the humanities to theories of aging', in J.E. Birren and V.L. Bengtson (eds), *Emergent Theories of Aging.* New York: Springer, pp. 19–40.

Nahemov, N. and Adams, B. (1974) 'Old age among the Baganda: continuity and change', in J.F. Gubrium (ed.), *Later Life Communities and Environmental Policy.* Springfield, IL: Charles C. Thomas.

Neysmith, S. and Edwardh, J. (1983) 'Ideological underpinnings of the World Assembly on Aging', *The Canadian Journal on Aging,* 2: 125–36.

Nigeria Population Commission (NPC) (2004) *The Elderly: Nigeria Population Census Analysis.* Abuja, Nigeria: NPC.

Nilsson, J., Grafstroem, M, Zaman, S., and Kabir, Z.N. (2005) 'Role and function: aspects of quality of life of older people in Bangladesh', *Journal of Aging Studies,* 19: 363–74.

Nxusani, N.C. (2004) 'Late-life migration and adjustment of older persons. Between the Eastern and the Western Cape', in M. Ferreira and E. van Dongen (eds), *Untold Stories: Giving Voice to the Lives of Older Persons in New South African Society: An Anthology.* Cape Town: The Albertina and Walter Sisulu Institute of Ageing in Africa, University of Cape Town.

Nyanguru, A.C. and Peil, M. (1993) 'Housing and the elderly in Zimbabwe', *Southern African Journal of Gerontology,* 2: 3–9.

Nyanguru, A.C., Hampson, J., Adamchak, D.J., and Wilson, A.O. (1994) 'Family support to the elderly in Zimbabwe', *Southern African Journal of Gerontology,* 3: 22–6.

Ohuche, N.M. and Littrell, J.M. (1989) 'Igbo students' attitudes towards supporting aged parents', *International Journal on Aging and Human Development,* 29: 259–67.

O'Rand, A.M. (1990) 'Stratification and the life course', in R.H. Binstock and L.K. George (eds), *Handbook of Aging and the Social Sciences,* 3rd edn. San Diego: Academic Press, pp. 130–48.

O'Rand, A. (2003) 'Cumulative advantage theory in life course research', *Annual Review of Gerontology and Geriatrics: Focus on Economic Outcomes in Later life,* 22: 14–30.

Palmore, E. and Manton, K (1974) 'Modernization and status of the aged: international correlations', *Journal of Gerontology,* 29: 205–10.

Peil, M., Bamisaiye, A., and Ekpenyong, S. (1989) 'Health and physical support for the elderly in Nigeria', *Journal of Cross-Cultural Gerontology,* 4: 89–106.

Phillipson, C. (1982) *Capitalism and the Construction of Old Age.* London: Macmillan.

Phillipson, C. (1998) *Reconstructing Old Age: New Agenda in Social Theory and Practice.* London: SAGE.

Phillipson, C. (2002) 'Globalization and the Future of Ageing: Economic, Social and Policy Implications' Keynote Paper presented at the Valencia Forum, 3 April 2002.

Phillipson, C. (2006) 'Aging and globalization: issues for critical gerontology and political economy', in J. Baars, D. Dannefer, C. Phillipson, and A. Walker (eds), *Aging, Globalization and Inequality*. Amityville, NY: Baywood, pp. 43–58.

Povlika, L. and Longino, C.L. (2006) 'The emerging postmodern culture of aging and retirement security', in J. Baars, D. Dannefer, C. Phillipson, and A. Walker (eds), *Aging, Globalization and Inequality: The New Critical Gerontology*. Amityville, NY: Baywood, pp. 183–204.

Qureshi, H. and Walker, A. (1989) *The Caring Relationship: Elderly People and Their Families*. Basingstoke: Macmillan.

Riley, M.W. and Riley, J.W., Jr. (1994) 'Structural lag', in M.W. Riley, R.L. Kahn, and A. Foner (eds), *Age and Structural Lag*. New York: Wiley, pp. 15–36.

Riley, M.W., Foner, A., and Waring, J. (1988) 'Sociology of age', in N. Smelser (ed.), *Handbook of Sociology*. Beverly Hills, CA: SAGE.

Robine, J.-M. and Michel, J-P. (2004) 'Looking forward to a general theory on population aging', *Journal of Gerontology: Medical Sciences*, 59A(6): 590–7.

Rostow, W.W. (1960) *The Stages of Economic Growth*. Cambridge: Cambridge University Press.

Ryff, C. and Marshall, V.W. (eds) (1999) *The Self and Society in Aging Processes*. New York: Springer.

Sagner, A. and Mtati, R.Z. (1999) 'Politics of pension sharing in South Africa', *Ageing and Society*, 19: 393–416.

Sangree, W. H. (1992) 'Grandparenthood and modernisation: the changing status of male and female elders in Tiriki, Kenya and Irigwe, Nigeria', *Journal of Cross-Cultural Gerontology*, 7: 331–61.

Scharf, T. and Smith, A.E. (2003) 'Older people in urban neighbourhoods: addressing the risk of social exclusion in later life', in C. Phillipson, G. Allan, and D. Morgan (eds), *Social Networks and Social Exclusion*. Aldershot, Ashgate, UK, pp. 162–79.

Sen, A.K. (1993) 'Capability and well-being', in M.C. Nussbaum, and A.K. Sen, (eds), *The Quality of Life*. Oxford: Clarendon Press, pp. 30–53.

Shapiro, E. and Kaufert, J. (1983) 'The role of international conferences – a theoretical framework', *Canadian Journal on Aging*, 2: 43–9.

Shelton, A. (1972) 'The aged and eldership among the Igbo', in D. Cowgill, and L. Holmes (eds), *Aging and Modernization*. New York: Appleton-Century-Crofts, pp. 31–50.

Sidorenko, S. and Walker, A. (2004) 'The Madrid International Plan of Action on Ageing: from conception to implementation', *Ageing and Society*, 24: 147–66.

Simmons, L.W. (1945) *The Role of the Aged in Primitive Society*. New Haven, CT: Yale University Press.

Temple, L. (2007) 'Intergenerational approaches. Promoting solidarity', *Ageways*, 69. London: HelpAge International.

Togonu-Bickersteth, F. (1989) 'Conflicts over caregiving: discussion of filial obligation among adult Nigerian children', *Journal of Cross-Cultural Gerontology*, 4: 35–48.

Togonu-Bickersteth, F. and Akinnawo, E.O. (1990) 'Filial responsibility expectations of Nigerian and Indian university studentss', *Journal of Cross-Cultural Gerontology*, 5: 315–32.

UNAIDS (2008) *Report on the Global AIDS Epidemic:* Joint United Nations Programme on HIV/AIDS (UNAIDS). Geneva: UNAIDS.

United Nations (1982) *Report of the World Assembly on Aging, Vienna, 26 July to 6 August*. United Nations, New York.

United Nations (Division for Social Policy and Development) (1999) 'Fourth Review and Appraisal of the Implementation of the International Plan of Action on Ageing: Summary of Findings'. http://www.un.org/esa/socdev/age4ra01.htm

United Nations (2000) *Millennium Declaration*. A/RES/55/2 . September, 18, New York: UN.

United Nations (2002) *Report of the Second World Assembly on Ageing*. New York: UN.

United Nations Development Programme (UNDP) (2009) *Human Development Report 2009. Fighting Climate Change: Human Solidarity in a Divided World*. New York: Palgrave Macmillan for UNDP.

United Nations HABITAT (UN HABITAT) (2008) *State of the World's Cities 2008/2009: Harmonious Cities*. Nairobi, Kenya: UN HABITAT.

United Nations Population Division (UNPD) (2005) *Living Arrangements of Older Persons Around the World*. New York: UNPD.

United Nations Population Division (UNPD) (2006) *Population Ageing 2006 Chart*. New York: UNPD.

United Nations Population Division (UNPD) (2007) *World Population Ageing 2007*. New York: United Nations. www.un.org/esa/population/publications/WPA2007/ES-English.pdf. Accessed January 28, 2008.

United Nations Population Division (UNPD) (2008a) *World Population Prospects: The 2006 Revision*. New York: UNPD. http://esa.un.org/unpp/

United Nations Population Division (UNPD) (2008b) *World Urbanization Prospects: The 2007 Revision*. New York: UNPD. http://esa.un.org/unupindex.asp

van der Geest, S. (1997a) 'Between respect and reciprocity: managing old age in rural Ghana', *Southern African Journal of Gerontology*, 6: 20–5.

van der Geest, S. (1997b) 'Money and respect: the changing value of old age in rural Ghana', *Africa*, 67(4): 534–59.

van der Geest, S. (2002) 'Respect and reciprocity: care of elderly people in rural Ghana', *Journal of Cross-Cultural Gerontology*, 17: 3–31.

van der Geest, S. (2004) '"They don't come to listen": the experience of loneliness among older people in Kwahu, Ghana', *Journal of Cross-Cultural Gerontology*, 19(2): 77–96.

van der Geest, S. (2007) 'Complaining and Not Complaining: Social Strategies of Older People in Kwahu, Ghana', *Global Ageing*, 4(3) 55–66.

Walker, A. (1981) 'Towards a political economy of old age', *Ageing and Society*, 1: 73–94.

Walker, A. (1983) 'Care for elderly people: a conflict between women and the state', in J. Finch and D. Groves (eds),

A Labour of Love: Women, Work and Caring. London: Routledge and Kegan Paul, pp. 106–28.

Walker, A. (1990) 'The Economic "Burden" of Aging and the Prospect of Intergenerational Conflict" *Ageing and Society* 10(4): 377–396.

Walker, A. (2006) 'Reexamining the political economy of ageing: understanding the structure/agency tension', in J. Baars, D. Dannefer, C. Phillipson, and A. Walker (eds), *Aging, Globalization and Inequality: The New Critical Gerontology*. Amityville, NY: Baywood, pp. 59–80.

Walker, A. and Deacon, B. (2003) 'Economic globalization and policies on aging', *Journal of Societal and Social Policy*, 2(2): 1–18.

World Bank (1994) *Averting the Old Age Crisis*. Washington, DC: World Bank.

World Bank (2002) *Constructing Knowledge Societies: New Challenges for Tertiary Education*. Washington, DC: World Bank.

World Bank (2006) *World Development Report 2007: Development and the Next Generation*. Washington, DC: World Bank.

World Bank (2010) 'Country classification'. http://go.worldbank.org/K2CKM78CC0

World Health Organization (WHO) (2002) *Active Ageing: A Policy Framework*. Geneva: WHO.

World Health Organization (WHO) (2006) *The Health of the People: The African Regional Health Report*. Brazzaville: WHO Regional Office for Africa.

World Health Organization (WHO) (2008) *The WHO Multicountry Study on Global Ageing and Adult Health*. http://www.who.int/healthinfo/systems/sage/en/index.html

Zimmer, Z. (2007) 'HIV/AIDS and the living arrangements of older persons across the sub-Saharan African region', Institute of Public and International Affairs (IPIA) Working Paper 2007–11–21, IPIA, University of Utah. www.ipia.utah.edu/workingpapers.html

Zimmer, Z. and Dayton, J. (2005) 'Older adults in sub-Saharan Africa living with children and grandchildren', *Population Studies*, 59: 295–312.

32

Population Ageing and Old-age Insurance in China

Zeng Yi and Linda K. George

INTRODUCTION

Fertility in China has declined dramatically from more than six children per woman in the 1950s and 1960s to about 1.7 children per woman today, which is about 15 per cent lower than that in the United States. Average life expectancy at birth for both sexes combined in China has increased from about 41 years in 1950 to 68.4 years in 1990, 71 years in 2000 (UN, 2005), and 73 years in 2005, and will continue to increase. In the next 20–30 years, the large cohorts of baby boomers, those born in the 1950s and 1960s, will enter old age. Thus, the population of China, the most populous country in the world with more than 1.3 billion people, is ageing at an extraordinarily rapid speed and on a large scale.

This chapter on population ageing and old-age insurance in China is organized into four sections. The first section describes the major socioeconomic characteristics of the Chinese older population and old-age care today. The second section presents and discusses forecasts of trends of population ageing in China in the first half of the 21st century. The third section focuses on the serious challenges and related policy recommendations concerning the old-age insurance programme in rural China, where ageing problems will be much more serious than in the urban areas. The last section concludes the essay with some remarks.

THE MAJOR SOCIOECONOMIC CHARACTERISTICS OF THE OLDER POPULATION AND OLD-AGE CARE IN CHINA

The data resources used in this section are the most recent Chinese census, conducted in 2000, and the Chinese Longitudinal Healthy Longevity Survey (CLHLS). The CLHLS survey areas include 22 provinces, sharing 85 per cent of the total population in China. Using the comprehensive and internationally comparative questionnaires for healthy ageing studies, the CLHLS has conducted face-to-face interviews with approximately 71,100 older persons in five waves of data collection (1998, 2000, 2002, 2005, and 2008–09). Of these, 13,953 respondents were centenarians, 18,281 were nonagenarians, 20,732 were octogenarians, 14,636 were younger elders aged 65–79, and 3490 were middle-aged controls aged 40–64. At each wave, the survivors were re-interviewed, while the deceased and those lost to follow-up were replaced by additional participants. Data on mortality and health status before dying for the 18,300 participants (age range 65–112) who died between waves were collected in interviews with a close family member of the deceased (see Zeng et al., 2002, for details).[1] For the purpose of the chapter, we employ only a small portion of the available data from the recent wave of the Chinese Longitudinal Healthy Longevity Survey conducted in 2005.

Living arrangements and family support

Based on the 2000 census data, more than a third (37 per cent) of Chinese men and two thirds (67 per cent) of women aged 65+ are widowed. The proportion of the population not living with a spouse increases dramatically with age due to high rates of widowhood at advanced ages; the divorce rate among older persons in China is very low. Many more older women than men are widowed because of the gender differential in mortality at older ages. The proportion of older men and women living alone was 8 and 10 per cent, respectively, in 2000. Note that older women are more likely to be widowed and thus to live alone. At the same time, older women are also more economically dependent. Therefore, the disadvantages of women in terms of marital status and living arrangements are substantially more serious than those of men at old ages (Zeng and George, 2000). A majority of both older men (60 per cent) and older women (69 per cent) live with children or grandchildren. Among the older men and women who live with offspring, a majority live with both children and grandchildren. Multi-generational households are one of the main living arrangements for Chinese older persons (Zeng and Wang, 2003).

In the cultural context of Chinese society, attitudes about supporting older parents are quite different from those in modern Western societies. Filial piety (*xiao*) has been a cornerstone of Chinese society for thousands of years and is still highly valued. The philosophical ideas of filial piety include not only respect for older generations but also the responsibility of children to take care of their old parents, which is stated clearly in the Chinese constitution and law protecting the rights of older persons. Our research has shown that, as compared to their urban counterparts, rural elders are significantly more likely to be widowed and rely on their children (Zeng and Wang, 2003). However, rapid population ageing and increased migration of young people induced by economic growth have jeopardized the family's ability to serve as a resource to its older members, especially in rural areas. Rural elders will be more likely to live separately from their children who have migrated to the urban areas and even to provide supervisory care for juvenile grandchildren. Thus, rapid economic development and urbanization have weakened the effects of filial piety, a key precondition for altruistic family support in Chinese families, as younger adults pay more attention to their career development and nuclear family members (Zhang, 2004). Additionally, the rural baby boomers, who were born in the 1950s and 1960s and will be advancing in age in the next few decades, are subjected to China's restrictive fertility policy and thus are likely to have two children or only one child. Furthermore, when they reach oldest-old age (80+) after 2035 or so, their children will also be ageing and many may also have left their home villages. Obviously, it will become increasingly impossible for the Chinese elders to rely entirely on their children and family for old-age support, especially for the oldest old and those living in rural areas. In the 'Future trends ...' section below we present projections of the living arrangements of older persons in rural and urban areas of China for the next few decades to quantitatively demonstrate those trends.

Economic status and care dependency

It is well known that income data collected in surveys are often unreliable because some people are unwilling to reveal their incomes. For this reason, we will mainly use self-reported economic status other than income per se. These data are from the most recent wave of the CLHLS collected in 2005.

About 71 per cent of the young old (aged 65–79) and 74 per cent of the oldest old (aged 80+) in rural areas reported that their financial support was sufficient to meet their daily needs. The corresponding figures for the urban young old and oldest old were 82 and 83 per cent, respectively. About 94 per cent of the young old and 92 per cent of the oldest old in rural areas had a separate bedroom of their own (or shared with their spouses), in contrast to 91 and 87 per cent for the urban older persons. The economic status of older persons in rural areas is substantially worse than that of their urban counterparts although more elders in rural areas had their own bedrooms, primarily due to much less expensive cheaper housing.

Figure 32.1 shows that the percentage of Chinese women who receive pensions is much lower than that for their male counterparts, although the proportion of older people receiving pensions is low for both sexes, especially those in rural areas (see 'old age insurance...' section below). The majority of Chinese elders rely mainly on their children for financial support. As noted earlier, women are more financially disadvantaged than men, and rely on their children more than men (Figure 32.2). The gender differentials in primary source of financial support are enormous; government at all levels, and Chinese society more broadly, needs to pay serious attention to the enormous gender differentials in pension support for older persons. Note that the Figures 32.1 and 32.2, which are based on the cross-sectional data, show the age-related decline in pension support and the age-related increase in primary financial support

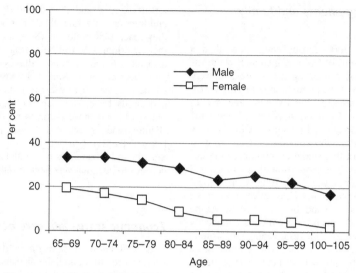

Figure 32.1   Percentage of men and women receiving a pension among the Chinese elderly, 2005.
Source: CLHLS 2005 wave dataset

from children. Such an age pattern, at least in part, reflects the cohort effects: compared to the oldest-old cohorts, the younger-old cohorts have relatively more pension support and rely less on financial support from children.

More than a quarter of young-old (27 per cent) and more than half of oldest-old (52 per cent) men reported that, during periods of sickness, their primary caregivers were their children or grandchildren. The corresponding figures for young-old and oldest-old women were 53 per cent and 74 per cent, respectively. Clearly, Chinese women rely more on children as caregivers than do men (Figure 32.3). Again, this is consistent with the fact that a much higher proportion of women than men are widowed.

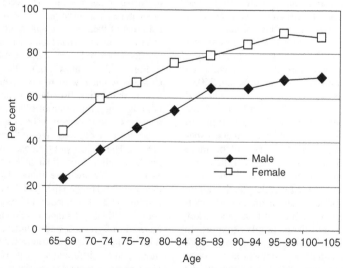

Figure 32.2   Percentage of elderly men and women whose primary financial support is from children, 2005.
Source: CLHLS 2005 wave dataset

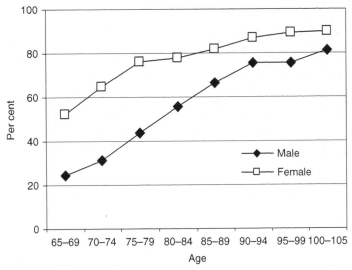

Figure 32.3   Percentage of elderly whose primary caregivers are children, 2005
Source: CLHLS 2005 wave dataset

Access to health services and long-term care

Based on the CLHLS survey conducted in 2005, about 94 per cent of the young old and 93 per cent of the oldest old in the urban areas reported that they could access adequate medical services when they were sick; the corresponding figures in rural areas are 89 per cent and 86 per cent, respectively. Note that the term 'medical service' used in the survey includes traditional Chinese medicine provided by local persons (who have either gained training or are self-taught), which is cheap and widely available even in poor and remote areas. Thus, we should not interpret the survey figures as indications of access to modern, high-quality health service facilities in China today.

In terms of financing health care, 28 per cent of the young old and 22 per cent of the oldest old in urban areas reported that most of their medical expenses were paid for by the government, collective enterprises, or health insurance in 2005. However, comparable figures were only 4.2 and 4.3 per cent for the elderly in rural areas. Over the past 2 years, the Chinese government has devoted tremendous effort and funds to increase medical care coverage by health insurance, especially the government-managed 'Cooperative Medicine System (CMS)' in rural areas. Thus, the percentage of the rural elders whose medical expenses are mainly paid by the government or collective enterprises or CMS in 2008 is expected to increase, although we have no data to confirm it yet.

Census data show that the proportions of females and males aged 65+ who lived in collective households (mostly nursing homes) in urban areas in 2000 were about 5 and 3 per cent, respectively. The corresponding figures for rural older men and women were 2 and 1 per cent, respectively. Given the extremely limited availability of long-term care facilities and the fact that a large majority of the older persons live with their children, especially those in rural areas, the major cause of institutionalization of older persons in China was childlessness (or absence of children). (See Chapter 43.)

FUTURE TRENDS OF POPULATION AGEING IN CHINA IN THE FIRST HALF OF THE 21ST CENTURY

Applying the most recent census and survey data (mainly collected around 2000) and analytical tools (Zeng et al., 2006), in this section we present future trends of Chinese population ageing and family structure for 2000–50. These projections have two unique features as compared to previous demographic projection studies concerning the future population in China. First, we simultaneously project the trends of population age/sex distributions and project family households, including living arrangements of older people. This is useful because the circumstances of families and households, including older persons, have major policy implications for population ageing, care needs, and provision. Secondly, we provide the projections for both rural and urban populations, taking into account the large rural–urban differentials in the demographic regimes, as well as the massive migration from rural to urban areas resulting from economic and social development.

Based on our analysis of the urbanization process since 1982, we assume that the proportion of the population that is urban residents will grow from 36 per cent in 2000 to 75 per cent in 2050. We also assume that the age distribution of the rural–urban migrants will be the same as that observed in the 2000 census. Details of our estimates and assumptions about the most likely current and future medium mortality and medium fertility levels in China are presented in Tables 32.1 and 32.2.

Fastest increase in proportion and huge number of older persons

Under the likely scenarios of medium fertility and mortality, the Chinese population will continue to increase from 1.27 billion in 2000 to a likely peak of 1.48 billion in 2038, and then gradually decline to 1.46 billion in 2050. The very large size of the older population is a unique characteristic of population ageing in China. In 2000, there were 87 million persons age 65 and older. By the years 2030 and 2050, there will be 238 million and 338 million older people in China, respectively.

Although the proportion of persons aged 65+ in China is not currently large (6.9 per cent in 2000), the speed of population ageing will be extremely fast in the first half of the 21st century. Under the

medium fertility and medium mortality assumptions, Chinese aged 65 and older will account for about 16.4 and 23.9 per cent of the total population by 2030 and 2050, respectively (see also UN, 2005).

In European societies, the population ageing transition has taken place over a century or more. In China, however, this change will take place within a few decades. As a result, China will reach more or less the same level of population ageing as in most developed countries by the middle of this century. Indeed, the proportion of older persons in China will increase much faster than in almost all other countries in the world. According to the UN population projections (UN, 2005), it will take about 20 years (from 2016 to 2036) for the proportion of the population aged 65+ to increase from 10 to 20 per cent of the total population in China, compared to 22 years in Japan (1984–2006), 59 years in Germany (1951–2010), 67 years in Sweden (1947–2014), and 66 years in the United States (1971–2037). The ageing process of the Chinese population will be even faster than that of Japan, which is regarded as a country with a very rapid rate of population ageing (Ogawa, 1988).

Even more rapid increase of oldest-old persons aged 80 and older

There were about 12 million Chinese oldest old (aged 80 and older) in 2000, but the number of oldest old will climb rapidly to about 27, 65, and 107 million in the years 2020, 2040, and 2050, respectively. The average annual increase in the proportion of the oldest old between 2000 and 2050 will be about 4.5 per cent. Between 2000 and 2040, the proportion of the oldest old among

Table 32.1 Life expectancies at birth under the medium mortality assumption

	Rural			Urban		
	2000	2020	2050	2000	2020	2050
Men	68.0	70.8	75.0	72.0	74.6	78.6
Women	72.0	74.8	78.9	76.0	78.6	82.5

Source: Zeng et al. (2008): Appendix C

Table 32.2 Rural and urban period total fertility rate (TFR), and weighted average period TFR of rural and urban combined (using per cent of rural and urban populations as weights)

	2000	2012	2030	2035	2050
Rural	1.9	2.09	2.09	2.27	2.27
Urban	1.15	1.67	1.67	1.80	1.80
Total	1.63	1.89	1.83	1.96	1.92

Source: Zeng et al. (2008): Table 1

the older population aged 65+ will increase by approximately 1.7 percentage points per decade. But in the 10 years from 2040 to 2050, that share will increase by 11.5 percentage points, mainly because China's baby boomers, born in the 1950s and 1960s, will fall into the oldest-old age category at that time.

Despite the uncertainties in accurately forecasting the oldest old population, it is certain that the oldest old will increase tremendously in the next few decades in China (also see Mayer et al., 1992: 81–2). Clearly, in the next few decades, especially by the middle of this century, China will face serious economic and societal challenges as a result of population ageing.

Future perspectives of living arrangements of the Chinese older persons

Our projections show that the proportion of households with at least one person aged 65+ (we call such households *elderly households*) will increase dramatically in China in the next few decades. By 2050, the overall percentage of elderly households (including households with only elder(s) as well as two- and three-generation households with at least one elder) is expected to nearly double as compared to the figure in 2000 (see Table 32.3). In 2030 and 2050, the percentage of households with one elder living alone will be 2.2 and 4.1 times as high as that in 2000; the percentage of households with one old couple without other family members living together will be 2.2 and 3.0 times as high as that in 2000.

Note that in our household and population projections, we have assumed that the preference for co-residence of old parents and adult children will decline rather slowly. Thus, the large increase in the percentage of the elderly households and older persons living alone is mainly due to the effects of fertility. On the one hand, fertility

decline substantially increases the overall proportion of older persons among the total population; on the other hand, fertility decline results in a much smaller resource of offspring, which is one of the determinants of co-residence between older parents and children. In other words, in China's future, substantial numbers of older persons may not be able to co-reside with children, even if they wish to do so, due to the shortage of children.

Substantially more serious problems of ageing in rural areas than in urban areas

Although fertility in rural areas in China is substantially higher than in urban areas, ageing problems will be much more serious in rural areas because of the continuing massive migration of rural young adults to urban areas. Persons aged 65+ are expected to grow to comprise a third of the total population by the middle of this century in the rural areas, which is much higher than that (21 per cent) in the urban areas. After 2030, the percentage of oldest old among the total population in rural areas is expected to be twice as high as in urban areas. By 2050, the percentage of those aged 65+ living in empty-nest households in rural and urban areas will be 5.8 and 3.9 times as high as in 2000. The percentage of the oldest old aged 80+ living in empty-nest households in 2050 in the rural and urban areas will be more dramatic: 15 and 8.8 times as high as in 2000.

A key underlying assumption of these projections is that the age distribution of the rural–urban migrants in the next few decades will be the same as that observed in the 2000 census. An important implication is that, if Chinese rural–urban migration continues to consist mainly of young people with ageing parents remaining in rural areas, the percentage of older persons in general and of the oldest old in particular will be too high for rural society to manage in the next few decades. Thus, China

Table 32.3 Percentages of households with at least one elderly person among the total number of households under the medium-fertility and medium-mortality assumptions

Household types	2000	2030	2040	2050
One person only	2.54	5.51	8.06	10.37
One couple only	2.74	6.06	8.08	8.16
One couple with at least one child	0.03	3.69	5.62	5.59
Single parent with at least one child	0.06	4.86	8.90	10.68
Three or more generations with one or two elderly parents	18.61	11.06	10.02	9.48
Subtotal	23.98	31.18	40.68	44.28
Total	100	100	100	100

Source: Zeng et al. (2008): Table 2

faces an urgent need to develop and adopt policies to encourage rural-to-urban family migration or family reunification after the young migrants settle in urban locales; this may avoid the 'elderly village' phenomenon spreading throughout rural areas and prevent the resulting serious social problems.

OLD-AGE INSURANCE PROGRAMME IN RURAL CHINA

In China, a public pension system was introduced in 1952, but is available only to state-owned enterprise employees in urban areas; its coverage in the late 1990s included about 140 million persons (Poston and Duan, 2000: 721). Farmers in rural areas do not have a retirement pension, and thus continue to work until their health fails. In general, with amount of coverage depending on location, China provides the 'Five Guarantees' of food, clothing, shelter, medical care, and a funeral for both rural and urban old persons who are childless, disabled, or who lack other close relatives on whom they can rely (Poston and Duan, 2000: 721). As the 'Five Guarantees' programme is only applicable to very few elders who are not able to work and have no resource of family support, it is a kind of aid for the disabled but cannot be considered as an old-age insurance for the older population.

As discussed earlier, the problems of the rapid ageing of the population will be much more serious in Chinese rural areas than in urban areas. However, the pension system in rural China is still extremely poor. This section will review the promising initial development of the old-age insurance programme in rural China in the early and middle 1990s and the unfortunate stagnation since the end of the 1990s. We will also provide our policy recommendation for this strategic issue for China.

In the early 1990s, the pilot programme of old-age insurance in rural areas in China was first launched in the Shandong province. It allows individuals aged 20–60 to voluntarily contribute premiums for old-age insurance, and then start receiving pensions at age 60. Part (usually less than 40 per cent) of the premium can be paid by the community collective fund if possible, but individuals pay most of their premiums. The amount of the monthly premium is flexible. The state gives favourable policies, such as high interest rates and compensation in case of inflation, to help ensure an increase in the value of the old-age insurance premium. The programme in the Shandong province was very successful and quickly spread to other provinces. According to the statistics from the Ministry of Civil Affairs, by the end of 1995, the programme had been implemented in 1608 counties in all 30 provinces. The number of participants was 61.2 million, and the participation rate among the population aged 20–60 was 14 per cent. By the end of 1999, 2100 counties in all provinces had implemented the rural old-age insurance programme; there were about 80 million participants, and about 890,000 peasants aged 60+ started to receive monthly payments from the old-age insurance programme.

The participation trend of the rural old-age insurance programme was promising through 1999 or so. Unfortunately, it has stagnated after 1999. The operation of the programme for those who have already participated continues, but recruitment of new participants has almost stopped. The official saying for such a stagnated situation is 'Zhen Dun Gai Ge' (consolidate and reform). By the end of 2004, the number of participants had dropped to 54 million, reduced by one-third as compared to 1999. About 10 per cent of the counties completely discontinued the rural old-age insurance programme.

Several complicating factors caused these unfortunate circumstances. The most important reason was that some policymakers at high levels had not yet realized the strategic importance of the rural old-age insurance programme. They argued that China was still a less developed country and that it was too early to develop an old-age insurance programme in rural areas. They were more concerned about current economic development, rather than the future welfare of the society, and tended to assume that family can always support older persons in the rural areas. Some officers even regarded the rural old-age insurance programme as an 'extra burden' for both peasants and government.

We believe that overlooking the importance of old-age insurance in rural areas is a serious mistake for three main reasons. First, as discussed earlier, future elders, especially the forthcoming baby-boomer oldest old in rural areas, will not have enough family support resources to rely on; an old-age insurance programme is necessary to enable them to have good quality of life. A second reason relates to the government's restrictive policies on childbearing. If the government says, 'Rural old age support should rely mainly on family,' peasants can say, 'If I do not have enough children, especially sons, how can I rely on my family for old age support?' This will consequently result in son-preference induced sex-selective abortion and dangerous rising trends in the sex ratio at birth and excess female infant mortality. Thirdly, compared to the European countries' experiences of establishing rural old-age insurance programmes 80–100 years ago, when their gross domestic product (GDP) per capita was much lower than China's in 1999 (see Table 32.4), there is no reason to argue that it is too early to develop an old-age insurance programme in rural China.

Table 32.4 Historical experiences of some European countries

	Year when the rural old-age insurance programme was established	Per cent of GDP per capita as compared to that of China in 1999 (standardized comparison)
Denmark	1891	79.3%
Sweden	1913	99.9%
Portugal	1919	46.6%
Spain	1947	73.3%

Source: Zeng (2005)

Another important factor that caused the stagnation of the rural old-age insurance programme was the restructuring of governmental agencies that occurred around the end of last century, which moved the department of rural social insurance from the Ministry of Civil Affairs to the Ministry of Labour and Social Security. The Ministry of Civil Affairs has a sophisticated network that reaches down to the village level, so it is plausible for them to organize and mobilize peasants to participate in the old-age insurance programme. The new Ministry of Labour and Social Security has no such network; it is difficult for them to mobilize rural people to participate in the old-age insurance programme.

We strongly believe that the Chinese government has a responsibility to promote, lead, and manage the old-age insurance programme for peasants, which is extremely important in responding to the challenge of serious ageing problems in rural China that will arise in the coming decades. Giving state resources (such as tax exemption) to only the urban old-age insurance programme and excluding rural people from the government-managed programme of old-age insurance is unfair, since both rural and urban residents make contributions to government revenues and state welfare. Leaving rural old-age support entirely to families will not be practical in the coming decades because of the current low fertility in many rural areas and the continuing rural-to-urban migration of young people. If there is no hope for social insurance for old-age care, rural people may have to resort to having more children, especially sons. This will certainly result in difficulties for the family planning programme, which aims to maintain relatively low fertility. This will also increase the dangerous trend of rising sex ratio at birth because farmers have no other way than relying on sons for old-age care. Lack of old-age insurance and the continued increase of the sex ratio at birth in rural areas would cause societal instability.

As the Ministry of Human Research and Social Security (MHRSS) has no down-to-village network, we propose that the State Population and Family Planning Commission (SPFPC) implement the social work (including propaganda and

mobilizations, etc.) of the rural old-age insurance programme, while the MHRSS remain responsible for the financial management of the programme. Such an arrangement would combine the welfare programme of old-age insurance with the policy and regulation of birth control. This policy proposal is based on the following considerations. First, many theoretical and empirical studies/practices in China have proven that the establishment of an old-age insurance system is closely related to and is useful for implementing changes in traditional fertility attitudes and son preference, which are the SPFPC's duties. Secondly, investment in future old-age support is one important component of family planning from both the individual and governmental points of view. The SPFPC has been trying very hard in past years to integrate birth control with other socioeconomic development programmes. The new client-centered and quality-focused approach to family planning programmes (Gu, 2000; Simmons et al., 2000) is one nice example. It is time for the SPFPC to extend its work from only one aspect of family planning (birth and the reproductive health of mothers) to another aspect of family planning: namely, old-age insurance for all adults. Such an extension will make the SPFPC's work match its name. Peasants will appreciate the SPFPC's caring for their future, thus improving the SPFPC's image and providing feedback, which may help to increase efficiency. Thirdly, the SPFPC has already accumulated some experience in old-age insurance as a reward for rural couples who firmly promised to have only one child. Thus, it may not be too difficult for the SPFPC network to implement the old-age insurance programme for all adults in rural areas. A fourth reason is the structural strength of the SPFPC network. In addition to its family planning programme offices extending down to all villages, there are 80 million members of the family planning associations as part of the SPFPC network. There is no doubt that the SPFPC network is much stronger than the Ministry of Civil Affairs (MCA) network is; the SPFPC can definitely do a more efficient job of implementing a rural old-age insurance programme than the MCA did in the 1990s, if appropriate policy guidance is in place.

The adequate policies should include at least the following two issues. First, tax exemption for the old-age insurance premium must be given to peasants by the government; this is not yet done in rural areas. Secondly, the SPFPC should not be responsible for the financial management of the old-age insurance funds; it is not the strength of the SPFPC. Responsibility for increasing the values of premium funds must be taken by the MHRSS and government appointed national banks.

CONCLUSION

China, the most populous country in the world, is ageing at a rapid speed and on a large scale, especially among the oldest old (aged 80+). This unavoidable trend is determined by the demographic facts that fertility in China has declined dramatically from more than six children per woman in the 1950s and 1960s to about 1.7 children per woman today, significantly lower than that in the United States. At the same time, life expectancy at birth for both sexes combined in China has increased from about 41 years in 1950 to 73 years in 2005, and will continue to increase in the future. The large cohorts of baby boomers born in the 1950s and 1960s will become old in a couple of decades.

These changes have direct implications for living arrangements. For example, the proportion of elderly households (those with at least one person aged 65+) will increase dramatically in China. By the year 2050, the proportion of those aged 65 or older living in empty-nest households without co-residing children among the total population (rural and urban combined) will be 4.4 times as high as that in 2000. It is clear that Chinese family households will be ageing rapidly and substantially in the first half of the 21st century.

Although fertility in rural areas in China is much higher than that in urban areas, the problems of ageing in population and family households will be much more serious in rural areas than in urban areas. Such anticipated trends are based on the assumption that the age distribution of the rural–urban migrants in the future will be the same as that observed in the 2000 census: namely, that almost all rural–urban migrants will be young people. Our study strongly suggests that China needs to adopt policies to encourage rural-to-urban family migration or family reunification after the young migrants are settled in urban areas, to avoid the 'elderly village' phenomenon in rural areas, which portends serious social problems in the future.

Yet the projections also indicate that a demographic window of opportunity is open in the next two decades, due to a large labour force, decreasing numbers of children, and proportions of older persons that are not yet burdensome. During this 'golden-age' period, it is possible for China to mobilize large amounts of individual savings and state capital to build a solid financial and institutional base of social security programmes, especially the old-age insurance programme, in both rural and urban areas. In this period, prompt governmental action is imperative, and there are indications that the Chinese government is becoming responsive. In 2007, the Chinese government stated in its official policy guidance paper that 'We will explore and establish old age insurance programme in rural areas,' which was a substantial step forward, as compared to the statement of 'exploring and establishing old age insurance programme in rural areas where needed conditions are met,' released a couple of years earlier. With this promising new policy guidance, we expect that actions will be taken quickly and the rural old-age insurance programme will be developed before too long. This is strategically important because the demographic window of opportunity will close around 2030, after which time it will be too late to start to resolve China's serious looming social and economic problems.

ACKNOWLEDGEMENT

The research reported in this chapter is supported by NIA/NIH (R01 AG023627-01) and China Natural Science Foundation (70533010).

NOTE

1 The 1998 baseline, 2000, 2002, and 2005 follow-up healthy longevity survey datasets are distributed domestically and internationally by the Peking University Center for Healthy Aging and Family Studies (http://www.pku.edu.cn/academic/ageing/ev/index) and the Center for the Study of Aging and Human Development at Duke University (http://www.geri.duke.edu/china_study). At this time of writing, the 2008–09 wave is still ongoing in the final stage of completion. Thus, the figures for the 2008–09 wave and the total sample size for the five waves are not final and will be updated in the near future.

REFERENCES

Gu, B. (2000) 'Reorienting China's family planning program: An Experiment on quality of care since 1995', Paper presented at the annual meeting of the Population Association of America, Los Angeles.

Mayer, G.C., Barbara, B.T., and Kinsella, K.G. (1992) 'The paradox of the oldest old in the United States: an international comparison', in R.M. Suzman, D.P. Willis, and K.G. Manton (eds), *The Oldest Old*. Oxford: Oxford University Press, pp. 58–85.

Ogawa, N. (1988) 'Aging in China: demographic alternatives', *Asia-Pacific Population Journal*, 3: 21–64.

Poston, D.L. and Duan, C.C. (2000) 'The current and projected distribution of the elderly and eldercare in the People's Republic of China', *Journal of Family Issues*, 21: 714–32.

Simmons, R., Gu, B., and Ward, S. (2000) 'Initiating reform in the Chinese family planning program', Paper presented at the annual meeting of the Population Association of America, Los Angeles.

United Nations (2005) *World Population Prospects: The 2004 Population Revision*. New York: United Nations.

Zeng Y. (2005) 'Population aging, pension deficits and old age insurance program in China', *Economic Quarterly*, No. 3, 1043–66.

Zeng, Y. and George, L. (2000) 'Family dynamics of 63 million (in 1990) to more than 330 million (in 2050) elders in China', *Demographic Research*, 2(5).

Zeng, Y. and Wang, Z. (2003) 'Dynamics of family and elderly living arrangements in China: new lessons learned from the 2000 census', *The China Review*, 3(2): 95–119.

Zeng, Y., Vaupel, J.W., Xiao, Z., Zhang, C., and Liu, Y. (2002) 'Sociodemographic and health profiles of oldest old in China', *Population and Development Review*, 28(2): 251–73 .

Zeng, Y., Land, K.C., Wang, Z., and Danan, G. (2006) 'U.S. family household momentum and dynamics: extension of ProFamy method and application', *Population Research and Policy Review*, 25(1): 1–41.

Zeng, Y., Wang, Z., Leiwen, J., and Gu, D. (2008) 'Projection of family households and elderly living arrangement in the context of rapid population aging in China – a demographic window of opportunity until 2030 and serious challenges thereafter.' *GENUS: An International Journal of Demography*, LXIV (1–2): 9–36.

33

Ageing in a Global Context: The Asia-Pacific Region

David R. Phillips, Alfred C.M. Chan, and Sheung-Tak Cheng

INTRODUCTION: ASIA-PACIFIC – A REGION WITH A SHARED IDENTITY?

The Asia-Pacific is a rather ambiguously described region which has wholly or in part been termed at various times the 'Asia(n) Pacific', 'the Pacific rim', 'Pacific Asia', 'East Asia' and 'East and Southeast Asia' (geographically perhaps the most precise term) and, Eurocentrically, 'the Far East' (Phillips, 2000). It stretches from Japan and China in the north to Indonesia in the south, and some definitions include Australasia although, in this chapter, we do not cover Australia, New Zealand, or the Oceania island states explicitly (see, however, Chapter 40). There are also numerous political, economic, and strategic regional groupings, such as ASEAN and APEC, along with regional offices of the United Nations and other international agencies such as the WHO, UNFPA, UNESCAP, and HelpAge International. Nevertheless, the Asia-Pacific region has evolved as a subglobal system of commonality and competition, a recognizable entity to many people living, working, and researching in the area.

Various forces of modernization and rapid economic development over recent decades have emphasized its distinctive regionalization in the global economy, while others have tended to promote diversity. Demographic transition, urbanization, and economic change have been major factors in the ageing of the populations (Goodman and Harper, 2006; Maidment et al.,1998; Maron, 2006; Phillips, 2000; UNESCAP, 2007). However, demographic change and ageing are by no means

uniform across the Asia-Pacific region. It includes the demographically oldest country in the world, Japan, which is facing new challenges of slow or even negative population growth, and several other low-fertility countries which are rapidly becoming demographically aged – China, Hong Kong, Taiwan, the Republic of Korea, and Singapore. But it also has many relatively youthful countries such as Vietnam, Cambodia, Laos, and Indonesia, where population policies still often concern family planning and reproductive health although even they are increasingly taking an interest in ageing issues.

The region's cultural heritage and contemporary cultural mosaic have been shaped under several different civilizations and religions, including Confucianism, Buddhism, Christianity, and Islam. A common sociocultural characteristic through much of the region is the high value placed on family integration and consensus in social relations to maintain harmony among members of groups, with an expectation of community welfare often rising above individual interests. The region's economies are also diverse, and socioeconomic changes have great implications for population ageing, family, and state care for older persons.

Publications on ageing in the region are relatively few but are steadily growing in number. Phillips (1992, 2000) provides regional overviews and specific country chapters, Yoon and Hendricks (2006) focus on selected countries (including India and Australia), and Hughes and Fu (2009) look at selected countries, issues, and future challenges; the UNESCAP (United Nations Economic and

Social Commission for Asia and the Pacific) and other organizations have produced reports and papers on ageing, social security, and access to social services (see Phillips and Chan, 2002a, 2002b, 2002c; UNESCAP, 2002a, 2002b, 2002c). There are several follow-up reports on the Madrid 2002 International Congress on Ageing, as well as the *Macao Plan of Action on Ageing* (this was the first UN region with such a plan, dating from 1999) and its own Shanghai Implementation Strategy for the Madrid plans (outlined below). The *Asian Journal of Gerontology and Geriatrics* (formerly *The Hong Kong Journal of Gerontology*) carries papers of clinical and social interest while, among others, the *Asia-Pacific Population Journal* published by UNESCAP regularly carries papers on ageing-related issues. The UNESCAP also produces annual population data reference sheets. UNFPA has prepared an overview of population ageing in East and Southeast Asia that usefully compares these subregions demographically with other world regions (Mujahid, 2006). The UN *Regional Dimensions of the Ageing Situation* has a chapter looking at ageing trends and policy priorities in the region. Cheng et al., (2009) also review ageing issues in the region.

DEMOGRAPHIC TRENDS IN THE ASIA-PACIFIC REGION

The Asia-Pacific (East and Southeast Asia) in mid-2008 was home to over 2100 million people, roughly one-third of the world's total population. Approximately 8 per cent were aged 65 and over, although this percentage varies considerably, with Japan having about 22 per cent aged 65+ and Brunei, Cambodia, Laos, Malaysia, the Philippines, and demographically-small East Timor (Timor Leste) having only about 3–4 per cent in the age group (see Table 33.1 and Population Reference Bureau, 2008; UNESCAP *Population Data Sheets*, annual). The worldwide population aged 65 or over in 2008 was approximately 500 million, of whom about 52 per cent – over half – lived in Asia excluding the Near East. Over one-third (37 per cent) of the world's 65+ population lived just in the East and Southeast Asian countries, the Asia-Pacific. Many of the countries in the Asia-Pacific region are ageing demographically rather faster than the Western nations have done historically. Most developing countries, including those in Asia, are doubling their older populations in a compressed time span of 20–25 years. China, for example, is expected to double its older population from 7 per cent to 14 per cent in just 26 years, from 2000 to 2026 (National Institute of Aging, 2007). Globally, the impact of population

ageing will be most felt in Asia in coming decades (Cheng and Heller, 2009; Cheng et al., 2008).

INCREASING EXPECTATION OF LIFE AND DECLINING FERTILITY RATES

Many of the region's countries have impressive longevity and include three of the world's most long-lived populations, in Japan and the Hong Kong and Macao SARs of China. In general, increasing longevity, usually indicated by the theoretical measure expectation of life at birth (ELB), does contribute to the ageing of populations. However, it does this at a gradual rate and, more importantly, the principal demographic driver of ageing has been falling fertility. The populations of many countries in the Asia-Pacific region have moved from high birth and death rates to low birth and death rates and rising longevity (Kinsella and Phillips, 2005; Phillips, 2000; Seetharam, 2006; UNESCAP *Population Data Sheets*, annual; Yoon and Hendricks, 2006).

Simply speaking, with fewer babies being born, there are fewer people at a younger age and proportionately more at older ages. Family planning campaigns and social change in many Asia-Pacific countries over the past three decades have had spectacular results. Falls in the total fertility rates (TFRs), combined with very low crude birthrates (emerging over a short period) have meant rapid demographic ageing. Hong Kong and Macao have at the moment the lowest TFRs in the world, at a probably unsustainably low level at or below 1, well below the 'natural replacement rate' of 2.1 children per woman. Almost all the major countries in the region, especially populous China, have TFRs below this level, although there are important large-population exceptions in countries such as Indonesia (2.3) and the Philippines (3.3). McDonald (2007) and others have argued that a slow decline in fertility rates to around 1.7–1.9 births per woman does not automatically create problems with, say, future labour supply. However, when fertility rates fall suddenly and also remain very low (below 1.5 births per woman) the fall in future labour force sizes can be substantial. Fertility also tends to remain low, rarely again exceeding this level, the so-called 'low fertility trap'. This has been encountered by several countries in the region, including Japan, Hong Kong, and Singapore, which have been seeking ways to increase their fertility, albeit with little success. A related and potentially explosive demographic element in many parts of the region, especially China, is the demographic imbalance, with substantially more baby boys being born than girls.

Table 33.1 Key ageing data for selected Asia-Pacific countries

Country or area and region	Mid-2008 population (millions)	Annual growth rate (percentage)	Crude birth rate (per 1000)	Total fertility rate	Life expectancy at birth (years) Males	Life expectancy at birth (years) Females	Per cent aged under 15	Per cent aged 65+	Ageing Index (2006)
EAST ASIA	1,558	0.5	12.6	1.7	72	76	19	9	62.3
China	1,324.7	0.6	13.2	1.7	71	75	19	8	53.5
Democratic People's Republic of Korea	23.5	0.4	13.4	1.9	65	69	25	8	46.8
Hong Kong, China	7.0	0.8	8.2	1.0	79	85	13	13	108.8
Japan	127.7	0.1	8.4	1.3	79	86	13	22	189.1
Macao, China	0.6	1.1	7.9	0.9	78	83	13	7	62.1
Mongolia	2.7	1.0	18.5	1.9	64	70	29	4	19.2
Republic of Korea	48.6	0.5	9.0	1.2	75	82	18	10	69.3
SOUTH-EAST ASIA	586	1.3	19.1	2.3	68	72	29	6	27.5
Brunei Darussalam	0.4	2.1	21.7	2.3	75	80	30	3	16.5
Cambodia	14.7	2.0	28.5	3.4	57	62	36	4	14.7
Indonesia	239.9	1.2	18.9	2.2	68	72	29	6	30.2
Lao PDR	5.9	1.7	27.0	3.3	63	66	44	4	13.1
Malaysia	27.7	1.8	18.7	2.6	72	77	32	4	20.1
Myanmar	49.2	0.9	18.3	2.1	59	65	27	6	26.8
Philippines	90.5	2.0	24.1	3.2	69	74	35	4	18.1
Singapore	4.8	1.3	10.0	1.3	78	82	19	9	68.1
Thailand	66.1	0.5	12.7	1.6	68	75	22	7	46.9
Vietnam	86.2	1.4	17.5	2.1	70	73	26	7	25.9

Sources: based on UNESCAP *Population Data Sheets 2006/2007* and Population Reference Bureau 2008 *World Population Data Sheet*

The long-term effects of this relatively new trend are hard to predict, but consequences for family structure, social integration, and care of older persons in the future may be serious.

Across Asia as a whole, and in many individual countries, the group aged 65 and over is expected to outnumber those aged below 15 at around 2050. Japan has already faced this in late 1990s and will be joined by other countries, including Hong Kong in about 2008, and Macao, Singapore, and the Republic of Korea, by about 2015. By 2050, population stability or decline are also expected in certain countries (Japan, the Republic of Korea, Taiwan, Singapore, and Macao).

At older ages, too, the feminization of ageing is very evident, principally because of the longer life span of women in East and Southeast Asian countries, where females on average typically outlive males in life expectancy by 4 or 5 years or more (Table 33.1). Today, females make up well over 50 per cent of the total older population and usually over 60 per cent of the olds old in all 15 Asian countries surveyed by the UNFPA (Mujahid, 2006). A final but equally important demographic feature in many countries of the region is this emergence of the oldest old (people aged 80 or 85+) as a growing segment of the elderly population. Whereas only around 1 per cent were aged 80+ in 2000, by 2050 this is likely to be 6 per cent region-wide.

The role of mortality

In spite of the prominence of fertility declines, mortality is becoming an increasingly important factor in the demographic ageing of populations (Kinsella and Phillips, 2005; NIA, 2007). The speed of decline of death rates at advanced ages ('increasing longevity') will play a major role in determining future numbers of the very old population. In this respect, many countries of Asia are doing well (Caldwell and Caldwell, 2006) although there remain significant anomalies in inter-country mortality rates (and probably also in some intra-country and urban–rural rates). Clearly, East Asia is the subregion with the most substantial gains in life expectancy and some parts of Southeast Asia have yet to catch up (with the exceptions of Singapore and Thailand).

Based on UNESCAP data, of the five countries with the longest life expectancy at birth, four – Japan, Hong Kong, Macao, and the Republic of Korea – are East Asian, with Singapore as the fifth, followed by Brunei. Among the lowest are the poorer Southeast Asian countries (Laos, Cambodia, Myanmar, and Indonesia). This reflects the not unusual deterministic relationship between real per capita income and life expectancy

(Caldwell and Caldwell, 2006; Maddison, 2003). An important area for health gains will be the reduction of male–female mortality differences and, as noted, almost everywhere, females outlive males, often by as many as 5 or even 7 years (in, for example, Japan, Republic of Korea, Thailand, Hong Kong, Singapore, and China). The exceptions are to be seen in South Asia. In the Asia-Pacific, the health of older men (and of the lifetime health of working males) should also be a target for health programmes. The WHO (2007), focusing on gender, notes several issues arising from the generally greater longevity of females, including barriers to health care, lengthy widowhoods, lack of carers, and the need for palliative care. However, some suggest that the socioeconomic disadvantage of older women may have been overemphasized and that contemporary research indicates a complex and varied situation both in terms of the country and measures of economic support and well-being that are examined.

KEY SOCIOECONOMIC ISSUES AND THEIR GERONTOLOGICAL IMPLICATIONS

Smaller household size and smaller, older households

Intergenerational co-residence and extended families have been traditional in many Asia-Pacific countries and this has been maintained in some if not all. However, almost all countries show some family size decline and a growth of the nuclear family. The UNDESA (2005) found that between 3.3 per cent (Singapore) and 13 per cent (Japan) of Asia-Pacific countries' older persons were living alone around the year 2000. Perhaps China exemplifies the potential impacts of smaller families most starkly, where a combination of economic development, intra-country migration for work, and population policy have led to smaller families and/or family fragmentation. Today, it is common to identify a '4-2-1' family structure in China (four grandparents, two children, and one grandchild). The reality often is that families, especially in urban areas where about one-third of China's population live, are likely to comprise three persons: husband, wife, and one child. The associated difficulties for extended family care of older members are thus a cause for concern and, consequent upon the growth of nuclear families, many older parents live separately from their adult children and their grandchildren. Whereas ageing and fertility declines do vary somewhat across the nation, the most developed and most populous eastern region has the highest share of population falling under the one-child rule and the lowest fertility levels. Overall, more than 60 per cent of Chinese couples are likely to end up with only one child (Gu, 2007), with the concomitant consequences noted here (and official relaxation of the One-Child policy to become a Two-Child policy was announced in some cities in 2009). Another feature is a growing gender imbalance in which many more male than female babies are being born.

A regional report on ageing in East and Southeast Asia (Mujahid, 2006) does suggest family support is in decline, citing reductions of co-residence with adult children as evidence. However, it also recognizes that in many settings in the region, declines have been modest and traditional family ties largely remain strong. In addition, developments in technology and communications can enable indirect contacts to be maintained and substituted, as discussed below. At the same time, advances in transport have in some circumstances facilitated migrant children's return at times of urgent need, while financial support across almost any distance has been facilitated by electronic transfers of remittances, assuming suitable financial systems exist where older persons live. Distance and difficulties of travel remain as obstacles, especially in the larger countries that have substantial migration for work, such as to China's coastal provinces, leaving many older relatives behind in the villages. Nevertheless, the significance and meaning of 'separated' living arrangements for the welfare of older parents are undergoing transformation. A key factor is that physical separation need not be automatically assumed to be total loss of family support and, conversely, co-residence does not always mean adequate support for older persons.

Research in Java, a densely populated part of Indonesia, based on 2002 national survey data, found the majority of older persons in all districts did co-reside with at least one child. This ranged from 57 to 70 per cent and varied as to whether the older person was defined as head of household (the child living with them) or they lived in the child's household. Contrary to expectations, it was found that the percentages of older persons living with children were higher in more economically advanced districts, rather than rural areas, where it seemed that older people were more likely to be living without children (Arifin, 2006). Such findings emphasize the complexity of the co-residence issue and cautions against making simplistic assumptions.

Filial piety and family care

Filial piety can be interpreted in a number of ways. It may be regarded as a fairly straightforward

duty (especially in Chinese societies) of children, traditionally meaning sons, to look after their parents in return for care received when they were being brought up. It can also be much more complex, involving various aspects of obedience, honour, and care provision, a two-way relationship that endures through generations (Cheng and Chan, 2006a; Phillips, 2000, 2002). While research-based evidence is scarce, many in the public and political arenas in the region assert that intra-family support and relations are becoming less strong. This is often blamed on the infiltration of supposedly Western (but probably universal) trends such as individualism, privacy, high divorce and remarriage rates, right-based notions, and greater provision of formal care. Spouses are increasingly the most common persons providing care in the family, while sons and daughters often provide limited material and emotional support at a distance (e.g., using phone calls or emails). Sometimes today, filial piety might be substituted by financial arrangements rather than actual personal care, especially among migrant workers who send remittances to their parents and older relatives, often in rural areas. Within the Madrid International Plan of Action on Ageing (MIPAA), promoting intergenerational solidarity and reciprocity is a major objective. This could be interpreted in some ways as encouraging the practice of filial piety and, as noted below, this has been fairly widely seen as a policy response in the region.

Advancing health and well-being into old age

A priority policy direction of the MIPAA is advancing health and well-being into old age, as good health is a vital individual and community asset. The Asia-Pacific region clearly illustrates the worldwide trend from predominantly acute and communicative illnesses towards chronic and non-communicable types (McCracken and Phillips, 2005; WHO, 2006). This calls for new approaches to healthcare provision and it is widely recognized that preventive and primary approaches to healthcare are the most appropriate for meeting these health challenges of population ageing (WHO, 2008). Many developing and intermediate countries here do not have the infrastructure to deliver modern high-quality secondary and tertiary hospital-level care to all their populations and are increasingly focusing on community-based models for health care. Indeed, for the foreseeable future, it will be prudent for poorer countries in particular, perhaps such as Laos,

Cambodia, Vietnam, Indonesia, the Philippines, and others, to concentrate their resources on health promotion and disease prevention, and on setting up effective primary healthcare systems, especially for rural areas. Some, such as Thailand, are striving to extend healthcare access at a nominal charge to all generations, although this is costly to the government and burdens the healthcare system.

Primary health care (PHC) is often more appropriate than distant tertiary care for older persons as it provides care that is accessible, community-based, and often culturally acceptable. For the chronic diseases and mobility problems that affect many older people, community-based long-term care (LTC) and PHC support are more appropriate than higher-level hospital technology. The acceptability and personal preferences for local, accessible PHC has been reaffirmed in a five-country qualitative study of older consumers and their carers in Cambodia, India, Indonesia, Singapore, and Vietnam (HelpAge International, 2007a). In particular, it was confirmed as highly appropriate for dealing with the increasing prevalence of chronic disease amongst older age groups, such as hypertension, diabetes, heart disease, and others, which will form the major burden of disease in the future. It can also support the quality of life of older persons near to their homes, but they in general had low expectations of current PHC and low levels of health knowledge. People were not accessing services, mainly because of the cost of health care. Improved PHC can address this as well as the difficulties of accessing remoter tertiary-type services. Therefore, the study clearly shows that governments should re-emphasize these services as socially, clinically, and cost-effective, and should especially enhance their quality and the ways in which they can provide health education for older people and their communities. Some countries, such as China, still have home visits by doctors. In 2000, some 36 per cent of older persons received visits at home and this was especially characteristic of the oldest of the old. Rural older people were much more likely to have received a home visit– (42 per cent), as compared to just under 16 per cent of urban older persons (He et al., 2007). Thailand, via its home healthcare scheme, attempts to provide healthcare visits for the less mobile, those discharged from hospital, with chronic illnesses or at risk, via interdisciplinary home healthcare teams based in hospitals and extending field visits to people's homes (Ministry of Social Development and Human Security, Thailand, 2007). These countries may be the exception rather than the rule, although home visits should be an essential feature of community-based care networks for older people and their families.

LONG-TERM CARE: TRENDS AND POLICIES

LTC in most but not all Asia-Pacific countries is more broadly interpreted than in much of the West. It encompasses formal and informal care and generally develops along two main forms, residential care and home-based or community-based care, especially by families. In view of demographic ageing, how to extend and support LTC, especially home- and community-based forms, is arguably the region's major challenge in health care for older persons. Despite the increasing recognition of ageing, there is still a lack of coherent policy for LTC, especially integrated support, in many countries. Such a policy should address not only demands for institutional care but also support home- and/or community-based LTC. Without this, the rising demand for institutional care will likely overwhelm even the most affluent countries. To the best of our knowledge, only a few countries such as the Republic of Korea and Japan have dedicated policies or legislation on LTC. Japan uses a social insurance model and benefits are typically in kind (e.g., home and nursing care). Others (such as Hong Kong, Singapore, and Australia) tend to incorporate LTC into related policies (such as disability allowances under social security).

The Chinese government has started to allocate more funds and to create new opportunities for entrepreneurship in health services, partly following China's social-welfare reform since the 1990s. Public funding for LTC of older persons is still limited but other sources are appearing and providing an alternative to family care and the stretched state sector. These include a growing number of private old people's homes, as well as the country's former government-sponsored homes for the aged, which previously catered exclusively for older people with no children and no other means of support (Kaneda, 2006). However, there are still relatively few of these and they are often too expensive for the majority of older people and their families and standards vary considerably. Community-based formal and informal LTC services for older persons have also began to emerge in China, especially in urban areas (Wu et al., 2005; Zhan et al., 2006). Lack of a trained workforce in caregiving for older people is limiting the development of China's LTC system. Certain local and other agencies are now providing limited, basic training in LTC for unemployed workers, but there is a need for more in-depth training programmes offering the range of caregiving skills. The need to develop undergraduate training in geriatric medicine is recognized and there are plans for more geriatric units (Kaneda, 2006).

In general, however, much needs to be done in most Asia-Pacific countries to finance and organize sustainable LTC programmes. A crucial component of LTC is provided by family members and relatives, for example in Thailand (Kespichayawattana and Jitapunkul 2009). However, there is generalized concern that Westernization is reducing the desire or ability of families to care for frail older members (Ng et al., 2002; Oh and Warnes, 2001). Initiatives to strengthen informal care systems are being developed in some countries such as recognized skill-based training for caregivers, including Singapore and Hong Kong. In many countries, training for both professional and informal carers on how to care for dependent older persons should be a future priority. In most, this is especially needed in palliative care and end-of-life decisions.

Strengthening informal care

In line with traditional values, family and wider informal care is seen as a major and desirable source for older people's well-being in almost all countries. In some places, this is associated with policies advocating 'ageing in place' and 'community care', with older persons being encouraged to remain living in their homes for as long as possible, assisted with community support services – formal and informal – when needs arise. In other places, families are left to cope more or less on their own resources. It is clear that both formal and informal social networks providing support are important for older people's subjective (psychological) well-being (SWB), but there is increasing evidence that SWB is also affected by the internal and external living environments; thus, careful coordination of urban planning and services is essential (Ong and Phillips, 2007; Phillips et al., 2004, 2005, 2008).

Where funding for community care services does exist, such programmes generally rely on public finance either via general taxation or a LTC budget vote (as in Japan). However, it is clear that the current modes and delivery of community support services often do not match the needs of the family and elderly members very well and/or they are too expensive to be tailor-made to specific individual needs. Worse, perhaps, is that most of these services are provided, perhaps unintentionally, in place of more appropriate forms of community care. Therefore, and also because of older persons' preferences, many more advanced Asia-Pacific countries have been advocating the bolstering of family care. Given the expectation of future older populations being older, perhaps frailer, and more demanding because of rising expectations,

income, and education, family care or community support services will require higher-level skills and much greater availability. Even those countries wanting to rebuild family care in order to reduce the burden on institutional care have to incorporate a more structured approach, with higher levels of caring skills, training, and support systems for informal caregivers. In some places, the 'younger-old' group aged 65–75 may be a source to help in this respect. Volunteers, as discussed below, may also prove to be a crucial supply of community-based labour, and some countries with existing volunteering systems within the region could initiate training programmes leading to formally recognized qualifications.

A generalized lack of political support for welfare states in Asia has sometimes been attributed to the region's strong family tradition (filial piety in particular) and those advocating more formal assistance, especially residential care, fear being accused of undermining Asian values. However, a heavy reliance on family care can have both positive and negative aspects. Family care can be seen as an ideal but, in reality, it can often be only partial and amateur, if well-meaning, especially in more serious cases of restricted activities of daily living (ADLs) or dementias. In the Republic of Korea, family responsibilities have long been emphasized but have even been said at times to have deterred the development of formal support and policy for older persons (Choi, 2000, 2002). There is a feeling that the same attitudes are held in some other countries in the region, such as Malaysia and Brunei, where the development of residential care and nursing homes might have been delayed because of the social stigma of a family placing its elderly parents into someone else's care. In the Republic of Korea, the rapid decline in fertility over recent years, and especially after the Asian economic crisis of 1997, has led to it being called the most rapidly ageing society in the world. The causes in this conservative country are complex and varied, so solutions to a perceived problem are not easy. The Rupublic of Korea government has attempted to develop a comprehensive proposal to the twin phenomena of low fertility and population ageing, explained in the *Saeromaji Plan 2010* (Eun, 2007). This focuses on three areas; creating a favourable environment for childbirth and rearing of children; foundations for improving the quality of life in an aged society; and human resources in a low-fertility and aged society. This plan is clearly echoed in the MIPPA responses for many countries in the region and it is clear these three areas will be of paramount importance in the next two decades.

One fairly common response in anticipation of probable future declines in family and community ability or wish to provide care for older persons sees some countries introducing initiatives to try to preserve traditional Asian values, notably the concept of filial piety. Examples include priority allocation of public housing units, tax incentives to children caring for an elderly parent, or even resort to implementing legal requirements for the care and maintenance of parents (Singapore and China are sometimes cited as implementing these). Volunteers are of growing importance in expanding caring networks, both in the care of older persons and in older people becoming volunteers, especially in more-developed ESCAP member countries. As noted, very low and even falling fertility rates are causing increasing concern, as these will mean ever-smaller families with lower abilities to provide LTC or any support, as well as wider implications for the workforce. In the Republic of Korea, for example, a focus of the 2005 'Basic Law for Population Policy and Ageing Society' launched a Presidential Committee on the subject, with the *Saeromaji Plan 2010* (mentioned above) looking at many ways to use women's and older people's potential and foster a family-friendly culture. Regionally, major initiatives stemming from this plan focus on the current low fertility, changes in population structure, and possible ways to create an environment conducive to increasing birth rates and enhancing child rearing (such as the introduction of child allowances), also in the context of sustaining economic development and competitiveness. This is perhaps the most common demographic conundrum facing most East Asian countries.

A particular feature affecting family and community ability to care is seen in the region's countries with a high prevalence of communicable diseases such as HIV/AIDS or where parents are long-term absent from homes because of migration, violence, and other causes. Parts of Cambodia, Thailand, Vietnam, and some rural areas of China are witnessing young and middle-aged parents ill with AIDS or who have died earlier than their old-aged parents, leaving young children, sometimes themselves also infected with HIV. This has extended the traditional role of grandparenting, in which older persons play a role in the family when, say, both parents work and the grandparents take on child and household care, developing the intergenerational solidarity highlighted in the MIPAA (UN, 2007). Grandparents now often become the primary or sole caregivers for children. Whereas older persons themselves are relatively rarely infected with HIV, much more common is this indirect impact through illness and death of their grown-up children. Studies in Thailand and Cambodia show that older adults can end up caring for their own children and also being responsible for the education and development of grandchildren, as well as assuming an important role in education about the epidemic (Knodel and Zimmer, 2007).

CONCEPTS OF AGEING AND ASIA-PACIFIC PERSPECTIVES: SUCCESSFUL, ACTIVE, AND PRODUCTIVE AGEING

Successful ageing has been represented as three overlapping circles with 'avoidance of disease and disability', 'involvement in society', and maintaining high cognitive and physical functioning (Rowe and Kahn, 1998). These psychosocial concepts in some ways resemble the WHO's *Active Ageing Policy Framework*, in which three pillars (participation, health, and security) are seen as the determinants of active ageing. This is defined as 'the process of optimizing opportunities for health, participation and security in order to enhance quality of life as people age', and it applies to individuals as well as population groups (WHO, 2002: 12). It is perhaps a rather optimistic policy framework, but is nevertheless valid as a set of aims (see Chapter 35). A key feature of the concept is that 'active' refers to continued social, economic, cultural, civic, and family participation, not merely the ability to be physically active or part of the labour force. Like the concept of 'productive ageing' discussed below, older people who retire and those who are ill or with disabilities can remain active and participate in their families, neighbourhoods, and societies.

There have been relatively few published studies in the region of successful or active ageing. One study used data from the 2002 Survey of the Elderly in Thailand, which, although not explicitly aimed at active ageing, did capture information on the major relevant variables (Thanakwang and Soonthorndhada, 2006). The findings indicated that many older Thais did have moderate active ageing, especially better-educated, higher occupational status males, and younger-old and married older people. The study suggests that to promote active ageing, a focus on elderly women, older persons with chronic illness, and uneducated or lower-income people would be beneficial.

Excessive promotion of social participation is, however, not always felt to be positive, as it has the potential to increase feelings of uselessness and negative stereotyping and possibly the exclusion of some older persons. This could in part explain why some Asia-Pacific countries have among the world's highest rates of elderly suicide in the world, especially those with an East Asian cultural base (Hong Kong, Taiwan, the Republic of Korea, Singapore, and China). Preventing suicide among older people is an increasing need that requires training, awareness, and interventions at many levels (Chiu et al., 2003; Phillips, 2000). The Hong Kong Elderly Commission recognized this with a policy study of older persons' suicide in the late 1990s, emphasizing training and awareness amongst professionals and families. Indeed, this seemed essential since, in Hong Kong's case, many older persons who committed suicide had actually mentioned this possibility to friends or relatives, so that preventative measures might have been possible.

As well as being productive economically, often through continued work in the absence of formal retirement systems, older persons in the region contribute to many other areas such as family welfare, child care, and caregiving for other older persons. In addition, the 'silver market' of older persons, both as consumers and as a major target for services such as finance, housing, vacations, and leisure activities (including education), is increasingly recognized in the region (Hedrick-Wong, 2006). As in the West, the older population is being seen both as consumers and as a market for services for the rest of the economy and, in some countries such as Japan and China, in coming years, the silver market, as it is sometimes called, will be substantial. Middle-class older consumers in particular are growing in numbers and in the future will form a major market segment, especially in economies where birth rates and new younger consumers are falling. The older market may have slightly different consumer requirements, for example, as travellers. Some older persons may wish to have a longer but deeper understanding of the places they are visiting. Odyssey Travel, started more than two decades ago in Australia, is now a thriving university-linked organization specializing in lifelong learning and education travel for the over-45s.

Demographic trends (declining fertility rates) and economic trends (increasing wealth) make the silver market an important area for many businesses. In addition, knowledge transfer between older and younger workers has been noted (HSBC, 2007). Older people can also have consumer power and increasingly demand quality in goods and services, as do other consumers. In a study in Malaysia, Ong and Phillips (2007) have found that older adults are discerning consumers, able to discriminate and to select, especially on the basis of price and durability of products. They also often appear as effective as other age groups in asserting their rights as consumers.

SELECTED REGIONAL PRIORITIES IN AGEING IDENTIFIED BY DEVELOPMENT AGENCIES

In addition to some of the issues above, the 2002 UN Madrid International Plan of Action on Ageing (MIPAA) (UN, 2002, 2007) and regional follow-up meetings by development agencies for a 5-year review (MIPAA+5), especially a Macau UNESCAP meeting in October 2007 (UNESCAP, 2007), have also highlighted a number of issues within the Plan's identified priority directions. Indeed, the Asia-Pacific has had a plan of action on ageing for over a decade, stemming from a series of meetings in Macou (UNESCAP, 1999) and policy issues have increasingly been identified. In the Asia-Pacific context, the following are generally agreed to be important.

Social protection: retirement and old-age security

It is often observed that, unlike most Western countries, most developing countries, including many in this region, are having to deal with the challenges of population ageing before they have built up the resources to deal with them (Phillips, 2000). For such countries, the provision of state-funded social security and retirement protection can be effectively impossible under current circumstances, although the provision of low-cost social pensions is now openly considered (HelpAge International, 2007b). In 2006, just over half of the world's population were reported to be living on less than 2 US $ a day. In Asia, this rises to almost 60 per cent, and in East and Southeast Asia it is about 46 per cent. Many of those living in poverty or extreme poverty are older persons, especially in rural areas. When working, these people have earned very little, so it has been difficult for them to save enough funds to support themselves when old. As the *UN World Economic and Social Survey 2007* (UN, 2007) points out, few have access to pensions, and the notion of retirement as such does not exist for the unprotected. They either continue to work if fit enough or rely on their family or community, as there is no comprehensive social security or even basic safety nets in many countries. There are generally no universal benefits for older people as a group. Because of limited resources, some countries do target their social security programmes to very poor, destitute, and disabled persons, such as in Malaysia's elderly assistance scheme, targeted at those with no kin and no other sources of support (Ong et al., 2009).

There are several regional key issues in terms of retirement income and general areas of support. Some stem from the changing nature of family and residence mentioned above; others relate to the nature of employment in the region. Often, employment in agriculture, for example, was steady but did not easily build up cash reserves, so a continued support by the family was expected.

Similarly, many people work all their lives in the informal sector, where retirement protection is rare. Increasingly, with economic development, younger and middle-aged people are moving to wage-economy employment but few as yet have built long-term careers. Therefore, fragmented occupational structures are commonplace and lead to a lack of long-term retirement provision. Indeed, relatively few people have any comprehensive pensions and retirement schemes, with the exception of a small number of countries such as Japan and the Republic of Korea.

In several countries (such as the Hong Kong SAR, Malaysia, and at the poorer end, Cambodia), formal pension benefits are primarily limited to civil servants or employees of state-owned enterprises, to senior staff in major national and international corporations, or, in some countries, to the military. After much debate, Hong Kong belatedly followed Singapore's well-known Central Provident Fund and started a Mandatory Provident Fund (MPF) scheme in December 2000. This provides a good general example, as it will be many years before it benefits older people, since it is essentially an individual savings scheme that requires decades to build a substantial retirement fund. Moreover, it principally only covers those who work and pay contributions. It has also been seen as a very minimal fund, for which reasons the amounts of contribution and tax deductions were under reassessment in 2007. Similar remarks have been aimed at Malaysia's Employees Provident Fund (EPF), which provides only limited savings for retirement and does not compulsorily cover many people who work in the informal sector (Ong et al., 2009). In Cambodia, barely 5 per cent of older persons report having a pension, so employment and transfer payments from the family are the main sources of income (Cambodia National Committee for Population and Development, 2007). Regionally, however, with the growth of nuclear families and fewer children, older people must inevitably try to become more independent financially in the coming years. Therefore, pension provisions, especially comprehensive basic systems, are becoming paramount.

Even the most affluent countries in the region are already finding it difficult to formulate sustainable pension schemes, including Japan, which perhaps has the best-established system. The Japanese pension system is primarily pay-as-you-go with partial pre-funding and is funded by employees and employers combined contributing 13.58 per cent of their annual wages. Government subsidies then support approximately one-third of basic flat rate benefits. Reforms were proposed in 2004 to improve prospects for the scheme's solvency, with increases of employee contributions to a ceiling of 18.30 per cent in 2017 and annual benefit reductions over the next 20 years. It is thought that a typical couple would see benefits fall from 60 per cent to 43 per cent of retirement income by 2023. These reforms have of course met domestic criticism but have generally been felt to be needed by international observers.

Regionally, as elsewhere, various pension options are being considered. Clearly, universal retirement support is desirable but everywhere governments are retreating from such provision even when it is established. Today, a balance of various sources is being advocated. As most employment-based and personal pension schemes do not reach the most vulnerable, some sort of universal, non-contributory social pension schemes are needed. Indeed, the UN (2007) points out that the simplest minimum pension scheme for old-age income security would be a universal transfer equal to the poverty line for all above a certain age, in spite of the difficulties of defining such levels in specific countries. This could be non-contributory (essential in the poorest countries), and variously financed through general taxation, by a 'solidarity tax', or by some sort of earmarked tax. A major problem is, of course, in the poorest countries especially, where the tax base is narrow and unreliable, and therefore the sources of funds are uncertain. HelpAge International (2007b), in particular, emphasizes that minimum non-contributory social pensions for the poor have enormous benefits as they trickle down and support many members of families. Recent ILO data suggest that such schemes can reduce poverty by 35–40 per cent but only require about 1–2 per cent of gross domestic product (GDP). These social pensions choices are thus probably affordable, but vested interests today tend to promote mainly private pension funds. As Mark Gorman of Help Age International (2007b) suggests, 'The key choice in developing social pensions policy is whether social pensions should be a) means tested and restricted to vulnerable older people or b) universal transfers which raise the living standards of the widest possible section of the population' (2007b: 5). This is very important as some 80 per cent of older people in developing countries, which cover the bulk of the Asia-Pacific region's population, have no regular income and therefore are forced to work during old age or fall back onto their families.

As yet, there is not a comprehensive regional overview of the percentages covered by pensions of any type – social, private, or mixed – although Salditt et al. (2007) provide a summary table for some Asian countries of coverage of social security schemes for older persons. In general, evidence suggests the percentages receiving regular pensions are low. In Asia, it is estimated that only 9–30 per cent of the older population receives any pension or social security benefits (UNESCAP, 2004).

Things may be changing, though slowly. In addition, as Cheng et al. (2008) note, public–private sector partnerships are also becoming important in many countries in many areas of social protection (OECD, 2005). Indeed, the role of the private sector in pension provision is increasingly being discussed in many Asian countries, although a HSBC (2005) review of retirement covering five Asian countries found the role of the private sector is currently still generally small, if growing. Malaysia's EPF is a compulsory saving scheme for private sector employees, but only voluntary for the informal workers, and some funds are invested with outside managers. The Republic of Korea has been implementing reform of its national pension by developing a three-tier system, introduced in 1988, but already feared to run into deficit. The third tier would be an optional individual pension from the financial market, providing around a quarter of the retirees total pension, to supplement the national and occupational pensions schemes. A long-term business trend is emerging in the Asian region for public financial institutions to try to improve efficiency, reduce costs, and improve returns, which are often low, noted in Japan, China, Sri Lanka, and Malaysia. In Japan, in 2001, a new Government Pension Insurance Fund (GPIF) was set up as the investment management agency. The Hong Kong MPF is effectively outsourced to private investment fund managers. Therefore, strong regulation for the protection of investments and benefits, as well as maximizing returns for savers, are crucial. Whether the private sector involvement will militate against the development of universal social pensions is a concern for older people and current pensions savers.

The case of China

China, the most populous country in the world, has experienced tremendous social and economic changes, with enormous challenges to providing a safety net for retired workers, many of whom were formerly covered by state-owned enterprises and agriculture but who today are not covered. In the transition to a market economy, the 'iron rice bowl', cradle-to-grave system has effectively been dismantled. The pay-as-you-go pension funds of many state-owned enterprises, huge employers, are bankrupt and basically only civil servants and some urban workers in certain enterprises are now covered in reality. As the old pension system has declined, by the end of 2002, the social security covered only 14 per cent of the workforce, of which almost all were urban workers. But China, since 1997, is in the gradual process of building

the largest pension system in the world, across the nation but effectively based at the provincial and county levels (Salditt et al., 2007). Since formal pension coverage in rural areas is currently very small (and some 64 per cent of China's population, and even more of the older population, are in rural areas), as many as 85 million older persons in rural areas are not covered by social welfare, pensions, or adequate medical care. How to address this has become a major target for China's policy-makers, especially the provision for migrant workers in their retirement, made more crucial by the financial turmoil of 2009. The Organisation for Economic Co-operation and Development (OECD) suggests that the family is still the main source of income for half of those aged 60+ in rural areas (Salditt et al., 2007).

Whereas China has declared that enabling better social protection in poor rural areas is a matter of national priority, it is extremely difficult to manage an effective pension system for such a large and populous country. Demographic changes (ageing and the one-child policy) imply fewer future taxable workers to support more retirement beneficiaries. For instance, in the year 2001, 29 retirees would be supported by 100 workers in China, but this is expected to increase to 55 by around 2030 (Keran and Cheng, 2002). Like many other countries, China is increasing its outsourcing social security reserves to private industry and regulating private pension schemes in attempts to achieve greater adequacy in retirement benefits in the long run. Private savings, as the new 'third pillar' of retirement income, are currently heavily invested in stock market speculation by all levels of citizens. The household saving rate is relatively high, as in other parts of Asia, but because of low wages, absolute amounts are low. The OECD notes that China has relatively expensive formal pension contribution rates, low portability, low returns on investments, and low public trust in many public pension schemes. They further estimate a window of opportunity between now and 2015 for China to upgrade its pension systems (Salditt et al., 2007).

Gender equality and eliminating age discrimination

Throughout most of Asia, older women are often caregivers for life for their own and the extended family, but they often receive little formal support for these informal roles. For instance, among married older persons in Thailand, 71.2 per cent of currently married men, compared with 49.7 per cent of women, nominated their spouse to be the main personal care provider (Knodel et al., 2005;

Knodel and Chayovan, 2009). Women most often cited a child or a child-in-law as their main provider of assistance, regardless of marital status or stage of old age. This is a very common situation and, on marriage, a new wife often traditionally becomes responsible for her husband's older parents.

Historically, women in the region have been disadvantaged by lack of education, illiteracy, and dependency on men for land and income, and many still are in the same condition today in some countries. Lack of education, especially in the rural areas, isolation, and lack of formal support place widows at increased risk of physical and psychological ill-health (Sorkin et al., 2002; UNESCAP, 2002b). Women can also suffer on divorce and on the death of their spouse, as they can lose the protection of the spouse's family who, conversely, can then lose a major female carer if a divorce occurs.

It is possible that, in the focus on women's health and welfare, the well-being and health of older males can be neglected. Males on average have shorter life expectancies than women in all the countries in the region, often the difference being 5 years or even around 6 years as in Japan, Hong Kong, and Taiwan. Also, as men grow older, they may become less likely to maintain a broad social network and they can tend to rely considerably on immediate family members, especially their wives, for psychological and practical support. As they have often spent time working, men often come to rely on their wives for networks, maintaining friendships, home care, and for psychosocial support. Their traditional roles as household head in patriarchal family structures can ironically make them somewhat distant from their own children. It has been noted that men often suffer more psychologically than women when their spouses are incapacitated or die (Cheng and Chan, 2006b).

In spite of traditional Asian reverence for age, it seems that negative stereotypes of older persons are unfortunately rather common in the region and sometimes these may extend beyond, into mistreatment of older persons. Abuse of older persons ('elder abuse') is probably much more prevalent than any official figures suggest. Indeed, abuse often occurs within the family, in its many complex structures, and also in institutional care. Older persons may be unable or unwilling to report abuse, and often the neglect aspects of abuse are not identified as such by the parties involved. Research in Hong Kong suggests that as many as 20 per cent of older persons had suffered some sort of abuse and that 75 per cent of abusers were their own children, many of whom were living with their older parents. Although China does have some legislation that states children

have a duty to support and assist their parents, there are as yet no such legal requirements in Hong Kong, even though the media and government are promoting family care (Chan et al., 2007).

More generally in the region, gender discrimination affects primarily older women but age discrimination directly or indirectly affects everyone in any society, as it is a type of segregation. Negative stereotypes of older people can reinforce ageism and, unfortunately, illiteracy and low education can perpetrate the myth of the non-productive, dependent, and frail older person. The 2005 UNESCAP regional survey found that most countries claimed to be promoting positive images of ageing, typically through public education and media campaigns, but the impacts of such campaigns are generally long term and can be slow to materialize. The International Federation on Ageing and HelpAge International (2009) note that, while generalization is difficult, overt age discrimination has tended to reduce overall in Asia but it still persists in some direct ways and often in subtle or indirect ways. It also affects males and females differently. Older women in particular are vulnerable, due to their low skills and inability to generate their own sources of income, so they are totally reliant on their families, often with little or no formal external support being available.

Economic, social, and political participation and employment

There is a considerable gender and age gap in economic participation almost everywhere. In most of the Asian countries for which data are available, female labour force participation rates at age 50–64 are much lower that those of males, often by half or two-thirds (ILO, 2007). In China, for example, labour force participation rates at 50–54 are 93 per cent for males but only 59 per cent for females. At age 60–64, these figures have fallen to 68.7 per cent and 26.9 per cent, respectively. Similar, if not quite as spectacular, declines are to be seen in Thailand, the Philippines, the Republic of Korea, and Japan. In Malaysia and Singapore, declines are even greater and, at 60–64 in Singapore, only 49.6 per cent of males and 15.3 per cent of females were participating in the labour force in 2000 (ILO, 2007; Peng and Fausten, 2006). In the region in the future, this is clearly an area in which change is to be expected as better educated and more independent cohorts of females enter older age and may want to use their skills and knowledge outside the home, although exactly how this will develop is very hard to predict. If trends in Europe and America are followed, these participation rates in Asia may again decline because, as populations become wealthier, labour force participation rates for older men and women tend to fall, especially when older people become eligible for pensions and benefits (Clark et al., 2004).

Access to knowledge, information, education, and training is one of the key issues identified in the MIPAA. Crucial to the employment of older workers, both male and female, is their skills and training in the face of changing current and future occupational structures. However, it seems that bias makes training or retraining for older employees relatively rare in most developed countries in the Asia-Pacific although some, such as Singapore, Malaysia, and Hong Kong, are starting to develop this and it is expected to grow elsewhere. Recognizing labour shortages and to improve older people's employability, Singapore provides a range of preferential funding support for skills development and lifelong learning, although it is acknowledged that ageist notions are still hard to shake among many employers (Teo et al., 2006). This is common regionally and, at the moment, many older persons tend to be relegated to unskilled or semi-skilled tasks if they wish to remain working, as employers may feel they have limited, outdated skills or lack of information technology (IT) modern skills, and even basic literacy (Chan et al., 2003). However, the view that technological changes automatically disadvantaged older persons, and especially older workers, is increasingly being challenged. Developments are taking place in 'seniors' IT training and in the application of user-friendly technology in people's homes and lives in countries such as China, Singapore, Hong Kong, and others (Chan et al., 2003). Moreover, if patterns in the West are followed, older people will increasingly be seen as a source of stable, reliable employees who can take on a wide range of tasks.

Indeed, technological change can potentially have wider benefits to older people, particularly in communications (phone networks, email) and transportation, which can allow family members to maintain relationships and crucial services over geographical distances that previously required co-residence or physical proximity (Mujahid, 2006). As Knodel and Saengtienchai's (2007) research in Thailand shows, mobile (cell, hand) phones have improved the maintenance of contact and social support between elderly parents and their adult children who live or work away. This can help maintain family social networks and at least enable contact over long distances, which would previously have totally separated parents and children. However, in spite of increasing

opportunities for training and exposure to IT (Chan et al., 2003), some older adults are deterred by a lack of skills or access to, say, the internet, in engaging in the growing power of online political activism, as a comparison of China and the United States indicates (Xie and Jager, 2007).

The MIPAA also has an objective to promote full utilization of the potential and expertise of persons of all ages, in recognition that increased experience with age can bring benefits. However, this is not always recognized and legislation may be necessary to enhance the availability of jobs or work for older persons. Some countries (China, Singapore, Republic of Korea, and others) are raising their formal retirement ages gradually, but middle-aged and late-middle-aged persons also quite commonly face discrimination when seeking formal employment. Unfortunately, legal protection against age discrimination is quite rare in Asia. Some places, such as Hong Kong, provide financial incentives to employers of persons aged over 40 or 45, but these are usually of limited duration and impact. Other, countries such as Japan, have enacted anti-age-discrimination legislation to protect the rights of older people in employment and in service. Korea, though currently without formal anti-age-discrimination legislation, has introduced affirmative actions to promote the participation of older persons in employment but it foresees opposition from corporations in enacting laws prohibiting age discrimination. Its Aged Employment Promotion Law stipulates numerous jobs for which priority should be given to older applicants although, as these mainly involve low-status work (selling tickets, attending parking lots, etc.), it may even add to stereotyping.

Formal measures may be more crucial for the more-developed countries of the region, whereas the economies of some developing countries still often have a substantial agricultural sector in which labour is shared by all ages in extended families. Moreover, emigration by younger workers to urban industrial employment can in fact make the older workers the only ones available in some rural areas. Emerging labour shortages in some Asia-Pacific countries may also add to the perceived value of older workers, as is evident in some parts of the economies in Singapore, Hong Kong, and Japan, although again the issue of training and skills of older workers can be a problem.

Volunteering by older people is becoming an important phenomenon both amongst older persons in the region and for some non-governmental organizations (NGOs) and even formal organizations. For individuals, volunteering in unpaid or minimally reimbursed activities can help compensate for role losses and help to build social ties. If it enhances social well-being, it can contribute to overall successful ageing and bolster the social participation pillar of WHO's *Active Ageing Policy Framework*, referred to earlier. As future cohorts of older people in Asia will be both better educated and probably more healthy, the desire both to volunteer and to continue contributing in various ways are going to increase, including participating in political and pressure groups (Cheng et al., 2004; Chou et al., 2003). Indeed, older people are likely to become ever more politically active and influential, given their growing proportions in the populations. However, today, many Asian older persons, having grown up in a tradition of submissiveness, obedience, and deference, tend to accept what they are given and are currently as a group often politically and socially quiescent.

It is probably true that many Asian older people, especially poorer ones, may not yet be interested in pressure groups, the political process, or elections. However, in countries such as the Philippines, local organizations working with older persons can assist them in both arousing awareness and participating in pressure groups. Activist groups are pressing for housing, social, and pension benefits in many countries such as Hong Kong, China, and Japan. Indeed, the increasing active political participation of older people in Japan, where they form such an important percentage of the electorate, has focused increasing attention from all political parties on pension reform, health, and social welfare. In Thailand's November 2007 elections, one candidate allegedly bribed older male voters with Viagra, a novel way of recognizing the value of the older person's vote. In Vietnam, too, where 30 per cent of older people are below the poverty line and almost two-thirds have no pensions or health cover, Global Action on Aging reports there is increasing evidence that older persons are wanting their rights. A 'demand action campaign' was organized in 2007 with HelpAge International and, using website resources, positively highlighted the roles and contributions of older persons in Vietnam's development (Nguyen, 2008).

CONCLUSION: FUTURE CHALLENGES

What will the coming decades hold for this region? There will clearly be considerable growth in the numbers and percentages of older persons in many countries, especially in East Asia, and an important, if less spectacular, growth in percentages in most countries of Southeast Asia. This will bring many challenges to all concerned. It is predicted that some governments will react positively and some are doing so already, and many NGOs and other organizations are devoting energies to organizing societies for their ageing futures. Meeting the challenge also involves developing positive attitudes amongst older persons themselves and society at large, and there is some evidence of this emerging trend, as noted above. One important phenomenon to address is what is sometimes called 'moral panic', the overstated fear or over-frequently mentioned concern about the impacts and 'problems' of ageing, which is sometimes intentionally or unthinkingly aroused by politicians, economists, and even healthcare professionals. It can be taken up in the media, which can overestimate potential costs (in terms of health and welfare, for example) and the possible future 'social problems' caused by larger numbers of older persons with fewer children and young people to care for them. Such ageism can be unintentional, and is often ill-informed and speculatively based purely on numbers of older persons rather than qualitative factors. The potentially negative aspects of the human success story of demographic ageing and greater longevity can certainly be mitigated with sufficient planning and provision, and the regional reviews of the MIPAA indicate this is gaining ground.

In spite of everything, the family frequently remains the preferred official and popular mainstay of support for older people in much of the Asia-Pacific region. A major challenge is therefore how to bolster 'traditional Asian values' and enable families to continue to perform this role. Initiatives to support ageing in place and the use of older volunteers offer some solutions. Likewise, strategies to reduce poverty among older people are another important avenue. The extension of non-contributory social pensions, as suggested by HelpAge International (2007b), definitely holds the potential to alleviate elderly and family poverty among the lowest-income groups, even if the development of such schemes represents a huge challenge. The provision of cost-effective, culturally acceptable, and accessible primary health care, near to communities, will also help to address the major common ailments of older people. Optimistically, with adequate planning and investment in retirement protection and with improving health, social, and educational services, future cohorts of older persons in the Asia-Pacific region will be healthier, wealthier, and more self-sufficient than today's population. Therefore, the future emphasis must be on practical and affordable social, health, and income provision for older Asia-Pacific populations and for their families.

REFERENCES

Arifin, E.N. (2006) 'Living arrangements of older persons in East Java, Indonesia', *Asia-Pacific Population Journal*, 21(3): 93–112.

Caldwell, J.C. and Caldwell, B.K. (2006) 'Important issues in the continuing mortality revolution in the Asian and Pacific Region', *Asia-Pacific Population Journal*, Special Issue: 47–64.

Cambodia National Committee for Population and Development (2007) *Population Ageing in Cambodia: Planning for Social Protection*. Phnom Phen: Office of the Council of Ministers and UNFPA.

Chan, A.C.M., Cheng, S.-T., and Li, C. (2007) Protective legislation for older persons in Hong Kong. *Asian Journal of Gerontology and Geriatrics*, 2(3): 143–52.

Chan, A.C.M., Phillips, D.R., and Fong, F.M.S. (2003) *An Exploratory Study of Older Persons' Computer and Internet Usage in Hong Kong*. Monograph Series No. 3, Asia Pacific Institute of Ageing Studies, Lingnan University, Hong Kong.

Chan, A.C.M. and Phillips, D.R. (2005) *Report on the Regional Survey on Ageing (2005)*. Bangkok, Thailand: United Nations Economic and Social Commission for Asia and the Pacific.

Cheng, S.-T. and Chan, A.C.M. (2006a) 'Filial piety and psychological well-being in well older Chinese', *Journal of Gerontology: Psychological Sciences*, 61B: 262–9.

Cheng, S.-T. and Chan, A.C.M. (2006b) 'Relationship with others and life satisfaction in later life: Do gender and widowhood make a difference?', *Journal of Gerontology: Psychological Sciences*, 61B: 46–53.

Cheng, S.-T. and Heller, K. (2009) Global aging: challenges for community psychology, *American Journal of Community Psychology*, 44: 161–173.

Cheng, S.-T., Chan, A.C.M., and Phillips, D.R. (2004) 'Quality of life in old age: an investigation of well older persons in Hong Kong', *Journal of Community Psychology*, 32: 309–26.

Cheng, S.-T., Chan, A.C.M., and Phillips, D.R. (2008) 'Ageing trends in Asia and the Pacific', *Regional Dimensions of the Ageing Situation*. Department of Economic and Social Affairs. New York: United Nations, pp. 35–69.

Cheng, S-T., Phillips, D.R., and Chan, A.C.M. (2009) 'Asia-Pacific Region', in E.B. Palmore, F. Whittington and S. Kunkel (eds), *The International Handbook on Aging*. Santa Barbara, Ca.: Praeger, pp. 29–54.

Chiu, H.F.K., Takahashi, Y., and Suh, G.H. (2003) 'Elderly suicide prevention in Asia', editorial, *International Journal of Geriatric Psychiatry*, 18(11): 973–6.

Choi, S.J. (2000) 'Ageing in Korea: issues and policies', in D.R. Phillips (ed.), *Ageing in the Asia-Pacific Region*. London: Routledge, pp. 223–42.

Choi, S.J. (2002) 'National policies on ageing in Korea', in D.R. Phillips and A.C.M. Chan (eds), *Ageing and Long-term Care: National Policies in the Asia-Pacific*. Singapore: Institute of Southeast Asian Studies and Ottawa, International Development Research Centre, pp. 68–106.

Chou, K.-L., Chow, N.W.S., and Chi, I. (2003) 'Volunteering aspirations of Hong Kong Chinese soon-to-be-old adults', *Activities, Adaptation and Aging*, 27(3/4): 79–96.

Clark, R.L., Burkhauser, R.V., Moon, M., Quinn, J.F., and Smeeding, T.M. (2004) *The Economics of an Aging Society*. Malden, MA: Blackwell.

Eun, K.-S. (2007) 'Lowest-low fertility in the Republic of Korea: causes, consequences and policy responses', *Asia-Pacific Population Journal*, 22(2): 51–72.

Goodman, R. and Harper, S. (2006) 'Introduction: Asia's position in the new global demography', *Oxford Development Studies*, 34(4): 373–85.

Gu, B. (2007) 'Low fertility in China: trends, policy and impact', *Asia-Pacific Population Journal*, 22(2): 73–87.

He, W., Sengupta, M., Zhang, K., and Guo, P. (2007) *Health and Health Care of the Older Population in Urban and Rural China: 2000*. US Census Bureau, International Population Reports P95/07–2. Washington, DC: US Government Printing Office.

Hedrick-Wong, Y. (2006) *The Glittering Silver Market: The Rise of the Elderly Consumers in Asia*. New York: Wiley.

HelpAge International (2007a) *Primary Health Care for Older Persons: A Participatory Study in 5 Asian Countries*. Asia-Pacific HAI Network, Chiang Mai: HAI.

HelpAge International (2007b) *Social Cash Transfers for Asia: Ensuring Social Protection/Social Pensions in Old Age in the Context of Rapid Ageing*. National Committee for Population and Development, Cambodia, Report on the intergovernmental regional seminar, Bangkok, January 2007. Chiang Mai: HAI.

HSBC (2007) *HSBC Global Forum on Ageing and Retirement. 2007 Report: The Future of Retirement – the New Old Age – Global Report*. https://www.ageingforum.org/files/8/default.aspx. Retrieved August 14, 2007.

Hughes, R. and Fu, T.H. (eds.) (2009) *Ageing in East Asia: Challenges and Policies for the 21st Century*. London: Routledge.

International Federation on Ageing and HelpAge International (2009) *The Rights of Older Persons in Asia*. http://www.globalaging.org/elderrights/world/2009/humanrightsasia.pdf. Accessed March 19, 2009.

International Labour Office (ILO) (2007) *LABORSTA Internet*. http://laborsta.ilo.org/

Kespichayawattana, J. and Jitapunkal, S. (2009) Health and health care system for older persons, *Ageing International*, 33: 1–4, 28–49.

Kaneda, T. (2006) 'China's concern over population aging and health', Population Reference Bureau, http://www.prb.org/. Retrieved August 3, 2007.

Keran, M., and Cheng, H.-S. (2002) *International Experience and Pension Reform in China* (Issue Paper No. 16). Burlingame, CA: The 1990 Institute.

Kinsella, K. and Phillips, D.R. (2005) 'Global aging: the challenge of success', *Population Bulletin*, 60(1): 1–40.

Knodel, J. and Chayovan, N. (2009) Intergenerational relationships and family care and support for Thai elderly, *Ageing International*, 33: 1–4, 15–27.

Knodel, J., Chayovan, N., Mithranon, P., Amornsirisomboon, P., and Arunraksombat, S. (2005) *Thailand's Older Population: Social and Economic Support as Assessed in 2002*. Population Studies Center Research Report No. 05–571, Institute for Social Research, University of Michigan.

Knodel, J. and Saengtienchai, C. (2007) 'Rural parents with urban children: social and economic implications of migration for the rural elderly in Thailand', *Population, Space and Place*, 13(3): 193–210.

Knodel, J. and Zimmer, Z. (2007) 'Older person's knowledge and willingness to provide care in an impoverished nation:

evidence from Cambodia', *Asia-Pacific Population Journal*, 22(1): 11–28.

Maddison, A. (2003) *The World Economy: Historical Statistics*. Development Centre Studies, Paris: OECD.

Maidment, R., Mackerras, C., and Schak, D. (eds) (1998) *Culture and Society in the Asia Pacific*. London: Routledge.

Mason, A. (2006) 'Population ageing and demographic dividends: the time to act is now', *Asia-Pacific Population Journal*, 21(3): 7–16.

McCracken, K. and Phillips, D.R. (2005) 'International demographic transitions', in G. Andrews and D.R. Phillips (eds), *Ageing and Place*. London: Routledge, pp. 36–60.

McDonald, P. (2007) 'The emergence of low fertility as a policy issue', *Asia-Pacific Population Journal*, 22(2): 5–9.

Ministry of Social Development and Human Security, Thailand (2007) *Thailand's Implementation of the Shanghai Implementation Strategy (SIS) and the Madrid International Plan of Action on Ageing (MIPAA)*. Bangkok: Bureau of Empowerment for Older Persons, MSDHS.

Mujahid, G. (2006) *Population Ageing in East and South-East Asia: Current Situation and Emerging Challenges*. Bangkok: UNFPA Country Technical Services Team for East and South-East Asia.

National Institute on Aging (NIA) (2007) *Why Population Aging Matters: A Global Perspective*. Washington, DC: NIA.

Ng, A.C.Y., Phillips, D.R., and Lee, W.K.M. (2002) 'Persistence and challenges to filial piety and informal support of older persons in a modern Chinese society: a case study in Tuen Mun, Hong Kong', *Journal of Aging Studies*, 16: 1–20.

Nguyen, T.N.T. (2008) *Age Demand Action: Vietnam 2007*. HelpAge International et al. http://www.globalaging.org/agingwatch/events/ngos/vietnam.pdf. Accessed March 26, 2009.

Organization for Economic Co-operation and Development (OECD) (2005) *Summary Record of the OECD/IOPS Conference on Private Pensions*. April 27–28, 2005, Bangkok, Thailand.

Oh, K.M. and Warnes, A.M. (2001) 'Care services for frail older people in South Korea', *Ageing and Society*, 21: 701–20.

Ong, F.S. and Phillips, D.R. (2007) 'Older consumers in Malaysia', *International Journal of Ageing and Later Life*, 2(1): 83–115.

Ong, F.S., Phillips, D.R., and Tengku-Aizan, H. (2009) 'Ageing in Malaysia: progress and prospects', in R. Hughes and T.H. Fu (eds), *Ageing in East Asia: Challenges and Policies for the 21st Century*. London: Routledge, pp. 138–160.

Peng, X. and Fausten, D. (2006) 'Population ageing and labour supply in China from 2005–2050', *Asia-Pacific Population Journal*, 2(3): 31–62.

Phillips, D.R. (ed.) (1992) *Ageing in East and South-east Asia*. London: Edward Arnold.

Phillips, D.R. (ed.) (2000) *Ageing in the Asia-Pacific Region*. London: Routledge.

Phillips, D.R. (2002) 'Family support for older persons in East Asia: Demise or durability?', in United Nations Department of Economic and Social Affairs, *Sustainable Social Structures in a Society for All Ages* (Report No. ST/ESA/275). New York: UN, pp. 42–7.

Phillips, D.R. and Chan, A.C.M. (eds) (2002a) *Ageing and Long-term care: National Policies in the Asia-Pacific*. Singapore: Institute of Southeast Asian Studies and Ottawa, International Development Research Centre.

Phillips, D.R. and Chan, A.C.M. (2002b) 'Ageing in Asia and the Pacific: critical issues in national policies and programmes', in United Nations Economic and Social Commission for Asia and the Pacific, *National Policies and Programmes on Ageing in Asia and the Pacific: An Overview and Lessons Learned* (Social Policy Paper No. 9). New York: UN, pp. 1–41.

Phillips, D.R. and Chan, A.C.M. (2002c) 'Social services for older persons in Asia and the Pacific: trends and issues', in United Nations Economic and Social Commission for Asia and the Pacific, *National Policies and Programmes on Ageing in Asia and the Pacific: An Overview and Lessons Learned* (Social Policy Paper No. 9). New York: UN, pp. 85–110.

Phillips, D.R., Siu, O.L., Yeh, A., and Cheng, K. (2004) 'Factors influencing older persons' residential satisfaction in big and densely populated cities in Asia: a case study in Hong Kong', *Ageing International*, 29(1): 46–70.

Phillips, D.R., Siu, O.L., Yeh, A., and Cheng, K. (2005) 'The impacts of dwelling conditions on older persons' psychological well-being in Hong Kong: the mediating role of residential satisfaction', *Social Science and Medicine*, 60(12): 2785–97.

Phillips, D.R., Siu, O.L., Yeh, A., and Cheng, K. (2008) 'Informal social support and older persons' psychological well-being in Hong Kong', *Journal of Cross-Cultural Gerontology*, 23: 39–55.

Population Reference Bureau (2008) *2008 World Population Data Sheet*. Washington, DC: PRB.

Rowe, J.W. and Kahn, R.L. (1998) *Successful Aging*. New York: Pantheon.

Salditt, F., Whiteford, P., and Adema, W. (2007) *Pension Reform in China: Progress and Prospect*. OECD Social, Employment and Migration Working Papers No. 53. Paris: OECD.

Seetharam, K.S. (2006) 'Age-structure transition and development in Asia and the Pacific: opportunities and challenges', *Asia-Pacific Population Journal*, Special Issue: 65–86.

Sorkin, D., Rook, K.S., and Lu, J.L. (2002). 'Loneliness, lack of emotional support, lack of companionship, and the likelihood of having a heart condition in an elderly sample', *Annals of Behavioral Medicine*, 24: 290–8.

Teo, P., Mehta, K., Thang, L.L., and Chan, A. (2006) *Ageing in Singapore: Service Needs and the State*. London: Routledge.

Thanakwang, K. and Soonthorndhada, K. (2006) 'Attributes of active ageing among older persons in Thailand: evidence from the 2002 survey', *Asia-Pacific Population Journal*, 21(3): 113–35.

United Nations (2002) *Report of the Second World Assembly on Ageing*. New York: UN.

United Nations (2006) *Follow-up to the Second World Assembly on Ageing: Report of the Secretary-General* (Paper A/61/167 of the 61st General Assembly). New York: UN.

United Nations (2007) *World Economic and Social Survey 2007: Development in an Ageing World.* New York: UN.

United Nations Department of Economic and Social Affairs (UNDESA) (2005) *Living Arrangements of Older Persons Around the World.* Population Division, UNDESA. New York: UN.

United Nations Economic and Social Commission for Asia and the Pacific (UNESCAP) (1999) *Macao Plan of Action on Ageing for Asia and the Pacific.* New York: UN.

United Nations Economic and Social Commission for Asia and the Pacific (UNESCAP) (2002a) *Report on the Regional Survey on Ageing (June 2002).* Bangkok: UN.

United Nations Economic and Social Commission for Asia and the Pacific (UNESCAP) (2002b). *National Policies and Programmes on Ageing in Asia and the Pacific: An Overview and Lessons Learned.* Social Policy Paper No. 9. New York: UN.

United Nations Economic and Social Commission for Asia and the Pacific (UNESCAP) (2002c). *Ageing in Asia and the Pacific: Emerging Issues and successful practices.* Social Policy Paper No. 10. New York: UN.

United Nations Economic and Social Commission for Asia and the Pacific (UNESCAP) (2004) *Report of the Regional Seminar on Follow-up to the Shanghai Implementation Strategy for the Madrid and Macao Plans of Action on Ageing.* Bangkok: UN.

United Nations Economic and Social Commission for Asia and the Pacific (UNESCAP) (2005) *Report on the Regional Survey on Ageing.* Bangkok: UN.

United Nations Economic and Social Commission for Asia and the Pacific (UNESCAP) (2005/2006) *Population Data Sheets* (annual). Bangkok: UNESCAP.

United Nations Economic and Social Commission for Asia and the Pacific (UNESCAP) (2007) *The Macao Outcome Document of the High-level Meeting on the Regional Review of the Implementation of the Madrid International Plan of Action on Ageing.* Macao, China, October, 9–11. Bangkok: UN.

World Health Organization (2002) *Active Ageing: A Policy Framework.* Geneva: WHO.

World Health Organization (WHO) (2006) *Preventing Chronic Diseases: A Vital Investment.* Geneva: WHO. http://www.who.int/chp/chronic_disease_report/en/index.html. Accessed March 19, 2009.

World Health Organization (WHO) (2007) *Women, Ageing and Health: a Framework for Action. Focus on Gender.* Geneva: WHO.

World Health Organization (WHO) (2008) *Closing the Gap in a Generation: Health Equity Through Action on the Social Determinants of Health.* Geneva: WHO.

Wu, B., Carter, M.W., Goins, R.T., and Cheng, C.R. (2005) Emerging services for community-based long-term care in urban China: a systematic analysis of Shanghai's community-based agencies, *Journal of Aging and Social Policy*, 17(4): 37–60.

Xie, B. and Jager, P.T. (2008) 'Older adults and political participation on the Internet: a cross-cultural comparison of the USA and China', *Journal of Cross-Cultural Gerontology*, 23, 1: 1–15.

Yoon, H. and Hendricks, J. (2006). *Handbook of Asian Aging.* Amityville, NY: Baywood.

Zhan, H.J., Liu, G., Guan, X., and Bai, H. (2006) 'Recent developments in institutional elder care in China: changing concepts and attitudes', *Journal of Aging and Social Policy*, 18(2): 85–108.

34

The Significance of Grandparents to Grandchildren: An International Perspective

Peter Uhlenberg and Michelle Cheuk

INTRODUCTION

Grandparenthood is a socially recognized category in every human society, but the meaning and significance of grandparenthood is socially constructed. This chapter focuses on the significance of grandparents for children, and we use studies from a number of societies to explore this issue. These studies reveal that, despite vast social, economic, and political differences across societies, grandparents always make a difference in the lives of some children. This is not to say, of course, that all grandparents make a positive contribution to the lives of their grandchildren. Although hardly studied, we know that some grandparents harm children by being abusive or by creating stress in children's families, and some grandparents have no involvement with their grandchildren. Nevertheless, the evidence is quite clear that across a wide range of societies, grandparents overall make important contributions to the well-being of children. This is especially evident in situations where children are at most risk.

To appreciate the significant contributions of grandparents in contemporary societies, we begin by exploring how changing demographic conditions are affecting the availability of grandparents

to have relationships with grandchildren. As noted by Bengtson (2001), the growing significance of multigenerational bonds in families is contingent upon demographic forces that have altered the structure of kinship networks. The remainder of the chapter considers ways in which grandparents affect the lives of children. The specific areas examined are: grandparents as surrogate parents of children; grandparents as childcare providers; grandparents as socializers and role models for children; and grandparents as sources of economic support for children.

DEMOGRAPHIC REGIMES AND SUPPLY OF GRANDPARENTS AND GRANDCHILDREN

Each of the primary demographic variables – fertility, mortality, and migration – has important implications for grandparent–grandchild relationships. Indeed, fertility and mortality patterns determine the supply of grandparents for children and the supply of grandchildren for older people. And studies have repeatedly shown that geographic proximity is associated with the level of interaction between members of different generations. This section first examines how historical demographic changes have affected the availability of grandparents for children and grandchildren for older people. Then, implications of some major contemporary differences in demographic behavior across societies are discussed.

Mortality

The relevance of the dramatic decline in death rates over the last two centuries in developed countries for grandparent–grandchild relationships depends on whose perspective one is taking. From the perspective of older persons, declining mortality hardly affected the likelihood that they had grandchildren. Given similar fertility patterns, an individual who survives to age 60 or 65 is equally likely to have a grandchild whether mortality rates are high or low. However, there are two potentially significant implications of a population moving from high to low mortality levels for grandparents. First, as the death of children changes from being commonplace to exceptional, one might expect that the emotional involvement of grandparents with their grandchildren would increase. This argument has been used to explain the increasing intimacy in parent–child relationships in the modern era (Shorter, 1975), and it can easily be extended to grandparent–grandchild relationships. When six out of a 1000 newborns die before reaching adulthood, as in Sweden today, it is much safer for grandparents to invest in relationships with grandchildren than when over one-third do not survive, as in Sweden around 1800 (data from Human Mortality Database).[1] Secondly, declining adult mortality has increased the likelihood that the middle generation survives to mediate the relationship between grandparents and grandchildren. Under mortality conditions existing around 1850, about 40 per cent of the older people who had two daughters who both married and bore children would have seen one of those daughters die before her children were reared. The chance now that a woman would die between ages 25 and 50 is about 3 per cent in the United States and 2 per cent in Norway or the Netherlands (Uhlenberg, 2005). This change is potentially significant because in many cases a grandparent steps in to care for an orphaned grandchild, often assuming the role of surrogate parent. In fact, it was much more common at the beginning of the 20th century than at the end of the century for an older woman in the United States to function as the mother of her grandchildren (Uhlenberg, 2000).

Shifting attention to the perspective of grandchildren, declining adult mortality produced large historical changes in the supply of grandparents. Based on mortality conditions existing in the United States, it is estimated that even in 1900 more than 90 per cent of all 10 year olds would have had at least one living grandparent. But the average number of living grandparents increased substantially in the century after 1900. For example, the proportion of 10 year olds with all four grandparents alive increased from about 6 per cent in 1900 to 41 per cent in 2000. Even more impressive was the increase in living grandparents for young adults. For example, it is estimated that the proportion of 30 year olds with a grandparent alive more than tripled between 1900 and 2000 – from 21 to 76 per cent (Uhlenberg, 2005).

Recent data on existence of grandparents for children and young adults in several European countries further indicate how common it is for children and young adults to have grandparents in low-mortality societies. Studies in Norway found that 40 per cent of the children aged 10–12 have all four grandparents living, and that 10 per cent of the Norwegians aged 40–44 are still grandchildren (Hagestad and Uhlenberg, 2007). Similarly, in Germany in the 1990s, 36 per cent of 10 year-old children had four living grandparents (Lauterbach, 1995). In Britain, 80 per cent of 20 year olds have at least one grandparent living (Grundy et al., 1999). A study of urban adults in four European countries plus Israel in 2000–01 (the OASIS study) found that one-third of people in their thirties still had at least one grandparent living (Hagestad and Herlofson, 2007). The emergence of low mortality in modern societies has made it possible for most children to experience a relationship with grandparents that lasts well into their adult years.

Fertility

A transition from high to low fertility in a society has interesting implications for grandparent–grandchild relationships. Under conditions of high fertility, a grandparent who survives to old age will typically have a large number of grandchildren competing for his or her attention and resources. A child who shares a grandparent with numerous siblings and cousins is likely to have a less intense relationship with that grandparent than one when he/she is an only child or who has few or no cousins (Uhlenberg and Hammill, 1998). Historical data on the number of grandchildren that older people had is not available, but estimates of the number of sets of grandchildren for members of different cohorts approaching old age in the United States suggest that fertility has a large effect on the structure of intergenerational relationships. About one-fourth of the women approaching old age in the 1950s were grand-childless (had zero sets of grandchildren), while the other three-fourths were grandparents of the baby boom (Uhlenberg, 2005). For those who were grandmothers at this time, there was a large supply of grandchildren (the baby boomers). The situation was quite different by the late 20th century, when the new grandmothers were the mothers of the baby boom. Relatively few of these women were grandchildless and about 40 per cent had three or more sets of grandchildren. However, the number of children in each grandchild set tended to be small, reflecting the low fertility of women in the baby-boom cohorts. When baby boomers reach old age, the supply of grandchildren will again change. The proportion with more than two sets of grandchildren will decline to a historic low of only 20 per cent and the number who will be grandchildless will increase significantly. Furthermore, the number of grandchildren in each set will, on average, be small. Hence we can antici-pate a situation where grandchildren will be in short supply.

The fertility decline in the United States after the 1960s produced an environment in which people entering grandparenthood after 2000 will typically have relatively few grandchildren vying for their attention, and one in which children have relatively few cousins and siblings competing for their grandparents' attention. Because fertility decline in most other industrialized countries has greatly exceeded that in the United States, the shifting ratio of grandparents to grandchildren in these countries will be even more pronounced. Italy, with its extremely low birth rate, provides a good example of the magnitude of this change in a relatively short time period. Consider, for example, the changing ratio of the number of children under age 15 to the number of adults aged 50–69 (the age category that contains many of the grandparents of the children). In 1950 this ratio was 1.55, in 2000 it was 0.59, and in 2020 it is expected to be 0.41 (data from *World Population Prospects: The 2006 Revision* and *World Urbanization Prospects: The 2005 Revision*).[2] Clearly grandparents in Italy, and other low-fertility countries, will increasingly find grandchildren to be precious. The large demo-graphic changes altering intergenerational rela-tionships throughout Europe have brought together researchers from a number of countries in an EU-funded research network[3] on 'Grandparenthood and Intergenerational Relationships in Aging European Populations' to explore aspects of grand-parenthood.

The increasing scarcity of grandchildren for older people will also be dramatic in the Asian countries experiencing below-replacement fertility, (such as Japan, South Korea, and China). The one-child policy in China and the resulting rapid decline of fertility in that traditionally kinship-based society is stimulating research on grandpar-enthood in that country (e.g. see Chen and Liu, 2009). As the '4:2:1' family structure (four grand-parents, two parents, one child) becomes increas-ingly common in China, the place of grandchildren might be expected to change. When four grand-parents must share one grandchild, that grandchild will typically receive a great deal of attention.

Migration

Studies in the United States have repeatedly found that geographic proximity is associated with greater contact and closer relationships between grandparents and grandchildren (Uhlenberg and Hammill, 1998). Thus, historical changes in rates of geographic mobility might be expected to play a role in changing intergenerational relationships. Contrary to popular opinion, however, there is no evidence that distance between grandparents and grandchildren increased over time. Geographic mobility has not increased over the past century in the United States (Wolf and Longino, 2005) or in the Nordic countries (Sundstrom, 2009). However, in countries such as China where rapid urbaniza-tion is currently occurring, migration may have significance for intergenerational relationships (Chen et al., 2000).

A relatively unexamined issue is the conse-quence of international migration for grandparent–grandchild relationships. Children whose parents migrate from their home country may have lim-ited contact with their grandparents living in a different country. The number of children in this situation is large. In the United States in 2006, 21 per cent of all children had at least one foreign-born parent. A similar situation exists in Western European countries where large-scale immigra-tion is changing the ethnic composition of the population. In many of these countries more than 10 per cent of the children are living in immigrant families.

GRANDPARENTS AS SURROGATE PARENTS

Of all the ways that grandparents can significantly affect the lives of grandchildren, none could be more important than when they take on the role of the child's parent. Families in which grandparents live with and care for grandchildren and where the middle generation is missing are referred to as 'skipped-generation' households. Given the normative expectation in virtually every society that biological parents ought to function as social parents for children, it is likely that grandparents would assume the role of surrogate parents only under the extreme circumstance of a parent not being available. Several settings where these extreme situations are relatively common have received attention.

The most obvious situation where a skipped-generation household might occur is when children are orphaned. Under low-mortality conditions existing in all developed countries, the likelihood of a child being orphaned is very low. However, in African countries where AIDS has become a major killer of young adults, and where other causes of death also continue to be high, it is not uncommon for parents of dependent children to die. (In the literature on this subject, 'orphan' refers to a child who has lost even one parent.) In sub-Saharan Africa in 2003, more than 12 per cent of all children under age 18 had at least one parent dead, and 2.2 per cent were double orphans (UNICEF, 2004). In countries most affected by AIDS (such as Botswana, Swaziland, and Zimbabwe), more than 20 per cent of the children are expected to be orphans in 2010. The probability of being orphaned at some time before reaching age 18 is, of course, even higher than the cross-sectional prevalence rate among all children. Under these conditions where many children are orphaned, grandparents may play a critical role.

Both traditional extended-family arrangements and migrant labor also contribute to situations where grandparents are found in the role of surrogate parents. Zimmer and Dayton (2005) have analyzed data from 24 countries of sub-Saharan Africa in the 1990s that show the prevalence of older people (aged 60 and older) living in households with a grandchild. They found that almost half (46 per cent) of all older people in these countries, and 57 per cent of older women, live with a grandchild. To some extent this reflects traditional kinship practices where extended households are normative. But in almost one-fourth of these situations, older persons are living with a grandchild whose parents are not in the household – a skipped-generation situation. In most of the skipped-generation households, however, the children are not complete orphans. Rather, the majority of these households may reflect the African child fostering tradition where children are cared for by extended-family members. This has become especially important as many parents move to urban areas for employment, but leave their children with grandparents in the rural areas.

In Uganda, Malawi, and Zimbabwe, which have high rates of AIDS-related mortality, about 5 per cent of older adults are living with double-orphaned children (Zimmer and Dayton, 2005). However, the significance of grandparents as surrogate parents is better assessed from the perspective of children who are orphaned. Grandparents care for about 45 per cent of the orphans in Uganda, more than 50 per cent in Kenya, and around 60 per cent in Namibia and Zimbabwe (UNICEF, 2006). In other words, in countries most affected by AIDS, grandparents are the most likely relatives to care for orphans. This is not surprising because, as noted above, children in Africa frequently live with grandparents whether or not they are orphaned (Zimmer and Dayton, 2005). Grandparents who are raising their grandchildren may experience hardships, but there is evidence that orphans are better off living with grandparents rather than other relatives or nonrelatives (Case et al., 2004).

As noted, an important reason why grandparents in Africa become surrogate parents for grandchildren is migration by the middle generation from rural to urban places. Skipped-generation households for this same reason are also reported in Indonesia, Thailand, and China (Knodel and Saengtienchai, 2007; Pan and Lin, 1987; Richter, 1996; Schroder-Butterfill, 2004). This type of arrangement where the middle generation is alive but living elsewhere is usually perceived as temporary, although indefinite. It can be viewed as a family strategy that works to the advantage of all generations (Richter, 1996). By migrating to urban areas, the middle generation can increase their earnings and solve the problem of childcare by leaving their children with the older generation. The grandparents benefit by receiving the remittances that are generally sent by the parents of the grandchildren they are keeping. Also, keeping grandchildren tends to increase the ties between the oldest and middle generations. Studies in both rural Indonesia and rural Thailand found that about 10 per cent of persons aged over 60 headed skipped-generation households (Knodel and Saengtienchai, 2007; Schroder-Butterfill, 2004).

In developed countries, skipped-generation households most often arise due to children being born to young, unmarried mothers or to mothers who are unable to provide care for reasons such as imprisonment, mental or emotional problems, or drug abuse (Goodman and Silverstein, 2002). Grandparents' willingness to care for needy grandchildren reflects both widespread intergenerational solidarity (Bengtson and Roberts, 1991), and the state giving preference to grandparent custody of foster children over non-relative homes (Worrall, 2006). Burton and Bengtson (1985), however, caution against assuming that grandparents welcome the role of surrogate parent. In recent years a great deal of both scholarly and popular attention has been given to grandparents raising grandchildren in the United States (e.g., see Hayslip and Kaminski, 2005; Pebley and Rudkin, 1999). One impetuous for this attention came from reports that the number of children living in households headed by a grandparent was rapidly increasing. For example, the US Census Bureau produced a report showing that the proportion of children living in households maintained by a grandparent had increased from about 3 per cent in 1970 to about 6 per cent in 1997 (Bryson and Casper, 1999). In addition to these statistics, there were also studies showing that grandmothers rearing grandchildren were often poor and suffering from stress and health problems (see Hayslip and Kaminski, 2005).

Both the extent to which American children are being cared for by grandparents and the negative health effects of this arrangement for the grandparents are often exaggerated. First, among children who live in a grandparent's home, more than half also have a parent in the household. The proportion of children living in skipped-generation households increased from 1.4 per cent in 1970 to 2.0 per cent in 1996, but the level was the same in 2006 as it was in 1996 (US Census Bureau, 2006). Thus only about 2 per cent of all children live in skipped-generation households, and this percentage has not continued to increase in recent years. Secondly, although the proportion of children living with grandparents increased in the early 1990s, the current level is not high by historical standards. Children were more likely to lived in skipped-generation households around 1940 than in 1995 (Pebley and Rudkin, 1999), and this living arrangement for children was much more common in 1900 (primarily due to orphanhood) than it is today (Uhlenberg, 2000). Finally, most studies reporting health disadvantages associated with caring for grandchildren have significant methodological problems and, importantly, fail to consider benefits that grandchild care might bring (Hughes et al., 2007). Using a multivariate analysis of data from a large, longitudinal survey of older adults, Hughes et al. (2007: S114–15) found that: 'Grandmothers whose grandchildren move in showed declines in self-rated health, but those who continued with this arrangement saw a modest improvement, suggesting the negative effect of starting this kind of caregiving disappears as the arrangement continues.'

Even if only 2 per cent of American children are living with grandparents in skipped-generation households, however, surrogate grandparents make an important contribution to children at greatest risk. Among children who do not live with a parent, 44 per cent were living with a grandparent in 2006 (US Census Bureau, 2007). The role of grandparents in caring for black children is especially important. Over 5 per cent of black children are in skipped-generation households, and 54 per cent of black children not living with parents are living with a grandparent (US Census Bureau, 2007). A disproportionate number of grandparents raising grandchildren are single and/or poor, and a strong case can be made for designing social policies '… that support the profound expressions of intergenerational solidarity demonstrated daily by grandparents raising their grandchildren' (Roe and Minkler, 1998–99: 31). Also, it should be noted that a cross-sectional perspective on grandparents raising grandchildren significantly underestimates the proportion who care for grandchildren at some point in their lives – over 10 per cent of grandparents in the National Survey of Families and Households reported that they had at some time had 'primary responsibility' for raising a grandchild for at least 6 months (Fuller-Thomson et al., 1997). Not all of these grandparents had lived in skipped-generation households, but some grandparents in three-generation households have primary responsibility for raising grandchildren. Being a surrogate parent for a grandchild in a three-generation household can, in fact, create special difficulties. One study found that African-American women were more satisfied with their lives when they were custodial grandparents than when they were co-parenting grandchildren with a daughter (Goodman and Silverstein, 2006).

GRANDPARENTS ASSISTING WITH THE CARE OF GRANDCHILDREN

Across many societies grandparents help with the important societal task of caring for children. As discussed above, under extreme circumstances some grandparents provide the complete care of grandchildren. More common, however, is the situation where grandmothers assist their children in caring for the youngest generation. The role of grandparent as partial caregivers for grandchildren is widespread in both developed and developing societies. Sometimes this caregiving occurs in three-generation households where the oldest generation contributes to the household economy by supervising children so that their mother can work outside of the home. Very often, however, it is non-co-resident grandmothers who are engaged as either primary or back-up caregivers for grandchildren. This type of arrangement is a good example of the modified extended family that persists in contemporary societies, where the oldest generation maintains a separate residence but continues to be actively involved in the lives of their descendant kin (Rossi and Rossi, 1990). We begin this discussion by considering the significance of the babushka in Russia, and then examine grandparents as caregivers of children in several other societies.

The babushka, Russian grandmother, has held a prominent and venerated position in Russian history, and her importance in the family continues up to the present. As Russia experienced a series of societal upheavals in the 20th century – World War I, the 1917 Revolution, Stalin's work camps and political purges, World War II, and economic collapse following the disillusion of the Soviet Union after 1991 – the Russian family experienced great hardship and children were at risk. Under conditions where mothers tended to have full-time work and many fathers were absent because of divorce, death, or military service, families increasingly revolved around mother, child, and grandmother, with grandmothers providing much of the care for children (Rotkirch, 2004). The importance of grandmothers in providing care during the Soviet years is evident from data collected in the Moscow longitudinal survey of young adults born in the 1990s (Semenova and Thompson, 2004). One-third of the adults in this survey reported growing up in households with a grandparent present, and three-fourths had at least weekly contact with a grandparent. Furthermore, the care provided by these grandmothers was considered to be important. Semenova and Thompson (2004: 129) write: 'It is very striking how much more often there seems to have been a confiding intimate relationship between the child and its grandmother than with the parents'.

The vital contribution of grandmothers continued in the 1990s as the number of children in single-parent families increased, poverty increased, and provision of state-sponsored childcare decreased (Lokshin et al., 2000). The frequency of children living with unmarried mothers increased not only because high divorce rates persisted but also because the proportion of children born to unmarried women increased rapidly and the increasing death rates for males left more mothers widowed. Living with a mother in a three-generation household was the major way that unmarried mothers were able to solve the problem of childcare while they were employed. Data from the Russian Longitudinal Monitoring Survey show the large and growing importance of these arrangements, as 42 per cent of single parents in 1996 lived in households that included their child's grandparent,

compared to 32 per cent in 1992 (Lokshin et al., 2000).

In China, with a traditional patrilineal and patrilocal kinship system, it has long been normative for children to live with or near their paternal grandparents. But China experienced great social and economic change in recent decades. Among other things, a growing proportion of mothers have entered the labor force and non-parental childcare has become an important issue. What role do grandparents play in caring for children of Chinese women who work outside of the home when those children are considered to be members of the paternal grandparents' extended family? Using data collected in the China Health and Nutrition Study, Chen (forthcoming) was able to explore this question by selecting all households with a child under 6. The continuing significance of intergenerational co-residence is obvious, as about 44 per cent of the urban children in the study had a co-resident grandparent – the ratio of paternal to maternal grandparents living in the household was 9 to 1. Although not all co-resident grandmothers provided childcare, most do and thereby they make an important contribution to the household economy. In addition, almost 20 per cent of the children in the 1990s who were cared for outside of their parental homes were cared for in the house of a grandparent who lived nearby. Non-co-resident grandparents who cared for grandchildren provided, on average, over 30 hours of care per week, indicating that most were the primary childcare providers. Thus in China, as in Russia, grandmothers are providing a significant amount of the childcare that allows mothers with young children to be in the labor force. But in China it is paternal grandmothers who most often assume this role.

In recent years there has been a great increase in our understanding of patterns of childcare provided by grandparents in Europe (Dench and Ogg, 2002; Hagestad and Herlofson, 2007; Hank and Buber, 2009; Harper, 2005). Especially useful data on this subject comes from the 2004 Survey of Health, Ageing and Retirement in Europe (SHARE), which provides comparable data in 10 European countries (Attias-Donfut et al., 2005). A remarkably high proportion of grandparents were found both to be looking after grandchildren and to accept the norm that grandparents ought to help care for grandchildren. Among the 10,000 respondents in these countries who had a grandchild under age 15, 58 per cent of the grandmothers and 49 per cent of the grandfathers reported providing at least some care for a grandchild in the past year (Hank and Buber, 2009). Furthermore, nearly half the grandparents strongly agreed with the statement: 'Grandparents' duty is to help grandchildren's parents in looking after young grandchildren.' Across these countries, grandparents were more likely to be caregivers if they were younger (under age 70), healthy, and lived near their grandchildren. Also, older people were more likely to provide care if they were maternal grandparents, if they had a grandchild aged 10 or under, and if the mother of their grandchild was employed (Hank and Buber, 2009).

One of the most interesting findings coming from studies that use data from SHARE is the differences across countries in the 'regular' involvement of grandparents as care providers. About 40 per cent of the grandparents in Mediterranean countries (Spain, Italy, and Greece) looked after grandchildren on a weekly basis, compared to only 20 per cent in the Scandinavian countries (Denmark and Sweden). Why are there such large differences between Northern and Southern Europe? Two related differences between these regions have been suggested as explanations for this contrast. First, long-standing cultural differences between these regions in family norm regarding filial and paternal obligation have been observed (Reher, 1998). Adults in the Mediterranean region have been, and are, much more likely than those in Scandinavia to believe that children have a responsibility to provide care for their old parents and that grandparents have a responsibility to look after their grandchildren. It is more likely that grandparents will assist with child rearing when the culture supports the norm that this is a duty. Secondly, major differences in welfare-state regimes between the regions affect the need for employed mothers to seek assistance from their parents (Hagestad and Herlofson, 2007). In the generous welfare states of Sweden and Denmark, state-funded day-care for children is nearly universal. In contrast, there is very little state support for childcare in Italy, Spain or Greece. When non-family childcare is hard to find or expensive, working mothers often look to family members for the care for their young children. It is also relevant that a much higher proportion of grandmothers are available to be regular childcare providers in the Mediterranean region, where relatively few grandmothers are employed outside of the home.

A great deal of attention recently has been given to childcare arrangements in the United States, where more than half of all preschool children have mothers who are employed, but where publicly financed childcare is limited. As parents are forced to work out their own solution to their childcare needs, many prefer to turn to the children's grandparents (Brandon, 2000). In 2002, according to data from the US Census Bureau, 28 per cent of preschoolers with employed mothers were being cared for by grandparents (Johnson, 2005). This level of reliance on grandparents to provide care has changed little since 1985. It is common for employed mothers to use multiple childcare arrangements, and 46 per cent of young children with employed mothers who were cared for by a grandparent were also being cared for in some other arrangement. But grandparent caregivers clearly enable many mothers to be in the labor force, and they report giving, on average, 24 hours of care per week (Johnson, 2005).

In addition to caring for grandchildren with employed mothers, grandparents may also help in caring for grandchildren at other times. Indeed, using data from the National Survey of Families and Households, Guzman (2004) found that 54 per cent of grandmothers with young grandchildren living nearby were providing some type of childcare for them, but for only 14 per cent was that care restricted to when the mother was working. About one-fifth of the grandmothers and grandfathers reported giving both work- and non-work-related childcare, and another fifth gave only non-work-related care. Thus, many grandparents are assisting their children by caring for grandchildren after school or on weekends or school holidays.

It is also important to note that some grandparents can provide great help to children by assisting in the care of grandchildren who have special needs. A study of 22,000 children enrolled in kindergarten allowed an examination of how frequently grandparents had previously been their primary caregivers (Park et al., 2005). About half of the grandparents reported that they had at some time been a caregiver for a grandchild, and there was little difference by whether or not they had a grandchild with special needs. But the authors report, '... grandparents are about 28 per cent more likely to provide primary care for a child with a challenging impairment for which child care is likely to be an issue for the parents' (Park et al., 2005: 133). In other words, there is evidence of grandparents being especially responsive to their special needs, grandchildren, when other childcare arrangements cannot be found. A more in-depth study of 91 special needs children in Florida found that 44 per cent of the children were receiving care on at least a weekly basis from a grandparent (Green, 2001). Significantly, having a grandparent involved in the caregiving contributed to parental well-being by increasing positive emotional outlook and reducing levels of physical exhaustion. Although comparable data from other countries are not available, it is likely that grandparents providing assistance to grandchildren with special needs is a widespread phenomenon.

OTHER WAYS GRANDPARENTS MAKE A DIFFERENCE

This section looks at two additional ways in which grandparents may contribute to the well-being of children. First, grandparents are often in a position to play an important role in the socialization of children. No doubt this often occurs when grandparents are surrogate parents or caregivers, but it is also possible for grandparents who are involved with their grandchildren in other ways to contribute to their socialization. The second contribution of grandparents considered here is through intergenerational economic transfers. This is possible whether or not grandparents have direct involvement in the lives of their grandchildren.

Socialization and mentoring

A number of writers have noted the potentially significant role of grandparents in the socialization of young people by functioning as mentors and/or role models. The anthropologist Margaret Mead argued that in modern societies, grandparents can provide children with a sense of continuity by sharing their experiences of living through massive social change (Mead, 1974). (Mead also had thoughtful things to say about the important role of children as teachers of old people in periods of rapid change.) Bengtson picks up on this theme of grandparents as interpreters of history for children and writes, 'Grandparents may play an enormously important role in this building of reasonable connections among our past, present, and future' (1985: 24). Elder discusses how grandparents who have lived through difficult times might be in a unique position to encourage grandchildren who face challenging times by providing them with hope for the future (Elder and Conger, 2000). Along with others, these writers point to the potential significance of grandparents in helping their grandchildren develop in a successful way. However, to understand how important grandparents are for child development, it is necessary to move beyond these theoretical discussions to empirically examine how commonly grandparents actually make significant contributions.

The extent to which grandparents contribute to the successful development of children growing up in stable two-parent families is debatable. To be sure, expressions of positive sentiments about grandparents are widespread, and interviews with Norwegian 10–12 year olds show that nearly all of them acknowledged learning from their grandparents: practical skills; knowledge of history (Hagestad and Uhlenberg, 2009). There are a few studies suggesting that involvement with grandparents has

beneficial consequences for the behavior and development of young children (see discussion in Elder and Conger, 2000). Further, an analysis of data from a large survey of American adolescents found that, in response to an open-ended question asking if any non-parent adult had made a positive difference in their lives, about 7 per cent identified a grandparent (Taylor et al., 2009). Nevertheless, the important question about grandparents' possible contribution to successful development of children has not received much rigorous research attention.

Two recent studies by Silverstein have attempted to advance our understanding of possible long-term consequences of grandparent socialization for child development. The first study (Silverstein and Ruiz, 2006) asked whether involvement with grandparents could buffer the transmission of depression from mothers to their adolescent and young adult children. The findings give an affirmative answer – the tendency for intergenerational transmission of depression did not occur among grandchildren who had strong ties to grandparents. In the second study (Silverstein et al., 2003), longitudinal data are used to examine whether the level of involvement of children with their grandparents in 1971 had any effect on their self-esteem when they were adults 26 years later. This study found that for children who grew up in intact families, those who had involved grandparents when they were children fared no better than those who did not. On the other hand, having an involved grandparent had a substantial, positive effect on the self-esteem of young adults who came from disrupted families. This finding supports Elder's suggestion that for children in stable, nurturing families, grandparents may be 'socially redundant' (Elder and Conger, 2000). That is, they can add to existing family strengths, but have little independent influence. However, when faced with a family crisis, grandparents can make an important contribution by being involved with their grandchildren.

Recognizing the potential of grandparents to step in, support and help guide children through family crises, Hagestad (1985) has referred to such grandparents as the 'family national guard.' A common type of family crisis for children in the United States is parental divorce. There is substantial evidence that maternal grandparents do increase their involvement with grandchildren when there is divorce in the middle generation, although contact with paternal grandparents tends to decrease (Cherlin and Furstenberg, 1986; Douglas and Ferguson, 2003; Johnson, 1988). And there is reason to expect that grandparents who assist single parents in rearing children would, in general, help decrease harmful effects of divorce on children. One study showing a long-term positive effect of grandparents' involvement with grandchildren whose parents divorce was noted above, but again there is little additional solid empirical research to draw on. The extent to which involvement of grandparents in the socialization of children in various contexts can enhance their well-being in adulthood is a topic that needs to be examined.

Family transfers

Grandparents can have an impact on grandchildren not only through direct contact but also by their intergenerational economic transfers. These transfers may go directly from grandparents to grandchildren, or they may be indirect transfers that flow through the middle generation. The economic contribution to grandchildren, whether direct or indirect, can come through a bequest when the grandparent dies or through *inter vivos* transfers. Given the increasing longevity of older people, there is special interest in *inter vivos* transfers because they are most likely to be given at a time when parents are supporting dependent children. Summarizing studies from the United States, France, Germany, Norway, and Sweden, Kohli (2005) has found common patterns of intergenerational financial transfers across countries. Not only are *inter vivos* transfers common but also they almost always flow from the older generation to the younger one. This finding of the downward generational flow of resources points out that the notion of adult children providing economic support for their ageing parents is obsolete. In modern welfare states, where the old receive state old-age pensions, children are seldom supporting their parents. In contrast, older people are frequently using part of their pension income to assist children and grandchildren who have needs. Thus, public pensions not only free younger generations from the need of supporting the old but also allow the old to express solidarity between generations by supporting their children and grandchildren (Kohli, 2006). Although *inter vivos* transfers benefit grandchildren in general, they also tend to increase inequality among children. Children living in more wealthy families are more likely to have grandparents with abundant resources to pass on than are children living in poor families (Uhlenberg, 2009).

Data from the German Ageing Survey provide evidence of how frequently *inter vivos* transfers given by older people go to adult children compared to grandchildren (Hoff, 2007). Among those aged 62–67, it was twice as likely that transfers made in the past 12 months went to children as to grandchildren (28 versus 14 per cent). Many of the grandchildren of people in this age category were still dependents in their parents' homes, so the transfers to children often indirectly benefit them. However, grandparents past age 68 were about equally likely to make economic transfers directly to grandchildren as to children – about 20 per cent in each category. The importance of the indirect economic support going from grandparents to grandchildren is seen in Norway, where 40 per cent of the individuals over age 55 who received inheritances passed on part or all of it to their children or grandchildren (Hagestad and Herlofson, 2007). Gifts to grandchildren on special occasions are another way in which grandparents contribute economically to their grandchildren. In the United States, a 2002 AARP survey found that grandparents reported spending an average of $500 annually on their grandchildren (AARP, 2002). Thus, in various ways – direct transfers, indirect transfers, gifts – grandparents contribute to the economic support of their grandchildren.

CONCLUSION

Contemporary grandparents in developed countries have an unprecedented opportunity to play a significant role in the lives of children. Increasing longevity and decreasing fertility mean that most children have grandparents, and they have relatively few siblings and cousins with whom to share their grandparents. Furthermore, most grandparents with young grandchildren are healthy and economically secure, and many are retired. Grandparents in developing countries also often have the potential to make a critical difference in the lives of grandchildren: for example, when mothers have died, migrated from rural to urban areas, or entered the labor force. To determine how significant grandparents actually are for the well-being of children throughout the world, however, requires empirical studies that examine this question. These studies need to go beyond establishing that grandparents and grandchildren typically communicate positive attitudes toward each other. Existing studies provide some useful information on how grandparents impact the lives of children, but further research will be needed before we can adequately assess how different the lives of children would be if there were no grandparents.

Across diverse societies we find that grandparents often step in to care for children experiencing family crises. Grandparents are generally the preferred and often the most important source of care for children who cannot be cared for by parents. In societies where a large proportion of mothers with young children have entered the labor force, grandparents are often an important source of childcare. The downward flow of economic resources from grandparents to grandchildren is significant in modern societies where state pensions provide older people with steady incomes. Wherever it has been examined, grandchildren are found to have a high level of contact with grandparents, although the significance of this has received insufficient attention. It has been suggested that grandparents may be socially redundant in well-functioning families, but tend to be available for help in meeting needs of children when called upon. To advance our understanding of the significance of grandparents for children, new research must critically look at how often and under what circumstances grandparents who are able to help support their grandchildren actually do it.

But there is one more role that grandparents play in the lives of children that has not been mentioned. It is through grandparents that most children experience meaningful contact with old people. The family is the last age-integrated social institution (Hagestad and Uhlenberg, 2005), and without grandparents most children would not interact with old people. Suppose that kinship ties beyond the nuclear family disappeared (as some sociologists once thought they would), so the grandparent–grandchild relationship no longer existed. Under such a scenario, children would grow up without having any close relationship with an old person. Would such a situation affect how children develop? The answer to this question might provide the best clue as to how significant grandparents are in contemporary societies.

NOTES

1 Data from Human Mortality Database can be found at: http://www.mortality.org

2 Data from *World Population Prospects: The 2006 Revision* and *World Urbanization Prospects: The 2005 Revision* can be found at: htt://esa.un.org/unpp

3 Information on this research networks can be found at: http://old.gold.ac.uk/research/rtn/research-output.html

REFERENCES

AARP (2002) *The Grandparent Study 2002 Report.* Retrieved October 30, 2007. http://assets.aarp.org/rgcenter/general/gp_2002.pdf

Attias-Donfut, C., Ogg, J., and Wolff, F.C. (2005) 'Family support', in A. Börsch-Supan, H. Brugiavini, H. Jürges, et al. (eds), *Health, Ageing and Retirement in Europe: First Results from the Survey of Health, Ageing and Retirement in Europe.* Mannheim: MEA.

Bengtson, V.L. (1985) 'Diversity and symbolism in grandparental roles', in V.L. Bengtson and J.F. Robertson (eds), *Grandparenthood.* Beverly Hills, CA: Sage.

Bengtson, V.L. (2001) 'Beyond the nuclear family: the increasing importance of multigenerational bonds', *Journal of Marriage and Family,* 63: 1–16.

Bengtson, V.L. and Roberts, R.E.L. (1991) 'Intergenerational solidarity in aging families: an example of formal theory construction', *Journal of Marriage and the Family,* 53: 856–70.

Brandon, P.D. (2000) 'An analysis of kin-provided child care in the context of intrafamily exchanges: linking components of family support for parents raising young children', *American Journal of Economics and Sociology,* 59: 191–216.

Bryson, K. and Casper, L.K. (1999) 'Coresident grandparents and grandchildren', *Current Population Reports,* P23–198, US Census Bureau.

Burton, L.M. and Bengtson, V.L. (1985) 'Black grandmothers: issues of timing and continuity of roles', in V.L. Bengtson and J.F. Robertson (eds), *Grandparenthood,* Beverly Hills, CA: Sage.

Case, A., Paxson, C., and Ableidinger, J. (2004) 'Orphans in Africa: parental death, poverty, and school enrollment', *Demography,* 41: 483–508.

Chen, F. (2009) 'Patterns of grandparents caring for grandchildren in China.' in D.L. Poston Jr. and W.S. Yang (eds), *The Family and Social Change in Chinese Societies,* New York: Springer.

Chen, F. and G. Liu (2009) 'Population aging in China', in P. Uhlenberg (ed.), *International Handbook of Population Aging.* Dordrecht, the Netherlands: Springer.

Chen F., Short, S.S., and Entwisle, B. (2000) 'The impact of grandparental proximity on maternal childcare in China', *Population Research and Policy Review,*19: 571–90.

Cherlin, A.J. and Furstenberg, F.F. (1986) *The New American Grandparent: A Place in the Family, A Life Apart.* New York: Basic Books.

Dench, G. and Ogg, J. (2002) *Grandparenting in Britain.* London: Institute of Community Studies.

Douglas, G. and Ferguson, N. (2003) 'The role of grandparents in divorced families', *International Journal of Law, Policy and the Family,* 17: 41–67.

Elder, G.H. Jr. and Conger, R.D. (2000) *Children of the Land.* Chicago: University of Chicago Press.

Fuller-Thompson, Minkler, E., M., and Driver, D. (1997) 'A profile of grandparents raising grandchildren in the United States', *The Gerontologist,* 37: 406–11.

Goodman, C. and Silverstein, M., (2002) 'Grandmothers raising grandchildren: family structure and well-being in culturally diverse families', *The Gerontologist,* 42: 676–89.

Goodman, C. and Silverstein, M. (2006) 'Grandmothers raising grandchildren: ethnic and racial differences in well-being among custodial and coparenting families', *Journal of Family Issues,* 27: 1605–26.

Green, S.E. (2001) 'Grandma's hands: parental perceptions of the importance of grandparent as secondary caregivers in families of children with disabilities', *International Journal of Aging and Human Development,* 53: 11–33.

Grundy, E., Murphy, M., and Shelton, N. (1999) 'Looking beyond household: intergenerational perspectives on living kin and contacts with kin in Great Britain', *Population Trends,* 97: 19–27.

Guzman, L. (2004) 'Grandma and grandpa taking care of the kids: patterns of involvement', *Child Trends Research Brief, 2004–17.*

Hagestad, G.O. (1985) 'Continuity and connectedness', in V.L. Bengtson and J.F. Robertson (eds), *Grandparenthood.* Beverly Hills, CA: Sage.

Hagestad, G.O. and Herlofson, K. (2007) 'Micro and macro perspectives on intergenerational relations and transfers in Europe', in *Report from United Nations Expert Group Meeting on Social and Economic Implications of Changing Population Age Structures.* New York: United Nations Department of Economic and Social Affairs/Population Division.

Hagestad, G.O. and Uhlenberg, P. (2005) 'The social separation of old and young: a root of ageism', *Journal of Social Issues,* 61: 343–60.

Hagestad, G.O. and Uhlenberg, P. (2007) 'The impact of demographic changes on relations between age groups and generations: a comparative perspective', in K.W. Schaie and P. Uhlenberg (eds), *Social Structures: Demographic Changes and the Well-Being of Older People.* New York: Springer.

Hagestad, G.O. and Uhlenberg, P. (2009) 'Grandparents', in R.A. Shweder (ed.), *Chicago Companion to the Child.* Chicago: University of Chicago.

Hank, K. and Buber, I. (2009) 'Grandparents caring for their grandchildren: findings from the 2004 Survey of Health, Ageing and Retirement in Europe', *Journal of Family Issues,* 30: 53–73.

Harper, S. (2005) 'Grandparenthood', in M.L. Johnson (ed.), *The Cambridge Handbook of Age and Ageing.* Cambridge: Cambridge University Press.

Hayslip, B. and Kaminski, P.L. (2005) 'Grandparents raising their grandchildren: a review of the literature and suggestions for practice', *The Gerontologist,* 45: 262–9.

Hoff, A. (2007) 'Patterns of intergenerational support in grandparent–grandchild and parent–child relationships in Germany', *Ageing and Society,* 27: 643–65.

Hughes, M.E., Waite, L.J., LaPierre, T.A., and Luo, Y. (2007) 'All in the family: the impact of caring for grandchildren on grandparents' health', *Journal of Gerontology: Social Sciences,* 62B: S108–19.

Johnson, C.L. (1998) 'Effects of adult children's divorce on grandparenthood', in M. Szinovacz (ed.), *Handbook on Grandparenthood.* Westport, CT: Greenwood Press.

Johnson, J.O. (2005) 'Who's minding the kids? Child care arrangements: Winter 2002', *Current Population Reports,* P70–101, US Census Bureau.

Knodel, J. and Saengtienchai, C. (2007) 'Rural parents with urban children: social and economic implications of migration for the rural elderly in Thailand', *Population, Space and Place,* 13: 193–210.

Kohli, M. (2005) 'Intergenerational transfers and inheritance: a comparative view', *Annual Review of Gerontology and Geriatrics,* 24: 266–89.

Kohli, M. (2006) 'Aging and justice', in R.H. Binstock and L.K. George (eds), *Handbook of Aging and the Social Sciences,* 6th edn. San Diego, CA: Academic Press.

Lauterbach, W. (1995) 'Die gemeinsame lebenszweit von familiengenerationen', *Zeitschrift fur Sociologie,* 24: 23–43.

Lokshin, M., Harris, K.M., and Popkin, B.M. (2000), 'Single mothers in Russia: household strategies for coping with poverty', *World Development,* 28: 2183–98.

Mead, M. (1974) 'Grandparents as educators', *Teachers College Record,* 76: 240– 49.

Pan, Y. and Lin, N. (1987) 'A model of contemporary Chinese urban families', *Sociological Research,* 3: 54–67.

Park, J.M., Hogan, D.P., and D'Ottavi, M. (2005) 'Grandparenting children with special needs', *Annual Review of Gerontology and Geriatrics,* 24: 120–49.

Pebley, A.R. and Rudkin, L.L. (1999) 'Grandparents caring for grandchildren: What do we know?', *Journal of Family Issues,* 20: 218–42.

Reher, D.S. (1998) 'Family ties in Western Europe: persistent contrasts', *Population and Development Review,* 24: 203–34.

Richter, K. (1996) 'Living separately as a child-care strategy: implications for women's work and family in urban Thailand', *Journal of Marriage and the Family,* 58: 327–30.

Roe, K.M. and Minkler, M. (1998–99) 'Grandparents raising grandchildren: challenges and responses', *Generations,* 22: 25–32.

Rossi, A.S. and Rossi, P.H. (1990) *On Human Bonding: Parent–Child Relations Across the Life Course.* Hawthorne, NY: Aldine de Gruyter.

Rotkirch, A. (2004) '"Coming to stand on firm ground": the making of a Soviet working mother', in D. Bertaux, P. Thompson, and A Rotkirch (eds), *On Living Through Soviet Russia.* London: Routledge.

Schroder-Butterfill, E. (2004) 'Inter-generational family support provided by older people in Indonesia.', *Ageing and Society,* 24: 497–530.

Semenova, V. and Thompson, P. (2004), 'Family models and intergenerational influences: grandparents, parents and children in Moscow and Leningrad from the Soviet to the market era', in D. Bertaux, P. Thompson, and A Rotkirch (eds), *On Living Through Soviet Russia.* London: Routledge.

Shorter, E. (1975) *The Making of the Modern Family.* New York: Basic Books.

Silverstein, M. and Ruiz, S. (2006) 'Breaking the chain: how grandparents moderate the transmission of maternal depression to their grandchildren', *Family Relations,* 55: 601–12.

Silverstein, M., Giarrusso, R., and Bengtson, V.L. (2003) 'Grandparents and grandchildren in family systems: a social-developmental perspective', in V.L. Bengtson and A. Lowenstein (eds), *Global Aging and Global Challenges to Families*. New York: Walter de Gruyter Inc.

Sundstrom, G. (2009) 'Demography of aging in the Nordic countries', in P. Uhlenberg (ed.), *International Handbook of Population Aging*. Dordrecht, the Netherlands: Springer.

Taylor, M., Elder, G.H., Uhlenberg, P., and McDonald, S. (2009) 'Revisiting the grandparenting role: grandparents as mentors in adolescence and young adulthood', in M. Silverstein (ed.), *From Generation to Generation: Continuity and Discontinuity in Aging Families*. Baltimore: Johns Hopkins Press.

Uhlenberg, P. (2000) *Twentieth Century Patterns in Grandparent–Grandchild Coresidence*. Paper presented at Annual Meeting of the Gerontological Society of America, Washington, DC.

Uhlenberg, P. (2005) 'Historical forces shaping grandparent–grandchild relationships: demography and beyond', *Annual Review of Gerontology and Geriatrics*, 24: 77–97.

Uhlenberg, P. (2009) 'Children in an aging society', *Journal of Gerontology: Social Sciences*, 64B: 489–96.

Uhlenberg, P. and Hammill, B.G. (1998) 'Frequency of grandparent contact with grandchild sets: six factors that make a difference', *The Gerontologist*, 36: 681–5.

UNICEF (2004) *Children on the Brink 2004: A Joint Report of New Orphan Estimates and a Framework for Action*. New York: United Nations.

UNICEF (2006) *The State of the World's Children 2007*. New York: United Nations.

US Census Bureau (2006) 'America's families and living arrangements', *Current Population Survey (March)*. Retrieved September 18, 2007. http://www.census.gov/population/www/socdemo/hh-fam/cps2006.html

US Census Bureau (2007) *Historical Time Series: Living Arrangements of Children*. Retrieved September 18, 2007. http://www.census.gov/population/socdemo/hh-fam/ch7.csv

Wolf, D.A. and Longino, C.F., Jr (2005) 'Our "Increasingly mobile society"? The curious persistence of a false belief ', *The Gerontologist*, 45: 5–11.

Worrall, J. (2006) 'Challenges of grandparent custody of children at risk in New Zealand', *Families in Society*, 87: 546–56.

Zimmer, Z. and Dayton, J. (2005) 'Older adults in sub-Saharan Africa living with children and grandchildren', *Population Studies*, 59: 295–312.

35

A Social View on Healthy Ageing: Multi-disciplinary Perspectives and Australian Evidence

H. Kendig and C. Browning

INTRODUCTION

This chapter considers healthy ageing from the viewpoint of social gerontology and the complex array of disciplines and fields of enquiry in which the concept is enmeshed. Our view of social gerontology is that research is 'for' a social purpose: that is, to yield understandings and information that contribute to actions that enhance the well-being and interests of older people and ageing societies. Research is increasingly demonstrating that processes of ageing are amenable to a range of bio-psycho-social influences, with many of these being changeable and hence improvable. Constructive, proactive actions are required to address the unprecedented societal ageing that the United Nations has termed as the major world challenge over the 21st century.[1]

Our chapter reviews and interprets key social concepts and evidence on healthy ageing, the development of this knowledge, and areas for its application. It draws upon major review pieces in the international literature, as well as specialized sociological material, and aims to point readers towards sources for more in-depth information.[2] The discussion concentrates on the Australian experience of healthy ageing, which is broadly comparable to that of other advanced, industrial societies in what Baars et al. (2006) recognize as an increasingly global

context of ageing. Australia can be typified as a country with a European past – with the legacy of British culture and political institutions along with a disadvantaged Aboriginal population – and an increasing international and Asian future in the context of massive migration and increasing interdependence with Asian economies (see Chapter 40).

The next section of the chapter reviews the development of multi-disciplinary, international perspectives on healthy ageing and the social context behind these developments. The Australian experience is reviewed to show how the emergence of healthy ageing ideas and policies has been related to an expanding research base. The chapter examines international research on how the social dimension influences healthy ageing. We conclude the chapter with our own (optimistic) views on the potential for ageing people themselves, through their own actions and advocacy, to improve the social structures that facilitate or impede healthy ageing.

MULTI-DISCIPLINARY PERSPECTIVES ON HEALTHY AGEING

The quest for 'successful' ageing is arguably as old as humanity itself and is deeply embedded in individuals' consciousness and collective ideas of social advancement. A social sciences approach is centred on *human* understanding: that is, our awareness both of ourselves and the social world in which we live. A social scientist has a research-based understanding of social and cultural forces, including the opportunities that can be enhanced in people's lives as well as the social constraints that can be overcome. In reviewing paradigms of healthy ageing, we take an historical approach, given its value for appreciating how ideas and evidence evolve in a social context with social purposes and interest groups intertwined.

What we study is inextricably based in value choices and our sense of responsibility concerning social action. At the same time, career interests are bound up with the political economy of research funding: that is, the topics or perspectives that are a priority for the government, professional, and/or other interest groups who can pay for research or influence its distribution. The usefulness of knowledge can be enhanced by multi-disciplinary efforts. Research gains social value when findings are translated into policy, practice applications, and public awareness.

INTELLECTUAL AND SOCIAL ORIGINS OF HEALTHY AGEING

The scientific search for successful ageing emerged during the 1950s and early 1960s but the term healthy ageing was not explicitly named as such in the early research literature. Research on the social activity 'theory' of ageing suggested that keeping active and social participation were keys to ongoing psychological well-being (Bengtson et al., 2005). A countervailing view, 'disengagement theory', posited that morale was maintained through withdrawal from social activity proportionate to waning physical and psychological resources (Cumming and Henry, 1961). Parallel bodies of knowledge emerged from medical research on treatments for old-age diseases and biological research on longevity (the latter based largely on animal research). National gerontological societies have, over the past five decades or more, served as umbrellas for these various strands of largely discipline-based research (Achenbaum, 1995). In hindsight, there was relatively little integration or multi-disciplinary investigation in the early days apart from pioneering efforts such as the Duke University longitudinal studies of ageing from the 1960s onwards (Busse, 1993).

The idea of successful ageing emerged on the public agenda most conspicuously through the

work by Rowe and Kahn (1997) and their colleagues sponsored by the US-based Macarthur Foundation. This investigation, entitled 'Towards a new Gerontology', aimed to integrate biological, psychological, and social approaches to move beyond earlier work preoccupied with disability, disease, and chronological age. It examined the importance of lifestyle and other psychosocial influences on positive aspects of ageing. The social purpose was to raise aspirations and aim for successful (not just usual) ageing. The three components of successful ageing were posited to be 'avoiding disease', 'engagement in life', and 'maintaining high cognitive and physical function'. The Foundation supported empirical research that aimed to identify personal and social actions that could increase the chances of successful ageing.

The concept of successful ageing must be examined critically in the context of the individualistic value base of American culture (with its Calvinist theological influences). While individual responsibility can motivate constructive action, it can also risk various forms of blaming and marginalizing 'victims' who do not age 'successfully' (Holstein and Minkler, 2003; see also Chapter 39). As summarized below, successive reformulations of the idea have aimed to overcome this core limitation by redefining the idea with new terminology and foci in line with emergent social contexts. The concept may, however, translate less easily into alternative cultural settings: for example, Buddhist or Hindu contexts which may focus less on the material world but have more fatalistic or accepting attitudes (Kendig, 2004).

Another important concept has been that of productive ageing, which emerged in the early 1980s largely as a reaction against the ageism that devalued older people in the United States and failed to acknowledge their contributions in the paid labour force, volunteer activities, family assistance, and/or self-maintenance (Morrow-Howell et al., 2001). The meaning and forms of productive ageing can be taken as an instance of how the social value accorded to older people and the social context of ageing varies greatly across cultures and countries. While the concept helps to counter negative stereotypes, it is important to recognize the need to value people who may not be 'productive' in the conventional sense. Here, alternative approaches have included critical perspectives in gerontology focusing on political action, social justice, and political and economic forces as constituents of 'successful ageing' (Estes and Mahakian, 2001). A related idea is that of 'Conscious Ageing', which focuses on improving ageing experiences through the wisdom of older people, spiritual seeking, and life review (Moody, 2002). In the United Kingdom and New Zealand, policy discussion has centred on the banner of 'positive ageing'. Some researchers use the term 'resourceful ageing' to emphasize the importance of enabling older people to take control of their lives (Minichiello et al., 1996). A review of various theories of ageing demonstrates how new terms and approaches from a range of disciplines have addressed contemporary 'problems' of ageing and ways in which research evidence could inform action to improve ageing experiences (Bengtson et al., 2009).

Active ageing

Over recent years much of the research and policy discussion on healthy ageing has followed the widely accepted World Health Organization (WHO) definition: 'Health is a state of complex physical, mental, and social well-being and not merely the absence of disease or infirmity' (WHO, 1952:100). 'Active Ageing', as promulgated by the WHO Global Programme on Ageing (WHO, 2002: 12) '… is the process of optimizing opportunities for health, participation, and security in order to enhance quality of life as people age'. The active ageing framework emphasizes continued involvement in six areas of life: social, physical, economic, civic, cultural, and spiritual life.

The active ageing framework approach recognizes that over our life span we set 'developmental trajectories' that heavily influence our capacities, resources, and vulnerabilities in later life. While functional capacities typically decline with age, there is considerable variability. The health and social sciences are learning that there are many opportunities for enhancing levels of functioning in mid-life and for preventing disability and maintaining independence into old age. Walker (2002) proposed that at different points in the life span the promotion of active ageing needs different priorities and approaches. For example, at retirement older people need choice in activities and encouragement to continue participation in society. At later stages, older people and their carers may need to establish ways of managing illness and disability in active collaboration with their health and social care professionals.

Environmental gerontology

Whether or not people maintain health, functioning, and well-being in later life can depend heavily on how they are located within or adapt to the demands and supports of their housing, neighbourhood, and regional environments. Pioneering psychological research on the 'person–environment fit' in housing is guiding new directions in planning the built environment and professional interventions to improve independence and well-being for vulnerable older people (Kendig, 2003; Lawton and Nahemow, 1973; see Chapter 8). The WHO's (2007) global strategy for age-friendly cities aims to facilitate 'active ageing' through better provision of outdoor spaces, transport, housing, social participation and inclusion, civic participation, and employment strategies. Processes of urban and rural stability and change set a broader context within which independence and well-being can be facilitated or constrained (Phillipson, 2004).

Medical interfaces

While this chapter and book are concerned with social gerontology, medicine and public health provide the dominant paradigms for understanding healthy ageing. Public beliefs in medical treatment as the core of good health – and the centrality of general practitioners in most people's lives – are important social facts and they underpin the authority of medical professions and disciplines. The primary objectives of medical research and practice are to treat, ameliorate, and prevent disease and thus extend life and its quality (Ebrahim and Byles, forthcoming). Geriatric medicine for very old people requires expertise in managing multiple medical conditions and heightened sensitivities to illnesses, interactions between them, and the risks of polypharmacy. Their medical needs often combine with social vulnerabilities such as widowhood and reduced income.

There are essential intersections between medical and social paradigms of healthy ageing. 'Patients' self-management of their own chronic diseases, in partnership with health professionals, aims to slow disease progress and limit adverse consequences for independence and quality of life. Chronic illness is strongly age-related and its management is important for healthy ageing. The Australian Sharing Health Care Initiative funded projects to test the efficacy of self-management of chronic illnesses in both community and primary care settings (Feyer et al., 2003). As a result of this initiative the Federal government through Medicare, a universal health insurance scheme, now funds general practitioners to work in collaboration with other health professionals to implement self-management approaches and provide preventive care for older people. Similar approaches have been taken in the United Kingdom,

United States, and New Zealand (Lorig et al., 2008; Rea et al., 2007).

Public health and health promotion

Public health and the closely related field of epidemiology have a primary focus on populations rather than individuals and a strong emphasis on health promotion and disease prevention. There is a primary emphasis on reducing risk factors for disease, notably through health actions such as adequate physical activity. Important priority areas for health promotion for older people include adequate physical activity, nutrition, mental health, and injury prevention (Haber, 2007). The Centers for Disease Control and Prevention in the United States makes important connections between medical approaches and health promotion, including funding for the Healthy Ageing Research Network. The Network aims to generate and disseminate research and guidance relating to primary prevention of disease and for secondary prevention through ameliorating the impact of disease on functioning.[3]

Essential public health goals of high importance for older people are reducing the time spent in ill-health before death (compression of morbidity) and enabling continuing active life expectancy (delay of disability). The International Classification of Functioning, Disability, and Health (ICF) conceptualizes disability as any or all of impairments, activity limitations or participation restrictions, created by the interaction of health conditions and a wide range of environmental factors (WHO, 2001). The ICF thus provides a strong focal point and framework for understanding supportive environments and for enabling older people to maintain functioning and well-being notwithstanding disabilities.

The 'new public health framework' recognizes the importance of addressing health inequalities and how health-related behaviours are influenced by social determinants such as education, income, occupation, life events, and social networks. This framework has been led mainly by activists and advocates, with the World Health Organization's Ottawa Charter for Health Promotion (1986)[4] serving virtually as its founding manifesto. Victor Marshall's (1993) critique of Canadian ageing and health policy applied sociology to developing principles for healthy public policy for older people, of which he identifies four:

- a multi-sectoral focus (working largely outside the healthcare system)
- a commitment to equity (principles of fairness)

- a participatory approach (with people involved in setting goals for themselves)
- an ecological perspective (understanding humans in the context of their physical and social worlds).

Working in the Healthy Ageing Research Network in the United States, Marshall has collaborated with a social work researcher to develop strategies to promote active ageing. They begin by emphasizing the importance of people's health aspirations and needs; their efforts to change or cope with environments; and the centrality of health as a resource in daily life (Marshall and Altpeter, 2005). They present an 'improved' model of Rowe and Kahn's successful ageing model and underscore the importance of developing these ideas in an ecological context and in setting national lifestyle targets for 'healthy people.' In their model:

- the term 'healthy ageing' is used rather than 'successful ageing'
- the goal of healthy ageing is expanded beyond disease prevention to include avoiding injury and promoting health
- optimizing health is proposed as a realistic goal rather than to aim for 'high' functioning that can be unattainable in late life
- managing chronic conditions to facilitate self-care and independence is proposed as an important component of healthy ageing.

HEALTHY AGEING IN AUSTRALIA

This section illustrates how public recognition and action on healthy ageing in Australia has emerged, albeit slowly, along with inter-related developments in research funding and research. Early initiatives in healthy ageing were led largely by state governments, through organizations such as the Victorian Health Promotion Foundation (VicHealth), responsive to local constituencies with funding from tobacco taxes (Browning and Kendig, 2003). Through the 1990s, healthy ageing was proposed (but seldom incorporated) as central to population-based health promotion to reduce health inequalities and improve interventions for disadvantaged groups. In 2001, a *National Strategy for an Ageing Australia*,[5] launched by a newly established Minister for Ageing, included healthy ageing as one of its four main themes. Yet various programme and research initiatives foundered as a result of intergovernmental conflict over funding as well as competition from interests behind direct healthcare provision and mainstream medical research.

Efforts to support healthy ageing research increased after 2002 when the Australian Government established National Research Priorities (NRP), which aimed to better connect government research funding to national and social benefits of more clear value to the electorates. After extensive public debate and policy consideration, National Research Priorities were established, including 'Promoting and Maintaining Good Health'. This Health priority had four goals: (1) a healthy start to life; (2) ageing well, ageing productively; (3) preventive health care; and (4) strengthening Australia's social and economic fabric. While the NRP process was dominated initially by physical and medical scientists, the goals became more inclusive of social and policy interests after lobbying by the social sciences, humanities, and policy areas in government, reflected in the addition of Goal 4. The first draft of the ageing goal was defined in terms of degenerative illness in a recommendation from the National Health and Medical Research Council. The final version was as follows:

Ageing well, ageing productively *Developing better social, medical and population health strategies to improve the mental and physical capacities of ageing people.* The priority further noted that 'major shifts in cultural expectations and attitudes about ageing are necessary to respond constructively, at both an individual and population level. A healthy aged population will contribute actively to the life of the nation through participation in the labour market or through voluntary work. This goal supports the Government's *National Strategy for an Ageing Australia'*.[6]

A second important initiative was the *Promoting Healthy Ageing in Australia* Working Group established by the Prime Minister's influential Science, Engineering, and Innovation Council (PMSEIC) (2003). The Group was composed of medical and epidemiology experts, along with a social scientist, advocates for older people, and a policy department representative. After extensive debate, the Group presented to the Prime Minister and his Cabinet recommending:

... a vision for an additional 10 years of healthy and productive life expectancy by 2050. Research evidence indicates that there are effective actions than can be taken to enable people to live longer in good health, staying mentally and physically active, and able to participate and enjoy life until they die in advanced old age. The report also outlines a research agenda that would provide information to assist in achieving this vision (PMSEIC, 2003, iv).[7]

The research agenda underscored the importance of ageing as an opportunity and recommended a 'whole of life' approach to healthy ageing. It presented a research agenda for physical activity, nutrition, work, the social environment, and the built environment. It recommended the establishment of a national network for healthy ageing research and longitudinal surveys of healthy and productive ageing.

Under the Australian Government's Research Networks Programme, the Australian Research Council and the National Health and Medical Research Council subsequently funded a national NHMRC/ARC Research Network in Ageing Well (2005–10). The Network aims to advance Australian research on ageing by enhancing the quality, scale, and multi-disciplinarity of research; the development of a new generation of researchers in ageing; improving research translation and collaboration with 'end users'; and strengthening connections to leading international research programmes.[8] In late 2004 the National Health and Medical Research Council and the Australian Research Council jointly established the Ageing Well, Ageing Productively (AWAP) research grant funding programme.[9] The purpose was '... to foster research into ageing which crosses sectors, research disciplines and institutions to develop an authoritative evidence base to underpin more effective and well informed policy and practice.' A total of $10 million was devoted to 5-year programme grants (as contrasted with the far better funded dementia research programme directed mainly to biomedical research and research on consumers and carers). Topics funded under AWAP included policy reforms and practice innovations in working longer, healthy brain ageing; addressing polymorbidity; policy and services for older indigenous Australians; predictors of ageing well among men and women; and modelling ways to compress morbidity and optimize healthy ageing.

Additional research programmes have a strong ageing component. The ongoing Australian Longitudinal Survey of Women's Health, funded mainly by the Australian Department of Health and Ageing, provides a wealth of data on women in the older, middle, and younger cohorts.[10]

The 45 and Up Study, sponsored by the New South Wales (NSW) State government and a coalition of government and private organizations, is following the health of 250,000 men and women aged 45 and over across the coming decades.[11] A sub-study of 45 and Up is 'Understanding the impact of social, economic and geographic disadvantage on the health of Australians in mid to later life: What are the opportunities for prevention?'. This research is funded under the Preventive

Healthcare and Strengthening Australia's Social and Economic Fabric Research Grants 2006.[12]

Notwithstanding the multi-disciplinary ageing research under special research initiatives, healthy ageing research has fared less well in the funding programmes of the mainstream ARC and NHMRC. There are, however, two exceptions. First, the ARC's 'Linkages' programme supports applied research in collaboration with industry and other partner organizations that provide co-funding. Secondly, the NHMRC 'Ageing Panel' was established to improve the appropriateness of reviewing for research involving multiple disciplines and professions. Various government research consultancies have evaluated interventions and best practice but the findings often are not released. It remains unclear as to the longer-term impacts on funding as a result of the 'Ageing Well, Ageing Productively' NRP goal.

Direct action by consumer groups is also contributing to research and advocacy to advance healthy ageing. The Australian Council on the Ageing provide advocacy, community information, and programmes on a wide range of topics, including healthy ageing.[13] The National Seniors Productive Ageing Centre, co-funded by the Australian government, funds and partners in applied research that '… promotes the choices and capacity of Australians, as they age, to engage in valued activities, whether through work, learning, volunteering or community activity'.[14]

Programmes and policies

State governments, to varying degrees, fund research that will inform policy and service provision. For example, the Active Service Model is based in part on research consultancies conducted by local universities. The model uses a 'wellness' approach to the delivery of community services which values '… capacity building, restorative care and social inclusion to maintain or promote a person's capacity to live as independently and autonomously as possible' (p. 1).[15] The model builds on the evidence base from the healthy ageing research literature and the WHO Active Ageing Framework which demonstrates that older people have capacity for improvement given supportive social and physical environments and appropriate and accessible services (see Browning and Thomas, 2006, for a review of this literature and applications to service development).

The WATCH Project: Wellness Approach to Community Homecare in Western Australia is another example of a wellness approach to service provision (O'Connell, 2007) as is Homecare Re-Ablement in the UK.[16] These approaches value

the role of community engagement and social relationships as well as improvements in the health of older people. For older people they add to the services provided in primary health care and the chronic disease management approaches outlined earlier in the chapter. In Western Australia, *Silverchain* (a provider of community, residential, and health services) has developed services based on healthy ageing principles. These include the Home Independence Program that utilizes health professionals to improve health and independence through physical activity programmes, chronic illness self-management, medication management, and falls prevention. The Social Enablement Program helps older people improve their social networks.[17]

A broader approach through the primary healthcare system recognizes chronic illness and obesity as the biggest threats to healthy ageing. Doctors, however, have limited time to work with patients to change the behaviours that often contribute to the onset of these conditions and their associated morbidity. Interventions enabling behavioural change, such as an innovative Australian falls prevention programme based on improving self-efficacy, have demonstrated effective health promotion for vulnerable older people (Clemson et al., 2004). The health and community care systems need better integration to provide a simpler point of access for older clients. At the population level, we need to adopt health promotion approaches more seriously and actually spend money if we are to achieve the society goal of 'ageing well, ageing productively'.

Healthy ageing research in Australia

There is a significant Australian literature on healthy ageing as shown in the many related entries in the Australian Ageing Research Online.[18] A comparative book, *Lessons on Aging from Three Nations* (Carmel et al., 2007), included Australian chapters on health and well-being, psychological contributions to understanding of age-related cognitive ability, ageing widowed older women, living to age 100 years, developing intergenerational solidarity, and migration and ageing.

Australian research has examined how health and ageing vary depending on social positions and earlier life experiences. Work-related disease, injury, and death for mature age workers show major variations between occupations and industries as well as age and gender differences; poor health is a major factor in productivity and workforce losses among older workers (Schofield et al., 2008) and use of disability pensions. Working-class men in Australia are at high risk in terms of low levels of physical and social activity, unhealthy eating patterns, excessive drinking, and low well-being before and after retirement (De Vaus et al., 2007). Among older Australians, former occupation, education, income, and home ownership are independently related to physical and social activity – two of the most important health actions for healthy ageing (Kendig et al., 1998).

Gender differences over the life course – in family and other social roles, occupational status and risk, and access to financial and social resources – are profoundly significant for older Australians' health status, health behaviours, and well-being (Russell, 2007). Contextual factors (e.g., workforce opportunities) and underlying gender orientations are neither fixed over time nor across population groups, as women have made gains in education, workforce participation, and financial independence. Cross-sectional findings from the Australian Longitudinal Survey of Women's Health show that SES (socioeonomic status) differences in health appear to be wider for women in middle age than in old age (Mishra et al., 2004).

Marriage and parenthood are associated with positive health behaviours later in life (e.g. not smoking, modest alcohol consumption, and physical exercise) (Kendig et al., 2007). A lack of the beneficial social control influences of family through mid-life may contribute to the relatively poor health outcomes later in life for men who had never married or who were divorced or separated. However, a qualitative study of older homeless men found strong efforts to maintain healthy ways of living, notwithstanding obstacles such as poverty and inadequate facilities for preparing food (Quine et al., 2004).

In Australia, the spatial dimension to healthy ageing is important in terms of ongoing migration and urban–rural differences across a vast continent. Healthier people are likely to migrate voluntarily (Australian Institute of Health and Welfare [AIHW], 2008) and migrants, in proportion to their length of residence, tend to adopt lifestyles closer to those of the Australian-born citizen. Australians in regional, rural, and remote areas have 'excess' mortality (AIHW, 2008) but we do not know how much of this may be attributable to life stresses, environmental exposures, poor service access, and/or selective migration.

Indigenous Australians (2.4 per cent of the population) experience intense deprivation. Only 5 per cent are aged 60 years or more as a result of high birth rates and life expectancies estimated at 15–20 years less than other Australians (Cotter et al., 2007). Indigenous people experience the kinds and levels of disease that are broadly comparable to those in developing countries. Their levels of poor health are equivalent to that of non-indigenous people who are 20 years or more older. Cotter and colleagues conclude that indigenous people are marginalized because healthy ageing policies largely neglect them by taking action in the health sector to the exclusion of income, housing, and culturally appropriate aged care. Efforts to 'close the gap' in indigenous life expectancy are directed overwhelmingly to younger people, with less attention to those in mid and later life.

The Melbourne Longitudinal Studies on Healthy Ageing (MELSHA) programme aims to uncover predictors and consequences of healthy ageing in a cohort of older people who in 1994 were living in the community (Kendig et al., 1996).[19] In the baseline survey, the older people reported that their health ideals centred mainly around keeping active; the major benefits of good health were perceived to be a positive outlook, physical or social activity, or independence or absence of disease (Kendig, 1996). Respondents had a strong focus on positive health actions, notably physical activity, healthy eating, and social activity. Healthy actions were encouraged most by spouses (especially wives), with friends and adult children also being significant.

A qualitative investigation of older Australians reported that older people had 'health identities' and generally viewed themselves as successful 'survivors' whose good health was 'earned' by good health habits (Kendig, 1996; Walker-Birckhead, 1996). Informants stated that health was valued as the essential resource enabling them 'to continue to be the person they always have been'. A qualitative study of perceived ageism found that health professionals were the people most likely to make ageing people 'feel old' rather than 'normally ageing' and to threaten their positive sense of self (Minichiello et al., 2000).

Ongoing follow-up of the MELSHA survey participants has allowed examination of lifestyle predictors of successful ageing over 14 years of outcomes (Kendig et al., in press). Lifestyle-related predictors of survival (after taking account of demographic and health variables) were low strain and social activity at baseline. For entry to residential care, significant lifestyle-related risk factors were being underweight and having low social activity. For ageing well (continued independence with good morale), significant lifestyle predictors were physical activity, nutrition, not being underweight, social support, low strain, and not smoking. These lifestyle factors are potentially improvable and hence targets for health promotion late in life.

The Australian evidence base on ageing will increase substantially as findings are published from the healthy ageing research initiatives in progress, as reviewed above.

NEW DIRECTIONS IN HEALTHY AGEING RESEARCH

The variety of healthy or successful ageing concepts and purposes complicates the development of a coherent body of research-based knowledge. After reviewing international research findings, an Australian research team noted the inconsistent approaches and argued for setting an agreed definition of healthy ageing (Peel et al., 2004). This would be difficult to achieve, however, given the plurality of values and disciplines that underpin research and policy ideas on healthy ageing. We review below selected research approaches that we commend as being at the leading edge of healthy ageing research from a social perspective.

Well-being and adaptation

The psychological model of 'selective optimization with compensation', developed by Paul and Margret Baltes (1990) and their colleagues in the Berlin Longitudinal Study of Aging, observed how older people adjust their selection of life goals in line with their capacities; optimize goal achievement within these capacities; and compensate when they are unable to achieve goals. Health and well-being can persist through later life by means of these psychological adjustment processes, notwithstanding increasing health-related chronic life strains (Smith et al., 2002). A related literature on resilience can be viewed as the healthy ageing counterpart to vulnerability and it identifies psychological resources to successfully make late-life adjustments (Windle et al., 2008). The evidence is that in advanced old age it is still possible to achieve healthy ageing by addressing health constraints and by enabling a sense of control, security, and comfort.

Social structures and the life span

Sociological research on healthy ageing is directing increasing attention to understanding the influence of social class and other 'structural' factors earlier in life. Differential exposure to risks and protections over the life course results in cumulative advantage and disadvantage with '… associated questions of fairness in the distribution of opportunities and resources' (Dannefer, 2003: S327).

Blane et al. (2004) have shown that adverse environmental exposures in childhood can have persistent health effects through mid-life. A 17-year follow-up of the landmark Whitehall study in the United Kingdom (Britton et al., 2008) found that successful ageing – as indicated by cognitive capacities, absence of disease, and good functional health – was predicted by socioeconomic factors and key health behaviours in mid-life, including diet and exercise, as well as work support for men.

Health and well-being in later life are also influenced by subjective social status (each individual's interpretation) and lifelong accumulation of economic advantage (wealth) (Demakakos et al., 2008). Another UK study (McMunn et al., 2006) drew on sociological concepts of agency, social structure, and human needs/social capital to interpret health differences arising from the social roles of women in middle age. They concluded that health and well-being can be achieved when people's intentions and capacities (e.g. in health actions) are facilitated by enabling rather than constraining social structures.

Understanding the influence of period of history and social change provides further insights into the effects of social structure. Actions to promote healthy ageing for the future need to take account of the 'health trajectories' of the baby-boom cohort, as contrasted with the current cohort of older people. People now in their 70s were born in the 1930s: their formative years as children were during the social and economic dislocations of the Depression and World War II, and they began work and completed childbearing before the education and fertility revolutions of the 1960s. A study in the United States, drawing on cross-sequential analyses of the Health and Retirement Survey, found that the post-World War II birth cohort had lower self-rated health (as well as higher levels of obesity) in late middle age compared to the pre-war cohort at this age (Soldo et al., 2006).

Cross-cultural and comparative research

Societal influences on healthy ageing are seen most clearly in the major contrasts between countries in terms of their socioeconomic development and cultural traditions and values. The demographic transition (decreasing fertility and population ageing), the epidemiological transition (reducing mortality and declining infectious disease), and economic development are fundamentally changing the age and health profiles of many developing countries (Ebrahim and Byles, forthcoming).

Many Asian countries are experiencing rapid ageing and societal change, over several generations, that took developed countries several centuries (Kendig, 2004). Other countries, notably in Africa, have extensive poverty and devastating epidemics that impact on all age groups. An overview of contrasting country experiences is provided in *Global Health and Global Aging* (Robinson et al., 2007). Cultural context is essential for understanding the meanings of ageing, health, and ways of maintaining health and well-being: for example, the importance accorded to traditional versus Western conceptions of health and medicine. Rapid social change can widen intergenerational differences in terms of economic advantage, core values, and life experiences. Ageism has been found to be all-pervasive across Eastern as well as Western cultures, including Confucian-based Asian cultures where respect for elders and filial piety are normative (Cuddy et al., 2005). It is possible that ageism is one of the main features of global ageing among modern, capitalist nations in which individual social views predominate over traditional collectivist views.

Critical perspectives

Some of the limitations of the 'healthy ageing' approach have been challenged by theoretical debates in social gerontology. Critical gerontology, to take one example, has challenged the one-sidedness of knowledge based overwhelmingly on individual experiences of ageing, with scant attention to the social structures in which people live their lives (Baars et al., 2006). Critical perspectives recognize that views and experiences on ageing are socially constructed through economic and social processes that reflect deep power imbalances and inequalities between social groups. These structures typically are 'socially invisible' but they can be subjected to critical analyses that can inform actions leading to empowerment and control by older people.

Ageing and health is an important focal point for critical gerontology. Estes and Grossman (2007) emphasize the importance of understanding how ideologies, social institutions, and interest groups influence the 'life chances' of social groups over their life course. They critically examine the social institution of 'biomedicine' for defining ageing as a medical problem, individualizing ageing understandings, and commodifying ageing. They state that biomedical approaches obscure or ignore the importance for illness, health, and well-being of 'potentially modifiable social factors' such as income, education, housing environments, opportunities for meaningful human connection, and public financing for rehabilitation and health promotion (Estes and Grossman, 2007:130). They suggest that critical gerontology in ageing and health should address social inequalities, privatization, bio-medicalization of disability, the future of the welfare state, and globalization.

The value of a critical approach can be demonstrated by a recent critique of 'new standards to age well' emerging in British social policy and the World Assembly on Ageing (Biggs et al., 2008). Dominant ideologies imposing 'sameness' to older as well as middle generations, based on midlife preoccupations with work, can amount to a form of 'age imperialism' that denies ageing and age differences in needs, capacities, and orientations. If problems of ageing can be misrepresented by policymakers as problems of attitudes, this can amount to a 'new type of social ageism' that imposes on older people the goals and values of people in mid-life.

Social gerontology can play a part in understanding new approaches to healthy ageing such as anti-ageing medicine (Binstock et al., 2006; see also Chapter 36). The social base of this movement rests in consumers, most conspicuously ageing baby boomers, who seek to delay or even prevent ageing. The commercial base lies in the substantial industry in anti-ageing medicines and treatments. Binstock and colleagues review how some gerontologists are active contestants in 'boundary work' as to the social value, dangers, and scientific validity of the anti-medicine industry. More fundamentally, the vision for an 'ageless' society in which people might live to 150 years or more raises profound social and ethical issues. Binstock et al. remind us that, however far-fetched such a prospect might seem to be, it is difficult to predict the rapidity of developments in the biological revolution in science and its societal consequences.

CONCLUSIONS: RESEARCH AND SOCIAL ACTION FOR HEALTHY AGEING

This chapter has reviewed diverse perspectives on healthy ageing research in social gerontology with illustrations of recent approaches from the United Kingdom, the United States, and Australia. The development of more integrated multi-disciplinary research is yielding knowledge valuable to inform health promotion efforts. For example, the dominant medical and public health paradigms are strengthened by better understanding the psycho-social factors underlying behavioural risk factors and self-management of chronic disease. New 'critical' perspectives shed light on the 'structural' factors in work, economic resources, and environmental exposures that influence inequalities in health and other life outcomes.

Research on healthy ageing potentially could inform action to achieve important global goals during the uncertain decades ahead. The WHO (2008) *Closing the Gap in a Generation* report calls for achieving 'healthy equity through action on the social determinants of health'.[20] The report emphasizes the importance of early childhood development and gender inequalities and mentions the need to '… create conditions for a flourishing older life.' It recommends comprehensive societal actions that support health in all aspects of daily life, including our urban environments, workplace conditions, and inequalities of power and money. However, the essential focus on a good start for children and younger adults is not balanced by much attention to a life-span approach that acknowledges the value and potential for improving health in later life.

The UN Second World Assembly on Ageing (2002) set three priority directions to achieve 'a society for all ages': (1) the active participation of older people in development that would benefit all citizens; (2) the promotion of health and well-being as people age; and (3) the provision of enabling environments to support healthy ageing (see Kalache, 2007). The United Nations/ International Association of Gerontology and Geriatrics Research Agenda on Ageing for the 21st Century (2003, 2007) has the potential to guide research on ways ahead with these priority directions, and seek to resolve tensions between economic development and the perceived 'burden' of ageing populations. [21]

In Australia, the modest place of healthy ageing is illustrated by the health priorities enunciated in the Australia 2020 Summit convened by the then new Australian government '… to help shape a vision for the nation's future'.[22] The Summit's long-term health strategy' articulated important 'ambitions' for healthy lifestyles, health promotion and disease prevention, health inequalities, future challenges and opportunities, and health research. There was a strong focus on indigenous health, children, and youth. Productive ageing was mentioned as a health opportunity. It was recommended that '… health funding should be redirected to prevention to stop people from coming into the health system later in life with chronic diseases'.

How might one advance the cause of constructive approaches to healthy ageing? Within developed countries such as Australia, research can point the way towards reconstructing our social and economic institutions and expectations in line with emergent aspirations and imperatives. Political economy perspectives indicate that the productivity of older people can be enabled through social, market, and political pressures that re-engineer the ways in which we organize work, leisure, and education over the life course. Commitment to social and health opportunities over the life course can show how social investments in vulnerable groups earlier in the life span can yield returns through greater independence and productivity later in life. Understanding psycho-social influences on health can guide health promotion and interventions that enable continuing health, independence, and well-being. Comparative research can identify ways in which key ageing issues can be addressed more equitably and more effectively through restructuring our social and policy institutions.

In the midst of the interest struggles over scarce resources, one might well ask where we can turn for leadership towards achieving healthy ageing and research underpinning it. Governments and employers are already demonstrating some enlightened self-interest as per their support for research and programmes that can increase productivity and reduce healthcare costs. More fundamental leadership is emerging among older people themselves and their advocates, who seek to continue their own active contributions, independence, and well-being, and leave a constructive legacy for future generations. Research can help us to identify how to socially construct healthy ageing in ways that benefit diverse social groups and successive cohorts over their life course in an increasingly global world.

ACKNOWLEDGEMENTS

The research and ideas in this chapter have been developed with colleagues, including Shane Thomas, Lindy Clemson, James Nazroo, Yvonne Wells, Felicity Lorains, Rick Moody, and Ros Madden.

NOTES

1 United Nations Programme on Ageing and the International Association of Gerontology and Geriatrics, 2007 Research Agenda on Ageing for the 21st Century: http://www.un.org/ageing/documents/Ageing ResearchAgenda-6.pdf

2 For a more comprehensive review of research related to healthy ageing – including epidemiological, medical, and other aspects of ageing and health – we recommend the *Encyclopedia of Health and Aging* (Markides, 2007), *The Cambridge Handbook*

of Age and Ageing (Johnson, 2005), and *Global Health and Global Ageing* (Robinson et al., 2007)

3 Healthy Ageing Research Network: http//depts.washington.edu/harn/about_us.shtml

4 WHO Ottawa Charter: http://www.who.int/healthpromotion/conferences/previous/ottawa/en/

5 National Strategy for an Ageing Australia: http://www.ifa-fiv.org/attachments/062_Australia-2001-National%20Strategy%20for%20an%20Ageing%20Australia.pdf

6 National Research Priorities: http://www.dest.gov.au/sectors/research_sector/policies_issues_reviews/key_issues/national_research_priorities/priority_goals/promoting_and_maintaining_good_health.htm#2

7 Promoting Healthy Ageing in Australia: http://www.dest.gov.au/sectors/science_innovation/publications_resources/profiles/promoting_healthy_ageing_in_australia.htm

8 Research Network in Ageing Well: http://www.ageingwell.edu.au/

9 http://nrv.gov.au/grants/types/granttype/strategic/agewell.html

10 http://www.alswh.org.au/

11 http://www.45andup.org.au/

12 http://www.nhmrc.gov.au/grants/rounds/preventative.htm

13 Australian Council on the Ageing: http://www.cota.org.au/

14 National Seniors Productive Ageing Centre: http://www.productiveageing.com.au/

15 Victorian HACC Active Service Model: http://www.health.vic.gov.au/hacc/downloads/pdf/asm_discussion_paper.pdf

16 Homecare Re-Ablement: www.dhcarenetworks.org.uk/csed/Solutions/homeCareReablement/

17 Independence Programs: http://www.silverchain.org.au/Services/Home-Care/Independence-Programs/

18 Ageing Research Online: www.aro.gov.au

19 http://www.med.monash.edu.au/sphc/haru/programs/melsha.html

20 *Closing the Gap in a Generation:* http://whqlibdoc.who.int/hq/2008/WHO_IER_CSDH_08.1_eng.pdf

21 http://www.un.org/esa/socdev/ageing/research-agenda.html

22 Australia 2020: www.australia2020.gov.au.

REFERENCES

Achenbaum, W.A. (1995) *Crossing Frontiers: Gerontology Emerges as a Science.* Cambridge: Cambridge University Press.

Australian Institute of Health and Welfare (AIHW) (2008) *Australia's Health.* Canberra, ACT: author.

Baars, J., Dannefer, D., Phillipson, C., and Walker, A. (2006) *Aging, Globalization and Inequality.* Amityville, NY: Baywood.

Baltes, P. and Baltes, M. (1990) *Successful Aging: Perspectives from the Behavioral Sciences.* Cambridge: Cambridge University Press.

Bengtson, V.L., Putney, N.M., and Johnson, M.L. (2005) 'The problem of theory in gerontology today', in M.L. Johnson (ed.), *The Cambridge Handbook of Age and Ageing.* Cambridge: Cambridge University Press, pp. 3–29.

Bengtson, V.L., Gans, D., Putney, N.M., and Silverstein, M. (2009) 'Theories about age and aging', in V.L. Bengston, D. Gans, N.Putney, and M. Silverstein (eds), *Handbook of Theories of Aging,* 2nd edn. New York: Springer, pp. 3–24.

Biggs, S., Phillipson, C., Money, A.M., and Leach, R. (2008) 'The age-shift: observations on social policy, ageism, and the dynamics of the adult life course', *Journal of Social Work Practice*, 20(3): 239–50.

Binstock, R.H., Fishman, J.R., and Johnson, T.E. (2006) 'Anti-ageing medicine and science: social implications', in R. Binstock and L. George (eds), *Handbook on Aging and the Social Sciences,* 6th edn. San Diego, CA: Academic Press, pp. 436–55.

Blane, D., Higgs, P., Hyde, M., and Wiggins, R.D. (2004) 'Life course influences on quality of life in early old age', *Social Science and Medicine,* 58(11): 2171–9.

Britton, A., Shipley, M., Singh-Manoux, A., and Marmot, M. (2008) 'Successful ageing: the contribution of early-life and mid-life risk factors', *Journal of American Geriatrics Society,* 56: 1098–105.

Browning, C. and Kendig, H. (2003) 'Healthy ageing: a new focus on older people's health and wellbeing', in P. Liamputtong and H. Gardner (eds), *Health, Social Change and Communities.* Melbourne: Oxford University Press, pp.182–205.

Browning, C. and Thomas, S. (2006) *A Review of Successful Ageing and Related Concepts.* Victorian Department of Human Services.

Busse, E.W. (1993) 'Duke University longitudinal studies of ageing', *Zeitschrift fur Gerontologie und Geriatrie,* 26(3): 123–8.

Carmel, S., Morse, C.A., and Torres-Gil, F.M. (2007) *Lessons on Ageing from Three Nations: The Art of Aging Well. Vol.1.* Amityville, NY: Baywood.

Clemson, L., Cumming, R.G., Kendig, H., et al. (2004) 'The effectiveness of a community-based program for reducing the incidence of falls in the elderly: a randomized trial', *Journal of the American Geriatrics Society,* 52(9): 1487–94.

Cotter, P., Anderson, I., and Smith, L. (2007) 'Indigenous Australians: ageing without longevity', in A. Borowski, S. Encel, and E. Ozanne (eds), *Longevity and Social Change in Australia.* Sydney: UNSW Press, pp. 65–98.

Cuddy, A., Norton, M., and Fiske, S. (2005) 'This old stereotype: the pervasiveness and persistence of the elderly stereotype', *Journal of Social Issues,* 61(2): 267–85.

Cumming, E. and Henry, W. (1961) *Growing Old: The Process of Disengagement.* New York: Basic Books.

Dannefer, D. (2003) 'Cumulative advantage/disadvantage and the life course: cross-fertilizing age and social science theory', *The Journals of Gerontology*, 58B(6): S327–37.

Demakakos, D., Nazroo, J., Breeze, E., and Marmot, M. (2008) 'Socio-economic status and healthy: the role of subjective social status', *Social Science and Medicine*, 67: 330–40.

De Vaus, D., Wells, Y., Kendig, H., and Quine, S. (2007) 'Does gradual retirement have better outcomes than abrupt retirement? Results from an Australian panel study', *Ageing and Society*, 27: 667–82.

Ebrahim S. and Byles J. (forthcoming) 'Health of older people', in R. Detels, R. Beaglehole, M.A. Lansang, and M. Gulliford (eds), *Oxford Textbook of Public Health*. New York: Oxford University Press.

Estes, C. and Grossman, B. (2007) 'Critical perspectives in gerontology', in K.S. Markides (ed.), *Encyclopedia of Health and Aging*. Thousand Oaks, CA: Sage, pp. 129–33.

Estes, C.L. and Mahakian, J. (2001) 'The political economy of productive aging', in N. Morrow-Howell, J. Hinterlong, and M. Sherraden (eds), *Productive Aging: Concepts and Challenges*. Baltimore, MD: Johns Hopkins University.

Feyer, A., Francis, C., Quigley, R., Jessop, R., and Walsh, J. (2003) 'The sharing health care initiative: issues in design of the evaluation of a national program of demonstration projects for self-management of chronic conditions', *Australian Journal of Primary Health*, 9(3): 208–16.

Haber, D. (2007) *Health Promotion and Aging*, 4th edn. New York: Springer.

Holstein, M.B. and Minkler, M. (2003) 'Self, society and the "New Gerontology"', *The Gerontologist*, 43(6): 787–96.

Johnson, M.L. (ed.). (2005) *The Cambridge Handbook of Age and Ageing*. Cambridge: Cambridge University Press.

Kalache, A. (2007) 'The World Health Organisation and global aging', in M. Robinson, W. Novelli, C. Pearson, and L. Norris (eds), *Global Health and Global Aging*. San Francisco, CA: Jossey-Bass, pp. 31–46.

Kendig, H. (1996) 'Understanding health promotion for older people: sociological contributions', in V. Minichiello, N. Chappell, H. Kendig, and A. Walker (eds), *The Sociology of Ageing*. Melbourne: International Sociological Association. pp. 360–75.

Kendig, H. (2003) 'Directions in environmental gerontology: a multidisciplinary field', *Gerontologist*, 43(5): 611–15.

Kendig, H. (2004) 'The social sciences and successful aging: issues for Asia-Oceania', *Geriatrics and Gerontology International*, 4(1): S6–11.

Kendig, H., Browning, C., and Teshuva, K. (1998) 'Health actions and social class among older Australians', *Australian and New Zealand Journal of Public Health*, 22(7): 808–13.

Kendig, H., Dykstra, P.A., van Gaalen, R.I., and Melkas, T. (2007) 'Health of aging parents and childless individuals', *Journal of Family Issues*, 28(11): 1457–86.

Kendig, H., Pedlow, R., Browning, C., Wells, Y., and Thomas, S. (in press) 'Socio-medical predictors of entry to residential aged care: an Australian longitudinal analysis'.

Kendig, H., Helme, R., Teshuva,K., et al. (1996) *Health status of Older people Project: Preliminary Findings from a Survey of the Health and Lifestyle of Older Australians*. Melbourne: Victorian Health Foundation.

Lawton, M.P. and Nahemow, L. (1973) 'Ecology and the aging process', in C. Eisdorfer and M.P. Lawton (eds), *The Psychology of Aging and Adult Development*. Washington, DC: American Psychological Association, pp. 619–74.

Lorig, KR., Ritter, PL., Dost, A., et al. (2008) 'The expert patients programme online, a 1-year study of an internet-based self-management programme for people with long-term conditions', *Chronic Illness*, 4(4): 247–56.

Markides, K.S. (ed.) (2007) *Encyclopedia of Health and Aging*. Thousand Oaks, CA: Sage.

Marshall, V.M. (1993) 'A critique of Canadian ageing and health policy', *Journal of Canadian Studies*, 28(1): 153–61.

Marshall, V.M. and Altpeter, M. (2005) 'Cultivating social work leadership in health promotion and aging: Strategies for active ageing interventions', *Health and Social Work*, 30(2): 135–44.

McMunn, A., Bartley, M., and Kuh, D. (2006) Women's health in mid-life: life course social roles and agency as quality', *Social Science and Medicine*, 63: 1561–72.

Minichiello, V., Browne, J., and Kendig, H., (2000) 'Perceptions and consequences of ageism: views from older persons', *Ageing and Society*, 20: 253–78.

Minichello, V., Chapell. N., Kendig, H., and Walker A. (eds) (1996) *The Sociology of Ageing* . Melbourne: International Sociological Association.

Mishra, G., Ball, K., Dobson, A., and Byles, J. (2004) 'Do socioeconomic gradients in women's health widen over time and with age?' *Social Science and Medicine*, 58: 1585–95.

Moody, H.R. (2002) 'Conscious aging: a strategy for positive development in later life', in J. Ronch and J. Goldfield (eds), *Mental Wellness in Aging: Strength-based Approaches*. USA: Health Professionals Press.

Morrow-Howell, N., Hinterlong, J., and Sherraden, M. (2001) *Productive Aging: Concepts and Challenges*. Baltimore, MD: Johns Hopkins University Press.

O'Connell, H. (2007) *The WATCH Project: Wellness Approach to Community Homecare*. Perth: Community West Inc and Western Australian Department of Health, Home and Community Care.

Peel, N., Bartlett, H., and McClure, R. (2004) 'Healthy aging: How is it defined and measured?', *Australasian Journal on Ageing*, 23(3): 115–19.

Phillipson, C. (2004) 'Urbanisation and ageing: towards a new environmental gerontology', *Ageing and Society*, 24: 963–72.

PMSEIC (2003) *Prime Minister's Science, Engineering,and Innovations Council Promoting Healthy Ageing in Australia*. PMSEIC, Canberra, Australia.

Quine, S., Kendig, H., Russell, C., and Touchard, D. (2004) 'Health promotion for socially disadvantaged groups: the case of homeless older men in Australia', *Health Promotion International*, 19(2): 157–65.

Rea, H., Kenealy, T., Wellingham, J., et al. (2007) 'Chronic care management evolves towards integrated care in counties Manukau', *The New Zealand Medical Journal*, 120: 1252.

Robinson, M., Novelli, W., Pearson, C., and Norris, L. (eds) (2007) *Global Health and Global Ageing*. San Francisco, CA: Jossey-Bass.

Rowe, J. and Kahn, R.L. (1997) 'Successful ageing', *The Gerontologist*, 37(4): 433–40.

Russell, C. (2007) 'What do older women and men want? Gender differences in the "Lived Experience" of Ageing', *Current Sociology*, 55: 173–92.

Schofield, D., Fletcher, S., Earnest, A., Passey, M., and Shrestha, R. (2008) 'Where are older workers with chronic conditions employed?' *Medical Journal of Australia*, 188: 231–4.

Smith, J., Borchelt, M., Maier, H., and Jopp, D. (2002) 'Health and well-being in the young old and oldest old', *Journal of Social Issues*, 58(4): 715–32.

Soldo, B., Mitchell, O., Tfaily, R., and McCabe, J. (2006) *Cross-Cohort Differences in Health on the Verge of Retirement*. Population Aging Research Center. PARC Working Paper Series WPS 06-13.

Walker, A. (2002) 'A strategy for active ageing', *International Social Security Review*, 55: 121–39.

Walker-Birckhead, W. (1996) *Meaning and Old Age: Time, Survival and the End of Life*. Lincoln Papers in Gerontology No. 35, December.

Windle, G., Markland, D., and Woods, R. (2008) 'Examination of a theoretical model of psychological resilience in older age', *Ageing and Mental Health*, 12(3): 285–92.

World Health Organization (WHO) (1952) 'Constitution of the World Health Organization', in *World Health Organization Handbook of Basic Documents*, 5th edn. Geneva: WHO.

World Health Organization (WHO) (2001) *The International Classification of Functioning, Disability and Health (ICF)*. Geneva: WHO.

World Health Organization (WHO) (2002) *Active Aging: A Policy Framework*. Geneva: WHO.

World Health Organization (WHO) (2007) *Global Age-Friendly Cities: A Guide*. Geneva: WHO.

World Health Organization (WHO) (2008) *Closing the Gap in a Generation*. Geneva: WHO.

36

Social Dimensions of Anti-ageing Science and Medicine

Robert H. Binstock and Jennifer R. Fishman

INTRODUCTION

Ambitions and attempts to control ageing have been part of human culture since early civilizations (Gruman, 1966/2003). An obsession with immortality is a central theme in a Babylonian legend about King Gilgamesh who ruled southern Mesopotamia in about 3000 BC. In the 3rd century BC., adherents of the Taoist religion in China developed a systematic programme aimed at prolonging life (Olshansky and Carnes, 2001). Through the centuries, a variety of anti-ageing approaches have recurred. Among them have been alchemy, the use of precious metals (e.g., as eating utensils) that have been transmuted from baser minerals; 'shunamatism' or 'gerocomy' (cavorting with young girls); grafts (or injected extracts) from the testicles, ovaries, or glands of various animal species; cell injections from the tissues of newborn or fetal animals; consumption of elixirs, ointments, drugs, hormones, dietary supplements, and specific foods; cryonics; and rejuvenation from devices and exposure to various substances such as mineral and thermal springs (Gruman, 2003; Hayflick, 1994).

Anti-ageing aspirations and efforts flourish today, perhaps more than ever, in the forms of (1) commercial and clinical enterprises that offer anti-ageing products, regimens, and treatment and (2) research and development efforts of biogerontologists, – scientists who study the biology of ageing. Indeed, anti-ageing is now a topic regularly considered at gerontology meetings, nationally and internationally.

The goals of the commercial and clinical 'anti-ageing' enterprises are essentially to extend the time their customers and patients can live without the common morbidities of ageing such as wrinkling of the skin, hardening of the arteries, memory loss, muscle loss, visual impairment, and slowed gait and speech. Although biogerontologists generally share these objectives, they also have more ambitious aims. Many of them seek to achieve what historian Gerald Gruman (2003) has termed 'prolongevity' – a significant extension of average human life expectancy and/or maximum life span without extending suffering and infirmity.

This chapter does not focus on questions regarding the medical and scientific feasibility of such goals. Rather, it deals with some of the social dimensions of these anti-ageing activities. The next section summarizes the sociopolitical aspects of biogerontology's emergence as a scientific discipline. A following section considers anti-ageing entrepreneurs and clinicians as part of a social movement, which is followed by a section that examines the 'boundary work' biogerontologists and the anti-ageing movement have undertaken to maintain and enhance the legitimacy of their respective enterprises. The chapter concludes with a section that briefly delineates a series of social and ethical issues implied by actually achieving prolongevity.

THE EMERGENCE OF BIOGERONTOLOGY AS A SCIENTIFIC DISCIPLINE

The history of biomedical research on ageing is a classic story of a discipline's struggle for scientific legitimacy and funding. Scholars in the social studies of science have long been interested in the emergence of new scientific disciplines (Hedgecoe, 2003). The premise of this scholarship is that discipline-building is a social, political, and cultural endeavor (see e.g., Abir-Am, 1985; Bud, 1993; Gieryn, 1983). A new discipline may in fact develop around a new set of scientific discoveries, new methodologies, or new objects of inquiry. However, these scientific 'facts' alone are not enough to constitute a new discipline. Individuals, groups, and institutions need to work toward legitimation within the larger scientific and social arena, through garnering political support, allying themselves with credible and respected scientists, and convincing those around them (often through rhetorical strategies) that their discipline is indeed worthy of scientific inquiry (Abir-Am, 1985; Fujimura, 1996; Hedgecoe, 2003; van Lente and Rip, 1998). Another closely related activity that follows suit with discipline-building is that of 'boundary work', wherein members of a new discipline need to distinguish themselves from other disciplines around them (Gieryn, 1983). The story of biogerontology's emergence is one that followed this pattern, as members in the field tried to establish their work as a legitimate scientific discipline. This story is particularly interesting given the legacy of ill-repute that anti-ageing/prolongevity efforts garnered in the many prior years. This perception of anti-ageing research as not only scientifically inferior but also as an area of 'forbidden knowledge' (Kempner et al., 2005) made the fight to establish the discipline all the more difficult.

Modern biogerontology: the early years

In his monograph on the history of ideas about 'prolongevity', Gruman observed that the subject tends to be:

> ... relegated to a limbo reserved for impractical projects or eccentric whims not quite worthy of serious scientific or philosophic consideration. One reason for this neglect is that there is, in philosophy, science, and religion, a long tradition of apologism, the belief that the prolongation of life is neither possible nor desirable. ... Another reason is the fact that there are few subjects which have been more misleading to the uncritical and more profitable to the unscrupulous; the exploitation of this topic by the sensational press and by medical quacks and charlatans is well known.
>
> (Gruman, 2003: 6)

Gruman's observations regarding prolongevity fit rather well the perceptions of biomedical research on ageing held by many in the scientific community until recent decades. In her history of the development of US governmental support for research on ageing, published several decades ago, political scientist Betty Lockett observed: 'Those who would study aging in order to retard or halt the process have been considered on the fringe of biomedical research, looking for the fountain of youth ... a marginal area ... with so little backing from the scientific community' (Lockett, 1983: 5).

As Achenbaum (1995), Hayflick (1994), and Lockett (1983) detail, the early development of the modern research enterprise in the biology of ageing in the United States, and in geriatrics as well, was to a significant degree stimulated by the Josiah Macy Foundation. During the late 1930s it supported surveys on ageing and commissioned a seminal volume on *Problems of Aging: Biological and Medical Aspects* (Cowdry, 1939) that reviewed research knowledge and issues regarding how to prolong human life and how to reduce disabilities and chronic diseases in old age. The Foundation also funded a series of professional conferences that brought together researchers from a variety of disciplines and professions who formed a Club for Research on Ageing. In 1940, the US Surgeon General, who had attended a meeting of the Club, took the lead in establishing a small intramural research programme in gerontology under the auspices of the US National Institutes of Health (NIH). Over the next three decades the broad field of gerontology grew, but the development of the biomedical research enterprise in gerontology stagnated. To be sure, in 1945, the two dozen members of the Club for Research on Ageing incorporated themselves as a professional association, the Gerontological Society, to (among other purposes) 'promote the scientific study of aging' (Adler, 1958: 94). And the new organization (known since 1980 as the Gerontological Society of America (GSA)) began publishing a *Journal of Gerontology* and grew 100-fold over the next 25 years to comprise nearly 2400 members from a wide variety of academic disciplines and professions (Schutz, 2002). However, the NIH intramural research programme on ageing barely got off the ground during World War II as it was diverted by research devoted to the war effort. In 1948 it was designated as the Gerontology Branch of the National Heart Institute, was given a line item budget, and conducted physiological research on older men.

Although an NIH Gerontological Study Section for reviewing extramural research applications was created in 1946, it was abolished 3 years later. Lockett's research documents that even though the Gerontological Study Section approved a percentage of applications that was average for all study sections, it was perceived by some NIH officials as too favorably biased toward funding applications because there were so fewresearchers in the field of ageing that many of them were members of the Study Section and were reviewing their own proposals. In any event, gerontological applications were subsequently reviewed by other study sections that, according to one NIH staff member, downgraded gerontology research, and the percentage of approvals 'went from one extreme to another' (Lockett, 1983: 37).

In the 1950s and 1960s, extramural research on ageing gained little ground at NIH. During this period, in response to pressures from Congress, five regional multidisciplinary centers for ageing research and training were funded through NIH's programme project mechanism. However, only one of these centers (at Duke University) ultimately survived, and an internal NIH evaluation of the work of these centers was pointedly uncomplimentary concerning the quality of their gerontological research (Lockett, 1983). Meanwhile, a Senate Subcommittee on Problems of the Aging and Aged issued a report 'disparaging the quality of gerontologic research' (Achenbaum, 1995: 200).

When a National Institute of Child Health and Human Development (NICHD) was established in 1963, NIH programmes on ageing became part of NICHD's Adult Development and Aging Branch. Although the branch had an external peer review committee comprising a multidisciplinary roster of gerontological researchers, it only reviewed applications for programme projects and training and career development grants, not research grants. Over the next 10 years gerontologists expressed their disappointment with the NICHD arrangement, especially the low proportion of that institute's funds earmarked for research on ageing (Eisdorfer, 1968).

The institutionalization of research on ageing

By the late 1960s, frustrated by NIH's lack of funding for research on the basic mechanisms of ageing, biogerontologists set in motion the forces that ultimately led to the establishment of a separate National Institute on Aging in order to ensure that earmarked funds for gerontological research would be adequate. They drafted a bill in 1968 that called for a new NIH Institute with a 5-year research plan 'to promote intensive coordinated research on the biological origins of aging' (Lockett, 1983: 85). In order to gain the support of the Gerontological Society of America, however, the bill was quickly broadened to include the medical, behavioral, and social sciences (Binstock, 2003).

During the subsequent political processes that finally led to the establishment of NIA in 1974, themes suggesting the marginal status of

biogerontology persistently emerged. For one thing, the key political actor in the successful lobbying effort, Florence Mahoney, was an ardent pursuer of anti-ageing interventions. Mahoney was a powerful Washington 'insider' with politically elite connections, a long-time behind-the-scenes effective advocate for expanded government support for biomedical research. She was very interested in rejuvenation therapies offered by an institute in Bucharest, Romania and accustomed to taking serum treatments that were purported to slow or prevent ageing. As noted in her biography, Mahoney's 'accuracy in separating real science from charletan [sic] science was not precise; she occasionally backed a rejuvenation expert who had mastered promotion and mystique' (Robinson, 2001: 237). At the point when biogerontologists attempted to persuade her to lobby for a separate institute she was highly receptive because of her personal interest in anti-ageing interventions.

Throughout the protracted legislative history of NIA's establishment, from 1969 through 1974, various opponents of such an institute were quite candid regarding their negative view of the quality and promise of gerontological research. At a Senate hearing in 1971, for instance, an assistant secretary in the Department of Health, Education, and Welfare argued that the field of ageing was not ripe for the injection of major new resources because it lacked 'a substantial body of interested and competent research investigators, plus enough research leads, or promising ideas within the field to challenge the researchers to productive endeavors' (Lockett, 1983: 98). Similarly, in a House of Representatives hearing in 1972, the president of the Association of American Medical Colleges asserted that 'there is a paucity of trained researchers and valid ideas in the field of aging research' (Lockett, 1983: 122). And when one version of the bill passed in 1972, a memo from the Office of Management and Budget to President Nixon urged him to veto it – which he ultimately did – because an NIA 'could raise false expectations that the aging process can somehow be controlled and managed through biomedical research' (Lockett, 1983: 139).

Despite Nixon's veto – and consistent opposition from high-level NIH officials who apparently did not want to have a new institute carving out its own share of NIH appropriations (Lockett, 1983; US Senate Subcommittee on Aging, 1973) – Mahoney, a cadre of gerontologists, and several key members of Congress persisted in their efforts. In 1974, in the midst of calls for his impeachment, Nixon signed the legislation creating NIA (*Research on Aging Act of 1974*, 1974).

The establishment of NIA provided for biogerontology the kind of institutionalization that confers scientific stature and power (Cozzens, 1990). It began a process that legitimated research on ageing both as more of a 'mainstream' subject for biomedical research than the broader scientific community had regarded it, and as an appropriate area in which to invest sizable amounts of public funds. Since NIA began operation, a number of important scientific frontiers have been opened up in research on the fundamental biological process of ageing (see Masoro and Austad, 2006). Moreover, the overall NIA budget, which was only about $20 million in its first year of operation (Lockett, 1983), grew substantially during the next 30 years to reach over $1 billion by fiscal year 2007 (National Institute on Aging, 2007).

Although there are, of course, a number of distinguished European biogerontologists, nothing comparable to the NIA has been established in Europe. Some of them look to the US NIA for research support and often succeed. But, as Warner (2007) reports, other than in Belgium and Denmark, there have been no sustained initiatives by European governments or the European Union to fund biogerontological research on ageing.

ANTI-AGEING AS A SOCIAL MOVEMENT

Parallel to the modern emergence of biogerontology as a scientific discipline has been the development of an anti-ageing medicine social movement around the world. Mykytyn (2006a) characterizes anti-ageing medicine as a social movement in the sense that it involves a group of people bound together under a particular mission in opposition to the 'mainstream', where the mainstream in this instance refers primarily to mainstream gerontology and also to clinical medicine. However, unlike other health social movements, which are often characterized as a resistance to biomedicine from those outside of it – e.g., patients, activists, grassroots organizations (see e.g., Brown and Zavetoski, 2004; Epstein, 1996; Landzelius, 2006) – the anti-ageing medicine social movement has its roots in large part from within biomedicine, if perhaps a marginal wing of biomedicine. This unique aspect of the anti-ageing medicine movement is in part responsible for the ongoing boundary work between biogerontological scientists and the anti-ageing medicine practitioners.

The modern movement

The modern European anti-ageing medicine movement was spearheaded in the 1960s and 1970s by a Romanian woman, Anna Aslan, who established an institute in Bucharest that offered rejuvenation therapies and an elixir called Gerovital (Robinson, 2001), which is still widely marketed. Members of the European and Asian elite, including Nikita Khrushchev, visited the institute for treatments, and the Soviet Union established its own institute to study Gerovital and other chemicals. Today, various academies and centers on anti-ageing medicine can also be found in France, Belgium, and Japan, along with European-wide and Asian/Pacific organizations of this ilk (Robert, 2004). According to German sociologist Mone Spindler (2007), a substantial German-speaking anti-ageing movement is headed by Johannes Huber, an Austrian scientist, physician, and theologian. Huber, who is a controversial president of Austria's bioethics commission, develops, applies, and sells hormone treatments, dietary supplements, and predictive gene testing.

At the same time that Gerovital was marketed throughout Europe, Geritol – a similar product – was aggressively marketed in the United States. However, the use of anti-ageing products in the United States, particularly dietary supplements, soared especially in the years following the enactment of the Dietary Supplement Health and Education Act of 1994, which relaxed regulation of such products (US GAO, 2001). During the same period, several dozen anti-ageing books were published, such as *Grow Younger, Live Longer: 10 Steps to Reverse Aging* (Chopra, 2001). A refereed scientific publication, the *Journal of Anti-Aging Medicine* (subsequently renamed *Rejuvenation Research*), began publishing in 1998 and several non-refereed publications with similar sounding names also appeared. Dozens of websites like 'Youngevity: The Anti-Aging Company' marketed products such as 'The Vilcabamba Mineral Essence' to enable people to live their lives 'in a state of youthfulness' (Youngevity, 2003). There are no hard statistics on the size of the overall anti-ageing market in the United States but some estimates are available. A research report prepared by the Business Communications Company, Inc. (2005) estimated that the anti-ageing market in the United States alone would reach about $72 billion by 2009. It defines the market in terms of three categories (excluding exercise and physical therapy): appearance products and services; drugs and supplements targeting diseases of ageing; and products based on 'advanced technologies'. Whatever the magnitude of the market, it seems highly likely to grow further with the ageing of the US baby-boom cohort (76 million persons born between 1946 and 1964).

One particular element of the anti-ageing movement that has directly challenged the established gerontological community is the American Academy of Anti-Aging Medicine (A4M), which, despite its name, is international in scope. Founded in 1993, the organization claims it has 19,000 members from 90 countries (A4M, 2007).

The latest publicly available income tax returns show that it had accumulated net assets of $5.9 million by 2005 and had $2 million in income that year (Guidestar, 2007).

Although A4M is not recognized by the American Medical Association or the American Board of Medical Specialties, it has established certification programmes under its auspices for physicians, chiropractors, dentists, naturopaths, podiatrists, pharmacists, registered nurses, nurse practitioners, nutritionists, dieticians, sports trainers and fitness consultants, and PhDs. The organization puts on three annual anti-ageing conferences in the United States, as well as conferences in nations throughout the world. Its first 'World Congress' of anti-ageing medicine outside the United States was held in Paris in 2003 in partnership with French, German, Japanese, European, and Asian-Pacific anti-ageing societies and organizations (Robert, 2004).

A4M's conferences have been so financially successful that in 2007 the organization sold an 80 per cent stake in its conference business for $49 million to a London-based international media firm, Tarsus Group (Wilson, 2007). A4M states that it does not sell or endorse any commercial product or promote or endorse any specific treatment. But it actively solicits and displays numerous advertisements on its website for products and services (such as cosmetics, and alternative medicines and therapies), anti-ageing clinics, and anti-ageing physicians and practitioners, most of them listing certification by A4M.

Although what A4M terms 'the traditional, antiquated gerontological establishment' (Arumainathan, 2001) may disagree with many of the organization's messages and the measures it promotes, most elements of A4M's broadly-stated goals seem, on the surface, to be the same as those of many biomedical researchers and practitioners in gerontology and geriatrics. The stated mission of A4M is:

> The advancement of technology to detect, prevent, and treat aging related disease and to promote research into methods to retard and optimize the human aging process. ... A4M believes that the disabilities associated with normal aging are caused by physiological dysfunction which in many cases are ameliorable [sic] to medical treatment, such that the human life span can be increased, and the quality of one's life improved as one grows chronologically older (A4M: 2005).

This A4M mission is, in fact, very similar to a portion of the US NIA's mission. For instance, an important research goal in the most recent official NIA strategic plan is 'Unlocking the Secrets of Aging, Health and Longevity'; the plan declares that 'The ultimate goal of this effort is to develop interventions to reduce or delay age-related degenerative processes in humans' (National Institute on Aging, 2001).

Social and cultural considerations

Although there has clearly been consumer interest in interventions to prevent, arrest, or reverse ageing throughout human history, historian Carole Haber asks, 'Why this sudden resurgence in the notion that aging is an abhorrent disease that must be eliminated?' (Haber, 2001–02:13). She suggests that there may be several relatively unique social and cultural forces driving the contemporary enthusiasm for anti-ageing products and services. One factor is that anti-ageing interventions may have a special appeal to the large cohorts of older people because they grew up in an especially youth-oriented period in mass culture. Another factor is that recent scientific discoveries seemingly have potential relevance to slowing the rate of ageing in humans (see Masoro and Austad, 2006). Haber attributes 'the precise timing of this movement and the nature of its appeal' (Haber, 2001–02:13) to a third factor, the social context of concerns about the negative economic consequences for nations that have unprecedentedly large proportions of older persons. Cole and Thompson (2001–02) suggest that still another factor is a widespread individual fear of decline.

Alternatively, British gerontologist Merryn Gott notes that some anti-ageing marketers portray themselves as meeting the needs of older people who are creating a new model of the life course in which age divisions are blurred. 'From this perspective, older people are *empowering themselves* to resist old age – the age-resisting technologies are produced as a response to this need' (Gott, 2005). An additional influence, of course, is the long-term and increasing medicalization of human conditions and experiences previously considered to be non-pathological (Clarke et al., 2003). This phenomenon has been specifically noted in the field of gerontology as the 'biomedicalization of aging' (Estes and Binney, 1989) and chronicled with respect to the sociopolitical transformation of cognitive senility into Alzheimer's disease (Fox, 1989).

Mykytyn (2006b) locates contemporary interest in anti-ageing medicine in the United States to the promises and predictions of cutting-edge biomedical and scientific research, such as stem cell research, nanotechnology, and gene therapy. Anti-ageing medicine is thought to be feasible in the United States because of its reliance on the (rhetoric of) scientific breakthroughs. French gerontologist Leslie Robert (2004) suggests that one possible reason for the increasing interest in anti-ageing medicine worldwide is that many health-care professionals are feeling a financial pinch and are exploring alternative sources of income.

BOUNDARY WORK

The growth and popularity of the anti-ageing medicine social movement in recent years has provoked biogerontologists to distinguish themselves from it, in order to preserve their hard-won scientific and political legitimacy, as well as to maintain and enhance funding for their research. Their efforts to differentiate themselves from the anti-ageing movement are a classic example of what Gieryn (1983) termed 'boundary work', paralleling disputes in many other areas of science in which rhetorical demarcations are employed to maintain legitimacy and power. As Taylor (1996: 5) observes, 'Practicing scientists, consciously or otherwise, discursively construct working definitions of science that function, for example, to exclude various non- or pseudo-sciences so as to sustain their (perhaps well-earned) position of epistemic authority and to maintain a variety of professional resources'. Such is the case with biogerontology.

In the spring of 2002, three scientists who have undertaken research on ageing for many years – Jay Olshansky, Leonard Hayflick, and Bruce Carnes (2002a) – launched a war of words to discredit the burgeoning anti-ageing medicine movement. They published an article in *Scientific American* entitled 'No truth to the fountain of youth' which summarized a lengthier position statement endorsed by an international roster of 51 scientists and physicians that had already been posted on the magazine's website. The article declared that,

> The hawking of anti-aging 'therapies' has taken a particularly troubling turn of late. Disturbingly large numbers of entrepreneurs are luring gullible and frequently desperate customers of all ages to 'longevity' clinics, claiming a scientific basis for the anti-aging products they recommend and, often, sell. At the same time, the Internet has enabled those who seek lucre from supposed anti-aging products to reach new consumers with ease.
> (Olshansky et al., 2002a: 92)

It went on to assert that 'no currently marketed intervention – none – has yet been proved to slow, stop, or reverse human aging, and some can be downright dangerous' (Olshansky et al., 2002a: 92–3). They also presented their interpretations of various lines of biological research relevant to the underlying nature of ageing, and their promise, or lack of promise, for slowing the progression of ageing.

Shortly after the article appeared, the full position statement was also posted online at a website of the American Association for the Advancement of Science and the journal *Science*. It was then reprinted in the *Journal of Gerontology: Biological Sciences* (Olshansky et al., 2002b) and arrangements were made to have it published (in translation) in Chinese, French, German, Korean, and Spanish journals. The scientists' message also reached a very large audience when the *AARP Bulletin*, with a circulation of more than 35 million, made the *Scientific American* article the lead story in its next issue (Pope, 2002).

The internationally endorsed position statement was the most publicized but not the only effort to distance the field of gerontological science from anti-ageing medicine (see Fishman, et al., 2008). Although different types of strategies have been employed in these efforts, one common goal has been to ensure that the hard-won respectability attained by the community of gerontological researchers not be tainted by the anti-ageing movement. As the position statement acknowledges, 'Our concern is that when proponents of anti-ageing medicine claim that the fountain of youth has already been discovered, it negatively affects the credibility of serious scientific research efforts on aging' (Olshansky, et al., 2002b: B295).

One approach has been to discredit the anti-ageing medicine movement by disparaging it for making a 'quick profit' by fraudulently 'exploiting the ignorance and gullibility of the public' (Hayflick, 2001–02: 25). To this end, Olshansky, Hayflick, and Carnes constituted themselves as a committee to designate annual 'Silver Fleece Awards' (in the form of bottles of salad oil, labeled 'Snake Oil') in 'a lighthearted attempt to make the public aware of the anti-ageing quackery that has become so widespread here and abroad' (University of Illinois at Chicago, 2002). The first Silver Fleece Award for an Anti-Aging Organization, in 2002, was presented in absentia to A4M, which Olshansky characterized 'as responsible for leading the lay public and some in the medical and scientific community to the mistaken belief that technologies already exist that stop or reverse human aging.'

A second and more subtle rhetorical approach has been to mobilize the adjective 'legitimate' to modify research on ageing and thereby distinguish it from the anti-ageing movement. As biogerontologist Richard Miller explains, 'Scientists and their patrons – even those who have *legitimate* research interests in interventional gerontology – do not wish to be seen hanging out with snake-oil vendors (Miller, 2002: 167, *emphasis* added). Thus, the newsletter of the

International Longevity Center, headed by the founding director of NIA, declares, '*Legitimate* aging research is particularly important due to the prevalence of "anti-aging therapies" being peddled in the marketplace that are not based on any scientific evidence and could possibly be dangerous' (Nyberg, 2002: 1, emphasis added). The international position statement signed by the 51 scientists also presents this contrast: 'The misleading marketing and the public acceptance of anti-aging medicine is not only a waste of health dollars; it has also made it far more difficult to inform the public about *legitimate* scientific research on aging and disease' (Olshansky et al., 2002b: B293, *emphasis* added).

Not surprisingly, the various attacks on anti-ageing medicine have engendered very strong ripostes from A4M. Although some of the responses have been personal, they have been primarily aimed at discrediting gerontology for the purpose of legitimizing anti-ageing medicine. In a rejoinder to the press release announcing its receipt of the Silver Fleece Award, A4M characterized Olshansky as 'part of a "multi-billion gerontological machine" that, without any basis in truth or fact, seeks to discredit tens of thousands of innovative, honest, world-class scientists, physicians, and health practitioners' (A4M, 2002a: 1). In response to the 'No truth to the fountain of youth' article in *Scientific American*, A4M set forth 10 alleged 'gerontological biases' and purported to refute each of them by describing various articles and data (often in a misleading pseudo-scientific fashion). In conclusion, it asserted:

> Simply put, *the death cult of gerontology* [*emphasis* added] desperately labors to sustain an arcane, outmoded stance that aging is natural and inevitable. ... Ultimately, the truth on aging intervention will prevail, but this truth will be scarred from the well-funded propaganda campaign of the power elite who depend on an uninterrupted status quo in the concept of aging in order to maintain its unilateral control over the funding of today's research in aging (A4M, 2002b).

Meanwhile, some gerontologists have also undertaken boundary work against British biogerontologist Aubrey de Grey (de Grey and Rae, 2007), author of *Ending Aging*, because of his comparatively radical claims concerning the feasibility of achieving prolongevity. Since the early 2000s de Grey has vigorously been promoting SENS, a strategy for engineering negligible senescence in order to postpone ageing (de Grey et al., 2002). He asserts that it is 'inevitable, barring the end of civilization, that we will eventually achieve a 150-year mean longevity' (de Grey, 2002) and hypothesizes that 'there is a threshold rate of biomedical

progress that will allow us to stave off aging indefinitely' (de Grey, 2007: 330).

In a 2005 journal article de Grey took the biogerontological community to task for not maintaining 'an open mind' to SENS, and thereby delaying progress and 'costing lives' (de Grey, 2005). Once again, the fragile status of biogerontologists was threatened. A group of 28 self-described 'representative mainstream biogerontologists' criticized 'the publicity drawn to ageing research by the SENS/de Grey juggernaut' because it threatens to drag the public image of research on ageing back into the shadows of 'charlatanry' from which it has only escaped within the past 30 years (Warner et al., 2005).

SOCIAL AND ETHICAL IMPLICATIONS OF ANTI-AGEING RESEARCH

Meanwhile, even as the biogerontological community is striving to distinguish itself from the contemporary purveyors of anti-ageing products and services, and promoters of 'radical' gerontology, anti-ageing research is a mainstream activity sponsored and supported by NIA and other National Institutes of Health. A great deal of research has established, for instance, that dietary caloric restriction in various species of experimental animals increases average life expectancy and maximum life span, and slows age-associated changes. By 1999, NIA and the National Institute of Diabetes, Digestive, and Kidney Diseases regarded work in this area to be sufficiently important to jointly convene a Caloric Restriction Clinical Implications Advisory Group to explore the implications 'for the development of interventions to affect human age-related changes and diseases' (Hadley et al., 2001: 5). More than 50 scientists assembled for the occasion. Working in six panels, produced a substantial agenda of opportunities for research on the human implications, including aspirations to slow fundamental processes of ageing and extend maximum life span (Masoro, 2001). In line with this goal, some biogerontologists have been working on the development of pills that could mimic the anti-ageing effects of dietary caloric restriction (e.g., Lane et al., 2002).

Three anti-ageing paradigms

Regardless of whether their research is in the area of caloric restriction or other areas such as genetics or stem cells, the anti-ageing aspirations of biogerontologists in general can be summarized by three paradigms. The most conservative of these is commonly described as *compression of morbidity*, a term first promoted by a Stanford physician, James Fries (1980), 3 decades ago. The ideal envisioned by Fries is for all of us to lead long lives free of chronic disease and disability, and then die rather quickly as we reach the limits of the human species life span because we are 'worn out' from the fundamental processes of ageing. Compressed morbidity includes the possibility of increases in average life expectancy, but not in maximum life span for the human species. A more ambitious paradigm is *decelerated ageing* in which the processes of ageing are slowed and average life expectancy and/or maximum life span are increased. In contrast to the compression of morbidity ideal, late-life functional disabilities are not eliminated but occur at a more advanced age than has been the case historically. US biogerontologist Richard Miller suggests that it may be possible through decelerated ageing to 'produce 90-year-old adults who are as healthy and active as today's 50-year-olds' (Miller, 2002: 155), as well as 'increase the mean and maximal human life span by about 40 per cent, which is a mean age at death of about 112 years for Caucasian American or Japanese women, with an occasional winner topping out at about 140 years' (Miller, 2002: 164).

The most radical paradigm is *arrested ageing* in which the processes of ageing are reversed in adults. In contrast to slowing the rate of ageing, the goal of reversing ageing includes restoration of vitality and function to those who have lost them – akin to the rejuvenation theme that has been present in prolongevity myths and quests for millennia. An example is de Grey's SENS strategy, discussed above, which envisions such reversal achieved by periodically removing the damage inevitably caused by basic metabolic processes. Success in achieving arrested ageing would be tantamount to bringing about 'virtual immortality' – that is, an increase in healthy adult life span of such a great magnitude that the consequence would be societies in which no one dies except from accidents, homicides, and suicides, or from choosing to forego or being excluded from the interventions that bestow continuing vigorous life.

Anticipating the consequences of anti-ageing interventions

Although achievement of any of these biogerontological visions may seem improbable, history shows how developments in biomedical science, like the cloning of mammals, can catch society unawares by accomplishing what seemed to be 'the impossible', Anti-ageing science is another arena where the so-called impossible may come to fruition and have many important social and ethical implications.

If dramatic increases in healthy life expectancy and life span become feasible, what are the potential consequences for those who receive anti-ageing interventions and those who do not? How should the interventions be distributed in society? Serious ethical issues would be created if the interventions were not universally available, but allocated in accordance with wealth, social and political status, ascribed 'merit', nationality, or some other distinguishing criteria. Alternatively, if access to effective anti-ageing interventions were unlimited, what we now term the *ageing society* would become transformed into the *long-lived society* populated by numerous prolonged old persons. We would certainly witness radical changes in the nature of family life; labor, housing, and consumer markets; politics, public policies, and the law; i.e., in virtually every social institution. And as biogerontologist Leonard Hayflick (1994) has long feared, slowing or arresting ageing could have adverse ecological consequences due to worldwide overpopulation.

These and other potential consequences of effective anti-ageing interventions have much more profound and far-reaching implications than other current biomedical policy issues, such as the ethics of human cloning. If biogerontologists succeed in their aspirations to decelerate or arrest ageing, the consequent transformations in the nature of individual and collective life may well be drastic. Perhaps as a reflection of advances in biogerontological science and the increasing legitimacy of the discipline, the potential consequences of anti-ageing interventions have been seriously addressed in recent years, though not in forums that reach a wide public (e.g., see Post and Binstock, 2004).

Leon Kass, chairman of the US President's Council on Bioethics from 2001 to 2005, believes that 'the finitude of human life is a blessing for every human individual, whether he knows it or not' (Kass, 2001: 20). He argues that even if the human life span were increased by only 20 years, we would lose the benefits that finitude confers: (1) interest and engagement in life; (2) seriousness and aspiration; (3) beauty and love; and (4) virtue and moral excellence. Building on these long-held views, Kass set the agenda for his President's Council to issue a report in late 2003, entitled *Beyond Therapy*, that generally takes a dim view of efforts to attain prolongevity through biotechnology (President's Council on Bioethics, 2003).

Like Kass, the prominent American bioethicist Daniel Callahan has long been an opponent of prolongevity. The only deaths that he regards as 'premature' are those that occur before age 65 (Callahan, 2000). Presenting an astounding litmus test for the desirability of scientific and medical advances, Callahan argues that we should not seek much longer lives if they will not bring about any alleviation of the 'pathologies of civilized life' such as finding 'the key to world peace, eliminating poverty, stopping terrorism, achieving equitable access to health care for the world's entire population, and curbing domestic violence' (Callahan, 2003: 3). Among those who sharply disagree with Kass and Callahan is English bioethicist John Harris (2002), who thinks that anti-ageing efforts should go forward because he sees no coherent ethical objections.

As Stephen Hall (2003) makes clear in his book, *Merchants of Immortality: Chasing the Dream of Human Life Extension*, scientists and entrepreneurs will persist in their efforts to combat ageing as well as disease, with or without government funding, and with or without the approval of bioethicists, philosophers, and other critics. As they do so, it is probable that dialogues concerning the social dimensions of anti-ageing science and medicine will take place in broader forums than they have to date, reaching communities in addition to biogerontologists and bioethicists. Such discussions may help shape wisely the future of developments in anti-ageing science and their social consequences.

As a step in this direction, two members of the Gerontological Society of America (GSA) – a biogerontologist and a political scientist – formed a 60-persons multidisciplinary interest group on the Societal Implications of Anti-Aging Research that has been meeting since 2003 during the annual scientific meetings of the GSA. NIA, which for years has been providing its cachet and public funding for biogerontological science, has begun funding research on the ethical and policy implications of its work. However, some have urged that NIA and other public institutions also lead public dialogues on these issues. As Eric Juengst and his colleagues have asserted in *Science*, 'Our scientific institutions have an obligation to ensure that public discussion of anti-aging research is as deliberate and farsighted as the research itself' (Juengst et al., 2003). International proliferation of such forums to discuss the social implications of anti-ageing, including the implications for developing nations, would be highly desirable.

REFERENCES

Abir-Am, P. (1985) 'Themes, genres and orders of legitimation in the consolidation of new scientific disciplines: deconstructing the historiography of molecular biology', *History of Science*, 23: 73–117.

Achenbaum, W.A. (1995) *Crossing Frontiers: Gerontology Emerges as a Science*. New York: Cambridge University Press.

Adler, M. (1958) 'History of Gerontological Society, Inc', *Journal of Gerontology*, 13: 94–102.

A4M (American Academy of Anti-Aging Medicine) (2002a) 'The fleecing of academic integrity by the gerontological establishment', Retrieved June 13, 2002. http://www.worldhealth.net/html/fleecing_of_academic_integrity.htm

A4M (American Academy of Anti-Aging Medicine) (2002b) 'Official position statement on the truth about aging intervention', Retrieved June 13, 2002. http://www.worldhealth.net/html/truth/html

A4M (American Academy of Anti-Aging Medicine) (2005) 'The American Academy of Anti-Aging Medicine', Retrieved May 31, 2005.http://:www.worldhealth.net/p/96.html

A4M (American Academy of Anti-Aging Medicine (2007) 'Biotech e-Newsletter', September 7. Retrieved September 27, 2007.http://www.worldhealth.net/p/2007-09-07

Arumainathan, S. (2001) 'Intellectual dishonesty in geriatric medicine – truth versus fallacy: A4M sets the record straight on a campaign of disinformation challenging the facts of the science of anti-aging medicine', Retrieved November 3, 2003. http://www.worldhealth.net/resources/IntellDishonesty.pdf

Binstock, R.H. (2003) 'The war on anti-aging medicine', *The Gerontologist*, 43: 4–14.

Brown, P. and Zavetoski, S. (2004) 'Social movements in health: an introduction', *Sociology of Health and Illness*, 2: 679–94.

Bud, R. (1993) *The Uses of Life: A History of Biotechnology*. Cambridge, UK: Cambridge University Press.

Business Communications Co., Inc. (2005) 'Anti-aging products and services',Retrieved September 26, 2007.http://www.bccresearch.com/RepTemplate.cfm?reportID=465&RepDet=HLT/cat=phm&target=rep.detail.cfm

Callahan, D. (2000) 'Death and the research imperative', *New England Journal of Medicine*, 342: 654–56.

Callahan D. (2003) 'A new debate on an old topic', *Hastings Center Report*, 33(4): 3.

Chopra, D. (2001) *Grow Younger, Live Longer: 10 Steps to Reverse Aging*. New York: Harmony Books.

Clarke, A.E., Shim, J.K., Mamo, L., Fosket, J.R., and Fishman, J.R. (2003) 'Biomedicalization: technoscientific transformations of health, illness, and US biomedicine', *American Sociological Review*, 68: 161–94.

Cole, T. and Thompson, B. (2001–02) 'Anti-aging: Are you for it or against it?', *Generations*, 25(4): 6–8.

Cowdry, V. E. (1939) *Problems of Aging: Biological and Medical Aspects*. Baltimore, MD: Williams and Wilkins.

Cozzens, S.E. (1990) 'Autonomy and power in science', in S.E. Cozzens and T.F. Gieryn (eds), *Theories of Science in Society*. Bloomington, IN: Indiana University Press, pp. 164–184.

de Grey, A. (2002) 'Gerontologists and the media: The dangers of over-pessimism', *Biogerontology*, 1: 369.

de Grey, A. (2005) 'Resistance to debate on how to postpone ageing is delaying progress and costing lives', *EMBO Reports*, 6: S49–53.

de Grey, A., and Rae, M. (2007) *Ending Aging: The Rejuvenation Breakthroughs That Could Reverse Human Aging in Our Lifetime*. New York: St. Martin's Press.

de Grey, A., Ames, B. Andersen, B.N., Bartke, J.K., et al. (2002) 'Time to talk SENS: critiquing the immutability of human aging', *Annals of the New York Academy of Science*, 959: 452–62.

Eisdorfer, C. (1968) 'Patterns of federal funding for research in aging', *The Gerontologist*, 8(1, Part I): 3–6.

Epstein, S. (1996) *Impure Science*. Berkeley, CA: University of California Press.

Estes, C.L., and Binney, E.A. (1989) 'The biomedicalization of aging: dangers and dilemmas', *The Gerontologist*, 29: 587–96.

Fishman, J.R., Binstock, R.H., and Lambrix, M. (2008) 'Anti-aging science: the emergence, maintenance, and enhancement of a discipline', *Journal of Aging Studies*, 22:295-303.

Fox, P. (1989) 'From senility to Alzheimer's disease: The rise of the Alzheimer's disease movement', *Milbank Quarterly*, 67: 58–102.

Fries, J.F. (1980) 'Aging, natural death and the compression of morbidity', *New England Journal of Medicine*, 303: 130–6.

Fujimura, J. (1996) *Crafting Science: A Sociohistory of the Quest for the Genetics of Cancer*. Cambridge, MA: Harvard University Press.

Gieryn, T.F. (1983) 'Boundary-work and the demarcation of science from non-science: Strains and interests in professional ideologies of scientists', *American Sociological Review*, 48: 781–95.

Gott, M. (2005) *Sexuality, Sexual Health and Aging*. Berkshire, England: Open University Press.

Gruman, G. J. (2003) *A History of Ideas about the Prolongation of Life*. New York: Springer. (Original work published in 1966.)

Guidestar (2007) 'Guidestar: the national database for nonprofit organizations',Retrieved September 26, 2007.http://www.guidestar.org/pqShowGsReport.do?npoID=598448

Haber, C. (2001–02) 'Anti-aging: Why now? – a historical framework for understanding the contemporary enthusiasm', *Generations*, 25(4): 9–14.

Hadley, E.C., Dutta, C. Finkelstein, J., et al. (2001) 'Human implications of caloric restriction's effects on aging in laboratory animals: An overview of opportunities for research', *Journal of Gerontology. Biological and Medical Sciences*, 56A (Special Issue 1): 5–6.

Hall, S.S. (2003) *Merchants of Immortality: Chasing the Dream of Human Life Extension*. Boston: Houghton Mifflin.

Harris, J. (2002) 'Intimations of immortality', *Science*, 288: 59.

Hayflick, L. (1994) *How and Why We Age*. New York: Ballantine Books.

Hayflick, L. (2001–02) 'Anti-aging medicine: hype, hope, and reality', *Generations*, 25(4): 20–6.

Hedgecoe, A. (2003) 'Terminology and the construction of scientific disciplines: The case of pharmacogenomics', *Science, Technology, and Human Values*, 28: 513–7.

Juengst, E.T., Binstock, R.H., Mehlman, M.J., and Post, S.G. (2003) 'Antiaging research and the need for public dialogue', *Science*, 299: 1323.

Kass, L.R. (2001) 'L'chaim and its limits: Why not immortality?', *First Things*, 13: 17–24.

Kempner, J., Perlis, C.S., and Merz, J.F. (2005) 'Forbidden knowledge', *Science*, 307: 854.

Landzelius, K. (ed.) (2006) 'Patient organization movements and new metamorphoses in patienthood', *Social Science and Medicine* (Special Issue), 62(3).

Lane, M.A., Ingram, D., and Roth, G.S. (2002) 'The serious search for an anti-aging pill', *Scientific American*, 287(2): 36–41.

Lockett, B.A. (1983) *Aging, Politics, and Research: Setting the Federal Agenda for Research on Aging*. New York: Springer Publishing Company.

Masoro, E.J. (ed.) (2001) 'Caloric restriction's effects on aging: opportunities for research on human implications', *Journal of Gerontology. Biological and Medical Sciences*, 56A (Special Issue 1).

Masoro, E.J., and Austad, S.N. (eds) (2006) *Handbook of the Biology of Aging*, 6th edn. San Diego, CA: Academic Press.

Miller, R.A. (2002) 'Extending life: scientific prospects and political obstacles', *Milbank Quarterly*, 80: 155–74.

Mykytyn, C.E. (2006a) 'Anti-aging medicine: A patient/practitioner movement to redefine aging', *Social Science and Medicine*, 62: 643–53.

Mykytyn, C.E. (2006b) 'Anti-aging medicine: predictions, moral obligations, and biomedical intervention', *Anthropological Quarterly*, 79: 5–31.

National Institute on Aging (2001) Action *Plan for Aging Research: Strategic Plan for Fiscal Years 2001–2005*. Washington, DC: US Department of Health and Human Services.

National Institute on Aging (2007) *Budget*. Retrieved September 26, 2007. http://www.nia.nih.gov/AboutNIA/BudgetRequests//FY2008/obligation.htm

Nyberg J.P. (2002) 'The importance of aging research', *ILC Policy Report*, May, 1.

Olshansky, S.J., and Carnes, B.A. (2001) *The Quest for Immortality: Science at the Frontiers of Aging*. New York: Norton.

Olshansky, S.J., Hayflick, L., and Carnes, B.A. (2002a) 'No truth to the fountain of youth', *Scientific American*, 286(6): 92–5.

Olshansky, S.J., Hayflick, L., and Carnes, B.A. (2002b) 'Position statement on human aging', *Journal of Gerontology. Biological Sciences*, 57A: B292–7.

Pope, E. (2002) '51 top scientists blast anti-aging idea', *AARP Bulletin*, 23(43): 3–5.

Post, S.G., and Binstock, R.H. (eds) (2004) *The Fountain of Youth: Cultural, Scientific, and Ethical Perspectives on a Biomedical Goal*. New York: Oxford University Press.

President's Council on Bioethics (2003) *Beyond Therapy: Biotechnology and the Pursuit of Happiness*. New York: Harper Collins.

Research on Aging Act of 1974 (1974) USA Public Law Number 93-296.

Robert, L. (2004) 'The three avenues of gerontology: From basic research to clinical gerontology and anti-aging medicine: Another French paradox', *Journal of Gerontology: Biological Sciences*, 59A: 540–2.

Robinson, J. (2001) *Noble Conspirator: Florence S. Mahoney and the Rise of the National Institutes of Health*. Washington, DC: The Francis Press.

Schutz, C.A. (2002) 'Personal communication, based on organizational records', June 19, from the executive director of the Gerontological Society of America.

Spindler, M. (2007) 'Anti-ageing and spirituality – surrogate religion, spiritual materialism, post-modern Calvinist ethic?', Paper presented at the annual meeting of the British Society of Gerontology, Sheffield, England, September 6.

Taylor, C.A. (1996) *Defining Science: A Rhetoric of Demarcation*. Madison, WI: University of Wisconsin Press.

University of Illinois at Chicago (2002) 'Silver Fleece Awards target anti-aging hype', Office of Public Affairs, News Release, February 12. Retrieved June 12, 2002. http://tigger.uic.edu/htbin/cgiwrap/bin/newsbureau

US GAO (General Accounting Office) (2001) *Health Products for Seniors: "Anti-aging" Products Pose Potential for Physical and Economic Harm*. Washington, DC: US Government Printing Office, GAO-01-1129.

US Senate Subcommittee on Aging (of the Committee on Labor and Public Welfare) (1973) *Research on Aging Act, 1973*. Washington, DC: US Government Printing Office.

van Lente, H. and Rip, A. (1998) 'The rise of membrane technology: From rhetorics to social reality', *Social Studies of Science*, 28: 221–54.

Warner, H. (2007) 'Making the political case for biogerontology funding: A view from the trenches', Paper presented at the SENS 3 Conference, Cambridge, England, September 9.

Warner, H., Andersen, J., Austad, S. et al., (2005) 'Science fact and the SENS agenda', *EMBO Reports*, 6: 1006–8.

Wilson, D. (2007) 'Aging: Disease or business opportunity?', *New York Times*, April 15. Retrieved September 17, 2007. http://www.nytimes.com/2007/04/15/business/yourmoney/15aging.html?ex=1189483200&en=2b075b8de1c1b427&ei=5070

Youngevity (2003) *The Youngevity Story*. Retrieved May 24, 2003.http://www.youngevity.com/the_ygy_story_fs.htm

37

The New Ageing Enterprise

Harry R. Moody

INTRODUCTION

In this discussion we profile a series of organizations that display characteristics of the 'New Ageing Enterprise'. The organizations presented here are a subset of a larger population of enterprises that I profile elsewhere (Moody, 2008) that are exemplars in showing the way to prosper as enterprises in an ageing society, adding social value and benefit specifically to the subpopulation of older people in the process. The paradigm cases considered here are Erickson Retirement Communities, the Eden Alternative in long-term care, Elderhostel lifelong learning, the Experience Corp volunteer programme, and RetirementJobs.com. These paradigm cases are analyzed in comparison to seven other New Ageing Enterprise models: Beacon Hill Village, On Lok, Universities of the Third Age, the Red Hat Society, and Idealist.org. From the organizations profiled here we draw comparative lessons for ageing policy and organizational change, including the importance of positive ageing and age-affirmative branding; the role of social capital; and the power of leadership in organizational innovation.

There has long been a pervasive fear about population ageing in many circles in the United States and Europe (Moody, 1988a). One reason for gloom is a simple projection into the future of present tendencies: specifically, conditions where older people are regarded as passive consumers of public services, especially health care and pensions. Pessimists envisage bankruptcy and increasing retirees without pension support in old age. They conclude that we cannot afford an ageing society because the future will bring ever-growing numbers of older people who are sick and helpless,

unable to be productive members of society, doomed to loneliness and despair. Whether on the golf course or in the nursing home, passivity is taken for granted. Those on the Right suggest that this gloomy future demands a cut in public entitlement programmes to prepare now for coming disaster. Those on the Left, if they admit a problem at all, argue instead for modest reform of public programmes to meet ever-growing needs.

Both Left and Right tend to agree on 'needs' but differ on how these needs could be met. Overcoming such pessimism about population ageing is not easy. It will not happen until we can point to tangible examples of success and positive organizational responses, cases that illustrate the way in which a growing older population can be an opportunity, rather than a problem. The New Ageing Enterprise is an attempt to describe such cases and draw from these examples lessons for the future.

In this chapter, we review selected case studies of organizations, both business and non-profit, which have thrived by responding to needs in areas such as retirement housing, long-term care, worklife extension, voluntary action, and lifelong learning. Some of these respond to new consumer markets, such as housing, travel, and hospitality, while others represent ways in which an ageing population can become more productive through work, volunteer roles, and health promotion. All domains and organizations considered in this chapter represent aspects of positive ageing that might have been considered 'utopian' but have turned out to be eminently practical with a proven track record of success. The organizations profiled here have important lessons from their success, especially for the sustainability of enterprises both in business and the non-profit sector.

Overcoming pessimism

Robert Butler has pointed to what he calls 'the paradox of longevity:' the curious fact that, on the one hand, mass longevity is a great human achievement, but, on the other hand, many remain pessimistic about the sustainability of an ageing society (Butler, 2008). Across advanced industrialized societies we see this pervasive anxiety about the impact of population ageing (Peterson and Howe, 2004).

The enterprises discussed in this chapter present themselves as transcending this debate, promoting more positive images of ageing while delivering value to society. As with earlier discussion of so-called 'Silver Industries' (Moody, 2005), these organizations are contributing to a new 'social construction of age' and at the same time identify best practices for organizational innovation. After presenting the cases, we conclude with an analysis on some cross-cutting elements of the New Ageing Enterprises examined here and with further reflections on implications for social policy understood in the tradition of critical gerontology.

OLDER WORKERS

Old age in the 20th century was a time when mass retirement was possible as a normative expectation for the majority of society. But by the end of the century many wondered whether a 'leisure ethic' was appropriate for the ageing society of the future (Freedman, 2002). Some gerontologists, questioning the institution of mass retirement, instead urged a policy of 'productive ageing' (Morrow-Howell et al., 2001). One impact of the economic downturn beginning in 2008 has been a marked trend toward expectations about worklife extension; surveys suggest that a large majority of ageing baby boomers expect to work beyond the traditional retirement age. The challenge for the new Ageing Enterprise is this: will these older jobseekers find the jobs they expect (Hedge et al, 2006)?

RetirementJobs.com

RetirementJobs.com has become the leading career website for jobseekers in the 50+ age group (Lewis, 2006). Its website lists between 20,000 and 30,000 open positions refreshed several times each week. Most openings are in the retail industry, but many are also in financial services. Older jobseekers can go directly to the site and be confident of finding employers who are eager to hire older workers.

RetirementJobs.com offers a distinctive brand positioning that reflects an appeal to its niche audience, the 50+ worker. Advice and stories on the website are focused on the distinctive issues a mature worker is likely to encounter. All jobseekers visiting the site know that employers posting jobs on this site are at least open to talking to them. Substantial work experience here is an asset, not a liability, which can help build the confidence of mature jobseekers.

RetirementJobs is not the only web-based search company focused on older workers. For example, there is Workforce50.com and Retired Brains.com, which both certify that employers listing jobs actually want to hire older workers, not only for entry-level positions – e.g., flipping burgers at McDonald's – but for higher-level positions as well. Another site, ExecSearches.com, is targeted primarily at midlevel and executive positions in the government, health, non-profit, and education sectors. YourEncore.com aims for experienced scientists, engineers, and product developers who want time-limited assignments.

Idealist.org

Idealist.org is a web portal created in 1995 by the international non-profit group 'Action Without Borders'. Idealist.org serves as a web-based channel for those interested in non-profit organizations and issues and careers, and acts as a clearinghouse for both paid employment and volunteer activities in the non-profit world. Action Without Borders has a mission to connect people, organizations, and resources in order to 'help build a world where all people can live free and dignified lives'. The organization's methods have evolved over the years but the core focus has been on providing a meeting point for individuals and organizations seeking to improve their communities on both a local and global level.

By 1999, more than 20,000 people were receiving Idealist daily email alerts and more organizations were signing up. To support its work, Idealist began charging US-based organizations a $40 fee for job postings, departing from the free listing practice up until that point. The result was an ongoing revenue stream that enabled Idealist to enhance its programmes and still keep most services free of charge. Idealist has gone on to become the most successful non-profit job site on the web. Its business model has enabled it to be sustainable without depending on outside grants or donations, as most non-profit organizations are compelled to do.

The impressive results of both RetirementJobs and Idealist are encouraging as we think about the opportunities for older workers. But encouragement must be tempered by the enduring problem of age discrimination, which serves as a barrier to those who want employment in later life. Despite legal prohibitions, age bias seems strongly entrenched in other segments of the economy (Palmore et al., 2005). Ageism seems unlikely to disappear by virtue of its own 'phased retirement' and it remains a factor inhibiting managers from making use of older workers.

LIFELONG LEARNING

Lifelong learning is a key strategy for positive ageing both for individuals and for society. Because the older population is our only indefinitely renewable natural resource, public policy will need to view lifelong learning as an investment in human capital, not as a luxury or a private entertainment. Successful innovations in late-life learning will be those that prize and enhance a sense of personal agency and control, instead of passivity in old age (Moody, 2004). Two examples of New Ageing Enterprises display patterns of organizational innovation and vitality that respond to this promise of positive ageing.

Elderhostel

Elderhostel is a programme offering liberal education and travel for older people, chiefly in the United States. Indeed, it is now the world's largest educational travel organization, attracting nearly 200,000 participants each year. Elderhostel currently offers 10,000 programmes annually, in all 50 US states and in over 90 countries around the world.

Elderhostel was founded in 1975 by Marty Knowlton, a social activist and educator. Elderhostel began as an effort to provide later-life learning through the use of low-cost summer dormitory facilities, in keeping with what Howard Bowen called the 'economics of unused capacity.' Elderhostel programmes in the United States are typically 6 days long, with three classes each day, drawing on subjects from the liberal arts, broadly understood. There are no tests, grades, or other requirements of conventional education. International Elderhostel programmes are typically longer, usually up to 3 weeks, and may involve more travel. Whether domestic or international, formal classes in Elderhostel are complemented by field trips and cultural events to take advantage of the local environment.

Elderhostel's growth has been extraordinary. The programme grew from 220 participants in 1975 to 20,000 five years later (Mills, 1993). Despite its growth, Elderhostel has retained most elements of the original learning plan: a week or two of organized but informal learning activities sponsored by a host institution (college or university, and increasingly, environmental center, national park, museum, and so on). The national and international Elderhostel network is administered by a non-profit organization headquartered in Boston. Maintaining a stable structure and commitment to informal, agency-oriented learning has conferred huge advantages on Elderhostel. On the one hand, Elderhostel operates as a franchise, and the term 'Elderhostel' is a legally registered trademark.

Elderhostel remains a not-for-profit organization, though it operates in many ways as a business enterprise. For example, liberal education remains the core of Elderhostel's mission. Elderhostel is best understood as a 'non-profit business' and it offers scholarships to learners otherwise unable to attend its offerings. Although it now operates in 90 countries, Elderhostel remains an American innovation. But on the international scene-older adult education has also produced other remarkable examples of the New Ageing Enterprise.

University of the third age

The idea for a 'University of the Third Age' (U3A) was originally proposed in 1973 by Pierre Vellas and launched at the University of Toulouse in France. Vellas had in mind a new kind of educational enterprise for older adults: an initiative that would enhance the quality of life and strengthen intergenerational ties, while at the same time promoting research in the field of gerontology. Since its beginning, the U3A movement has spread to all continents, becoming a global phenomenon and comprising, literally, thousands of locally developed U3A programmes of remarkable variety (Swindell and Thompson, 1995).

Universities of the Third Age have followed different models but two ideal types predominate: the French model, based on close association with a traditional university; and the British model, operating more in the spirit of mutual aid and self-help. The French model was established earlier (1973) and the British somewhat later (1981). An American version, the Learning in Retirement Institute (LIR) actually predates both (1962). In the 1990s, the LIR movement received new momentum from the establishment of the Osher

Institutes for Lifelong Learning, which operate in more than 100 sites in the Unites States.

A similar process took place in Britain, where the Third Age Trust promoted a network of U3As. By the turn of the century, there were more than 400 local U3As established in the United Kingdom, with a total membership approaching 100,000. U3As inspired by the French model are affiliated with a formal university and tend to look to university resources and faculties for their support. Unlike Elderhostel or Osher Institutes in the United States, the U3As on the French model may be funded by the government, with modest support from local sources. By contrast, the British U3As, guided by a self-help philosophy, need only be loosely affiliated with a university.

It is ironic that two of the most spectacular successes of later-life learning in higher education – Elderhostel and U3A – have largely owed nothing to public policy of any kind. They have grown and flourished entirely without government funding or support. Yet these examples of the New Ageing Enterprise have lessons for policymakers. Lifelong learning has long been understood to be a domain of increasing importance in post-industrial societies, with a shift to 'information economies' and a demand for recurrent education. With population ageing in all developed countries, it is increasingly clear that lifelong learning must become a strategic arena for the future (OECD, 2005).

The lessons from Elderhostel and U3A could be of importance as we seek to fashion public policies in support of lifelong learning. Above all, Elderhostel and U3A have demonstrated that older adults can learn and want to learn. But a key fact here is that previous public policy has often turned out to be out of alignment with the needs and perceptions of older learners themselves. What characterizes New Ageing Enterprises like Elderhostel and U3A is the centrality of individual agency and self-determination: above all, a sense of intrinsic enjoyment in learning for its own sake and the pursuit of learning in ways that capitalize on life experience instead of diminishing such experience.

Voluntary action

There is a popular, pessimistic image of ageing where older people are isolated and selfish, unconcerned with younger generations, living lonely lives in age-segregated settings. But this image is grossly misleading. Here we look at two models of the New Ageing Enterprise very different from that gloomy image. Instead of isolation, we see a vibrant alternative: intergenerational collaboration and social networking,

exemplified in the Experience Corp volunteer programme and the Red Hat Society as vehicles for communal ties. Both of these models represent a revival of community and strengthening of social capital.

Experience Corps

Experience Corps is a signature programme created by the Civic Ventures organization. It is a volunteer network for Americans over 55 now operating in 19 major cities in the United States, including major urban centers such as Boston, San Francisco, Minneapolis, and Washington, DC. Two thousand Experience Corps members are currently serving as tutors and mentors helping children to read. They work in urban public schools and after-school programmes, where, along with basic skills, they help develop confidence for future success. Research has shown that Experience Corps can boost student academic performance, help schools and youth-serving organizations become more successful, strengthens ties between these institutions and surrounding neighborhoods, and enhance the well-being of the volunteers in the process.

Experience Corp combines several programme elements that have proved critical for its success. First, Experience Corps members make a substantial commitment, with each participant devoting a significant number of hours to tutoring and mentoring each week. Secondly, Experience Corps members receive rigorous training in early childhood education and literacy. Thirdly, Experience Corps members work in teams, developing supportive networks of colleagues. Experience Corps is now part of the AmeriCorp network of national service programmes and its budget comes from diversified sources, including foundations, the private sector, and other public resources.

One of the most pessimistic appraisals of American life was given by Harvard political scientist Robert Putnam in his influential book *Bowling Alone: The Collapse and Revival of American Community*. His book is a reflection on the fate of 'social capital' in the contemporary world, a theme developed by Pierre Bourdieu. Putnam argues that America is currently depleting its traditional social capital: that is, the collective value of social networks and habits that dispose people to do things with each other and for each other. In Putnam's words,

'For the first two-thirds of the twentieth century a powerful tide bore Americans into ever deeper engagement in the life of their communities, but a few decades ago – silently, without warning – that tide reversed and we were overtaken by a treacherous rip current. Without at first noticing, we have been pulled apart from one another and from our communities over the last third of the century'.

(Putnam, 2000)

Putnam attributes the cause of declining social capital to a variety of causes, but notes that this decline coincides with the passing of an older generation: specifically, the waning of the so-called 'greatest generation', now in their seventies and eighties. As baby boomers approach old age, Putnam fears, they will lack adequate habits to sustain our social capital.

But Experience Corps is a ray of hope, one of a dozen 'success stories' cited in *Better Together: Restoring the American Community*, written by Putnam and Lewis Feldstein (2003). The authors write:

'The reading scores of 75 per cent of Experience Corps students in Philadelphia have increased one grade level. Attendance among the students tutored has improved. Surveys of volunteers taken at the beginning of their participation in the pilot programme and at the end of the two-year pilot show a significant increase in their sense of purpose and energy and a significant decrease in loneliness.'

Other studies of Experience Corp volunteers revealed gains in health status, as well (Fried et al., 2004).

Experience Corp is designed to tap into the generativity and altruism of older adults, in order to strengthen public education by the power of volunteering. But volunteering is not the only way to find such camaraderie, as we will see in the following example of a New Ageing Enterprise.

The Red Hat Society

The Red Hat Society was inspired by the opening lines of a now-famous poem by Jenny Joseph: 'When I am an old woman, I shall wear purple with a red hat that doesn't go.' In 1998 Sue read those lines and was inspired to found a 'Red Hat Society' as a vehicle for older women to be 'outrageous', to play and to find the 'late freedom' displayed by some great artists in their later years. Since then, the Red Hat Society has grown to the point of having more than 1.5 million registered members in 40,000 chapters in the United States and around the world. By some estimates, the Red Hat Society is adding an average of 40–50 new chapters a day, not by advertising but by 'viral marketing' or word-of-mouth dissemination. Clearly, the Society represents a vehicle for age-based voluntary association that deserves closer attention.

The Red Hat Society embodies some of the anarchistic impulses that emerged in the decade of the 1960s. Its playfulness is likely to appeal to ageing baby boomer women nostalgic for the spirit of Woodstock. Red Hat, in fact, describes itself as a 'disorganization' whose goal is social interaction and play: it wants to encourage silliness as well as friendship for women aged 50 and above. Red Hatters customarily wear elaborately decorated hats and purple attire to their gatherings, such as tea parties. Women under age 50 can also be auxiliary members, wearing a pink hat and lavender attire until their 50th birthday. In a world where cultural images of ageing tend to be negative, the Red Hat Society offers a very different approach to later life.

Like other New Ageing Enterprises, the Red Hat Society has become a powerful brand name with a robust marketing dimension, including a line of romance novels and self-helps books such as *Designer Scrapbooks the Red Hat Society Way* (2005) and *The Red Hat Society Cookbook*. The Society has become a big business, with several websites such as the 'Red Hat Society Store', offering accessories, apparel, crafts, dress-up items, footwear, gifts, gourmet products, jewelry, stationery, media products, and, of course, hats and hat accessories.

The Red Hat Society offers playfulness as a compensation for the loss of self-esteem faced by ageing women as they confront the empty nest, declining health, widowhood, and the challenge of body image (Featherstone, 1995). Above all, the Red Hat Society has provided a means of socialization and connectivity for older women and a new approach to the long-standing gerontological challenge of the meaning of leisure in later life.

But the Red Hat Society should not be understood merely as a form of compensation. Its emergence also expresses certain ideals of positive ageing. Some studies suggest that membership in the Red Hat Society serves as an entrée into a temporary, communal world with its own distinctive sources of meaning. Evidently, Red Hat activities offer an opportunity for camaraderie and bonding through a sense of sisterhood and of being admitted to a social space with 'no rules' (Hutchinson et al., 2008). The authors of a recent study of the Red Hat Society concluded that

Leisure and health promotion professionals could utilize the Red Hat Society model to provide programmes for older women that are empowering. Providers might consider creating leadership programmes for older women to engage in the process of developing, implementing, and leading leisure-based programmes.

(Son et al., 2007)

POLICY PERSPECTIVES

In, *Bowling Alone*, Putnam distinguishes between two different forms of social capital: what he terms **bonding** capital and **bridging** capital. Bonding capital grows with socialization among people who are similar according to ethnicity, religion, socioeconomic background, and so on. The Black Church would be a prime example of social capital in a minority neighborhood. By contrast, bridging social capital arises from people socialization across barriers of different kinds. Participation in a multi-ethnic sports team might be an example here. Putnam believes that bonding capital and bridging capital strengthen each other and that both are required for societal maintenance.

Putnam specifically cites Experience Corp as a positive case of strengthened social capital helping to support a formal organization: in this instance, the public school system in inner-city settings. Experience Corp has elements of both bonding and bridging capital: bonding because both mentors and students are likely to be African-American; bridging because the volunteer programme engages retirees who may have higher socioeconomic levels than the students they are supporting. We see a similar pattern in the Red Hat Society. Red Hat participants, by definition, are older women: men and younger people are automatically excluded, and the exclusion is part of the bonding promoted by Red Hat membership. On the other hand, a voluntary association like Red Hat is likely to bring together women of very different backgrounds who might not otherwise meet each other.

From a policy perspective, Experience Corp has demonstrated the importance of volunteer groups in providing kinds of support that formal organizations are not able to provide on their own: one-to-one tutoring and mentoring relationships. By contrast, the Red Hat Society, at first glance, might seem to be a purely private association whose playful activities cannot claim serious attention. But the Red Hat Society underscores the profound and destructive influence of ageism in our society. Some forms of voluntary action can be critical in building self-esteem for groups who have been subject to discrimination or prejudice, and gender and age would be prime examples. Voluntary action, by strengthening social capital, helps to sustain the 'ties that bind' which make possible constructive public policy, whether in education or in overcoming ageism.

Retirement housing

Retirement communities are, in many respects, a distinctively American institution (Hunt, 1984) and they are likely to remain important. Dating back to the development of Sun City, retirement communities have attracted only a small proportion of older people. Yet they have had influence in shaping the way we think of the meaning of later life in relation to retirement housing. Here we consider two models of retirement housing that deserve closer attention.

Erickson Retirement Communities

Erickson Retirement Communities is a network of 20 retirement campuses, serving more than 20,000 residents in 11 states from Massachusetts to Texas. Erickson Retirement Communities have been inspired by ideals of active and positive ageing (Peck, 2006). Erikson began in 1983 with the explicit aim of making retirement living available to middle and moderate-income Americans (Adler, 2000). A critical element in its success has been its pioneering use of a 100% refundable entrance deposit, which serves to protect the residents' equity; a fee-for-service schedule, whereby residents pay only for services they actually want or need; and economies of scale (with up to 2000 residents at each site, reducing cost for amenities).

From the outset, founder John Erickson wanted his community to be affordable for middle-class Americans. Erickson stated that he believed that high-end retirement communities already existed but no one had yet built such communities for teachers or postal workers. The success of Erikson has shown that it is possible to create an affordable retirement inspired by ideals of positive ageing. But other approaches are inspired by the ideal of 'ageing in place'.

Beacon Hill Village

Beacon Hill Village is an upscale historic district in Boston where neighbors banded together to create a local community organization that would permit them to age in their homes. Instead of long-term care, they wanted a 'concierge' service that maximized their autonomy. In 2000 they created 'Beacon Hill Village', a non-profit association to provide them with services, ranging from in-house health and social services to pet care or computer support (Gross, 2006, 2007). Like Erickson, they 'unbundled' services and payment to create a package cheaper than assisted living or conventional home care.

The grassroots innovation represented by Beacon Hill Village was not the first effort of its kind. Naturally occurring retirement communities (NORCs) were recognized in the 1970s, appearing in urban high-rise apartment buildings such as Manhattan's West Side (Vladeck, 2004). Like Beacon Hill, NORCs appealed to those who wanted to 'age in place' and they obtained government assistance to achieve that goal. In some respects, the emergence of NORCs was a response to declining federal funding for senior housing in the last decades of the 20th century (Pine and Pine, 2002). NORCs, along with grassroots initiatives like Beacon Hill Village, are responding to a distinctive market segment: middle-class people who are not sick enough for Medicare, who have too much income for Medicaid services, and who are not rich enough for private individual care.

Since the vast majority of older people will not move into either public or private retirement housing, there is a big policy challenge around how to create and sustain livable communities where older people will continue to live in their own homes. Here is where the lessons from Beacon Hill and NORCs prove valuable. To date around 80 communities around the United States have experimented with providing public funding to support 'ageing in place' on the NORC model. Along with senior cohousing, these initiatives represent just a few of the experimental approaches now underway as there is a great call for retirement communities as a 'third way' for the third age (Peace and Holland, 2001).

Long-term care

It is not unusual for older people to say things like 'I'd rather die than go into a nursing home', expressing a widespread sentiment that long-term care is the 'end of the line', something we would rather not think about at all. The challenge is whether we can develop organizational models to provide long-term care in a way that affirms our positive values of life. Here we examine two exemplary models: On Lok and the Eden Alternative.

On Lok

On Lok is a comprehensive health plan serving frail older people living in the San Francisco Bay area. Its programme of housing and supportive services offers an alternative of community-based long-term care when nursing home care might otherwise prove necessary. Originally based in Chinatown, the name 'On Lok' means 'place of peace and happiness' in Chinese, its name reflecting the organization's mission and philosophy of care. On Lok Senior Health Services focuses on providing quality, affordable care services for 950 frail older people. On Lok's success has been attributed partly to its use of an interdisciplinary professional team who can engage in assessment and development of an individualized care plan

(Kornblatt et al., 2002). The aim is to promote independence by proving services across the entire continuum of care: primary and specialty medical care, adult day health care, in-home health and personal care, social work services, and hospital and nursing home care.

The On Lok approach has proved to be a model for national replication, known as the Programme of All-Inclusive Care for the Elderly (PACE). Instead of a conventional reimbursement approach, PACE operates through capitated financing, allowing a single average monthly payment with flexibility to provide services based on individual need rather than limited services reimbursable under Medicare and Medicaid fee-for-service systems (Rich, 1999).

The Eden Alternative

The Eden Alternative began in the early 1990s as an experiment in a single nursing home in upstate New York (Thomas, 1996). In 1991 geriatrician Dr. William Thomas created at a nursing home in rural upstate New York a habitat containing birds, dogs, cats, rabbits, and a flock of hens, and hundreds of indoor plants and gardens of flowers and vegetables. Children were also brought into the nursing home. Thomas said his goal was to decrease the plague of loneliness, helplessness, and boredom found in nursing homes. A decade and a half later, Eden and related culture change initiatives such as the 'Pioneer Network' have become a national and international movement on behalf of 'culture change' in nursing homes and other long-term care facilities (Thomas, 2007).

Thomas subsequently extended the Eden Alternative in a new direction called the Greenhouse Project, emphasizing a 'warm, smart and green approach' consisting of small, family-size homes for 6–8 residents, supported by paid caregivers who also serve as homemaker and friend with 24/7 back-up nursing support. In effect, the Greenhouse is intended to de-institutionalize long-term care, returning it to a more human scale, as proponents of community-based long-term care have long advocated.

The Eden Alternative is one of several efforts promoting humanistic culture change in long-term care. In the United States, others have included the Wellspring model and the Live Oak regenerative community model introduced by Barry Barkan. But these American initiatives were predated and inspired by other practices and initiatives along these lines have appeared in Australia, Canada, and Switzerland as well as the United Kingdom. Especially noteworthy is the 'person-centered approach' to dementia care pioneered by the late Tom Kitwood and the Bradford Dementia Group.

How far can such approaches go in transforming the culture of long-term care facilities? Adopting the Eden label is one thing; actually changing a facility's culture is another, and the change seems likely to take 2 years. Some studies suggest that an Eden Alternative facility costs somewhat more to build than a conventional facility, but not excessively so. But the real issue is not about cost or bricks-and-mortar or companion animals. Transformative change is more far-reaching and difficult and requires organizational leadership. Still, nursing home culture remains profoundly influenced by ownership and leadership. As long as a top-down, hierarchical management style predominates, culture change may not be successful. Adoption of the Eden Alternative model is faced by the challenge of educating sufficient numbers of nursing home staff and management in the visionary principles of Eden. There are other problems as well. Staff have complained about extra work demanded by caring for animals, and, understandably, not all facilities are equally eager to open their doors to the wider community. Facilities need to restructure their hierarchy, giving residents and staff more responsibility for making decisions. Such a transformation takes time.

The success of the Eden Alternative and On Lok should be seen in the context of the larger political economy of long-term care (Olson, 2003). For example, in the past few years, large private investment groups have acquired six of the ten largest nursing home chains, or 9 per cent of the total in the United States; private investment groups own smaller chains and are likely to acquire more companies in the future. Ominously, this trend toward corporate take-overs has been accompanied by declining quality of care. We must wonder: at a time when private investors are cutting staff in nursing homes, will they be interested in genuine 'culture change' represented by the Eden Alternative and On Lok? What Eden and On Lok have shown is that long-term care can be transformed in far-reaching ways. Whether that promise can be fulfilled is a question for the future (Baker, 2007).

CONCLUSIONS

Common elements of New Ageing Enterprises

There are some cross-cutting elements evident in the New Ageing Enterprise cases examined so far.

Positive ageing

New Ageing Enterprises build on strengths of ageing, not on a deficit model. Repeatedly, older people are seen as a source of value to society through work (RetirementJobs) or volunteerism (Experience Corp). Later life is viewed as a time of growth even under conditions of disability (Eden Alternative). The New Ageing Enterprise offers an optimistic vision of ageing as an 'Abundance of Life' (Moody, 1988b).

Age-affirmative branding

New Ageing Enterprises are brands based on something more than adaptation to age. They appeal to principles of growth over the life span through lifelong learning (Elderhostel) and intergenerational mentoring (Experience Corp). RetirementJobs emphasizes the value of mature workers to employers and society.

Ageless marketing

In keeping with the 'ageless marketing' approach propounded by David Wolfe (Wolfe and Snyder, 2003), New Ageing Enterprises appeal to what transcends age, such as learning and positive social engagement. The strategy of ageless marketing represents a fulfillfilment of gerontologist Bernice Neugarten's call for an 'age-irrelevant society', which was the official theme of the 1981 White House Conference on Ageing.

Blurred genres

New Ageing Enterprises go beyond the dichotomy of 'profit' versus 'non-profit'. For example, Erickson Retirement Communities has created its own foundation and non-profit university programme on behalf of housing and ageing. RetirementJobs has allied itself with the American Association of Retired Persons (AARP) and works actively against ageism in all forms.

Social capital

Social capital, as described by Robert Putnam, is as important as financial capital for New Ageing Enterprises. These organizations typically spend less than other companies on conventional advertising or marketing, relying instead on 'viral marketing' (Elderhostel) and promoting social ties at the local level. Morale and group cohesion is essential for success whether in volunteering (Experience Corp) or long-term care (Eden Alternative).

Economies of scale

Some New Ageing Enterprises are huge in scale: e.g., Elderhostel, the largest education-travel enterprise in the world. But these organizations also strive to retain an atmosphere of small-scale intimacy. Idealist, for example, complements its web-based communities with face-to-face interaction. Low cost is central to the 'value proposition' offered by New Ageing Enterprises.

Integrity of mission and values

In the style defined by Collins (2001) in *Good to Great*, New Ageing Enterprises have remained faithful to their original mission and values. The point is illustrated by the liberal arts orientation maintained by Elderhostel as well as by organizations like the Pioneer Network and Civic Ventures which have become major forces for changing public understanding of ageing. For New Ageing Enterprises, mission matters.

Product innovation

New Ageing Enterprises have not remained static over time. They have typically added new product lines responsive to new cohorts of older people. For example, Elderhostel created its 'Road Scholar' programme to appeal to ageing baby boomers. The Eden Alternative developed its Greenhouse Project to encourage community-based long-term care.

A Third Way for ageing policy?

The New Ageing Enterprise tries to draw lessons from incremental change at the organizational level. In *The Consequences of Modernity* (1990), Giddens has specifically criticized the attempt to propagate a single, comprehensive ideology or political agenda, instead favoring such incremental steps in which people can make improvements to the workplace or local community. On the positive side, Giddens has underscored the importance of a new 'life politics' or politics for self-actualization, arising under conditions of late and reflexive modernity. However, he has not extended that approach to the micro level in the analysis of organizational structure, as we have tried to do in the New Ageing Enterprise.

This approach, in essence, is midway between what is 'utopian' and what is 'realistic'. Some policy analysts have attempted to apply a version of the Third Way to ageing issues, calling for a path between the excesses of the free market and problems generated by state-run bureaucratic systems (Qureshi, 2001). Others have even considered the retirement community as a 'third way for the Third Age' (Peace and Holland, 2001). Senior cohousing and naturally occurring retirement communities could represent examples of such a Third Way strategy in practice.

This framework for a Third Way in ageing policy is precisely what is represented by the New Ageing Enterprise and what is illustrated by paradigm cases of organizational innovation discussed here. For example, Elderhostel represents the use of a market mechanism – essentially, an international travel agency – mobilized for non-profit purposes. The University of Third Age (U3A) represents the creation of a 'social space' for Third Age self-actualization through individual agency, as Peter Laslett called for. For both Elderhostel and U3A, individual agency remains of pivotal importance.

New Ageing Enterprises should not be seen as some kind of 'second best' alternative to public policy. Instead, they constitute utopian models and benchmarks for what public policy could become. Ernst Bloch spoke of the need for 'realistic utopias'. The Eden Alternative and Experience Corp represent 'utopian' efforts undertaken in settings – the nursing home and ghetto schools – that would otherwise seem unpromising for social change. Nursing homes and public education have often appeared as institutions that are oppressive and resistant to change. By contrast, other New Ageing Enterprises have aimed strategically for market niches ignored by others.

None of the organizations profiled here are overtly political enterprises. In that sense, they do not fit Giddens' Third Way agenda for political mobilization and citizenship in late modernity. But each of them offers important lessons and perspectives for public policy in the spirit of Giddens' characterization of a Third Way. Some, though not all of them, are described by the O'Neill's term 'Civic Enterprise' because they actively promote ideals of civic engagement. New Ageing Enterprises also display some surprising affinities with 'emancipatory' goals called for by some exponents of critical gerontology.

Critical gerontology and the New Ageing Enterprise

Critical gerontology, over the past three decades, has been inspired by hostility to commodification and rationalization, rejection of forms of instrumental domination that prevent genuine freedom in later life, whether domination originates in government bureaucracy or the marketplace. Critical gerontology remains an indispensable theoretical perspective in helping us imagine a future for ageing which is different from the past (Vincent and Downs et al., 2006). In practice, critical gerontology has been allied with a critical perspective known as the political economy of ageing. The perspective of political economy displays a deep and persistent hostility to market economics and its influence on ageing policy, particularly health care (Armstrong et al., 2001). Above all, there is a critique of neoliberalism and globalization.

Since I have in this discussion offered at least a qualified endorsement of some forms of market economics, such as Elderhostel or RetirementJobs, it is appropriate to consider whether market economics can be consistent with the perspective of critical gerontology. More specifically, are there forms of market economics in ageing which do **not** result in commodification, or what Habermas termed 'the colonization of the life world?' Can the market, under specific conditions, lead to values we could describe as emancipatory for later life?

An article of my own summarizing the agenda of critical gerontology concluded with these words:

> Critical gerontology urges us to question and reject what might be called the social engineering approach to gerontology whereby 'the elderly' appear as clients, that is, essentially as objects susceptible to instrumental control through social policy or professional practice. Instead, critical gerontology invites us to appreciate the last stage of life as an opportunity for freedom and then to reshape our institutional practices in pursuit of this ideal.
>
> (Moody, 2006: 274)

The point here is: we need more than critique. We need positive benchmarks to give us hope. The point is made by Dannefer and colleagues (2008), who offer another appraisal of critical gerontology and call for attention to elements often neglected: namely, attention to positive ageing and the domain of practice. Both these elements have always been part of the critical tradition which is based, as they note, 'on a vision of human possibility and a continuing nourishment of human wholeness realized through a dialectic of theory and practice' (2008:102). The challenge we confront is how to 'expand the horizon of emancipatory ideals' in a fashion which is more than merely utopian or imaginary. If we fail to do so, critical gerontology will remain, as Dannefer and colleagues say, in its 'comfort zone' of criticism and speculation. Criticism remains 'an essential and perennial task', but we need to go beyond 'the comfort of the negative moment and its incompleteness' to identify elements of hope.

In going beyond the negative moment, what is of central importance is the practice of freedom in later life. By this definition, it seems clear enough, for example, that Elderhostel participants are pursuing a form of freedom, with 10,000 possible programmes to choose among. Older people who find new jobs through RetirementJobs.com are not merely victims of ageism or structural hegemony but are using the connectivity of the Internet to obtain employment that draws on skills and life experience. Although most of us would not want to live in a nursing home, residents of facilities inspired by the Eden Alternative may find more freedom and fulfillment than they would as medicalized objects of instrumental control in conventional long-term care facilities.

What we see here is that New Ageing Enterprises have offered older people tangible experiences of positive ageing while meeting concrete needs such as housing, health care, or job opportunities. Whether that experience is mediated by the marketplace (Elderhostel, RetirementJobs) or by nonprofit organizations (Eden Alternative, Experience Corp) is **not** the question. The question rather relates to the role of individual **agency** or self-initiated action in contrast to some hegemonic structure (bureaucracy or market) that would otherwise inhibit freedom and self-fulfillment. When elder participants in these New Ageing Enterprise programmes 'vote with their feet', we cannot simply dismiss their responses as 'false consciousness'. On the contrary, their participation itself has helped to foster and sustain the life-world manifest in their activities themselves. These 'success stories' help us reflect on the dialectic of theory and practice in new ways and appreciate the diversity of possibilities for positive ageing.

Part of this reflection will include a reappraisal of the role of the marketplace and business, just as the success of micro-capitalism has done in the economics of developing countries. Business ventures described as part of the New Ageing Enterprise range from a web-based portal (RetirementJobs), to the franchise model (Elderhostel), to a privately held corporate model (Erickson). A more thorough analysis of the character of these ventures would suggest many ways in which they meet the profile defined by Jim Collins in *Good to Great* and match many of the criteria for what Paul Hawken has called 'natural capitalism'. For non-profits, as for business ventures, the key question is sustainability: Can the nonprofit enterprise move beyond dependence on foundation grants or the enthusiasm of a founder to develop a dependable and durable income stream? An important factor here is whether the non-profit enterprise develops its fee-based revenue stream and operates in a 'business-like' fashion while still remaining faithful to its non-profit mission.

Gilleard and Higgs (2000) conclude their book, *The Cultures of Ageing*, with these words: '...the aim of an increasingly commodified economy is to maximize people's ability to spend at each and every point in their life course'. What about poverty in later life? Their own solution to inequities in old age is for people earlier in the life course to have better jobs and therefore better retirement income. Gilleard and Higgs insist that they are trying merely to document this ever-advancing differentiation into commodified 'cultures in ageing'.

But is advancing commodification the only foreseeable scenario for an ageing society? The message from the New Ageing Enterprises is quite different. New Ageing Enterprises do not constitute endless 'commodification', which Habermas has called 'the colonization of the life-world'. Elderhostel, for example, is a travel market but is hardly best described as a bundle of commodities, unless we want to claim that anything mediated by a market has, ipso facto, become a commodity. Indeed, the very term 'commodity' tends to be a derogatory term, designating interchangeable items of diminishing price and value (e.g., computer chips). Enterprises like Universities of the Third Age or Experience Corp cannot remotely be described as 'commodified' in their relationship to older people. Indeed, New Ageing Enterprises tend to embody the 'Third-Ageism' and 'project of the self' that Gilleard and Higgs (2000) find so attractive as part of the 'cultural turn' celebrated in their book. But the cultural turn, and the primacy of agency, should not be equated with the marketplace, still less with commodification.

Since the original *Ageing Enterprise* by Carroll Estes appeared in 1979, the world has changed, which is why this article is titled as it is. That book advanced critical gerontology in historic ways, as have her subsequent contributions (Estes, 1998, 2001). But since 1979 a whole generation has passed and the conditions around the world have changed in substantial ways, which Gilleard and Higgs have documented in detail. Problems of poverty and disability have not disappeared, but new forms of human organization, whether business or non-profit, are being developed to respond creatively to the historical challenge and opportunities of population ageing, and are adding social value in the process.

The argument urged here is that we need **not** turn over these tasks to 'privatization' but should instead learn from, and apply, the lessons exemplified by New Ageing Enterprises. Just as Federal Express has lessons for the government-run postal system, and private universities have lessons for public ones, so New Ageing Enterprises can be seedbeds for new policies to help our public institutions respond to population ageing. Similarly, there is no reason why lessons from Elderhostel for late-life learning or the Eden Alternative as a prototype for policies to restructure long-term care could not be adopted by public policy. Often, public policy demands a political response to these opportunities.

It is not difficult to imagine a world where community colleges make low-cost late-life learning more widely available, or where the public ageing network adopts health promotion more aggressively. Indeed, there are steps already underway in this direction. In short, public versus private here is a false choice. What we face is the challenge in making all organizations more efficient, effective, and sustainable, as the New Ageing Enterprises have demonstrated.

REFERENCES

Adler, S. (2000) 'Middle class act: Erickson retirement communities' model makes continuing care affordable', *Contemporary Long Term Care*, 23(3): 28–30.

Armstrong, P., Armstrong, H., and Coburn, D. (eds) (2001) *Unhealthy Times: Political Economy Perspectives on Health and Care*. London: Oxford University Press.

Baker, B. (2007) *Old Age in a New Age: The Promise of Transformative Nursing Homes*. Nashville, TN: Vanderbilt University Press.

Butler, R.N. (2008) *The Longevity Revolution*. New York: Public Affairs.

Collins, G.A. (2003) 'Rethinking retirement in the context of an aging workforce', *Journal of Career Development*, 30(2): 145–57.

Collins, J. (2001) *Good to Great: Why Some Companies Make the Leap ... and Others Don't*. Boulder, CO: Collins Business.

Dannefer, D., Stein, P., Siders, R., and Patterson, R.S. (2008) 'Is that all there is? The dialectic of critique and the concept of care', *Journal of Aging Studies, 22:* 101–8.

De Grey, A. and Rae, M. (2007) *Ending Aging: The Rejuvenation Breakthroughs That Could Reverse Human Aging in Our Lifetime*. New York: St. Martin's Press.

Estes, C.L. (1979) *The Aging Enterprise: A Critical Examination of Social Policies and Services for the Aged*. San Francisco: Jossey-Bass.

Minkler, M. and Estes, C.L. (eds) (1999) *Critical Gerontology: Prespectives from Moral and Political Economy*. Amityville, New York: Baywood Publishing Company.

Estes, C.L. (2001) *Social Policy and Aging: A Critical Perspective*. Thousand Oaks, CA: SAGE.

Freedman, M. (2002) *Prime Time: How Baby Boomers Will Revolutionize Retirement and Transform America*. New York: Public Affairs.

Fried, L.P., Carlson, M.C., Freedman, M. et al. (2004) 'Social model for health promotion for an aging population: initial evidence on the Experience Corps Model', *Journal of Urban Health*, 81(1): 64–78.

Giddens, A. (1990) *The Consequences of Modernity*. Cambridge: Polity.

Gilleard, C. and Higgs, P. (2000) *Cultures of Ageing: Self, Citizen and the Body*. Upper Saddle River, NJ: Prentice Hall.

Gross, J. (2006) 'Aging at home: for a lucky few, a wish come true', *New York Times*, February 9, 2006.

Gross, J. (2007) 'A grass-roots effort to grow old at home', *New York Times*, August 14, 2007.

Hedge, J.W., Borman, W.C., and Lammlein, S.E. (2006) 'Aging workforce: realities, myths, and implications for organizations', *American Psychological Association*.

Hunt, M. (eds.) (1984) *Retirement Communities: An American Original*. Binghamton, NY: Haworth.

Hutchinson, S.L., Yarnal, C.M., and Staffordson, J. (2008) 'Beyond fun and friendship: the Red Hat Society as a coping resource for older women', *Ageing and Society*, 28(7): 979–99.

Kornblatt, S., Cheng, S., and Chan, S. (2002) 'Best practice: the On Lok Model of geriatric interdisciplinary team care', *Journal of Gerontological Social Work*, 40(1–2): 14–22.

Lewis, D.E. (2006) 'A job-search site for those who eschew retirement: website caters to a graying population', *Boston Globe*, September 11, 2006.

Mills, E.S. (1993) *The Story of Elderhostel*. New Hampshire: University of New Hampshire Press.

Moody, H.R. (1988a) 'Toward a critical gerontology: the contribution of the humanities to theories of aging', in J.E. Birren and V.L. Bengtson (eds), *Emergent Theories of Aging*. New York: Springer.

Moody, H.R. (1988b) *Abundance of Life: Human Development Policies for an Aging Society*. New York: Columbia University Press.

Moody, H.R. (1993) 'Overview: What is critical gerontology and why is it important?', in, T.R. Cole, W.A. Achenbaum, P.L. Jakobi, and R. Kastenbaum (eds), *Voices and Visions of Aging: Toward a Critical Gerontology*. New York: Springer.

Moody, H.R. (2004) 'Structure and agency in late-life learning', in E. Tulle (ed.), *Old Age and Agency*. New York: Nova Science Publishers, pp. 29–44.

Moody, H.R. (2005) 'Silver Industries and the New Aging Enterprise', *Generations*, 28:4: 75–8.

Moody, H.R. (2006) 'Critical theory and critical gerontology', in R. Schulz, L. Noelker, K. Rockwood, and R. Sprott (eds), *The Encyclopedia of Aging*. New York: Springer.

Morrow-Howell, N., Hinterlong, J., and Sherraden, M. (eds) (2001) *Productive Aging: Concepts and Challenges*. Baltimore, MD: Johns Hopkins University Press.

Olson, L.K. (2003) *Not-so-golden Years: Caregiving, The Frail Elderly, and the Long-Term Care Establishment*. Lanham, MD: Rowman and Littlefield.

Palmore, E.B., Branch, L., and Harris, D.K. (eds) (2005) *Encyclopedia of Ageism*. Biinghampton. NY: Haworth.

Peace, S.M. and Holland, C. (eds) (2001) *Inclusive Housing in an Ageing Society: Innovative Approaches*. London: Policy Press.

Peck, R.L. (2006) 'Staying alive: three takes on today's senior living', *Nursing Homes Long Term Care Management*, 55(8): 14–6.

Peterson, P. and Howe, N. (2004) *On Borrowed Time: How the Growth in Entitlement Spending Threatens America's Future*. Piscataway, NJ: Transaction.

Pine, P.P. and Pine, V.R. (2002) 'Naturally occurring retirement community-supportive service program: an example of evolution', *Journal of Aging and Social Policy*, 14(3–4): 181–93.

Putnam, R. (2000) *Bowling Alone*. New York: Simon and Schuster.

Putnam, R. and Feldstein, L. (2003) *Better Together: Restoring the American Community*. New York: Simon and Schuster.

Qureshi, H. (2002) 'Social and political influences on services for older people in the United Kingdom in the late 20th century', *Journals of Gerontology: Series A: Biological Sciences and Medical Sciences*, 57A(11): 705–11.

Rich, M.L. (1999) 'PACE model: description and impressions of a capitated model of long-term care for the elderly', *Care Management Journals*, 1(1): 62–70.

Son, J.S., Kerstetter, D.L., Yarnal, C.M., et al. (2007) 'Promoting older women's health and well-being through social leisure environments: what we have learned from the Red Hat Society', *Journal of Women and Aging*, 193–4: 89–104.

Swindell, R. and Thompson, J. (1995) 'International perspective on the university of the third age', *Educational Gerontology*, 21(5): 429–47.

Thomas, W.H. (1996) *Life Worth Living: How Someone You Love Can Still Enjoy Life in a Nursing Home: The Eden Alternative in Action*. St. Louis, MO: VanderWyk and Burnham.

Thomas, W.H. (2007) *What Are Old People For? How Elders Will Save the World*. St. Louis, MO: VanderWyk and Burnham.

Vincent, J. and Downs, M. (2006) *The Futures of Old Age*. London: SAGE.

Vladeck, F. (2004) *Good Place to Grow Old: New York's Model for NORC Supportive Service Programs*. New York: United Hospital Fund of New York.

Wolfe, D.B. and Snyder, R.E. (2003) *Ageless Marketing: Strategies for Reaching the Hearts and Minds of the New Customer Majority*. Chicago: Dearborn Trade Publishing.

Ageing and Social Policy

38

Social Policies for Ageing Societies: Perspectives from Europe

Thomas Scharf

INTRODUCTION

As in other world regions, nations across Europe are engaged in an ongoing restructuring and reform of their social policy systems with a view to meeting the challenges associated with demographic change. Alongside population ageing and shifting patterns of migration, changing social values and a range of economic and budgetary pressures have encouraged European societies to reconsider the foundations of their welfare states. Historically, Europe's nations have developed quite different and distinctive social policies in relation to ageing populations. Ageing policies are potentially wide-ranging, encompassing, for example, the areas of pensions and income maintenance, housing and planning, health care, informal and long-term care, and the broad field of social inclusion. While attention is paid to other themes, the central focus of this chapter is on pensions policy, because this represents the greatest source of public expenditure in relation to Europe's ageing populations and the main source of most older Europeans' retirement incomes (Naegele and Walker, 2007). The chapter addresses ageing policies within the 27 nations of the European Union (EU). Within the context of an enlargement process, which has seen the EU expand from a community of a handful of western European nations to one which stretches from the Atlantic to the borders of Russia, the European Commission, as the EU's executive body, has assumed a much

greater role in the coordination of social policies – once the exclusive domain of national governments. The chapter examines the nature of this changed role and its implications for national welfare states and the future development of ageing policies across Europe.

The chapter is organized in four main sections. First, a broad historical overview of the development of Europe's social policy systems is presented. The aim is to explore similarities and differences in welfare state development across a range of nations, highlighting the key factors that underpin social policy development. Secondly, notwithstanding the different trajectories of Europe's welfare states, we review some of the main ways in which researchers have sought to compare national social policy systems. This approach provides a framework for analyzing contrasting social and ageing policies across European societies. It forms the basis for a third section which analyzes public pension systems in contrasting nations, and discusses the degree to which such systems succeed in one of their main objectives, the alleviation of poverty in later life. Fourthly, consideration is given to the ways in which international actors, in this case the EU, have assumed growing importance in relation to developing and coordinating policymaking concerning current and future generations of older people. The chapter concludes with some thoughts about the ways in which social gerontology might respond to the opportunities presented by the shifting context of European decision-making in relation to ageing policies.

HISTORICAL PERSPECTIVES

In most western European nations, the origins of social security systems are to be found in the late 19th and early 20th centuries. During this time, laws were introduced to provide workers with a basic level of protection against the social risks associated with industrial accidents, illness, old age, and invalidity. Schmidt (2005) notes a certain regularity with which such income maintenance policies were adopted (Table 38.1). Policies addressing the risk of industrial accidents were generally introduced ahead of those insuring against loss of employment income related to old age, illness, and invalidity (Cousins, 2005: 80). Schemes designed to provide income at times of unemployment were generally adopted in European nations somewhat later. Schmidt (2005) argues that this pattern reflects the degree to which social policies represented a break with traditions of economic and political liberalism in

the industrializing Europe of the late 19th and early 20th centuries. Accident insurance schemes appeared to represent the least significant departure from liberal traditions, since they tend to reflect a traditional view that individuals should assume responsibility for their actions. By contrast, unemployment insurance schemes tended to face greater social and political resistance, since the degree of state intervention into the labour market necessitated by such policies posed a fundamental challenge to the principles of free-market liberalism. Within this context, old-age insurance, in the form of public pension schemes, occupies an intermediary position. On the one hand, many nations had already introduced a range of programmes designed to provide some form of retirement benefits to social groups on which states depended, including military personnel and senior civil servants (Ritter, 1986). In this context, it might appear a small step to extend such benefits to a broader population. On the other hand, the introduction of pension schemes nevertheless represents a major intervention by the state into the operation of the free market, and consequently a potential focus for resistance by a range of political, economic, and social forces.

Table 38.1 Introduction of social security systems in Western Europe

Country	Accident insurance	Health insurance	Old-age insurance	Unemployment insurance	Overall ranking
Belgium	1903	1894	1900	1920	3
Germany	1884	1883	1889	1927	1
Denmark	1898	1892	1891	1907	2
Finland	1895	1963	1937	1917	15
France	1898	1928	1910	1905	6
Greece	1914	1922	1934	1945	16
Great Britain	1897	1911	1908	1911	5
Ireland	1897	1911	1911	1911	7
Iceland	1925	1936	1909	1936	14
Italy	1898	1943	1919	1919	12
Luxembourg	1902	1901	1911	1921	8
Netherlands	1901	1931	1919	1916	11
Norway	1895	1909	1936	1906	10
Austria	1887	1888	1907	1920	4
Portugal	1913	1935	1935	1975	17
Sweden	1901	1891	1913	1934	9
Switzerland	1918	1911	1946	1982	18
Spain	1900	1942	1919	1919	13
Average	1905	1924	1917	1929	

Source: Schmidt (2005: 182).

In the light of current social policy debates, it is helpful to consider why some nations introduced income maintenance policies, including public pension schemes, ahead of others. Modernization theory, which links the emergence of welfare states to general developments in Western societies – for example, urbanization, industrialization, and increasing national wealth – has been shown to be useful in identifying broad similarities between nations (Cousins 2005; Flora and Alber, 1981; Kennett, 2001). However, as the data in Table 38.1 indicate, such theories are rather limited in their capacity to explain cross-national differences in the development of social policies (Skocpol and Amenta, 1986). The fact that nations such as Germany and Austria, which industrialized much later than Britain or France, were amongst the pioneers of compulsory social insurance schemes suggests that alternative explanations for the historical development of welfare states might be more fruitful. While acknowledging important elements of the modernization thesis, Hill (1996) places more emphasis on the complex interplay of at least six factors in explaining the historical development of national welfare systems (see also Cousins, 2005). These factors are as relevant to the development of ageing policies as they are to other spheres of social policy.

First, Hill (1996) notes that social policies reflect national concerns about the dangers posed to society by disadvantaged groups. However, nations vary in terms of the extent to which such groups might represent a risk at particular points in time. For example, while there was widespread concern across Europe during the 1920s in relation to the threat of social unrest associated with mass unemployment, especially in the aftermath of the 1917 Russian revolution, this concern was felt much more acutely in countries that lacked stable political systems. In relation to contemporary ageing policy, concerns about the economic costs associated with population ageing, the future viability of intergenerational contracts, or the position of informal carers continue to represent important motivations underpinning social policy development. In this sense, providing a greater degree of financial security to older people and their family carers by means of long-term care insurance policies, as has happened in a number of European countries since the mid-1990s, could be interpreted as a means of preventing such groups from becoming (further) disadvantaged.

A second factor contributing to the development of social policy relates to a concern about perceived national weakness. This extends to areas such as health and economic policymaking. For example, states wishing to secure, or extend, their borders may develop healthcare systems to ensure that the population has sufficient numbers of healthy (male) children surviving to adulthood and potential military service. This also implies a need to develop maternity services to guarantee a natural regeneration of the population. Equally, nations may be concerned about weak economic performance and this might generate a range of policies linked to education, training, and the regulation of labour markets. Welfare states themselves have increasingly been portrayed as an economic burden and as a factor that undermines economic performance. Thus, shifts from the late 1990s in pensions policies across Europe and an increased focus on delaying retirement can be seen as an attempt to address (anticipated) economic weaknesses in future decades (see further below).

Thirdly, Hill (1996) highlights the influence of the emerging unionized working classes on the development of social policies, and in particular the growing demand for egalitarian policies that serve to secure the allegiance of this group to the nation-state. Once the right to participate in elections was extended to all citizens, liberal and conservative forces risked losing power on a permanent basis in the face of burgeoning social democratic parties. In this respect, social policy can be interpreted as the state's attempt to buy off the politically motivated working-class movement by providing income at times of labour market inactivity. In democratic systems, once a basic level of social security has been provided, political parties have historically sought to secure electoral advantage by supporting policies that seek to extend the social rights of employees. For much of the 20th century, there was a general consensus across Europe's political systems that older people should benefit from societies' growing prosperity in the form of improved coverage of public pension systems. While older people themselves have tended not to act as a concerted political force in order to campaign for better pensions, this role has tended to be assumed by the labour movement on behalf of current and future generations of retired people.

Fourthly, social policy development also reflects concerns about the need to regulate the operation of free-market activities. In the absence of state intervention, it is likely that an unbridled market would generate a range of problems that would act to disadvantage particular social groups or potentially limit the state's economic competitiveness. For example, left to its own devices, the market might not provide adequate health and social care services to people with a range of chronic and acute health conditions. In relation to older people, the state may intervene to ensure the necessary supply of welfare services to people with long-term care needs who might otherwise prove unattractive to commercial insurance providers.

Fifthly, once established, national welfare states have been shown to generate their own momentum in terms of the development of social policies. Professional groups associated with the welfare state, such as doctors and nurses, teachers, and social workers, may represent powerful lobby groups within nations, and act collectively in order to influence the policymaking processes. In essence, this is one of the arguments developed by Estes (1979) in her influential study of ageing policy in the United States.

Finally, Hill (1996) suggests that altruism also plays an important role in determining the development of social policy. Whereas altruism alone may not explain emergence of welfare states, the role of charitable organizations or key individuals as advocates of social action is not to be ignored. Such actors can represent the social conscience of a nation, or help to identify a range of social problems that demand state intervention. Equally, altruistic attitudes held by different generations can significantly shape the direction of social policy. In relation to ageing, the evidence suggests that older people's attitudes towards public policy tend not to be motivated by sectional self-interest, but instead focus on altruistic views about the need to support other age groups (Logan and Spitze, 1995; United Nations Population Fund, 1998).

Such an analysis of the reasons why states introduce social policies is important in the context of comparative studies of ageing policies. While it can be argued that there are similarities between nations in relation to the state's involvement in social policies directed towards older people, and that such involvement is universal, it is evident that nations also differ. The development of social policy is prone to the influence of a complex range of factors that vary from policy to policy and country to country across time periods. These factors continue to be relevant in helping to explain state intervention in the field of social policy (Brooks and Manza, 2006).

POLICIES FOR OLDER PEOPLE AND EUROPEAN WELFARE MODELS

Despite variation in factors that underlie their development, there are a number of broad similarities between European nations' welfare systems. Indeed, it is often argued that there is a western European 'welfare model', and that this region's society and culture is at least in part defined by its comprehensive welfare systems (e.g., van Oorschot et al., 2008). This has given rise to a wealth of comparative studies, which seek to compare nations and social policies at different levels (see Clasen, 1999; Hill, 1996, 2006; Kennett, 2001). First, there are studies that seek to compare welfare states as a whole. This form of comparative study can focus on either small or large numbers of nations or on particular regions of Europe (e.g., Clasen, 2005; Ferrera, 2005a; Kautto et al., 2001; Mabbett and Bolderson, 1999). Secondly, numerous cross-national studies compare the characteristics of different types of social policy system. Such comparisons examine, for example, pension policies, health and social care services, or family policies in different national settings (Blank and Burau, 2004; Freeman, 2000; Pavolini and Ranci, 2008; Schludi, 2005; Tester, 1999). Finally, an increasing number of comparative studies address welfare state provision for particular social groups (e.g., Guo and Gilbert, 2007; Lewis, 2007; Sainsbury, 2006). This type of study also includes comparative research relating to ageing and older people. Such analyses encompass research concerning, for example, the social circumstances of older people as a whole as well as subgroups within an ageing population, including people belonging to a variety of national ethnic minority groups (e.g., Daatland, 2001; Frericks et al., 2006; Glendinning and Kemp, 2006; Motel-Klingebiel et al., 2005; Ogg, 2005; Patel, 2003; Rake, 1999).

An initial route into the comparative study of welfare states as a whole drew upon the analysis of a range of statistical data collected by such international organizations as the United Nations (UN), International Labour Organization (ILO) or Organization for Economic Co-operation and Development (OECD) (e.g., Flora and Heidenheimer, 1981; Wilensky, 1975). For example, it is possible to compare nations on the basis of the proportion of national wealth expended on social protection systems (Table 38.2) (e.g. Alsasua et al., 2007). However, such comparisons are prone to a variety of difficulties (de Dekan and Kittel, 2007). Issues arise concerning the degree of comparability of the data used and the extent to which the information addresses welfare costs associated with regional and local levels of government, especially within federal systems where social responsibilities may be devolved. Despite such problems, this type of analysis also has at least two uses. First, the data further emphasize the absence of a clear connection between per capita incomes and public expenditure on social protection systems. While European nations with a relatively low gross domestic product (GDP), such as Greece, Portugal, Spain, and the new democracies of central and eastern Europe, tend to spend below-average proportions of national income on their social protection systems, nations with higher GDPs do not always spend more on

Table 38.2 Total expenditure on social protection in the European Union: current prices (as percent of GDP)

Country	GDP per head in Purchasing Power Standards (EU-25 = 100)			
	1995	2000	2005	2005
EU (27 countries)	—	—	27.1	94.9
EU (25 countries)	—	26.5	27.3	100.0
EU (15 countries)	27.6	26.8	27.7	107.0
Belgium	27.4	26.5	29.7	116.8
Bulgaria	—	—	16.0	33.5
Czech Republic	17.4	19.5	19.1	73.3
Denmark	31.9	28.9	30.2	120.0
Germany	28.3	29.3	29.7	108.7
Estonia	—	14.0	12.7	58.9
Ireland	18.8	13.9	18.2	136.5
Greece	19.9	23.5	24.3	82.6
Spain	21.6	20.3	21.1	97.1
France	30.3	29.5	31.4	108.5
Italy	24.2	24.7	26.3	100.1
Cyprus	—	14.8	18.4	88.9
Latvia	—	15.3	12.4	47.7
Lithuania	—	15.8	13.1	51.0
Luxembourg	20.7	19.6	21.7	248.8
Hungary	—	19.3	21.9	61.6
Malta	16.1	16.9	18.4	72.9
Netherlands	30.6	26.4	27.9	124.5
Austria	28.8	28.4	28.8	122.1
Poland	—	19.7	19.7	48.4
Portugal	21.0	21.7	25.4	71.7
Romania	—	13.2	14.2	32.7
Slovenia	—	24.2	23.0	80.5
Slovakia	18.5	19.4	16.7	56.8
Finland	31.5	25.1	26.7	108.7
Sweden	33.6	30.1	31.5	113.1
United Kingdom	27.7	26.4	26.3	113.6

Source: Eurostat/ESSPROS.

social protection. Thus, Ireland and Luxembourg, as relatively wealthy nations in terms of per capita GDP, spend proportionately less on social protection than Slovenia or Portugal. Secondly, with regard to the geographical distribution of countries, it tends to be the nations of northern Europe that consistently spend more on social protection than those in the south and east. Recognition of such patterns initially encouraged social scientists to seek explanations for similarities and differences in the development and structure of welfare states.

Early explanations of differences in social spending (and the structure of welfare states) tended to focus on the role played by different political traditions in European nations. The influence of social democratic parties and the labour movement was perceived to be especially important, with researchers identifying a potential link between the degree of electoral support given to left-wing parties and levels of social protection expenditure (Flora and Heidenheimer, 1981). While this approach has merits in explaining the historically high levels of expenditure in Nordic nations, and the relatively low levels of spending in Anglo-Saxon nations, there were too many anomalous cases to sustain the model. A more enduring means of comparing national welfare states arose from Esping-Andersen's (1990) shift in focus away from examining *how much* of a nation's GDP is expended on welfare towards an assessment of *how* such resources are spent. Drawing on the notion of decommodification, as reflecting 'the degree to which individuals, or families, can uphold a socially acceptable standard of living independently of market participation' (1990: 37), Esping-Andersen's analysis of social security programmes in 18 OECD nations led to the identification of three distinct welfare state regime types:

- A *'liberal' welfare regime*, incorporating the European nations of Britain and Ireland, displaying low levels of decommodification. In such nations, social policy is characterized by a dominance of means-tested assistance, modest universal transfers, and relatively underdeveloped social insurance schemes.
- A *'conservative' regime*, with a strong corporatist dimension, found in nations such as Germany, Austria, Italy, and the Netherlands. In these countries, state social policy seeks to maintain existing differentials between social groups by associating welfare benefits to individuals' labour market participation rather than to rights arising from principles of social citizenship.
- A *'social-democratic' welfare regime*, encompassing the Nordic nations, characterized by a high degree of decommodification. This regime type is historically associated with universal social protection policies that provide benefits to all citizens regardless of their relationship to the labour market.

Esping-Andersen's (1990) analysis represented a major turning point in comparative social policy discussions, acting as an important staging post for further debate. Its basic premise is also borne out by Castles (1993, 1999) who adopts a different analytic approach, yet generates similar 'families of nations' in relation to their welfare state development. In particular, the idea of welfare regimes encouraged other researchers to develop alternative, albeit ultimately similar, models. In this context, Leibfried's (1993) four-fold typology of welfare systems in Europe has been widely used as a means of addressing similarities and differences between nations in relation to social policy:

- *Bismarckian*: in this category of welfare state, social security protection is linked to labour market participation and seeks to preserve employees' income levels both in and outside of the labour market. Such 'corporatist-conservative' welfare systems typically expect the family and other informal and voluntary sector organizations to provide protection for people with no or inadequate levels of social insurance cover. The six founding members of the European Community, including Germany and France, belong to this welfare state type.
- *Anglo-Saxon*: based on the Beveridge model of equal insurance protection for all, together with universal provision for education and health, under the 'liberal' welfare regime state benefits are often only available after a strict test of availability for work within the private labour market. The system is characterized by extensive use of means-tested benefits, reflecting both inadequate coverage of insurance protection and a desire to encourage private welfare coverage. This model applies to the United Kingdom and Ireland.
- *Scandinavian*: founded on a dominance of the state sector and principles of universalism, this 'social democratic' welfare regime type delivers state benefits and services to all citizens as a matter of right. As a consequence, nations with this form of welfare state, including Sweden, Norway, and Denmark, have relatively high levels of social expenditure.
- *Latin Rim*: according to Leibfried (1993), the nations of southern Europe represented a new category of welfare regime, characterized by low levels of social spending and high levels of poverty and deprivation. In countries such as Greece, Portugal, and Spain, state welfare protection was regarded as 'rudimentary', with undeveloped labour-market-based protection and limited universal state provision. Countries with such a welfare state regime tended to rely on informal and voluntary sector provision, in particular through the organized church.

There are important criticisms of the type of analysis undertaken by Esping-Andersen and Leibfried (Arts and Gelissen, 2002; Cousins, 2005). While social historians such as Baldwin (1996) are critical of the principle of making excessively broad comparisons between nations which have followed very different social, political, and economic trajectories, four other types of criticism have been levelled at researchers whose focus is on grouping nations together on the basis of their welfare systems. These relate first to the nature of the welfare policies considered in developing typologies of welfare regimes. In concentrating on income maintenance policies, the impact of other important forms of welfare provision, including education, health, and social care policies, tend to be overlooked. Rather different typologies are likely to emerge when the full range of national social policies is taken into consideration.

A second criticism from feminist researchers argues that welfare typologies inadequately reflect the 'gendered' nature of social policy (Kennett, 2001; Langan and Ostner, 1991; Lewis, 1992; Sainsbury, 2001). In this respect, Estes et al. (2003: 55) highlight 'the fallacy of the theoretical "universal citizen" under social security and other public policies of the state'. Similarly, the influence of other factors, including ethnicity, health status, and disability, are often ignored in developing regime typologies (Walker and Wong, 2005).

Thirdly, it is evident that welfare state typologies tend to become rather static and fail to accommodate shifts in social policy over time (Arts and Gelissen, 2002). This can be demonstrated most clearly with reference to Europe's 'Latin Rim' nations, which have experienced considerable social policy change since joining the EU in the mid-1980s (Ferrera, 2005b; Sotiropoulos, 2004). Equally, the post-communist nations of central and eastern Europe have yet to be adequately accommodated within welfare regime typologies (Deacon, 1993; Fenger, 2007; Naegele and Walker, 2007: 143). In this context, there are also doubts about whether or not particular nations fit adequately within their designated welfare regime type (Arts and Gelissen, 2002; Cousins, 2005). Finally, Goodin et al. (1999) make the necessary, if obvious, point that there can be a substantial difference between what welfare states offer in principle and what they provide in practice. Essentially, Goodin et al. (1999) argue that liberal welfare states fail to meet their objective of alleviating poverty, and that corporatist welfare states are not that successful in minimizing income instability.

PUBLIC PENSIONS IN COMPARATIVE PERSPECTIVE

Despite criticisms, welfare regime typologies continue to be influential and offer a potentially useful means of making comparisons between nations in relation to a range of social policy programmes. In this respect, Arts and Gelissen emphasize the value of welfare typologies as 'a means to an end – explanation – and not an end in itself' (Arts and Gelissen 2002: 140). Typologies facilitate the understanding of broad differences between nations in terms of the major social security systems, including ageing policies. For the purposes of this chapter, the value of a comparative approach to ageing policy is to be explored in relation to public pension systems in a selection of European nations.

In general, the major component of older people's income across Europe is composed of statutory public pensions and related state benefits. The material security offered through such provisions can be judged to have an important impact on the well-being not only of older people but also of those likely to retire in the future. In response to the ongoing demographic changes, as well as economic imperatives, nearly all European public pension systems are subjected to ongoing reform (Cousins, 2005; European Commission, 2008a). In broad terms, the aim of such measures has been to adapt welfare systems to actual and anticipated

'financial burdens' by cutting back on pension entitlements and benefits or by extending or removing altogether compulsory retirement ages (Naegele and Walker, 2007). Such 'burdens' arise as a result of demographic change and a restructuring of the labour market, marked by an historic trend towards early retirement and flexible labour markets. At first view, pension systems funded through the 'intergenerational contract' appear to rest on increasingly shaky foundations (Myles, 2002; Phillipson, 1996). Across Europe, savings in pension systems have been pursued with varying degrees of intensity (Taylor-Gooby, 1999). The degree to which individual nations have been able to reform public pension provision is itself in great part determined by the structure and characteristics of the welfare regime to which it belongs (Hemerijck, 2002). Thus, considerable change in the British pension system, especially since 1980 (Cousins, 2005; Phillipson, 2009), contrasts with less radical reforms in pension arrangements in countries such as Germany, Italy, and France (Busemeyer, 2005; Cousins, 2005; Scharf, 1998).

In general, all European employees belong to some form of compulsory pension scheme in recognition of the fact that old age represents a social risk to be addressed by society as a whole rather than by individuals. Typically, public pension systems require contributions to be paid by employees, their employers, and the state. The 'universal' Danish system represents something of an exception in this regard, being primarily funded through central taxation. However, there is substantial variation in the scale of contributions and the value of pensions ultimately derived from the different systems (Table 38.3). Under the Bismarckian regime, typified here by Germany, relatively generous pensions arise from a higher level of contributions to the pension insurance system. The close connection between employment biographies and pension incomes in this system tends to reinforce labour market inequalities in retirement. Thus, employees with lengthy, unbroken work histories systematically do better than those whose relationship with the labour market has varied across the life course. In practice, this tends to work to the disadvantage of many women and also people belonging to minority groups or migrant workers (Naegele and Walker, 2007; Scharf, 1998). While researchers have sought to make a case for a distinctive 'Latin Rim' welfare regime, it is evident that the pension systems of countries such as Spain, as presented here, largely resemble the insurance-based schemes of the Bismarckian nations. A key difference concerns the grouping together of all social insurance schemes into a single fund (as in the United Kingdom), and a greater emphasis placed in Spain on employer rather than employee contributions to social protection. In the

Table 38.3 Public pension systems in European comparison, 2007

	Sweden	Germany	Spain	UK	Poland
	Scandinavian	Bismarckian	Latin Rim	Anglo-Saxon	Post-communist
Welfare regime type					
Basic principles	Compulsory, universal public pension system consisting of: 1. Earnings-related 'pay-as-you-go'(PAYG) pension 2. Fully funded premium reserve system with individual accounts 3. Tax financed guaranteed pension for residents with low or no earnings-related pension	Compulsory social insurance scheme providing earnings-related pensions depending on contributions and duration of affiliation	Compulsory social insurance scheme financed by contributions covering employees and assimilated groups providing earnings-related retirement pensions depending on contributions and duration of affiliation	Contributory state pension scheme made up of a flat-rate basic state pension and an earnings-related additional state pension	Compulsory social insurance scheme financed by contributions covering employees and the self-employed providing earnings-related pensions depending on contributions and duration of affiliation
Funding					
Employee	Public pension system: 7% of earnings as general pension contribution	9.95% of earnings	Contributions cover all social protection schemes (excluding unemployment). Employees pay 4.7% of earnings	Contributions cover all insurance benefits. Employees pay up to 11% of earnings between €144 and €958	9.76% of earnings
Employer	10.21% of income	9.95% of earnings	23.6% of earnings	12.8% of weekly earnings above €144	9.76% of earnings
State	Part financing	Part financing	Financing of guaranteed amounts to reach minimum pension of contributory systems	Subsidy to cover deficit, if required	Subsidy to cover deficit, if required
Benefits					
Conditions for drawing full pension	Earnings-related pensions: No concept of 'full pension'. Guaranteed pension: 40 years' residence	No concept of 'full pension'	35 years of contributions	Basic state pension: contributions paid or credited for 44 years (men) and 39 years (women)	No concept of 'full pension'

Qualifying age	Flexible retirement age from 61 to 67 years. Possibility to work thereafter with employers' consent	65 years. From 2012 to 2029 standard retirement age to be increased to 67 years	65 years	Men: 65 years Women: 60 years (gradually rising to 65 from 2010–2020)	Men: 65 years Women: 60 years
Qualifying period	None for earnings-related pension. Three years' residence for guaranteed pension	5 years of contributions	15 years of contributions	10–11 years of contributions for basic state pension	Old-age pension with guaranteed minimum pension: men 25 years, women 20 years of contributory and non-contributory periods
Calculation basis	Earnings-related PAYG pension: calculated by dividing accrued pension assets by an annuity factor depending on average life expectancy for cohort, an individual's retirement age, and a 'norm' for (expected) average wage increases. Guarantee pension: full pension of €9,512 after 40 years' residence for an unmarried person. Full pension of €8,485 for a married person	Based on individual contribution history and relationship between insured person's annual income and average incomes of all employees	Based on individual contribution history. The pension value ranges from 50% with 15 contribution years to 100% with 35 contribution years. The pension is paid 14 times a year	Basic State Pension: flat-rate amount of €125 per week (paid pro-rata if number of qualifying years is less than the requisite number)	For persons born before 1949: based on relationship between insured person's annual income and average incomes. For persons born after 1949: based on pension assets accumulated in an individual's account and anticipated remaining life expectancy at retirement
Minimum pension	No statutory minimum pension. Guarantee pension for those with a small or no pension	No statutory minimum pension	Minimum pension: €493.22, or €606.06 per month with dependant spouse, for people aged 65 and over	Minimum of 25% of full rate of basic state pension, normally payable if contributions paid for 10–11 years	€ 156 per month
Up-rating	Guarantee pension adjusted annually in line with inflation. Earnings-related pension adjusted annually in line with incomes	Pensions adjusted annually in line with incomes. Since 2005, a 'demographic factor' also applied	Automatic annual adjustment according to anticipated rate of inflation	Annual adjustment at least in line with inflation	Annual adjustment in line with inflation

Source: MISSOC (Mutual information system on social protection) (2007) Comparative Tables, Directorate-General for Employment, Social Affairs and Equal Opportunities European Commission.

Scandinavian nations, with Sweden as the example used, alongside a tax-funded guaranteed minimum pension that is provided as a right to all citizens based on a residence requirement, recent reforms have sought to encourage individuals to take greater responsibility for their retirement income. As a result, the Swedish system has introduced a fully funded premium reserve system with individual accounts which coexists with a more traditional earnings-related 'pay-as-you-go' (PAYE) scheme. In the Anglo-Saxon welfare regime, represented here by the United Kingdom, relatively limited contributions to a general national insurance scheme that underpins all social security benefits is associated with the provision of a rather modest basic state pension. Under this system, the market, in the form of alternative pension types and private savings or investments, offers the main means of providing financial security in later life (Hills, 2004: 249). The post-communist nations of central and eastern Europe, with Poland used as an example, have tended to adopt insurance-based schemes along the lines of the Bismarckian model rather than systems based on universal principles. However, Fenger (2007) regards these as belonging to a qualitatively different welfare regime type. Underpinning variations between the welfare states of the post-communist nations and those of western Europe are fundamental differences in the social situation which have yet to be overcome in the transition process (Fenger, 2007).

Such diversity in public pension systems raises a number of issues for potential policy reforms. In particular, against a background of ongoing demographic change and concerns about meeting the costs of increased longevity, some nations might appear to be better placed to adjust their pension schemes in a manner that increases their long-term financial sustainability. Thus, it can be argued that it is more straightforward to introduce fundamental pension reform in nations where the principles of social insurance are underdeveloped, than in those countries where individual employees accrue entitlements to pension benefits through their (often lengthy) record of contributions to public pension systems. In this respect, pension reform in countries such as Germany, Austria, and Italy has proved particularly difficult in recent years. By contrast, the residual nature of provision in the United Kingdom and Ireland has encouraged policymakers to enact significant reforms in the past two decades that amount to a hollowing out of (the already limited) state pension provision. Despite such differences between nations, EU member states have typically drawn on a range of measures in order to make their public pension systems more sustainable in the face of demographic change. This includes, for example, increasing statutory retirement ages, removing incentives for early retirement, changing the basis on which pension incomes are calculated, and encouraging employees to make alternative pension arrangements (European Commission, 2008a; Naegele and Walker, 2007: 152).

The foregoing discussion of structural differences in relation to Europe's pension systems tells us relatively little about the adequacy of these incomes. Older people with inadequate pension incomes are prone to poverty and may be vulnerable to different forms of social exclusion (Scharf et al., 2002). It is notoriously difficult to generate robust measures of poverty in cross-national research. Not only do countries adopt different views about the conceptualization and measurement of poverty but also there are weaknesses in the way in which relevant data are collected (Spicker, 2001). Nevertheless, it is useful to present an overview of recent data relating to the degree to which older people in the EU experience poverty (Table 38.4). These data arise from the analysis of Zaidi et al. (2006) EUROSTAT's CRONOS database which draws on a range of nationally representative surveys such as the European Community Household Panel (ECHP), the EU Statistics on Income and Living Conditions (EU-SILC), and various national household budget surveys. The findings broadly correspond with earlier data from the Luxembourg Income Study (Hauser, 1999: 119). In international comparisons, poverty is typically judged to exist where a person lives in a household whose net equivalized income is at a level below 60% of overall median household income.

In 2006, just under one-fifth of people aged 65 and over – equivalent to around 13.3 million individuals – were living in poverty in the 25 EU member states. The distribution of poverty across the EU nations varies considerably. While poverty affected less than 10 per cent of older people in the Netherlands, Luxemburg, Poland, and the Czech Republic, over a quarter of people aged 65 and over in Greece, Portugal, Spain, Ireland, and Cyprus had incomes below 60 per cent of median household income. This suggests that the welfare state regimes of the Bismarck nations and the post-communist states of central Europe are generally better placed to reduce the risk of poverty in later life than those of the Latin Rim or Anglo-Saxon nations. In all EU countries, poverty is more commonly experienced by women and also increases with age. Thus, women aged 75 and over, many of whom are widowed, tend to be amongst Europe's most disadvantaged citizens in terms of their financial circumstances (European Commission, 2008a; Naegele and Walker, 2007: 148; Zaidi et al., 2006).

Table 38.4 Poverty rates for people aged 65 and above, EU countries, 2003

Country	At-risk-of-poverty rate* (%)	Population at risk of poverty (000s)
Cyprus	52	44
Ireland	40	176
Spain	30	2,112
Portugal	29	504
Greece	28	539
United Kingdom	24	2,268
Belgium	21	370
Malta	20	9
Slovenia	19	56
Austria	17	213
Denmark	17	135
Estonia	17	37
Finland	17	135
France	16	1,561
Italy	16	1,743
Germany	15	2,167
Latvia	14	52
Sweden	14	215
Lithuania	12	61
Slovakia	11	68
Hungary	10	156
Netherlands	7	154
Luxembourg	6	4
Poland	6	294
Czech Republic	4	57
EU25	**18**	**13,350**
EU15	**19**	**12,156**
New member states	**9**	**902**

* Poverty measure based on 60% of equivalized median household income.

Source: Zaidi et al. (2006).

INTERNATIONAL INFLUENCES ON SOCIAL POLICY: AGEING POLICY IN THE EUROPEAN UNION

Increasingly, the social policies of EU member states are prone to the influence of international organizations. Despite the pronounced structural differences in nations' welfare systems, discussed above, the future of social policy within the EU is likely to be based on a greater degree of coordination and integration. Alcock (1996) refers to such developments as a 'one-way street', since member states that embark upon a process of economic and social union may find it difficult, if not impossible, to withstand the pressures that lead to greater conformity and convergence of policy-making.

In the European context, the changing role of the European Union's institutions has influenced the development of social policies in a number of ways. This contrasts with the relatively limited role played by such institutions in shaping national social policy for much of the post-war period. One could argue that social policy has always been a key dimension of plans for a more integrated Europe, with social policy harmonization representing a professed aim of the original European Economic Community (EEC). In this respect, the Treaty of Rome (1957), which established the EEC, included a number of social policy measures relating, for example, to the free movement of labour and the provision of equal pay for men and women. However, in practice, progress on harmonizing European Community member states' social policies was confined to reaching agreement on broad policy goals for much of the 1960s and 1970s. Moreover, the growing influence of neoliberal economic and social policy thinking at the beginning of the 1980s challenged the basis for any form of supranational intervention into what were seen, especially in the United Kingdom, as largely domestic matters. The resulting policy blockage was overcome by the Single European Act (1986), which confirmed the need to 'improve the Community's economic and social situation by extending common policies and pursuing new objectives'.

Acceptance of the policy to establish a single market by 1992 was associated with a need to reconsider the slow progress on social policy, leading to the introduction of the, largely symbolic, Community Charter on the Fundamental Social Rights of Workers in 1989. The Social Charter, as it became known, identified a range of social rights for European Community citizens, including the right to 'adequate social protection for both those in and out of work' and 'proper retirement pensions', and essentially expressed the future ideal of EC social policy. The Maastricht Treaty (1992), which laid the foundation for the creation of a European Union in which persisting economic barriers to free trade would be removed, significantly strengthened supranational involvement in member states' social policymaking by reducing the ability of individual member states to resist collectively taken decisions. This was taken a step further with the Lisbon Treaty, which established the open method of coordination (OMC) for social policy within the EU.

By developing social policy initiatives around particular issues it is anticipated that EU member states will ultimately adopt more common practices and thereby reduce policy barriers between nations. In 2006, coordination of social policies took a further step forward with member states agreeing to a set of common objectives for social protection and social inclusion. EU member states are currently committed to cooperating in the broad areas of social inclusion, pensions reform, and the modernization of healthcare and long-term care systems. In relation to pensions policies, a series of common principles have been adopted that aim to safeguard the future viability of national pension arrangements. These principles seek to ensure, for example, that pension systems can continue to deliver adequate retirement incomes, that they can be financially sustainable, and that they can reflect the changing needs of European societies (European Commission, 2008a; Naegele and Walker, 2007: 162).

Evidence of a more coordinated EU strategy in relation to social policy can also be seen in recent work around social inclusion (Atkinson, 2002), with member states initially producing a National Action Plan on Social Inclusion every 2 years and, since 2008, presenting National Strategic Reports every 3 years aimed at demonstrating progress towards meeting common objectives on social protection and social inclusion (European Commission, 2008b). On the one hand, these various action plans and strategic reports provide a useful summary of measures taken by the 27 EU member states to reduce poverty and social exclusion. On the other hand, in relation to ageing policy, they provide a basis for examining the degree to which older people are identified as a key target group for social policy interventions at national level.

While initial National Action Plans provided nations with scope to address a broad range of issues that addressed the multifaceted nature of social exclusion, recent documents appear to adopt a rather more limited view of ageing policy. For example, the UK National Action Plan for 2001–03 addresses measures designed to tackle disadvantage associated with low incomes, poor housing, ill health, social care needs, and vulnerability to crime in later life (Department for Work and Pensions, 2001). The equivalent plan from Germany identifies the potential risks posed by the exclusion of older people from access to new technologies and a failure to claim state benefit entitlements (Federal Republic of Germany, 2001). In 2008, by contrast, EU member states tended to concentrate much more on a narrow range of measures designed to maintain employment rates amongst older workers and to extend people's working lives (European Commission, 2008b). Thus, the Czech Republic report for 2008–10 highlights various measures designed to promote active ageing, lifelong learning, and active employment policies (Czech Republic, 2008). The Netherlands report for the same period follows a similar approach, whilst also making a strong case against early retirement: 'the Dutch government considers it irresponsible to continue giving the impression that early retirement is the standard by giving (continued) fiscal support for such schemes' (The Netherlands, 2008: 46). Such a strategy reflects what Levitas (2005) refers to as a 'social integrationist discourse' of social exclusion – one which regards participation in the labour market as being the prime route to social inclusion. This type of approach to ageing policy tends to draw attention away from forms of exclusion in later life that reach beyond work and employment, including, for example, disadvantage arising from age discrimination, limited material resources, lack of access to services, or one's place of residence (Scharf et al., 2004).

CONCLUSIONS

In relation to social policy, this chapter has shown how national welfare states have evolved according to a wide range of influences. Despite similarities between European nations in terms of the state's involvement in social policy, and recognition that such involvement is universal, it is evident that nations also differ. The development of social policy is influenced by a complex range of factors that vary from policy to policy and country to country across time periods. The diverse pathways that led, and still lead, to the development of welfare states continue to exert a major influence on contemporary social policy, and this includes nations' ageing policies. Although Europe's nations have experienced different paths to the welfare state, researchers such as Esping-Andersen (1990) and Leibfried (1993) have nevertheless shown that it is possible to group nations together according to the broad characteristics of their social policy systems. In this chapter, key similarities and differences between EU nations representing contrasting welfare regime types were illustrated in relation to public pension policies. Amongst the major impacts of differing approaches to pension provision are variations in older people's risk of living in poverty. Drawing on the work of Zaidi et al. (2006), it was shown that the risk of poverty ranges from less than

10 per cent in countries like the Czech Republic and the Netherlands to more than one-quarter in Spain and Ireland. Finally, the chapter considered the growing role of supranational actors in shaping the social policies of EU member states. In particular, the European Commission's open method of coordination has encouraged EU nations to adopt common strategies to render their pension policies more financially sustainable in the face of ongoing demographic change. This approach has also been adopted in the sphere of social inclusion policies. However, recognition of the complex and multidimensional nature of exclusion in later life that was evident in national policymaking at the beginning of the 21st century appears to have given way in recent years to a much narrower focus on achieving inclusion by promoting labour market participation.

Against this background, it is evident that there are a range of opportunities that could usefully be pursued in future gerontological studies. Three potential themes are highlighted as areas that merit further attention in social gerontology. First, there is scope to consider the historical and ongoing development of ageing policies across European nations. Drawing on Hill's (1996) approach, research could usefully focus on the factors that underpin policy innovation. For example, while all European nations are facing similar demographic pressures, the pace of policy change appears to vary from country to country. This applies most obviously to pensions policy, but is also evident in other areas of ageing policy, including long-term care, health, housing and planning, and age equality measures. Research which explores the influence of national and international political actors in shaping ageing policies, including the EU, may help to explain such policy variation. The EU member states' National Action Plans on Social Inclusion and subsequent strategy documents provide an excellent source for gerontology researchers seeking to explore nations' policy priorities in relation to their older populations. In similar vein, research which addresses cross-national variation in the impacts on social policymaking of the global economic downturn that began in 2008 would be useful in illustrating the extent to which different nations' ageing policies are able to withstand market pressures.

A second area that merits further research concerns the development and refinement of welfare regime models that pertain to a broader range of ageing policies. While such models are relatively well developed in relation to income maintenance and social care policies, other areas of ageing policy have received rather less attention. This applies, in particular, to policies that fall into the broad domain of social inclusion and exclusion.

There is some work in this area at national level, especially in the United Kingdom (e.g., Phillipson and Scharf, 2004), but such studies are relatively few and far between. Given a growing EU focus on promoting social inclusion, there is scope to explore further the ways in which member states frame policies in relation to older citizens. Such research would be helpful in identifying the extent to which inclusion policies either conform to or reach beyond existing welfare regime models. In this context, the ways in which Europe's welfare states provide social protection to increasingly diverse older populations might also challenge existing welfare regime models. Again, at national level there is a growing focus on the ways in which social policies affect subgroups of older people, including men and women, the oldest old, people providing informal care, people belonging to black and minority ethnic communities, and those with a range of health conditions. By shifting the focus of research away from broad policy measures towards the experiences of particular groups of older people, it might be possible to develop alternative categorizations of national welfare regimes.

Finally, the analysis of pension systems in different European countries highlights considerable variations in older people's vulnerability to poverty. Studies which chart the development of poverty across nations are likely to become increasingly important as future cohorts of older people reach retirement. Yet even amongst current cohorts of pensioners, there is considerable scope to develop studies of material disadvantage. Such studies could focus, for example, on the conceptualization and measurement of poverty in contrasting European nations. This would reach beyond statistical approaches that identify people as living in poverty according to the level of household incomes towards alternative approaches based on the lifestyles that people's incomes permit. The lifestyles approach, founded on the work of researchers such as Townsend (1979) and Gordon et al. (2000), is capable of drawing attention to the ways in which poverty restricts older people's ability to participate in what may be regarded as 'normal' social activities. Such activities are prone to temporal and cultural variation, and consequently provide opportunities for researchers to explore common and distinctive patterns across nations. This is also true for studies that draw on the experiences of older people living on low incomes. Quantitative approaches are necessarily limited in what they can say about the lives of people at risk of poverty in later life. Qualitative research which explores the influence of poverty of daily life is helpful in bringing the voices of disadvantaged older people to the fore, and may therefore have a greater impact in the development of policies designed to alleviate material disadvantage in later life.

REFERENCES

Alcock, P. (1996) *Social Policy in Britain: Themes and Issues.* London: Macmillan.

Alsasua, J., Bilbao-Ubillos, J., and Olaskoaga, J. (2007) 'The EU integration process and the convergence of social protection benefits at national level', *International Journal of Social Welfare*, 16(4): 297–306.

Arts, W. and Gelissen, J. (2002) 'Three worlds of welfare capitalism or more? A state-of-the-art report', *Journal of European Social Policy*, 12(2): 137–58.

Atkinson, A.B. (2002) 'Social inclusion and the European Union', *Journal of Common Market Studies*, 40(4): 625–43.

Baldwin, P. (1996) 'Can we define a European welfare state model?', in B. Greve (ed.), *Comparative Welfare Systems: The Scandinavian Model in a Period of Change.* London: Macmillan, pp. 29–43.

Blank, R.H. and Burau, V. (2004) *Comparative Health Policy.* Basingstoke, UK: Palgrave Macmillan.

Brooks, C. and Manza, J. (2006) 'Why do welfare states persist?', *Journal of Politics*, 68(4): 816–27.

Busemeyer, M. (2005) 'Pension reform in Germany and Austria: system change vs. quantitative retrenchment', *West European Politics*, 28(3): 569–91.

Castles, F.G. (1993) *Families of Nations: Patterns of Public Policy in Western Democracies.* Aldershot: Dartmouth.

Castles, F.G. (1999) *Comparative Public Policy: Patterns of Post-war Transformation.* Cheltenham, UK: Edward Elgar.

Clasen, J. (ed.) (1999) *Comparative Social Policy: Concepts, Theories and Methods.* Oxford: Blackwell.

Clasen, J. (2005) *Reforming European Welfare States: Germany and the United Kingdom Compared.* Oxford: Oxford University Press.

Cousins, M. (2005) *European Welfare States: Comparative Perspectives.* London: Sage.

Czech Republic (2008) *National Report on Strategies for Social Protection and Social Inclusion 2008–2010.* Prague: Ministry of Labour and Social Affairs.

Daatland, S.O. (2001) 'Ageing, families and welfare systems: comparative perspectives', *Zeitschrift für Gerontologie und Geriatrie*, 34(1): 16–20.

Deacon, B. (1993) 'Developments in East European social policy', in C. Jones (ed.), *New Perspectives on the Welfare State in Europe.* London: Routledge, pp. 177–97.

de Deken, J. and Kittel, B. (2007) 'Social expenditure under scrutiny: the problems of using aggregate spending data for assessing welfare state dynamics', in J. Clasen and N.A. Siegel (eds), *Investigating Welfare State Change: The 'Dependent Variable Problem' in Comparative Analysis.* Cheltenham: Edward Elgar, pp. 72–105.

Department for Work and Pensions (2001) *United Kingdom National Action Plan on Social Inclusion 2001–2003.* London: Department for Work and Pensions.

Esping-Andersen, G. (1990) *The Three Worlds of Welfare Capitalism.* Cambridge: Polity Press.

Estes, C.L. (1979) *The Aging Enterprise.* San Francisco: Jossey Bass.

Estes, C.L., Biggs, S., and Phillipson, C. (2003) *Social Theory, Social Policy and Ageing: A Critical Introduction.* Buckingham: Open University Press.

European Commission (2008a) *Monitoring Progress Towards the Objectives of the European Strategy for Social Protection and Social Inclusion.* Brussels: European Commission.

European Commission (2008b) *Joint Report on Social Protection and Social Inclusion 2008: Social Inclusion, Pensions, Healthcare and Long-Term Care.* Brussels: European Commission.

Federal Republic of Germany (2001) *National Action Plan to Combat Poverty and Social Exclusion.* Document 14/6134. Berlin: Federal Parliament.

Fenger, H.J.M. (2007) 'Welfare regimes in central and eastern Europe: incorporating post-communist countries in a welfare regime typology', *Contemporary Issues and Ideas in Social Sciences*, 3(2). Retrieved March 3, 2009, from http://journal.ciiss.net/index.php/ciiss/article/view/45

Ferrera, M. (2005a) *The Boundaries of Welfare: European Integration and the New Spatial Politics of Social Solidarity.* Oxford: Oxford University Press.

Ferrera, M. (ed.) (2005b) *Welfare State Reform in Southern Europe: Fighting Poverty and Social Exclusion in Italy, Spain, Portugal and Greece.* Abingdon: Routledge.

Flora, P. and Alber, J. (1981) 'Modernization, democratization, and the development of welfare states in western Europe', in P. Flora and A.J. Heidenheimer (eds), *The Development of Welfare States in Europe and America.* New Brunswick, NJ: Transaction, pp. 37–80.

Flora, P. and Heidenheimer, A.J. (eds) (1981) *The Development of Welfare States in Europe and America.* New Brunswick, NJ: Transaction.

Freeman, R. (2000) *The Politics of Health in Europe.* Manchester: Manchester University Press.

Frericks, P., Maier, R., and de Graaf, W. (2006) 'Shifting the pension mix: consequences for Dutch and Danish women', *Social Policy and Administration*, 40(5): 475–92.

Glendinning, C. and Kemp, P. (eds) (2006) *Cash and Care: Policy Challenges in the Welfare State.* Bristol: Policy Press.

Goodin, R.E., Headey, B., Muffels, R., and Dirven, H.-J. (1999) *The Real Worlds of Welfare Capitalism.* Cambridge: Cambridge University Press.

Gordon, D., Addman, L., Ashworth, K., et al. (2000) *Poverty and Social Exclusion in Britain.* New York: Joseph Rowntree Foundation.

Guo, J. and Gilbert, N. (2007) 'Welfare state regimes and family policy: a longitudinal analysis', *International Journal of Social Welfare*, 16(4): 307–13.

Hauser, R. (1999) 'Adequacy and poverty among retired people', *International Social Security Review* 52(3): 107–24.

Hemerijck, A. (2002) 'The self-transformation of the European social model(s)', in G. Esping-Andersen (ed.), *Why We Need a New Welfare State*. Oxford: Oxford University Press, pp. 173–214.

Hill, M. (1996) *Social Policy: A Comparative Analysis*. London: Prentice Hall/Harvester Wheatsheaf.

Hill, M. (2006) *Social Policy in the Modern World: A Comparative Text*. Oxford: Blackwell.

Hills, J. (2004) *Inequality and the State*. Oxford: Oxford University Press.

Kautto, M., Fritzell, J., Hvinden, B., Kvist, J., and Uusitalo H. (eds) (2001) *Nordic Welfare States in the European Context*. London: Routledge.

Kennett, P. (2001) *Comparative Social Policy: Theory and Research*. Buckingham: Open University Press.

Langan, M. and Ostner, I. (1991) 'Gender and welfare: towards a comparative framework', in G. Room (ed.), *Towards a European Welfare State*. University of Bristol, Bristol: SAUS, pp. 127–50.

Leibfried, S. (1993) 'Towards a European welfare state? On integrating poverty regimes into the European Community', in C. Jones (ed.), *New Perspectives on the Welfare State in Europe*. London: Routledge, pp. 133–56.

Levitas, R. (2005) *The Inclusive Society? Social Exclusion and New Labour*, 2nd edn. Basingstoke: Macmillan.

Lewis, J. (1992) 'Gender and the development of welfare regimes', *Journal of European Social Policy*, 2(3): 159–73.

Lewis, J. (ed.) (2007) *Children, Changing Families and Welfare States*. Cheltenham, UK: Edward Elgar.

Logan, J.R. and Spitze G. (1995) 'Self-interest and altruism in intergenerational relations', *Demography*, 32(4): 353–64.

Mabbett, D. and Bolderson, H. (1999) 'Theories and methods in comparative social policy', in J. Clasen (ed.), *Comparative Social Policy: Concepts, Theories and Methods*. Oxford: Blackwell, pp. 34–56.

Motel-Klingebiel, A., Tesch-Roemer, C., and von Kondratowitz, H.-J. (2005) 'Welfare states do not crowd out the family: evidence for mixed responsibility from comparative analyses', *Ageing and Society*, 25(6): 863–82.

Myles, J. (2002) 'A new social contract for the elderly?', in G. Esping-Andersen (ed.), *Why We Need a New Welfare State*. Oxford: Oxford University Press, pp. 130–72.

Naegele, G. and Walker, A. (2007) 'Social protection: incomes, poverty and the reform of pension systems', in J. Bond, S. Peace, F. Dittmann-Kohli, and G. Westerhof (eds.), *Ageing in Society*, 3rd edn. London: Sage, pp. 142–66.

Ogg, J. (2005) 'Social exclusion and insecurity among older Europeans: the influence of welfare regimes', *Ageing and Society*, 25(1): 69–90.

Patel, N. (ed.) (2003) *Minority Elderly Care in Europe: Country Profiles*. Leeds: Policy Research Institute on Ageing and Ethnicity.

Pavolini, E. and Ranci, C. (2008) 'Restructuring the welfare state: reforms in long-term care in Western European countries', *Journal of European Social Policy*, 18(3): 246–59.

Phillipson, C. (1996) 'Intergenerational conflict and the welfare state: American and British perspectives', in A. Walker (ed.), *The New Generational Contract*. London: UCL Press, pp. 206–20.

Phillipson, C. (2009) 'Pensions in crisis: aging and inequality in a global age', in L. Rogne, C. Estes, B. Grossman, B. Hollister, and E. Solway (eds), *Social Insurance and Social Justice*. New York: Springer, pp. 319–40.

Phillipson, C. and Scharf, T. (2004) *The Impact of Government Policy on Social Exclusion among Older People: A Review of the Literature*. Social Exclusion Unit, Office of the Deputy Prime Minister. London: Stationery Office.

Rake, K. (1999) 'Accumulated disadvantage? Welfare state provision and the incomes of older women and men in Britain, France and Germany', in J. Clasen (ed.), *Comparative Social Policy: Concepts, Theories and Methods*. Oxford: Blackwell, pp. 220–46.

Ritter, G.A. (1986) *Social Welfare in Germany and Britain*. New York: Berg.

Sainsbury, D. (2001) 'Welfare state challenges and responses: institutional and ideological resilience or restructuring?', *Acta Sociologica*, 43: 257–65.

Sainsbury, D. (2006) 'Immigrants' social rights in comparative perspective: welfare regimes, forms in immigration and immigration policy regimes', *Journal of European Social Policy*, 16(3): 229–43.

Scharf, T. (1998) *Ageing and Ageing Policy in Germany*. Oxford: Berg.

Scharf, T., Phillipson, C., and Smith, A.E. (2004) 'Poverty and social exclusion: growing older in deprived urban neighbourhoods', in A. Walker and C. Hagan Hennessy (eds), *Growing Older: Quality of Life in Old Age*. Maidenhead, UK: Open University Press, pp. 81–106.

Scharf, T., Phillipson, C., Smith, A.E., and Kingston, P. (2002) *Growing Older in Socially Deprived Areas: Social Exclusion in Later Life*. London: Help the Aged.

Schludi, M. (2005) *The Reform of Bismarckian Pension Systems: A Comparison of Pension Politics in Austria, France, Germany, Italy and Sweden*. Amsterdam: University of Amsterdam Press.

Schmidt, M.G. (2005) *Sozialpolitik in Deutschland: Historische Entwicklung und internationaler Vergleich*, 3rd edn. Wiesbaden: VS Verlag für Sozialwissenschaften.

Skocpol, T. and Amenta, E. (1986) 'States and social policies', *Annual Review of Sociology*, 12: 131–57.

Sotiropoulos, D.A. (2004) 'The EU's impact on the Greek welfare state: europeanization on paper?', *Journal of European Social Policy*, 14(3): 267–84.

Spicker, P. (2001) 'Cross-national comparisons of poverty: reconsidering methods', *International Journal of Social Welfare*, 10: 153–63.

Taylor-Gooby, P. (1999) 'Policy change at a time of retrenchment: recent pension reform in France, Germany, Italy and the UK', *Social Policy and Administration* 33(1): 1–19.

Tester, S. (1999) 'Comparative approaches to long-term care for adults', in J. Clasen (ed.), *Comparative Social*

Policy: Concepts, Theories and Methods. Oxford: Blackwell, pp. 136–58.

The Netherlands (2008) *National Strategy Report on Social Protection and Inclusion, The Netherlands 2008.* The Hague: Ministry of Social Affairs and Employment.

Townsend, P. (1979) *Poverty in the United Kingdom.* Harmondsworth, UK: Penguin.

United Nations Population Fund (1998) *The State of World Population 1998. The New Generations.* New York: United Nations Population Fund.

van Oorschot, W., Opielka, M., and Pfau-Effinger, B. (eds) (2008) 'The culture of the welfare state: historical and theoretical arguments', in W. van Oorschot and W. Clunk (eds), *Culture and Welfare State: Values and Social Policy in Comparative Perspective.* Cheltenham, UK: Edward Elgar, pp. 1–28.

Walker, A. and Wong, C.K. (eds) (2005) *East Asian Welfare Regimes in Transition.* Bristol: Policy Press.

Wilensky, H.L. (1975) *The Welfare State and Equality: Structural and Ideological Roots of Public Expenditure.* Berkeley, CA: University of California Press.

Zaidi, A., Makovec, M., Fuchs, M., et al. (2006) *Poverty of Elderly People in EU25.* Vienna: European Centre for Social Welfare Policy and Research.

39

Globalization, Social Policy, and Ageing: A North American Perspective

Carroll L. Estes and Steven P. Wallace

INTRODUCTION

This chapter begins with a discussion of globalization and related ageing issues including the response of various international agencies and forums (e.g. the World Health Organization and the United Nations). This review is occurring within the larger context of the aggressive stance of major institutions of global financial capital such as the World Bank (WB), the International Monetary Fund (IMF), and the World Trade Organization (WTO) that have been seeking a restructuring (if not full demise) of the welfare state. The chapter then describes the political and ideological warfare around the sanctity of the market that has shaped social policy in the United States and the new forms of ageism that have arisen, beginning in the 1980s. The view from advocates of privatization is that global and societal crises of demographic ageing make the welfare state unsustainable in the United States and elsewhere. The institutionalization of larger processes of rationalization and privatization (Rogne et al., 2009) have been pivotal in the efforts of market ideologists to implement state policies of structural adjustment, which accelerated during the 8 years of the George W. Bush presidency and then slowed during the Obama administration. Two relevant examples of such structural adjustment efforts are briefly examined in this chapter: (1) efforts to privatize Social Security and

Medicare (the universal, federally administered health insurance programme for those aged 65 and over and for the younger severely disabled) and (2) the case of long-term care. The 'risk shift' from the state to the individual is further highlighted and the chapter concludes with an assessment of the challenge of globalization to ageing and old-age policy.

Understanding social policy and ageing in the contemporary scene requires attention to the state and to the competing forces of capital and labour that engage in continuous struggles to frame the discourse and thereby shape the direction and largesse of state policy. The state plays a significant role in social provision for ageing populations because of its power to (a) allocate and distribute scarce and crucial resources; (b) mediate conflict between different segments of society, including those bounded by race, ethnicity, class, gender, and age, and (c) alleviate (or not) conditions that potentially threaten the social order or status quo (Estes and Associates, 2001: 7). In the globalizing world, the role of the state itself is contested. In addition, there is a struggle for the soul of the nation-state that is manifested in the relative favouritism accorded to the needs of market capitalism versus the social needs of human beings in the society.

Older persons, especially older women, are more directly dependent upon the substance of state policy than are most other age groups. This is because the economic and health security of elders is built upon retirement schemes and the provision of medical and other old-age services that are secured through the state and/or the private sector according to state law. Each of these systems of provision is determined by the strength and dominance of different political, economic, and cultural interests in the nation-state and in the world.

GLOBALIZATION AND AGEING

Growing old is increasingly viewed in a transnational context of international organizations and cross-border migration that creates new conditions and challenges for older persons and their families. There is a growing tension between a nation-state's policies on ageing and those formulated by global organizations and institutions. Ageing is no longer solely a national issue (Estes and Phillipson, 2002). Increasing life expectancy is usually viewed as a societal achievement, but also as a socioeconomic burden of crisis proportions by adherents of 'apocalyptic demography' (Robertson, 1999). This view, common in the United States and elsewhere, assumes that ageing populations will burden public policies to the point of creating disastrous social consequences. Politicians, think tanks, and major economic institutions have proffered dire warnings of impending national bankruptcy, underinvestment in children, and the overwhelming of available family support (Jackson and Howe, 2008; Lamm, 2002). Older people have become scapegoats for political problems such as rising federal deficits that were caused by tax cuts, rising military spending, and the bank bailouts and economic stimulus funding of 2008 and 2009 (Quadagno, 1999; Rogne et al., 2009; Schulz and Binstock, 2006). In this context, societal adaptations to population ageing represent merely one issue. Nevertheless, the cause of economic stability is used to justify continuing attacks on the social contract, the welfare state, and social insurance, especially Social Security and Medicare.

The ageing of societies creates major concerns for older women (see Chapter 10). In all societies, women outlive men; by very old age, the female-to-male ratio is generally 2:1 (United Nations, 2009). This is a formidable challenge because women are caregivers for people of all ages, especially for children and, increasingly, for grandchildren. For example, among populations where HIV/AIDS prevalence is high, older women are essential caregivers of their adult children and their orphaned grandchildren. Although unpaid,

women's caregiving work generally ceases only when they are physically and/or mentally unable to provide it and in need of care themselves (Estes and Zulman, 2008). As a result, older women worldwide experience greater economic deprivation and insecurity in comparison with older men (Gornick et al., 2009). Thus, older women are highly vulnerable to governmental upheavals and restrictions of safety-net policies.

Response to ageing by the international community: the World Health Organization (WHO), the United Nations (UN), and others

The UN publication *World Ageing Situation* (Desai, 2000) calls for revolutionary thinking in which ageing is viewed as a lifelong and society-wide phenomenon that permeates all social, economic, and cultural spheres, compelling 'policy interventions that include social and human, as well as economic, investments.' Regrettably, neither the WHO nor the UN as a whole appear poised to implement either revolutionary thinking or action. Both the WHO and the UN have adopted an overarching general objective of 'active ageing' – 'the process of optimizing opportunities for health, participation and security in order to enhance the quality of life as people age' (World Health Organization, 2007: 5); this underpinned by the paradigm of 'successful' and 'productive' ageing (Butler and Brody, 1995; Holstein and Minkler, 2003; Rowe and Kahn, 1987).

According to the WHO publication *Towards Policy for Health and Ageing*, 'the challenge for the developing world is two-fold: investing in "healthy ageing" from a public health perspective and making medical interventions more cost-effective and more widely available' (WHO, 2001). This approach might be viewed as overly narrow since more than medical interventions are needed to improve the lives and health of older people, especially in developing countries. After conducting focus groups with older adults around the world, the WHO report *Global Age-Friendly Cities* (WHO, 2007) takes a broader view of the conditions needed for active ageing that include social inclusion, the built environment, and civic participation. The approach, none the less, continues to be individualistic and focuses on the person–environment fit, with no attention to community- and societal-level issues such as the extent of income inequality and social solidarity that impact the aged population. In the context of globalization, pressures for privatization, the power of international financial markets and medical–pharmaceutical markets, and the biomedicalization of ageing, it is likely that the demography of ageing will become an excuse to impose on the world's poor 'prefabricated, selectively chosen, market- and technology-driven, externally monitored, and dependency-producing programs' (Banerji, 2002: 738).

The Second World Assembly on Ageing (United Nations, 2002) proposed a framework, the so-called 'Madrid Plan of Action', that supports dual goals of economic development and poverty reduction as the core of ageing policies. This approach emphasizes the importance of active ageing, intergenerational solidarity, and the necessity of developed countries helping developing countries. The framework is also infused with discussions of universal human rights, including non-discrimination, access to and control over adequate economic resources, and freedom from maltreatment and violence. In Latin America this framework was further elaborated in 2007 in the Brasilia Declaration (Economic Commission on Latin America and the Caribbean, 2008). The primary focus of the rights discussed in Brasilia, however, continues to be individual or occasionally family rights and not larger communal rights involving the distribution of wealth, power, and life chances over the life course.

The United States and other developed countries (even the United Kingdom) support free-market-oriented policies that embody the most individualistic principle of justice, based on a utilitarian philosophy where maximizing the sum of individuals' health and wealth is the primary goal. This is reflected in regularly reported data on single national-level measures of life expectancy and gross domestic product (GDP). These measures ignore the distribution of health and wealth, making them inadequate – even detrimental – to ensuring equal opportunities for all (United Nations, 2002). The policies are contradictory since the privatization and free-market principles have been pushed furthest in less developed nations that are least able to buffer the resulting economic insecurity, while the citizens of developed nations that promote these policies have more effectively resisted many of those same policies in their own counties.

From a public health perspective, the international documents do not reflect 'health services as a component of intersectoral action in wider fields, such as . . . adequate access to potable water, sanitation, (and) proper housing' (Banerji, 2002: 737). And the international organization that has a mandate to focus on public health, the WHO, devotes limited attention to ageing issues. These trends are mirrored in the United States where the leading governmental public health

agency, the US Centers for Disease Control, only has a small and underfunded programme on ageing. The leading US governmental agency on ageing, the Administration on Ageing, only has a tiny and underfunded programme specifically on health promotion, although a significant component of its funding goes to nutrition programmes.

GLOBALIZATION AND THE RESTRUCTURING OF THE WELFARE STATE

The promotion of privatization and the restructuring of the welfare state is an essential part of an intentional global strategy of financial capitalism to get nations to divest themselves of public (and defined) benefits in favour of privatized pension and health schemes (Estes and Associates, 2001; Phillipson et al., 2009; Svihula and Estes, 2009). The effort is to increase the reliance on private capital markets for pensions and health insurance, and to create new markets to generate profits in the provision of services. This neoliberal agenda is being promoted by organizations such as the World Bank, International Monetary Fund, and policies and actions of the World Trade Organization (Scholte, 2005), the actions of whom diminish the likelihood of robust welfare states in the present and the future. This is particularly significant in view of the economic meltdown that started in 2008 with the dramatic reversal in stock markets and banking worldwide and the millions of mortgage foreclosures and serious unemployment in the United States that has spread globally. Nevertheless, these international institutions have not taken their eye off the issue. An IMF staff paper on the recent world financial crisis notes, 'We should not forget that the main threat to the long-term viability of public finances in rapidly-ageing countries comes from the trend increase in the net cost of publicly funded pension and health entitlements . . .' (Spilimbergo et al., 2008: 9).

It is clear that these international financial institutions (and the financial capital enterprises that they represent) would obtain enormous wealth and power through privatization; and it is these institutions that have claimed that no country can afford to support older people through publicly guaranteed retirement and health programmes (Feldstein, 2005). Beginning during Reagan's presidency and continuing, these institutions have exploited 'the ageing of the population' in their efforts to coerce governments to privatize their public pension and health systems – that is to move away from systems based on social solidarity (where all citizens share financial risk) to systems of individual capitation (where each person is at individual risk).

Phillipson and colleagues (Estes and Phillipson, 2002; Phillipson, 2006; Phillipson et al., 2009) have identified the problems that globalization presents for the development of social policy on ageing, in particular that globalization produces a form of disempowerment of citizens within the nation-state without commensurate citizen leverage on the global scene that is dominated by transnational organizations. There is clearly a need for a new politics of old age under these global conditions, especially in view of the relative weakness of citizen groups in this landscape (Phillipson, 2006). Yet, there are very few organizations in ageing that are working against the negative social consequences of globalization. Generally, with a few exceptions, older people in the United States are not engaged in struggles for justice at the global level. The American Association of Retired Persons (AARP), an exceptionally large membership group, engages in some global ageing issues, but not from a social justice perspective. Other organizations in the United States that have interests in global ageing include professional and trade organizations that focus on promoting their own professional and business interests, and the National Institute on Aging of the National Institutes of Health that has a narrowly scientific interest in global ageing demography and disease.

A negative and militaristic view of the link between globalization and ageing comes from a segment of the international defense community in the United States. Haas (2007) contends that altering Social Security and Medicare policy is crucial to security and the dominance of the United States in international power relationships. In Global ageing: opportunities and threats to American security, Haas poses an inevitable trade-off between national security and the human needs of the American population:

> To pay for the massive fiscal costs associated with its ageing population, the U.S. will in all likelihood have to scale back the scope of its international policies . . . .The economic effects of an ageing population will likely deny even the U.S. the fiscal room necessary to maintain the extent of its current global position, let alone adopt major new international initiatives. [In order to be] better protected [in] its international power dominance . . . . America should reduce Social Security and Medicare payments to wealthier citizens, raise the retirement age . . . maintain largely open immigration policies to help keep its median age relatively low, and above all restrain the rising costs of its healthcare system.
>
> (Haas, 2007: 10)

It is noteworthy that Haas' calculus of what is undermining the revenue base that he considers essential for international dominance excludes the costs of a potentially endless (possibly pointless) war on terror and the Bush tax cuts (and latter-day bailouts) for corporations and the rich. Haas appears to be calling for a robust hyper-capitalist imperialism intertwined with a thriving militarism built on a bedrock of ageism and a blind eye to human social needs.

In a contrasting view, Vincent links the fear of population demography to the politics of state welfare systems and the interests of (private) pension-fund capitalism. He argues that: '. . . the changing demographic agenda is best understood as reflecting the ideological concerns – economic, military, and political – of dominant elites' (Vincent, 2006: 259). Vincent rejects the view that declining fertility rates and the ageing of the world's population inevitably produce: 'an inequity between generations and the potentiality for "age wars"' (Vincent, 2006: 259). Instead, he poses three 'critical gerontological questions: . . . in what circumstances do population changes become social issues; who is defining those problems; and to what purpose?'

Significantly, the global transnational capitalist infrastructure is already in place that is committed to advancing policies to enrich private capital as part of the restructuring of the welfare state. Its financial institutions (many of which are themselves in serious financial crisis) have been challenging the rights and benefits of working people and the multitudes of redundant workers displaced by the capitalist system, including the old. While the statistical averages about older people in the United States suggest they are advantaged in comparison with older people in less developed nations, they also hide significant inequalities. Among developed nations, older women in the United States are among the very poorest (Estes and Wallace, 2006; Harrington Meyer and Herd, 2007). The life expectancy of African-Americans in selected urban areas is 15.4 years shorter than that of Asian-American men, and in late middle age is similar to that of those in sub-Saharan Africa (Murray et al., 2006). And despite the nearly universal coverage of the older population by Medicare, one in 10 low-income seniors in US rural areas delayed seeking medical care because of the cost (US AHRQ, 2007). These inequities among the ageing population in the United States show the need for a more, not less, robust welfare state.

Central to the chain of relationships are the varied ways in which economic globalization marginalizes large numbers of people by reducing public spending on social services and de-links economic reform from social policy. This type of marginalization manifests a gendered dimension inasmuch as women are among those most directly affected. Neoliberal market-based globalization and ideology are layered on top of pre-existing 'rigid hierarchies of patriarchy [that] work to impoverish women.' Markets further ingrain and deepen 'poverty on a gendered basis' (Mittelman and Tambe, 2000). The twin ideologies of gender and globalization separately, and in combination, exacerbate the inequalities of an already-stacked deck against women, as both women's work and hardship are dramatically increased – with women pressed to take on the lowest-paying jobs while continuing to care for their children, families, and elders (Mittelman and Tambe, 2000). Among the most significant effects of globalization on older women is the reduction in the role of the state with regard to the economic and health security of the people.

Globalization has allowed wealthy countries to externalize some of the costs of their ageing populations to developing countries through the chain of caregiving that exists (Isaksen et al., 2008). The inadequate state support of caregiving leads many families to rely on low-cost immigrant labour to support disabled older adults (and young children). Many of the immigrant women who work in that sector are forced to leave dependent children and elders behind in the care of other family members. The result is a weakening of the social fabric of the sending families and communities, even though they often benefit materially from remittances (Isaksen et al., 2008). According to the 2007 American Community Survey for example, among personal care and home care aides in California, about half are immigrants and 85 per cent are female. Two-fifths have household incomes near (below 200 per cent) or below the official poverty line. Among maids and housekeepers the exploitation is even more striking: about 80 per cent are immigrants, 90 per cent are women, and over 60 per cent live in or near poverty (Ruggles et al., 2008). The global care chain of exploitation also extends to more skilled workers such as nurses, whose educational expenses are absorbed by sending countries such as the Philippines, on top of the families that are left behind absorbing the additional care work (Brush et al., 2004; Yeates, 2004).

At its most extreme, the state entirely abdicates responsibility for social welfare of a segment of the aged. There are an estimated 13 million undocumented immigrant residents in the United States, two-fifths of whom are women, and almost all of whom are in working families (Passel, 2006). These workers pay into, but are not eligible for, Social Security and Medicare when they reach old age. The result is that the state benefits from taxes they pay – an estimated $7–12 billion

annually into Social Security alone (Porter, 2005) and private companies benefit from cheap labour, but the workers are abandoned in their old age to their families and own savings. The flow of highly exploitable labour is a direct consequence of the economic pressures of internationalization and the weakened labour standards fostered by international institutions.

AGEISM AND OLD-AGE POLICY

Ageism is a major element influencing social policy in the United States (Estes and Portacolone, 2009). It is pernicious in its social and individual consequences. In its contemporary form, ageism is 'the denial of basic and civil rights of elders' (Butler, 2006). Maggie Kuhn (1984: 5–7) linked ageism to 'deep, insidious, paternalism' that 'infects us when we reject ourselves and despair at our own powerlessness, wrinkled skin and physical limitations.' Ageism is manifested both structurally and ideologically. Structurally, ageism influences the agenda setting, formation, and implementation of public policy. Ideologically, ageism bolsters the imagery of elders as unproductive persons who are undeserving of the benefits that they have earned and paid for over many decades.

Ageism is 'a human rights violation no less than racism or sexism' (Butler, 2006); yet it is being effectively nurtured in unrelenting attacks on older persons and older generations in the interest of larger political and economic goals of corporate and global capitalist hegemony of power and profit. This reinvigorated form of ageism is embedded in the labelling of elders as 'greedy geezers'; as a 'demographic tsunami' that the nation cannot afford, and who drain resources needed for capitalist development and productivity gains (ergo, profit) in the global economy. The name-callers have captured centre stage, successfully employing the media in framing its messages of the inevitability of 'demography as destiny,' although such portrayals run directly counter to arguments that 'demography is not destiny' (Friedland and Summer, 1999, 2005).

The scare tactics around demography are paradoxical in view of two demographic facts: (1) the population of the United States is younger than that of most other developed nations that have (and are able to afford) more generous welfare states (e.g., the United Kingdom, Germany, France, and Japan); and (2) in 2006 the total fertility rate in the United States was the highest it had been since 1991 at the 2.1 babies per woman which is the population replacement rate

(Martin et al., 2009). This is a crucial fertility benchmark that can help keep retirement programmes such as Social Security solvent by supplying a steady stream of new workers to pay into the system to support retirees (Stein, 2007). Schulz and Binstock (2006) refute the prognostications of the 'merchants of doom' and their 'phony threat[s] of population ageing,' offering a strong defence of the nation's need for (and ability to pay for) its bedrock programmes of social insurance (see Chapter 3).

In summary, the cumulative effects of ageism constitute a form of violence that is being perpetrated on older individuals, families, and generations. Yet there appears little public awareness or outrage that ageism is rampant throughout the policy discourse in the United States (Estes et al., 2009b). Such overt and vicious attacks would not be publicly tolerated against children or other racial or ethnic groups in contemporary discourse. It is noteworthy that this new ageism appears not only to be 'politically correct,' but also has been the cornerstone of the fight by the Right against social insurance in the United States.

ATTACKS ON SOCIAL INSURANCE AND THE SOCIAL MOVEMENT FOR PRIVATIZATION: THE CASE OF SOCIAL SECURITY AND MEDICARE

Starting with the gathering strength and institutionalization of Reaganism in the 1980s, scholars from the American Enterprise Institute (AEI) and The Cato Institute set their sights on privatizing Social Security, publicly announcing a 'Leninist Strategy' to do just that in the *Cato Journal* (Butler and Germanis, 1983). The strategy is to build a movement which creates a focused political coalition that is successful in isolating and weakening its opponents. Indeed, they noted that:

> Social Security reform requires mobilizing the various coalitions that stand to benefit from the change . . . the business community, and financial institutions in particular . . . the strategy must be to propose moving to a private Social Security system in such a way as to . . . neutralize . . . the coalition that supports the existing system. But then, as Lenin well knew, to be a successful revolutionary, one must also be patient and consistently plan for real reform.
>
> (Butler and Germanis, 1983: 556)

From this opening salvo in 1983 to the present, presidents and Republican congressional leaders have floated proposals for the partial or full privatization of the once-sacrosanct Social Security and Medicare programmes (Svihula and Estes, 2007, 2008, 2009). Conservative think tanks and economists propagate a coherent set of principles framing the necessity and strategy for privatization. The privatization projects of Cato, Heritage and the American Enterprise Institute build upon arguments about the 'unsustainability', of the capitalist economy (and by inference, democracy), should the state be asked to pay out the Social Security benefits from the Trust Fund that its citizens have earned and paid into for many decades. Privatization ideas flow from a steady stream of ideological pronouncements about market superiority and the ideology of individual responsibility.

Throughout his two-term presidency, George W. Bush asserted the necessity and inevitability of privatization, in spite of the fact that his administration reluctantly acknowledged that privatization would worsen Social Security solvency issues (Baker and Weisbrot, 1999; Ball, 2000; Smeeding et al., 1999). Bush Presidential commissions were appointed with the requirement of developing privatization reforms, and Bush Presidential budgets submitted to Congress for 2007, 2008, and 2009 included the nearly $1 trillion costs of privatization and other crippling mandates for reform.

Although the 2008 presidential election sent Democrat Barack Obama to the White House, and Democratic majorities to Congress, there remains a serious threat of budget cuts, privatization, and other measures that would eviscerate Social Security. This is reflected in the almost unanimous Republican resistance to Obama's stimulus plan and a continued drumbeat on the need for 'entitlement reform' (Falcone, 2009), which in the United States are code words for privatization and entitlement cutbacks. Medicare is no less at risk under such a scenario, especially given that there is little certainty that the universal healthcare measures that Obama has promised will survive the politics emanating from the economic meltdown and government spending on an economic stimulus.

The most significant move towards the privatization of social programmes in the United States is in Medicare. In a major paradigmatic shift, the 2003 Medicare Modernization Act (MMA) initiated the privatization of the nation's only public universal healthcare plan for the elderly and severely disabled – Medicare (Geyman, 2004). The MMA added prescription drug coverage to Medicare for the first time, but it did so by departing from the uniform, national structure of Medicare and instead subsidized private insurance companies that offer individual coverage through an endless variety of different plans. To soften pharmaceutical company opposition, it barred Medicare from negotiating drug prices. And the bill augmented the subsidy of privately managed care plans that provide clinical care to some Medicare recipients such that the private plans in 2009 received an average of 114 per cent of what similar beneficiaries spend in the traditional fee-for-service Medicare programme, a $12 billion overpayment (MedPAC, 2009). The state-subsidized private-managed care corporations are competing to draw older beneficiaries away from the public Medicare programme for their medical services. Worse, the MMA has segmented Medicare's universal risk-pool among private insurers and the government, thus impairing its major mechanism to achieve cost efficiency. As a consequence of its design, different Medicare beneficiaries now have a different range of drug benefits, formularies, and costs. The MMA also added provisions instituting automatic caps on federal funding. Since it provides no federal cost-containment provisions for drug costs, it has predictably led to rising out-of-pocket costs for many elders (Hoadley et al., 2008).

Commodification and privatization: the case of long-term care

Although long-term care (LTC) was a part of the Clinton healthcare reform (Estes et al., 2003), it has since been largely absent from the policy scene in the United States. The story of LTC from President Reagan to the present is the continuing refusal of the state to provide meaningful LTC benefits to older and disabled people except for those who impoverish themselves and then become eligible for public assistance through Medicaid, and then disproportionately for nursing home care. The overall trend has been one of (1) state policy and financing for the commodification of services (the buying and selling of ageing services in the for-profit market); (2) the rationalization and bureaucratization of care via structures designed to increase efficiency, e.g., acquisitions, mergers, managed care, and contracting out; (3) the medicalization of care for the ageing in ways that have accelerated capitalist expansion and globalization of the medical services and technologies aimed at acute rather than chronic or social care needs of elders (Estes et al., 2000), producing a $3 trillion medical–industrial complex that exceeded 16 per cent of the US economy's GDP in 2007 (Hartman et al., 2009); and (4) the for-profit conversion and consolidation of a beleaguered network of traditionally non-profit home and community-based

service organizations (e.g., home health and hospice care) (Estes and Associates, 2001).

The history and financing of LTC in the United States has resulted in a fragmented array of services that relies heavily on out-of-pocket payment and privately provided services (Wallace et al., 2007). Combined with the trends towards commodification, rationalization, and medicalization, many older adults and their families encounter 'no-care zones' where appropriate services do not exist or the available patchwork public programmes will not cover the care. These no-care zones are exacerbated by policies that continue to push older adults out of hospitals quicker and sicker as well as other changes in policies that are designed to save the public treasury by shifting care onto family and friends (Estes, 1993; Wallace et al., 2007).

Although there has been some interest in LTC, with Senator Kennedy's development of a federal bill, it is proposed as a voluntary programme. The continuing resistance of both political parties and their respective administrations to providing a federal policy solution to the problem of LTC means that the actual policy has been one of informal care or informalization (Binney et al., 1983; Estes, 1979; Estes and Zulman, 2008), which is part of a larger austerity strategy derived from the needs of both the state and capital for women (regardless of their labour force participation) to continue to perform large, debilitating, and unending amounts of unpaid servicing work, particularly in the care of the aged. This is in spite of the fact that informal caregivers already provide about 80 per cent of all such care (Estes and Zulman, 2008).

This stasis in LTC is consistent with efforts to restore and regulate family life (and particularly the lives of women) that resonate with the deep concerns of both the state and corporate sectors, in conjunction with the religious Right, to: (1) minimize state costs and corporate expenses (e.g., payroll taxes) for elder entitlements and (2) shift more of the burden on to families (and, for evangelicals, to restore patriarchal family arrangements). Such policies enforce the continuing supply of women's free labour necessary for the reproduction and maintenance of the labour force and the winnowing down of the welfare state (Estes and Associates, 2001).

The devolution of risk and responsibility from the state to the individual

In the United States, the devolution of responsibility from the federal to the state and local levels, and down to the private individual and family has been a theme from the Nixon presidency to the present (Estes and Gerard, 1983; Estes and Linkins, 1997). The old are even given individual responsibility for their own successful (or unsuccessful) ageing and productivity in old age (Estes et al., 2001b). As noted earlier, these themes of productivity and individual healthy ageing are echoed in some of the documents on ageing of the well-respected WHO and UN organizations.

The devolving (if not eradication) of state responsibility (policy and fiscal) and replacing of it with individual responsibility is a blow against the 'social,' the collective, and communal values undergirding policy. This shift to individual responsibility is intentionally oblivious to the structural sources (over which individuals have little control) of trends in unemployment, contracting out, corporate greed, bankruptcies and malfeasance, terrorist attacks, and disappearing employment coverage of retiree and health benefits.

Hacker (2006) describes this embrace of individualism as 'the Personal Responsibility Crusade.' He observes that it has produced increasing levels of income instability, psychological costs, and pain due to the erosion of the employment-based structure of retirement and health benefits of US workers and other serious economic security challenges attendant to the issues described above. In *The Great Risk Shift*, Hacker illuminates the fact that the erosion of broad risk pools, the expansion of individually borne risk, and massive social (systemic, structurally induced) risks 'occur to many people at once and thus are particularly difficult for private insurers to cover' (Hacker, 2006: 180). In such situations, social insurance is the best means to ensure both economic security and the expansion of opportunity. In contrast to the dominant rhetoric of inevitable trade-offs or zero-sum game, Hacker and others posit an essential connection between economic security *and* economic opportunity and growth (see also Schwarz, 2003). Hacker flips the usual question and asks how economic security can enhance economic growth. He contends that government is appropriately the risk manager, and that this basic institution for risk management and pooling is essential. The commercial sector does not and cannot serve as a risk pooler for the whole because it survives and grows by making a profit rather than being able to provide protection for an entire population. The financial bottomline for stakeholders is the guiding principle along with the necessity to identify and mitigate risk. For example, in commercial health care, individuals who cannot afford to pay according to their risk (experience rating or underwriting in health insurance) are excluded or must pay more. In contrast, the bottom line of the state

is its people, in addition to its economic and political system. Medicare and Social Security were both created because of the failure of the private market to work to insure the nation's elders and disabled (Geyman, 2004).

CONCLUSION

Older people, women, minorities, and the poor have been largely absent from influential debates of the World Bank – against public pensions – and the World Trade Organization – for the commercialization of care services. The major participants in these debates have been governments from rich countries, seeking to deregulate (even abolish) government provision of services, and corporations, wanting to expand into lucrative areas of work worldwide (Estes et al., 2003; Vincent, 1999; Vincent et al., 2002). Major players in the international trade of health services include health insurance companies, drug companies, and medical equipment suppliers.

Critics of globalization have been mobilized in areas of human rights, ecology, women's rights, race and ethnic justice, and worker rights. Elder rights advocates are invisible, except for the largely uncritical formal positions articulated in United Nations and WHO documents that offer little guidance or evidence of commitment to the goals of universal, collective, and social obligations enacted through government programmes. Although not 'wrong' in their entirety, current UN and WHO efforts are no match for the active efforts of the WTO, the IMF, and the World Bank to privatize government provision of social care and retirement support for the aged. The opening of markets (i.e., privatization) of such services is now commonly inserted as a condition of development loans and debt relief to developing countries, in which it is known as 'structural adjustment.'

Important issues concern the extent to which all older persons and women of all generations will be a major (or even minor) voice in the social movements around the new global economy and efforts to reshape the institution of old age and retirement that are occurring across different nation-states (Estes and Phillipson, 2002). This is part of a larger question of globalization – the influence of politics in constructing the present and the future. Globalization as a process is both an historical transition, opening new 'spaces', and an opportunity for the development and testing of political power and strategy involving the balance between consent and coercion (Sassoon, 2001).

Organizations of older people need to link with larger organizations and forums working on the global justice agenda. The upsurge of political activity among pensioners in a number of countries (Walker and Maltby, 1997) offers a potentially important platform upon which to build an age and generation-integrated social movement for social change. The joining of the movements of opposition to the worst abuses of globalization is essential and the role of older-people's organizations is pivotal because older persons not only have much to lose should there be widespread privatization of public health and retirement programmes but also are the guardians of the next generations of children and grandchildren who will be hurt most by privatization schemes.

With the forces of financial collapse gripping the United States, there is a disturbing reservoir of cleavage, disadvantage, and distrust that has been stoked during the past 8 years, rather explicitly along the lines of race, class, gender, generation, disability, and immigration status. The twin fears of 'the end of work' and 'the end of retirement' have entered the national lexicon in conjunction with millions unemployed and joblessness growing at an alarming pace. The struggles will be paramount between capital and labour and the divisive fights over the role of the state in ensuring the social needs of the people are addressed. It is not an exaggeration to observe that the right to employment and to organize workers is at stake – and with it the threatened loss of security, human dignity, and the American dream for all generations. Such conditions clearly imperil the lives of the old and young alike. The vital role of the state is unveiled, always, in cases of the failure of the market. However, the dominant market rhetoric has desensitized the nation's leaders to imperatives of bedrock values such as the common good, the collective, the communal, and the inevitable interdependence of our peoples. One price of the ideological success of Reagan's mantra that 'government is the problem and the market is the solution' is a legitimacy crisis of the state.

In the United States, there is a 'crisis of confidence' in the banking and market system (Krugman, 2009b) tantamount to a legitimacy crisis *of capitalism*. As research shows us, crises – however they come about (socially constructed and objectively rendered) – provide the nation's most powerful elites the opportunity for bold and radical action (Edelman, 1964, 1977). However, such crises also provide an opportunity for the opposition and the grassroots to mobilize. A giant window of potential social change has opened (Krugman, 2009a). As with the Depression of the 1930s, the worldwide economic crisis at the end of the first decade of the 2000s may help mobilize groups that have been exploited and oppressed due to their class, gender, race, ethnicity, or immigration status, among others. The working people

of the nation are poised for the battle of the century for the soul of democracy (Estes et al., 2009a). The failure of the state to address the needs of the people for work and for basic economic and health security across the life course, especially because the needs are so real and deep, and the fears and anger so raw, could engender a major legitimacy crisis *of democracy*.

The question is how the Obama presidency and the Congress will structure and implement the state's response to the three major arenas of crisis that test the United States now: the legitimation crisis of capital, the legitimation crisis of the state, and the legitimation crisis of democracy (Estes, 2008). The future of social insurance is, at base, an issue of social justice. The issues starkly underscore the crucial importance of social insurance and the peril of the choices that will be made concerning the economic and health security of elders and all present and future generations in the United States and those that are likely to shape those adopted by other nations around the globe.

REFERENCES

Baker, D. and Weisbrot, M. (1999) *Social Security: The Phony Crisis.* Chicago: University of Chicago Press.

Ball, R.M. (2000) 'Getting the facts straight', in R. Ball (ed.), *Insuring the Essentials.* New York: Century Foundation, pp. 247–71.

Banerji, D. (2002) 'Report of the WHO Commission on Macroeconomics and Health: a critique', *International Journal of Health Services,* 32: 733–54.

Binney, E.A., Estes, C.L, and Humphers, S. (1983) 'Informalization and community care', in C.L. Estes, J.H. Swan, and Associates (eds), *The Long Term Care Crisis.* Newbury Park, NJ: Sage, pp. 155–70.

Brush, B.L., Sochalski J., and Berger, A.M. (2004) 'Imported care: recruiting foreign nurses to U.S. health care facilities', *Health Affairs,* 23: 78–87.

Butler, R.N. (2006). 'Combating ageism: a matter of human and civil rights', in *Ageism in America.* New York: International Longevity Center – USA.

Butler, R. and Brody, J.A. (eds) (1995) *Strategies to Delay Dysfunction in Later Life.* New York: Springer.

Butler, S. and Germanis, P. (1983) 'Achieving a Leninist strategy', *Cato Journal,* 3: 547–56.

Calasanti, T.M. and Slevin, K.F. (2006) *Age Matters: Realigning Feminist Thinking.* New York: Routledge.

Desai, N. (2000) *The World Ageing Situation.* New York: United Nations.

Economic Commission on Latin America and the Caribbean (2008) *Brasilia Declaration, Second Regional Intergovernmental Conference on Ageing in Latin America and the Carribean, Towards a Society for All Ages and Rights-based Protection*. United Nations, ECLAC, Santiago, Chile.

Edelman, M. (1964) *The Symbolic Use of Politics*. Urbana, IL: University of Illinois Press.

Edelman, M. (1977) *Political Language: Words that Succeed and Policies that Fail*. New York: Academic Press.

Estes, C.L. (1979) *The Aging Enterprise*. San Francisco, CA: Jossey-Bass.

Estes, C.L. (1993) 'The ageing enterprise revisited', *Gerontologist*, 33: 292–8.

Estes, C.L. (2008) 'The politics of aging: the legitimation crisis of the state, capitalism, and democracy', paper presented at the American Public Health Association Annual Meeting, San Diego, CA.

Estes, C. L. and Associates (2001) *Social Policy and Aging: A Critical Perspective*. Thousand Oaks, CA: Sage.

Estes, C.L. and Gerard, L. (1983) 'Governmental responsibility: issues of reform and federalism', in C.L. Estes, R.J. Newcomers and Associates, (eds.), *Fiscal Austerity and Aging: Shifting Government Responsibility for the Elderly*. Beverly Hills, CA: Sage, pp. 41–58.

Estes, C.L. and Linkins, K.W. (1997) 'Long-term care and the race to the bottom?', *International Journal of Health Services*, 27: 427–32.

Estes, C.L and Phillipson, C. (2002) 'The globalization of capital, the welfare state, and old age policy', *International Journal of Health Services*, 32: 279–97.

Estes, C.L. and Portacolone, E. (2009) 'Maggie Kuhn: social theorist of radical gerontology', *International Journal of Sociology and Social Policy*, 29: 15–26.

Estes, C.L. and Wallace, S.P. (2006) 'Older people', in B.S. Levy and V.W. Sidel (eds), *Social Injustice and Public Health*. Oxford: Oxford University Press, pp. 113–29.

Estes, C.L., and Zulman, D.M. (2008) 'Informalization of long term caregiving: a gender lens', in C. Harrington, and C.L. Estes (eds), *Health Policy*. Boston, MA: Jones and Bartlett, pp. 142–51.

Estes, C.L., Alford, R., and Egan, A. (2001a) 'The transformation of the nonprofit sector', in C.L. Estes, and Associates (eds), *Social Policy and Aging: A Critical Perspective*. Thousand Oaks, CA: Sage, pp. 61–91.

Estes, C.L., Mahakian J.L., and Weitz, T.A. (2001b) 'A political economy critique of "productive aging"', in C.L. Estes, and Associates (eds), *Social Policy and Aging: A Critical Perspective*. Thousand Oaks, CA: Sage, pp. 187–200.

Estes, C.L., Swan J.H., and Associates. (1993) *The Long-term Care Crisis: Elders Trapped in the No-care Zone*. Newbury Park, CA: Sage.

Estes, C.L., Wallace, S., and Linkins, K. (2000) 'Political economy of health and aging', in C.E. Bird, P. Conrad, and A.M. Fremont (eds), *Handbook of Medical Sociology*. Upper Saddle River, NJ: Prentice-Hall, pp. 129–42.

Estes, C.L., Wiener J.M., Goldberg, S.C., and Goldenson, S.M. (2003) 'The Politics of long term care under the Clinton health plan: lessons for the future', in P.R. Lee and C.L Estes (eds), *The Nation's Health*. Sudbury, MA: Jones and Bartlett, pp. 213–20.

Estes, C.L., Rogne, L., Grossman, B., Solway, E., and Hollister, B.A. (2009a) 'From the audacity of hope to the audacity of action', in L. Rogne, C.L. Estes, B. Grossman, B.A. Hollister, and E. Solway (eds), *Social Insurance and Social Justice: Social Security, Medicare and the Campaign Against Entitlements*. New York: Springer, pp. 435–30.

Estes, C.L., Rogne, L., Grossman, B., Solway, E., and Hollister, B.A. (2009b) 'We're all in this together: social insurance, social justice, and social change', in L. Rogne, C.L. Estes, B. Grossman, B.A. Hollister, and E. Solway (eds), *Social Insurance and Social Justice: Social Security, Medicare and the Campaign Against Entitlements*, New York: Springer, pp. 19–27.

Falcone, M. (2009) 'Republican Senate Leader sings bipartisan tune', *New York Times The Caucus Blog*, January 23.

Feldstein, M. (2005) 'Structural reform of social security', *Journal of Economic Perspectives*, 19: 33–55.

Friedland, R.B. and Summer, L. (1999) *Demography is not Destiny*. Washington, DC: National Academy on an Aging Society.

Friedland, R.B. and Summer L. (2005) *Demography is not Destiny, Revisited*. Washington DC: Center on an Aging Society, Georgetown University.

Geyman, J.P. (2004) 'Privatization of medicare: toward disentitlement and betrayal of a social contract', *International Journal of Health Services*, 34: 573–94.

Gornick, J.C., Sieminska, E., and Smeeding, T.M. (2009) 'The income and wealth packages of older women in cross-national perspective', *Journal of Gerontology: Social Sciences*, 64b: 402–14.

Haas, M.L. (2007) 'Global aging: opportunities and threats to national security', *Public Policy and Aging Report*, 17: 7–11.

Hacker, J.S. (2006) *The Great Risk Shift*. New York: Oxford University Press.

Harrington Meyer, M. and Herd, P. (2007) *Market Friendly or Family Friendly? The State and Gender Inequality in Old Age*. New York: Russell Sage Foundation.

Hartman, M., Martin, A., McDonnell, P., Catlin, A., and the National Health Expenditure Accounts Team (2009) 'National Health spending in 2007: slower drug spending contributes to lowest rate of overall growth since 1998', *Health Affairs*, 28: 246–61.

Hoadley, J., Thompson, J., Hargrave, E., Cubanski, J., and Neuman, T. (2008) *Medicare Part D 2009 Data Spotlight: Premiums*. Menlo Park, CA: Kaiser Family Foundation.

Holstein, M.B. and Minkler, M. (2003) 'Self, society, and the "new gerontology"', *Gerontologist*, 43: 787–96.

Isaksen, L.W., Devi, S.U., and Hochschild, A.R. (2008) 'Global care crisis: a problem of capital, care chain, or commons?', *American Behavioral Scientist* 52: 405–25.

Jackson, R. and Howe, N. (2008) *The Graying of the Great Powers: Demography and Geopolitics in the 21st Century*. Washington, DC: Center for Strategic and International Studies.

Krugman, P. (2009a) *The Conscience of a Liberal*. New York: W.W. Norton and Co.

Krugman, P. (2009b) *The Return of Depression Economics and the Crisis of 2008*. New York: W.W. Norton and Co.

Kuhn, M. (1984) 'Challenge to a new age', in M. Minkler and C.L. Estes (eds), *Readings in the Political Economy of Aging*. Amityville, NY: Baywood, pp. 7–9.

Lamm, R.D. (2002) 'The moral imperative of limiting elderly health expenditures', in S.H. Altman and D.I. Shactman (eds), *Politics for an Aging Society*. Baltimore, MD: Johns Hopkins University Press, pp. 199–216.

Martin, J.A., Hamilton, B.E., Sutton, P.D., Ventura, S.J., and Menacker, F. (2009) *Births: Final Data for 2006*. Hyattsville, MD: National Center for Health Statistics.

MedPAC (2009) *Report to the Congress: Medicare Payment Policy*. Washington, DC. Medicare Payment Advisory Commission.

Mittelman, J.H. and Tambe, A. (2000) 'Global poverty and gender', in J.H. Mittelman (ed.), *The Globalization Syndrome*. Princeton, NJ: Princeton University Press, pp. 74–89.

Murray, C.J.L., Kulkarni, S.C., Michaud, C., et al. (2006) Eight Americas: investigating mortality disparities across races, counties, and race-counties in the United States. *PLoS Med*, 3(9): e260. doi:10.1371/journal.pmed.0030260

Passel, J.S. (2006) *The Size and Characteristics of the Unauthorized Migrant Population in the U.S.* Washington, DC: Pew Hispanic Center.

Phillipson, C. (2006) 'Aging and globalization: issues for critical gerontology and political economy', in J. Baars, D. Dannefer, C. Phillipson, and A. Walker (eds), *Ageing, Globalization and Inequality*. New York: Baywood, pp. 43–58.

Phillipson, C., Estes, C.L., and Portacolone, E. (2009) 'Aging in health and development: the role of international organizations in population aging' in A. Gatti and A Boggio (eds), *Health and Development: The Role of International Organizations*. New York: Palgrave Macmillan, pp. 155–67.

Porter, E. (2005) 'Illegal immigrants are bolstering social security with billions', *New York Times*, April 5.

Quadagno, J. (1999) 'Social security and the myth of the entitlement "Crisis", in J.B. Williamson, D.M. Watts-Roy, and E. Kingson (eds), *The Generational Equity Debate*. New York: Columbia University Press, pp. 140–56.

Robertson, A. (1999) 'Beyond apocalyptic demography: toward a moral economy of interdependence', in M. Minkler and C.L Estes (eds), *Critical Gerontology: Perspectives from Political and Moral Economy*. Amityville, NY: Baywood, pp. 75–90.

Rogne, L., Estes, C.L., Grossman, B.R., and Hollister, B.A. (eds) (2009) *Social Insurance and Social Justice: Social Security, Medicare and the Campaign Against Entitlements*. New York: Springer.

Rowe, J.W., and Kahn, R.L. (1987) 'Human aging: usual and successful', *Science*, 237: 143–9.

Ruggles, S., Sobek, M., Alexander, T., et al. (2008) *Integrated Public Use Microdata Series: Version 4.0* [Machine-Readable Database]. Minneapolis, MN: Minnesota Population Center [producer and distributor].

Sassoon, S. (2001) 'Globalisation, hegemony and passive revolution', *New Political Economy*, 6: 5–17.

Scholte, J.A. (2005) *The Sources of Neoliberal Globalization*. Geneva, Switzerland: UN Research Institute for Social Development.

Schulz, J.H. and Binstock, R.H. (2006) *Aging Nation: The Economics and Politics of Growing Older in America*. Westport, CN: Praeger.

Schwarz, J.E. (2003) *Freedom Reclaimed: Rediscovering the American Vision*. Baltimore, MD: Johns Hopkins University Press.

Smeeding, T., Estes, C.L., and Glasse, L. (1999) *Social Security Reform and Older Women: Improving the System (*Paper No. 22*)*. Syracuse, NY: Syracuse University.

Spilimbergo, A., Symansky, S., Blanchard, O., and Cottarelli, C. (2008) 'Fiscal policy for the crisis', *IMF Staff Position Note*, International Monetary Fund, Washington, DC. http://www.imf.org/external/np/pp/eng/2008/122308.pdf

Stein, R. (2007) 'US fertility rate hits 35-year high, stabilizing population', *The Washington Post*, December 21.

Svihula, J. and Estes, C.L. (2007) 'Social security politics: ideology and reform', *Journals of Gerontology: Social Sciences* 62: S79–89.

Svihula, J. and Estes, C.L. (2008) 'Social security privatization: an ideologically structured movement', *Journal of Sociology and Social Welfare*, 35: 75–104.

Svihula, J. and Estes, C.L. (2009) 'Social security privatization: the institutionalization of an ideological movement', in L. Rogne, C.L. Estes, B. Grossman, B.A. Hollister, and E. Solway, (eds), *Social Insurance and Social Justice: Social Security, Medicare and the Campaign against Entitlements*. New York: Springer, pp. 217–31.

United Nations (2002) 'Second World Assembly on Ageing adopts Madrid Plan of Action and political declaration', in *Second World Assembly on Ageing*. Madrid, Spain.

United Nations (2009) *World Population Prospects: The 2008 Revision*. UN Department of Economic and Social Affairs, Population Division, New York.

US AHRQ (2007) *National Healthcare Disparities Report, 2007: Appendix D: Data Tables*. Rep. 08-0041, Agency for Health Care Research and Quality, Rockville, MD.

US Census Bureau (2004) *Global Population Profile, 2002*. Washington, DC: US Government Printing Office.

Vincent, J. (1999) *Politics, Power, and Old Age*. Aldershot, UK: Ashgate Books.

Vincent, J., Patterson, G., and Wale, K. (2002) *Politics and Old Age*. Aldershot, UK: Ashgate Books.

Vincent, J.A. (2006). 'Globalization and critical theory: political economy of world population issues', in J. Baars, D. Dannefer, C. Phillipson, and A. Walker (eds),

Aging, Globalization and Inequality. New York: Baywood, pp. 245–71.

Walker, A. and Maltby, A. (1997) *Ageing Europe.* Buckinghamshire: Open University Press.

Wallace, S.P., Abel, E., Pourat, N. and Delp, L. (2007). 'Long-term care and the elderly population', in R. Ancdersen, T. Rice, G. Kominski (eds), *Changing the U.S. Health Care System, 3rd edn.* San Francisco, CA: Jossey-Bass, pp. 341–62.

World Health Organization (2001) *Towards Policy for Health and Ageing.* Geneva: World Assembly on Aging.

World Health Organization (2007) *Global Age-Friendly Cities: A Guide.* Geneva: World Health Organization.

Yeates, N. (2004) 'A dialogue with "global care chain" analysis: nurse migration in the Irish context', *Feminist Review,* 77: 79–95.

40

Social Policies for Ageing Societies: Australasian Perspectives

Michael Fine and Sally Keeling

INTRODUCTION

Demography, geography, and the legacies of colonial history in the South West Pacific

Australia and New Zealand are each located on the global periphery, in the South West Pacific. Twinned island state nations separated by the Tasman Sea, they are divided not only by national boundaries but also by important local differences and rivalries arising from their near common history from the time they were settled as British colonies in the late 18th and early 19th centuries. While marked by significant but instructive divergences, the courses they have followed since independence in the early 20th century have nevertheless continued in broad parallel. Their uniqueness and global interest as ageing societies arises from their commonality as pastoral, industrial, and, later, post-industrial migration societies, located well away from the centres of metropolitan power in Europe and North America. Their economies, dominant culture, and political institutions are derived from the British and European backgrounds, as is the majority of their population. Both countries also share a history of recent colonial takeover of the land of native peoples (Denoon et al., 2000). In each case, a distinct dynamic of nation building has meshed with global processes to produce what Castles and

Mitchell once termed a 'fourth world' of welfare capitalism – similar in some aspects to the liberal approach to the welfare state evident in the major English-speaking countries, but with unique Australasian twists (Castles and Mitchell, 1990).

In this chapter, an initial consideration of demographic and geographic factors and trends in Australasia (effectively Australia and New Zealand) turns next to the politics of population ageing, before reviewing social policy developments of the later 20th century. Structural and constitutional differences are explored in terms of their relevance to the policy design and development process in each country. Two key examples of how these differences have played out in the fields of income support and aged care are presented.

Building on the early acknowledgement of the need to provide income support for those excluded from the labour market by age, observers might agree with Castles (1985) that the guarantee of a state-funded aged pension combined with a fair, legally guaranteed wage early in the 20th century signalled the beginnings of the 'wage earners' welfare state'. Through this approach, which served as a template for future developments in social policy over the 20th century, a minimal standard of living was ensured through the guarantee of a fair family wage for working families. Based on the model pioneered by the old-age pension, social benefits were available on a 'means tested' basis (i.e., dependent on income being below a defined minimum level) to those unable to support themselves through employment or the income received by a family wage earner.

From the 1980s, however, each country has also implemented neoliberal reforms of the welfare system, implementing major changes in the way in which older people receive income support, and other forms of collective support, including health and welfare services. Over the course of the 20th century, the economies of each country expanded, as did the amount and extent of state support and intervention in social life. This has been accompanied by a change in approach from providing support for a marginal and dependent group to the promotion of an ideology of self-provision and responsibility. In line with public health and health promotion principles, significant emphasis is also placed on a range of other personal and lifestyle adaptations to ageing, including the advancement of notions of healthy or active ageing, encouragement of social participation, and the reinforcement of family responsibility and informal care. These changes reflect both the traditions and institutional structures of liberalism and social democracy, responding to the impact of significant global economic forces.

Table 40.1 Life expectancy (years) in Australia at birth and at age 65, 1901 to 2003–05

Years	At birth		At age 65	
	Males	Females	Males	Females
1901–10	55.2	58.8	11.3	12.9
1920–22	59.2	63.3	12.0	13.6
1946–48	66.1	70.6	12.3	14.4
1960–62	67.9	74.2	12.5	15.7
1980–82	71.2	78.3	13.8	18.0
1994–96	75.2	81.1	15.8	19.6
1995–97	75.6	81.3	16.1	19.8
1996–98	75.9	81.5	16.3	20.0
1998–2000	76.6	82.0	16.8	20.4
2003–05	78.5	83.3	18.1	21.4
Indigenous Australians 1996–2001	59.4	64.8	10.7	12.0

The methodology used to calculate this table has changed since 1995. Data on population and deaths averaged over 3 years are now used to minimize year- to-year statistical variations.

Age 65–69 for indigenous Australians.

Source: Australian Bureau Statistics (2005)

AGEING AND LIFE EXPECTANCY

Life expectancy in the 20th century increased dramatically for the immigrant populations and their descendents in each country, but lagged well behind for indigenous peoples. An overt comparison between measures of social well-being between New Zealand and Australia (Ministry of Social Development, 2006) shows clear parity on life expectancy measures, despite significant divergence on a range of other social indicators between the two countries.

As shown in Table 40.1, average life expectancy at birth in Australia rose by over two decades, from 55.2 years in 1901–10 to 78.5 in 2003–05 for males, while female life expectancy increased from 58.8 years to 83.3 over the same period (Australian Bureau of Statistics (ABS), 2005). Amongst the Australian Aboriginal population, which made up approximately 2.2 per cent of the total Australian population in 2001, however, poor health outcomes and high infant mortality have prevailed, so that in the early years of the 21st century the life expectancy of Australian Aborigines at best approximated that experienced by the general population in the 1920s or that experienced in the Third World (Cotter et al., 2007). Problems with statistical collection of data on the indigenous population compound the real

social, economic, and health problems experienced. Whereas there is some evidence that life expectancy amongst Aborigines in Australia has also increased in recent years (Hetzel, 2000), it is clear that old age has quite different meanings in the two populations. In recognition of this, a formal statistical convention has been adopted by Australian government departments in reporting services to older people, referring to those aged 65 and above, except in the case of people of indigenous background, amongst whom those aged 55 and over are counted as 'aged'.

A mark of differentiation between Australian and New Zealand's historical and contemporary demography is the experience of the indigenous population. New Zealand prides itself on a foundation document known as the Treaty of Waitangi, signed in 1840 between the Crown and the majority of the Maori tribes. The Treaty, however, did not avert a turbulent period of land wars and significant population impacts in the 19th and early 20th century, or significant health and socioeconomic inequalities through to the present day (Ellison-Loschmann and Pearce, 2006; King, 2003; Mein-Smith, 2005). Yet, there was dramatic improvement in the 5 years up to 2000–02, when the most recent life expectancy gains for Maori reduced the gap between the Maori and non-Maori populations, although it remains significant.

Female life expectancy at birth for non-Maori in 2000–02 was 81.1 years, compared to 73.2 for Maori women – a difference of 7.9 years; the figures for males were 77.2 for non-Maori and 69.0 years for Maori (Table 40.2). In recognition of this differential, New Zealand health services informally acknowledge that a more relevant marker for age-related research and service planning purposes might be age 55 rather than age 65, for Maori and for the Pacific Islanders who now make up a rapidly growing sector of the New Zealand population, due to rapid immigration from the Pacific in the post-war period. There is increasing research since Koopman-Boyden (1993) noted some of the particular dimensions of Maori ageing, complicated as it is by intermarriage and also now by tribal and regional variation, with recent Treaty settlements with the Crown.

POLICIES FOR POPULATION AGEING

Little attention was paid to population ageing for most of the 20th century. Interest in demography has traditionally been high in the settler societies of Australasia, but it was absolute population numbers thought necessary for a growing society (most directly affected by fertility rates and immigration), not the age profile of the population that counted. The situation began to change in the

second half of the century. In Australia, the situation of neglect experienced by aged pensioners and others in the period following World War II led to the publication of a groundbreaking local study of the plight of disadvantaged older people in the 1950s (Hutchinson, 1956) and to a series of other publications in the years that followed (Sax, 1970; Stoller, 1960). Along with the interest of policymakers in ageing, these studies focused on issues of immediate importance, most notably the needs for aged care services and the high rates of poverty amongst older people. As overseas examples and demographic research began to demonstrate the potential impact of population ageing, political interest in population ageing grew markedly in the 1980s and has become central to the redesign of social policies in the 21st century.

As life expectancy increased over the 20th century, the proportion of the population aged 65 and over also rose. In Australia those aged 65 and over grew from 4.0 per cent in 1901 to 12.6 per cent of the population in 2002. Demographic projections indicate further increases, to almost one in five people in 2021, and then to over one in four by 2051 (see Table 40.3). As in other developed nations, the increase reflects not only the extension of life expectancy but also fluctuations in fertility and the long-term trend towards a reduced birth rate. These growth factors are mitigated to some extent by the impact of vigorous immigration programmes that have served to effectively lower the average age of the population

Table 40.2   Life expectancy (years) in New Zealand at birth and at age 65, 1901 to 2004–06

Years	At birth			At age 65		
	Males	Females	Maori[a]	Males	Females	Maori
1901[b]	58.8	63.7		12.9	16.9	
1911	61.9	68.6		14	17.9	
1921	63.4	72.1		15.5	19.2	
1931	69.5	75.2		17.4	20.3	
1950–52	67.2	71.3	54.0	12.8	14.8	10.5
1960–62	68.4	73.8	59.0	12.8	15.5	10.7
1980–82	70.4	76.4	65.1	13.3	17.1	11.3
1995–97	74.4	79.7	66.6	15.6	19.1	11.7
2000–02	76.3	81.1	69.0	16.7	20.0	12.7
2004–06	77.9	81.9		17.8	20.5	

a Comparisons over time and between Maori and non-Maori should be interpreted with caution because of changes in data sources, e.g., a new death registration form was introduced in 1995.
b Data from 1901–31 based on life expectancy of cohort.
Source: Cohort Life Expectancy http://www.stats.govt.nz/analytical-reports/new-zealand-65plus-population.htm, Tables 3.04 and 3.05; Life Expectancy at Selected Ages http://www.stats.govt.nz/analytical-reports/nz-life-tables-2000-2002/default.htm Table 2.01. New Zealand's 65+ Population: A statistical volume (2007) Statistics New Zealand. Based on key employment statistics from OECD Employment Outlook, www.oecd.org/employment/keystatistics

Table 40.3   Proportion of the population in select age groups, Australia, 1901–2101

Age group	Year						
	1901	1947	1971	2002	2021	2051	2101
0–14	35.1	25.1	28.7	20.3	16.1	14.0	13.8
15–64	60.8	66.8	63.0	67.1	64.9	58.9	57.2
65+	4.0	8.1	8.3	12.6	19.0	26.1	28.9

Source: ABS 2006: 114; Table 5.16 in Borowski and Olsberg, 2007. Based on key employment statistics from OECD Employment Outlook, www.oecd.org/employment/keystatistics

(ABS, 2006; Borowski and Olsberg, 2007). The result has been that while the proportion of those aged 65+ grew and that of those aged < 15 fell, the proportion aged 15–64 has remained relatively stable, at around two-thirds of the total population. This is projected to decrease significantly later in the 21st century.

As is apparent from the evidence presented in Tables 40.1 and 40.2, population ageing in Australia and New Zealand has been a gradual process spread across the 20th and 21st centuries. In this way, the Australasian demographic transition is unlike the rapid ageing of the industrialized economies of northern Asia, such as China and Japan, in which a dramatic shift took place within the compressed time span of the final decades of the 20th century. Due, in a large part, to the long-term impact of immigration on the population profiles, the age profile of Australasia is also younger than that of most Western European nations. The age profile of the Australasian populations at present most closely resembles that of the small number of other relatively affluent immigration countries of the United States and Canada (Borowski and Olsberg, 2007). By the mid 21st century, however, Australasia's populations will be very old, like those of most developed nations (Hayward and Zhang, 2001).

The proportion of the population aged 65 or over doubled over the first half of the 20th century, rising in Australia from 4 per cent in 1901 to 8.1 per cent by 1947. Reflecting a lower rate of immigration, this proportion reached around 9 per cent in New Zealand by 1951, having climbed from 4 per cent in 1901. In each country the process of population ageing took place so gradually in the first half of the 20th century that it appears to have been barely an issue for policymakers. The major exception to this in Australia was the preparation of legislation for the *Health and Age Pensions Insurance Act* in 1938, which intended to ensure a minimal level of support would be available for the numbers of older people clearly unable to find employment in the decade of the Great Depression. Due to the diversion of finances to defence in the years immediately following, the law was never enacted (Kewley, 1973) but remains a historic curio that points to an emerging awareness of social policy needs associated with health and ageing. Interestingly, parallel developments also took place in New Zealand in the pre-war years (Saville-Smith, 1993).

Political indifference towards population ageing largely continued through the 1950s, the period perhaps best remembered for the baby boom that followed World War II. As a result of the increased numbers of births, the proportion of older people in Australia actually fell from 8.5 per cent of the total population in 1966 to 8.3 per cent in 1971 (Borowski and Olsberg, 2007). Nevertheless, further steps towards the identification of the aged as a distinct population group were taken in the health field with the incremental development of a separate aged care service system in the 1950s. This commenced in Australia under Prime Minister Robert Menzies, who led a Conservative national government. As hospitals began to specialize in high-technology acute care, a need for separate facilities for older, chronically ill patients became apparent. Aged care services, along with the first national health insurance programmes, were path-breaking initiatives insofar as the national, rather than the state governments, took prime responsibility (Fine and Stevens, 1998).

Developments in the late-20th century

Population ageing began to be acknowledged as a significant concern to governments in both New Zealand and Australia in the final two decades of the 20th century. By the 1980s, economic restructuring that flowed from the breaking of traditional links to the British economy saw the potential costs of support for large aged populations an increasing preoccupation of policymakers. As the national economies of Australasia were opened up to global competition in the 1980s and 1990s, many of the traditional public monopolies were corporatized or privatized, with the entitlements of the ageing population cited by academics and governments as a key justification for restructuring (Thomson, 1991). Social policy moved from an emphasis on nationally funded public assistance pensions and service supports to ones based on an ideology of self-provision in old age. This was most keenly expressed in the field of income support, but was also evident in other fields of social policy such as aged care, health care, and housing. The new policy directions being pursued have served to mark out the dependent aged population as a threat to future national well-being and have sought to restructure policies to encourage self-provisioning and to ensure that claims on public resources remained manageable.

Despite consistently high rates of immigration, demographic prospects changed dramatically with a decline of the birth rate in the late 1960s and 1970s. As those who had migrated to Australasia grew older, the initial effects of the mass post-war immigration programmes that delayed the effects of population ageing ceased to have this impact (Davey, 2003; McDonald and Kippen, 1999). As shown in Tables 40.1 and 40.2, the population profile shifted at this time from a comparatively young population to that of an older, declining one (Pollard and Pollard, 1981; Rowland, 2003). Political attention to the issue of population ageing emerged in response to the financial pressures that arose from income support programmes. Changes that loosened the eligibility test for the Age Pension in Australia in 1969, 1973, 1975, and 1978, marked the beginning of what has been called 'a fundamental shift in the widely accepted role of the age pension' (Borowski and Olsberg, 2007: 193).

A consequence of the new interest was an awakening of policy interest in the broader issue of population ageing. This was a key feature of Australian debates around the introduction of national superannuation in the mid-1980s, under the (Bob) Hawke Labour government (Borowski and Olsberg, 2007; Clare and Tulpule, 1994) and was again invoked by the newly elected John Howard Conservative coalition government in 1996 in an audit-based review of public finance (NCA National Commission of Audit, 1996). In each case, a well-publicized case was made for sweeping fiscal and financial reforms to protect the future Australian government and economy. A number of other reviews of the implications of population ageing were also undertaken by sections of the Commonwealth government.

These exercises became institutionalized through the Howard government's *Charter of Budget Honesty Act 1998*, which required publication of an 'intergenerational report' to assess the 'long-term sustainability of current Government policies over the 40 years' (Treasury: 2002: ii) following the report's publication, taking account of the financial implications of demographic change. The first *Intergenerational Report* (IGR1), released in 2002, was based on an assessment of government finances and the prospects of the

Australian economy, combined with projections of Australia's ageing population over the following four decades. This reported that while the current economy provided a sound basis for strong future economic growth:

> A steadily ageing population is likely to continue to place significant pressure on Commonwealth government finances. In addition, on the basis of recent trends it seems likely that technological advancement, particularly in health care, and the community's expectation of accessing the latest health treatments will continue to place increased demands on taxpayers' funds.
>
> (Treasury, 2002: 1)

The projections and calculations presented in the IGR1 report were then used to provide a rationale for the government's existing priorities intended to enable strong economic growth to sustain revenue generation capacities while reducing growth in government spending. To this end, a number of key priorities were nominated. These included:

- maintaining a balanced public budget;
- developing an 'efficient and effective medical health system, complemented by widespread participation in private health insurance' (Treasury, 2002: 1);
- containing growth in the Pharmaceutical Benefits Scheme (PBS)[1] through increased user charges;
- requiring increased payments by residents of the residential aged care system and through the use of market mechanisms in social programmes;
- preserving a targeted 'social safety net' that encourages working-age people to seek employment and remain employed;
- supporting the participation of older people in the labour force;
- maintaining a retirement incomes policy that promotes private saving for retirement and reduces future demand for the (publicly funded) Age Pension (Treasury, 2002).

In short, the ageing population was portrayed as a reason for entrenching and extending the use of market-based approaches to social policy, and particularly in the health sectors of both countries (Ashton, 2000; Howe, 2000).

These issues and the effects of demographic change on future economic growth continued to be reviewed in other major speeches, reports, and budget papers, including the consultative document, *Australia's Demographic Challenges,* released in 2004, and the research report from the Productivity Commission, *Economic Implications of an Ageing Australia* (2006). A second *Intergenerational Report* (IGR2) was released in April 2007 (Treasury, 2007). The conclusions were more optimistic than in IGR1, reflecting both the more positive results from projections and demographic assumptions underpinning the conclusions, and the impact that a long resources boom had had on the Australian economy. The following extract from the executive summary of IGR2 provides a synopsis of the link between social and economic policy and population ageing that the Australian Treasury sees for the first five decades of the 21st century:

> Over the next 40 years, the ageing of the popula-
> tion (specifically the impact of relatively fewer
> people of traditional working age) is projected to
> slow economic growth, with real GDP per person
> rising more slowly than in the past 40 years: 1.6
> per cent per year on average over the next 40
> years compared with 2.1 per cent over the past 40
> years... . At the same time, spending pressures in
> areas such as health, age pensions, and aged care
> are projected to rise, due to demographic and
> other factors... . As a consequence, net debt is
> projected to re-emerge and rise rapidly, reaching
> around 30 per cent of GDP by 2046–47.
>
> (Treasury, 2007: vii)

Demographic challenges continued to be acknowledged. The tone and conclusion of the review were nonetheless more optimistic than previous reports. The optimism reflects the experience of successful economic growth and fiscal management, along with the acknowledgement that support for older people must remain a key electoral strategy. In contrast to the earlier rhetoric of the prohibitive costs of population ageing, a series of initiatives saw budgetary generosity extended on an unprecedented scale in the form of financial concessions to those middle- and high-income earners commonly referred to as 'self-funded retirees'. The reforms, referred to as 'Simpler Super', provided for the exemption of superannuation pensions and the old-age pension from tax for all Australian citizens aged 60 or over, as well as the abolition of tax on lump sum payments. The generous treatment of contributions to private pension (superannuation) saw this form of saving effectively become tax free from July 2007 (Parliamentary Library, 2008). Critics, such as Denniss (2007), argue that the approach, popular with high-income earners, is regressive and inequitable, and that it has a much greater cost to government, in terms of taxation forgone, than increasing payments through the old-age pension.

Policies in New Zealand

Across the Tasman Sea, New Zealand's experience shows significant parallels in the emergence of a political and policy awareness of the impacts of an ageing population. Saville-Smith (1993) outlined the early recognition at the end of the 19th century of the need for old-age pensions and support for health and care services in what was then a very young country. In the post-war period, New Zealand had its version of a clearly marked baby boom, and it has been the ageing of this cohort that has largely driven the growing consciousness of age-related issues (Pool et al., 2003, 2007).

Koopman-Boyden's 1993 collection of contributions exploring the implications of *New Zealand's Ageing Society*, considered three main areas of policy – housing, income support, and health care – along with family and community services. In each field, significant differentiation within the older population was identified reflecting gender lines and along the divisions arising from Maori cultural background and engagement with the political process. By 2006, a New Zealand group of researchers and policy analysts took a future-looking perspective, envisaging and projecting opportunities and risks arising out of the implications of the ageing of the population. Based on demographic trends and the long-term projections for retirement income, a number of areas were identified as risks: labour market and workforce issues; higher fiscal costs; slower economic growth; shortages in skilled labour; inadequate levels of formal and informal elder care; greater inequality of well-being among older people; and risks arising from policy shifts and discontinuities (Boston and Davey, 2006: 374). On the opportunity side, the researchers identify maximizing the potential of an older population, and celebrating its positive aspects. The extension of life expectancy and the prolongation of active and independent life is a major achievement; the contribution of older people in both the paid workforce and the unpaid family care and community service sectors should be highly valued (Boston and Davey, 2006: 382).

In New Zealand, as elsewhere, the development of an awareness of the financial effects of an ageing population has been accompanied by a parallel recognition of the growing political importance of older voters. Levine and Roberts (1993) chart this historically for New Zealand, but there has been limited analysis of how this has continued in the subsequent period. The issue of the fiscal implications of superannuation has maintained a high profile throughout New Zealand's transition within its electoral system, from a simple majority style of government based on the 'first past the post' system of voting to a mixed-member proportional style that requires complex post-election coalition building.

THE POLITICS OF AGEING

Population ageing presents something of a paradox in the 21st century, at least in liberal democracies such as those of Australasia: on the one side, new and growing costs; on the other, an expanding electorate for governments. Neither can be neglected. Not surprisingly, while there have been significant policy reforms across all portfolio areas in both countries in recent years, policy provisions targeted towards older people have escaped the stigmatization of 'welfare' as well as the ensuing cutbacks that have affected other groups, notably the unemployed, migrants, single parents, and the indigenous population (Disney, 2004). This is not simply the result of the national government responding to demographic statistics and projections. The politics of ageing in Australasia reflects the interplay of interest and pressure groups, particularly the influence of associations of retired persons, pensioners, and various provider organizations in the aged care field, and also the much greater pressures brought to bear by corporate interests concerned with workforce, taxation, and markets (Encel and Ozanne, 2007).

As Encel and Ozanne note, 'grey power' and the 'grey vote' are phrases often invoked by conservative commentators when warning of the negative financial consequences and excessive political impacts that population ageing will have. The criticism simplifies and misrepresents the political power of older voters, however, because it is based on a misrepresentation of the aged as a homogenized and unified interest group. Despite the fact that older voters share a broad age category in common, significant divisions exist that extend well beyond the lifestyle and disability differences evident between the active 'young old' (the third age) and the 'old old', those above 85, who are far more likely to need care. In Australia and New Zealand, differences in lifestyles and political interests are evident, based on many of the same lines of schism that characterize younger voters, including home ownership, source of income, and level of education. These factors are reflected indirectly through voting behaviour, as well as more directly through lobbying and other political campaigns undertaken by aged interest groups.

Electoral research in Australia has found that in recent years a majority of older voters have supported conservative parties, with more than 60 per cent of those aged over 55 voting for the coalition (conservative) parties in two-party preferred terms.[2] This preference is more marked among women than men. Opinion polling also suggests that older electors are less likely than younger voters to change their votes (Borowski and McCormack, 2005). Yet it would be wrong to single older voters out as somehow unique in this regard, as evidence suggests that older voters also appear to be important in changing governments, as occurred in Australia in 2007, when large numbers of older people voted for a new Labour government, matching the mood of the broader electorate.

In many ways, pressure groups involving older people and organized campaigns around issues such as pensions, services, and housing have a greater potential to shape policy than voting behaviour of older voters alone might suggest. Amongst membership organizations representing older people, considerable differences are evident in the political orientation and policy prescriptions. The Australian Pensioners and Superannuants Federation (APSF), of which the membership includes significant numbers of older people reliant on the old-age pension, advocates policies that tend to be more progressive and left-leaning than the Australian Retired Persons Association (ARPA), which is essentially a group composed of wealthier 'self-funded' retirees. National Seniors is a more recently formed and well-organized group that is also widely seen as representing higher-income groups. This latter group is also more active in Queensland than in most other states, as membership politics tends to have a strong local and regional focus. Recent attempts in Australia to form a single membership organization, comparable to the American Association of Retired Persons (AARP) in the United States, have failed (Ozanne, 2007).

CONSTITUTION, POLICY CULTURE, AND POLITICAL DESIGN

Although older people are often portrayed as a sectional interest, population ageing affects nearly all areas of public policy. In identifying and responding to it, Australian and New Zealand governments have placed an emphasis on the costs of supporting an increasingly aged population. Reforms to social policies have, in turn, been conditioned by those taking place as part of the wider processes of economic restructuring associated with globalization and financial deregulation. Domestic politics, particularly the alternating periods of rule by conservative and social democratic governments, have also been important determinants of policy in both countries. The federal structure of Australia, in which constitutional power is divided between the Australian Federal (Commonwealth) and State governments, has made policy complex and restrained implementation of many of the more extreme reforms associated with marketization and the increased use of competition as key components of policy. The more unified, less-complex constitutional structure of New Zealand, in turn, has meant that policy reforms have encountered fewer obstacles. Consequently, New Zealand has tended to be more innovative in social policy than Australia. This openness to change was apparent in the expansion of entitlements in the post-war period, as well as with the introduction of sweeping market-based reforms of social welfare provisions in the 1980s and 1990s, which was markedly more advanced in New Zealand than across the Tasman Sea in Australia where the complexity of parliamentary structures slowed such reform (Alford and O'Neill, 1994; O'Connor et al., 1999).

The New Zealand experience of welfare reconstruction in the late 20th century has attracted significant international attention, and has been well charted by Kelsey (1993; 1995), who captures this process in the title of her book *Rolling Back the Welfare State*. Her analysis highlights the reversal in policy from New Zealand being pioneers in the development of a comprehensive welfare framework, providing 'cradle to the grave' support (Davey, 2003), to becoming pioneers in welfare re- (or de-) construction, 100 years later.

On both sides of the Tasman Sea, governments have sought to promote positive health and social participation through explicit strategies, known by different labels. New Zealand adopted the term 'positive ageing', which first became public language from a 1997 Prime Ministerial Taskforce on Positive Ageing. The Positive Ageing Strategy was launched in 2001 and continues as an annual feature of public policy, reporting at a national and cross-government level, and includes local government (Ministry of Social Development, 2007). The objectives of the Positive Ageing Strategy provide a framework for continuing policy and service development in all sectors. The *Health of Older People Strategy*, for example, is subtitled, *Health Sector Actions to 2010 to Support Positive Ageing* (Ministry of Health, 2002).

In Australia, the term 'positive ageing' has been used alongside that of 'active ageing', which clearly links to the World Health Organization (WHO) ideology (WHO, 2002). The approach has been adopted at both national and state levels. For example, the government of West Australia uses an Active Ageing framework to advance a wide range of strategies for which responsibility is carried out in some instances by state government departments, and in others by contracted non-governmental organizations. The 'Health and Wellbeing' priority set out under the policy framework, for example, supports the 'Depression Initiative', the 'Stay On Your Feet' campaign, and 'Research into Transitional Stages of Ageing' as funded programmes. Unfunded strategies include the 'Statewide Falls Policy', the 'Living Longer Living Stronger' initiative, and the 'Carers Recognition Bill'. Other priority areas are identified as 'Employment and Learning', 'Community Awareness and Participation', 'Protection and Security', and 'Planning and the Built Environment'. The West Australian Active Ageing framework gives expression to the vision for the Active Ageing Strategy, which aims to ensure that: in 10 years' time, increasing numbers of older Western Australians are measurably healthier, more physically active, and growing numbers are valued active participants in the workforce and in community and cultural life. Strong, mutually beneficial intergenerational connections promote a sense of belonging and security. Attitudes to ageing are positive across the community (Department for Communities, Western Australia, 2004).

A culture of sport (many might say sports fanaticism) and a celebration of fitness is shared by New Zealand and Australia. This may reflect the fact that physical fitness was a quality demanded in pioneer societies. It was also through sports such as cricket and rugby union that each country first was able to demonstrate significant achievements on the international stage. Both countries have promoted programmes of active participation by older men and women through a range of mechanisms throughout the 20th century (Grant, 2001). Recreational walking for exercise is perhaps the most common activity, as it needs little in the way of facilities or membership and can be undertaken throughout the year. Lawn bowls is an important team sport amongst older people in both countries, with significant facilities being found in almost every suburb, country town, and village. Other activities widely pursued by older people include sports such as golf, fishing, and sailing in both countries; hiking (referred to locally as tramping) and mountain climbing in New Zealand; and swimming, tennis, and body-surfing in Australia.

Data from an ABS nationwide survey undertaken in 2005–06 show that levels of participation in sport and active recreational activities decline with age. Nonetheless, 50.8 per cent of males and 48.2 per cent of females aged 65 or above participated in organized sport or planned recreation involving strenuous physical activity on a regular basis. This compares with a participation rate of 66 per cent for all men and 65.7 per cent for all women aged over 15. The five most popular activities amongst older people, ranked in terms of the participation rate amongst that age group, were walking for exercise (29.1 per cent), lawn bowls (5.6 per cent), golf (5.4 per cent), aerobics/fitness (5.4 per cent), and swimming (4.2 per cent). Carpet bowls, an activity most common amongst those with mobility limitations, was reported to be played regularly by 1.2 per cent of those aged 65 or above (ABS, 2007: 12). In both countries, the phenomenon of 'grey nomads' is a well-known third age pursuit, as retired couples and individuals travel the country in camper vans and caravans. Health and cultural policies play in on this disposition to activity, promoting 'active ageing' through a range of programmes for seniors – although in both countries there is also criticism of the varying and generally inadequate levels of financial commitment shown to them.

Other systems of concessions, facilities, and legal entitlements provide support for seniors that help sustain the engagement of active citizens. State governments in Australia, for example, have long subsidized public transport for pensioners, extending these concessions to all seniors since the late 1980s. Concessional rates on telephones, household electricity, and gas similarly mitigate the effects of low-income levels in many households. New Zealand's solid stance of universalism has historically not offered targeted subsidies to particular age groups, although the 2008 Budget does introduce some plans to move in this direction. The lifelong learning movement has taken root in both New Zealand and Australia, combining low levels of formal public support with voluntary effort (Rimmer, 2007). Each country introduced anti-discrimination legislation in the late 1970s, providing a minimum level of legal protection against some of the more blatant forms of discrimination, such as forced job loss. Yet those seeking work above the age of 45 continue to report problems in almost all fields of employment (Encel and Ranzijn, 2007). New Zealand has recently been recognized by the OECD (Organization for Economic Co-operation and Development) as having high levels of labour market participation of those in the over 65-year-old age groups, and has not had high levels of so-called 'early retirement' reported in west-European countries (Davey and Cornwall, 2007; see also Chapter 41).

We focus below on the key areas of income support and aged care as brief case studies of the approach to policy development for ageing in Australasia.

INCOME SUPPORT

Income from employment or self-employment remains the main and preferred means of financial support for most individuals and families in Australasia. The necessity to develop income support arrangements for those unable to continue in employment as a result of old age was recognized early in both countries. New Zealand and Australia were amongst the first countries in the world to implement an aged pension as a right of citizenship to those aged 65 or above without an alternative income. Pioneering legislation was introduced in New Zealand in 1898, granting an old-age pension to men aged 65 and women 60 and over, subject to a financial means test (Saville-Smith, 1993). A similar bill was enacted in New South Wales in 1901 and was extended in 1909 in legislation by the new Australian Federal Government that granted an aged pension to eligible Australian citizens (Kewley, 1973). In each instance, a defining feature was the financial means test. Not surprisingly, at the beginning of the 20th century both countries were widely recognized as international leaders in the field of what we now call social policy.

These policies, based on social assistance principles, remain central to the design of retirement income support in both countries in the 21st century. By the mid-1970s, however, eligibility criteria had been loosened in Australia, and what had once been a residual programme targeted at the needy had come to be widely regarded as a social right. Attempts to tighten eligibility, to reduce the cost to government associated with the population ageing at the time, were unpopular and not very successful.

Significant additions to the range of options in each country introduced in the second half of the 20th century provided retirees with important options, at the same time adding markedly to the complexity of income support arrangements arising from what is now commonly described in terms of the three pillars of income support. The Age Pension, now set in Australia at the rate of 25 per cent of average male weekly income, represents a second pillar that operates alongside the first, that of an independent income through earnings or investment. A third pillar, compulsory 'occupational superannuation' (mandatory contributory pensions) for all employees and self-employed, was introduced in the 1980s by the Hawke Labour government (Borowski and Olsberg, 2007; Olsberg, 1997). This requires payment by both employee and employer. Initially funded by employer contributions, set at a level of 3 per cent for each worker whose income was determined by centralized wage fixing processes, this was extended to all employees in 1992 under the *Superannuation Guarantee (SG) Charge Act.* The level of contributions also increased progressively, growing to 9 per cent in 2002. By that year, almost all full-time and three in every four part-time workers were covered.

A feature of the Australian programme of occupational superannuation has been the development of large non-government savings and investment funds, which have grown to become major sources of investment capital for Australia. These funds are operated by non-profit Industry Funds, commonly set up by trade unions, or by private financial bodies, typically controlled by insurance companies and banks (Mann, 2001). As the World Bank pointed out in showcasing Australia's retirement income system, the SG programme has also had a significant effect on the long-term viability of the Australian system of public finance, primarily through the reduction in unfunded commitments to retirement income, which would otherwise have been paid through the old-age pension (World Bank, 1994). Yet significant problems remain. For individuals and couples reliant on compulsory occupational superannuation or the old-age pension, the inadequacy of income replacement continues to constrain lifestyle options in retirement. For government, the limited amounts available through the SG charges mean that a significant proportion of retirees continue to depend on the Age Pension. Unless significant reforms are introduced, the direct cost of retirement income support to the Australian government is projected to rise from 2.5 per cent of GDP (gross domestic product) in 2006–07, to 4.1 per cent in 2036–37, and to continue to rise in subsequent years (Treasury, 2007).

The New Zealand pattern differs from the Australian experience. In particular, the development of large-scale pension funds is markedly less evident in New Zealand. After many years in New Zealand of playing 'political football' on matters of superannuation, particularly between the two major political parties, the establishment of the Office of the Retirement Commissioner (ORC) in 1995 has contributed strongly to a growing bipartisan and public awareness of age-related public policy issues, particular retirement income. As St John and Willmore (2001) have argued, 'Two legs are better than three'. Despite the fact that the New Zealand model for old-age support does not conform to the World Bank's ideal of three pillars, it has been a durable, fiscally responsible, and comprehensive system that merits international attention (Else and St John, 1998). The introduction in 2007 of the *Kiwisaver* scheme further supports the two-pillar approach, with an emergent third pillar mechanism for employer-subsidized superannuation, without the compulsory mechanisms now in place in Australia. The ORC (2008) has given support to a politically neutral voice in the New Zealand arena and their website, information services, and periodic Retirement Income Reviews are highly regarded as promoting a balanced approach to public and private provision for income support in old age.

AGED CARE

In the early years of the 20th century, long-term care for older people was predominantly provided by family members. When this was not available, the indigent were forced to rely on the system of 'indoor-relief' – large, workhouse-like institutions, such as the Lidcombe Homes for Old Men and Old Women that developed in Australia in the 19th century (Dickey, 1980). By World War II, those without family who were old and chronically ill could also be found kept in the public and charitable hospitals, which developed as centres for medical treatment but often served as long-stay facilities for those who could not be cured (Fine and Stevens, 1998). By the 1950s, a specialized system of care services funded by the Commonwealth government began to emerge, based on the development of residential facilities. Public subsidies to both private for-profit and non-profit services became available from 1963 to those who needed long-term support but were unable to receive ongoing care in hospitals. Access was provided to a distinct set of residential care facilities, where the need for care exceeded the capacity of the family to provide support. These are today officially referred to as high- and low-care facilities, but are probably still best known by their more established titles of nursing homes and hostels, the latter sometimes also referred to as 'homes for the aged'.

With slight terminological variation, and in the context of an 'unstable and uncertain policy environment' (Ashton, 2000: 73), New Zealand has also had two levels of residential care throughout the post-war period to the present. Admission must follow 'needs assessment', as well as a form of means testing, to review eligibility for public funding subsidy. Those with a lower level of assessed need (which often includes social support needs with limited clinical health service inputs required) can be cared for in a 'rest home', while 'hospital-level care' is provided for those with a continuing care need that requires 24-hour access to registered nursing staff. Specialist registered facilities for care of people with advanced dementia are also available, but usually only in major centres. Consistent with the incremental age-related prevalence of dementia, a significant proportion of those in residential care have cognitive problems, along with mobility, health, and social care needs.

Attempts have been made in both countries to promote community care, but it was only in the 1980s that an effective national programme of support became available. In Australia this occurred with the development of the Home and Community Care Program (HACC), introduced in 1985. HACC services are generally task-specific, providing specialized forms of assistance such as Meals on Wheels, Local Home Nursing Services, Day Care, and Home Care. Assistance is commonly the responsibility of small, locally-based organizations. Since the 1990s, other innovative aged care services have been developed, including the Community Aged Care Packages (CACP) programme, which provides packages of assistance based on that available in low-level residential care to people who remain in their own home. A similar programme, Extended Aged Care in the Home (EACH) is now also available to provide nursing home levels of service to those who remain at home (AIHW, 2007; Fine, 2007). Despite perceptions of the decline of the family, informal care provided by spouses, partners, and other family members remains by far the most prevalent form of support in the early 21st century, with over 80 per cent of older people requiring assistance receiving it from family members alone (ABS, 2003). As if to reinforce the importance placed on family support, family carers are given strong representation, with carer payments (a public pension payment equivalent to that of the Age Pension) available to those unable to be employed elsewhere due to their care commitments.

The expansion of community care in the 1980s in Australia was part of reforms introduced by the *Labor* government intended to constrain nursing home costs by diverting those who do not need such care into alternative, home- and community-based provisions. These included the introduction of the Aged Care Benchmark of 100 residential care beds per 1000 people aged 70 years or older. This has since been modified to 110 places, including CACP provisions. Other changes included restrictions on access to nursing homes through the introduction of tightened entry criteria and standardized assessment procedures and the implementation of multi-disciplinary Aged Care Assessment Teams (ACATs) to screen applicants for residential care and determine if alternative and less costly provisions might be feasible. The *Aged Care Reform Strategy,* as the approach was known, provided an expanded range of services to people who required support to remain living independently in their own homes. The funding of residential care is met by the Australian government, while the HACC programme is shared by the Commonwealth and State governments

(Gibson, 1998; Howe, 1997; Kendig and Duckett, 2001).

In New Zealand, the promotion of community care, particularly through the development of home-based services such as Home Care, follows clearly from the concept of 'ageing-in-place' as defined in the Positive Ageing Strategy of 2001 (Schofield et al., 2006). The Health of Older People Strategy (Ministry of Health, 2002) was developed as a national plan, with a goal of achieving an 'integrated continuum of care' by 2010. To a large extent, this plan became diverted by concurrent and continuing restructuring in the public health sector, described by the various writers in Gauld (2003) as 'continuity amid chaos', as funding for health service delivery to older people was devolved to New Zealand's 21 District Health Boards according to a population-based formula.

Nevertheless, throughout this period there have been continuing national attempts to retain consistent policy messages. For example, there have been reviews and updates of the eligibility for residential care subsidy through:

- asset and income testing amendments;
- the development of and support for restorative models in home care delivery;
- increments in the funding for wage rates and training of care workers, in both home and residential care;
- moves to standardization and national consistency in needs assessment;
- systematic analysis of evidence for 'best practice' in key aspects of health service delivery for older people

The 2008 Budget outlined a 4 year programme of national implementation of the Guidelines for Assessment Processes for Older People (New Zealand Guidelines Group, 2003), which includes adoption of the MDS-HC (Minimum Data Set-Home Care) as a key component of national quality improvement in this sector.

In both New Zealand and Australia, public funding supplemented by limited or regulated charges to service users is a key feature of aged care. In Australia, attempts were made by the Howard government, elected in 1996, to reduce and restructure the extent of the Commonwealth's financial commitment to aged care by extending the commercialization of residential aged care services and increasing direct payments by service users (Fine and Chalmers, 2000). These met with limited success. Plans requiring most users to contribute entry payments for high-level residential care services equivalent to the cost of their family home (comparable to the 'accommodation bonds' that had been charged to long-term residents of low-level residential care) led to a public outcry when they were implemented in October 1997. Guidelines were subsequently changed to enable new residents to pay a means tested daily fee rather than a single large entry payment, maintaining and extending the principle of consumer co-funding of services, but reducing the financial benefit to nursing home owners that large contributions from residents on entry would have involved. In a move that many regard as encouraging the development of a publicly supported market, contracts for the provision of HACC services are increasingly being put to competitive tender from 2004 (Productivity Commission, 2006).

To assess the capacity of government to cover the additional costs of aged care associated with population ageing, the Hogan Review was commissioned in 2002 by the Howard government. It concluded that 'the Australian Government will not be able to maintain its share of responsibility for the funding of aged care services for older people ... without running up significant deficits' (Hogan, 2004: 116). The Review suggested that there was a strong case to tighten means testing of incomes and to make a number of other changes that would effectively increase the total contribution of most service users and open it up to make it a much more deregulated market in which a number of corporate players compete. Government would continue to have a role, but its role in funding would be much more limited than at present, reduced to providing a welfare safety net for a small number of older people without assets, income, or any personal capacity to pay (Hogan, 2004: 117–29). Changes of this magnitude were not implemented by 2007 and are no longer under consideration.

As the need for care increases strongly with age, the increase in the numbers of people aged 85 and above (the 'old old'), which well exceeds the level of growth of all older people, is of most concern in terms of the future need for care. One of the greatest of these challenges is to meet the significant increase in the demand for long-term care and the increased need for skilled and dedicated staff that this entails (Department of Health and Ageing (DHA), 2005; Hugo, 2007). Despite mixed evidence of trends in disability, the numbers of people needing ongoing care will increase significantly, although some results point to a possible modest reduction in the prevalence of disability. Others suggest stability or even a possible increase in prevalence (Fine, 2007: 105–40; Freedman et al., 2004; Jacobzone et al., 1998). Even assuming a reduction in the age-specific disability rates of 0.25 per cent a year, projections show that the need for care will continue to increase sharply as a result of the high rates of growth of the population of 'old old' with its higher rates of disability (Hogan, 2004: 89).

Hugo has calculated that in Australia, in order to meet demand for aged care accommodation alone, the numbers of nursing staff and direct care workers in 2003 will need to double by 2011, and increase by over 300 per cent by 2021 and 400 per cent by 2031 (Hugo, 2007). A problem in both countries has been the low wage rates paid to staff in aged care services. For New Zealand, there has been a long-standing recognition that the low pay rates within the care sector, as part of gender equity in employment (Burns et al., 1999), has continued to be a factor working against recent attempts to maintain a well-trained workforce, building both quality and capacity. At a time in which competition from other industries for staff will be at unprecedented levels, it is not known how, or whether, the need for many more personnel will be met. Current reviews of workforce planning linked to the *National Aged Care Workforce Strategy* (DHA, 2005) in Australia, together with data modelling studies projecting increasing shortages of informal carers (Jenkins et al., 2003; Percival and Kelly, 2004), indicate the importance attached to this topic. Formal figures on the availability of informal carers are elusive for New Zealand, but the situation appears to be comparable in both countries – with future population ageing the availability of informal care will decrease.

CONCLUSION

This analysis and presentation has drawn together parallel social policy trends and developments, reflecting some shared circumstances arising from geographic and post-colonial forces throughout the 20th century, while accented by significant points of divergence and difference between the two major countries of Australasia.

As these populations age, policies intended to provide for the future are being shaped and reconfigured by the exigencies of exposure to international markets. Despite the attractions of European social models, outcomes are determined by the realities of history as laid out in the existing policy frameworks. But exposure to a competitive globalized economy is loosening the conditions set out through the institutions of government and society and developed over the past two centuries. The outcomes for the peoples of New Zealand and Australia who age in the 21st century will be shaped not only by the success of responses to climate change but also by the impact of the parallel responses to demographic change in the South West Pacific.

NOTES

1 The Pharmaceutical Benefits Scheme is a programme, introduced in the late 1940s, through which significant pharmaceutical products are reviewed and made available to the public at heavily subsidized prices. The programme is particularly significant for older people, amongst whom a high proportion rely on ongoing medication (for more detail, see AIHW, 2008: 383)

2 Preferential voting is used in Australia. This ensures the winning candidate in each electorate receives a majority of all votes, either as first choice of each voter or in 'two-party preferred' terms as preferences are allocated from other candidates.

REFERENCES

ABS (2003) *Disability, Ageing and Carers: Summary of Findings*. Cat No. 4330.0. Canberra: Australian Bureau of Statistics.

ABS (2005) *Deaths, Australia 2005.* Cat No. 3302.0. Canberra: Australian Bureau of Statistics.

ABS (2006) *Population Projections*. Cat No. 3222.0. Canberra: Australian Bureau of Statistics.

ABS (2007) *Participation in Sports and Physical Recreation, Australia 2005-06*. Cat No. 4177.0. Canberra: Australian Bureau of Statistics.

AIHW (2007) *Australia's Welfare 2007*. Canberra: Australian Institute of Health and Welfare, AusInfo.

AIHW (2008) *Australia's Health 2008*. Cat. No. AUS 99. Canberra: Australian Institute of Health and Welfare.

Alford, J. and O'Neill, D. (eds) (1994) *The Contract State*. Geelong: Centre for Applied Social Research, Deakin University.

Ashton, T. (2000) 'New Zealand: long-term care in a decade of change', *Health Affairs,*19(3): 72–85.

Borowski, A. and McCormack, J. (2005) 'The contemporary politics of ageing: the 2004 federal election', paper presented at the annual conference of the Australian Association of Gerontology, Surfers' Paradise, November.

Borowski, A. and Olsberg, D. (2007) 'Retirement income policy for a long-lived society', in A. Borowski, S. Encel, and E. Ozanne (eds), *Longevity and Social Change in Australia.* Sydney: UNSW Press, pp. 189–218.

Boston, J. and Davey, J. (eds) (2006) *Implications of Population Ageing: Opportunities and Risks*. New Zealand: Institute of Policy Studies, Victoria University of Wellington.

Burns, J., Dwyer, M., Lambie, H., and Lynch, J. (1999) *Homecare Workers: A Case Study of a Female Occupation.*

Gender Earnings Gap Research Series. Wellington, NZ: Ministry of Women's Affairs.

Castles, F. (1985) *Working Class and Welfare*. North Sydney: Allen and Unwin.

Castles, F. and Mitchell, D. (1990) *Three Worlds of Welfare Capitalism or Four?* Public Policy Program, Discussion Paper No. 21. Canberra: Australian National University.

Clare, R. and Tulpule, A. (1994) *Australia's Ageing Society.* Economic Planning Advisory Council Background Paper No. 37. Canberra: Australian Government Publishing Service.

Cotter, P., Anderson, I., and Smith, L.R. (2007) 'Indigeneous Australians: ageing without longevity', in A. Borowski, S. Encel, and E. Ozanne (eds), *Longevity and Social Change in Australia.* Sydney: UNSW Press, pp. 65–98.

Davey, J. (2003) *Two Decades of Change in New Zealand: From Birth to Death 5.* New Zealand: Institute of Policy Studies, Victoria University of Wellington.

Davey, J. and Cornwall, J. (2007) *Maximising the Potential for Older Workers*. http://www.victoria.ac.nz/nzira/publications/recent_publications.aspx. (Accessed October 30, 2008).

Denniss, R. (2007) 'Crisis of cash or crisis of confidence: the costs of ageing in Australia', *Journal of Australian Political Economy,* June (59): 30–47.

Denoon, D., Mein-Smith, P., and Wyndham, M. (2000) *A History of Australia, New Zealand, and the Pacific.* Blackwell History of the World Series. Oxford: Blackwell Publishers.

Department for Communities, Western Australia (2004) *Active Ageing Strategy. Generations Together: 2004–2008 Report.* Government of Western Australia, Perth. http://www.community.wa.gov.au/NR/rdonlyres/2AF5F433-C008-4E2D-BC8D-8A141D965A9C/0/Active AgeingStrategy_Report20042008.pdf. (Accessed October 30, 2008).

DHA (2005) *National Aged Care Workforce Strategy.* Aged Care Workforce Committee. Canberra: Department of Health and Ageing.

Dickey, B. (1980) *No Charity There: A Short History of Social Welfare in Australia.* Melbourne: Thomas Nelson.

Disney, J. (2004) 'Social policy', in R. Manne (ed.), *The Howard Years*. Melbourne: Black Ink Agenda, pp. 208–10.

Ellison-Loschmann, L. and Pearce, N. (2006) 'Improving access to health care among New Zealand's Maori population', *American Journal of Public Health,* 96(4): 612–17.

Else, A. and St John, S. (1998) *A Super Future? The Price of Growing Older in New Zealand.* Auckland: Tandem Press.

Encel, S. and Ozanne, E. (2007) 'The politics of ageing', in A. Borowski, S. Encel, and E. Ozanne (eds), *Longevity and Social Change in Australia.* Sydney: University of New South Wales Press, pp. 296–315.

Encel, S. and Ranzijn, R. (2007) 'Age and employment', in A. Borowski, S. Encel, and E. Ozanne (eds), *Longevity and Social Change in Australia.* Sydney: University of New South Wales Press, pp. 142–66.

Fine, M. (2007) 'Uncertain prospects: aged care policy for a long-lived society', in A. Borowski, S. Encel, and E. Ozanne (eds), *Longevity and Social Change in Australia*. Sydney: University of New South Wales Press, pp. 265–95.

Fine, M. and Chalmers, J. (2000) 'User pays and other approaches to the funding of long term care for older people in Australia', *Ageing and Society*, 20(1): 5–32.

Fine, M. and Stevens, J. (1998) 'From inmates to consumers: developments in Australian aged care since white settlement', in B. Jeawoddy and C. Saw (eds), *Successful Ageing: Perspectives on Health and Social Construction*. Sydney: Mosby, pp. 39–92.

Freedman, V.A., Crimmins, E., Schoeni, R.F., et al. (2004) 'Resolving inconsistencies in trends in old-age disability: report from a technical working group', *Demography*, 41(3): 417–41.

Gauld, R. (ed.) (2003) *Continuity Amid Chaos: Health Care Management and Delivery in New Zealand*. Dunedin, NZ: University of Otago Press.

Gibson, D.M. (1998) *Aged Care: Old Policies, New Solutions*. Melbourne: Cambridge University Press.

Grant, B. (2001) ' "You're never too old": beliefs about physical activity and playing sport in later life', *Ageing and Society*, 20(6): 777–98.

Hayward, M.D. and Zhang, Z. (2001) 'Demography of aging: a century of global change', in R.H. Binstock and L.K. George (eds), *Handbook of Aging and the Social Sciences*. San Diego: Academic Press, pp. 69–85.

Hetzel, B.S. (2000) 'Historical perspectives on indigenous health in Australia', *Asia Pacific Journal of Clinical Nutrition*, 9(3): 157–63.

Hogan, W. (Chair of Enquiry Task Force) (2004) *Review of Pricing Arrangements in Residential Aged Care*. Canberra: Department of Health and Ageing.

Howe, A. (1997) 'The aged care reform strategy: a decade of changing momentum and margins for reform', in A. Borowski, S. Encel, and E. Ozanne (eds), *Ageing and Social Policy In Australia*. Melbourne: Cambridge University Press, pp. 301–26.

Howe, A. (2000) 'Rearranging the compartments: the financing and delivery of care for Australia's elderly', *Health Affairs*, 19(3): 57–71.

Hugo, G. (2007) 'Contextualising the "crisis in aged care": a demographic perspective', *Australian Journal of Social Issues*, 42(2): 169–82.

Hutchinson, B. (1956) *Old People in a Modern Australian Community: A Social Survey*. Melbourne: Melbourne University Press.

Jacobzone, S., Cambois, E., Chaplain, E., and Robine, J.-M. (1998) *Long Term Care Services to Older People: A Perspective on Future Needs; the Impact of an Improving Health of Older Persons*. Paris: OECD.

Jenkins, A., Rowland, F., Angus, P., and Hales, C. (2003) *The Future Supply of Informal Care, 2003 to 2013: Alternative Scenarios*. Canberra: Australian Institute of Health and Welfare.

Kelsey, J. (1993) *Rolling Back the State: Privatisation of Power in Aotearoa/New Zealand*. Wellington: Bridget Williams Books.

Kelsey, J. (1995) *The New Zealand Experiment: A World Model for Structural Adjustment?* Wellington: Auckland University Press/ Bridget Williams Books.

Kendig, H.L. and Duckett, S. (2001) *Australian Directions in Aged Care: The Generation of Policies for Generations of Older People*. Australian Health Policies Institute, Commissioned Paper Series 2001/05. Sydney: University of Sydney.

Kewley, T.H. (1973) *Social Security in Australia, 1900–1972*, 2nd edn. Sydney: Sydney University Press.

King, M. (2003) *The Penguin History of New Zealand*. Auckland: Penguin Books.

Koopman-Boyden, P.G. (ed.) (1993) *New Zealand's Ageing Society: The Implications*. Wellington: Daphne Brasell Associates Press.

Levine, S. and Roberts, N. (1993) 'Elderly people and the political process', in P.G. Koopman-Boyden (ed.), *New Zealand's Ageing Society: The Implications*. Wellington: Daphne Brasell Associates Press, pp. 230–54.

Mann, K. (2001) *Approaching Retirement: Social Divisions, Welfare and Exclusion*. Bristol: Policy Press.

McDonald, P. and Kippen, R. (1999) *The Impact of Immigration on the Ageing of Australia's Population*. Canberra: Department of Immigration and Multicultural Affairs.

Mein-Smith, P. (2005) *A Concise History of New Zealand*. New York: Cambridge University Press.

Ministry of Health (2002) *The Health of Older People Strategy: Health Sector Actions to 2010 to Support Positive Ageing*. Wellington: Ministry of Health. http://www.moh.govt.nz/publications/hops. Accessed October 30, 2008.

Ministry of Social Development (2006) *Social Report 2006*. Wellington, New Zealand: Ministry of Social Development. http://www.socialreport.msd.govt.nz/comparisons/australia.html. Accessed October 30, 2008.

Ministry of Social Development (2007) *Positive Ageing Indicators Report*. Wellington: Ministry of Social Development.

NCA (1996) *Report to the Commonwealth Government*. Canberra: National Commission of Audit, Australian Government Publishing Service.

New Zealand Guidelines Group (2003) 'Assessment processes for older people: an evidence-based best practice guideline'. http://www.nzgg.org.nz/guidelines/dsp_guideline_popup.cfm?guidelineCatID=32&guidelineID=30. Accessed October 30, 2008 .

O'Connor, J.S., Orloff A.S., and Shaver, S. (1999) *States, Markets, Families. Gender, Liberalism and Social Policy in Australia, Canada, Great Britain and the United States*. Cambridge: Cambridge University Press.

Olsberg, D. (1997) *Ageing and Money: Australia's Retirement Revolution*. Sydney: Allen and Unwin.

ORC (2008) Wellington, New Zealand. http://www.retirement.org.nz/about_us.html. Accessed October 30, 2008.

Ozanne, E. (2007) 'The politics of ageing', paper presented at the Longevity Symposium, Policy Implications of Victoria's Ageing Population, University of Melbourne, November.

Parliamentary Library (2008) *Chronology of Superannuation and Retirement Income in Australia*. Library of the Parliament of Australia, Background note. http://www.aph.gov.au/

library/pubs/BN/2008-09/Chron_Superannuation.htm. Accessed October 30, 2008.

Percival, R. and Kelly, S. (2004) *Who's Going to Care? Informal Care and an Ageing Population.* Report prepared for Carers Australia by the National Centre for Social and Economic Modelling. Canberra: National Centre for Economic and Social Modelling.

Pollard, A.H. and Pollard, G.N. (1981) 'The demography of ageing in Australia', in A.L. Howe (ed.), *Towards an Older Australia.* St Lucia: University of Queensland Press, pp. 13–34.

Pool, I., Dharmalingam, A., Bedford, R., Pole, N., and Sceats, J. (eds) (2003) *Population and Social Policy,* Special Issue of *New Zealand Population Review,* 29(1). Wellington: Population Association of New Zealand.

Pool, I., Dharmalingam, A., and Sceats, J. (2007) *The New Zealand Family from 1840: A Demographic History.* Auckland: Auckland University Press.

Productivity Commission (2006) *Report on Government Services 2006: Part F Community Services.* Melbourne: Australian Government Productivity Commission. http://www.pc.gov.au/gsp/reports/rogs/2006/communityservices. Accessed October 30, 2008.

Rimmer, S. (2007) 'Lifelong education and lifelong learning', in A. Borowski, S. Encel, and E. Ozanne (eds), *Longevity and Social Change in Australia.* Sydney: University of New South Wales Press, pp. 316–33.

Rowland, D. (2003) 'An ageing population: emergence of a new stage of life?', in S. Khoo and P. McDonald (eds), *The Transformation of Australia's Population 1970–2030.* Sydney: University of New South Wales Press, pp. 238–65.

Saville-Smith, K. (1993) 'The state and the social construction of ageing', in P.G. Koopman-Boyden (ed.), *New Zealand's Ageing Society: The Implications.* Wellington: Daphne Brasell Associates Press, pp. 76–94.

Sax, S. (ed.) (1970) *The Aged in Australian Society.* Sydney: Angus and Robertson.

Schofield, V., Davey, J., Keeling, S., and Parsons, M. (2006) 'Ageing in place', in J. Boston and J. Davey (eds), *Implications of Population Ageing: Opportunities and Risks.* Wellington: Institute of Policy Studies, Victoria University of Wellington, pp. 275–306.

St John, S. and Willmore, D. (2001) 'Two legs are better than three: New Zealand as a model for old age pensions', *World Development,* 29(8): 1291–305.

Stoller, A. (ed.) (1960) *Growing Old: Problems of Old Age in the Australian Community.* Melbourne: Cheshire.

Thomson, D. (1991) *Selfish Generations: The Ageing of New Zealand's Welfare State.* Wellington: Bridget Williams Books.

Treasury (2002) *Intergenerational Report, 2002–03.* 2002–03 Budget Paper No. 5. Canberra: Department of Treasury and Finance.

Treasury (2007) *Intergenerational Report 2007.* Canberra: Department of Treasury, Australia. http://www.treasury.gov.au/igr. Accessed October 30, 2008.

WHO (2002) *Active Ageing: A Policy Framework.* http://www.who.int/ageing/active_ageing/en/index.html. Accessed October 30, 2008.

World Bank (1994) *Averting the Old Age Crisis.* New York: Oxford University Press.

41

Cross-National Trends in Work and Retirement

Philip Taylor

INTRODUCTION

This chapter examines the changing face of work and retirement as governments and employers face up to the prospect of ageing workforces.[1] Labour force ageing is high on the agenda of policymakers in most developed countries, and is a frequent topic of academic and media debate. The virtues of older workers are now extolled against a background of a predicted crisis of social security systems resulting from population ageing and the supposed dependency burden this will place on a dwindling number of younger people (OECD, 2006a).

Demographic, economic, social, and political trends in many societies are encouraging the public and other policymakers and interested citizens to develop and propagate the notion of 'active ageing' (WHO, 2002). This chapter reviews the current status of policymaking concerned with age and employment and how this needs to be adapted to align with the varied circumstances and characteristics of different individuals and societies. It considers trends in the employment of older workers, how policymakers are envisioning a flexible end to working life, and their prospects of success in selected countries (Australia, Finland, Germany, Japan, the Netherlands, and the United States), drawing upon the findings of a number of research projects.[2] This is supplemented by analysis of waves of the European Working Conditions Survey (EWCS)[3] that examines trends and preferences in terms of part-time working among older workers. The chapter begins with a brief discussion of population ageing and the labour market situation of older workers in each country, before moving on to analyze developments in public policy. It concludes by setting out some principles for the development of public policy on age and work, specifically as it concerns later-life transitions.

CHANGING PERSPECTIVES ON THE PLACE OF OLDER WORKERS IN LABOUR MARKETS

In order to properly understand the present situation of older workers, and to fully appreciate how public policy shapes their lives, some context is required. A policy development since the late 1990s has concerned the idea of prolonging working lives, presented as a means of reducing pressures on social welfare systems (Chiva and Manthorpe, 2008; Loretto et al., 2007; Smeaton and Vegaris, 2009). This approach contrasted with public policy in the 1970s and 1980s that focused on the need to remove older workers from the labour market to reduce high unemployment among younger workers and other social groups.

In the 1980s and 1990s, the restructuring of Western industrialized economies was accompanied by a dramatic fall in labour force participation rates among older workers (Kohli et al., 1991). Until recently, public policies in many countries, particularly in Western Europe, fostered (often deliberately) early retirement, while labour market policy was aimed almost exclusively at tackling youth unemployment (Gruber and Wise, 1999). Early retirement, for labour market reasons, took various forms and was frequently encouraged by the social actors involved. Some industrial countries provided generous early retirement benefits, contributing to a certain sense of voluntarism among those taking them. By contrast, in other countries, 'early retirement' was experienced as a form of unemployment (Casey and Laczko, 1989). The result has been the emergence, in many European countries, of an expectation of early retirement, with older workers experiencing the devaluation of their skills in the workplace. According to Guillemard and Argoud (2004: 177–8), in France, 55 has become 'the normal age for definitively leaving the labour market', with workers in their 40s now viewed as 'nearly old' and facing reduced employment prospects. Contrast this situation with the example of post-World War II Britain when reconstruction, economic expansion, and labour shortages resulted in government efforts to promote the employment of older workers (Macnicol, 2006; Tillsley and Taylor, 2001).

The fortunes of older workers have been and continue to be strongly influenced by the ebbs and flows of market forces and government policy. In recent decades, older workers have had a greater likelihood of both losing their jobs and experiencing considerable problems re-entering the labour market. With increasing policy interest in the issue, the question arises as to whether we are on the verge of a new era of employment characterized by a prolongation of working life in organizations newly enlightened as to the benefits of employing and retaining older people. While research certainly points to some interest among older people in retiring later, perhaps while reducing working hours (e.g., Loretto et al., 2005; McNair, 2006), even a cursory glance over many years of research would temper optimism that many older workers have real choice over the circumstances in which they work or retire (McGoldrick and Cooper, 1980; Walker, 1985; Walker and Taylor, 1993), or that the attitudes and practices of employers are undergoing a permanent shift in favour of older workers. Rather, research makes it clear that their prospects depend on to a large extent on market conditions, which should make us sceptical that their improved circumstances will persist if economies experience significant downturns, and raises important questions about the changing position of older workers in a globalizing labour market. They may, in fact, be viewed as a reserve labour force whose prospects are strongly tied to economic fluctuations (Taylor, 2006).

POPULATION AGEING AND THE LABOUR MARKET

As a result of declining or stable fertility rates and an increase in life expectancy, the populations of most nations are set to age markedly over the next 50 years. Table 41.1 shows the increasing proportion of the population aged over 60 and over 65 at various dates for the period from 1980 to 2050 for the countries discussed in this chapter. By 2010, roughly between a fifth and a quarter of the populations of these countries will be aged over 60, with the United States having a somewhat younger age profile and Japan having one that is somewhat older. In the decades that follow, populations will age markedly. This would suggest that the labour forces of these countries will also have a higher proportion of workers drawn from the older age groups.

Table 41.1 Population aged 60 and over 65

Country	Population over 60 (% total pop.)					Population over 65 (% total pop.)				
	1980	2000	2010	2030	2050	1980	2000	2010	2030	2050
Australia	13.7	16.2	19.2	26.1	28.4	9.6	12.1	13.4	20.0	22.6
Finland	16.4	19.9	24.6	31.6	31.6	12.0	14.9	17.0	25.3	25.6
Germany	19.3	23.2	25.3	34.4	35.3	15.6	16.4	19.8	26.1	28.4
Japan	12.9	23.1	29.3	34.2	37.6	9.0	17.1	21.5	27.3	31.8
Netherlands	15.7	18.4	22.6	33.4	34.5	11.5	13.8	15.8	25.6	28.1
UK	20.1	21.0	23.5	30.0	31.3	15.1	16.0	17.1	23.1	24.9
USA	15.6	16.4	18.7	26.4	27.8	11.2	12.5	13.2	20.6	21.7

Source: World Labour Report 2000, ILO

Population ageing has run alongside continuing problems faced by older workers in the labour markets of the main industrialized economies. Their position is summarized in a review of OECD (Organization of Economic Co-operation and Development) countries that drew the following conclusions:

- Labour market mobility in terms of new hires is lower for older workers.
- While rates of job loss are similar for younger and older workers, the latter are more prone to experience long-term unemployment.
- Shift to economic inactivity is generally permanent across older age groups (OECD 2006a: 36–8).

On the other hand, there is also evidence that, after decades of increasingly early labour market withdrawal, important changes are underway. Table 41.2 shows trends in labour force participation rates among older men and women in selected countries between 1979 and 2007, with 15 countries of the European Union (EU-15) included as a further point of comparison. As noted above, 'early retirement', or 'early exit', as it is often described (Kohli et al., 1991), has been a significant feature of the labour market experiences of older workers. For example, in Australia and the European countries, there was a substantial decline in labour force participation (those classified as employed or unemployed) rates among older men. While there has also been a downward trend in the United States, this has been less marked. In Japan, there has been a slight decline, although from a higher level of participation. However, importantly, there is evidence that this decline went into reverse, and markedly so in three of the selected European countries – Finland, Germany, and the Netherlands – in the period from the mid-1990s up to the economic recession beginning in 2008. In Australia and the United States, increases since

the mid-1990s have been more modest, although starting from a much higher level than these European countries. A notable feature of participation rates for older workers is that despite an upturn in some countries, levels are only just returning close to those of 1979. The figures for the EU-15 also illustrate why the European Union has implemented a number of policy initiatives concerning prolonging working life in recent years, including the European Equal Treatment Directive, and the Barcelona and Stockholm targets for the employment of older workers (European Council 2001, 2002).

Table 41.2 also shows that labour force participation among older women is increasing. However, as with men, it also shows that their participation among the European countries took a considerable period of time to get close to that of Japan and the United States. In Australia, labour force participation among older women has more than doubled since 1979. However, it is also important to point out that much of this shift in patterns of older female participation represents a cohort effect of increasing female labour force participation overall, which has tended to mask early exit among women.

Declining labour force participation among older workers has been attributed to a number of economic, political, and social factors. Older men have been over-represented in industries which have either become more capital-intensive, or from which jobs have been exported, and under-represented in industries experiencing employment and/or output growth (Jacobs et al., 1991; Jorgensen and Taylor 2008; Trinder, 1989). During periods of economic expansion and contraction, when labour demand has tended to grow and recede, the status of older workers has altered accordingly. In programmes of downsizing, older workers are affected disproportionately (Leppel and Heller Clain, 1995), and during recessions, early retirement has been used to tackle youth

Table 41.2 Labour force participation rates among men and women aged 55–64 between 1979 and 2007

Country	Men						Women					
	1979	1983	1990	1995	2000	2007	1979	1983	1990	1995	2000	2007
Australia	69.5	62.0	63.2	60.8	61.2	67.8	20.3	20.5	24.9	28.6	36.1	48.8
Finland	56.3	54.1	47.1	41.6	48.1	59.2	41.3	47.4	40.8	42.9	45.2	58.3
Germany	66.9	63.1	55.9	52.7	52.4	65.8	28.4	26.3	24.7	28.1	33.5	48.9
Netherlands	65.3	54.2	45.8	41.4	50.8	63.3	14.4	14.4	16.8	18.6	26.4	41.1
Japan	85.2	84.7	83.3	84.8	84.1	84.9	45.4	46.1	47.2	48.5	49.7	52.5
UK	–	71.5	68.1	62.4	63.3	68.9	–	–	38.7	40.8	42.6	50.1
USA	72.8	69.4	67.8	66.0	67.3	69.6	41.7	41.5	45.2	49.2	51.9	58.3
EU-15	–	–	55.4	51.5	53.0	58.4	–	–	25.7	27.0	31.0	40.4

Source: OECD Employment Outlook (various)

unemployment (Kohli et al., 1991; Trinder, 1989). Several factors may explain higher labour force participation among Japanese older workers. These include the possibility of receiving a pension while working, low-income replacement rates from receiving a pension as opposed to earnings from work, and improving health among older people (Koshiro, 1996).

In 2001, the European Council of Stockholm defined a quantitative and highly ambitious target by determining that by the year 2010 the employment rate of older workers (aged 55–64) should be 50 per cent (it was 26.3 per cent in 2000) (European Council, 2001). Table 41.3 shows trends in employment/population ratios[4] among men and women aged 55–64. It demonstrates progress in Europe, but a wide gap between it and Japan and the United States. Regarding men, Finland, Germany, and the Netherlands have experienced substantial increases in employment/population ratios between 1995 and 2007, albeit to levels that are only just returning to those of the early 1980s in the case of Germany and the Netherlands. In the United Kingdom, the pattern is the same, but the increase is more modest. In Japan, rates have remained steady. Regarding women, Finland, Germany, and the Netherlands have experienced marked increases in employment/population ratios since 1995. In the United Kingdom and the United States, increases in female employment rates have been less dramatic, with a largely stable picture in the case of Japan.

A NEW CONSENSUS ON 'ACTIVE AGEING'

In recent times, early retirement has largely been rejected, with the aim of extending working lives now being a major policy objective in many countries, even if the extent and pace of reform

varies significantly (European Commission, 2003). In policy circles, a new consensus is emerging around the notion of 'active ageing', which was defined by the World Health Organization as 'the process of optimizing opportunities for health, participation and security in order to enhance quality of life as people age' (WHO, 2002: 12). According to the OECD (1998), this will necessitate a greater emphasis on prevention, making inexpensive policy interventions at an earlier life stage, and thereby reducing the need for later remedial action. Earlier interventions facilitate actions that are less fragmented and that are concentrated at critical transition points in life and also enable less constrained choices and greater responsibility at the level of individuals. It has been argued that a common strategic framework for reform is needed, as changes in one area can offset reforms in another and may also cut across traditional programme boundaries (Auer and Fortuny, 2000).

The following sections briefly consider, first, the evolution of national-level public policy towards older workers; secondly, how closely these policies match OECD objectives, and, thirdly, evidence on the effects of policy towards older workers.

PUBLIC POLICIES TOWARDS OLDER WORKERS

Population ageing and how it will influence future labour supply features prominently in European, Japanese, and Australian debates about economic stability, growth, and social welfare. The significance of changing demography for developed economies and the policy responses has also been questioned, with some commentators (e.g. Mullan, 2002; Sigg, 2005) highly sceptical that it will be the harbinger of the kinds of economic and social

Table 41.3 Employment/population ratios among men and women aged 55–64 between 1979 and 2007

Country	Men						Women					
	1979	1983	1990	1995	2000	2007	1979	1983	1990	1995	2000	2007
Australia	67.4	59.6	59.2	55.3	58.3	65.9	19.8	19.9	24.2	27.4	35.3	47.5
Finland	54.3	51.4	46.3	34.9	43.7	55.1	39.0	44.1	39.7	33.1	40.9	54.8
Germany	63.2	57.4	52.0	47.2	46.4	59.4	26.8	24.0	22.4	24.4	29.0	43.4
Netherlands	63.2	46.1	44.5	39.9	49.9	60.4	14.0	13.2	15.8	18.0	25.8	39.6
Japan	81.5	80.5	80.4	80.8	78.4	81.5	44.8	45.1	46.5	47.5	47.9	51.2
UK	–	64.3	62.4	56.1	59.8	66.1	–	–	36.7	39.3	41.4	49.0
USA	70.8	65.2	65.2	63.6	65.7	67.4	40.4	39.4	44.0	47.5	50.6	55.6
EU-15	–	–	52.3	47.2	48.9	55.1	–	–	24.3	25.6	28.4	38.1

Source: OECD Employment Outlook (various)

catastrophes as some foresee (e.g., Jackson, 2002).

Nevertheless, among the countries highlighted in this chapter, there is a broad consensus on the economic and social benefits of extending working lives via the closing of early retirement pathways, along with the encouragement of and support for later working (OECD, 2006a). Demographic change and the associated issue of how to control the financing of public pension systems have been central to this, but other factors have come into play: first, a shift of responsibility in areas such as early retirement and pension provision from employers towards the individual; secondly, concerns about skills and labour shortages; thirdly, evidence that early retirement schemes created few job opportunities for younger workers; fourthly, a general move from passive to active labour market policies; and finally, a growing recognition of the problem of age discrimination in labour markets (Macnicol, 2006; OECD, 2006a; Taylor, 2002, 2006; World Bank, 1994). At the same time, there are factors working against the reintegration of older workers: for example, relatively high levels of youth unemployment in some countries, increasing levels of work intensity, and the persistence of an early exit culture, resulting in continuing pressure for early retirement (Taylor, 2006).

The logic and utility of early retirement started to be questioned in the mid-1990s as policymakers, concerned with economic competitiveness and looking ahead to a worsening social welfare burden due to demographic ageing, began to turn to older workers to once again take their place among the workforce. Signalling a sharp diversion from the recent past, outwent supposedly outmoded beliefs concerning the benefits of early retirement. Instead, extending working lives became the policy objective (Phillipson, 2006).

A range of measures, at the level of the firm and individual, are aiming to encourage later retirement, promote skills acquisition, and generally improve the employability of older workers. The measures adopted include efforts to limit the extent of early exit, making the drawing of a pension only possible at later ages, and providing incentives for deferring the receipt of a pension. Central to current debates about working later is the notion of flexible retirement, characterized as a gradual letting go rather than an abrupt severing of the link between employee and employer, often in the form of part-time working. This has been presented as providing major advantages for governments, business, and older workers, with the potential to allow organizations to retain talented individuals for longer periods and to enable a gradual withdrawal from the labour market. Individuals obtain the benefits of reducing hours

and retaining an attachment to the labour market. For governments, the benefits are also clear – increased tax revenues and reduced social welfare payments.

In the above context, a number of new policy approaches are emerging, although the outcome of many remains uncertain. In this section, a number of these are reviewed, drawing on examples from our selected countries. In Australia, the *Pension Bonus Scheme* was introduced in 1998, which provided an additional payment of 9 per cent on top of the standard pension for those remaining in employment beyond age 65. In 2002, this was supplemented by providing a lump sum payment in lieu of the pension increase. To date, take-up has been modest, with a likely reason being that the financial incentive is insufficient to tempt very many people to continue working (Encel, 2008).

Regarding its stance on older workers, Finland has been much lauded in European policy circles for policies such as the *Finnish Programme on Ageing Workers (FINPAW)*. This was a joint initiative of the Ministries of Social Affairs, Labour, and Education, which also involved local authorities, the Social Insurance Institution, the Institute of Occupational Health, and pension companies. The aim of the programme was to address the whole work environment rather than isolated features, developing good practice around retention, as well as adapting employment services to the needs of older workers (Hirsch, 2007). FINPAW was further supported by the introduction of pension reforms in 2005, designed to raise the length of working lives by two to three years through improved incentives to work longer. These work and pension reforms have, however, attracted criticism, for example, from the OECD (2006b) that has emphasized the need to limit pathways to early retirement. In 2004, nearly 7 out of 10 new retirees in Finland left employment early on some form of unemployment or disability benefit. In this context, the OECD (2006b) argue the case for more ambitious employment objectives for Finnish older workers, with unemployment and disability benefits re-focused on their original purpose and not used as instruments for early retirement.

In Germany, in recent years, a range of reforms have focused on raising the age of exit from the labour force, including closing off early exit pathways, increasing the retirement age (to 67 by 2029), and introducing new labour market programmes. Of particular note is the work of the *Hartz Commission*, established in 2002, which bought forward proposals for a radical reform of labour market policy. In particular, the activating policy approach that was proposed emphasized the personal contribution to economic integration on the part of the unemployed. In all, four laws resulting from its activities were implemented (Hartz, I, II, III, and IV) (Frerichs and Taylor, 2005). Modification to unemployment insurance was an important feature of work arising from the Commission. Prior to the Hartz IV reforms, there were three types of support mechanisms. Unemployment insurance provides a relatively generous payment to which an unemployed person is entitled for up to 12 months. Previously, those who remained jobless beyond this period moved on to a special unemployment scheme. Although less generous than the insurance scheme, it was more generous than social welfare and an individual could remain on this programme indefinitely. The third scheme is welfare, the least generous form of provision. Under Hartz IV, the middle layer was abolished such that, after 12 months, the unemployed person moved directly on to welfare, the intention being to increase incentives to search for work. Evidence of a tacit acknowledgement that, given their weaker position in the labour market, some older workers have been severely disadvantaged by this law, comes perhaps from discussions among the Social Democratic Party (SPD), which introduced the reform, extending the eligibility of unemployment pay from 12 to 18 months for those aged 45 and over (Münchau, 2007).

In Japan, legislation passed in 2004 requires that employers actualize extension of employment up to age 65 between 2006 and 2013 (Oka, 2008). The response most commonly adopted in large firms has been to extend employment beyond the mandatory age at 60 but to leave present employment systems largely intact (Fujimura, 2001). Many firms have adopted a system of continued employment after mandatory retirement, although often at the discretion of the employer (see below for one such approach taken by a major Japanese corporation). An inquiry committee of the Ministry of Health, Labour and Welfare recommended in the summer of 2007 that the government's next policy target should be extension of employment to age 70. Also in Japan, an earnings test applied to pension income that discouraged employment after the age of 60 was substantially raised in 1995 (Kimura and Oka, 2001; Koshiro, 1996).

In the Netherlands, firms are moving away from early retirement schemes to pre-pension schemes that are capital funded. The government has emphasized the need to discourage early retirement, especially among those aged 55–65. To achieve this, policy objectives include making paid employment more attractive, preventing involuntary retirement, and giving the responsibility for funding early retirement to individual workers (Ministry for Social Affairs and Employment, undated). One element of this policy

was the ending, in 1999, of an exemption for unemployed people aged 57.5 or over from the requirement to work. They are now required to register at an employment office and must accept suitable employment opportunities (Ministry for Social Affairs and Employment, 2001). However, in response to such initiatives, individuals may simply adjust their retirement planning in order that they still retire early (Taylor, 2002).

In the United Kingdom, the introduction of more generous State Pension deferral options has increased the rewards for working longer,[5] although the number opting to do this has been low (Pensions Commission, 2005). However, there have been calls for greater promotion of its availability, and concern expressed that it might only be accessible to people on middle incomes who can afford to forgo a pension and remain economically active (Select Committee on Work and Pensions, 2006). Also, the earliest age from which a non-State Pension can be taken will increase from 50 to 55 by 2010 (Department for Work and Pensions, 2005). The Pensions Commission (2005) considered the issue of retirement age, concluding that a change to the State Pension Age (SPA) could offset issues arising from population ageing; namely, an increase to 68 (from 65) by the middle of the century and, rising with life expectancy, maintaining the average length of time spent in retirement. In response, Parliament has passed legislation increasing the SPA to 66 by 2026 and 68 by 2046.[6]

In the United States, the age at which a social security pension can be claimed is gradually being raised to 67 with penalties for early retirement.[7] Also, limits on what a person can earn before their benefits are affected have been relaxed, with a gradual increase in the retirement credit paid to workers delaying retirement until age 70 (Rix, 2001). Pension reforms in the United States, particularly the trend towards defined contribution (DC) over defined benefit (DB) plans, is likely to result in much greater heterogeneity in the ages at which people retire. Of course, in the former, the risks associated with possible investment losses lie with the recipients, whereas in the latter, a specific amount is guaranteed by the sponsor (Taylor et al., 2000). People who have made better, or luckier, financial decisions, and are in a position to contribute more to their defined contribution pensions may fair well and be in a position to retire early. On the other hand, others may opt to consume rather than save and end up with less in their DC accounts, thus being forced to work longer, whereas under a DB plan those resources would be protected (Phillipson, 2009; Taylor, 2002). Significant numbers of eligible American workers do not participate in the voluntary 401(k) retirement plans funded through pre-tax payroll deductions, particularly low-income workers (Munnell and Sunden, 2004). Given evidence that access to a DB plan may increase the likelihood of early retirement (Dulitzky, 1999), the DB – DC shift may serve to fulfil the policy objective of prolonging working lives.

Ending mandatory retirement has been an additional policy approach, having the potential to provide older workers with greater choice concerning the timing of their retirement. However, in Australia, the abolition of mandatory retirement in all states by 1999 (Encel, 2000) has apparently had little effect. The rate of involuntary retirement continues as before, with employers finding alternative ways to retire older workers, while the rate of voluntary retirement encouraged by superannuation also continues to be high. In the United States, similarly, in the past few years, there has been a decline in early retirement (before age 65), but this may be due to the elimination of mandatory retirement (since most people retire long before this might become an issue and therefore few are affected) and more to the decline of DB pension schemes.[8]

Although the effect of its removal elsewhere has been slight, and given that few people remain in work beyond their early 60s, the abolition of mandatory retirement ages has been a topic of considerable recent debate in the United Kingdom. After deliberating for some time as part of the process of responding to the European Equal Treatment Directive of 2000, the British government decided on a default retirement age of 65, at which point an individual worker may put a request to their employer that they be allowed to remain in employment. However, while the employer is obliged to consider any request in good faith, it is within their rights to decline. This measure will be subject to review. Meanwhile, the retention of a mandatory retirement age has been challenged legally.[9]

A more flexible approach to retirement has also come in measures to promote gradual retirement. There would appear to be a strong case for policies that offer a phased transition from work to retirement. For employers, gradual retirement allows skill and knowledge retention; for older workers, it may facilitate an easier adjustment to retirement. Yet it has often not had the success its proponents had anticipated. Thus, while Finland has operated a part-time pension, enabling gradual retirement since 1987 (Ilmakunnas and Ilmakunnas, 2006), a number of problems have emerged, including low take-up, high earners benefiting more than other groups, and problems in reorganizing jobs to accommodate part-time pensioners. Taylor (2002) concludes that the net effect on participation rates may be small, given that without this measure roughly equivalent numbers of

workers would have remained in full-time work or exited via full early retirement.

This situation contrasts with Japan, where versions of gradual retirement are common and take-up has been relatively high, although older workers cannot choose whether to switch to another employment contract, in contrast with Finland. An important issue to emerge in Japan is that of institutionalized ageism. The case of a major Japanese manufacturing company is one example of a re-employment scheme implemented in response to the increase in the eligibility age for Japan's public pension. Under this scheme, a relatively low wage on re-employment is supplemented by pension income, leaving an individual better off than if they had retired at 60. Workers can work until age 65, although with annual contract reviews. However, the nature of the scheme appears inconsistent with the principles of active ageing, in that it could be viewed as simply shifting older workers into publicly subsidized, poorly paid work. While it may be a stepping-stone towards later retirement, it may also be said to be ageist, as those over the age of 60 are treated differently from other workers (Taylor et al., 2002).

In Germany, a version of gradual retirement has existed for some time. The official aim of the partial retirement law (Altersteilzeitgesetz [ATG]), which was enacted in 1996, was to ease the transition from work to retirement via a reduction in working time. In the majority of cases it is not used for this purpose, but instead for staff reductions. Most beneficiaries opt for a particular variant, known as the 'block model', which allows them to retire permanently without first reducing their working hours, effectively making it a full early retirement scheme, in line with the wishes of workers and employers. The law is in fact best viewed as a modified instrument for early retirement (Frerichs and Taylor, 2005).

In the United States, the numbers of older workers, particularly women, in some form of 'bridge employment' between a career job and full retirement are significant and growing, although formal company programmes are rare. Thus, workers usually obtain such employment of their own volition. Job mobility is often downward, although not exclusively so (Rix, 2001; Taylor et al., 2000). Cahill et al. (2006), examining retirement patterns among a cohort of retirees aged 51–61 in 1992 during a 10-year period, report that a majority of older Americans with career jobs phase their retirement, rather than ceasing work abruptly. The utilization of bridge jobs was found to be more common among younger people, those without DB pension plans, and those at both the lower and upper ends of the wage distribution.

THE LAST POST: FLEXIBLE RETIREMENT OR INFLEXIBLE WORKING?

Surveys increasingly demonstrate a willingness amongst older workers to continue working under certain conditions: namely, if they can reduce or work more flexible hours. What are the realities of flexible working for older people? Is it the good news story policymakers and commentators would have us believe? Clearly, not universally so, as observed by Platman (2003), whose research among older freelance workers in the media industry found that they were vulnerable to job insecurity and financial risk due to diminishing networks and skills. For others, undoubtedly, flexibility offers certain benefits, but often neglected in current debates is consideration of those for whom a gradual switch from work to non-work is not an option. An indication of the size of this phenomenon comes from the author's analysis of the European Working Conditions Survey for the years 2000 and 2005 for members of the former EU-15. It was found that part-time working among older workers is on the increase. But in stark contrast to the gradual retirement rhetoric, among the 55–59 age group and those currently part-time workers there has been an approximate doubling of those wishing to increase their working hours or become full-time workers between 2000 and 2005. A similar but stronger pattern emerged for 60–64 year olds. These findings are suggestive of significant constraints on the choices of older workers and indicate that a singular public policy position of one-way transitions from full-time to part-time work and on to retirement is misguided. The present policy position may also be viewed as perhaps being drawn from age-based stereotypes concerning the preferences and needs of older workers. The purpose here is not to argue against the principle of flexible retirement but to point out that its current conceptualization is simplistic and that evidence points to limitations in its utility for policymakers, employers, and workers.

ASSESSING THE EFFECTS OF PUBLIC POLICIES ON AGE AND WORK

The forces of the market on the one hand and public policy on the other interact to shape the employment and retirement trajectories of older workers. While it is not easy to disentangle the effects of public policy and national economic performance, it can be speculated that strong economic growth and changes in public policy may

both have played a role in the improving situations of older workers in Finland, the Netherlands, and the United Kingdom, whereas, despite policy efforts, sluggishness in the German and Japanese economies for over more than a decade may have disadvantaged older workers in these two countries.

As most of the policies discussed above are new, and against a changing economic backdrop, assessing effects is problematic. The ending of mandatory retirement appears not to have been effective. Regarding gradual retirement, the schemes on offer appear to have had limited influence, although is it early days in terms of evaluation. It may even be posited that some gradual retirement schemes have promoted early retirement, not facilitated a more gradual withdrawal from the labour market. Certain forms of gradual retirement schemes could be viewed as embedding rather than removing age barriers. A more pragmatic view is that such schemes accept the existence of age barriers in the labour market and at least offer (some) older workers opportunities to remain economically active.

FRAMING PUBLIC POLICY TOWARDS OLDER WORKERS

Based on this examination, the final section of this chapter sets out some basic principles for the development of public policies on flexible retirement (Taylor, 2002). In the first place, policies on age and the labour market must be capable of meeting the needs of diverse groups. For example, pension reforms could disadvantage some people, forcing them to remain economically active and, if they lack abilities that are valued in the marketplace, into a form of prolonged unemployment, with the potential for a quality of later life that falls short of what proponents of active ageing would wish for them. By contrast, those who are better off will continue to retire early or to have access to a wider range of jobs. Thus, it is important that an adequate safety net is retained where employment is an unrealistic option. A significant extension to working life depends on a range of individual, organizational, economic, and societal factors and while this may be achievable for some, prospects for others might be remote (Frerichs and Taylor, 2005). Those who are long-term unemployed or disabled have remote employment prospects and a working late rhetoric will probably achieve little more than stir anxiety about loss of social security benefits. While early retirement is currently unfashionable in policy circles, it offers the only prospect of a dignified exit to many older people (Taylor, 2008).

Secondly, the need for the integration of public policies on age and employment is emphasized in policy circles, but where perhaps even the most integrated initiatives have been deficient is in terms of emphasizing 'work'. There would be value in policies on age being better integrated in order that policy efforts in one domain do not to undermine those in another. For instance, how older women will sustain work, caring, and community engagement roles while combining these with leisure does not seem to have been much considered. Rather, narrow economic imperatives to reduce early retirement and increase labour force participation have taken precedence over wider social ones.[10]

Thirdly, while there has been a tendency to consider the needs of 'older workers', a shift to a life-cycle or life-course approach would emphasize measures that focus on minimizing the risk of an older individual losing a job or making an unsuccessful transition to retirement and beyond. One approach is to increase labour market flexibility, which could enable workers to move to less-demanding jobs, but with due account taken of what this might mean in reality. As discussed above, flexibility that is a one-way street of reduced working hours does not meet the aspirations of all older people.

Fourthly, as older workers' positions in labour markets have become ever more precarious in recent years, there has emerged an increasing need to support them in managing associated risks through assistance with career and retirement planning and access to training. This will be aided by clarity and consistency in social security provision and pension policy. There is a need to get the incentive structure right and to link this to employment policy so that older workers are encouraged and supported to remain economically active if they so wish.

CONCLUSION

This chapter has argued that the current policy interest in the employment of older workers is not novel in historical terms. In recent times they have been welcomed into the labour market as economies have grown, only to be rejected subsequently during economic downturns. At present, a general public policy shift towards their inclusion can be observed. Whether this represents the beginning of a long-term change in their fortunes or is the familiar result of short-term political expediency is as yet unclear. Most observers of this volte-face,

with early retirement being the policy objective until relatively recently, have been unerringly uncritical, tying together current gerontological perspectives on the benefits of 'active ageing' with apparently self-evident economic and social realities concerning dwindling labour supplies and rising welfare burdens. Critical commentaries on the likelihood of many older people achieving active ageing and, if they do, how it will be manifested, have been rare. For instance, the question remains as to whether a prolonged recession would result in a reversal of the apparent labour market gains made by older workers in recent years in some countries. Another seemingly plausible scenario is that much of business, perceiving a threat to labour supply from demographic ageing, and competing in a globalizing market place, will endeavour to become more efficient, doing more with the labour it already has, or choose to relocate to regions of the world where there is an abundance of skilled workers *available at low cost*. While governments (currently) and age campaigners might prefer to paint a picture of newly enlightened companies welcoming willing cohorts of older workers to swell the ranks of their workforces, the reality may be that the history of older workers is also their future. Far from being at the vanguard of an employment revolution involving choice and flexibility, a plausible scenario is that many older workers will continue to face the now familiar problem of diminishing opportunities and, with it, prospects of a happy old age.

NOTES

1 The author is grateful to Chris Phillipson, Juhani Ilmarinen, Masato Oka, and Sara Rix who commented on this chapter as it was prepared.

2 The chapter draws on the author's research, which was funded by the Joseph Rowntree Foundation, the Anglo-German Foundation, the International Longevity Centre-UK, and the European Foundation for the Improvement of Living and Working Conditions. The research, carried out in different phases between 2001 and 2005, has consisted of extensive literature reviews coupled with visits to a selected number of countries: Australia, Finland, Germany, Japan, the Netherlands, the United Kingdom, and the United States. These countries were chosen because policymaking towards older workers was already quite well advanced or was emerging rapidly. Interviews were conducted with academic experts, policymakers, and practioners in order to obtain up-to-date information on the situations of older workers in the labour markets of each country and policymaking regarding age and employment.

In the cases of Finland, Germany, and the Netherlands, these data have been supplemented by reports prepared by national experts.

3 http://www.eurofound.europa.eu/ewco/surveys/index.htm

4 The employment-to-population ratio is defined as the proportion of an economy's working-age population that is employed.

5 http://www.dwp.gov.uk/mediacentre/pressreleases/2005/apr/state_pens_rules.asp

6 http://www.publications.parliament.uk/pa/cm200607/cmhansrd/cm070116/debtext/70116-0005.htm

7 There have always been penalties for early retirement, but because early retirement payments must be paid for more years, workers will get a lower benefit at age 62 with the higher retirement age than when this was set at age 65.

8 In fact, since before mandatory retirement was eliminated workers had the right to work until 65 (1967 Age Discrimination in Employment Act) and then 70 (1976 amendments).

9 http://business.timesonline.co.uk/tol/business/law/article4809180.ece

10 http://www.publications.parliament.uk/pa/cm200506/cmselect/cmworpen/1068/106813.htm

REFERENCES

Auer, P. and Fortuny, M. (2000) 'Ageing of the labour force in OECD countries: economic and social consequences', ILO, http://www.ilo.org/public/english/employment/skills/older/download/ep00-2.htm. Accessed December 30, 2008.

Cahill, K.E., Giandrea, M.D., and Quinn, J.F. (2006), 'Retirement patterns from career employment', *The Gerontologist*, 46: 514–23.

Casey, B. and Laczko, F., (1989) 'Early retired or long-term unemployed? The situation of non-working men aged 55–64 from 1976 to 1986', *Work, Employment and Society*, 1(4): 509–26.

Chiva, A. and Manthorpe, J. (2008) *Older Workers in Europe*. Buckingham: McGraw-Hill/Open University Press.

Department for Work and Pensions (2005) 'Opportunity age', http://www.dwp.gov.uk/opportunity_age/. Accessed December 30, 2008.

Dulitzky, D. (1999) *Incentives for Early Retirement in Private Pension and Health Insurance Plans*. Washington, DC: Urban Institute.

Encel, S. (2000) 'Mature age employment: a long-term cost to society', *Economic and Labour Relations Review*, 11(2): 233–45.

Encel, S. (2008) 'Looking forward to working longer in Australia', in P. Taylor (ed.), *Ageing Labour Forces: Promises and Prospects*. Cheltenham, UK: Edward Elgar.

European Council (2001) *Presidency Conclusions*. Stockholm, March 23 and 24. Brussels.

European Council (2002). *Presidency Conclusions*. Barcelona, March 15 and 16. Brussels.

European Commission (2003) 'The Stockholm and Barcelona targets: increasing employment of older workers and delaying the exit from the labour market', http://europa.eu.int/comm/employment_social/employment_analysis/work/exit_en.pdf

Frerichs, F. and Taylor, P. (2005) *The Greying of the Labour Market: What Can Britain and Germany Learn from Each Other?* London: Anglo-German Foundation for the Study of Industrial Society.

Fujimura, H. (2001) 'Revision of pension system and employment issues involving workers in their early 60s', *Japan Labour Bulletin*, July: 6–12.

Guillemard, A-M and Argoud, D. (2004) 'France: a country with a deep early exit culture', in T. Maltby, B. De Vroom, M.L. Mirabille, and E. Overbye E. (eds), *Ageing and the Transition to Retirement. A Comparative Analysis of European Welfare States*. Aldershot, UK: Ashgate, pp. 165–85.

Gruber, J. and Wise, D. (1999) 'Social security, retirement incentives and retirement behaviour: an international perspective', *Employee Benefit Research Institute Issue Brief 209*, EBRI.

Hirsch, D. (2007) 'Sustaining working lives: the challenge of retention', in W. Loretto, S. Vickerstaff, and P. White (eds), *The Future for Older Workers*. Bristol: The Policy Press, pp. 103–21.

Ilmakunnas, P. and Ilmakunnas, S. (2006) 'Gradual retirement and lengthening of working life', Helsinki School of Economics and HECER, MPRA Paper No. 1860, http://mpra.ub.uni-muenchen.de/1860/

Jackson, R. (2002) 'The global retirement crisis', *The Geneva Papers on Risk and Insurance*, 27(4): 486–511.

Jacobs, K., Kohli, M., and Rein, M. (1991) 'Testing the industry mix hypothesis of early exit', in M. Kohli, M. Rein, A.-M. Guillemard, and H. van Gunsteren, H. (eds), *Time for Retirement: Comparative Studies of Early Exit from the Labour Force*. Cambridge: Cambridge University Press, pp. 67–96.

Jorgensen, B and Taylor, P. (2008) 'Older workers, government and business: implications for ageing populations of a globalising economy', *Economic Affairs*, 28(1): 18–23.

Kimura, T. and Oka, M. (2001) 'Japan's current policy focus on longer employment for older people', in V.W. Marshall, W.R. Heinz, H. Krüger, and A. Verma (eds), *Restructuring Work and the Lifecourse*. London: University of Toronto Press, pp. 348–59.

Kohli, M., Rein, M., Guillemard, A., and van Gunsteren, H. (1991) *Time for Retirement: Comparative Studies of Early Exit from the Labour Force*. Cambridge: Cambridge University Press.

Koshiro, K. (1996) 'Policies for a smoother transition from work to retirement', *Journal of Aging and Social Policy*, 8(2–3): 97–113.

Leppel, K. and Heller Clain, S. (1995) 'The effect of increases in the level of unemployment on older workers', *Applied Economics*, 27: 901–6.

Loretto, W., Vickerstaff, S., and White, P. (2005) *Older Workers and Options for Flexible Work.* EOC Working paper series. Manchester: Equal Opportunities Commission.

Loretto, W., Vickerstaff, S., and White, P. (eds) (2007) *The Future for Older Workers.* Bristol: The Policy Press.

Macnicol, J. (2006) 'Age discrimination in history', in L. Bauld, K. Clarke, and T. Maltby (eds), *Social Policy Review 18, Analysis and Debate in Social Policy, 2006.* Bristol: The Policy Press, pp. 249–68.

McGoldrick, A. and Cooper, C. (1980) 'Voluntary early retirement – taking the decision', *Employment Gazette,* August: 859–64.

McNair, S. (2006) 'How different is the older labour market? Attitudes to work and retirement among older people in Britain', *Social Policy and Society,* 5(4): 485–94.

Times, April 27 http://www.ft.com/cms/s/0/db7f63b4-d58a-11da-93bc-0000779e2340.html?nclick_check=1. Accessed January, 29, 2009.

Ministry for Social Affairs and Employment (2001) *The Preventive Approach in a Nutshell.* Brussels: The Hague.

Ministry for Social Affairs and Employment (undated) *The Old Age Pension System in the Netherlands: A Brief Outline.* Brussels: The Hague.

Mullan, P. (2002) *The Imaginary Time Bomb.* London: Tauris Publishers.

Münchau, W. (2007) 'The death of Hartz IV', http://www.eurointelligence.com/Article.620+M582e49425cb.0.html. Accessed December 30, 2008.

Munnell, A.H. and Sunden, A.E. (2004) *Coming Up Short: The Challenge of 401(k) Plans.* Brookings: Institution Press.

OECD (1998) *Maintaining Prosperity in an Ageing Society.* Paris: OECD.

OECD (2006a) *Live Longer, Work Longer: A Synthesis Report.* Paris: OECD

OECD (2006b) *Economic Survey of Finland 2006.* Paris: OECD.

Oka, M. (2008) 'Japan: toward employment extension for older workers', in P. Taylor (ed.), *Ageing Labour Forces: Promises and Prospects.* Cheltenham, UK: Edward Elgar.

Pensions Commission (2005) *A New Pension Settlement for the Twenty-First Century: The Second Report of the Pensions Commission.* London: The Stationery Office.

Phillipson, C. (2006) 'Extending working life: problems and prospects for social and public policy', in L. Bauld, K. Clarke, and T. Maltby (eds), *Social Policy Review 18.* Bristol: Policy Press, pp. 221–48.

Phillipson, C. (2009) 'Pensions in crisis: aging and inequality in a global age', in L., Rogne, C., Estes, B., Grossman, B. Hollister, and E. Solway (eds), *Social Insurance and Social Justice.* New York: Springer, pp. 319–40.

Platman, K. (2003) 'The self-designed career in later life: a study of older portfolio workers in the United Kingdom', *Ageing and Society,* 23(3): 281–302.

Rix, S. (2001) 'Restructuring work in an aging America: what role for public policy', in V.W. Marshall, W.R. Heinz, H. Krüger, and A. Verma (eds), *Restructuring Work and the Lifecourse.* London: University of Toronto Press, pp. 375–96.

Select Committee on Work and Pensions (2006) http://www.publications.parliament.uk/pa/cm200506/cmselect/cmworpen/1068/106813.htm#n495. Accessed April 15, 2008.

Sigg, R. (2005) 'A global overview on social security in the age of longevity', paper presented to Expert Group Meeting on Social and Economic Implication of Changing Population Age Structures, Mexico City, August–September 2005.

Smeaton, D. and Vegaris, S. (2009) *Older people Inside and Outside the Labour Market: A Review.* Research Report 22. Manchester: Equality and Human Rights Commission.

Taylor, P. (2002) *New Policies for Older Workers.* Bristol: The Policy Press.

Taylor, P. (2006) *Employment Initiatives for an Ageing Workforce in the EU-15.* Office for Official Publications of the European Communities, Luxembourg.

Taylor, P. (2008) *Ageing Labour Forces: Promises and Prospects.* Cheltenham, UK: Edward Elgar.

Taylor, P., Encel, S., and Oka, M. (2002) 'Older workers – trends and prospects', *Geneva Papers on Risk and Insurance,* 27(4): 512–31.

Taylor, P. Tillsley, C., Beausoleil, J., and Wilson, R. (2000) *Factors Affecting Retirement.* London: Department for Education and Employment.

Tillsley, C. and Taylor, P. (2001) 'Developing strategies for managing third age workers', in I. Glover and M. Branine (eds), *Ageism, Work and Employment.* Aldershot, UK: Ashgate, pp. 311–28.

Trinder, C. (1989) *Employment after 55.* London: National Institute for Economic and Social Research.

Walker, A. (1985) 'Early retirement: release or refuge from the labour market?', *Quarterly Journal of Social Affairs,* 1(3): 211–19.

Walker, A. and Taylor, P. (1993) 'Ageism versus productive ageing: the challenge of age discrimination in the labour market', in S. Bass, F. Caro, and Y. Chen (eds), *Achieving a Productive Ageing Society.* London: Auburn House, pp. 61–80.

WHO (2002) *Active Aging: A Policy Framework.* Geneva: World Health Organization.

World Bank (1994) *Averting the Old Age Crisis: Policies to Protect the Old and Promote Growth.* Oxford: Oxford University Press.

42

Continuous and Long-term Care: European Perspectives

Caroline Glendinning

INTRODUCTION

This chapter examines arrangements for public funding and provision of long-term care services for older people within the countries of western, southern, and eastern Europe and Scandinavia – broadly, the member countries of the enlarged European Union (EU). However, both long-term care policy develpments as well as published English-language research and policy analysis are considerably more extensive in some of these countries than in others. In particular, there is extensive English-language literature on long-term care in the Nordic countries (particularly Sweden, Denmark, Norway, and Finland) and western European countries (France, Germany, the Netherlands, and the United Kingdom); a little on the countries of southern Europe (Spain and Italy); but very little on the new EU member states of eastern and south-east Europe.

Even among those EU countries where policy and research on long-term care are relatively well-documented in English, there is nevertheless very considerable diversity in funding and institutional arrangements for long-term care. This diversity includes how resources for funding long-term care are generated; the criteria used to access and allocate these resources; and the nature of the services and other forms of provision that are funded from these resources. Such diversity raises the question of whether it is in fact possible to identify any distinctive 'European' perspective or pattern to continuous and long-term care arrangements. This question is lent added significance because, unlike other regional groupings of countries, Europe has

in the EU a powerful supranational body that exerts extensive control over many areas of economic and political life within its constituent member states. The chapter will therefore also consider the role of the EU in relation to continuous and long-term care policies and provision, and the extent to which any convergent patterns or trends can be identified.

First, the demographic and economic context of long-term care in Europe is described. Secondly, the different approaches to the funding and provision of long-term care within the countries of Europe are summarized. Rather than providing detailed descriptions, the aim here will be to illustrate the extraordinary diversity of policies and approaches that exist within a single global region. This diversity is further illustrated by short case study descriptions of long-term care arrangements in three countries – Denmark, Germany, and England – to illustrate how these different approaches are combined within individual countries. Thirdly, the chapter discusses some emergent common themes that appear to characterize policies in at least some European countries. The chapter concludes with a brief discussion of the potential for greater convergence between countries, given the supranational status of the EU.

BACKGROUND, DEMOGRAPHICS, AND COUNTRY POLICIES

The age structure of the European population is older than that of any other world region and is set to age further during the next few decades. By 2020, almost one quarter of the population in several European countries will be aged 65 and over; in many of these countries the proportions and numbers of people aged 85 and over are growing even more rapidly. The age structure of the overall population is as important as the absolute numbers of older and very old people. In 2001 it was estimated that the EU old-age dependency ratio (the numbers of people aged 65+ over the numbers of working age people aged 15–64) would more than double, from 24 per cent in 2000 to 49 per cent by 2050. In other words, the EU as a whole is expected to move from having four to only two people of working age for every person aged 65+ by 2050. Within this European average, however, striking differences between individual countries are apparent. In 2000, Ireland had the lowest dependency ratio of 17 per cent, compared with ratios of 25 per cent in Belgium, Greece, France, Spain, Sweden, and Italy. At the other end of the spectrum, by 2050 Spain and Italy are expected to have higher than average dependency ratios, of around 60 per cent.

Even more significant, from the point of view of the potential demand for and expenditure on long-term care, is the anticipated rise in the proportions of people aged 80+. By 2050, 37 per cent of all over 65s will be aged 80+, although, again, there is considerable divergence around this figure. Thus, in Ireland by 2050 it is expected that only 27 per cent of older people will be aged over 80, but the proportions are expected to be higher than average in Austria, Italy, and Denmark, at 42 per cent, 39 per cent, and 39 per cent, respectively (European Commission, 2001).

As well as these variations in current and projected demographic patterns, current levels and patterns of spending on long-term care services for older people as percentages of countries' gross domestic product (GDP) also vary widely. In 2004, across the 25 countries of the enlarged EU an average 0.5 per cent of GDP was spent on care allowances, supported accommodation, and personal care. However, this average masked differences ranging from 0.1 per cent of GDP in Estonia, Greece, Italy, Latvia, and Lithuania, to 1.1 per cent in Austria and 1.7 per cent in Denmark.[1] Overall, levels of public spending on long-term care are relatively low compared with other areas of age-related expenditure such as health care and pensions. Public expenditure on long-term care would undoubtedly be much higher were it not for user co-payments and for the very significant contributions of informal carers to the total volume of care provision (Ovseiko, 2007). Even so, projections of expenditure on long-term care in Germany, the United Kingdom, Spain, and Italy between 2000 and 2050 indicate that this is likely to more than double in each country, though these projections are highly sensitive to assumptions about future rates of disability and dependency, the unit costs of services, and the availability of informal care (Comas-Herrera et al., 2006). Although improvements in efficiency are in principle also possible, in practice their impact on future public expenditure is likely to be limited because of the labour-intensive nature of formally organized long-term care services.

Overall, across the countries of Europe, correlations between the age structure of a country's population (especially the proportions of people aged 80+) and demand for spending on long-term care for older people as a percentage of national GDP is weak. The relationship between demographic trends and demand for long-term care is mediated by factors such as the health status, marriage patterns, household composition, and living arrangements of older people (Hussein and Manthorpe, 2005). The relationship between demand for long-term care and levels of public expenditure are in turn mediated by cultural, political, and institutional factors. The impacts of these latter factors on patterns of funding and provision will be illustrated in the next section of this chapter.

DIVERSITY ACROSS EUROPE: ONE SYSTEM OR MANY?

Identifying common and divergent patterns in the approaches of different welfare states in relation to long-term care is far more difficult than in other areas of social and welfare policy (Esping Anderson, 1990; Lewis, 1992). Indeed, as Karlsson et al. (2007) point out, reforms to long-term care have generally built on the existing institutional arrangements of individual countries, rather than borrowed from the models of other countries.

Moreover, 'care policies never did and actually do not vary systematically with the type of welfare regime' (Pfau-Effinger, 2005: 324). One reason why continuous and long-term care does not conform to conventional models of welfare regimes is that much of it is unpaid, invisible, and highly gendered. As noted above, the help and support provided by close relatives and friends is essential to the sustainability of formal long-term care arrangements – indeed, in many countries, measures to support informal caregiving are integral to overall long-term care arrangements. Comparative analysis therefore needs to take account of how far the policies of different welfare states acknowledge this informal care work and seek to redistribute it more equally between women and men (Lewis, 1992, 2006). A second reason behind the difficulty in discerning common patterns in policies and structures for long-term care across different European countries is that in many countries these originated in residual, means-tested schemes that acted as a last-resort safety net in the event of both market and family failure (see, e.g., Means and Smith, 2008): indeed, in some countries such as Italy they still do. In other countries, the pressures on these schemes caused by population ageing have been major drivers of reform. This consideration also indicates that provision for long-term care may intersect with and prompt changes in the dynamics of central–local government relationships and responsibilities. Thirdly, to the extent that local and regional governments continue to have responsibility for some or all of long-term care funding and service provision, this may introduce further, within-country, variations.

Fourthly, cultural values and traditions permeate social structures and institutions, public discourses, and the normative beliefs and actions of individuals alike. Thus, how individuals and families behave in relation to the care of their elderly relatives and friends, what they think are the 'proper' ways to behave, and how these beliefs and values shape – and are shaped by – welfare priorities, structures, and delivery systems are less tangible factors that contribute to differences between countries. The influence of values and traditions at all these levels is likely to be high, given the normative nature of care (Pfau-Effinger, 2005).

It is arguable, therefore, that arrangements for continuous and long-term care within any one country reflect both institutional structures and traditions within that country's welfare state as a whole; and cultural values, norms, and beliefs, particularly about the way in which 'care' is provided and who it is provided by. Furthermore, both institutional and cultural factors will affect the nature, scope, and trajectory of any contemporary reforms. It is this position of continuous and long-term care policies, on the margins of national, local, and informal welfare structures and norms, culture, and beliefs, that leads to wide diversity, even within a single global region.

DIMENSIONS OF DIVERSITY

The following section illustrates the diversity of approaches to funding and providing long-term care across Europe; these are summarized in Table 42.1.

These approaches encompass:

- *How revenue for publicly funded long-term care is generated.* Revenue sources can include general national taxation (for example, England, Scotland, and Austria); local, municipal-level taxation (for example, Denmark and Sweden); social insurance contributions from employees and employers (for example, Germany and the Netherlands); and means-tested user co-payments or other user contributions (for example, Germany, Austria, and England). Where regional or local authorities have devolved responsibility for raising revenue for continuous and long-term care provision, this can result in variations in levels of funding and provision *within* a single nation, as is the case in the United Kingdom (with variations between England and Scotland), Spain, and Italy. In the case of Italy, regional variations exist in both levels of services and eligibility criteria for services

Table 42.1 Different approaches to funding and providing long-term care

Dimension of long-term care	Range of mechanisms
Raising resources	• National taxation • Local taxation • Social insurance contributions (employer/employee) • User co-payments
Governance – locus of responsibility for distributing resources/ensuring provision is available	• National governments • Local governments • Local governments within national guidelines
Mechanisms for allocating resources	• Standardized national eligibility criteria and decision-making • Individualized needs-led assessment
Form in which resources are allocated	• Services • Cash payments with no restrictions on how they are used • Vouchers to be spent on specific (range of) services
Nature of support for family caregiving	• Assumed to be available with minimum support • Explicitly encouraged/supported as part of long-term care provision

(Gori, 2000). In no European country does private insurance play any significant role (Glendinning et al., 2004). The redistributional effects of different approaches to long-term care funding depend at least in part on the progressivity of the underlying system by which resources are generated.

- *Where responsibility lies for ensuring adequate levels and quality of long-term care provision.* In Germany and the Netherlands this is a responsibility of national social insurance systems; in Scandinavia, with its long traditions of local municipal autonomy (Sundström and Johansson, 2005), responsibilities lie with municipalities; this can also lead to considerable variations in levels of provision between municipalities. In England and Scotland, local authorities have responsibility for ensuring the levels and quality of long-term care, but within common legal, quality, and performance frameworks set by their respective national governments.
- *How public funding for long-term care is allocated.* This dimension covers the ways in which eligibility for, or access to, publicly funded long-term care is assessed. Some countries, such as France, Germany, and Austria, have national eligibility criteria and employ a single national assessment tool that is administered relatively uniformly across the country. Such assessment tools tend to be based on measures of individual disability and cognitive functioning. In other countries such as England, Italy, Denmark, and Sweden, eligibility depends on more individualized, needs-led assessments that allow some discretion in the interpretation of individual circumstances, including the help that is available from close relatives and friends.
- *The form in which public funding for long-term care is allocated.* A key distinction is between provision in the form of cash payments (for example, Austria and Italy) or in the form of services (for example, Sweden, France, and Denmark). This distinction is, however, becoming less clear. Thus England, Scotland, the Netherlands, and Flanders have all introduced cash-based alternatives ('direct payments' or 'personal budgets') to in-kind service provision. The German long-term care social insurance scheme offers a choice between a cash payment or a 'service assignment' benefit – the latter has been described as a 'voucher' for approved services (Evans Cuellar and Wiener, 2000), while a similar option (an 'individual budget' that could be deployed in the form of services or cash) was piloted in England between 2005 and 2007 (Glendinning et al., 2008). The use of vouchers or cash payments as the method of allocating resources for long-term care is discussed further below.

- *The role of informal care in the provision of publicly funded long-term care.* Across Europe as a whole, it has been estimated that the prevalence of informal care is five times that of formal services (Daly and Rake, 2003). However, although obligations, bonds, and solidarity between generations remain considerable across European countries, there are nevertheless differences between countries in the strength of these bonds and in how they are manifested in levels and types of emotional and instrumental help (Lowenstein and Daatland, 2006). There are also major differences in the extent to which countries encourage, acknowledge, and reward such care, and in the different mechanisms that are used to provide such support. In some countries (for example, Germany, Ireland, and Italy), long-term care arrangements reflect continuing assumptions that families will provide the majority of long-term care. Indeed, in the Netherlands the 'customary care' (Pijl and Ramakers, 2007) obligations of household members have recently been spelt out in administrative guidance; publicly funded long-term care no longer covers these responsibilities. In contrast, in Denmark relatives are not expected to provide personal care; this remains a municipal responsibility. In England, the care provided by relatives is usually taken into account in assessing an older person's need for long-term care, although the needs of carers themselves are also considered and supported through separate services and social security benefits. Although many long-term care systems also provide support for family carers, there is a distinction between countries (for example, Germany and Austria) where such support is 'routed' through the entitlements and allowances paid to the older person (Ungerson, 2003) and countries where carers themselves have direct access to support in their own right (England and Ireland) (see Glendinning, 2006).

Although the main dimensions of the different approaches to long-term care across Europe are covered above, there appears to be little co-variation along these dimensions; it is not the case that a particular approach to raising resources is always associated with a specific method for allocating those resources. Thus, standardized, national eligibility criteria are commonly associated with social insurance-based systems (such as in Germany); but such eligibility criteria are also found in taxation-financed schemes, as in the case of France and Italy (Glendinning et al., 2004). The following summaries of long-term care in Denmark, Germany, and England illustrate how widely these different dimensions can vary, independently of each other.

Denmark

In Denmark, long-term care is highly decentralized (Sundström and Johansson, 2005), with the 98 municipalities being legally responsible for both funding and providing community nursing, social care, and institutional care. Most of the revenue for long-term care comes from the income taxes raised by each municipality. Municipalities do receive some additional funding from central government, which tends to be used to promote the expansion of specific services or to compensate for differences in local tax bases and demography. Municipalities have considerable discretion over the allocation of resources between particular services, within budgetary guidelines set by central government (including the ceilings on local taxation). Public spending on long-term care is high and coverage of services is extensive.

Denmark was one of the first industrialized countries to adopt an explicit policy of community care, with a clear commitment during the 1980s to developing alternatives to institutional provision. The 1987 Act on Housing for Older and Disabled Persons prohibited the construction of any more nursing homes and prompted an extensive building programme of sheltered and adapted housing; between 1985 and 1998 the number of sheltered and adapted dwellings increased by 331 per cent (Stuart and Weinrich, 2001). During the same period, the use of institutional care decreased significantly (Platz and Brodhurst, 2001), as did overall public spending on long-term care, particularly on services for the over 80s (Stuart and Weinrich, 2001). Even very severely disabled older people now live in their own homes or sheltered housing, with admission to institutional care predominantly restricted to people with dementia.

National legislation spells out the welfare state's responsibilities to older people; family care is considered an addition to, not a substitute for, that provided by municipalities. The 1998 Social Services Act creates a statutory duty on municipalities to offer domiciliary services to anyone unable to perform regular activities of daily living (ADLS). Within this framework, each municipality develops services to meet its particular local circumstances, resulting in wide local variations in the range and levels of services. Local services include adapted or specialist housing; home-based domestic, personal care and nursing; round-the-clock home care; transport to treatment facilities; day centres; meals on wheels; and preventive activities in and outside the home. Practical (domestic), personal, nursing care, and rehabilitation services are all free of charge to users.

Applicants for services are entitled to an individual needs assessment carried out by a nurse, home help, or manager. The assessment takes into account the capacity of a partner to provide domestic help, but not the help provided by adult children or relatives outside the household. Admission to a nursing home depends on the decision of a municipal admissions board, which considers a range of professional views and whether admission could be avoided by the provision of domiciliary services. There are no national criteria governing nursing home admissions, although the Association of Municipalities has been concerned about a lack of consistency in assessments and admission criteria.

Home care and home nursing staff work in integrated teams, delivering support to people in their own homes, specialist housing, and nursing homes alike (Lund Pederson, 1998). Increasingly, home help (domestic) services are contracted out to private (for-profit and non-profit) firms; in some municipalities older people needing only domestic help are offered a cash payment or voucher to purchase their own services, including the option of paying a relative to undertake domestic tasks (Platz and Brodhurst, 2001). Since 2002, older people have been able to choose between private or public providers of publicly funded domestic help and since 2003 this choice has been extended to the provision of personal care. Municipalities must now ensure that a number of alternative providers are available, along with the public provider. Ideally all providers should be able to offer both domestic and personal care, although in practice many private firms offer only domestic help. Home help services nevertheless continue to be free of charge, although private firms can charge for extra services like window cleaning. Private provision is more common in larger, urban areas, and more likely to be chosen by new service users and those needing only practical, domestic help (Rostgaard, 2006). Although both wages and job satisfaction among care workers are high, workforce capacity is a problem; recent measures have included improving levels of education and professionalism and recruitment among recent immigrants and students (Hussein and Manthorpe, 2005).

Germany

In Germany, the introduction of a compulsory, national long-term care insurance scheme in 1995 had multiple aims. The scheme sought to create a financially and politically sustainable solution to the funding of long-term care; to reduce financial burdens on the health insurance scheme and local authorities responsible for social assistance, which had hitherto borne most of the costs of long-term care; to develop a market in home care provision; and to support family care. Long-term care insurance is compatible with the insurance-based structure of German social welfare (Clasen, 1994) and provides universal coverage, significantly reducing stigma for older people who previously had to 'spend down' their assets before claiming for social assistance for long-term institutional care.

Long-term care insurance is a 'pay-as-you-go' scheme, with current contributions funding current benefits. Funding comes from compulsory contributions from gross salary (although employees pay a higher proportion of these costs than employers). In 2008 contributions were raised from 1.7 per cent to 1.95 per cent of salary costs for people with children and to 2.2 per cent for people without children. Contributions for people receiving unemployment insurance or social assistance are paid in full by the respective funds. Initially, half the contributions of retired people were paid by their retirement insurance, but since 2004 retired people must pay their own contributions in full. Because membership of care insurance, like health insurance, is mandatory, almost the entire population is covered; non-employed family members are covered by the breadwinner's contributions.

Both eligibility criteria and benefits are determined by the insurance principle that people requiring similar levels of assistance with specified ADLS should be treated equally across the country; no account is taken of individual needs or circumstances. Eligibility is determined through a test of 'care dependency'; three levels of 'care dependency' reflect the severity and extensiveness of care needs. At each of these three levels, benefits can be paid in the form of a cash allowance, which is usually given to a family carer; or in the form of service 'assignments'; or as mixture of the two (Schunk, 1998). Despite its lower value, the cash payment has consistently proved more popular (by about 80:20); it is widely assumed that some or all of it is paid to family carers or contributed to the shared household income (Schunk and Estes, 2001).

For those entitled to long-term care insurance, other benefits include funding for respite care to give family carers 4 weeks break each year; specialist equipment; and retirement and accident insurance contributions for family carers. Additional benefits introduced in 2008 include extra cash payments for people with dementia; unpaid leave from work for up to 6 months for carers; and additional funding for care management and respite care services. These measures provide additional support for family carers, although the latter have no entitlement at all to any benefits in their own right. Nevertheless, there are high levels of satisfaction with the scheme among both beneficiaries and carers (Geraedts et al., 2000).

Intended consequences of the insurance scheme include a significant increase in the number of home care provider organizations and an increase of 60,000–70,000 workers employed in the home care sector, mainly in private, for-profit organizations.

However, at least some of these organizations are relatively unstable, with high turnover. Moreover, there is little consensus over definitions and standards of quality in formal services and the fragmentation of funders and providers makes any common principles unlikely (Arntz et al., 2007). There have also been concerns about the acute shortage of care management services that can provide impartial information and advice on appropriate formal services and also about the biases against older people with cognitive impairments inherent in the test of 'care dependency' (von Kondratovitz et al., 2002).

Long-term care insurance has proved a highly effective method of controlling the public expenditure costs of long-term care. Neither contributions nor benefits were increased for 15 years until 2008, although the actual costs of both domiciliary and institutional care did so. Consequently, the numbers of older people who have to 'top up' their insurance benefits, particularly to meet the costs of institutional care, increased. Although long-term care insurance has not experienced the same actuarial pressures as the German pensions and health insurance schemes, it has nevertheless been affected by high unemployment that has reduced anticipated levels of contributions to the scheme and also by increased costs.

England

In the case of England, public funding for long-term care comes from (mostly national) general taxation. However, responsibilities for allocating these resources are fragmented and embedded within the mainstream budgets of three policy sectors: funding for nursing care provided within institutions and in the community comes from the National Health Service budget; social security benefits for people needing extra care or supervision and for some family carers are allocated by the Department for Work and Pensions; and local authority adult service departments are responsible for residential and domiciliary social care. Access to support provided through these separate funding streams depends upon different sets of eligibility criteria (Glendinning, 2007). However, expenditure through these channels amounts to only about two-thirds of total spending on long-term care; charges and fees paid by older people themselves make up the remaining 35 per cent, of which around half comes from means-tested user co-payments and half from private purchase (Comas-Herrera et al., 2004). In particular, a test of assets (including the value of a house) determines eligibility for public funding for institutional care in nursing and residential care homes. As a consequence, about a quarter of all residents pay all their own fees (Wanless, 2006) and a further third contribute some private resources to 'top up' their local authority funding to meet the actual costs of a home placement (Office of Fair Trading, 2005).

Access to local authority-funded residential and domiciliary care depends on a multi-professional assessment of disability and support needs. There have been attempts to integrate separate multiple assessments of medical, personal, and nursing care needs (Department of Health (DH), 2001) and to reduce local variations in assessment processes and eligibility thresholds (DH, 2003). However, eligibility thresholds are linked to the financial situation of individual local authorities and therefore vary between localities. Increasing financial pressures have raised thresholds in many local authorities, so that by 2007 older people needed to be experiencing 'substantial' or 'critical' risks to their well-being to qualify for domiciliary or residential-based personal care in around three-quarters of English local authorities (Community Care, 2007).

Since the early 1980s, residential and nursing home care has increasingly been supplied by private sector providers and the market is now dominated by some large, for-profit providers; in 2005 about 20 per cent of residents lived in homes owned by the 10 largest independent providers (Scourfield, 2007). The shift from local authority to private provision of home care services is both more recent, and dramatic; in 1992, only 2 per cent of number of hours of home care were delivered by the private sector; by 2005 this had increased to more than 73 per cent – a market which was nevertheless described in an inspection report as 'fragmented and unstable' (CSCI, 2006).

As eligibility criteria for personal care have tightened, so home care services have been increasingly targeted on older people with higher levels of need. Between 1992 and 2005, the numbers of households receiving home care fell from 500,000 to 354,500, but the average number of hours of care provided to each household increased from 3.2 to 10.1 a week (CSCI, 2006). The overall proportion of older people receiving local authority-funded home care is now low by international standards (Wanless, 2006). Although there has been some investment in rehabilitation services to support hospital discharge, and pilot initiatives to provide low-level support to older people, preventive services remain seriously underfunded (CSCI, 2006).

From 2001, older people have been able to choose a cash-based 'direct payment' of an equivalent value to their home care services with which to purchase their own support arrangements. However, older people's take-up of this option remains very low, compared to younger adults (Poole, 2006). Between 2005 and 2007, a more flexible 'individual budget' option was piloted in 13 local authorities; this option also has the potential for introducing greater equity in the allocation of resources between older people and between older and younger disabled people. However, extensive evaluation found little evidence of benefits to older people and lower levels of well-being among older individual budget holders than a comparison group of older people receiving standard services (Glendinning et al., 2008).

England is relatively unusual among European countries in having a long-established and extensive legislative framework of support specifically for family carers. Since 1995, carers have had an unconditional right to an assessment of their own support needs; since 2006 this has been underpinned by a commitment that carers and those without care responsibilities should have equal opportunities to participate in training, employment, and leisure activities. Carers with no more than minimal earnings are also eligible for a nationally administered Carer Allowance, giving them rights to an income (albeit very low) that is independent of the person for whom they are caring.

Despite improvements in support for long-term care, dissatisfaction has been expressed by older people's organizations and others about the levels of public funding for long-term care, the conditions under which older people can access this funding, and the consequent inequities between different groups of older people. Concerns increased in 2002, when Scotland introduced a policy of free nursing and personal care for older people. Notwithstanding anxiety about its long-term affordability, and popular confusion about the scope of 'personal' (as distinct from domestic) care, the policy is popular among older people and their families (Bowes and Bell, 2007). Nevertheless, despite two major reports and a Green Paper in a decade (Royal Commission on Long-Term Care, 1999; Wanless, 2006; HM Government, 2009), the English government has been reluctant to make major changes to either the level or distribution of public funding for long-term care.

COMMON CROSS-CUTTING THEMES/TRENDS

The previous section has shown how arrangements for long-term care are embedded within the welfare systems of individual countries; hence, it is difficult to identify any common, distinctively European approach. Indeed, even greater diversity would be apparent if case studies of arrangements in southern and eastern Europe were presented. Nevertheless, a number of cross-cutting, common themes can be identified and two, in particular, are discussed below. Again, it is important to emphasize that these themes are not necessarily distinctively European, but may also characterize long-term care arrangements in other regions as well.

(Re)drawing the boundaries of welfare-state responsibilities

In many European countries, new arrangements or alterations to existing arrangements are explicitly limiting the scope of welfare-state responsibilities for continuous and long-term care, in order to accommodate new demographic pressures within limited (or no) increases in public expenditure. However, the precise nature of these changes varies between countries and there are, moreover, significant exceptions; the introduction of long-term care insurance in Germany, for example, can be seen as representing a major expansion of social rights for older people (while at the same time containing costs).

One retrenchment strategy is to target services on only those older people with the highest levels of need for help. This has been the case in Sweden, which has a tradition of extensive services in kind funded from general taxation, but where services are now increasingly targeted on older people who have no close kin, are very frail, and live alone. Indeed, older people without acute needs or those who have children or other family members living nearby are now denied public help (Sundström and Johansson, 2005). Other research has shown that the inability to perform ADLS and cognitive impairment are the strongest predictors of home help receipt, while older people living with others are allocated significantly fewer hours of home help than those living alone (Meinow et al., 2005). In Italy too, with its much more fragmented and residual public provision for long-term care, 'services are increasingly provided as a "last resort" to people whose condition has seriously deteriorated' (Gori, 2000: 264). In the majority of English local authorities, as previously noted, older people must be at critical or substantial levels of risk before they can receive domiciliary or residential care. One consequence of these strategies is that opportunities for publicly funded services to adopt a preventive function, or to support family caregivers by substituting formal services for some of their care, are significantly reduced.

A second strategy is to restrict access to publicly funded care to only the poorest older people, essentially (re)turning long-term care to a means-tested, residual welfare function. Again, this strategy has been adopted in both Sweden and Italy, and also in England, where only those older people with minimal assets can access publicly funded institutional care. Not only do means-tested policies reduce total public expenditure but also they may reduce demand from some people who are unwilling to undergo means testing or find publicly funded services give poor value for money.

Thirdly, the range of services or activities included within publicly funded long-term care can be reduced. Thus, in Denmark, it is now unusual for help with domestic tasks to be provided by municipal home help services, unless an older person is also receiving help with personal care (Platz and Brodhurst, 2001). In the Netherlands, responsibility for funding domestic help has recently been transferred from the AWBZ social insurance scheme to the municipalities, where the provision of such help is discretionary – although the cost-effectiveness of this transfer has been questioned (Pijl and Ramakers, 2007).

Fourthly, a widespread strategy is to encourage, sustain, or increase family caregiving responsibilities. This was a key objective behind the introduction of the cash benefit option in the German long-term care insurance scheme. With a traditional culture of family care, the cash allowance enabled families to purchase assistance and, at least initially, applications for nursing home admission reduced (Wegner, 2001). In the Netherlands, the absence of informal care was made a criterion for accessing benefits in 2004, when a series of measures was instituted that defines and enforces the 'customary care' that household and family members are expected to give to each other (Pijl and Ramakers, 2007).

Finally, in many countries cash allowances are attractive options for containing expenditure. However, the provision of cash allowances also has other rationales and these are discussed below.

Care allowances and vouchers for long-term care

Cash payments or vouchers play an increasingly central role in arrangements for continuous and long-term care within Europe. They have a variety of underpinning rationales; in the context of any single long-term care system, several of these rationales may be evident. In some countries, particularly those with relatively underdeveloped community-based services, care allowances can offer support for family care or incentives for the development of formal home care services. The former objective is apparent in Ireland

(Timonen et al., 2007) and Italy, where 'allowances are provided to the elderly on the verge of institutionalization' (Gori, 2000: 266). In such situations, care allowances can counter biases towards institutional care and its associated spiralling costs.

Again in situations where community-based services are in short supply, care allowances may be intended to stimulate the development of a diverse range of formal services that can respond to the needs of individual older purchasers. Care allowances, vouchers, and similar hypothecated cash payments enable new resources to be directed at provider organizations who, according to the logic of market theories, are incentivized to expand their capacity and compete with each other for customers, thereby both enhancing the range and quality of services and reducing costs. This was one rationale for the introduction of the 'care assignment' entitlement option within German long-term care insurance, in order to break the former 'virtual cartel' of traditional provider organizations (Schunk, 1998). In Finland, home care service vouchers are also intended to increase the numbers of private home care provider agencies (Timonen et al., 2007). In the Spanish region of Valencia, the introduction of vouchers for nursing home care aimed, amongst other things, to increase the supply of publicly funded rooms and hence equality of access (Tortosa and Granell, 2002).

However, such precise objectives may be more difficult to achieve with cash payments which have no restrictions on their use. Thus, where care allowances are not restricted to spending on formal services, they can also stimulate increases in informal and 'grey' caregiving labour, particularly from migrants who are employed by families at less than market rates to provide live-in care to older people; these developments are particularly marked in Italy (Bettio et al., 2006) and Austria (Kremer, 2006; Österle and Hammer, 2007).

Thirdly, care allowances are consistent with discourses of consumerism and choice. Depending on the level of the allowance, they can also allow older people the choice of paying relatives or friends on a flexible basis. This consumerist rationale underpins the Personal Budget in the Netherlands – a cash alternative to the services otherwise provided under the AWBZ long-term care insurance scheme, which allows recipients the opportunity to receive care closely tailored to their needs and preferences; and direct payments and the individual budget pilots in England. In both countries, pressures to introduce this cash-based choice option came initially from younger disabled people, but take-up by older people actually remains very low.

Care allowances are, however, not unproblematic and widespread concerns have been expressed about the institutionalization of very low paid care work by female relatives (Germany, Italy, and Austria) or migrant workers (Austria) and about the difficulty of regulating the quality of care provided under such arrangements. Nevertheless, care allowances offer prima facie opportunities for cost control, especially when allocated on the basis of standardized, national assessment and eligibility criteria. Whether used to pay for informal care or to employ (migrant) carers, care allowances invariably fund much more care than would be provided by formal services for the same amount. Moreover, the levels of care allowances can be pegged; in Germany, levels were frozen for 15 years and increases requir Federal government legislation. This enhances their potential for costcontainment (Schunk, 1998) – in effect by shifting responsibilities for meeting any funding gap from the public sector back to the family (Pijl, 2000).

The Scottish exception

However, neither of the trends described above are universal. Scotland has devolved responsibility for health and social care policies and limited tax-raising powers. In 2002, Scotland introduced a complex package of funding reforms that included the provision of free (that is, non-means-tested) personal care services for older people. This led to an increase in demand for services, with the overall numbers of people receiving local authority-funded home care increasing by 10 per cent by 2005. There is no evidence that informal carers are withdrawing their support, although they may be providing less personal care and concentrating instead on offering social support, outings, and similar activities. The policy of free personal care continues to command wide political support and two-thirds of Scots claim a willingness to pay an increase in income tax to fund it (Bell et al., 2007). However, there are wide variations between local authorities in the costs and budgetary impact of the policy; the collection and recording of data on service use needs to improve in order to better monitor demand and costs (Bell et al., 2007). Until these improvements are put in place, it may be difficult to allay concerns about the long-term financial sustainability of the policy (Dickinson et al., 2007).

FUTURE PROSPECTS – TOWARDS GREATER CONVERGENCE?

This chapter has illustrated the diversity of approaches to funding and delivering long-term care services within Europe. This final section returns to a question raised at the start of the chapter: How is it that such diversity of arrangements persists in the context of a powerful supranational body, the European Union? What role does the EU play in influencing current arrangements for long-term care within its member states and what role might it play in future? To what extent is the current diversity of arrangements likely to continue; or is it likely that there will be greater harmonization between member states in the coming decades?

The EU has no legal competencies in the policy arena of long-term care; its legal responsibilities are restricted to economic policies and the linked movement of goods, services, capital, and workers. However, two developments are particularly significant: the 2000 EU Charter of Fundamental Rights and the impact of population ageing on the future economic competitiveness of the EU. These developments reflect concerns about the potential impact of population ageing on member states' publicly funded long-term health and social care systems and about the tensions between flexible skilled labour markets and high levels of responsibility for family caregiving. In relation to the latter concern, the EU has increasingly stressed the importance of the effective use of women's skills in a competitive, knowledge-based economy. Increased female labour market participation is seen as a means of improving competitiveness and the tax base of European welfare states (Lewis, 2006). Even women and older workers, both groups likely to be affected by care responsibilities, have target employment rates of 60 per cent and 50 per cent, respectively.

This immediately raises the question of how the increased labour market participation of women is to be reconciled with traditional gender-based responsibilities for care, a question which immediately also resonates with arguments for greater gender equality in the workplace. A range of policy options have been proposed, including 'caretaker accounts' – dedicated sums, allocated to the individual, to be used to support caregiving or buy care services; and the redistribution of working time over the entire life course (see Lewis, 2006). However, further analysis is needed to test the appropriateness of such proposals for the provision of care to frail older people; their impact on gender (in)equality; and for the risk of rendering the care of older people a predominantly private, unsupported, family responsibility.

In order to address some of the gaps created by the EU's limited legal competencies, in 2006 the integrated Open Method of Coordination (OMC) was introduced, aimed at 'strengthening EU capacity to support Member States in the drive for greater social cohesion in Europe' (Council of the European Union, 2007: 3). The OMC provides an additional framework for sharing experiences, ideas, and approaches and identifying best transferable practice in areas of policy that impact on social cohesion and social exclusion. These policies now include health care and long-term care; a 2007 Council of the European Union report drew attention to the disparities in funding capacity, coverage, and provision and the high personal costs and long waiting times often experienced in accessing long-term care services. This recognition may lead to the development of EU-wide proposals and policies, although their adoption by members states will remain voluntary.

At the same time, cross-national lobby groups, particularly those representing older people and family carers, are increasingly active in attempting to influence debate and policy at EU levels. The activities of these lobby groups include the creation and support of special interest groups of Members of the European Parliament and provide many informal opportunities for debate about the policy approaches within and between different member states; for sharing information about research on the outcomes of different policies; and for promoting the exchange of ideas and best practice at EU level.

CONCLUSION

In conclusion, considerable diversity exists between the countries of Europe in arrangements for funding and providing long-term care. This diversity reflects the fact that long-term care is embedded within multiple institutional and cultural arrangements and traditions within countries. Significant among these are the tensions and dynamics of central–local government responsibilities and relationships; and shifts in the boundaries between formal and informal, paid and unpaid care. While some common trends – particularly that towards cash payments for care – can be identified, their underpinning rationales and exact nature continue, to a greater or lesser extent, to reflect specific country circumstances.

In future, European Union policies that aim to increase the proportion of working age people in paid employment and contain pressures on publicly funded health and care systems may exert a growing common influence across European countries. However, it is not clear that this will necessarily lead to greater convergence in long-term care arrangements. Because these policies will also have an impact on the supply of informal, unpaid care, this may in turn prompt countries to devise new solutions to the resulting care crisis.

If the analysis of this chapter is correct, these solutions are likely once again to reflect to a greater or lesser extent the institutional and cultural structures and traditions of individual countries. Moreover, while the OMC provides less formal opportunities for policy learning and transfer between countries, these are likely to be diffuse and indirect and again subject to differential impact within individual European countries. The prospects for greater convergence therefore seem uncertain.

NOTE

1 http://epp.eurostat.ec.europa.eu

REFERENCES

Arntz, M., Sacchetto, R., Spermann, A., Steffes, S., and Widmaier, S. (2007) *The German Long-Term Care Insurance: Structure and Reform Options.* Discussion Paper 2625. Born: Institute for the Study of Labour.

Bell, D., Bowes, A., and Dawson, A. (2007) *Free Personal Care in Scotland: Recent Developments.* York: Joseph Rowntree Foundation.

Bettio, F., Simonazzi, A., and Villa, P. (2006) 'Change in care regimes and female migration: the "care drain" in the Mediterranean', *Journal of European Social Policy*, 16(3): 271–85.

Bowes, A. and Bell, D. (2007) 'Free personal care for older people in Scotland: issues and implications', *Social Policy and Society*, 6(3): 435–46.

Clasen, J. (1994) 'Social security', in J. Clasen and R. Freeman (eds), *Social Policy in Germany.* Hemel Hempstead: Harvester Wheatsheaf.

Comas-Herrera, A., Wittenberg, R., and Pickard, L. (2004) 'Long-term care for older people in the United Kingdom: structure and challenges', in M. Knapp, D. Challis, J.L. Fernández, and A. Netten (eds), *Long-Term Care: Matching Resources and Needs.* Aldershot, UK: Ashgate.

Comas-Herrera, A., Wittenberg, R., Costa-Font, J., et al. (2006) 'Future long-term care expenditure in Germany, Spain, Italy and the United Kingdom', *Ageing and Society*, 26(2): 285–302.

Community Care (2007) *Eligibility Criteria Depriving Older People of Gain Services: Thresholds on the Rise.* Downloaded from www.communitycare.co.uk, August 10, 2007.

Council of the European Union (2007) *Joint Report on Social Protection and Social Inclusion 2007* 6694/07. Brussels: Council of the European Union.

CSCI (2006) *Time to Care.* London: Commission for Social Care Inspection.

Daly, M. and Rake, K. (2003) *Gender and the Welfare State: Care, Work and Welfare in Europe and the USA.* Cambridge: Polity Press.

DH (2001) *National Service Framework for Older People.* London: Department of Health.

DH (2003) *Fair Access to Care Services. Guidance on Eligibility Criteria for Adult Social Care.* London: Department of Health.

Dickinson, H., Glasby, G., Forder, J., and Beesley, L. (2007) 'Free personal care in Scotland: a narrative review', *British Journal of Social Work*, 37: 459–74. (Advance access publication March 28, 2007.)

Esping Anderson, G. (1990) *The Three Worlds of Welfare Capitalism.* Cambridge: Polity.

European Commission (2001) *Budgetary Challenges Posed by Ageing Populations.* European Union Economic Policy Committee EPC/ECFIN/655/01-EN final.

Evans Cuellar, A. and Wiener, J. (2000) 'Can social insurance for long-term care work? The experience of Germany', *Health Affairs*, 19(3): 8–25.

Geraedts, M., Heller, G.V., and Harrington, C.A (2000) 'Germany's long-term care insurance: putting a social insurance model into practice', *The Millbank Quarterly*, 78(3): 375–401.

Glendinning, C. (2006) 'Paying family care-givers; evaluating different models', in C. Glendinning and P.A. Kemp (eds), *Cash and Care: Policy Challenges in the Welfare State.* Bristol: Policy Press.

Glendinning, C. (2007) 'Improving equity and sustainability in UK funding for long-term care: lessons from Germany', *Social Policy and Society*, 6(3): 411–22.

Glendinning, C., Chalis, D., and Fernández, J.L. (2008) *Evaluation of the Individual Budget Pilot Programme. Final Report.* York: Social Policy Research Unit, University of York.

Glendinning, C., Davies, B., Pickard, L., and Comas-Herrera, A. (2004) *Funding Long-Term Care for Older People: Lessons from Other Countries.* York: Joseph Rowntree Foundation.

Gori, C. (2000) 'Solidarity in Italy's policies towards the frail elderly: a value at stake', *International Journal of Social Welfare*, 9: 261–9.

HM Government (2009) *Shaping the Future of Care Together.* Cm 7673, London: The Stationery Office.

Hussein, S. and Manthorpe, J. (2005) 'An international review of the long-term care workforce: policies and shortages', *Journal of Aging and Social Policy*, 17(4): 75–94.

Karlsson, M., Mayhew, L., and Rickayzen, B. (2007) 'Long-term care financing in four OECD countries: fiscal burden and distributive effects', *Health Policy*, 80: 107–34.

Kremer, M. (2006) 'Developments in Austrian care arrangements', in C. Glendinning and P.A. Kemp (eds), *Cash and Care: Policy Challenges in the Welfare State.* Bristol: Policy Press.

Lewis, J. (1992) 'Gender and welfare regimes', *Journal of European Social Policy*, 2(3): 159–73.

Lewis, J. (2006) 'Care and gender: have the arguments for recognising care work now been won?', in C. Glendinning and P.A. Kemp (eds), *Cash and Care: Policy Challenges in the Welfare State*. Bristol: Policy Press.

Lowenstein, A. and Daatland, S.O. (2006) 'Filial norms and family support in a comparative cross-national context: evidence from the OASIS study', *Ageing and Society*, 26(2): 203–24.

Lund Pederson, L. (1998) 'Health and social care for older people in Denmark', in C. Glendinning (ed.), *Rights and Realities: Comparing New Developments in Long-Term Care for Older People*. Bristol: Policy Press.

Means, R. and Smith, R. (2008) *From Poor Law to Community Care: The Development of Welfare Services for Elderly People, 1939–1971*, 4th edn. Bristol: Policy Press.

Meinow, B., Kåreholt, I., and Lagergren, M. (2005) 'According to need? Predicting the amount of municipal home help allocated to elderly recipients in an urban area of Sweden', *Health and Social Care in the Community*, 13(4): 366–77.

Office of Fair Trading (2005) *Care Homes for Older People in the UK: A Market Study*. London: Office of Fair Trading.

Österle, A. and Hammer, E. (2007) 'Care allowances and the formalization of care arrangements: the Austrian Experience', in C. Ungerson and S. Yeandle (eds), *Cash for Care in Developed Welfare States*. Basingstoke, UK: Palgrave Macmillan.

Ovseiko, P. (2007) *Long-term Care for Older People, Ageing Horizons Brief*. Oxford: Oxford Institute of Ageing.

Pfau-Effinger, B. (2005) 'Welfare state policies and the development of care arrangements', *European Societies*, 7(2): 321–47.

Pijl, M. (2000) 'Home care allowances: good for many but not for all', *Practice*, 12(2): 55–65.

Pijl, M. and Ramakers, C. (2007) 'Contracting one's family members: the Dutch care allowance', in C. Ungerson and S. Yeandle (eds), *Cash for Care in Developed Welfare States*. Basingstoke, UK: Palgrave Macmillan.

Platz, M. and Brodhurst, S. (2001) 'Denmark', in T. Blackman, (ed.), *Social Care and Social Exclusion: A Comparative Study of Older People's Care in Europe*. Basingstoke, UK: Palgrave.

Poole, T. (2006) *Direct Payments and Older People*, Background Paper. Wanless Social Care Review. London: Kings Fund.

Rostgaard, T. (2006) 'Constructing the care consumer: free choice of home care for the elderly in Denmark', *European Societies*, 8(3): 433–63.

Royal Commission on Long-Term Care (1999) *With Respect to Old Age*, Cm 4192. London: The Stationery Office.

Schunk, M. (1998) 'The social insurance model of care for older people in Germany', in C. Glendinning (ed.), *Rights and Realities: Comparing New Developments in Long-Term Care for Older People*. Bristol: Policy Press.

Schunk, M. and Estes, C. (2001) 'Is German long-term care insurance a model for the United States?', *International Journal of Health Services*, 31(3): 617–34.

Scourfield, P. (2007) 'Are there reasons to be worried about the "cartelization" of residential care?', *Critical Social Policy*, 27(2): 155–80.

Stuart, M. and Weinrich, M. (2001) 'Home- and community-based long-term care: lessons from Denmark', *The Gerontologist*, 41(4): 474–80.

Sundström, G. and Johansson, L. (2005) 'The changing balance of government and family in care for the elderly in Sweden and other European countries', *Australasian Journal on Ageing*, 24 Supplement, June: S5–11.

Timonen, V., Convery, J., and Cahill, S. (2007) 'Cash-for-care programmes in four European countries', *Ageing and Society*, 26(3): 455–74.

Tortosa, M.A. and Granell, R. (2002) 'Nursing home vouchers in Spain: the Valencia experience', *Ageing and Society*, 22(6): 669–88.

Ungerson, C. (2003) 'Commodified care work in European labour markets', *European Societies*, 5(4): 377–96.

von Kondratowitz, H-J., Tesh-Römer, C., and Motel-Klingebiel, A. (2002) 'Establishing Systems of care in Germany: a long and winding road', *Ageing: Clinical and Experimental Research*, 14(4): 239–46.

Wanless, D. (2006) *Securing Good Care for Older People: Taking a Long-Term View*. London: Kings Fund.

Wegner, E. (2001) 'Restructuring care for the elderly in Germany', *Current Sociology*, 49(3): 175–88.

43

Long-term Care in China and Japan

Yun Zhou and Yuzhi Liu

BACKGROUND

As East Asian neighbors, China and Japan have a long history of contact with each other. Judging by developmental stages, Japan is currently classified as a developed country and China as a developing one. Japan has completed the demographic transition, and China has almost done so. Japan has a longer life expectancy and lower fertility rate, although China's fertility rate is rapidly declining due to the national population policy.

Despite these and other important differences, both countries have large older populations, and are ageing societies. The different demographic regimes in the two countries pose different social tasks, yet many of the age-related challenges are similar: both countries have to consider how to take care of the large size of their older population and develop a best or suitable social policy for older people. In this chapter, we will discuss ageing trends, needs for long-term care among the older populations, and social or government reaction to the needs of older people in both China and Japan.

CHINA

Ageing in China

According to five censuses conducted in China, the percentage of older people increased from 4 per cent in 1953 to almost 7 per cent in 2000 (the threshold for a society to be identified as an ageing society), and to almost 8 per cent in 2005 (see Chapter 5). Although the percentage of older people in the total population is not as high as many other countries, given the absolute size of the Chinese population (1.3 billion in 2000), the percentages put China as the most populous country in the world, not only by total population but also as an ageing population (see Chapter 5 and 32). In this most populous country, about 46 per cent of older people live in urban areas and 54 per cent in rural areas, according to a Statistical Communique of the People's Republic of China on the 2008 National Economic and Social Development.[1]

As noted elsewhere in the handbook, several features characterize change in the Chinese elderly population (see Chapter 32). First, the rate of population ageing has been growing since the 1950s, and has now made China an ageing society. Secondly, the older population itself is ageing. As in other countries, mortality decline among the population aged 80+ has grown more rapidly than in other age groups. Thirdly, regional differences mean that the speed and extent of ageing in China tends to be greater (due to fertility declines and increases in life expectancy) in Eastern than in Western China. Fourthly, unlike developed countries, the age structure of the rural Chinese population makes the ageing problem more serious than in urban China. And last, as in other countries in the world, feminization of later life is also a phenomenon in China.

In the context of an ageing population, long-term care has become a major issue in social and health policy. As many individuals are living longer, they will need help and care from their families and society, especially at older ages. Traditionally, older relatives have always been taken care of by family members. This traditional expectation is diminishing due to several significant trends: the decline in fertility, which is leading to a change in the overall age structure of society; the increase in workforce participation, especially of females; changes in living arrangements (from patrilocality to neolocality); and finally, changes in attitudes toward old-age care. All of these trends mean that the elderly in contemporary China cannot expect to count on their children for their needed old-age care as in previous generations. The realization that traditional forms of care may be inadequate to meet the care needs of older people has fueled interest in long-term care in China.

'Long-term care' is a new concept in China, and one that has no official or widely accepted definition. Usually, people take it for granted without imputing any specific meaning. Nevertheless, many Chinese understand that older people, often including aged parents or grandparents, may need help and care for basic daily needs in later life (Tian, 2005).

There are currently several channels of long-term care for older people: (1) care by a family member (or hired helpers) at home (traditional care); (2) care by professionals in welfare institutions (e.g., nursing home) or medical institutions (social care); and (3) care at home by persons from specialized organizations or institutions (social care) (Wu and Qin Quin, 2007). Although Chinese older people have various choices of care, their family is still the major force for old-age care in China (Sun, 2002). Xu and Zhe (2007) project that in the next 50 years, when 'baby boomers' born in the 1950s and 1960s enter old age, family care for older persons may not be viable on anything like the scale it has been, and the need for institutional care will have increased dramatically.

Some scholars propose dividing long-term care into two categories: 'market service' and 'non-market service' (Tian, 2005). Currently, there is a clear gap between the supply and demand for social institutions for older people. According to a survey by the Ministry of Civil Affairs of China in 1997, 12 per cent of the older adults surveyed intended to use institutional services; however, available institutions were inadequate to meet this level of demand (Gu, 2000). The contemporary demand for long-term care in China entails change not only in quantity but also in quality and in the types of services demanded (Pei, 2004). Older people using long-term care services are usually those who cannot visit doctors conveniently, who have rather high income, and whose ADLs (activities of daily living) have deteriorated (Li et al., 1998). A study of residents in 67 elder homes in Tianjin China found that images of institutions for older people are positive in terms of facility, medical, and direct care conditions among the old. Among other factors, marital status and financial ability are the major concerns influencing older adults' decision to use the facility (Zhan et al., 2006).

The gap between supply and demand leads to another important issue in long-term care in China: the initiation of a long-term care system or long-term care insurance system. Although China does not have a system as such, in people's minds the system should be able to minimize the problems of lack of resources of caregiving and financial difficulties that older people and their families may face in seeking care (Jing, 2006).

The need for long-term care

Although long-term care has been a major topic of discussion in China, few studies have looked into the real need for care among older people, or the quality of care delivered in long-term care settings. Lack of national data and the relatively recent emergence of these issues may account for the limited availability of material. Data from the national Chinese Longitudinal Healthy Longevity Survey (CLHLS) have become available,[2] and provide a basis for estimating the care needs or demands for long-term care among the older people. The survey randomly selected half of the counties/cities in 22 provinces of China, whose populations together constitute about 85 per cent of the total population in China and covered older people in the area over a 10-year period, from 1998 to 2008 (for more information about the survey, see Zeng, 2004; Zeng et al., 2001, 2007). Analyses by Gu (2008) and Zhang et al. (2006) suggest that the data in these surveys are reliable. Among the 15,636 older people who responded to the survey in 2005, there were more females than males, more rural residents than urban residents and more oldest-old than young-old older people (younger than 80 years old). Relevant findings regarding old-age care from the survey include the following:

1 *Almost one-fifth of the surveyed older people need help for their activities of daily living (ADLs).* The ADLs here include bathing, dressing, in-house activities, using the bathroom, continence, and feeding. The percentage of older people who need help for at least one type of these six activities was 18 per cent. The results of this survey suggest that a substantial number of older people need some daily care.

2 *There are age and sex difference in the need for long-term care.* In the age group 65–79, only about 3 per cent of the older people need care,

but the percentage increased to 42 per cent for the age group over 100 years (Table 43.1). Gender differences in care needs are also evident, with a consistent finding that more females than males need care. For example, 22 per cent of females but only 12 per cent of males need assistance with at least one ADL.

3 *Sources of financial support among the older people with care needs are limited.* When older people need care from people other than their family members, they must draw upon financial resources, especially if they are cared for in institutions, whether public or private ones. According to the CLHLS, less than 18 per cent of older people with care needs live on their pensions, whereas almost two-thirds (65 per cent) receive financial support from their children. The limited and dependent nature of non-familial financial support available to older people raises serious problems for the provision of care, since it means that the care of older people may depend on the economic condition of their children. In rural areas, older persons who have real difficulties in their life (e.g., are not able to work and have no financial resources and no family members or whose family members cannot take care of them) receive government support. The supports are called 'five guarantees' (Wu-bao), comprising guarantees for food, cloth, dwelling, medical care, and burial.[3]

Clear urban–rural differences exist in the provision of support by children. According to the CLHLS, more than half of older people in urban areas but more than three–quarters in rural localities depend on their children for financial support. Male–female differences in financial support by children in urban areas are larger than that in rural areas. In rural China, most older men and women are financially dependent upon their children. However, in urban China, more older people, men

especially, live on their pensions alone. Women are more likely to depend on their children; for those childless and below the poverty line, some government pension will be provided.

These differences in residence and gender result from the working experiences of older people earlier in their lives. When young, most women, both in urban and rural areas, stayed home to take care of their children and their aged parents-in-laws and never worked outside of the family. In rural areas, fewer males worked for a salary, and thus were not entitled to receive a pension. Therefore, most contemporary older Chinese women, and most rural Chinese, both male and female, do not qualify for pensions because they did not participate in a salary-based labor market. This is a very serious social security issue and the government is working on a social security system for all citizens of China.

The limited sources of finance can also be seen in low participation rates in public medical plans. Among older people with care needs in the CLHS, few had basic medical insurance plans (about 9 per cent). If they needed medical treatment or care from medical or social institutions, they would have to fund themselves, with the result that care needs would often not be met, leading to considerable hardship.

4 *Family members are still the major source of caregiving.* Most older people in the survey with care needs were living with their family. The percentage living with their family in rural areas was higher than that of urban areas and that of living alone was also high in rural areas (Table 43.2). The top six types of caregivers were son, daughter-in-law, daughter, grandchildren, spouse, and live-in non-family caregivers. Among the caregivers, over 50 per cent of care was provided by sons and their wives instead of their daughters. Family members thus played an important role in the care of older people.

Table 43.1 Percentage of older people with care needs by age and sex

Age (Years)	Male (N)	Female (N)	Both
65–79	3.19 (81/2536)	2.56 (63/2464)	2.88 (144/5000)
80–89	10.80 (205/1898)	15.07 (295/1957)	12.97 (500/3855)
90–99	18.59 (308/1657)	26.33 (596/2264)	23.06 (904/3921)
100+	33.72 (201/596)	43.82 (992/2264)	41.71 (1193/2860)
Total	11.89 (795/6687)	21.75 (1946/8949)	17.53 (2741/15636)

Note: Parentheses denote number of elderly who have care needs/number of elderly in the age group by gender.

Figures in Table 43.2 also show that there are few gender differences in nursing home placement, although the proportion residing in nursing homes in urban areas was twice that in rural areas.

Public attitudes toward long-term care

Although Chinese families are continuing to take much of the responsibility for their elders' care, with most older people continuing to live with family members rather than in institutions, there is a widespread acknowledgment that both the family members and elders should be given more choices for their care needs. One choice is the *social institution for the elderly* (SIEs), through which care is provided by public or private institutions when the family cannot provide care, or when there is no family. Social welfare institutions (including SIEs) are officially defined as 'institutions, operated by the state, organizations, and individuals, providing nursing care, rehabilitation and managed services, for older people, the handicapped, orphans, and foundlings' (Office of China National Committee on Aging and China Association on Aging, 2004: 195–96). Such institutions were established in China as early as the 1950s – then called *Jing-lao-yuan* (seniors home) (Chen, 1999) – and since 1999 have been operated under the supervision of the Ministry of Civil Affairs; they are approved and managed by the Department of Civil Affairs at county or higher-level government.

In 2000, when the government acknowledged the challenging burden of long-term care to the government and society, the State Council presented a document produced by the Ministry of Civil Affairs entitled 'An Opinion on Socialization of Social Welfare'. In the document, the government stated:

'From consideration of long-run and overall situation, we need to mobilize and rely on social forces to promote socialization of social welfare, and speed up the development of social welfare … . Socialization of social welfare means diversification of sources of investment, users, and types and ways of services of social welfare'.
(Office of China National Committee on Aging and China Association on Aging, 2004: 186–5)

The document outlined goals for increasing availability of institutional beds in urban areas and increasing the number of social welfare institutions in rural areas.

To promote the development of SIEs, the Chinese government has provided special benefits to private institutions, including discounted prices for electricity, benefits for telephone and telecommunication fees, and exemption from corporate income taxes (Office of China National Committee on Aging and China Association on Aging, 2004: 173–4).

For older Chinese living in rural areas (the majority), the government issued a separate interim provision defining the 'senior's home' ('*Jing-lao-yuan*') as a rural collective welfare unit, and promoted enterprises, public institutions, organizations, and individuals to found or support rural senior's homes. Most clients in rural senior homes are widowed and childless.

Changes in social institutions for the elderly

Although the number of SIEs in China has not changed greatly, the number of beds available within them has risen dramatically over the past two decades. In 1989, there were only about 687,000 beds, but the number had increased to over 1 million in 1999 and passed 2.5 million in 2007, almost four times the number of beds in 1989, with most of this increase occurring after 2000.

Table 43.2 Living arrangement of the older people with care needs by residence and gender in per cent (numbers in parentheses) (N = 2741)

Living arrangement	Urban males (N)	Urban females (N)	Subtotal	Rural males (N)	Rural females (N)	Subtotal
With family	88.4 (418)	88.2 (891)	88.3 (1309)	92.2 (297)	90.0 (842)	90.5 (1139)
Alone	5.9 (28)	6.1 (62)	6.1 (90)	5.6 (18)	7.9 (74)	7.3 (92)
Nursing home	5.7 (27)	5.6 (57)	5.7 (84)	2.2 (7)	2.1 (20)	2.1 (27)
Total	100 (473)	100 (1010)	100 (1483)	100 (322)	100 (936)	100 (1258)

Source: The national Chinese Longitudinal Healthy Longevity Survey

With an increase in beds, there has been a corresponding increase in the number of people using the service. In 2007 the number of older people using SIEs increased to almost 1.7 million, which represented nearly a four-fold increase from 1989. Although a causal connection cannot be drawn between the number of institutions and the number of older people using the services, the two factors appear to be quite closely related to each other. The needs of older people clearly have stimulated the development of SIEs, and an increase in number of beds of the institutions has attracted more older people to use the facilities.

At the same time, while the number of older people using the facilities increased, occupancy has been only around 70 per cent of available beds. Even though SIEs are thus operating below capacity, the percentage of older people using the facilities to the total ageing population is rapidly growing. Based on population data, Table 43.3 indicates that the number of beds available per 1000 older people more than doubled (11 to 24 beds per 1000 older people) in the 19 years from 1989 to 2007.

As indicated by the third column of Table 43.3, the ratio of older people using the facilities has risen even more rapidly, especially since 1999. Since then, usage has more than quadrupled, from about 0.4 per cent to 1.6 per cent.

Among the surveyed older people who were in SIEs, about 60 per cent of them reported were there because they did not have children, or that their children were not able to take care of them, another 26 per cent said that they lived in SIEs to minimize the care burden of their children, 9 per cent of older people wanted to communicate with people of their own age, and about 3 per cent did not have their own houses and did not want to

share houses with their children. In sum, it seems clear that SIEs are growing rapidly in popularity. However, the extent to which older people will utilize the SIE as a choice for their old age if they have enough care sources from their families is unclear.

Long-term care in China: concluding comments

The absolute size of the older Chinese population is substantial compared with that of China in the past, as well as compared with other countries, with an especially dramatic increase in the numbers of older women. Although 'long-term care' is a new concept in China, people recognize the need for such care, as a result of the lengthening of the life course and deteriorating health condition at advanced age.

As more individuals are living longer in failing health conditions, they will need help and care from their families and society. Estimates are that about 18 per cent of people aged 65 and over have care needs. At present, long-term care in China is still a family matter, but increasingly with some assistance from the society. The majority of older people with care needs are living with families both in rural and urban areas; however, more urban older adults (5.7 per cent) live in nursing homes compared with rural older adults with similar care needs. Lack of family caregivers appears to be the main reason for older people using social institutions for the elderly. To meet the demand for SIEs, the number of beds is increasing and ratio of the number of beds to the total older population is also growing.

Table 43.3 General characteristics of social institution for the elderly (SIE) beds and the older people using SIEs

Year	Number of beds per 1000 older people (65+)	Ratio of older people using SIE to the total elder population (per cent)
1989	10.5	0.37
1994	11.8	0.46
1999	10.7	0.43
2004	14.9	0.99
2007	23.6	1.59

Source: Data of 1989–99 are from Zhou and Chen, 2007; data of the other years are from *China Civil Affairs' Statistical Yearbook*, 2005 (p. 144) and 2008 (p. 300) (Ministry of Civil Affairs of China, 2005/2008)

JAPAN

Ageing in Japan

The situation in Japan is different from that in China in terms of its history of population ageing and the size of the elderly population. In Japan, population ageing is not a new phenomenon. The increase in the percentage of the population aged 65+ was small until 1970, when it reached 7 per cent; the proportion tripled to 21 per cent by 2005 (see Chapter 5).[4] The first characteristic of the aging process in Japan is the steady increase of the over-65 population, which has accelerated even more rapidly in the last two decades. Since 1990, the increase of population aged 65+ has ranged from 2 to 3 percentage points per year.

These increases in the percentage of older people to the total population also mean a dramatic increase in the absolute number of the older population in Japan.

The second characteristic of the ageing process in Japan is the 'ageing of the ageing population', which has been equally dramatic. Over the last 25 years of the prior century, the percentage of the oldest-old population (80+) increased rapidly, from 1 per cent of the total population in 1975 to over 11 per cent in 2000 (United Nations, 2002). The number of centenarians increased from 548 in 1975 to 13,036 in 2000 and 25,554 in 2005 (National Institute of Population and Social Security Research, 2008). And the last characteristic of the ageing process in Japan, as elsewhere, is the low sex ratio among the older population, indicating an excess of females. As in other highly developed societies, the sex ratio of the older population in Japan has been consistently lower than 100 (United Nations, 2002). Among the oldest-old population, the number of women is twice that of men.

When a population ages, it is likely to be characterized by higher rates of morbidity and of chronic rather than acute diseases. Moreover, chronic conditions mean that care needs may last for an extended period of time due to gradual deterioration of health with ageing. Thus, the need for long-term care among the older population is high.

The need for long-term care

Some characteristics of the care needs of older people in Japan can be summarized as follows:

1   *About one-quarter of those aged 65+ years old have difficulties in their life due to poor health status.* In Japan, almost 50 per cent of older people report not feeling well and 25 per cent of them reported that their lives are affected by their health status (Ministry of Health, Labour and Welfare, 2007). More females are restricted by their health status than are males; this is a trend that persists in all age groups. Overall, about 11 per cent of the population aged 65+ had difficulties with their ADLs. The percentage of females was higher than that of males (12 vs 9 per cent) (Ministry of Health, Labour and Welfare, 2007). These proportions indicate the need for support or care from others, if not long-term care.
    In 2000, when Japan started a national long-term care insurance system, about 11 per cent of the total population aged 65 and over (2.5 million people) needed support or care of some kind from others for the rest of their lives.[5] The number gradually increased to 4.2 million in

2005 (15 per cent of those aged 65 and over), reflecting both the gradually expanding use of the system as well as the reality of a rapidly growing older population with health needs.

2   *Home is the preferred place to stay in old age and family members are the most chosen category of caregivers.* In response to a government survey that asked where the respondent would 'want to get care', 45 per cent of older persons expressed that 'they will try hard to stay in their own home and to be taken care of there'. However, fully one-third (33 per cent) considered 'special nursing homes for the elderly or long-term health care facilities for the older people'. The top three reasons given for utilizing facilities for care were as follows (multiple answers): 'Do not want to bother family members (77 per cent); can get professional care (36 per cent); and family members are working and do not have enough time to take care of the elderly (26 per cent)' (Cabinet Office, 2003). Among caregivers of family members, most older people choose their spouse as first choice as caregiver (Cabinet Office, 2003); males are likely to choose their wives as the caregiver. By contrast, females are more likely to choose their daughters as the preferred caregiver. The family is still very important for individuals in old age and many family members still recognize the traditional norms of familiar responsibility for old-age care. For example, 49 per cent of the respondents answered 'it is natural to take care of parents'. At the same time, 36 per cent of them agreed with the statement 'You do not have to take care of your parents by yourself just because you are their children', indicating the changes from the traditional ideology of old-age care (Cabinet Office, 2003 [Figure 17 in the report]; see also Chapters 15 and 32).

3   *About one-third of the persons aged over 65 need rather intensive care.* Among older people with care needs, 22 per cent need day-long care from their caregivers and 8 per cent of them need about half-day care each day (Ministry of Health, Labour and Welfare, 2007). These figures indicate the intensive care needed, often entailing heavy care work by caregivers. When a family has aged parents or grandparents with care needs, members of the family will spend a lot of their time providing care. However, there is an important paradox here: most caregivers of older adults are also old themselves. For example, 27 per cent of the caregivers are 60–69 years old, 20 per cent are 70–79, and 9 per cent are over 80 years old (Ministry of Health, Labour and Welfare, 2007). Within the family, caregiving usually occurs within the same or adjacent generations; i.e., between husband and wife, or children and parents.

4   *Most older Japanese do not have financial problems.* Because of the pension and medical

systems in Japan, most older Japanese do not have many financial problems. According to six government-sponsored surveys in Japan conducted between 1980 and 2005 (Cabinet Office, 2005, Table 28), on average, 48 per cent of the respondents reported no financial problems at all in their lives, while the proportion reporting significant financial problems never exceeded 6 per cent. The financial resources of the Japanese elderly come from a variety of sources (Table 43.4). Their major financial resource is the public pension, and reliance on it has been rising since 1980. Consequently, Japanese older people have a rather stable life income, and the financial role of children in their lives is not that important. The older people may depend on their children for their daily care but not financial support. As indicated in Table 43.4, the proportion receiving public pension increased from 65 per cent in 1980 to over 90 per cent in 2005; contributions from children as well as earnings show substantial declines over the same period.

Major response of the government to the needs of long-term care

In 2000, the establishment of a long-term care insurance system (or nursing-care insurance system, *kaigo-hoken-seido*) made coverage available for every Japanese aged 40 and over. Despite the breadth of coverage across the older population, a strict screening process has been used to determine the eligibility to use those services for individuals over 65+ years old covered by the insurance. Degree of care provided is divided into six categories, beginning with 'support required' for frail older people, and extending through five levels of care for those bedridden or with dementia. Older people are able to get care services at home or at facilities. When they use the service, individuals pay a partial fee at a fixed rate (10 per cent of the cost of the insured services). Older

people may be able to choose whether to use services at home or in institutions. Because of the variety of in-home services provided by the insurance system, Japanese older people may stay at home while getting services usually one may only get at institutions (e.g., visiting nurses; bathing services) and they may arrange short-term stays at facilities. These services not only help older people but also reduce the burden of caregivers. Providing care services at home also may reduce the public cost of services at institutions. In 2006, among 3.4 million older people (65+) using the long-term care insurance system, 28 per cent were males and 72 per cent were females. Of them, 77 per cent were getting home services and 23 per cent were getting services from institutions for the older people (Ministry of Health, Labour and Welfare, 2007).

Changes in social institutions for older people

Institutions to deal with old-age problems in Japan are classified as 'welfare institutions for the aged', including (1) 'nursing homes for the aged', (2) 'special nursing homes for the aged', (3) 'low-cost homes for the aged', (4) 'welfare centers for the aged', and (5) 'daily service centers for the aged'. Older people are able to utilize all these facilities for their activities and old-age care. The first three types of facilities provide various types of care for the old living in institutions according to their needs.

The first three types of the institutions have been sites of significant change. The number of institutions for older people and number of seniors using facilities has been steadily rising. Between 1970 and 2006, the population of 65+ people increased four times, but the number of institutions increased ninefold. Although information on the number of beds in institutions is not available, the number of older adults entering institutions

Table 43.4 Financial sources for life among Japanese older people (percentage, multiple answers)

Financial Source	1980	1985	1990	1995	2000	2005
Salary from work	41.0	34.3	34.1	35.0	33.4	27.7
Public pension	64.6	77.0	81.2	84.0	84.9	90.6
Private pension	8.4	5.4	7.8	7.5	11.1	7.1
From savings	11.4	16.6	22.7	21.4	22.1	23.8
From property	15.6	14.5	13.9	11.4	8.2	6.5
From children	29.8	21.8	18.9	15.4	12.0	10.0
On welfare	1.7	1.4	1.4	0.7	1.0	0.5
Other	4.8	4.0	3.2	3.8	3.2	3.3

Source: Cabinet Office, Government of Japan, 2005

has been rising, from about 75,000 individuals in 1970 to over 535,000 individuals in 2006 – a more than seven-fold increase (Table 43.5). This increase in the number of older adults in the institutions may be explained partly by changes in attitude toward places for old age, but perhaps even more by the expansion in the number and types of facilities available to serve the needs of older persons. With an increase in number of institutions, older people in Japan are having more choices for their old-age care.

The proportion of persons over age 65 in institutions is very low, but it doubled from 1 per cent to 2 per cent over the 35 years from 1970 to 2006 (Table 43.5). Considering the nature of the institutions, it seems likely that older people in these institutions are those who have difficulties in their daily life and need additional care that family members are not able to provide.

Long-term care in Japan: concluding comments

The degree and seriousness of population ageing in Japan poses important challenges. Japan has developed strong pension, social security, and medical systems: most older Japanese do not have major financial problems in their lives. However, about one-quarter of Japanese over age 65 had difficulties in their life due to health problems and about one-third need rather intensive care. Care needs are met through a combination of family members as well as social institutions catering for older people. In Japan, a new type of long-term care insurance system was put into practice in 2000. This compulsory insurance for individuals over 40 is helping many older people, especially those with care needs, in their daily lives. Using the insurance system, older Japanese are able to choose to stay at home or to stay in different types of facilities for the elderly. Only a small percentage of Japanese older adults are using the facilities as a permanent residence. Home is still their best or preferred choice of place to stay in their old age.

SUMMARY

In China and Japan, care for ageing populations poses major societal challenges that cause concerns for individuals, policymakers, and the government as a whole. However, Japan faces these issues with a stronger economic foundation and a developed infrastructure to support older people. China has to deal with these challenges with fewer public economic resources to help or compensate the older people, especially those who need the help. This difference in economies may affect the lives of older people in the two countries. For example, most Japanese older people live on a universal public pension and medical system. In addition to their relatively fewer financial worries, Japanese older people are covered by a new public long-term care insurance system. The insurance system guarantees that older people will be able to meet their old-age care needs. They can obtain care services in their own homes or at facilities, depending on the category of care they are classified under the insurance system. For Chinese older people, financial circumstances vary greatly between urban and rural residents. Urban residents, who worked when they were young, are likely to have pensions as well as savings. By contrast, rural residents generally have no pension and must rely on their savings, if any, and thus also on their children for financial support. If present trends continue, more older people in China will depend on pensions and their own savings for their old age in the future, a result of the improvement of financial status among the young population today.

Table 43.5 Changes in institutions for the elderly in Japan

Year	Number of institutions	Number of persons residing in institutions	Per cent of older people using SIEs to the total elder population
1970	1014	75,056	1.02
1975	1594	117,842	1.33
1980	2181	157,425	1.48
1985	2843	201,044	1.61
1990	3505	241,931	1.62
1995	4699	307,497	1.68
2000	6856	416,176	1.89
2004	8181	497,483	2.00
2006	8737	535,583	2.01

Source: Number of institutions and number of elderly in the institutions are from '*Statistical Annual Report of Social Security*' for 1970–85 (www.ipss.go.jp), that of 1990–2000 are from *Japan Statistical Yearbook*, 2008; 'Elderly in the institutions to elderly over age 65+' are calculated based on population from *Japan Statistical Yearbook, 2008*

Economic and financial differences are important when comparing the situation of older people in China and Japan. However, these differences do not change the desired and actual role of family in older peoples' lives. In both of the countries, family members are still the most wanted and dependable source for old-age care. And in both countries, the most popular and preferred forms of care are care within one generation (husband and wife) and between two generations (parents and children).

In Japan, with various and abundant public resources for old-age or long-term care, the government and public try to help older people with long-term care needs so they can stay in their familiar homes during old age for as long as possible. Some services previously available only at facilities are now available at home. In China, with the limited and slow development of public facilities for older people, the government has tried to encourage and support the development of nursing homes. The purposes are to meet the needs of long-term care of the older people and to provide more choices of old-age care to the elderly population and their families. Some Chinese scholars are discussing the possibility of setting up a long-term care insurance system in China, as that used in Japan and other developed countries.

Both home care and institutional care are important for an ageing society. Despite the challenge, the ideal or harmonious model of old-age care continues to be that older people are cared for by their family members at their own homes and in their own communities with the assistance and support from public or governmental programmes and services. Institutional facilities to compensate the long-term care needs of older people that cannot be met by their families are continuing to expand. Both China and Japan are now working hard to develop long-term care systems and to provide services to the old with care needs for their old age, leading to the hope that older people in both China and Japan will have an even better life in the near future.

NOTES

1 http://www.stats.gov.cn/english/newsandcomingevents/t20090226_402540784.htm

2 http:web5.pku.edu.cn/ageing/English/indexe.htm

3 http://dbs.mca.gov.cn/article//ncwb/zcfg/200711/20071100003488.shtml

4 http://www.stat.go.jp/data/nenkan/index.htm

5 http://www8.cao.go.jp/kourei/whitepaper/w-2007/zenbun/html/j1232000.html

REFERENCES

Cabinet Office. Government of Japan (2003) 'Survey on old-age care', http://www8.cao.go.jp/survey/h15http://www8.cao.go.jp/survey/h15/h15-kourei/index.html

Cabinet Office. Government of Japan (2005) 'Sixth survey on life of elderly and consciousness: an international comparison', http://www8.cao.go.jp/kourei/ishiki/h17_kiso/pdf

Chen, H. L. (1999) 'Civil affairs', in *National Statistics Bureau* (ed.), *Fifty Years of New China*. Beijing: China Statistics Press.

Gu, D. (2008) 'General data assessment of the Chinese Longitudinal Healthy Longevity Survey in 2002', in Y. Zeng, D. Poston, D.A. Vlosky, and D. Gu (eds), *Healthy Longevity in China: Demographic, Socioeconomic, and Psychological Dimensions*. Dordrecht: Springer.

Gu, J. (2000) 'Improving policies and make elderly to enjoy the community and social services', *Population Research*, 2: 59–62.

Jing, T. (2006) *Long-term Care Insurance*. Beijing: University of International Business and Economics Publishing House.

Li, S., Huang, M., and Yi, G. (1998) 'Studies on long-term care needs among elderly in Wuhan', *Chinese Journal of Hospital Administration* 2: 24–26.

Ministry of Civil Affairs of China, Department of Finance and Administration (2005/2008) *China Civil Affairs' Statistical Yearbook*. Beijing: China Statistical Press.

Ministry of Health, Labour and Welfare. (2007) *White Paper on the Aging Society*. www8.cao.go.jp/kourei/whitepaper) (http://www8.cao.go.jp/kourei/whitepaper/w-2007/zenbun/19index.html)

National Institute of Population and Social Security Research. (2008) *Population Statistics of Japan*. www.ipss.go.jp

Office of China National Committee on Aging and China Association on Aging. (2004) *Yearbook of Works on Aging* (1982–2002). Beijing: Hualing Publishing House.

Pei, X. (2004) 'The development of long-term caring service in the aged city and its problems', *Journal of Shanghai Polytechnic College of Urban Management*, 6: 35–7.

Statistical Annual Report of Social Security, various years. http://www.ipss.go.jp/

Sun, J. (2002) 'Policy issues of long-term care among elderly in China', *Beijing Observation*, 8: 41–3.

Tian, S. (2005) 'An analysis on long-term care needs and service uses among Chinese elderly', *Chinese Journal of Public Health Management*,1: 71–3.

United Nations. (2002) *World Population Aging: 1950–2050*. www.un.org/esa/populations/worldaging19502050

Wu, B. and Qin, X. (2007) 'Community care of elderly in Urban China – Shanghai as an example', *Population Research*, 5: 61–70.

Xu, Q. and Tang, Z. (2007) 'Long-term care in China: current status and future trend', *Population and Economics*, 2: 6–12.

Zeng, Y. (2004) 'Chinese Longitudinal Healthy Longevity Survey and some research findings', *Geriatrics and Gerontology International*, 4: S49–52.

Zeng, Y., Gu, D., and Land, K.C. (2007) 'The association of childhood socioeconomic conditions with healthy longevity at the oldest-old ages in China', *Demography*, 43: 497–518.

Zeng, Y., Vaupel, J.W., Xiao, Z., Zhang, C., and Liu, Y. (2001) 'The Healthy Longevity Survey and the active life expectancy of the oldest old in China', *Population: An English Selection*, 13(1): 95–116.

Zhan, H.J., Liu, G., and Guan, Y. (2006) 'Willingness and availability: explaining new attitudes toward institutional elder care among Chinese elderly parents and their adult children', *Journal of Aging Studies*, 20: 279–90.

Zhang, W., Gu, D., Zeng, Y., and Liu, Y. (2006) 'Data quality evaluation of the Foruth round follow-up survey of Chinese Longitudinal Healthy Longevity Survey in 2005', working paper (in Chinese), CHAFS, 2006/7

Zhou, Y. and Chen, M. (2007) 'A study on nursing homes in China', *Population Journal*, 4: 19–24.

44

Ageing and Quality of Life in Europe

Alan Walker

INTRODUCTION

The main purpose of this chapter is to provide an overview of the current state of knowledge on the quality of life (QoL) of older people in Europe. Of course, in the space of one short chapter it is possible only to scratch the surface of a burgeoning literature. The endeavour is worthwhile, nonetheless, because there is an important story to be told about the development of a European perspective on QoL in old age that will be of interest to a global audience. The absence of a distinct *European perspective on ageing* has begun to be corrected in recent years, with an increasing number of comparative studies. The key drivers of change here are, first, the scientific communities and their appetite for European collaboration, culminating in the launch of the *European Journal of Ageing* in 2004; secondly, there is the European Union (EU) and its Framework Research Programmes encouraging comparative work. As well as specific scientific projects, there have been initiatives to coordinate ageing research in Europe, and this chapter will report on some of that work. The chapter, first, considers the various approaches to, or models of, QoL; secondly, it summarizes the current state of knowledge about QoL in old age; thirdly, it reports the results of European efforts to prioritize future research in this field. Most of the references are to European research given the emphasis of the chapter, but non-European references are not excluded artificially when they are needed.

QUALITY OF LIFE: DIMENSIONS AND SCOPE

Quality of life is a somewhat amorphous, multilayered, and complex concept, with a wide range of components – objective, subjective, macro-societal, micro-individual, positive, and negative – which interact (Lawton, 1991, Tesch-Römer et al., 2001). It is a concept that is difficult to pin down scientifically and there are competing disciplinary paradigms. Three central limitations of QoL are its apparent open-ended nature, its individualistic orientation, and its lack of theoretical foundations (Walker and van der Maesen, 2004). The widely acknowledged complexity of the concept, however, has not inhibited scientific inquiry. As Fernández-Ballesteros (1998a) has shown, in the final third of the last century, there was a substantial increase in citations of QoL across five different disciplinary databases. While the growth was significant in the psychological and sociological fields, in the biomedical one, starting from a lower point, it was 'exponential' (for example, increasing from one citation in 1969 to 2424 in 1995 in the 'Medline' database). This reflects the fact that, in many countries, discussions of QoL have been dominated by health issues, and a subfield, health-related quality of life (HRQoL), has been created, reflecting the longstanding pre-eminence of medicine in gerontology (Bowling, 1997; Walker, 2005).

Another key factor behind this growth in scientific inquiry is the concern among policy makers about the consequences of population ageing, particularly for spending on health and social care services, which has prompted a search for ways to enable older people to maintain their mobility and independence, and so avoid costly and dependency-enhancing institutional care. These policy concerns are not peculiar to Europe but are global (World Bank, 1994); nor are they necessarily negative because the new policy paradigms such as 'a society for all ages' and 'active ageing', both of which are prominent in the 2002 Madrid International Plan of Action on Ageing, offer the potential to create a new positive perspective on ageing and a major role for older people as active agents in their own QoL. A significant part of the impetus for this positive approach comes from within Europe (Walker, 2009).

MODELS OF QUALITY OF LIFE

Given the complexity of the concept and the existence of different disciplinary perspectives, it is not surprising that there is no agreement on how to define and measure QoL and no theory of QoL in old age. Indeed, it is arguable whether a theory of QoL is possible because, in practice, it operates as a meta-level construct that encompasses different dimensions of a person's life. Nonetheless, a theory would not only lend coherence and consistency but also would strengthen the potential of QoL measures in the policy arena (Noll, 2002). As part of the European FORUM project, Brown and colleagues (2004) prepared a taxonomy and systematic review of the English literature on the topic of QoL. In this, Bowling (2004) distinguishes between macro (societal, objective) and micro (individual, subjective) definitions of QoL. Among the former, she includes the roles of income, employment, housing, education, and other living and environmental circumstances; among the latter, she includes perceptions of overall QoL, individuals' experiences and values, and related proxy indicators such as well-being, happiness, and life satisfaction. Bowling also notes that models of QoL are extremely wide-ranging, including potentially everything from Maslow's (1954) hierarchy of human needs, to classic models based solely on psychological well-being, happiness, morale, life satisfaction (Andrews, 1986; Andrews and Withney, 1976; Larson, 1978), social expectations (Calman, 1984) or the individual's unique perceptions (Brown et al., 2004; O'Boyle, 1997). She distinguishes eight different models of QoL which may be applied, in slightly adapted form, to the gerontological literature:

- Objective social indicators of standard of living, health, and longevity, typically with reference to data on income, wealth, morbidity, and mortality. Scandinavian countries have a long tradition of collecting such national data (Andersson, 2005; Hornquist, 1982). Recently, attempts have been made to develop a coherent set of European social indicators (Noll, 2002; Walker and van der Maesen, 2004) but, as yet, these have not been applied to subgroups of the population.

- Satisfaction of human needs (Maslow, 1954), usually measured by reference to the individual's subjective satisfaction with the extent to which this has been met (Bigelow et al., 1991).

- Subjective social indicators of life satisfaction and psychological well-being, morale, esteem, individual fulfilment, and happiness, usually measured by the use of standardized, psychometric scales and tests (Bradburn, 1969; Clarke et al., 2000; Lawton, 1983; Mayring, 1987; Roos and Havens, 1991; Suzman et al., 1992; Veenhoven, 1999).

- Social capital in the form of personal resources, measured by indicators of social networks, support, participation in activities, and community integration (Bowling, 1994; Knipscheer et al., 1995; Wenger, 1989, 1996).

- Ecological and neighbourhood resources covering objective indicators such as levels of crime, quality of housing, and services and access to transport, and subjective indicators such as satisfaction with residence, local amenities and transport, technological competence, and perceptions of neighbourliness and personal safety (Cooper et al., 1999; Kellaher et al., 2004; Mollenkopf et al., 2004; Scharf et al., 2004). Recently, this approach to QoL has become a distinct subfield of ecological or architectural gerontology, with German researchers playing a prominent role (Mollenkopf and Kaspar, 2005; Wahl and Mollenkopf, 2003; Wahl et al., 2004; Weidekamp-Maicher and Reichert, 2005).

- Health and functioning, focusing on physical and mental capacity and incapacity (for example, activities of daily living and depression) and broader health status (Beaumont and Kenealy, 2004; Deeg et al., 2000; Verbrugge, 1995).

- Psychological models of factors such as cognitive competence, autonomy, self-efficacy, control, adaptation, and coping (Brandtstädter and Renner, 1990; Filipp and Ferring, 1998; Grundy and Bowling, 1999).

- Hermeneutic approaches, emphasizing the individual's values, interpretations, and perceptions, usually explored via qualitative or semi-structured quantitative techniques (Bowling and Windsor, 2001; Gabriel and Bowling, 2004a; O'Boyle, 1997; WHOQOL Group, 1993). This model, which is growing in its research applications, includes reference to the implicit theories that older people themselves hold about

QoL (Fernández-Ballesteros et al., 1996, 2001). Such implicit theories and definitions may be of significance in making cross-national comparisons by providing the basis for a universal understanding of QoL (and will be revisited later).

A common feature of all of these models identified by Brown et al. (2004) is that concepts of QoL have invariably been based on expert opinions rather than those of older people themselves (or, more generally, those of any age group). This limitation has been recognized only recently in social gerontology but has already led to a rich vein of research (Farquhar, 1995; Gabriel and Bowling, 2004a, 2004b; Grundy and Bowling, 1999). This does not mean, however, that QoL can be regarded as a purely subjective matter, especially when it is being used in a policy context. The apparent paradox revealed by the positive subjective evaluations expressed by many older people living in objectively adverse conditions, such as poverty and poor housing conditions, is a long-standing observation in gerontology (Walker, 1980, 1993). The processes of adjustment involved in this so-called 'satisfaction paradox' have been the focus of interest in recent research (Mollenkopf et al., 2004; Staudinger and Freund, 1998). As Bowling (2004) notes, there may be a significant age-cohort effect behind the paradox, as older people's rating of their own QoL are likely to reflect the lowered expectations of this generation, and they may therefore rate their lives as having better quality than a person in the next generation of older people in similar circumstances would do (Schilling, 2006).

Empirical research is required to test whether or not the satisfaction paradox is a function of a particular age-cohort. Nonetheless, the caution concerning subjective data on older people's QoL is particularly apposite in a comparative European context where expectations may differ markedly on the north/south and east/west axes (Mollenkopf et al., 2004; Polverini and Lamura, 2005; Weidekamp-Maicher and Reichert, 2005). For example, there are substantial variations in standards of living between older people in different European countries: in the 'old' EU-15, the 'at risk' of poverty rate among those aged 65 and over varied, in 2001, from 4 per cent in the Netherlands to over 30 per cent in Greece, Ireland, and Portugal (European Commission, 2003).

A recent review of QoL in old age in five European countries found a fairly widespread national expert consensus about the range of indicators that constitute the concept, particularly in the two countries with the most developed systems of social reporting, the Netherlands and Sweden, in which objective indicators were dominant (Walker, 2005). The southern European representative, Italy, does not consistently distinguish older people's QoL from the general population and frequently does not differentiate among the older age group. In all five countries, health-related QoL is the most prevalent approach in gerontology. Also, while there is no consensus on precisely how QoL should be measured, there is evidence of some cross-national trade in instruments, such as the adaptation of the Schedule for the Evaluation of Individual Quality of Life (SEIQOL) for use in the Netherlands (Peeters et al., 2005).

UNDERSTANDING QUALITY OF LIFE IN OLD AGE

In the light of the wide spectrum of disciplines involved in research on QoL in old age and their competing models, is it possible to draw any conclusions about how it is constituted? The answer is yes, but, because of the lack of either a generally agreed definition or a way to measure it, such conclusions must be tentative. First of all, although there is no agreement on these two vital issues, few would dissent from the idea that QoL should be regarded as a dynamic, multifaceted, and complex concept which must reflect the interaction of objective, subjective, macro, micro, positive, and negative influences. Not surprisingly, therefore, when attempts have been made to measure it, QoL is usually operationalized pragmatically as a series of domains (Grundy and Bowling, 1999; Hughes, 1990).

Secondly, QoL in old age is the outcome of the interactive combination of life-course factors and immediate situational ones. For example, prior employment status and mid-life caring roles affect access to resources and health in later life (Evandrou and Glaser, 2004). Fernández-Ballesteros and her colleagues (2001) combined both sets of factors in a theoretical model of life satisfaction. Recent research suggests that the influence of current factors such as network relationships may be greater than the life-course ones, although, of course, the two are interrelated (Wiggins et al., 2004). What is missing, even from the interactive approaches, is a political economy dimension (Baars et al., 2006). Quality of life in old age is not only a matter of individual life courses and psychological resources but also must include some reference to the individual's scope for action – the various constraints and opportunities that are available in different societies and to different groups, for example, by reference to factors such as socioeconomic security, social cohesion, social inclusion, and social empowerment

(Walker and van der Maesen, 2004). Hence, a consideration of the overarching and framing macroconditions, which is a matter of course in general QoL research, should also become accepted practice in research on QoL in old age (see Heyl et al., 2005).

Thirdly, some of the factors that determine QoL for older people are similar to those for other age groups, particularly with regard to comparisons between mid-life and the third age. However, when it comes to comparisons between young people and older people, health and functional capacity achieve a much higher rating among the latter (Hughes, 1990; Lawton, 1991). This emphasizes the significance of mobility as a prerequisite for an active and autonomous old age (Banister and Bowling, 2004; Mollenkopf et al., 2005), as well as the role of environmental stimuli and demands, and the potential mediating role of technology, in determining the possibilities for a life of quality (Mollenkopf and Fozard, 2004; Wahl et al., 1999). In practice, with the main exception of specific scales covering physical functioning, QoL in old age is often measured using scales developed for use with younger adults. This is clearly inappropriate when the heterogeneity of the older population is taken into account, and especially so with investigations among very frail or institutionalized older people. Older people's perspectives and implicit theories are often excluded by the common recourse to predetermined measurement scales in QoL research. This is reinforced by the tendency to seek the views of third parties when assessing QoL among very frail and cognitively impaired people (Bond, 1999). Communication is an essential starting point to involving older people and understanding their views, and recent research suggests that this can be achieved successfully among even very frail older people with cognitive impairments (Tester et al., 2004).

Fourthly, the sources of QoL in old age often differ between groups of older people. The most common empirical associations with QoL and well-being in old age are good health and functional ability, a sense of personal adequacy or usefulness, social participation, intergenerational family relationships, the availability of friends and social support, and socioeconomic status (including income, wealth, and housing) (Bengtson et al., 1996; Gabriel and Bowling, 2004a, 2004b; Knipscheer et al., 1995; Lehr and Thomae, 1987; Mayer and Baltes, 1996; Tesch-Römer et al., 2001). Still, different social groups have different priorities. For example, Nazroo and colleagues (2004) found that black and ethnic minority elders valued features of their local environment more highly than their white counterparts. Differences of priority have been noted in Spain between older people living in the community and those in institutional care, with the former valuing social integration and the latter the quality of the environment (Fernández-Ballesteros, 1998b). Other significant priorities for older people in institutional environments are control over their lives, the structure of the day, a sense of self, activities, and relationships with staff and other residents (Tester et al., 2004). This emphasizes the importance of the point made earlier about the need to communicate with frail older people in order to understand their perceptions of QoL: although some recent research has begun to address this (Gerritsen et al., 2004), the quality of the lives of the very old is still a relatively neglected area of gerontology. Comparative European research also points to different priority orders among older people in different countries – for example, the greater emphasis on the family in the south compared to the north (Polverini and Lamura, 2005; Walker, 1993). Another example of variations within Europe is the greater impact of objective living conditions on subjective QoL in former socialist countries, like East Germany and Hungary, compared to the more developed and affluent countries of most of the northern, western, and southern parts of Europe (Mollenkopf et al., 2004).

Fifthly, while there are common associations with QoL and well-being, it is clear that subjective self-assessments of psychological well-being and health are more powerful than objective economic or sociodemographic factors in explaining variations in QoL ratings (Bowling and Windsor, 2001; Brown et al., 2004). Two sets of interrelated factors are critical here: on the one hand, it is not the circumstances per se that are crucial but the degree of choice or control exercised in them by an older person; on the other hand, whether or not the person's psychological resources, including personality and emotional stability, enable that person to find compensatory strategies – a process that is labelled 'selective optimisation with compensation' (Baltes and Baltes, 1990). There is some evidence that the ability to operationalize such strategies, for example, in response to ill health, disability, or bereavement, is associated with higher levels of life satisfaction and QoL (Freund and Baltes, 1998). Feelings of independence, control, and autonomy are essential for well-being in old age. Moreover, analyses of the Basle Interdisciplinary Study of Ageing show that psychological well-being is more strongly associated with a feeling of control over one's life than with physical health and capacity among the very elderly than among the young-old individuals (Perrig-Chiello, 1999).

QUALITY OF LIFE IN OLD AGE: WHAT WE KNOW

Putting together a vast amount of scientific research, it is possible to highlight the core components of QoL in old age, which, incidentally, are confirmed by older people's own definitions. There are six broad groups of factors.

Psychological variables

Psychological variables include, in particular, personal control and mastery but also cognitive adjustment, social expectations and comparisons, optimism–pessimism, and resilience. Mastery was found to be a major predictor for all dimensions of well-being in Daatland and Hansen's (2007) Norwegian study (age range 40–79). Older people had nearly the same level of well-being as those in their mid-life even when their sense of mastery was lower. Given the same level of mastery, the older people had in fact higher well-being on all measures (except positive affect). These findings suggest a persistent positive effect of instrumental control. Personal control seems to be an important contributor to well-being even in very old age, when capabilities decrease and environmental constraints weigh heavily.

Findings from the European ENABLE-AGE study on very old people (aged 80–89) living alone in urban districts (Iwarsson et al., 2004) show that besides meaningful bonding to the home and high usability and accessibility, housing-related control beliefs were linked to the maintenance of independence in daily living and well-being. Conversely, a lack of personal control over the environment is linked to increased perceived environmental stress and depression among older adults (Disch et al., 2007). Taken together, findings such as these support the notion that a sense of actual control over important life domains, one's environment, and/or desirable outcomes add considerably to well-being among older people. It may be even more important for autonomy and self-respect among very old and vulnerable people when individual competencies decrease and environmental circumstances are, or become, stressful. In the case of changes that are entirely out of personal control, such as the loss of a partner or the occurrence of a severe health impairment, cognitive adjustment may reduce mental incongruence and, by this, help to maintain QoL.

Health and functional status

In a multitude of studies, health has proved to be of prime importance for QoL, both as a significant predictor emerging from scientific analyses and as a salient aspect of life according to older people's own definitions. At the same time, there are interesting differentiations and changes. For example, QoL in terms of both life satisfaction and positive affect is higher among healthy than among ill older people. However, there is a similar change over time in these aspects, and while health is considered important by most older people, this is less so for ill than for healthy people. Moreover, older people rated their QoL higher than was to be expected in view of their score on a standard health-related QoL measurement instrument. After making an inventory of aspects of life important to them hence, the relationship between health and QoL may not be as strong in older age as has been assumed. The reason that physical health decreases in its significance in the case of illness might be the psychological process of cognitive dissonance or mental incongruence, an adaptive strategy to losses of important aspects of life that cannot be regained (Freund and Baltes, 1998).

Social relations, support, and activity

The fundamental role that the manifold dimensions of social relations play in QoL is widely acknowledged. Older people themselves mentioned social relationships, social roles, and activities in the first place when answering open-ended survey questions and in-depth interviews on the constituents of the 'good things' that gave quality to their lives (Bowling, 2005). Also, the older participants of the Longitudinal Ageing Study Amsterdam (LASA) considered a good marriage among the three most important aspects of life (besides physical and mental health) (Deeg et al., 1993).

Social support appears to be particularly salient in the case of those experiencing structural disadvantages as they are commonly shared across ethnic subgroups within developed countries. The family, in particular, seems to enhance QoL under disadvantaged macro-structural conditions. In the face of meso-structural conditions such as deprived neighbourhoods, social support can work like a buffer (Disch et al., 2007). Many of the older residents living in low-income housing in environmentally stressful contexts had strong social support systems that many of them derived from their building networks. Those who had the highest social support experienced no environmental stress/depression, whereas those in the environmental stress/depression group had the lowest support.

Economic circumstances and independence

As many previous studies on the general population have shown (Diener et al., 2003; Veenhoven, 1996), financial circumstances are the most important predictors for life satisfaction besides health status. Older people seem to be more satisfied with their financial situation than younger ones, though, and the predictive power of the income level, for both satisfaction with the financial situation and the level of the subjective well-being, decreases with advancing age. However, this should not be interpreted to the effect that financial resources are losing their importance for a good QoL in old age. Instead, the objective significance of sufficient earnings increases because the more health impairments that arise and the more fragile social support networks become, the more important is the availability of other supporting resources. Thus, it is not the absolute level of income that plays the most important role in the subjective evaluation of financial resources, but rather the living standard it enables. In other words, the key issue is whether or not the available economic resources suffice to attain a satisfactory living standard, including, for instance, participation in social life (despite mobility restrictions) or affording the rising costs of health care or nursing care.

The level of income affects many domains of life. For example, the heaviest explanatory parameter for overall residential satisfaction of older people living in the Madrid region was the perception of their own economic resources and the household in which they live (Rojo-Pérez et al., 2007). This subjective aspect was underpinned by objective conditions insofar as wealthier, higher-class people live in relatively more modern and better equipped houses. Probably due to their better economic resources, they could afford a house in a neighbourhood according to their wishes – and, consequently, were more satisfied with their residential environment. Satisfaction with income was also revealed to be an important predictor for QoL in the MOBILATE study (Mollenkopf et al., 2005). Interestingly, this factor affected significantly the cognitive dimension of life quality (satisfaction with life in general) in all European regions under study but was less or not at all important for its emotional dimension (positive affect).

Whether older people have sufficient financial resources at their disposal to enable them to maintain a satisfactory standard of living is largely dependent on the country they live in and the welfare system prevailing in that country. Motel-Klingebiel (2007) demonstrated through his research in three European countries that, to some extent, the levels and, in particular, the variations of QoL among older people are significantly influenced by the countries' differing welfare systems. In such a comparative perspective, England (as an example of a liberal welfare system) showed the lowest level of objective resources. Older people did best in Germany (representing a conservative-corporatist regime) and somewhat less so in Norway (representing the social-democratic welfare regime typical of the Scandinavian countries). Moreover, Germany and Norway revealed the lowest variability in objective income measures, whereas England showed the highest variability on all indicators used for assessing QoL of older people. Nevertheless, England's older people do not seem to feel deprived when asked for a subjective appraisal of their QoL. This raises the important issue of older people's frames of reference when evaluating their QoL. Regardless of welfare regime, this research found a higher degree of variation in QoL among older than younger age groups and, consistently, physical health was the most important single domain for overall QoL in old age (Motel-Klingebiel, 2006).

Environmental conditions

Closely connected with financial circumstances are the options for choosing where to live, a connection often neglected in QoL research although older people themselves emphasize the importance of home and neighbourhood.

Indoor and outdoor environments can constitute major resources for older people's QoL. Based on Lawton's (1991) theoretical approach towards person–environment relationships, Wahl and colleagues (2007) provide empirical evidence that both objective and subjective components have to be considered to understand better QoL outcomes such as autonomy, life satisfaction, and emotional well-being (see Chapter 8). Likewise, Disch and colleagues (2007) show that the structural characteristics of buildings and neighbourhoods affect the residents' QoL. At the same time, their findings indicate that residents with more positive social support experienced higher QoL. If the social environment is compromised, mental health problems and negative perceptions of the built environment increase.

The importance of good housing and an appropriate neighbourhood increases when severe illness or chronic diseases make continued functioning in daily life more critical. Particularly for older people who are receiving care, the physical environment cannot be excluded if the care is to be effective in promoting their QoL. Hence, it is important to consider personal aspects, on the one hand, and to extend individualized person–environment system approaches to the meso and macrolevels of analysis, on the other hand, in order to understand the complex nature of the relationships between environmental factors and QoL.

Leisure activities and mobility

Two further components which are only rarely addressed in generic QoL scales and research turn out to be of great importance to older people: activities and mobility. Both aspects are closely interconnected, and their significance for an autonomous and meaningful life in old age becomes obvious in the light of the age-related increase in mobility restrictions. This applies especially to modern societies where mobility is not only a fundamental precondition for overcoming the growing distances between functional areas but also constitutes a highly appreciated societal value.

Objective and subjective aspects of out-of-home activities and mobility were significant predictors of satisfaction with life and emotional well-being among the older adults participating in the MOBILATE study (Mollenkopf et al., 2006). In Bowling's (2005) study, too, the lay models of QoL emphasized the importance of leisure and social activities, including those enjoyed alone. Furthermore, based on their review of available research findings on material well-being, Weidekamp-Maicher and Naegele (2007) state that in very old age satisfaction with mobility (alongside satisfaction with one's state of health and social networks) exceeds income in the subjective evaluation of QoL. Finally, according to analyses of the longitudinal LASA data (Deeg, 2007) the importance of meaningful spending of time increases for ill older adults. Therefore, aspects of activity and mobility need to be included in future QoL approaches.

PRIORITIZING FUTURE RESEARCH ON QUALITY OF LIFE IN OLD AGE

The final part of this chapter turns from a consideration of what we know to an outline of what more we need to know and do with regard to QoL in old age. There are many open research questions. For example:

- Why are levels of satisfaction and well-being in general so high among older people?

- Why is health less important among ill than among healthy older people?
- Which role does age and ageing play for their subjective QoL?
- What really matters in very old age or in the case of chronic illness and the need for care?
- What exactly is the role of social network resources in relation to QoL in late life?
- To what extent does intra-group supportiveness – for instance among ethnic minorities – arise out of necessity?
- What is the significance of the residential context among both older people who live on their own and those who live dependently in a residential institution?
- Which physical and social conditions are suited to support the person's QoL?
- What is the interrelationship between the two?
- While empirical research indicates that care has a role in the production of QoL for frail older people, the issues are when, how, and under what conditions is this so?
- And, on a more general level, which personal resources and which environmental conditions are contextually most or least important for QoL?

More research is needed to determine the strength and contextual salience of each of the variables using a clearly defined QoL model.

Some further knowledge gaps concern cohort-related aspects. For instance:

- What is the frame of reference of today's older people's evaluations of their lives – and with whom and at what times will future generations compare their situation?
- What will QoL be for future cohorts of older people in the light of demographic change, structural uncertainty, precarious jobs, long-term unemployment, cuts in pension levels, and reduced welfare provision?
- Will they be able to cope or compensate for changing environments and resources?

The questions raised here correspond with the research gaps and priorities that emerged in two European Framework Programme projects which have focused specifically on QoL in old age: the FORUM on Population Ageing Research and the European Research Area in Ageing, ERA-AGE. The FORUM project (2002–04) conducted a series of scientific workshops on three topics – QoL; health and social care; and genetics, longevity, and demography – aimed at identifying knowledge gaps and prioritizing research from a European-wide perspective. The outcomes of the FORUM process command a high level of consensus among both scientists and key research end-user groups. The ERA-AGE project (2004–08) is designed to promote long-term coordination of national research programmes and to promote interdisciplinary research and international collaboration in the field of ageing across Europe. A wide range of recommendations were made by the FORUM project and ERA-AGE, but here the focus will be only on four sets of them in the QoL field: environmental resources; sociodemographic and economic resources; health resources; and personal resources, social participation, and support networks. (The full set of recommendations, including those covering the topics of health and social care and genetics, longevity, and demography, and those intended for national and European research funders and policymakers can be viewed on the FORUM and ERA-AGE websites.[1]

Environmental resources

The environment (at all levels) should be treated as a key component and dynamic context of QoL in old age. The scientific discussion about its role envisaged a three-dimensional framework, linking together individual factors (from health and personal ability to life story), psychological and social factors (security, loneliness, autonomy, attachment, diversity, cohort, ethnicity, culture, gender, and material resources), and environmental factors (migration, transport, accommodation, technology, neighbourhood, and the natural world). Within this framework, the urgent priorities for research in the environmental dimension include a deeper understanding of:

- the spatiality of ageing and the experience of interior and exterior space in later life across different countries and regions
- the relationship between living arrangements and the community, neighbourhoods, and care services
- the environments that are accessible or inaccessible for older people, and the intergenerational dimension of integration/segregation within public and private spaces
- how older people with learning difficulties/ intellectual disabilities and older people with dementia are ageing in place.

There is also a need to balance knowledge about older people living in 'special' settings such as residential and nursing homes with research on those living in 'ordinary' ones. Moreover, more evaluations of practical environmental interventions are necessary to provide knowledge on how to improve the lives of older people. This holds especially for technological developments that have an immense impact upon different spheres of the everyday life of older people because, with advancing age, the significance of mobility, environmental stimuli and demands, and the potential of technology as prerequisites for a life of quality increases. Finally, there is a substantial knowledge gap about the impact on older peoples' QoL of major crises related to environmental issues such as climate change, heat waves, power supply shortages, and so on.

Sociodemographic and economic resources

Four key priority issues were highlighted with regard to sociodemographic and economic resources. First, QoL research needs to explore further the question of diversity. There is a need to understand the causal factors behind inequalities between countries and social groups, including the interrelationship with experiences gained earlier in the life course, the extent to which some circumstances and experiences are universal, and how the priority order of factors determining quality varies between different groups of older people. Given the changes in male and female life-course trajectories, it is important to investigate issues such as gendered changes in working life, the experience of long-term and discontinuous employment, changes in pension policy, the transition to retirement, and the impact of these on QoL. Secondly, it is important to focus research on the economic status of future cohorts of older people and the relationship between ageing and income and other material resources. New knowledge is required on how the income needs of older people change as they age, their perceptions of income, and how these change over time. Too little is known about wealth and inheritance, including the economic power of older people in society and within families, and how wealth is transmitted between generations. The absence of reliable data on this topic means that new research is needed to collect comparative information on wealth and goods in kind at both the individual and household levels. Thirdly, further research is required on employment in later life and the transition to retirement. For example, what are the economic incentives to continue to work in later life? What is the relationship between work, age of exit from the labour market, pensions, and inheritance? What effect has retirement on QoL and subjective well-being, and what is the role of different local, regional, and national policies and welfare systems in shaping the standard of living, social inclusion, and QoL in old age? Fourthly, more knowledge is needed about 'active ageing'. How does active ageing relate to the policies and politics of statutory retirement in Europe? What does active ageing mean beyond working? How is active ageing defined in different countries – what are the differences and what is their relevance to policy? What strategies and policies are needed to promote a form of active ageing that enlarges well-being?

Health resources

In the field of health resources two different sets of research priorities were identified. First, reviews are needed of the existing conceptual and empirical research relating to the concept of QoL covering not only subjective QoL but also all aspects relevant for individual agency (such as resources and competence). To prepare for comparative research, it is also necessary to review analyses of policy, health systems, societal structure, and cultures. In addition to the need for preparatory reviews, there were five specific field research priorities:

- Aspects of prevention, rehabilitation, and disease management in healthcare systems and their effects on health behaviour and QoL.
- Quality of life of older people with chronic disease.
- Inequalities in health and QoL related to structural factors such as income, gender, ethnicity, and age.
- Historical health trends within and between cohorts and generations (comparisons between the young-old individuals who have become healthier over time and the old-old individuals who have developed new forms of frailty such as dementia).
- The relationships between migration and ethnicity and health and social care systems, including research on both ethnic and cultural variations in attitudes towards and use of services and on the roles that migrants fulfil in different national health and social care systems such as in-house domestic carers in Italy and Greece and employees in residential and nursing homes in Germany and the United Kindom.

Personal resources, social participation, and support networks

A large number of priorities were highlighted in the field of personal resources, social participation, and support networks, a small selection of which are reported here. More focus is needed on individual and societal changes in the second half of the life course, both at the micro and macro

levels, as well as on the changing objective living conditions and how older people subjectively perceive and adapt to these. These changes impact on dependency, care issues, employment, economic and social resources, retirement, lifelong learning, and other important issues. Furthermore, these consequences have implications on inequalities and social exclusion in later life. Therefore, there is an urgent need to integrate research with policy and interventions studies.

- More research is required on the needs, characteristics, and the risk of marginality among particularly vulnerable groups such as ethnic minorities, the very old and frail, and older people suffering from chronic disease and/or dementia and other intellectual disabilities.
- The impact on QoL of factors such as bereavement, retirement, disability, low income, living alone (especially older women), age-friendly or age-unfriendly attitudes towards older people, elder abuse, migration, and so on.
- The interaction between societal modernization, mechanization, life-course trajectories, family change, and intergenerational relationships, including new family forms, on the one hand, and the resources of older people for coping and adapting to the risks and challenges associated with later life, on the other.

Methodological issues

With respect to methodological issues, again, a large number of recommendations were made in the course of the two European coordination projects. The main ones are referred to here. First of all, there is a need for further theoretical work on the models of QoL and the instruments used to measure it. In particular, the implicit theories held by older people concerning the quality of their lives must be incorporated into a basic definition of QoL. In other words, investigators should ensure that their models are grounded in lay perspectives, standards, and norms, and not purely in theoretical constructions. Thus, a model is required for use in both descriptive and evaluative research that captures individual agency and perspectives on what constitutes quality and well-being with other relevant factors as preconditions. Secondly, such theory development needs to be undertaken by disciplines working in collaboration, moving beyond the common emphasis on health and functioning, which is prevalent in much of the QoL literature, so that the different factors shaping QoL – from genetics to pensions – can be incorporated. Thirdly, comparative QoL research is greatly inhibited by the wide variations in the type and quality of data available on this topic in different countries. Thus, there is an urgent need for comparable approaches and measures to be adopted if the full potential of past, ongoing, and future research is to be realized. Such a harmonization may consist of both the post-harmonization of existing data and pre-harmonization aimed at developing comparable instruments. Fourthly, there is a need for coordinated longitudinal and repeated cross-sectional studies on the dynamics of QoL. Such research is required urgently to assess and distinguish cohort effects, effects of ageing, and the impact of changing values and expectations in QoL. Most existing national longitudinal studies concern one historic cohort in which ageing-related changes in QoL are studied (an exception is LASA in the Netherlands, which adds new cohorts at specific time intervals). But, given generational and social changes, a cohort-sequential design is necessary to distinguish these from those changes associated with ageing. Fifthly, in view of the unique spread of nations and cultures in Europe as well as in other parts of the world, it is vital that definitions and methods are cross-cultural and dynamic. Cross-national studies should include both standardized instruments plus additional culture-specific items considering cultural peculiarities. Finally, more attention should be given to the heterogeneity of ageing and the aged. Frequently, average data conceal differences between specific groups or conditions. The lack of information on ethnic minority elders and of people in need of care has already been mentioned. Similarly, many findings may not generalize to countries with differing living standards and welfare-state arrangements.

Theoretical approaches

The most striking observation that is prompted by both reviewing the literature and participating in European projects such as FORUM and ERA-AGE is how little research and conceptual thinking is shared among this community of scientists. The only theoretical approaches that were used commonly are Lawton's (1991) and Veenhoven's (2000) multidimensional models of QoL.

Apart from these, there is a general agreement that a basic definition and comprehensive model of QoL are urgently needed. Such a model should incorporate different perspectives (individual, societal, and social policy) and conceptualizations (at the societal and objective level to those referring to the individual and subjective levels) and enable research on the societal level as well as on the individual level. For that very reason, the basic dimensions included in a model of QoL should reflect science, social policy, and the views of older people. There is also consensus about the process-oriented character of QoL and hence the need to take individual, societal, and historical changes into account. Furthermore, theoretical work is needed to clarify and give reasons for methodological key concepts and operationalizations, and for indicators and scales.

CONCLUSION

Although the notion of QoL may be criticized easily for its amorphous nature, there is no doubt that it is a broad-based multidisciplinary concept and one that is the focus of increasing interest among gerontologists. As noted previously, an important driver of this interest is the policymaking process. Several strands of recent research in this field may be emphasized. Most important of all, there is a discernible shift away from the application of health-related proxies for QoL – functional capacity, health status, psychological well-being, social support related to incapacity, morale, dependence, coping with and adjustment to disability – without reference to the ways in which older people in general, or specific groups of older people or service users, define their own QoL or the value they place on the different components used by the 'experts'. In practice, older people are remarkably consistent, across a wide range of studies, in the domains they identify as being important for the quality of their lives: familial and other relationships and contact with others, emotional well-being, religion/spirituality, independence, social activities, finances and standard of living, and their own health and the health of others (Brown et al., 2004).

The danger with the previous approach to assessing QoL in old age, which has dominated both scientific and professional worlds, was that it tended to homogenize older people rather than recognize inequality, diversity, and differences based, for example, on age, gender, race and ethnicity, and disability. A key element in this homogenization is the prevailing use of statistical techniques that focus on means and general coefficients of association rather than on internal sample differentiation (see Singer and Ryff, 2001 for a review of statistical methods addressing diversity). Also inherent in this paradigm was a conception of older age as a distinct phase of the life course, one that is detached from middle age and earlier phases (Bond, 1999; Gubrium and Lynott, 1983). In its place, have gradually appeared interpretive approaches that aim, among other things, to build on the implicit theories of QoL held by older people themselves. In particular, two complementary approaches to assessing QoL from the perspective of older people are, on the one hand, from life-span development psychology, attempts to understand subjective meanings of QoL within the context of the person's life course and, on the other, the operationalization of QoL as a multidimensional phenomenon reflecting lay perspectives (Bowling et al., 2002; Grundy and Bowling, 1999). Combining the strengths of these two approaches operationally calls for both quantitative and qualitative research methods.

Comparative research is necessary not only to share knowledge and good practice but also to provide a critical perspective on the portability of different models of practice. Comparisons are needed of QoL in old age in different countries because the existing aggregate data provide only a superficial view, and such studies must relate QoL to the national cultural and institutional context. Comparative research will also help to avoid ethnocentric value biases in definitions of 'the good life'. Finally, with regard to multi- and interdisciplinary collaboration, European scientists in the FORUM and ERA-AGE projects emphasized the importance of disciplinary identities but also stressed the need to integrate knowledge to produce broader models of QoL. The essential point is that the nature of the collaboration should be determined by the specific research question and, therefore, a range of different sorts of multi- and interdisciplinary working may be envisaged. Thus, a combination of comparative and multidisciplinary research is required in order to advance our understanding of QoL in later life.

ACKNOWLEDGEMENT

I am grateful to Heindrun Mollenkopf for her permission to use our joint work in this chapter.

NOTE

1 Websites (http://www.shef.ac.uk/ageingresearch and http://era-age.group.shef.ac.uk/).

REFERENCES

Andersson, L. (2005) 'Sweden: quality of life in old age I', in A. Walker (ed.), *Growing Older in Europe*. Maidenhead: Open University Press, pp.105–27.

Andrews, F.M. (1986) (ed.) *Research on the Quality of Life*. Michigan: University of Michigan Press.

Andrews, F.M. and Withey, S.B. (1976) 'Developing measures of perceived life quality: results from several national surveys', *Social Indicators Research*, 1: 1–26.

Baltes, P.B. and Baltes, M.M. (eds) (1990) *Successful Ageing: Perspectives from the Behavioural Sciences*. New York: Cambridge University Press.

Baars, J., Dannefer, D., Phillipson, C., and Walker, A. (eds) (2006) *Aging, Globalisation and Inequality*. Amityville, NY: Baywood.

Banister, D. and Bowling, A. (2004) 'Quality of life for the elderly: the transport dimension', *Transport Policy*, 11: 105–15.

Beaumont, J.G. and Kenealy, P.M. (2004) 'Quality of life – perceptions and comparisons in healthy old age', *Ageing and Society*, 24: 755–70.

Bengtson, V., Rosenthal, C., and Burton, L. (1996) 'Paradoxes of family and aging', in R. Binstock and L. George (eds), *Handbook of Aging and the Social Sciences*. San Diego: Academic Press, pp. 263–87.

Bigelow, D.A., McFarlane, B.H., and Olson, M.M. (1991) 'Quality of life of community mental health programme clients: validating a measure', *Community Mental Health Journal*, 27: 43–55.

Bond, J. (1999) 'Quality of life for people with dementia: approaches to the challenge of measurement', *Ageing and Society*, 19: 561–79.

Bowling, A. (1994) 'Social networks and social support among older people and implications for emotional well-being and psychiatric morbidity', *International Review of Psychiatry*, 9: 447–59.

Bowling, A. (1997) *Measuring Health*. Buckingham: Open University Press.

Bowling, A. (2004) 'A taxonomy and overview of quality of life', in J. Brown, A. Bowling, and T. Flynn *(eds), Models of Quality of Life: A Taxonomy and Systematic Review of the Literature*. University of Sheffield, FORUM Project.

Bowling, A. (2005) *Ageing Well: Quality of Life in Old Age*. Maidenhead: Open University Press.

Bowling, A. and Windsor, J. (2001) 'Towards the good life', *Journal of Happiness Studies*, 2: 55–81.

Bowling, A., Banister, D., Sutton, S., Evans, O., and Windsor, J. (2002) 'A multidimensional model of the quality of life in older age', *Ageing and Mental Health*, 6: 355–71.

Bradburn, N.M. (1969) *The Structure of Psychological Well-being*. Chicago: Aldine Press.

Brandtstädter, J. and Renner, G. (1990) 'Tenacious goal pursuit and flexible goal adjustment: explication of age-related analysis of assimilative and accommodative strategies of coping', *Psychology and Ageing*, 5: 58–67.

Brown, J., Bowling, A., and Flynn, T. (2004) *Models of Quality of Life: A Taxonomy and Systematic Review of the Literature*. University of Sheffield, FORUM Project. http://www.shef.ac.uk/ageingresearch.

Calman, K.C. (1984) 'Quality of life in cancer patients – a hypothesis', *Journal of Medical Ethics*, 10: 124–7.

Clarke, P.J., Marshall, V.W., Ryff, C.D., and Rosenthal, C.J. (2000) 'Well-being in Canadian seniors: findings from the

Canadian Study of Health and Aging', *Canadian Journal on Aging*, 19: 139–59.

Cooper, K., Arber, S., Fee, L., and Ginn, J. (1999) *The Influence of Social Support and Social Capital in Health*. London: Health Education Authority.

Daatland, S.O. and Hansen, T. (2007) 'Well-being, control and ageing: an empirical assessment', in H. Mollenkopf and A. Walker (eds), *Quality of Life in Old Age*. Dordrecht: Springer, pp. 33–47.

Deeg, D. (2007) 'Health and quality of life', in H. Mollenkopf and A. Walker (eds), *Quality of Life in Old Age*. Dordrecht: Springer, pp. 195–214.

Deeg, D.J.H., Bosscher, R.J., and Broese van Groenou, M.I. (2000) *Ouder Warden in Nederland*. Amsterdam: Thela Thesis.

Deeg, D.J.H., Knipscheer, C.P.M., and Van Tillburg, W. (1993) 'Autonomy and well-being in the ageing population: concepts and design of the Longitudinal Aging study Amsterdam (LASA)', *Trendstudies No. 7*, Netherlands Institute of Gerontology, Bunnick, the Netherlands.

Diener, E., Oishi, S., and Lucas, R.E. (2003) 'Personality, culture, and subjective well-being: emotional and cognitive evaluations of life', *Annual Review of Psychology*, 54: 403–25.

Disch, W. Schensul, J., Radda, K., and Robison, J. (2007) 'Perceived environmental stress, depression and quality of life in older, low income, minority urban adults', in H. Mollenkopt and A. Walker (eds), *Quality of Life in Old Age*. Dordrecht, Springer, pp. 151–66.

European Commission (2003) *Draft Joint Inclusion Report, Statistical Annex*, COM (2003), 773 final. Brussels: European Commission.

Evandrou, M. and Glaser, K. (2004) 'Family, work and quality of life: changing economic and social roles through the lifecourse', *Ageing and Society*, 24: 771–92.

Farquhar, M. (1995) 'Elderly people's definitions of quality of life', *Social Science and Medicine*, 41: 1439–46.

Fernández-Ballesteros, R. (1998a) 'Quality of life: concept and assessment', in J.G. Adair, D. Belanger, and K.L. Dion (eds), *Advances in Psychological Science*. East Sussex, UK: Psychology Press, pp. 387–406.

Fernández-Ballesteros, R. (1998b) 'Quality of life: the differential conditions', *Psychology in Spain*, 2: 57–65.

Fernández-Ballesteros, R., Zamarrón, M.D., and Marciá, A. (1996) *Calidad de Vida en la Vejez en Distintos Contextos*. Madrid: IMERSO.

Fernández-Ballesteros, R., Zamarrón, M.D., and Ruiz, M.A. (2001) The contribution of socio-demographic and psychosocial factors to life satisfaction', *Ageing and Society*, 21: 25–43.

Filipp, S.H. and Ferring, D. (1998) 'Regulation of subjective well-being in old age by temporal and social comparison processes? *Zeitschrift für Klinische Psychologie – Forschung und Praxis*, 27: 93–7.

Freund, A.M. and Baltes, P.B. (1998) 'Selection, optimization and compensation as strategies of life management: correlations with subjective indicators of successful ageing', *Psychology and Aging*, 13: 531–43. Erratum (1999) 14: 700–2.

Gabriel, Z. and Bowling, A. (2004a) 'Quality of life in old age from the perspectives of older people', in A. Walker and C. Hagan Hennessy (eds), *Growing Older: Quality of Life in Old Age*. Maidenhead: Open University Press, pp.14–34.

Gabriel, Z. and Bowling, A. (2004b) 'Quality of life from the perspectives of older people', *Ageing and Society*, 24: 675–92.

Gerritsen, D., Steverink, N., Ooms, M., and Ribbe, M. (2004) 'Finding a useful conceptual basis for enhancing the quality of life of nursing home residents', *Quality of Life Research*, 13: 611–24.

Grundy, E. and Bowling, A. (1999) 'Enhancing the quality of extended life years', *Ageing and Mental Health*, 3: 199–212.

Gubrium, J. and Lynott, R. (1983) 'Rebuilding life satisfaction', *Human Organisation*, 42(1): 33–8.

Heyl, V., Wahl, H.-W., and Mollenkopf, H. (2005) 'Visual capacity, out-of-home activities and emotional well-being in old age: basic relations and contextual variation', *Social Indicators Research*, 74: 159–89.

Hornquist, J. (1982) 'The concept of quality of life', *Scandinavian Journal of Social Medicine*, 10: 57–61.

Hughes, B. (1990) 'Quality of life', in S. Peace (ed.), *Researching Social Gerontology*. London: Sage, pp. 46–58.

Iwarsson, S., Wahl, H.-W., and Nygren, C. (2004). 'Challenges of cross-national housing research with older persons: lessons from the ENABLE-AGE project', *European Journal of Ageing*, 1(1): 79–88. DOI 10.1007/s10433-004-0010-5.

Kellaher, L., Peace, S.M., and Holland, C. (2004) 'Environment, identity and old age: quality of life or a life of quality?', in A. Walker and C. Hagan Hennessy (eds), *Growing Older: Quality of Life in Old Age*. Maidenhead: Open University Press, pp. 60–80.

Knipscheer, C.P.M., Jong Gierveld, J. de, van Tilburg, T.G., and Dykstra, P.A. (1995) (eds), *Living Arrangements and Social Networks of Older Adults*. Amsterdam: VU University Press.

Larson, R. (1978) 'Thirty years of research on the subjective well-being of older Americans', *Journal of Gerontology*, 33: 109–25.

Lawton, M.P. (1983) 'Environment and other determinants of well-being in older people', *The Gerontologist*, 23: 349–57.

Lawton, M.P. (1991) 'Background: a multidimensional view of quality of life in frail elders', in J.E. Birren, J. Lubben, J. Rowe, and D. Deutchman (eds), *The Concept and Measurement of Quality of Life in the Frail Elderly*. San Diego, CA: Academic Press.

Lehr, U. and Thomae, H. (eds) (1987) *Formen Seelsichen Alterns*. Stuttgart: Enke.

Maslow, A. (1954) *Motivation and Personality*. New York: Harper.

Mayer, K.U. and Baltes, P. (eds) (1996) *Die Berliner Altersstudie*. Berlin: Akademie-Verlag.

Mayring, P. (1987) 'Subjektives wohlbefinden im alter', *Zeitschrift für Gerontologie*, 20: 367–76.

Mollenkopf, H. and Fozard, J. L. (2004) 'Technology and the good life: challenges for current and future generations of aging people', in H.-W. Wahl, R. Scheidt, and P. Windley (eds), *Aging in Context: Socio-physical Environments* (*Annual Review of Gerontology and Geriatrics* (2003), 23: 250–79). New York: Springer, pp. 250–79.

Mollenkopf, H. and Kaspar, R. (2005) 'Elderly people's use and acceptance of information and communication technologies', in B. Jaeger (ed.), *Young Technologies in Old Hands – An International View on Senior Citizens' Utilization of ICT*. Copenhagen: DJOF Publishing, pp. 41–58.

Mollenkopf, H., Kaspar, R., Marcellini, F., et al. (2004) 'Quality of life in urban and rural areas of five European countries: similarities and differences', *Hallym International Journal of Aging*, 6: 1–36.

Mollenkopf, H., Marcellini, F., Ruoppila, I., Széman, Z., and Tacken, M. (eds) (2005) *Enhancing Mobility in Later Life – Personal Coping, Environmental Resources, and Technical Support: The Out-of-home Mobility of Older Adults in Urban and Rural Regions of Five European Countries*. Amsterdam: IOS Press.

Mollenkopf, H., Baas, S., Kaspar, R., Oswald, F., and Wahl, H.-W. (2006) 'Outdoor mobility in late life: persons, environments and society', in H.-W. Wahl, H. Brenner, H. Mollenkopf, D. Rothenbacher, and C. Rott (eds), *The Many Faces of Health, Competence and Well-Being in Old Age: Integrating Epidemiological, Psychological and Social Perspectives*. Dordrecht: Springer, pp. 33–46.

Motel-Klingebiel, A. (2006) 'Quality of life and social inequality in old age', in Daatland, S.O. and Biggs, S. (eds), *Ageing and Diversity*. Bristol: Policy Press, pp.189–222.

Motel-Klingebiel, A. (2007) 'Quality of life in old age, inequality and welfare state reform: a comparison of Norway, Germany and England', in H. Mollenkopf and A. Walker (eds), *Quality of Life in Old Age*. Dordrecht: Springer, pp. 85–100.

Nazroo, J., Bajekal, M., Blane, D., and Grewal, I. (2004) 'Ethnic inequalities', in A. Walker and C. Hagan Hennessy (eds), *Growing Older: Quality of Life in Old Age*. Maidenhead: Open University Press, pp. 35–59.

Noll, H.H. (2002) 'Towards a European system of social indicators: theoretical framework and system architecture', *Social Indicators Research*, 58: 47–87.

O'Boyle, C.A. (1997) 'Measuring the quality of later life', *Philosophy Transactions of the Royal Society of London*, 352: 1871–9.

Peeters, A., Bouwman, B., and Knipscheer, K. (2005) 'The Netherlands: quality of life in old age I', in A. Walker (ed.), *Growing Older in Europe*. Maidenhead: Open University Press, pp. 83–104.

Perrig-Chiello, P. (1999) 'Resources of well-being in elderly: differences between young and old and old old', in C. Hummel (ed.), *Les Science Sociales Face au d'fi de la Grande Viellesse*. Geneva: Questions d'Age, pp. 45–7.

Polverini, F. and Lamura, G. (2005) 'Italy: quality of life in old age I', in A. Walker (ed.), *Growing Older in Europe*. Maidenhead: Open University Press, pp. 55–82.

Rojo-Pérez, F., Fernàndez-Mayoralas, G., Rodríguez-Rodríguez, V., and Rojo-Abuín, J.-M. (2007) 'The environments of ageing in the context of the global quality of life among older people living in family housing', in H. Mollenkopf and

A. Walker (eds), *Quality of Life in Old Age*. Dordrecht: Springer, pp. 123–50.

Roos, N.P. and Havens, B. (1991) 'Predictors of successful aging: a twelve year study of Manitoba elderly', *American Journal of Public Health*, 81: 63–8.

Scharf, T., Phillipson, C., and Smith, A.E. (2004) 'Poverty and social exclusion: growing older in deprived urban neighbourhoods', in A. Walker and C. Hagan Hennessy (eds), *Growing Older: Quality of Life in Old Age*. Maidenhead: Open University Press, pp.81–106.

Schilling, O. (2006) 'Development of life satisfaction in old age: another view on the "paradox"', *Social Indicators Research*, 75: 241–71.

Singer, B. and Ryff, C. (2001) 'Person-centred methods for understanding aging: the integration of numbers and narratives', in R. Binstock and L. George (eds), *Handbook of Aging and the Social Sciences*. San Diego, CA: Academic Press, pp. 44–65.

Staudinger, U.M. and Freund, A. (1998) 'Krank und "arm" im Hohen Alter und trotzdem Guten Mutes?', *Zeitschrift für Klinische Psychologie*, 27: 78–85.

Suzman, R.H., Willis, D.P., and Manton, K.G. (eds) (1992) *The Oldest Old*. Oxford: Oxford University Press.

Tesch-Römer, C., von Kondratowitz, H.J., and Motel-Klingebiel, A. (2001) 'Quality of life in the context of intergenerational solidarity', in S.O. Daatland and K. Herlofson (eds), *Ageing, Intergenerational Relations, Care Systems and Quality of Life*. Oslo: Nova, pp. 63–73.

Tester, S., Hubbard, G., Downs, M., MacDonald, C., and Murphy, J. (2004) 'Frailty and institutional life', in A. Walker and C. Hagan Hennessy (eds), *Growing Older: Quality of Life in Old Age*. Maidenhead: Open University Press, pp. 209–24.

Veenhoven, R. (1996) 'Average level of satisfaction in 10 European countries: explanation of differences', in W.E. Saris, R. Veenhoven, A.C. Scherpenzeel, and B. Bunting, (eds), *A Comparative Study of Satisfaction with Life in Europe*. Budapest: Eotvos University Press, pp. 243–53.

Veenhoven, R. (1999) 'Quality-of-life in individualistic society', *Social Indicators Research*, 48: 157–86.

Veenhoven, R. (2000) 'The four qualities of life: Ordering concepts and measures of the good life', *Journal of Happiness Studies*, 1: 1–39.

Verbrugge, L.M. (1995) 'New thinking and science on disability in mid- and late life', *European Journal of Public Health*, 1: 20–8.

Wahl, H.W. and Mollenkopf, H. (2003) 'Impact of everyday technology in the home environment on older adults' quality of life', in K.W. Schaie and N. Charness (eds), *Impact of Technology on Successful Aging*. New York: Springer.

Wahl, H.-W., Mollenkopf, H., and Oswald, F. (1999) *Alte Menschen in ihrer Umwelt*. Wiesbaden: Westdeutscher Verlag.

Wahl, H.-W., Scheidt, R., and Windley, P. (eds) (2004) *Annual Review of Gerontology and Geriatrics, 23, Aging in Context: Socio-physical Environments*. New York: Springer.

Wahl, H.-W., Mollenkopf, H., Oswald, F., and Claus, C. (2007) 'Environmental aspects of quality of life in old age: conceptual and empirical issues', in H. Mollenkopf and

A. Walker (eds), *Quality of Life in Old Age*. Dordrecht: Springer, pp. 101–22.

Walker, A. (1980) 'The social creation of poverty and dependency in old age', *Journal of Social Policy*, 9: 75–91.

Walker, A. (1993) *Age and Attitudes*. Brussels: European Commission.

Walker, A. (2002) 'A strategy for active ageing', *International Journal of Social Security*, 55: 121–39.

Walker, A. (2005) *Growing Older in Europe*. Maidenhead: Open University Press.

Walker, A. (2009) 'The emergence and application of active ageing in Europe', *Journal of Ageing and Social Policy*, 21: 75–93.

Walker, A. and van der Maesen, L. (2004) 'Social quality and quality of life', in W. Glatzer, S. von Below, and M. Stoffregen (eds), *Challenges for Quality of Life in the Contemporary World*. The Hague: Kluwer.

Weidekamp-Maicher, M. and Naegele, G. (2007) 'Economic resources and subjective well-being in old age', in H. Mollenkopf and A. Walker (eds), *Quality of Life in Old Age*. Dordrecht: Springer, pp. 65–84.

Weidekamp-Maicher, M. and Reichert, M. (2005) 'Germany: quality of life in old age I', in A. Walker (ed.), *Growing Older in Europe*. Maidenhead: Open University Press, pp. 33–54.

Wenger, G.C. (1989) 'Support networks in old age: constructing a typology', in M. Jeffreys (ed.), *Growing Old in the Twentieth Century*. London: Routledge, pp. 166–85.

Wenger, G.C. (1996) 'Social networks and gerontology', *Reviews in Clinical Gerontology*, 6: 285–93.

WHOQOL Group (1993) *Measuring Quality of Life*. Geneva: World Health Organization.

Wiggins, R.D., Higgs, P., Hyge, M., and Blane, D.B. (2004) 'Quality of life in the third age: key predictors of the CASP-19 measure', *Ageing and Society*, 24: 693–708.

World Bank (1994) *Averting the Old Age Crisis*. Washington: World Bank.

45

Later Life and Imprisonment

Azrini Wahidin and Ronald H. Aday

INTRODUCTION

For the first time in history, nations around the globe are faced with the dilemma of managing prisons with increasingly large populations of older people. For legitimate reasons, prison officials responsible for making decisions about this group are raising concerns about how best to respond to what is now viewed as a major challenge for prison management. Although a number of countries have commissioned studies to investigate and make policy recommendations, the body of knowledge on elderly prisoners and the issues posed to prisons systems in meeting their special needs remains limited. From an international perspective, prisons have been slow to respond to the physical and mental needs of older prisoners. As a consequence, a comparative analysis between countries can be an important first step in identifying best practice models and emerging policies. The aim of this chapter is to assess issues relating to older people in prison by examining the responses of two countries – the United States and the United Kingdom. The two countries represent different stages in the development of policies and correctional/prison facilities for the older prison population. The chapter will review some of the issues raised from experiences of managing the needs of prisoners in later life. It will examine the range of issues and challenges facing policymakers and correctional/prison facilities in managing the health and social care needs of an ageing prison population. Finally, the chapter will conclude with a series of policy recommendations addressing the needs of the ageing prison population.

Although the crimes committed by older offenders mirror those of young offenders, the older prisoner cohort is different in terms of their health and social care needs, individual adjustment to institutional life, maintenance of kinship networks, and resettlement needs. In consequence, they pose specific challenges to the prison system regarding custody, rehabilitation, and release. For the purpose of this chapter, the term 'older' or 'offender in later life' or 'elder' will be used interchangeably to denote a person aged 50 or over detained in a correctional/prison institution.

AGEING AND IMPRISONMENT

The issue of older offenders and prisoners in later life has attracted limited research and policy studies, with neglect from gerontologists and criminologists alike. The explanation frequently given for the lack of statistical information on this topic is that at present the numbers of older prisoners are too small to yield significant information, with the implication that this justifies excluding and ignoring the rights of elders in prison. Much of the debate on older offenders has been around how to define 'old' in the context of the prison population (Cullen et al., 1985; Phillips, 2005). Definitions of 'elderly', 'elder', or 'older' can produce information that at first appears contradictory. Official statistics on the age breakdown of offences and prison statistics in the United Kingdom (see Home Office, 1997a, 1997b) use a wide spectrum of ages between 21 and 59 or simply give figures for prisoners aged 21 and above. Some researchers have defined older prisoners as those 65 years of age and older (Newman, 1984), 60 (Kratcoski and Babb, 1990), or 55 (Goetting, 1983, 1992). However, studies such as those by Phillips (1996),

Eastman (2000), Wahidin (2002, 2004, 2009), Aday (2003), Howse (2003a), Prison Reform Trust (2009), and Mann (2008), together with statutory bodies such as the American Department of Justice and prison units for older prisoners in the United Kingdom, have used 50–55 as the threshold age to define when one becomes an older prisoner.

At the same time, assessment of the care and support issues relating to custody for an ageing prison population are only just beginning to develop. Discussion has begun to emerge in the United Kingdom, following the first report to be commissioned by Her Majesty's Chief Inspectorate HMCIP Team[1] on older prisoners entitled, *No Problems – Old and Quiet (HMCIR, 2004)*, and the later report, *Older Prisoners in England and Wales – A follow-up to the 2004 Thematic Review* (HMCIR, 2008).[1] Research on the older prisoner, however, remains limited both in quality and quantity. The majority of research to date has focused on the relationship between older people and the possibility of them being victims of crime (Bachman, 1993). Over half a century ago, Pollak wrote:

> The old criminal offers an ugly picture and it seems that scientists do not like to look at it for any considerable amount of time ... .Criminologists have touched the problem of old age criminality only occasionally, and if so, very briefly (1941: 213).

This statement has, until very recently, held true for the United Kingdom, as Brogden and Nijhar argue, '[t]here are criminologies of the young, of women, of ethnic minorities but – especially in the UK – no criminology concerned with the experience of older people' (2000: 5). Research by Aday and Webster (1979), Phillips (1996), and more recently by Howse (2003b), Wahidin (2004), Crawley and Sparks (2005), and Mann (2008) has begun to correct this. However, the literature available on older prisoners is still restricted to predominantly American-based research (Aday, 1995; Anderson and Morton, 1989; Newman, 1984). The work of Aday (Aday, 1994a, 1994b; Aday and Webster, 1979) in the United States has been of particular importance in addressing the increase in older people committing crime and the challenges the ageing prison population poses to correctional facilities, and is discussed in some detail below.

federal or state prisons or in local jails. Around 500,000 people aged 50 and above are arrested each year in America. The 'greying' of American's prisons became especially noticeable during the 1990s (Aday, 1994a). For example, the number of prisoners 50 years of age and older in federal and state institutions more than tripled from 33,499 in 1990 to more than 125,000 in 2002 (Corrections Yearbook, 2003). This growth has continued with the prison population aged 50 and over increasing to more than 178,000 by 2007 (American Correctional Association, 2008). In 2007, this age group comprised 11.6 per cent of the total prison population – nearly triple the 4.9 per cent figure of 1990. To further illustrate the exponential growth of this subgroup of prisoners, older men and women prisoners comprise over 12 per cent of the total prison population in 18 states – a growth from just seven states in 1990. Lifers and prisoners with 20+ year sentences now constitute about one-quarter of the total prison population (Corrections Yearbook, 2003).

Research indicates that the type of offences committed by older prisoners are similar to those committed by younger prisoners (Aday, 1994a; Kerbs, 2000). The majority of older offenders are unmarried, male (95 per cent), and have fewer than 12 years of formal education. In the United States, the exception is in the Southern States where older black prisoners outnumber their white counterparts. Just below 50 per cent of older prisoners in the United States are first-time offenders (primarily murder and sex crimes), these usually committed against relatives or close acquaintances (Beck, 1997). Formerly regarded as 'model citizens', these prisoners frequently have difficulties adjusting to life in prison, abiding by prison policies, living with a potentially violent population, and being away from family and former friends. The difficulties associated with imprisonment can leave some feeling guilty and unsure about what the future might bring and anxious about surviving in a total institution (Acoca, 1998; Aday, 1995; Bachman, 1993). As a result, many begin to exhibit symptoms of depression, withdrawing from prison staff and prisoners, changes in sleep and eating patterns, and suicidal ideations (Aday, 2003). Remorseful for the crimes committed, other 'new elderly' offenders are appreciative of the free food, shelter, and clothing they now have, and adjust rather well to institutional living (Aday, 2003).

OLDER PRISONERS IN THE UNITED STATES

Figures show that as of December 31, 2006 in the United States, 2,258,983 prisoners were held in

OLDER PRISONERS IN THE UNITED KINGDOM

Out of the 81,724 prisoners who were held in prisons in England and Wales on March 31, 2008,

6,977 people were age 50 and above, representing 8.5 per cent of the prison population (Prison Reform Trust, 2009); the majority were serving sentences between 4 years and 'life'. The 60 + age group has become the fastest growing age group in the prison population (Ministry of Justice, 2007), with the number of men more than tripling between 1996 (699) and 2008 (2242) (Prison Reform Trust, 2009). This compares to one and a half times increase among the under 60s prison population. The majority of men in prison aged 60 and over (56 per cent) have committed a sexual offence: among those 60–69 years, 52 per cent have been imprisoned for sex-related offences, and among the over 70s it is 73 per cent (Prison Reform Trust, 2009). At the end of August 2007, the oldest male prisoner was 92, while 454 were over 70 years of age (Prison Reform Trust, 2009).

From 1999 to 2008, the older prison population more than doubled from 3000 to over 6000. This increase in the older prison population is not explained by demographic change but is a consequence of harsher sentencing policies that have resulted in courts sending a larger proportion of criminals aged over 50 to prison to serve longer sentences (Howse, 2003b; Wahidin, 2006; Wahidin and Aday, 2005). This has been especially the case in relation to sex-related offences, including men in later life charged with 'historical offences' (offences committed two/three decades ago) and drug traffickers (Ministry of Justice, 2007). The women's prison population in England and Wales in 2008 stood at 4,390, representing 5 per cent of the total prison population. Out of the 316 women aged over 50 who are in prison in England and Wales, nearly half are foreign nationals (44 per cent), with many serving sentences for importing drugs (Prison Reform Trust, 2009).

MANAGEMENT CHALLENGES OF THE AGEING PRISON POPULATION: RESPONSES IN THE UNITED STATES

Prisons have not traditionally been constructed to house older persons, or to respond to the changing physical and social needs which ageing is likely to bring. As a result, health and social care tends to be the most critical concern for older prisoners and those responsible for managing their needs while in prison. Most correctional/prison departments and facilities view the rising cost of providing adequate health care as the biggest challenge in meeting the needs of an ageing prison population (Morittz, 2004). Ageing prisoners come into the system bringing a variety of high-risk

behaviours requiring immediate attention. In terms of healthcare needs, research has shown prisoners are likely to have an earlier onset of chronic health and social care needs than the general population[2] (Aday et al., 2004; HMCIR, 2008; Howse, 2003a; Prison Reform Trust, 2009). The most common age-related illnesses are arthritis, hypertension, cardiovascular, musculoskeletal, and respiratory conditions. As a whole, they have a higher incidence of chronic disease and significant functional disability compared to similar age groups on the outside (HMCIR, 2004). If, as studies suggest, younger prisoners have high rates of smoking, drug and alcohol use, and poor diet, it is likely that as they grow old in prison there will be an increase in the prevalence of related diseases, such as ischaemic heart disease and respiratory conditions (Bridgwood and Malbon, 1995). One estimate, based on a study in the United States, is that health care and security for prisoners over the age of 60 typically cost in the region of $70,000 (around £35,000) per annum (Shimkus, 2004): that is three times as much as for younger prisoners. Despite making up only 8 per cent of the total prison population in the United States, prisoners over age 50 were responsible for 19 per cent of the costs paid for ambulatory surgery episodes, 17 per cent of costs for non-emergency room episodes, 31 per cent of costs for ancillary care episodes, 20 per cent of costs for specialty care episodes, and 29 per cent of costs for inpatient care episodes (Florida Corrections Commission, 2001).

There are additional services that the various American states provide beyond what they would for a non-offender citizen. Once a prisoner is incarcerated, national health care programmes such as Medicaid and Medicare benefits[3] are no longer accessible and each state is legally responsible to provide health care. If prisoners are not housed in a healthcare facility or a special geriatric unit, there are additional costs such as transporting an older prisoner with an armed guard to the appropriate facility. Due to the debilitating conditions that may accompany the ageing process, older prisoners are frequently housed where they have the availability of healthcare staff and emergency care 24 hours each day. Medical professionals are needed in some cases for the basic activities of daily living (ADLs) such as bathing, feeding, physical therapy, medication management, and rehabilitation. Numerous states also offer chronic care clinics with the hope of encouraging health promotion activities. Some older prisoners that are too frail and too weak to attend to their own personal needs are more likely to receive treatment in a nursing home environment or in an infirmary (Anno et al., 2004). The vast majority of prison systems now require prisoners to provide a medical co-pay. For those systems that utilize health maintenance organizations (HMOs) to provide prison health care, a co-pay plan is mandated for prisoners in a similar way as for individuals living in the community. The medical co-payment is a required fixed fee for each visit to see a clinical nurse or doctor.

The 1976 *Estelle vs Gamble* ruling in the United States stated that prisons have an obligation to provide for the medical and personal needs of all prisoners, including the approximately 2500 who die in prison each year in the United States (Byock, 2002). Compassionate release from prison is considered an important alternative to prison hospice care. While laws vary from state to state, 43 states have reported the availability of compassionate release (Anno et al., 2004). For example, when the State of Virginia abolished parole in 1994, it also created a possible loophole for older prisoners. Prisoners aged 60 or older who have served at least 10 years of their sentence, or those aged 65 and older who have been incarcerated for at least 5 years are allowed to petition the parole board for release. Over a period of 10 years, not a single older prisoner has received early release (Hammack, 2004). Moreover, America's courts do not mandate prisons to release terminally ill, older or infirm prisoners, but some federal and state prisons do provide compassionate release for prisoners who have medical records and physicians' statements documenting their prognoses (Aday et al., 2009). Sending minimal risk, terminally ill prisoners home to die reduces prison medical expenditures (Yates and Gillespie, 2000), but placing prisoners in the care of others is not always possible. For example, the Texas Criminal Justice Department reported that two elderly prisoners in their 70s suffering from chronic heart and lung failure required around-the-clock intensive medical care, costing taxpayers nearly $1 million per month (Morittz, 2004; National Institute of Corrections, 1997). Prison officials could not release the two men to a nursing home where their medical bills would be lower because under Texas law, it forbids the early release of those convicted of sex-related crimes. In many cases, ageing relatives often do not have the strength, stamina, or time adequately to support a frail elderly prisoner, and nursing staff are generally reluctant to assume the liability of caring for former prisoners who have committed heinous offences (Aday, 2003). Therefore, prison officials must provide in-house health services and treatment programmes for prisoners who have no other option but to spend their remaining days behind bars.

In the United States, there are a range of examples of how the correctional system is addressing the growing crisis by creating specialist facilities such as those at Louisiana State Penitentiary (Angola Prison) and Oregon Department of Corrections geriatric unit (Anno et al., 2004), for older men. These correctional institutions have wheelchair access, hospital-style beds, hoists, toilets, showers, a therapeutic gym equipped on site with a pooltable configured at a lower height to accommodate wheelchairs that comply with the American Disability Act of 1990 (ADA). Close-captioned television and specially equipped phones are available for the hearing impaired. According to prison officials in the Oregon Department of Corrections, expenditure is significantly reduced when housing older offenders in an environment where specially trained healthcare staff can recognize and treat problems before they become severe. In 51 states, provisions are made for older prisoners, ranging from being grouped or placed in geriatric facilities, having access to specificaly tailored programmes for the older offender, chronic care clinics on site, and hospice/end-of-life programmes (Colsher, et al., 1992; Mezey et al., 2002). It is evident that an increasing number of prison systems do routinely house older prisoners apart from the general population, and offer them unique programming or services. In specific states (i.e., Alabama, Georgia, Florida, Oklahoma, Wisconsin, Illinois, Kentucky, West Virginia, Virginia, Tennessee, Louisiana, Pennsylvania, Mississippi, North Carolina, Texas, Ohio, Wisconsin, and New Mexico), stand-alone facilities or secure nursing homes have been established to accommodate the increasing number of older prisoners (see Aday, 1999, 2006; American Correctional Association, 2001; Neff, 1997). In a number of other states, prisoners over the age of 50 are either grouped together or housed in separate medical units. In some cases, these units may mix older prisoners with younger disabled ones. As long as these conditions remain in place, prison healthcare costs will continue to increase dramatically.

In an increasingly pressurized prison system, the needs of older offenders are likely to be overlooked unless there is specific provision – as the numbers of older prisoners increase, the issues this group poses are likely to become more acute. The final sections of this chapter examine some of the key policy issues to be addressed.

SEGREGATION VERSUS INTEGRATION

The United States has been at the forefront of delivering special programmes addressing the needs of older offenders (Aday and Rosenfield, 1992; Krajick, 1979). In this sense, 'special programmes' constitutes the distinctive treatment of the older prisoner housed in an age-segregated or in an age-sensitive environment. Elder housing placements are typically based on a clinical criteria based on medical need. Rather than relying strictly on age, most States take the length of sentence and physical condition into consideration when prisoners are classified, custody graded, and given work programmes or housing assignments (Flynn, 1992, 2000). The main question for prison administrators concerning ageing offenders in prison is whether to mainstream or segregate this population. One argument is that segregated housing provides a concentration of specialized staff and resources for the elderly, thereby reducing costs (Florida Corrections Commission, 2001). Previous research supports the notion that participation in a specific group increases self-respect and increases capability to resume community life once released. A choice of age segregation or age integration provides older prisoners with the opportunity for forming peer networks, while at the same time reducing vulnerability and violence they may encounter in the mainstream of prison life. Fattah and Sacco state: 'Concern for their safety and the need to protect them against victimisation, exploitation and harassment outweigh any stabilising effect their integration may have' (1989: 101).

It is imperative that the prison system provides not only comprehensive opportunities for older prisoners while in prison and appropriate resettlement programmes but also alternatives to the traditional custodial framework in which elders find themselves growing old. What is needed is the flexibility of having accommodation and provision reserved, without creating a separate prison or experiencing exclusion from the main prison environment. Aday argues that 'like the elderly in the free world, they are familiar with life in the general population and perceive that it has a mark of independence' (2003: 146). The needs of elders in prisons are substantial, and this is not an exhaustive list but can include: physical, mental and preventative health care; custody classification to special housing, educational, vocational or recreational programmes, physical exercise, and rehabilitation programming; dietary considerations; and long-term geriatric and nursing care. An overriding theme within the integration versus segregation debate is that the way forward is to provide flexible accommodation, not through *segregation*, but through *integration*, within a framework of tolerance, understanding, and adaptability.

In identifying and recognising the needs of older people in prison, we should also be turning our attention to older people's experiences of the criminal justice system, and address how older people are processed from court to prison. In reflecting on the needs of the older prisoner, it is important to consider training criminal justice

personnel to deal with the specific issues raised by older prisoners. For example, in relation to the sentencing process for the older prisoner, would it be fairer if we took into account the probable years remaining in the offender's life[4] when deciding a sentence length? It can be argued that a 15-year sentence for a 65-year-old person is virtually a life sentence, while a 25-year-old person who spends 15 years in prison still has a 30-year life expectancy after s/he leaves prison. This practice condemns the older offender to spend a greater percentage of her or his remaining life in prison. This disparity could be reduced by giving older offenders sentences that represent the same percentage of their remaining lives as those given to younger persons. For example, the average 25-year-old male can expect to live for 46.9 more years. If such a person were convicted of a crime that carries a 20-year prison term, he would spend approximately 43 per cent of his remaining life behind bars. A 65-year-old male is expected to live 14.2 more years. A 20-year sentence would thus represent 141 per cent of this defendant's remaining life, a de facto life sentence. By contrast, 43 per cent of his life would be only 6.1 years (see James, 1992). In *State v. Waldrip*, the judge reduced a 67-year-old defendant's sentence for voluntary manslaughter from 5 years to life to 5–10 years, recognizing that even the minimum term of 5 years could theoretically be a life sentence because of the defendant's age (James, 1992). It can be argued that if an older person does not have her or his sentence reduced, s/he will experience a greater punishment than a younger person sentenced for committing the same crime. Special arrangements for elderly prisoners, such as Angola Prison Hospice in America, can make prisons seem more like nursing homes. This raises the question of the necessity of keeping certain frail and infirm elderly persons behind bars, since the infirm elderly person is least likely to commit crimes in the future. The alternative would be to incorporate an early release scheme. Only by exploring the possibilities that addresses age-specific issues can we begin to create alternatives. At one level, it can be argued that it is only through well-funded alternatives to custody changes in sentencing and a concerted effort to divert offenders from custody that this can be achieved.

MANAGEMENT CHALLENGES OF AGEING PRISON POPULATIONS: THE RESPONSE OF THE UNITED KINGDOM

In the case of the United Kingdom, it is evident from the review ' *No Problems – Old and*

Quiet: Older Prisoners in England and Wales' (HMCIR, 2004) that people aged 50+ are a significant group within the prison population. However, the subsequent report (HMCIR, 2008) found that many of the key recommendations made in the earlier document had not been acted upon. For example, one of the key areas identified concerned the extent to which the prison environment was failing to reflect the needs of those with age-related impairments and disabilities. The Inspectorate Team found that in the majority of the prisons there were no separate regimes for older prisoners and that many were excluded from a range of activities and remained locked in their cells during the day. Another key area for concern was the general level of health of older prisoners and healthcare provision. In some cases, prison healthcare centres were being used inappropriately to house older and/or disabled prisoners. Mental health difficulties are also a major issue. Over half of all elderly prisoners have been diagnosed with a mental illness, the most common being depression, which can itself emerge as a result of imprisonment (Prison Reform Trust, 2009).

The reports from the Inspectorate Team also highlight the lack of adequate resettlement programmes for offenders in later life. Prison Service Order 2300 (para.1.12) states inter alia, that account must be taken of the diversity of the prisoner population and the differences in resettlement needs, and that specific cohorts of the prison population (e.g., elderly prisoners) may need to be catered for in different ways, however Aday et al., (2009), Crawley and Sparks (2006) and Mann (2008) have highlighted that older men and women in prison often experience anxiety as release becomes more imminent. Many elderly offenders – especially men who are convicted of sexual offences – feel that they are more vulnerable to assault when released. Many feel that they have nothing to go out to and that for them 'time is running out' (Aday et al., 2009; Wahidin, 2005). Crawley and Sparks (2006) found that some older offenders exhibited a profound sense of fear and despair at the prospect of dying in prison. So the question that must be asked is: 'What sort of life is left for those who *know* that a life after prison would never be a possibility?' Thus for older men and women in prison, release and resettlement is not an unproblematic issue but a highly complex one. The two key issues facing the older offender due for release are: first, the lack of clarity from prison and probation staff *as* to where they are going to live, with *whom* they will be living, and *how* they are going to get there. Secondly, many elderly prisoners have little idea as to what they are supposed to do once released, or what (if anything) has been arranged for them when they get out. The majority of prisons in England and Wales have virtually no resettlement schemes geared for the elderly offender, and no account is taken of the need for older prisoners to manage, often by themselves, with disability or illness, or loneliness and isolation (Gallagher, 1990; Howse, 2003b). At the time of writing (2009) there is no national strategy to develop such courses for older prisoners to ensure equality of access for this age group. It is important to note that due to the relative compliant nature of this prisoner group, their specific resettlement needs are being overlooked. In the above studies, the knowledge that time is running out makes both the prison experience and the resettlement process for older men and women different to that of the younger population.

The UK experience suggests continued reliance on the initiative of committed prison officers, with an assumption that the care of older prisoners, including their social care, is a matter of the health services rather than that of the prison service. Since 2004, prisons in England and Wales have been subjected to the Disability Discrimination Act (DAA), which requires the prison service to take all reasonable steps to ensure that prisoners with disabilities can access services. In consequence, the prison service has issued orders (PSO 2855 and PSO 8010) detailing the steps prisons should take. The National Service Framework (NSF) for Older People (Department of Health, 2001) also identifies the need for prisons to provide for the health and social care needs of prisoners over 60. Yet it is evident from the official reports in this area that few prisons are reaching the standards required in legislation, though progress could be identified in some cases (HMCIR, 2008; Prison Reform Trust, 2009).

This increase in the proportion of elders is having far-reaching effects on all components of the criminal justice system. Once in prison, as illustrated above, the vulnerabilities of age are exacerbated by the lack of age-related facilities. Furthermore, the lack of continuity of programmes from the outside, such as health care, structured activities for the non-working prison community, and an 'adequate' living allowance for men and women who are of pensionable age in prison, increases the pains of imprisonment as the disparity between the working younger prison population and the non-working population is magnified (Hancock and Sunderland, 1997). This was illustrated by a former Chief Inspector of Prisons Sir David Ramsbotham, who states:

As I go around the prison estate I am finding an increased number of elderly prisoners, all of whom are classified as being retired, which means that they do not qualify for work. Without qualifying for work they do not get wages and, therefore, they live in pretty impoverished circumstances. Some of them need special facilities, including medical facilities, and these too are lacking.

(Eastman, 2000)

Prisoners in later life require improved health services, better pensions, different types of housing, and a variety of aids when they become infirm. But they also need a reason for using these things. As Phillipson argues: 'In our society the purpose of life in old age is often unclear ... .Old age is seen as a "problem" with the elderly viewed as dependents, worse still they are often described as a non-productive burden upon economy' (1982: 166). It is not surprising that elders in prison experience isolation and alienation when they are denied access to the sources of meaning that are valued by the society in which they live. The lack of help and rehabilitation can only exacerbate the almost inevitable poverty that elders will face as a result of their imprisonment. The Thematic review on older prisoners by HM Inspectorate of Prisons, published in December 2004, found little evidence that older offenders' individual needs were either being met or that provision was being made for them. The report concluded by stating that 'prisons are primarily designed for, and inhabited by, young and able-bodied people; and in general the needs of the old and infirm are not met (HMCIR, 2004).

Unless the prison service of England and Wales begins to recognize the needs of the older offender, mistreatment and neglect will be a pervasive facet of prison life. For those elders who are already incarcerated as well as those who are to be imprisoned, there must be clearly articulated policies addressing their special needs while in custody and as they prepare for release. A discussion as to the possible scope of these forms the final section of this chapter.

FUTURE ISSUES AND RECOMMENDATIONS

As the number of older offenders within the criminal justice system increases, developing social policies to respond effectively to this group will become critical. The programmes and policies now in place vary from country to country and this will most likely continue. Economic resources, sentencing guidelines, policy priorities, and the variation in the number and diversity of older offenders contribute to these differences. Some have suggested that the elderly offender should be treated differently than his or her younger counterpart at all stages of the criminal

justice system (Aday, 2003). In particular, given the mental and physical characteristics of the older offender, the purpose of legal sanctions may be different, leading to a de-emphasis upon restraint, deterrence, and rehabilitation (Mara, 2002). Such an alternative would not be simply lenient justice, but a separate and distinct system that differs from the current adult system in philosophy, purpose, and technique (James, 1992).

To alleviate some of the problems associated with imprisonment, the prison authorities should be turning their attention to literature relating to residential homes or assisted living facilities (Aday, 2003; Atherton, 1989; Coleman, 1993; Hockey, 1989). There are many simple measures which could be taken that would allow elders control over their immediate physical environment: for example, installing doors and windows that they could open easily and radiators that they could adjust themselves; replacing the harshness of the prison corridors with appropriate carpet tiles; use of electricity sockets that would allow all older prisoners the opportunity to listen to the radio; televisions with teletext for the hard of hearing; electric hoists; and replacing the glare of the strip light with something less harsh. Such measures would at once make prison a less hostile and more accessible place. In addition, due to the impairment of sight, hearing, memory, and reflexes, as well as the general slowing of movement and mental responsiveness, elders need to be cared for by staff members who are specifically trained in the needs of elders in prison. Mental and physical assessment, counselling services, and other programming will be necessary. For prisoners who will spend the rest of their lives in prison, managing their health care will become a critical issue, as will dealing sensitively with end-of-life issues (see Chapter 48). Prison officials will be faced with the problem of finding suitable work and recreational activities, so that prisoners can pass the time in reasonably good health. Of course, prisoners who have spent a greater portion of their lives incarcerated will need intensive discharge planning and community placement orientation. Locating family or community agencies who will accept ageing prisoners eligible for parole will be a challenge.

The ageing prison population poses a number of dilemmas, and deserves recognition both among those interested in the well-being of those in later life and those executing prison policy. Age, in time, will be considered as one of the biggest issues that will continue to affect the criminal justice system and prison health care in the future. In many ways, geriatric policies and programming is still in the developmental stage. While it is obvious that the criminal justice system is becoming more sensitive to the special needs of ageing offenders, barriers continue to exist, which interfere with the ability for correctional/prison facilities to respond more effectively. Most states and local governments are faced with the rising costs of medical care and overcrowded jails and prisons. With the continued increase in criminal activity among the elderly population as a whole, learning more about the relationship between crime and ageing, and about institutional adjustment, recidivism, and release seems imperative.

The limited knowledge concerning the elderly, and the absence of relevant policies and planning in this area, lead one to suggest that the criminal justice system should be turning its attention to:

- An examination of existing formal and informal practices regarding elders, as the first step in developing an explicit and integrated set of policies and programmes to address the special needs of this group across jurisdictions. This will enable a national strategy to be implemented and good practice to be identified.
- Developing a comprehensive and gender-sensitive programme for older prisoners that fosters personal growth and accountability and value-based actions that lead to successful reintegration into society.
- Preparing all personnel of the criminal justice system to understand and appropriately address elder-specific topics and issues as discussed in the chapter.

In terms of being able to address the needs of elders in the criminal justice system, correctional units should be able to institute the following:

- Adoption of the age of 50 as the chronological starting point in a definition of the older offender.
- Compiling of comprehensive data on the over 50s from arrest to custody, through to re-entry into wider society.
- Introduction or expansion of specific programmes, policies, and facilities geared towards the needs of older people.
- Identification of the costs of long-term incarceration of infirm prisoners and the potential risks of early release or extended medical furlough for this population.

CONCLUSION

This chapter has presented some of the issues and challenges of an ageing prison population by focusing on the developments being made in the United States and the United Kingdom for the

elderly prisoner. It is only by examining the work that is currently being done by the United States and the United Kingdom that we can begin to identify policies, programmes, and prison facilities that have been specifically designed to reflect the needs and experiences of an older prison population. It is by turning our attention to these countries that this chapter has begun to identify practice and policies which are currently in place that address the needs of an ageing prison population. Moreover, it is only by addressing the needs of the older prison population that we can begin to implement best practice and prevent further accusations of injustice and lack of care for the prisoner in later life. Although the older prison population is still statistically nominal compared to other prison population groups such as young offenders, the numbers are growing at an exponential rate in the United States and in England and Wales. Thus, in order to comply with the Human Rights Convention, policymakers must address the needs of the ageing prison population as identified in this chapter or be accused of discrimination on the basis of age and, worse, contravening legislation, and of violating peoples' human rights.

ACKNOWLEDGEMENT

We would like to thank Professor Chris Phillipson for his suggestions and guidance in writing this chapter.

NOTES

1 The purpose of Her Majesty's Inspectorate team is to provide independent scrutiny of the conditions for and treatment of prisoners. Her Majesty's Inspectorate of Prisons for England and Wales (HMI Prisons) in an independent inspectorate that reports on conditions for and treatment of those in prison, young offender institutions, and immigration removal centres. The Chief Inspector reports to the government on the treatment and conditions for prisoners in England and Wales and other matters.

2 Prison Reform Trust (2003) *Growing Old in Prison*. London: Prison Reform Trust.

3 Medicaid and Medicare health insurance programmes based in the United States.

4 Cristina Pertierra (1995) presents a series of cases brought to the American Court of Appeal in which elderly offenders, under the Eigtht Amendment, have clamied that, given their ages and life expectancies, the sentences imposed amount to life imprisonment, and are thus disproportionate to the crimes.

REFERENCES

Acoca, L. (1998) 'Defusing the time bomb: understanding and meeting the growing health care needs of incarcerated women in America', *Crime and Delinquency*, 44: 49–70.

Aday, R. (1994a) 'Aging in prison: a case study of new elderly offender', *International Journal of Offender Therapy and Comparative Criminology*, 1(38): 79–91.

Aday, R. (1994b) 'Golden years behind bars: special programs and facilities for elderly inmates', *Journal of Federal Probation*, 58(2): 47–54.

Aday, R.H. (1995) *A Preliminary Report on Mississippi's Elderly Prison Population*. Parchment, MS: Mississippi's Department of Corrections.

Aday, R.H. (1999) 'Golden years behind bars: a ten-year follow up', paper presented at the annual meeting of the Academy of Criminal Justices Sciences, Orlando, FL.

Aday, R.H (2003) *Ageing Prisoners: Crisis in American Corrections*. Westport, CT: Praeger.

Aday, R.H. and Rasenfield, H.A. (1992) 'Providing for the geriatric inmate: implications for training', *Journal of Correctional Training*, 12(20): 14–16.

Aday, R. and Webster, E. (1979) 'Aging in prison: the development of a preliminary Model', *Offender Rehabilitation*, 3: 271–82.

Aday, R.H., Krabil, L., and Wahidin, A. (2004) 'A comparative study of health care needs of the female ageing offender in the USA and the UK', paper presented at American Society of Criminology Conference 2004, Nashville. Unpublished paper.

American Correctional Association (2001) *Directory of Correctional Facilities*. Lanham, MD: American Correctional Association.

American Correctional Association (2008) *Directory of Adult Correctional Facilities*. Lanham, MD: American Correctional Association.

Anderson, J.C. and Morton, J.B. (1989) 'Graying of the nation's prisons presents new challenges', *The Ageing Connection*, 10: 6–18.

Anno, B.J., Graham, C., Lawrence, J., and Shandsky, R. (2004) *Correctional Health Care: Addressing the Needs of Elderly, Chronically Ill and Terminally Ill Inmates*. Washington, DC: National Institute of Corrections, US Department of Justice.

Atherton, J. S. (1989) *Interpreting Residential Life – Values to Practice*. London: Routledge.

Bachman, R. (1993) 'The double edged sword of violent victimisation against the elderly: patterns of family and stranger perpetration', *Journal of Elder Abuse and Neglect*, 5(4): 59–79.

Beck, A.J. (1997) 'Growth, change, and stability in the U.S. prison population, 1880–1995', *Corrections Management Quarterly*, 1(2): 1–14.

Bridgwood, A. and Malbon, G. (1995) *Survey of the Physical Health of Prisoners*. London: HMSO.

Brogdan, M. and Nijhar, P. (2000) *Crime, Abuse and the Elderly*. Devon: Willan.

Byock, I.R. (2002) 'Dying well in corrections: why should we care?', *Journal of Correctional Health Care*, 12: 27–35.

Coleman, P. (1993) 'Adjustment in later life', in J. Bond, P. Coleman, and S. Peace (eds), *Ageing in Society – An Introduction to Social Gerontology*. London: Sage, pp. 35–45.

Colsher, P.L., Wallace, R.B., Loeffelhotz, P.L., and Sales, M. (1992) 'Health status of older male prisoners: a comprehensive survey', *American Journal of Public Health*, 82: 881–4.

Corrections Yearbook (2003) *Prison Population Statistics*. New York: Criminal Justice Institute.

Crawley, E. and Sparks, R. (2005) 'Hidden injuries? Researching the experiences of older men in English prisons', *Howard Journal for Penal Reform*, September, 4: 25–45.

Crawley, E. and Sparks, R. (2006) 'Is there life after imprisonment? How elderly men talk about imprisonment and release', *Criminology and Criminal Justice*, 6: 63–82.

Cullen, F., Wozniak, J., and Frank, J. (1985) 'The rise of the new elderly offender: Will a new criminal be invented?', *Crime And Social Justice*, 23: 151–65.

Deaton, D., Aday, R., and Wahidin, A. (2009) 'The effect of health and penal harm on ageing female prisoners' Views Of Dying in Prison', *Journal of Death and Dying: Omega*, 60(1): 51–70.

Department of Health (2001) *National Service for Older People*. London: Department of Health.

Eastman, M. (2000) 'Discovering the older prisoner – meeting the social care needs of older prisoners', Better Government for Older People, London. unpublished paper.

Fattah, E.H. and Sacco, V.F. (1989) *Crime and Victimisation of the Elderly*. New York: Springer.

Florida Corrections Commission (2001) *Annual Report Section: Status Report on Elderly Offenders*. Tallahassee, FL: Florida Corrections Commission.

Flynn, E. (1992) 'The graying of america's prison population', *The Prison Journal*, 16: 77–98.

Flynn, E. (2000) 'Elders as perpetrators', in M. Rothman, B. Dunlo, and P. Entzel (eds), *Elders, Crime and the Criminal Justice System*. New York: Springer, pp. 72–90.

Gallagher, E. (1990) 'Emotional, social, and physical health characteristics of older men in prison', *International Journal of Aging and Human Development*, 31(4): 251–65.

Goetting, A. (1983) 'The elderly in prison: issues and perspectives', *Journal of Research, Crime and Delinquency*, 5: 291–309.

Goetting, A. (1992) 'Patterns of homicide among the elderly', *Violence and Victims*, 7: 203–15.

Hammack, B.W. (2004) 'Aging prisoners behind bars', *Roanoke Times*, P. A1. America. September 2, 2004: 5.

Hancock, R. and Sutherland, H. (1997) *Costs and Distributional Effects of Increasing the Basic State Pension*. London: Age Concern.

Hockey, J. (1989) 'Residential care and the maintenance of social identity: negotiating the transition to institutional life', in M. Jefferys (ed.), *Growing Old in The Twentieth Century*. London: Routledge, pp. 201–18.

Her Majesty's Chief Inspectorate Review (HMCIR) (2004) *No Problems – Old and Quiet: Older Prisoners in England and Wales*. London: HMSO.

Her Majesty Chief Inspectorate Report (HMCIR) (2008) *Older Prisoners in England and Wales: A Follow Up to the 2004 Thematic Review*. London: HMIP.

Home Office (1997a) *Understanding the Sentencing of Women*. Research Study 170. London: The Research and Statistical Directorate, London: HMSO.

Home Office (1997b) *The Prison Population in 1997: A Statistical Review* . Research Findings No. 76. London: HMSO.

Howse, K. (2003a) *Growing Old in Prison*. London: Prison Reform Trust.

Howse, K. (2003b) *Growing Old in Prison: A Scoping Study on Older Prisoners*. London: Centre for Policy on Ageing and the Prison Reform Trust.

James, M. (1992) 'Sentencing of elderly criminals', *American Criminal Law Review*, 29: 1025–44.

Kerbs, J. (2000) 'The older prisoner: social, psychological and medical considerations', in M. Rothman, B. Dunlop, and P. Entzel (eds), *Elders, Crime and the Criminal Justice System – Myth, Perceptions, and Reality in the 21st Century*. New York: Springer.

Krajick, K. (1979) 'Growing Old in prison', *Corrections Magazine*, 5(1): 32–46.

Kratcoski, P.C. and Babb, S. (1990) 'Adjustment for older inmates: an analysis by institutional structure and gender', *Journal of Contemporary Criminal Justice*, 6: 139–56.

Mann, N. (2008) 'Doing harder time? The experiences of an ageing prison', Unpublished PhD, Essex University.

Mara, C. M. (2002) 'Expansion of long-term care in the prison system: an aging inmate population poses policy and pro-grammatic questions', *Journal of Aging and Social Policy*, 14(2): 43–61.

Mezey, M., Dubler, N.N., Mitty, E., and Brody, A. A. (2002) 'What impact do setting and transitions have on the quality of life at the end of life and quality of the dying process?', *The Gerontologist*, 42 (Special Issue III): 54–67.

Ministry of Justice (2007) *Offender Management Caseload Statistics*. London: Ministry of Justice.

Moritz, J. (2004) 'Elderly inmates costing millions', Ft. Worth Star Telegram, March 21, 2004. p.1, 1A.

National Institute of Corrections (1997) *Prison Medical Care: Special Needs of Populations and Cost Control*. Longmont, CO: National Institute of Corrections.

Neff, J. (1997) 'The old's folk's slammer', *World Press Review*, 44(2): 30–4.

Newman, E. (1984) 'Elderly offenders and American crime', in E. Newman, D. Newman, and M. Gewirtz (eds), *Elderly Criminals*. Cambridge: Gunn and Hain.

Pertierra, J.C. (1995) 'Do the crime: do the time: should elderly criminals receive proportionate sentences?', *Nova Law Review*, Winter: 1–5.

Phillips, J. (1996) 'Crime and older offenders', *Practice*, 8(1): 43–55.

Phillips, J. (2005) 'Crime and older people: the research agenda', in A. Wahidin and M. Cain (eds), *Ageing, Crime and Society*. Cullompton: Willan, pp. 53–71.

Phillipson, C. (1982) *Capitalism and the Construction of Old Age*. London: Macmillian.

Pollack, O. (1941) 'The criminality of old age', *Journal of Criminal Psychopathology*, October: 213–35.

Prison Reform Trust (2009) *Doing Time: The Experiences and Needs of Older People in Prison, London*. A Prison Reform Trust Briefing. London: Prison Reform Trust.

Shimkus, J. (2004) 'Corrections copes with care for the aged', *Correct Care*, 18(3): 1–16.

Wahidin, A. (2002) 'Reconfiguring older bodies in the prison time machine', *Journal of Aging and Identity*, 7(3): 177–93.

Wahidin, A. (2004) *Older Women in the Criminal Justice System Running Out of Time*. London: Jessica Kingsley.

Wahidin, A. (2005) 'Managing the needs of older offenders: re-awakening the criminological imagination', Leeds University, British Society of Criminology, unpublished paper.

Wahidin, A. (2006) 'No problems-old and quiet: imprisonment in later life', in A. Wahidin and Cain, M. (eds) (2006) *Ageing, Crime and Society*. Cullompton: Willan.

Wahidin, A. (2009) 'Older offenders, crime and the criminal justice system', in C. Hale, K. Hayward, A. Wahidin, and E. Wincup (eds), *Criminology*. Oxford: Oxford University Press.

Wahidin A. and Aday, R. (2005) 'The needs of older men and women in the criminal justice system', *Prison Service Journal*, 160: 13–23.

Yates, J. and Gillespie, W. (2000) 'The elderly and prison policy', *Journal of Aging and Social Policy*, 11(2–3): 167–75.

46

Ageing and Urban Society: Growing Old in the 'Century of the City'

Chris Phillipson

INTRODUCTION

Two dominant forces will do much to shape social life in the 21st century: namely, population change on the one side, and urbanization on the other. UN/HABITAT (2008: x) have labelled the 21st century as the 'century of the city'. Already, half of the world's population reside in urban areas and by the middle of the century most regions of the developing world will be predominantly urban. Katz et al. (2008: 474) view the present century as the 'urban age', one that is unfolding at a 'dizzying pace and with a scale, diversity, complexity, and level of connectivity that challenges traditional paradigms and renders many conventional tools and practices obsolete'.

The characteristics of contemporary urbanization may be defined in a variety of ways, but the main elements are:

- *scale* – with the growth of very large cities with populations of 10 millions or more now housing 5 per cent of the world's population (Burdett and Rode, 2008)
- *speed of urbanization* – especially in the developing world, which absorbs an average of 5 million new urban residents every month and is responsible for 95 per cent of the world's urban population growth (UN/HABITAT, 2008: xii)
- *mobility of populations* – with the migration of young adults from rural areas and declining industrial centres

- *complexity* – with urban areas functioning as centres of production and consumption, and as nodes within transnational networks of people and goods (Blokland and Savage, 2008).

The changes associated with urbanization must be further related to the rise of global cities, defined as those that command economic and political influence at a global level (Sassen, 2001). Indeed, Soja and Kanai (2008: 54) view contemporary urbanization as not just an adjunct to the globalization process but also: 'its primary driving force, stimulating innovation, creativity and economic growth while at the same time intensifying social and economic inequalities ...' They conclude that: 'Not only is urbanization increasingly reaching everywhere, everywhere is increasingly reaching into the city, contributing to a major reconfiguration of the social and spatial structures of urbanism and creating the most economically and culturally heterogeneous cities the world has ever known'.

The consequence of the above developments is that the study of ageing is inexorably bound up with understanding the lives of older people within the context of urban environments. This chapter explores this issue as follows: first, there is an assessment of some of the main features of contemporary urbanization; secondly, research evidence for the impact of the urban environment on older people is reviewed, with a particular focus on processes relating to social exclusion; and thirdly, the chapter considers the range of policies that might be developed to provide greater security to older people living in urban environments.

OLDER PEOPLE AND CITIES

Cities grow as well as decline in complex ways, both processes raising challenging issues for groups such as older people. Despite this, the association between urban change and problems in later life has yet to be fully addressed in research in social gerontology. Notwithstanding the resurgence of interest in environmental issues and ageing (see Chapter 8), links to changes affecting urban areas remain underexplored. Yet the argument developed in this chapter is that understanding the forces behind urban change will make a substantial contribution to understanding the lives of older people.

The significance of the urban dimension itself reflects the interaction between the spatial concentration of populations (with two-thirds of the world's population residing in cities by 2030) and the impact of the changes associated with migration and demographic change (Rodwin and Gusmano, 2006). Cities, as suggested above, are themselves undergoing radical change, notably through the process of globalization, which is promoting accelerated growth in some urban centres while contributing to economic and social decline in others (Office of the Deputy Prime Minister, 2006a).

Cities combine images of mobility and change, together with those of loss and abandonment. In *London: The Biography*, Peter Ackroyd (2000) notes the extent to which metaphors of incarceration have persisted throughout the history of London, illustrated in periods such as the Great Plague in the 17th century and World War II in the 20th century. The image of confinement still carries force for many urban dwellers, notably with fears aroused by particular neighbourhoods, or the perceived dangers attached to moving around particular areas at certain times of the day or night (Sampson, 2009). Moreover, the city may present physical and institutional barriers to groups such as those with a disability of some kind, separating them from the mainstream of economic and social life (Gleeson, 2001).

Reflecting on this last point, Beck (1998) views the modern city as characterized by an *'architecture of apartheid'* (author's emphasis) organized around the needs of 'productive elites'. Global cities are in fact faced with major contradictions in the 21st century: for example, between the demands of a 'hyper-mobile' professional minority on the one side, and groups such as those 'ageing in place', single women living alone and the homeless, on the other side.

Older people are, though, an increasingly important part of urban environments. Rodwin and Gusmano (2006: 22), analyzing demographic trends in London, New York, Paris, and Tokyo, highlight population projections for 2015 which suggest inner Tokyo will have 35 per cent of its population aged 60 and over, Paris (20 per cent), Manhatten (18 per cent), and Inner London (14 per cent). Champion (2008) suggests that the major urban areas of the United Kingdom will have around one in four of their populations aged 60 and over by 2029.

The trends affecting urban areas are, however, complex and subject to considerable variation. Contrasting examples are provided by, on the one side, cities with declining populations caused by a shrinking manufacturing base – these are located mainly but not exclusively in the Global North. Such cities are likely to have populations with higher than average proportions of older people but with declining levels of investment, deteriorating public services, and poor quality public and private housing. Power and Houghton (2007: 195) note how decline may be hastened through more secure working families moving to new developments in the suburbs, leaving behind 'older, poorer and disproportionately minority ethnic neighbourhoods in still declining city neighbourhoods'.

On the other side, are those cities that expanded (at least up until the beginning of the 2008 recession) through rapid industrialization in the Global South or through new finance and technology-based industries in the Global North. Katz et al. (2008: 476) make the point that:

> Hundreds of millions of rural residents in China, Brazil and India and elsewhere [have] moved in droves to cities. These rural-to-urban migrants are pulled by the tantalizing prospect of jobs and opportunity, driven by the harsh realities of rural life and, particularly in Africa, displaced by horrific wars and civil conflicts.

The pace of urbanization is best illustrated by the case of China, with many of its cities achieving growth rates of more than 10 per cent per year. In 2003 alone, China put up 28 billion square feet of new housing – one eighth of the housing stock of the United States (Campanella, 2008). Campanella (2008) and Meyer (2008) note how much of this development resulted in the destruction of traditional urban and rural neighbourhoods. Some of the fastest-growing cities have substantial populations of older people – Shanghai with 15 per cent of its population aged 65 years and over; Chongqing (11.1 per cent); Bejing (11.1 per cent) (all 2004 figures) – with this group being among those most directly affected by forced relocation to housing estates located on the periphery of urban centres (Shin, 2008).

Another type of urbanization has come with the rise of what Davis (2006) refers to as 'second-tier cities and smaller urban areas'. He notes that if the so-called 'mega-cities' have captured much of the research and policy focus, three-quarters of future world population growth in fact will be in these smaller cities, where 'there is little or no planning to accommodate ... people or provide them with services' (UN-HABITAT cited in Davis, 2006: 7). An even bigger issue in the Global South is the predominance of slums, affecting one of three people living in cities in the developing world. In the case of sub-Saharan Africa nearly two-thirds of city dwellers live in what are officially defined as slum neighbourhoods (UN-HABITAT, 2008). If the nature and characteristics of slum development varies enormously both within and across different countries, the reality is similar in terms of a vastly depleted urban infrastructure unable to support vulnerable populations in general and population ageing in particular.

From this review of some of the general characteristics of urbanization, the chapter now examines the impact of urban change on older people, drawing in particular on research evidence from the United Kingdom and the United States.

URBAN CHANGE AND OLDER PEOPLE

An important question for research concerns the extent to which urban change promotes experiences of 'inclusion' or 'exclusion' among groups such as older people. The concept of social exclusion was developed through the 1990s and is a 'shorthand term for what can happen when people or areas suffer from a combination of linked problems such as unemployment, poor skills, low incomes, discrimination, poor housing, high crime, bad health and family breakdown' (Social Exclusion Unit, 2001:10). Scharf et al. (2002) have emphasized the spatial dimension to social exclusion, drawing on Perri 6's (1997) view that: '[Social exclusion] is a useful term in societies in which there is a growing polarisation of access and opportunity, so that often small areas – a housing estate, an inner or outer urban area – are effectively cut off from life around them'. This idea is further developed by Madanipour et al. (1998: 22) who refer to the multidimensionality of social exclusion and its impact on particular types of location:

Social exclusion is defined as a multi-dimensional process, in which various forms of exclusion are combined: participation in decision-making and political processes, access to employment and material resources, and integration into common cultural processes. When combined, they create acute forms of exclusion that find a spatial manifestation in particular neighbourhoods.

The idea of people being 'excluded' in some way from particular environments is especially associated with the literature on the impact of urban deprivation (see, e.g., Scharf et al., 2002), where the concept of exclusion has been most often applied (Social Exclusion Unit, 2001). Although the impact of rural disadvantage among older people should also be emphasized (Scharf and Bartlam, 2006), the evidence to date has tended to feature exclusionary processes in densely populated urban settings (Office of the Deputy Prime Minister (ODPM, 2006b). On the basis of the available empirical data, at least three dimensions of social exclusion in urban settings can be emphasized: first, as a consequence of neighbourhood change; secondly, arising from generic pressures operating in the urban environment; and, thirdly, through the impact of globalization on perceptions of place and identity.

Social exclusion and neighbourhoods

The area dimension of social exclusion has been a distinctive feature of British research, reflected for example in the work of the Labour government's *Social Exclusion Unit* (SEU, 2001; ODPM, 2006b). As implied earlier, the neighbourhood element may represent a much more important aspect of exclusion than is the case with other age groups. Oswald et al. (2005) note that the immediate home environment becomes more important to older people due to increased physical difficulties that decrease the range of their spatial activities. In comparison with younger age groups, the present generation of older people are much more likely to have lived in the same community for a considerable portion of their lives. For example, taking the 39 *New Deal for Community* (NDC) areas in England (urban areas characterized by severe deprivation), 43 per cent of the residents of all ages had lived in the locality for *less* than 5 years; only 22 per cent had lived in the area for more than 20 years, and most of them were elderly people (Neighbourhood Renewal Unit, 2003). A study of localities with NDC characteristics found that 79 per cent of people aged 60 and over had lived in their neighbourhoods for 20 years or more, and nearly one-half (47 per cent) had been in the area for 40 or more years (Scharf et al., 2002).

Studies of the same communities at different times have indicated that older people derive a strong sense of emotional attachment from both their home and the surrounding community (Phillipson et al., 2001; Townsend, 1957). Indeed, Rowles (1978: 200) makes the point that 'selective intensification of feelings about spaces' might represent 'a universal strategy employed by older people to facilitate maintaining a sense of identity within a changing environment'. This idea is reinforced by Rowles and Ravdal (2002: 87) who argue that the 'selective and repeated mental reconstruction of these places in consciousness ... provides a sense of reinforcement of the self'.

Yet discussion of potential environmental impacts on self-identity raises particular concerns in terms of the situation of older people in deprived and/or rapidly changing urban areas. In their study of residents living on two estates in London, Cattell and Evans (1999) comment that older people derived an important part of their identity from their similarity with one another. Such desire for similarity is understandable: at one level it is about feeling acknowledged by those with similar attributes; at another, it is about being surrounded by people with a similar history. In many urban areas, however, the desire for 'sameness' may be difficult to realize, most notably in 'zones of transition' with a rapid turnover of people and buildings. A similar situation to this may also arise for older people living in what Power (2000: 12; see also, Lupton, 2003) describes as 'nonviable' estates – those unpopular urban neighbourhoods characterized by low housing demand and subsequent abandonment of housing by all but the poorest and least mobile residents. Part of the problem here may be that the advantages of the inner city for some (ethnic diversity, access to cultural resources) may also translate into disadvantages for others (destruction of familiar buildings, environmental deterioration). It is also clear that older people can be highly selective in how they view the consequences of profound urban change, and this may translate into often negatively charged perceptions about those around them. A significant result of the rapid change experienced in some urban neighbourhoods may be an undermining of older people's sense of identification with the local community, and an expression of dissatisfaction with the local neighbourhood (Dench et al., 2006; Solnit and Schwartzenburg, 2000).

On the other hand, social exclusion may also operate in neighbourhoods that are not threatened by economic decline but are undergoing various forms of gentrification (Butler and Robson, 2003). This aspect remains under-researched but has been identified by Phillipson et al. (2001) and Savage et al. (2005: 44), who commented in relation to one gentrifying Manchester locality that, 'there is no sense of a past, historic, community that has moral rights on the area: rather the older

working-class residents, when they are seen at all, are seen mainly as residues'. The use of the term 'residues' is perhaps suggestive of the divisions between older residents and the more recent arrivals (see also, Ogg and Bonvalet, 2007). But the issue of difference is almost certainly one of age *and* social class: older working-class residents lacking the resources to match the lifestyles of younger middle-class residents (discussed further below). This point was also brought out by Phillipson et al. (2001: 112) through the example of a working-class widow living in what had become a middle-class estate – her situation exemplified isolation and alienation in a relatively prosperous neighbourhood.

Environmental change and older people

Exclusionary processes within neighbourhoods may be exacerbated by generic problems associated with urban environments. A survey in the United Kingdom found that 2.5 million people over age 65 had recently fallen on defective kerbs and flagstones, with half requiring medical attention (Harding, 2007). Older people may be especially vulnerable to problems arising from poor-quality housing (Hunt and McKenna, 1992). Particular types of urban housing have been linked to mental health problems in later life. Research in the United States found that elderly residents living in high-rise dwellings were more depressed, had higher rates of psychiatric disorder, and were more socially isolated than those living in detached homes in the community (Husaini et al., 1991). The UK Department for Communities and Local Government (2008: 97) summarize some of the issues here as follows:

> Just as our homes have not been built with an ageing population in mind, neither have our neighbourhoods, streets and public spaces. Seemingly trivial problems, such as poor paving and street clutter, or lack of benches and toilets, can become significant barriers to moving around the neighbourhood, especially as we grow older. This can make a trip outside the home a daunting prospect. And, for many older people, this can translate into a lack of confidence, or even fear, which prevents them from leaving home.

Environmental crises affecting cities have also illustrated the vulnerability of groups such as older people. Although there is limited empirical research on this theme, there have been studies in the United States and France of the problems arising from major environmental change, during, for example, extreme heat waves. Klinenberg (2002) examined the 1995 heat wave in Chicago that over 1 month alone killed around 600 people, of whom three-quarters were aged 65 or more years. As well as the specific acute factors that caused such high mortality, Klinenberg pointed to the abiding or chronic attributes of the urban environment that reduced the quality of life of elderly residents:

In recent years, a number of studies have shown that older people living in violent and deteriorated urban areas tend to be more isolated and afraid of crime than those in more robust regions. Among the mechanisms producing this concentrated fear and isolation in ecologically depleted and politically underserved places are the lack of local commercial venues and service providers to draw people into the streets; barriers to physical mobility, such as broken stairs, crumbling sidewalks, and poor lighting; the psychological impact of living amongst signs of disorder; indifferent government agencies who neglect the local infrastructure; and the decrease of trusting and reciprocal relationships in areas with high levels of crime.

(Klinenberg, 2002:55)

Generic issues were also identified by Ogg (2005) in his analysis of a heat wave in France during 2003 that resulted in an estimated 15,000 deaths, most of whom were older people. Ogg cited several French studies that demonstrated that the highest mortality rates were in urban areas, particularly the Paris and Lyon conurbations. While it was suggested that the support networks of older people were mobilized to greater effect in rural than urban areas, the data were inconclusive. Ogg (2005) concluded that, as with the Chicago experience, the French heat wave raised important questions about the quality of life of older people living in densely populated urban areas. He argued that:

These environments are often not adapted to the needs of older people and they can be one of the primary causes of social exclusion. Spatial and mobility-related aspects of citizenship are increasingly recognised as important dimensions of social inclusion ... and older people in inner cities often face many disadvantages related to access to services (org, 2005: 35).

Globalization and 'ageing in place'

A third influence on inclusion/exclusion concerns the impact of globalization on definitions and perceptions of place. Saskia Sassen (2000a) has referred to the challenge of recovering the meaning of place in the context of global telecommunications and the intensifying of transnational and translocal dynamics (see also, Eade, 1997). But research on older people suggests that, globalizing processes notwithstanding, the relationship between people and place is even more important at the beginning of the 21st century than it was a century or more ago. Older people ageing in place within cities may be the first in their families to achieve a sense of residential stability – living in the same house for three, four, or even five decades (Phillipson et al., 2001). This is in contrast to the 19th century and early 20th century when, as Charles Booth observed in his survey of the London poor: 'the people are always on the move; they shift from one part of it [London] to another "like fish in a sea"' (Davin, 1996).

The paradox here is that globalization produces both huge migrations and population displacements on the one hand, but on the other hand increased numbers of people (older people especially) maintaining a strong sense of attachment to particular places (Phillipson et al., 2001). This sense of attachment to place or 'investment', as Massey (1984) has termed it, has a number of dimensions. Gender interacting with age is one important element. Gerontologists have defined older women as often playing the role of 'kinkeepers', sustaining the family not only through care-work but also with activities such as letterwriting, telephoning, and remembering birthdays. But research also suggests that they may act as 'neighbourhood-keepers' as well, vigilant about the changing fortunes of the localities in which they have invested much of their lives (Campbell, 1993; Phillipson et al., 2001).

Ethnicity will be another dimension interacting with globalization and changing definitions of place. Older people from minority groups may be especially vulnerable to the pressures of adapting to urban living (especially if they are first-generation migrants from predominantly rural areas). They will almost certainly experience more acutely than most the housing pressures characteristic of urban areas in many European cities (UN/HABITAT, 2008). The character of globalization is thus likely to generate both new challenges for urban areas but also to bring fresh social groups and issues for investigation for gerontological research.

In a more general commentary on globalization, Sassen (2000b) has identified the way in which large cities concentrate both the leading sectors of global capital along with a growing share of disadvantaged populations (see also, Rodwin and Gusmano, 2006). Cities, she argues, have become a strategic terrain for a series of conflicts and contradictions – among which the management and support of vulnerable populations is certainly one of the most acute. An important question here concerns the extent to which the construction of the modern (or late-modern) city as the 'site for the new consumerism' (Savage et al., 2003: 149) results in social exclusion for groups such as older people. Rodwin et al. (2006: 7) make the point that while world cities offer extensive cultural and entertainment opportunities, they are expensive places in which to live. They illustrate this point by citing a study of New York City which found that only one-in-20 older households had sufficient money to take full advantage of the quality of life offered by the city. Comparable data are not available for British cities, although a relevant finding from the English Longitudinal Study on Ageing (ELSA) for the Social Exclusion Unit was that a larger percentage of older people living in London than in the rest of the country were multiply excluded (ODPM, 2006b). This is consistent with an analysis of global cities that emphasizes the increasing divergence of the lifestyles and opportunities of wealthy and poor residents, which is itself a manifestation of growing inequalities linked to social class, ethnicity, and, in some respects, age.

An additional dimension of social exclusion in cities may be the extent to which the environment is itself perceived as alienating and discordant with older people's biographies and values. Savage et al. again provided support for this contention from older residents' own statements. Their respondents of all ages viewed the city 'as a space largely hollowed out from social relationships, as a physical shell whose visual surfaces they scan for meanings' (Savage et al., 2005: 129). Although supporting evidence from other studies is still fragmentary, these expressions raise an important issue about how different social groups experience and regard the visual images and the opportunities provided by the changing city landscape. Much of the literature on older people's experience of urban living has focused on their engagement with (or disengagement from) the physical environment of cities, viewed as geographical sites with facilities and opportunities (see, e.g., Phillips et al., 2005). But an equally important dimension (and potential source of social exclusion) is the way in which cities are appropriated symbolically by particular groups in pursuit of their interests – commercial, social, cultural, and political. This draws us into the need for what Castells (2002) referred to as 'urban semiotics', the interpretation or reading of urban change (and of particular cities) for the meanings that they convey for different generational groups. The research question here concerns the way in which both the *visual* and *physical* attributes of urban centres are changing in ways that are experienced as excluding by certain groups of older people (as well as others).

URBANIZATION AND THE CHALLENGE OF AGEING POPULATIONS: IMPLICATIONS FOR PUBLIC POLICY AND RESEARCH

The emphasis in much of the above has been on the problems facing older people living in cities and urban environments. Yet a more positive dimension also needs to be highlighted: namely, that the energy and diversity of city life can help fulfil the potential of old age. Davis (2002: 101) makes the point that:

> Cities have incredible, if largely untapped, capacities for the efficient use of scarce natural resources. Above all they have the potential to counterpose public affluence (great libraries, parks, museums and so on) as a real alternative to privatized consumerism, and thus cut through the apparent contradiction between improving living standards of living and accepting the limits imposed by ecosystems and finite natural resources.

The future of older age will, in fact, to a large degree be determined by the extent to which living in cities is made a tolerable and enjoyable experience. Of course, cities can be disabling and threatening environments at any age. The difference is that at 75 or 85 years of age, people may feel an even greater sense of being trapped or disadvantaged by urban decay. Older people need, therefore, to be a central part of building a sustainable and inclusive urban environment (Scharf et al., 2002). Awareness of the speed of change affecting urban environments has generated new visions and ideas about the most appropriate way in which planning might develop. From the 1960s, writers such as Jane Jacobs (1961) and Richard Sennett (1970) argued the case for protecting the diversity of city life. In Britain, Rogers and Power (2001) developed fresh perspectives on urban planning, which emphasized a sharing of spaces for the collective good and reversing urban sprawl and suburbanization. Katz et al. (2008) have put forward an 'agenda for the urban age', one which aims to rediscover the qualities and benefits of city life which they suggest were largely destroyed in the 20th century.

At present, the extent to which ageing populations are also *urban* populations receives limited acknowledgement in the research and policy literature (e.g., Burdett and Rode, 2008; UN-HABITAT, 2008). But the intersection between the two will be a critical issue for the framing of public policy in the 21st century. What kind of research and policy agenda will need to be developed as a result? Here, five main themes might be identified:

- exploring links between urban sociology and social gerontology

- understanding different responses among older people to urban change
- extending the discussion about the basis for 'age friendly cities'
- acknowledging the importance of environmental change
- developing new research methods for understanding the lives of older people in urban areas.

The first theme concerns the case for linking work in urban sociology with that in social gerontology. The argument here is that most studies of older people are by accident or design studies that involve ageing in urban environments. But the relationship between the two is rarely addressed in any systematic form. Studies of poverty, loneliness, vulnerability to crime, housing, and related matters are interesting topics in themselves but they invariably nest within urban settings; these almost certainly influence the development of the topic under discussion. Demonstrating how old age is influenced by urban processes such as regeneration, property development, and the decline and rise of new industries is one aspect. Equally, it is important to consider how older people themselves and the ageing of localities will itself influence the character of our cities.

A second issue concerns variations in the way in which older people respond to urban change. Although much of the discussion – as noted above – emphasizes the problems facing older people in the city, urban living may also represent opportunities and advantages for those moving into retirement. Ogg and Bonvalet (2007) make this point when examining residential preferences among the baby-boom generation (those born between 1945 and 1955) living in inner city London and Paris. They highlight in particular the experience of those who chose to move to the city when starting their careers in their 20s and 30s. Among this group are the 'pioneers' of gentrification within inner cities; they benefited from the rise in property values and from urban regeneration. Some in this group may well have 'second homes' in the country, with dividing time between 'the city' and 'the country' becoming a preferred strategy to leaving the urban environment altogether. The city may then retain its appeal for those who moved earlier in their lives from provincial towns or rural areas. Conversely, 'local inhabitants', who were born in and who have spent most of their life living in and around a particular urban area, may be more divided about the changes affecting their locality. Nonetheless, even among this group, despite concern with changes in the population and the apparent loss of social cohesion, attachment to life in an urban environment appears strong (Ogg and Bonvalet, 2007; see also, Scharf et al. (2002)).

A third issue is the need to further develop discussions launched by the World Health Organization (2007) on planning what have been called 'age friendly cities'. This approach has developed a number of valuable recommendations concerning the need to improve the physical environment of cities and to promote improved transportation and housing (see also, the debate around 'lifetime neighbourhoods' promoted by the UK Department for Communities and Local Government, 2008). At the same, this discussion is largely disconnected from influences on urban environments in the Global North, where private developers remain the dominant influence on urban planning. The result, according to Harvey (2008: 31), is that the: 'Quality of urban life has become a commodity, as has the city itself, in a world where consumerism, tourism, cultural and knowledge-based industries have become major aspects of the urban political economy'. Blokland and Rae (2008: 38) argue that such processes are leading to a different type of urbanism, one that is: 'confirming rather than challenging inequalities within cities and the various enclaves that can be found there – ranging from gated communities and gentrified neighbourhoods on the one hand to ghettos and poor enclaves on the other – and between central cities and their suburbs'.

One approach in response to the above would be to link the discussion about 'age friendly cities' to ideas about urban citizenship and rights to the benefits which living in a city brings. Painter (2005:9), for example, cites the work of Henri Lefebvre, who explored issues relating to citizenship and rights in an urban context. Lefebvre:

> ... stressed the use-value of the city over its exchange value, emphasizing that citizens have a right to make use of the city, and that it is not just a collection of resources to enable economic activity. The uses of the city by citizens should be seen as valid ends in themselves, not merely as a means to produce economic growth. ... The right to the city is the right to live a fully urban life, with all the liberating benefits it brings. [Lefbvre] believed the majority of city residents are denied this right because their lives are subordinated to economic pressures – despite being *in* the city, they are not fully *of* the city.

This last point applies especially well to older people, who may find that despite having contributed to the urban environment in which they have spent most of their life, it offers few resources and many obstacles to achieving a fulfilling life in old age. Addressing how 'urban citizenship' can be extended into an explicit set of rights applicable to older people is an important agenda, the development of which might fulfil the potential of some of the discussion around 'age friendly cities' and 'lifetime neighbourhoods'.

A fourth issue concerns linking the debate around environmental change with that concerned with urbanization and population change. The vulnerability of older people in periods when urban environments are challenged, through extremes of temperature, has already been highlighted. But other problems may also be cited. Air pollution is a major hazard, especially in newly industrializing countries in the Global South. The World Health Organization (WHO) estimates that more than 1 billion people in Asia alone are exposed to outdoor air pollutant levels that exceed WHO guidelines, leading to the premature death of half a million people annually. Older people, especially those with chronic health conditions – exacerbated or caused by environmental degradation – will be among the worst affected in terms of their quality of life. Looking ahead, rising sea levels associated with climate change may bring particular risks for older people living in cities. Fourteen of the world's 19 largest cities are port cities located along a coastline or river delta. In Asia, the dominance of port cities is even greater: 17 of the region's 20 largest cities are coastal, or on a river bank or in a delta. Many of the world's most prominent global cities (e.g., Mumbai, Shanghai, New York City) will be among the most exposed to surge-induced flooding in the event of sea level rise (UN-HABITAT, 2008: 141). The consequences for their substantial populations of elderly and very elderly people are immense, and will require detailed planning and assessment. Older people are especially vulnerable in periods of environmental crisis, with the potential for displacement from their home, from relatives, and services and support (Rodwin and Gusmano, 2006). These aspects were clearly demonstrated in crises such as Hurricane Katrina in the United States (Bytheway, 2006) and the 2003 heat wave in France. In both cases, elderly people were disproportionately affected compared with other age groups, but failed to received the specialist help and assistance required.

Finally, in keeping with the approach taken in this article, given the rapid changes to many urban centres (notably those associated with 'world' or 'global' cities), new approaches to understanding older people's relationship to urban change – and city development in particular – are urgently required. Following the argument in Phillipson and Scharf (2005:73), there is a strong case for an 'urban ethnography' that captures the disparate experiences of living in cities now subject to intense global change and strongly influenced by complex patterns of migration. Sassen (2000a: 146) has pointed to the need for detailed fieldwork as a 'necessary step in capturing many aspects of the urban condition', and this seems especially important in studying the impact of urban change on specific groups of older people. Urban sociology was founded (through the work of the Chicago School from the 1920s) upon detailed studies of experiences of urban life, particularly of disadvantaged and insecure people from different migrant populations. Ethnographies would bring to the surface the attitudes, motivations, and experiences of older people who are 'ageing in place', and deepen our understanding about both the way in which cities are changing and of the positive and negative contributions that these are making to the quality of daily life in old age (Newman, 2003; Scharf et al., 2002).

CONCLUSION

These various agendas emphasize the importance of placing the lives of older people within the context of the challenges posed by urbanization. When cities face environmental threats or experience population decline, major risks are posed for their most vulnerable residents. When the 'formal' urban infrastructure breaks down, it may cause considerable damage to the 'informal' networks and bonds that sustain older people. But cities, as has been argued, also have the potential to enhance the quality of life – for all age groups. A new focus within gerontology on the strengths and challenges of urban living is urgently required.

REFERENCES

Ackroyd, P. (2000) *London: The Biography.* London: Chatto and Windus.

Beck, U. (1998) *Democracy Without Enemies*, trans. M. Ritter. Cambridge: Polity Press.

Blokland, T. and Rae, D. (2008) 'The end to urbanism: how the changing spatial structure of cities affected its social capital potentials', in T. Blokland, and M. Savage (eds), *Networked Urbanism.* Aldershot, UK: Ashgate, pp. 23–41.

Blokland, T. and Savage, M. (2008) (eds) *Networked Urbanism.* Aldershot, UK: Ashgate.

Burdett, R. and Rode, P. (2008) 'The urban age project', in R. Burdett and D. Sudjic (eds), *The Endless City.* London: Phaidon, pp. 8–31.

Butler, T. and Robson, G. (2003) *London Calling.* Oxford: Berg.

Bytheway, B. (2006) 'The evacuation of older people: the case of Hurricane Katrina', Paper presented at the Annual Conference of the Royal Geographical Society and the Institute of Geography, London.

Campanella, T. (2008) *The Concrete Dragon*. New York: Princeton Architectual Press.

Campbell, B. (1993) *Goliath*. London: Methuen.

Castells, M. (2002) 'Urban sociology in the twenty-first century', in Susser, I. (ed.), *The Castells Reader on Cities and Social Theory*. Oxford: Blackwell, pp. 390–406.

Cattell, V. and Evans, M. (1999) *Neighbourhood Images in East London: Social Capital and Social Networks on Two East London Estates*. York: Joseph Rowntree Foundation/York Publishing Services.

Champion, A. (2008) 'The changing nature of urban and rural areas in the UK and other European countries', http://eprints.ncl.ac.uk/file_store/nclep_221224851528.pdf. Accessed March 13, 2009.

Davin, A. (1996) *Growing Up Poor*. London: Rivers Oram.

Davis, M. (2002) *Dead Cities*. New York: The New Press.

Davis, M. (2006) *Planet of Slums*. London: Verso.

Dench, G., Gavron, K., and Young, M. (2006) *The New East End*. London: Profile Books.

Department for Communities and Local Government (2008) *Lifetime Homes, Lifetime Neighbourhoods*. London: Communities and Local Government.

Eade, J. (ed.) (1997) *Living the Global City: Globalization as a Local Process*. London: Routledge.

Gleeson, B. (2001) 'Disability and the open city', *Urban Studies*, 38: 251–65.

Harding, E. (2007) *Towards Lifetime Neighbourhoods: Designing Sustainable Communities for All*. London: International Longevity Centre/Department for Communities and Local Government.

Harvey, D. (2008) 'The capitalist city', *New Left Review*, 53: 23–42.

Hunt, S. and McKenna, S. (1992) 'The impact of housing quality on mental and physical health', *Housing Review*, 41: 47–9.

Husaini, B., Moore, S., and Castor, R. (1991) 'Social and psychological well-being of black elderly living in high rise for the elderly', *Journal of Gerontological Social Work*, 16: 57–78.

Jacobs, J. (1961) *The Death and Life of Great American Cities*. New York: Vintage Books.

Katz, B., Altman, A., and Wagner, J. (2008) 'An Agenda for the Urban Age', in R. Burdett and D. Sudjic (eds), *The Endless City*. London: Phaidon, pp. 474–83.

Klinenberg, E. (2002) *Heatwave: A Social Autopsy of Disaster in Chicago*. Chicago: University of Chicago Press.

Lupton, R. (2003) *Poverty Street*. Bristol: Policy Press.

Madanipour, A., Cars, G., and Allen, J. (eds) (1998) *Social Exclusion in European Cities: Processess, Experiences and Responses*. London: Jessica Kingsley.

Massey, D. (1984) *Spatial Divisions of Labour: Social Structure and the Geography of Production*. London: Methuen.

Meyer, M. (2008) *The Last Days of Old Beijing*. New York: Walker and Company.

Neighbourhood Renewal Unit (2003) The National Evaluation. Annual Report 20002/3. Research Report No. 7, New Deal for Communities, Office of the Deputy Prime Minister. Whetherby: North Yorkshire.

Newman, K. (2003) *A Different Shade of Gray*. New York: New Press.

Office of the Deputy Prime Minister (2006a) *State of the English Cities*. Urban Research Summary 21. London: ODPM.

Office of the Deputy Prime Minister (2006b) *A Sure Start to Later Life: Ending Inequalities for Older People*. London: Social Exclusion Unit.

Ogg, J. (2005) *Heat Wave*. London: The Young Foundation.

Ogg, J. and Bonvalet, C. (2007) 'Ageing in inner cities: the residential dilemmas of the baby boomer generation', *International Journal of Ageing and Later Life*, 2: 61–90.

Oswald, F., Hieber, A., Wahl, H-W., and Mollenkopf, H. (2005) 'Ageing and person–environment fit in different urban neighbourhoods', *European Journal of Ageing*, 2: 88–97.

Painter, J. (2005) *Urban Citizenship and Rights to the City*. Durham: Durham University International Centre for Regional Regeneration and Development Studies.

Phillips, D.R., Siu., O.L., Yeh, A., and Cheng, K. (2005) Ageing and the Uraban Environment, in G.J. Andrews, and D.R. Phillips (eds), *Ageing and Place*. London: Routledge.

Phillipson, C. (2004) 'Urbanisation and ageing: towards a new environmental gerontology', *Ageing and Society*, 24(6): 963–72.

Phillipson, C. and Scharf, T. (2005) 'Rural and urban perspectives on growing old: developing a new research agenda', *European Journal of Ageing*, 2(1): 67–75.

Phillipson, C., Bernard, M., Phillips, J., and Ogg, J. (2001) *The Family and Community Life of Older People*. London: Routledge.

Power, A. (2000) *Poor Areas and Social Exclusion*. London: CASE Paper 35, Centre for Analysis of Social Exclusion, London School of Management.

Power, A. and Houghton, J. (2007) *Jigsaw Cities*. Bristol: Policy Press.

Rodwin, V. and Gusmano, M. (eds) (2006) *Growing Older in World Cities*. Vanderbilt Nashville, TN: University Press 1–25.

Rodwin, V., Gusmano, M., and Butler, R.N. (2006) 'Growing older in world cities: implications for health and long-term care policy', in V. Rodwin, and M. Gusmano (eds), *Growing Older in World Cities*. Nashville, TN: Vanderbilt University Press, pp. 1–15.

Rogers, R. and Power, A. (2001) *Cities for a Small Country*. London: Faber.

Rowles, G. (1978) *Prisoners of Space? Exploring the Geographical Experience of Older People*. Boulder, CO: Westview.

Rowles, G. and Ravdal, H. (2002) 'Ageing, place and meaning in the face of changing circumstance', in R. Weiss, and S. Bass (eds), *Challenges of the Third Age: Meaning and Purpose in Later Life*. Oxford: Oxford University Press.

Sampson, R.J. (2009) 'Disparity and diversity on the contemporary city: social (dis)order revisited', *British Journal of Sociology*, 60: 1–31.

Sassen, S. (2000a) 'New frontiers facing urban sociology at the millennium', *British Journal of Sociology*, 51: 143–59.

Sassen, S. (2000b) *Cities in a World Economy*. London: Pine Forge.

Sassen, S. (2001) *The Global City*. Princeton, NJ: Princeton University Press.

Savage, M., Warde, A., and Ward, K. (2003) *Urban Sociology, Capitalism and Modernity*, 2nd edn. London: Macmillan.

Savage, M., Bagnall, G., and Longhurst, B. (2005) *Globalization and Belonging*. London: Sage.

Scharf, T. and Bartlam, B. (2006) *Rural Disadvantage: Quality of Life and Disadvantage Amongst Older People. A Pilot Study*. Cheltenham: Commission for Rural Communities.

Scharf, T., Phillipson, C., Smith, A., and Kingston, P. (2002) *Growing Older in Socially Deprived Areas*. London: Help the Aged.

Sennett, R. (1970) *The Uses of Disorder: Personal Identity and City Life*. New Haven: Yale University Press.

Shin, H.B. (2008) *Driven to Swim with the Tide? Urban Redevelopment and Community Participation in China*. Centre for Analysis of Social Exclusion, Working Paper 130. London: London School of Economics.

Social Exclusion Unit (2001) *Bringing Britain Together: A National Strategy for Neighbourhood Renewal*. Social Exclusion Unit. London: Stationery Office.

Soja, E. and Kanai, M. (2008) 'The urbanization of the world', in R. Burdett, and D. Sudjic (eds), *The Endless City*. London: Phaidon, pp. 54–69.

Solnit, R. and Schwartenburg, S. (2000) *Hollow City*. London: Verso.

Townsend, P. (1957) The Family of Old People. London: Routledge and Kegan Paul.

UN/HABITAT (2008) *State of the World's Cities 2008/2009*. London: Earthscan.

World Health Organization (2007) *Global Age-Friendly Cities: A Guide*. Geneva: WHO 6, P (1997) 'Social exclusion: time to be optimistic', in I. Christie, and H. Perry (eds), *The Wealth and Poverty of Networks*. London: Demos.

47

Technology and Older People

Claudine McCreadie

INTRODUCTION

Technology, in some form, has been integral to the majority of humankind's history. Items such as tools, boats, carts, printing, machinery, and weapons, were all designed to enable a task to be undertaken more efficiently (with less expenditure of time and energy) and more effectively (achieving a better result). During the 19th and 20th centuries, the scope of technology increased dramatically, affecting most areas of human activity – notably through the development of industrialized products. Technology is now an essential part of everyday life in all countries, to varying degrees, of the world. The wealthier a country is, the more likely its citizens are to depend on a huge and constantly changing range of technology in their day-to-day activities.

For a person in their 90s in the early 21st century, their world at birth had not yet seen the advent of television, and telephones and radios were still new. All domestic work was done by hand – or by several pairs of hands for those who were affluent. Although typewriters were beginning to come into use, virtually all records were handwritten and most communications with anyone at any distance were by post. These points are reminders that it is easy to confuse *age* differences with *cohort* differences. We grow up with technology, but technology changes, sometimes in revolutionary ways (Charness and Czaja, 2005). Human beings are constantly adapting to change of all kinds. As we age, we have variously to adapt to changes, such as those associated with our ageing body, retirement from paid work, disability, ill health, our past life, and the impact of bereavement. Technological change is both integrated with, and superimposed upon, these various developments running through the course of our life.

How human beings adapt and respond to social change is the special interest of social scientists. Social change rarely has a uniform impact on all groups in society, and the human costs generally fall most heavily on disadvantaged groups. Older people may fall disproportionately into this category, at least in financial and educational terms. Recurrent concerns that are particularly relevant to the implications of technology for ageing are stratification, social capital, organizational behaviour, and people's sense of personal and social identity. 'Stratification' refers to systematic social divisions, by income, social class, education level, occupation, and status. Factors such as age, gender, and ethnic background intersect with these dimensions of inequality. Insofar as access to technology is affected by income, the extent of inequality among older people may be highly pertinent to their response to current technological change (Jones et al., 2008). 'Social capital' refers to the ability of individuals to secure benefits by virtue of their membership of wider social networks – family, neighbours, friends, locality, organizations to which people belong in different ways. Older people place considerable importance on social capital in their assessments of quality of life (Walker and Hagan Hennessey, 2004). Insofar as technology promotes, or reduces, contact with others, it is of great value for older people.

Organizations – whether these are supermarkets, government departments, banks, hospitals, or social welfare departments – impact on the populations they serve by the manner in which they deliver services. Rapid change in technologies, for example, through automated telephone systems, ordering and paying for goods and services with credit and debit cards, and accessing substantive information on everything from medical conditions to the side effects of drugs, are altering the relationships between users and producers of services. The implications of these changes for older people, as users of services, may be considerable, both by placing greater responsibility on the user for ensuring delivery, and by giving them the potential to be more fully informed and therefore demand more of services. How this works out will depend substantially on the factors mentioned above that promote or reduce inequality.

This chapter provides a particular focus on the application of Information and Communication Technology (ICT) in the lives of older people, but relates this to broader issues surrounding access to technology in the home and beyond. The material covered in this chapter suggests that developments relating to ICT raise four key questions. First, what is the *scope* of technology in its impact on everyday life, and the particular aspects that may address a range of older people's needs? Secondly, what factors operate to *exclude* people, particularly older people, from the benefits of new technology? Thirdly, what are the likely human *costs*, particularly to older people, of new technology? Fourthly, how can older people increase their involvement in the *shaping* of technology? These points will be considered in this chapter as part of a general review of the place of technology in everyday life in old age.

APPLYING TECHNOLOGY TO THE LIVES OF OLDER PEOPLE

Technology has penetrated the lives of older people in a variety of ways. Jones et al. (2008) highlight that the importance of older people as consumers is reflected in ownership of a range of household goods. Technology, in other words, in the form of consumer goods such as refrigerators, washing machines, microwaves, and televisions, has become a progressively more important feature of daily life. Rapid developments in ICT are resulting in the increasingly pervasive use of mobile communications and personal computers, developments that also have significant applications to questions linked to the safety and security of people in their own homes as well as in the delivery of services (Loader et al., 2009; Sixsmith, 2006).

There is a risk that the study of technology from the standpoint of older people places undue emphasis on issues of disability and care provision rather than focusing on technology in everyday life, in which illness and declining capacity may play a part. The following list of terms frequently used in the field illustrates, however, the broad scope and relevance of technology as applied to the lives of older people:

- *Ambient Intelligence*: the provision of information while people are mobile (Antona et al., 2007 in Roe, 2007: 158).
- *Assistive Technology*: products and services designed with the aim of promoting independence for older people and people with disabilities.
- *Digital Age:* describes the effects of the rapid fall in cost, and rapid expansion of digital devices such as computers and telecommunications such as mobile/cell phones.
- *E-health*: health care that uses interactive communications networks (Fisk, 2003:198).
- *Ergonomics*: applied science addressing the design of human–machine–environment interactions with an emphasis on the effective use of human strengths and weaknesses in order to optimize system performance, promote wellbeing, and minimize risk or injury.
- *Gerontechnology*:

... the study of technology and aging for the improvement of the daily functioning of [elderly] people. ... Core concepts in gerontechnology are (1) the integration of older adults into a changing society by directing technological developments at them; (2) the adequate modification of the technological environment of older adults' so that it enhances rather than limits their ambitions and aspirations; (3) giving older adults full control over their technological environment, for example allowing them to decide the tasks in their living environment which should be automatized.
(Melenhorst et al., 2007: 254)

- *Human–Computer Interaction*: the study of the interaction between people and computers.
- *Inclusive Design/Design for all/Universal Design*: designing products to facilitate their use by the widest possible range of individuals.
- *Information Technology/Information and Communication Technology*: the use of computers for accessing, storing, and processing information securely.
- *Persuasive Technology*: 'A class of technologies that are intentionally designed to change a person's attitude or behaviour' (Ijsselsteijn et al., 2006: 1).
- *Robotics*: A robot is an electromechanical system under some form of computerized control that gives the illusion that it has some agency or intent of its own.
- *Smart Technology*: the combination of ICT with 'industrial' products. A 'Smart House' refers to the provision of a range of automated services controlled by a computer.
- *Telecare*: 'the application of information and communication technology to promote and

enable independent care in the community and home setting' (Emery et al., 2002: 29).

- *Telemedicine*: the practice of medicine at a distance (Fisk, 2003: 196).

TECHNOLOGY IN RELATION TO THE SPECIAL NEEDS OF OLDER PEOPLE

A number of the above definitions apply to the special needs of older people arising from problems associated with declining physical and/or mental capacity. To illustrate this point, this section focuses on *assistive technology*, the use of *robotics*, and the application of *telecare* in the area of risk management and assessment. The first of these, assistive technology, has traditionally been linked with medical and rehabilitation engineering and is primarily associated with short-term recuperation from injury or illness, or long-term functional support (Newell, 2003). The broader definition given in the list above recognizes that disability is properly seen as a product of an interaction between the individual and his or her environment. This approach reinforces Newell's (2003) argument that assistive technology can increasingly address a 'mainstream' market, responding to a range of disabled and older users. The advent of sensors and computers has created the potential for alarm devices of all kinds that, apart from their traditional applications (e.g., burglar and smoke alarms), can be used to address special needs, for example, among older people with a cognitive impairment (Cash, 2003). A gas supply can be turned off automatically if left on, just as the water in the bath can be prevented from overflowing, and a buzzer can sound in the room of a carer if someone in another room gets out of bed during the night (see, further below).

Lansley et al. (2004), in a study examining the scope for adapting different types of housing to accommodate the changing needs of older people, categorized assistive technology into three different types: portable, fixed, and electronic. *Portable* assistive technology includes those items that are independent of housing – e.g., wheelchair, furniture, walking aids, and kitchen aids. Occupational therapists have traditionally referred to this as community equipment or 'aids to daily living'. *Fixed* assistive technology includes items that are specific to a particular property because they have to be installed – lifts, showers, grab rails, hoists, and ramps are typical examples. These have generally been referred to as housing adaptations. Finally, *electronic* assistive technology comprises all items requiring an electricity supply or battery operation, such as door and window openers, alarms, and communication devices. All these

technologies have the potential to reduce the impact of disability – and arguably to redefine disability (Brink, 1997). Being able to shop online, for example, makes walking to the shops less essential for the maintenance of everyday life.

Assistive technologies may also be a *substitute* for human care (Lansley et al., 2004), and reduce consumption of health and social care services (Mann et al., 1999). They may offer the potential of increasing *choice* for the individual, doing a task more efficiently, and offering significant help to carers, paid care workers (in both institutional and domestic environments), and other family members. An important question in relation to assistive technology as it relates to older people is how far many of these items can be developed as useful mainstream technology, rather than being part of 'special needs' provision (Fisk, 2003; Newell, 2003).

A second illustration of how ICT may be particularly salient to old age concerns the use of robotics by older people. Robots are automated devices that make use of sensors to 'react' in a variety of ways. Robotic technology is increasingly available from lawn mowers and vacuum cleaners at one level, to surgery for gall bladder removal at another. Robots for cleaning and lawn mowing might arguably be seen as ideal mainstream technology for many older people. Other developments in robots are more specifically geared to care and rehabilitation. A Japanese robot has been designed that can help people to walk and one that can 'conduct meaningful relationships with human beings' (Dethlefs, 1999). By its computer link, the robot can communicate news, weather reports, and other information (Dethlefs, 1999). Robots are likely to become an increasingly feasible way of helping with a number of demanding tasks performed by caregivers, for example helping someone with a disability in and out of a bath, or bed (Dario, 2005).

The third area – 'telecare' services – refers to the application of ICT to help people live independently in their own homes. Technology in the form of ICT is also increasingly applied to maintain the safety and security of elderly people in their own homes as well as to assist in the delivery of services. Loader et al. (2008) note the distinction drawn by Barlow between telecare systems that are designed for *risk management* and those primarily aimed at *assessment and information sharing*. Telecare associated with managing risk and providing security in the home has taken a number of forms. Sixsmith and Sixsmith (2008) refer to 'first' and 'second generation' systems. The former refer to community alarms where a person raises an alarm in a call centre by pushing a button (or pulling a cord), with a call centre arranging an appropriate response. The authors note that the UK market for this type of technology is 'perhaps the most well developed worldwide … with approximately 1.5 million users'

(Sixsmith and Sixsmith, 2008: 231). However, 'second generation' systems have evolved to respond to situations where individuals are unable – through, for example, cognitive impairment – to recognize a problem and/or initiate a response:

Typically, such systems attempt to identify unusual or 'abnormal' patterns of activity, for example if a person is motionless for an extended period of time. Fall detectors have been developed which detect sudden movements or changes in position that may indicate the person has fallen. Such second generation systems comprise:

- alarm button, telecommunications link, control centre, records system for monitoring alerts (the first generation functionality)
- sensors for passively monitoring the person's movement (e.g., ... door opening, pressure sensors for bed or chair occupancy...)
- environmental sensors for smoke, flood, temperature, gas etc
- intelligent home base unit or hub to link in home sensors together
- advanced record system logging new data from sensors (Sixsmith and Sixsmith, 2008: 231)

In respect of assessment and information sharing, activities in the United Kingdom and other countries include extending medical care in the home through remote monitoring, or consultations by telecommunications (Fisk, 2003; Loader et al., 2009). Chronic illnesses, such as diabetes, heart conditions, asthma, and hypertension, are among those that can be monitored in people's own homes, or in care settings. The development of electronic care records can facilitate access, not only by different members of multidisciplinary team but also by the older person themselves or by their carer. Important issues of confidentiality are raised (Norris, 2002) as well as the potential for harmful, as well as beneficial, consequences. In the field of social care, Brink (1997) suggests that in future older people may be able to choose, for example, to have a needs assessment at a distance, rather than use a local service (or this might be introduced as a cost-saving device).

OLDER PEOPLE AS USERS AND CONSUMERS OF TECHNOLOGY

Differences in attitudes towards, and the use of, technology are often ascribed to chronological age, but this is a self-evidently simplistic view. Older people in fact use technology all the time – especially through their use of household goods and equipment such as telephones, remote controls for television, microwaves, and, increasingly, personal computers. Social and personal factors such as education, income, and personal preference will affect how people view the relevance of particular types of technology (Loader et al., 2008). Older people also play many different roles – as volunteers, grandparents, friends, and carers – and variously participate in a range of social networks. All these bring them into contact with technology over and above what they might use in their home and may influence their own views. Charness (2003) identifies five factors as necessary conditions in the successful use of technology by older people: design, access, motivation, ability, and training. The issue of design will be considered in the following section. The remainder of this part of the Chapter focuses on four 'user-related' issues.

In the first place, older people may want to access both 'mainstream' and 'special needs' technology. In the case of 'mainstream' technology, economic theory would suggest that the price of the good, the consumer's income, the availability of substitute goods, and consumer preferences are of prime importance in explaining access. Jones et al. (2008) demonstrate the extent to which income is an important factor in determining access to technology in the home. It may be that it is not the only factor, since a high income usually denotes a longer time spent in education. It may also mean that the older person's adult children themselves have higher incomes and can afford to buy new technology for their parents. In economically developed countries of the world, ownership of technology in domestic settings has increased over the past 30 years, which can be attributed to both rising incomes and the falling price of a range of technologies. Katz and Aakhus (2001) have pointed to the connection between mobile (cell) phone penetration rate and cost per minute of using a mobile (cell) phone. Within any given country there is a divide between those at the top and bottom of the income distribution, which can be illustrated in relation to ownership of mobile (cell) phones (Mann et al., 2004) or personal computers. In Great Britain, for example, ownership of a home computer and the associated access to the Internet, increasingly a 'normal' part of daily living, are related to both age and income group. McCreadie and Stuchbury (2006) showed that in Great Britain in 2004–05, there were actually a higher proportion of 'well-off' households (earning more than £500 weekly) with heads aged over 80 that had Internet access than there were households with younger heads (16–49 years) in the lowest income group (earning less than £300 weekly). The point is that the trend to declining use with age is greatly modified when income is taken into account. Access to assistive ('special needs') technology may also depend on income, but it also depends on information provision on one hand, and is closely linked to health and social care provision and service delivery on the other (Wright et al., 2005).

Attitudes to the ownership and use of different kinds of technology are also the product of a number of sociodemographic variables in addition to age and income, such as gender, education, ethnicity, and wider social network, including peer group. Family members – children, and particularly, grandchildren – use mobile (cell) phones and email contact routinely. They may, as a result, influence the way older people use technology in general, and information technology in particular. The importance of technology in maintaining social connections has been stressed in research undertaken in France (Bouchayer and Rozenkier, 1999). In relation to everyday technology, German researchers (Wahl and Mollenkopf, 2003) found both positive and negative attitudes among older people. When people are active problem solvers and the technical device is useful in solving their problem, people were positive about its use. Roelands et al. (2002) in Belgian research also found support for this pragmatic approach to technology.

Czaja et al. (2006) proposed a complex model of attitudes to using computers, combining sociodemographic and attitudinal variables with cognitive abilities, themselves mediated by age and education. They found among a sample of adults aged between 60 and 91 (n = 1204), despite the fact that participants were healthy and fairly well educated, there were still significant age differences in computer and Internet use. Anxiety about using the computer was associated with less use of technology in general and computers in particular, and anxiety was more prevalent among female respondents. But having allowed for attitudes and cognitive ability, Czaja et al. (2006) still found that there were unexplained factors in relation to older adults' use of technology and suggest that this may be 'perceived need' (2006:32). This accords with the research of Selwyn (2004) on older adults' use of computers, and the proposed model of McCreadie and Tinker (2005) around the acceptability of a wide range of assistive technology. Their conclusion, based on face-to-face interviews with 67 older people, was that acceptability depends on the interaction between a 'Felt Need for Assistance' (itself the product of the individual's disability, housing, preferences, living arrangements, and carer input) and the attributes of the technology – efficiency, reliability, simplicity, safety, and aesthetics (McCreadie, 2004). The importance of involving older people in the development of technology is increasingly recognized (see Clarkson et al., 2003).

This was done successfully in relation to the development of a stair climbing aid (McCreadie et al., 2002) and way-finding technology (McCreadie et al., 2006). However, it can also be argued (Mann, 2003) that negative attitudes to ageing and disability in society are carried over to and imposed upon those products that are specifically meant to compensate for loss of functional ability, and in turn influencing their acceptability.

As people age, they experience, to diverse degrees, a decline in their sensory, cognitive, and physical abilities. Some technology may usefully compensate for some of these deficits – this is often a function of assistive technology – spectacles being a very common example. The possibility of the text function of mobile (cell) phones becoming increasingly useful in countering hearing impairment is another illustration. Contrary to many stereotypes, McCreadie (2005) found, in the preliminary stages of research on way-finding technology, that the most avid user of a mobile phone for texting was an 85-year-old woman. Other technology may challenge deficits. Getting into a car can be increasingly difficult with ageing joints. Differences in learning, spatial ability, processing speed, accuracy, memory, vision, and dexterity may all affect older people's capacity to adapt easily to computer and mobile (cell) phone technology. Researchers into human factors have consistently made 'good practice' recommendations to technology designers (Fozard, 2003) (see Table 47.1). Notwithstanding these, instructions and packaging remain difficult to read on a range of goods (Weale and McCreadie, 2006). Similar recommendations have been made for attention and memory, but there is arguably more scope in these areas for a focus on interventions that can delay or prevent these deficits (Fozard, 2001).

As seen in Table 47.1, a repeated recommendation in relation to compensating for hearing loss is that older people receive training in using a hearing aid. Technology varies in the demands that it makes on people's mental and physical capacities. An important factor in relation to the use of computers is that people (of all ages) need education and training to use them – comparable, although to a lesser extent, to the training required to drive a car. Like driving a car, computer use requires skills that have to be learnt and, as the technology changes and its scope increases, the updating of these skills. Thus, there are implications for learning at all ages. Is this an individual responsibility or one for families, volunteers (for example, students linked to older people in localities), or for paid personnel? What are the implications for older people living in residential or healthcare settings? Czaja and Barr (1989) found that older people's competence in using computers was closely related to the kind of training they received,

Table 47.1 Repeated recommendations for compensating vision and hearing, loss in older age

Compensating age-related difficulties by improved design: repeated recommendations	
Vision	Hearing
Increase colour contrast	Increase volume, decrease background noise
Reduce glare	Avoid high-frequency signals
12 point font for 65+ years; 18 point font for 85+ years	Combine fitting of hearing aids with user training

Source: Adapted from Fozard (2003)

as well as to design (Czaja and Sharit, 2003). Older computer users are 'typically slower to acquire new skills than younger adults and generally require more help and "hands on" practice', but with training of the right kind, performance improves (Charness and Czaja, 2005: 665). Similar findings in relation to the time required to learn how to use more complex technology were reported in research using personal digital assistants (PDAs) for reminding people about taking medication (Mayhorn et al., 2005). Brink points out that 'exposure to new technologies is necessary to develop confidence and know-how' and that step-by-step instructions may also be important (Brink, 1997: 9) and Czaja et al. (2006) report that training should focus on the reduction of anxiety – allowing enough time and opportunity for students to develop at their own pace.

Finally, housing structure and design are critical, both in relation to people's capacity to access technology (without an electricity supply, much contemporary technology cannot operate), as well as in relation to their need for it. For example, a person living in a bungalow does not require technology to help climbing stairs, while a person using a wheelchair may benefit substantially from automated door and window openers. House design creates 'architectural disability' and the movement to 'lifetime homes' in the United Kingdom and elsewhere attempts to minimize this as far as possible, thereby obviating the need for technology to compensate for architectural design limitations on the one hand, and making provisions for assistive technology, like hoists, or lifts, on the other (Department for Communities and Local Government, 2008).

'Smart homes' offer the possibility of applying information technology to automate and coordinate routine activity in the home and link devices to one another by some form of central control. For example, instead of switching a light on as you enter a room, the light comes on automatically as you go in, and 20 minutes later the curtains close, the heating comes on, and, at the appointed hour, the TV news comes on. These applications are not widespread in domestic settings, although common in office buildings in relation to heating and air conditioning. On the other hand,

devices such as burglar and smoke alarms, and passive infrared lighting that is triggered through sensing body heat, are widely used. Older people may well benefit from increased automation in their homes for routine activities like drawing curtains. However, the focus of such applications has too often been exclusively on 'special needs'. Institutional care presents further opportunities for the application of technology, both mainstream and assistive, but evidence from the United States suggests that its potential is very far from being realized (Freedman et al., 2005).

TECHNOLOGY AND OLDER PEOPLE: CRITICAL ISSUES

Discussions around technology and its application to improving the lives of older people raise a number of important issues. This section considers four main areas. First, are older people excluded from using technology? Secondly, do we shape or are we shaped by technology? Thirdly, is technology designed in a user-friendly way for older people? Fourthly, what are the ethical issues raised by developments in technology?

Are older people excluded from technology?

Older people use many kinds of technology in line with the rest of the population. To the extent that ICT is a part of everyday life, like cars or television, issues of accessibility are bound up with disparities in income and opportunity, nationally as well as globally. DiMaggio and colleagues argue that establishing equality of use of the Internet is crucial: 'to ensure that less well-to-do or technically sophisticated citizens are not excluded from the political, economic and social opportunities that the Internet increasingly provides' (2001: 328). Older people require special attention, *not* because of chronological age, but because (a) of their position in the income distribution; (b) their education and working life being situated in a context of contrasting technology to the present time; and (c) the likelihood of their having 'special needs' not addressed by mainstream consumer products. Chronological age must not be confused with the social and economic characteristics that accompany it.

The UK government has attempted to make it possible for more people to participate in the 'digital age' by opening up public access through libraries and adult education. There have also been comparable voluntary sector initiatives. Policies such as these help address issues of exclusion and there may be very real benefits from socially organized provision of ongoing support, cost sharing, security against things going wrong with the computer, and updating, the equipment – quite necessary in a fast-moving world. But the issue of access also concerns the geographical spread of the older population and the availability of an infrastructure of transport, since older people in lower-income households are less likely to have access to a car. In care settings, there may be considerable scope for provision of a communal computer, with volunteer assistance to enable residents to email family members, play card games, search out information, and generally maintain connections with the wider world. There seems little reason why such a facility could not also be open to older people still living in their own home. Inequalities in access, however, are not just relevant within particular countries and their income distributions. Between different countries, there are likely to be significant inequalities, as

can be seen from Table 47.2, where in most countries of the world it may be assumed that older people have very limited access to contemporary information technology.

Does technology shape us, or do we shape technology?

It is easy to be 'swept along' by the potential of technology and by the enthusiasm and visions of those on the cutting edge of innovation and development (Ijsselsteijn et al., 2006; Loader et al., 2009; Roe, 2007). As Selwyn has pointed out: 'the ability to use Information and Communications Technology is now assumed by most commentators to be a prerequisite to living in the "information age"' (2004: 370). The evidence, in relation to the implications of the Internet, however, appears to be that 'the Internet's impact is more limited than either the utopian or dystopian visions suggests' (DiMaggio et al., 2001: 327). DiMaggio and colleagues argue that the nature of that impact will vary 'depending on how economic factors, government regulation and users collectively organize the evolving internet technology' (2001: 328). Dickinson and Gregor (2006) reviewed a range of empirical studies investigating whether computer use improves the well-being of older people. They concluded that no such relationship is demonstrated by the research because of the diversity of older people and the powerful independent effects of social contact that occur through

Table 47.2 Percentage of Internet users by selected countries, 2000 and 2006, with percentage aged 60 and over, 2005

Country	Internet users as per cent of population		Total population in 2000, millions	Per cent of Population aged 60 and over, 2005	
	2000	2006		Women	Men
Brazil	2.9	17.2	169.5	10	8
Canada	40.3	67.8	32.4	20	16
Chile	26.2	42.8	15.8	13	10
China	1.7	10.4	1370.0	12	10
Finland	37.1	62.3	5.2	24	18
Germany	29.2	61.2	82.2	28	22
Iran	3.8	10.8	69.4	7	6
Israel	18.2	45.8	6.98	15	12
Jamaica	2.3	39.6	2.6	11	10
Japan	37.1	67.2	126.9	29	24
Kenya	0.7	3.1	30.3	4	4
Senegal	0.1	5.0	10.4	5	4

Source: Internet use, www.internetworldstats.com;
population figures, http://unstats.un.org/unsd/demographic/products/socind/popcomp.htm. Accessed 9.5.08

training and other social aspects of computer use. They question the premise that older people need to be part of the digital revolution, pointing to the potential negative implications of new technology, as well as noting findings that older people regard social relationships of primary importance in relation to their quality of life (Walker and Hagan Hennessey, 2004). Selwyn concludes that: 'rather than trying to change older adults, older adults should be involved in changing ICT to be more of an attractive, interesting, or useful option for many older adults' (2004: 382).

Is technology designed in a user-friendly way for older people?

Charness cites the view of one critic that 'the world is not a well-designed place' and poses the question, 'well designed for whom?' (2003: 16). He reiterates the familiar point that older people are marked by their diversity, but points to the importance of social context – older men, for example, are more likely to be living with someone else than are older women, and therefore may be joint rather than 'solo problem solvers'. Furthermore, there may be important gender issues in relation to design. How many guides to technology, to take one example, are written by and for women? Charness (2003) goes on to raise the question of whether, for a given product, the best design for younger people will be the best design for older people. Proponents of 'inclusive design' would argue that the best design for older people is also likely to be the best design for younger people. While there is much variation, a look at catalogues and a visit to some showrooms, to examine 'assistive technology', can fill the consumer with considerable despondency. The association with special needs has meant that much design is 'medicalized' and only available to a limited extent in shops and 'normal' commercial channels. Thus, social alarms, worn around the neck, are generally made of white plastic with a red button. By no stretch of the imagination could they be deemed a fashion accessory, yet somehow older people are expected to wear them (McCreadie, 2004). Raised toilet seats, often very helpful when it is harder to bend to the standard lower height, exemplify some of the worst in assistive technology design. Market forces have failed significantly in this instance to produce a range of attractive versions that offer choice.

However, the growing interest in 'inclusive (universal) design', while not entirely able to reconcile the tensions between 'mainstream' and 'special needs' products, is increasingly identifying the commercial rationale of addressing the needs of consumers of *all* ages.

What ethical issues are raised by developments in technology?

The scope of ethical considerations is arguably social as well as individual. Issues of accessibility and inclusion are ethical issues, relating to the share of individuals, particularly those who are least advantaged, in the resources of society (Rawls, 1999). Current technology increasingly substitutes for human activity in a number of spheres. The Internet enables us to book our own tickets, sort out queries about products, handle our financial affairs, and so on, without contact with another human being. As pointed out above, the human implications are not *necessarily* benevolent.

There are important ethical questions about the substitution of technology for human care. Technology has the potential to enable people to do things for themselves that otherwise they would need help with. Having a shower is preferable to many older people rather than having human help to get into and out of a bath because they value the independence that this brings. It may also be highly beneficial for family carers and paid care workers, an increasingly important issue, as mutual care in older age becomes more the norm. But there also has to be balanced consideration of how far this process can go. Perhaps the most important aspect of ethics is that people are enabled to make an informed choice. In Italian research about the use of robots in the home, older respondents were more concerned than younger people about the safety issues (Scopelliti et al., 2004).

Key ethical issues concern consent around the deployment of technology. These are notably most acute in relation to people with forms of cognitive impairment (Sixsmith, 2006). The dangers and risks involved, for example, by people 'wandering', make the notion of a tracking device that monitors their movements an intuitively attractive one, but it clearly raises considerable problems in terms of consent. Similarly, if a care home manager suspects that one resident is going into the room of another and removing possessions, would they be justified in installing a closed circuit television camera to monitor what is going on in the room? Many similar situations raise moral dilemmas for those involved and the principles, used by clinicians, of beneficence, non-maleficence, and autonomy in decision making wherever possible, are probably the most useful guide in practice (Magnusson and Hanson, 2003; see also

Chapter 49). Confidentiality is another key ethical issue that arises out of the greater ease of information transfer – this may be a particularly important consideration in relation to an increase in the use of telemedicine.

CONCLUSION: FUTURE DIRECTIONS

It is striking that textbooks and handbooks on gerontology have invariably not included technology as a topic, that most discussion of older people and technology is in terms of their dependency and 'need for care', and that the scientific community follow this lead in applying for funding.[1] The least ageist perspectives are evident in the design community, and particularly among those who have seen the relevance of the concept of inclusive design (Coleman et al., 2003). Bernard and Phillips identified the lack of recognition in gerontology literature of technology's significance for today's world, arguing that it should be at the 'centre of social policy' (2000: 49), for three reasons: technology is intergenerational, in that it affects us all; it pervades every aspect of contemporary life; and it can facilitate communication and 'empower people as they shop, vote and seek expert help "online" in all areas of policy' (2000: 49). Following this, some final questions for gerontologists in all countries might include the following. To what degree have gerontologists thought adequately about technology and technology change? What is the relationship between mainstream and special needs? How far, and in what circumstances, is a special needs approach required for technology used by older people? What are the issues around inequality, education, and lifelong learning that need to be addressed if older people are to be genuine participants in the 'digital age'? How can gerontologists link most appropriately with other disciplines, notably technology researchers? What help can gerontologists give these communities? What is the relationship between gerontologists and the market? How do gerontologists respond to the special needs approaches embraced by some companies? How do theories in gerontology address the issues of interface between older people and technology? How can gerontologists contribute to shaping technology for the benefit of older people?

Like many topics in gerontology, what appears at first sight to be a relatively contained area of thought and investigation turns out to be a topic that has huge multidisciplinary implications with associated challenges for research and understanding. The issue of technology, in a range of contexts, is likely to develop as a key topic for research and debate within gerontology. This chapter has outlined a potential framework for developing work around this important area of research.

NOTE

1 The Ambient Assisted Living (AAL) Joint Programme, supported by 23 European member states and associated states, will oversee a major expansion in research studying the role of ICT in improving the lives of older people. AAL has initial funding over the period 2008–13 and includes the aim of fostering innovative ICT-based products and services supporting older people at home, in the community, and at work. For further information, contact www.aal-europe.eu/about-aal.

REFERENCES

Antona, M., Burzagli, L., Emiliani, P.L., and Stephanidis, C. (2007) 'The ISTAG scenarios: a case study', in P.R.W. Roe (ed.), *Towards An Inclusive Future: Impact and Wider Potential of Information and Communication Technologies.* Brussels: COST, pp. 158–87.

Bernard, M. and Phillips, J. (2000) 'The challenge of ageing in tomorrow's Britain', *Ageing and Society,* 20(1): 33–54.

Bouchayer, F. and Rozenkier, A. (1999) *Technological Developments, the Dynamics of Age, and Ageing of the Population. Progress Report.* Paris: Caisse Nationale d'Assurance Vieillesse.

Brink, S. (1997) 'The twin challenges of information technology and population ageing', *Generations,* 21(3): 7–10.

Cash, M. (2003) 'Assistive technology and people with dementia', *Reviews in Clinical Gerontology,* 13: 313–19.

Charness, N. (2003) 'Commentary: access, motivation, ability, design, and training: necessary conditions for older adults success with technology', in N. Charness and K. Warner Schaie (eds), *Impact of Technology on Successful Aging.* New York: Springer, pp. 15–27.

Charness, N. and Czaja, S.J. (2005) 'Adaptation to new technologies', in M.L. Johnson (ed.), *The Cambridge Handbook of Age and Ageing.* Cambridge: Cambridge University Press, pp. 662–9.

Clarkson, J., Coleman, R., Keates, S., and Lebbon, C. (2003) *Inclusive Design: Design for the Whole Population.* London: Springer.

Coleman, R., Lebbon, C., Clarkson, J., and Keates, S. (2003) 'From margins to mainstream', in J. Clarkson, R. Coleman, S. Keates, and C. Lebbon (eds), *Inclusive Design. Design for the Whole Population.* London: Springer. pp. 1–25.

Czaja, S.J. and Barr, R.A. (1989) 'Technology and the everyday life of older adults', *Annals of the American Academy of Political and Social Science*, 503: 127–37.

Czaja, S.J. and Sharit J. (2003) 'Practically relevant research: capturing real world tasks, environments, and outcomes', *The Gerontologist*, 43 (special issue 1): 9–18.

Czaja, S.J., Charness, N., Fisk, A.D., et al., (2006) 'Factors predicting the use of technology: findings from the Center for Research and Education on Aging and Technology Enhancement (CREATE)', *Psychology and Aging*, 21(2): 333–52.

Dario, P. (2005) 'Biorobotics for longevity', *Gerontechnology*, 4(1): 1–4.

Dethlefs, N. (1999) 'Issues in the development of robotics technology for aged care in Japan', *Australian Journal on Ageing*, 18(4): 174–8.

Department for Communities and Local Government (2008) *Lifetime Homes, Lifetime Neighbourhoods: A National Strategy for Housing in an Ageing Society*. London: Department for Communities and Local Government.

Dickinson, A. and Gregor, P. (2006) 'Computer use has no demonstrated impact on the well-being of older adults', *International Journal of Human-Computer Studies*, 64: 744–53.

DiMaggio, P., Hargittai, E., Russell Neuman, W., and Robinson, J.P. (2001) 'Social implications of the Internet', *Annual Review of Sociology*, 27: 307–36.

Emery, D., Hayes, B.J., and Cowan, A.M. (2002) 'Telecare delivery of health and social care information', *Health Informatics Journal*, 8: 29–33.

Fisk, M.J. (2003) *Social Alarms to Telecare: Older People's Services in Transition*. Bristol: Policy Press.

Fozard, J.L. (2001) 'Gerontechnology and perceptual motor function: new opportunities for prevention, compensation, and enhancement', *Gerontechnology*, 1(1): 5–24.

Fozard, J.L. (2003) 'Using technology to lower the perceptual and cognitive hurdles of aging', in N. Charness and K. Warner Schaie (eds), *Impact of Technology on Successful Ageing*. New York: Springer.

Freedman, V.A., Calkins, M., and van Haitsma, K. (2005) 'An exploratory study of barriers to implementing technology in United States residential long-term care settings', *Gerontechnology*, 4(2): 86–100.

Ijsselsteijn, W., de Kort, Y., Midden, C., Eggen, B., and van den Hoven, E. (2006) *Persuasive Technology*. Berlin: Springer.

Jones, I.R., Hyde, M., Victor, C.R., et al. (2008) *Ageing in a Consumer Society*. Bristol: Policy Press.

Katz, J.E., and Aakhus, M.A. (2001) *Perpetual Contact: Mobile Communication, Private Talk, Public Performance*. Cambridge: Cambridge University Press.

Lansley, P., McCreadie, C., and Tinker, A. (2004) 'Can adapting the homes of older people and providing Assistive Technology pay its way?', *Age and Ageing*, 33(6): 571–6.

Loader, B., Hardey, M., and Keeble, L. (2008) 'Health informatics for older people: a review of ICT facilitated integrated care for older people', *International Journal of Social Welfare*, 17: 46–53.

Loader, B., Hardey, M., and Keeble, L. (2009) *Digital Welfare for the Third Age: Health and Social Care Informatics for Older People*. London: Routledge.

Magnusson, L. and Hanson, E. (2003) 'Ethical issues arising from a research, technology and development project to support frail older people and their family carers at home', *Health and Social Care in the Community*, 11(5): 431–9.

Mann, W.C. (2003) 'Assistive technology', in N. Charness and K. Warner Schaie (eds), *Impact of Technology on Successful Aging*. New York: Springer, pp. 177–87.

Mann, W.C., Ottenbacher, K.J., Fraas, L., Tomita, M., and Granger, C.V. (1999) 'Effectiveness of assistive technology and environmental interventions in maintaining independence and reducing home care costs for the frail elderly', *Archive of Family Medicine*, 8: 210–17.

Mann, W.C., Helal, S., Davenport, R.D., et al. (2004) 'Use of cell phones by elders with impairments: overall appraisal, satisfaction and suggestions', *Technology and Disability* 16: 49–57.

Mayhorn, C.B., Lanzolla, V.R., Wogalter, M.S., and Watson, A.M. (2005) 'Personal Digital Assistants (PDAs) as medication reminding tools: exploring age differences in usability', *Gerontechnology*, 4(3): 128–40.

McCreadie, C. (2004) 'Devices and desires: identifying the acceptability of assistive technology to older people', in S. Keates, J. Clarkson, P. Langdon, and P. Robinson (eds), *Designing a More Inclusive World*. London: Springer, pp. 91–100.

McCreadie, C. (2005) Older pedestrians, mobile phones and new way-finding technology: first stage of new research, *Gerontechnology* 4(1): 5–14.

McCreadie, C. and Stuchbury, R. (2006) 'Who can afford computers?', *Working with Older People* 10(4): 15–18.

McCreadie, C. and Tinker, A. (2005) 'The acceptability of Assistive Technology to older people', *Ageing and Society*, 25(1): 91–110.

McCreadie, C., Seale, J., Tinker, A., and Turner-Smith, A. (2002) 'Older people and mobility in the home: in search of useful assistive technologies', *British Journal of Occupational Therapy*, 65(2): 54–60.

McCreadie, C., Raper, J., Gunesh, A., et al., (2006) 'Persuasive technology for leisure and health: development of a personal navigation tool', in W. Ijsselsteijn et al. (eds), *Persuasive Technology*. Berlin: Springer, pp. 187–90.

Melenhorst, A.-S., Rogers, W., and Fisk, A. (2007) 'When will technology in the home improve the quality of life for older adults', in Wald, H.-W, Tesh-Romer, C., and Hoff, A., (ed.), *New Dynamics in Old Age*. Amityville, NY: Baywood, pp. 253–270.

Newell, A. (2003) 'Inclusive design or assistive technology?', in J. Clarkson, R. Coleman, S. Keates, and C. Lebbon (eds), *Inclusive Design*. London: Springer. pp. 172–81.

Norris, A.C. (2002) *Essentials of Telemedicine and Telecare*. Chichester, UK: John Wiley.

Rawls, J. (1999) *A Theory of Justice*, revised edn. Oxford: Oxford University Press (first edn 1972).

Roe, P.R.W. (2007) *Towards an Inclusive Future: Impact and Wider Potential of Information and Communication Technologies*. Brussels: COST.

Roelands, M., Van Oost, P., Buysse, A., and Depoorter, AM. (2002) 'Awareness among community-dwelling elderly of assistive devices for mobility and self-care and attitudes towards their use', *Social Science and Medicine*, 54: 1441–51.

Scopelliti, M., Giuliani, M.V., D'Amico, A.M.D., and Fornara, F. (2004) 'If I had a robot at home … people's representations of domestic robots', in S. Keates, J. Clarkson, P. Langdon, and P. Robinson (eds), *Designing a More Inclusive World*. London: Springer.

Selwyn, N. (2004) 'The information aged: a qualitative study of older adults' use of information and communications technology', *Journal of Aging Studies*, 18: 369–84.

Sixsmith, A. (2006) 'New technologies to support independent living and quality of life for people with dementia', *Alzheimer's Care Quarterly*, July/September: 194–205.

Sixsmith, A. and Sixsmith, J. (2008) 'Ageing in place in the United Kingdom', *Ageing International*, 32(3): 219–35.

Walker, A. and Hagan Hennessey, C. (eds) (2004) *Growing Older: Quality of Life in Old Age*. Maidenhead, UK: Open University Press.

Wall, H.-W, and Mollenkopf, H. (2003) 'Impact of everyday technology older adults' quality of life', in Schaie, K.W., and Chamess, N. (eds), *Impact of Technology on Successful Aging*. New York: Springer, pp. 215–241.

Weale, R.A. and McCreadie, C. (2006) 'Vanishing legibility: daily departures from best practice', *Gerontechnology* 5(4): 239–43.

Wright, F., McCreadie, C., and Tinker, A. (2005) *Improving the Provision of Information about Assistive Technology for Older People*. London: Institute of Gerontology, King's College London.

48

End-of-Life Issues

Liz Lloyd

INTRODUCTION

The aim of this chapter is to analyze key themes concerning the end of life in old age and to consider how these can contribute to gerontological knowledge. Drawing on international data, trends in mortality are identified, including age at death, causes of death, and place of death. These trends are analyzed for their significance for understanding the social conditions of ageing and dying. Secondly, themes from the study of death and dying are considered in relation to ageing, with a particular focus on what is understood by a 'good death' and how age influences this understanding. Thirdly, a discussion of issues in end-of-life care and support for older people considers the inter-relationship between the social status of older people and the circumstances in which they die.

The chapter focuses on the complex and inter-connected factors that shape the end-of-life course in old age. Socioeconomic and geopolitical structures, health and social care systems, family forms and functions, cultural and religious norms and practices, as well as individual lifestyles, resources, and relationships all have a bearing on the circumstances in which older people die. Around the world there are trends in common as well as significant differences.

Until recently gerontologists have not shown a great deal of interest in issues of death and dying. This is partly explained by the dominance in gerontology of the need to combat negative assumptions about ageing and to emphasize that old age is not all about decline and death. At the same time, until relatively recently, research into death and dying has focused on cancer deaths rather than the complex chronic illnesses that often lead

to death in old age, and this has reinforced a separation in the two fields of study. A further point to consider is that information about the lives and deaths of older people is not always easy to obtain, particularly in less socioeconomically developed countries, and does not lend itself to international comparisons because of different conventions concerning death registration and certification.

Reducing premature deaths, prolonging healthy active life expectancy, and delaying the onset of disease are key policy goals at national and international levels. A range of practices, from the relatively outlandish, such as cryogenics, through more mainstream science, such as the human genome project, to the more mundane 'healthy lifestyle' practices, such as exercise, smoking cessation, and healthy diets, can all be understood in relation to prevalent attitudes towards death (Boia, 2004; Olshansky and Carnes, 2001). The trend towards increased old-age mortality throughout the previous century might therefore be regarded as a triumph that reflects better standards of living and medical advances. However, the reaction has not been unequivocally positive and demographic trends have generated concerns over pressures on healthcare systems.

These concerns raise important and wide-ranging questions. What is meant by a good death in old age and how can this be achieved? What kind of care is most appropriate when an older person is facing death at a near but uncertain time? Should age and proximity to death have a bearing on the distribution of resources for health care? Should efforts to extend the length of life now give way to improving the quality of life in its final stages? In this chapter the aim is to explore such questions, drawing on available evidence from research and practice in a number of disciplines. The discussion is inevitably selective and the intention is to focus particularly on the issues that are most pertinent to the relationship between ageing and dying.

PATTERNS OF MORTALITY IN AN AGEING WORLD

Patterns of mortality around the world present a complex picture concerning the age at which people die, the causes of death, and the place of death. Examination of these factors reveals significant social inequalities, both between and within countries, and highlights the importance of age to understanding mortality trends.

Age at death

The World Health Organization estimates that by 2025 63 per cent of all deaths in the world will be among the people aged over 65s. There is a strong association between the overall socioeconomic status of a country and the likelihood of deaths occurring in old age rather than prematurely. In high-income countries, the 20th century saw greater increases in life expectancy than in the whole of previous history.[1] According to the Global Forum for Health[2] almost 85 per cent of deaths in high-income countries occur after the age of 60, whereas in low to middle-income countries only 45 per cent of deaths occur in this age group. At the same time, there are also variations between countries that have a similar socioeconomic status, which demonstrates that policy decisions make a difference to people's chances of living to old age. Mathers et al. (2001) identify a strong association between healthy life expectancy and government healthcare expenditure as a percentage of gross domestic product (GDP).

In their examination of global mortality trends, McMichael et al. (2004) identify three groupings of countries. First is a group of countries with rapid gains in life expectancy at birth, such as in Chile, Mexico, and Tunisia, where trends are converging on developed countries. This grouping also includes some African countries, where there are substantial gains in life expectancy, although absolute levels remain low. Secondly, countries where gains in life expectancy are slower or plateauing, including high-income countries such as France and Denmark. Thirdly, is a grouping, including former Eastern bloc countries such as

Russia, as well as some sub-Saharan African countries such as Zimbabwe, where life expectancy is stagnating or falling, affecting primarily younger to middle-aged people. A mixture of factors explain the fall, including social upheaval, violence, and heavy alcohol and tobacco consumption as well as the HIV pandemic. These are very broad groupings and inequalities within countries need to be taken into account. McMichael et al. (2004) argue that in many of the richest nations socioeconomic inequalities in mortality have increased over the past 20 years.

It is important to point out that trends in each of these groupings have implications for the circumstances in which older people die. For example, increases in middle-aged mortality affect employment patterns and the availability of family carers for older people when they are dying. The effect of the HIV pandemic on older people's lives and family roles has been profound, affecting their own support and security at the end of life (Knodel and Saengtienchai, 2004; McIntyre, 2004; see also Chapter 31).

Causes of death

Because of the ageing of populations it is expected that there will be a substantial worldwide shift in the distribution of deaths from communicable to non-communicable diseases. By 2030 it has been projected that almost 70 per cent of all deaths world-wide will be from non-communicable diseases, including ischaemic heart disease, cerebrovascular disease (stroke) and chronic obstructive pulmonary disease (Mathers and Loncar (2006)). Obtaining information about causes of death is not straightforward because of inaccuracies and variations in recording individual deaths. For example, in some countries Alzheimer's disease has recently been recognized as the primary cause of death, whereas in others it is still seen as an underlying or contributory cause. These differences may appear insignificant but they matter because they have an impact on whether a person is seen as living with or dying from a disease and on the kind of care that is seen as appropriate.

The practice of establishing a cause for every death raises the question: *Is old age a cause of death?* This question is more complex than might at first appear. How deaths are recorded reflects a range of factors, including the level of resources available in individual countries as well as political priorities, legal conventions, and cultural norms. One point of view is that in modern societies, death, like old age, has become overmedicalized and that the practice of establishing and elaborating on causes and contributing causes of death has played a major part in this process. Since all human beings must die, a death in old age can be regarded as a natural event – the normal course of events because the individual has lived for a full lifespan. On the other hand, information about causes of death is crucial to the allocation of resources for health care. The attribution of old age as a cause of death can mask underlying health problems that might otherwise be given a higher priority. To treat causes of death in old age differently from premature deaths risks disadvantaging older people as patients and expose them to neglect. Determining the cause of death can also play a part in protecting vulnerable older people from abuse and homicide. The practice of establishing the cause or causes of an individual's death can therefore provide a form of protection of older people's rights (Hawley, 2003). In addition, the practice of recording underlying and contributory causes provides useful data about complex health conditions that require greater integration of care.

One cause of death amongst older people that receives surprisingly little attention is suicide. Rates of death from suicide are higher in people aged over 65s than in any other group, particularly in richer countries. As with other age groups, the reasons are multidimensional, related to isolation, depression, widowhood or divorce, and ill-health, but older people are more likely to have experienced these (Brogden, 2001). The actual rate of suicide in later life is likely to be higher than that reported because the high levels of medicinal drugs consumed by older people may mean that the intention to kill oneself is interpreted as a mistake in dosage.

Older people are also at greater risk of death from a range of external threats, including violence, wars, and environmental threats. The high rate of old-age mortality arising from the exceptional heat wave in France in August 2003 illustrates this point (Belmin et al., 2007; Ogg, 2005). The deaths of around 15,000 people, many older people, were attributed to this heat wave. This episode highlights the importance of public policy interventions in preventing crises from environmental hazards and protecting vulnerable older people. The ineffectiveness and poor coordination of public services in this case were widely regarded as contributory factors to the high numbers of deaths.

A related point concerns the quality of housing occupied by older people. It was noteworthy that many of the deaths were in care homes and that these were often poorly designed and ill-equipped to deal with unusually high temperatures. The higher risk of death from hypothermia in the United Kingdom than in Scandinavia also raises

questions about the role of housing and fuel policies in preventing unnecessary deaths, and demonstrates the complex interplay of physiological factors, which can increase older people's risk to environmental threats, and political factors, which have a bearing on older people's capacity to cope (see also Laake and Sverre, 1996).

Place of death

For most of the 20th century Western societies[3] saw a trend away from deaths at home towards deaths in hospital. This trend has been subject to critical comment, often focused on the isolation of people dying in institutions. As Elias expresses it:

> Never before in the history of humanity have the dying been removed so hygienically behind the scenes of social life … (1985: 23).

As life expectancy increases, death is increasingly disassociated from the daily lives of younger people. This raises the question: Is the place of death an inevitable outcome of socioeconomic development? The picture is in fact very mixed. Overall, there is a relationship between level of development and place of death but there are also important variations, and age is a crucially important influencing factor. At the individual level, the place of death is influenced by age, cause of death, gender, and ethnic origin as well as whether the person who is dying lived in a rural or urban environment. At the societal level, influencing factors include the organization of health services, policy priorities, and levels of knowledge about the diseases of old age as well as cultural expectations about 'the proper place' to die. It should be pointed out that for the vast majority of the world's older population, because of the absence of accessible health services, there is no choice other than to die at home, reliant on the care and support of family and community.

Towards the end of the 20th century in Western countries there was a further age-related trend towards deaths in care homes. In the United States, for example, the rate of in-hospital deaths declined from a high of 54 per cent in 1983 to 41 per cent in 1998 when 24 per cent of deaths of people aged 75–84 and 45 per cent of people aged 85+ were in nursing homes (Flory et al., 2004). In the United Kingdom, hospitals continue to be the most common place of death, but older people are increasingly likely to die in a nursing home (Tomasini, 2005). This trend is linked to the increased number of private sector care homes that followed the community care reforms of the 1990s.

In contrast, analysis of data from the Chinese Longitudinal Healthy Longevity Survey by Gu et al. (2007) showed that 92 per cent of people aged between 80 and 105 died at home, 7 per cent in hospital, and 1 per cent in institutions. Being resident in an urban area, having a higher socioeconomic status, and having more accessible formal care services all increased the likelihood that an older person would not die at home. The current trend in place of death in the Republic of Korea is *towards* deaths in hospital, and older people are more likely than younger people to die at home. Yun et al. (2006) argue that the major determining factor in the Republic of Korea is the availability of hospital services. The higher the availability of hospital beds, the more likely it is that people will die in hospital.

Older women have been disproportionately affected by the trends in high-income countries towards dying in care homes. This reflects the higher numbers of women who are widowed and therefore less likely to have someone to care for them at home at the end of life (Davies and Seymour, 2002). In Belgium, 34.3 per cent of deaths of people aged over 80 were in care homes and 28.1 per cent of these deaths were of women compared with 11.7 per cent of men (Cohen et al., 2006). In Japan, also, the trend towards deaths in care homes has affected women more than men (Shinoda-Tagawa and Ikegami, 2005). Whether or not a person who lives in a care home will also die in a care home will be influenced by the nursing home's own resources and willingness to provide end-of-life care, without which it would be more likely that an older person would die in hospital (Klinkenberg et al., 2005).

Variations in place of death are also evident between ethnic groups. Flory et al. (2004), for example, point out that in 1980 the overall rate of inpatient deaths was the same between white and African Americans (54 per cent) but by 1998 the rate for white Americans had dropped to 40 per cent compared with 48 per cent for African Americans. Gelfand et al. (2004) questioned why Mexican Americans are reluctant to use hospices and found a diverse set of explanations, including cultural and religious preferences, unequal geographical distribution of provision, and the inaccessibility, cultural inappropriateness, or insensitivity of services.

Recently, the policy's aim of a number of countries has been to promote deaths at home. This can be understood partly as a reaction to the institutionalization and medicalization of care, since deaths at home are often taken as an indication of a better quality of end-of-life care. Studies in the United States and Europe demonstrate a marked difference between the numbers of people who express a wish to die at home and the numbers that actually do, the main determining factor being the presence of a family carer, which, because of their longer life expectancy further affects women disproportionately. Taylor and Carter (2004) also point to possible gender bias on the part of professional service providers in the United Kingdom, which reduces women's chances of dying at home.

Whether or not a death outside hospital is less institutionalized than a death inside hospital is debatable. Flory et al. (2004) make the important point that the trend away from hospital might indicate not that there is a trend towards a more 'natural' death but that the type of care available in nursing homes and domestic settings might have come to resemble hospital care more closely, so that it becomes unnecessary to admit people to hospital at the end stage of life. A further question arises about the motivation of policymakers. Are deaths at home promoted as a way of reducing the cost of long-term care at the end of life? In Sweden there has been a drive to relocate deaths out of hospital and into local communities through increased investment in home-based services, and this has radically altered people's chances of dying at home. However, Jeppsson Grassman and Whitaker argue that this policy is partly ideological – in keeping with prevalent discourses of de-institutionalization, 'local belonging, networks and civic participation for community and for care' – and partly political, being part of the deregulation of Swedish welfare and changed expectations about the roles and responsibilities of families, and voluntary organizations, in providing unpaid care for very elderly people at the end of life (2007: 262).

Gu et al. (2007) suggest that there are three stages in the evolution of place of death. In the first stage, most people die at home because of the lack of alternatives and underdeveloped medical technologies. In the second stage, more people die in hospitals because improved medical techniques and more accessible healthcare resources make survival more likely. In the third stage, quality of care at the end of life is emphasized more strongly than added years of life and the type of care offered by the hospice movement is preferred over that of the hospital.

This model provides a useful overview of the relationship between place of death in old age and levels of socioeconomic development but the variations within countries described above show that a wider range of factors need to be taken into account. Whereas there is evidence to support the view that there is preference for hospice care in countries at the third stage, it is also evident that older people are disadvantaged in their access to hospice care. A death at home is widely regarded as desirable but might reflect characteristics of the first stage, if older people are expected to rely more on the unpaid support of their families, or of the second stage, if this is combined with hospital care at times of acute illness and at the time of death itself.

A 'GOOD' DEATH: WHAT ARE THE IMPLICATIONS FOR DEATH IN OLD AGE?

The global policy aim of eliminating premature deaths is a powerful indication that old age is widely regarded as the 'right time' to die. A premature death, when an individual dies biologically before achieving his or her full social potential, is perceived as more tragic than a death in old age, when an individual has 'had a good innings'. There is no sense that the individual has been 'robbed' of life, as is frequently said of a premature death. A death in old age is also more likely to have been prepared for, with one's affairs having been put in order. For Tornstam (1996), old age is when an individual can develop 'gerotranscendence', when concern with the self and the ageing body is transcended and death is accepted as part of a process of maturation.

Yet, deaths in old age are frequently not good. In old age, if the cause of death results in a long process of dying and dependency for care on others, an older person might be regarded as socially dead before their biological death. This is particularly so where there is cognitive decline, when it is not unusual for those close to the older person to feel they are already bereaved, as though the person who is dying in the biological sense is someone other than the one they knew.

In his research in Ghana, van der Geest (2004) explored the idea of a 'peaceful' death. For his research participants a peaceful death entailed first being at peace with others, having reconciled differences and resolved conflicts. Secondly, the dying person should be at peace with his or her own death. Death at the end of a life well-spent can be accepted – even welcomed, as is sleep at the end of a hard day's work. Thirdly, a peaceful death would be from 'natural causes' rather than from disease, with pain and distressing symptoms, or from accidents or violence, which were regarded as punishment. Fourthly, a peaceful death would be at home, and if deaths occurred away it was important to bring the body back home. The fifth and final aspect of a peaceful death was that others around the dying person would be at peace with

the death. Van der Geest notes that the characteristics of a good death in Ghana – social, psychological, and spiritual, with an emphasis on dying at the right time after a long and productive life and in the right space, at home, surrounded by family – bear a striking resemblance to those of other cultures.

Within relatively developed Western societies, perceptions of what constitutes a 'good death' may be summarized as follows:

- The unique physical, psychological, social, and spiritual needs of the individual who is dying are given attention in a holistic way.
- Pain and other distressing symptoms are eliminated or controlled.
- The dying person is accompanied and given comfort.
- The dying person is aware of their impending death and able to discuss this with their family and those providing treatment and care.
- The dying person is able to exercise choice and control as far as possible over the place of death and forms of treatment or decision not to be given treatment.
- The family and others close to the dying person are given support and comfort both prior to the death and subsequently in their bereavement.

Good for whom?

For a death to be considered good the preferences of a range of people need to be satisfied, including those of the individual, their family, and, more broadly, the society they live in. These do not necessarily coincide – indeed they might be in conflict. Death by natural causes is generally more likely to be considered as good rather than death by accident, homicide, or suicide. On the other hand, physician-assisted death might be regarded by an individual older person and their family as good – at least better than a long and painful death by natural causes – but the societal view might be that this is a form of murder.

In his seminal study of death and dying in old age in the Scottish city of Aberdeen, Rory Williams (1990) identified two types of good death: the quick, painless death and a death within the bosom of an affectionate family. The first kind might be desirable for the individual who is dying but not for the bereaved relatives who would be unprepared. There was broad agreement that a death would be bad if the elderly person was socially dead before being physically dead, particularly where there was cognitive decline.

A further point is that even where there is broad agreement about what would make a death good it does not necessarily follow that there is the capacity to ensure this happens. Jeppsson Grassman and Whitaker's Swedish study, discussed above, identified how, contrary to expectations, the Church of Sweden could not provide spiritual support to parishioners who were dying, except where there was an already existing relationship, because often churches simply did not know who was dying in their parish. Unless older people had been involved with the church at an earlier stage of the life course, they were not able to have their spiritual needs met at the end of life.

Awareness, choice, and control

Within Western contexts, awareness, choice, and control are key elements of a good death but age has an impact on their achievement. The trend in the West has been towards greater openness between doctors and patients and this has increased awareness amongst older people and their families about an impending death. But, in old age, defining an illness as 'terminal' is not easy and health professionals are less likely to raise the issue of death with older people. A further point is that forms of communication between professionals and patients that have developed in Western contexts are not universally applicable. Saldov et al. (1998) observed that Japanese-American elders and their families in Hawaii had a highly nuanced view of communication about the dying process and preferred non-verbal over verbal forms because it was thought that they helped to maintain harmonious family relationships.

Giving individuals greater choice and control over treatment decisions at the end of life has become a policy goal as well as a campaigning issue for older people's organizations in Western countries (Help the Aged, 2002). The development of advance directives, or 'living wills', which set out a person's wishes about how to be treated, indicates that choice and control are important goals even where an older person loses mental capacity (see Chapter 49). However, Waddell and McNamara (1997) make the important point that these goals reflect the individualistic nature of Western cultures and that within less individualistic cultures elsewhere the needs of the individual older person are not so easily conceptualized as separate from those of the collective group.

Reflecting on Gu et al.'s (2007) typology of place of care, it is clear that choice and control are not possible where there are no alternatives to family care, nor where deaths are institutionalized in hospitals. Deaths in hospices might be regarded as most likely to promote individual choice and control. However, McNamara (2001) argues that the involvement of families in caring for people in hospices places limits on the exercise of individual choice and control. It can be difficult for an individual to opt for a form of care that is unacceptable to others. Thus, despite its widespread appeal as an abstract goal, the exercise of individual choice and control at the end of life is not straightforward in practice. Older people with more resources and the capacity to control these will be in a much stronger position to exercise choice and control than those without. At the same time, there is evidence to suggest that older people do exercise a degree of choice and control over the timing of their deaths. Lawton (2000), for example, observed how some terminally ill people employed strategies such as refusing to eat or drink so as to hasten their death.

Outstaying your time and being a burden

It is often assumed that the shift towards deaths in old age from chronic and degenerative diseases will result in demand for health care over a longer period of time and drive up the cost of health care to the detriment of younger people. However, there is a lack of sound comparative data to support this view. Seale (2005) points out how deaths at an earlier stage of the life course, such as from HIV/AIDS or tuberculosis, may also be preceded by long-term dependency and symptoms. Dixon et al. (2004) conducted a retrospective cohort study of hospital admissions in England and concluded that there was no discernable increase with increasing age in the time spent in hospital in the period before death. Thus, it is not age per se that generates costs but proximity to death, and the costs of care are greatest amongst older people because older people make up the largest proportion of the dying. The view that the ageing of populations will inevitably drive up the costs of care is, therefore, questionable in fact. In addition, we might question why it is that in countries with ample resources there should be concerns about the cost of care at the end of life, particularly in view of the policy aim of extending life expectancy.

Are these views about the burdensomeness of older people a consequence of modernization? Brogden (2001) argues that there never was a 'golden age' in which older people were revered but, on the contrary, that ageism has existed in all societies past and present. Logue (1990) argues that, in Asian cultures, despite strong cultural norms concerning 'filial piety', care might be given grudgingly out of a sense of obligation rather than willingly out of a sense of love. Van der Geest also identified ambiguous attitudes towards older people in Ghana, where, living to old age was sometimes interpreted as 'refusing to die' (2004: 907). Similar attitudes are evident elsewhere, even in societies that are considered to revere older people (Kelley, 2005; Kreager and Schröder-Butterfill, 2007). A crucial point to stress, however, is that the strengthening relationship between old age and death creates the conditions in which discourses of burdensomeness flourish with significant impact on older people's sense of self-worth and dignity.

Dignity at the end of life

The concept of dignity has particular relevance at the end of life in old age. Since dignity is a social and cultural construct, it follows that there are clear cross-cultural differences in how dying with dignity is understood. Hence, for some, bearing pain stoically might be regarded as dignified, whereas for others suffering pain is an indignity (Leming and Dickinson, 2002). In Western contexts, dignity is inextricably linked with autonomy. As a policy statement by UK Help the Aged expresses it: *'A good death is one in which people are enabled to die with dignity and a sense of completion, retaining their autonomy'* (Help the Aged, 2002). However, the term dignity is used in many and contradictory ways. For example, the UK organization 'Dignity in Dying' (formerly the Voluntary Euthanasia Society) promotes the right to physician-assisted deaths and emphasizes individual choice and control. In direct opposition to this is the 'Care not Killing Alliance', which argues that dignity should be promoted through palliative care and control of the type of pain and suffering that are frequently invoked as the rationale for assisted deaths.

From their UK research, Woolhead et al. (2004) concluded that the key dimensions of dignity for older people are identity, respect, recognition, autonomy, and independence, all of which are highly significant to an analysis of death in old age. The process of dying poses a challenge to older people's dignity because it is at this stage of the life course that dependence on others for support becomes inevitable. Serious illness and loss of mental capacity pose a challenge to older people's identity. Research in Australia by Minichiello et al. (2000) showed how older people went to great lengths to avoid being seen to have 'given up' because this would damage their carers' attitudes towards them. In these circumstances, the loss of independence led to a lack of respect and recognition. The issue that arises from this is whether the loss of identity, autonomy, and independence *inevitably* entails a loss of dignity. Is it possible for care to maintain or enhance older people's dignity at the end of life, when they have lost autonomy and become dependent on others?

CARE AND SUPPORT AT THE END OF LIFE

In this section the focus is on the contexts of care. The ways in which the dying are cared for are considered, with attention to the significance of age as an influencing factor. The potential for improving older people's chances of a good death and the factors that are likely to impede this are discussed.

The dying trajectory: predicting the course of death

The concept of the dying trajectory describes both the length of time it takes for a person to die and also the 'shape' of that process. The trajectories of deaths from non-communicable diseases are likely to be longer and more complex than those from acute infections. Murray et al. (2005) point out that within the question *'How long have I got?'* often asked by individuals with a life-threatening disease is another often unspoken question *'What will happen?'* Discerning accurately the point at which a person is 'dying from' rather than 'living with' a disease poses a problem in terms of predicting the course of the illness and death and this has an impact on how people are informed about what will happen and how they are cared for.

Murray et al. (2005) identify three common trajectories. The first, frequently found in deaths from cancer, is where there is a relatively short period of decline that is reasonably predictable. The second, typical in heart failure or chronic obstructive pulmonary disorders, is where a person will have long-term health problems accompanied by periodic episodes of serious illness which they survive but to which they eventually succumb. The third trajectory is a prolonged and steady dwindling of health, typical in Alzheimer's disease, which might end fairly suddenly after an acute episode of infection or a fractured neck of femur. Indeed, pneumonia is referred to as the 'old man's friend' because it can curtail suffering from long-term illness. Predicting the length and shape of a dying trajectory highlights the interrelationship of physiological and psychosocial aspects of dying in old age. Uotinen et al. (2005), for example, identified how older people's *subjective perceptions* of age were a strong predictor of mortality, whilst Bond et al (2006) found that *self-rated health* (in combination with other co-variates) has the capacity to predict death.

Prolonging or hastening death

The extension of late-life expectancy has been highly significant since the late 20th century. The role played by medical interventions in extending and shaping older people's dying trajectories is important but there are variations in medical practices, which reflect differences in attitudes as well as in legal codes. For example, when the insertion of a feeding tube where an individual is unable to eat or drink normally is more commonplace in Japan than in the USA and Europe (Kosaka et al., 2003). Whether such interventions are always beneficial is debatable. Whilst they can help to maintain older people's nutrition during an acute illness episode they can also lead to a longer, more distressing dying process for older people and their families. Amella et al. (2005) make the important point that decisions about whether to intervene or not are often made at stressful times without clear appreciation and discussion of the issues entailed. They also argue that decisions can be clouded by cultural and religious factors or mistrust of professionals. At the same time, health professionals might pursue treatment for fear of litigation by bereaved relatives. Without a clear terminal diagnosis medical interventions are more likely than would be the case where there is a shared understanding of a patient's terminal condition and the need for palliative care.

Avoiding a prolonged and painful death provides a rationale for euthanasia or physician-assisted death, which is practised in few parts of the world but which has generated a great deal of interest. In the Netherlands, for example, it has been possible since 1973 for a physician to assist a patient to commit suicide, as long as strict guidelines are followed. The arguments concerning physician-assisted death are too numerous and complex to examine here, but there are a number of age-related issues. For example, the high numbers of suicides amongst older age groups points to the need for a compassionate approach which would avoid painful self-violence. In the Netherlands the rate of suicide is lower than in comparable countries (Brogden, 2001), which suggests that physician-assisted suicide is a much-needed service. On the other hand, many older people's organizations oppose physician-assisted deaths on the grounds that older people's social position and the perceptions that they are a burden would place them under increased pressure to end their lives prematurely.

Palliative care

The philosophy of palliative care, particularly within the hospice movement, has been highly influential in shaping ideas about the possibilities for a good death. The World Health Organization defines palliative care as:

> An approach that improves the quality of life of patients and their families facing the problems associated with life-threatening illness, through the prevention and relief of suffering by means of early identification and impeccable assessment and treatment of pain and other problems, physical, psychosocial and spiritual' (WHO, 2002: 84).

Interest in palliative care is worldwide. Indeed, the European Region of the World Health Organization calls for palliative care to be recognized as a human right (Davies and Higginson, 2004). Wright et al. (2006) conducted a worldwide study that demonstrated a strong link between levels of socioeconomic development and palliative care provision. They also point out that countries at similar levels of socioeconomic development have very different approaches to end-of-life care. Costa Rica, for example, is alone amongst Central American countries in having relatively well-developed palliative care services, demonstrating that policies make a difference. However, palliative care is often a lower priority than other spheres of health care: fewer than 15 per cent of countries in Wright et al.'s (2006) study had palliative care integrated into their health services.

Extending palliative care and reducing inequalities in access are important goals but there are widespread age-related inequalities. In spite of the high proportion of deaths in old age in high-income countries, the numbers of older people receiving palliative or hospice care is well below that of younger people (Grande et al., 2006). A related question concerns the applicability of contemporary palliative care services to the diseases of old age, which, as argued above, do not always follow the trajectory associated with terminal cancer. Davies and Higginson (2004) argue that, in the context of ageing populations, models of palliative care need be flexible enough to apply over a longer period of illness and not just at a defined point just before death. Thus, for older people to benefit, palliative care should not only be extended but also reconceptualized to encompass their longer, more complex, and varied dying trajectories.

Spiritual care at the end of life

Religious organizations have a long history of care of the dying. The hospice movement began within a Christian context and its continuing role demonstrates that even within secular societies there remains a desire for spiritual care. Organized religion can offer a bulwark against insecurities and suffering at the end of life. It can also offer protection by instilling in carers a sense of moral obligation to provide care and to treat the dying person with kindness. However, spirituality is not synonymous with religion. For MacKinlay (2005), spirituality entails the human need for meaning in life and relationships with others. She maintains that there is a need to reclaim the spiritual dimension of care at the end of life because the medicalization of the dying process associated with modern life has led to a neglect of spiritual needs.

This view points to the relevance of palliative and hospice care to death in old age but Lawton (2000) raises an important question concerning hospices. She argues that hospices do not have a sufficiently rounded understanding of *suffering* at the end of life, and that this calls into question their capacity to provide spiritual comfort. In her study she identified a tendency in hospices to equate suffering with physical pain and to overlook the broader existential and relational aspects. This point reinforces the need for ongoing development of palliative and hospice care, in order to ensure that spiritual well-being is given due attention as an aspect of a good death.

Care at the end of life: who provides it?

Care at the end of life is provided by family members and a range of volunteers as well as by paid healthcare professionals and staff. As discussed, without a co-resident family carer it is very difficult to die at home and, given demographic trends, it is likely that nursing homes will continue to play an increasingly important role in caring for the dying.

The trend towards deaths in nursing homes highlights the nature and extent of global socio-economic inequalities and also shows that not only are there differences between countries but also that these differences are inextricably linked and mutually reinforcing. Countries with the least-developed healthcare systems face the loss of key health workers because of the demand for more care staff in long-term care services in countries where numbers of people reaching very advanced ages are greatest. Moreover, in these services migrant workers frequently experience poor pay and low status, raising moral and political questions about the recruitment practices of care home providers (Angel, 2007; Global Health Watch, 2005).

Low-income countries also face greater pressures on family carers because of the undeveloped state of health services and because of particular pressures created by the HIV pandemic, although there are differences between countries in the ways that these pressures are managed. A study of long-term care in developing countries by Brodsky et al. (2003) identified that whereas the family remains the predominant source of care in the home, volunteer support from communities was needed in an increasing number of countries. In others, traditional healers were being trained to take on new roles in long-term care for older people. Emerging themes from this study include the importance of good relationships between professional services, on the one hand, and family and community support, on the other, and the influence of resources on the types and locations of care. The importance of resources for care at the end of life is evident in all contexts: the lack of adequate hospital care creates pressure on families in Indonesia but so too does the lack of adequate resources for home care in the United Kingdom.

We might question why it is that end-of-life care is regarded as a separate and distinctive sphere of practice rather than being understood as part of the overall system of support for older people who become sick and disabled. Long-term care for older people is often evaluated in terms of its capacity to promote or restore independence and its potential role at the end of life is rarely considered. Long-term care could play a part in the development of more flexible forms of palliative care discussed above. A more fluid relationship between long term care and palliative care has significant potential to promote well-being through longer dying trajectories, not just in the period immediately before death.

CONCLUSION

In this chapter a number of common trends and concerns have been considered, including the goal of extending life expectancy and the growing incidence of chronic disease as a cause of death. These trends place demands on healthcare systems to adapt and on families to maintain or extend the care they give their older members at the end of life.

The prevalent view that traditional societies treat their older people with more respect than Western countries is open to challenge, as the discussion of burdensomeness demonstrated. Logue (1990) argues that in most societies, whatever their state of development, older people are likely to become isolated when they become dependent and the burden of care outweighs the value of their assets.

Evidence suggests that as societies modernize, attitudes towards dependency do not change. Indeed, given the high value placed on individual independence in Western cultures they are likely to become more entrenched and when resources are limited it becomes all too easy for dependent people to be perceived as a burden. Contemporary demographic trends mean that burdensomeness is strongly associated with old age and felt most keenly at the end of life. Under contemporary conditions, limits on resources for health and social care place older people in a highly vulnerable position because of competing priorities. The strength of the demographic relationships between old age and death has implications for gerontology in terms of the way that dependency and the need for care in old age are understood (Lloyd, 2004).

In the light of the issues discussed in this chapter, we might question whether there is cause for optimism concerning the end of life in old age. What can be said is that there is broad agreement about the conditions needed for a good death, but creating these will require a changed view of the role of care. The relationship between health and care services, on the one hand, and family care, on the other, appears to be a crucial factor in determining whether an older person will have a 'good death'. Family care can play an important role in overcoming the negative effects of institutionalized deaths but family care requires support and resources in order to overcome the risk that older people will be seen as too burdensome. Elias (1985) referred to the isolation that accompanies frailty in older people as the early isolation of the dying. The need for care at the end of life throws into sharp relief our social nature as human beings and reminds us of the importance of relationships at all stages of the life course. Creating the conditions for a good death in old age is in everyone's interests.

NOTES

1 The categorization of countries into high-, middle-, and low-income groups is based on World Bank (2000) data on gross national income (GNI) per capita in US dollars. The groups are: low income, $905 or less; lower middle income, $906–$3595; upper-middle income, $3596–$11,115; and high income, $11,116 or more.

2 www.globalforumhealth.org

3 The term 'Western societies' is used to denote not only the advantageous economic position but also the political and cultural contexts characteristic of countries in North America, Europe, as well as Australia and New Zealand.

REFERENCES

Amella, E.A., Lawrence, J.F., and Gresle, S.O. (2005) 'Tube feeding: prolonging life or death in vulnerable populations?' *Mortality*, 10(1): 69–81.

Angel, J. (2007) 'Immigration effects on health care for older people' in K .W. Schaie and P. Uhlenberg, (eds), *Social Structures: Impact of Population Changes on the Well-being of Older Persons.* New York: Springer, pp. 123–57.

Belmin, J., Auffray, J-C., Berbezier, C., et al. (2007) 'Level of dependency: a simple marker associated with mortality during the 2003 heatwave among French dependent elderly people living in the community or in institutions', *Age and Ageing*, 36: 298–303.

Boia, L. (2004) *Forever Young: A Cultural History of Longevity.* London: Reaktion Books.

Bond, J., Dickinson, H.O., Matthews, F., Jagger, C., and Brayne, C. (2006) 'Self-rated health status as a predictor of death, functional and cognitive impairment: a longitudinal cohort study', *European Journal of Ageing*, 3: 193–206.

Brodsky, J., Habib, J., and Hirschfield, M. (eds) (2003) *Long-term Care in Developing Countries: Ten Case Studies.* Geneva: World Health Organisation.

Brogden, M. (2001) *Geronticide: Killing the Elderly.* London: Jessica Kingsley Press.

Cohen, J., Bilsen, J., Hooft, P., et al. (2006) 'Dying at home or in an institution: using death certificates to explore the factors associated with place of death', *Health Policy*, 78: 319–29.

Davies, E. and Higginson, I.J. (eds) (2004) *Palliative Care: The Solid Facts.* Copenhagen: World Health Organization.

Davies, S. and Seymour, J. (2002) 'Historical and policy contexts', in J. Hockley and D. Clark (eds), *Palliative Care for Older People in Care Homes.* Buckingham: Open University, pp. 4–33.

Dixon, T., Shaw, M., Frankel, S., and Ebrahim, S. (2004) 'Hospital admissions, age and death: a retrospective cohort study', *British Medical Journal*, 328:1288 (29 May).

Elias, N. (1985) *The Loneliness of the Dying.* London: Continuum International.

Flory, J., Young-Xu, Y., Guroi, I., et al. (2004) 'Place of death: US trends since 1980', *Health Affairs*, 23(3): 194–200.

Gelfand, D.E., Balcazar, H., Parzuchowski, J., and Lenox, S. (2004) 'Issues in hospice utilization by Mexicans', *Journal of Applied Gerontology*, 23(1): 3–19.

Global Health Watch (2005) *Global Health Watch 2005–2006: An Alternative World Health Report.* New York: Zed Books.

Grande, G., Farquhar, M.C., Barclay, S.I.G., and Todd, C.J. (2006) 'The influence of patient and carer age in access to palliative care services', *Age and Ageing*, 35(3): 267–73.

Gu, D., Liu, G., Vlosky, D.A., and Yi, Z. (2007) 'Factors associated with place of death among the Chinese oldest old', *Journal of Applied Gerontology*, 26(1): 34–57.

Hawley, C. (2003) 'Is it ever enough to die of old age?', *Age and Ageing*, 32(5): 484–86.

Help the Aged (2002) *Making Decisions around the End of Life.* Help the Aged Policy Statement. London: Help the Aged.

Jeppsson Grassman, E. and Whitaker, A. (2007) 'End of life and dimensions of civil society: the Church of Sweden in a new geography of death', *Mortality*, 12(3): 261–80.

Kelley, L.S. (2005) 'Growing old in St Lucia: expectations and experiences in a Caribbean village', *Journal of Cross-Cultural Gerontology*, 20: 67–78.

Klinkenberg, M., Visser, G., Broese van Groenou, M.I., et al. (2005) 'The last 3 months of life: care, transitions and the place of death of older people', *Health and Social Care in the Community*, 13(5): 420–30.

Knodel, J. and Saengtienchai, C. (2004) 'AIDS and older persons: the view from Thailand', in P. Lloyd-Sherlock (ed.), *Living Longer: Ageing, Development and Social Protection.* London: Zed Books.

Kosaka, Y., Satoh-Nakagawa, T., Ohrui, T., et al. (2003) 'Tube feeding in terminal elderly care', *Geriatrics and Gerontology International*, 3: 172–74.

Kreager, P. and Schröder-Butterfill, E. (2007) 'Gaps in the family networks of older people in three Indonesian communities', *Journal of Cross-Cultural Gerontology*, 22: 1–25.

Laake, K. and Sverre, J.M. (1996) 'Winter excess mortality: a comparison between Norway and England plus Wales', *Age and Ageing*, 25: 343–48.

Lawton, J. (2000) *The Dying Process: Patients' Experiences of Palliative Care.* London: Routledge.

Leming, M.R. and Dickinson, G.E. (2002) *Understanding Dying, Death and Bereavement*, 5th Edn. Orlando: Harcourt.

Lloyd, L. (2004) 'Mortality and morality: ageing and the ethics of care', *Ageing and Society*, 24(2): 235–56.

Logue, B.J. (1990) 'Modernization and the status of the frail elderly: perspectives on continuity and change', *Journal of Cross-Cultural Gerontology*, 5: 345–74.

MacKinley, E. (2005) 'Death and spirituality', in M. Johnson (ed.), *The Cambridge Handbook of Age and Ageing.* Cambridge: Cambridge University Press, pp. 394–402.

Mathers, C.D. and Loncar, D. (2006) 'Projections of global mortality and burden of disease from 2002–2030', PLoS Med 3(11):e442,doi:10.1371/journal/pmed.0030442.

Mathers, C.D., Sadana, R., Salomon, J.A., Murray, C.J.L., and Lopez, A.D. (2001) 'Health life expectancy in 191 countries, 1999', *The Lancet*, 357: 1685–91.

McIntyre, D. (2004) 'Health policy and older people in Africa', in P. Lloyd-Sherlock (ed.), *Living Longer, Aging and Social Protection.* London: Zed Books, pp. 160–83.

McMichael, A.J., McKee, M., Shkollnikov, V., and Valkonen, T. (2004) 'Mortality trends and setbacks: global convergence or divergence?', *The Lancet*, 363: 1155–59.

McNamara, B. (2001) *Fragile Lives: Death, Dying and Care.* Buckingham: Open University Press.

Minichiello, V., Browne, J., and Kendig, H. (2000) 'Perceptions and consequences of ageism: views of older people', *Ageing and Society*, 20(3): 253–78.

Murray, S., Kendall, M., Boyd, K., and Sheikh, A. (2005) 'Illness trajectories and palliative care', *British Medical Journal*, 330: 1007–11.

Ogg, J. (2005) *Heatwave: Implications of the 2003 French Heat Wave for the Social Care of Older People.* Young Foundation Working Paper No. 2. London: The Young Foundation.

Olshansky, S.J. and Carnes, B. (2001) *The Quest for Immortality: Science at the Frontiers of Aging.* New York: W.W. Norton and Company.

Saldov, M., Kakai, H., McLaughlin, L., and Thomas, A. (1998) 'Cultural barriers in oncology: issues in obtaining medical informed consent from Japanese–American elders in Hawaii', *Journal of Cross-Cultural Gerontology*, 13: 265–79.

Seale, C. (2005) 'The transformation of dying in old societies', in M.L. Johnson (ed.), *The Cambridge Handbook of Age and Ageing.* Cambridge: Cambridge University Press, pp. 378–386.

Shinoda-Tagawa, T. and Ikegami, N. (2005) 'Resident and facility characteristics associated with the site of death among Japanese nursing home residents', *Age and Ageing*, 34(5): 515–18.

Taylor, D. and Carter, S. (2004) *Valuing Choice–Dying and Home.* London: Marie Curie Cancer Care.

Tomasini, C. (2005) 'The demographic characteristics of the oldest old in the United Kingdom', *Population Trends,* 120: 15–22.

Tornstam, L. (1996) 'Gerotranscendence – a theory about maturing in old age', *Journal of Ageing and Identity*, 1: 37–50.

Uotinen, V., Rantanen, T., and Suutama, T. (2005) 'Perceived age as a predictor of old age mortality: a 13-year prospective study', *Age and Ageing*, 34: 368–72.

Van der Geest, S. (2004) 'Dying peacefully: considering good death and bad death in Kwahu-Tafo, Ghana', *Social Science and Medicine*, 58: 899–911.

Waddell, C. and McNamara, B. (1997) 'The stereotypical fallacy: a comparison of Anglo-Chinese Australians' thoughts about facing death', *Mortality*, 1(2): 149–61.

Williams, R. (1990) *A Protestant Legacy: Attitudes to Death and Illness among Older Aberdonians.* Oxford: Clarendon Press.

Woolhead, G., Calnan, M., Dieppe, P., and Tadd, W. (2004) 'Dignity in older age: what do older people in the United Kingdom think?', *Age and Ageing*, 33: 165–70.

World Bank (2000) *World Development Report 2000/2001: Attacking Poverty*. http://go.worldbank.org/51C10OSNO0

World Health Organization (2002) *National Cancer Control Programme: Policies and Managerial Guidelines*, 2nd edn. Geneva: WHO.

Wright, M., Wood, J., Lynch, T., and Clark, D. (2006) *Mapping Levels of Palliative Care Development: A Global View*. Lancaster University, International Observatory on End of Life Care.

Yun, Y.H., Lim, M.K., Choi, K., and Rhee, Y.S. (2006) 'Predictors associated with the place of death in a country with increasing hospital deaths', *Palliative Medicine*, 20: 455–61.

Ethics and Old Age: The Second Generation

Martha Holstein

INTRODUCTION

Ethics is a disciplined and systematized reflection on our moral practices (Walker, 2003). It is a means to test critically our moral values, judgments, responsibilities, aims, and actions. A normative enterprise, it is about the 'oughts' in our lives, allowing us to evaluate the relations that connect people to one another, helps to reveal human wrongs, and to suggest ways to remedy them (Held, 2006), and to help us make wise decisions when values conflict. Ethical reflection offers a means to analyze arguments, examine different ways in which choices can be justified, while holding up to critical analysis 'what everyone knows'. It also suggests to those of us who work in practical arenas some core values to inform our work. Hence, over these past 20 or 30 years, we have integrated into practice a solid core of value-rich content (substantive values) that support the values of professions such as social work, medicine, law, and counseling.

We have also developed approaches that help resolve value conflicts that are inevitable when we cannot do everything, or when organizational needs and professional values clash, or when the contexts in which we work constrain what we perceive to be our ethical obligations to clients or patients. We tend to be at our best in our direct work with individuals and least practiced when it comes to issues that are grounded in social, economic, and political contexts and difference. In addition, we are often better at encouraging certain kinds of autonomy than identifying and supporting justice-based claims.

Many other issues have received inadequate attention from ethicists who think about old age. These issues include broader societal questions that ask if and how emerging cultural constructs about old age are morally significant (Holstein and Minkler, 2003) or how our ageing bodies influence our moral standing. Additionally, although most of the professions involved in ageing are committed to social justice as a central concern, we have only rarely explored the ethical meanings of class, gender, and race inequalities that infuse the ageing experience. This chapter will focus on the major developments in ethical thinking about ageing and old age that have evolved over the past 30 years. It will use long-term care to illustrate the need for continued work. However, it will not, given the limits of space, be able to address the social and political questions mentioned above that deserve searching inquiry. The chapter will open with a brief conceptual overview as a means to situate both author and text.

A PERSPECTIVE: A PERSONAL AND CONCEPTUAL ORIENTATION

There is no neutral starting place for ethical reflection and analysis (Meyers et al., 2004; Walker, 2003). Who we are affects what we see, how we think, the judgments we reach, and hence the actions that become possibilities for us. My own commitment to feminist ethics and critical gerontology, for example, means that I foreground and take as ethically significant issues that arise when women are in situations of unequal power that subtly but consistently disadvantage them. Awareness of how class and race influence our moral standing in old age also influences my thinking. For feminist ethicists, intimate relationships such as giving and receiving care, questions about dependency and vulnerability, and about justice within families are ethical foci. Doing ethical work as a feminist means that I include emotion as a relevant feature of the ethical landscape and that abstract principles and rules have less power than trying to determine what to do in particular situations that involve significant and often long-standing relationships among people. It also means that while I view autonomy as important, I do not see it as a property of isolated individuals but as the product of, and bound up with, relationships (Stoljar and McKenzie, 2000: 2). This background also leads me to accept that we do the best we can 'all things considered' but that, despite our best efforts, we often are left with uncertainties, which I accept as fundamental when 'reasonable people struggle together to reach judgments' (Pritchard, 2006: 7). Unfortunately, I don't believe we can be assured of a 'right' answer, but that fact does not absolve us from trying to work through the difficulties we face. Uneasiness about the usefulness of familiar moral theories, principles, and ideas in addressing practical situations in professional ethics is not uncommon (Kuczewski, 1999; Lindemann, 2006).

Along with new theoretical or quasi-theoretical insights, we are faced with issues that arise because we are likely to be working in organizational settings with others who see and think about ethical issues in different ways. This fact of contemporary life calls for an eclectic approach to ethical analysis and the search for integrity-preserving compromises (Goodstein, 2000). For these reasons, Moody (1992), Johnson (1999), Cooper (2004), Hugman (2005), and others support using a 'communicative ethic' that has its origins in the thinking of Jurgen Habermas, but has been adapted for use in practice settings. It involves information, deliberation, and negotiation (Johnson, 1999), in which there is a give and take among equal participants who strive to reach agreement that all can accept even if that agreement would not be their first choice.

As these approaches become more familiar, it is important for each of us to 'know ourselves' ethically (Abramson, 1996), to develop the courage to voice our commitments and concerns and to find ways to see that compromise is not necessarily a threat to our integrity (Goodstein, 2000). To this end, we might consider adopting what has been called an ethics of responsibility (May, 1996) that redefines integrity to encompass a commitment to the group of which we are a part – and its commitment to us – and thus signal our willingness to listen to others, to be open to their arguments, and to be prepared to support our own normative judgments with reasons. It also, quite often, means recognizing that emotions have a place in ethical deliberation, both as a signal that problems exist and as a guide to action (Goodstein, 2000; Held, 2006; May, 1996). Moreover, in the tradition of feminist scholarship, a critically based ethics 'links conclusions about how to live with attempts to put those conclusions into practice' (Nussbaum, 1997: 208), thus joining the political and the ethical (Lloyd, 2006).

THE JOURNEY TO THE PRESENT: AN OVERVIEW AND CRITIQUE OF ETHICS AND AGEING

For older people, ethical work that has been undertaken during the last two decades has placed certain substantive values at the forefront of our thinking: for example, values about keeping confidences, telling the truth, and respecting older people as important decision-makers about their own lives. First among equals, however, *autonomy* has been the value upheld as primary. While not ruling out 'best interests' or beneficent judgments, the rules regarding informed consent, which is the enactment of autonomy in practice settings, apply to older people no differently than to younger people unless it is clear that they are unable to make decisions on their own behalf. This feature of control has been extended to end-of-life care primarily through the use of advance directives, known in the United States as Durable Power of Attorney (DPA) for health care. Such instruments have been developed to try to assure that an individual's medical care choices will be carried out when he or she is no longer able to communicate them. The DPA, created by the Patient Self-Determination Act (PSDA) (1990), names a proxy decision-maker, making it the strongest of these instruments. Given its limits – a snapshot view of what a person may have wanted at a certain point in time – efforts are now being made to focus on values rather than primarily on decisions. Skepticism persists, however, whether for most people end-of-life care has been greatly improved (Teno et al., 2007). One particular decision – asking and receiving physician assistance with dying – is not on the political agenda.

In its early years (the 1970s and 1980s), it was common to think of bioethics as 'applied' ethics. In other words, familiar theories – Kantianism,

Utilitarianism, and the Social Contract – would be applied in practice settings. This approach emerged because philosophers, mostly male, and mostly American, came to dominate bioethics; unsurprisingly, they transferred what was well-established in the academic setting to the practice one. Hence, the idea that moral thinking was detached, universal, and impartial held sway. This perspective, intended to assure that personal feelings, biases, preferences, etc., would not 'muddy' moral analysis, seemed to define the bioethical enterprise.

By the 1980s, the text, *Principles of Biomedical Ethics*, by Thomas Beauchamp and James Childress (2009), first published in 1979, introduced four basic principles – respect for autonomy, beneficence, non-maleficence, and justice – that have played a major role in the evolution of thinking about bioethics, which remains the primary terrain of ethics and ageing. By asking us to weigh and balance these mid-level principles, that is, 'finding reasons to support beliefs about which moral norms should prevail' (Beauchamp and Childress, 2009: 20) when we encounter an ethical conundrum in biomedicine, this approach gave a structure to moral intuitions and seemed to capture prevailing ideas about what ought to count when making medical care decisions. This method for addressing ethical problems in medicine adopts these four principles as 'general guidelines for the formulation of more specific rules' (Beauchamp and Childress, 2009: 12). These rules are substantive, such as confidentiality, procedural, such as rules for organ distribution, and about authority, such as who decides. In practice settings, clinicians, social workers, and other practitioners repeatedly invoke them when facing ethical dilemmas in which two (or more) conflicting actions can be defended on ethical grounds.

The above rules were first used in the clinic or the hospital intensive care unit and later transferred to the nursing home and community care settings. Hence, 'doing' ethics was organized around the notion of a 'dilemma' where values conflicted and the possibility of a solution was promised (Jennings, 2006). Ethical analysis focused on 'patient competency and self-determination, on the nature and limits of caregiver obligation, on threats posed by professional paternalism, institutional self-interest, and the imperatives of high tech medicine' (Collopy et al., 1990). The patient, and later the long-term care client, was the decision-maker unless incompetent or unable to make decisions. While efforts were made to address the demands placed on others as the result of patient or client choices (Blustein, 1993; Collopy et al., 1990), in practice, client choice reigned relatively unchallenged.

As experience would show, this impartial, universal approach to 'doing' ethics was generally unable to satisfactorily address, for example, the 'household' issues that arose in work with older people. Problems such as who was to care for whom, what to do when family members disagreed, or when the responsibility for care fell completely on one person, seemed to need something beyond principles to guide individuals, families, and professionals as they sought to make wise choices in the face of loss and other elements of the ageing condition. Nonetheless, the mindset that called for applying abstract principles and rules carried a particular authority, an authority that defined what it means to do an ethical analysis: 'There is a certain logic to a procedure that asks us to order, weigh, or reconcile the differing values and interest of morally autonomous, rational and competent individuals' (Cole and Holstein, 1996: 482).

Because this practice emerged in the American context, where individualism and independence are central to national self-identity, *principlism*, as it came to be known, quickly elevated autonomy, understood as self-direction, to the first principle among equals, a place that it still holds. As a result, the individual has generally taken priority over the collective – the focus has less often been on changing the context, such as the public policies that help define the possibilities actually available to older people, or even defining the context, than on using individual strategies for bettering conditions (Capitman and Sciegaj, 1995; Lloyd, 2006). Thus, the absence of social or economic conditions that made autonomy very nearly impossible for large numbers of older people received far less attention than did individual choice, however limited those choices might have been in practice.

Another difficulty was the 'self' that came to dominate thinking – individuals who were detached and free of obligations that weren't chosen became the 'subject' of ethics. This view of the self did not fit well with either the older person, whose infirmities and complicated life created many of the problems that called for attention, or with the life-world of the caregiver, whose responsibilities severely constrained her or his ability to choose. By limiting ethical thinking to people who were free, independent, and at least putatively equal to one another, ethics was unable to satisfactorily account for people who were legitimately dependent because of ill health, age, or other features of their lives. Because moral theorizing assumed a certain kind of person, it was inadequate when faced with moral concerns that arose in situations of legitimate dependency and vulnerability. Instead the theoretical conceptions developed for people engaged in symmetrical, equal relationships were applied to other, very different relationships where they had little relevance (Walker, 2003). This effort obscured 'the moral significance of our day-to-day relationships which are frequently involuntary and unequal and thus [we have] failed to see how those attributes apply in the . . . wider society' (Held, 2006: 13). Considering all the unequal relationships that persist in our hierarchical and class-based society, it might be argued that sustained analysis of their moral elements might make a difference for all who are involved.

By the mid-1980s, the principle of autonomy was extended to people who lacked capacity to make decisions for themselves. Authorized proxy decision-makers were instructed to decide as that person would have decided had they been able to act for themselves. Acting benevolently – or in an elder's best interests – was a distinct second best. The focus on individual autonomy often led health professionals to view families skeptically, as less than trustworthy transmitters of the interests of their loved ones (Levine and Zuckerman, 1999).

Although autonomy commits us to an acceptance of advance planning for disability, not all questions about proxy decision-making are settled. What about the person with Alzheimer's disease who cannot speak a coherent sentence but laughs and smiles a lot and then develops a massive infection requiring intravenous antibiotics? Which of the following counts: the views she expressed when she was not cognitively impaired or her current experiential state when making healthcare decisions (Dresser, 1986; Dworkin, 1993)? What happens in the presence of family disagreement even if there is an appointed proxy?

In the United States, the Retirement Research Foundation's initiative 'Enhancing Autonomy in Long-Term Care', launched in 1984, almost single-handedly defined the work to come in subsequent years. This development created a critical mass of individuals who, for the first time, focused concentrated attention on ethics as they applied to older people in need of long-term care services. It also supported empirical work that revealed the limited choices available in such settings. Researchers, for example, uncovered multiple ways in which nursing homes disregarded client/patient autonomy (Agich, 1990; Lidz et al., 1992), while Bart Collopy (1988) contributed a conceptual analysis of autonomy, recognizing that the inability to act on our choices does not mean denying the right to choose. In what remains a classic account of autonomy in long-term care, Collopy called attention to issues that are still inadequately addressed, such as the interrelation between competency (or incapacitated choice)

and autonomy, the right to be left alone against the need for positive action that makes real choice possible, and the distinction between short-term and long-term autonomy.

American nursing homes now post a 'Patient Bill of Rights'. They less often address the companion piece – responsibilities of living in a closed community. Admissions agreements are improved (Ambrogi and Leonard, 1988) and patients are invited to participate in 'care planning'. In community-based care, autonomy is also the most frequently articulated value. This commitment sets the stage for common ethical conundrums such as individual choice vs safety, causing Kane and Levin (2001) to ask how one avoids interfering with life goals while meeting one's professional obligation to promote health and safety. As they observe, the 'rights of a consumer to take informed risks are modified by the moral, legal, and regulatory responsibilities' of health professionals and care organizations' (2001: 221). In an effort to address these concerns, strategies for assessing risk have been developed (Fireman and Dornberg-Lee, 2003) while negotiated risk agreements (Kane and Levin, 2001) permit facilities, usually assisted living, to protect themselves from litigation, while granting considerable freedom to individuals.

A less-developed area in ethics concerns the person who seemingly – and often dangerously – disregards his or her well-being but refuses any intervention. Labeled 'self-neglect', this behavior tends to produce the standard response that if individuals have the capacity to make their own decisions, beyond trying to persuade him or her to accept help, the social service provider must accept the choices the person makes. This issue requires further study and analysis, focusing on compromised capacity, longer- and shorter-term autonomy, the choices available to people, and the role of emotions such as compassion in working with the individual to determine the most appropriate action, all things considered.

The relationships between families and their elder members have received significant attention (Arras, 1995; Blustein, 1993; Nelson, 1992) over the past 10-15 years. Despite the deep reliance on autonomy, many ethicists are acknowledging that we usually make important decisions in dialogue with others we love or who will be affected by our decisions. Hardwig (1992) has taken the most extreme position in this regard by putting family interests and patient rights on an equal footing. Others (Arras, 1995; Blustein, 1993; Nelson, 1992) have adopted more modest stances, calling attention to the moral significance of intimacy and the legitimate interests of family members who are caring for their loved ones. High (1991), for example, reminded us that decision-making, especially healthcare decision-making, involves moral dialogue, most often grounded in the unique moral community that is the family. Families are more than conduits of the older person's wishes. Arras (1995) has convincingly argued that families' interests matter; they ought not be dismissed on conflict of interest grounds. This recognition of the family extends to the end of life. An elder's decision to die at home rarely affects him or her alone. Thus, there are important questions that must be considered. How can the interests of all who may be involved intimately in the older person's life be taken into account (Ellingson and Fuller, 2003; Kuhn, 2003)? What would an ethics of accommodation rather than an ethics of autonomy (Collopy et al., 1990) look like if it were to account for elders, families, formal carers, and communities? What would it mean to see the relevant stakeholders – older person, family members, health and social service providers – in a single vision, all included in deciding what to do both preventively and reactively (McCullough et al., 1995)?

In this 'preventive ethics' approach, the key stakeholders, including the older person, meet regularly to decide on courses of action that are open to regular adjustments in the fluid situation that reflects long-term care (see below for a further discussion of this approach). Negotiated consent, characterized by the 'clash and balancing of competing interests' (Moody, 1992), may be the best approach when love and compassion rather than autonomy become the most important values (Cole and Holstein, 1996). While we may not need an impartial, universally applicable principle to support the actions that are chosen, these open processes still call for reasonable explanations or rationales that support the choices that we make (Moody, 1992; Pritchard, 2006).

Thus, by the early 1990s, the new discipline of bioethics (with its focus on temporally isolated, procedural approaches to questions about death, dying, and medical care decision-making) framed the new discourse on ethics and ageing (Moody, 1992). With minimal challenges to the medical context and the policy apparatus that supported hospitals and medical care, changes occurred, most importantly in the one-on-one relationships between physician and patient and between social service professionals and clients. Informed consent became the central enactment of autonomy in the medical setting. Later, as language transformed the patient into the consumer and then the customer, without analysis of the moral significance of these changes, medicine became seen as a contractual relationship between putative equals. Unfortunately, this position did not account for the actual situation in hospitals: unrecognized and

so unacknowledged power relationships permitted their effects to go unaddressed. It also permitted busy hospital or nursing home staff or community-based social workers to adopt a 'minimalist ethics' (Fox and Swazey, 1994) that suited their training, time constraints, and their professional codes.

MORE QUESTIONS ARISE

Kane and Caplan (1990), in their studies of autonomy in nursing homes, found that residents worried less about major decisions, like termination of treatment, than the opportunity to make private phone calls, or to preserve private space either for visitors or themselves. Agich (1990) reinforced the observation that what really mattered to people in long-term care settings was the chance to live in habitual ways, which allowed them, to the extent possible, to preserve a sense of self in spite of loss. Care providers can play a significant role in this effort to make everyday life a source of self-preservation, which Agich describes as 'interstitial' or 'actual' autonomy. This means 'acknowledg[ing] the essential social nature of human development' (Agich, 1990: 12), a point that has been further developed by feminist philosophers (Kittay, 1999; Parks, 2003; Tronto, 1993). This view of autonomy understands individuals as concrete and not as generalized others for whom choice is not an abstractly given right but rather a meaningful reflection of their identity. Given this understanding of actual autonomy, to respect individuals means that 'we attend to their concrete individuality, to their affective and personal experiences' while also learning 'how to acknowledge their habits and identifications' (Agich, 1990: 14). It means, to start with, that we offer not merely choice to people, but meaningful choice. These enlarged ethical obligations and the practical demands on carers affirm the notion that the good precedes the right. The right to choose is meaningless in the absence of an idea of the good and the possibility to realize that good. Yet, for people in long-term care settings, rights are granted without any assurance that they will be able to live in ways that they would consider good despite their limitations.

That we live our lives coherently and purposefully matters at any age. For many older people, the effects of chronic illness and the social devaluation that accompanies frailty and inactivity threaten their self-respect and what Charles Taylor (1984) called 'horizons of meaning'. Both are critical. In Taylor's view, dignity, in the sense of 'commanding (attitudinal) respect', (1984: 15) grounds self-respect. Social devaluation threatens our dignity at its most fundamental level. But, along with our profound need to feel respected, is the need for a framework that shapes our conception of the good in the absence of which our life is 'spiritually senseless' (1984: 18). It is this sense of making qualitative distinctions – that some way of life is infinitely higher than others – that becomes increasingly difficult when we become old in societies as diverse as the ones in which we live. Extant cultural norms give little or no guidance once we become frail or 'not young'. Yet, this search for a viable self, for recognizing and having 'goods that command our awe' in conditions of frailty and dependency, is essential for remaking our identity when so much that has been familiar is eroding. The moral is thus far more demanding than granting rights to make choices that may not have any connection with our horizons of meaning.

A SPECIFIC CONTEXT: LONG-TERM CARE

In recent years, as ethicists and others have come to study long-term care more closely, it has become increasingly clear that the models for addressing ethical problems developed in acute care settings cannot be transferred directly to long-term care settings. From micro issues of individual decision-making, particularly in regard to autonomy and safety, to issues related to public policy and social justice, justice within families, and the moral implications of vulnerability and dependency, long-term care creates its own moral demands.

Vulnerability and dependency

In societies that are devoted almost single-mindedly to independence and self-control, it is not surprising that vulnerability, which implies some if not all loss of control and power over many circumstances of our daily lives, has not received the attention it deserves (Hoffmaster, 2006). The condition of vulnerability takes individuals far from the Kantian 'autonomous man' that has so dominated ethical thinking. Recall the ancient Socratic question about how to lead a good life. This question applies to individuals with functional and other disabilities as well as to the more able-bodied. Social and moral ideals that are focused on independence and individualism do not mesh well with actual vulnerability and dependency. Yet, in today's society it is difficult to give these almost ubiquitous conditions moral meaning for fear that attention to them will denigrate the person for not living up to the social ideal of independence. Can we, however, care about ethics and ageing without thinking 'deeply and candidly' about what equality and dignity mean for all sorts of people, including those who have varying degrees of physical and mental capacity? (Walker, 2003).

If we do not address the above questions, we risk isolating people who are dependent and hence vulnerable, setting them apart from the strong who will give care without necessarily needing to care. A feminist ethics of care embraces a basic value that 'proper care for others is a good, that humans in society should strive to enhance the quality of life in the world so that people can live as well as possible' (Tronto, 1995: 142). Compare this sentiment to one based on a market system of care that strives for efficiency and rests on a contractual relationship between provider and customer and on the achievement of instrumental tasks. Jan Baars (2006) aptly describes it as 'pit-stop models of service' which 'may be adequate in terms of maintenance and repair, but not care, especially long-term care' (2006: 33). These market mechanisms do not contribute to solidarity, a normative foundation for policy for which I argued elsewhere (Holstein, 2005).

In the United States, public support for long-term care has been historically located in the welfare sector. Even though Medicaid today pays 42 per cent of the costs of long-term care, primarily financing institutional care, the programmes that serve clients and families are generally starved for resources. In the United Kingdom, long-term care has been subject to privatization and delivered, as in the United States, by low-wage workers (Player and Pollock, 2001). The clock, rather than the actual autonomy needs of clients, generally governs activities. Hence, choice often means selecting one home care agency over another or, in some circumstances, using a cash voucher to hire a care worker. Most often even this choice is limited, since the potential user of the service has very little information about the agency or the individual who will be caring for them in the most intimate of ways.

As a result, the likelihood of meshing actual and ideal autonomy is tied to social class. Individuals able to pay privately can, if they have sufficient resources, ignore the clock and seek meaningful choices. As Agich (1990) reminds us, 'Being able to identify with one's choices is a prerequisite for true autonomy' (1990: 15). While individuals may have lost control over bathing or dressing, they have control over how much help they get and from whom. They have the opportunity, within the limits of their physical and cognitive functioning, to continue developing and expressing their individuality. Families, perhaps freed from the daily responsibilities of caregiving, then have the chance to engage in soul mending, and other meaning-giving activities.

For those reliant on public-funded assistance, overburdened family members and poorly paid carers are often unable to care in ways that go beyond the instrumental. Ethical values such as attentiveness, responsibility, responsiveness (Tronto, 1998) or competence, compassion, and care are difficult to enact. Further more, when instrumental care dominates, who can listen to stories and socially construct or re-construct identities threatened by loss and change?

People needing long-term care share another feature of their lives. They are most often cared for by women family members, who provide three-quarters of the care in the community. Some older people also receive care from paid home care workers, about 99 per cent of whom are women. Wages are low and benefits are few. Essentialized and billed as 'natural', their work is simultaneously praised and demeaned (Abel, 1991; Twigg, 2004). A former colleague of mine described caregivers as 'saints' while making it quite clear that he couldn't (or wouldn't) do what these saints did. None of this, of course, is new. We have known, in both Europe and America, that women provide paid and unpaid care and that the primary care receivers are also women. For most families, choice is a myth. A choice is not really free, or autonomously made, if the options for good and dependable alternatives are either non-existent or very limited. Nor is fully autonomous choice possible when deeply rooted cultural expectations reinforce the fact that women have fewer acceptable reasons for not giving care than do men (Jecker, 2002; Holstein, 2007). Thus, these 'choices' of women can hardly be labeled as such if men are not called upon to make comparable choices. If the consequences of caring were neutral perhaps the problem would not seem so significant but they are not neutral because people who give care can never be equal to those who do not give care (Kittay, 1999). Caregiving is not 'employment at will'; it makes it difficult, if not impossible, to live according to one's life plans and it generates long- and short-term financial as well as physical and mental health problems. Careers, for example, are often interrupted, wages and future pension benefits are sacrificed (in countries where, like the United States, caregiving years earn no social security or pension benefits), and the risks of poverty in old age increased. Although perhaps not always the case, since some carers have the resources to seek care for themselves, it is common and familiar. Women are thus placed at serious disadvantage to men, a disadvantage that accumulates over time.

Yet, women (and many men) are devoted caregivers. They provide care even if prior relationships were stormy or even abusive. This fact says something about the power of filial obligation (Brakeman, 1995). It also says something about the inadequate provision of care by the state. In the United States, the care provided by family members, if translated into dollars, amounts to over $300 billion a year (Arno et al., 1999). The burden has increased as the state has sought to save public dollars: 'Cost containment . . . is largely the shifting of the costs of care to patients and families' (Levine and Zuckerman, 1999: 148). Thus, without the commitment of family caregivers, the state's burden would be overwhelming. The state's obligation to carers requires recognition. Care for elderly parents (bracketing the care of spouses), who need assistance, is not a private matter deserving only some small assistance from the state but rather it is a public matter calling for broad risk-sharing.

Decision-making and autonomy

McCullough and his colleagues suggest that 'concepts such as autonomy, safety, and independence are drawn too starkly and too abstractly in the bioethics literature to be adequate to the complex and shifting realities of long-term care decision-making' (1995: 6). Life situations often change dramatically and in ways that prior experiences may have ill-prepared the older person. Trial and error may be the most effective strategy for coming to understand what one's values are in new and difficult circumstances (Kuczewski, 1999).

As described above, notions of autonomy as developed for acute care settings have more limited value in the long-term care setting. This observation does not imply that it is acceptable to simply override the person's wishes. To quote Agich once again, '"giving" a frail elder a range of choices or "letting" the elder choose may be ethically less compelling than helping the elder to live in the face of frailty, loss, and ultimately death' (1990: 17). Autonomy may best be reflected in adaptation to change, a process in which carers may be actively engaged. While often constrained by the instrumental nature of their work or by the clock, most caregivers would prefer supporting an individual's value commitments and identifications if only there were time and if only they, the caregivers, felt respected for the work that they do.

More practically, however, day-to-day decision-making – often in very complex situations – is a central feature of long-term care. Older people and those around them are in multiple roles, very different than the patient–physician relationship that dominates acute care settings. At one moment, the 83-year-old woman is a client; minutes later she is a mother, grandmother, neighbor, friend. These relationships each have 'their own principles that reflect role-specific duties as well as more general concepts that are conducive to mutual self-discovery among the community members' (Kuczewski, 1999: 18). Decision-making itself is also more complicated. It involves quotidian matters like finances, where pets will go, and family work schedules in a context where the older person may be experiencing diminished capacity and suffering from multiple medical conditions. Decisions tend to be made incrementally over time with elder, family members, doctors, social workers, and often others involved. No longer is decision-making vested in the physician–patient dyad. (McCullough and Wilson, 1995).

Other features of long-term care further complicate efforts to apply moral rules and principles to the situations that we face. Family relationships are usually decades old and so are the problems. There may be few families who behave in the rational, consensual way that would facilitate good care. A significant incidence of cognitive impairments with coexisting medical conditions often complicate how decisions are made. And probably one of the most difficult issues we face is the fact that, often, there are no good choices. The older person will not be recapturing his or her health or even old way of life. 'Safe' accommodations are often experienced as overly regimented and unable to respond to habitual ways of being. Living alone, on the other hand, especially for the person with cognitive impairments, may be truly dangerous.

Moreover, while we tend to focus on moments of choice – moving to a nursing home, terminating treatment, violating confidentiality because of perceived danger to the client, telling the truth to a patient, or honoring a daughter's wish not to take away her mother's hope – in fact, all of long-term care involves ethical concerns. How we give a person a bath, the respect we show (or don't show) for the old body, the dignity-enhancing (or dignity-eroding) ways in which we talk and listen to the older person are all ethical in nature. Imagine for a moment exposing your culturally abject body to the eyes of a stranger as she is helping you with your bath. In this asymmetrical relationship, where trust is so essential and the potential for power abuse so possible, trust, an elemental moral value, raises the task of bathing to a deeply moral relationship (see Twigg 2000, 2004). Long-term care involves relationships, gratitude, reciprocity, love, and fairness, and so it is, above all, about morality.

Despite all these complications, decisions need to be made and actions need to be taken. What then

does it take to facilitate the process of self-discovery and the identification of 'morally desirable, or at least morally permissible, actions and practices . . .' (Jagger, 1995: 179). Situations that arise in long-term care require 'sensitivity, flexibility, discretion, and improvisation to find precisely what responds to the very particular' (Walker, 1992: 28–9). How do we do this? McCullough and Wilson (1995), as noted above, recommend a process they call preventive ethics. By anticipating what might come next, all stakeholders are better prepared to respond appropriately. In this model, one:

- identifies stakeholders
- seeks factual agreement of the elder's condition
- elicits the values of the elder and the family and on this basis seeks their evaluations of the elder's conditions and realistic alternatives for managing them, including the issue of caregiver burden and costs
- weighs benefits and harms
- considers limited obligations in order to promote and protect the interests of others
- invites reflection on how alternatives affect self-identity of elder and family member and the relationships they wish to protect
- makes recommendations, recognizing that they are provisional
- reviews plans and decisions regularly .

Kuczewski also embeds his casuistic or case-based approach in the ongoing situation, suggesting that 'routine daily life and social institutions embody moral principles' (1999: 19). He argues that a basic ethical framework for elder care must include candor, as a sign of respect, and responsibility for narrative integrity so that the meaning of an elder's life is preserved. This latter concept resembles Agich's sense that one of the most important ways to honor autonomy is to facilitate the changes to live in familiar and meaningful ways in spite of the many changes that may be occurring.

ETHICS AS CRITICAL PRACTICE: NEXT STEPS

I have argued for a contextual view of ethics that is enacted in our daily lives, in our practices and policies, and in our relationships with others. Rooted in our daily lives, ethics is part of the 'everyday experiences of thoughtful people' who are an 'essential resource for, and check on, the reflections of [others] joined in inquiry, including philosophers' (Pritchard, 2006: 8). It is less about theory than it is about how to live in spite of loss and change. It recognizes that context, understood in social and political terms, most often operates as a constraint on what we are able to do. Awareness of context, like power, is critical if ethics is to be a force for social change.

This understanding of ethics, like critical gerontology, is descriptive, analytical, value laden, and action-oriented. A phrase recently caught my attention. Though directed at the erosion of social work as a force for progressive social change, the author described social work practice as 'the dog that didn't bark even when its soul appeared to be stripped out' (Stepney, 2006: 1). I see this happening when we complacently take as given the neoliberal orientation that relies on the market for arenas of life, such as care, where it doesn't fit and so does harm. It becomes instrumental and task driven rather than person-centered, despite the lively rhetoric about client-centered care (see Baars, 2006, for a critique of this 'colonization'). A critical ethics analyzes universal policies and practices for their differential impact on individuals and groups and builds a bridge between analyses and action.

A critical ethics establishes claims upon society that allow us to meet our responsibilities to ourselves and to others and establishes the moral grounds for such claims. It insists that one cannot be a responsible social or health professional in the absence of resources to meet our obligations well (Lloyd, 2006; Tronto, 1993). It criticizes our current insistence on discussing public life from a vision of autonomous, equal, rational actors each pursuing separate ends. This is a faulty vision of the self and serves older people poorly. Instead, based on a feminist ethics of care, it would start with 'a vision of interdependent actors, each of whom needs and provides care in a variety of ways and each of whom has other interests and pursuits that exist outside the realm of care' (Tronto, 1993: 168).

Critical reflection permits us to 'unpack dominant discourses and the assumptions that sustain them' (Stepney, 2006: 10). I touched on some ways this can work above. A critical perspective 'takes all views as provisional, open to criticism' (McCullough, 2005: 1). To so engage is the 'way' of the humanities. A critical ethics can help assess cultural, social, and political aspects of ageing by identifying the normative features of seemingly non-normative areas, like images of ageing. Ethical thinking can expose these areas to an analysis that challenges universalistic assumptions and proposes alternative policies or norms that take our differences as well as our commonalities seriously. While policies cannot take individuals as their focus, they can attend to groups, like women or ethnic and racial minorities (Clement, 1996). It would recognize that 'generalizations and idealizations tended to . . . mirror conditions and positions more likely to be familiar

to, or entertained as possibilities by, some people rather than others' (Walker, 2003: 14).

To enact a critically grounded ethics means confronting deeply rooted societal issues. For one, it calls upon us to accept dependency as part of human life and the meaning this fact has for our commitment to human rights. In Western society, human rights are important sources of human dignity. For people, who are dependent because of cognitive or physical limits, common notions of negative rights – the right to be left along – can leave them feeling abandoned. A more substantive notion of positive rights – to care, for example – is rarely sufficiently available. The inability to claim such rights can be a source of humiliation, an oft-ignored moral wrong (Margalit, 1996). This inability to claim basic rights even while honoring individuals and their choices occurs, in part, because this focus on the individual has often occluded the way social forces operating at the macro level profoundly influence what happens at the micro level (Baars, 2006). This interaction penetrates all aspects of long-term care. It shapes social attitudes toward ageing and old age, and influences the chances to live decently when old. Individualism has meant that decision-making in the clinical realm has taken priority over the social and cultural context in which these decisions are embedded and which significantly affect the range of choices we actually have, the ways we are seen and treated. I close then with an urgent plea that we see ethics as an ally in whatever efforts we make to help more people achieve a good old age. At the end of life, as at the beginning, we need love and support as much or more than we need the chance to decide. And in those areas where decision-making is important, context – the system between moments of choice – is critical.

REFERENCES

Abel, E. (1991) *Who Cares for the Elderly? Public Policy and the Experiences of Adult Daughters.* Philadelphia: Temple University Press.

Abramson, M. (1996) 'Reflections on knowing oneself ethically: toward a working framework for social work practice', *Families in Society: Journal of Contemporary Human Services.* CEU article No. 61: 195–202.

Agich, G. (1990) 'Reassessing autonomy in long-term care', *Hastings Center Report,* 20(6): 12–17.

Ambrogi, D. and Leonard, F. (1988) 'The impact of nursing home admission agreements on resident autonomy', *The Gerontologist,* 28(Suppl): 82–9.

Arno, P., Levine, C., and Memmot, M. (1999) 'The economic value of informal caregiving', *Health Affairs,* 18(2): 182–8.

Arras, J. (1995) 'Conflicting interests in long-term care decision making: acknowledging, dissolving, and resolving conflicts', in L. McCullough and N. Wilson (eds), *Long-Term Care Decisions: Ethical and Conceptual Dimensions*. Baltimore, MD: Johns Hopkins University Press, pp. 197–217.

Baars, J. (2006) 'Beyond neomodernism, antimodernism, and postmodernism: basic categories for contemporary critical gerontology', in J. Baars, D. Dannefer, C. Phillipson, and A. Walker (eds), *Aging, Globalization, and Inequality: The New Critical Gerontology*. Amityville, NY: Baywood, pp. 17–42.

Baier, A. (1994) *Moral Prejudices: Essays on Ethics*. Cambridge, MA: Harvard University Press.

Beauchamp, T. and Childress, J. (2009) *Principles of Biomedical Ethics*, 6th edn. New York: Oxford University Press (originally published in 1977).

Blustein, J. (1993) 'The family in medical decision making', *Hastings Center Report*, 23: 6–13.

Brakeman, S.V. (1995) 'Filial responsibility and long-term care decision making', in L. McCullough and N. Wilson (eds), *Long-Term Care Decisions: Ethical and Conceptual Dimensions*. Baltimore: Johns Hopkins University Press, pp. 181–96.

Capitman, J. and Sciegaj, M. (1995) 'A contextual approach for understanding individual autonomy in managed community long-term care', *The Gerontologist*, 4: 533–43.

Clement, G. (1996) *Care, Autonomy, and Justice: Feminism and the Ethic of Care*. Boulder, CO: Westview Press.

Cole, T. and Holstein, M. (1996) 'Ethics and aging', in R. Binstock and L. George (eds), *Handbook of Aging and the Social Sciences*, 4th edn. San Diego: Academic Press, pp. 481–97.

Collopy, B. (1988) 'Autonomy in long-term care: some crucial distinctions', *The Gerontologist*, 28(Suppl): 10–17.

Collopy, B. (1995) 'Safety and independence: rethinking some basic concepts in long-term care', in L. McCullough and N. Wilson (eds), *Long-Term Care Decisions: Ethical and Conceptual Dimensions*. Baltimore: Johns Hopkins University Press, pp. 37–154.

Collopy, B., Dubler, N., and Zuckerman, C. (1990) 'The ethics of home care: autonomy and accommodation', *Hastings Center Report*, 20(Special supplement): 1–16.

Cooper, D. (2004) *Ethics for Professionals in a Multicultural World*. Upper Saddle River, NJ: Pearson/Prentice Hall.

Dresser, R. (1986) 'Life, death and incompetent patients', *Arizona Law Review*. 28(3): 373–405.

Dworkin, R. (1993) *Life's Dominion: An Argument about Abortion, Euthanasia, and Individual Freedom*. New York: Knopf.

Ellingson, S. and Fuller, J. (2001) 'A good death? Finding a balance between the interests of patients and caregivers', in M. Holstein and P. Mitzen (eds), *Ethics and Community-Based Elder Care*. New York: Springer, pp. 200–7.

Fireman, D., Dornberg-Lee, S., and Moss, L. (2001) 'Mapping the jungle: a proposed method for decision-making in geriatric social work', in M. Holstein and P. Mitzen (eds), *Ethics and Community-Based Elder Care*. New York: Springer, Co, pp. 145–65.

Fox, R. and Swazey, J. (1984) 'medical morality is not bioethics: medical ethics in China and the United States', in R. Fox (ed.), *Essays on Medical Sociology*. New Brunswick, NJ: Transaction Books, pp. 645–71.

Goodstein, J. (2000) 'Moral compromise and personal integrity: exploring the ethical issues of deciding together in organizations', *Business Ethics Quarterly*, 10(4): 805–19.

Hardwig, J. (1990) 'What about the family?', *Hastings Center Report*, 20: 5–10.

Held, V. (2006) *The Ethics of Care: Personal, Political, and Global*. New York: Oxford University Press.

High, D. (1991) 'A new myth about families of older people', *The Gerontologist*, 31: 611–18.

Hoffmaster, B. (2006) 'What does vulnerability mean?', *Hastings Center Report*, 36(2): 38–45.

Holstein, M. (2005) 'A normative defense of universal age-based public policy', in R. Hudson (ed.), *The New Politics of Old Age Policy*. Baltimore: Johns Hopkins University Press, pp. 23–41.

Holstein, M. (2007) 'Long-term care, feminism, and an ethics of solidarity', in R. Pruchno and M. Smyer (eds), *Challenges of an Aging Society: Ethical Dilemmas and Political Issues*. Baltimore: Johns Hopkins University Press, pp. 156–74.

Holstein, M. and Minkler, M. (2003) 'Self, society and the "new" gerontology', *The Gerontologist*, 43(6): 787–96.

Holstein, M. and Mitzen, P. (eds) (2001) *Ethics and Community-Based Elder Care*. New York: Springer.

Hugman, R. (2005) *New Approaches in Ethics for the Caring Professions*. New York: Palgrave/Macmillan.

Jennings, B. (2006) Unpublished talk, delivered at the University of North Carolina, Charlotte, NC, October 2006.

Johnson, T.F. (ed.) (1999) *Handbook of Ethical Issues in Aging*. Westport, CT: Greenwood Press.

Kane, R. and Caplan, A. (eds) (1990) *Everyday Ethics: Resolving Dilemmas in Nursing Home Life*. New York: Springer.

Kane, R.A. and Levin, C. (2001) 'Who's safe? Who's sorry? The duty to protect the safety of HCBC consumers', in M. Holstein and P. Mitzen (eds), *Ethics in Community-Based Elder Care*. New York: Springer, pp. 217–33.

Kittay, E.F. (1999) *Love's Labor: Essays on Women, Equality, and Dependency*. New York: Routledge.

Kuczewski, M. (1999) 'Ethics in long-term care: Are the principles different?', *Theoretical Medicine*, 20: 15–29.

Kuhn, D. (2001) 'Is home care always the best care?', in M. Holstein, and P. Mitzen (eds), *Ethics and Community-Based Elder Care*. New York: Springer, pp. 187–99.

Levine, C. and Zuckerman, C. (1999) 'The trouble with families: toward an ethic of accommodation', *Annals of Internal Medicine*, 130: 148–52.

Lidz, C., Fischer, L., and Arnold, R. (1992) *The Erosion of Autonomy in Long-Term Care*. New York: Oxford University Press.

Lindermann, H. (2006) *An Invitation of Feminist Ethics*. Boston: McGraw-Hill.

Lloyd, L. (2006) 'A caring profession? The ethics of care and social work with older people', *British Journal of Social Work*, 36: 1171–85.

May (2006) *The Socially Responsive Self: Social Theory and Professional Ethics.* Chicago: University of Chicago Press.

McCullough, L. (2005) 'The critical turn in clinical ethics and its continuous enhancement', *Journal of Medicine and Philosophy*, 30: 1–8.

McCullough, L. and Wilson, N. (eds) (1995) *Long-Term Care Decisions: Ethical and Conceptual Dimensions.* Baltimore: Johns Hopkins University Press.

McCullough, L., Wilson, N., Rhymes, J., and Teasdale, T. (1999) 'Ethical issues in long-term care', in T.F. Johnson (ed.), *Handbook on Ethical Issues in Aging.* Westport, CT: Greenwood Press, pp. 305–25.

Meyers et al. (2004) – p 2

Moody, H.R. (1992) *Ethics in an Aging Society.* Baltimore: Johns Hopkins University Press.

Nelson, J. (1992) 'Taking families seriously', *Hastings Center Report.* 22: 6–12.

Nussbaum, M. (1997) *Cultivating Humanity: A Classical Defense of Reform in Liberal Education.* Cambridge, MA: Harvard University Press.

Parks, J. (2003) *No Place like Home? Feminist Ethics and Home Health Care.* Bloomington, IN: University of Indiana Press.

Player, S. and Pollock, A (2001) 'Long-term care: from public responsibility to private good', *Critical Social Policy*, 21(2): 231–55.

Pritchard, M. (2006) *Professional Integrity: Thinking Ethically.* Lawrence, KS: University of Kansas Press.

Stepney, P. (2006) 'Mission impossible? Critical practice in social work', *British Journal of Social Work*, 36(8): 1289–307.

Taylor, C. (1984) *Sources of the Self: The Making of Modern Identity.* Cambridge, MA: Harvard University Press.

Teno et al. (2007) 'Association between advance directives and quality end of life care: a national study', *Journal of the American Geriatrics Society*, 55(2): 189–94.

Tronto, J. (1993) *Moral Boundaries: A Political Argument for an Ethics of Care.* New York: Routledge.

Tronto, J. (1995) 'Care as a basis for radical political judgments', *Hypatia*, 405(2): 141–9.

Tronto, J. (1998) 'An ethics of care', *Generations*, 22(3): 15–20.

Tronto, J. (2001) 'An ethic of care', in M. Holstein and P. Mitzen (eds), *Ethics and Community-Based Elder Care.* New York: Springer, pp. 60–8.

Twigg (2000) *Bathing, the Body and Community Care.* London: Routledge.

Twigg, J. (2004) 'The body, gender, and age: feminist insights in social gerontology', *Journal of Aging Studies*, 18: 59–73.

Walker, M.U. (1992) 'Feminist ethics, and the question of theory', *Hypatia*, 7(3): 23–39.

Walker, M.U. (1998) *Moral Understandings: A Feminist Study in Ethics.* New York: Routledge.

Walker, M.U. (2003) *Moral Contexts.* Lanham, MD: Rowman and Littlefield.

The Politics of Ageing

Susan A. MacManus
with the assistance of Andrea L. Polk
and David J. Bonanza

INTRODUCTION

The ageing of the world's population, the economic downturn of the global economy in the early years of the 21st century, and the growing propensity of politicians and political campaigns to engage in identity politics, segmenting their constituents by age, race, and gender, have greatly expanded the theoretical and methodological frameworks used by scholars to study the politics of ageing. While the traditional focus of the politics of ageing studies has been on the political orientations, attitudes, and behavior of individuals, old-age-based political action organizations, and 'the politics of government action to establish and revise policies toward older individuals' (Binstock and Quadagno, 2001: 333), newer research is investigating the practical side of politics and policymaking as well. Studies examine, for example, ways of segmenting the older electorate and the technologies that make that possible. However, the difficulties of distinguishing between cohort, lifecourse, and period effects in political orientations and public policy formation remain, as do the challenges associated with precisely defining what, for political purposes, is 'old.'

This chapter reflects the general thrust of research on the politics of ageing around the globe. To present a meaningful level of detail, we focus on a specific case, that of the United States, in order to discuss enduring themes and issues of the politics of age, including voting patterns, campaign techniques and strategies, and retiree recruitment efforts and impacts. The chapter is divided into six main sections. The first section deals with key global issues and trends discussed in the politics of ageing. The second section focuses on political trends and issues in the USA. The third section details participation in electoral politics (voting), and the fourth section, participation more broadly construed, including volunteering and other forms of civic engagement. The fifth section discusses identity politics, especially in the U.S. context of political strategy and tactics aimed at exploiting social location and personal identity to gain political support. A brief sixth section discusses community-level responses to population ageing.

AGEING AND POLITICS: KEY GLOBAL POLICY DEBATES

In many countries, the ageing of the workforce is predicted to result in generational battles over budget priorities in education, housing, and related areas (Alvarez, 2002). The battles are already more intense in some parts of the world than others, producing what some call a global 'demographic divide' (Haub, 2007). In countries with larger ageing populations, retirement-related policies (pensions, retirement age, even immigration) have been key political issues (Aaron, 2000; Zaidi, 2008; see also Chapter 39).

Such issues become framed and defined by the character of economic circumstances. During times of economic boom, models of public sector resource allocation are more likely to find – or prescribe – intergenerational cooperation. The opposite is true during economic downturns, such as that experienced in the mid-to-late 2000s. When times are tough and resources are scarce, it is often older citizens who go on the offensive and complain about intergenerational injustices, while the reverse may be true in periods of economic expansion. Seniors see themselves and their cohort as victims of ageism in the workplace with the introduction of short-time working and redundancies, both of which may disproportionately affect those aged 50 and over.

This pattern has been observed in European countries, notably England, and in the United States. Yet this dynamics may not operate the same way in other societal contexts. In impoverished, famine- and disaster-ridden rural areas of Third World nations, older people, especially women, often encounter age discrimination, and have few political or social networks to advocate for them (Global Actions on Aging, 2008).

Conversely, in many Western and Eastern European countries, economists and public administrators call for the adoption of public policies allowing older workers to work longer to counter economic downturns attributable to population ageing (World Bank, 2007; Zaidi, 2008). During economic downturns, the public may give greater scrutiny to government expenditures. Questions arise as to: (1) how fair public policies are across and within different generations; (2) how effective decision-makers and policies are at reaching specific age cohorts; and (3) whether responses to needs are made in a timely, resourceful way. According to Street (2007: 7): 'Getting policies right requires careful planning, the capacity to evaluate the efficiency and equity of all social programmes, and sufficient political will to pursue important goals of accommodating both current and future...needs, not just for older individuals, but for all ...'

Such concerns are evident within the current European context (see Chapter 38). More specifically, European Union (EU) and World Bank leaders have warned Eastern European countries against lagging in their efforts to make pension systems financially sustainable and failing to take proactive measures for financing long-term care. Pointing to demographic, economic, and political transitions that have the potential to shrink the region's population by almost 24 million by 2025, the World Bank (2007) has recommended raising retirement ages and/or changing benefit rates in Lithuania and the Slovak Republic (and lowering retirement ages for Albania, Romania, Serbia, and Turkey).

Recommendations for EU member states made by the EU Economic Affairs Commission call for: (1) consolidating public finances to create some surplus to deal with the ageing population and declining workforce problem; (2) raising employment rates, especially amongst women, youth, and older workers; and (3) reforming pension, healthcare, and long-term care systems.[1] Other proposals include providing more flexible working arrangements ('flexicurity') and easing immigration

restrictions to enable the recruitment of younger workers from neighboring countries. (The immigration proposal is as controversial in Europe as the recruitment of retirees can be in the United States.)

Public policy experts anticipate the most serious generationally based policy confrontations will occur in parts of the world with high growth rates in both their oldest and youngest cohorts (e.g., Africa and the Middle East; see Campbell, 1979; Global Action on Aging, 2008). High fertility rates in these areas:

> Will result in continued population growth, exacerbating the demographic risks of political instability... .Civil unrest and political violence in these areas will continue to demand worldwide attention and resources at a time when wealthier nations face increased demands from their own ageing populations and may be unable to muster sufficient political will to address global issues.
> (Hayutin, 2007: 16–17; Urdal, 2006).

There are those who believe an ageing population might very well affect the world's balance of power since 'virtually every great power in history has possessed either a relatively large or expanding population, or both' (Haas, 2007: 7). It is estimated that by 2050, at least 20 per cent of the populations of today's powerful nation states will be over 65 (Diaz, 2006). Consequently, the degree to which resources normally reserved for militaries in these nations are redirected to help support retirement and healthcare programmes for older citizens may change the world's list of superpowers. Such domestic costs may also reduce many nations' ability to participate in international cost-sharing with key allies or to improve international relations via financial aid pacts.

There is, however, as previously noted, considerable debate over the degree to which resource pressures will force drastic shifts in public policy, especially in developing countries (Altman and Schactman, 2002; Schultz and Binstock, 2006). Scholars continue to disagree over whether 'simple economic projections that show catastrophic effects of aging' are sound in light of major demographic, economic, social, and technological changes that are occurring across the globe. They debate whether the retirement of the baby-boomer generation will create labor shortages and higher wages, which will, in turn, likely result in 'increased labor force participation, the immigration of workers from developing countries and longer working lives (supported by improved health as well as increased longevity)' (Bloom and Canning, 2007: 21).

From this general overview of the politics of ageing, we turn to examine key features of political activity in the United States, with particular attention to the consequences arising from changing patterns of voter participation and political identification.

POLITICAL TRENDS AND ISSUES: DEVELOPMENTS IN THE UNITED STATES

By 2030, the number of Americans aged 65 and older will more than double to 71 million and comprise some 20 per cent of the US population (Centers for Disease Control and Prevention and The Merck Company Foundation, 2007). By 2050, there will be 81 million persons aged 65 and older (Gamboa, 2008). This population is, however, divided along class, gender, ethnic, health, and related lines. Indeed, the health, wealth, and educational status of seniors vary considerably from state to state. Even within a state, there is likely to be considerable variation in the size and makeup of the senior population, making it difficult for state legislatures to enact effective 'one size fits all' policies, even when it comes to a specific age cohort. The so-called 'baby boom' generation (born roughly between 1946 and 1960), some 77 million strong, are the next big wave of retirees, one likely to bring substantial changes to the political and community activism hitherto characteristic of older people.

At the same time, there is also a senior divide – between the 'young old' and the 'old old' – attention to which has increased as a consequence of the growing number of centenarians (Aaron, 2000). As elsewhere, the rapid growth of the oldest-old age group has reignited discussions of what is old (Gonyea, 2005; O'Rand, 2005), sparked debates over end-of-life decisions (Christopher, 2003; Hudson, 2003; Peres, 2003; Sabatino, 2003; Tilly and Wiener, 2003) and disability policies (Ansello, 2004; Kane, 2004; Putnam, 2004; Steuerle et al., 2004), and raised questions of whether entitlement programmes like Social Security or property tax exemptions should be need-based (Meyer, 2005).

The rapid growth of the older population has prompted states and communities to re-examine everything from housing (Golant, 2004; Liebig, 1998; Pynoos and Nishita, 2005), transportation (Davis and Peterson, 2005; Dobbs and Carr, 2005; Staplin and Freund, 2005), and healthcare delivery systems (Wiener, 2006) to driver licenses (Molnar and Eby, 2005) and communication formats (fonts, signage size, etc., MacManus, 2000). Seniors comprise a higher-than-average proportion of the residents in key political states like Florida, Pennsylvania, Georgia, and Arizona.

However, looking ahead, some demographers have predicted that baby boomers will not retire to the same states as their parents and grandparents (Cava, 2007). More will 'age in place,' effectively causing suburbs to grow grayer and communities with a significant commercial sector to focus on recruiting younger working-age residents (Frey, 2007).

Ageing dynamics affect the nation's criminal justice system (Bureau of Justice Statistics, 2000; Steffensmeier, 2000), as those with life sentences age in jail and require expensive health care (see Chapter 45). Escalating incidences of elder abuse have taxed justice system resources (Branch, 2002; Fulmer et al., 2002; Quinn and Heisler, 2002). Age issues are also interwoven into technological innovations sparked by federal and state grants and tax incentive policies (Applebaum and Straker, 2005; Charness, 2005; Rogers and Fisk, 2005).

However, the most attention has been focused on the sustainability of large entitlement programmes aimed primarily at older people (cf. Grogan, 2005; Herd and Kingson, 2005; Ikegami, 2006; Moon, 2005). Generational equity in entitlements has become a much more important issue of late and is likely to continue escalating politically (cf. Cox, 2004; Schultz and Binstock, 2006). Surveys consistently show that younger Americans have little faith that Social Security will be there for them when they reach retirement age. They have also become hostile toward taxes in recent years, a pattern that is directly affecting state and local governments, even though younger Americans are still less likely to vote in non-presidential election years than their elder counterparts.

Government income security programmes continue to be of interest, especially to low income seniors (because their benefits constitute a higher portion of their total income) and those baby boomers about to retire with insufficient savings but high debt levels (Copeland, 2007). Any proposal aimed at restructuring Social Security will likely generate groups of protestors. Baby boomers, a key group within the electorate and on the cusp of retirement, are often more adamant against changes than seniors who have been well-represented by effective advocacy groups in recent years.

SENIOR POLITICAL PARTICIPATION

Age is one of the best predictors of political participation, especially in democratic societies (cf. Binstock, 2000; Jennings and Markus, 1988; MacManus, 2000; Williamson et al., 1983).

As noted by Goerres in his study of voting in Europe (2007: 90): 'Higher turnout among older age groups, after basic controls for education and gender, has been a consistent finding in many years of research.' This pattern exists across countries in spite of differences in 'electoral systems, party systems, socioeconomic development, and democratic experience.' This is attributed to habit, civic duty, and living longer in an area, thus 'habituating patterns of social behavior and complying with social norms are universal human propensities that exist everywhere' (Goerres, 2007: 91).

At one time, studies of the politics of ageing were almost exclusively focused on either the economic needs of poor seniors or their growing political clout, or both (Binstock, 2005). Reports by world and regional organizations such as the United Nations documented the extent of impoverishment among older residents in many poor, underdeveloped countries. Attention to the growing power of seniors at the ballot box, more common in industrialized and developed democratic countries, prompted candidates to target seniors because of their high turnout rates and their political cohesiveness.

Increasingly, seniors are a less monolithic voting bloc (cf. Binstock, 2005; Campbell, 2003a, b; MacManus, 2005; Schulz and Binstock, 2006). Generational replacement has changed the partisan and ideological composition of the electorate, and public policy successes and failures have resulted in the emergence of new issues. For example, in the United States, what was once a solidly Democratic voting bloc (the 65–75 year-old cohort) is now less cohesive from a partisan perspective (Hudson, 2005). Advocacy groups, like the American Association of Retired Persons (AARP), that were formed to represent a single age group – 'seniors' – now focus their attention on building bridges across different groups of seniors – 'young old,' and 'old old,' as well as across multiple generations.

Following the above, there is a growing propensity to differentiate the ideological leanings (liberal, moderate, conservative), participatory patterns, and political successes of various generations. One popular classification (Carlson, 2009) identifies seven 20th-century US generations: The New Worlders (1871–1889); The Hard Timers (1890–1908); The Good Warriors (1909–1928); The Lucky Few (1929–1945); The Baby Boomers (1946–1964); Generation X (1965–1982); and The New Boomers (sometimes called Generation Y) (1983–2001). Another commonly-cited five generation classification is: G.I (born 1921–1924), Silent (1925–1945), Boomer (1946–1964); Generation X (1961–1981); and Millennial

(1982 to present). While demographers may differ somewhat in how they define and label generations,[2] they concur that each generation has different political orientations and outlooks.

On the other hand, the difficulty of using generations to describe political behavior and policy preference differences must also be recognized. The issue here lies in determining whether intergenerational differences are a consequence of cohort, life-course, or period effects, as well as shifts in the internal composition of cohorts. For example, are observed generational differences due to 'historical circumstances affecting a particular birth cohort' (cohort effect) or do they 'reflect the common traits and interests developed through the process of aging' (life-course effect) or are they driven by 'social trends and events that affect all people during specific historical periods' (period effect)? (Binstock and Day, 1996: 363).

In the world of politics, the disproportionately greater reliance on public opinion surveys taken at a single point in time (cross-sectional data) makes it difficult to 'distinguish between cohort and life-course effects' while panel studies which track birth cohorts over time (longitudinal data) increase the likelihood of 'confound[ing] period with life-course effects' (Binstock and Day, 1996: 363). Disentangling cohort, life-course, and period effects is particularly difficult when an age group or generation is quite diverse. What we do know is that 'a birth cohort – diverse in economic and social class, gender, race, ethnicity, religion, education, health status, family status, residential locale, political attitudes, partisan attachments, and many other characteristics – does not suddenly become politically homogenized when it reaches the old-age category' (Binstock, 2006: 383).

Changes in parisan identification patterns of older Americans

In the United States, the gradual generational replacement of the staunchly Democratic Depression-era cohort with a more evenly divided younger old cohort has created an increasingly partisan-divided, but less predictable, senior electorate (Hudson, 2005; Kohut, 2008). The most politically cohesive age cohort is the youngest (the Millennials). This cohort is heavily Democratic, driven in that direction by the War in Iraq and the economic downturn of the 2000s.

The younger portion of the senior electorate is healthier, wealthier, and better educated than the older segment. The young-old group contains a higher percentage of retired working women, with their own pension benefits. The young old are less economically dependent upon the federal government (and more likely to be invested in the stock market) than the oldest old.

In the United States, senior voters have other unique participation attributes. They are more likely to *vote a complete ballot from top-to-bottom.* They vote on all races – national, state, and local – and on issues at the bottom of the ballot. This pattern has earned them the label 'super voters.' Senior voters *rely on a broader range of media (electronic and print) for information about candidates and issues.* Polls by the Pew Research Center consistently show older voters are much more likely than younger voters to be newspaper readers, watch TV news programmes with a political orientation, and listen to news on the radio. Older voters are also more likely to read organizational newsletters and direct-mail pieces sent to their home by candidates. In contrast, younger people rely more on the Internet and comedy TV shows for political news. Nearly three times as many people aged 18–29 go on the Internet to get election news as turn to newspapers. Nearly the opposite is true among those over age 50 (Pew Research Center, 2008), although Internet use among seniors is on the upswing. Overall, seniors get their political news from a wider variety of the more traditional news sources than the youngest voters. In general, 'retired people are more politically conscientious because they feel political decisions the most, being more involved in paying taxes and the like, and they are more informed about politics as a whole' (Bain, 2004).

Older voters in the United States *more strongly identify with a political party and see sharper differences between the two major parties* than their younger counterparts. They have more explicit likes and dislikes toward each party, possibly because they have had more years of experience with the political party system (Binstock, 2005; Binstock and Day, 1996; Glenn and Hefner, 1972; MacManus, 2000, 2005). Seniors *fill the ranks of campaign contributors and volunteers.* Some studies have shown that 70 is the average age of contributors to political direct-mail campaigns (more contributions are still made by mail than online, although online contributors are somewhat younger). Older persons are also more willing to work in political campaign offices, although a bit less likely to participate in highly active activities such as precinct walking or sign waving at a busy intersection. Moreover, older persons are *more knowledgeable of how government works at all levels,* less shy about contacting public officials to share their opinion or get action on some issue, and *less reticent to make a statement before elected officials* at a formal meeting of a governmental body (Binstock, 2005; Campbell, 2003a, b;

MacManus, 1996, 2000). They also tend to be better-informed about the intricacies of issues and *more knowledgeable about the timing of the political process.*

Finally, seniors have stepped up their protests against ageism and discrimination against the disabled. Historically, studies have found an inverse relationship between age and protesting and civil disobedience. Agnello (1973: 251) suggests that 'Growing older means an exchange of unconventional for more traditional forms of political behavior.'

If experiences in the United States can be taken as indicative, these generalizations may not apply so easily to some subpopulations, such as those that feel particularly marginalized. This may be the case for the gay, lesbian, bisexual, and transgender population, for example. Older members of the disabled community have become more involved in protest activities and 'sit-ins' or 'wheel-ins' in recent years. Age discrimination cases are on the upswing (Macnicol, 2006; McCann, 2004; see also Chapter 17). Concerns about age- and disability-based discrimination are also on the rise in Europe where analysts have proposed easing mandatory early-retirement policies letting workers, including women, stay employed longer and called for policies promoting the employment of persons with disabilities (Zaidi, 2008: 12).

VOLUNTEERISM, CIVIC ENGAGEMENT, AND ADVOCACY

Recently, scholars have begun to pay more attention to volunteerism and civic activism as critical forms of participation (Achenbaum, 2006; Holstein, 2006; Hudson, 2006; Reilly, 2006; National Council on Aging's RespectAbility project, 2006; Schwabenland, 2006). These activities are a measure of what is called a community's 'social capital' – social connectedness or social networks. 'Rather than being identified with the "deficit model of aging" centered on needs and benefits, the civic engagement movement finds in older adults a population fully capable of being productive and contributing to American life' (Hudson, 2006: 2).

In the United States, volunteerism rates are higher in the suburbs and rural areas than in the more populous urban core. Women volunteer more than men and middle-age persons more than younger or older generations (Jackson, 1996), although *older volunteers on average put in a considerably higher number of hours than younger generations.* Volunteering often gets one involved in local politics and can be a launching pad for running for county, city, or school board offices. This helps account for the growing number of seniors who decide to run for local political offices.

New concerns have been raised regarding use of seniors as volunteers. Some worry about inattention to the health status of volunteers (and litigation related to it) (Weinstein, 2007). Others are concerned about gender and class biases in the recruitment of volunteers, the undervaluing of senior volunteers, and their political cooptation by shrewd politicians with a personal agenda (cf. Holstein, 2006; Hudson, 2006).

The old adage that there is strength in numbers has proven true when it comes to the effectiveness of senior-based organizations. The Working Group on the Empowerment of Older Persons in its report to the United Nations Program on Aging and Development treated senior empowerment as fundamental to social justice – an equity issue. 'Members felt strongly that, where possible, coalitions should be formed as a means of collective empowerment and of promoting intergenerational solidarity, with special attention given to older women and to the use of older volunteers' (Greengross, 1995: 206).

Without a doubt, age-based interest, or advocacy, groups are seen as vital to empowering seniors internationally (cf. Olson, 2004 – Asia; McKenzie, 1995; Pratt, 1995; Thursz et al., 1995), in developing countries (cf. Chawla and Kaiser, 1995; Rao, 1995), and in specific countries (cf. Sodai, 1995 – Japan; Hastrup, 1995 – Denmark; Zaki, 1995 – Pakistan; Moller, 1995 – South Africa; Pratt, 1995 – Canada, Great Britain, the United States). These groups aim at righting the wrongs associated with poverty, illness and disease, educational inadequacies, and age discrimination, an important step toward improving social and economic development around the globe.

In the United States, interest groups have been active and influential in American politics since the nation's founding (cf. Cigler and Loomis, 2006). The two largest age-based groups, AARP and the National Council of Senior Citizens, were both formed over a 3-year period (1958–1961), as was the National Council on Aging (Pratt, 1995; Campbell, 2003a, b). Over the years, the number of senior-based groups has proliferated, reflecting the cohort's growing diversity – socioeconomic and political (Achenbaum, 2006).

Many scholars attribute the rising political clout of seniors to the effectiveness of advocacy-based interest groups in promoting economic equity-oriented programmes like Social Security, Medicare, and Medicaid reforms in the 1960s and 1970s (cf. Binstock, 1972; Hudson, 1998; Pratt, 1993). Specifically, Campbell (2003a: 1) suggests

that 'public policies can confer resources, motivate interest in government affairs by tying well-being to government action, define groups for mobilization, and even shape the content and meaning of democratic citizenship.'

Over the years, the political involvement of seniors and their advocacy groups has effectively improved the economic circumstances of many of the nation's elderly (cf. Smeeding et al., 2006). Although once the nation's most impoverished age group, poverty rates for those aged 65+ are now roughly equivalent to those of the general population.

As the composition of the senior electorate has changed in its political and economic makeup, so has the emphasis of political powerhouse organizations like the AARP, which have come under attack for caring only about seniors, particularly on the volatile issue of Social Security. In 2008, AARP launched its 'Divided We Fail' platform with more of an intergenerational emphasis: 'We believe that the opportunity to have access to health care and long-term financial security is a basic need that all Americans share. We believe it is the foundation for future generations.'[3] The organization has called for strengthening Social Security without burdening future generations. It has turned to extensive television advertising during news-related programmes in an effort to energize support among politically attentive Americans.

IDENTITY POLITICS AND AGE-BASED MICRO-TARGETING

In the United States, micro-targeting has become a major staple of modern-day political campaigns and public policymaking. It is defined as identifying key slices of the electorate, and then developing highly tailored messages to reach each of them. According to Levy (2008: 00):

> The process involves gathering elaborate information on voters (... a 'data DNA profile') that can include public items like party affiliation, ZIP code-based assumptions on income level and housing, and fairly detailed consumer preferences such as which car you drive, where you vacation and which entertainment you prefer... .That information is augmented by surveys that link those traits and behaviors to attitudes on political and social issues.

Micro-targeting often taps into what is referred to as *identity politics*. According to Heyes:

> The phrase 'identity politics' has come to signify a wide range of political activity and theorizing

founded in the shared experiences of injustice of members of certain social groups. Rather than organizing solely around belief systems, programmatic manifestoes, or party affiliation, identity political formations typically aim to secure the political freedom of a specific constituency marginalized within its larger context. Members of that constituency assert or reclaim ways of understanding their distinctiveness that challenge dominant oppressive characterizations, with the goal of greater self-determination.

(Heyes, 2007: 1)

Within the senior population, gender, race/ethnicity, and sexual orientation are often found to be major explanations of the non-monolithic nature of older generations' political orientations and behavior. Regarding gender, women outnumber men in the 65 years and over population (Lock, 1993). In the United States, there are 21 million older women compared to 14 million older men (Hetzel and Smith, 2001; Smith and Spraggins, 2001). Women's life expectancy is higher, although women of all ages are more likely than men to have acute and chronic health conditions (cf. Harrington Meyer, 2001). Although labor force participation rates of older women trail those of older men and younger women (Nyce and Schieber, 2004), workforce participation of older women has been increasing steadily in developed countries (Dobriansky et al., 2007) with growing calls for more in traditional societies (World Bank, 2007; Zaidi, 2008). The intersection of sex and age (sexism and ageism) has sparked a number of studies regarding the political activism of women (Coyle, 2001; Reger, 2005; Ryan, 2001). The more women have been affected by inequality of opportunity in the work force, the more involved they have become in politics in democratic societies.

The ageing of society, along with changes in the family structure, have also increased the activism of those concerned with caregivers (the bulk of whom are female), and with the economic plight of single and divorced women (see Chapters 10 and 39). However, experiments with long-term care involving family members as paid caregivers have been applauded by some but opposed by others concerned about elder fraud (cf. Kunkel and Nelson, 2005).

From a partisan perspective, older women are more heavily Democratic in comparison with older men and baby-boomer females. This is true for a number of reasons. First, a higher percentage of older women are dependent upon government income security programmes (Kramarae and Spender, 2000). For black and Hispanic older women, Social Security comprises 80 per cent of their income (Harrington Meyer, 2007). Secondly,

marital status greatly affects the poverty rate of elder women. Over one-fifth of unmarried older women have income levels below the poverty line – double the rate for all persons aged 65 or older (Holden and Hatcher, 2006). Historically, lower-income persons have identified with the Democratic Party.

In terms of race and ethnicity, the oldest cohorts are less racially and ethnically diverse than younger ones (Wilmoth and Longino, 2007). However, with generational replacement will come more diversity, leading demographers to project that by 2026, 25 per cent of retirement aged persons will be African American, Hispanic or Asian (Angel and Angel, 2006). The racial divide among seniors is wide, particularly when it comes to health status, income, and retirement benefits (Angel et al., 2007; LaVeist, 2003; Whitfield et al., 2006). In the early 2000s, poverty rates among black and Hispanic seniors were 2.5 times those of whites. Gender disparities were even greater: the poverty rate of 'old-old' black women (aged 75 and older) is 10 times that of 'young-old' (65–74) white men. Factors contributing to the lagging economic circumstance of seniors of color include 'low wages, intermittent work histories, family responsibilities, inadequate pension coverage, poor financial literacy, and discrimination' (Hudson, 2002: 1; see also Flippen, 2005). Others would add to that list ' distinct cultures, languages, and migration histories' (Villa, 1998: 212; Frisbie, 1982).

Marital status differences also exist across the races, greatly affecting Social Security benefits (Herd, 2002; Taylor et al., 1997). Black women are much more likely to be single parents than white women. In terms of political activism, older black women usually vote at higher rates than older black men; the reverse is true within the Hispanic communities (Torres-Gil et al., 2000). This pattern is reflective of the differences in societal structures: matriarchal (black) vs patriarchal (Hispanic) (Campbell, 2003a; Desipio, 1996; Hudson, 2002; Taylor et al., 1997). There are, however, few partisan differences across the genders; minorities tend to vote Democratic, although the pattern is weaker among Hispanics and Asians.

As noted earlier, political activism organized around transgender, intersex, lesbian, gay, racial/ethnic, and old-age issues has intensified. As a result, late-life liberal political activism is on the upswing (Bennett and Bennett, 1996; Waldner et al., 2004). Older gay, lesbian, and transgendered voters in the United States have been at the forefront of protests calling for governments to permit civil unions and gay marriage. They are predominantly Democratic in their partisan preference. The growing political clout of the gay community has also prompted new political battles over the classification of a typical family structure (cf. Settersten, 2007) and the revamping of income security programmes like Social Security (cf. Harrington Meyer, 2007; see also Chapter 17).

COMMUNITIES STARTING TO PLAN AHEAD

In many communities with sizable senior populations, leaders from the public, private, and non-profit sectors have begun joining forces to plan and produce innovations that will create 'ageing-friendly' locales. It will be a rather long process. Most communities have not yet modified land use regulations, housing policies, transportation policies, or opportunities for community involvement – many of which were initially put in place more than half a century ago when life spans, work patterns, and social networks were quite different. (see Lehning et al., 2007.)

With the growing size of the 65+ population, interjecting youth into the lives of ageing persons through intergenerational programmes will be an even higher priority for governments than it already is (see Chapters 15 and 34). Newer volunteerism and civic engagement models include key intergenerational components (cf. Morrow-Howell et al., 2003). The most successful intergenerational programmes to date have featured seniors mentoring young students and/or volunteering in local schools – serious business. However, multi-generational programmes are increasingly evident at senior centers and at more unconventional places like science centers (Morgan and Ellis, 2007) and museums (Rathbone, 2007). As they age, baby boomers, the leading edge of the computer revolution, may not want to be left behind technologically.

CONCLUSION

The ageing of the world's population is affecting a vast array of policies, ranging from the social safety net, pensions, immigration, international trade and aid, economic development and retiree recruitment, transportation modes, housing, healthcare equipment and delivery systems, medical research priorities, consumer protection and employment patterns, to communication technologies and civil rights. All are regulated or overseen in some way by governments; each is of interest to those who follow the plight of older persons in our society.

As is often the case in the world of public policy, innovations tend to bubble from the grassroots up rather than from the top down, regardless of the political system. As this chapter has shown, the ageing of the world's population is greatly affecting the politics of neighborhoods, local governments, states, and nations as tough choices must be made. But the major debates about 'demographics as destiny' and intergenerational justice remain largely unresolved.

The changing age composition of many nations in the world has reignited the '*demographics is destiny*' debate. The issue is whether such changes intensify intergenerational *conflict* or produce higher levels of intergenerational *cooperation*. To date, studies focusing on *generational equity* – the fairness of the distribution of public goods and services across generations – have come to different conclusions. Some have found that older people have received a disproportionately high amount of public resources relative to children through the expansion of the welfare state – entitlement programmes, such as Social Security, Medicaid, and Medicare. They see the situation as less than optimal – a formula for *intergenerational conflict*.

In contrast, others envision ageing politics as moving in a more positive direction – more *intergenerational cooperation*. Scholars in this vein base their optimism on the potential restructuring of the healthcare system, different retirement patterns of baby boomers (working longer), and the emergence of an intergenerational coalition formed by advocacy groups representing the old and the young.

The difficulty that public policymakers have is that each vision yields different policy prescriptions and there is increasingly less agreement on what is 'old.' Applying the insights from political science to further understand social change and generational politics remains an important area for development within social gerontology.

NOTES

1 EurActiv.com, 2008
2 For a slightly different, more controversial, classification, see William Strauss and Neil Howe, (1991) *Generations: The History of America's Future, 1584 to 2069*. New York: William Morrow.
3 DividedWeFail.org

REFERENCES

Aaron, H. (2000) 'The centenarian boom: providing for retirement in a long-lived America', *The Brookings Review*, 18(2): 22–5.

Achenbaum, W.A. (2006) 'Civic ventures: looking backward, planning forward', *Public Policy and Aging Report,* 16(Fall): 9–12.

Agnello, T.J., Jr. (1973) 'Aging and the sense of political powerlessness', *The Public Opinion Quarterly,* 37(2): 251–9.

Altman, S.H. and Shactman, D.I. (2002) *Policies for an Aging Society.* Baltimore, MD: The Johns Hopkins University Press.

Alvarez, R.C. (2002) 'The promise of e-Health – a Canadian perspective', *eHealth International,* 1(September): 1–4.

Angel, J.L. and Angel, R.J. (2006) 'Minority group status and healthful aging: social structure still matters', *American Journal of Public Health,* 96: 1152–9.

Angel, J.L., Jimenez, M.A., and Angel, R.A., (2007) 'The economic consequences of widowhood for older minority women', *The Gerontologist,* 47: 224–34.

Ansello, E.F. (2004) 'Public policy writ small: coalitions at the intersection of aging and lifelong disabilities', *Public Policy and Aging Report,* 14(Fall): 1, 3–6.

Applebaum, R.A. and Straker, J. (2005) 'Long-term care challenges for an aging America: improving technology and changing the system's culture as critical parts of the solution', *Public Policy and Aging Report,* 15(4): 1, 3–7.

Bain, N. (2004) 'Elderly poll workers may cause problems', *The Hilltop Student Newspaper for Howard University,* September 17.

Bennett, L.M. and Bennett, S.E. (1996) 'Changing views about gender equality in politics: gradual change and lingering doubts', in L.L. Duke (ed.), *Women and Politics: Have the Outsiders Become Insiders?* Englewood Cliffs, NJ: Prentice-Hall.

Binstock, R.H. (1972) 'Interest-group liberalism and the politics of aging', *The Gerontologist,* 12: 265–80.

Binstock, R.H. (2000) 'Older people and voting participation: past and future', *The Gerontologist,* 40(1): 18–31.

Binstock, R.H. (2005) 'The contemporary politics of old age policies', in R.B. Hudson (ed.), *The New Politics of Old Age Policy,* Baltimore, MD: Johns Hopkins University Press.

Binstock, R.H. (2006) 'Older voters and the 2004 election', *The Gerontologist,* 46(3): 382–4.

Binstock, R.H. and Day, C.L. (1996) 'Aging and politics', in R.H. Binstock, and L.K. George (eds), *Handbook of Aging and the Social Sciences.* San Diego, CA: Academic Press.

Binstock, R.H. and Quadagno, J. (2001) 'Aging and politics', in R.H. Binstock and L.K. George (eds), *Handbook of Aging and the Social Sciences.* San Diego, CA: Academic Press.

Bloom, D.E. and Canning, D. (2007) 'Demographic change, fiscal sustainability, and macroeconomic performance', *Public Policy and Aging Report,* 17(Fall): 1, 18–23.

Branch, L.G. (2002) 'The epidemiology of elder abuse and neglect', *The Public Policy and Aging Report,* 12(Winter): 19–23.

Bureau of Justice Statistics (2000) 'Elderly crime victims: national crime victimization survey', *The Public Policy and Aging Report,* 10 (Winter): 14–16.

Campbell, A.L. (2003a) 'Participatory reactions to policy threats: Senior citizens and the defense of social security and Medicare', *Political Behavior,* 25(1): 29–49.

Campbell, A.L. (2003b) *How Policies Make Citizens: Senior Citizen Activism and the American Welfare State.* Princeton, NJ: Princeton University Press.

Campbell, J.C. (1979) 'The old people boom and Japanese policy making', *Journal of Japanese Studies,* 5(2): 321–57.

Carlson, Elwood (2009). '20th Century U.S. Generations', *Population Bulletin* 64(1), 1–18.

Cava, M.R.D. (2007) 'New home in old age: seniors start over in different cities to be near families', *USA Today,* April 12: 1D-2.

Centers for Disease Control and Prevention and The Merck Company Foundation (2007) *The State of Aging and Health in America 2007.* Available at www.cdc.gov/aging.

Charness, N. (2005) 'Age, technology, and culture: gerontopia or dystopia?', *Public Policy and Aging Report,* 15(Fall): 20–3.

Chawla, S. and Kaiser, M.A. (1995) 'The aged and development: mutual beneficiaries', in D. Thursz, C. Nusberg, and J. Prather (eds), *Empowering Older People: An International Approach.* Westport, CT: Auburn House.

Christopher, M.J. (2003) 'The new place of end-of-life issues on the policy agenda', *Public Policy and Aging Report,* 13(Winter): 23–6.

Cigler, A.J. and Loomis B.A. (2006) *Interest Group Politics.* Washington, DC: CQ Press.

Copeland, C. (2007) 'Increasing debt risk of those age 55 or older, 1992–2004', *Public Policy and Aging Report,* 17(Spring): 20–3.

Cox, C.B. (2004) *Community Care for an Aging Society: Issues, Policies, and Services.* New York: Falmer Press.

Coyle, J.M. (ed.) (2001) *Handbook on Women and Aging.* Westport, CT: Praeger Publishers.

Davis, E.S. and Peterson, M.F. (2005) 'Identification of at-risk drivers: Professional and reimbursement issues', *Public Policy and Aging Report,* 15(Spring): 21–3.

Desipio, L. (1996) *Counting on the Latino Vote: Latinos as a New Electorate.* Charlottesville, VA: University of Virginia Press.

Diaz, F.G. (2006) 'Interview: future labor, fiscal and social policy reforms Mexico should make', *AARP Global Aging Issues,* February.

Dobbs, B.M. and Carr, D. (2005) 'Screening and assessment of medically at-risk drivers', *Public Policy and Aging Report,* 15(Spring): 6–13.

Dobriansky, P.J., Suzman, R.M., and Hodes, R.J. (2007) *Why Population Aging Matters: A Global Perspective.* Washington, DC: National Institute on Aging, National Institutes of Health, March.

EurActiv.com. (2008) 'Almunia warns of looming demographic crunch in Europe', February 5. Available at www.euractiv.com/en/socialeurope/almunia-wars-looming-demographic-crunch-europe. Accessed June 21, 2008.

Flippen, C.A. (2005) 'The oldest old and a long-lived society: challenges for public policy', in R.B. Hudson (ed.), *The New Politics of Old Age Policy.* Baltimore, MD: Johns Hopkins University Press.

Frey, W.H. (2007) *Mapping the Growth of Older America: Seniors and Boomers in the Early 21st Century.* Washington, DC: Brookings Institution, May.

Frisbie, W. (1982) *Household-Family Structure and Socio-economic Differentials: A Comparison of Hispanics, Blacks, and Anglos.* University of Texas, Austin, TX: Texas Population Research Center Papers.

Fulmer, T., Paveza, G., and Guadagno, L. (2002) 'Elder abuse and neglect: policy issues for two very different problems', *The Public Policy and Aging Report,* 12(Winter): 15–18.

Gamboa, S., Associated Press (2008) 'Older population to more than double', February 11. Accessed at www.breitbart.com, February 11.

Glenn, N.D. and Hefner, T. (1972) 'Further evidence on aging and party identification', *The Public Opinion Quarterly,* 36(1): 31–47.

Global Action on Aging (2008) 'Rural aging issues around the world', globalaging.org. Accessed June 21.

Goerres, A. (2007) 'Why are older people more likely to vote? The impact of ageing on electoral turnout in Europe', *British Journal of Politics and International Relations,* 9(1): 90–121.

Golant, S.M. (2004) 'Do impaired persons with health care needs occupy U.S. assisted living facilities? An analysis from six national studies', *Journal of Gerontology,* 59B(2): S68–S79.

Gonyea, J.G. (2005) 'The economic well-being of older Americans and the persistent divide', *Public Policy and Aging Report,* 15(3): 1, 3–11.

Greengross, S. (1995) 'Conclusion of the working group on the empowerment of older persons', in D. Thursz, C. Nusberg, and J. Prather (eds), *Empowering Older People: An International Approach.* Westport, CT: Auburn House.

Grogan, C.M. (2005) 'The politics of aging within Medicaid', in R.B. Hudson (ed.), *The New Politics of Old Age Policy.* Baltimore, MD: Johns Hopkins University Press.

Haas, Mark L. (2007) 'Global aging: opportunities and threats to American security', *Public Policy and Aging Report,* 17(Fall): 7–11.

Harrington Meyer, M. (2001) 'Gender, generations, and chronic conditions', *The Public Policy and Aging Report,* 11(Winter): 1, 8–10.

Harrington Meyer, M. (2007) 'Changing marital rates and stagnant social security policy', *Public Policy and Aging Report,* 17(Summer): 11–14.

Hastrup, B. (1995) 'Establishing a seniors' organization in Denmark', in D. Thursz, C. Nusberg, and J. Prather (eds), *Empowering Older People: An International Approach.* Westport, CT: Auburn House.

Haub, C. (2007) 'Global aging and the demographic divide', *Public Policy and Aging Report,* 17(Fall): 1, 3–6.

Hayutin, A.M. (2007) 'Graying of the global population', *Public Policy and Aging Report,* 17 (Fall): 12–17.

Herd, Pamela (2002). 'Care credits: race, gender, class, and Social Security reform', *Public Policy and Aging Report* 12(3), 13–18.

Herd, P. and Kingson, E.R. (2005) 'Reframing social security: cures worse than the disease', in R.B. Hudson (ed.), *The New Politics of Old Age Policy.* Baltimore, MD: Johns Hopkins University Press.

Hetzel, L. and Smith, A. (2001) 'The 65 years and over population: 2000', *Census 2000 Brief.* Washington, DC: US Department of Commerce, Economics and Statistics Administration, US Census Bureau, October.

Heyes, C. (2007) 'Identity politics', *Stanford Encyclopedia of Philosophy.* Available at http://plato.stanford.edu/entries/identity-politics, June 21, 2008.

Holden, K. and Hatcher, C. (2006) 'Economic status of the aged', in R.H. Binstock and L.K. George (eds), *Handbook of Aging and the Social Sciences.* San Diego, CA: Academic Press.

Holstein, M. (2006) 'A critical reflection on civic engagement', *Public Policy and Aging Report,* 16(4): 1, 21–26.

Hudson, R.B. (1998) 'Privatizing old-age benefits: re-emergent ideology encounters organized interest', in J.G. Gonyea (ed.), *Re-Securing Social Security and Medicare: Understanding Privatization and Risk.* Washington, DC: Gerontological Society of America.

Hudson, Robert B., ed. (2002). 'Getting ready and getting credit: Populations of color and retirement security', *Public Policy and Aging Report* 12(3), 1–2.

Hudson, R.B. (2003) 'End-of-life care: issues and options', *Public Policy and Aging Report,* 13(1): 2.

Hudson, R.B. (2005) *The New Politics of Old Age Policy.* Baltimore, MD: Johns Hopkins University Press.

Hudson, R.B. (2006) 'Terms of engagement: the right and left look at elder civic activism', *Public Policy and Aging Report,* 16(4): 13–18.

Ikegami, N. (2006) 'Long-term care insurance in Japan', AARP global aging issues, May.

Jackson, V.R. (1996) *Volunteerism in Geriatric Settings.* Binghamton, NY: Haworth Press.

Jennings, M.K. and Markus, G.B. (1988) 'Political involvement in the later years: a longitudinal survey', *American Journal of Political Science,* 32(2): 302–16.

Kane, R.A. (2004) 'Coalitions between aging and disability interests: potential effects on choice and control for older people', *Public Policy and Aging Report,* 14(Fall): 15–18.

Kohut, A. (2008) 'The widening gap', Pew Research Center, Special to the *New York Times,* May 9.

Kramarae, C. and Spender, D. (2000) *Routledge International Encyclopedia of Women Global Women's Issues and Knowledge.* New York: Routledge.

Kunkel, S.R. and Nelson, I.A. (2005) 'Consumer direction: changing the landscape of long-term care', *Public Policy and Aging Report,* 15(Fall): 13–16.

LaVeist, T.A. (2003) 'Racial segregation and longevity among African Americans: an individual-level analysis', *Health Services Research,* 38(December): 1719–34.

Lehning, A., Chun, Y., and Scharlach, A. (2007) 'Structural barriers to developing 'aging-friendly' communities', *Public Policy and Aging Report,* 17(Summer): 15–20.

Levy, S. (2008) 'Campaigns get personal', *Newsweek,* April 28. Accessed at www.newsweek.com/id/132853/out/print, June 21, 2008.

Liebig, P.S. (1998) 'Housing and supportive services for the elderly: intergenerational perspectives and options',

The New Politics of Old Age Policy. Baltimore, MD: Johns Hopkins University Press.

in J.S. Steckenrider and T. Parrott (eds), *New Directions in Old Age Policies*. Albany, NY: SUNY Press.

Lock, M. (1993) 'Ideology, female midlife, and the greying of Japan', *Journal of Japanese Studies,* 19(1): 43–78.

MacManus, S.A. (1996) *Young v. Old: Generational Combat in the 21st Century*. Boulder, CO: Westview Press.

MacManus, S.A. (2000) *Targeting Senior Voters: Campaign Outreach to Elders and Others With Special Needs*. Boulder, CO: Rowman and Littlefield.

MacManus, S.A. (2005) 'Florida's senior voters in election 2004: results, top issues, reforms, and new concerns', *Public Policy and Aging Reports,* 15(Winter): 10–14.

Macnicol, J. (2006) *Age Discrimination: An Historical and Contemporary Analysis*. New York: Cambridge University Press.

McCann, L.A. (2004) 'Age discrimination in employment: why its predicted demise is off the mark', *Public Policy and Aging Report,* 14(3): 7–10.

McKenzie, H. (1995) 'Empowering older persons through organizations: a case study', in D. Thursz, C. Nusberg, and J. Prather (eds), *Empowering Older People: An International Approach*. Westport, CT: Auburn House.

Meyer, M.J. (2005) 'The hidden benefits of property tax relief for the elderly', *Elder Law Journal,* 12(2): 417–21.

Moller, V. (1995) 'Research as a tool for empowerment', in D. Thursz, C. Nusberg, and J. Prather (eds), *Empowering Older People: An International Approach*. Westport, CT: Auburn House.

Molnar, L.J. and Eby, D.W. (2005) 'A brief look at driver license renewal policies in the United States', *Public Policy and Aging Report,* 15(2): 1, 13.

Moon, M. (2005) 'Sustaining Medicare as an age-related program', in R.B. Hudson (ed.), *The New Politics of Old Age Policy*. Baltimore, MD: Johns Hopkins University Press.

Morgan, R.E. and Ellis, D.W. (2007) 'The longevity revolution: new opportunities for science centers', *Public Policy and Aging Report,* 17(Winter): 1–6.

Morrow-Howell, N., Hinterlong, J., Rozario, P.A., and Tang, F. (2003) 'Effects of volunteering on the well-being of older adults', *The Journals of Gerontology, Series B: Psychological Sciences and Social Sciences*, 58B(May): S137–S45.

National Council on Aging (2006) 'References on civic engagement', from the RespectAbility Project, Older Americans and Civic Engagement in the 21st Century, *Public Policy and Aging Report,* 16(4): 27–30.

Nyce, S.A. and Schieber, S.J. (2004) 'Demographics matter: the economic reality of an aging society', *Public Policy and Aging Report,* 14(3): 11–15.

Olson, L.L. (2004) 'The politics of aging, Asian style', paper presented at the 2004 Annual Meeting of the American Political Science Association, September 2–5. Available online at www.allacademic.com/meta/p61759_index.html

O'Rand, A.M. (2005) 'When old age begins: implications for health, work, and retirement', in R.B. Hudson (ed.), *The New Politics of Old Age Policy*. Baltimore, MD: Johns Hopkins University Press.

Peres, J.R. (2003) 'End-of-life care: How do we pay for it?', *Public Policy and Aging Report* (Winter): 1, 3–6.

Pew Research Center for the People & the Press (2008) 'Internet now major source of campaign news'. Accessed at http://pewresearch.org/pubs, March 21, 2009.

Pratt, H.J. (1993) *Gray Agendas: Interest Groups and Public Pensions in Canada, Britain, and the United States*. Ann Arbor: University of Michigan Press.

Pratt, H.J. (1995) 'Seniors' organizations and seniors' empowerment: an international perspective', in D. Thursz, C. Nusberg, and J. Prather (eds), *Empowering Older People: An International Approach*. Westport, CT: Auburn House.

Putnam, M. (2004) 'Issues in the further integration of aging and disability services', *Public Policy and Aging Report,* 14(4): 1, 19–23.

Pynoos, J. and Nishita, C.M. (2005) 'The changing face of senior housing', in R.B. Hudson (ed.), *The New Politics of Old Age Policy*. Baltimore, MD: Johns Hopkins University Press.

Quinn, M.J. and Heisler, C.J. (2002) 'The legal system: civil and criminal responses to elder abuse and neglect', *The Public Policy and Aging Report,* 12(Winter): 8–14.

Rao, M. (1995) 'Older persons: issues concerning their empowerment and participation in development', in D. Thursz, C. Nusberg, and J. Prather (eds), *Empowering Older People: An International Approach*. Westport, CT: Auburn House.

Rathbone, J.A. (2007) 'Weaving threads of a common identity: non-formal intergenerational education and the community museum of Ollantaytambo, Peru', *Together;* 12(2): 7, 9.

Reger, J. (2005) *Different Wavelengths: Studies of the Contemporary Women's Movement*. London: Routledge.

Reilly, S.L. (2006) 'Transforming aging: the civic engagement of adults 55+', *Public Policy and Aging Report,* 16(4): 1, 3–8.

Rogers, W.A. and Fisk, A.D. (2005) 'Aware home technology: potential benefits for older adults', *Public Policy and Aging Report,* 15(Fall): 28–30.

Ryan, B. (2001) *Identity Politics in the Women's Movement*. New York: NYU Press.

Sabatino, C.P. (2003) 'De-balkanizing state advance directive law', *Public Policy and Aging Report,* 13(Winter): 1, 7–12.

Schultz, J.H. and Binstock, R.H. (2006) *Aging Nation: The Economics and Politics of Growing Older in America*. Westport, CT: Praeger Publishers.

Schwabenland, C. (2006) *Stories, Visions and Values in Voluntary Organizations*. Burlington, VT: Ashgate Publishing Company.

Settersten, R.A. Jr. (2007) '10 reasons why shake-ups in the life course should change approaches to old-age policies', *Public Policy and Aging Report,* 17(Summer): 1, 21–7.

Smeeding, T.M., Williamson, J., Sierminska, E., Gormick, J., and Brandolini, A. (2006) 'Income and poverty in the United States in comparative perspective: the role of income and wealth in guaranteeing economic security in old age', *Public Policy and Aging Report,* 16(3): 23–7.

Smith, D.I. and R.E. Spraggins (2001). *Census 2000 Brief: Gender: 2000*. Washington, D.C.: U.S. Department of Commerce, Economics and Statistics Administration, Bueau of the Census. Accessed at http://www.census.gov/population/www.cen2000/briefs.html.

Sodai, T. (1995) 'Tradition impedes organizational empowerment in Japan', in D. Thursz, C. Nusberg, and J. Prather (eds), *Empowering Older People: An International Approach*. Westport, CT: Auburn House.

Staplin, L. and Freund, K. (2005) 'Public and private policy initiatives to move seniors forward', *Public Policy and Aging Report*, 15(2): 1, 3–5.

Steffensmeier, D. (2000) 'Sentencing the senior-citizen offender: age bias or warranted leniency?', *Public Policy and Aging Report*, 11(1): 21–4.

Steuerle, C.E., Carasso, A., and Cohen, L. (2004) 'How progressive is social security when old age and disability insurance are treated as a whole?', The Urban Institute Policy Briefs: Straight Talk on Social Security and Retirement Policy, May 1.

Strauss, W. and Howe, N. (1991) *Generations: The History of America's Future, 1584 to 2069*. New York: William Morrow.

Street, D. (2007) 'Too much, too little, just right? Policy disconnects in an aging society', *Public Policy and Aging Report*, 17(Summer): 7–10.

Taylor, R., Jackson, J., Chatters, L. (eds) (1997) *Family Life in Black America*. Thousand Oaks, CA: SAGE.

Thursz, Daniel, Charlotte Nusberg, and Johnnie Prather, eds. (1995). *Empowering Older People: An International Approach*. Westport, CT: Auburn House.

Tilly, J.A. and Wiener, J.M. (2003) 'End-of-life care for the Medicaid population', *Public Policy and Aging Report*, 13(Winter): 17–22.

Torres-Gil, F., Villa, V.M., and Portillo, M. (2000) 'The politics of aging in a diverse California', Paper No. 964, UCLA School of Public Affairs, California Policy Options. Available at http://repositories.cdlib.org/uclaspa/cpo/964

Urdal, H. (2006) 'A clash of generations? Youth bulges and political violence', *International Studies Quarterly*, 50: 607–29.

Villa, Valentine M. (1998). 'Aging policy and the experience of older minorities', in Janie S. Steckenrider and Tonya M. Parrot, (eds). *New Directions in Old-Age Policies*. New York: State University of New York Press, pp. 211–234.

Waldner, L., Dobratz, B., and Buzzell, T. (eds) (2004) *Politics of Change Volume 13: Sexuality, Gender and Aging (Research in Political Sociology)*. San Diego, CA: Elsevier.

Weinstein, H. (2007) 'Age prejudice case to cost firm millions', *Los Angeles Times*, reprinted in *The Tampa Tribune*, October 6.

Whitfield, K., Angel, J., Burton, L., and Hayward, M. (2006) 'Diversity, disparities, and inequalities in aging: implications for policy', *Public Policy and Aging Report*, 16(Summer): 16–22.

Wiener, J.M. (2006) 'It's not your grandmother's long-term care anymore', *Public Policy and Aging Report*, 16(Summer): 28–35.

Williamson, J.B., Evans, L., and Powell, L.A. (1983) 'Politics of aging: power and policy', *Contemporary Sociology*, 12(4): 395–6.

Wilmoth, J. and Longino, C. (2007) 'Demographic trends contributing to structural lag and policy stagnation', *Public Policy and Aging Report*, 17(Summer): 1, 3–6.

World Bank (2007) 'World Bank warns eastern European countries on ageing problem', EurActiv.com, June 22. Available at www.eurativ.com/en/enlargement/world-bank-warns-easter-european-countries-ageing-problem. Accessed June 21, 2008.

Zaidi, A. (2008) 'Features and challenges of population ageing: the European perspective', *Policy Brief*, European Centre, March 1.

Zaki, S.M. (1995) 'Older persons in Pakistan: their major problems and empowerment strategy', in D. Thursz, C. Nusberg, and J. Prather (eds), *Empowering Older People: An International Approach*. Westport, CT: Auburn House.

Author Index

Subject Index